THE SHELL GUIDE
TO
IRELAND

by

LORD KILLANIN, M.A., M.R.I.A.

and

MICHAEL V. DUIGNAN, M.A.

Professor of Celtic Archaeology,
University College, Galway

SECOND EDITION

Ebury Press
in association with George Rainbird
London 1967

First published 1962
Reprinted 1964
Second edition, revised and reset, 1967
Revised 1969

© *Irish Shell and BP Ltd, 1962, 1967*

Designed and produced by
George Rainbird Ltd
Marble Arch House, 44 Edgware Road,
London W2.
Printed and bound by
Hely Thom Ltd, Dublin

7181 4031 1

Contents

Colour Plates

Preface

For this new edition of *The Shell Guide to Ireland* the original work has been revised and brought up to date in the light of experience in using it and of the helpful comments of readers. The book remains, therefore, a general guide which pays particular attention to antiquities and to things of historic, artistic, and literary interest. Since the first edition appeared, an archaeological survey of the Republic has, at long last, got under way, and the survey of Northern Ireland has continued to make progress; but until a complete survey of all the monuments in Ireland appears the perfect guide book cannot be written.

The main part of this *Guide* is presented in the form of a gazetteer; that is to say, the items are grouped under alphabetically ordered principal centres – usually towns and villages. Under each principal centre will be found, not only a description of the noteworthy features of the place itself, but also references to places (usually townlands) within convenient reach of it. These sub-entries, as they may be called, though they are not distinguished by any form of heading, are arranged in order following the points of the compass, normally working clockwise, i.e. from north via east, south, and west, about the chosen centre. In some cases it has seemed convenient to group some of the sub-entries under a sub-centre, working clockwise round the sub-centre. Where this expedient has been adopted, the sub-entries have been "paragraphed" by means of dashes. Thus the mileage and compass-bearing immediately following a dash refer back to the sub-centre, not to the place or feature mentioned in the sentence immediately before the dash. See, for example, page 366, where Rusheen crossroads in the entry MACROOM is treated as a sub-centre: Parknalicka is two miles north-north-west of Rusheen crossroads, not of Knockglass. Sub-entries, whether or not they are grouped under a sub-centre, can be located quickly by reference to the index at the end of the book; if you do not know the name – e.g. of something noticed from the road – refer to the sub-entries under the nearest principal centre in the gazetteer.

It should be noted that the compass-bearings are, for the most part, approximations, and that the mileages, with certain self-evident exceptions, represent distances by road or track, not straight across country.

The maps in the *Guide* are included as a visual index of the main entries in the gazetteer. It is assumed that each user of the *Guide* will have maps of a scale suited to his purpose, but even the possessor of the Ordnance Survey six-inch sheets must be prepared to invoke local guidance when looking for some of the lesser-known monuments. Maps to various scales can be obtained from booksellers or from the Government Publications Sale Office, G.P.O. Arcade, Dublin 1, and H.M. Stationery Office, 80 Chichester St, Belfast 1. The Ordnance Survey of Northern Ireland's one-inch maps show a fair proportion of ancient monuments of all periods. Attention is also drawn to the Ordnance Survey of Ireland's *Map of Monastic Ireland*. For Dublin, the same

Survey's 2½-inch *Map of Dublin* (with index to streets) can be recommended; for Belfast, the "Geographia" *Postal Plan of Belfast*.

In the spelling of place-names the forms used by the Ordnance Surveys have usually been adopted. In the spelling of personal names, whose orthography has naturally fluctuated through the centuries, absolute consistency has not been attempted. In the English rendering of surnames in O the misleading apostrophe has been omitted: e.g. O Neill, not O'Neill. When such names are given in their Irish form the mark of length is included: e.g. Ó Néill.

Monuments in State ownership or care are "National Monuments" in the Republic, "Ancient Monuments" in Northern Ireland. For convenience, the term "Nat. Mon." has been used to cover both, and this term has been somewhat loosely applied, not only to monuments in State care, but also to monuments in the ownership or custody of local authorities and to monuments for which Preservation Orders (prohibiting injury or destruction) have been issued by the State.

Mention of a house, building, garden, monument, work of art, or anything else, in private ownership does not imply public right of access. As those houses and public places which are open to the public frequently change their entrance fees and times of admission, intending visitors should enquire beforehand at some convenient Tourist Office or obtain the current "Houses and Gardens" pamphlet from An Bórd Fáilte.

Since the first printing of this edition the following houses have been opened to the public:
Adare Manor and demesne, Adare
Bermingham House and gardens, Tuam
Clonalis House, Castlerea, Co. Roscommon
Castletown House, Celbridge
Derrynane House (Derrynane Abbey), Caherdaniel
Knappogue Castle, Quin (?), Co. Clare
Longfield House, Goold's Cross, Cashel
Lough Cutra Castle, Gort
Lough Rynn, Mohill
Tullynally Castle ("Pakenham Hall"), Castlepollard
47 Mountjoy Square, Dublin (Mr and Mrs John Molloy)
The following houses are no longer open to the general public:
Dunsany Castle, Dunshaughlin
Dungory Castle, Kinvara

At Camp Hill, Omagh, the ancestral homestead of the Mellons, an American banking family, has been restored and opened to the public. Mount Congreve Gardens, Waterford, may now be visited only by prior arrangement. Permits to visit Glenveagh Castle, Kilmacrenan, must be obtained from the Estate Agent, Church Hill, Co. Donegal (Tel. Church Hill 7).

For brevity, and in accordance with long-established usage, the dioceses, cathedrals, parish churches, etc., of the Roman Catholic Church are referred to simply as "Catholic", and those of the Church of Ireland (Anglican Communion) are usually referred to as "Protestant". Since the Church of Ireland is the only Protestant Church in the country with a diocesan-parochial organization, and since non-episcopalian Protestant churches and institutions are named specifically Methodist, Presbyterian, etc., as the case may be, no confusion should arise.

Information concerning golf and fishing facilities is included in the Appendices, but the most up-to-date details about all tourist facilities, including accommodation, travel, and sport, can be obtained from Bórd Fáilte Éireann (Irish Tourist Board), Baggot Street Bridge, Dublin 2, or from the Northern Ireland Tourist Board, 10 Royal Avenue, Belfast 1. These two bodies publish annually revised information on all matters of tourist interest. Enquiries about youth hostels should be addressed to An Óige, 39 Mountjoy Square South, Dublin 1, or to the Youth Hostel Association of Northern Ireland, Bryson House, 28 Bedford St, Belfast 2.

The authors have not hesitated to give free rein to personal opinions and foibles in respect of things social, political, historical, religious, and artistic; it should be emphasized that the sponsors of the *Guide* are in no way responsible for such opinions and foibles.

It is not possible to thank all who helped with the original work or who submitted corrections and suggestions for this edition. Particular thanks, however, are due to the following who provided us with expert information or assisted us in checking facts beyond our control: Mr C. B. E. Brett; Dr Maurice Craig; the Rev. Dr P. K. Egan; Professor E. Estyn Evans, The Queen's University, Belfast; Mr Dermot Foley, Central Library Council, Dublin; Mr R. Neville Hadcock; the late Mr P. J. Hartnett, Archaeological Officer, Bórd Fáilte Éireann; Mr John Hunt; the late Dr H. G. Leask, sometime Inspector of National Monuments, Dublin; Mr John Lewis-Crosby, National Trust, Northern Ireland; Mr Raymond McGrath, Chief Architect, Office of Public Works, Dublin; Professor G. F. Mitchell, Trinity College, Dublin; the late Very Rev. Mgr Michael Moloney; the late Mr Frank O Connor; Professor Michael J. O Kelly, University College, Cork; the late Professor Seán P. Ó Ríordáin, University College, Dublin; Mr Cathal O Shannon; Miss E. Prendergast, National Museum of Ireland; Mr Etienne Rynne, National Museum of Ireland; the Rev. L. Taheny, O.P.; Mr T. Trench; Mr James White, Director of the National Gallery, Dublin; Mr Seán F. White; and many owners of private houses and estates and directors of public institutions.

It is also not possible to acknowledge all the printed sources consulted, but special mention must be made of the following: Maurice Craig's *Dublin 1660–1860*, indispensable to the student of Dublin architecture; *A preliminary survey of the ancient monuments of Northern Ireland* (H.M.S.O., 1940); Máire Mac Neill's admirable *The festival of Lughnasa*, which appeared just in time to be consulted when preparing this edition; R. A. S. Macalister's *Corpus inscriptionum insularum Celticarum*, from which most of the lapidary inscriptions have been taken.

This *Guide* was originally made possible by the encouragement given by Mr T. A. Crawford-Young, at that time Managing Director of Irish Shell and BP Limited, and his enthusiasm continues with his successor, Mr B. A. Nolan. Generous cooperation has been given by Dr T. J. O'Driscoll and the staff of Bórd Fáilte Éireann (the Irish Tourist Board), and by Mr R. Frizzell of the Northern Ireland Tourist Board. We have also had the cooperation of Mr Percy Le Clerc, Inspector of National Monuments, and his staff at the Office of Public Works, Dublin, and of Mr G. J. Falkiner, formerly of the Ministry of Finance, Northern Ireland. Generous help has been given by the directors and curators of national and provincial museums throughout Ireland, by the directors and curators of the national and municipal art galleries, and particularly by the Library staff of University College, Galway. Finally, the first edition could not have been completed without the assistance of Mrs Ruth Cannon, who was responsible for typing a very difficult and intricate manuscript.

In a work of this kind inaccuracies and discrepancies are perhaps inevitable. Corrections and suggestions for future editions should be addressed to the authors at Shell-BP House, 13–16 Fleet Street, Dublin 2.

1967
Killanin
M. V. Duignan

HISTORICAL INTRODUCTION

Prehistoric Ireland

Hunters and Fishers

Two skeletons found in 1928 in Kilgreany cave, Co. Waterford, show us that about the close of Late Glacial times, perhaps before 9000 B.C., Final Palaeolithic hunters were living in the south of Ireland. We know nothing else about them, but the animals on which they preyed may well have included the great Irish Elk (Giant Deer) – now long extinct – and the reindeer.

Shortly after 6000 B.C., by which time Ireland was an island, Mesolithic hunter-fishers were living in the densely wooded Bann valley, as well as by the Antrim seashore close to inexhaustible supplies of excellent flint. Because of the abundance of their flints at Larne, these people have been called Larnians. We are still uncertain of their origins and know little of their culture; but in the course of the next three thousand years or so we find them spreading coastwise as far west as the mouth of Lough Foyle and as far south as Dalkey near Dublin. Cross-country they seem to have penetrated as far as Lough Gara on the borders of Cos. Roscommon and Sligo. At their camping places on the Leinster coast we find them accompanied by the hunting dog, though the food they ate by the sea was mostly shell fish in rich variety.

Farmers and Tomb-builders

Before 3000, perhaps as early as 3500, Neolithic stock-raisers and grain-growers had joined the hunter-fishers in the heavily forested island. Their pottery and other evidence show that these first Irish farmers belonged to the so-called Western Neolithic cultural complex which, spreading northwards from the mainland, flooded so much of the British Isles in the later fourth and earlier third millennia B.C.

While it is in the south that we might expect to find the earliest signs of the presence of the neolithic farmers, the evidence to date suggests that they reached the north no later than the south. That evidence demonstrates the co-existence of two contrasting neolithic provinces. In the southern two-thirds of the island, south that is of a line from Clifden Bay in the west to Dundalk Bay in the east, the Western Neolithic is represented by a few scattered ritual and settlement sites (the most notable on the light limestone soils about Lough Gur) of varying date, none of which need represent the initial stage of colonization there; likewise by a very few (Late Neolithic?) single-burial graves such as pit-graves (which may be under the floor of the dwelling) and stone cists (which may be under round mounds). The origins and relationships of this southern neolithic complex have yet to be unravelled.

In the northern third of the island is a Western Neolithic province distinguished first and foremost by long-cairn collective-burial chamber tombs of the kind here called court graves (alias court cairns). Remains of some three hundred of these survive, widely distributed, but noteworthy for marked concentrations in the neighbourhood of certain ports; half a dozen outliers have been recorded in south Galway, north Clare, north Tipperary, south Kilkenny, and south-west Waterford. The specialists are still divided as to the homeland of the tomb-builders. Some would bring them from Britain to east Ulster via ports like Carlingford Lough; others visualize them as coming from Atlantic France, by-passing the southern two-thirds of Ireland, and landing on the northern shores of Connacht.

Inside the court-grave province, probably in mid-Ulster, there developed a simpler form of tomb, the portal grave (portal dolmen), whose funerary deposits confirm its architectural kinship with the court grave. These portal graves – about one hundred and fifty survive – spread widely throughout the court-grave province, and south of it as well, particularly down through the eastern counties as far as Co. Waterford. From eastern Ireland they spread to Britain.

A major complication was added to the Irish Neolithic by the arrival (c. 2500 B.C. ?) of a fresh, and itself complex, collective-tomb element, one characterized by round-cairn passage graves. Commonly cruciform, the Irish passage graves include some of Europe's most impressive prehistoric monuments (see Newgrange). Their first builders, who also colonized Anglesey, came up the Irish Sea to enter the country in the Liffey–Boyne area. Thereafter passage graves and their simple-polygon relatives – about one hundred all told – spread mainly north-westwards into the court-grave province as far as Sligo Bay. A scatter of tombs through the eastern half of Ulster as far as Fair Head marks a second substantial penetration of the court-grave province. From west Wicklow isolated outliers trail southwards into Cos. Kilkenny, Tipperary, and Limerick.

The builders of the passage graves favoured hill-top sites, and often grouped their tombs in cemeteries where the clustering of satellites about major monuments is a recurring feature. In each of these respects, as likewise in the matter of their hieratic art, the passage graves present noteworthy contrasts with every other class of Irish chamber tomb.

The passage graves themselves, and their art, suggest that Brittany was the home of the new colonists. At the same time, some of the grave goods point beyond Brittany to Iberia, where the Atlantic passage graves originated. Unlike the court graves and the portal graves, the passage graves continued in use (or were re-used) in the Bronze Age. Indeed, their arrival in Ireland may be said to herald the coming of metallurgists, for, while metal objects have never been recorded in an Irish passage-grave context, the passage-grave builders of southern Iberia were acquainted with copper, and some at least of the Irish tombs were in the neighbourhood of copper deposits. (One of the passage stones at Newgrange seems to have been dressed with a metal claw.) Moreover, Irish passage-grave art includes motifs which recur among the rock-scribings so abundant in the copper-bearing region of south Kerry and south-west Cork. These southern scribings (cup-marks, cup-and-circle devices, concentric circles, "map-patterns", etc.) find their closest counterparts in the Galician region of Portugal and Spain, and suggest the arrival in Munster of metallurgists from that quarter.

In its Irish environment, where it was open to influences from native mesolithic traditions as well as from various quarters overseas, the Neolithic gradually assumed a local complexion and developed into a new amalgam. In their turn, the Neolithic farmers and tomb-builders influenced the ancient hunting and food-collecting societies which, as a result, spread much more widely through the wooded interior of the island, adopting neolithic ideas and equipment, and generating vigorous "secondary" neolithic cultures whose traditions are still discernible in the Bronze Age.

Metallurgists, Traders, and Warriors

At an advanced stage of the Irish Neolithic it was overtaken by the arrival of Beaker Folk, their traces being found in all four provinces. The newcomers may have arrived in two waves, a small one (before 2000 B.C. ?) from Atlantic Europe (Brittany ?), a much stronger one, around or after 2000, from Holland and the Rhine (and Central Europe ?) by way of Britain.

Whereas in Middle Europe and in Britain generally the Beaker Folk are among the representatives of the Single-burial tradition, in Iberia, Britanny, the Channel Islands, and part of Scotland their distinctive beakers are found in collective-burial tombs. In Ireland Beaker ware – both early and late – has been found in eight (of fifteen) excavated collective-burial tombs belonging to the wedge-shaped gallery-grave class (*below*). While this is too small a sample for any valid generalizations, it is noteworthy that, as yet, not one Beaker single-burial has been found in Ireland. Most of the Irish finds of Beaker have, in fact, come from widely scattered habitation sites, much of the pottery in the Lough Gur area occurring in the later levels of sites said to have been occupied without a break from Neolithic to Bronze Age times. Ritual sites, too, have yielded Beaker, sometimes in quantity. Among such sites is an embanked stone circle (*see* Grange *under* Lough Gur) which also yielded neolithic-type and Bronze Age pottery. These and other considerations (such as the occurrence of copper or bronze objects in four of the eight Beaker collective tombs) suggest that in Ireland, as elsewhere, the Beaker Folk had to do with the first exploitation of local metal resources. They may well have been responsible for the "Copper Age" or initial phase of the Irish Bronze Age. Beaker traditions certainly contributed to the Irish Bronze Age proper.

The short-cairn wedge-shaped gallery graves, about two per cent of which have yielded Beaker, are at once the most numerous (some four hundred surviving examples) and most widespread of the Irish chamber tombs. The main distribution lies in the south-west, the west, and the north; but a few tombs occur in east Leinster. Once again we are dealing with tombs whose counterparts may be found in north-west France. The Irish tombs continued to be built and used well into the Bronze Age.

The replacement, from about 2000 B.C. onwards, of edged implements of stone by implements of metal was necessarily long drawn out, and brought with it no cultural revolution, no fundamental change in the basic economy established by the neolithic farmers. As soon as that economy had become capable of supplying the food for prospectors and metal-workers it had been only a question of how soon Ireland's gold and copper resources, exceptionally abundant for North-west Europe, would lure prospectors and exploiters from regions, like South-West and Middle Europe, where the demand for metal was steadily increasing. Inevitably, therefore, when her own Bronze Age proper began (in the seventeenth century?) Ireland quickly became a major focus of metal manufactures and trade.

The Galician rock-scribings of Munster suggest an Iberian contribution to early Irish metallurgy. Some early Irish metal types do the same. Others mirror Beaker connections with Britain, yet others contacts with Middle Europe. Before very long, however, Ireland began to make her own distinctive contributions to Bronze Age Europe and Irish craftsmen-traders were peddling their wares in many lands – Britain, Iberia, France, the Low Countries, Central Germany, the West Baltic area – where their competitors sometimes found it worth their while to imitate Irish products. Prominent in this early Irish export trade were lunulae (crescentic neck ornaments of Portuguese ancestry) and "sun-discs" of sheet gold, halberds (weapons of Middle European ancestry) of copper, and axes of bronze. In exchange Ireland acquired special products (daggers, axes, halberds, amber, beads of glass and of faience) – as well as new techniques – from Portugal, Britain, Central Europe, the Baltic, and the eastern Mediterranean. After a time Irish ininitiative seemingly weakened, and in the fifteenth century or thereabouts the Irish metal industry is markedly influenced by Central European ideas reaching her, in the main, via Southern England.

The brilliant earlier phase of the Irish Bronze Age proper ended in the fourteenth century, to be followed by a couple of centuries during which the skill of the local craftsmen was devoted to the progressive development of established metal types rather than to the devising of new ones, centuries that is, in which the invigorating connections with the mainland seemingly slackened and were feebler than was the case in Southern Britain. Thereafter, however, came (c. 1200–900 B.C.) a truly vigorous and wealthy period which strongly reflects the lively stimulus of the Nordic Bronze Age of Denmark and North-west Germany on Southern England. These centuries are marked by a revitalizing and reorganizing of Irish industry (exemplified by new techniques, by an elaboration of the craftsman's equipment, and – perhaps – by a new trading system); by an abundance of repoussé and bar-gold ornaments (torques, ear-rings, bracelets, pins, etc.) in which Nordic influences are conspicuous, East Mediterranean and West European not insignificant; and by the adoption of new bronze types (notably the socketed axe and – towards the end – the leaf-shaped slashing sword) which thereafter figure prominently in the archaeological record. While the socketed axe, of Central European ancestry, reached Ireland via Britain, the first swords seem to have come from France.

Between the tenth century and the eighth intimate connections with the English Channel area led to a further reorganization of the Irish metal industry. (Accompanying the first signs of manufactures on an unprecedented scale is a significant increase in the number of slashing swords.) Then, in the eighth century, comes the climax of the Irish Late Bronze Age.

The Late Bronze Age, like the ensuing Early Iron Age critical for the emergence of the Gaelic Ireland of history, remains obscure in several important respects, largely owing to the paucity of known settlements and burials and to the fact that the pottery available is not commensurate with the exotic metal types.

One outstanding feature of the Late Bronze Age is the evidence for a technological and industrial revolution that is linked with a much wider range of contacts with the outside world, not so much now with Britain as with West-central Europe, North Germany, South Scandinavia, Iberia, and the Mediterranean. Of particular note are the connections with Denmark, and with Central Europe of the Late Urnfield phase of the Bronze Age and of the initial (Hallstatt) phase of the Celtic Iron Age. It is sometimes assumed that the intrusive metal types imply a succession of invasions; but, in the earlier stages at any rate, the exotic types in question can be explained by trade relations involving, at most, the arrival of smiths belonging to Continental schools.

Thanks to the external stimuli, the output of the Irish metal industry now reached its peak, a peak characterized by the enormous output of the gold and armament industries, by technological innovations (e.g. the making of shields and buckets of sheet bronze), and by an extended range of artificer's tools. At the same time a noteworthy increase in the number and size of hoards buried in the earth by merchants and metal-founders suggests a likelihood that life had become less secure, a suggestion strengthened by some few fortifications (all very late ?) as well as by the increase in the output of weapons of war. Round about 600/500 B.C. a fresh exotic element is revealed by the first of forty-odd bronze swords indicating contacts with the Hallstatt world. These swords join with a few personal ornaments in signalling the approach of the Iron Age.

Despite its recurring phases of close contact with the outside world, the Irish Bronze Age, viewed as a whole, provides little evidence of substantial immigrations after the arrival of the Beaker Folk, for much of the pottery of the earlier phases – Food Vessels and Cinerary Urns – can be traced to local Neolithic-Beaker origins. Thus the Irish Bowl variety of Food Vessel, frequent in the earlier Single-burial graves, represents a fusion of native Neolithic and incoming Beaker traditions. However, the Yorkshire Vase type of Food Vessel points to immigration from Britain via Ulster; as does also the encrusted variety of Cinerary Urns found with so many of the cremations typical of the developed Bronze Age; but these two classes of pottery likewise have their roots in the insular Neolithic. (In its turn the Irish Bowl spread to north and west Britain, where it exerted its own influence.) A small group of late collective tombs, the V-shaped passage graves of the Tramore district whose counterparts are found in the Scilly Isles and in France, points to immigration from Europe.

By and large the later Bronze Age pottery carries on the established traditions. The few innovations assignable to the closing phases are imperfectly understood. Of these the most conspicuous are large urns of Knocknalappa and Flat-rimmed Ware. Knocknalappa urns seem to have been suggested by Late Urnfield sheet-bronze buckets which found their way to both Britain and Ireland in the eighth century and were speedily imitated in insular workshops. The Flat-rimmed Ware is held to belong to a family already present in seventh century Britain and likewise thought to indicate contact with Late Urnfield Europe.

In Ireland, as elsewhere, a noteworthy contrast between the Neolithic and Bronze Ages is provided by the evidence for social grading and for the ever increasing rôle of warfare. In the Neolithic, apart from whatever may be implied by the collective-burial tombs, we have little that points unmistakably to social grading. By contrast, already in the earlier Bronze Age we have occasional Single-burial dagger- and other graves which recall, however feebly, the rich "chieftains' graves" of con-temporary Wessex, Brittany, and Saxony. The Neolithic record includes no weapons primarily devised for combat, no fortifications, no defended homesteads. On the other hand, in the Bronze Age the dagger and the clumsy halberd are early con-spicuous, and are soon joined by the spear, the dirk, and the stabbing sword (rapier), all three evolved from the dagger, itself perhaps initially a personal hunting and eating knife. In time the spear (like the dagger and the arrow not solely a fighting weapon) acquires an added importance which is expressed by new varieties as well as by increasing numbers. In the later Bronze Age the warlike evidence rises to a prehistoric climax revealed by the abundance and quality of the weapons and by a few, very late, fortifications. Among the weapons, spears and slashing swords take pride of place, but with them go shields – sometimes ornate – of sheet-bronze, leather, and wood, shields which are among the signs of contact with Mediterranean and Urnfield Europe. The extravagance of a few spears and the quality of the best shields unite with the abundance of gold ornaments and of bronze buckets and cauldrons to suggest the presence of a warrior aristocracy, precursors of the Iron Age heroes of Emain Macha (*see under* Armagh) and Cruachu (*see* Rathcroghan). For all that, in the Final Bronze Age the farmer was still the prop and support of the whole economic and social fabric, his surplus wheat, barley, cattle, sheep, and pigs supplying the wherewithal for craftsman, merchant, and warrior alike.

As yet we know little about the homesteads of the Neolithic and Earlier Bronze periods. Our clearest picture comes from Munster, particularly from the limestone slopes about Lough Gur. There farmers, from Neolithic into Bronze Age times, and herdsmen lived on the same sites in isolated dwellings of several kinds, rect-angular, round, and irregular. While the wall footings might be of stone, the walls themselves seem always to have been of timber or wattle or other organic material. One rectangular house was an aisled, timber-post structure of a kind known also in Devon and the Isle of Man. Some of the Lough Gur houses were enclosed by stone-kerbed ring walls. In Carrigillihy, near Glandore, an oval dry-masonry hut stood in a small oval enclosure bounded by a massive wall of dry masonry; the pottery resembled early Bronze Age ware found at Lough Gur. In Rathjordan, Lough Gur, and on the shore of Lough Gara (near Boyle) small circular crannógs – "artificial islands" – and lake-shore house-sites have been discovered. Neolithic and earlier Bronze Age lake-dwellings have also been found in Ulster; but it is uncertain if these were crannógs in the accepted meaning of the term. At a few places in Ulster crannógs and waterside settlements (little groups of circular timber-post huts, etc.) belonging to users of the Cinerary Urn have recently been discovered.

The dwellings of the later Bronze Age also included crannógs and other waterside settlements. In Ballinderry, Co. Offaly, remains were found of a roomy rectangular structure supported by a substantial framework of excellent joinery. A crannóg in Lough Gara is thought to have had about ten small circular huts, each with a central hearth.

Undefended homesteads leave little above ground to excite the imagination of the layman, to whom funerary and ritual monuments normally make a more immediate appeal. A few classes of such Neolithic and Bronze Age monuments have already been mentioned. A few others merit passing reference, e.g. derivative and degenerate chamber tombs, non-chambered cairns and tumuli, ritual circles, stone alignments, and standing stones (pillarstones).

The derivative and degenerate tombs include such impressive monuments as those of Sess Kilgreen and Knockmany near Clogher, tombs whose hieratic art links them with the passage graves.

The non-chambered mounds, of several classes, vary considerably in scale. Some cover single burials on the ground; others cover single burials in short cists or in pits; yet others are cemetery mounds containing single-burial graves of various kinds. (Flat cemeteries too are known, particularly in the mature Bronze Age.) While the cemetery cairn and tumulus seem to be confined to the Bronze Age, the low ring-barrow appears to be represented in all periods from the Neolithic onwards. As the Bronze Age advanced, whatever the type of funerary monument in use, cremation became the prevailing burial rite.

Like the funerary monuments, the ritual circles – "open air temples" – found in all four Provinces include some impressive monuments, though nothing comparable to the greater circles of Britain. Some are circles of stones (pillarstones or boulders), others are earthen rings; yet others are circles of earth and stones. Some have an external fosse, some an internal one; yet others have no fosse. A few have a central chamber tomb, or cairn, or tumulus, or other grave; others have a central stone which may mark a grave; yet others have no visible central feature of any kind. Some stone circles have stone outliers; some have tangent or other alignments. At Beaghmore near Cookstown stone circles combine with alignments and small cairns in a complex covering several acres. In parts of Cork and Kerry there are numerous small stone circles with a single recumbent stone; they may have outliers. Very few Irish circles have been excavated; fewer still have yielded satisfactory dating evidence. The great circle in Grange, Lough Gur, yielded Neolithic as well as Beaker and Food Vessel sherds. Drombeg recumbent-stone circle near Glandore enclosed a central dedicatory pit-burial with a Bronze Age type of urn. Earthen circles, including the kind known as "henges" in Britain, are also found in Ireland. None have been examined.

Little as we know about the Irish ritual circles, we know even less about the pillarstones and alignments. Some pillarstones mark Bronze Age graves, others had an uncertain cult significance. Comparable monuments, but with ogham inscriptions or Christian symbols, or both, were still being erected in protohistoric and early historic times. Ireland has nothing which compares with the concentrations of alignments found in Brittany or on Dartmoor, or with the famous English "avenues" of standing stones.

Kings and Heroes

Gaelic epic, which mirrors the Ireland of the closing centuries of the prehistoric Iron Age, shows us a country of chariot-riding kings and heroes whose aristocratic culture displays many of the features reported in Classical accounts of the Continental Celts. The archaeological evidence, such as it is, of the Irish Iron Age proper, is consistent with the testimony of the Heroic tales.

Although the Irish Iron Age lasted several centuries – perhaps from the third century B.C. to the firm establishment of Christianity, say about 500 A.D. – it is but meagrely represented in the archaeological record. Once again we are hampered by the paucity of known dwelling places and burials. Once again there is no unambiguous evidence of significant immigration.

Archaeologically speaking, the outstanding feature of the period is the highly sophisticated abstract ornament applied to fine metalwork and to a few stone carvings. This ornament is in the La Tène style characteristic of the specifically Celtic phase of the European Iron Age. That phase opened on the Middle Rhine in the later fifth century B.C. By the third century La Tène immigrants were beginning the first of a succession of movements into Britain, and there are signs of Irish contacts with several phases of their culture.

Some of the La Tène manifestations in Ireland, notably the decorated cult-stones of Turoe (see under Loughrea), Castlestrange (see under Athleague), Killycluggin (see under Ballyconnell), and Mullaghmast (now in the National Museum), have no counterpart in Britain and may represent direct connections between Ireland and Europe – conceivably only Continental craftsmen working for native clients. A few stray metal finds also suggest possible Continental contacts of one kind or another.

On the other hand, a small series of ornate sword scabbards is generally taken to imply an influx of warriors from northern Britain into Ulster in the later first century B.C. (Details of the Turoe stone itself could also be interpreted as reflecting first century links with Britain.) Some argue, however, that the earliest La Tène metalwork in Ulster represents the same third century movement from Europe as does the first insular style of La Tène work in Britain. However they originated, the scabbards combine with other parade equipment, including trappings for pairs of ponies, to indicate the presence of chariot-riding warriors in Ireland.

One of the many striking contrasts between the British Iron Age and the Irish is presented by the abundance of hill forts in Britain and their rarity in Ireland. Few as are the Irish forts – less than a couple of dozen all told – we still know little factual about them. One of them is the Emain Macha of Irish epic, a royal seat which may still have been flourishing as late as the fifth century A.D. (see Navan Fort under Armagh). Others (see Tara, Greenan Elly under Derry, and Dún Ailinne under Kilcullen) are associated with early historic dynasties.

The so-called ringfort, the classic farmstead of early Irish history, was already known in the prehistoric Iron Age. Normally the visible remains consist of a bank set inside its quarry ditch and enclosing a circular farmyard (about one hundred feet in diamater) in which had stood dwelling house and outhouses; on rocky terrains the bank of earth, or of earth and stones, was of necessity replaced by a rampart of dry masonry. Only a very small percentage of "ringforts", those with strong or multiple ramparts, deserves the name "fort".

The crannóg too was known in the Irish Iron Age, but we are still without particulars of the excavated examples.

In the course of the centuries Irish traditions and the Irish environment combined with external stimuli to modify and attenuate the La Tène elements in the later Iron Age material, stimuli from abroad which operated through raiding and trading in the Roman provinces and, towards the end, through Gaelic colonies in Wales and in Scotland. By the close of the Iron Age the Gaelic-speaking nation of early history had evolved, a nation needing only the inspiration of Christianity to play an important rôle in Dark Age Europe, a nation with a distinctive civilization that is all the more fascinating because it is archaic in so many respects. Major roots of that civilization lie in the Celtic Iron Age, whence its distinctive social and political institutions, its art, its epic literature, derive. Its patriarchal warrior aristocracy, only finally overthrown by the Tudors, preserved to the last something of the heroes of Emain and Cruachu. Its poets, maintained to the end by that aristocracy, were in a real sense the heirs of the druides, vates, and bardi of La Tène Europe.

Gaelic Ireland, *c.* 500-1165

"Island of Kings"

The Romans omitted Ireland from their conquests. No Germanic migrants violated her shores until the Viking age. Gaelic Ireland, therefore, presents us with the unique example of an archaic, Iron Age, Celtic society operating unchanged – save in so far as it has been affected by Christianity – in the light of history. Therein lies much of its fascination.

The primary aggregate of Gaelic society was the *túath*, a tiny pastoral and agricultural community ruled by a king (*rí*). The precise number of *túatha* at any particular stage seems impossible now to determine, but most of the two-hundred-odd "baronies" still shown on the Ordnance Survey sheets represent ancient *túatha*.

The *túatha* tended to cluster together in "over-kingdoms" acknowledging the superiority of the king of the dominant *túath*. (Many of the ecclesiastical dioceses organized in the twelfth century represent over-kingdoms of that time.) The over-kingdoms in turn grouped together in major federations. Heroic literature, which mirrors the conditions obtaining towards the close of the prehistoric Iron Age, shows us five such major federations, "the Five Fifths of Ireland", viz. Ulaid (whence "Ulster") in the north, Mide (whence "Meath") in the eastern midlands, La(i)gin (whence "Leinster") in the south-east, Mumha (Mumhain, whence "Munster") in the south, and Connachta (whence "Connacht", "Connaught") in the west.

"The Field of Royal Niall"

When – in the later sixth century – the fogs obscuring the earlier historic centuries begin to clear, two of the "Fifths" have undergone major changes. The Midlands have been parcelled out among the southern branches of a dynastic stock called Uí Néill ("The Descendants of Niall") after Niall Nine-Hostager who died about 427 (?). The Ulster federation has been reduced to little more than the area of the three small dioceses which today represent its principal historic kingdoms: the diocese of Down representing Dál Fiatach, or Ulster proper; the diocese of Dromore representing Uí Echach; the diocese of Connor representing Dál nAraidi and Dál Riada. (Dál Riada, in north Antrim, has a particular interest in that its ruling stocks had overflowed in the fifth century into Scotland, much of which thereafter belongs to the Gaelic world.) The rest of the North, from the Bann westwards to the Atlantic, is now in the hands of the northern branches of the Uí Néill and their tributary Airgíalla (Oirghialla, whence "Oriel", "Uriel") kinsfolk, Ulster's Heroic Age capital, Emain Macha (*see* Navan Fort *under* Armagh) having been destroyed by these conquerors from the Midlands in the previous century (*c.* 450 ?). Together with the Airgíalla, the Southern and Northern Uí Néill constitute a new "Fifth" which covers the Midlands as well as the North, a "Fifth" which is the largest and most powerful federation in the country. The acknowledged head of this federation bears the title King of Tara (*see* Tara) and is pre-eminent among the over-kings.

Though a St Adomnán (*see* Raphoe), writing in the seventh century, can describe a sixth-century King of Tara as "ruler of all Ireland consecrated by the authority of God" (*see* Rathmore *under* Antrim), the King of Tara in fact is not even titular King of Ireland. He may, it is true, overawe Connacht and Leinster, but he is accorded no primacy by the jurists. Neither is his superiority recognized by the second-greatest federation Munster, whose over-king, the King of Cashel is also the head of a widely distributed royal stock, the Eóghanacht. (Unlike the Uí Néill, the Eóghanacht have a strong sense of dynastic solidarity, and succession to their over-kingship is remarkably peaceful.)

The notion of a supreme King of Ireland long remained foreign to the Gaelic mind, to which the Church could impart no political message, no Roman ideas of order and unity. (Rather was it Gaelic society which remoulded the organization of the Church to its own image.) This is something which admits of no single, simple explanation. In addition to the weight of traditions constantly expounded by jurist and poet, we have to reckon with the operation of the law of succession which, at one and the same time, fragmented the Uí Néill, incited faction among them, and caused the Kingship of Tara to oscillate between the strategic "heart-land" of Meath and the remote, marginal domains of the Northern Uí Néill. Nor must we overlook the effects on a relatively prosperous and relatively civilized country of centuries of immunity from external aggression. It is only when that immunity has ceased that the idea of a national monarchy, prompted perhaps by the example of the Emperor Charlemagne (with whose court Ireland was in contact), is seen in active operation.

Gaelic Society

For the ordinary everyday purposes of life it was the *túatha*, not the over-kingdoms or the major federations, which mattered. Each *túath* was an aristocratic hierarchical community. As its head stood the king, president of the public assembly of freemen and commander of the armed hosting of freemen. In pagan times he had been a sacred personage of divine ancestry, and at his inauguration had been mystically wedded to the local goddess by ancient fertility rites. In modified form such rites survived as long as traditional Gaelic kingship survived at all.

Below the king were stratified grades of noblemen. Every nobleman was the vassal (*céle*, companion) of the king, or of some other social superior, who was his lord (*flaith*) and protector. His own rank was determined by the amount of his property, or the number of his vassals, or his function in society, as well as by his birth. Together, the royal and noble grades formed the warrior aristocracy of the *túath*; the aristocracy whose pedigrees were preserved by the genealogists and on whose patronage the literati and superior craftsmen depended, the aristocracy whose final defeat and dispersal in the seventeenth century cleared the way for the anglicization of the island.

Supporting the social superstructure were the free commoners, lesser landowners who tilled the soil and raised livestock, paid food-rent to the king, had a voice in the public assembly of the *túath*, served with the armed hosting, and were normally vassals of some nobleman or other.

Intercalated between the free commoners and the nobles, but associated more closely with the latter, were "the men of art" (*áes dána*), jurists, poets, leeches, superior craftsmen, historians, harpers, clerics, Latin scholars, in a word all whose superior knowledge or skill had raised them above their birth. At the foot of the social scale were various servile and semi-servile classes, including tenants-at-will, serfs bound to the soil, and slaves.

Save where they had been secured to him by formal treaty, the freeman, whether noble or commoner, had no legal rights outside the bounds of his ancestral *túath*. Within the *túath* his rights came to him, not as an individual, but as a member of a blood-group called *fine* (family, legal kin, friends) which was the Gaelic counterpart of the Indo-European "great family". At the head of the *fine* was the patriarchal *áige fine*, Gaelic counterpart of the Roman *paterfamilias*. In a society where the administration of justice was not a function of the "state", a prime function of the blood-group was to protect and avenge its members. With the development of *célsine* (*see below*) this function of the *fine* tended to become obsolete. For this and other reasons the rigid organization of the *fine* withered gradually away. Previously a five-generation group, the *fine* has already been reduced to the four-generation *derb-fine* ("certain family") in the oldest stratum of customary law, where it is the normal unit for all major legal purposes such as inheritance, the sharing of liabilities, and the pursuit of blood-feuds to protect its members; it is also the ultimate land-owning unit, with a contingent interest in the ancestral real property of all its members. By the middle of the eighth century the *derb-fine* has been replaced for most purposes by the three-generation *gel-fine* ("clear family"). By the second half of the ninth century the jurists themselves no longer understand the original organization of the *fine*.

The normal freeman owned his own private parcel of land. This he would have inherited from his father, and would in due course leave to his sons, to be divided equally among them. His *fine*, however, had a contingent interest in his ancestral land, so that he could not alienate it, or burden it with liabilities, without the consent of the adult members. To his daughters he could leave only chattels and land acquired otherwise than by inheritance.

Kingship, like real property, ultimately belonged to the *fine*. Unlike property, it could not be divided. The king therefore had to be chosen – how precisely we know not – from the "sacred" royal stock, in practice from the *derb-fine* of a previous ruler. The method of choice operated so as to favour succession through collaterals rather than in the direct line. This occasioned endless strife and, in the case of the Kingship of Tara, hindered the emergence of a national monarchy. On the other hand, invaders, when they came, found it next to impossible to exterminate the ramified dynasties that opposed them.

While the Gaelic polity engendered strife and disorder, the pre-Viking warfare was seldom serious, for it was limited, at all levels, by ritual, taboo, and legal convention, which combined to maintain the established political and social structure: warriors grounded their arms once their king had fallen; the victor did not normally dethrone the "sacred" dynasty of the vanquished, or annex even part of its territory; "sanctuaries" immune from attack – monastic settlements and the lands of the *áes dána* – were numerous; legal enactments safeguarded women, clerics, and children.

Célsine: Gaelic "Feudalism"

Every freeman was normally the *céle* (companion, client, vassal) of a social superior who was his *flaith* (lord). Initially the contract between lord and vassal had been strictly personal, contractual, and terminable; it could, moreover, be impugned by the vassal's *fine*. In time, however, the relationship tended to become hereditary. The essence of the contract was the advancing of a fief (normally of livestock, but occasionally of land) by the lord to the vassal. The latter became thereby the lord's debtor, bound to pay him interest, and his "companion", bound to do him homage, to render him personal services such as accompanying him to war and on public occasions, and to provide him with one night's *cóe* or entertainment (the "coshering" so sharply denounced by the English) in the period between New Year's Day and Shrove. On the other hand, the lord became the vassal's protector, bound to support him in all his causes.

The relationship is clearly but the Gaelic version of that ancient system of the commendation of the weak to the protection of the strong which spread far and wide in late Roman and post-Roman Europe to culminate in the fully feudal relationship of lord and vassal. In Gaelic Ireland the institution and development of such a relationship point, not only to the absence of state justice, but also to the decay of tribal institutions, in particular to the decay of the *fine* as the protector and avenger of its members.

Gaelic Literati

Classical accounts of the Continental Celts name the *druidis, vatis,* and *bardus* (druid, seer, and bard) as the principal exponents of Celtic oral tradition and litera- ture. While all three were concerned with the poetic art, the druid's primary concern was with religion, the seer's with prophecy and divination, the bard's with the making of poems praising his patrons "as regards birth, bravery, and wealth".

All three survive in early Gaelic Ireland, though time and circumstance have altered their relative importance and their social functions. The druid (*druí*) is now but an easily discomfited magician, doomed to disappear from the scene. The bard (*bárd*) retains his ancient office, but acts also as the chanter of compositions by the seer, who is himself not above adapting the bard's "crooked lays" to his own pur- poses. (Between the thirteenth and seventeenth centuries the bard's influence as a maker of praise-poems exerts a tremendous influence on the struggle for Gaelic survival and provokes the bitter hostility of the foreigner.) The seer (*fili*; less usually *fáith=vatis*) has become the lord of the learned and literary world. Originally a diviner and weaver of spells, he is now professional story-teller, antiquary, jurist, and court poet. As story-teller he is a weaver of new tales as well as master of the traditional canon. As jurist he is at once assessor, arbitrator, and custodian-teacher of the corpus of customary law. As antiquary (*senchaid*) he is expert in *senchas,* which comprises the history, topographical lore, and antiquities of the Gael. As court poet he is a maker of didactic and mantic verse recounting the pedigrees and achievements of his patrons and their ancestors. He is also an expert in Irish grammar, in "etymology", in ogham, and in the secret language of his order. A heathen odour still clings to his office, and all fear his satire, not only for the loss of face occasioned by its recital throughout all the Gaelic lands, but also for the blisters it can raise on the victim's very countenance, or the death it may bring.

The Coming of Christianity

By the opening of the historic period Ireland is substantially Christian, the first country outside the Roman world to be won for the new faith; but the beginnings of Irish Christianity are hidden from us. The first recorded missionary, Palladius, had been sent from Rome in 431 as bishop "to the Irish believers in Christ". By that time much of the South and East may already have been Christianized by emigrants returning from Britain, as well as by British missionaries. Of the work of Palladius himself, and of the missionaries who, presumably, had preceded him, we know nothing, for the fame of all has been eclipsed by that of Bishop Patrick, a Romanized British Celt who, taken to Ireland as a youthful slave, had dedicated his adult life to the conversion of his captors. Patrick's mission is usually dated to the period 432–61, but these dates are still the subject of controversy, as is also the field of Patrick's labours. According to ancient tradition Patrick established his principal church at Armagh, close to Emain Macha, the capital of the prehistoric Fifth of the Ulaid.

Other missionary bishops were: Secundinus (Sechnall) of Dunshaughlin (Domh- nach Sechnaill) near Tara, who died in 447/8; Auxilius of Killossy (Cell Auxli, Cell Aussaili) near the Leinster royal seat at Naas, who died in 459/60; Iserninus of Old Kilcullen (near the Leinster royal hill-fort called Dún Ailinne) and of Aghade (near Rathvilly, another Leinster royal seat), who died in 468.

The coming of Christianity was of tremendous cultural consequence. The remote, peripheral, island was reintegrated into the West European fabric. The artistic repertoire was enlarged with new media and enriched with new motifs and new techniques that stimulated the last, and finest, flowering of insular Celtic art. To the Church Ireland owes her first true architecture, to the Church her introduction to the treasury of Mediterranean thought and letters, to the Church that early written literature in the Gaelic vernacular which is one of the boasts of her heritage.

"Island of Saints" – Primitive Monasticism

The expansion of the heathen Germanic nations, in particular their conquests in Britain and Gaul, had severed Ireland's connexions with Latin Europe and left the Irish mission-field to the churches of Celtic Britain. It was kindred British, not alien Roman, influences which were decisive in shaping the Irish ecclesiastical structure, in fitting it to the inchoate Gaelic polity. In their isolation the insular churches, set in closely related social and cultural environments, inevitably developed Celtic eccentricities of organization, discipline, and practice. Some ecclesiastical institutions atrophied, others became distorted, yet others acquired an exaggerated significance. When, in the seventh and eighth centuries, the Irish Church emerges into daylight, we find that a wave of monasticism has well-nigh obliterated all traces of the primitive episcopal framework, and that the typical focus of regional jurisdiction is no longer the episcopal see, but the monastery ruled by a priest-abbot. (There are bishops, but their office is now purely sacramental.) In addition, the Irish Church adheres to an outmoded method of computing the date of Easter, and to an outmoded tonsure. Curiously enough, it is these minor eccentricities of the computus and the tonsure which rouse the ire of the orthodox abroad.

The phenomenal growth of Irish monasticism in the sixth and seventh centuries was primarily due to the influence of the great British saints, some of whom founded monasteries in Ireland and attracted Irish disciples to Wales, whence they returned home to found new monasteries themselves. Foremost among such Irish founders were Éanna ("Enda") of Killeany in Aran, who died about 530, and Finnian of Clonard, "Tutor of the Saints of Ireland", who died in 549. Other celebrated founders were: Colum (Columba) of Derry and Iona best known as Columcille, Comgall of Bangor, Finnian of Moville, Colum (Columba) of Terryglass, Ciarán of Clonmacnois, Ciarán of Seir, Kevin of Glendalough, Brendan The Navigator of Clonfert, Mo-Ling of Timolin, and Finnbárr of Cork. Three all-Ireland women saints were Brigid of Kildare, Íde of Kileedy, and Samthann of Clonbroney. Men and women such as these fired the imagination of thousands and inspired them to follow in their footsteps, so that in a brief space the Gaelic lands were covered with hundreds of monastic and anchoritic foundations. Houses – however widely dispersed – which revered a common founder tended to form leagues under a supreme abbot, leagues to which the name *paruchia* (Ir. *fairche*) was transferred from the moribund dioceses. The greater the prestige of the founder, the greater the prestige of his *paruchia*. The fame of Columcille could, for a time, overshadow that of Patrick, the hegemony of Iona eclipse that of Armagh.

"Exiles for Christ"

For the Gaelic saints, passionately attached to home and kindred, to go into exile "for the love of Christ" was to make the supreme sacrifice, to suffer martyrdom. And so we find them sailing away in their frail boats to the Orkneys, to the Faroes, and even to distant uninhabited Iceland, as well as to Britain, France, the Germanies, and Italy. The best known names in the countless roll of these "exiles for Christ" are those of Columcille (Columba) of Iona, Colmán (Columbanus) of Bangor, Luxeuil, and Bobbio, Aidan of Lindisfarne, Fursa of Cnoberesburgh and Peronne, Gall (Gallus) of St Gallen, Fergal ("Vergilius") of Aghaboe and Salzburg, and Cilian (Kilian) of Würzburg.

Columcille left his beloved Ireland in 563 "to make a pilgrimage for Christ" in

Irish Scotland (Dál Riada), where he settled on the barren, but strategic, island of Iona. His monastery there became a base for the conversion of Pictland and of Northumbria, a prop of the Gaelic monarchy in Scotland, and a clearing-house through which important cultural and artistic influences passed – in both directions – between Ireland and England. (Scottish Dál Riada was as Irish a kingdom as any in Ireland, Iona as Irish a monastery as, say, Clonmacnois.)

About 635 King Oswiu of Northumbria applied to Iona for missionaries, Iona sent him Aidan, a monk-bishop who fixed his see on the island of Lindisfarne. Before his death (651) Aidan saw Christianity firmly established north of the Humber. From Northumbria the Iona mission spread into Mercia and to the Middle Angles, even into Sussex and Essex. Contacts with representatives of the Augustinian mission to England inevitably led to wranglings about tonsures and the date of Easter. The issue was brought to a head in 663 at the Synod of Whitby, where the intransigence of the Iona party led to the withdrawal of Aidan's successor, Bishop Colman of Lindisfarne, together with the more stubborn of his Irish and English disciples (see Mayo), from Northumbria. Their departure marked the end of Ireland's spiritual hegemony in the northern half of England. It did not put an end to Irish missionary activities in England, or to Irish influence in non-controversial spheres.

On the European mainland the great Irish name is that of the Colmán, alias Columbanus, who set out from Bangor with the traditional company of twelve disciples in 590. In Burgundy he founded monasteries at Annegray, Luxeuil, and Fontaine. Expelled after twenty years by an offended king, he eventually made his way to Bregenz on Lake Constance, and there preached the Gospel to the heathen Alemanni. From Bregenz, too, he was driven away and, in 614, crossed over the Alps to Bobbio. There he founded his last monastery and there he died the following year. Irish influence and Irish connexions remained potent at Bobbio throughout the seventh and eighth centuries, and occasional Irish contacts persisted down to the eleventh.

Columbanus revived religion wherever he went. He gave a special impetus and direction to European monasticism and was responsible for the European adoption of the practice of private and frequent confession. His letters and poems reflect the relatively high quality of Latin studies in the Ireland of his day.

St Fursa, whose celebrated Visions of Heaven and Hell were to influence medieval European literature, spent the earlier part of his exile at Cnoberesburgh (Burgh Castle, Suffolk). About 640/44 he passed over to France, where his brothers (Ultán and Foíllán) founded famous monasteries at Péronne ("Péronne of the Irish"), Lagny-sur-Marne, Nivelles, and Fosse.

Other Irish exiles made their way to the heathen and semi-heathen lands beyond the Rhine: Thuringia, Franconia, Swabia, Bavaria, and Carinthia. Here the best-known Irish names are those of St Cilian of Würzburg and St Fergal of Salzburg. Cilian was martyred with two Irish companions in 689. Fergal, who had been abbot of Aghaboe, appears about 743 at the court of Pippin the Short, whence he was sent to Salzburg, where he became abbot of St Peter's. St Boniface, English apostle of Germany, sought to have him condemned as a heretic, but he became bishop of Salzburg and ruled the diocese for more than forty years.

The Viking onslaught (p. 28) gave a fresh impetus to the dispersion of Irish monks and to the multiplication of Irish monasteries and hospices in Europe. Now, however, in the ninth and tenth centuries, the typical Irish exile is the Latin scholar rather than the ascetic or the missionary; Clemens Scottus ("The Irishman"), Latin scholar and Alcuin's successor as head of Charlemagne's celebrated palace school; Dícuil, grammarian, geographer, astronomer, and teacher in the palace school; Sedulius Scottus, a Leinster scholar active between 848 and 858 at Liège, Metz, and Cologne, where he proved himself an outstanding Ciceronian and an accomplished maker of gay drinking songs; Johannes Scottus (Eriugena), intellectual giant of his age, who appears at the court of Charles the Bald in 845.

"Island of Scholars" – Monastic Culture

The Irish monasteries quickly won international renown for their scholarship, so that the descriptions "Irishman" (*Scottus*) and "scholar" came to be synonymous, and that princes, nobles, prelates, priests, and monks flocked from overseas for training in the several branches of Christian learning as well as in the religious life. Students from Anglo-Saxon England were particularly numerous, among them several whose names were to become famous in English history.

The texts and treatises studied being in Latin, a good grounding in that language was a primary requirement. The study of Latin awakened an interest in profane Latin literature, including the writings of Cicero, Horace, and Virgil, an interest so fruitful that some of the Irish scholars have to be numbered among the foremost Classical scholars of their time, while others rank among the finest Latin poets of the Carolingian age. The true genius of that age was John The Irishman (Johannes Scottus, alias Johannes Eriugena), poet, grammarian, philosopher, and theologian; a superb Latinist, an excellent Greek scholar, and a master dialectician. The attainments of such men are fully appreciated only when we recall that Ireland, unlike Britain and France, had never formed part of the Roman Empire and thus had no tradition of Latin culture.

A unique feature of the Latin culture of the Irish monasteries was the fact that it proved in no way inimical to the development of a written literature in the Gaelic vernacular. On the contrary, it was monks who adapted the Latin alphabet and Latin verse-forms to Gaelic requirements and who created the vernacular written literature. St Columcille was a famous protector of the *filí*, and an elegy on him by one of them, Dallán Forgaill, is the oldest securely dated (597) Irish poem we have. St Colmán of Cloyne was himself the author of some of the oldest surviving examples of the new verse. That lovely ancient tale, *The Voyage of Bran*, was first committed to writing in the monastery of Bangor. The *céle Dé* movement (p. 27) of the eighth and ninth centuries has left us a body of personal lyrics, intimate nature poems which still delight. Clonmacnois and Terryglass have left us the oldest of our collections of secular tales. Not until the introduction of Continental Rules and Orders in the twelfth century did the written canon – as we may call it – of Gaelic secular lore finally pass into the guardianship of the famous secular families who conserved it throughout the rest of the Middle Ages. And even they conserved that canon as it had been arranged in the monastic codices.

The arts, too, owed much to the monasteries. Most of the finest metalwork of the period, exemplified by such masterpieces as the Ardagh Chalice (National Museum, Dublin), was produced for them and, like the other manifestations of ecclesiastical art, reflects their foreign connexions. Metalwork was an ancient, pre-Christian craft. So, too, was the stone-carving exemplified by gravestones, cross-slabs, and High Crosses (*below*). Both these crafts were probably practised in monastic ateliers; proof, however, is lacking. Book-painting, on the other hand, was an entirely new, and essentially monastic, art; and here there is no doubt about who produced it. The supreme masterpiece is the *Book of Kells* (Trinity College, Dublin).

The early monastery differed markedly from the highly organized monastery, with buildings of well-developed architecture, which was diffused throughout middle and western Europe from Carolingian times onwards. In essence it was but an adaptation to monastic purposes of the larger ringfort, and its primitive character accorded well with the ascetic temper of the early Irish Church: an enclosure ringed by one or more ramparts of earth or stone; within it one or more tiny churches or oratories, of the simplest form and, at first, of timber wherever possible; a series of rude huts for the monks; similar structures for kitchen and refectory, as also for library, workshops, and school, where such existed; a series of crosses and cross-pillars; a cemetery with gravestones which might be decorated with delightful cross-patterns and whose inscriptions are normally in Irish, not Latin; from the tenth century onwards a lofty, free-standing, conical-roofed, circular belfry (Round Tower) whose impregnable strength and remote doorway made it also a convenient refuge when danger threatened. In time the timber churches were translated into stone, to give small, ill-lit, and usually single-chamber, buildings whose remains are normally devoid of ornament. However, a seventh century description of the church at Kildare, with its glowing shrines, its painted pictures, and its hangings, reminds that such remains are but fleshless skeletons of the dead. (So, too, for all their elaboration of ornament, are the remains of the Romanesque churches associated with the twelfth century reformation.)

Some monastic sites are noteworthy for their High Crosses, great freestanding crosses of stone whose elaborate carvings were doubtless picked out in colour. An early group, exemplified at Kilclispeen near Carrick-on-Suir, is characterized by predominantly abstract, overall ornament. A second group, nobly represented at Monasterboice, dates from the ninth or tenth centuries and may be linked with the *céle Dé* movement (*below*); it is characterized by panelled figurations of Scriptural themes.

Monastic Decay; The *céle Dé* Movement

The missions abroad had quickly drawn attention to the eccentricities of the early monastic churches, and the Easter Controversy had led to the eclipse of Iona at the synod of Whitby and to the withdrawal of Colmán of Lindisfarne from the English mission. The same controversy had involved Colmán of Luxeuil with the bishops of Burgundy. The irony of the situation was that the two namesakes had been defending positions already being abandoned at home.

Of greater moment than a wrongly calculated Easter, or an outlandish tonsure, were the evils which sprang from the Gaelic social system, and from the growth of the monasteries in privilege, wealth, and power. Some of the greater monasteries, notably those with schools, scriptoria, and ateliers, gradually grew into town-like centres inhabited by craftsmen, farmworkers, lay-tenants, and the like; that is to say, developed into corporations whose economic and political significance was bound to attract the attention of secular potentates. And always in the background was the concept of the continuing interest of the founder's *fine* in the headship of a monastery, of the continuing interest of the patron's *fine* in its landed property. Small wonder if the headship of the monasteries tended to become hereditary and to fall into the hands of lay members of the ruling stocks.

While the decay of primitive simplicity and piety was enormously aggravated by the Viking wars (p. 28), it was not caused by them. In the later eighth century, well before the first recorded Viking raids, monastic offices were already passing from father to son, and monasteries were already engaging in battle, even with other monasteries, to safeguard their material interests.

Reaction to such evils found expression in the *céle Dé* ("culdee") movement, which came to the fore in the eighth and ninth centuries, a movement characterized by anchoritic asceticism, puritanical idealism, and strict supervision by spiritual superiors. With these were combined choral duties and care of the poor, of the sick, and of travellers. The Viking wars arrested the natural development of the movement and, by the time they had subsided, few culdee houses survived. In its heyday, the movement had been of great significance for art and literature, and has left as its memorials the great High Crosses of the ninth and tenth centuries and a remarkable body of personal lyrics (nature poems).

Norse Pirates and Traders

Ireland's freedom from serious foreign aggression ended in 795 with a Viking raid on Lambay Island. Two centuries of devastation and destruction followed.

At the outset the heathen ravagers came in small independent bands, and confined their "tip-and-run" forays to the seaboard. The attack entered on a more serious phase with the arrival, in 837, of a large fleet on the Boyne and Liffey, which became bases for plundering expeditions deep into the heart of the country. That year, too, a great Viking, Thorgestr ("Turgesius"), assumed the leadership of the scattered raiding parties. Even more ominous, Vikings set up a semi-permanent camp near the mouth of the Liffey. Two years later, Thorgestr brought a fleet to Lough Neagh and ravaged the North. In 841 he occupied Armagh, by then the ecclesiastical capital of Ireland. That same year, the Viking camp by the Liffey became a permanent settlement, soon to grow into the seaport town of Dublin. In 844 Thorgestr established himself on Lough Ree, from which he wasted Meath and Connacht. The great monasteries of Inis Cealtra, Lorrha, Terryglass, Clonfert, and Clonmacnois, all were pillaged, Thorgestr's wife, Ota, pronouncing pagan oracles from the principal altar at Clonmacnois. The following year, Melaghlin I (Máel-Shechlainn, "Malachy") of Meath captured Thorgestr and drowned him.

In 847, Melaghlin succeeded to the kingship of Tara. His reign (847–62) was to prove a landmark in Irish history. About this time, Scandinavian activity in both Britain and Ireland was rising to a climax. Worse, Melaghlin found himself faced more than once with alliance between Gaelic king and Norse plunderer, even with alliances between Uí Néill rivals and the Norse. He proved himself the outstanding Irish king of the century, and raised the Uí Néill kingship of Tara to its greatest height, compelling Munster in 859 to concur in the transfer of the important kingdom of Ossory to the hegemony of Meath and, of greater moment still, to acknowledge for the first time the supremacy of a king of Tara (*see* Rahugh *under* Tullamore). The next year Munster forces marched alongside those of Connacht, Leinster, and Meath in Melaghlin's campaign against rebellious Tír Eóghain.

By this time, Dublin was on the way to finding a place in Gaelic polity, and alliance – often by marriage – with the heathen was becoming a normal feature of the policy of the Gaelic kings. On the Norse side, trade was assuming an ever increasing importance, though raiding and plundering still took place as opportunity offered. The Battle of Killineer (near Drogheda) in 868 marks a critical stage in the Norse-Irish struggle, as well as exemplifying the new Norse rôle in Irish affairs. Here, Melaghlin's successor, Áedh Finnliath of Tír Eóghain (862–79), who himself had not scrupled to join with Norse Dublin against Melaghlin, was confronted with a Leinster-Dublin-East Meath combination. He won the day, and was able to follow up his success by destroying for ever the Scandinavian strongholds in the North. Nevertheless, the disruption of the old order was now far advanced, and in 873, 876, 878, and 879 Áedh was unable to convene Aonach Tailteann (*see* Teltown *under* Donaghpatrick). Thereafter, the great annual assembly of the Uí Néill federation lapsed repeatedly.

The forty years after 876 were marked by a comparative lull in major Norse activity, a fresh phase of which opened with the arrival (914, 915) of fleets which set up a new raiding base at Waterford. In 919 came the disastrous Battle of Dublin, where the King of Tara (Niall Glúndub, eponymous successor of the O Neills of Tír Eóghain) was slain. This was followed by widespread campaigns of plundering and wasting based on new settlements (Limerick, Cork, and Wexford) as well as on old. Luckily for Ireland, about this time (918–54) the Dublin Norse were dissipating their strength in efforts to get control of the Scandinavian kingdom of York.

The Norse wrought untold harm to Ireland, Mercilessly efficient, they were trammelled in their search for lands and booty by neither Christian principle nor Gaelic convention, but slaughtered and laid waste all about them. Having learnt to counter like with like, the Irish kings soon began to apply Viking methods to their traditional quarrels also, and to discard the shackles which had rendered those quarrels harmless. From the ninth and tenth centuries onwards Gaelic battles too became ruthless; all over the country weaker stocks were forcibly subjected to stronger; ecclesiastical liberties were invaded; kings were dethroned and replaced by "strangers in sovereignty"; long-established landowning families were displaced by the kindred of conquerors; ancient federations were broken up. In the end the old Gaelic order was wrecked, and the strongest king in the country could make himself high-king of all.

Organized religion suffered too: the monasteries, treasure-houses of art and nurseries of Latin learning and of Gaelic civilization, were foremost among the victims of the Scandinavian plunderers – and of their Irish emulators; secularization of the greater foundations was intensified; hundreds of minor houses and churches were turned into lay hereditaments claiming monastic privileges and exemptions.

(There was, of course, a credit side to the account: the Scandinavian contribution to Irish trade, to Irish town life, and, in the twelfth century, to Irish art styles. The seaport towns, however, had their sinister aspect, for they prepared the way of the Normans and provided them with secure bases through which periodically to renew their strength.)

One of the first signs of a serious break in the established Gaelic tradition was the challenge (944) to the declining, now faction-ridden, Eóghanacht supremacy in Munster by Cennétig, king of the obscure Dál Chais (eastern Clare). Twenty years later Cennétig's son and successor, Mahon, captured Cashel and made himself, in effect, over-king of Munster. Three years after that, Mahon and his brother, Brian Boru, routed the Limerick Norse at Solohead (near Tipperary) and sacked their city. The sequel was the collapse of both Eóghanacht and Norse power in Munster (976–8) and the unchallenged supremacy of Brian Boru in the South by 979.

Brian's triumph in Munster coincided with the accession (980) of Melaghlin II of Meath to the Kingship of Tara. Rivalry between the two kings was inevitable. They were, however, for a time evenly matched, and it was not until 997 that Melaghlin surrendered the claims he had inherited from Melaghlin I and acknowledged Brian's supremacy in the southern half of Ireland, including Leinster. The two kings signalized their accord by joint action against the Norse settlements the following year.

King Máel-Mórdha of Leinster proved no more submissive to Brian than he or any of his predecessors had been to the Kings of Tara. He found a ready ally in Norse Dublin, which by now had become more or less a permanent dependency of Leinster. Brian, however, trapped the Leinster-Dublin army in Gleann Máma on the western side of the Wicklow mountains and won a resounding victory (999) which he followed up by plundering Dublin, and by forcing Máel-Mórdha to give the customary hostages for good behaviour.

Brian's way was now clear for a final contest with Melaghlin. The tussel between them dragged on until 1002, when Melaghlin, unable to rally Uí Néill support, bowed to the inevitable. The northern kings, however, though riven by dissension, would have none of Brian, and it required several expeditions against them to enforce their submission. By 1005, however, Brian was strong enough to go to Armagh, the ecclesiastical capital, there to present himself in the great church as *Imperator Scottorum*, "Emperor of the Irish". Only Tír Chonaill refused to submit.

Brian was the most famous king in early Irish history, and the legends which grew around him make him first and foremost a life-long leader of resistance to the Norse. They also credit him with active measures to restore religion, learning, and civilization, and with endeavouring in every way to undo something of the damage the Scandinavians had wrought. The account may be exaggerated, but the achievement must have been substantial. In the political sphere his one innovation was the nominal high-kingship. In fact he seems to have respected the traditional rights of the over-kingdoms. Notwithstanding this, Leinster continued to chafe at the bit and in 1013 set about organizing a widespread rebellion against him. The midlands were soon the scene of moves and countermoves, in the course of which Melaghlin attacked Dublin territory. Leinster sprang to Dublin's aid and forced Melaghlin to appeal to Brian for help. The latter harried Leinster and Ossory with Munster-Connacht forces and blockaded Dublin, but had in the end to withdraw without satisfaction. Both sides then set about gathering forces for a decisive encounter.

Brian's call for support was answered only by two of the South Connacht kingdoms, by the Mór-máer (Earl) of Marr in Scotland, and by Melaghlin; and Melaghlin withdrew before battle was joined at Clontarf outside Dublin on Good Friday 1014. On the opposing side were ranged the forces of North Leinster and Dublin, reinforced by Norse contingents from Man and the Orkneys. The battle – the greatest in early Irish history – lasted all day and was stubbornly contested. It ended in complete victory for the high-king's army; but Brian himself, his son Murchad, and his grandson Turloch were slain.

Reorganization of the Church

When the Scandinavian tempest died away in the eleventh century, there set in a new phase of Irish pilgrimages to Rome and other holy places abroad, and of Irish monastic foundations on the Continent (even in Rome itself). In this way Irish kings, as well as ecclesiastics, made contact with the Cluniac and Hildebrandine movements which were reorganizing monasticism and freeing bishops and popes from subservience to secular rulers to raise them to unprecedented heights of authority. Irish participation in the movements quickly followed, kings and churchmen uniting to improve private morals, to cleanse and revive monasticism, and to provide the country with a normal diocesan system. To help in the undertaking they invited the assistance of the great European orders of monks, notably of the Tironian, Savigny, and Cistercian Benedictines and of the Canons Regular of St Augustine. Ominously enough, the assistance sometimes came from monasteries in Normandy and in Norman England.

To the establishment of the diocesan system the Norse settlements, now Christian, made a significant contribution, for their first bishops, as well as being the first bishops in Ireland to rule clearly defined dioceses, ominously acknowledged the primacy of Canterbury, and that despite the fact that they were all native-born Gaels.

Giolla Easbuig ("Gilbert"), who became bishop of the Norse diocese of Limerick in 1105, appears to have been the initiator of Hildebrandine reforms in Ireland. His active zeal led to his appointment as papal legate, in which capacity he presided in 1111 over a synod held at Rath Breasail in the presence of Muircheartach O Brien, contender for the high-kingship. Other reforming synods followed, the last being the synod of Kells (1152) which gave the Irish Church its enduring diocesan system under the primacy of Armagh. (It was not without significance that obstacles had been placed in the way of the papal legate a latere, Cardinal Paparo, on his journey across England.)

The greatest of the Irish reformers was undoubtedly St Máel M'Aedhóig ("Malachy") Úa Morgair (see Bangor and Armagh). His journeys to Rome as representative of the Irish bishops brought him into contact with the Augustines of Arrouaise and with St Bernard of Clairvaux, and so led to the introduction of both Arroasians and Cistercians into Ireland. Canons Regular of St Augustine are said to have been in Armagh by 1126. Máel M'Aedhóig seems to have introduced them to Bangor, Downpatrick, and Saul about 1135–40. Benedictines were brought from Savigny in Normandy to Carrick (Erynagh; *see under* Downpatrick) as early as 1127 by Niall Mac Dunleavy, King of Ulster, and St Mary's Abbey, Dublin, was founded for the same order in 1139. Tironians are said to have been at Holy Cross Abbey (*see under* Thurles) and at Fermoy before 1135. In 1142 Máel M'Aedhóig brought the first Cistercians to Mellifont. In 1158 steps were taken to organize the remaining Columban monasteries in a single congregation under the abbot of Derry. The Norman invasion wrecked this particular project, and all the surviving monasteries of ancient foundation seem to have become houses of Augustinian Canons Regular.

This eleventh and twelfth century reformation made a distinctive contribution to the arts, the most important development being in architecture. The need for diocesan cathedrals stimulated the adoption of the Romanesque style – in a distinctively Irish guise. The first dated example, Cormac's "Chapel" at Cashel (1127–34) exemplifies not only the Continental and English influences at work, but also the small size of the buildings needed to meet the social and economic conditions of the time. Despite its unique towers, this tiny cathedral is only a nave-and-chancel structure. Indeed, the small, aisleless, nave-and-chancel church appears to have been the utmost of which the twelfth century Irish mason was capable (and in many of the Romanesque churches the chancel is an addition). In due course, the great Orders, notably the Augustinians and the Cistercians, introduced Transitional-style monasteries, cathedrals, and churches of the highly organized, elaborate kinds to which they were accustomed. To do so, they had to bring over experienced masons; but the Irish craftsmen soon imparted a local stamp to buildings which, by European standards, were modest in size.

Closely related to the Romanesque churches was a new style of sculpture well represented (at such places as Cashel, Kilfenora, and Tuam) by High Crosses which are characterized by large figures and by Scandinavian (Urnes) style ornament. Urnes influence is also a feature of the art-metalwork of the time, outstanding examples of which are the Cross of Cong (National Museum, Dublin) and St Manchán's Shrine (Boher Church, *see under* Clara).

The vitality of the contemporary literati is also well attested. Secular and religious literature were gathered into great bibliotheca like the so-called *Book of Leinster*, compiled by an abbot of Terryglass, and *Lebor na hUidre* ("The Book of the Dun Cow"), compiled at Clonmacnois. In this period, too, ballad poems made their first recorded appearance, Finn tales found their way into the canon of upper-class literature, and early Gaelic story-telling reached its culmination in *Acallamh na Senórach* ("The Colloquy of the Ancient Men").

The Close of the Gaelic Epoch

Brian's high-kingship marked the end of the old Gaelic order. Unfortunately, with Murchad and Turloch dead, there was no one in Dál Chais capable of filling Brian's place, and his high-kingship collapsed. Not until 1073 could any real attempt be made to replace it. In that year, Dál Chais having recovered the hegemony of Munster, Turloch Mór O Brien (Ó Briain – "descendant of Brian"), found himself strong enough to enforce the submission of Meath and Connacht. An attempt to enforce the submission of the North led to his defeat at Ardee, a defeat, however, which could not prevent him from installing a kinsman in the kingship of Teallach Óg in Tír Eóghain itself, just as he installed his son Muirchertach in the Norse kingship of Dublin. These were classical examples of "strangers in sovereignty".

Turloch's death in 1086 was followed by more than twenty years of intermittent struggling for supremacy between Dál Chais and Tír Eóghain. Then a new actor,

Connacht, moved to the front of the stage. By an obscure process, the O Conor kings of Connacht had been advancing in strength and winning control of lands outside their domestic territories. By 1118, King Turloch Mór O Conor was strong enough to partition Munster between the Eoghanacht and Dál Chais. This division of the southern over-kingdom into Desmond (South Munster) and Thomond (North Munster) was to prove as lasting as it was fatal. Turloch next (1125) invaded Meath and partitioned that strategic kingdom between three local rulers of his own choice; this partitioning, too, was to prove disastrous for Gaelic Ireland. Dynastic rivalries in Leinster enabled him to lead his armies at will through that kingdom, and to emulate Turloch O Brien by imposing first (1126) his son Conor, later (1127) a North Leinster prince, on the Norse of Dublin. He also endeavoured to impose his son on Leinster itself, and later, on Meath. His most faithful adherent was Tiernan O Rourke of Breany, one of the stronger and expanding sub-kingdoms of Connacht (=roughly Cos. Leitrim and Cavan). Him he rewarded with large tracts of Meath. Further designs on Meath were indicated by the erection (1129) of a fortress ("the first castle in Ireland") to command the Shannon crossing at Athlone, gateway to the Midlands. Athlone lay outside the historic lands of the O Conors, as also did Tuam, which about this time became the royal seat of Connacht and was soon to become the ecclesiastical capital as well. The zenith of Turloch's power was reached in 1152, when he presided as high-king over the national synod of Kells in the presence of the papal legate.

When Turloch's reign came to a close in 1156, Muirchertach Mac Lochlainn asserted the claims of Tír Eóghain to the high-kingship. Leinster had acknowledged him as far back as 1145, but Connacht and Munster resisted him at first. In 1161, however, Connacht too submitted, the price being Muirchertach's acknowledgement of Connacht supremacy in the western half of Meath. Five years later, Muirchertach was overthrown, in consequence of a crime which shocked his supporters, and Rory O Conor, son of Turloch and his successor on the throne of Connacht, became high-king. As such, he presided in 1167 over the national synod of Tlachtga (Hill of Ward, near Athboy) and in 1168 over a national assembly at the site of Aonach Tailteann. The downfall of Gaelic Ireland was at hand, but no one in Ireland had eyes for the portents long visible.

Medieval Ireland, 1165–1690

The Coming of the "Franks"

By his misdeeds and his ambitions Dermot II (Dermot Mac Murrough) of Leinster had made many enemies. Of these the most dangerous were the O Conors of Connacht, whose Mac Lochlainn rival he had supported. The accession of Rory O Conor led inevitably to Dermot's dethronement, and in 1166 he fled to Henry II of England, his mind full of a childish project for recovering Leinster and seizing the high-kingship.

For Henry, Dermot's naïve appeal for help was indeed timely. A decade or so previously, within a couple of years of the Synod of Kells (p. 315), the Norman bishops and "religious men" of England had combined with the magnates to get ready an army for the purpose of invading Ireland and making Henry's brother king. Henry had had the project deferred, but in 1155–6 had himself sought papal permission to conquer Ireland, professing a Hildebrandine purpose, viz. the proclamation of the truths of religion among a rude and barbarous people. Overzealous Irish reformers had already reported to Rome the "enormities of the vices" of their people. Not surprisingly, therefore, Pope Adrian IV, animated by Hildebrandine ideals and political notions worthy of a St Bernard, had readily acceded to Henry's request and had invested him with the government of Ireland. (Had not Alexander II, for comparable reasons, authorized William the Conqueror's invasion of England ninety years earlier?)

The time not being ripe, Henry II had heretofore neither published his papal commission nor taken any steps to implement it. Now, however, he gave Dermot leave to recruit volunteers. These Dermot found in south Wales, at that time full of Normans of broken fortune or of none. For his principal lieutenant he chose Richard de Clare, Earl of Pembroke, better known as Strongbow. To him he promised the hand of his beautiful daughter, Aoífe, and the succession to the kingship of Leinster, this latter in utter disregard both of Gaelic law and of the loyalty of some of his kinsfolk; lesser recruits he enlisted with the promise of lesser prizes. In the history books Dermot's allies are conventionally labelled "Anglo-Normans". To the Irish chroniclers, they were "Men from overseas", "Foreigners" or, more precisely, "Franks". And Franks, i.e. French, their leaders were in language, customs, and institutions, if not wholly in blood. (Henry II himself was French, and French the kings of England and their officials in Ireland were to remain until well into the fourteenth century.) The rank and file of Dermot's allies were mostly Welsh and Flemings.

In 1167 Dermot returned home with the foreign vanguard. The obtuse high-king was content to accept his hostages and leave him in possession of Hy Kinsella, his ancestral kingdom in south Leinster (capital, Ferns). Dermot, of course, was merely biding his time, while Rory's attention was absorbed by the Synod of Tlachtga (over which he presided that same year) and by the revival of Aonach Tailteann (over which he presided in 1168). Even the arrival of substantial reinforcements for Dermot in 1169 failed to rouse Rory from his stupor, and it was the coming of Strongbow in 1170 with two hundred armoured knights and a thousand men-at-arms which first spurred him to action. But even then the enemy struck faster.

Dermot and his allies had promptly stormed Waterford, where Aoífe was married to Strongbow. Dublin was their next objective. King Rory had meantime blocked the normal route to Dublin from the South. Dermot simply came another way, and on 21 September 1170 the vital seaport was in Leinster-Norman hands.

Dermot now announced his intention of making himself high-king, but he died suddenly on 1 May 1171. Backed by Dermot's adherents in Hy Kinsella, Strongbow set about making good his own illegal claim to Leinster. He soon found himself sore pressed. King Rory mustered an Irish army; Earl Asgall of Dublin recruited Norse mercenaries; Waterford revolted. Fortunately for the Normans, the Norse struck at Dublin prematurely and were cut to pieces. Rory nevertheless blockaded the city for two months. When all seemed lost a despairing sortie found the Irish hosting off guard and dispersed it.

In the meantime, Henry II of England, alarmed at the facile success of his barons in Leinster, had rushed across to thwart any notions they might have of setting up an independent kingdom and to hoodwink the Irish kings and prelates into peaceful acknowledgement of his papal grant. His first act on reaching Ireland was to confirm Strongbow's title to Leinster, but as a fief to be held of the Crown of England. At the same time he reserved to that Crown the vital Norse seaports. Dublin was to remain until 1921 the seat of England's power in Ireland.

Almost at once the Gaelic kings began to come in and make their submission, influenced, no doubt, by Adrian's Bull and by the naïve belief that they were simply exchanging one high-king for another. Only the high-king himself and the Northern Uí Néill kings of Tír Eóghain and Tír Chonaill held aloof. Acceptance of their submissions bound Henry to respect the rights of the Gaelic kings himself and to protect them against attack by others. Henry, however, had his own concept of honour.

The Irish Church too, at a synod held in Cashel, obeyed the papal instructions and acknowledged Henry's authority. The synod also decreed a number of reforms. Most of these had been initiated before ever Henry set foot in the country.

The following year Pope Alexander III commended the Irish rulers for submitting peacefully to Henry, instructed the bishops to support his authority, and formally conferred on him the Lordship of Ireland.

Before leaving Ireland Henry appointed one of his followers, Hugh de Lacy, to be Justiciar of Ireland, i.e. representative and principal law officer of the English Crown. At the same time, in defiance of law and honour, he granted to him the whole of the former kingdom of Meath. The Irish kings were having their first lesson in English statecraft, a lesson they were singularly slow to learn.

The Conquest, 1171–1280

Henry's bad faith in regard to Meath, soon to be repeated in the case of other kingdoms, was promptly emulated by the invading barons. And so began a long-sustained policy of deceit, aggression, and murder which in eighty years was to make the invaders masters of three-fourths of Ireland. At the outset the credulous Irish – lightly armed, occasional fighters who wore no armour, and whose foolish custom it was to disperse their short-term levies once a battle had been won or a fortress overthrown – were no match for the seasoned forces of the enemy, an enemy who employed murderous bowmen as well as mail-clad cavalry and men-at-arms, an enemy who promptly secured every foothold by erecting a motte castle. The persistence of Irish credulity is well exemplified by the Treaty of Windsor, 1175, whereby King Rory at last submitted to Henry who, for his part, undertook to maintain Rory in the high-kingship as well as in the kingship of Connacht.

In the long run the speed and extent of the conquest were to prove its undoing. At first, however, all seemed more than well, and great tracts of the richer lands quickly fell to the invaders. These they organized into feudal manors, planted with castles, monasteries, villages, and towns, and colonized with tenants lured from England with the offer of special privileges and easy tenures.

In 1177 Henry II created his younger son, John, Lord of Ireland. At the same time, shamelessly disregarding his obligations, he granted Desmond (i.e. South Munster) to Robert Fitz Stephen and Milo de Cogan and Thomond (i.e. North Munster) to Philip de Braose, reserving to the Crown the cities of Cork and Limerick. King Dermot Mac Carthy of Desmond was forced to surrender Cork and seven of his best cantreds, and to promise tribute for the twenty-five cantreds left to him. Donal Mór O Brien of Thomond, on the other hand, proved too strong to be disturbed.

That same year, 1177, John de Courcy, a venturous young freebooter, overran the little kingdom of Ulster (Cos. Down and Antrim) with dazzling rapidity, planting motte castles all over the place. The venture had been undertaken without licence from Henry II who, however, made no attempt to honour his obligations by either checking or recalling de Courcy. The latter, therefore, set himself up as more or less independent Prince of Ulster and, with future conquests in mind, "granted" the Tír Eóghain seaboard (in Co. Derry) to the Norman Lord of Galloway.

Eight years later the young Lord of Ireland paid his first visit to his new dominion and trusting Gaelic rulers came to him to reaffirm their submissions. John's entourage included three men who were to found great Anglo-Irish families and lordships: Bertram de Verdun, John's Seneschal; Theobald Walter, his Butler; and Walter de Burgo. To them and to others John proceeded to grant vast territories including south-east Uriel as well as Ormond (East Munster) and other parts of the kingdom of Thomond. The attack on Thomond was resumed when Donal Mór died in 1194. Among those who shared in the spoil were Theobald Walter, ancestor of the Butlers of Ormond, Thomas fitz Gerald, ancestor of the Earls of Desmond, and Walter de Burgo (ancestor of the Burkes), who was already planning the conquest of Connacht.

When he succeeded his father, John endeavoured to secure effective authority for the English Crown in Ireland. With this object in view he set up a royal administration and courts of law; tried to create a new, subservient baronage; conceded Connacht to King Cathal Crovderg O Conor, Rory's successor, and what was left of Thomond to Donnchad O Brien; sought to make the Church an instrument of state by the appointment of non-Irish, feudal prelates; clipped the liberties of the Norman lordships of Leinster and Meath; and expelled de Courcy from Ulster, which he made into an earldom for Hugh II de Lacy.

This policy inevitably aroused discontent among magnates heretofore unbridled, and drove some of them into rebellion. In 1210 John had himself to conduct a campaign against de Braose and the de Lacys. At its conclusion he held a council of his barons, at which English law was extended to Ireland and many Gaelic rulers made formal submission. But the kings of Tír Eóghain and Tír Chonaill were not among them. About this time the O Neills and O Donnells were getting a hold on the succession to the Northern Uí Néill kingships, and they were to maintain their ancestral kingdoms for another four hundred years.

The Norman attempts on these kingdoms had heretofore ended in failure, but just now new and graver threats were mounting against them. Castles were being erected on their southern and eastern marches, and de Courcy's grant of the Tír Eóghain seaboard to the Lord of Galloway was confirmed by John's Justiciar. Away to the south the FitzGeralds and others were overrunning faction-ridden Desmond and girdling it with castles. By 1215 only Thomond, Connacht, Tír Chonaill, Tír Eóghain, and western Uriel remained outside the "English land".

The turn of Connacht came in 1227, when Richard de Burgo obtained a shameful grant of the western kingdom. De Burgo's first efforts proved abortive, but in 1235 he mounted a supreme attack supported by the Justiciar and the whole feudal levy. King Felim O Conor salvaged what he could of the wreckage by submitting to de Burgo, who left him the O Conor domain in Roscommon. The rest of the Connacht lowlands was at once parcelled out among the victors, de Burgo retaining for himself the limestone plains of Galway and Mayo. On the conquered lands the usual manors, villages, and towns were founded, and colonies of Welshmen, Flemings, and other foreigners established. In less than a century the countryside was to revert to the Gaelic order, but towns like Galway were to remain enduring citadels of English royal authority and of foreign speech.

Tír Eóghain was attacked in 1238, but with little result, and three years later Brian O Neill overthrew the last Mac Lochlainn to rule that kingdom. From 1241 until 1605 the proud names of Tír Eóghain and O Neill were to remain synonymous. In 1247 Tír Chonaill was invaded from Connacht for the second time. This attempt likewise failed, as did five further attacks between 1248 and 1257 on one or other of the two neighbouring kingdoms. The attack of 1257 was made memorable by the presence in the Tír Chonaill army of galloglas (*gall-óglách*, foreign soldier), mail-clad Norse-Gaelic mercenaries from the Kingdom of Argyll and the Isles (the Lordship of the Isles). The Irish kings were now beginning to employ standing armies of galloglas, whose hereditary captains received estates by way of payment. The importation of Hebridean fightingmen was to continue for three centuries, so that they came to form an appreciable element of the Gaelic-speaking population. In time the Norman magnates too, and the Dublin government itself, saw fit to employ them.

In 1258 Tír Eóghain moved into the forefront of the Gaelic resistance, for in that year Aodh O Conor of Connacht and Tadhg O Brien of Thomond formally acknowledged the ancestral claims of Brian O Neill to the high-kingship of Ireland.

Unfortunately, Donal Óg O Donnell of Tír Chonaill elected to signalize his accession by holding aloof from the combination, in breach of an O Neill–O Donnell
alliance which had operated since 1201. Despite O Donnell's defection and O Brien's
death, O Conor and O Neill invaded Ulster in 1260, only to be disastrously routed
in the epic First Battle of Down (14 May 1260). Despite this set-back, O Neill power
continued to grow and in 1264 Brian's successor, Aodh Buidhe, ancestor of
the Clann Aodha Bhuidhe ("Clannaboy") O Neills, extended Tír Eóghain
sovereignty over Uriel (the Monaghan–Fermanagh region). After his time O Neill
of Tír Eóghain calls himself *Rex Ultoniae – Rí Uladh*, "King of (Great) Ulster",
i.e. king of the whole of the prehistoric Fifth, not just of the tiny historic Ulster.

The year after the Battle of Down, Finghin (of Rinn Róin; *see under* Kinsale)
MacCarthy won a resounding victory in Desmond. He and his brothers having
begun to raze the Anglo-Norman castles there, John fitz Thomas FitzGerald rallied
the whole feudal levy against them. At Callan near Kenmare, on 24 July 1261, the
MacCarthys routed the Norman host with heavy loss. Nine years later Aodh
O Conor and Turloch O Brien won a comparable victory over de Burgo and the
Justiciar at Athankip near Carrick-on-Shannon. Eight years after that King
Donnchad again routed the invaders of Thomond at Quin. The tide was on the
turn at last.

Decline of the Colony and Gaelic Resurgence, 1280–1400

The first attempt to conquer the whole of Ireland had resulted in a threefold division
of the island which was to endure until the Tudor conquest: (a) an ever-shrinking
"English land", or "land of peace", i.e. the few shires effectively controlled by
Dublin; (b) the Liberties of the feudal magnates who acknowledged the English
Crown, but were opposed alike to encroachment on their privileges and to government from England, and who inclined more and more to Gaelic speech and ways;
(c) the unconquered Gaelic kingdoms which, during the next two centuries, were to
recover much ground at the expense of both the feudal Liberties and the "English
land".

To this stalemate a variety of causes had contributed, among them the speed and
thinness of the conquest, the absorption of the English Crown in domestic strife and
Continental wars, the thwarting of English Crown policy by the self-seeking Anglo-
Irish baronage, the repeated passing by marriage of great feudal fiefs to absentee
lords unable to defend them, the revolt of cadets against such transferences, the
impossibility of extinguishing any Gaelic ruling stock because the *derb-fine* always
provided heirs capable of continuing the kingship, and the creation of Gaelic
standing armies.

A major crisis for the Norman colony arose from Scotland's victory over England
at Bannockburn (1314). In pursuance of a projected Scottish-Irish-Welsh alliance
against the common foe, Edward Bruce brought a veteran army to Ireland in May
1315. He was promptly joined by King Donal of Tír Eóghain and other adherents,
Gaelic and Norman, and a year later was solemnly invested as King of Ireland on
Knocknamelan near Dundalk (1 May 1316). The king of Tír Eóghain and other
Gaelic princes addressed a celebrated Remonstrance to Pope John XXII, indicting
the behaviour of the English kings and the Norman baronage in Ireland, and informing him that they had made Bruce their king. The Pope replied by excom-
municating Bruce and his adherents. In the meantime Bruce was campaigning more
or less at will through Ulster, the Midlands, and Leinster, his successes setting off
a chain of local uprisings against the Normans. Of these the most serious was in the
West, where Thomond and Gaelic Meath joined forces with the King of Connacht,
only to be disastrously routed outside Athenry, by the baronage of Meath and
Connacht, 10 August 1316.

This reverse was offset the following month by the arrival of King Robert of Scotland at the head of a large army. In February 1317 the Bruces marched on Dublin, only to be baulked by lack of a siege train. They then marched back and forth at will as far as Limerick, wasting the countryside and destroying many small towns as well as villages and castles, but achieving nothing of military value.

In the hope of holding the loyalty of the Norman magnates, Edward II of England had created Edmund Butler Earl of Carrick in September 1315 and Thomas FitzGerald (baron O Faly) Earl of Kildare in April 1316. Now, in April 1317, Edward's Lieutenant, Roger Mortimer, Earl of March and absentee claimant of the lordships of Trim and Laois, brought a strong army to Ireland. The Earl of Kildare joined forces with him and helped him to overawe the new King of Connacht and to force Edward Bruce back into Ulster to await further reinforcements from Scotland.

1318 bid fair to redress the balance in Bruce's favour, for, on 10 May, Muircheartach O Brien of Thomond, by a decisive victory at Dysert O Dea, turned back the Norman tide which for forty years had been threatening to engulf his kingdom. On 14 October, however, Bruce was slain at Faughart near Dundalk. With him fell Gaelic Ireland's last hope of an independent monarchy.

The Bruce episode shook the whole Anglo-Norman colonial fabric. Many inland towns and settlements were destroyed for ever. Great areas were recovered for Gaelic civilization, a fact well exemplified by the restoration in 1327 of the Mac Murrough kingdom of Leinster that had been in abeyance since the death of Dermot II in 1171. The Norman magnates too were enlarging their privileges by maintaining standing armies of native Irishmen, and by exacting from their "English" tenants services which aggravated the exodus set off by the 1315–18 campaigns. And the English Crown was powerless to check them, or even to punish those who had joined Bruce. The growing power of the magnates is reflected in the creation of the Earldom of Ormond (1328), with great privileges, for James Butler, Earl of Carrick, and of the Earldom of Desmond (1329), with palatine jurisdiction over Kerry, for Maurice, son of Tomás an Ápa, FitzGerald. The Earls of Desmond were to lead the Home Rule Party of the "Middle Nation" and to incline more and more to Gaelic culture. The Earls of Ormond, on the other hand, were eventually to lead the English Party among the colonists. (Butler policy can be explained in part by Butler-Geraldine rivalry, in part by three notable Butler marriages: the first earl of Ormond himself married a grandaughter of Edward I, thereby acquiring rich estates in England and making his descendants "cousins" of the King; the fifth earl was to marry a sister of Thomas Beaufort, Duke of Somerset; the seventh earl's heiress married Sir Thomas Boleyn, grandfather of Anne Boleyn, the mother of Elizabeth I of England.)

The year 1333 was marked by a grave blow to the English interest. William de Burgo, "Brown" Earl of Ulster and Lord of Connacht, was murdered in the course of a family feud. The title to his vast possessions passed to his infant daughter, who was to convey it by marriage to the absentee Duke of Clarence, from whom it would descend to the absentee Mortimers and so, ultimately, to the English Crown. In the meantime the Earldom of Ulster was leaderless against the northern Irish, who made the most of their opportunities. Their great hour came in 1375, when Niall O Neill of Tír Eóghain, great-grandson of Brian of the Battle of Down, routed the feudal levy of Ireland at the Second Battle of Down. Of the Norman supremacy established in Ulster by John de Courcy only Carrickfergus now remained. In less than fifty years after the "Brown" Earl's death the ancient Uí Néill stocks dominated the whole of the North as never before, and Tír Eóghain had pushed its eastern frontier across the Bann into Ulster itself, where the Clannaboy O Neills were to remain the foremost stock until the seventeenth century.

In Connacht too the Gaelic order made a spectacular recovery. There, semi-

Gaelicized de Burgo cadets seized the "Brown" Earl's lordship and established the Norman-Gaelic families known to history as Mac Uilliam Íochtair (Lower Mac William Burke, in Mayo) and Mac Uilliam Úachtair (Upper Mac William Burke, alias Clann Riocáird – Clanrickard, in Galway). The lesser barons also became Gaelicized, while the ancient Gaelic stocks recovered substantial portions of their patrimony. In effect, the whole of the West, apart from the town of Galway, was won back to Gaelic speech and culture.

Even in the Midlands the Gaelic tide was turning. Here the most notable successes were won by the O Mores of Laois, the O Connors of Éile, and the O Kennedys of north Ormond.

In 1361 Lionel, Duke of Clarence and husband of the "Brown" Earl's heiress, came to Ireland as Lieutenant of the English king. The sole enduring relic of his five years of effort to hold back the tide were the notorious, unenforceable, Statutes of Kilkenny designed to prevent the colony, its laws, language (now largely English), and culture from succumbing to Gaelic arms and Gaelic civilization. The statutes were themselves an admission of a factual threefold division of the island between the "Irish enemies", the "degenerate English", and the "land of peace". By implication, four-fifths of the island are abandoned to the "Irish enemies" and "English rebels", though the feudal titles to them are not surrendered and, centuries later, will be unjustly resurrected as opportunity offers (see Leighlinbridge).

The reign (1375–1418) of Art Óg Mac Murrough of Leinster, with its widespread assaults on the dwindling "land of peace", presented English authority with a crisis of such magnitude that Richard II felt impelled to resolve it himself. Richard's threefold aim was to induce "the wild Irish" – other than the unspeakable Mac Murrough – to submit with honour on a guarantee of just treatment, to win back the "Irish [i.e. Norman] rebels", and to consolidate the shrinking "English land" and plant it with fresh colonists. For the success of this last, Mac Murrough and his vassals should quit Leinster and settle on lands to be won from the "king's rebels and enemies".

To give effect to this ambitious programme Richard came in person in 1394 with the largest English army (perhaps 10,000 men) to land in medieval Ireland. Blockaded by land and sea, his forces pinned down by a network of garrisons, his land laid waste, Mac Murrough was compelled to accept Richard's terms. Eighty other Gaelic rulers hastened to make formal submission to the English king. But it was all a sham, for Richard had hardly reached home when Mac Murrough, Desmond, O Neill, O Brien, and the rest took up arms once more. Three years after Richard's departure his Lieutenant, cousin, and heir, Roger Mortimer, Earl of March and pretender to the vanished earldom of Ulster and the lost lordships of Connacht, Meath, Laois, and Ossory, was routed and slain by Leinster Irish at Kellistown near Tullow. Richard came back to Ireland (1399), resolved to be avenged and to finish Mac Murrough. This time, however, the Leinster king beat him all along the line and, before he had accomplished anything, Richard was called home by Bolingbroke's usurpation. Art Óg had, indeed, "wrecked English unity for a hundred years". The English king's Lordship of Ireland collapsed, not to be restored until Tudor times, for from 1399 to 1534 the effective authority of the English Crown in Ireland was hedged into the little Pale, outside of which Gaelic kings and Norman magnates ruled the land. A succession of these magnates nominally represented the Lord of Ireland, but they behaved as independent princes.

Anglo-Norman Home Rule;
Gaelic Resurgence continues, 1400–1534

Fifteenth century England's preoccupation with foreign and dynastic wars played into the hands of the Irish potentates, Gaelic and Norman. Some of the more spectacular manifestations of Gaelic resurgence were in the North. Thus in 1423 Tír Eóghain, Tír Chonaill, and Ulster combined to rout Henry VI's Lieutenant at Dundalk, and in 1430, with Tír Eóghain at the zenith of its power, Eóghan O Neill, as "King of Ulster", was receiving the submissions of Midland Normans as well as of Midland Gaels. Hand in hand with political recovery went a religious revival exemplified by the Observant movement among the Augustinian, Franciscan, and Dominican friars, for it was the Gaelic lands which first, and most widely, adopted the Observant reforms.

Among the Normans, by now speakers of English (and Irish) rather than French, the counterpart of the Gaelic resurgence was the Home Rule movement which had manifested itself as far back as 1326, when – so his enemies later alleged – Maurice of Desmond had engaged in the first of many conspiracies to make himself King of Ireland, and which now, under the leadership of the fourth earl of Ormond (1405–52), took a constitutional course. Ormond supported the House of Lancaster, and was several times head of the King's government in Ireland. Not unnaturally, "Lancastrian Constitutionalism" was welcomed by him and his supporters, the more readily since it could be used to their own advantage. From Ormond's viceroyalty of 1441–4 onwards it was the Home Rule Party that ruled Ireland, controlled its parliament, shared the offices of state, and exercised the prerogatives of the Lord of Ireland.

In the Wars of the Roses the earls of Desmond and Kildare, backed by their Gaelic relatives and allies, actively espoused the Yorkist cause. Like Ormond, they too made the most of their opportunities to advance the Home Rule cause, and when Richard of York fled for refuge to Ireland the colonial parliament constrained him (1460) to acknowledge the independence of the "land of Ireland", save only for the personal link with the English Crown. When Richard returned in triumph to England, he left Kildare as his Deputy in Ireland.

By 1465 the English Pale had shrunk to Dublin and the nearer parts of Louth, Meath, and Kildare. The ever-present fear of successive English kings, even Yorkist kings, was that some feudal magnate or other would set himself up as King of Ireland with the support of Gael and Norman. In 1467 Edward IV sought to forestall such a disaster by sending over Sir John Tibetot to assert the royal authority. Tibetot shocked the Anglo-Norman colony by having Desmond and Kildare attainted for treason, felony, and alliances with the Irish. Desmond was at once beheaded, but Kildare made his escape to England.

This shrewd blow at the Home Rule party proved premature, for the Yorkist cause was still in need of support from Ireland. Three years later Kildare was appointed Justiciar, not by the English government, but by the colonial parliament of Ireland. The only real consequence of Tibetot's brutal action was the permanent estrangement of the House of Desmond from the English Crown.

In the days of their supremacy (1470–1534) the Earls of Kildare were Kings of Ireland in all but name, clothing their doings with legality by acting with the authority of a subservient parliament. The zenith of their power, and the zenith of colonial Home Rule, was attained under the eighth earl, Gearóid Mór – Gerald the Great – whose sister and daughters allied him by marriage with three great Norman and four great Gaelic stocks, among the latter the O Neills of Tír Eóghain. With such backing he was safe even from Lancastrian Henry VII. Nevertheless, the advent of the Tudors and the introduction of firearms spelled the doom of feudal earl and Gaelic king alike.

It was Yorkist conspirators and impostors who opened Henry VII's eyes to the dangers threatening the new absolute monarchy of England from a Home Rule and Yorkist Ireland and from the continuing erosion of the English Pale. Clearly the immediate necessity was to secure the English bridgehead and to nullify the colonial parliament. Both objectives were secured in the brief Deputyship (1494–6) of Sir

Edward Poynings, whose "packed" parliament adopted the necessary measures, including a sweeping Act of Resumption (which gave the Crown the appointment of all officers of state) and the notorious "Poynings' Law". The latter was to hamstring every Anglo-Irish parliament until 1782 by providing that no parliament could thereafter assemble without prior English approval of its proposed enactments and unless it was summoned under the Great Seal of England. Poynings' parliament also re-enacted the Statutes of Kilkenny, with the significant exception of those against the use of the Irish language.

Poynings' task completed, Kildare was restored, and retained in office until his death (1513). He was succeeded as Lord Deputy by his heir, Gearóid Óg (Young Gerald), third successive earl of Kildare to hold the chief governorship. But Cardinal Wolsey, Henry VIII's chief minister, and the zealous Butlers were bent on the downfall of the House of Kildare, and filled Henry's ears with endless complaints against Gerald's rule. Henry therefore replaced him for two years (1520–22) by the Earl of Surrey, who advised a new conquest and a new English plantation as the only solution of the Irish problem. Henry preferred to restore Kildare and to adopt a policy of Surrender and Regrant whereby the Gaelic magnates (and those Old English whose titles to their land were poor in feudal law) were to be induced to surrender their land to the Crown and receive it back as estates-in-tail.

In 1534 Kildare was summoned to London, for the third time, to answer the charges of his enemies, leaving as his deputy his eldest son, Silken Thomas. Thomas was deliberately goaded into rebellion by false rumours of his father's death in the Tower. Though O Conor Faly and O Carroll of Éile rallied to their kinsman's support, the rebellion was speedily crushed by a great English army equipped with heavy guns. The earl died, Silken Thomas and his five uncles were executed, and the sole survivor of the ancient and powerful house of Kildare was a fugitive boy of ten.

The Tudor Conquest, 1534–1603

With much of Leinster subjugated and, by a legal fiction, forfeit to the Crown, more active policies directed to the subjugation of the whole island seemed feasible. Their implementation was to prove slow, arduous, and costly.

The first steps were to give Henry VIII control of the Church and to provide him with capital by dissolving the monasteries; the next to make him King of Ireland, free from the shackles of papal grants of simple lordship. And so the state "Church of Ireland" was called into being in 1537, the "Kingdom of Ireland" in 1541. (In 1555 Pope Paul legitimized the Kingdom of Ireland for Henry's daughter, "Bloody Mary".) From first to last (1541–1800) the Kingdom of Ireland was governed from England through English viceroys and officials responsible to London. From first to last (1537–1869) the state Church of Ireland was the church of a minority, for Protestantism was something alien introduced by New English officials and planters.

His legal titles acknowledged, Henry VIII was, on the whole, content to let events drift to their logical outcome. While the ultimate Anglicization of the whole island was an explicit objective of both his secular and his ecclesiastical policy, he was normally content to allow the Gaelic magnates (once they had acknowledged the Crown by treaties of surrender and regrant) to rule their countries by Gaelic law. Not until the reign of Mary was the next major step taken, the adoption of the long debated plantation policy.

In 1556 the inland Leinster territories of Laois and Uí Failghe were shired as Queen's County and King's County, and the eastern two-thirds granted to English and Welsh settlers. For Laois a Crown title through the Mortimers was fabricated. For Uí Failghe, O Conor Faly's share in the rebellion of Silken Thomas afforded the lawyer's pretext. The victims fought desperately to retain their ancestral lands and only finally laid down their arms in 1603.

English attention was next directed to Tír Eóghain. Conn Bacach O Neill had, in a disingenuous game of bluff, acknowledged Henry VIII and had accepted the title Earl of Tyrone (1541–2). On Conn's death (1559), however, his second son, Seaán an Díomais (John the Proud), had, in accordance with Gaelic law, been installed as O Neill, as King of Tír Eóghain. Elizabeth I ordered him to be crushed forthwith. Seaán gave arms to the common folk – "the first that ever did so of an Irishman" – and could not be brought to bay. Attempts to have him murdered miscarried. Neither could he be cajoled or deceived. In the end it was the O Donnells who broke Great O Neill, the Mac Donnells of Antrim who murdered him (1567). The English at once had him attainted, the title O Neill pronounced extinguished, and – somewhat prematurely – the land of Tír Eóghain declared forfeit to the Crown.

In the meantime the attack was switched to the old earldom of Ulster, for which also a Crown title through the Mortimers was devised. The Clannaboy O Neills and the Mac Donnells were declared to have no rights there, and schemes were set afoot for planting the Ards peninsula (1572) and Glens of Antrim (1574) with English settlers. The projects had to be abandoned, but not before the Earl of Essex had perpetrated loathsome massacres.

About the same time Desmond was attacked, the 15th Earl made prisoner for engaging in battle (Affane, 1565) with his traditional enemy, the Earl of Ormond, and the palatinate jurisdiction of Kerry abolished. About this time too the possessions of the Old English in Munster (and elsewhere) began to be threatened by Devon-Somerset adventurers like Sir Peter Carew (see Leighlinbridge) and Sir Walter Raleigh. In 1569 the Pope at long last excommunicated Elizabeth I for her share in making England Protestant, whereupon Desmond's cousin, Sir James Fitzmaurice, headed an Old English revolt in defence of the Catholic religion and of ancestral property. The rebels were soon joined by Gaelic lords like MacCarthy Mór. In Wicklow too, and in Laois-Uí Failghe, men sprang to arms. No major actions took place, but when several Munster castles had been taken with merciless slaughter the revolt died away, Fitzmaurice surrendering in 1573 and departing for the Continent.

In 1579 Fitzmaurice returned and tried to rally the south in defence of Catholicism, but very few joined him. In Leinster, however, the indomitable O Mores and O Conors of Laois-Uí Failghe rose once more; likewise O Byrne of Wicklow, soon to be joined by James FitzEustace, Viscount Baltinglass. In Munster the rising was countered with horrifying savagery, the whole land laid desolate, and the hapless, hunchback 15th Earl of Desmond driven to rebellion and destruction. Abandoned by Philip II of Spain, on whom they had pinned their hopes, the insurgents were overwhelmed. All was over by 1583.

The way now seemed clear for the plantation of Munster. Accordingly 210,000 acres of the best land were confiscated for settling with Protestant English owners and tenants. (The opportunities for swindling on a grand scale were eagerly seized. Sir Walter Raleigh, for example, ended up with 40,000 ill-gotten acres.) Nevertheless, as an effort at colonization the Plantation proved a failure, for very few English tenant farmers were attracted to Munster at this stage.

By this time the English Governor of Connacht was steadily encroaching on the southern marches of Tír Chonaill and Tír Eóghain. For twenty-five years, against a background of widespread plotting to organize a national, Catholic confederacy supported by Spain, Great Hugh O Neill (Earl of Tyrone, 1587) had cunningly, patiently, and tortuously maintained a minimal loyalty to the English Crown. The English seizure (1594) of Enniskillen and the Gap of the Erne forced him at last to choose between open war and surrender. So began the Nine Years' War. Having no artillery with which to reduce the English towns, O Neill adopted Fabian tactics, engaging the enemy only when compelled to do so, and playing for time by repeated truces and parleys; for time until Spanish help should come, or James VI of Scotland ascend Elizabeth of England's throne; for time to convert a struggle for self-preservation into a confederacy for the salvation of Catholic Ireland.

The first five years of war gave O Neill and Red Hugh II O Donnell a series of spectacular victories; victories which brought most of the country over to them, including Munster, where the Plantation was swept away and the Súgán (Strawrope) Earl of Desmond restored for a space to a portion of his patrimony. In 1600, however, Lord Mountjoy arrived with the greatest army ever sent from England. His savagely effective policy of repression and devastation soon crushed the revolt in the south. Within eighteen months O Neill and O Donnell had been hemmed into their own territories by a chain of forts and entrenchments; but they still held out, their hopes on Spain. At long last the Spanish aid arrived – at the opposite end of Ireland. The English and Irish armies hurried south to Kinsale, and there the issue was decided by a resounding English victory on Christmas Eve, 1601.

Thereafter Mountjoy harried the North almost at will until Tír Eóghain and Tír Chonaill surrendered at last on 30 March 1603. Gaelic Ireland had made its greatest effort and had failed.

The Final Conquest, 1603–90

Though the vanquished were pardoned by James I, the earldom of Tyrone restored to O Neill, and the earldom of Tyrconnell conferred on Red Hugh's successor, Rory, the Northern princes were no longer independent Gaelic rulers. Their territories were shired (as Cos. Donegal, Tyrone, Derry, and Armagh) and subjected to English law; Gaelic law and Gaelic tenures were abolished. In addition, the Dublin junta never ceased to plot Tyrone's destruction. Only by flight could he and O Donnell hope to save themselves and their families, and so, on 14 September 1607, they sailed away, never to return.

The "Flight of the Earls" was promptly declared to be treason and made a pretext for finding the six western counties of the modern Province of Ulster forfeit to the Crown. By chicanery of every kind nearly 500,000 acres of the best land were taken from their owners and thrown open for planting with Protestants from England and Scotland, the City of London Companies obtaining large estates. Only some 300 old freeholders were conceded grants under the articles of plantation, though of course thousands of Gaelic tenants remained. Similar, if smaller, plantations were carried out in parts of Leinster and Connacht. Like the Ulster Plantation, these were a violation of the Act of Oblivion and Pardon (1604) which had terminated the Nine Years' War.

The violence, suffering, degradation, and interdenominational hatred inseparable from the several sixteenth and seventeenth century plantations only prepared the ground for violent efforts at recovery and revenge as soon as opportunity offered, which efforts in their turn would engender further violence, suffering, and hatred. In the long view, however, perhaps their worst feature was the enlargement of the agrarian proletariat by the depression of a substantial body of ancient freeholders. It was in these confiscations and plantations that the oppressive features of the landlordism of eighteenth and nineteenth century Ireland had their roots.

Despite the plantations, the great majority of Irish landowners, as of the population at large, was still Catholic. But it had grave causes for fear: Protestants, aliens by birth and speech as well as by religion, had control of parliament and the state; a plantation of Connacht threatened; further confiscations were in the air, imperilling even Old English magnates who had become Protestants; Munster was falling into the clutches of English "carpet-baggers" like Robert Boyle, "Great"

Earl of Cork; Catholics were barred from public office, the legal profession, and the university, and were forbidden to keep schools; a Court of Wards had been set up to ensure the Protestant upbringing of minors. In general, however, James I, and after him Charles I, adopted a policy of "connived indulgence" towards the majority, and all might have ended well enough but for the rise of Nonconformist parliamentarianism in Britain and the repeated cheating of the Irish Catholics in the matter of royal Graces (i.e. the amelioration of injustices) promised by Charles I in return for subsidies. In 1638 the Scottish Presbyterians rose against Charles and the following year the Dublin government fell into the clutches of Puritan Lords Justice, who finally blocked the Graces and seemed bent on driving the country to rebellion so as to justify further spoliation of the natives. And rebellion came. It started in October 1641 with the rising of the Old Irish of Ulster, led by Sir Felim O Neill, and of Leinster, led by Rory O More of Laois, but soon spread to the Old English lords of the Pale, to Munster, and to Connacht. Tragically, if understandably, the first upsurge of those so recently and so cruelly wronged was the occasion of atrocities on the planters, particularly in the North. These atrocities were grossly exaggerated by calculated propaganda and were later made the pretext for barbarous treatment of the vanquished. The insurgent demands appear to us today as scarcely excessive: civil and religious rights for all, redress of injustices arising from the confiscations, the freeing of parliament from the shackles of Poynings' Law.

The course of the ensuing Eleven Years' War was bedevilled by a complexity of sometimes shifting interests: Royalist v. Parliamentarian, Catholic v. Protestant, Episcopalian Protestant v. Dissenting Protestant, Old Irish and Old English v. New English, Old Irish v. Old English. It was the Old Irish who provided the best of the Catholic armies, the army of Ulster, and the best Catholic general, Eóghan Rúa O Neill, nephew of Great Hugh. Nevertheless, it was the Old English faction which dominated the government and parliament of the Catholic Confederacy (Confederation of Kilkenny). The choice of Kilkenny, capital of the Butler country, as the seat of the Confederation, gave an undue influence to the Butler interest, and thus to Charles I's Lord Lieutenant, the Protestant Earl (later Marquis and Duke) of Ormonde, whose sole purpose was to make Ireland a stronghold of the Crown in its struggle with the English Parliament, and to keep the country dependent on England – on a Parliamentarian England if necessary.

In 1649–50, O Neill being dead, Cromwell butchered his way through Leinster and Munster and the Confederation dissolved. Thereafter the Catholic-Royalist armies were beaten one by one, the war coming to a close in 1652. By the time it had ended famine, plague, and the sword had reduced the population to a mere 500,000.

The victors allowed the Irish leaders and troops to take service abroad, and then set about crushing the defenceless nation for ever. The Catholic Church was suppressed; thousands of common folk were shipped to the West Indies practically as slaves; the "Irish Papist" landowners – save those who took to the hills and woods as "rapparees" – were herded into parts of Connacht and Clare; 11,000,000 acres of land were apportioned out among new Protestant settlers; the towns, too, were colonized with new Protestants. In this way a substantial Protestant and English minority was added to the population and Protestants came to dominate, not only the landowning classes, but also the urban, commercial, industrial, and professional life of the country.

The restoration of Charles II (1660) merely confirmed the Cromwellian settlers in power and possessions. The king had been well served by the Catholic Irish exiles, but only a minority of these recovered anything of their estates. (A few were given compensation in New England, the pioneers of the great Irish migrations to the Americas in search of freedom and opportunity.) However, the king's policy of "connived toleration" meant that the worst anti-Catholic laws were seldom enforced.

Under James II the "Old English" Catholic party came to power, and in 1687 a member of that party, Richard Talbot (Earl of Tyrconnell, 1685), became Lord Lieutenant. Civic rights were restored to the majority, the army and the legal profession opened to them. Such elementary justice awakened the resentment of the newly come Protestants, and when Talbot proceeded to raise a Catholic army to maintain the Stuart Crown they began to fear for their rights as well as for their privileges. Accordingly, when the Williamite rebellion broke out in England most of the Protestants in Ireland sided with the rebels. Catholic Ireland, on the other hand, naturally rallied round King James against the Protestant ally of the Pope. In 1689 James came to Ireland and summoned the Patriot Parliament, whose Catholic majority proceeded to disendow the Church of Ireland and to undo the Cromwellian Confiscation in such a way as to cause injustice to some Protestants. James then took the field against the northern rebels, who had seized Derry and Enniskillen. His attempt on Derry failed and a Williamite army landed at Carrickfergus to outmanoeuvre him on the Boyne (July 1690). Though James then left the country, his adherents continued the struggle with French help. The decisive action took place at Aughrim, near Ballinasloe (12 July 1691), where the Jacobite field army was broken, with heavy losses among the Old Irish and Old English aristocracy. The war ended with the Treaty of Limerick, on 3 October 1691. The Jacobite army then sailed away to France, leaving the nation leaderless and defenceless. The English conquest of Ireland was complete.

Modern Ireland, 1691–1921

The Rise and Fall of the "Protestant Nation", 1691–1801

The Williamite victory was followed by further confiscations, so that by 1700 only one seventh of the land remained in Catholic ownership. Even this small fraction was to be further whittled away by the operation of the Penal Laws enacted against Catholics between 1695 and 1727 in violation of the Treaty of Limerick. The worst aspect of the revolution thereby completed was not the transfer of the land to a small minority, but the replacement of a patriarchal system, in which the lord was primarily the lord of dependants who looked to him for protection, by a system in which he was an absolute lord of land to be exploited solely in his own interest.

The population was by now quite a medley: Old Irish, Old English, Elizabethan and Stuart Planters, Cromwellians, and Williamites, with the Catholic (Gaelic and Old English) element much the largest. The victorious Protestant minority was divided into two hostile halves, the episcopalian Church of Ireland on the one hand, the Nonconformists on the other. From 1691 onwards the Episcopalians constituted that "Ascendancy" whose plebeian aristocracy aroused the contempt of the blood-conscious Gael, the hostility of the democratic Nonconformist.

The Catholic majority was deprived of political and civic rights and was excluded from public office, the legal profession, the army, and several branches of trade and manufacture. Its Church was forbidden by law. It was not permitted to educate its children either at home or abroad. The Catholic peasant was among the most oppressed in Western Europe: weighed down by taxes and tithes as well as by rack rents and forced labour, exposed to capricious eviction, and demoralized by poverty and unemployment. The old aristocracy was gone, the leaders of the people and the patrons of the poets and poetry that had so long fanned the flame of Gaelic resistance. For a time the bardic schools and the bardic profession managed, indeed, to survive by the liberality of the countryside; but soon, if he would live, the poet had to reach for the spade, or stoop to *sráid-éigse* – the demeaning balladry of the market-place. Then the polished literary language, the classical metres, and the traditional themes ceased to be cultivated, their place taken by a new literature in the peasant language, a literature whose themes were the unfortunate "Dark Rosaleen" (Ireland) and the joys and sorrows of the oppressed. In some districts the poets continued for a while to vie with one another in "Courts of Poetry" meeting in farmhouse or inn, but their normal stage was the market-place or, preferably, the peasant's fireside, where captive listeners absorbed their outpouring into the fibre of their being. In this way the last Gaelic struggle for the soul of the nation was prolonged into the nineteenth century, when the advice of political leaders and the struggle for survival in an age of hunger and emigration induced the masses to jettison the last treasure of their Gaelic heritage, a treasure which had come to seem a badge of servitude at home and which proved an impediment to advancement abroad.

The democratic Nonconformists, too, had their galling religious and civic grievances. They, too, were helots; helots to the same oligarchy as the Catholic peasantry. Inevitably, their thoughts turned towards combination with the majority, to the alarm of the English interest. Unfortunately for Irish democracy – so it was to prove – Ulster custom gave the Presbyterian tenant rights denied to his Catholic neighbour. Moreover, the starveling Catholic was often tempted to outbid the Presbyterian when leases came to be renewed. Selfish landlords thus had reasons for replacing Presbyterian by Catholic tenants. The natural resentment of the dispossessed occasionally found expression in outbursts of anti-Catholic violence.

More important at first, however, than such sectarian conflict, was the stream of Presbyterian emigration to New England, a stream set off by wholesale rent-raising in 1718. From their American havens of religious and political equality the exiles passed back democratic ideals to their kinsfolk in Ulster, and it was among these that Irish republicanism first took root. In the outcome sectarianism was to triumph in Ulster, and the story of Irish democracy is largely the story of the slow, agonizing, but wondrous resurrection of the indomitable explosive older peasantry which, surmounting every obstacle, surviving every disaster, broke in succession sectarian tyranny, landlordism, and the entire English system in Ireland. The nation as a whole – including the non-Catholics – has benefited by the victory.

The episcopalian oligarchy had its own grievances and, once its fears of a Jacobite counter-revolution had been stilled, began to air them. Foremost among its champions was a Dublin-born Englishman, the immortal Jonathan Swift (1667–1745), who to personal disappointment added a bitter indignation against social wrong. His indignation was not, however, typical of episcopalian Protestants, and the oligarchy's complaints were primarily concerned with its own pocket. The oligarchy's venal, unrepresentative parliament had no real power. Neither had it a voice in appointments to the great offices of Church or State, which were filled with English-born nominees of the London government. In addition, Irish trade, largely in Protestant hands, was hampered by restrictions imposed in the interests of England. Towards the middle of the eighteenth century there began to emerge among the Protestants a Patriot Party which by 1770, under the leadership of Henry Grattan, was agitating in the name of the "Protestant Nation" for a "free Constitution and freedom of trade".

The rising tide of rebel successes in America prompted limited concessions (1774, 1778) to the Catholic middle class as well as to the few surviving Catholic landowners, and the admission (1780) of Nonconformists to public office. When France, Holland, and Spain joined in the American war against England, fear of invasion was added to the dread of risings by the Presbyterian and Catholic peasantry. England therefore consented to the raising of Protestant volunteers to defend the country. These the Patriot Party promptly employed to wring from her a relaxation of the restrictions on trade (1779) and the acknowledgement of legislative independence (1782).

The Protestant colony now had its free parliament, "Grattan's Parliament", but that parliament had no control over the Dublin government, which continued to be a junta manipulated from London. Moreover, the parliament was as venal as it was unrepresentative, and it resisted every attempt at electoral reform. It is true that the period of Grattan's Parliament was one of great prosperity for the upper and middle classes. But the masses continued to be exploited in the same old evil way. Small wonder if the Catholic peasantry proved indifferent to the fate of the legislature, or sought to defend itself against local tyrants by the Whiteboys, Defenders, and other terrorist societies. Small wonder if the competition for farms called forth rival secret societies among the Presbyterians.

In the meantime increasing agitation for parliamentary reform and for Catholic emancipation, and the spread of French and American republicanism, were turning the thoughts of the Dublin junta to complete union with Great Britain as the only hope of preserving the power and privileges of the Ascendancy. At the same time disagreements between the Dublin and London parliaments were awakening English fears for the link between the two kingdoms, fears which were magnified by the rapid growth of the Irish population and the outbreak of war with the French Republic (1793).

It was about this time that the democratic movement found a leader in Theobald Wolfe Tone, a young Protestant lawyer who had been attracted by the French doctrines of liberty and equality. In 1792 Tone became secretary of the Catholic Committee – a timid organization for pleading the Catholic cause – and he helped it to secure the parliamentary vote for Catholics and other concessions (1793). In 1791 he and other Protestants, "interpreters of the new America and the new France", founded in Belfast the Society of United Irishmen, a secret society for the promotion of a "brotherhood of affection, and a communion of rights, and a union of power among Irishmen of every religious persuasion". It was the continued rejection of the demands for parliamentary reform and Catholic emancipation which turned the United Irishmen into a revolutionary organization and sent Tone to France to seek the aid of the new republic there.

The United Irishmen had become particularly strong among the Presbyterians of Ulster. And yet it was now that sectarian feuds in the North began to come to a head with the "Battle of the Diamond" (Co. Armagh) and the foundation of the "Orange Order" pledged to maintain Protestant ascendancy.

In December 1796 Tone set sail from France with a large French army which was only prevented by ill luck from putting ashore in Bantry Bay. (A projected Franco-Dutch expedition was forestalled by the British naval victory at Camperdown the following year.) The Dublin junta now took steps to disarm the United Irishmen and to set off the threatened revolution at half-cock by provoking premature risings. Yeomanry and militia were let loose on the countryside to disarm the peasantry and to cow them by flogging, burning, torture, and other atrocities. In this way Ulster was substantially disarmed in 1797. Despite these set-backs, the Directory of the United Irishmen made plans for a national rising on 23 May of the following year, 1798, designating as commander of their forces gallant young Lord Edward Fitz Gerald, son of the Duke of Leinster and cousin of Charles James Fox (through whom he had made contact with the English republicans). The government, forewarned, seized the Leinster leaders, 12 March 1798, Fitz Gerald alone evading arrest. Nevertheless, on 24 May, sporadic, uncoordinated risings of poorly armed peasants took place in parts of Leinster and of north-east Ulster. Two days later the only formidable rising broke out – among the Old English peasantry of Wexford. Here too the insurgents displayed desperate courage, and the fighting lasted into July. Though the Wexfordmen had chosen a Protestant landlord to lead them, their rising was represented to Ulstermen as essentially a Catholic affair, and this contributed to the ultimate estrangement of Ulster from the democratic cause.

The Rising also played into the hands of those who were bent on the Union. The entire oligarchy took fright. So, too, did the Catholic hierarchy, which had good reason to dislike Jacobinism. To make doubly sure of the hierarchy, the English Prime Minister, Pitt, let it be expected that a United Kingdom would grant Catholic emancipation, abolish the payment of tithes to the minority State Church, and provide state salaries for bishops and parish priests. The Catholics of Dublin might protest as loudly as they would, and the Orange Order too, for there now remained but one obstacle to the Union, the oligarchy's own parliament. And most of its votes were for sale! On 7 June 1800 the Act of Union was passed, and Henry VIII's (and Pope Paul IV's) "Kingdom of Ireland" came to its shameful end on New Year's Day, 1801. Simultaneously the Church of Ireland was united to the Church of England.

The Rise of Irish Democracy, 1801–1921

The expectations of the Catholic bishops were disappointed, and Ireland's entry into the United Kingdom had to be marked by renewal of the agitation for the emancipation of the majority. At this juncture Catholic Irish democracy found its first great leader in Daniel O Connell, the Liberator. O Connell, a Gael of the Gaels, found the Irish peasants slaves. He left them men.

The close of the Napoleonic wars brought widespread poverty, unemployment, and evictions. Partial famines in 1817 and in 1821–2 added to the misery of the fast-increasing population. The proud, harassed victims of landlordism knew but one means of self-defence: agrarian crime and counter-terror. The government knew but one cure for social ills: further oppression. And indeed from 1796 to 1837 the whole social-political fabric was sustained by an uninterrupted, official, reign of terror; the shadow of the gallows hung over every parish; the oligarchy snatched at every device, including sectarian strife, to retain its power.

It was under these conditions that O Connell, aided by the parish clergy, set to disciplining the tortured explosive peasantry, to organizing them within the law so that they might bring overpowering weight to bear on the law without risking the law's brutality. He spoke to their hearts, and to their hearts they took him while he guided their steps in the tortuous, alien paths of constitutional agitation and English party politics.

The first demonstration of their new-found manhood came at the Waterford election of 1826, when the electors, heedless of the vengeance of their landlords, returned a liberal Protestant. Two years later the peasants of Clare elected O Connell himself. The law barred his entry to the House of Commons, but the Claremen sent him back a second time. And behind them stood the millions of Catholic peasants! The British Government capitulated; Catholic emancipation was grudgingly conceded in 1829.

O Connell's victory automatically freed the Presbyterians from their civic and political disabilities. Nevertheless, by now anti-Papist agitators had worked their will on the instinctive fears of the Presbyterians, and the Liberator, whose struggle against oppression won the admiration and support of enlightened opinion everywhere else in Europe, was not welcome in Ulster.

By alliance with the Whigs O Connell began to secure some measure of social justice for his people, including the ending of Protestant terrorism (1837). When, however, the Tories ousted the Whigs (1841) it quickly became clear that Ireland had little hope of even elementary social justice under the Union. O Connell, spurred on by the rise of the Young Ireland movement, therefore embarked on a gigantic campaign for "Repeal of the Union", i.e. for the setting up of an Irish legislature with limited powers. His efforts to overawe the Government by a series of "Monster Meetings" quickly raised national feeling to fever pitch, but the

Government called out troops and artillery to prevent what was to be the greatest meeting of all (8 October 1843). O Connell called off the meeting to save his followers from slaughter. The Repeal movement collapsed. Four years later the Liberator himself was dead.

For a brief space his place was taken by Young Ireland, a militant movement of romantic nationalists – Protestants and Catholics – whose *Nation* newspaper gave Ireland her first romantic, nationalist literature in the fast-spreading English tongue.

At this stage the peasants were overwhelmed by catastrophe, the Famine of 1845–7. Hundreds of thousands perished of hunger and cholera; hundreds of thousands fled to penniless safety in Britain and America. Between 1845 and 1850 the population fell from 8½ million to 6½, and since that time the drain of emigration has never ceased.

This disaster, the greatest of its kind ever to befall a European nation in a time of peace, was the final condemnation of the Union, and in 1848, a year of European revolutions, Young Ireland made a futile despairing effort at insurrection under the leadership of William Smith O Brien, a Protestant aristocratic landlord of ancient Gaelic lineage. With this fiasco the Young Ireland movement in turn collapsed, but it passed on its ideal of the union of "Orange" and "Green" in a sovereign nation, a union symbolized by its republican tricolour flag – which today flies over twenty-six of the Irish counties.

While the Tories refused any substantial redress of Irish grievances, they did make some minor concessions, among them the Queen's Colleges (1845) of Belfast, Cork, and Galway, designed to answer the Nonconformist and Catholic demands for university education. The Catholic bishops and O Connell rejected the colleges as "Godless", and only the Belfast foundation prospered. (In 1854 the bishops set up a Catholic University in Dublin with John Henry Newman as first rector. The British Government refused to recognize it, and in 1908 the surviving departments, together with the Queen's Colleges of Cork and Galway, were absorbed into the new National University of Ireland.)

The four or five decades after the Famine saw continuing distress, with much rural unemployment and wholesale evictions. The peasantry sought to defend themselves by their traditional terrorist combinations, only to provoke the inevitable Coercion Acts. To add its sectarian poison to the witch's brew, the Orange Order had by now become firmly entrenched in the North. Nationalist efforts to secure moderate concessions by constitutional means continued to prove unavailing, and republicanism, aimed both at the abolition of the landlord system and at complete separation from Britain, raised its head once more. In 1858 exiles in America founded the Irish Republican Brotherhood, a secret oathbound society dedicated to the principles of Wolfe Tone. Under the name "Fenians", its members set about preparing for a revolution to which veterans of the American Civil War (in which Irish-born generals and soldiers had played brilliant and heroic parts on both sides) would make expert contributions. Though the movement succeeded in recruiting a great number of adherents, the rising (1867) was easily crushed. But the Irish Republican Brotherhood survived to organize the underground, physical-force arm of the later constitutional movement for land reform and Home Rule.

About this period the Irish cause found a noble English champion in Gladstone, whose liberal principles were grounded in a Christian sense of justice. In 1869 Gladstone disestablished the Protestant state church which, resuming its pre-Union name, Church of Ireland, has ever since governed itself. The following year he carried a Land Act ameliorating the peasants' condition.

That same year an Ulster Protestant lawyer, Isaac Butt, founded the Home Rule Association to press for Home Rule within the United Kingdom. In 1873 a strong Home Rule party entered the House of Commons. Four years later the leadership of the party passed to Charles Stewart Parnell, a young Protestant landlord from

Wicklow. Parnell proved to be the second great leader of Irish democracy. No suppliant pleading for favours, but a proud aristocrat asserting his people's rights, his personality and tactics won the love and veneration of the nationalist majority. He had able lieutenants, most notable of them Michael Davitt, who in 1879 founded the Land League and forged the weapons of the boycott and "No Rent". Under Parnell and Davitt the constitutional movement for peasant proprietorship and Home Rule filled the stage, with distress, evictions, and peasant violence supplying a lurid back-cloth. In the wings, ready to intervene should constitutional agitation fail yet again, stood the Irish Republican Brotherhood. In 1881 Gladstone, in alliance with Parnell's Irish Party, carried an Act securing the tenant's right to fixity of tenure and substantially reducing his rent. Even the landlords now began to see the wisdom of selling out to their tenants, and a series of later Land Acts (1887, 1891, 1903) effected the social revolution.

In 1885 Gladstone embarked on his last great crusade. His Home Rule Bill was, however, rejected by the House of Commons, and the Conservatives returned to power. In 1890 tragedy overtook Parnell: he was convicted of adultery. Gladstone's Nonconformist supporters were shocked and he was compelled to refuse further cooperation with the Irish leader. The Irish nationalist movement thereupon split into two factions; and then Parnell died suddenly at the age of forty-five (1891). In 1892 Gladstone introduced his second Home Rule Bill, only to have it defeated in the House of Lords. In Ireland there followed a decade of political stagnation, during which the Irish Republican Brotherhood maintained its secret revolutionary organization.

In non-political fields, on the other hand, there were at this time many signs of renewed life. In 1893 the Gaelic League was founded to stem the rapid decay of the Irish language. About the same time a new generation of writers in English was beginning to write the most brilliant chapter in Anglo-Irish literature. About this time too, the ill-paid workers of the towns began to organize trade unions to protect themselves from exploitation. In 1899 Arthur Griffith began to propound the gospel of Sinn Féin (We Ourselves): passive resistance to British rule, the revival of Irish industry, and abstention from the Westminster Parliament. His aim was "government by the King, Lords, and Commons of Ireland".

The return of the Liberals to power at Westminster in 1906 made Home Rule a live issue once more. In 1911 the power of the House of Lords was curtailed, and the way at last seemed clear for the third Home Rule Bill, which passed the Commons in 1912 and was due to come into effect in 1914. But the British and Irish opponents of Home Rule found a most effective leader in Sir Edward Carson, M.P. for Trinity College, Dublin. Carson worked on the fears of the Protestants, raised the Ulster Volunteers to resist the law, and named a "Provisional Government" which would take over Ulster if the Home Rule Act were put into operation. Nationalist Ireland countered these seditious illegalities by raising the Irish Volunteers "to secure and maintain the rights and liberties common to the whole people of Ireland", the Irish Republican Brotherhood (which itself included Ulster Protestants) having a hidden hand in the business.

The outbreak of the first world war gave the British Government an excuse for putting the Home Rule Act into abeyance. Most Nationalists supported the "struggle for the freedom of Belgium and small nations", but a minority, including the Republican Brotherhood, held aloof in anticipation of an opportunity to strike for Irish freedom. Among the Republican leaders were Patrick Pearse (Dublin-born son of an English father), James Connolly (leader of the Socialist wing of the trade-union movement just then emerging from the testing fires of a series of great lock-outs and strikes), and Bulmer Hobson (a Belfast Quaker). In alliance with Connolly's Irish Citizen Army, the Republican Brotherhood prepared for a wide-spread insurrection. The insurrection broke out on Easter Monday 1916, but was more or less confined to Dublin, and was crushed in less than a week. But thirty months later a new (Sinn Féin) republican party swept the polls. The Sinn Féin members of parliament constituted themselves a national assembly (Dáil Éireann), ratified the 1916 proclamation of the Irish Republic, and set up a "government" claiming *de jure* authority over the whole island. Guerrilla warfare soon broke out between the Irish Republican Army and the forces of the Crown. In 1920 the British amended the Home Rule Act so as to establish two Irish parliaments with limited powers, one for the six north-eastern counties ("Northern Ireland"), the other for the remaining twenty-six counties ("Southern Ireland"). Dáil Éireann rejected this solution of the Irish Question and the struggle continued until the following year. Britain then improved her offer by conceding full Dominion Status to the "Twenty-six Counties" ("The Irish Free State") while insisting on allegiance to the Crown and on the maintenance of the special position of the "Six Counties" as an integral part of the United Kingdom (but with a local parliament and government in control of agriculture, social services, education, police, etc.). The partitioning of the country – and of Ulster itself – was hateful to Nationalist Ireland. There was strong dislike also of the British Crown. In the event, Dáil Éireann ratified the Anglo-Irish Treaty, but by so slender a majority that civil war proved inevitable. Peace finally came when the Republicans cached their arms (1923).

As a part of the United Kingdom the "Six Counties" were actively involved in the second world war, whereas the independent "Twenty-six Counties", though at one in heart and principle with the democracies, remained neutral. But neutrality was no obstacle to prompt assistance for bombed Belfast, or to generous post-war succour for the hungry and homeless peoples of devastated Europe.

In 1948 the "Twenty-six Counties" seceded from the British Commonwealth and became a sovereign republic calling itself "Ireland" (*Éire* in Irish). Thanks to its traditions of nationalism, democracy, and individual liberty, the republic has been able to play a valuable role in the councils and affairs of the United Nations, and this in turn would seem to have contributed to the post-war diminution of sectarianism in Northern Ireland and to improved relations between the Belfast and Dublin governments. In 1965, after more than forty years of aloofness, the two Irish premiers exchanged visits for the first time, and rational cooperation between North and South in matters of common concern may henceforth be expected, a cooperation made easier by the 1966 Free Trade agreement between Dublin and London.

Gazetteer

ABBEY, Co. Galway (Map 5, C2), on the Portumna (8 m.)–Gort (22 m.) road, at the foot of Slieve Aughty, takes its name from the adjacent Franciscan friary of Kinalehin, alias Kilnalahan. A monastery founded before 1252 by John de Cogan for Carthusians was abandoned about 1340 and was taken over by the Franciscans about 1370. There are Burke memorials in the ruins.

A short distance N. is Lady's Well.

3½ m. WSW., in the former demesne of Marble Hill, are three or more gallery graves (condition various).

3 m. NNW. is Duniry (*q.v.*).

ABBEYDORNEY, Co. Kerry (Map 4, D3), is a village on the Tralee (5 m.)–Ballyduff (8 m.) road.

N. of the village are remains of the small Cistercian abbey, Mainistear Ó dTórna, from which it takes its name. Dedicated to the Blessed Virgin, it was colonized from Monasternenagh (*see under* Croom) in 1154; the name of the founder is unknown. Gilla Críst O Conarchy, first Abbot of Mellifont, afterwards Bishop of Lismore and Papal Legate, died here in 1186. The remains date largely from the 14th cent.

ABBEYFEALE, Co. Limerick (Map 4, D3), is a small market town on the Newcastle West (13 m.)–Castleisland (14 m.) road, close to the junction of the Feale and Allaghaun rivers. It takes its name from a Cistercian abbey founded beside the Feale by Brian O Brien in 1188, annexed to Monasternenagh as a cell (*see under* Croom) in 1209 and later affiliated to Margam in Glamorganshire. In the market-place is a statue of the Rev. William Casey (1844–1907), parish priest and leader of his people in the grim struggle against landlordism.

1½ m. NW. on the N. bank of the Feale are fragmentary remains of the 14th cent. Geraldine castle of Portrinard.

ABBEYKNOCKMOY, Co. Galway (Map 1, E5), a hamlet on the Galway (18 m.)–Mountbellew Bridge (8 m.) road, takes its name from the nearby Cistercian abbey of Collis Victoriae founded in 1190 by King Cathal Crovderg O Conor of Connacht and colonized from Boyle. The abbey remains (Nat. Mon.) comprise church, chapter-house, etc. The aisled church was a Transitional–Early Gothic structure on the Cistercian cruciform plan, with rib-vaulted chancel and with two E. chapels in each transept. Three of the arches of the crossing have been walled up, perhaps to take the weight of a central tower added in the 15th cent. On the N. wall of the chancel can be discerned traces of paintings which included the *Holy Trinity, Martyrdom of St Sebastian*, and *The Three Dead and Three Living Kings*. Numerous graffiti are visible on the plaster of the chancel walls and elsewhere. On the plaster of the S. chapel can be discerned painted inscriptions in Irish (MS. hand). The fine window of the chapter-house has traces of colouring.

ABBEYLEIX, Co. Laois (Map 6, A4), is a village on the Portlaoise (13 m.)–Durrow (6 m.) road. It takes its name from vanished Mainistear Laoighse, the Cistercian abbey De Lege Dei, dedicated to the Virgin Mary, which was founded in 1184 by Cú-Coigríche O More on the site of an early monastery at Old Town (2 m. SW.) and was colonized from Baltinglass (*q.v.*). It is a centre for fishing the Nore and its tributaries.

The village was built by Viscount de Vesci about the middle of the 18th cent. Its well laid out, tree-shaded streets, Protestant church, Market House, and pleasant houses provide a good example of the work of an "improving" landlord of the period. Like many another place, Abbeyleix decayed after the Union, and today it slumbers placidly in its bower of trees.

Immediately SW. is the beautiful demesne (open to pedestrians only) of Abbeyleix House, home of Viscount de Vesci. The house (1773–7/8) is usually attributed to Sir William Chambers, but Viscount de Vesci thinks it is more probably by James Wyatt. In the garden are: the effigy (Ossory armour), from a 1502 tomb in the Cistercian abbey, of Melaghlin (son of Eoghan) O More, Lord of Laoighis; the grave slab (by William O Tunney, 1513) of William O Kelly; and a fragment of a medieval font. These may be seen only by appointment.

6 m. NE., in Ballyroan, is an Anglo-Norman motte.

3½ m. SE. is Ballinakill (*q.v.*).

ACHILL, Co. Mayo (Map 1, B4), is a large, mountainous island – joined to the mainland by a bridge across Achill Sound – between Blacksod Bay and Clew Bay, 17½ m. NW. of Newport. Its fine cliff scenery, excellent beaches, and colourful moors make it a holiday resort of singular beauty.

Achill Sound has given its name to the chief shopping village. Bathing, boating, and fishing may be had here. Motor and sailing boats may be hired for viewing the spectacular cliffs of the W. coast, visiting Achillbeg, and for deep-sea fishing (tunny and porbeagle shark). The main road to the NW. and W. across the island affords splendid views.

From Achill Sound village: 4 m. NW., in Bunacurry, a by-road leads N. to Valley (3¾ m.), a lake-ringed settlement near Ridge Point, the N. extremity of the island; ¼ m. W. are extensive sand dunes piled up from Gubnahardia and Barnynagappul strands. Between the strands is Caraun Point, with traces of a stone ringfort.

6¾ m. NW. a branch road leads N. to Doogort on the N. coast at the foot of Slievemore. Doogort comprises Doogort village proper, at the E. end of Pollawaddy cove, and the Missionary Settlement to the SW. of it. The former is an old island village, the latter now primarily a holiday resort. The name of the settlement recalls its origin (1834) in the unhappy campaign of the Rev. E. Nangle to proselytize the poverty-stricken Catholic islanders. There is a good bathing beach at Pollawaddy, and boats may be hired there for visiting the impressive Seal Caves (2 m.) under Slievemore. Slievemore (2,204 ft) is a picturesque cone of quartz and mica, which rises abruptly from the ocean. A splendid view is to be had from the summit (most readily reached from the graveyard on the E. slope). – 2 m. SW., alt. 100 ft on the S. slope of Slievemore, is a very ruinous gallery grave (Pagan Cemetery). 35 yds ESE. is a dubious chamber tomb. Some 500 yds NW., on the S. side of the old road in Doogort West, is Giants Grave, a ruined chamber tomb. 600 yds NW. of the latter, alt. 500 ft, is Keel East Cromlech, a ruined cairn with elliptical court and three-chamber gallery grave; the site commands a fine view; 120 yds W. is Cromlech Tumulus, a very dubious chamber tomb. Less than ½ m. W. of the Doogort West Giants Grave and on the S. side of the same road, close to the old village of Slievemore, is Keel East Giants Grave, a ruined cairn with elliptical court. Slievemore village nowadays serves as a *buaile,* i.e. is occupied only during the summer pasturing season. The ridge rising from the old Signal Tower W. of the village leads to Saddle Head and Croaghaun (*see* Keel, *below*).

9 m. WNW., at the NW. end of Trawmore, a very fine 2-m. strand, is Keel village. Boating, bathing, and sea fishing may be had here. At the SE. end of the strand begin the Cliffs of Menawn (highest point, 800 ft), best viewed by boat. Behind them rises Mweelin (1,530 ft), which affords excellent views of the Galway–S. Mayo coast. It may be climbed from Dookinelly near the SE. end of Trawmore. The walk S. along the cliffs and moors in the direction of Dooega Head (318 ft) is very fine.

11 m. WNW. is Dooagh, a village beside Dooagh Strand. 1½ m. W., on the slope of Croaghaun, is Corrymore House, once occupied by Captain Boycott (*see* Lough Mask House, *under* Ballinrobe). 1¾ m. W. is beautiful little Keem Bay, with an excellent small beach sheltered on the S. by Moyteoge Head, on the N. and W. by the great mass of Croaghaun. Croaghaun (2,192 ft) affords not only very fine cliff scenery – best viewed, of course, by boat – but also a splendid panorama. The ascent (two hours) from Corrymore House is simple enough, but should not be attempted in stormy or misty weather,

and the seaward edge of the mountain should always be treated with caution. Near the summit the whole mountain has been shorn away by the Atlantic and falls very steeply for 1,950 ft to the water, 2¼ m. NNE. of the summit is Roennacorragh, alias Saddle Head (512 ft). Instead of returning by Corrymore House, the energetic may prefer the fine circuit: Keel – Dooagh – Croaghaun – Saddle Head – Slievemore village – Keel. From Saddle Head the route follows the ridge SE. and E. past the old Signal Tower to Slievemore village and so to the Doogort–Keel road.

4½ m. WNW. are Mweelin village and mountain (1,530 ft). The latter offers rewarding views. A fine cliff walk leads N. to Menawn Cliffs (*see* Keel *above*).

2¼ m. S., beside Achill Sound itself, are the featureless ruins of Kildavnet, alias Kildownet, a small 12th/13th cent. church; in the earlier part of the last century it was used as a Catholic church. About 350 yds S. is the well-preserved tower of a small castle (Nat. Mon.) associated with Gráinne Ní Mháille (*see* Clare Island); a fragment of the miniature bawn survives.

4½ m. S. is Achillbeg Island. Half-way down the W. coast is Doon Kilmore, one of the most elaborate of Irish promontory forts. The outer neck of a complex peninsula has been cut off by a ditch and stone-revetted rampart. Inside this is Kilmore, a ringfort-type enclosure with graves, remains of huts, and a bullaun; presumably an early hermitage. To the W. are two smaller promontories with defence works across the necks. The larger, SW., promontory, the Dún, is trivallate. The smaller promontory, the Daingean, has remains of a medieval castle.

ADAMSTOWN, Co. Wexford (Map 6, C6), is a village on the Clonroche (6 m.)–Taghmon (7 m.) road. There are remains of a castle and a church (Romanesque fragment).

ADARE, Co. Limerick (Map 5, B4), is a model village in a setting of rich quiet beauty where the Limerick (10 m.)–Rathkeale (7 m.) road crosses the Maigue at the head of the tideway. The village owes its attractive, if exotic, appearance to Edwin, 3rd Earl of Dunraven (1812–71), an Oxford Movement convert to Catholicism, one of the best of the "improving" landlords of his time, and an authority on early Irish architecture.

Nothing is known of the history of Adare prior to the early 13th cent., when the Norman, Geoffrey de Marisco, had a manor there. Subsequently a small town grew up in the shelter of the Kildare castle (*below*). Tomás Ó Glasáin, poet, lived in the 18th cent. village, while between 1733 and 1759 another poet, Fr. Nicolás Ó Domhnaill, was five times guardian of the Penal-times Franciscan community. He had been Professor of Philosophy at Louvain and head of the Irish Franciscan college there. He presided several times over the Croom "Court

J. Allan Cash

Adare

of Poetry" and was "Sheriff" of the Cork "Apollonian Court".

Holy Trinity Church incorporates the nave, crossing (with low tower over), chancel, and N. transept of the church of the White Monastery, a house of Trinitarian Canons of the Order of the Redemption of Captives. The only certain house of the Order in Ireland, the monastery was allegedly founded in 1230 by Lord Ossory and restored, or enlarged, in 1275; it was dedicated to St James. The church ruin was re-edified for the Catholic parishioners by the 2nd Earl of Dunraven. In 1852 the 3rd Earl had the nave lengthened, the E. end of the chancel rebuilt, the Lady Chapel, sacristy, and S. porch added, and battlements (modelled on those at Jerpoint Abbey) placed on the tower, all to the designs of P. C. Hardwick. Subsequently he added the new nave and N. aisle (also by Hardwick) which fill most of the medieval cloister court. Hardwick also designed the Convent of Mercy and the school which incorporate the remnants of the W. cloister range. The Lady Chapel altar incorporates medieval alabaster roundels: *Annunciation, Visitation, Crowning of the Virgin*. In the sacristy is part of a late medieval polychrome altar triptych with scenes from the life of Our Lady; it was brought from France by the 2nd Earl of Dunraven. In the convent are two 17th cent. wooden figures (*St Joseph, Virgin and Child*) said to have belonged to the Franciscans who ministered at Adare in Penal times. SW. of the convent is the monastery columbarium.

Adare Manor demesne is open to pedestrians at all times (admission 1/3; tickets at the Dunraven Arms Hotel). The Tudor Gothic residence, seat of the Earls of Dunraven (not open to public), was erected from 1831 onwards to the designs of the 2nd Earl (1782–1850); from 1850 onwards to the designs of Hardwick (S.

and W. fronts, garden terraces, a geometric garden, etc.); Pugin designed a couple of fireplaces and a scheme of decoration for the dining room. The Earls of Dunraven descend from Thady Quin, who leased the castle and lands of Adare from the Earl of Kildare in 1683. The poet, Seán Ó Tuama (1706–75, *see* Croom), fallen on evil days, was a servant ("keeper of hens") to the then Mrs Quin; he wrote a satire on her, *Bean na cleithe caoile*.

In the demesne, on the N. side of the Maigue, are the now neglected ruins of a Franciscan friary dedicated to St Michael the Archangel, in 1464. In 1466, church, sacristies, cloister, and cemetery were consecrated for friars of the Strict Observance. The completion of the friary extended over many years, Anglo-Norman and Gael contributing to every phase. Thomas, 7th Earl of Kildare (d. 1478), and his wife, Johanna (daughter of the 3rd Earl of Desmond), provided the nave and chancel, the window glass, and one side of the cloister. Donal, son of O Daly Fionn, and his wife, Sadhbh O Daly, provided a second side of the cloister; Rory O Dea a third. Conor O Sullivan (d. 1492) gave the bell tower. The S. transept (Chapel of the Blessed Virgin) was the gift of Margaret Fitzgibbon (d. 1483), wife of the poet, Cú Uladh O Daly; its E. chapels the gifts of Sir John of Desmond (d. 1536) and of ". . . Luogh of Tulach Aoibhinn" and Margaret "Mauricii Thomae fusci". The dormitory was the gift of Donnchadh (d. 1492), son of Brian Dubh O Brien, and of Anina, daughter of Donnchadh O Brien of Ara, while the infirmary was the gift of Edmund fitz Thomas Fitzgerald, Knight of Glin (*sic*), and his wife, Honorina O Mahony (d. 1503). The refectory was provided by Morianus O Hickey, who also gave one range of choir stalls. Johanna O Felan, wife of Fitzgibbon of Mahoonagh, lengthened the

J. Allan Cash

Franciscan friary, Adare

chancel. – A tablet E. of the chancel marks the spot where John Wesley preached.

400 yds W. of the friary are the overgrown remains of "Desmond's Castle". The first builder is unknown, but in the 14th, 15th, and 16th centuries the castle belonged to the Earls of Kildare. Forfeited by Silken Thomas's rebellion (1536) and granted to the Earl of Desmond (1541), it was recovered by the Kildares. It figured in the wars of the later 16th and early 17th centuries and was dismantled by the Cromwellians. The inner ward was defended by a water fosse and – like the outer ward – by a crenellated curtain. Adjoining the main gate (c. 1200 and later) of the outer ward is a Great Hall (cellar basement) of about 1200 (Transitional windows as at Monasternenagh, Croom) with 15th cent. S. wing (latrine). E. of the hall was its kitchen, etc. Further E. are the ruins of a second (later 13th cent.?) Great Hall (aisled; buttery at E. end); it had its own kitchen further E. The square keep was a characteristic Norman work of its period (c. 1200). Taken as a whole, the castle is one of the most interesting examples of feudal architecture in the country, which makes its present condition all the more regrettable.

N. of the castle are the overgrown, neglected remains of the manorial parish church of St Nicholas of Myra. This was a much altered, nave-and-chancel structure of various 13th cent. (chancel) to 16th cent. (E. end; priest's residence) dates. N. of it are the densely overgrown remains of a 15th cent. chantry chapel (undercroft); the chaplain's quarters were over the E. end. (The name "Desmond's Chapel-of-Ease" is modern.)

NE. of the village are the Protestant parish church and school, re-edifications (1807–14 by the Ecclesiastical Commissioners, 1852–4 by Caroline, dowager Countess of Dunraven) of the Black Abbey, an Augustinian friary founded before 1315 by the 1st Earl of Kildare and which adopted the Observant reform in 1472. (In 1807 the ruins were presented to the Protestant parishioners by the 1st Earl of Dunraven. The Ecclesiastical Commissioners swept away the 15th cent. crenellations of the E. gable of the church and needlessly replaced the piers of the 14th cent. aisle, "not the only instance of barbarism. . . sanctioned by the Ecclesiastical Commissioners" (Edwin, 3rd Earl of Dunraven; some of the recent conservation work on the church is also unhappy). Noteworthy details of the church are: the sedilia and aumbry, the W. window and the cornice (figures of beasts, etc.) of the aisle. The tower is a 15th cent. insertion. The beautiful small cloister, too, is 15th cent.; the N. and E. ambulatories are 1831 rebuildings by the 2nd Earl of Dunraven. The E. and W. ranges have disappeared. W. of the site of the W. range is an 1826 Dunraven mausoleum. The N. range had vaulted apartments below. In 1814 the upper floor (dormitory) was re-roofed for use as a school. (A most unhappy feature is the stove-pipe recently installed.) At the NE. angle of the claustral buildings are remains of the friary gatehouse. 300 yds S. of the friary (inside the demesne) are the ruins of the friars' columbarium.

2½ m. S. (by the Croom road) of Adare, in Dunnaman, are the remains of small Teampall na Trionóide (Trinity Church). Nearby is the stump of a 16th cent. castle tower with a sheila-na-gig.

The road SW. to Rathkeale passes through The Palatinate, so called from Calvinist refugees planted there early in the 18th cent. by Lord Southwell, after the French conquest of the Rhenish Palatinate. Their descendants still retain their German surnames (pronounced with an Irish twist), but have been largely absorbed by the Catholic majority.

1½ m. SW. the road passes the small manorial castle of Clonshire with a twice-enlarged tower. Nearby are the ruins of Templenakilla, a small, early church with trabeate W. door and Transitional E. window. ½ m. further W. are the ruins of 15th cent. Garraunboy Castle (small tower in a rectangular bawn with D-shaped angle-turrets).

6 m. NW. is Currah Chase (*see under* Askeaton).

ADRIGOLE, Co. Cork (Map 4, C5), is a seaside village on the Glengarriff (11 m.)–Castletown Bearhaven (9 m.) road, at the foot of the Caha Mountains.

The roads N. to Lauragh (*q.v.*) via the Tim Healy Pass (1,084 ft), NE. to Glengarriff, and SW. to Castletown Bearhaven, are noted for their splendid scenery. The Castletown Bearhaven road skirts the lower slopes of Hungry Hill, highest peak (2,251 ft) of the Caha Mountains; the peak gave its name to Daphne du Maurier's novel. On the slope is a fine waterfall.

AGHABOE, Co. Laois (Map 6, A4), is situated on the Borris-in-Ossory (4 m.)–Durrow (8 m.) road, to the S. of the main Dublin–Limerick road.

St Cainneach moccu Dalann, companion of Columcille and the "Kenneth" of Scottish churches (*see* Kilkenny; *also* Drumachose *under* Limavady), founded a celebrated monastery here, and here he died and was buried (559/600). In time this monastery supplanted Seir Kieran (*see under* Birr) as the principal church of Ossory, and it was not until the synod of Ráth Breasail that it, in turn, was supplanted by Kilkenny (*q.v.*). Like so many Irish monasteries, it had a turbulent history. It was plundered in 913, rebuilt 1052, burnt 1116, rebuilt yet again, as an Augustinian priory, in 1234. Towards the close of the 12th cent. Strongbow granted "half the vill" and much neighbouring territory to Adam de Hereford. The rich manor was one of the last places held by the English in Upper Ossory at the time of the 14th cent. Irish resurgence. In 1346 Aghaboe was burnt by Dermot Mac Gillapatrick (Fitzpatrick), on which occasion the shrine and relics of St Cainneach were destroyed. From 1349 until the Tudor conquest the place remained in Mac Gillapatrick hands. A turret of the medieval priory church survives at the Protestant parish church, which occupies the site of the Augustinian choir and incorporates windows from the church of the nearby Dominican friary, which was founded in 1382 by Mac Gillapatrick. The remains of the friary include a late 15th cent. aisleless church and the small Phelan's Chapel. Some of the church windows are at Heywood

House, Ballinakill (*q.v.*). 150 yds from the Protestant church a square earthwork marks the site of the Anglo-Norman castle. Nearby is the hill-top motte of Monacoghlan.

Ledwich, the 18th cent. antiquary, was vicar of Aghaboe.

AGHAVANNAGH, Co. Wicklow (Map 6, D4), is a remote mountain hamlet at the junction of roads from Baltinglass (16 m.) and Aughrim (7 m.) with the old Military Road (not for cars) from Glenmalure (*q.v.*) to Tinahely. Gaunt Aghavannagh House, now an An Óige (Youth) Hostel, was one of the chain of posts guarding the Military Road (*see* Glencree *under* Enniskerry; Glenmalure; Laragh; *and* Glen of Imaal *under* Donard). It was later the shooting lodge of Charles Stewart Parnell (1846–91), and later still the country residence of John Redmond (1858–1918), leader of the Irish Party at Westminster. Aghavannagh is a good place from which to climb Lugnaquilla (3,039 ft), highest mountain in Leinster. Climbers should take due precautions against losing their way in the mists which can descend unexpectedly on the mountain.

AGLISH, Co. Waterford (Map 5, D6), is a village on the Cappoquin (7 m.)–Ardmore (11 m.) road. Close by is a fragment of a small Transitional church with part of a small stone cross.

3 m. N., at Kilmolash, are the remains of a church of various dates; it is called after St Mo-Laisse. In the chancel step is a broken, defaced, ogham stone with three inscribed crosses. 1 m. NE. are the ruins of Clogh Castle, a square bawn with angle-turrets. 4 m. NE. is Kilgreany cave, where the oldest human skeletons in Ireland (Late Glacial Age) were found in 1928.

3½ m. S. is Kilmore Rath, a great kidney-shaped earthwork.

2 m. W., in Dromore townland, 1 m. S. of Villierstown, is Kiltera, an ancient cemetery with two ogham stones. A third ogham stone has been removed to the National Museum.

3½ m. NW. is Dromana House, seat of the Villiers Stuarts. Demesne and gardens are justly famous. At the historic Waterford election of 1826 the Catholic voters elected Henry Villiers Stuart of Dromana, a liberal Protestant, in place of Lord George Beresford. In revenge the Beresfords evicted hundreds of their tenants. Dromana Castle was the birthplace of the celebrated Old Countess of Desmond, said to have been 140 years of age at her death (1604). Sir Walter Ralegh was entertained at the castle by Sir James Fitzgerald.

AHASCRAGH, Co. Galway (Map 5, C1), is a village on the Ballinasloe (7 m.)–Mountbellew Bridge (9 m.) road. Neighbouring big houses include Castlegar (Sir George Mahon, Bt) to the E., and Clonbrock (about 1780, Hon. Ethel Dillon), to the W.

2 m. NE., in Castlegar, is St Cúán's Well, with an 18th/19th cent. *Crucifixion* slab (Nat. Mon.).

3 m. E. are the remains of Eglish "Abbey", a Carmelite friary founded about 1396 by Uilliam Ó Cormacáin, Bishop of Elphin.

3 m. W., in Clonbrock demesne, are ruins of a castle.

ALLENWOOD, Co. Kildare (Map 6, B3), 8 m. W. of Clane and 10 m. SE. of Edenderry, has a peat-fired power station exploiting the great Bog of Allen.

3 m. W., in Lullymore East, on an "island" in the bog, is an early monastic site: circular enclosure with graveyard (early gravestones) at the centre.

ANASCAUL, Co. Kerry (Map 4, C4), is a hamlet on the main Tralee (20 m.)–Dingle (11 m.) road. The road S. and then E. along the N. shore of Castlemaine Harbour is noted for its scenery. The name of South Pole Inn commemorates the participation by a former owner in Scott's expedition to the South Pole.

½ m. N., on the W. side of the river in Annagap, is Lisnakilla, a large bivallate enclosure (early church site).

4 m. N. (via Ballyandreen), in Dromavally, alt. 1,500 ft on Reamore and Beenoskee, above the cirques of Lough Anscaul, are three cairns in a line; the central one is flanked by two long graves, that on the W. being Cuchulainn's Bed, that on the E. Cuchulainn's Grave. To the NE. are remains of Cuchulainn's House and six pillarstones.

3 m. NNE., in Ballinahunt, is a cross-inscribed ogham stone.

1½ m. NE., at an ancient church site in Ballinvoher, Rathduff, is an ogham stone with three crosses.

1¼ m. E., in Ballintermon, is a cross-inscribed ogham stone.

3 m. SE., at Inch, is a beautifully situated 3-mile beach backed by dunes.

3 m. SW. are the remains of Minard castle (Knights of Kerry). Thomas Ashe (1885–1917) (*see* Ashbourne, Co. Meath) was a native of Minard East.

¾ m. W., at a well in Ballinclare, is an early cross-slab.

1 m. W. is Doonclaur ringfort.

2 m. W., in Gortacurraun, is an early cross-pillar.

2 m. NW., in Knockane, are remains of a large tumulus with cist graves; to the SE., in a field fence, is a boulder with a chi-rho cross.

ANNAGHDOWN, Co. Galway (Map 1, D5), on the shore of Lough Corrib, 12 m. N. of Galway (via the Headford road; turn W. at Corandulla crossroads, 7 m.), is the site of a monastery attributed to St Brendan of Clonfert who, it is said, died there in 577 after setting his sister, St Brigid, over a nearby nunnery. (But the nunnery appears to have been a 12th

J. Allan Cash

Parish church, Antrim (C. of I.)

cent. foundation.) In the 12th cent. the monastery adopted the rule of the Canons Regular of St Augustine. In the same century there was also a convent (St Mary's) of Arrouasian Augustinian nuns. This appears to have died out around the turn of the 12th/13th cent, and may have become a house of Premonstratensian canons before 1224.

About 1188/9 Annaghdown became the see of a diocese corresponding to O Flaherty's Country, which at that time still lay to the E. of the great lake. About 1325/6 the diocese was reabsorbed by Tuam, but a succession of English and Irish titular bishops is recorded in the following century.

The remains at Annaghdown comprise cathedral, "nunnery", Augustinian priory (Nat. Mons.), castle and holy wells.

The cathedral, perhaps rather a Premonstratensian church, is a simple rectangular building. It may well occupy the site of an earlier church (or churches). It has a Gothic doorway in the N. wall and a Late Romanesque–Transitional E. window purloined from the chancel of the nearby priory. The high quality and delightfully delicate carvings of this window reward examination. In its later days the building served as a Protestant parish church; hence the unsightly windows in the S. wall.

The scant remains of the "nunnery" lie NW. of the cathedral, and may, in fact, represent the *Cella Parva* of Premonstratensian canons established at Annaghdown before 1224, perhaps on the site of a nunnery. The nuns seem to have left the place about that time, perhaps for Inishmain (*see under* Ballinrobe). The featureless remains include a relatively long, nave-and-chancel church of Premonstratensian type.

The ruins of the priory are by the lake shore, W. of the cathedral. The remains are, for the most part, those of a 15th cent. monastery most of whose architectural features (including the cloister walks) have disappeared. Sheltered in a garderobe on the S. side may be seen excellent Romanesque pilasters from a doorway or chancel arch. The church, on the N. side of the cloister garth, is of at least three periods: an early period represented by parts of the N. wall, a middle period represented by the chancel, and a late (15th cent.?) period represented by the W. extension. The small chancel was an excellent Transitional structure. (According to some, the cathedral E. window was taken from this chancel. Its dimensions match those of the void in the E. wall.)

The 15th cent. tower of the castle rises above the lake to the SE. of the priory. Nearby are St Brendan's Well and St Cormac's Well.

ANNALONG, Co. Down (Map 3, D6),

is a small fishing village and summer resort on the coast of the lovely Mourne country, 7½ m. S. of Newcastle and 5¾ m. NE. of Kilkeel.

1¼ m. W., by the roadside in Moneydorragh More, is a 9 ft pillarstone. 1½ m. WSW., in Ballyveaghbeg, is Carn, a long cairn with wrecked chamber tomb.

6 m. WNW. is Silent Valley (*see under* Kilkeel).

ANTRIM, Co. Antrim (Map 3, C4),

the little town which gives its name to the county, lies at the NE. corner of Lough Neagh (where the Six Mile Water enters the lake) 17 m. NW. of Belfast and 11 m. S. of Ballymena. The Six Mile Water is a good trout stream.

The town derives its name from Aentrebh, a monastery believed to have been founded in the 5th/6th cent., but of which little remains and even less is known. In 1643 the town was burnt by Scottish Covenanters under General Munroe. In 1798 it was attacked, without success, by insurgent United Irishmen led by Henry Joy McCracken. The Protestant parish church of All Saints (Church St) began as an Elizabethan rectangular structure with S. transept (1596). It was enlarged in 1816, when the tower was added, and again in 1869. A small window in the old transept has rich Continental glass, put there in the 18th cent. The monuments include one by Flaxman to the 4th Earl of Massereene (d. 1816).

At the W. end of the main street is a good, small Town Hall of 1726. Nearby is the entrance to Antrim Castle demesne (Viscount Massereene). Here are a motte-and-bailey and the ruins of a house built in 1602, rebuilt in 1816, and burnt down in 1922.

In Pogue's Entry is the cottage home (restored) of the Rev. Alexander Irvine, author of *My lady of the chimney corner*.

1 m. N., in the grounds of Steeple House (Antrim Rural District Council), is a well-preserved Round Tower (Nat. Mon.); there is a bullaun in a rock nearby. These are the only visible remains of the ancient monastery of Aentrebh. The tower has a trabeate doorway with a "Celtic" cross in relief above, and is 92½ ft high. The cap is a "restoration" into which has been built a carved architrave.

2 m. E., near Rathmore school, is Rathmore Trench, claimed to be that Ráth Mór of Magh Líne which was a seat of the kings of Dál Araide in the 6th and 7th centuries and the scene of a bloody battle with Northumbrian invaders in 684. It is an oval ringfort with a large souterrain (inaccessible). An Anglo-Norman motte has been added at the E. end;

Ulster Museum, Belfast (photo: R. J. Welch)

Double bullaun, Antrim

the castle was burnt by Edward Bruce in 1315. About ¾ m. N. is another ringfort, Rathbeg, perhaps that Ráth Becc of Magh Líne where, in 565, Díarmait mac Cerrbeóil, *totius Scotiae regnator*, *Deo auctore ordinatus* (thus Adamnán), was murdered by Áed Dub, son of Suibne Áraide and overking of Ulster (= Cos. Antrim and Down). William Orr, United Irishman (hanged 1797), was born in Farranshane nearby. 2 m. ENE. of Rathmore is Donegore, where a church and graveyard mark an ancient ecclesiastical site. Sir Samuel Ferguson (1810–86), poet and antiquary, is buried here. NE. of the churchyard is Donegore Moat (Nat. Mon.), partly artificial. Originally, perhaps, a prehistoric burial-mound, it is thought to have been adapted as a motte by the Anglo-Norman invaders of Ulster. Close by is a rock-hewn souterrain, now partly closed up, which has yielded finds of the early historic period. Neolithic pottery is said to have come from a cavern beside the motte. On the summit of Donegore Hill (789 ft) is a prehistoric cairn. 2 m. N. of the hill, near the summit of Browndod Hill (alias California; 868 ft), is a fine four-chamber court cairn (Nat. Mon.) excavated in 1934.

5¼ m. ESE. (on the Belfast road) is Templepatrick (*q.v.*).

1½ m. SE. Muckamore cemetery marks the site of a monastery founded about 550 by St Colmán (mac Beognai) moccu Sailne, alias Colmán Eala (*see* Lynally *under* Tullamore), joint patron of the diocese of Connor (*see under* Ballymena), who died 610/11. In the Middle Ages the monastery became a house of Augustinian Canons Regular. 1¼ m. SSE. of the cemetery, in Ballyharvey Lower, is a motte with crescentic bailey (Nat. Mon.).

1¾ m. SSW., in Deerpark, is a motte-and-bailey with stone-revetted ditches; relic of a Roger de Courcy castle?

ANTRIM, THE GLENS OF, Co. Antrim (Map 3, C2–D3), noted for their scenery, are the coastal valleys between Larne Lough and the Bush: Glenarm, Glentaise, Glencloy, Glenariff, Glenballyemon, Glenaan, Glendun, Glencorp, Glenshesk. Most of them debouch on the famous Antrim Coast Road (*see under* Larne), while five of them may also be reached by roads across the hills from Ballymena to Glenarm, Carnlough, and Cushendall. In this *Guide* the relevant particulars will be found under the nearest town or resort: Ballycastle, Carnlough, Cushendall, and Glenarm.

The region of the Glens – the Glynn(e)s of English documents – corresponds, more or less, to the Dál Ríada of early history, the little kingdom whose 5th cent. rulers united the Gaelic colonies of SW. Scotland under their sway, so laying a foundation for the future kingdom of Scotland. Throughout the whole of history the narrow seas hereabouts have been a highway for repeated comings and goings of settlers on either shore. Throughout most of history the

inhabitants of both shores shared a common Gaelic speech and culture, as well as a common religion. (Unlike the Lowland Scots settlers of 17th cent. Ulster, the "Scots of Antrim" were not aliens in a foreign land.)

At the Anglo-Norman invasion most of Antrim was rapidly overrun, to become part of the Earldom of "Ulster". In the following century the Norman Bisets, expelled from Galloway in 1242, obtained Rathlin and lands about Glenarm (from the Earl?). About 1400 the Mac Donnells of the Hebrides and Argyll made their appearance. The Mac Donnells took their name from a grandson of Sumarlidi (Gaelicized, *Somhairle*), the 12th cent. Gaelic–Norse ruler of the Hebrides, Argyll, and Cantire, whose kingdom (the "Lordship of the Isles"), under the suzerainty of Norway until 1265, maintained its independence of the Scottish Crown until 1493.

From the outset, Mac Donnells had been in the forefront of the galloglas (p. 35) recruited by Irish rulers to resist the Normans. Then in 1399 Eóin (Iain) Mór Mac Donnell, brother of King Donal of the battle of Harlaw, married the Biset heiress of the Glynns, so reuniting the Dál Ríada region with SW. Scotland. From this marriage stemmed the Mac Donnells of Islay and Antrim. As early as the 14th cent. a Mac Donnell had married an O Kane of Co. Derry. In the 15th, the Mac Donnells of Antrim begin to intermarry with the great house of O Neill of Tír Eoghain.

About 1499/1500 Alasdar Carrach Mac Donnell, great-great-grandson of Eóin Mór, fled from the wrath of James IV of Scotland to his Antrim heritage, and James V gave him an army to secure his hold of the Glynns and to annex the Mac Quillan (de Mandeville) country known as the Route (from the Glynns to the Bann). About 1540 Alasdar's son, James, succeeded to the headship of the Mac Donnells of the Isles. His brothers, Colla and the redoubtable Somhairle Buidhe (Lord of the Glynns, the Route, etc.), remained in Antrim. Somhairle's son, Sir Raghnall (Randall), was an ally of his cousin and father-in-law, Great Hugh O Neill, but forsook him after the battle of Kinsale. James I rewarded him with a grant of the Glynns, etc., in 1603, the Viscounty of Dunluce in 1618, and the Earldom of Antrim in 1620. Colla's famous great-grandson, Alasdar "Colkitto" (= son of Colla Ciotach), came to Ireland when his family was driven from Colonsay. In 1644 he commanded the Irish troops sent by Raghnall Óg, 2nd Earl of Antrim, to aid royalist Montrose. He was killed at Knocknanuss (*see under* Kanturk) in 1647.

ARAN ISLANDS, Co. Galway (Map 1, C6), three in number (the small, uninhabited Brannock Islands not included), viz. Inishmore, Inishmaan, Inisheer, lie NW.–SE. across the mouth of Galway Bay. They are most readily reached by small steamer from Galway, but may also be reached by sailing-boat from

Kilkieran (*see under* Carna), Doolin (*q.v.*), Casla Bay, and other places on the mainland (by arrangement with local boatmen).

The islands consist for the most part of exposures of limestone karsts, continuations of the exposures of Burren, Co. Clare (*see* Ballyvaghan). They have long been celebrated in antiquarian and folklore circles. More recently they have become deservedly popular with those in search of pleasant, restful vacations. Accommodation, simple but good, is available at various centres. There are several good, small beaches.

The relative isolation of the islands has preserved something of the traditional way of life: Irish is the normal speech of the great majority (though the non-Irish-speaking visitor will find sufficient English for his needs); the canvas-covered currach, handled with superb skill, is still the standard boat; traditional costume is worn by many, especially on Inishmaan. Noteworthy items of local costume are the rawhide shoes (*brógaí urleathair*; tourist literature calls them by the exotic name "pampooties"), admirably adapted to the island rocks; the superb, hand-knitted, white sweaters of infin-

Irish Tourist Board

An Aran currach

itely varied pattern; the finger-braided *crios* or girdle of coloured wools. (The tourist trade in *criosanna* has, unfortunately, led to the introduction of untraditional colours obtained from synthetic dyes.)

In archaeological circles the islands are celebrated for their prehistoric forts of dry-stone masonry. In Irish literary legend these are associated with the Fir Bolg (Belgic Celts), but nothing factual is known about them.

In Irish history the islands are celebrated for their early eremitical settlements, most notably that founded by St Éanna (Enda; d. about 530), who appears to have introduced monasticism, in the strict sense, into Ireland, and who numbered among his disciples several of the most famous of the early Irish saints. (He had been trained in the British monastery of Candida Casa, Whithorn, Galloway.) Remains of several of these monastic settlements survive.

The civil history of the islands is obscure. During the Middle Ages the O Briens and O Flaherties contended for them. In 1587 they passed into effective English control.

John Millington Synge (1871–1909) drew the attention of the literary world to the islands (*Aran Islands*, 1907); his play *Riders to the Sea* is set on Inishmaan.

In 1934 Robert Flaherty, distinguished American film director, made his splendid *Man of Aran* on the islands, the entire cast being island folk. The island life depicted was that of an older generation.

Liam O Flaherty, the distinguished author, is a native of Gortnagapul, Inishmore.

The following list of the principal resorts, antiquities, etc., covers Inishmore, Inishmaan and Inisheer, in turn.

INISHMORE

Kilronan, capital and port of the islands, is a village on the NW. side of Killeany Bay, near the E. end of Inishmore. It is linked by road to the chain of villages along the N. side of the island from Bungowla in the W. (6½ m.) to Killeany in the SE. (1½ m.). The village takes its name from the monastery of St Rónán, of which the only relic is Toberonan, a holy well. There are small beaches to the E. and S.

1½ m. SW. is Kilchorna, an ancient ecclesiastical site with two clocháns (one called Teampall Mór, The Great Church) and a holy well. ½ m. SSE. are remains of a clochán. ½ m. SSW., in the top of a low cliff near Pollnabriskenagh Cove, is a "puffing hole" eroded by the sea.

1 m. NW. is Monasterkieran (St Ciarán's Monastery), alias Mainistear Chonnachtach – Connacht Monastery, with ruins of a Transitional church, four early cross-pillars, four early cross-slabs, an ancient sundial and St Kieran's Well; all Nat. Mons. (One of the cross-pillars is in a field to the E. of the church; three of the cross-slabs are at or near a mound across the lane from the church.) Nearby is a

Commissioners of Public Works in Ireland

Oghil Fort, Inishmore

prehistoric chamber tomb (Nat. Mon.). – ½ m. W. is Templesoorney (*see* Oghil, *below*). 1½ m. WNW. is the village of Oghil. There are remains of a small stone ringfort on the N. side of the village. 800 yds NE. are the fragmentary remains of Templesoorney (Teampall Assurnaidhe, Assurnaidhe's Church, a small primitive structure), and St Soorney's Bed (Nat. Mons.). 150 yds NW. of these is St Soorney's Well, to the W. of which is St Soorney's Bush (Nat. Mons.). – ¼ m. SSE., to the E. of the old lighthouse, is Oghil Fort (Nat. Mon.), over-restored. One of the great forts of the islands, it has two concentric, dry-masonry ramparts, the inner one terraced. In the inner enclosure are remains of two clocháns. The fields to the W. and S. are littered with ancient remains (*see* Cowrugh, *below*).

½ m. W. of Oghil is Cowrugh village. To the SSW. is a holy well. To the S. of this is the small 15th cent. church (Nat. Mon.), Teampall an Cheathrair Álainn, Church of the Four Comely Saints (SS Fursa, Brendan of Birr, Conall, and Bearchán). At the E. gable is the Leaba, or Bed, of the four saints (Nat. Mon.). S. of the church is a holy well (Bollán an Cheathrair Álainn). A couple of fields W. are graves marked by plain pillarstones. 300 yds S. of the church is ruinous Clochán a' Phúca; 400 yds SW. is Dermot and Grania's Bed, a gallery grave (Nat. Mon.). To the W. of the bohereen leading to it are ancient clochán sites (Nat. Mons.), etc. Not far away, obscured by field fences, are the defaced remains of a very large, multivallate, stone ringfort with traces of

clocháns in the central enclosure (200×110 ft). The whole region between this fort and Oghil Fort is littered with ancient remains, hut-sites, small ringforts, a chambered mound, etc. (The high field fences obscure the monuments and make exploration difficult.)

2 m. W. of Cowrugh is Kilmurvy village. To the E. is the excellent small strand of Portmurvy. (The two cottages by the pier were built by Robert Flaherty when making *Man of Aran*.) A short distance SW. of Kilmurvy are Templemacduagh (Nat. Mon.), an early cross-pillar, Tobermacduagh holy well, and a fragment of an enclosing cashel (Nat. Mon.). Church and well are dedicated to St Colmán mac Duach (*see* Kilmacduagh). The church is a small, pre-Romanesque structure with *antae*; its chancel a plain Romanesque addition. The battlemented chancel parapet is a 15th cent. addition. In the N. face of the N. nave wall is the figure of a horse. 100 yds S., on the E. side of the bohereen leading to Dún Aonghus, is little Templenaneeve, Church of the Saints (Nat. Mon.); there are traces of an enclosing cashel (Nat. Mon.). ½ m. SW. of Templenaneeve, spectacularly sited on the edge of a 300-ft cliff is far-famed Dún Aonghus (Nat. Mon.), one of the finest prehistoric monuments in W. Europe. For all its size and interest, it does not figure in island folklore, and a hundred years ago only one old man could be found who remembered its name (pronounced Doon Eeneece); today the islanders call it Dún Angus, a name they have learned from antiquarians and tourists ignorant of Irish.

(Aonghus was a chief of the Fir Bolg in medieval literary legend.) The fort, which covers some 11 acres, comprises three "concentric" enclosures defended by stout walls of dry masonry: outer enclosure, 1,174×650 ft; middle enclosure, 400×300 ft; inner citadel, 150 ft in diameter. The middle wall is covered by a remarkable abatis (or *chevaux-de-frise* of jagged, limestone uprights), which also embraces an outwork at the NW. gateway through the wall. The terraced innermost wall, built in three sections and 12 ft 9 in. thick, is now 18 ft high. (The outer part rose above the inner.) Much of the walls had collapsed when conservation was undertaken by the Office of Public Works in 1881. Unfortunately, the work was carried out without judgement, and no records were made of the fort as it then stood. Many of the flights of steps, etc., date from that time. The innermost rampart affords a splendid view of the island and of the Connemara coast. – 2 m. N. of Kilmurvy, to the N. of the Onaght road near Sruffaun, is Clochán na Carraige (Nat. Mon.), a late clochán, oval without, rectangular within. The disposition of the doors and other features link it with the traditional Irish peasant house.

1¾ m. NW. of Kilmurvy is Onaght village. Here the miscalled Seven Churches (Nat. Mons.) mark an ancient site dedicated to St Breacán. There are remains of two small churches, Temple Brecan and Teampall an Phoill. Temple Brecan is a nave-and-chancel structure of various dates. Built into the W. wall (inner face) is an early gravestone inscribed: OR[ŌIT] AR II CANOIN ("A prayer for two canons"); by the N. wall of the nave is an early cross-slab inscribed TOMAS AP[STAL] ("Thomas the Apostle"). Close to the church, on the SW., is Leaba an Spioraid Naoimh ("Holy Ghost Bed"), a penitential station with fragments of a figured High Cross (*Crucifixion*, interlacing, etc.) and portion of an early cross-slab inscribed S[AN]C[T]I BRE[CA]NI. Nearby to the W. is an early gravestone: ORAIT AR ANMAIN SCANDLAIN ("A prayer for the soul of Scannlán"). Nearby, to the SE., is Leaba Bhreacáin, another "station". To the N. of Leaba an Spioraid Naoimh is an early cross-slab. N. of the church are the ruins of late 15th cent. monastic houses. In the SE. corner of the churchyard are some early graves; the gravestones include one inscribed OR[ŌIT] DO MAINACH ("A prayer for Maínach"). Another cross-slab here is inscribed UII ROMANI, presumably referring to the seven martyr sons of Symphorosa; their cult was known in Ireland. Prostrate on the rock in the field to the SE. is a fractured High Cross (Nat. Mon.) with elaborate interlaces, etc. N. of the monastery are another *leaba* and fragments of an ornamented cross with a rude *Crucifixion* (Nat. Mons.). Nearby are a "castle" and square fort (Nat. Mons.). ½ m. SSE. of Onaght village is Dún Onaght (Nat. Mon.), a massive, univallate, stone ringfort (restored) with terraced rampart and three house-sites. ENE. of the fort is the ancient ecclesiastical site of Kilcholan (Nat. Mon.); in the enclosure are three pillarstones, 200 yds NW. of the fort is a rectangular clochán; nearer the fort is another.

1½ m. SE. of Kilronan is Killeany village. Here are the ruins of Arkin Castle (Nat. Mon.), a Cromwellian fort; a Round Tower and four churches (including a Franciscan friary of 1485) were demolished to provide the material. 150 yds S. is the ancient monastic site of Cill Éinne, from which the village takes its name. The scant remains (Nat. Mons.) include the stump of a Round Tower, parts of a High Cross with zoomorphic and other ornament, an "altar", Dabhach Éinne (alias St Eany's

Commissioners of Public Works in Ireland

Dún Aonghus, Inishmore

Well), and foundations of the Franciscan friary. On a rock-terrace 200 yds SW. is Teampall Mionnáin, alias Temple Benan (St Benignus's Church), with remains of clocháns and vestiges of a cashel (Nat. Mons.). The church is a diminutive structure with trabeate W. door. Built into the SE. angle is an early gravestone inscribed CARI. To the SW. is a portion of an early cross-slab. An early gravestone is inscribed: OR[ÓIT] AR MAINACH ("A prayer for Maínach"). To the NW. is a clochán-site (Priest's House, alias Monk's House). – ½ m. ESE. of Killeany, by Trawmore, is Tighlagheany (Teaghlach Éinne, Enda's Household), holiest place in Aran with, says tradition, the graves of 120 saints. All that remains here is a small early church (Nat. Mon.) with E. *antae* and some 15th cent. features. In it are part of a figured High Cross, St Eany's Grave, and some early gravestones. Two of the latter are inscribed: BEN[DACHT] DIE F[OR] AN[MAIN] S[AN]C[T]AN ("The blessing of God on the soul of Sanctán") and OROIT AR SCANDLAN ("A prayer for Scannlán"). Nearby is St Enda's Leaba. 400 yds SW. are remains of a clochán. – 1½ m. SE. of Killeany, overlooking Gregory Sound, are the ruins of Turmartin Tower (Nat. Mon.). Some 300 yds SW. are "puffing holes" in the rock surface.

1½ m. W. of Killeany (via the cliffs), at Bensheegipson, is the great promontory fort called Doocaher (Nat. Mon.); it, too, has been restored. Outside the massive stone rampart are remains of *chevaux de frise* with traces of hut-sites. In the shelter of the rampart are remains (restored) of several clocháns. There were formerly rows of hut-sites SW. of these.

INISHMAAN

Near the slip at the middle of the E. coast, SW. of Trawletteragh, are the ruins of Kilcanonagh church (Nat. Mon.) and Tobercanonagh holy well; the church is a small, primitive structure with trabeate W. doorway. On a rock-terrace to the W. is Doonfarvagh, alias Mur (Nat. Mon.), a stone ringfort; the rampart is terraced.

The first village to the W. of the landing place is Moher (Mur). 300 yds NNE. is Dermot and Grania's Bed, a chamber tomb (Nat. Mon.).

About the centre of the island, at the W. end of Ballinlisheen village, are: Templemurry, a small 15th cent. church which was incorporated in the 19th cent. church; traces of Templeshaghtmacree (Church of the King's Seven Sons, Nat. Mon.); Labbanakinneriga (St Cinneirge's Bed, Nat. Mon.); and Tobernakinneriga (St Cinneirge's Well).

400 yds W. of Templemurry is Dooconor, Dún Conchuirn (Nat. Mon.), a magnificent oval stone fort with an outer bailey and a small forework at the entrance. The massive rampart (restored) of the fort proper is terraced and has wall chambers; it encloses a number of hut-sites (restored). 50 ft N. are remains of a

Commissioners of Public Works in Ireland
Cross-shaft, Tighlagheany, Inishmore

clochán. In the same townland is Dunbeg, a ringfort (Nat. Mon.).

INISHEER

Close to the landing place is Knockgrannia, an ancient circular cemetery (Nat. Mon.).

In the sands SE. of the landing place are the ruins of Teampall Chaomháin (Nat. Mon.), an early church with later W. chamber and Gothic chancel. A pátrún is held here on 14 June. Buried in the sands to the NE. is St Caomhán's Grave.

On the rocky hill S. of the landing place is fragmentary O Brien's Castle, alias Furmina Castle (Nat. Mon.), a 15th cent. tower set in a stone ringfort (Great Fort ; Nat. Mon.). Near the hill-top to the S. are traces of Cahernaman fort. ½ m. S. of the latter are remains of An Chill Bheannuighthe, alias Cill na Seacht nInghean, alias Dún an Chreagáin Chaoil (Nat. Mon.), a cashel with the "Grave of the Seven Daughters"; there is an early cross-slab here.

NW. of the post office is a small cairn. A few fields away is a ruined chamber tomb.

800 yds W. of the landing place are the ruins of Cill Ghobnait (Nat. Mon.), a small church with trabeate W. door. In the enclosure are remains of a clochán and two bullauns. ½ m. SW. of this, overlooking Foul Sound, is Clochán Éinne (Enda's Clochàn), with Tobar Éinne (Enda's Well) 150 yds to the N.

ARDAGH, Co. Limerick (Map 4, E3), is a village on the Newcastle West (4 m.)–Shanagolden (7 m.) road, at the foot of Slieveluachra.

At the W. end of the village, beside the road in Reerasta South, is a large, overgrown, and partly defaced ringfort (Nat. Mon.). The celebrated Ardagh chalices and brooches, now in the National Museum, were discovered here in 1868.

The country round Ardagh is rich in ringforts and small circular earthworks.

1½ m. NE. is Cahermoyle House, 1870 successor of the home of William Smith O Brien (1803–64), leader of the abortive Young Ireland rebellion of 1848. William was the second son of Sir Edward O Brien (1773–1856), brother of the 13th Baron Inchiquin of Dromoland (see under Newmarket-on-Fergus) and opponent of the Union. Sir Edward had married the heiress of Cahermoyle, descendant of a Cromwellian grantee, Smith. William was father of Charlotte Grace O Brien (see under Foynes) and grandfather of Dermot O Brien (1866–1945), President of the Royal Hibernian Academy. The house (recently destroyed by fire and rebuilt) is now a novitiate of the Oblates of Mary Immaculate. Not far away is a massive stone ringfort (defaced).

1¼ m. WSW., at the edge of the gorge of the little Daar River, close to Dunganville bridge, is a well-preserved bivallate ringfort with souterrains and a wet fosse. The site commands a fine view.

Commissioners of Public Works in Ireland
Inishkeel cross-shaft, Ardara

ARDARA, Co. Donegal (Map 2, B3), is a village on the Killybegs (12 m.)–Glenties (5 m.) road, where the Owentocker flows into Loughros More Bay. It is noted for its homespun tweed, embroidery, and knitting industries. It is a good centre for fishing the Owenea and local lakes, as well as the Owentocker, and for exploring beautiful SW. Donegal (see Glencolumbkille and Carrick). The Church of the Holy Family has a rose window (1954) by Evie Hone: *Christ among the Doctors.*

The (minor) road to Glencolumbkille (14 m.) climbs beautiful Glengesh to the 900-ft saddle between Croaghavehy (1,228 ft) and Crocknapeast (1,649 ft), and then descends the Owenteskiny valley. It is a rewarding, if none too easy, drive (gradients of one in six, as well as very sharp bends).

2 m. E., in Doochill North, is Carn, a disturbed court cairn.

5½ m. W., in Maghera on Loughros Beg Bay, are caves accessible at low tide; nearby is Eassaranka, a waterfall. The coastal scenery to the W., around Slievetooey, is splendid. Footpaths follow the coast to Glencolumbkille. Others cross the summits of Slievetooey (1,515 ft, 1,458 ft and 1,500 ft).

3½ m. WNW., in Newtownburke, are three early cross-slabs, one 20 yds S. of the road to

Loughros Point, the second 50 yds N. of the road, the third 400 yds away on a hillside. 1½ m. NE., in Kilcashel graveyard, to the N. of Lough Aleen, is St Conall's Cross, a primitive stone cross with a cross incised on it.

4 m. NNW. is Kilclooney bridge (*see under* Naran-and-Portnoo*).

ARDEE, Co. Louth (Map 3, B7), is a market town where the Drogheda (15 m.)–Carrick-macross (12 m.) road crosses the little Dee River.

Ardee takes its name from Áth Fhir Diadh, Fear-Diadh's ford, now crossed by the bridge. The name has inspired the well-known story of the mythical Cú Chulainn's single combat with Fer Diad, interpolated into *The Cattle Raid of Cooley*.

About 1186 Prince John of England, as Lord of Ireland, granted the barony of Ardee to Gilbert Pipard, who seemingly aspired to conquer Uriel as far W. as Fermanagh, but by 1302 the Pipards had given up hope of retaining Ardee against the Irish. In the period 1402–25 the surrounding country was formally abandoned by the English to the Mac Mahons of Uriel. The town, however, remained in English hands. In 1539 Conn O Neill and Manus O Donnell burned the place. In 1641 it was seized and held for a time by Sir Felim O Neill. From October to November 1689, James II had his headquarters here.

The principal monument in the town is Ardee Castle, now the Court House (Main St). This 13th cent. square keep is reputed to have been built by Gilbert Pipard's brother, Roger. In its day it was an important border-fortress of the English Pale. After the Restoration it was granted to Theobald Taafe, Earl of Carlingford (1639–77; *see* Smarmore Castle *below, and under* Carlingford). Permission to view may be had from the Town Clerk.

In Market St is Hatch's Castle, so called after the Cromwellian family that lived there until 1940. This, too, is a 13th cent. structure.

St Mary's Protestant Church (1789, 1812) incorporates the S. nave arcade and other fragments of a medieval church (presumably the collegiate parish church, but thought by some to have been the church of Ardee's medieval Carmelite friary). The church also has a medieval font (from Mansfieldtown near Castle-bellingham). In the churchyard is part of a stone cross with a *Crucifixion* on the W. face and a *Virgin and Child* on the E. face.

St Mary's Catholic Church (1829) is thought to occupy part of the site of the priory-hospital of St John the Baptist (Augustinian Crucifers) founded in 1207 by Roger Pipard.

Near the railway station is a fragment of the medieval town wall.

¾ m. S. of the town is Castleguard, alias Dawson's Fort, alias The Priest's Mount, motte of Gilbert Pipard's castle of Ardee.

4½ m. N. is much altered and enlarged 17th cent. Louth Hall, until recently the seat of Baron Louth (Plunkett family; *see* Beaulieu

under Drogheda). Blessed Oliver Plunkett (1629–81), martyred Archbishop of Armagh, found refuge here with his kinsfolk; his hiding-place is still pointed out. In the demesne are the shattered remains of a figured cross set up in 1601 in memory of Oliver, 4th Baron Louth, by his widow, Ienet Dowdall (*see also under* Duleek). ¾ m. N. of Louth Hall is Tallanstown motte.

3½ m. NE. is Mapastown motte with nearby remains of a manorial church.

3 m. ENE., via the Castlebellingham road, is Roodstown Castle (Nat. Mon.), a small 15th cent. tower with two angle turrets. ¾ m. E. is Drumcashel motte.

2 m. SSE., in Kildemock, are remnants of medieval St Catherine's Church, sometimes known as The Jumping Church. A storm in February 1715 caused part of the W. gable to shift inwards from its foundation, but popular belief soon explained the "jump" as a miracle to exclude the grave of a heretic who had been buried within the church.

4 m. SSW. is Smarmore Castle, sometime seat of the Anglo-Norman Taafes who became Viscounts Taaffe of Corran in 1628 and Earls of Carlingford in 1661. Though Jacobites, they were not deprived of their peerage by William III. Several members of the family sought refuge abroad with the "Wild Geese"; two of them (Francis, 1639–1704, and Nicholas, 1677–1769) became Austrian field marshals, while the 12th Viscount was Prime Minister of Austria (1879–93). John Taafe (1787–1862), poet and commentator on Dante, was also a member of this family. The castle is a 14th cent. square keep with modern wings. ¼ m. N. are remains of a medieval manorial church.

6 m. SW., at Woodtown, is a well preserved sector of the English Pale.

6 m. WNW. is Crowmartin motte.

6 m. NW., Aclint bridge (motte nearby) crosses the Lagan, alias the Glyde, at the ford where Elizabeth's ill-starred favourite, Robert Devereux, Earl of Essex, parleyed with Great Hugh O Neill, 7 Sept. 1599. The ensuing truce was signed at Lackan Castle, home of Garret Fleming, 2 m. SW. The castle was the birthplace of Garret's famous son, Christopher, who published the *Life* and *Works* of St Columbanus and other early Irish ecclesiastical documents. Sent to Prague in 1630 as first superior of the Irish Franciscan college there, he was murdered by Hussites in 1631.

ARDFERT, Co. Kerry (Map 4, C3), on the Tralee (5 m.)–Ballyheigue (6 m.) road, was the site of a monastery founded by the celebrated St Brendan the Navigator (d. 577; *see* Clonfert). In the 12th cent. it became the see of a diocese now absorbed into that of Kerry. The medieval remains are among the most interesting in Co. Kerry. St Brendan's Church (1853–4) is by J. J. McCarthy.

The principal monument is the scandalously neglected St Brendan's Cathedral (Nat. Mon.),

Plate 1. The National Stud, Kildare

a mid-13th cent. rectangular structure (details excellent) with S. nave aisle, to which a S. transept (with E. chapel) and a NE. chapel, or sacristy, were added in the 15th cent. Interesting features are the incorporated fragment (doorway flanked by blind arcading) of the W. wall of a 12th cent. Romanesque church, the fine lancet windows of the choir (which was separated from the nave by a timber rood loft), and two episcopal effigies. There was a Round Tower near the NW. angle of the church until 1771.

NW. of the cathedral are the ruins (Nat. Mons.) of Temple-na-Hoe and Temple-na-Griffin. Temple-na-Hoe was a small, Late Romanesque, nave-and-chancel church; the unusual ornaments include quoin-shafts with carved capitals. Temple-na-Griffin was a small, simple, 15th cent. church. Opposite the graveyard stile is an ogham stone (partly defaced) which formerly stood in a field opposite the Protestant church.

The house called Ardfert Abbey, to the E., was the Georgian home of the Talbot Crosbies (Earls of Glandore). N. of the house are the ruins (Nat. Mon.) of a Franciscan friary founded in 1253 by Thomas Fitzmaurice, 1st Baron of Kerry. The remains include late-13th cent. nave and chancel, 14th/15th cent. S. transept, W. tower, cloister, etc. There are many ringforts in the area.

2¾ m. E., in Tubridmore, is Tobernamolt, alias Wethers' Well, the most frequented holy well in Kerry today (Sat. before Midsummer). Nearby is St Íde's Grave. Íde's prayers called forth the well, in whose waters St Erc baptized the famous St Brendan. The arcaded tomb slab with three weepers (popularly SS Erc, Brendan and Íde) came from Ardfert friary. Sufferers from rheumatism, etc. used to bathe in the well; hence the little "dressing house".

1 m. NW. is Mc Kenna's Fort, a univallate

Commissioners of Public Works in Ireland

Effigy, St Brendan's Cathedral, Ardfert

ringfort where Sir Roger Casement (1864–1916) was arrested on Good Friday, 1916, after landing at nearby Banna strand from a German submarine.

1½ m. N., close to the summit of a ridge in

Commissioners of Public Works in Ireland

Franciscan friary, Ardfert

Arcading of St Declan's Church (the Cathedral), Ardmore

Killeacle, is a circular earthwork (120 ft diameter) with central pillarstone (8 ft); WSW. is Caherferta ringfort.

5 m. SW. is Round Castle (*see under* Fenit).

1¼ m. WSW. is Rathcrihane, a ringfort with souterrain (Nat. Mon.), which gives its name to the townland.

ARDFINNAN, Co. Tipperary (Map 5, D5), is a wool-manufacturing and market village where the Clonmel (10 m.)–Mitchelstown (17 m.) road crosses the Suir. The Suir up-river to Cahir (following the W. bank) and down-river to Clonmel (following the E. bank) is noted for its scenery. The name of the village commemorates St Fíonán Lobhar, who founded a monastery here in the 7th cent. (the Protestant church stands on the site). On a precipitous rock commanding the river-ford are remains of a strong castle wrecked by the Cromwellians. Prince John of England built a castle here in 1185, but the oldest part of the extant castle is a fragment of a late 13th cent. round keep.

2 m. NW., in Rochestown, are the ruins of a medieval church. The sheila-na-gig in the E. gable was the first of these curious carvings to be published and has given its name to the entire series.

1¼ m. SW., in Monroe West, are the scant remains of Lady's Abbey, a Carmelite friary. The church was a 14th/15th cent. building with later S. transept.

2 m. S., in Raheen, are the ruins of Bally-bacon 13th cent. church. There is a medieval carved font here.

5 m. SE., near the mouth of the lovely Nier valley, are remains of New Castle and its manorial church. 1 m. NE. of the village is a remnant of Molough "Abbey": remains of the church and traces of the conventual buildings. A nunnery dedicated to St Brigid was founded here in the 6th cent. by the daughters of Cinaed, King of the Déise, whose seat was at Crohan to the SW. of New Castle; in the 14th cent. it was revived by the Butlers of Cahir. 3½ m. SE. of New Castle are the ruins of the Prendergast castle of Curraghcloney. 3 m. E. of New Castle, in Tooracurragh, Co. Waterford, is a prostrate pillarstone with inscribed cross.

ARDGLASS, Co. Down (Map 3, D5), is a fishing village and small resort 7 m. SE. of Downpatrick. It occupies the site of a Viking settlement, and its importance in medieval times is attested by the remains of five 14th–16th cent. fortified merchants' houses: King's Castle (the largest), Margaret's Castle, Cowd Castle, Horn Castle (incorporated in 1790 Ardglass Castle, now the Golf Club), and Jordan's Castle (alias Castle Shane). Jordan's Castle (Nat. Mon.) houses the F. J. Bigger collection of antiquities.

¾ m. NNE., in Ardtole, are the ruins of a medieval church dedicated to St Nicholas of Myra (Nat. Mon.). A cross-slab from here is preserved at Dunsfort Catholic church about 1½ m. NE.

4½ m. NNE. is Ballyhoran Bay with a good beach. There is another beach 1 m. further, in Killard.

2¼ m. WSW. is Killough, a well laid out fishing village. Some 2 m. SSW., near St John's Point, St John's Well and remains (Nat. Mon.) of a pre-Romanesque church mark an early monastic site. The older graves in the church-yard were disposed radially, as at Kilnasaggart (*see under* Newry) and Kildreenagh (*see under* Valencia Island). 5 m. W., in Rathmullan, is a motte-and-bailey.

ARDMORE, Co. Waterford (Map 5, D6), is a pleasant, small seaside resort with a good strand, 14 m. SW. of Dungarvan and 6 m. E. of Youghal. It is a convenient base for exploring the S. Waterford coastal region. There are interesting sea caves in Ardmore Head and Ram Head, to the E. and S. of the village.

The " pre-Patrician " abbot-bishop, St Déaglán (Declan), of whom very little is known, founded a monastery here which became one of the principal ecclesiastical centres of the kingdom of the Déise (Decies). Though it was not recognized as an episcopal see at the 12th cent. reorganization of the Irish Church, some 12th–13th cent. bishops are known by name. Some time after 1210 the diocese was merged with Lismore (*q.v.*).

In the later Middle Ages the bishops of Waterford had a castle at Ardmore. In 1495 it was seized by Perkin Warbeck, who left his wife there when he marched on Waterford. In 1642 the castle was occupied by 114 Confederate Catholic troops, accompanied by 200 women and children. 40 more – of whom only two had muskets – stationed themselves in the nearby Round Tower. They were attacked by a superior force with artillery, under Lord Broghill, and two days later surrendered. Broghill hanged 117 of the defenders.

On the hill-slope S. of the village, St Declan's Church (alias the Cathedral), St Declan's House (alias Tomb), and the Cloigtheach, or

Commissioners of Public Works in Ireland

Fall of Adam and Eve, St Declan's, Ardmore

Round Tower (Nat. Mons.), mark the site of Déaglán's monastery.

The three-period Cathedral (said to have been erected by Máel-Ettrim Ó Duibherathra (d. 1203) before he became bishop) is a nave-and-chancel church. The Romanesque arcading (with figure carvings) of the W. gable is unique

Commissioners of Public Works in Ireland

Round Tower and St Declan's Church, Ardmore

in Ireland. The subjects include *The Fall, The Judgment of Solomon*, and *The Adoration of the Magi*. The chancel arch, of early-13th cent. date, has Transitional capitals, etc. The side-wall arcades may have held paintings. Stored in the nave are the original capstones of the Round Tower and seven early gravestones. In the chancel are stored two ogham stones; the S. stone, which was found used as a building stone in St Declan's Tomb, has two inscriptions. The basin and base of an octagonal 15th cent. font from the cathedral are preserved in the nearby Protestant church. (The basin was originally supported by four ribbed columns.)

St Declan's House, which is said to contain the saint's grave, is an important "station" of the annual pilgrimage (24 July). The roof, upper gables, and N. door are modern. St Déaglán's Grave, a stone-lined pit in the floor, was formerly covered by a flagstone which, like the filling of the grave, has vanished as a result of centuries of relic-collecting.

The beautiful Round Tower (95 ft 4 in.) is perhaps the finest, and latest, in Ireland. Five of the internal corbels have grotesque carvings.

On the lawn of Monea House is Cloch Daha, the base of a stone cross which formerly stood by the roadside opposite the Protestant church. On Ash Wednesday the young men of Ardmore used to set up a tow-crowned rod in it and make the old maids dance round it while spinning the pendant tow. Afterwards they seated the maids on old logs and dragged them through the village.

At the S. end of the strand is St Declan's Stone, a conglomerate erratic which, so goes the tale, carried the saint's bell and vestments across the waves from Menevia in Wales and, by coming ashore at Ardmore, indicated Déaglán's place of resurrection. To crawl under the stone, a feat impossible to those in a state of sin, is held to cure rheumatism.

½ m. SE. of the village is a fragment of Teampall an Dísirt, alias Dysert Church, successor of the *desertulum* ("little hermitage") mentioned in Déaglán's *Life*. Nearby is St Declan's Well, repaired in 1798. The remains here include a rudely built stone chair, three rude stone crucifixes, and a shallow tank in which pilgrims used to bathe their limbs.

½ m. SW., in Ardoginna, is Gort an Dúinín promontory fort.

2 m. W., in the ancient churchyard of Grange, a cross-inscribed ogham stone serves as marker of a modern grave.

5½ m. W., on the E. side of Youghal Harbour, is Monatray strand (*see* Youghal).

ARDPATRICK, Co. Limerick (Map 5, B5), a hamlet on the Kilmallock (5½ m.)–Fermoy (18¾ m.) road, 3 m. SW. of Kilfinnane, is situated at the foot of the Ballyhoura Mountains. St Patrick is said to have founded a church here, whose monastic successor is represented by the stump of a Round Tower, remnants of a contemporary church with *antae*

and a plain, Romanesque S. door (with Gothic insertion), etc. This monastery was the seat of "Patrick's *maor*" for Munster, whose function was to collect Munster contributions to Armagh; the O Langans were hereditary coarbs. On 1 April 1129, Ceallach, reformer and 1st Archbishop of Armagh, died here (he was buried at Lismore). Nearby are Rian Bó Phádraig (the "Slug of St. Patrick's Cow's Horn"), an ancient, entrenched roadway; also remains of an ancient field system.

The Ballyhoura Mountains (1,702 ft) have many legends of Fionn mac Cumhail and the Fiana; a cairn on the summit is legendarily the tomb of Fionn's son, Oisín (Fionn and Oisín are the Fingal and Ossian of Macpherson's celebrated 18th cent. literary forgeries).

2 m. SE., in Glenosheen (Gleann Oisín), is the demesne of Castle Oliver. Nothing remains of 18th cent. Castle Oliver, birthplace of notorious Lola Montez (Marie Gilbert, 1818–61), who danced her way into the lunatic affections of Ludwig I of Bavaria, got control of the country, and provoked the revolution of 1848. Clonodfey House, in the demesne, is a Victorian Gothic structure. On the hill is a Famine-times folly.

5 m. SE., in Abbey, are remains of a church of various dates.

2 m. W., at Mount Russel, is Oscar's Bed, a prehistoric chamber tomb.

ARDRAHAN, Co. Galway (Map 5, B2), is a hamlet on the main Galway (17 m.)–Limerick (44 m.) road, 8 m. N. of Gort. The surrounding countryside is rich in ancient remains of all periods. On an earthwork (bretasche) beside the village stand the fragmentary remains (Nat. Mon.) of a square-keep castle of about 1250, one of the fortresses of the Anglo-Norman invaders of Connacht. The nearby churchyard occupies an early monastic site with the stump of a Round Tower (outside the W. wall of the graveyard) and fragments of a medieval church. The countryside is very rich in ringforts.

1 m. ENE., in the SE. angle of Cregaclare crossroads, is the Doon, a large trivallate ring-fort (tree-planted and overgrown) with several souterrains (inaccessible). In the field on the opposite side of the road is a pillarstone. ½ m. SW. is Cregaclare (ruined), sometime seat of Lord Clanmorris, whose family mausoleum may be seen at a ruined Penal-times Catholic chapel ½ m. SW. 1½ m. NE. of the Doon, close to the S. side of the road in Fiddaun, is a ring-barrow; 1 m. further NE., in Monksfield, is a second; 1¼ m. ENE. of this, on the N. side of the road, is Lakyle Motte, a ring-barrow. 2 m. N. of the Monksfield barrow is Ballynamannin (*see* Craughwell).–1 m. E. of the Doon, in Furzy Park, is a ring-barrow; 1¼ m. ESE., in Rathbaun, is a second; 2 m. ESE., in Furzy Park, close to the N. side of the Loughrea road, is a trivallate ringfort with a ring-barrow to the NNW. Less than 1 m. ENE. of these last, on the N. side of the road, are the remains of

Isertkelly (Díseart Cheallaigh) church; about 600 yds SE. of the church, in Castlepark, is the 16th cent. tower (Nat. Mon.) of a Mac Hubert Burke castle; noteworthy interior details. – 3 m. SE. of the Doon, in Grannagh, is a small ring-barrow. Close by is a ringfort which affords a delightful view of the verdant pastures of Castleboy at the foot of Slieve Aughty.

1¼ m. S. is Laban. The nondescript parish church has its place in the story of 20th cent. Irish church art. When Edward Martyn of Tullira (*below*) wished to commission family windows for the church, he discovered that Continental and English factories had a monopoly of the "art" of the resurgent Catholic Church in Ireland. For Martyn it was self-evident that art is the function of artists, and that "the artists of Ireland should decorate the churches". Accordingly, he commissioned the English artist, Christopher Whall, a disciple of William Morris, to do windows for Laban and for Loughrea cathedral (*q.v.*), stipulating that the "actual work" on the Loughrea windows should be done in Ireland. Whall sent A. E. Childe over to Dublin to execute the Loughrea windows. Martyn's zeal helped to have Childe appointed (1903) teacher of stained glass in the Dublin Metropolitan School of Art, and stimulated Sarah Purser to found the famous Túr Gloine studio (*see* Pembroke St *under* Dublin, South-East). The Laban windows in question are five single lights: St Anne (?), St Robertus, Naomh Peadar (the poorest), Naomh Eilís, Naomh Andrís; the first two are undated, the others are 1900; all have a Túr Glóine look. The altar baldachino looks like a William Scott design, its capitals and bases like the work of Michael Shortall (*see* Loughrea cathedral).

1¼ m. SE. is Tullira Castle (Lord Hemphill), home of Edward Martyn (1859–1923; *see also* Doorus House *under* Kinvara), playwright, poet, author, and admirable patron of the arts, who figures prominently in the lives and writings of his contemporaries, W. B. Yeats, Lady Gregory, George Moore, *et al* (e.g. George Moore's *Hail and Farewell*). The house was re-built – despite Yeats's protests – in a "Tudor" style at a time (1882) when Martyn was very much under the influence of William Morris. It incorporates the tower of a Burke castle which passed to the Martyns early in the 17th cent. (*see* Dungory castle *under* Kinvara).

1¾ m. W. is Owenbristy crossroads. 500 yds N., in Rooaunmore, is a fine square "fort". ¾ m. SSE., in Drumharsna, is Seán Ballach's Castle (Nat. Mon.); it served as a British outpost, 1920–21.

4½ m. SSW. (via Laban) is the tower of Lydican castle (Nat. Mon.).

ARKLOW, Co. Wicklow (Map 6, D4), is a fishing port and popular seaside resort on the estuary of the Avoca (properly the Avonmore) 16 m. S. of Wicklow and 11 m. NE. of Gorey. The town has long been noted for the building

Irish Tourist Board

An Arklow potter

of small wooden ships and boats, including the Arklow "nobbies". In more recent times it has developed a flourishing pottery. There are good bathing beaches S. and N. of the town, as also at Johnstown (3 m.) and Ennereilly (4 m.) further to the NE.; boating facilities both at the harbour and on the river. A variety of delightful walks can be made in the beautiful Avoca valley and along the shore (NE. via the North Strand, Porter's Rocks, and Johnstown to Ennereilly; S. via the South Strand to Arklow Rock, 411ft, which affords fine views of mountains and coast). The town is also a convenient base for touring some of the celebrated Co. Wicklow beauty spots, e.g. Glendalough (*q.v.*), Glenmalure (*q.v.*), the Clara valley (*see under* Laragh), Meeting of the Waters (*see under* Rathdrum).

In Viking times the Norse had a settlement at Arklow. From them the place derives its English name (Irish, An tInbhear Mór).

In 1185/9 Prince John granted the town, castle, and manor of Arklow to William Marshal and Theobald fitz Walter, ancestor of the Butlers. The town was burned by Edward Bruce in 1315. Thereafter East Wicklow was gradually recovered by the Irish, and by the beginning of the 16th cent. the towns of Arklow and Wicklow were the only places remaining in English hands. In 1641 the castle was taken by Confederate Catholics, who held it until 1649, when they burned it down on the approach of Cromwell. On 9 June 1798, the Wexford Insurgents, incompetently if bravely led by Father Michael Murphy, made a reckless assault on the town in their effort to link up with the United Irishmen of Dublin. After 2½ hours of very fierce fighting Father Murphy was killed at the head of his men, who were dispersed with heavy loss. It was the decisive battle of the Rising.

The Catholic church is by Patrick Byrne (1783–1864). In a field adjoining the parish priest's house are remains of a Dominican friary founded in 1264 by Thomas fitz Walter. Of the 13th cent. Butler castle only fragments of the curtain and of one corner tower survive. Nothing survives of Arklow's medieval Cistercian house. The only modern building of note is the large, English-looking, Protestant church (1900) by Sir Arthur Blomfield; it has a three-light window (*Ascénsion*; 1922) by Harry Clarke. In front of the Catholic parish church is a 1798 memorial.

3½ m. N. are the remains of Temple Michael church.

7 m. N. is Brittas Bay (*see under* Wicklow).

2 m. NE. is Ennereilly (Inbhear Daoile), where there is a good small beach backed by dunes. Bishop Dagan, nephew of St Kevin, built a church here at the mouth of the little Redcross (Daoil) River.

3½ m. SSW., to the SW. of Arklow Rock, are St Iver's Well and remains of Ballinabanoge church.

2¼ m. NW., on the N. bank of the Avoca (properly Avonmore; *see under* Rathdrum), are Shelton Abbey and its beautiful demesne (noted for rhododendrons), formerly seat of the Earls of Wicklow, now a State forestry school. The Tudor-style house is by Sir Richard Morrison (1767–1849) and his son William Vitruvius Morrison, architect of Kilruddery, Bray. A chemical factory has recently been erected in the demesne by Nitrigin Éireann.

6 m. NW. is Woodenbridge. Nearby the Avoca and Aughrim (Gold Mine) rivers unite in a beautiful "meeting of the waters" beneath the wooded heights of Kilcarra and Ballyarthur. A good secondary road leads NW. up the attractive valley of the Aughrim River to Aughrim (*q.v.*). To the SW. rises Croghan, alias Croghan Kinsella (1,995 ft), whose streams have yielded placer gold from time to time. Some gold mining was carried out here round the turn of the 18th cent.

1½ m. NNW. are the remains of Kilbride church.

ARLESS, Co. Laois (Map 6, B4), is a village on the Carlow (6 m.)–Stradbally (10 m.) road.

The Grace family, descended from Raymond le Gros who accompanied Strongbow to Ireland, has a curious mausoleum here, modelled on St Doolagh's Church, Co. Dublin (*see under* Portmarnock).

ARMAGH, Co. Armagh (Map 3, B5), capital of its county and primatial city of Ireland, is an important road junction on the Belfast (37 m.)–Enniskillen (50 m.) and Dundalk (28 m.)–Derry (73 m.) roads. It is one of the more attractive towns in Ireland, with good Georgian–Regency buildings and houses.

The name of this historic town, Ard Macha (Macha's Height), preserves the memory of the goddess, Macha, who was also associated with Eamhain Macha (*see* Navan, *below*). It was, doubtless, the still enduring fame of Eamhain which led St Patrick to choose Armagh to be the site of his principal church (445?). Bishop Cormac (d. 497) made the church of Armagh a monastic one, and for some centuries thereafter the offices of bishop and abbot were united in the same person, the episcopal functions becoming, as elsewhere in Ireland, subordinate to the abbatial. From at least the 8th cent. onwards the bishop-abbots of Armagh, as the heirs of Patrick, claimed primatial authority over the whole Irish Church, though their claims must have been largely nullified by the power of such famous monastic federations as that of Iona. In 1004 Armagh's primacy was formally acknowledged by High-King Brian Boru. Meanwhile Armagh had suffered from Scandinavian raiders (nine or ten raids between 832 and 943). Consequences of those disturbed centuries were the separation of the abbatial from the episcopal office, and its seizure by the Úa Sínaich family; from 957 until 1134 it was held as a hereditary possession by members of this family, all laymen. During these same centuries, however, the *céle Dé* movement (*see* Tallaght) had spread to Armagh, and genuine religion always had its representatives there. (The *céle Dé* community survived until 1570/80.) Not unfittingly, it was an Úa Sínaich who led the post-Viking reform movement in the North.

From an early date Armagh had its monastic school, and it, too, played its part in the post-Viking renaissance, so that in 1162 the Synod of Clane saw fit to decree that no one who was not an alumnus of Armagh should be master of studies in any Irish monastic school. Seven years later High-King Rory O Conor endowed the Armagh school so as to provide instruction for the students of Ireland and Scotland. (The plundering of Armagh by the Anglo-Normans in 1184, 1185 and 1189 dealt the embryonic university a blow from which it never recovered.)

When Cellach ("Celsus") Úa Sínaich succeeded to the abbacy in 1105 he was still a layman, but promptly took holy orders. On the death of the bishops in the following year he had himself consecrated in his stead, thus once more uniting the episcopal and abbatial offices. Until his death in 1129, Cellach was, in effect if not in name, Archbishop-Primate of Ireland. As his successor he nominated the celebrated St Máel M'Aedhóig ("Malachy") Úa Morgair who, with the aid of the secular power, finally broke the Úa Sínaich stranglehold on Armagh. In 1137, his victory assured, Máel M'Aedhóig retired to the bishopric of Down, leaving as his successor in Armagh Gilla-meic-Liag ("Gelasius"), Abbot of Derry. At the Synod of Kells (1152) Gilla-meic-Liag received his pall as first canonical Archbishop of Armagh and Primate of all Ireland from the papal legate, Cardinal Paparo.

From the 14th cent. onward, the English Crown contrived the appointment of archbishops only of non-Gaelic stock. Such arch-

The Archbishop's Palace, Armagh

bishops could exercise only restricted jurisdiction outside the English Pale, and therefore made Termonfeckin (*q.v.*) their normal place of residence. It was not until the 16th cent. campaigns against the O Neills (for which its strategic position dictated an unfortunate rôle) that Armagh passed into effective English (by now Protestant) control. The 16th and 17th cent. wars and the victory of Protestantism have left us but few relics of either the ancient or the medieval ecclesiastical capital, and the most important of these are now elsewhere: the *Book of Armagh* (*see* Ballymoyer *under* Newtown Hamilton) in Trinity College library, the Bell of St Patrick's Will and its superb shrine in the National Museum, the *Gospels of Máel-Brigte Úa Máel-Úanaigh* (1138) in the British Museum.

The town is dominated by the two cathedrals, which crown rival hill-tops.

St Patrick's Protestant Cathedral occupies the site of St Patrick's principal church, which was erected inside a bivallate hill-fort given to him by "a certain rich and honourable man named Daire". The rings which enclosed the fort may still be traced: the inner, via the gardens at the rear of Vicars Hill–Callan St–Abbey St–Market St–Castle St back to Vicars Hill; the outer, by a dip in Abbey St and Market St some 60–70 ft outside the inner ring. The cathedral, though its walls have a medieval core, is in effect the work of the English architect, Lewis Cottingham, who "restored" (1834–7) the long-suffering fabric for Archbishop

Lord John George Beresford. The medieval cathedral, built by Archbishop O Scannail about 1261–8, had been repaired in the 14th and 15th centuries, turned into an English strong-point and wrecked by the Irish in the 16th cent., re-edified for Protestant use early in the 17th cent., and burned by the Irish at the outbreak of the Eleven Years' War. It had been several times repaired and altered between 1663 and 1802, Thomas Cooley and Francis Johnston being among those who had laid hands on it. Cottingham's idea of restoration included the removal and dispersal of most of the surviving medieval carvings.

Inside the cathedral are monuments to Sir Thomas Molyneux (1661–1733) by Roubilliac, to Dean Drelincourt (d. 1722) by Rysbrack, to Archbishop Stuart (d. 1822) by Sir Francis Chantrey, and to Archbishop Robinson (Lord Rokeby; d. 1794) by Nollekens; also 17th cent. monuments of the Caulfields of Charlemont (*q.v.*). At the W. end of the N. aisle are the shaft and broken head of a High Cross which formerly stood in Market St to the E. of the cathedral. (It is said to have been brought to Armagh from Raphoe in 1441.) The figure subjects include the following. E. Face: *Temptation of Adam and Eve, Noah's Ark, Sacrifice of Isaac, Crucifixion*; W. Face: *Annunciation to the Shepherds* (?), *Baptism of Christ, Christ in Glory*; N. Side: *The Three Children in the Fiery Furnace, The Raven brings bread to Paul and Anthony*; S. Side: *David and the Lion, Jacob and the Angel*. In the N. Transept is a small collection of medieval and pre-Christian (?) carvings. The regimental colours in the cathedral are those of the Royal Irish Fusiliers. There is also a French flag taken at the Battle of Ballinamuck (*q.v.*), 1798. Under the E. end of the cathedral is a small crypt of uncertain date. In the church-yard are fragments of a stone cross which, says a local tradition, belonged to the monument of High-King Brian Boru, who was brought to Armagh for burial after the battle of Clontarf, 1014. (A tablet in the outer face of the W. wall of the N. transept marks the reputed position of his grave.) Medieval Armagh had many stone crosses – at least six in 1166.

The cathedral ring-enclosure formerly con-tained several ancient buildings: The Sabhal, or Barn, on the site of the present N. transept; the Church of the Elections, at the S. side of the. chancel; the Abbot's House, later the Arch-bishop's Court, to the N. of the cathedral; the Round Tower (site unknown); the House of Writings, or Library, near the present Public Library; the Augustinian monastery of SS Peter and Paul (founded in 1126 by St Máel M'Áedhóig's recluse-tutor, Íomhar O Hagan), on the site of the Archbishop Alexander Memorial Hall in Abbey St; St Brigid's Church, some 30 yds NE. of the present St Malachy's Church in Chapel Lane.

NW. of the cathedral, in Callan St, is the Public Library (1771) founded by Archbishop Robinson. The original building (by Thomas Cooley) – librarian's residence and a long hall with a gallery – was completed in 1771, the W. staircase entrance being added in 1820. The library has valuable collections of MSS. and books. Off Abbey St is the Old Presbyterian Church (1722), now the Y.M.C.A. The wrought-iron gates (1750) are an interesting example of the work of the Thornberrys of Richhill (*see* Hillsborough). Between the Pro-vincial Bank and the Unionist Club, Abbey St, is the site of the ancient Church of St Columcille.

SE. of the cathedral, in Dobbin St, is the entrance to the fine, Georgian Archbishop's Palace. Not far from the gate are remains (Nat. Mon.) of a Franciscan friary founded in 1264 by Archbishop O Scannail. The first buildings are attributed to a Mac Donnell leader of the galloglas of O Neill of Tír Eoghain. Gormlaith O Donnell, wife of Áedh Mór O Neill, was buried in the friary in 1353. In 1561 the friary was destroyed by Seaán the Proud O Neill to prevent its becoming an English strong-point. The Palace was designed about 1770 for Arch-bishop Robinson by Thomas Cooley. Francis Johnston (1761–1829), Armagh's distinguished architect son, very skilfully added the third storey and built the chapel. There is an interest-ing collection of portraits of the Protestant primates from 1582 onwards, also a number of important royal portraits. The chapel is an excellent little Classical temple; the sensitive interior details are typically Johnston. An obelisk in the decayed demesne commemorates

Primate Robinson's friendship with the Duke of Northumberland.

The Technical School, Market St, was built as the town Market House in 1815 to the design of Francis Johnston.

The Bank of Ireland, Scotch St, built in 1812 for the Dobbin family, is attributed to Francis Johnston. It occupies the site of Teampall na Fearta, alias Fearta Martar, legendarily St Patrick's first church and the burial place of the saint himself (*see* Downpatrick) and of his "sister", Lupita.

To the E. of Upper English St is The Mall, an early 19th cent. promenade. At the N. end is the classical County Courthouse (1809), also by Johnston, who complained that the builder spoilt the portico by attenuating the columns for convenience of transport. On the E. side is a good, late Georgian, terrace by Johnston's nephew, John Skipton Mulvany. Nearby is the County Museum, which incorporates an attrac-tive Classical-temple schoolhouse of 1833. The archaeological and folk collections are interest-ing; also the exhibits relating to the Orange Order and to the rival Ancient Order of Hibernians. There is also a collection of Francis Johnston papers and notebooks.

The NE. corner of The Mall opens on College Hill, called after the Royal School founded by James I in 1608. In 1773 the school was removed from Abbey St to its present site, where the original buildings – completed in 1774 at the expense of Archbishop Robinson – formed a quadrangle with covered passage in front, schoolroom at the back, and the head-master's and pupils' lodgings in either wing. On the opposite side of the road is Armagh Obser-vatory, founded in 1793 by Primate Robinson and still flourishing. (It works in co-operation with the Dublin Institute for Advanced Studies.) The dignified buildings, by Francis Johnston, were not completed until 1825.

St Patrick's Catholic Cathedral was begun in 1840, but the Great Famine called a halt to the undertaking, which was not resumed until 1854 and was completed only in 1873. The original architect, Thomas J. Duff of Newry (*see* St Colman's Cathedral, Newry, *and* St Patrick's Church, Dundalk), had designed a Perpendicular church with a low central tower as well as two W. ones. The resumed work was entrusted to J. J. McCarthy, who gave us the existing, better, loftier, Decorated building. In accordance with an unfortunate fashion still, unhappily, with us, the lavish interior decora-tions and appointments (1900–1904) were en-trusted to Italian "artists". The carillon has thirty-nine bells.

2¼ m. N., on the borders of Tullyard and Cabragh, is Béal an Átha Bhuidhe, alias the Yellow Ford, scene of Great Hugh O Neill's signal victory over Marshal Sir Henry Bagenal in 1598 (*see under* Blackwatertown).

6 m. NE. is Richhill Castle, an interesting gabled house of 1655–96. The superb wrought-iron entrance gates of about 1745, thought to

R. E. Scott

St Patrick's Catholic Cathedral, Armagh

be the work of the Thornberry brothers of Richhill, were removed to Government House, Hillsborough (*q.v.*), in 1936.

5 m. SE. is Carnavanaghan (*see under* Markethill).

4 m. S., in Killyfaddy, is the Dane's Cast, a travelling earthwork running NE.–SW. It is thought to have formed part of the defences of the ancient "Fifth" of Ulster (*see* Navan Fort, *below, and* Scarva). Other stretches survive in the neighbouring townlands of Lisnadill, Latmacollum, and Killycapple.

1¼ m. SW., by the Callan in Tullymore, is Niall's Mound, alias O Neill's Mound, reputedly a cenotaph marking the place where King Niall Caille was drowned, 846.

2 m. W., in Navan (An Eamhain), is Navan Fort (Nat. Mon.), an 18-acre hill-fort enclosed by a bank (largely defaced) set (as at Tara and Knockaulin, Kilcullen) outside its ditch. The site commands an extensive prospect. On the summit of the enclosure is a univallate tumulus covering a low cairn. SE. of this are traces of a ringfort. These scant remains are all that survive of the Isamnium of Ptolemy's *Geography*, the Eamhain Macha of Irish mythology and heroic literature. Eamhain was the seat of the overkings of the ancient "Fifth" of the Ulaid destroyed by the 5th (?) cent. expansion of the Uí Néill of Tara. Thereafter Ulster was confined to Cos. Antrim and Down, while for some centuries the Eamhain region formed part of Uriel. In the 9th cent. however, this part of Uriel was absorbed by the O Neill kingdom of Tír Eoghain, and with Tír Eoghain it remained until the Tudor conquest. In the celebrated *Ulster Cycle* of heroic tales, the King of Eamhain is the mythological Conchobar mac Nesa, who dwells and feasts with his heroes, Cú Chulainn, Cú-Roí, and the rest, in one of the three halls of Eamhain, viz. Cráebrúad (The Red Branched) whose name survives in that of adjoining Creeveroe. The fame of Eamhain endured throughout the centuries, and as late as 1387 Niall Óg O Neill, who claimed to be King of all Ulster, built a house there to entertain the literati of Ireland. – ½ m. NW. of Navan Fort, in Tray, are the King's Stables, a ringfort with sunken floor.

7 m. W. is Tynan (*see under* Middletown).

2 m. WNW. (½ m. N. of Navan Fort), in Ballybrolly, is the Druid's Ring (Nat. Mon.), a circle of thirty boulders; a chamber tomb stood at the centre. In the next field was a similar monument.

ARMOY, Co. Antrim (Map 3, B3), is a village 6½ m. S. of Ballycastle, 1 m. W. of the main road to Belfast (49 m.). Close to the Protestant church is the stump of a Round Tower (Nat. Mon.), all that survives of a monastery which succeeded a church confided, we are told, by St Patrick to Bishop Olcán (*see* Dunseverick *under* Bushmills).

Armoy is a convenient centre for visiting the N. Glens of Antrim (Glenshesk, Glenaan and Glendun).

2 m. ENE., in Tullaghora (Tullaghore), are two ancient stone crosses (Nat. Mons.).

7 m. SSW. is Knockaholet Moat (Nat. Mon.), remnant of a motte-and-bailey castle. The ditch-enclosed motte has been sited centrally inside an earlier oval earthwork so as to provide a bailey at either end.

ARVAGH, Co. Cavan (Map 2, D6), is a small village on the Cavan (8 m.)–Longford (17 m.) road, 2 m. N. of pretty Lough Gowna.

2½ m. NE., near the foot of Bruse Hill, is Coranea Mass Rock, a relic of Penal times. Near the N. foot is Finn Mac Cool's Finger Stone, a pillarstone. Easily climbed Bruse Hill (856 ft) affords fine panoramas of the Cavan lake country and the Sligo–Leitrim highlands.

3½ m. NW. is Drumhart court cairn.

ASHBOURNE, Co. Meath (Map 6, D2), is a village on the Dublin (13 m.)–Slane (16 m.) road.

In 1916 a sharp skirmish took place 1 m. N. between a strong party of Royal Irish Constabulary and local insurgents led by Thomas Ashe, the village schoolmaster (1959 memorial by Peter Grant). The following year Ashe died in Mountjoy Prison, Dublin, as a result of forcible feeding when on hunger-strike.

"But down the pale roads of Ashbourne
Are heard the voices of the free"
Francis Ledwidge

1¼ m. S. is an 1880 obelisk (interesting panels) to the memory of Charles Brindley of Stafford, for thirty-five years (1843–78) Huntsman of the Ward Hounds. The Huntsman's House is noteworthy.

It is from Ashbourne that the Gibson barons take their title. William, the second baron (d. 1947), always wore a saffron kilt – in the fond belief that it was Ireland's national costume – and insisted on speaking Irish in the House of Lords.

ASHFORD, Co. Wicklow (Map 6, D4), is a small village beautifully situated by the River Vartry on the Newtown Mount Kennedy (8 m.)–Wicklow (4 m.) road. It is a convenient centre for exploring the eastern Wicklow Mts as well as the attractive local countryside with its fine demesnes. Beside the village is Mount Usher, whose noted gardens are open to the public except on Sat., Sun., and Bank Holidays.

2½ m. NNE., in Courtfoyle, is a medieval square fortification with a water-ditch and traces of a masonry revetment. It was an O Byrne stronghold in the 16th–17th centuries (*see* Ballyraine Middle *under* Arklow). In the adjacent townland of Moorstown is a 7-ft pillarstone.

1½ m. SE. is the village of Rathnew. St Ernín, alias M'Earnóg (d. 634/5), of Portmarnock (*q.v.*) founded a church here. The only remains are fragments of a church and a bullaun in the old graveyard.

3 m. SW. is Glenealy State Forest.

1½ m. NW., on the S. side of the Vartry, are the featureless remains of Kilfea, a small church with clay-bonded walls; there are traces of an enclosing wall or bank. 220 yds SE. is Tobar Bride, a holy well still resorted to.

2 m. NW. is the beautiful Devil's Glen, a rugged 2-m. defile where the Vartry tumbles down a fine fall. Paths and walks afford splendid views. The glen was one of Joseph Holt's retreats after 1798.

1½ m. NNW. is classical Ballycurry House (1805) by Francis Johnston.

2¾ m. NNW. are the overgrown remains of Killiskey church.

ASKEATON, Co. Limerick (Map 5, A4), is a small market town on the Limerick (16 m.)–Tarbert (19¼ m.) road. After the Anglo-Norman invasion the place was among those granted to Hamo de Valognes, who built a castle about 1197/9. Early in the 14th cent. the manor was acquired by the Earls of Desmond, whose great castle, on an island (the ancient Inis Geibthine) in the River Deel, adjoins the bridge. The remains (Nat. Mon.) comprise two courts or wards. The upper ward is on a limestone outcrop scarped into a sort of motte in the 13th cent.; in it are a lofty, narrow tower and remains of a tall 16th cent. house. On the W. side of the lower ward are ruins of a splendid 15th cent. Great Hall raised on the remnants of an older one by the 7th (?) Earl of Desmond; the S. end has remains of a chapel. After the second battle of Monasternenagh, 1579 (*see under* Croom), Garret, 15th (Rebel) Earl of Desmond, shut himself up in the castle. Malby, the English Governor of Connacht, marched on Askeaton but, having

no artillery to batter the castle, contented himself with firing the town and friary, butchering the friars, and wrecking the ancestral tomb of the Desmonds. On 3 April 1580, English under Pelham appeared before the castle with artillery. The terrified garrison abandoned their charge, which thenceforth remained an English stronghold. It was twice unsuccessfully blockaded by Great Hugh O Neill's ally, James, Súgán Earl of Desmond (for 247 days in 1598). In 1642 it was taken by Confederate Catholic troops, and it remained in Confederate hands till the Cromwellian victory in 1652. The Cromwellians dismantled it.

On the E. bank of the river are remains of the medieval parish church of St Mary and of Rock Abbey (Nat. Mon.). The "abbey" was a Franciscan friary founded before 1400, probably by Gearóid *file*, 4th Earl of Desmond, and restored in the 15th cent. by James, the 6th earl. It adopted the Observantine reform in 1497. The place was wrecked by Malby in 1579, but the friars returned in 1627 and re-edified it in 1643. They finally abandoned it on the approach of the Cromwellians. The original friary consisted of a rectangular church and the usual buildings round a cloister (on the S. side). Additions included a sacristy, aisled N. transept, belfry (removed), and a large refectory to the S. of the cloister. The cloister is a beautiful example of the friary type; at the NE. angle (N. ambulatory) is a carving of St Francis, showing the Stigmata. In the chancel are fine sedilia and the figure of a bishop.

The remains (fragments of belfry and chancel) of St Mary's Augustinian priory are close to the Protestant parish church. Aubrey de Vere (*see* Currah Chase, *below*) is buried in the Protestant churchyard.

6 m. NE. is Killulta (*see under* Pallaskenry).

5 m. SE. is Currah Chase, ancestral home of the de Vere family. The fine late-18th cent. house was destroyed by fire in 1941. It was the birthplace of Aubrey de Vere (1814–1902), poet.

2 m. SW. is Ballycullen House, a Georgian house. In Lismakeery, the adjacent townland to the S. and SE., is Lismakeery, a fine ringfort with remains of a stone revetment. Beside it are the ruins of a late-15th cent. church.

ATHBOY, Co. Meath (Map 6, B2), is a market village on the Trim (8 m.)–Oldcastle (16 m.) road.

There was a battle here in 1022 between the Norse of Dublin and Melaghlin II, in which the latter was victorious. In the Middle Ages Athboy was a small walled town, a strong-point of the English Pale. In 1643 it was captured by Eóghan Rúa O Neill.

The Protestant parish church stands on part of the site of a Carmelite friary, whose 15th cent. W. tower it incorporates. At the church door, exposed to the elements, is a late 15th cent. tomb with effigies of an armoured knight and his wife; the panels include a *Resurrection*. Nearby are fragments of the town wall.

3 m. N. (1 m. SW. of Fordstown) is Girley where, in 695, Finshnechta the Festive, King of Tara, and his son, Breasal, were routed and slain by rival kinsfolk. There are remains of a medieval church. In the churchyard is part of the head of a small ringheaded cross with fret and other patterns.

3 m. NE., on the Navan road, are the ruined early-15th cent. castle and manorial church (Nat. Mon.) of Rathmore. Some time before 1443, Sir Thomas Plunkett, third son of Christopher of Killeen and Dunsany (*see under* Dunshaughlin), married the heiress of Rathmore, Mary Cruise. Either he or Mary's father (d. 1423) built the church, which was dedicated to St Laurence. It is a nave-and-chancel structure with a small bell-tower at the SW. angle, a three-storey sacristy-cum-priest's house, and a N. porch (1519). Over the E. end of the nave was a wooden rood-loft, which may have had a chapel on either side of the chancel arch. On the N. side of the chancel is the elaborate tombstone of Sir Christopher Plunkett (d. 1531) and Katherine Preston, his wife. A broken slab on the S. side commemorates John Bligh of London, a Cromwellian Adventurer who got possession of Rathmore in 1657. In the S. wall of the chancel are a piscina and fan-vaulted sedilia. The E. window is good. Parts of the base of the high altar survive; the carving is typical of a 15th cent. workshop which supplied altar-tombs to several churches in Cos. Meath and Dublin. The figures include one of St Laurence the Deacon, and the coats of arms include those of Plunkett, Fleming, Bellew, Bermingham, and Cusack. In the sacristy is the mensa of a 15th cent. double tomb with the effigies, in high relief, of an armoured knight and his lady. These probably represent Sir Thomas Plunkett (d. 1471) and Mary Cruise. Near the N. porch is the figured shaft of a 15th cent. font: *Baptism of Christ, Ecce Homo, St Peter, St Paul, St Brigid*. The porch was erected in 1519 by Sir Christopher Plunkett and Katherine Preston, as was the sculptured cross of which a portion (Nat. Mon.) may be seen to the N. of the church. The subjects on the latter represent SS Patrick, Laurence, and Brigid.

1 m. E. is the Hill of Ward, formerly called Tlachtga and the meeting place of an *aonach*, or great public assembly, which met at Samhain (31 Oct.). The site of the assembly is presumably marked by the much disturbed multivallate ring-work (a ringfort?; Nat. Mon.; fine view). In 1168 High King Rory O Conor presided over a national synod of kings and prelates which enacted "good decrees regarding veneration for churches and clerics and for the good government of the tribes and túatha"; 13,000 horsemen are said to have thronged the roads leading to the hill on that occasion. In 1172 Hugh de Lacy murdered Tiernan O Rourke, King of Breany, at a conference here. In 1649 Cromwell's army encamped on the hill.

1½ m. SSE. is Ballyfallon, birthplace of Father Eugene O Growney (1863–99), author of a celebrated Irish primer. He had learned his Irish from local native speakers.

5 m. SSE. is Kildalkey, where remains of a medieval church mark the site of a foundation of St Mo-Luóg's.

ATHENRY, Co. Galway (Map 5, B2), is a small market town on the N. road from Ballinasloe (25 m.) to Galway (15 m.), 11 m. NW. of Loughrea. It is the best centre for hunting the County Galway Hunt ("Galway Blazers") country. (The Blazers' kennels are at Craughwell, 5 m. S.)

The town was founded by Meiler de Bermingham, to whom William de Burgo, Anglo-Norman conqueror of much of Connacht, granted the place about 1235. Meiler also built the first castle and founded the Dominican friary. On 10 Aug. 1316, a great battle was fought outside the town between young King Felim O Conor, ally of Edward Bruce, and the Anglo-Normans of Connacht and Meath, led by William Liath de Burgo and Richard de Bermingham. The Irish endured the murderous fire of the Anglo-Norman bowmen all day long, but were routed in the end. King Felim and 60 Irish princes and lords were among the 8,000 slain, and the victors walled the town out of the profits of the arms and armour taken from the fallen. In 1574 the town was sacked by the sons of the Earl of Clanricard; three years later they attacked it again and wrecked the new walls and buildings. In 1596 the town was stormed and sacked by Red Hugh II O Donnell.

Considerable lengths of the town wall survive, also five of its flanking towers, but only one of its gates.

At the NE. corner of the old town stands the imposing de Bermingham castle (Nat. Mon.). The gatehouse and much of the towered curtain have gone, but the great three-storey keep of about 1250 is well preserved, The ground floor of the keep is vaulted on three square pillars; the floor above, the hall or principal apartment of the castle, was entered by a handsome Early Gothic doorway which was approached by an outside flight of steps; the roof-gables are medieval additions.

Nearby to the S. are the ill-kept ruins (Nat. Mon.) of the church of the Dominican friary of SS Peter and Paul, founded in 1241 by Meiler de Bermingham, who made it the family place of burial. Though an Anglo-Norman foundation, it owed much to native Irish patronage: the refectory was built by Felim O Conor (d. 1265), son of Cathal Crovderg; the dormitory by Eóghan O Heyne; the chapter-house by Conor O Kelly. In the early 14th cent. the choir was extended and the N. aisle and transept added. A century or so later a bell tower (vanished) was inserted between nave and chancel. A disastrous fire of 1423 entailed large-scale rebuilding (notice the inferior character of the alterations to the aisle and transept arcades and of the 16th cent. E. window inserted inside the remains of its nobler predecessor). Being in the land of the Irish, the friary was specifically exempted from Henry VIII's dissolution of the monasteries. In 1574, however, it was dissolved and granted to the town. That very year, town and friary were sacked by Clanricard's sons. Early in the 17th cent. the friars returned, and remained in possession until the Cromwellian victory of 1652. About 1750 the conventual buildings were demolished to make way for a military barracks, whose occupants wrecked the funerary and other monuments.

The Protestant parish church, SW. of the castle, occupies the site of the chancel of St Mary's Church founded in the 13th cent., made collegiate (with eight priests under a warden) by Archbishop O Murray of Tuam in 1484 (see St Nicholas's Church, Galway), and burned by Clanricard's sons in 1574. Fragments of the medieval nave and transepts survive, while two nave columns serve as churchyard gateposts. Outside the gateway, on a modern stepped pediment, is the head of a 15th cent. cross with Crucifixion and other figures. Nearby, in Nicolroe St, is the ruined N. gate of the medieval town.

3 m. NNW., to the E. of the Tuam road, is Castle Ellen, formerly home of the Lamberts and birthplace of Edward Carson's mother, Isabella Lambert.

5 m. NNW., on the W. side of the Tuam road, in Kilskeagh, is overgrown Cahermore, a ringfort 600–650 ft in diameter.

4 m. NE., to the W. of the Tiaquin road, is fragmentary Temple Moyle, a friary of Franciscan Tertiaries. In the adjoining townland to the W. Tighsaxon (Teach Sacsan) is a fragment of another friary of Franciscan Tertiaries, founded by one of the Burkes about 1441. Teach Saxan ("English House"), alias Teampall Geal, was an early monastery founded by Balan, brother of Berecheart of Tullylease (see under Drumcolliher).

6 m. SE. in Kiltullagh North is the ruined birthplace of Count Patrick D'Arcy (properly O Dorsey), 1725–79, Jacobite, French soldier and scientist, and Member of the French Academy. His great-nephew, John D'Arcy, founded Clifden (q.v.). Kiltullagh parish church has good Stations of the Cross by Evie Hone.

8 m. ESE., in a demesne bereft of its trees, is Raford, a rather gaunt house of 1797; it has a good galleried hall.

ATHLEAGUE, Co. Roscommon (Map 2, B7), is a village 5 m. SW. of Roscommon on the Ballygar (5 m.) road to Galway. There are ruins of a castle (of about the same date as Roscommon castle, q.v.) built to command the crossing of the Suck. In popular legend it is the "Fort of the Earls", a trench across the middle being pointed out as evidence of a partition between rival claimants who had failed to settle the issue with the sword.

2 m. NW., beside the avenue in derelict Castlestrange demesne, is the Castlestrange Stone (Nat. Mon.), a granite boulder covered with incised Iron Age spiral patterns.

ATHLONE, Co. Westmeath (Map 5, D1), is an important communications centre on the main Dublin (78 m.)–Galway (56 m.) road, at the principal Leinster–Connacht crossing of the Shannon. Today the larger portion of the town lies on the E. bank of the river, but the original town grew up in the shadow of the strong castle which commands the crossing from the W. bank. The town has always been an important garrison post. It also has a thriving cotton-weaving mill, and is an important regional centre for fairs and markets. It is a convenient base for visiting (ideally by boat) Clonmacnois (q.v.) and exploring Lough Ree (q.v.). During the summer months frequent lake and river cruises are available.

Because of its strategic position, Athlone has figured prominently in the history of Irish warfare. In the 10th and 11th centuries, before any town had grown up, the kings of Hy Many (Uí Maine) had their chief seat in the vicinity of the present castle. Early in the 12th cent. the expanding power of the O Conor kings of Connacht absorbed the place into their kingdom, and in 1129 Turloch Mór O Conor, King of Connacht and High-King of Ireland, "the Augustus of the West of Europe", built a fort to protect the bridge he had thrown across the river to provide ready access to Meath. Bridge and fort were repeatedly destroyed and replaced by the rival interests concerned during the following thirty years. At some time before 1199 the Anglo-Norman invaders had seized the vital crossing. They built a motte-castle on the W. bank, which has remained the kernel of all subsequent fortresses. In 1199 Cathal Crovderg O Conor burned the bawn of the castle and carried off much booty from the newcomers. In 1210 John de Gray, the English Justiciar, erected the strong castle which still survives. Though it has suffered much since then, and has been repeatedly altered, the core is still made up of the 12th cent. motte and de Gray's massive 13th cent. decagonal donjon. In 1641 the town was held successfully for twenty-two weeks against the Confederate Catholics of Connacht, but in February 1642 the English garrison and colonists were forced to withdraw, and the command of the town and castle was taken over by Viscount Dillon of Costelloe. The town suffered severely in the course of the war and never really recovered. In 1650 it was taken by the Cromwellian general, Sir Charles Coote II, at the second attempt. In July 1690, it was attacked by 10,000 Williamites under Douglas, but the sturdy Jacobite defence, led by Col. Richard Grace, forced the attackers to withdraw after a week's bombardment. The following June it was attacked by 21,000 Williamites led by Jodert de Ginkell. These were opposed by a garrison of 1,500 Jacobites under the command of Col. Nicholas Fitzgerald (with the Jacobite field army under St Ruth standing to nearby). The main attack centred on the bridge and the Connacht town, which was pounded by fifty cannon and eight mortars. These fired 50 tons of powder, 600 bombs, 12,000 cannon balls, and many tons of stones, in the course of the heaviest and most devastating bombardment in Irish history. It was during this attack that Custume (who has given his name to the adjacent military barracks) and his fellow volunteers heroically broke down the bridge in the face of the Williamite fire. After ten days gallant defence the Williamites made a brave, surprise crossing by way of the deep ford below the bridge. St Ruth failed to employ the Jacobite field army, and the defence of the town collapsed. The Jacobites then withdrew to the W. (see Aughrim, Co. Galway).

Little of interest survives in the Leinster part of the town. The Franciscan friary occupies the site of one founded before 1241. After the Dissolution the friars found a place of refuge in Coill an Iubhair (Killenure) near Glassan, and it was there that Brother Michael O Clery, chief of the Four Masters, copied a *Life* of St Cíarán of Saighir from a MS. belonging to Aodh Óg Ó Dalacháin of Liscloony, and a *Life* of St Rúadhán of Lorrha from a MS. belonging to Eochaidh Ó Síaghail of Fercáll, 26 Feb. 1628. There too he completed his *Succession of the Kings of Ireland* and his *Naomhshenchas Érenn*, 4 Nov. 1630. In St Mary's Protestant Church is a fragment of a monument to Sir Mathew de Renzi (d. 1634), a native of Cologne. He gave, we are informed, "a great perfection to this nation by composing a grammar dictionary and chronicle in the Irish tongue".

On the Connacht bank of the river is the castle. It was badly battered in the siege of 1691, and its appearance has not been enhanced either by repairs and modifications or by the warehouse which masks the river front. The unfortunate 1937 parish church of SS. Peter and Paul is by Ralph Byrne. The railway station (Galway road), by John Skipton Mulvany, nephew of Francis Johnston, is a good piece of early railway architecture. Further W. are the savagely defaced remains of fortifications constructed early in the 19th cent. to hold the bridgehead against threatened French invasion (see Shannonbridge).

Among the natives of Athlone who have achieved celebrity were Richard Rothwell (1800–1868), the painter; T. P. O Connor ("Tay-Pay", 1848–1929), journalist and Nationalist M.P.; and John, Count McCormack (1884–1945), the noted tenor, who was born in The Bawn, off Mardyke Street. Cartron, in the parish of St Peter's, was the home of Tadhg Ó Neachtain, Gaelic poet (d. 1729).

5 m. NE., near Glassan, are the ruins of Waterstown House, by Richard Cassels; an octagonal, spired dovecot raised on arches survives.

11 m. NE., in the Goldsmith country, is Auburn (q.v.).

3 m. ENE., on the hill N. of Bealin post office, is a High Cross (Nat. Mon.) said to have come from an ancient well near Twyford House. The carvings consist for the most part of spirals and interlaced zoomorphs, but include a figured panel with a hunting scene. The inscription, OROIT AR TUATHGAIL LAS DERNATH IN CHROSSA ("A prayer for Túathgal by whom this cross was made"), is thought to date the cross to about 800. 3 m. E. is Mount Temple, alias Ballyloughloe (see under Moate).

7½ m. WNW. is Brideswell, Co. Roscommon (q.v.).

ATHY, Co. Kildare (Map 6, B4), is a market town where the Kilcullen (15 m.)–Castlecomer (17 m.) road – the old highway from Dublin to the South – crosses the Barrow.

Though the ford from which it takes its name was always an important passage, the town is a Norman creation, the first lords of the feudal manor being the de St Michaels. In the later 13th cent. the manor, along with that of Woodstock (below), passed by marriage to the House of Kildare. In 1300 the town was burned by the Irish, and seven years later it was sacked by Edward Bruce. About a hundred years later, Henry V's Lieutenant in Ireland, Sir John Talbot, "Scourge of France", repaired and fortified the bridge. In 1420 James "White" Earl of Desmond and Lieutenant of the King of England, slew "many of the kin and the terrible army of O More" at the Red Moor of Athy. The partisan sun stood still for three hours to facilitate the slaughter of the Irish. In 1642 the town was held by Ormonde against the Confederate Catholics, but fell to Eoghan Rua O Neill in 1645. Five years later it was taken by the Cromwellians.

There are some remains (E. end of town) of the 14th cent. parish church of St Michael; none of St John's Priory of Augustinian Cruciferi, founded before 1216 (?) by Richard de St Michael, Lord of Rheban; none of the medieval Dominican friary (probably also a de St Michael foundation). The Court and Market House (now a fire station) is a good late-18th cent. building. The Dominican church (1963–5; by John Thompson & Associates) is of unusual interest: a pentagon with hyperbolic paraboloid roof; statues and high-altar crucifix by Bridget Rynne, high-altar plaque by Breda O Donoghue, and windows and Stations of the Cross designed by George Campbell, R.H.A.; the Stations are rather spoilt by the windows. White's Castle (Nat. Mon.), on the bridge, is a 16th cent. replacement of Sir John Talbot's fortification.

½ m. N., on the W. side of the river, are the remains of Woodstock castle, 15th cent. Kildare successor of Richard de St Michael's castle of c. 1250. In 1649 it was badly damaged by Confederate Catholic besiegers.

3¾ m. NE., on the Kilcullen road, is the great Moat of Ardscull, 55 ft high; there are remains of Cromwellian fortifications. 1½ m. NNW. is Skerries where, on 26 Jan. 1316, Edward Bruce defeated the army of the English Crown commanded by Edmund Butler, Earl of Carrick, and John Fitzgerald, Lord O ffaly. 2½ m. S. is Inch castle, built by the de Vescis in the 13th cent. and enlarged by the 6th Earl of Kildare in 1420.

1 m. S., in Ardree, site of an Anglo-Norman settlement, is the motte of Dunboris.

5 m. SE. is Kilkea (*see under* Castledermot).

4½ m. S., on the W. side of the Barrow in Co. Laois, is Kilmoroney motte (erected by Robert de Bigarz?). 4 m. SSW. is Killabban, where remains of a 12th (?) cent. nave-and-chancel church mark the site of a foundation by St Abbán moccu Corbmaic, apostle of Leinster (*see* New Ross).

4 m. SW. are the ruins of the castle of Ballyadams. At the Norman invasion the manor fell to the de Poers, but was recovered by the O Mores in the 14th cent. At the Tudor plantation of Laois–Uí Fáilghe the manor was leased to John ap Thomas Bowen (Ap Owein). Called Seón an Phíce (John of the Pike) by the Irish, Bowen was notorious for his cruelty. In 1643 Castlehaven, the Royalist general, summoned the castle to surrender under threat of bombardment, but Sir John Bowen, Parliamentarian provost marshal of Leinster and Meath, dissuaded him: "I will cover that part, or any other your Lordship shoots at, by hanging both my daughters in chairs". The remains of the castle comprise turreted tower and post-1550 Bowen wings. ¾ m. WSW. the remains of a nave-and-chancel church mark the site of the ancient foundation, Kylmohydde, alias Kilmokidy. From the Plantation until *c*. 1780 the church served the Protestant parish. In the chancel are: the fragmentary remains of "Seón an Phíce's Tomb", actually the 1631 double-effigy altar tomb of Sir Robert Bowen (d. 1621) and his wife, Allis Harpole (d. 1634) – the weepers represent the children and two daughters-in-law of Sir Robert; also the broken tombstone of Thomas and Walter Hartpoole, "Brittanes born". Walter, whose low-relief effigy fills the slab, was Protestant Dean of Leighlin and died in 1597.

AUBURN, Co. Westmeath (Map 2, C7), properly Lissoy, is a hamlet on the Ballymahon (6 m.)–Athlone (9 m.) road. It is the "Sweet Auburn" of Goldsmith's *Deserted Village*, for it was here, where his father was rector, that the poet first went to school (*see also* Ballymahon *and* Elphin).

A short distance NE. is The Three Jolly Pigeons, a pub named after the inn in *She Stoops to Conquer*. Although Goldsmith nominally set his works in England, there can be no doubt that he had his boyhood Irish home always in mind: "If I go to the opera, I sit and sigh for the Lissoy fireside and Johnny Armstrong's 'Last Goodnight' – or if I climb Hampstead Hill, I confess it is fine, but then I had rather be placed on the little mount before Lissoy Gate, and there take in, to me, the most pleasing horizon of nature."

3 m. NW., at Bethlehem, on the shore of Lough Ree (*q.v.*), are the remains of Ireland's first Poor Clares' nunnery. Founded in Dublin in 1629, the community was expelled in 1630 and was brought here (to a Dillon property?) in 1631 by Abbess Cecily Dillon. In 1642 the nuns fled to Galway, where a wooden statue of the Virgin and Child from Bethlehem is still preserved in the Poor Clares' convent.

AUGHER, Co. Tyrone (Map 2, E4), is a village on the Enniskillen (25 m.)–Dungannon (19 m.) road, about 2 m. NE. of Clogher (*q.v.*).

At the W. end of the village is Spur Royal Castle, erected by Lord Ridgeway about 1615 on the site of an older fortress. It is a square Plantation castle with a triangular tower at the middle of each side. Burned in 1689, it was restored in 1832, when the wings were added. Of the original bawn only the circular SW. tower survives.

4 m. NE., about 1 m. W. of Ballynasaggart bridge, is beautifully sited Errigal Keerogue (Aireagal Do-Chíaróg, Aireagal Do-Shean-Chíaróg; Do-Chíaróg's Cell, Do-Chíaróg the Elder's Cell), site of an early monastery founded by St Cíarán, alias Do-Chíaróg. There are remnants of St Kieran's Church (Nat. Mon.) and traces of a Round Tower, as well as part of a primitive stone cross (Nat. Mon.) and St Kieran's Well (*see* Favour Royal, *under* Aughnacloy). Ballynasaggart, 1 m. E., is thought to be the site of a Franciscan friary founded by Conn, son of Henry O Neill, in 1489. In the Protestant church are two stone fonts (Nat. Mons.), the simpler of which may have come from the friary or from Errigal Keerogue.

2½ m. SE., in Derrycloony, is Relicnapain, a ruinous chamber tomb.

2 m. NW., near the summit of Knockmany (700 ft), is Annia's Cove (Nat. Mon.), a large round cairn with a degenerate passage grave which has been somewhat altered in modern times. Three of the uprights carry concentric circles and other symbols. The chamber has recently been enclosed in a protective housing. (Open to the public 1 April–30 Sept., Sats. and Suns., 2–7 p.m.). The tomb is named after the goddess Aine. There is a comparable tomb 7 m. NE. at Sess Kilgreen (*see under* Ballygawley).

AUGHNACLOY, Co. Tyrone (Map 3, A5), is a market village on the Monaghan (12 m.)–Omagh (21 m.) road.

St James's Protestant Church was built in 1736 by Acheson Moore, the spire being added in 1796 by his daughter, Mrs Malone.

4 m. NE., near Glasdrummond Cottage, is Glasdrummond court cairn (Nat. Mon.).

2½ m. E., in Edengeeragh, is Lismalore, a bivallate ringfort.

3 m. WNW., in Lismore, is Favour Royal (Moyenner), a large rectangular bawn with

circular angle towers; it was built in 1611 by Sir Thomas Ridgeway. Here are preserved a fragment of a stone cross (Nat. Mon.) said to have been taken from St Kieran's Well, Errigal Keerogue (*see under* Augher), and a "stone chair" found on Ashban Mountain S. of Clogher.

AUGHRIM, Co. Galway (Map 5, C2), is a small village off the main (i.e. S., or Loughrea) road from Ballinasloe (4 m.) to Galway (37 m.). It takes its name from the nearby ridge, scene of the battle of 12 July 1691, which decided the Jacobite–Williamite war and the course of Irish history. The memorial cross recently erected at the site of the castle had lain incomplete for half a century or more at the edge of a street in Ballinasloe, the promoters having fallen out at the time of the "Parnell Split"!

After the fall of Athlone (*q.v.*), St Ruth drew up the Jacobite army on an admirably chosen and prepared position. His lines followed the high ground from the castle, whose fragmentary remains stand beside the road at the N. end of the village, as far S. as the neighbourhood of Tristaun bridge (1¾ m.). The Jacobites stood up well to several assaults, but a series of blunders and mischances, including St Ruth's death at the crisis of the battle, turned expected victory into complete rout.

William J. Mac Nevin (1763–1841), member of the United Irishmen and father of American chemistry, was a native of Aughrim parish. Among the Williamite Protestants settled about Aughrim were the Ringlings, ancestors of the famous American circus family.

¾ m. S., on the highest point (338 ft) cf Attidermot Hill (Gallows Hill), is Aughrim Fort, alias Gen. St Ruth's Fort, a small ringfort (Nat. Mon.); 250 yds NE. is the spot where, tradition says, St Ruth was killed by a cannonball; to the SE. is Lisbeg, a second ringfort (Nat. Mon.). ½ m. S. of Aughrim Fort are the site of Kilcommadan church and St Ruth's Flag(stone).

1 m. SE. is Bloody Hollow, where furious fighting took place between Jacobite and Williamite (Huguenot) infantry.

1¾ m. E. (to the E. of Urraghry House) is Urraghry Hill (279 ft), centre of the Williamite line.

AUGHRIM, Co. Wicklow (Map 6, D4), is a village on the Rathdrum (9 m.)–Tinahely (8 m.) road, just below the confluence of the Ow and the Derry Water. It is a convenient road junction for the explorer of the S. Wicklow mountain region. A good road SE. leads down the pretty Aughrim valley to Woodenbridge (*see under* Arklow) and the lovely Avoca valley (*see under* Rathdrum). A second road, to the NE., reaches the Avonbeg at Ballinaclash (*see under* Rathdrum). A third climbs N. and NE. across the hills to Greenan and the beautiful Clara valley (*see under* Laragh). A fourth climbs the Ow valley NW., via Roddenagh bridge and the old

Military Road, to Aghavanagh (*q.v.*). The main road SW. to Tinahely ascends the Derry Water valley to Lugduff, where it crosses over the divide into the valley of the Derry River.

BAILIEBOROUGH, Co. Cavan (Map 3, A7), is a market town on the Virginia (9 m.)–Carrickmacross (16 m.) road. The parish church has Stations of the Cross by the contemporary painter, George Collie.

2½ m. S. is the ancient graveyard of Moybolgue, with nearby the well-preserved remains of a motte-and-bailey.

6 m. SW., in Beagh (Glebe), are the remains of the cottage birthplace of Gen. Philip Sheridan (1831–88), Commander of the United States Army and one of the great generals of history.

1½ m. NW. is Bailieborough Castle, home of the Youngs.

BALBRIGGAN, Co. Dublin (Map 6, D2), is a small manufacturing town and minor seaside resort on the Dublin (20 m.)–Drogheda (11 m.) road. It is noted for its hosiery (whence the Americanese "Balbriggans"). The little Delvin (Oilbhine) River (2 m. NW.), which flows through a pretty valley, is a good brown trout stream. It was at the estuary of this river that St Patrick is said to have met and christened his disciple and successor, St Benignus (*see* Kilbannon *under* Tuam). Fine sandy beaches extend all the way N. from the estuary past Gormanston, Mosney, Laytown, and Bettystown to the mouth of the Boyne, a distance of 6 m. The Catholic parish church has two two-light windows by Harry Clarke: *Raising of Lazarus* (1921) and *Visitation* (1922).

To the NNW. are the remains of the chapel and outbuildings of Bremore Castle, a Barnewall stronghold. St Mo-Laga (*see* Labbamolaga *under* Mitchelstown), disciple of St David of Wales and a noted beekeeper, founded a monastery called Lann Beachaire (Lambecher), Monastery of the Beekeeper, somewhere in Bremore. ½ m. N. of the castle, on a low headland by the sea, are the remains of five tumuli (a passage-grave cemetery?).

2 m. SSW. is Balrothery, where the Protestant church has a bell-tower of about 1500. Balrothery was the meeting place of the council of local feudatories, to each of whom was assigned a hereditary grazing plot for use when attending the council. These Knights' Plots at the village remained in the possession of their descendants down to our own day.

6 m. WSW. is The Naul, a hamlet on the S. side of the Delvin. The parish church has a two-light Harry Clarke window: *Sacred Heart, Our Lady* (1926). The Delvin flows through the picturesque Vale of Roches, where there are a number of caves. N. of the hamlet, on a cliff (*An Aill* – Naul) overlooking the glen, are remains of Roches Castle, said to have been built by the de Genevilles. 1 m. NW., in Fourknocks, Co. Meath, are three tumuli (Nat. Mons.).

Irish Tourist Board
Cross in old churchyard, Balbriggan

The largest (Fourknocks I), of layered turves and shingle, covered a cruciform passage grave some of whose passage and chamber stones have typical passage-grave scribings (including anthropomorphs). The scribings, and some of the grave goods, suggest Iberian connections. In passage and side chambers were the remains, cremated and uncremated, of more than 65 individuals. In Middle Bronze Age times food-vessel, urn, and other burials had been inserted in the covering mound. (Passage and chambers have been skilfully re-roofed by the Office of Public Works.) The second mound (Fourknocks II) was ringed by a rock-cut fosse and covered a crematorium trench, as well as a low fosse-enclosed cairn: Burials with passage-grave artefacts had been pushed into the "passage" of the crematorium; neolithic flints and sherds had been incorporated in the mound, into the top of which food-vessel and urn burials had been intruded. The third mound (Fourknocks III) covered a food-vessel cremation in a central cist. About 1½ m. NW., in Micknanstown, are remains of a "henge" and of a fosse-ringed tumulus.

3 m. NW. is Gormanston, from which the Prestons, Viscounts Gormanston, took their title. Sir Robert Preston, Chief Justice of the Common Pleas in the English colony, purchased the manor in 1363. The Prestons always supported the interests of their ancestral England, but adhered to the Old Faith at the Reformation and, until the advent of O Connell, were usually numbered among the leaders of the oppressed Catholic majority. Thomas Preston, uncle of the 6th viscount and a distinguished soldier in the Spanish service, was appointed general of the Confederate Catholic Army of Leinster in 1642. He was defeated near New Ross by Ormonde in 1643, but later captured the important castle of Ballinakill, Co.

Laois. His failure to co-operate wholeheartedly with Gen. Eóghan Rúa O Neill was responsible for the failure of the Confederate siege of Dublin (held by the royalist Ormonde) in 1646. On 6 Aug. 1647, he was disastrously routed by the Parliamentarian, Michael Jones, at Dungan Hill near Summerhill (q.v.). Created Viscount Tara by Charles II in 1650, he commanded the defence of Galway during the Cromwellian siege, but escaped to France before the capitulation. The Preston properties at Gormanston were confiscated by the Cromwellians, but were recovered at the Restoration, only to be lost again at the Williamite revolution. In 1800 they were given back to the 12th viscount, who restored the castle. Adjoining it are the ruins of a domestic chapel erected in 1687 by the 7th viscount. In 1947 the castle was purchased by the Franciscans, who built (1955-7) the large boarding school by John Thompson. 1¾ m. SW. of the castle is the village of Stamullin, Co. Meath. It takes its name (Tech meic Mellén, later Teach Mealláin) from an early monastery founded by Mellén's Son. There are ruins of a medieval nave-and-chancel parish church dedicated to St Patrick. On the S. side of the chancel is the roofless chantry chapel of St Sylvester, founded by the 2nd Viscount Gormanston (d. 1532); beneath it is the Preston family vault. 1½ m. NNW. of the castle is Sarsfieldstown cross (see under Julianstown).

BALLA, Co. Mayo (Map 1, D4), is a village on the Castlebar (7 m.)–Claremorris (8 m.) road. A broken Round Tower (Nat. Mon.) and a medieval altar in a shamefully neglected graveyard mark the site of a monastery founded in the 7th cent. by St Crónán, alias Mo-Chúa. To the W. of the graveyard are Tobar Mhuire, alias the Blessed Well, and the ruins of a 17th cent. shelter for the blind and lame who resorted to the well on Patron Day (15 Aug.).

3 m. S. is Mayo, from which the county takes its name. Now a mere hamlet, it occupies part of the site of a famous early monastery. When the Irish party was defeated at the Synod of Whitby, (p. 25), Bishop Colmán of Lindisfarne withdrew from the English mission to Iona, and thence to Ireland. His adherents included thirty English monks who followed him to Inishbofin (see under Clifden), where he set up a monastery. Disputes having arisen between the Irish and English brethren, Colmán transferred the latter to a new monastery at Mayo, thereafter called Mag nEó na Sachsan (Mayo of the English). The monastery, which won the praise of Bede, retained its English character for a considerable period. (One of Alcuin's letters, 773–86, is addressed to Bishop Leuthfriht of the monastery, a second, 792–800, is addressed to the fathers of the monastery; the best known name connected with the place is that of St Gerald (d. 732), an Englishman.) In time the monastery became a college of secular canons which, about 1370, adopted the Augustinian Rule and survived until the Dissolution. All

Plate 2. Muiredach's Cross, Monasterboice, Co. Louth

that remains today are fragments of ecclesiastical buildings and the trace of a great circular enclosing wall or vallum.

BALLAGHADERREEN, Co. Roscommon (Map 2, A6), is a small market town on the Roscommon (25 m.)–Charlestown (10 m.) road. St Nathy's Cathedral (Catholic diocese of Achonry) is a mediocre Gothic Revival structure.

1½ m. NE. is the old parish church of Kilcoleman.

3¾ m. NE., in Clogher, Co. Sligo, is Cashelmore, a stone ringfort (Nat. Mon.). ½ m. NE. is Toberaraght, St Áracht's Well (*see* Killaraght *under* Boyle); there is a *Crucifixion* carving here. ½ m. ENE. are remains of Cashelnamonastragh, site of an early monastery. 2¼ m. ENE., on Lough Gara, is Coolavin, home of Mac Dermot of Coolavin.

BALLINA, Co. Mayo (Map 1, D3), is a busy market town and small seaport on the estuary of the Moy (Killala Bay), 37 m. SW. of Sligo, 10 m. N. of Foxford, and 39 m. ESE. of Belmullet. The largest town in the county, it is also the cathedral town of the Catholic diocese of Killala. At Ardnaree, on the Co. Sligo bank of the river, are the ruins of an Augustinian friary founded by the O Dowds about 1375 (?).

¾ m. SW., by the roadside beyond Cockle St, is Cloghogle, remnant of a chamber tomb (Nat. Mon.). In 1838 John O Donovan "identified" this with the tomb of the Four Maols (Maol Cróin, Maol Seanaidh, Maol Da-Lua, Maol Deoraidh) who were said to have murdered a Bishop Cellach of Killala (*q.v.*) and to have been executed on Ardnaree, east of the river.

4 m. N. via a minor road (5½ m. via the main Killala road) are the ruins of Rosserk "Abbey" (Nat. Mon.), the best preserved Franciscan Tertiary friary in Ireland. Founded before 1441 by one of the Joyces, it was burned in 1590 together with the friaries of Moyne and Rathfran (*see under* Killala) by the English Governor of Connacht, Sir Richard Bingham. The remains comprise a typical friary church (with 2-chapel S. transept) and conventual buildings; the cloister garth has no ambulatories. Across the hill to the SSW. is a roofed-in holy well resorted to on 15 Aug. (Feast of the Assumption). 3¼ m. NNW. is Moyne friary (*see under* Killala).

4½ m. NE., in Co. Sligo, are the ruins of Castle Connor. ½ m. NE. are the remains of the medieval church of Killanly.

7 m. NE. is the pleasant little seaside resort of Inishcrone (*q.v.*).

8 m. E., in Carrowcrom, are a wedge-shaped gallery grave and some pillarstones (Nat. Mons.).

4 m. SE., on the W. shore of Ballymore Lough, are the remnants of little Kildermot church (Nat. Mon.).

5 m. W. is Deel castle (*see* Castle Gore *under* Crossmolina).

4¾ m. WNW. are the ruins of the Mac William (Burke) castle of Rappa.

1 m. NNW. is the ancient site of Kilmoremoy (the great church of the Moy), where St Patrick's disciple, Olcán, founded a church. There are remains of an ancient church and of an enclosing rampart. Near the centre of the enclosure is the Liag, a cross-inscribed rock-surface which some would identify with the Lia na Manach of the *Tripartite Life* of St Patrick. Outside the graveyard is a holy well.

BALLINAFAD, Co. Sligo (Map 2, B5), is a village on the Boyle (6 m.)–Sligo (20 m.) road at the foot of the Curlew and Bricklieve mountains and at the SW. corner of Lough Arrow. It is a convenient centre for fishing the lough, which in the mayfly season is well worth visiting.

The small four-towered Castle of the Curlieus (Nat. Mon.) was built about 1610 by Captain St John Barbe. It was captured in 1642 by the insurgent Irish.

¾ m. N. is Aghanagh, which has given its name to the townland and the parish. St Patrick founded a church here, which he entrusted to his disciple, Maine. There are remains of a simple, pre-Romanesque church, with inserted plain Romanesque N. door and Gothic S. window. NW. is Tobar Mhaine, "Maine's Well".

2 m. N., by the shore of Lough Arrow are Hollybrook House and demesne. Hollybrook, alias Ballyhely, is the setting of the romantic adventures of Carleton's *Willy Reilly and his fair Colleen Bawn*. A nearby bohereen leads W. from the main road to the Bricklieve Mountains (highest point 1,057 ft), where, in Mullaghfarna, Carrowkeel, Carricknahorna East, Carricknahorna West, Tully, and Treanscrabbagh, are an ancient village site, fourteen chambered cairns, and two dolmen-like structures. The chamber tombs constitute the important passage-grave cemetery of Carrowkeel. One of the tombs (Cairn E, in Carricknahorna West), is of exceptional interest, in that it combines the long cairn and ritual forecourt of the court cairn with a cruciform passage grave. The burials in the tombs were mostly cremations. The scanty grave goods included characteristic passage-grave types: long bone pins, Carrowkeel Ware, etc. The village site is on the NE. spur of the mountain, in Mullaghfarna, where the stone footings of forty-seven circular huts, 20–42 ft in diameter, have been identified. If these were the dwellings of the cairn builders, they would represent the only known village of their period in Ireland.

4 m. N. is Castle Baldwin (Nat. Mon.), a small, L-shaped, 17th cent. fortified house. From the nearby crossroads a road leads 4 m. W. and S. to the Carrowkeel passage-grave cemetery (*above*). 2 m. NE. of Castle Baldwin is Heapstown cairn (*see under* Riverstown). – 3½ m. E. is Ballindoon "Abbey" (*see under* Riverstown). – 2½ m. NNW. is Tawnagh church (*see under* Riverstown).

BALLINAGH, alias Bellinagh, Co. Cavan (Map 2, D6), is a village on the Cavan (5 m.)–Granard (12 m.) road.

4½ m. E., in Carrickboy, the foundations of a church and an early cross-slab mark the site of an early monastery and of the medieval parish church of Denn. Above the graveyard is the Saint's Grave, alias the Flags of Denn, a ruined prehistoric chamber tomb (?). At the Protestant church in Denn Glebe (1 m. NE.) is the shaft of a High Cross with interlacing, etc.

4½ m. ESE. (1½ m. S. of Denn) the Worm Ditch, a bank and ditch, marks a mile-long quarter-circle on the W. and S. slopes of Ardkillmore hill.

6 m. SE. (1½ m. S. of the Worm Ditch) is Pollareagh Giants Grave, a chamber tomb.

5½ m. SW., in Middletown, is a prehistoric chamber tomb; ¾ m. E., in Drumhawnagh East, is another.

BALLINAKILL, Co. Laois (Map 6, A4) is a village on the Abbeyleix (3½ m.)–Ballyragget (7 m.) road.

The important castle here (slight remains) was taken by the Confederate Catholic general, Thomas Preston (*see* Gormanston *under* Balbriggan) in 1646. Severely battered by Fairfax's Cromwellians, it was rebuilt in 1680, but never re-occupied.

The Market House was built for Lord Stanhope, a former proprietor.

1 m. NNE. is Haywood House (1773; rebuilt after a fire, 1950). Formerly home of the Trenches; it is now a Salesian missionary college. The Italianate sunk garden is by Sir Edward Lutyens. By the avenue is a 19th cent. folly with windows from the Dominican friary at Aghaboe (*q.v.*) and part of a 1522 tomb.

3 m. NE. is Dysert Gallen, an early anchoritic site.

2 m. ENE., in Moat, is a motte.

2½ m. SSW., on the Owveg, are the remains of Rosconnell nave-and-chancel church, 13th cent. but partly rebuilt in 1646. 1½ m. NW. is Fermoyle (Formhaol na bhFian) with a ringfort 300 ft in diameter.

BALLINAMORE, Co. Leitrim (Map 2, C5), is a village on the Killeshandra (13 m.)–Drumshanbo (15 m.) road.

¼ m. N., in Fenaghbeg, are Dermot and Grania's Bed (a prehistoric chamber tomb) and a pillarstone. In Mullaghnameely, the townland to the N., is St Everan's Well. Longstones townland, to the NE., takes its name from a series of pillarstones.

3 m. SW. is Fenagh, site of an early monastery of St Caillín's, patron of the O Rourkes of Breany (*see* Dromahaire). The place was burnt in 1360. In the Middle Ages the O Roddys were the hereditary coarbs, and in 1516 Tadhg O Roddy had the *Book of Fenagh* (now in the Royal Irish Academy) copied by Muirghes O Mulconry out of "an old book of Caillín's". It contains a catalogue of the lands, privileges,

etc., of the monastery, as well as a collection of wonders, etc., alleged to have been performed by the saint, and its purpose is obviously to maintain the value of the emoluments in the interest of the coarbs. The O Roddys were also hereditary custodians of St Caillín's Bell, alias Clog na Rí, so called because of the kings alleged to have been baptized from it. The bell, which dates from the 12th/13th cent., is now preserved at the parish priest's house at Foxfield. The remains at Fenagh comprise two churches (Nat. Mons.). The one is an aisleless, rectangular structure with a good 14th/15th cent. E. window and sculptured gable-brackets. The W. end is barrel-vaulted, and presumably had living-quarters above. At the SE. external angle is a mausoleum erected in 1671 for Eóghan Duignan of Castlefore (*below*) and his wife and heirs, by his brother, Tórna Duignan, Rector of Fenagh. The second church, 150 yds NE., is also barrel-vaulted at the W. end and has a curious "corridor" along the S. side. ¼ m. SW. of Fenagh, to the W. of the road, in Commons, is Giants Graves, a two-court cairn.

7 m. SW. is Castlefore, formerly seat of the senior line of the Duignans, hereditary historiographers to the O Farrells of Annaly, the Mac Dermots of Moylurg, the Mac Donaghs of Corann, and the Mac Donaghs of Tirerrill. (*See* Boyle, Ballymote, Ballyfarnan, Kilmactranny.) Peregrine Duignan, one of the Four Masters (*see* Donegal), was born here.

BALLINAMUCK, Co. Longford (Map 2, C6), is a village ¾ m. NE. of the Arvagh (8 m.)–Newtown Forbes (9 m.) road.

Here took place the last encounter of the daring French invasion of 1798. Gen. Humbert, having marched the 160 miles from Castlebar through Cos. Sligo and Leitrim to Ballinamuck, with his small force of French troops and untrained insurgents, was forced to turn and accept battle with superior British forces under Lord Cornwallis. He drew up his line on the lower slopes of Shanmullagh, overlooking Ballinamuck. The French surrendered after a brief engagement, but the Irish fought with desperate bravery, and no quarter was shown to them. The battle is commemorated by a statue near the village. 3 m. N., in Tubberpatrick graveyard, are memorials to Gunner Magee and his cousins, who manned Humbert's two guns with extraordinary heroism, and to Gen. Blake, executed after the battle.

BALLINASLOE, Co. Galway (Map 5, C2), at the crossing of the River Suck, on the Athlone (15 m.)–Galway (40 m.) road, is the principal market town of E. Galway. It is a good coarse-angling centre. Its great October Fair is still the largest livestock fair in Ireland (In the peak year, 1856, 20,000 cattle and 99,685 sheep were offered for sale.) In the days of cavalry and horse transport it was also the largest horse fair in Europe. The local limestone quarries were once famous too. (They supplied the masonry for a street of shop fronts in New York.)

Though there was previously a small settlement in the shadow of the castle (*below*), the town is esentially an 18th cent. creation of the Trench family, who in 1716 increased their property here by purchasing the estate of the Spensers, descendants of Cromwellian grantee William Spenser (himself a grandson of the poet, Edmund Spenser; *see* Kilcolman *under* Doneraile). Before the English conquest the district had formed part of the O Kelly territories.

At the E. end of Church St (on the E. side of the Suck) are the remains of Creagh medieval church. The nearby Church of Our Lady of Lourdes has two single-light porch windows (*Annunciation, Nativity, St Joseph* etc.) by Patrick Pye. Nearby, to the W., is the Mental Hospital for Cos. Roscommon and Galway. The entrance facade of the original building (1838) is good, if rather jail-like; the new gate-lodge is altogether unworthy of it. A short distance W., beside the Suck, a 19th cent. dwelling, Ivy Castle, masks the towered bawn of the castle which guarded the vital Suck crossing in late medieval times. The original fortress here was probably built by the local O Kelly. In 1572 it was held by the Earl of Clanricard. In 1579 it was taken over by the Crown, put in a state of defence, and made the residence of the English Governor of Connacht, Sir Anthony Brabazon, whose father-in-law had acquired confiscated lands in the neighbourhood. In 1651–2 it was held against the Cromwellian, Ireton, by another Anthony Brabazon, who had espoused the Confederate Catholic cause.

The Catholic parish church of St Michael (1852–8) is by J. J. McCarthy, whose 1846 design was revised by Pugin. The high altar (with *Dead Christ*) is by Albert Power; it has an excellent tabernacle door (*Christ at Emmaus*) in gold, silver, and enamels, by Mia Cranwell. The chancel mural paintings (1921), *SS Brendan and Greallan*, are by Joseph Tierney. The painting (on canvas) of the *Holy Trinity* over the chancel arch was by Harry Clarke, who was awarded an Aonach Tailteann prize. (Having deteriorated, its "restoration" was recently entrusted to a housepainter.) The church has two good windows: one of two lights, *St Rose of Lima* and *St Patrick*, by Harry Clarke (1924); the other, *The Holy Family*, by Patrick Pollen (1958). The church also has Dun Emer Guild vestments, banners, and carpets.

On the W. side of the town is Garbally, formerly seat of the Trenches, Earls of Clancarty, now St Joseph's College, diocesan-school (boys) of Clonfert. The house (1824) is a late Georgian mansion of local limestone. The school collection of paintings includes works by modern Irish artists. The library has some rare books and MSS. The altars in the chapel (former ballroom) are by Albert Power as is also the garden statue of St Joseph.

7 m. NNE., in Sraduff, ½ m. S. of Taghma-connell graveyard, Co. Roscommon, is St Ronan's Well. There is a late, rude *Crucifixion* slab here. 2 m. N., on Sheep Hill, Rocklands, is Standing Stone, shaft of a 17th cent. cross.

1¾ m. SE., on the E. bank of the canal in Pollboy, is The Teampaillín, ruin of a medieval parochial church.

4 m. SSE., via the Portumna road, in Clontuskert, are the interesting remains of St Mary's Priory. St. Baodán founded a monastery here in 805, which in the 12th/13th cent. became a priory of Canons Regular of St Augustine (Arrouaisian Congregation), who·served many of the parochial churches of the diocese of Clonfert. The principal patrons were the O Kellys, and in the decadent days of the later 15th cent. the office of prior became rather a family monopoly of theirs. In 1413 the priory and its contents were destroyed by fire. Rebuilt, it survived until the Dissolution and beyond. After the Dissolution the priory and its possessions were granted to the Earl of Clanricard who, however, shielded the canons. In the early part of the 17th cent. the priory was in part re-edified. Its final destruction doubtless dates from the Cromwellian victory. Little more than traces of the claustral buildings remain, but the church is better preserved. In its original form this was a rectangular Transitional structure. Additions and alterations included a 14th/15th cent. rood-screen of Sligo "Abbey" type (only fragments survive), a 15th cent. N. transept or chapel, a Perpendicular W. door of 1471 (with figures of SS Michael, John the Baptist, Catherine of Alexandria, and St. Augustine), and an interesting holy water stoup. The inscription over the door commemorates Bishop Maitiu Mac Craith of Clonfert and Pádraic Ó Neachtain, "canon of this house". In 1637 the priory was re-edified on a reduced scale. The relics of this restoration include the wall shutting off the chancel (date over doorway) and the oven at the NE. corner of the claustral buildings.

4 m. SW. is Aughrim (*q.v.*).

6 m. W. is Kilconnell (*q.v.*).

2 m. NW., in Kilclooney (Ceall Chluaine), the ruins of a medieval parish church mark the site of a foundation by St Greallán, 5th/6th cent. apostle of the district. In the 16th cent. the O Higginses had a bardic school hereabouts.

7 m. NW. is Ahascragh (*q.v.*).

BALLINCOLLIG, Co. Cork (Map 5, B6), is a village and former British artillery depot in the beautiful valley of the Lee, 5¼ m. W. of Cork (Macroom road). It is a convenient centre for fishing the Bride as well as the Lee.

Gen. Patrick Roynane Clebourne, one of the greatest Confederate commanders of the American Civil War, was born (1828) in Ballincollig, where his father was a physician. He advocated emancipation of the American slaves and was a member of the Fenian Brotherhood (p. 48).

1¾ m. ENE. are Carrigrohane castle and church (*see under* Cork).

Ballinderry Middle Church

1 m. SW. are the ruins of Ballincollig castle, a large rock castle of the Barrets, dating from the reign of Edward III. It was garrisoned both by Cromwell and by James II. There are remains of an irregular bawn with flankers, and of a tower with unusually small rooms; also traces of a great hall and of a moat.

3 m. WSW., on the River Bride, is Ovens, which takes its name (Uamhanna) from a 670-yd labyrinthine limestone cave in a quarry near the bridge. 3½ m. WSW. of the bridge are the ruins of Kilcrea castle and "abbey", both built by Cormac Láidir Mac Carthy (d. 1495; *see* Blarney). The castle ruins comprise tower, small court, and turret; the moat has been partly obliterated by the railway. The "abbey", a Franciscan friary, dates from 1464; it was dedicated to St Brigid. The Mac Carthys were able for a time to stave off the dissolution of the friary, but in 1584, and again in 1599, it was raided by English troops from Cork. (The 1584 raiders smashed the statuary, defaced the wall paintings, and carried off the church plate, including a very fine crucifix with gold and silver panels of the Evangelists.) In 1650 the friary was turned into a strong-point by the Cromwellians. The remains (Nat. Mon.) have been largely despoiled of their ornamental details and grossly overcrowded with burials. They represent a typical Irish medieval friary: on the N. the conventual buildings grouped around a small cloister (ambulatories gone; sacristy-scriptorium unusually well lit); on the S. a church comprising nave with S. aisle, bell-tower (inserted), choir, and aisled S. transept

with two E. chapels. In the SE. angle of th nave is the tomb of Art O Leary of Raleigh Macroom, sometime officer of the Hungaria army. He was slain as an outlaw by Englis troops near Carriganimmy, 4 May 1773, and fo some years his remains were forbidden burial i any churchyard. His widow, Eileen Dub O Connell of Darrynane (*see under* Caher daniel), aunt of the great Liberator, mourne him in a celebrated *caoineadh* which has bee finely rendered into English by Frank O'Conno A well-known Irish translation of *The Travels o Sir John Mandeville*, now at Rennes, in Brittan appears to have been written for the Franciscar of Kilcrea. – 4¾ m. SW. of Ovens bridge, i Garranes, is Lisnacaheragh (*see under* Crooks town).

5 m. W., in Mullaghroe, is a bivallate rin fort with berm inside the outer bank.

4½ m. WNW., near Inishcarra, is the lowe of the two dams which have flooded the Le valley for 18 miles (Lee hydro-electric project The upper dam is near Carrigadrohid (*see unde* Coachford).

BALLINDERRY, LOWER, Co. Antri (Map 3, C5), lies on the Lurgan (7 m.)–Glenav (5 m.) road, near the SE. corner of Loug Neagh.

1 m. WNW., by Lough Beg, alias Portmo Lough, the remains of Ballinderry Fir Church, alias Portmore Church, and tw bullauns mark an early monastic site. Th church is that "half ruined church of Kilulta where Jeremy Taylor (1613-67), afterwar

Protestant bishop of Dromore, "often preached to a small congregation" at the time he found refuge from the Cromwellians in Lord Conway's nearby house of Portmore. It was at Portmore that Taylor wrote (1659) the preface to *Ductor Dubitantium*, dedicated to Charles II, and Sallow Island in the lough was a favourite retreat of his.

1½ m. E. is Ballinderry Middle Church, built (1666-8) for Jeremy Taylor. Thanks to 1896 restoration, this is an unusually well-preserved example of Protestant church architecture in the Ireland of its day; noteworthy pulpit, pews, etc.

BALLINEEN-ENNISKEAN, Co. Cork

(Map 5, A7), are twin Bandonside villages on the Cork (29 m.)–Dunmanway (8 m.) road. They are convenient centres for fishing the Bandon and the Brinny. The Bandon WSW. to Manch bridge (3¼ m.) is very pretty.

4½ m. NE. of Enniskean, in Killaneer, is Cromlech, a chamber tomb; ¾ m. NNE. is a second; 1½ m. N. of the latter, in Bengower, are a third Cromlech and a pillarstone.

1½ m. ENE. of Enniskean is Palace Anne, a very ruinous and ivy-covered 17th cent. house.

3 m. NW. of Enniskean, in Sleenoge, is the unusual, 68-ft (topless) Cloigtheach, or Round Tower, of Kinneigh; the first 18 ft are hexagonal, the doorway trabeate. It marks the site of a monastery founded by St Mo-Cholmóg.

1½ m. WNW., in Gortaleen, is the Giants Grave, a chamber tomb; there are many pillarstones in the district. 3 m. NNW. of Kinneigh, in Capeen West, is Cahervaglier, alias Cahermoygilliar (Nat. Mon.), a bivallate ringfort with a collapsed trabeate gateway in the inner stone-faced rampart; it contains a collapsed stone hut and a souterrain. The following mileages are calculated from the fort: 1½ m. NNE., near the summit of Slieveowen, is Leaba Eóghain, a wedge-shaped gallery grave (roofless). – 4 m. NE., in Knockane, are remains of three chamber tombs. – 1½ m. E., in Cappeen East, is O Boughalla's Bed; ¼ m. S. are O Boughalla's Grave and a pillarstone. – 4½ m. NW., at Carriganaffrin, Coolaclevane, is Leaba na Muice, alias Carraig na gCat, a wedge-shaped gallery grave (ruined).

1 m. S. of Ballineen, in Curraghcrowley West, is a large, five-chamber, rock-cut souterrain.

2 m. SE. are the remains of Derrylemlary castle.

4¼ m. SW. (1 m. SSW. of Manch bridge) are the ruins of the 1585 O Hurley castle of Ballynacarriga (Nat. Mon.). This castle has a good sheila-na-gig in the external wall, high up, but quite visible.

1½ m. W. is Fort Robert, formerly Connorville, birthplace of Fergus O Connor (1794–1855), leader of the Chartist Movement in England. O Connor was a nephew of Arthur O Connor, the 1798 Republican leader. His father, Roger, was also implicated in the disturbances of 1798, but as a monarchist with crazy aspirations to the Irish crown. He fortified Connorville, but took no stronger measures. Though a Protestant, Fergus O Connor took a leading part in the Co. Cork agitation against tithes and joined O Connell's Repeal Movement. In 1832 and 1834 he was elected M.P. for Co. Cork despite the entrenched Whig and Tory landlords; in 1835 he was unseated. The following year he tried, without success, to oust O Connell from the leadership of the Repeal Movement. Soon afterwards he took up Chartism, and in 1847 was elected M.P. for Nottingham.

BALLINGARRY, Co. Limerick (Map 5, B4), is a small village on the Croom (8 m.)–Newcastle West (9 m.) road, 5½ m. SE. of Rathkeale. Pádraig Ó Fionnghalaigh, poet, was schoolmaster here in 1771. The Lacy castle commanding the hill-pass was repaired as a dwelling in 1821, and in 1827 served as a barracks during the "Rockite" land troubles; later still it served as a hospital.

4 m. ENE. are the ruins of Kilmacow church; to the S., in a ring-enclosure, was "Abbey", perhaps the Cill Mo-Chúa from which the place takes its name. 3 m. NNE. of this are St Kieran's Well and the ancient church site of Kilfinny; the nearby castle ruins comprise bawn and two towers.

To the E. rises Knockfeerina (Cnoc Fírinne; 948 ft), a volcanic eruption through the sandstone. The hill is one of the most celebrated Otherworld seats in Munster (seat of the god, Donn Fírinne) and formerly had its annual Lughnasa assembly. The cairn (Buachaill Bréige) on the summit, removed by Ordnance Survey sappers, was replaced by the local peasantry. On the N. slope is the Giants Grave, alias Fawha's Grave, a wrecked chamber tomb. On the W. hill, alt. 775 ft, is Lios na bhFian (the Ordnance Survey's Lissnaberne), a bivallate ringfort with very deep fosse.

4½ m. SW. is the ancient church site of Cloncagh (*see under* Newcastle West).

BALLINROBE, Co. Mayo (Map 1, D5), is a small market town where the Galway (31 m.)–Castlebar (18 m.) road crosses the Robe, 4 m. E. of Lough Mask. It is a convenient centre for fishing Loughs Carra, Mask and Corrib.

The parish church has nine windows by Harry Clarke, all 1926: *SS Fursey and Fechin; Colman and Brendan; Gormgall and Kieran; Enda and Jarlath; Assumption* and *Coronation of B.V.M.; Presentation in the Temple* and *Immaculate Conception; Ecce Homo* and *Jesus blesses a young man; Baptism of Christ* and *Ascension; SS Patrick, Brigid, Columcille*.

On the N. edge of the town, close to the Claremorris road, are remains of the church of an Augustinian friary founded about 1313, probably by one of the de Burgos. It was in the friary that Émonn Albanach de Burgo (ancestor of Mac William Íochtair; *see* Lough Mask Castle *below*) seized his rival cousin

Émonn na Féasóige (son of the "Red" Earl of Ulster and ancestor of the Clanwilliam Burkes of Limerick–Tipperary) on Low Sunday, 1338, and had him drowned in Lough Mask. This foul stroke marked an important stage in the Gaelicization of the vast de Burgo lordships.

3½ m. SE., close to the Kilmaine road, is Lisnatreanduff, a large ringfort. Between this and Kilmaine are many ringforts and tumuli. 3½ m. S. is The Neale (see under Cong).

2 m. SW., to the W. of the Clonbur road in Carn townland, is a large dilapidated cairn, Carn Bowen (Buoin).

4½ m. SW., on Lough Mask, is Inishmaine. St Cormac founded a monastery here in the 7th cent., according to legend on the site of the fort of King Eógan Bél of Connacht (d. 537). In the 12th/13th cent. the monks became Canons Regular of St Augustine. Máel-Ísa O Conor, grandson of King Turloch Mór and prior of the monastery, died there in 1223/4. The monastery is represented today by the ruins of an interesting little Transitional church (Nat. Mon.) with details in the Cong (q.v.) style. The "transepts" are 13th/14th (?) cent. additions. NE. of the church is the remnant of a small 15th cent. gatehouse. 1 m. SW. of the monastery, on Inishowen, is an unusual bivallate circular earthwork which had a ring of contiguous tall pillarstones on the edge of the inner bank. Several of these still stand. The site commands a delightful view of Lough Mask and the mountains. – Near the W. shore of Inishmaine are the ruins of a unique sweat house: two crypt-like sweating chambers with high-pitched stone ceilings.

4 m. SW. are the ruins of Lough Mask Castle. The first "castle of Lough Mask" was built by Maurice Fitzgerald (see Sligo) in the 13th cent. The existing castle is a MacWilliam (Burke) fortress of 1480. It was re-edified in 1618 by Sir Thomas Burke, last MacWilliam Íochtair. Nearby Lough Mask House was the residence of Captain Charles Boycott (1832–97), Lord Erne's agent. Because of his treatment of the tenants he was ostracized (1880) by tenants, workers, and tradesmen; the English vocabulary thus acquired a new word, "boycott".

4½ m. SW. (1½ m. E. of Lough Mask Castle), in Carn, is great, ruined Eochy's Cairn (passage-grave type; Nat. Mon.); it is set in an oval enclosure bounded by remains of a ditch and bank.

BALLINSKELLIGS, Co. Kerry (Map 4, B5), a village and quiet little resort on the W. side of Ballinskelligs Bay, 10 m. SSW. of Cahersiveen and 8 m. NW. of Waterville, is the market centre of one of the last pockets of Irish speech in Co. Kerry. Nearby is a station of the U.S. Direct Cable. Boating, bathing, and sea fishing may be had from the pier or from the fine beaches. To the SW. rises Bolus (1,350 ft). 8 m. WSW., off Bolus Head, are the Skelligs (q.v.). The roads circling the bay to Hogs Head, SSW. of Waterville, are noted for their scenery.

On Ballinskelligs Point are remains of a Mac Carthy castle. By the shore to the S. are the sea-eroded remains (13th cent. and later) of Ballinskelligs "Abbey" (Nat. Mon.), a priory of Canons Regular of St Augustine, to which the monks of the Great Skellig are said to have removed.

2½ m. N., in the ancient burial ground of Killurly, is a prostrate ogham stone.

2½ m. NE., in Meelagulleen, is Labbyder-mott, a ruined wedge-shaped gallery grave.

2 m. SW., on the slope of Bolus, are the remains of Killerelig, alias Kildreelig, an interesting little anchoritic monastery. They comprise a diminutive ringfort-type enclosure with remains of a Gallarus-type (see under Ballyferriter) oratory, two clocháns, two rectangular structures, a cross-pillar, a souterrain, etc., and, outside the entrance, the remnant of a tiny dry-masonry oratory with a cross-pillar inside. A short distance W. are remains of clocháns, etc.; in the next field is a holy well. 800 yds NE. of the monastery are remnants of a small stone ringfort and a prostrate pillarstone. Some 200 yds further up the slope is an alignment of four pillarstones; the site commands a fine view.

3 m. NW. is the picturesque mountain-saddle of Coom, affording fine views of the Skelligs and other islands, etc. 1 m. S. (by road) of the saddle, in Leabaleaha, are remains of a complex megalithic monument with a "dolmen" (cup-marks), a pillarstone, etc.; in the next field to the S. is a small stone circle with internal pillarstone; 700 yds E., in Coom, are remains of a wedge-shaped gallery grave.

4½ m. NW., in Rathkieran, the ruins of Killemlagh church (Nat. Mon.) mark the site of an ancient monastery founded by St. Fíonán Lobhar, after whom nearby St Finan's Bay is called. The church was Romanesque, but the W. door has been destroyed. Sufferers from scrofulous diseases used to come to the ruins in search of a cure. In later Penal times a Catholic Mass-house was built against the N. wall; it remained in use until our own day. 150 yds S., in the field called Keelmalomvorny, is the Pagan's Grave, remnant of a prehistoric chamber tomb; it is called after one Maol-Mhórna, who is said to have endeavoured to procure the assassination of St Fíonán. – ½ m. N. is a pair of pillarstones. – ¾ m. W., beyond Keel Point, in Cloghanecanuig, is Doonecanuig, alias The Doon, a small promontory fort; there are interesting erosion arches in the sea cliff. – 1¼ m. NE. of Killemlagh, commanding a fine view of the Skelligs, is the ancient anchoritic site of Killabuonia. On the uppermost of three terraces are remains of a diminutive oratory of the Gallarus (see under Ballyferriter) type, a cross-pillar, and some graves. The Priest's Grave, SW. of the church, is a ruined shrine-shaped tomb; it has a circular opening in the W. gable. Another grave is marked by a small stone cross. On the middle terrace the remains of nine clocháns survived until about 1853, clustered round the ruins of a larger structure; today there survive only two clocháns, in addition to traces of two rectangular structures. To the NNW., close to the top terrace, are remains of another clochán. On the lowest terrace are St Buonia's Well and Cross; in the next field to the S. are remains of a double clochán. Pilgrims resort to the well and the Priest's Grave on Fridays, Saturdays, or Sundays. – A short distance E. is the Giants Grave, a wrecked chamber tomb. – 1 m. SE. of Killabuonia, in Cools, alias Coolnacon, is a pillarstone. – 4 m. NE. of Killabuonia, in Killoluaig, is the neglected early eremitical site from which the townland takes its name; there are remains of a shrine-shaped tomb, a broken cross, and a pillarstone, etc.

6 m. NW., in Ballynabloun Demesne, are the remains of the ancient nunnery of Temple Cashel; the tiny oratory was of the Gallarus (*see under* Ballyferriter) type. The zig-zag road up Coumaneaspuig, to the NW., commands magnificent views. 4 m. NW. of Temple Cashel, on Doon Point in Reencaheragh townland, is a promontory fort with a medieval gatehouse ("Reencaheragh Castle") and other additions. The cliff scenery hereabouts is good. 1½ m. ENE. is Portmagee (*see under* Cahersiveen).

BALLINTOBER, Co. Mayo (Map 1, D4), lies just ¾ m. E. of the Ballinrobe (7 m.)–Castlebar (11 m.) road. Here are the remains of a small abbey founded beside the site of an early monastery in 1216, by Cathal Crovdearg O Conor, King of Connacht, for Canons Regular of St Augustine. It was dedicated to the Holy Trinity. The "sanctuary and crosses were diligently finished in honour of Patrick, Mary, and St John the Apostle" before 1225. The nave of the church was rebuilt, following a fire, in 1265. In 1653 the church was unroofed, and the placed wrecked, by the Cromwellians; the central tower collapsed at a later date. The ruined church continued to be used for public Mass throughout Penal times, and in 1846 an untutored attempt was made to re-edify it. The Great Famine put a stop to the undertaking. In 1889 the chancel, crossing, and transepts were re-roofed under the direction of George C. Ashlin, whose projected reconstructions of tower and nave were not carried out for lack of funds. Generally speaking, this "restoration" must be regarded as unsatisfactory from the aesthetic, as well as from the practical, point of view. The original church was an aisleless, cruciform building with low tower over the crossing, and with the E. part laid out on the Cistercian plan, i.e. with E. chapels in the transepts. The delicate Late Romanesque–Early Gothic details of windows, capitals, etc., are characteristic of a group or school of masons active in Connacht round the turn of the 12th/13th cent. (Cong, Inishmaine, Knockmoy, Boyle, Corcomroe, *et loc. al.*). The existing altar-rail is made up of fragments of the 15th cent. cloister arcade. The sacristy is a 17th cent. annexe erected as a mausoleum for the Viscounts Mayo. In it may be seen the battered remains of the elaborate Renaissance tomb of Tiobód na Long (Theobald of the Ships) Burke (d. 1629), son of Gráinne Ní Mháille (*see* Clare Island) by her second husband; he was created Viscount Mayo in 1627. Of the claustral buildings (Nat. Mon.) only fragments survive. These, however, include a chapterhouse doorway in the Cong style. Excavations in 1963 have uncovered remains of two or three successive cloister ambulatories. The nave has been restored and the fragments of the cloister arcade reassembled. Through the generosity of the Church of Ireland, the 15th cent. W. door, taken to Hollymount in the last century, has been returned to the abbey. To the NW. are remains of a church, relic of the earlier monastery(?). 200 yds SE. is Tober Patrick, whence the place derives its name (Baile Tobair Phádraig, Baile an Tobair).

2½ m. SE., incorporated in a farmstead, are the remains of Castle Burke, alias Kilvoynell Castle, a MacEvilly (Staunton) stronghold given to Miles Burke, 4th Viscount Mayo, under the Acts of Settlement. The 5th viscount sold it to the Brownes of Westport.

7 m. SE., near the NE. corner of Lough Carra, are the ruins of Burriscarra church and "abbey" (Nat. Mons). The latter was founded by the Stauntons, alias MacEvillys, for Carmelites in 1298 and was abandoned in 1323. At the invitation of the MacEvillys it was taken over by Austin friars in 1430. The remains are largely early-14th cent.; the nave aisle is an addition. 1 m. SW., by Lough Carra, are the tower and bawn of Castlecarra (Nat. Mon.), a MacEvilly castle. In 1678 it passed to the Lynches under the Acts of Settlement. The first castle here was built by Adam de Staunton about 1238.

9 m. SE., overlooking Lough Carra, are the ruins of Moore Hall, Georgian home of the Moore family whose best known members were: John Moore (d. 1799), President of the Republic of Connaught on the occasion of the French invasion of 1798; George Henry Moore (1811–70), M.P. for Mayo, 1847–57, 1868–70, one of the leaders of the Tenant-Right Movement; and George Moore (1852–1933), novelist. Lough Carra has been well described in the opening pages of George Moore's *The Lake*; local places and persons figure in his celebrated trilogy, *Ave, Salve, Vale*. When he died his remains were cremated, inurned in a "Food Vessel", and buried under a cairn on Castle Island at the N. end of the lough. – Towerhill House (Blake family), 2 m. NE. of Moore Hall, is a good Georgian house. In the demesne is a tumulus. The countryside is rich in ringforts and tumuli.

BALLINTOBER, alias Toberbride, Co. Roscommon (Map 2, B6), a village on the

Roscommon (12 m.)–Castlerea (6 m.) road, takes its name from a holy well dedicated to St Brigid. NW. of the village are the ruins of a great keepless castle of about A.D. 1300, with twin-towered gatehouse and polygonal corner towers. It has been suggested that it is an Irish version of the Norman castle at Roscommon, but it may itself be Norman (built by William de Burgo, cousin of the "Red" Earl of Ulster?). From early in the 14th cent. until 1657 it was in the possession of the O Conors, being from 1385 onwards the property of O Conor Don. Between 1385 and 1500 it figured prominently in the local wars. In 1579, after the battle of the Curlieus, it was attacked by Red Hugh O Donnell, who breached the wall with Spanish guns and forced Hugh O Conor Don to recant his allegiance to the English crown. During the early 17th cent. it was the chief meeting-place of the Catholic leaders and clergy of the county. It was here the Catholic nobility and gentry of Connacht met in 1641 to consider participation in the Eleven Years' War (the War of the Three Kingdoms). In 1642 a Parliamentarian force under Lord Ranelagh and Sir Charles Coote I defeated the Irish assembled at Ballintober, but failed to take the castle. At the Cromwellian transplantation the castle was assigned to Lord Kilmallock, but in 1677 it was restored to O Conor Don. Soon afterwards it was mortgaged, and after a time passed for ever from the O Conors.

In the churchyard is the 1636 mausoleum of O Conor Don, burial place of Charles O Conor of Bellanagare (*q.v.*).

3 m. NW. is Emlagh (*see under* Castlerea).

BALLINTOGHER, Co. Sligo (Map 2, B5), is a hamlet on the Collooney (6 m.)–Manorhamilton (12 m.) road.

The Catholic church is by Vincent Kelly. The Protestant parish church dates from 1715.

1½ m. NE., in Gortlownan, is the "Mote" (Nat. Mon.; natural?). A bohereen leading N. from Gortlownan crossroads ends on the S. shore of Lough Gill close to Yeats's "Lake Isle of Innisfree". ¾ m. N. of Gortlownan crossroads are remains of the medieval church of Killery where, in 1346, Úalgharg O Rourke of Breany sought sanctuary from the O Conors and Mac Donaghs. They burned the place about his ears and slew him. In the churchyard is the "Straining Thread", reputed to cure sprains.

2 m. WSW., in Carricknagat, are two chamber tombs (Nat. Mons.). 1½ m. WNW. of these is Doonamurray, a univallate, stone-faced ringfort; O Donnell occupied it in 1516. ¾ m. N. of this fort, to the S. of Lough Dargan, is a fragment of Castle Dargan, a castle built early in the 15th cent. by Conor Mac Donagh on the site of a cliff-top ringfort. 150 yds E. of the N. end of the lake is Arnasbrack court cairn (*below*).

1 m. NNW. is Cashelore, alias Castleore (Caiseal óir), alias Bawnboy Fort (Nat. Mon.), an oval, stone ringfort; 400 yds SE. are the remains of a prehistoric chamber tomb (a court cairn?). 1½ m. W., in Carrownagh, is Leaba Dhiarmada agus Ghráinne, alias the Druids' Altar, a court cairn; 800 yds further W., in Arnasbrack, is Giant's Grave, alias Clogher-more, alias Cloch Mhór, a ruined court cairn. ½ m. SW. is Castle Dargan (*above*).

BALLINTOY, Co. Antrim (Map 3, B2), is a small village on the coast road from Bally-castle (7 m.) to Bushmills (8 m.). It is a convenient base for exploring the magnificent coast between Kinbane (White Head) and the Giant's Causeway (*see under* Bushmills), which the National Trust is doing so much to conserve. Late Bronze Age–Early Iron Age remains have been found in nearby cliff caves.

⅓ m. W. of the harbour, on a sea promontory in Ballintoy Demesne, is Dundrif, motte of a de Mandeville manor.

1½ m. ENE. is offshore Carrickarade (Carrickarede), noted for its fishermen's rope footbridge.

1¼ m. SW. (¼ m. SSE. of Mount Druid rectory), in Magheraboy, is the Druid Stone (Nat. Mon.), a chamber tomb set in a small, round cairn covering deposits with flints, Western Neolithic sherds, etc.

1½ m. WSW., and 300 yds S. of the White Park Bay road, in Clegnagh, is Cromlech, a small chamber tomb. About ½ m. SW., in Lemnagh Beg, is Cloghaboghill, a ruinous round cairn with a chamber tomb. ¾ m. WNW. of the latter is the entrance to White Park Bay (Nat. Trust), with a lovely, mile-long beach backed by dunes. 1 m. NW. of the entrance to the bay, and 300 yds W. of Portbraddan, remains of Teampall Lasrach (St Lasair's Church) and an ancient cross-slab mark the site of an early monastery. 2 m. WNW. of the entrance to White Park Bay is Dunseverick (*see under* Bushmills).

BALLINTRA, Co. Donegal (Map 2, B4), is a village on the Ballyshannon (7 m.)–Donegal (7 m.) road.

½ m. E., in the demesne of Brown Hall, are The Pullins, a series of interesting caves through which the River Blackwater flows. The demesne was devastated by "Hurricane Debby" (1962) and the caves are at present inaccessible.

¾ m. S., in Ballymagrorty, is Racoon (Ráth Chuinghe), where St Patrick is said to have founded a church. The site is represented by a flat, rectangular mound. Bishop Assicus, "St Patrick's goldsmith", whom the saint had placed in charge of a religious community at Elphin, Co. Roscommon, fled to a hermitage on Slieve League (*see under* Carrick, Co. Donegal). Discovered after seven years and induced to return to his post, he died on the way back at Racoon, where a vulgar 1956 monument has been intruded into the mound to mark his grave. The Seven Bishops of Racoon are commemorated in the oldest extant Irish martyrology (797–808), that of Oengus

Céle Dé (*see* Coolbanagher *under* Port Laoise). On a neighbouring hill, Ard Fothaid, Domnall, King of Tara 626–42, had his royal seat. The barony takes its name, Tirhugh (Tír Áeda), from his father, Áed mac Ainmirech. Also in Ballymagrorty was the church where the Mac Robhartaighs (after whom the townland is named) kept the Cathach (*see* Academy House, Dawson St., Dublin SE.), whose hereditary custodians they were.

2½ m. SW. (1 m. W. of Ballymagrorty schoolhouse) is Lurgan Carn: a neolithic (?) ring enclosure with a chambered cairn; the hill (492 ft) commands a splendid panorama.

1 m. SW. (via the Rossnowlagh road), in Ballymagrorty Scotch, is Giants Grave, a chamber tomb.

3½ m. SW. is Rossnowlagh (*see under* Ballyshannon).

2 m. NW. is Drumhome, site of a Columban monastery. The only relic is the E. wall of a church at the foot of Mullinacross Hill.

BALLITORE, Co. Kildare (Map 6, C4), is a decayed village to the W. of the Kilcullen (9 m.)–Castledermot (8 m.) road. It originated as a Quaker settlement. Abraham Shackleton (1697–1771), a Yorkshire Quaker, founded a school here in 1726, of which the most illustrious pupil (1741–4) was Edmund Burke. Mrs Mary Leadbeater (1758–1828), grand-daughter of Shackleton, friend of Burke, and author of many works important as social documents, lived at Ballitore. There are several ringforts and Fitzgerald castles in the area, including Uslee castle on the Kilcullen road.

The parish church of SS Mary and Laurence (*c.* 1860) is by J. J. McCarthy, foremost Irish architect of the Gothic Revival.

2 m. S., on the Carlow road, is Timolin, site of an early monastery founded by St Mo-Ling (*see* St Mullins). In the Protestant church is the mid-13th cent. effigy of an armoured knight supposed to be Robert fitz Richard, Lord of Norragh and ancestor of the de Valle (Wall) family. He founded a convent for Arroasian nuns at Timolin. ½ m. further S. is Moone, site of a 6th cent. Columban monastery of which the most important relic (Nat. Mon.) is St Columcille's Cross, an unusually slender granite High Cross (9th cent.) found buried in the ground in 1835 and pieced together and re-erected, the base and head in 1850, the shaft in 1893. The subjects include the following: E. face: *Crucifixus, The Fall, Sacrifice of Isaac, Daniel in the Lions' Den;* S. side: *The Children in the Fiery Furnace, Flight into Egypt, Multiplication of the Loaves and Fishes;* W. face:

Commissioners of Public Works in Ireland

The Multiplication of the Loaves and Fishes, from the High Cross at Moone, Ballitore

Commissioners of Public Works in Ireland

The Flight into Egypt, from the High Cross at Moone, Ballitore

Crucifixion, Twelve Apostles; N. side: *SS Anthony and Paul Break Bread in the Desert, Temptation of St Anthony*. Close by are the fragments of a second cross. There is also a fragment of a Franciscan friary founded in 1258 by Sir Gerald Fitzmaurice. Not far off is the 15th cent. tower of Moone castle.

1¼ mí. SE., in Simonstown West, is an 8-ft granite pillarstone.

3 m. SW., on the Athy road, is Burtown House, an early Georgian house.

1 m. W. is the celebrated hill of Mullaghmast (563 ft). On the summit is Ráth Maisten, alias Rathmore, more popularly The Rath of Mullaghmast. Here, on New Year's Day 1577, the chiefs of Laoighis and Uí Fáilghe were treacherously massacred by the English and their O Dempsey allies. The Bloody Hole is the reputed scene of the slaughter. Garret Óg, 11th ("Wizard") Earl of Kildare, is supposed to sleep in the Rath, emerging every seventh year to ride around The Curragh (*see also* Kilkea

Commissioners of Public Works in Ireland

Combat of lions and serpents, from the High Cross at Moone, Ballitore

Castle *under* Castledermot). Daniel O Connell held a famous "Monster Meeting" in the adjacent "Meeting Field", 1 Oct. 1843. ¼ m. S. of the Rath, not far from the road, is the Long Stone of Mullaghmast, an artificially grooved granite pillarstone (*see* Punchestown, *under* Naas).

BALLYBAY, Co. Monaghan (Map 3, A6), is a small market town on the Castleblayney (8 m.)–Newbliss (11 m.) road. Coarse fishing may be had in local lakes.

4 m. NE., in Lennan, is a prehistoric chamber tomb with scribings on one upright.

BALLYBOFEY, Co. Donegal (Map 2, C3), is a small market town on the Donegal (18 m.)–Letterkenny (14 m.) road. It is situated on the S. bank of the River Finn, opposite the village of Stranorlar.

Isaac Butt (1813–79), founder of the Irish Home Rule movement, is buried in the Protestant graveyard. He was born in Glebe House, 7½ m. NW. in Glenfinn (*below*).

The road SW. to Donegal passes through Barnesmore Gap (499 ft) between Croaghconnallagh (1,724 ft) and Barnesmore (1,491 ft). 5½ m. SW. via this road, on the S. slope of Croaghanierin and about 100 ft over Lough

Commissioners of Public Works in Ireland

The Twelve Apostles, from the High Cross at Moone, Ballitore

Mourne, is the large stone ringfort called Cashelnavean (Stone fort of the Fiana). S. of the road, at the NE. end of Lough Mourne, is the Giant's Bed, a chamber tomb.

The road NW. to Glenties and Dungloe climbs the wild, picturesque valley of the Finn (Glenfinn) to Lough Finn, where it bifurcates, the right-hand branch crossing Carbat Gap to Doochary and Dunglow, the left-hand branch following the valley SW. to Glenties. Some 7–9 m. NW. of Ballybofey, on the N. side of Glenfinn (townlands of Brockagh, Cloghanmore, and Kiltyfergal) are three prehistoric chamber tombs. There is a pretty Salmon Leap at Cloghan Lodge.

BALLYBOGHILL, Co. Dublin (Map 6, D2), is a hamlet on the Dublin (13 m.)–The Naul (12 m.) road. The district – from 1175 onwards the property of St Mary's Abbey, Dublin – is alleged to take its name from the Bachall Íosa (see Christ Church Cathedral under Dublin SW.). But the name *Balibachel* is recorded before that relic was brought to Dublin (1177). There are some remains of the medieval parish church.

2 m. ESE. is Grace Dieu, site of one of the most famous nunneries (Augustinian) of the English Pale (see Lusk). At the Dissolution the English colony in Ireland pleaded in vain for the convent on the grounds that there "the womenkind of the most part of the whole Englishry of this land be brought up in virtue, learning, and in the English tongue and behaviour". The nuns retired to Portrane (see under Donabate), and the convent and its possessions were granted to the Barnewalls, who dismantled the buildings in 1565 to provide materials for Turvey House, Donabate (q.v.). Traces of a cloister court and a few gravestones, etc., are all that survive. A short distance E. is St Brigid's Well; to the SW. is Lady Well.

1½ m. NW. are remains of Westphalstown medieval nave-and-chancel church.

2¼ m. NW., in Cottrelstown, are remains of St Michael's Church; to the S. are St Michael's Well and, further S., St John's Well.

BALLYBRITTAS, Co. Laois (Map 6, B4), is a small village on the Monasterevin (3½ m.)–Port Laoighse (9 m.) road.

4 m. W. is Emo Court (1790–1800), built for the Earl of Portarlington to the designs of James Gandon. Now the Jesuit novitiate, it has a noteworthy collection of paintings, stained glass, and sculpture (by Evie Hone, Francis Kelly, Oisín Kelly, Patrick Pye, and others). The demesne, which is noted for its fine timber, in particular the Wellingtonias, now belongs to the Department of Lands (Forestry Division). In Emo Catholic church is a recumbent effigy of Alexandrina Octavia, Countess of Portarlington (d. 1874), by Sir Joseph Edgar Boehm, the Austro-Hungarian who became Sculptor-in-Ordinary to Queen Victoria.

BALLYBUNNION, Co. Kerry (Map 4, D2), is a popular little seaside resort with a fine beach at the mouth of the Shannon, 9 m. NW. of Listowel. There are caves (visited by Tennyson in 1842) in the sea cliffs.

SW. of the village, in the enclosure (Castle Green) of a promontory fort, are the remains of Ballybunnion Castle. There is a complex souterrain beneath Castle Green.

NW. of the village, on the S. side of lovely little Doon Cove, is a large promontory fort with remains of later Pookeenee Castle inside the fosse.

1¼ m. N., at Doon Point, are a promontory fort and fragments of a Geraldine castle. The headland commands a delightful view.

1¾ m. N., at Tonalassa in Bromore West, is a promontory fort. Offshore to the S. rises the Devil's Castle, a fine 100-ft sea-stack.

3 m. NE. is Knockanore Hill (880 ft), affording fine views of the Shannon estuary.

5 m. S. is the village of Ballyduff. 1 m. SE., in Rattoo House demesne, are a 92-ft Round Tower (roof restored) and remains of a small church (Nat. Mons.), relics of an early monastery. Near the demesne gate are remains of Rattoo "Abbey", founded about 1200 as the Hospital of St John the Baptist (Augustinian Canons Regular Hospitaller), but which afterwards became a house of the Arroasian Canons and was dedicated to SS Peter and Paul.

BALLYCASTLE, Co. Antrim (Map 3, C2), a market town and popular seaside resort 27 m. N. of Ballymena, stands at the junction of Glentaise and Glenshesk to the N. of Knocklayd (1,695 ft) and its great prehistoric cairn, Carn-na-truagh, which may cover a passage grave. The town takes its name from a castle built by Sir Randall MacDonnell, 2nd Earl of Antrim, fourth son of Somhairle Buidhe. There are good sandy beaches here. The Carey and Glenshesk rivers offer good brown trout fishing. By the shore is the cottage from which Marconi transmitted his first wireless message (to Rathlin), 1905. The coast in the vicinity offers fine cliff scenery and interesting geological formations.

1 m. E. are the ruins of Bunamargy Friary (Nat. Mon.; Bun na Mairge=Mouth of the Margey, the Margey being the river formed by the confluence of the Carey and Glenshesk rivers). A Franciscan Tertiary friary founded by Rory MacQuillan about 1500, it was burned down in 1584, when the MacDonnells attacked English troops garrisoned there. In 1626 it passed to the Franciscan First Order and survived until 1642. The remains include a gatehouse and fragments of the claustral buildings, as well as an aisleless preaching church, the S. transept of which has been converted into a MacDonnell mausoleum (1621–66). Among those buried here are Somhairle Buidhe (Sorley Boye) MacDonnell himself (d. 1590), his son, the 1st Earl of Antrim (d. 1636), and Randall, 2nd Earl (d. 1682). The latter's tomb has in-

Stone-revetted crannóg, Lough na Cranagh, Ballycastle

scriptions in Irish (very rare), Latin, and English. There is an interesting Mac Naghten tomb of 1630 in the S. wall of the church, while near the E. end is the grave of Francis Stewart, Catholic bishop of Down and Connor (d. 1749). A small, crude cross at the W. end of the church is said to mark the grave of Julia Mac Quillan, the "Black Nun".

¾ m. NW., on a promontory (200 ft), are the ruins of Dunineny (*dún an aonaigh*, fort of the public assembly) castle, one of the earliest Mac Donnell strongholds in Antrim. Somhairle Buidhe Mac Donnell resided here from his accession in 1558 until his death in 1589. 2½ m. further W., offshore on Kenbane (Ceann Bán, White Head), are remains of a castle built in 1547 by Somhairle's brother and predecessor as chief of the Mac Donnells, Colla Dubh Mac Donnell, who died here in 1558.

5½ m. NE. is Benmore, alias Fair Head (636 ft). The interesting geological formations between town and head include coal measures worked in the 18th and 19th centuries. Below Fair Head is Carraig Uisneach, rocks which legend would link with the mythological tale of Déirdre and the Sons of Uisneach. 500 yds SW. of the head is Lough Doo. 300 yds SW. of the lough and 50 yds from the cliff edge is a passage grave. ¼ m. SE. of the lough is Lough na Cranagh, with an oval crannóg having a dry-masonry revetment. About ½ m. W. is Doonmore, a motte-and-bailey carved out of a basalt outcrop; traces of stone defences survive.

2 m. SE., in Churchfield, is Culfeightrin "Old Church" (Nat. Mon.), a fragment with a fine 15th cent. window. In the graveyard are two pillarstones.

2½ m. SE., on the W. side of Glenshesk, are the remains of The Gobán Saor's Castle, traditionally a castle put up by the Gobán in a single night, actually the ruins of a church which may be the successor of one founded by St Patrick. Glenshesk was the scene of two Mac Donnell defeats, one (1565) at the hands of Seaán the Proud O Neill, the other (1583) at the hands of the Mac Quillans.

BALLYCASTLE, Co. Mayo (Map 1, C2), is a village and little resort at the foot of Ballinglen, 9 m. W. of Killala and 30 m. E. of Belmullet. There are sand dunes and a small beach (Trabaun) 1 m. N. on Bunatrahir Bay.

¾ m. WNW., in Ballyglass townland, is a court cairn with a large elliptical court entered from the side and having a segmented gallery at each end. 250 yds S. are the remains of a court cairn with oval court and facade. 1¼ m. WNW., in Ballyknock, are remains of a portal dolmen; 300 yds WNW. are remains of another.

5 m. NNE. is Downpatrick Head (126 ft). Here are the ruins of St Patrick's Church, a holy well, a small ancient stone cross, and other stations to which pilgrims resort on Garland Sunday (last Sunday in July). Here, too, is Pollnashantinny, a puffing hole with subterranean channel to the sea. On the larger promontory are traces of a promontory fort. Just off the head is spectacular Doonbristy, an isolated cliff rock with a promontory fort. ½ m. S. of the church, on the SW. slope of the hill, is Tobar Phádraig, a holy well.

2½ m. NE. are the ruins of Kilbride church and an early cross-pillar.

3¾ m. ESE., in Barnhill Upper, is a court cairn. 1 m. SE., alt. 200 ft in Rathoonagh, are remnants of a court cairn. ½ m. SE. of this are remains of another. 1 m. SW. of the latter, alt. 700 ft, is the hill-top cairn of Seefin.

2 m. S. are Ballinglen pillarstone and castle (remnant).

5 m. S., alt. 200 ft, is Creevagh More "Burial Ground", a ruined court cairn very much overgrown.

6 m. SSE., in Ballybeg, are the Cloghabracka, a full-court cairn with antecourt.

2 m. NW., in Doonfeeny Upper, are two old graveyards separated by a bohereen. In one are remains of a church, in the other traces of a circular enclosure in which stands a slender, 18-ft pillarstone with an elaborate pattern of two crosses low down on the W. face. On the hillside to the NW. is Ráth Uí Dhubhda, alias the Fairy Fort.

From Ballycastle W. to Belderg (10 m.) the road runs between Maumakeogh (1,247 ft) and the wild cliff coast which is worth exploring.

4 m. NW., alt. 500 ft on the NE. spur of Maumakeogh, in Behy, is The Roomeens, a transeptal court cairn with horseshoe-shaped court. The grave goods included Western Neolithic pottery.

7 m. NW., and ½ m. N. of the road, is Port Conaghra promontory fort. ¾ m. SSW. of this, and not 200 yds N. of the road, is Cashlaunicrobin, alias Foherglass promontory fort.

10 m. NW. is Belderg. The river has good salmon fishing. The cliff scenery to the W. is very fine.

BALLYCLARE, Co. Antrim (Map 3, C4), is a linen town on the Larne (11 m.)–Antrim (11 m.) road.

1¼ m. N. is Ballyeaston, birthplace of the grandfather of Andrew Jackson, 17th President of the U.S.A. The Johnston cottage is to be restored as a memorial.

BALLYCONNEELY, Co. Galway (Map 1, B5), is a hamlet on the isthmus between Ballyconneely Bay and Mannin Bay, 9 m. NW. of Roundstone and 6 m. SSW. of Clifden.

½ m. N. is Mannin Bay with its beautiful beaches, including Coral Strand.

2 m. SW. are remains of the small, late church of Bunowen (St Flannan's). The derelict "castle" nearby was commenced in 1838 by Richard Geoghegan, descendant of a Cromwellian transplantee from Co. Westmeath; the stones were taken from a ruined O Flaherty castle by the seashore to the SE. To the SW. is Doon Hill; the derelict 1939–45 coast watching post is on the site of a "folly" (mentioned by Thackeray) which was built (1780) by Richard Geoghegan to commemorate the winning of freedom of trade by Grattan's Volunteers. Less than ½ m. W., near the road to Bunowen quay, in Aillebrack, is the Well of the Seven Daughters (see under Rinvyle; also Inisheer, Aran Islands). To the W., in Aillebrack, Creggoduff, and Keerhaunmore, 2 m. of sand dunes flank a lovely beach with extensive shellmiddens, 1 m. SW. of the beach, in Keerhaunmore, is Tobercallin (St Caillín's Well), a bullaun. Off the SW. tip of the peninsula are

Doonawaul islet (with remnants of clocháns, etc.) and, 1 m. further SW., Chapel Island (with St Caillín's Well and remains of little St Caillín's Church). To the W. of the latter, on Ilaunamid, is Slyne Head lighthouse.

BALLYCONNELL, Co. Cavan (Map 2, D5), is a Border village at the foot of Slieve Rushen (1,279 ft), on the road from Belturbet (7 m.) to Swanlinbar (11 m.).

The Protestant church dates from the early 17th cent.; the tower was added in 1814. A Romanesque door or window head (from Toomregon Round Tower ?; *below*) has recently been brought to the church. In the churchyard are remains of two diamond-shaped redoubts, relics of fortifications constructed in the Williamite war.

4 m. SE., in Ballyhugh, overlooking Lough Dungummin, is a promontory fort with rockcut ditch and remains of a stone rampart. In a thicket to the S. is a double-court cairn with roofless chambers. 1 m. S., in Carn, is Carndallan, an enormous ruined cairn which apparently covered a passage grave. It is set towards the end of a large rectangular enclosure bounded by a low bank.

2½ m. S., in Mullynagolman and not far from Togher Lough, traces of a church and Round Tower mark the site of the early monastery of Toomregon (Túaim Drecon) celebrated in Irish literary legend. According to that legend Cenn Faelad *Sapiens* (d. 679), grandson of Baetán, King of Tara, and cousin of King Oswiu of Northumbria (who came to Ireland to study), was severely wounded at the battle of Mag Roth (*see* Moira, Co. Down) in 637, so that his "brain of forgetting" was cut out. He was brought to Toomregon to be healed by Abbot Briccéne, a famous surgeon. At Toomregon "there were three schools, a school of Latin learning, a school of Irish law, and a school of Irish poetry. And everything Cenn Faelad would hear of the recitations of the three schools by day he would have it by heart at night. And he fitted a pattern of poetry to these matters, and wrote them on slates and tablets, and set them in a vellum book". Prof. Eóin Mac Néill interpreted this legend as reflecting the first reduction of traditional Irish law to writing, but other scholars do not agree.

3 m. SW., in Killycluggin, is a stone circle having outside it the shattered remnants of a phallic stone ornamented with incised Iron Age Celtic patterns. Comparable, if finer, stones are at Castlestrange, Co. Roscommon (*see under* Athleague), and Turoe, Co. Galway (*see* Bullaun *under* Loughrea; one found at Mullaghmast, Co. Kildare, is now in the National Museum), but nowhere else in these islands, though the type is known on the Continent. In Kilnavert, the adjacent townland to the SW., are (*a*) two small stone circles side by side, (*b*) the remains of a low chambered cairn inside a circular enclosure demarcated by a rock-cut ditch, (*c*) the remains of a gallery grave in an oval

cairn enclosed by a circular bank of earth, and (*d*) two pillarstones, one 20 ft N. of the latter, the other 150 yds to the SE. Magh Sléacht, celebrated in Irish literary legend as the seat of a fictitious high-idol of Ireland (a pillarstone inside a stone circle, to which the name Crom Crúaich was attached) overthrown by St Patrick, is generally supposed to have been the plain round about Kilnavert and Killycluggin.

BALLYCOTTON, Co. Cork (Map 5, D6), a fishing village and small resort on Ballycotton Bay, 7 m. SE. of Cloyne and 8 m. S. of Castlemartyr, is a noted centre for deep-sea angling. Excellent bathing may be had in nearby coves and rock pools, as well as at Garryvoe – Ballylongane strand, 4 m. N. The road round Ballycotton Bay, via Shanagarry – Garryvoe – Ballymakeagh – Knockadoon Head – Ballymacoda, to Youghal, is noted for its scenery; likewise that W. to Whitegate via Churchtown and Inch.

2 m. NNW., on the Cloyne road, is Shanagarry House. The out-offices incorporate fragments of a courtyard house built by Admiral Sir William Penn, who had been granted the castle and manor of Macroom by Cromwell. At the Restoration these were restored to Donagh Mac Carthy, Viscount Muskerry, and Penn received the Power castle and lands of Shanagarry in part exchange. (Some remnants of the Power castle survive.) In 1667 Penn sent his son, William (of Pennsylvania), to Ireland to administer his estates. William resided at Shanagarry. It was on the occasion of a visit to Cork that he became a Quaker. Descendants of Admiral Penn held the Shanagarry estate until 1903.

BALLYCROY, Co. Mayo (Map 1, B3), is a hamlet on the Mallaranny (9 m.)–Bangor Erris (12 m.) road.

2 m. NE., in Bunmore West, are the remains of Teampall Éanna, an early church, with Tobar Éanna, a holy well, nearby.

2¼ m. S., in Castlehill, in the second field S. from the old castle site, is a pillarstone with crosses on the E. and W. faces.

2 m. SSW., in Kildun, is a mound (Nat. Mon.) with two pillarstones. One pillarstone has a ringed cross on the W. face, the other has a diamond pattern on the W. face. Local legend makes the mound the grave of Donn, son of Míl.

4 m. NW. are the remains of Doona castle, said to have been another of Gráinne Ní Mháille's castles (*see* Clare Island).

BALLYFARNAN, Co. Roscommon (Map 2, B5), is a village on the Sligo (19 m.)–Drumshanbo (10 m.) road at the foot of Kilronan Mt (1,081 ft).

2½ m. SE., on the N. shore of Lough Meelagh, are the ruins of the church of Kilronan of the Duignans, erected in 1339 by Fearghal Muimh-neach Duignan, and dedicated to St Lasair, who, with her father, St Rónán, is said to have founded the first church here (6th/7th cent.). The Late Romanesque S. door of the ruin derives from a 12th/13th cent. church. (St Lasair is also associated with Aghavea, Co. Fermanagh, and Killasser, Co. Mayo.) The local branch of the Duignans became erenachs, or hereditary lay proprietors, of the foundation in addition to being historiographers to the Mac Dermots. *The Book of the Duignans*, alias the *Annals of Kilronan*, alias the *Annals of Connacht*, an important chronicle of the period A.D. 900–1563, used by the Four Masters, was compiled in their school. Kilronan was the ancestral burial place of the Mac Dermot Roes. The celebrated songwriter and harpist, Turlough O Carolan (1670–1738), was buried in their tomb at the N. side of the church. He had died at Alderford, the home of Mac Dermot Roe, just outside Ballyfarnan. An enormous concourse, including ten harpers, attended his four-day wake, which gave rise to still-told tales. In the later 18th cent. his skull was displayed in a niche in the churchyard. Among O Carolan's compositions was the melody to which *The Star-spangled Banner* is sung. NW. of the church are the remains of a prehistoric chamber tomb. Nearby is Tobar Laisre, Lasair's Well.

BALLYFERRITER, Co. Kerry (Map 4, B4), is a village and summer resort near Smerwick Harbour, 8½ m. NW. of Dingle and 3½ m. NE. of Dunquin.

1 m. NNE., in Cloonties, is a gallery grave.

1½ m. N. is the beautiful strand of Smerwick Harbour (formerly the Haven of Ardcanny).

2½ m. N. is Smerwick village. 500 yds SE., commanding a fine view, are the remains of Dún an Óir (Nat. Mon.), constructed by a party of James Fitzmaurice's Italians and Spaniards who landed in the bay, 12 Sept. 1580. English land and sea forces under Lord Deputy Grey and Admiral Winter attacked the fort, 7 Nov. After three days' bombardment the fort capitulated. The officers were spared, but some 600 common soldiers and 17 Irish men and women were butchered in cold blood. Previous to the surrender the Italian commander had delivered up Father Laurence Moore, Oliver Plunket, and an English Catholic, William Wollick. These, refusing to acknowledge the religious supremacy of Elizabeth I, were savagely tortured and mutilated before being hanged. Because foreigners were the victims, the Massacre of Smerwick has attracted much attention from historians and propagandists; but it was in conformity with normal Elizabethan practice in Ireland. The remains of the fort include an eroded mainland outwork with two bastions, as well as an inner rock-fort cut off by a rock-cut trench. 1¼ m. N. of Smerwick village, on Beendermot (tip of the peninsula), is Dermot and Grania's Bed. Beendermot (501 ft), Been-

managah (462 ft), and Beenhenry (448 ft), alias
The Three Sisters, have fine cliffs.

1¾ m. ENE., in Reask, the remains of two
clocháns, a cross-inscribed stone, an early
cross-slab, two early cross-pillars (one with
elaborate, incised cross-pattern), and an ancient
burial ground mark the site of an early anchoritic monastery.

¾ m. E. are remains of Ballineanig castle. ¾ m.
S. of the castle, in Ballineanig Church Quarter,
are the ruins of Ballywiheen church (Nat.
Mon.); there are two early cross-slabs here
(one broken). Three fields WSW., in Ballywiheen, is a 17-ft pillarstone. Two fields SW. of
this are St Mo-Laga's Well and a pillarstone.
¼ m. WSW. of the well, on the W. side of the
bohereen around Ballineanig Hill (Ballyferriter,
1¼ m.), is an ancient church site with remains of
a dry-stone oratory of Teampall Geal (see
Ballymorereagh under Dingle) type and an
early incised stone cross (Nat. Mons.). ¼ m. S.
of the latter is Cathair na gCat (Nat. Mon.), a
stone ringfort; fragments of a well-known
ogham stone have been deposited here for
safety.

2½ m. E., in Emlagh East, is a ringfort (Nat.
Mon.). 1¼ m. E., in Lateevemore, is the ancient
church site of Templenacloonagh. The enclosure is marked by traces of a cashel. In it
stand the shell of a tiny church or oratory and
two early cross-pillars. 1¾ m. (by road) NNE.,
is the celebrated church of Gallarus (date unknown), a corbel-roofed, dry-masonry structure
(Nat. Mon.); an early cross-pillar (Nat. Mon.)
is inscribed COLUM MAC DINET. ¾ m. NW.
are the ruins of Gallarus castle (Nat. Mon.),
a Fitzgerald castle commanding a lovely view.
1 m. E. of the castle, in Caherdorgan South, is
Boen, a stone ringfort with three ruined clocháns and a souterrain; to the E., NE., and SE. is
the Saints' Road. 400 yds NE., in Caherdorgan
North, is a stone ringfort with four ruined
clocháns (Nat. Mon.). 400 yds N. of the latter
is the Chancellor's House (Nat. Mon.). Some
350 yds NE. of the Chancellor's House the road
passes between the Cow Stone (W.) and the
Thief Stone (E.), two pillarstones. A short distance N. is Kilmalkedar village. Here are (a)
15th cent. St Brendan's Fothrach or House,
(b) St Brendan's Oratory, (c) Kilmalkedar

Cross-pillar at Reask, Ballyferriter

Gallarus cross-pillar, Ballyferriter

Gallarus church, Ballyferriter

church (Romanesque), (*d*) the Alphabet Stone (an ogham stone), (*e*) a stone cross, (*f*) the Keelers (a stone), and (*g*) a sun dial – all Nat. Mons.; also St Brendan's Well. The "oratory" was a structure of the Gallarus type. The Romanesque church (some details reminiscent of Cormac's Chapel, Cashel) was a developed form of the same sort of structure, i.e. had a corbelled barrel-vault roof; the chancel is a Transitional enlargement of the Romanesque original. The whole Gallarus–Caherdorgan–Kilmalkedar area is embarrassingly rich in antiquities (21 churches, 15 "oratories", 12 large crosses, 9 "penitential stations", and 76 holy wells have been listed).

$3\frac{1}{4}$ m. SE. is Rahinnane castle (*see under* Ventry).

$\frac{1}{2}$ m. SW., in Ballyferriter townland, is a stone circle; beside it is Toberacloghaun.

2 m. NW., on the NW. side of sandy Ferriter's Cove, Ballyoughter South, are the fragmentary remains of Ferriter's Castle (1460). (The best known of the Ferriters was the gallant poet-scholar, Piaras Feiréir, last Kerry commander to submit to the Cromwellians. His safe-conduct was dishonoured, and he was hanged on Martyrs' Hill, Killarney, 1653.) The castle stands in earlier works cutting across the neck of Doon Point. 180 yds W. is a second line of defence across the peninsula. At the ex-

tremity of Doon Point are hut-sites. The site commands a panorama of great beauty. WNW. of Ferriter's castle is Sybil Point, from which very fine cliffs extend NE. past the Three Sisters to Carrigbrean (3 m.; *see* Smerwick, *above*).

BALLYGAWLEY, Co. Tyrone (Map 3, A5), is a village on the Omagh (12 m.)–Dungannon (10 m.) road.

$3\frac{1}{2}$ m. W. is Errigal Keerogue (*see* Augher).

2 m. NW., on the S. slope of Slievemore (1,035 ft), is Ballygawley House, which incorporates some remains of a castle built by Sir Gerald Lowther and destroyed by Sir Felim O Neill of Kennard (Caledon) in 1641. 1 m. SW., in Sess Kilgreen, is "The Fort" (Nat. Mon.), a degenerate passage grave resembling that on Knockmany (*see under* Augher); concentric circles and other prehistoric hieratic devices are still visible on one of the rear uprights. In the next field, behind Woodvale Cottage, is a stone (Nat. Mon.) with similar devices; it is said to have been the capstone of a destroyed chamber tomb. Behind Sess Kilgreen post office are two pillarstones, perhaps the remains of a chamber tomb. In Glenchuil, next townland to the W., is "The Fort", a wrecked burial cairn; one of the stones has fifteen cup marks. $\frac{3}{4}$ m. N. of Glenchuil bridge, alt. 500 ft, is Shantavney

Irish Giants Grave, a round cairn with a wrecked circular chamber.

⅓ m. N., in Green Hill Demesne, are the remains of a round cairn.

BALLYHAISE, Co. Cavan (Map 2, D5), on the Cavan (4 m.)–Clones (17 m.) road, is a village which has a good 18th cent. Market House.

Ballyhaise House (now an agricultural school) is a fine mansion built about 1750 by Brockhill Newburgh to the design of Richard Cassels. It is vaulted on all floors, each room separately.

4 m. N. is Redhills village. Killoughter Protestant church has a three-light window (*The Sower*) by Catherine A. O Brien (1954). 4½ m. NNE., in Drumavrack, is a dual-court cairn.

5¾ m. NE., in Magherintemple, the site of a medieval parish church is marked by a hill-top graveyard at the centre of a very large oval earthwork (Neolithic?). Down to the 16th cent. this was the site of a great fair.

BALLYHAUNIS, Co. Mayo (Map 1, E4), is a small market town on the Claremorris (11 m.)–Castlereagh (11 m.) road.

At the E. end of the town is an Augustinian priory which incorporates fragments of the church of an Augustinian friary dedicated to the Blessed Virgin Mary. The friary was founded, about 1430, by the Jordan Duff MacCostellos (alias Nangles) on the site of a castle or manor house. In the Convent of Mercy chapel are five single-light windows (1924–5) by Michael Healy: *The Good Shepherd, St Brigid, St Patrick, St Ita, St Columcille*.

9 m. N., on the N. shore of Urlaur Lough, are the ruins of Urlaur "Abbey", a Dominican friary dedicated to St Thomas. It was founded in 1430 by Edmund MacCostello and his wife, Fionnúala, daughter of O Conor Don.

2 m. WNW., on a commanding site in Island townland, is a tumulus with an ogham stone ("Braghlaghboy Ogham Stone").

5½ m. NW. the ancient churchyard of Aghamore marks the site of an early monastery. In the next field is a rude cross with an incised design and traces of an inscription.

2 m. NNW., in Coolnaha South, 300 yds NE. of Annagh castle, is a low earthen ring in which stands a pillarstone with a ringed cross on one face.

6½ m. NNW., in Cappagh, is a dual-court cairn.

BALLYHEIGE, Co. Kerry (Map 4, C3), is a quiet little resort on the Tralee (11 m.)–Ballybunnion (16 m.) coast road. Ballyheige Bay has an excellent sandy beach. The drive NW. to Kerry Head and around Maulin Mountain (719 ft) affords magnificent views of the Kerry and Clare coasts.

Derelict Ballyheige Castle, NW. of the village, was built for the Crosbies of Ardfert to the design of Sir Richard Morrison (1767–1849). It was burnt down by Republicans in 1922. There are many ringforts with souterrains in the district.

3½ m. W., at the foot of Trisk Mountain (701 ft) in Glenderry, are (a) the defaced remains of St Macadaw's Church, (b) a cupped pillarstone with incised, red-painted cross, (c) a charmed stone ball, and (d) St Macadaw's Well. (Also in Glenderry are ancient hut-sites with souterrains.) 1½ m. NW., on Kerry Head, is Cahercarbery Beg, a promontory fort; ½ m. N. is Cahercarbery More, a larger promontory fort.

5 m. N., on "a huge rock in the middle of the sea", are the complex traces of Ballingarry, alias Ballincaheragh, castle. The Cantillons had a castle here from 1280 onwards. They lost it for their part in the Desmond rebellion. In 1602–3 it was held by Gearóid Rúa Stack against English land and sea forces. At the outbreak of the 1641-52 war local English planters, led by Col. David Crosbie, withdrew into the castle, which they enlarged and strengthened. They held out for five years. On the mainland are remnants of a turret and of two diverging covered ways constructed by Crosbie; to the rear are other earthworks. In the isolated inner ward are traces of many houses. The lovely coast hereabouts is little known to tourists.

BALLYJAMESDUFF, Co. Cavan (Map 2, D6), a market town between Virginia (6 m.) and Cavan (10 m.), is the subject of Percy French's ever-popular ballad "Come back, Paddy Reilly, to Ballyjamesduff".

5½ m. SW., near Mountnugent, on an islet off the shore of Lough Sheelin, are the remains of Crover castle, built by Thomas, son of Mahon O Reilly, in the late 14th cent. 2 m. SE. of Mountnugent is Dungummin, Lower (*see under* Oldcastle).

BALLYLIFFIN, Co. Donegal (Map 2, D1), is a small resort 6 m. NW. of Carndonagh and ½ m. away. Pollan Strand.

2¾ m. N., at the NW. corner of Doagh Isle peninsula, are remains of the O Doherty castle of Carrickbraghy: a 16th (?) cent. square tower with an added circular tower and fragments of a 16th/17th cent. bawn.

3½ m. ENE., in Magheranaul, is Cloghtogle, a gallery grave with a holed portal slab; to the NE. is St Buchan's Burial Ground; further NE. is a pillarstone. 1¼ m. NW., in Carrowreagh, alias Craignacally, is the Altar, alias the Mass Stone, a boulder covered with prehistoric scribings.

3 m. SE., on the S. slope of Tullynabratilly, alias Knockaughrim, alias Coolcross Hill, is Dermot and Grania's Bed, a ruined chamber tomb. 2 m. SW., in Cloontagh, near Ard, Magheramore, is Clochtogle, a chamber tomb with cup marks and enormous capstone.

1¾ m. SSW. is Clonmany (*q.v.*).

BALLYLONGFORD, Co. Kerry (Map 4, D2), is a village at the head of Ballylongford

Bay, Shannon estuary, 5 m. WSW. of Tarbert and 8 m. N. of Listowel.

1 m. N., on the E. shore of the inlet, are the ruins (Nat. Mon.) of Lislaughtin "Abbey", a friary founded in 1477 by O Conor Kerry for Franciscans of the Strict Observance. The long church has a short, aisled, S. transept and noteworthy sedilia. A fine processional crucifix (Ballylongford Cross) in the National Museum probably belonged to this friary.

2 m. S., in Ballyline West, is the Giants Grave, a chamber tomb.

2 m. NNW., in the channel between the mainland and Carrig Island, are the remains (Nat. Mon.) of Carrigafoyle castle (O Conor Kerry). The fine 86-ft tower stood at the centre of a bawn which enclosed a dock for boats. There were outworks on the mainland. In March 1580, the castle was held by the Italian engineer, Captain Julian, with 50 Irish and 16 Spaniards, for the Earl of Desmond against an English force under Sir William Pelham. Julian had every cranny in the rock filled with smooth masonry, but Pelham's artillery, brought up by sea, battered down the bawn, and the place was stormed after two days. Pelham hanged all the survivors and sent the Earl of Desmond's plate to the Queen. The castle also figured in the Tyrone (1600) and Cromwellian (1649) wars; it was finally wrecked by the Cromwellians. The tower commands a very fine view. – On Carrig Island are remains of Carrig "Abbey", Friars Well, and a fine early 19th cent. battery (Corran Point).

6 m. WNW. is lovely Beal Strand. The road SW. from Beal to Ballybunnion offers fine views. 3 m. WSW. of Beal, on Dooneen Point, is Lissadooneen, a promontory fort. A few fields E. is a pair of pillarstones.

BALLYMAHON, Co. Longford (Map 2, C7), is a village where the Mullingar (19 m.)–Lanesborough (12¾ m.) road crosses the River Inny.

In 960, Mahon, King of Thomond (Dál gCais), defeated Fergal, son of Ruarc, King of Breany and Connacht, near Ballymahon.

Oliver Goldsmith (1728–74), essayist, poet and playwright, was born near Pallas about 1 m. N. of the road to Abbeyshrule, and Ballymahon itself was probably his last home in Ireland. There is a memorial window to him in Forgney church, 2½ m. SE. of Ballymahon. The area chiefly associated with Goldsmith lies, however, to the SW. of Ballymahon (see Auburn, Co. Westmeath).

1 m. E. are the demesne and Georgian house of Newcastle, former home of the King-Harmans. Two other interesting houses in the area are Doorly Hall (Jessop family; 4 m. NE. on the Edgeworthstown road) and Castlecor House (1½ m. W.), a miniature Windsor Castle built by Dean Cults-Harman of Waterford.

4 m. NE. of Ballymahon is the hamlet of Abbeyshrule. SE., on the E. bank of the Inny, are remains of the Cistercian abbey (Flumen Dei) from which it takes its name (Irish, Mainistear na Sruthra). The abbey was founded about 1200 by O Farrel and was colonized from Mellifont. Burned in 1476, it was subsequently repaired. The sadly neglected remains include the choir and part of the nave of an aisleless 12th–13th cent. church (Transitional details) with later modifications. The tower at the SE. angle of the vanished E. cloister range is probably post-Reformation. In the graveyard NNE. of the abbey is the broken shaft of a small, early cross with a five-strand plait and other patterns. This is the only early cross in the county.

Mosstown House, Ballymahon

Commissioners of Public Works in Ireland

3 m. W. is Gorteen, native place of Leo (John Keagan Casey, 1846–70), author of "The Rising of the Moon", "Máire my Girl", and other ballads.

8 m. NW. are the remains of Abbeyderg Augustinian abbey (13th cent.).

6¼ m. NE. is derelict Mosstown House (17th cent., but much altered. In 1641 Mosstown was unsuccessfully defended against the insurgent Irish by the Newcomens, who had better fortune when they resisted the Jacobites half a century later).

BALLYMENA, Co. Antrim (Map 3, C4), is a manufacturing and commercial town on the Belfast (28 m.)–Coleraine (27 m.)–Ballycastle (27 m.) road. It is a predominantly Presbyterian town, founded for Scottish settlers in the 17th cent. by William Adair from Kinhilt. Those of the inhabitants who have emigrated have converged largely on Toronto, Canada (among them Timothy Eaton, founder of the great store). The prosperity of the town dates from the introduction of the linen industry about 1730/32. The only buildings of interest are the Linen Hall and the Town Hall. In the porch of St Patrick's Church, Castle St, is preserved an early grave-slab from Kirkinriola (*below*) with the inscription OR[Ō]IT DO DEGEN ("A prayer for Degen"). On a ridge in the S. suburbs is Harryville Motte (Nat. Mon.), a 40-ft high motte with a rectangular bailey on the E. It is one of the finest surviving Anglo-Norman earthworks in Ulster.

Ballymena is a convenient centre for visiting the beautiful Glens of Antrim (*q.v.*), and the neighbourhood is rich in remains of antiquarian interest.

1¾ m. NNE. is Drumfane "Moat" (Nat. Mon.), a motte-and-bailey. 1½ m. N. the ruined church of Kirkinriola (more correctly Kilconriola) marks the site of an early monastery.

8 m. NE. is Ticloy Hill; ½ m. S. of the summit are the remains of a court cairn with a single chamber and a shallow forecourt.

3½ m. SE., in Ballymarlagh, is a Neolithic court cairn (Nat. Mon.).

5 m. SE. is Connor, site of an early monastery which has given its name to the diocese. The monastery was founded by Bishop Óengus mac Nisse (St Mac Nisse; d. 514). The second patron was St Colmán Eala (*see* Muckamore *under* Antrim *and* Lynally *under* Tullamore). The trunk of Díarmait mac Cerrbeóil, King of Tara, who was murdered near Rathmore (*see under* Antrim) in 565, was buried at the monastery (his head was brought to Clonmacnois). In 1315 Edward Bruce routed Richard III de Burgo, "Red" Earl of Ulster, at Connor. In 1453 the diocese was united with that of Down. – ½ m. W. is Kells, site of the *disert* of Connor and, later, of the Augustinian abbey of St Mary (Teampall Muire). The abbey survived until the 16th cent. The only relic of the early monastery is the shaft of a High Cross preserved at the rectory.

1½ m. WSW. is Galgorm castle, a Plantation castle and bawn built by Sir Faithful Fortescue in 1618–19. It was renovated in 1832. Beyond the demesne is Gracehill, a Moravian settlement with central square, founded in 1746.

3 m. NW., in Cullybackey, is the house (Nat. Mon.) in which Chester Alan Arthur (1830–86), 21st President of the U.S.A., was born.

BALLYMOE, Co. Galway (Map 2, B7), is a small village on the Dunmore (15 m.)–Castlerea (5 m.) road, 13 m. NW. of Roscommon.

4 m. SE. are the ruins of Glinsk castle (Nat. Mon.), a fine late-17th cent. fortified house attributed to Sir Ulick Burke, a prominent Jacobite. 1 m. W., in the ruined church of Ballynakill, is a good early-16th cent. effigy of a mailed knight from a Burke tomb. There is also a rude carving of the Crucifixion.

BALLYMONEY, Co. Antrim (Map 3, B3), is a linen and agricultural centre on the Ballymena (19 m.)–Coleraine (8 m.) road.

3 m. NNE., in Conagher (Conacher), off the road to Dervock, is the family home of William McKinley, 25th President of the U.S.A. The old dwelling long served as an outhouse, the fittings having been sold to Americans.

6½ m. SSE. and 1¾ m. SE. of Finvoy, alt. 650 ft on the Long Mountain, Craigs, is The Broadstone, a three-chamber court cairn (Nat. Mon.).

7 m. SE. is Dunloy. In Ballymacaldrack, ¾ m. SSE. of the village, under the E. slope of the Long Mountain (alt. 400 ft), is Dooey's Cairn, an unusual oval court cairn excavated in 1935. Behind the single chamber was a boulder-lined (cremation?) trench, in the floor of which were three pits. In one of these were several cremations. The finds included Neolithic pottery, flint arrowheads, and stone axes.

BALLYMORE, Co. Westmeath (Map 2, C7), is a village on the Mullingar (16 m.)–Athlone (15 m.) road. The principal de Lacy (later de Verdon) seignorial manor in West Meath was here, and some remains of the castle survive.

½ m. N. is Lough Sewdy (alias Sunderlin), which gave its name to the Anglo-Norman manor. In pre-Norman times the O Melaghlins appear to have had a fort at the site of the "Camp", at that time a peninsula on the S. shore of the lake, and Hugh de Lacy's motte castle (1184) was doubtless on the same site. Edward Bruce spent Christmas there in 1315. (The strongest position in the locality, it was garrisoned by the English in 1641 and by the Jacobites in 1690.) In 1648 Eoghan Rúa O Neill, marching with the Catholic Army of Ulster to the relief of Athy, routed a strong Ormondist force between Shinglis (N. of the lake) and Ballymore. Oileán Mór island is mentioned as a crannóg in 11th and 12th cent. annals.

S. of the village is a remnant of Plary convent

(dedicated to the Virgin Mary), founded in 1218 by the de Lacys for Cistercian nuns. About ½ m. away was an Augustinian priory whose church was for a short time made cathedral of the diocese of Meath by Henry VIII.

4½ m. E. is Killare, where the remains of a church, to the S. of the crossroads, mark the site of Cell Fháir (Cell Áir), one of the principal monasteries of Bishop St Áed mac Bric, a prince of the Uí Néill (see Rahugh *under* Tullamore *and* Slieve League *under* Carrick). A *sui liag*, or master physician, he was highly reputed for his power of healing, and was invoked particularly by those who suffered from headaches. In time, popular tradition invested him with some of the attributes of the ancient sun-god Áed. NE. of the crossroads is the motte of the "castle of Cell Áir", erected in 1184 by Hugh de Lacy, but destroyed in 1187 and never rebuilt. NW. of the crossroads are Bride's Well and remains of a church. 6 m. SW. of the crossroads is Knockast (*see under* Moate).

5 m. E. is the Hill of Ushnagh (Uisneach). From the summit (602 ft) no less than twenty of the thirty-two counties of Ireland are visible in clear weather. As the accepted centre of Ireland, the hill was a place of sanctity in pagan times, and seems to have been the seat of a fire cult with a great May Day (Bealtaine) festival. St Patrick is said to have founded a church on the hill. In 984 Brian Boru occupied the hill as a challenge to the King of Tara, Melaghlin II. In 1111 a synod was held at Uisneach to plan the rearrangement of the dioceses of the kingdom of Meath. In 1414 Sir John Stanley, the English king's Lieutenant in Ireland and an enemy of the Gaelic poets, plundered Niall Ó Huiginn (O Higgins), a member of Ireland's foremost family of hereditary poets, at Uisneach. Whereupon Niall made satires on him "and he lived only five weeks after them". To avenge Stanley's death his successor, John Talbot, "Scourge of France", despoiled many of the poets of Ireland, including Díarmait O Daly of Meath. – On the Hill of Ushnagh are the following ancient remains. In *Kellybrook townland* on the SW. slope, to the N. of the Ballymore-Mullingar road: (a) An overgrown ringfort with central cairn and traces of buildings. (b) NW. of this ringfort is the Cat Stone, a large erratic at the centre of a low earthen ring 62 ft in diameter. This has been identified with the Aill na Míreann (Rock of the Divisions) of Irish literary legend, called Umbilicus Hiberniae by Giraldus Cambrensis. In *Ushnagh Hill townland:* (a) ENE. of the Kellybrook ringfort is a hillock enclosed by a low ring-bank; near the summit is a prostrate pillarstone. (b) NE. of this is St Patrick's Well. (c) NW. of the well is a small, D-shaped, earthen enclosure with central mound. (d) NW. of the latter, at the summit, is St Patrick's Bed, a rectangular platform of stones despoiled by the Ordnance Survey

sappers when setting up their trigonometrical station on the hill-top. (e) NW. of the Bed is a small ring barrow. (f) On the N. slope of the hill is Rathfarsan, a bivallate ringfort. In *Togherstown townland:* NE. of Rathfarsan are (a) A tree-covered tumulus, 9 ft high and 96 ft in diameter, and (b) a bivallate ringfort with secondary radial walls subdividing the area between the ramparts; excavation revealed traces of rectangular houses in both the outer and inner enclosures and two souterrains in the latter; the few finds indicated a date in the early historic period. (c) ESE. of the ringfort is an overgrown rectangular enclosure. In *Mweelra townland:* ¼ m. E. of St Patrick's Bed is a mound of earth and stones said to have contained a cist grave. In *Rathnew townland:* On the SE. eminence of the hill are the remains of (a) a bivallate, conjoint ringfort of dry masonry; the larger, E., part is subdivided by three straight walls and has remains of a souterrain and of a seven-compartment house of stones and earth; in the W. part are remains of a rectangular house of stones and earth with a souterrain beneath it; the line of an ancient roadway approaching the site from the S. may be traced as far as the Ballymore-Mullingar road. Inadequate excavations (1925–8) revealed that this site had had a complex functional and structural history: beneath the E. part of the fort were traces of a circular ritual (?) enclosure represented by ditches, pits, post-holes (and two burials ?). The ringfort itself possibly dates from the 2nd cent. A.D., but there is no justification for the excavator's claim that the E. house was the "palace of Tuathal Techtmar". (b) SE. of this ringfort are the remnants of a cairn (?), and (c) SE. of the cairn is a small ring-barrow. (d) ENE. of the barrow is a rectangular enclosure 27 × 24 ft.

1½ m. SE. is Clare Hill (433 ft), probably the Cláthra where Medbh's army is described as camping in *Táin Bó Cualnge*. On the summit are remains of a strong castle set on a large raised platform.

3½ m. WSW. is Drumraney, site of a castle of the Dillons, the Anglo-Norman family which was granted (about 1185) lands in Co. Westmeath at the expense of the Mac Eochagáins. There were other Dillon castles at Ardnagragh and Killaniney. Bryanmore Hill was the setting of Bruiden Da Choca, one of the five mythological festive halls of early Irish literature; on the hill are the remains of a ringfort.

BALLYMORE EUSTACE, Co. Kildare (Map 6, C3), is a Liffeyside village on the eastern Naas (7 m.)–Baltinglass (15 m.) road, 1½ m. W. of the great Liffey Valley reservoir. It takes its name from the Anglo-Norman FitzEustaces (*see* Harristown *and* Castlemartin *under* Athy, *and* Clongoweswood *under* Clane) who, 1373–c. 1524, were hereditary constables of the Archbishop of Dublin's manor here "among the Irish enemies".

In the Protestant church is an early-16th cent. armoured FitzEustace tomb effigy from New Abbey, Old Kilcullen (*see under* Kilcullen); it was for long in Barrettstown Castle (*below*).

In the old churchyard are a granite High Cross (the 1689 inscription is, of course, an addition), a smaller granite cross, and remains of an ancient church. There are several fine houses and demesnes by the Liffey.

2 m. N. is Barrettstown Castle, an early-19th cent. house incorporating a medieval tower (altered); now the property of Elizabeth Arden.

2½ m. NE. is Russborough House (*see under* Blessington).

1½ m. S., on a hill-top in Broadleas Common, are The Piper's Stones, a large stone circle, of which twenty-seven complete stones and twelve fragments survive. ¼ m. NW., in Longstone townland, is The Long Stone, a prostrate pillarstone (13½ ft) of granite; the enclosing earthen ring (cf. Longstone Rath, Furness, *under* Naas; *also* Punchestown, *ibid.*) has been removed. The small crosses are thought to have been incised since the stone fell.

3 m. S. is Hollywood, Co. Wicklow (*q.v.*).

2 m. W., on the N. bank of the Liffey in Coghlanstown, the remains of St James's Church and its graveyard lie inside what was a large bivallate ring-enclosure (an early monastic site ?). In the graveyard are a granite cross base and a fragment of a 17th cent. FitzEustace commemorative cross. ½ m. E. of the graveyard is a small roadside granite cross (from the graveyard ?).

BALLYMOTE, Co. Sligo (Map 2, B5), is a village on the Ballaghaderreen (16 m.)–Sligo (15 m.) road. It takes its name from an early-13th cent. Anglo-Norman motte (Rathdoony) 1¼ m. to the W.

At the N. end of the village are the remains of the "Abbey", a small Franciscan Third Order friary. At the W. end of the village are the ivy-smothered ruins (Nat. Mon.) of the remarkable castle built about 1300 by Richard de Burgo, "Red" Earl of Ulster. This was a square, keepless fortress with twin-towered gatehouse, massive drum towers at the angles, and lesser D-towers in the curtain walls. By 1338 it had fallen to the O Conors and by 1380 to the Mac Donaghs, who held it for two centuries, though in 1567 it was still claimed by O Conor Sligo. The celebrated literary codex, *The Book of Ballymote*, was compiled about 1400 by Duignans and others for Tomaltach Óg (son of Tadhg, son of Donnchadh, son of Diarmait) Mac Donagh, Lord of Corann, partly "in his house [i.e. castle] of Ballymote". In 1584 Ballymote was taken by Sir Richard Bingham, English Governor of Connacht. In 1598 the Mac Donaghs recovered the castle. That same year the great Red Hugh O Donnell made it his Connacht headquarters. It was here he

assembled his forces en route to Kinsale in 1601. In 1603 his successor, Rury O Donnell, surrendered the castle to the Crown. From 1633 to 1635 it was a Crown fortress in the custody of Sir John Taafe (*see* Carlingford, Co. Louth), who had been created Baron Ballymote and Viscount Taafe of Corran and granted Mac Donagh lands by Charles I. The Taafes held it in the Royalist interest until 1652, when they surrendered to the Cromwellians. At the outbreak of the Williamite war it was seized for James II by Counsellor Terence Mac Donagh. In 1690 the Jacobite commander was an O Conor! The castle was attacked in 1690 by a thousand Williamites under Balldearg O Donnell, grandnephew of the notorious renegade, Niall Garbh, and O Conor was forced to surrender. Shortly afterwards the fortifications were dismantled and the moat filled up.

In Carrowcauley, alias Earlsfield, ¾ m. N. of the village, is Sidheán an Gháire, "The Fairy Mound of Laughter", a conical tumulus.

The country about Ballymote is rich in ringforts, many of which have souterrains.

3 m. E., on the Hill of Doo in Doomore, is a large cairn.

1¼ m. SSE., in Tieveboy, is the early church site of Emlaghfad where Columcille is said to have founded a monastery.

4 m. SE. is Keshcorran (1,182 ft), which affords wide and splendid panoramas. On the summit is a great cairn. In the mountain are seventeen small caves in which were found the remains of animals such as reindeer, Irish elk, cave bear and arctic lemming, as well as traces of ancient human occupation. Keshcorran figures in the literary legends of Cormac mac Airt and of Díarmait and Gráinne. (One cave in the W. escarpment is Umhaigh Chormaic mhac Airt, "Cormac mac Art's Cave", for here the she-wolf reared him. ¾ m. N. of this, in Cross, is Tobar Chormaic, "Cormac's Well", where Cormac's mother delayed his birth, as witness a stone with the imprint of the infant's head.) The greatest of Co. Sligo's Lughnasa celebrations was held on Garland Sunday in front of the caves of the W. escarpment; it survives in attenuated form. – In 971 the battle of Keshcorran took place between Vikings and a Connacht army. The latter was defeated, and the dead were brought for burial to the ancient monastery of Toomour (1 m. SE. of Kesh village). In the churchyard are three early crossslabs. The founder of the monastery was Bishop Luguid. The remains of the older church here are known locally as The Altar; the name, Grave of the Kings, sometimes attached to them, is a 19th cent. invention.

4½ m. SW., in Rinnardogue, are remains of Cloonameehan, alias Bunnamaddan, "Abbey", a Dominican friary founded in 1488 by Eóghan Mac Donagh.

6 m. SW., in Kilturra, are Toberaraght (St Áthracht's Well), and a small cross-inscribed pillarstone.

4 m. NW., near Temple House, are some re-

mains of Teach an Teampla, a preceptory of the Knights Templars. When the Templars were suppressed (1312) the place became a dependency of St John's Hospital at Rinndown (*see under* Lecarrow). The castle was destroyed by Aedh O Conor of Connacht in 1271, but was later rebuilt.

BALLYNAHINCH, Co. Down (Map 3, C5), is a small town and agricultural centre on the Dromore (10 m.)–Downpatrick (11 m.) road. S. of the town is Montalto House, formerly residence of the earls of Moira.

Ballynahinch figured in the 1798 insurrection, when the heights around Montalto were held by the United Irishmen under Henry Monro against General Nugent. The insurgents were driven to Slieve Croob, 6 m. SW. (*below*), Monro himself being captured and subsequently executed at Lisburn (*q.v.*).

James Robb (d. 1723), the Scots architect of Waringstown House and Church (*see under* Lurgan) and of Killyleagh Castle (*q.v.*), died at Ballynahinch. Born in Edinburgh, he was an apprentice assistant of Inigo Jones and came to Ireland at the Restoration as Chief Mason of the King's Work.

Slieve Croob (1,755 ft), between Ballynahinch and Castlewellan, dominates the centre of Co. Down, and its slopes afford fine prospects. The river Lagan has its source on the NE. slope. The Twelve Cairns (little heaps of stone made from the spoil of a large prehistoric cairn) at the summit were until recently a place of Lughnasa celebrations (singing, dancing, etc.) on Domhnach Deireannach, alias Blaeberry Sunday, alias Lammas Sunday (first Sunday of August/last Sunday of July).

3 m. SW., in Dunbeg Upper, is Dunbeg (Nat. Mon.), a small hill-fort.

12 m. SW., via Dromara and Finnis, is Leganạnny Dolmen (*see under* Castlewellan).

3 m. NNW. is Magheraknock Fort, another small hill-fort.

BALLYNAHINCH, Co. Galway (Map 1, B5), 7 m. ESE. of Clifden and 42 m. NW. of Galway (via Oughterard; 51 m. via Casla and Screeb), takes its name from a small castle-crowned island (a crannóg?) in Ballynahinch Lake.

The district is of surpassing loveliness, with the magnificent Beanna Beóla, alias the Twelve Bens (Bencorr, 2,336 ft), the monarchs of the landscape. Ballynahinch Lake, at the foot of Benlettery's quartzite cone (1,904 ft), is the southernmost of the chain of waters (Ballynahinch Lake, Derryclare Lough, Lough Inagh) which girdle the Bens on the S., SE., and E. The circuit of the mountains is a delightful tour, but those who leave the main roads, or climb, meet with even greater rewards.

Ballynahinch Castle Hotel, a much altered 18th cent. house superbly sited over the Owenmore, was the home of the Martin family, the best-known member of which was Richard (Humanity Dick) Martin (1754–1834), M.P., friend of the Prince Regent, and one of the promoters of the R.S.P.C.A. The vast Martin estates – largely mountain and moor – made him one of the greatest landlords in the West, and it was he who built the greater part of the house, which figures in Thackeray's *An Irish Sketch Book* and Maria Edgeworth's *Letters*. The property passed from the Martins as a consequence of the Great Famine. (Charles Lever's *The Martins of Cro Martin* is based on the story of the family.) It was acquired in 1926 by the Jam Sahib of Nawanagar – Ranjit Sinjhi, the cricketer; in 1945 it was converted into an hotel.

Before falling to the Martins, the Ballynahinch estate had belonged to the O Flahertys and, before them, to the O Keelys. One of the O Flahertys founded a Carmelite friary in 1356; no trace survives. Donal O Flaherty, first husband of Gráinne Ní Mháille ("Granuaile", *see* Clare Island) built the small castle in the lake; the stones are said to have been taken from Toombeola "Abbey" (*below*).

6 m. E. are Glendollagh ("Glendalough") and its lough (Garroman), well stocked with fish. At the NE. end of the lough rises Lissoughter (1,314 ft), which offers a lovely panorama of mountain and lake. 2¼ m. NE., at Tullywee bridge, a footpath climbs NE. to Maumeen (2¾ m.; *see* Cur *under* Maum).

6 m. SE. is Cashel, which takes its name from the ancient ringfort-type burial ground on the hill above the hotel. Near the burial ground is Tobar Conaill, St Conall's Well.

3 m. S., on the W. bank of the Owenmore, are remains of Toombeola "Abbey", late-16th cent. church of a Dominican friary, dedicated to St Patrick, which was founded in 1427.

6½ m. SW. is Roundstone (*q.v.*).

BALLYPOREEN, Co. Tipperary (Map 5, C5), is a village on the Clogheen (5 m.)–Mitchelstown (8 m.) road, at the foot of the Knockmealdown–Kilworth mountains. For tours in these mountains *see* Kilworth *under* Fermoy, Lismore, *and* Clogheen. The parish church has a Michael Healy window, *St Patrick* (1918).

2½ m. N., in Coolagarranroe, are the celebrated "Mitchelstown Caves". (Their misleading modern name is due to the fact that Coolagarranroe was part of the estate of the Kingstons of Mitchelstown.) The caves comprise two groups, Uaimh na Caorach Glaise, alias Desmond's Cave, and New Cave. Desmond's Cave (rope or ladder necessary) is so called because the Sugán Earl of Desmond sought refuge there, only to be betrayed by the White Knight (*see* Kilmallock) in 1601; the E. chamber is the largest cave-chamber in the British Isles. The New Cave (guide available), discovered in 1833, comprises 1½ m. of passages and chambers with splendid stalagmite and stalacteti formations. Several of the chambers have been given the usual silly names ("House of Lords", etc.) by the 19th cent. gentry. 2 m. NE. is Burncourt (*below*).

4 m. NE., in Burncourt, formerly Clogheen, is An Cúirt Dóighte, alias Burncourt Castle (Nat. Mon.), a great embattled house built in 1641 by Sir Richard Everard of Ballyboy, Clogheen, as the *caput* of his new manor of Everard's Castle. Sir Richard was a member of the Supreme Council of the Confederation of Kilkenny, and was one of those hanged by Ireton when Limerick capitulated in 1651; his great house had been captured and burnt by Cromwell the year before. 1½ m. NW. of Burncourt village is pretty Glengarra, which affords a fine ascent of Galtymore (3,018 ft; magnificent views).

6 m. S., in the Knockmealdowns, is the beautiful Araglin valley (*see* Kilworth *under* Fermoy, *and* Lismore).

BALLYRAGGET, Co. Kilkenny (Map 6, A5), is a village at the intersection of the Abbeyleix (10 m.)–Kilkenny (11 m.) and Castlecomer (6 m.)–Freshford (5 m.) roads. It takes its name from the Anglo-Norman le Raggeds, who had lands here in the 13th cent. The tower (still roofed) and fossed bawn of a 15th/16th cent. Butler castle still survive in good condition. Tradition attributes the castle to Mairgréad Ní Ghearóid, wife of Sir Piers Rua Butler, Earl of Ossory and Ormond. In the late 16th cent. the castle was the chief seat of the Butlers, Viscounts Mountgarret. Richard, 3rd Viscount, was President of the Supreme Council of the Confederation of Kilkenny. A branch of the Mountgarret Butlers resided in the castle until 1788, when it passed to the Kavanaghs of Borris. James Butler (1742–91), Archbishop of Cashel and author of the well-known *Butler's Catechism*, was a son of James Butler (d. 1746/7) of Ballyragget. In 1798 the castle served as a British military post.

½ m. S. of the village are the ruins of the ancient parish church of St Patrick, Donoughmore.

1 m. N., overlooking the Nore, in Moat (Moat Park), is Tullabarry motte-and-bailey.

2 m. N., in Gorteenara, are the ruins of Kilminan (Cill Mo-Fhínáin) church; 200 yds SE. are Tubber Finawn holy well and a small fossed enclosure.

7 m. N. is Rosconnell (*see under* Ballinakill, Co. Laois).

2½ m. E., in Toormore, is Corrandhu Hill, where Eóghan O More of Laois seized "Black" Thomas Butler, Earl of Ormond and Lieut.-Gen. of Elizabeth I's forces, 10 April 1600. At the summit of the hill (836 ft) is an oval, bivallate enclosure (defaced) in which prehistoric burials have been found.

3½ m. SSE. is Foulksrath castle, now a youth hostel. The de la Frenes were succeeded here by the Purcells in the 15th cent. In Shanganny, next townland to the E., are remains of Coolcraheen church (St Nicholas's) and fragments of a 1629 Purcell tomb which include a *Virgin and*

Child panel. 1 m. S. of Foulksrath is Swifte's Heath, a 17th–18th cent. house acquired by Dean Swift's cousin, Godwin, *c.* 1720.

1½ m. SSW., to the N. of the old church site of Grangemacomb, is a fine ringfort.

3 m. SSW. the ruined Protestant church of Rathbeagh incorporates fragments of medieval St Catherine's Church. On the brink of the Nore is Rathbeagh, an oval "henge" or earthwork with rampart outside the fosse. This is thought to be the Ráith Bhethaigh named as the burial place of legendary Éremón, son of Míl.

1¾ m. WNW., in Ballyconra, are the ruins of Barney (properly Barony) Church. It has a plain, Romanesque chancel arch and N. window; the chancel (handsome Gothic piscina) was converted into a mausoleum by the Mountgarret Butlers, who lived at Ballyconra House about 1721–1840. The original Ballyconra House was the home of the Clarke family, to which belonged James Henry Clarke (1765–1818), Duc de Feltre, Minister of War to Napoleon and, later, Marshal of France.

BALLYSADARE, Co. Sligo (Map 2, B5), is a village prettily situated at the head of Ballysadare Bay, on the Collooney (2 m.)–Sligo (5 m.) road. It takes its name from the falls and rapids (Eas Dara) on the Owenmore.

700 yds N. of the bridge, on the W. bank of the river, close to the last waterfall, are the remains of a monastery founded in the 7th cent. by St Féichín of Fore (*q.v.*; *see also* Árd Oileán *and* Cong). There are ruins of three small buildings including Teampall Mór Féichín, a pre-Romanesque church with a Romanesque doorway in the S. wall. In the 12th/13th cent. the community adopted the Rule of the Canons Regular of St Augustine, and built a new priory some 300 yds to the W., where part of a 13th cent. church ("The Abbey") survives. The last abbot, Conchubhar Ó Siaghail (O Shiel; member of a family of hereditary physicians, some of whose members were also exponents of Gaelic literature and learning), was made first post-Reformation bishop of Elphin by Henry VIII at the request of O Donnell.

2¼ m. N. are the remains of the parish church of Kilmacowen; nearby are Tobar Phádraic holy well and a stone with the "imprint of the Saint's knee".

BALLYSHANNON, formerly Belashanny, Co. Donegal (Map 2, B4), is a seaport and market town at the head of the Erne estuary, on the Sligo (27 m.)–Donegal (14 m.) road. The falls at the river-mouth were called Assaroe (Eas Ruaidh) after the god Áed Rúad, whose seat was nearby Síd Áeda, now Mullaghnashee (*below*). The river-crossing has always been of strategic importance, and has figured prominently in history. (It was here, e.g., that the celebrated Red Hugh O Donnell threw back an English force led by Sir Conyers Clifford in 1597.) In the Middle Ages the O Donnells made themselves masters of the crossing, and held it until the final collapse of the Gaelic North. The area was thereafter "planted", and Ballyshannon received a charter of incorporation in 1611.

The Erne has long been known for its salmon fishing, and the new hydro-electric scheme (dams and power houses between Ballyshannon and Belleek, *q.v.*) makes provision for the passage of salmon to their spawning grounds.

William Allingham (1824–89) was a native of Ballyshannon (birthplace in Mall marked by tablet). His best known poem is probably "Adieu to Belashanny and the winding banks of Erne". He is buried in St Anne's churchyard on Mullaghnashee (NW. of the town), which, says tradition, was the place of residence of Conall Gulban, son of Niall Nine Hostager and great-grandfather of St Columcille. Conall was King of Tara as well as of Cenél Conaill, and it was from him that Cenél Conaill and Tír Chonaill took their names.

Of the medieval O Donnell castle only a fragment (N. of market-place) survives.

¾ m. S., via the Garrison road, in Sminver, a small graveyard and fragments of a church mark the site of a monastery founded by the O Clerys in 1178. There is an O Clery tomb here.

¾ m. NW., in Abbey Island by the estuary, are remains of the Cistercian abbey of Assaroe founded by Flahertach O Muldory, King of Tír Chonaill, and colonized from Boyle (*q.v.*) in 1178. In 1398 it was sacked by Niall Óg O Neill. The English occupied the abbey on the occasion of their 1597 attack on Ballyshannon. Miscellaneous fragments of 12th cent. and later dates are to be seen in the graveyard, graveyard wall, and adjacent farm buildings. Nearby to the SW. is a cave where Mass was said in Penal times.

3½ m. NW., close to the W. side of the Rossnowlagh road in Kilbarron, are the ruins of a small, medieval church, successor of St Barron's 6th cent. foundation. A bohereen S. of the church leads SW. to the remains (in Cloghbolie) of Kilbarron Castle, which was the seat in turn of the O Sgingins and their O Clery successors. The O Sgingins were hereditary historiographers of Tír Chonaill. Their office and its endowments passed by marriage to the O Clerys. Michael O Clery, chief of the Four Masters, was born in the castle about 1580. ¾ m. SE. of the castle, in Kilbarron, is Giants Grave, a prehistoric chamber tomb.

5 m. N. is Rossnowlagh with very fine Belalt Strand (2 m.). In Coolbeg, ½ m. SSW. of the strand,is Giants Grave, a prehistoric chamber tomb. A small collection of local antiquities, bygones, etc., is housed in Rossnowlagh Franciscan friary.

4 m. NE., to the W. of Ardpattan Lough, in Twomilestone and Ardpattan townlands are the Two-mile Stone (a prehistoric pillarstone) and two stone ringforts; also hut-sites and ancient field walls connected with them.

BALLYVAGHAN, Co. Clare (Map 1, D6), is a village and small fishing port on the S. shore of Galway Bay, 31 m. S. of Galway and 10 m. N. of Lisdoonvarna. It is a convenient centre for exploring the fascinating Burren country, whose karsts are so well known to geologist, botanist, and antiquarian. The circuit Ballyvaghan–Blackhead–Ballynalacken–Lisdoonvarna–Corkscrew Hill–Ballyvaghan (28 m.) offers a rewarding variety of coast and mountain scenery.

1½ m. NE., in Bishopsquarter, are the ruins of Drumcreehy Church, a nave-and-chancel structure with a Transitional E. window and Perpendicular N. door.

7 m. NE. is New Quay (*see under* Corcomroe Abbey).

7 m. E. is Corcomroe Abbey (*q.v.*).

2½ m. SSW., on the W. side of the Corrofin road in Ballyallaban, is Cahermore, a stone ringfort with remains of houses, medieval gateway (cf. Cahermacnaghten, *below*), etc. 1½ m. SE., on the SW. slope of Ballyallaban Hill, in Berneens, is Dermot and Grania's Bed, a wedge-shaped gallery grave. Three other gallery graves are visible ½ m. S., in Gleninsheen; one of these, Cromlech, is well preserved. 2 m. S. of the Gleninsheen tombs, to the E. of the road in Poulnabrone, is Cromlech, a fine portal dolmen. ¾ m. S. of this, in Caherconnell, is the stone ringfort from which the townland takes its name. 1¼ m. NE. of Caherconnell crossroads the side road enters Cragballyconoal; 150 yds N. of the road is Cromlech, a ruined gallery grave in a long mound; 500 yds NNE. is another cairn with a wedge-shaped gallery grave (also Cromlech). – 1 m. SSW. of Caherconnell crossroads, in Poulawack, is a cemetery cairn (Nat. Mon.) excavated by Harvard archaeologists in 1934: Food Vessel, Urn, and other burials (including Beaker?). 4 m. SW. of the cairn is Noughaval (*see under* Kilfenora). – 1¼ m. SSE. of the cairn, in Poulacarran, are the ruins of St Cronan's Church, a parish church of *c.* 1500 marking an early monastic site; St Cronan's Well cures sore eyes (*see* Termon *under* Carran). 1 m. (cross-country) ESE. of the church, in Fanygalvan, is a long mound (Cromlechs) with remains of a wedge-shaped gallery grave and two other tombs. NE. of this mound are two small cairns; N. of the first, in Cahermackirilla, is a third. – 1¾ m. SSE. of St Cronan's Church, in Deerpark, is Cromlech, a wedge-shaped gallery grave. 2½ m. SW. is Leamaneh (*see under* Kilfenora).

1½ m. SW., in Newtown, is an unusual castle tower: circular, rising from a pyramidal base. 1½ m. SW. are the ruins of Rathborney parish church. About 1½ m. W. of the church, in Faunarooska, are two wedge-shaped gallery graves (ruinous). About ½ m. (cross-country) NW. in Derrynavahagh, is one of the best gallery graves in Burren.

3½ m. SW., at the foot of Corkscrew Hill, are the ruins of Craggan castle (O Loughlin).

4 m. SW. the road to Lisdoonvarna climbs

Corkscrew Hill, which affords delightful views
N. to Galway Bay. 2 m. S. of the Corkscrew
is Cahermacnaghten (Nat. Mon.), a stone ringfort castellated in the later Middle Ages. As
late as the 17th cent. the O Davorens had a
school of Irish jurisprudence here, at which An
Dubhaltach Óg Mac Fhirbhisigh (see Lacken
under Inishcrone) received part of his training.
2 m. SSE. is Ballymurphy castle.

BALLYWALTER, Co. Down (Map 3, D5),
is a village on the E. coast of the Ards peninsula
11 m. SE. of Bangor.
¾ m. NNW. are the fragmentary ruins of
Templefinn, alias White Church, a medieval
parish church. At the east gable are three
Anglo-Norman grave slabs.
3 m. S., in Ballyhalbert, alias Talbotstown,
is a conspicuous motte. John de Courcy
founded a Benedictine abbey at Ballyhalbert in
1180, but no trace of it remains.
3 m. SW., in Inishargy churchyard is an
Anglo-Norman gravestone.
1½ m. NW., in the grounds of Dunover
House, is an imposing motte.

BALTIMORE, Co. Cork (Map 4, D6), 7 m.
SW. of Skibbereen, is a small fishing port with
a reputation for the building of fine boats and
yachts. It is a good sea-angling centre and the
port for Sherkin Island (below) and Clear
Island (q.v.).
In 1537 the place was sacked by the men of
Waterford, in revenge for the seizure of a
Waterford ship. In 1631 it was raided by
Algerine pirates, who carried off some 200 of
the inhabitants. The event is commemorated in
Thomas Davis's ballad, The Sack of Baltimore.
Overlooking the harbour are the remains of the
O Driscoll castle of Dunashad.
Offshore to the N. is Ringahogy Island, from
which fine views may be had.
To the SW. is Sherkin Island, with many
quiet coves. At the E. end of the island are the
ruins (Nat. Mon.) of Farranacouth "Abbey",
a small friary founded 1460/70 by either
Finghín or Dermot O Driscoll for Franciscans
of the Strict Observance. It also was sacked by
the Waterford men in 1537. This was a typical
Irish friary, with claustral buildings on the N.
and church on the S. The sacristy and bell-
tower are 16th cent. additions, as are also,
perhaps, the E. chapels of the S. transept. ¼ m.
N. are the scant ruins of the O Driscoll castle
of Dún na Long.
2½ m. ENE., in Ballymacrown, is Kill Burial
Ground; there is a rude, ring-headed cross here.

BALTINGLASS, Co. Wicklow (Map 6, C4),
is a small market town on the W. side of the
Wicklow massif, where the River Slaney and
the Dublin (37 m.)–Tullow (11 m.) road make
their way between Tinoran Hill (1,023 ft) and
Baltinglass Hill (1,256 ft).
While the place figures in early legend and
tradition by reason of its ancient highway

(Bealach Conglais – Baltinglass), its history
really commences with Dermot Mac Murrough's foundation (about 1148) of the Cistercian abbey of Vallis Salutis, whose ruins
(Nat. Mon.) lie some 400 yds N. of Main St.
At the Dissolution, Thomas Fitz Eustace, Lord
of Kilcullen (q.v.; see also Ballymore Eustace),
was granted the abbey and its lands and was
created Viscount Baltinglass. When the Fitz
Eustace estates here were forfeited (1586), by
the rebellion of the 3rd Viscount Baltinglass,
they were granted to the Stratfords. John
Stratford (Earl of Aldborough, 1777), who
represented the borough in the Dublin Parliament, enlarged and improved the town.
Baltinglass Abbey was a daughter foundation of Mellifont Abbey (q.v.), and itself sent
out colonies to Maune (see Abbeymahon under
Courtmacsherry), Jerpoint (see under Thomastown, Co. Kilkenny), Abbeyleix (q.v.), and
Monasterevan (q.v.). The remains comprise
fragments of the church and traces of the
cloister. The former was a typical Cistercian
church, with E. chapels (two, projecting separately) in each transept and an aisled nave. The
alternately square and cylindrical nave piers
stand in a screen-wall which shuts off the aisles.
The ornamental details of bases and capitals,
like those of the fragments of the N. door, the
W. window, and the processional door to the
cloisters, are of modified Irish Romanesque
type. The narrow tower at the crossing was a
later medieval insertion. In more recent times
the presbytery (chancel), crossing, and E. end
of the nave were walled off to serve as the
Protestant parish church. To the S. of the abbey
are some remains of a Fitz Eustace castle.
¾ m. SE., close to the N. side of the Red
Wells road, is Lathaleere Cromlech, a ruined
gallery grave in a mound. 1 m. E., on a ridge
in Deerpark, beside Deerpark House, is a
tumulus.
4 m. NNE., to the W. of the Little Slaney, is
the decayed village of Stratford-on-Slaney, laid
out (c.1783) and built for Edward Stratford,
2nd Earl of Aldborough, who provided houses
and bleach greens for a cotton manufactory,
built a church and a chapel, and encouraged
settlers. From 1785/6 to about 1850 cotton and
linen printing were carried on in the mills to
the SE. of the village. In their heyday these
employed up to a thousand workers. – 400 yds
SE., at the junction of the Dublin and Kiltegan
roads, is Ballintruermore pillarstone.
5¾ m. NE., in Castleruddery Lower, are the
Druidical Circle and a motte (Nat. Mons.).
The circle is enclosed by an earthen bank, and
the entrance is flanked by two white quartz
portal stones (see Tornant Upper and Brewel
Hill under Dunlavin). ½ m. SE. the motte
guards a river-crossing now spanned by Bally-
hubbock bridge (1798). The road ESE. from
Castleruddery crossroads leads to the Glen of
Imaal (see under Donard).
1¼ m. ENE., on Baltinglass Hill (1,256 ft), is
Rathcoran, a great hill-fort whose twin banks

and fosse follow the 1,181–1,187-ft contour. Near the summit of the hill, commanding a broad prospect, are remains of a chambered cairn which covered two passage graves and three other tombs; six stones bear spiral and other signs. Less than 600 yds NW. of Rathcoran is Rathnagree, a bivallate ringfort 600 ft overall. In the same townland (Tuckmill Upper) is a pillarstone.

6 m. ENE. (via Tuckmill and Kill crossroads), on the summit of Brusselstown Hill (1,328 ft), is Brusselstown Ring, a contour hill-fort commanding a very fine view. On the SE. slope of the hill, to the S. of the road, are remains of Castlequarter church and castle. 2½ m. SW. of the Ring is Kilranelagh (below).

4 m. E., in Boleylug, on the SE. slope of Baltinglass Hill, is Moatamoy, a large motte.

4¾ m. ESE. (via Red Wells crossroads), in Talbotstown Lower, is Tobernacristhamaun; ¾ m. NE., in Talbotstown Upper are remains of Talbotstown Fort, a quadrangular, moated house-site which perhaps marks the *caput* of the medieval barony of Talbotstown. – 1¾ m. N., in Colvinstown Upper, are St. Brigid's Well and remains of Kilranelagh church. The latter marks one of the oldest Christian sites in SW. Wicklow. In the churchyard are the Gates of Glory, two orthostats with intervening sill. Coffins for burial were formerly carried between the uprights. ½ m. N., in Cloghnagaune, is St Brigid's Headstone, a perforate pillarstone formerly the resort of votaries; ENE. is St Brigid's Chair; beyond that, in Moorstown, St Brigid's Well – 1½ m. E. of Kilranelagh, in Boleycarrigeen, is Crossoona Rath (Nat. Mon.); in the rampart is an ogham stone. Nearby are the Griddle Stones, a circle of eleven complete stones with the stump of a twelfth. 80 yds E. is a ruined tumulus with remains of a large cist. – 1½ m. SE. of Tobernacristhamaun, in front of Humewood Castle, Barraderry East, is a stone with grooves and cup-and-circle markings. Humewood Castle (property of Mme Weygand – née Hume – daughter-in-law of Marshal Weygand) is an 1845, Scottish Baronial-cum-Norman house; ornamental lakes in grounds. It was at Humewood that Michael Dwyer, the 1798 hero, surrendered to Col. Hume in 1804.

5 m. NNW. is Grange Con House demesne; noted for its herd of white fallow deer.

BANAGHER, Co. Offaly (Map 5, D2), is a village on the E. bank of the Shannon, 7 m. NW. of Birr and 17 m. SE. of Ballinasloe.

Anthony Trollope (1815–82) was stationed here as Post Office surveyor in 1841, and it was here he wrote his first two novels, both with Irish settings, viz. *The Kellys and the O'Kellys* (1848) and *The Mac Dermot of Ballycloran* (1843–7). The Rev. A. B. Nicholls, Rector of Birr, who married Charlotte Brontë in 1854, died here in 1906. Sir William Wilde (1815–76), father of Oscar Wilde and husband of "Speranza", was a pupil at the Royal School (now closed).

The ruined church and its shamefully-kept graveyard mark the site of an early monastery. The shaft of a High Cross from the monastery is now in the National Museum. On the banks of the Shannon are a fine early-19th cent. fortified bridgehead, batteries, etc., commanding the crossing from Connacht.

1½ m. SE., to the W. of the Birr road, are the remains of the large Mac Coghlan stronghold of Garry Castle. 1¾ m. SSE., to the W. of the Cloghan–Borrisokane road, in Garrycastle, is the site of an ancient convent with Saints' Well (Tobar na Naomh), Eye Well (Tobar na Súl), Head Well, etc.; formerly a Lughnasa station.

BANBRIDGE, Co. Down (Map 3, C5), is a market and linen town beside the River Bann, on the main Newry (14 m.)–Belfast (24 m.) road. It came into existence following the building of a stone bridge across the river in 1712 and is built along a curious main street sunk into a cutting.

Opposite the Protestant church is a statue of Captain Francis Crozier (1796–1848), a native of the town, who was second-in-command to Sir John Franklin on his last voyage in search of the North-West Passage.

¾ m. S. is Lisnatierny (alias Tierny Fort), a strong, multivallate ringfort.

3 m. W. are Lisnagade and Lisnavarragh forts (*see under* Scarva).

BANDON, Co. Cork (Map 5, B7), properly Bandonbridge, a small market town and a well-known angling resort on the Cork (19 m.)–Bantry (38 m.) road, is the junction of roads from Kinsale (12 m.), Timoleague (8 m.), Clonakilty (13 m.), Ballineen (10 m.), and Crookstown (10 m.). It is the chief centre for fishing the Bandon and the Brinny.

The town was founded by Richard Boyle, "Great" Earl of Cork (*see* Youghal *and* Lismore), who acquired vast Munster estates – often by dubious means – in 1608, after the expropriation of the Mac Carthys, O Mahonys, O Driscolls, Desmond Geraldines, and other ancient stocks. He planted his ill-gotten lands with English Protestants and proceeded to exploit the mineral and timber resources on a large scale.

Some fragments remain of the town wall (dismantled in 1688). One of its gates is alleged to have borne the Christian inscription:

"Turk, Jew, or Atheist
 May enter here;
 But not a Papist."

To which a local wit added:

"Who wrote it, wrote it well;
 For the same is written on the Gates of Hell."

At the Court House may be seen the 18th cent. town stocks.

The Protestant parish church, at Kilbrogan to the N. of the town, dates from 1610.

4¼ m. N., in Castlenalact, is a prehistoric stone alignment; in the next field to the N. is a

chamber tomb. 3¾ m. E. is Cashel Fort (*below*).
– 2½ m. NW. is Lisnacaheragh (*see under* Crookstown).

5 m. NE., in Clashanimud, is Cashel Fort, a bivallate hill-fort (Nat. Mon.).

5 m. E., at the picturesque junction of the Bandon and the Brinny, are the remains of Downdaniel castle, a 15th cent. stronghold of Barry Óg. It was purchased in 1612 by the East India Company, which founded a settlement here for smelting iron ore.

1 m. W., in the former demesne of Castle Bernard, are ruins of an O Mahony castle.

6½ m. W. is the early monastic site, Kilcolman, a subdivided, circular enclosure. In the larger division are remains of a church; in the smaller is a cemetery.

4 m. WNW., in Derrycool, is Cromlech, a chamber tomb.

BANGOR, Co. Down (Map 3, D4), is a prosperous industrial town and seaside resort on the S. shore of Belfast Lough, 13 m. E. of Belfast.

A convenient base for exploring the Ards (*see under* Newtownards), it has two beaches (Bangor Bay and Ballyholme Bay), beautiful gardens (Castle Park, 125 acres), golf (four courses in the immediate vicinity), bathing, boating, yachting (Royal Ulster Yacht Club), sea fishing, and all the other amenities of a major holiday resort. The lovely, well-timbered countryside towards Holywood (*q.v.*) and Clandeboy (*below*) offers a variety of pleasant walks. Near the E. end of Ballyholme Bay is the entrance to a National Trust coastal strip with a fine walk round Ballymacormac Point to Groomsport (1½ m.), where Schomberg, the Williamite general, landed in 1689.

Bangor has a long and illustrious history. It was here that St Comgall (alias Mo-Choma) moccu Áraide, the master of St Columbanus of Luxeuil and Bobbio and the close friend and collaborator of St Columcille, founded (about 555/9) the abbey which, until the Vikings came, was one of the glories of Ireland, "a place truly sacred, the nursery of saints" (St Bernard of Clairvaux).

Comgall is said to have studied under Fintán of Clonenagh (*see under* Mountrath), Finian of Clonard (*see under* Kinnegad), and Mo-Bhí of Glasnevin (*see under* Dublin, NE.). Though Bangor was in Ulster, Comgall was always regarded as patron of Dál Áraide (roughly the diocese of Connor), and when the Vikings raided Bangor in 842 it was to Antrim (*q.v.*) and the protection of the king of Dál Áraide that Comgall's relics were taken.

Many of the great saints and scholars of the 6th cent. were trained at Bangor. Particular attention appears to have been paid to historical studies in the monastery school which, seemingly, was situated on Cranny Island in Strangford Lough. The earliest Irish chronicle has been plausibly attributed to Abbot Sinlán, alias Mo-Shinu moccu Mín (d. 610), who is said

to have learned the whole Computus by heart from a Greek. A pupil in the school, Mo-Chuaróc moccu Neth-Semon, committed it to writing from Sinlán's dictation. *The voyage of Bran*, one of the oldest, most famous, and most beautiful of Irish poems, was probably shaped in the monastery.

Repeated Viking attacks led to the decay of the abbey. In 1124 the great reformer, St Máel M'Áedhóg Úa Morgair (*see* Armagh), succeeded to the abbacy and set about reviving the monastery. His introduction of Continental architecture aroused local ire ("We are Irish, not Gauls. What is this frivolity?"). About 1127 the place was ravaged by the King of the Northern Uí Néill, and abbot and monks fled to Munster (*see* Lough Currane *under* Waterville). In 1137 Máel M'Áedhóg resigned the primacy, to which he had been called in 1129 (*see* Armagh), and, setting up a new diocese for the little kingdom of Ulster, fixed his see at the abbey of Bangor, to which he introduced Arroasian Canons Regular of St Augustine. He died at Bangor in 1148. Twenty-nine years later John de Courcy, Anglo-Norman "Prince of Ulster", transferred the see to Downpatrick (*q.v.*). By 1469 the Arroasian monastery at Bangor was so decayed that Pope Paul II caused a Franciscan to be installed as abbot. Less than a century later (1542) the monastery was dissolved by Henry VIII. Its possessions were ultimately granted to Sir James Hamilton, 1st Viscount Clandeboye, by James I.

Nothing remains of the buildings of the early monastery, and the only relics are a handsome bronze bell and a cross stele now in the Town Hall museum, a cross-shaft in Clandeboye chapel (below), and the *Antiphonary of Bangor*, a small service-book now in the Ambrosian Library, Milan, whither it was brought from Bobbio.

Bangor Abbey Church, W. of Castle Park, incorporates the tower (mantled in ugly pebble-dashing and disguised by 17th/18th cent. spire and balustrade) which stood between nave-and-chancel of the Arroasian church. In the church are medieval fragments; also 17th–18th cent. memorials, including a Hamilton–Mordaunt memorial by the Dutch sculptor, Peter Scheemakers (1691–1769).

The Town Hall museum, Castle Park, has a small collection of local antiquities, bygones, etc.

The Belfast Bank, Bingham Lane, is an attractive 18th/19th cent. building.

Near the harbour is Bangor Castle (Nat. Mon.), a small 1637 Scottish-style tower built by Lord Clandeboye as a customs house.

3 m. SW. is Clandeboye (entrance via Clonlig village and Clandeboye golf course), the fine house and demesne of the Marquess of Dufferin and Ava, descendant of Sir James Hamilton, 1st Viscount Clandeboye. The public is admitted to Sunday service (12 noon) in the chapel; on weekdays the chapel may be seen only by appointment with the Agent. In the grounds is

a prehistoric chamber tomb. Helen's Tower (admission by permit from the Agent) was built by the 1st Marquess (d. 1902) to house a famous library, now dispersed; it is named after his mother, Helen, Lady Dufferin, the poetess.

BANTRY, Co. Cork (Map 4, D5), is a market town near the head of magnificent Bantry Bay, 20 m. W. of Dunmanway, 10 m. SSE. of Glengarriff, and 31 m. SW. of Macroom. It is the principal centre for fishing the Mealagh, Durrus (Four Mile Water), and Ballylickey rivers, etc. It is also a convenient centre for touring some of the finest regions of the SW. The hills to the E. and SE. offer magnificent panoramas. Recommended tours: (a) The Seefin peninsula, to the SW. between Bantry Bay and Dunmanus Bay, via Glenalin crossroads–Kilcrohane–Ahakista–Durrus–Bantry (35 m.); (b) Bantry–Durrus–Dunmanus–Three Castles Head–Toormore–Skull–Ballydehob–Bantry (50 m.); (c) the Beare peninsula (see under Kenmare); (d) Bantry–Ballylickey–Pass of Keamaneigh–Ballingeary–Inchigeela – Macroom – Killarney – Kenmare – Glengarriff–Bantry (108 m.).

Bantry Bay, formerly a station of the British Atlantic fleet, was twice entered by French fleets: in 1689 to aid James II, and in December 1796, to aid a Republican insurrection. The great 1796 fleet was dispersed by storm and only sixteen vessels made the bay (Wolfe Tone was on board the *Indomptable*). These, after sustaining more than a week of storms, returned to France without putting their troops ashore.

T. M. Healy (1885–1931), leader of the Irish Party at Westminster and first Governor-General of the Irish Free State, was a native of Bantry. The Tim Healy Pass (see under Adrigole) was so named in his memory.

On the façade of the Catholic parish church are two statues by Séamus Murphy, contemporary Cork sculptor.

Immediately SW. of the town, in a beautifully sited demesne, is Bantry House, home of the White family. The good Georgian house (stone and brick) was built for Richard White, 1st Earl of Bantry. Its treasures included until recently great ceiling canvases (never put in position) by Guardia. From Easter to mid-Oct. the house is open to the public, Mon. and Thur., 10 a.m.–1 p.m.; Tue., Fri., Sat., 3 p.m.–6 p.m.; and the gardens are open Mon. to Sat. inclusive, 10 a.m.–6 p.m.; admission to house and gardens, 2/6; to gardens only, 1/-.

2 m. N., to the SW. of Ballylickey bridge, are the ruins of Reenadisert Court. 3¼ m. NE. of the bridge is Kealkil crossroads: ¼ m. N., at the crossing of the Owvane, are the ruins of Carriganass castle, a 15th/16th cent. stronghold of O Sullivan of Bear (see Dunboy under Castletown Bearhaven). In Kealkil townland are two pillarstones and a small recumbentstone circle of W. Cork type, beside which is a small ring cairn covering a circle of radial standing-stones; excavation yielded no dating evidence. In Breenymore, next townland to the S., is a circle (Nat. Mon.) of fourteen stones (several prostrate).

Bantry House and Bay

Irish Tourist Board

7 m. NE., in Coomleagh East, are the two survivors of an alignment of pillarstones; one is prostrate, the other has a defaced ogham inscription.

9 m. ENE. is Castle Donovan (*see under* Drimoleague).

8½ m. SSW., in Dunbeacon, ¼ m. W. of the by-road crossing the shoulder of Mount Corin, is an eleven-stone circle. In a field on the E. side of the road, in Coolcoulaghta, is a very fine pair of pillarstones (Galláin); there was a third stone S. of them.

1 m. SW., to the S. of the road in Kilnaruane, is an early cross-pillar (Nat. Mon.) with figured and other panels.

9 m. SW. (via Carrigboy and Durrus) is Dromnea Well: 400 yds ESE. are pillarstones; 440 yds SSW. is the site of O Daly's Bardic School. 4½ m. SW., in Caherurlagh, is Ballyroon holed stone (Nat. Mon.).

1¾ m. W. is Whiddy Island. There are three 19th cent. redoubts here, relics of the British naval station. At the S. end of the island are the remains of Kilmore church. At the N. end are the ruins of Reenabanny castle (O Sullivan Mór).

BARRINGTONSBRIDGE, Co. Limerick (Map 5, B4), is a village 7 m. E. of Limerick.

¾ m. E. are the ruins (Nat. Mon.) of the small Romanesque church of Clonkeen, sole relic of a monastery founded in the 6th/7th cent. by St Mo-Díomóg. 2½ m. SE., in Abington, alias Abbey Owney, alias Woney (Uaithne), is the site of Mainistear Uaithne, a Cistercian abbey founded by Theobald fitz Walter, ancestor of the Butlers, and colonized from Furness, Lancs., about 1206. The buildings were destroyed in 1647 by Parliamentarians led by the notorious Murrough "the Burner" O Brien. More recent vandals have destroyed the remains of the Renaissance monument (by Patrick Kerin, 1618) of Sir Edward Walsh, son of Peter Breathnach of Grange (*see* Fiddown *under* Piltown).

4½ m. NE., in Cappanahannagh, is Tuaim an Fhir Mhóir, a prehistoric chamber tomb (roofless).

4½ m. ENE. are St Columba's Abbey and school (Benedictine), Glenstal. The nucleus of the abbey is the great Norman-style "castle" (incomplete) designed by William Bardwell for Sir Matthew Barrington (1788–1861): ward, square "keep", circular "donjon", etc.; many eclectic features, including a copy of the Romanesque doorway in Killaloe cathedral; the figures flanking the principal door represent Edward the Confessor and Queen Eleanor. The disappointing new abbey church has four three-light windows by Patrick Pye: *St Patrick on Croagh Patrick* (1960); *The calling of St Peter, SS Peter and Paul, St Paul meets the Romans* (1961); *Marriage feast of Cana, The Women of Apocalypse XII, The Heavenly Jerusalem* (1964); *The Banquet on Mount Sion, The Cloud descends on the Tent of the Ark, The Holy City* (1964);

also a three-light window by Patrick Pollen, *SS Malachy of Armagh, Bernard, Columcille* (1960).

BECTIVE, Co. Meath (Map 6, C2), is a hamlet on the E. side of the Boyne, 6 m. S. of Navan and 7 m. NE. of Trim.

¼ m. WNW., on the W. bank of the river, are the ruins of Bective Abbey (Nat. Mon.). The first daughter house of Mellifont (*q.v.*), it was founded in 1146 by Murchadh O Melaghlin, King of Midhe, and was dedicated to the Blessed Virgin Mary. In the late 12th or early 13th cent. the abbey was entirely rebuilt. In 1195 Hugh de Lacy's headless trunk was reinterred at the abbey, his head going to St Thomas's Abbey, Dublin. A dispute arose between the two monasteries, nominally for possession of the complete remains, essentially for certain lands which went with them. In 1205 the Pope had to appoint a conclave of prelates and "other discreet and venerable persons" to decide the issue. In its day Bective Abbey was very powerful, and the abbot was *ex officio* one of the fifteen spiritual lords of parliament. By the 15th cent., however, a decline had set in, and the buildings had to be remodelled on a significantly reduced scale. After the Dissolution they were turned into a fortified mansion. Of the original O Melaghlin abbey nothing at all survives. Of the 12th/13th cent. buildings there remain the chapter-house with central column (the kitchen of the post-Dissolution house), part of the W. range, and fragments of the aisled cruciform church. In the 15th cent. the church was shortened on the W., the aisles removed, new S. and W. ranges erected inside the lines of the old cloister, and a smaller cloister built. The S. and W. alleys of this latest cloister survive; the arcades have good and interesting details (*see also* Johnstown church *under* Navan). The remains of the post-Dissolution fortified mansion have their own interest (the great hall was an adaptation of the monks' refectory; the tower was raised over part of the S. cloister range). Mary Lavin, author of *Tales from Bective Bridge*, etc., lives nearby. ¾ m. N., on the W. side of the Boyne near the little Clady River, are the scant ruins of Clady church, a small 13th cent. nave-and-chancel edifice with a later S. transept.

¾ m. N. is Balsoon. James Ussher (1581–1656), Protestant archbishop of Dublin and distinguished scholar, resided here for a time. There are remains of a medieval church in an ancient graveyard.

1¼ m. NNE., on the E. side of the Boyne, are the ruins of Asigh, alias Assey (Áth Sighe) castle, a square tower with circular flankers at the E. and W. angles. On the slope between it and the river are the remains of a small pre-Romanesque church. 1¼ m. ENE. is Ballinter House (*see under* Navan).

3½ m. N. is Ardsallagh (*see under* Navan).

1¼ m. SW., on a commanding height to the E. of the Boyne, is a remnant of the Cusack castle of Trubley, or Tubberville. It was of the same type as Assey castle.

BELCOO, Co. Fermanagh (Map 2, C4), is a Border village on the Enniskillen (14 m.)–Manorhamilton (14 m.) road. It is situated on the isthmus between Upper and Lower Loughs Macnean, in beautiful country (*see* Blacklion).

¼ m. N. of the railway station is Drumcoo pillarstone, known locally as Crom Cruaich. On one face are rudimentary representations of a girdle and two legs (*see* Killinagh *under* Blacklion). Not far away is Belcoo cairn, a grass-covered mound.

2½ m. NE. (alt. 850 ft), is Carrickmacflaherty Giants Grave (Nat. Mon.), a much ruined court cairn.

6 m. NE. is Boho (*see under* Enniskillen).

1¼ m. E. are Templenaffrin church ruins (Nat. Mon.) and bullaun.

1¼ m. SE. is Inishee, an islet in Lower Lough Macnean with a great artificial mound (Battle). Melaghlin Magrannel of Muintear Eólais, Co. Leitrim, was imprisoned here in 1429 by the O Rourkes, taken from them by Rory Maguire, and ultimately released by O Donnell.

4 m. SE. are Killesher and the Marble Arch (*see under* Enniskillen).

1 m. NW. is Holywell village. Here are (*a*) Templerushin, alias Holywell Church (Nat. Mon.); (*b*) penitential stations (three bullauns) still visited between Garland Sunday (the last Sunday of July) and 15 Aug.; and (*c*) St Patrick's holy well (Dabhach Pádraig), described in Camden's *Britannia* as the best cold bath in Ireland and as being resorted to for the cure of paralytic and nervous complaints. A small stone cross in the graveyard is reputed to have been the head of a cross which stood in the village. – 1½ m. WNW. is Kilrooskagh Dolmen (Nat. Mon.), a prehistoric chamber tomb with a large, earthfast capstone. – 1¾ m. NW., in Toppan, are Clogherstuckane pillarstones and stone circle.

BELFAST (Map 3, C4), is 101 m. NNE. of Dublin and 74 m. ESE. of Derry. Capital of Northern Ireland since the partitioning of Ulster in 1921, it is Ireland's greatest seaport and commercial and manufacturing centre (linen, ship-building, engineering, cordage, tobacco, rayon textiles, etc.). It is the seat of the General Assembly of the Presbyterian Church in Ireland, and the cathedral city of the Catholic diocese of Down and Connor. The Church of Ireland dioceses of Connor and of Down-and-Dromore share an extra, non-diocesan, cathedral in the city, which is also the seat of a flourishing university.

While a typical 19th cent. industrial city, Belfast is unusually fortunate in its setting – where the Lagan flows to beautiful Belfast Lough, between the low Castlereagh hills (600 ft) and the loftier Black Mountain–Priest's Hill–Divis –Wolf Hill–Squire's Hill–Cave Hill range (825–1,574 ft). The opportunities for outdoor relaxation afforded by hills and lough (*see also* Carrickfergus, Holywood, Bangor) are supplemented by good parks and by facilities for outdoor games (e.g. eight golf courses).

The name of Belfast – *Béal Feirsde* "mouth of (approach to) the sandspit" (crossing the River Lagan) – first appears in late-15th cent. references to a Clannaboy O Neill castle commanding the Lagan crossing. (The principal Clannaboy seat and inauguration place was at Castlereagh, on the SE. edge of the modern city.) The city owes its origin to Sir Arthur Chichester, sometime commander of the English garrison at Carrickfergus (*q.v.*) – then the only town and seaport in all this region. In 1603 Chichester secured for himself a grant of the Clannaboy castle and the neighbouring townlands. (He was one of the arch-contrivers of the 17th cent. spoliation of the Northern Irish, and of the Ulster Plantation which brought so much misery and suffering to the dispossessed. His brother, Edward, was ancestor of the Marquesses of Donegall, and also of the Lords O Neill, whose family assumed the Clannaboy surname in 1855.) By 1611 a little town was beginning to arise around Chichester's castle. Two years later, for all its diminutive size, the town was incorporated by James I as a parliamentary borough. For close on two centuries it remained a small market centre, with a mere 8,500 inhabitants as late as 1750. But by 1800 the great advance was under way: 20,000 inhabitants in 1800, 230,000 in 1880, about 500,000 today. The first decisive step was the establishment (1778) of a cotton industry based on coal-fired factories; the second, the establishment (1851) of the Queen's Island shipyard; the third, the replacement of the cotton industry (crippled by the American Civil War) by a linen industry likewise based on the factory system. (Heretofore the Irish linen industry had been basically a cottage industry.)

In the later 18th cent. the little market town was the centre of a liberal and democratic, social-political reform movement among Ulster Protestants, notably among the Presbyterians. And so, in 1783, we find the local Volunteers, Protestants all, parading in honour of the opening of Belfast's first Catholic "Mass-house". The movement was strongly influenced by the American and French Revolutions, and by Paine's *The Rights of Man* (1791). Its active organs were the Northern Whig Club and the Secret Committee of a local Volunteer Club. It was the latter which, through Cork-born Thomas Russell (who had come to Belfast in 1790 as an ensign in the 64th Regiment), brought Wolfe Tone to Belfast in 1791 and made the town the cradle of the Society of the United Irishmen and of Irish Republicanism. Among the leaders of the movement were: Samuel Neilson (1761–1803; *see also under* Rathfryland), proprietor-editor of the *Northern Star* and originator of the United Irishmen idea; Henry Joy MacCracken (1767–98), founder of Belfast's first Sunday School, member of the Executive of the United Irish- men, and leader of the Antrim rebels in 1798; Robert and William Simms, co-founders of the United Irishmen; and Dr William Drennan (1754–1820), poet, first President of the United Irishmen, and a founder of the Belfast Academ- ical Institution – his liberalism baulked at Catholic Emancipation.

Catholic Emancipation, the Orange Order, and the 19th cent. erosion of the State Church's position of privilege and power, combined to magnify Protestant fears of the Catholics while diminishing the political and social differences between Presbyterian and Church of Ireland Protestants. By the 1880's, for all that Belfast Protestants continued to share in the leader- ship of Irish Republicanism, the city had become the stronghold of interdenominational Protestant resistance to Home Rule ("Home Rule is Rome rule"). From time to time sectarian violence still raises its unchristian head, but the visitor to Belfast can count on kindliness from citizens of every creed.

Outstanding dates in Belfast's history

1613.   Charter of incorporation
1771–4. Charitable Institute (Clifton House)
1778.   Cotton industry introduced
1783.   White Linen Hall founded; First Catholic church
1788.   Linen Hall Library
1791.   Society of United Irishmen founded
1807.   Academical Institution founded
1845.   Queen's College founded
1851.   Queen's Island shipyard
1888.   City status
1898.   St Anne's Cathedral commenced
1902–6. City Hall
1908.   Queen's University instituted
1912.   Anti-Home-Rule "Covenant"
1921.   Capital of Northern Ireland
1921–32. Parliament House, Stormont
1964.   First visit of a Dublin prime minister to Stormont

The focal centre of the city is Castle Junction, where Donegall Pl., Royal Ave., Castle St, and Castle Pl. meet in the heart of the shopping quarter. Most of the distances given below are reckoned from here.

Like Castle St and Castle Pl., Castle Junction preserves the memory of the Chichester castle commanding the Lagan crossing. Castle Pl. and High St follow the curve of the little Farset (called after the Lagan sandspit) as it makes its way – today entirely underground – to the Lagan; at the end of the 18th cent., ships still sailed up to the quays at the foot of High St. The Ulster Club (1863), Castle Pl., is by Sir Charles Lanyon (1813–89), a Sussex-born engineer who spent his working life in Ireland and who, in his day, had a near monopoly of Belfast's architectural business (from 1860 to 1872 in partnership with W. H. Lynn): Northern

Bank, Custom House, Prison, Deaf and Dumb Institute, Queen's College. Henry Joy Mac Cracken was hanged from the Market House, High St (at the corner of Cornmarket), 17 July 1798.

At the E. end of High St, is St George's Church, 19th cent. successor of the "English Church", Belfast's first Church of Ireland parish church. The fine portico was taken from Lord Bristol's palace at Ballyscullion, Co. Derry (*see under* Bellaghy). The church, which was named after King George III, was erected (1813–16) to the design of John Bowden, but the interior is a wholesale remodelling to the design of W. J. Barre; it is spoilt by unworthy glass. Henry Joy MacCracken was buried in the churchyard. Nearby, at the junction of Victoria St and Queen's Sq., is the Albert Memorial (1867–9), a Gothic-Revival clock tower prob- ably by Newry-born W. J. Barre, who intro- duced the Gothic Revival to Ulster; the statue is by W. H. Lynn. To the E. is Lanyon's classical Custom House (1857); the vigorous stone carving is by Thomas Fitzpatrick: tympanum, *Britannia with Mercury and Neptune*; entrance figures, *Industry, Commerce, Manufacture, Peace.* ¼ m. N. of the Custom House, in Corporation Sq., is the Sinclair Seamen's Church (1857) by Lanyon. It has a "maritime interior in the Moby Dick style".

N. of Castle Junction, on the E. side of Royal Ave., is Rosemary St, with Belfast's most charming church, The First Presbyterian Church, a mellow brick ellipse of 1783 (by Roger Mulholland; chancel an addition). The façade, completely and coarsely reconstructed in 1833, has been quite spoilt by removing the window glazing bars and by the choice of horrid paint. Features of the interior are: ceiling, galleries, curved passages, and box pews; the glass is deplorable (two 1929 windows by Wilhelmina Geddes have, unfortunately, been destroyed). There is a memorial by P. Mc- Dowell, R.A., to William Tennent (1759–1832). Robert Patterson, F.R.S., (1802–72), naturalist and zoologist, was a member of the congrega- tion. To the E., in Waring St, are the Com- mercial Buildings (1820) whose elevation is one of the best compositions in the city. The Belfast Bank (1845), by Lanyon, was modelled on Barry's Reform Club, London.

¼ m. N. of Castle Junction, Royal Ave. joins York St (large 19th cent. linen mill, now part of Gallahers' great tobacco factory), Donegall St, and Clifton St. SE. of the intersection is St Anne's Cathedral, joint extra cathedral of the Protestant dioceses of Connor and Down- and-Dromore. This disappointing Romanesque basilica was commenced in 1898 to the designs of Sir Thomas Drew; apse and ambulatory completed 1955–9. The W. portals, a 1914–18 War Memorial with sculptures of *Sacrifice, Victory, Peace,* are by Sir Charles Nicholson. The capitals of the interior represent *Free- masonry, Theology, Ship-building, Medicine, Science, Music, Agriculture, Arts,* etc. The

Plate 3. A country road near Killarney

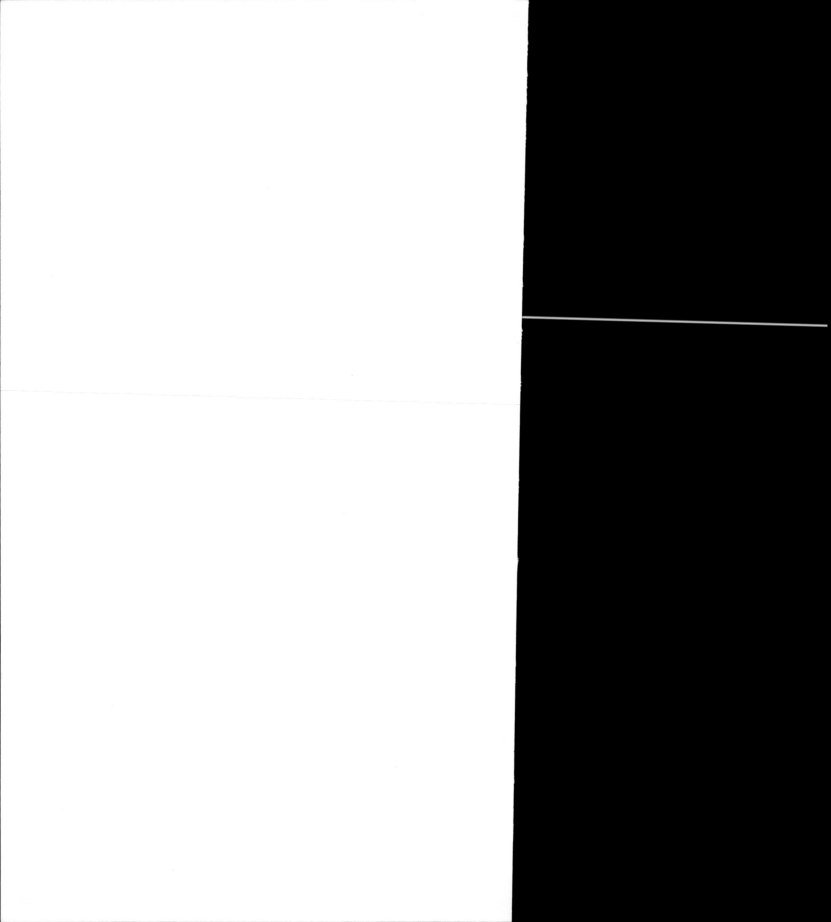

St George's Church, High Street, Belfast

Northern Ireland Tourist Board

baptistery is by W. H. Lynn, its mosaics by Gertrude Stein, the angel heads of the font by Rosamund Praeger. Lord Carson (1854–1935), Dublin-born leader of the opposition to Home Rule, is buried in the cathedral.

In Upper Donegall St is St Patrick's Church. In a side chapel is a mural painting by Sir John Lavery, who was born in nearby North Queen St.

In North Queen St is Clifton House. Near the gateway is a short terrace of late Georgian houses. Clifton House (1771–4), alias the Belfast Charitable Institute, is a home for the aged and infirm. It was erected on the edge of the town by the Belfast Charitable Society as a hospital and poorhouse. Henry Joy Mac-Cracken's uncle, Robert Joy, was one of the most energetic promoters, and his sister, Mary Ann MacCracken, was a lifelong active member of the Ladies' Committee. Dr William Drennan, first President of the United Irishmen, was a member of the Committee. The building, Belfast's most important Georgian monument, is an attractive, if amateurish, essay. In its original form it enclosed three sides of an open square, and had open arcades to the wings. Robert Joy had a large hand in the design, which was submitted to Thomas Cooley for advice. The entrance hall and Board Room have interesting portraits and relics. The Black Hole was for the incarceration of "sturdy vagrants and beggars". NW. of Clifton House, in Henry St, is the Charitable Society's New Burying Ground (1797), whose melancholy, mouldering tombs include those of: William Steel Dickson (1744–1824), "Patriot, Preacher, Historian *Dochum onóra na hÉireann*"; William Drennan, M.D. (1754–1820); Mary Ann Mac-Cracken, "beloved sister of Henry Joy Mac-Cracken 1770–1866 *Díleas go h-éag*".

200 yds S. of Castle Junction is Donegall Sq. On the N. side is the Linenhall Library, founded in 1788 by the Belfast Society for Promoting Knowledge; Thomas Russell of the United Irishmen was the first librarian; he was executed in 1803 for complicity in Emmet's Rebellion. The City Hall (1902–6, by Sir Brumwell Thomas) occupies the site of the White Linen Hall erected at the S. edge of the town in 1783. It is a vast, ostentatious, Renaissance-style affair with "sugar-icing" interiors. A 1951 mural, by Luke, commemorates the town's 1613 charter. The Queen Victoria and Sir Edward I. Harland statues in the garden are by Brock, the Dufferin monument by F. W. Pomeroy. The Methodist Church (1850; by Isaac Farrell of Dublin) on the E. side of the square has a good Classical portico (stucco). Around the corner, in May St, is the Egypto-Grecian Victoria Hall, built as a music hall in 1840 by Peter Lundy, turned into a church and renamed in 1887. Facing it is May Street

Presbyterian Church, an 1829 Classical building by W. Smith. To the S., in Alfred St, is St Malachy's Church, an 1844 Tudor-Gothick essay by Thomas Jackson. The S. side of Donegall Sq. retains a few good Georgian façades.

From the NE corner of Donegall Sq., Chichester St leads E. to the markets and the Royal Courts of Justice, 1933 " Official Classical " by J. G. West.

At the SW. corner of Donegall Sq. is Bedford St. The Ulster Hall, the city's largest public hall, was commenced to the designs of W. J. Barre. It was the scene of momentous anti-Home Rule meetings. Belfast's Group Theatre has its home here.

From the NW. corner of Donegall Sq. Wellington Pl. leads to College Sq. East and Fisherwick Pl. At the corner of Fisherwick Pl. and Howard St is Church House (by Young and Mackenzie, 1905), seat of the Presbyterian General Assembly. There are three Wilhelmina Geddes windows here: four-light *Prodigal Son, Virgins, Talents, Good Samaritan* (1916); *Pilgrim's Progress* (1929); *Go ye forth, teach ye all nations* (1929). In College Sq. uncouthly obscured by the City of Belfast College of Technology, is Belfast's best-known school, the Royal Belfast Academical Institution (familiarly known as "Inst"), founded in 1807 by the Presbyterians. (Its college department–extinct–was the precursor of the Queen's University.) The austere brick buildings (1810) are by Sir John Soane, whose original design was for a grandiose two-court building of stone. The school roll includes the names of Lord Kelvin (1824–1907), celebrated scientist, who was born in Fisherwick Pl. and whose father was mathematics master at "Inst", and Viscount Bryce (1838–1922), statesman and scholar. Nearby in College Sq., North, are good terrace houses of *c.* 1825–40, including the Old Museum (1831; by William Duff and Thomas Jackson. Founded by the Belfast Natural History (and Philosophical) Society, the Old Museum was the first museum in Ireland built as such. Its chaste architecture derives directly from Athenian Stewart and Resett. Nearby Regency Christ Church (1833) is by William Farrell, architect of Colebrook and Portaferry House; the fantastic three-decker pulpit (1878) is by William Batt.

A short distance W. of Castle Junction is Chapel Lane. St Mary's Church is the successor (1868; by John O Neill) of Belfast's first (1783) Catholic "chapel" or "Mass-house", to whose erection both Presbyterians and Church of Ireland Protestants had contributed.

½ m. NW. of Castle Junction, the Townsend St Presbyterian Church (1878; by Young and Mackenzie) has a two-light window by Wilhelmina Geddes: *Faith, Hope, Charity* (1914).

½ m. W. of Castle Junction, in Derby St, is St Peter's Church (completed 1866), grimy, twin-spired, Gothic-Revival pro-cathedral of the Catholic diocese of Down and Connor. It was designed by Father Jeremiah M'Auley, but completed by John O'Neill. The interior demands forbearance. This is the heart of the Falls Rd Catholic quarter (denominational segregation of the working-class population has long been a feature of Belfast social conditions). ½ m. SW. of St Peter's, in Falls Rd, is St Mary's Dominican Convent; the chapel has a single-light window (1948) by Evie Hone, *Our Lady of Mercy and Dominican Saints.*

1¼ m. SSW. of Castle Junction (via Donegall Sq. and Great Victoria St) is the Queen's University of Belfast, founded in 1845 as one of the three Queen's Colleges (*see* Cork *and* Galway) for the university education of those not belonging to the State Church (Church of Ireland) and raised to independent university rank in 1908. Best financed of the Irish universities, it is now second only to University College, Dublin, in point of student numbers (*c.* 5,000), and its rapidly expanding faculties are turning this quarter of Belfast into a *cité universitaire.* The original "Redbrick Tudor" buildings (1849), in University Rd, are by Lanyon. The 1949 Whitla Hall is by J. McGeagh. Adjoining Whitla Hall are the Botanic Gardens (thirty-eight acres; open daily, 8 a.m.–sunset) and the Ulster Museum (1929). The latter (by J. C. Wynnes) is another of Belfast's "Official Classical" buildings, happily never completed; extensions (designed by Francis Pym of London) in the current idiom are projected. The museum houses an art gallery (works by Turner, Lawrence, Steer, Sickert, Jack Yeats, Belfast-born Sir John Lavery, and Belfast-schooled Wilhelmina Geddes), as well as interesting archaeological, natural history, technological, and historical collections. (Open Wed. 10 a.m.–9 p.m.; other weekdays, 10 a.m.–6 p.m.) Between Stranmillis Rd and Malone Rd are the David Keir Buildings (1958) housing the university's Zoological Museum and Departments of Chemistry, Biology, and Civil Engineering; there is a Redwing figure by F. E. McWilliam in the central court. Close by is the Ashby Institute (1954–64); by Cruickshank and Seward) housing the Departments of Mechanical and Electrical Engineering. St John's Church (1894; by Henry Seaver), nearby in Malone Rd, has one window by Wilhelmina Geddes (*The leaves of the trees were for the healing of the nations*; 1920) and three by Evie Hone: *St Brigid* (1948; in porch), *Rose Window* (1947–8), and *St Columba* (1948). ENE. of the University, in College Park, is the Presbyterian General Assembly's Theological College, a Romano-Doric building (1853) by Lanyon. The nearby Presbyterian Student's Centre (1962) is by Robert McKinstry. The University Rd Methodist Church (1865) is by W. J. Barre. In University Ave. is the Christian Science First Church; by Clough Williams-Ellis.

½ m. E. of Castle Junction are Queen's Bridge and Queen Elizabeth Bridge. (The latter was opened by Queen Elizabeth in 1966.) The bridges link the heart of the city with Newtownards Rd and the E. suburbs. ¾ m. NNE. of

Stormont, Belfast

the bridges is Queen's Island with its famous shipyards and engineering works (Harland and Wolff), largest single unit of its kind in the world (300 acres, over 11,000 workers); on twenty-four occasions these yards have headed the world's output of shipping tonnage. ¾ m. E. of Queen's Bridge is St Patrick's Church (1893; by S. P. Close), Newtownards Rd; good Gothic-Revival tower. ¾ m. SE., to the S. of Newtownards Rd, is a 40-acre ropeworks, one of the largest in the world. ⅜ m. E. of St Patrick's, in Witham St, is the City of Belfast Transport Museum with interesting exhibits. (Open, Wed. and Sat. 10 a.m.–9 p.m.; other weekdays, 10 a.m.–6 p.m.; admission, 1/-.) 1 m. ENE., in Holywood Rd, Dundela, is St Mark's Church (1878; by William Butterfield, "uncomfortable genius" of the English Gothic Revival). One of Belfast's finest churches, it has a three-light window (1932) by Michael Healy: *SS. Luke, James, Mark.* 2¼ m. E. of Queen's Bridge, Sandown Rd joins the S. side of Newtownards Rd. Near the S. end of Sandown Rd, close to Knock burial ground, is a Norman motte.

3½ m. E. of Queen's Bridge, on Newtownards Rd, is one of the best of recent Protestant churches in Ireland, St Molua's Church (1961–2), by Denis O'D. Hanna. The disappointing apse mural, *Christ Enthroned in Majesty*, is by Desmond Kinney. The good bronze *Jesus the Carpenter* over the door of the parish hall is by James Mac Kendrey.

On the opposite side of Newtownards Rd, in 300 acres of parkland, is Stormont, seat of the Parliament and Government of Northern Ireland, i.e. of the "Six Counties" partitioned from Ulster in 1921 (as a result of the resistance to Home Rule) and assigned limited Home Rule within the United Kingdom. The 1963 administration building, Dundonald House, is by

Gibson and Taylor. A ¾-m. processional way, Prince of Wales Ave., climbs from Newtownards Rd to Parliament House. This massive "Official Classical" essay (1921–32), by Sir Arnold Thornley of Liverpool, was the gift of the British Government and was opened by King George V. The statue of Lord Carson at the junction of Prince of Wales Ave. and Massey Ave. is by L. S. Merrifield.

1½ m. E. of the Stormont entrance gate, at Dundonald village, is Dundonald Fort (Nat. Mon.), a Norman motte. 1¾ m. E. in Greengraves, is a very fine portal dolmen (The Kempe Stones; Nat. Mon.).

2½ m. S. of Castle Junction, via Ormeau Rd (Lagan-side Ormeau Pk, 137 acres) is Knockbreda Parish Church (1747), sole survivor of Richard Cassels's three churches (the others were in Sligo and Castlebar): short cruciform with apsidal chancel and transepts. The exterior has been spoilt by ugly belfry louvres and the all-too-familiar cementing of the wall faces. The austere, typically Church of Ireland, interior remains attractive, despite the 19th cent. windows. 2½ m. SW., in Ballynahatty, is the Giant's Ring (Nat. Mon.), a seven-acre ritual enclosure bounded by a 15-ft bank; off-centre is a chamber tomb. Bronze Age burials have been found in the fields on the N. At one time the enclosure served as a race course. 2½ m. SSE., to the SE. of Ballylesson village, is Farrell's Fort, a trivallate ringfort which some claim to be the "Rath of Drumbo" mentioned in 11th cent. annals. 1½ m. SW., at Drumbo, the stump of a Round Tower and remains of a church (Nat. Mons.) mark the site of an early monastery founded by St Mo-Chumma.

3 m. SW. of Castle Junction (via the old Lisburn road), at Balmoral, are King's Hall and the show grounds of the Royal Ulster

The Kempe Stones: Portal dolmen near Dundonald, Belfast

Agricultural Society. It was here that the "Covenant" against Home Rule was signed, 9 April 1912. 1¾ m. further is Dunmurry, a village rapidly being engulfed by industrial estates. The First Presbyterian (Unitarian) Church (1779) is a good example of an "Ulster barn church".

6 m. NW. of Castle Junction is Ballyutoag (*see under* Templepatrick).

10 m. NW. of Castle Junction is Lyles Hill (*see under* Templepatrick).

3½ m. NNW. of Castle Junction (via Antrim Rd), on the slope of Cave Hill (Ben Madighan; 1,182 ft), the grounds of Belfast Castle, Hazelwood, and Bellvue combine to form Belfast's largest (290 acres) municipal park and pleasure gardens; various vantage points afford splendid views. Belfast Castle (1867; probably by Lanyon's partner, W. H. Lynn), sometime seat of the Marquess of Donegall, was presented to the city by Lord Shaftesbury in 1934. In Bellvue are the city's Zoological Gardens and Amusement Park (13 acres; open Mon. to Sat., 10 a.m.–dusk; Sun., 2 p.m.–dusk). The ascent (several paths) of Cave Hill, at least as far as Mac Art's Fort, is rewarding. The fort, said to be called after Brian mac Airt O Neill of Clannaboy (slain in 1601 by Lord Deputy Mountjoy), seems to have been a promontory fort on the basalt cliff. (It was at the fort that, in 1794, Wolfe Tone and his Belfast comrades made the famous vow "never to desist in our efforts until we have subverted the authority of England over our country".) Nearby are five artificial caves.

BELLAGHY, Co. Derry (Map 3, B4), is a village on the Randalstown (10 m.)–Maghera (6 m.) road.

There are remains of a Plantation bawn (Vintners' Company of London) with one round and two rectangular flankers.

1½ m. E., in the grounds of Ballyscullion House, are the remains of a palace built by Placidio Columbini (by Francis Sandys?) for Lord Bristol, Bishop of Derry (*see* Downhill *under* Coleraine), and destroyed about 1810. The portico has been incorporated in St George's Church, Belfast.

2 m. SE., on Church Island, a peninsula in Lough Beg, are the remains of a medieval monastic church; the tower and spire were added in 1788 by Lord Bristol. To the S. is a font, still the resort of pilgrims.

BELLANAGARE, Co. Roscommon (Map 2, B6), is a village on the Rathcroghan (4 m.)–Frenchpark (2½ m.) road.

¾ m. N., in Ballaghcullia, is Caltragh, a circular, early church site which, as so often, was bisected by a N.–S. cross-wall.

1½ m. N. is Hermitage House, sometime seat of O Conor Don (representative of the ancient dynasts of Rathcroghan; *q.v.*) and home of the celebrated Charles (Cathal) O Conor of Bellanagare (1710–91), Irish scholar and antiquary. Charles is buried in the family mausoleum at Ballintober, Co. Roscommon (*q.v.*; *see also* Mounttown *under* Kilmactranny).

½ m. ESE., in Drummin, is a ring-work with an ogham stone at the rampart.

BELLAVARY, Co. Mayo (Map 1, D4), is a village on the Castlebar (6 m.)–Foxford (7 m.) road.

2¼ m. NE. is Strade, birthplace of Michael Davitt (1864–1906), Fenian and leader of the struggle for land and other social reforms. There is a hideous plaque commemorating him close to the ruins of a friary founded by Jordan de Exeter, lord of Athlethan, for Franciscans, but transferred to the Dominicans in 1252/3 by Jordan's son, Stephen, at the instance of his wife, Basilia Bermingham of Athenry. In the church are remains of a fine, figured, high altar and other sculptures. A beautiful 15th/16th cent. tomb, with Flamboyant tracery and figures of Christ (displaying the Five Wounds) and saints, has been appropriated by a Ballaghaderreen family. In the vaulted sacristy are some medieval gravestones. In the adjacent townland, Knockshanbally, is Giants Grave, a wedge-shaped gallery grave (ruined) in a cairn.

BELLEEK, Co. Fermanagh (Map 2, B4), is a Border village on the River Erne some 4 m. below Lower Lough Erne, and on the Ballyshannon (5 m.)–Enniskillen (24 m.) road. The old Protestant parish church is at Cliff, just over the Border in Co. Donegal.

Belleek is renowned for its lustre-finish china. The clay came originally from Castle Caldwell (*below*). The pottery is open to the public. The rapid Lower Erne has long been famous for its salmon and sea-trout fishing, though these have deteriorated since a celebrated High Court judgement declared that there was a public right of fishing in the tidal waters. The falls at Belleek have recently been harnessed to serve the Erne hydro-electric scheme (*see* Ballyshannon).

3 m. E., on the S. shore of Keenaghan Lough, the ruins of Tivealough "Abbey" (Nat. Mon.) mark the site of an ancient monastery.

9½ m. ENE. (via road bridge) is Boa Island (*see under* Pettigoe).

6 m. NE. is Castle Caldwell. The original castle, now in ruins, was built in 1612 by the Blennerhassets. In 1662 the property passed to the Caldwells. A stone fiddle at the castle gate inscribed:

"On firm land only exercise your skill
That you may play and safely drink your
    fill"

commemorates a fiddler of theirs who fell from a pleasure boat in 1770. Near the former railway station are the ruins of a Protestant church built in 1641 by Sir Francis Blennerhasset and later adapted as a private chapel by the Caldwells.

BELMULLET, Co. Mayo (Map 1, B3), is a small decayed seaport at the neck of the Mullet, 39 m. W. of Ballina and 48 m. NW. of Castlebar. It is a convenient centre for exploring the cliffs and antiquities of the windswept Mullet peninsula (sole Irish nesting place of the great phalerope) and the NW. Mayo coast. Along the

W. coast of the Mullet are extensive areas of sand dunes and several pleasant beaches.

6¾ m. N., on offshore Illandavick islet, is Erris Head. Magnificent views may be had from the cliffs above Danish Cellar, 1 m. SE. of the Head. To the NNW., on a high headland, is Dún Fiachrach, a promontory fort.

5½ m. NW. are the last remnants of Doonamo (Nat. Mon.), a cliff-top fort with slight traces of *chevaux-de-frise* (*see* Dún Aonghus *under* Aran Islands). ¾ m. S. is the fortified shore-rock of Doonaneanir. On the adjoining promontory to the S. is Eanir's Grave, a low four-sided mound kerbed with stones. 2 m. SSW. of Eanir's Grave, on the N. side of Portnafrankagh, is Port Point promontory fort with remains of huts and souterrains.

5 m. NW. (c. 3 m. S. of Doonamo) is the old graveyard of Termoncarragh; there is a late limestone cross with *Crucifixion*.

4½ m. WNW., in the sand dunes, less than 1 m. E. of the ruins of Bingham Lodge and about 1½ m. N. of Leacht Áir Iorrais (*below*), is the ancient Kilmore which gives its name to the parish of Kilmore Erris. The site is a small circular enclosure divided by a N.–S. cross-wall (*see* Duvillaun More, *below*). At the N. end of this is a large pillarstone. About the middle of the E. sub-enclosure is a cross-slab. S. of it are some small, circular, stone-crowned mounds. A local tale has it that "people in Kilmore churchyard are buried standing".

5½ m. SW., by the sea, 2 m. W. of Binghamstown, are the remains of Cross "Abbey", a small medieval church with some early cross-pillars. From the 14th cent. onwards the "abbey" was a priory (dedicated to the Blessed Virgin Mary) dependent on Ballintober Abbey, but the original foundation was attributed to St Brendan. 1½ m. offshore is Inishglora with remains (Nat. Mon.) of a monastic settlement founded by St Brendan the Navigator (d. 577). These comprise: traces of a monastic cashel (or dry-masonry ring wall); St Brendan's Cell; St Brendan's Chapel; Templenafear, alias Teampall na Naomh Monastery; fragmentary Templenaman Nunnery; several early cross-slabs and pillars; and seven pilgrims' "stations", five of them in the W. half of the island. St Brendan's Cell was one chamber of a triune, beehive, stone house. St Brendan's Chapel was a diminutive corbel-roofed structure of dry masonry.

3¾ m. WSW., in the sandhills, is Leacht Áir Iorrais, an oval platform of earth enclosed by a penannular ditch and slight bank. On it is a small cairn. Close by are other remains. (The sandhills in this area are littered with remains of various kinds.) 1½ m. N. is Kilmore (*above*).

8½ m. S., close to the ruins of Bingham Castle, is a tumulus or motte.

11 m. S., by the seashore, 600 yds E. of Termon, is Kilbeg, alias The Relig. There is an early cross-slab here. 3½ m. WSW. is Fallmore (*below*).

14 m. SSW., at Fallmore, the SW. tip of the

Mullet, are the ruins of St Derivla's Church (Nat. Mon.), St Derivla's Bed (or Grave), and early cross-pillars. The church is a small, primitive structure with a simple, Romanesque W. door on whose N. jamb is some much-weathered, interlaced ornament, while the arch is bordered within and without by incised lines. St Derivla's Bed, NE. of the church, is a small enclosure with an early cross-slab. 300 yds N. of the church is St Derivla's Dabhach or "Vat", a holy well reputed to have curative powers. The view from Fallmore S. towards Achill is very beautiful. – 2¾ m. offshore, SW. of Fallmore, is the small island of Duvillaun More (accessible only in very calm weather) abandoned nearly sixty years ago. Here are remains of a small, early anchoritic settlement, including a small circular enclosure subdivided, like Kilmore Erris (*above*), by a curved N.–S. cross-wall. In the E. sub-enclosure are remains of a small corbel-roofed oratory. Immediately to the S. of this is the Tomb of the Saint, at the head of which stands a slab with a remarkable, primitive, yet stylized, *Crucifixion* on the W. face and a ringed Maltese cross on the E. face. S. of the enclosure is a line of five collapsed beehive huts. SW. of the enclosure is a well. – 4 m. offshore, NW. of Fallmore, is Iniskea North, with remains (Nat. Mon.) of an early anchoritic settlement. SW. of the deserted modern village are the ruins of St Columcille's Church, a tiny, dry-masonry structure with lintelled doorway. A cross-slab which stood to the SW. has been removed to the National Museum. E. of the deserted village are three dunes in line from N. to S. These are (N.–S.): Bailey Dóighte, Bailey Mór, Bailey Beag. NW. of Bailey Dóighte, and between it and Bailey Mór, are remains of ancient houses, etc. ESE. of Bailey Beag is a circular, raised platform. On the Baileys were corbel-roofed huts of slabs and dry masonry. Associated with those on the Bailey Mór are nine early cross-slabs, cross-pillars, and cross fragments; a tenth has been removed to the National Museum. The most interesting has incised on it a remarkable, primitive *Crucifixion*. On the circular platform SE. of Bailey Beag is yet another cross-slab (a second slab found here has also been taken to Dublin. – On Inishkea South are: to the S. of the harbour, a tall cross-slab with an elaborate spiral and fret pattern; to the N. of the harbour, two concentric circles of small stones with a cross-pillar at the centre.

6 m. SE. of Belmullet, on the N. side of the Castlebar road in Glencastle, alias Glencashel, is Dún Domhnaill, a rock fort closing the Gates of Erris, with fine views to the NW. At the W. end of the rock was Domhnall's Grave.

BELTRA, Co. Sligo (Map 2, A5), is a village on the Sligo (12 m.)–Ballina (25 m.) road, close to a beautiful inlet of Ballysadare Bay.

1½ m. N. is the fine Georgian mansion, Tanrego House. Close by, in Tanrego West, are the ruins of a Mac Swiney castle. Also in Tanrego West are remains of three prehistoric chamber tombs (including two court cairns) and other megalithic graves. In Tanrego East is Cromlech, a wrecked chamber tomb.

2½ m. W. is Longford House, where Lady Morgan (Sydney Owenson; *c.* 1783–1850) wrote her first novel, *The Wild Irish Girl*. Near the site of Longford castle (O Dowds) are the ruins of a 17th cent. chapel with figure carvings.

BELTURBET, Co. Cavan (Map 2, D5), is a market town on the River Erne between Cavan (10 m.) and Enniskillen (30 m.).

On Turbet Island is a low, overgrown motte dating from the abortive Anglo-Norman attempt (1211) to penetrate the heart of the North (*see* Kilmore, Granard, Cavan).

4 m. SSW. is Drumlane, site of a 6th cent. monastery founded by St M'Aodhóg("Mogue"), reputedly a disciple of St David of Wales, and founder of the celebrated monastery of Ferns (*q.v.*; *see also* Rossinver *under* Kinlough). In the Middle Ages Augustinian Canons were introduced from Kells. The remains (Nat. Mon.) comprise the lower part of a fine 12th cent. Round Tower and ruins of a long, aisleless church. The church was burnt down in 1246 and repaired at various dates between then and the 18th cent. In the S. wall are two tomb recesses. Outside the N. wall is a medieval grave-slab with interlacings, etc; it is said to mark the grave of one of the O Farrelly coarbs. To the S. of the church the site of the conventual buildings is marked by a complex of banks and ditches.

BENBURB, Co. Tyrone (Map 3, B5), is a village on the River Blackwater, 8 m. S. of Dungannon and 10 m. NW. of Armagh.

At the E. end of the village is a Protestant church built by Sir Richard Wingfield in 1618 and alleged to incorporate medieval fragments from the early monastic site at Clonfeacle nearby (*see also* Blackwatertown). It was repaired in 1815, and its tower was added in 1837. It contains a memorial to Captain James Hamilton, killed at the battle of 1646 (*below*).

Somewhere near the village Seán the Proud O Neill had his "chief house", a castle burned down in 1566, but restored, for Turloch Luineach O Neill resided there frequently until 1573. It subsequently fell into disrepair, and was used as a quarry by the English when building their fort at Blackwatertown, 1¾ m. E. (In 1610 Turloch O Neill petitioned the Crown for a grant of the castle, but was given instead Knocknacloy castle, a short distance W.) The actual site of Seán the Proud's castle may have been that now occupied by the Plantation castle (Nat. Mon.) built about 1615 by Sir Richard Wingfield, a former Marshal of Ireland, in a strong, cliff-top position 200 ft above the Blackwater in Benburb Demesne. This castle is said to have been sacked by the insurgent Irish in 1641 and dismantled soon after 1646. A house was built in the SW. corner towards the end of the 18th cent. Further rebuilding took place in the 19th cent. The remains are those of a quadrangular bawn with rectangular towers at the NE. and NW. angles and a small, circular tower at the SE. corner. The rectangular flankers served as dwellings as well as defences. 200 yds SE. is an artificial mound. (Benburb House is now a Servite priory.)

Benburb is celebrated in history as the scene of General Eóghan Rúa O Neill's brilliant victory in 1646 over a strong English and Scots army under Gen. Munroe.

1¼ m. N. is Sessiamagaroll Fort (Nat. Mon.), a large ringfort with an oval mound, or motte, on the W. side. It is traditionally associated with the O Neills.

2 m. SW., in the ancient graveyard of Eglish (Co. Armagh), are the heads of two High Crosses with solid, recessed rings.

½ m. W. is Drumflugh, where, in 1597, Great Hugh O Neill defeated Lord Deputy Brough. The latter was killed and his second-in-command, the Earl of Kildare, died of his wounds.

4 m. NW. is Cadian sweat house (Nat. Mon.).

BIRR, Co. Offaly (Map 5, D2), is a prosperous market and former garrison town on the small Camcor River just above its confluence with the Little Brosna. It is an important road-junction at the intersection of the main Roscrea (12 m.)–Tullamore (23 m.) road with roads to Banagher (7 m.), Portumna (16 m.), Nenagh (23 m.), and Roscrea (12 m.).

St Brénainn (Brendan; son of Neman), d. 572/3, disciple of St Finian of Clonard, founded a monastery here which was celebrated in its day, but of which little is known. In 697 a National Assembly met there to adopt St Adamnán's famous law for the protection of non-combatants and to adopt the orthodox reckoning of Easter. The *Gospels of Mac Regol*, alias the Rushworth Gospels, now in the Bodleian, were written and painted by Mac Regol úa Magleni, scribe, bishop, and abbot of Birr, who died in 822. In the following cent. the book was at Harewood, Yorks. – In the later Middle Ages the O Carrolls of Éile had their principal castle at Birr. In 1620, after the confiscation of the O Carroll territories, the district was granted to Laurence Parsons, a native of Leicestershire, with whom the history of the town such begins, and after whom it was for a time named Parsonstown. In 1641 the castle was held for the Parliamentary party by William Parsons, but was captured by a Confederate Catholic force under Preston the following year. It remained in Confederate hands until 1650, when it was taken by the Cromwellian general, Ireton. The Parsons of the day being a Williamite, the castle and Parsons properties were declared confiscate by James II's Patriot Parliament, but were recovered after the Battle of the Boyne and successfully held against the attack of Patrick Sarsfield, Earl of Lucan. The castle (to the W. of the town) is still the Irish seat of the Parsons family (Earls of Rosse).

The 1st Earl (1749–1807) was prominent in Grattan's Volunteers. The 2nd Earl (1758–1841) was an opponent of the Union, an advocate of Catholic Emancipation, and an amateur architect. The 3rd Earl (1800–1867) was internationally famous as an astronomer: discoverer of the spiral nebulae. His wife, Mary Wilmer Field, was a pioneer photographer. The 4th Earl (1840–1929) was also an astronomer; his brother, Charles, invented the steam turbine.

The castle was enlarged (after an 1823 fire) by the 2nd Earl himself: courtyard facade, "Strawberry Hill" saloon, etc. It has (besides family portraits) pictures by Cuyp, Carracciolo, Kneller, Russell, Hoare, and others; also furniture from the Royal Pavilion, Brighton. The demesne, with ornamental lake, beautiful gardens, and arboretum, owes much to the 1st and 2nd earls. Gardens open daily: May to Sept. 3–6, Oct. to April 3–5; or by special arrangement; permits at Estate Office (Lodge Gate).

In the 19th cent., Birr was the scene of a short-lived local schism in the Catholic Church when Father Crotty said Mass in English instead of Latin. His chapel is now used as a store. It was at Birr, too, that the County Galway Hunt acquired the nickname of "The Blazers". In their carousal following an Invitation Meet to hunt the Ormonde country, Dooley's hotel was burnt to the ground.

Joseph Stirling Coyne (1803–68), dramatist and contributor to Vol. I of *Punch*, was born at Birr. He compiled the well-known *Scenery and Antiquities of Ireland*, illustrated by W. H. Bartlett. The Rev. A. B. Nicholls (d. 1906), widower of Charlotte Brontë, was for a time Rector of Birr (*see* Banagher).

The town is well laid out, with the four principal streets opening off a square (Emmet Sq.). It has some good 18th–19th cent. houses and terraces, notably in Oxmantown Mall and St John's Mall. The two parish churches are Gothick essays by the 2nd Earl of Rosse, the Catholic church being the first full-scale post-Reformation parish church in the diocese of Killaloe; it served for a time as cathedral.

The column in Emmet Sq. (for which a statue of St Brendan is proposed) was erected (1747) to commemorate the notorious Duke of Cumberland, who defeated the Scottish Jacobites at Culloden. The story has it that fears of a mutiny by Highland troops prevented its erection in an English garrison town.

In St John's Mall is an 1876 statue of the 3rd Earl of Rosse; by John Henry Foley.

There are good Georgian houses in the neighbourhood, including Thomastown (1730), 5 m. NE., beside Rath village, and Gloster, 8 m. S. (*see under* Roscrea).

6 m. SE., near Clareen, is Seir Kierán (Saighir Cíaráin), site of an important monastery founded by St Ciarán (Old Ciarán, to distinguish him from his more celebrated namesake of Clonmacnois), patron of the ancient kingdom of Ossory (Ossraige, a tribal name) in

which Saighir was situated. The place may
previously have been a pagan sanctuary; a perpetual fire is said to have burned there (see
Kildare, Cloyne, and Inishmurray). Until supplanted by Aghaboe (q.v.), Saighir was the
chief monastery of Ossory and the burial place
of its kings. About 1200 the monastery was
reorganized as a house of Canons Regular of
St Augustine. The 25-acre site of Ciarán's monastery is marked by earthworks, church ruins,
four early gravestones (one inscribed OR[ÓIT]
DO CHERBALL ("A prayer for Cerball"),
part of a small, plain, stone cross, and the sculptured base of a 10th cent. High Cross (Nat.
Mons.). The subjects on the latter include The
Fall and a battle scene. The Protestant parish
church incorporates ancient fragments, including a weathered figure of St Ciarán on the W.
gable.–About ½ m. S. of Clareen crossroads are
St Ciarán's Bush and Stone. The bush has been
left to grow undisturbed in the middle of the
roadway. – 3½ m. S. of Clareen, on the Roscrea
road, is Leap castle (see under Roscrea).

7 m. SW. is Knockshigowna (see under
Borrisokane).

BLACKLION, Co. Cavan (Map 2, C5), is a
small village between Upper and Lower Lough
Macnean, on the Belcoo (½ m.)–Dowra (12 m.)
road.

3½ m. S., alt. 800–850 ft in Burren, are five
chamber tombs (condition various), including
two wedge-shaped gallery graves. ¼ m. SE., in
Legalough, are remains of a court cairn, of a
wedge-shaped gallery grave, and of a round
cairn.

4 m. S., in Moneygashel, are remains of
three cashels or stone ringforts. The central
cashel is 80 ft in diameter, has a rampart 9 ft
thick with internal and external stairways, and
a souterrain (largely blocked up). Inside the
S. cashel is a beehive-shaped stone sweat house.
(The country between Blacklion and Dowra
has a number of abandoned sweat houses of
different kinds. Generally speaking, they fell
into disuse about 50 or 60 years ago.)

6¼ m. S. (1¼ m. SE. of the central fort in
Moneygashel), on the S. slope of Tiltinbane,
are remains of the White Cairn. About 1 m. to
the SW. is Log na Sionna, the source of the
Shannon. The valley of the Owenmore river to
the S. joins a road from Dowra in wild Glan-
gevlin, the last place in Co. Cavan where Irish
survived as a living language. From Glan-
gevlin the road climbs the saddle between
Cuilcagh (2,188 ft) and Benbrack (1,652 ft) to
the Bellavalley Gap (1,100 ft), from which
roads descend to Ballyconnell, Swanlinbar, and
Ballinamore.

1½ m. W., on the S. shore of Upper Lough
Macnean, is the promontory of Killinagh.
Here are St Brigid's Stone and two smaller
erratics; all three have cursing stones resting in
bullauns or other depressions on their upper
surfaces; in the 19th cent. there were cursing
stones (ten in number) only on St Brigid's

Stone. According to tradition, the pillarstone
sometimes called Crom Cruaich, which stands
in Drumcoo, Co. Fermanagh (see under Belcoo), originally stood in Killinagh beside St
Brigid's Stone. In a thicket close to the latter
is St Brigid's House, alias The Queen's Bed,
perhaps a prehistoric chamber tomb. Beyond
it are remains of a church (12th cent.?), said
to belong to a monastery founded by SS
Brigid and Laighse.

BLACKWATERTOWN, Co. Armagh (Map
3, B5), is a village 2½ m. S. of Charlemont and
1¾ m. E. of Benburb, with some remains of a
fort which the English compelled Great Hugh
O Neill to sanction in 1584. O Neill's siege of
the fort in 1598 culminated in the defeat of an
English relieving army under Sir Henry Bagenal
at the Battle of the Yellow Ford (see under
Armagh).

The derelict warehouses are relics of the ill-
fated Ulster Canal.

SW. of the Blackwater bridge St Patrick's
Church, Tullydowey, marks the ancient mon-
astic site of Clonfeacle. A stone cross (Nat.
Mon.) survives.

BLANCHARDSTOWN, Co. Dublin (Map
6, D7), is a village on the Dublin (6 m.)–Navan
(24 m.) road.

2¼ m. W. is Clonsilla Protestant church:
Evie Hone window (St Fiacre, 1937).

1½ m. E., on a hill commanding a delightful
prospect, is Dunsink Observatory, from 1782
to 1921 the observatory of Trinity College,
Dublin, and since 1947 the School of Astro-
nomical Physics of the Dublin Institute for
Advanced Studies. The buildings still retain
something of their quiet, 18th cent. charm. The
greatest name connected with the Observatory
is that of Sir William Rowan Hamilton (1805-
65), who published his celebrated Lectures on
Quaternions in 1835.

2 m. NW., ½ m. NE. of Mulhuddard (Mul-
laghiddart) bridge, are the 15th cent. tower and
fragments of the 14th cent. nave and chancel of
the parish church of the Blessed Virgin Mary.
In the churchyard is buried Richard Bellings,
Secretary to the Supreme Council of the Catholic Confederation of Kilkenny and supposed
author of Vindiciae Catholicorum Hiberniae.
The hill (299 ft) affords a fine view of the rich
lowlands and distant mountains. Nearby to
the SW. is Lady Well, formerly a place of
popular pilgrimage on 8 Sept.

BLARNEY, Co. Cork (Map 5, B6), is a
woollen-manufacturing village on the N. bank
of the beautiful Shournagh river, 5 m. NW. of
Cork. The Shournagh and Martin rivers offer
fairly good trout fishing. The Muskerry Hunt
has its headquarters here. The countryside is
rich in ancient remains.

SW. of the village is fine Blarney Castle
demesne whose 18th cent. delights are sung in
Richard Millikin's The Groves of Blarney. The

Blarney Castle

first castle at Blarney seems to have been an English royal fortress. In the 14th cent. it is found in the custody of the Lombards of Cork. The Lombards were expelled by the Mac Carthys when they recovered this part of Desmond (*see under* Cork, History), and Blarney became one of the principal seats of the Mac Carthys of Muskerry. In 1446 Cormac Láidir Mac Carthy (*see* Kilcrea *under* Ballincollig) built the great castle whose 85-ft keep still stands on a rock over the Croomaun. Beneath it are two caves, one of them partly artificial. The view from the parapet is very fine. Just below the battlements is the famous Blarney Stone,

"A stone that whoever kisses
O, he never misses to grow eloquent"
(Father Prout)

The origin of the ridiculous, and relatively modern, custom of kissing the stone is unknown. – The Mac Carthys contrived to retain their hold on Blarney until the Cromwellian confiscation, when the place was granted to Lord Broghill, son of Richard Boyle (*see* Lismore *and* Youghal). At the Restoration the Mac Carthys recovered possession, only to lose it for ever at the Williamite revolution, when Donnchadh Mac Carthy, 3rd Earl of Clancarty, followed James II into exile (*see* Carrignavar

under Cork). Blarney was then acquired by the Jefferyes family, from which it passed by marriage to the Colthursts, who built the nearby 19th cent. mansion. Not far from the castle is Rock Close, a beautiful dell with trees and a circle of great stones – a piece of 18th cent. landscape gardening.

For centuries the Mac Carthys of Blarney maintained a bardic school. With the downfall of the Gaelic order it withered away. The last official head of the school was Tadhg Ó Duinnín (d. 1726), who was driven to take up farming for a living. He later became a priest (*see* Doneraile). After him the school was unofficially continued, first by Diarmuid mac Sheáin Bhuí Mac Carthy in the Blarney neighbourhood, then by Liam an Dúna Mac Cairteáin (1668–1717) at Whitechurch (*see* Glennamought bridge *under* Cork).

2¾ m. N. is Garrycloyne church; ½ m. N. are the remains of Garrycloyne castle. – 2 m. NW. of the church, in Newcastle, is a prehistoric stone alignment. – 4¼ m. NW. of the church, in Garryadeen, is Tobar Laichtín, St Laghteen's Well (*see* Donaghmore *under* Coachford).

7 m. NNE., in beautiful Glencam, is a prehistoric chamber tomb.

2 m. NE., in Curraghnalaght, is a standing stone.

3¾ m. WSW., in Cloghroe, are traces of a Mac Carthy castle built inside a ringfort.

2 m. W. is decayed St Anne's Hydro. The Kursaal has pleasantly fantastic woodwork.

3½ m. W. are the ruins of Cloghphillip, a Barrett castle transferred by deed to the Mac Carthys of Muskerry in 1488.

2½ m. NW., in Loughane East, is Lisnaraha, a very fine bivallate ringfort; nearby is a pair of pillarstones; a second large ringfort here is sub-rectangular in plan. 2¾ m. N., is the Newcastle alignment (*above*). – 4 m. NW. is Garraun North Cromlech (*see under* Coachford).

BLASKET ISLANDS, THE, Co. Kerry

(Map 4, A4), lie off Dunmore Head at the SW. tip of the Dingle Peninsula. The principal islands of the group are The Great Blasket, Inishtooskert, Inishnabro, and Inishvickillane.

Two Armada ships, the *Santa Maria de la Rosa* and the *San Juan de Ragusa*, sank in the Sound, 10 Sept. 1588.

On The Great Blasket are ruins of an early church (Nat. Mon.). Prior to its recent depopulation, the island was a noted resort of folklorists and students of the Irish language, and an interesting account of island life, as seen through sympathetic English eyes, is available in *Western Island* by Robin Flower, the distinguished English Celticist who, like Professor Kenneth Jackson of Edinburgh, made an important collection of the folklore of the islands. Flower also translated into English Tomás Ó Criomhthainn's (Tomás O Crohan) remarkable autobiography, *The Islandman*, a classic piece of Irish writing. Other island autobiographies are Maurice O Sullivan's *Twenty Years Agrowing* (English translation by George Thomson), and Peig Sayer's *Peig*.

Inishtooskert is an uninhabited sheep-pasture. There are remains (Nat. Mons.) of an early anchoritic settlement, comprising the ruins of a small church dedicated to St Brendan the Navigator, three stone crosses, and four clocháns (and traces of others).

On Inishvickillane the ruins of a small church (St Brendan's Oratory) and of several clocháns, an early cross-stone, and an early gravestone inscribed OR[ŌIT] DO MAC-RUED Ú DALACH, mark the site of an. early anchoritic settlement (Nat. Mon.). An ogham stone which stood in front of the church is now in Trinity College, Dublin.

BLESSINGTON, Co. Wicklow (Map 6,

C3), called Burgage until 1683, is a village on the Dublin (18 m.)–Baltinglass (19 m.) road.

The manor of Blessington was created in 1669 by Charles II for Michael Boyle, Archbishop of Dublin and cousin of the 1st Earl of Cork. Boyle laid out the one-street village and built the Protestant parish church (about 1682; memorial to Boyle by William Kidwell, the Dublin statuary, who died in 1736) as well as a great brick mansion in Blessington demesne NW. of the village. (The mansion was destroyed by fire about 1760.) In 1778 the manor devolved on Lord Hillsborough, later 1st Marquess of Downshire (*see* Hillsborough, Co. Down). In 1798 the village was attacked by the Insurgents and "every good house" burned to the ground. In the churchyard is St Mark's Cross (Nat. Mon.; formerly St Baoithín's Cross), a 14-ft granite cross from the early monastic site (now submerged) of Domhnach Imleach (founder St Mo-Lomma) in Burgage More.

Adjoining the village on the E. is the great lake of the Liffey hydro-electric works. It was formed by flooding the valleys of the King's River and the Liffey. The circuit of the lake is attractive. A tolerable road crosses the lake at Baltiboys to join the Hollywood–Wicklow Gap–Glendalough road (*see* Hollywood) in the valley of the King's River. Baltiboys was the birthplace (1898) of Dame Ninette de Valois, creator of the Sadler's Wells Ballet.

2¾ m. ENE., in Threecastles, is the 14th cent. keep (Nat. Mon.) of a castle.

6½ m. NE., to the NE. of Kilbride, in Ballyfolan, is a small tumulus of earth and stones with remains of an enclosing stone circle (?); to the W. is a prostrate slab. 3 m. SE. of Ballyfolan crossroads, on the lower slope of Seefingan (2,364 ft), N. of the Liffey, is a large chambered cairn. About 1 m. from this, on the summit of Seefin (2,043 ft), is a round cairn (Nat. Mon.), covering a cruciform passage grave which has six sub-chambers or recesses; two of the passage uprights have lozenge patterns.

4½ m. ESE., in the NE. corner of Lackan townland (alt. 1,300 ft), between Lugnagun Hill (1,464 ft) and Sorrel Hill (1,975 ft), is a small, ruined, chambered cairn (a passage grave?).

4 m. SE., in Lacken, is the early monastic site, Temple Boodin, with St Boodin's Grave. ½ m. ENE. is St Boodin's Well, alias Father Germaine's Well, once famed for its cures; sores and limbs were bathed in the stream. In 1902 the well was dedicated to Our Lady of Mount Carmel, and a bathing place was erected.

3 m. SSW. is Russborough House (Sir Alfred Beit), one of Ireland's notable Palladian country houses (not open to the public). It was designed by Richard Cassels and Francis Bindon of Clooney, Co. Clare, for Joseph Leeson (1st Earl of Milltown), a wealthy Dublin brewer. The interior includes some splendid apartments with riotous stucco. Sir Alfred Beit has an excellent collection of paintings and *objets d'art* here.

5 m. SW. the Hollywood road crosses the Liffey at Poll an Phúca, where the river, having forced its way through a narrow gorge, plunges 150 ft in three stages. At the foot of the middle fall is the Púca's pool which has given its name to the picturesque cataract. (The Púca was a malicious sprite.) A convenient path leads down from the bridge to various vantage points. The new dam above the bridge has reduced the volume of the falls considerably, most of the

water being now led underground to the Liffey power-house. – ¾ m. SE., in Ballysize Lower, is an ancient granite cross.

BORRIS, alias **BORRIS IDRONE**, Co. Carlow (Map 6, B5), is an attractive Georgian village on the Carlow (16 m.)–New Ross (14 m.) road. It is prettily situated to the E. of the River Barrow, at the head of the valley between the Blackstairs Mountains and Brandon Hill, and is a good base for climbing Mount Leinster (*see under* Bunclody).

Borris House, to the W. of the village, is the seat of the Mac Murrough Kavanagh family, descendants of the Mac Murrough Kavanagh kings of Leinster. A remarkable 19th cent. member of the family was Arthur Mac Murrough Kavanagh (1831–89), who, though born with only rudimentary limbs, learned to ride and to shoot, was a world traveller, and a Member of Parliament.

4 m. NE., at Killoughternane (Fortchern's Church), are the remains of the 12th cent. White Chapel (Nat. Mon.), a simple rectangular structure with *antae* at each gable and a small, plain, Romanesque E. window; the W. doorway has been removed. The Fortchern in question is sometimes supposed to be St Patrick's disciple of that name.

3 m. SW. is Ullard, Co. Kilkenny (see under Graiguenamanagh).

BORRIS-IN-OSSORY, Co. Laois (Map 5, D3), is a village on the Mountrath (9 m.)–Roscrea (8 m.) road. Sited in the mouth of one of the main passes into Munster, it was of considerable strategic importance in the Middle Ages and was a major coaching centre in the pre-railway period.

2 m. N. are the remains of the Morres castle of Mondrehid.

2½ m. SW., at Skirk, are the motte and bailey of an early Anglo-Norman castle. The bailey, which is circular and has a pillarstone at the centre, appears to be a prehistoric ritual site adapted to medieval military use.

2 m. NW. is Clonfertmulloe, site of the principal monastery of Luguid moccu Ochae (544–609), alias St Mo-Lúa. A disciple of St Comgall of Bangor, he was credited with the founding of a hundred monasteries. The only ancient remains at Clonfertmulloe are a wall-fragment, St Mo-Lúa's Grave (marked by a rough stone at either end), an early gravestone nearby, St Mo-Lúa's Trough, and St Mo-Lúa's Stone. This last, a boulder with five bullauns, is a few hundred yards from the graveyard; the Trough has been mounted on a pedestal at Ballaghmore Catholic church. St Mo-Lúa's Bell is now in the British Museum.

BORRISOKANE, Co. Tipperary (Map 5, C3), is a market village on the Nenagh (11 m.)–Portumna (9 m.) road.

7½ m. N. is Lorrha (*q.v.*).

3½ m. NE. are the remains of Uskane church.

6¼ m. NE. (1½ m. N. of Ballingarry), in Lismacrory, are two tumuli (Nat. Mons.).

6 m. E. (2 m. E. of Ballingarry) is Knockshigowna (Cnoc Sídhe Úna), celebrated in folklore as the Otherworld seat of Úna, "fairy queen" guardian of the O Carrolls of Éile. The hill (699 ft) commands a splendid panorama and was a place of Lughnasa celebrations on Garland, alias Fraughan (*fraochán*, bilberry), Sunday.

6 m. SE. is Cloghjordan village, birthplace of Thomas Mac Donagh (1878–1916), poet and one of the signatories of the Proclamation of the Irish Republic, 1916. The Church of SS Michael and John has a two-light window (*Blessed Virgin, St Joseph*) by Evie Hone (1953).

4¾ m. SW., in Ardcroney, are the ruins of a small castellated church; the nave had a vaulted stone roof. ¼ m. N. are remains of Laghtcarn, a burial cairn.

6¾ m. WSW., via Newchapel, are the ruins of Kilbarron "Abbey", a plain, Romanesque, nave-and-chancel church with traces of a later W. tower; in the nave is a late cross-slab. – 2 m. SW. (via Kilbarron Quay), on Ilaunmore, an island of Lough Derg, is the site of an early monastery. ½ m. SW. of the site is a pillarstone. – Kilbarron castle was an O Kennedy stronghold.

7 m. WNW., beside Lough Derg, is Drominagh castle, an O Madden stronghold which came into the possession of the O Kennedys. 2¾ m. NE. is Terryglass (*see under* Portumna).

BORRISOLEIGH, Co. Tipperary (Map 5, D3), is a village at the E. end of the pass between the Devil's Bit and Slievefelim ranges. Roads from Thurles (8 m.) and Templemore (6 m.) join here to follow the pass to Nenagh (12½ m.). There are remains of a Burke castle.

1½ m. NW., in Glenkeen, are remains of a two-period church in which is an early 17th cent. monument by Patrick Kerin to one, Walter Burke; W. of the church is Glenkeen Well. Church and well probably mark the site of Kilcuilawn (Cill Chuileáin), founded in the 7th cent. by St Cuileán. Bearnán Cuileáin, alias Obair na Naomh, an ancient bell of bronzed iron encased in fragments of a 12th cent. reliquary, is said to have been found "some centuries ago" in a hollow tree at Kilcuilawn holy well; it is now in the British Museum. 4¾ m. NW. of the church is Latteragh, site of a monastery founded by St Odhrán *Magister* (d. 549). At the Anglo-Norman conquest of Ormond a round castle was built here and a colony established. In 1304 the settlement was destroyed by Turloch O Brien of Thomond. O Sullivan Béara passed the 7th night of his epic retreat from Glengarriff to Domahaire at Latteragh, 31 Dec. 1602. The only remains at Latteragh today are fragments of a 12th cent. church re-edified on a reduced scale in the 15th cent.

BOYLE, Co. Roscommon (Map 2, B6), is a market town where the Carrick-on-Shannon

(10 m.)–(Sligo (26 m.) road crosses the pretty River Boyle by a good, though rustic, Palladian bridge.

On the N. side of the town are the fine ruins (Nat. Mon.) of the 12th–13th cent. Cistercian abbey named Mainister na Búaille after the river. (The town took its name, properly Abbey Boyle, from the monastery.) A daughter house of Mellifont, the abbey was founded in 1148 at Greallach Dinach; was transferred thence to Druim Conainn; thence to Buninny, Co. Sligo; and finally, in 1161, to Boyle. The name of the founder is unknown, but the Mac Dermots of Moylurg were important patrons, gave members and abbots to the monastery, and had their family burial place there. The abbey was probably the most important in medieval Connacht, supplying bishops to several dioceses and numbering among its abbots members of the most illustrious families of the West: O Conors, O Haras, and others, as well as Mac Dermots. Among the illustrious dead buried here was the most famous religious poet of medieval Ireland, Donnchadh Mór O Daly (d. 1244), who is thought by some to have been abbot of the monastery.

The abbey was plundered by Anglo-Norman invaders led by Richard de Burgo and Maurice Fitzgerald, the English Justiciar, in 1235. It figured prominently in local history down to the Dissolution. In 1659 the buildings were occupied by Cromwellians, who did much damage to them.

The remains of the abbey, though fragmentary in places, are among the most beautiful and best preserved in Ireland. They comprise gatehouse with porter's lodge, cloister, kitchen, cellars beneath the refectory, sacristy, and noble church. The church (consecrated 1218) is of various dates, and is a most interesting example of the transition from Romanesque to Gothic in Ireland. To the late 12th cent. belong the barrel-vaulted chancel (the lancet windows are early-13th cent. replacements), the transepts (each with two barrel-vaulted chapels), and the crossing (the tower was increased in height in the 15th cent.). Work on the nave commenced only after an interval. The whole S. arcade is Western Transitional, though the three W. bays are an extension of c. 1205–18. The whole N. arcade has blunt-pointed arches, though here, too, the five E. bays are earlier than the three W. The carvings of the arcade capitals – men, beasts, foliage – repay study; all belong to the latest phase of the building. The aisles were intended to carry barrel vaults, but these were never erected.

N. of the town rises the Curlieu (867 ft). The road to Ballinafad (q.v.) affords beautiful views of Lough Key (below) and Lough Arrow. In 1599 Sir Conyers Clifford, English President of Connacht, attempted to advance across the mountain from Boyle, but was hurled back by Red Hugh O Donnell and O Rourke.

2½ m. NE. the Boyle flows into lovely Lough Key. Castle Island (Carraig Locha Cé, alias Carraig Mhic Dhiarmada) was for centuries a seat of Mac Dermot of Moylurg. Here, in 1541, Tadhg Mac Dermot feasted the literati of Ireland. Here, too, and at Mac Dermot's house at Cloonybrien in the parish of Ardcarn, the well-known *Annals of Loch Cé* were abstracted from the *Book of the Duignans* (*see* Ballyfarnan; *also* Castlefore *under* Ballinamore) for Brian, son of Rory Mac Dermot, in the years about 1589 by Duignan and other scribes. On Trinity Island are the ruins of Trinity "Abbey", a Premonstratensian priory founded in 1215 by Maoilín O Mulconry, member of the principal family of historiographers in Connacht. Here the so-called *Annals of Boyle* were compiled. The grave of Sir Conyers Clifford is still pointed out. W. B. Yeats once had a project for a community on the island. On Hog's Island are the remains of a church. On the S. shore of the lake is the beautiful demesne (now a public park) of Rockingham. Rockingham House was remodelled by John Nash for Lord Lorton in 1810, but was burned down in 1863 and again in 1957. To the S. of the main avenue are the remains of a medieval church.

4 m. E., on the site of an early monastery, is the Protestant parish church of Ardcarn: 1934 window, *SS. Patrick, Brigid, Barry*, by Evie Hone. Also in Ardcarn are a grass-grown cairn and a trivallate stone ringfort.

4½ m. SW., via the Frenchpark (*q.v.*) road, is Killaraght where St Adhracht(a), daughter of Talan, took the veil from St. Patrick. The cell, cross, and well are still held in veneration (*see* Toberaraght *under* Ballaghaderreen). In the same townland is a large grassy cairn.

6 m. SW., in Ardsoreen (Co. Sligo), is an interesting rectangular ringfort.

1 m. W. is Asselyn (Eas Uí Fhloinn, O Flynn's waterfall), where there are remains of a medieval church. The waterfall was originally Eas mic Eirc, and the first church here was attributed to St Columcille, who is said to have placed Mo-Chonna mac Eirc over it.

2 m. W., to the N. of the Sligo railway, is the fine portal dolmen of Drumanone. 4 m. further W. is Moygara castle (*see under* Kilfree).

BRAY, Co. Wicklow (Map 6, D3), a popular seaside resort on the Dublin (13 m.)–Wicklow (19 m.) road, is one of the most beautifully situated towns in these islands. It is also a convenient base for exploring some of the more celebrated beauty spots of Co. Wicklow, e.g. Powerscourt (*see under* Enniskerry), the Glen of the Downs (*below*), the Devil's Glen (*see under* Ashford), Glendalough (*q.v.*), Avoca valley (*see under* Rathdrum *and* Arklow).

The town is essentially the creation of the 19th cent. railway entrepreneur, William Dargan, and itself has nothing to offer the tourist interested in history or antiquities.

Christ Church (C. of I.) is by the English architect, William Slater.

At the S. end of the mile-long Esplanade, Bray Head (791 ft) rises steeply from the sea. It affords splendid views of mountain, lowland, and sea, as well as some fine walks, including the Cliff Walk to Greystones. On the N. side of the hill is a public park of 75 acres. Near the pathway leading to the Eagle's Nest are the ruins of Ráithín a' Chluig church (Nat. Mon.), a small structure of c. 1200.

¾ m. N. is Cork Abbey, now a glass factory belonging to Solus Teoranta. The 18th cent. residence has stucco by Michael Stapleton.

4 m. N. are Killiney Hill and Killiney Strand (*see under* Dalkey).

¾ m. S., in the grounds of Oldcourt House, is a tower (restored) of Oldcourt castle. Close to a stream in the grounds is the base of a stone cross with traces of panelled figures.

1 m. S., in the lovely valley between Bray Head and the Little Sugar Loaf (1,120 ft), is Kilruddery, seat of the Earl of Meath. The "Elizabethan" mansion was built in 1820 to the design of Sir Richard Morrison (1767–1849) and his son, William Vitruvius Morrison (1794–1838). Demesne and gardens are open to the public 11 a.m.–6 p.m. each Thur. between 1 May and 1 Oct.

½ m. SW., at the foot of the Little Sugar Loaf, is Hollybrook (Sir Edmond Adair Hodson). The mansion (1834) is the successor of the house in which lived sportsman Robin Adair, hero of a well-known ditty to the lovely air of *Eibhlín a Rúin*. The gardens are noted for their luxuriant shrubs.

1¼ m. SW., at the foot of the Rocky Valley, is the hamlet of Kilmacanoge, with remains of the church which gives the place its name. This is the best point from which to climb the Great Sugar Loaf (1,659 ft), a steep but simple quartz cone which affords magnificent prospects. A delightful walk or drive of 12 m. is Bray – Kilmacanoge – the Rocky Valley – Powerscourt waterfall (*see* Enniskerry) – Powerscourt Demesne – Dargle valley – Bray.

7 m. SW. is the Glen of the Downs (*see under* Delgany).

1½ m. WSW., in Fairy Hill graveyard, Kilbride, is an early cross-pillar. ½ m. further WSW. are the remains of Kilbride church. In the field behind the church are two small, broken crosses. 1 m. WSW. is St Valery, Fassaroe (*see under* Enniskerry).

2 m. W. (via Little Bray), in the valley of the Bray river, are the remains of Ballyman church, rebuilt in the 12th/13th cent. Traces of an enclosing stone vallum (destroyed about 1860) are discernible. W. is St Kevin's Well.

3¼ m. NW. is Carrickgolligan (912 ft). The walk hither via Little Bray, Old Connaught, and Ballyman, offers delightful views. The chimney on the summit was connected by a mile-long flue with Ballycorus lead works.

BRIDESWELL, Co. Roscommon (Map 5, C1), on the Athlone (7½ m.)–Mount Bellew Bridge (17 m.) road, takes its name (Tobar Brighde) from a well formerly reputed for its cures and for a great *pátrún* which commenced

on Garland Friday (last Friday of July). Five "stations" mark the places of religious exercises. Of these the chief is the well itself: the waters flow through a bath house (roofless) erected in 1625 by Sir Randall Mac Donnell, 1st Earl of Antrim (*see* Antrim, Glens of), whose countess was cured of barrenness at the well.

2 m. WNW., in Cam(ma), a bullaun and the remains of a simple, early church with Transitional (good E. window) and later additions, mark the site of Cammach Brighde, one of the seven principal monasteries of Uí Maine. 2½ m. W., in Commeen, is Díseart churchyard with remnants of a small Transitional church (with 15th/16th cent. windows), etc. S. of the churchyard a 1639 cross commemorates Phelim O Conor and his wife, Sara.

BRIDGETOWN, Co. Wexford (Map 6, C6), is a village on the Rosslare (8 m.)–Duncormick (5 m.) road.

The country here, between Wexford Harbour and Bannow Bay (the baronies of Forth and Bargy), was among the earliest in Ireland to be colonized by the Anglo-Normans with settlers from Britain. It was always strongly held by the relatively isolated colonists, as witness the numerous castles. Furthermore, the colonists intermarried only with their own kind. So this area was neither reconquered nor assimilated by resurgent Gaelic Ireland in the 14th and 15th centuries. Indeed, until quite modern times, the inhabitants retained their own distinctive dialect, the most ancient English speech in Ireland. Moreover, though they rejected the Reformation, they remained stubbornly loyal to the English Crown, their loyalty being at times strangely rewarded. At the Cromwellian confiscation much of the land in the baronies was granted to Ludlow's Horse, and Col. Ludlow himself, together with Captains Ivory, Nunn, and Claypole, all got handsome estates here. In 1798 the exasperated peasantry, though so largely of ancient English stock, took a conspicuous part in the insurrection.

3 m. NE. are the remains of Mayglass church, burned down in 1798. A tablet commemorates the unfortunate Beauchamp Bagenal Harvey of Bargy Castle (*below*), Protestant landlord and local leader of the United Irishmen and of the insurgent Catholic peasantry in 1798. After the collapse of the rising he fled to the Saltee Islands (*q.v.*), but was tracked down and brought to Wexford, where his head was mounted on the Sessions House and his body thrown into the river. His remains were afterwards buried at Mayglass.

4 m. ESE. is much modified Bargy Castle (still occupied). It was built by the Rosseters (*see* Rathmacknee *under* Wexford) in the 15th/16th cent. In general character it resembles the castles of Slade (*see* Fethard, Co. Wexford) and Rathmacknee. 1 m. E. is Butlerstown castle. – ½ m. S., in Tomhaggard, are remains of a small late-14th cent. church.

BROUGHSHANE, Co. Antrim (Map 3, C3), in the foothills of Slemish Mountain, is 4 m. E. of Ballymena, on the road to Carnlough (13½ m.).

Whitehall, 1 m. N., was the birthplace of Field Marshal Sir George White, V.C. (1835–1912), defender of Ladysmith in the Boer War. Sir George's son, Capt. Jack White, D.S.O., became a prominent Irish Republican.

2 m. NE., in Ballymena (Broughshane) townland, is an imposing motte-and-bailey.

3 m. ENE., in Magheramully, are the remains of Skerry Church and "St Patrick's Footmark". The church is popularly believed to occupy the site of the home of Miliuc, to whom, according to legend, St Patrick was sold as a boy slave; the E. end served as mausoleum of the Clannaboy O Neills from the 15th to the 18th cent. "St Patrick's Footmark" is a hollow in a stone, from which, says legend, the Angel Victor, after a visit to Patrick, ascended to heaven, leaving the mark of his toe on the stone.

8 m. ENE. is Ticloy Hill (*see under* Ballymena).

5 m. ESE. is Slemish Mountain (Sliabh Mis; 1,437 ft), where, says legend, the boy slave Patrick herded Miliuc's swine for six years.

BRUFF, Co. Limerick (Map 5, B4), is a village on the Limerick (15½ m.)–Killmallock (5 m.) road.

2½ m. NNE. is Lough Gur (*q.v.*).

3 m. E. (½ m. N. of the Hospital road) is Kilballyowen House, an 18th cent. O Grady residence.

3¾ m. E. is Knockainy (*see* Hospital).

1 m. S. is the ruined Kildare Fitzgerald, later Foxe, castle of Ballygrennan, a complete bawn with 16th cent. tower and remains of 17th cent. houses.

3 m. NW., over an area of some 500 acres in Caherguillamore deer park and neighbouring fields, are remains of a medieval settlement (fields, roads, house-sites). Excavation has dated two of the houses to the 14th–16th cent. They were essentially of the same type as the traditional peasant house which survived to our own day. More ancient remains in the area include remnants of a prehistoric chamber tomb as well as ringforts, etc.

BRUREE, Co. Limerick (Map 5, B4), is a village on the Ballingarry (9 m.)–Kilmallock (4 m.) road, which here crosses the Maigue by a good six-arch bridge. It is a well-known hunting centre. On the W. side of the river, in Ballynoe, are remains of Bruree Castle, Upper.

Petty kings of the Dál gCais had their seat hereabouts from the 7th to the 9th cent. (whence the name Brugh Ríogh, *brugh* of the kings). These were replaced by Eóghanacht kings of the Uí Fidgeinte line, one of whom, Donnabhán, figured in the treacherous slaying of Brian Boru's famous brother, Mahon, A.D. 976, and was himself slain by Brian two years later. In 1178 the Uí Fidgeinte were driven out of Co.

Limerick by Donal Mór O Brien. Their expulsion left a vacuum which the Anglo-Normans were only too ready to fill after Donal's death (1194).

¼ m. W., between the Castletown road and the river, in Lotteragh Upper, is a ringfort (with terraced central mound ?). To the NW., at the bend of the river, is a bivallate ringfort. 500 yds N. is the unusual Bruree Castle, Lower. Its ringfort-like lower bawn had three turrets; as well as the main tower, there is also a lofty gate-tower; a third tower was levelled early in the 19th cent.

½ m. W., in Ballynoe, is Eagle Mount (Mounteagle), alias Lios a' deocha, a "platform ringfort" with a low pillarstone on the steep, high mound.

4½ m. NE., in Rathcannon, are the ruins of a castle of the earls of Kildare, later of the Caseys: bawn with square tower to NW. and later house to the W.

BUNCLODY, Co. Wexford (Map 6, C5), long called Newtownbarry after James Barry, who came into possession of it in 1708, is a village on the Enniscorthy (12 m.)–Tullow (12 m.) road. It is charmingly situated.

"By the streams of Bunclody where all
    pleasures do meet"

i.e. where the little Clody joins the Slaney at the foot of the Blackstairs Mountains (Mt Leinster, 2,610 ft, Black Rock Mountain, 1,975 ft).

This is the best base for climbing Mount Leinster. A road climbs the valley of the Clody, between Black Rock Mountain and Kilbrannish Hill (1,336 ft), to Corrabut Gap (1,050 ft) on the saddle between Mt Leinster and Croaghaun (1,499 ft). From here a rough road leads S. to the Nine Stones and the Black Banks, whence the final ascent is straight and steep. The road over the Corrabut Gap goes on to Myshall, or to Muine Bheag, (*q.v.*), or to Borris, Co. Carlow (*q.v.*).

Bunclody was attacked in 1798 by a body of insurgents led by Father Kearns, in an unsuccessful effort to break out of Co. Wexford.

3 m. N. is Clonegall (*q.v.*).

1 m. S., in the graveyard at Kilmyshall, are remains of a church with a simple, Romanesque W. door.

BUNCRANA, Co. Donegal (Map 2, D2), is a small port and holiday resort on the E. shore of Lough Swilly, 14 m. NW. of Derry and 19 m. S. of Ballyliffin.

½ m. NW. is the 14th/15th cent. tower (rebuilt in 1605 by Hugh O Doherty; modified later in cent.) of a castle of the O Dohertys, lords of Inishowen. The castle was burned by the English on the occasion of Sir Cahir O Doherty's rebellion (1608), and thereafter was granted to Sir Arthur Chichester (*see* Belfast), who leased it to Henry Vaughan. The Vaughans lived in it till 1718, when Sir John Vaughan built the adjacent house of materials quarried

Commissioners of Public Works in Ireland

Stele with ribbon cross and figures, Fahan

from the castle bawn, etc. (Sir John was probably also the builder of the interesting six-arched bridge.) According to local tradition, it was to the castle that Wolfe Tone was brought when taken prisoner in 1798 (*see* Rathmullan).

1 m. N. on Crockacashel (Croc a' chaisil), Ballynarry, is a ruinous prehistoric chamber tomb.

1½ m. NW., in Ballynarry, is Porthaw holy well. ¼ m. N. is (Father) Hegarty's Rock, where a priest is said to have been slain in Penal times. Nearby is his "grave", a prehistoric chamber tomb (?).

4 m. NE. is Kinnagoe Giants Grave, a prehistoric chamber tomb. To the E. are Split Rock and a cairn.

3 m. E., on the S. slope of Druminderry, Meenkeeragh, are pillarstones; ¼ m. N. is another.

¾ m. SE., in Gransha, is a pair of pillarstones; two fields further S. is another pair. 1¼ m. S. is the Giant's Den, a ruined chamber tomb.

3¼ m. S., on Gollan Hill, Lisfannan, is the ruined stone fort, Caiseal na Bearnan; it stands on the edge of a precipice. On the NE. slope of the hill are the Friar's Grave (a small cairn) and a holy well; on the summit is a cairn.

4¼ m. S. is Fahan (Fahan Mura), a pretty little resort convenient to Lisfannan golf-links and having a regular ferry-service with Rathmullan (*q.v.*). Fahan Mura takes its name from St Mura, patron of the O Neills and first recorded abbot (early 7th cent.) of a Columban (?) monastery here. From the time of the early monastery there survive a cross-slab (built into the road wall near the entrance to the graveyard) and St Mura's Cross (Nat. Mon.), a magnificent work of early Irish (7th cent. ?) art. The latter is a flat stele 7 ft high, with an arm projecting slightly on either side. On the W. face is a superb cross, of broad interlaced ribbons, flanked by two standing figures of ecclesiastics on whose robes have been read traces of an inscription in Irish: BENDEXT AR ARDEBSCOB MARGAU ÚA RINDAGAIN ——SIR RIG TADGAIN ("A blessing on the high bishop, Margau úa Rindagáin ... king Tadgán" ?). On the E. face is a ribbon cross of different design with two birds above it. On the N. edge is inscribed a Greek rendering of the version of the *Gloria Patri* approved by the Council of Toledo in 633: "Glory *and honour* to the Father and the Son and the Holy Ghost." Other important relics and art treasures belonging to the monastery, and still surviving, are St Mura's enshrined bell (Wallace Collection, London) and St Mura's enshrined *bachall*, or staff (National Museum, Dublin). The monastery appears to have been reduced to the status of a parish church in the Middle Ages. There is a window (*St. Elizabeth of Hungary*) by Evie Hone (1948) in Fahan Protestant church. – 2½ m. S. is Inch, formerly a large island in Lough Swilly, now joined to the mainland as a result of drainage works. In Carnaghan, at the centre of the island, is the King's Grave, a large cairn enclosing a roofless portal dolmen and a large, secondary cist grave; a Food Vessel was found here. At the W. boundary of Carnaghan is another portal dolmen (the Ordnance Survey's "Standing Stones"). In Castlequarter, on the S. tip of the island, are the ruins of a strongly sited castle said to have been built about 1430 by Neachtan O Donnell for his father-in-law, O Doherty. In 1454 Rúairí O Donnell tried to burn alive in the castle his rival, Donal O Donnell. – 3 m. E. of Fahan church, in Crislaghmore, is a prehistoric chamber tomb. In adjoining Monreagh, alias Barr of Kilmackilvenny, is a cairn.

BUNDORAN, Co. Donegal (Map 2, B4), is a popular seaside and golfing resort on the Ballyshannon (4 m.)–Sligo (29 m.) road. It is a convenient centre for exploring the lovely region of lakes and mountains between Lower Lough Erne and Lough Gill.

There is a short strand here, and a deep rockpool (Roguey Pool) with diving boards.

1 m. N. is the fine 1½-m. Tullan Strand, backed by the sand dunes of Finner. On Finner Hill is Flaherty's Stone, a chambered cairn. Several chamber tombs were destroyed at the

laying out of Finner Camp. At the S. end of Tullan Strand are the Fairy Bridge, the Pigeon Hole, and the Wishing Chair, rock-formations curiously eroded by the sea.

In the cliffs to the W. of the town is the Lion's Paw Cave.

1 m. W., on the sea coast, are remains of Magheracar Giants Grave, a prehistoric chamber tomb; a few hundred yds SW. is a pillarstone.

1½ m. W. is the River Drowes, a good salmon and trout river. Near Bundrowes (Foot of the Drowes), in the refugee Franciscan community of Donegal (*q.v.*), the *Annals of the Four Masters* were compiled (1630–36).

5 m. W. is the River Duff, a good trout and salmon river.

6 m. W. is Bunbeg Strand (Co. Sligo).

2¼ m. S. is Kinlough, Co. Leitrim (*q.v.*).

BUNMAHON, Co. Waterford (Map 6, A7), is a fishing village, with a good small beach, 10 m. WSW. of Tramore and 5 m. E. of Stradbally. The cliffs nearby rise to 200 ft. There are many old copper mines in the area.

1 m. SW. is Illaunobric, alias Dane's Island, with a strongly sited promontory fort (very difficult of access).

2½ m. NNW. is Ballylaneen churchyard, burial place of Tadhg Gaelach Ó Súilleabháin (1715–95). His Latin epitaph was composed by his friend and fellow-poet, Donnchadh Rúa Mac Conmara.

BUNRATTY, Co. Clare (Map 5, B4), is noteworthy for the keep of a great O Brien castle (Nat. Mon.) commanding the crossing of the little Ratty River, alias Owenogarney, 8 m. NW. of Limerick and 6 m. SE. of Newmarket-on-Fergus. Following on the Anglo-Norman invasion of the O Brien kingdom of Limerick, alias Thomond, Robert de Muscegros built (about 1250) a castle here whose motte-and-bailey may be seen to the N. of the O Brien castle. In 1277 Sir Thomas de Clare, who had received a speculative grant of Thomond from John of England, built the first stone castle at the river-crossing, and a small town grew up about it. In 1285, 1296, 1298, and 1299 the castle was unsuccessfully attacked by the

Bunratty Castle

Plate 4. The Cliffs of Moher, Co. Clare

Irish. When, in 1318, Richard de Clare, son and heir of Sir Thomas de Clare, was routed and slain at Dysert O Dea, his widow fired the castle and town, and sailed away, never to return. The place was thereafter granted by Edward II of England to James Bellafago, but in 1325 and 1331 it was seized by adherents of the Earl of Desmond, and in 1332 the castle was captured and destroyed by Desmond's ally, King Muirchertach O Brien of Thomond. In 1353 a new castle was built by the English Justiciar, Sir Thomas de Rokeby. Two years later this castle was captured by Murchadh O Brien, and from that date until the 17th cent. Bunratty remained in Irish hands. The existing structure was erected about 1460 (by one of the Mac Namaras?). In the early part of the following cent. it is found in the possession of the O Briens, later Earls of Thomond, who remained its owners until 1712. In 1642, and again in 1645, Brian, 6th Earl of Thomond, handed the castle over to the Parliamentarians. In the latter year the English commander was Admiral William Penn, father of William Penn of Pennsylvania (*see* Shanagarry *under* Ballycotton). The castle was soon blockaded by a Catholic Confederate force under Lord Muskerry, who forced its surrender after some two months. All that remains are fragments of the curtain and the large, massive, rectangular keep of three storeys with four complex angle turrets, those on the N. and S. sides being linked by broad arches. The original entrance, in the N. face, leads into a vaulted hall, into the S. wall of which has been inserted a sheila-na-gig. Beneath the hall is a vaulted cellar, above it a once splendid upper hall with traces of elaborate 16th cent. stucco. In the SE. turret is a chapel with rich stucco ceiling. In its heyday the castle and its gardens were remarkable for their beauty, winning the praise of Rinuccini, the Papal Nuncio, in 1646: "In Italy there is nothing like the palace and grounds of the Lord Thomond, nothing like its ponds and park with its three thousand head of deer."

In 1954 the ruined keep was purchased by Viscount Gort and admirably restored (with subventions by Lord Gort and Bórd Fáilte) by the Office of Public Works. Only the reconstruction of the roofs and battlements is conjectural. It was, however, suggested by contemporary work elsewhere in Ireland. The castle, which houses Lord Gort's collection of medieval furniture, paintings, tapestries, and glass, is managed by the Shannon Airport Development Company. Hours of Admission: April to Sept., 10 a.m.–9.30 p.m.; Oct. to March, 10 a.m.–5.30 p.m.; admission 2/6 (children, 1/–). Nearby, the Shannon Airport Development Company is erecting a series of cottages of traditional type with traditional furnishings.

250 yds W. of the castle (behind Bunratty Castle Hotel) are the remains of a 16th cent. church; nearby, to the SW., is a fragment of a dovecot.

BUSHMILLS, Co. Antrim (Map 3, B2), is a small town on the Ballycastle (12 m.)–Portrush (6 m.) coast road, 12 m. N. of Ballymoney. Billy church has three one-light windows by Michael Healy (*Resurrection*, 1925; *Virgin Mary*, 1929; *Ecce Homo*, 1935).

2½ m. WNW., on the road to Portrush and near the little seaside resort of Portballintrae, is Dunluce Castle (Nat. Mon.), romantically situated on a high, sea-tunnelled rock and probably occupying the site of an earlier fort (*dún*). The early history of the castle is unknown, but its erection is usually ascribed to Richard de Burgo, or one of his followers, about 1300. In the early 16th cent. it was a Mac Quillan (=de Mandeville) fortress, but the Mac Quillans were ousted by Somhairle Buidhe Mac Donnell (*see* Antrim, Glens of). In 1565 Seaán the Proud O Neill forced the Mac Donnells to surrender it to him, but two years later Somhairle was back. In 1584 Lord-Deputy Perrott took it with the aid of artillery, but Somhairle quickly returned, and it continued to be occupied by his descendants, the Earls of Antrim. In 1639 part of the domestic quarters fell into the sea, carrying a number of servants with it. In 1641 the castle was unsuccessfully besieged by the insurgent Irish. In 1642 the Scottish Covenanter, General Munroe, arrested there the 2nd Earl of Antrim, whose guest he was. After the Eleven Years' War the Earls of Antrim ceased to reside in the castle, and it gradually fell into decay. – The extensive remains are of different periods. The Scottish-style gatehouse appears to be 16th/17th cent. The S. curtain, SE. tower and NE. tower are 13th/14th cent. In the upper court are the ruins of an early-17th cent. house. Between it and the S. curtain are remains of a 16th cent. loggia. In the yard between the house and the NE. tower is a rock-cut souterrain older than the castle. The buildings of the lower court were probably the quarters of the garrison. On the mainland are the remains of a large 17th cent. courtyard house ascribed to the Duchess of Buckingham, wife of the 2nd Earl of Antrim.

2½ m. N. is the Giant's Causeway (Nat. Trust), a remarkable geological phenomenon. Enormous quantities of basalt have cooled into thousands of polygonal (three- to nine-sided) columns. These present many curious and spectacular formations, to which fanciful, and often silly, names were given in the 19th cent.: The Giant's Chair, The Giant's Grandmother, The Giant's Organ, The Amphitheatre, The fan, The Mitre, and so forth. Since 1963 the Causeway (together with ten miles of cliff walks) has been open to the public. The nearby caves, especially those of Portcoon and Runkerry, are worth a visit by boat.

4½ m. NE. (about 2½ m. E. of the Causeway and 2 m. W. of Whitepark Bay), on a flat, steep-sided rock, are the scanty remains (Nat. Mon.) of Dunseverick (Dún Sobhairce, Sobhairce's Fort) Castle. St Patrick is said to have visited and blessed the dún and to have there consecrated St Olcán of Armoy (*q.v.*). In 870, and again in 934, the fort was stormed by the Vikings. The early history of the castle itself is obscure. In the 16th cent. it was held by a branch of the O Cahans (O Kanes), apparently under the Mac Quillans. It was captured by Seaán the Proud O Neill in 1565, but was recovered by the O Cahans. It was finally destroyed by Cromwellian forces, the last O Cahan of Dunseverick, Giolla Dubh, being executed in 1653 for his part in the national resistance. The remains seem to belong to a 16th cent. gatehouse.

BUTTEVANT, Co. Cork (Map 5, B5), is a small market town beside the Awbeg River, on the Cork–Limerick road 8 m. N. of Mallow and 8 m. S. of Charleville (Ráthluirc).

The town was founded by the Anglo-Norman (de) Barrys, who seized Mac Carthy territory hereabouts in the 12th/13th cent. Its English name has no connection with the Barry warcry, *Boutez-en-avant*, but is simply *botavant* (*botavaunt*), Norman-French name for a defensive outwork. Its Irish name is Cill na Mullach, the *mullach* of which, though not the name of the river, suggested the "gentle Mulla" of Edmund Spenser's *Colin Clouts Come Home Againe* (written in the Ballyhoura Mountains; *see* Kilcolman castle *under* Doneraile):

"Mulla, the daughter of old Mole so hight
The nymph which of that water course
    hath charge,
That springing out of Mole, doth run
    down right
To Buttevant, where spreading forth at large
It giveth name unto that cittie
Which Kilnemullah cleped is of old."

The head of the Barrys was created Viscount Buttevant in 1555, Earl of Barrymore in 1627 (*see* Carrigtohill). In 1691 the Williamites burned the town, and it has never wholly recovered. In 1831 it was purchased by Lord Doneraile.

The earliest recorded steeplechase took place at Buttevant in 1752, the course being from the church to the steeple of St Leger church (4½ m.).

The principal relic of medieval Buttevant is the ruined church (Nat. Mon.) of the Franciscan friary of St Thomas, founded in 1251 by David Óg Barry. It comprises choir, nave, and S. transept with a single E. chapel. A tower which stood at the junction of nave and choir fell in 1814. In the N. and S. walls of the nave are the recesses of two early Barry tombs; in the N. wall are pillars from the cloister arcade. Unusual features are the crypt and sub-crypt beneath the chancel. The ornamental details of the church, more elaborate than those of any other Franciscan house in Cork, indicate two well-defined periods; original 13th cent. work in sandstone, and 15th cent. work in limestone. The adjacent Catholic parish church is a Gothick structure (1831–7) by Charles Cotterel of Cork. The belfry incorporates Caisleán

Chaoimhín, alias Killeens Castle, part of a medieval tower attributed to the Earls of Desmond. At the S. end of the town are remains of one of the towers, etc., of Lombard's Castle, called after the Lombards who figure in the 16th cent. affairs of the town. On a riverside rock S. of the town are the tower and bawn of the medieval castle of the Barrys.

1 m. S. are the remnants of Ballybeg "Abbey" (Nat. Mon.), a priory of Augustinian Canons Regular, dedicated to St Thomas. It was founded in 1237 by Robert de Barry. Apart from the late, castle-like tower, the church is 13th cent. (the W. end late-13th). ESE. is the priory dovecot.

1 m. NE., in Lacaroo, is Cnocán na mBuach-aillí, a tumulus; not far away is Cnocán na gCailíní, a tumulus half demolished by 1824 roadmakers.

3½ m. NE. is Kilcolman castle (*see under* Doneraile).

4 m, SW. are remains of the ancient church of Kilmaclenine, called after St Colmán mac Lénéne of Cloyne(*q.v.*). To the NW., on a large, flat, limestone outcrop, is The Motte, remnant of the medieval castle of le Caryg, which belonged to the bishops of Cloyne. Nearby are the ruins of Kilmaclenine Castle, a 1640 embattled house of the Barrys. ESE. of the church is Acuthoge, a chambered cairn or tumulus. The chamber contained a skeleton accompanied by a bronze sword, beads, etc. 5½ m. SW. of the church is Lohort Castle (*see* Cecilstown *under* Kanturk).

7 m. WNW. is Liscarroll (*q.v.*).

CABINTEELY, Co. Dublin (Map 6, E7), is a suburban village on the Dublin (8 m.)–Bray (7 m.) road.

1¼ m. SSW. is Tully, alias Tullagh (Teallach na nEasbog), site of an early-6th (?) cent. foundation of one of the several SS Brigid (perhaps Brigid, daughter of Léinín, *see* Killiney). The remains (Nat. Mon.) comprise the ruined, Transitional chancel of a church whose earlier nave has almost disappeared, two stone crosses, and two early gravestones. The NW. cross, by the roadside, is a plain High Cross; it has been left insulated *in situ* by the lowering of the road level. The W. cross (in the field to the S.) was a fine, figured cross of the 13th (?) cent.; on the E. face is the figure of an ecclesiastic (bishop ? ; abbess ?), on the W. face a human mask; close by is a boulder socketed to serve as the base for another cross. One of the early gravestones (in the chancel) bears concentric circle and herring-bone patterns like some at Killegar (*see* Enniskerry), Rathmichael (*see* Loughlinstown), and Ballyman (*see* Bray); a trunnion, or rudimentary arm, projects from each side. The other, SW. of the ruin, has a ringed cross in high relief on a "herring-bone" background.

1 m. SW., in the grounds of Glendruid, is Brenanstown Dolmen (Nat. Mon.), a splendid portal dolmen with granite capstone.

CAHERDANIEL, Co. Kerry (Map 4, B5), is a hamlet near the N. side of the entrance to Kenmare Bay (Kenmare River), on the Kenmare (18½ m.)–Waterville (8¾ m.) road. It takes its name from a fine, small, stone ringfort ½ m. to the W., on the slope of Tullig, alias Cahernageeha, Mountain (1,640 ft). The road along the Kenmare River to Derreenaulif and beyond affords delightful views.

2 m. ENE., on the slope of Coad Mountain (1,093 ft), are the ruins of Kilcrohane (St Criomthann's Church), which gives its name to the parish; to the NW. is Toberavila holy well, called after a holy tree which stood nearby. ½ m. NNW., at Carrigcrohane, are St Crohane's Hermitage and Tobercrohane; nearby are old copper mines; to the NE. is Windy Gap (1,263 ft), which affords a fine, if stiff, walk to lovely Loughs Isknagahiny and Currane (see under Waterville).

3¾ m. E. are the ruins of Castle Cove (Nat. Mon.). The nearby cove has small, beautifully sited beaches. 2½ m. NE. is Póna na Stéige, alias Staigue Fort (Nat. Mon.), a fine, univallate, stone ringfort with an elaborate system of stairways leading to the terraces of its 13-ft-thick rampart (in which are two small chambers).

1½ m. SW. is Darrynane Abbey (Nat. Mon.), ancestral home (see Carhan House, under Cahersiveen) of Daniel O Connell (1775–1847). Victim of decay and of recent ill-advised restorations, it houses many interesting – if hideously Victorian – relics of the Great Liberator. On the seashore is an ogham stone. Offshore, in Darrynane Bay, is Abbey Island which may be reached on foot at low tide. There are remains of a monastery – the real Darrynane Abbey – founded by St Fíonán Cam, but which became a dependency of Dairinis (see under Youghal) in the Middle Ages. 5 m. SW. is Scariff Island, with remains of a small church.

3½ m. W. the road to Waterville climbs Coumakista Pass (683 ft), which affords fine views of the Kenmare River and Ballinskelligs Bay. In Coumatloukane, near the summit of the Pass, is the Bóirdín (Boardeen), a ruined chamber tomb; the capstone is said to bear Bronze Age scribings. Below the pass, to the NW., is Loher (see under Waterville).

CAHER ISLAND, Co. Mayo, alias **CATHAIR PHÁDRAIG**, alias **CATHAIR NA NAOMH** (Map 1, B4), lies 5 m. SW. of Roonah Quay (see under Louisburgh).

In a hollow to the W. of the landing place at Portatemple are remains of a small, early eremitical monastery. Fragments remain of a cashel, or enclosing wall of dry-built masonry. At the E. side of the enclosure, in front of a chamber in the cashel, are the ruins of Temple-patrick, a diminutive oratory of dry masonry renovated in the 14th/15th cent. E. of the oratory is Labapatrick, a grave covered by an early carved slab and having a carved head-stone. In and about the E. end of the enclosure are thirteen leachtaí, square platforms or heaps of stones, which served as pilgrims' "stations". Twelve are marked, each by a stone slab, plain or carved; but the principal leacht, to the E. of the oratory, has two carved slabs and one plain slab. A fourteenth leacht stands on the opposite side of the gully leading down to Portatemple. All in all, there are fourteen early cross-slabs and pillars in and about the enclosure. 200 yds to the SE. are Caherpatrick, a small enclosure, and Bohernaneeve, an ancient track. ½ m. NW. of the oratory is Tobermurry, St Mary's holy well.

CAHERSIVEEN, Co. Kerry (Map 4, B4), is a small market town beside the Valencia River, at the foot of Bentee (1,245 ft). It is 10 m. N. of Waterville and 7 m. SW. of Glenbeigh.

1 m. ENE., on the Killorglin road, are the ruins of Carhan House, birthplace of Daniel O Connell, the Liberator (see Darrynane Abbey under Caherdaniel).

2 m. SW. is the ferry to Valencia Island (q.v.). ¾ m. N. is the ancient anchoritic site, Killobarnaun, alias Killavarnaun, with remains of a small, Gallarus-type (see under Ballyferriter) oratory. 1¾ m. W. are the ruins of the 15th cent., Mac Carthy Mór castle of Ballycarbery; it has some interesting carvings. ¾ m. N. of the castle, in Kimego West, is Cahergal (Nat. Mon.), a Staigue-type (see under Caherdaniel) ringfort with ruined clochán and rectangular house. ¼ m. NW. of Cahergal is the stone ringfort, Leacanabuaile (Nat. Mon.), which has remains of four dry-stone huts, and two chambers in the terraced rampart. Excavation has dated it to the 9th–10th cent. 300 yds N. of Leacanabuaile is Cathair na gCat, a large, stone ringfort.

3¾ m. NE., in Killurly West, is Glaise Chúmhra, a holy well dedicated to St Fursa. This is the starting point of an ancient pilgrims' path to the summit of Knocknadobar (2,267 ft), a former Lughnasa station which offers magnificent views. There are five standing stones on the S. slope of the mountain.

7 m. NE., on a commanding site with splendid prospects, in Caherlehillan, are remains of a univallate stone ringfort which gives its name to the townland. In a small ancient graveyard by the roadside to the S. are two early cross-pillars, one with the outline of a bird incised above the cross, etc. ¼ m. W. of the fort (700 yds by road) is Leac na Scríbhneoir-eachta, another scribed stone; bonfires used to be lit on it. Some 350 yds NE. of the fort is a ruined, wedge-shaped gallery grave; 300 yds further NE. is a second, 700 yds NE. of the latter, on Beenmore, in Gortnagulla, is a boulder with Bronze Age scribings and a small triple cross.

4 m. ENE., in Ballynahow Beg, is a stone with Bronze Age scribings.

2 m. S., alt. 400 ft on Bentee, in Letter, is Ceallúrach, a small, ancient, ringfort-type

House ruins, Leacanabuaile fort, Kimego West, Cahersiveen

anchoritic site with an ogham stone in the rampart. 1½ m. ESE. are the remnants of Killoe, another anchoritic site. About 1 m. E. of Killoe, to the N. of the road, in Canburrin, is a pillarstone; further up the slope of Bentee is a prehistoric chamber tomb; in a roadside field is an ogham stone. Some 600 yds S. of the road, in Killogrone, is the ancient anchoritic site which gives the townland its name: a sub-rectangular enclosure with remains of clocháns and small rectangular structures; near the centre is a cross-inscribed ogham stone (upside down).

6¼ m. S. (via Aghnagar bridge, 3 m. S. of Letter ceallúrach, *above*), in Aghatubrid, is the ancient anchoritic site, Kilpeacan: a sub-rectangular enclosure with remains of rectangular structures and a tall, cross-inscribed, ogham stone; 50 yds S., beside a spring, is a clochán. 1½ m. E., to the S. of the road, in Cloghane-carhan, are the remains of Keeldaragh, an ancient, ringfort-type, anchoritic settlement with remains of buildings, souterrains, and a cross-slab; in the E. entrance is an ogham stone.

10 m. WSW. is Portmagee, a small resort; there is a ferry to Valencia Island. The coastal scenery to the E. and W. is very good. To the NW. is Illaunloughan, an islet with remains of an ancient anchoritic settlement: tiny oratory, clochán, souterrain, shrine-shaped tomb.—4½ m. E. is Killoluaig (*see under* Ballinskelligs).

CAHIR, Co. Tipperary (Map 5, D5), is a small market town charmingly situated at the E. foot of the Galty Mountains, where the main Dublin (126 m.)–Cork (50 m.) and Limerick (40 m.)–Waterford (43 m.) roads cross the Suir, 11 m. S. of Cashel and 17 m. NE. of Mitchelstown. The town is a convenient centre for exploring the beautiful Glen of Aherlow (*see also* Tipperary *and* Galbally) and for climb-

ing the Galtys (*see* Mitchelstown *and* Ballyporeen). The Suir valley affords delightful walks and tours, upriver to Golden (*see* Cashel) and downriver to Ardfinnan (*q.v.*) and Clonmel. Adjoining the town on the SW. is the beautiful demesne of Cahir Park (open to the public); a noteworthy feature is the charming *cottage orné*.

On a rock-island in the Suir is an impressive 15th–16th cent. Butler castle, the largest castle of its period in Ireland. Though somewhat incorrectly restored (1840), it gives a good idea of the greater feudal castles of Ireland. The towered curtain encloses two wards or courts, a great hall, and a massive square keep. In Elizabeth I's reign the castle was "the bulwark for Munster, and a safe retreat for all the agents of Spain and Rome". Elizabeth's Lord Lieutenant, Robert Devereux, Earl of Essex, attacked it in May 1599. His artillery was too much for the garrison, which fled after a siege of two or three days. In 1647 the castle surrendered after an even briefer defence to Murrough "the Burner" O Brien, Parliamentarian Lord President of Munster. In 1650 it surrendered to Cromwell without firing a shot. The Butlers of Caher descended from Séamus Gallda, son of James, 3rd Earl of Ormond (d. 1405), by his niece and mistress, Katherine, daughter of Gearóid *Iarla*, 3rd Earl of Desmond. Like other junior branches of their house (*see* Pottlerath *under* Callan), they inclined towards the Gaelic way of life, and a fragment of an Irish poembook compiled 1566–76 for Theobald, 3rd Baron Cahir, still survives (R.I.A. MS. 23 F 1). Unlike the Earls of Ormond, they contrived to remain Catholics, and at the same time to retain, or recover, their titles and estates. The family became extinct in the male line in 1858.

In Church Rd, at the E. side of the town, are some remains of the medieval parish church; it served as a Protestant church until 1820. The Gothick Protestant church, at the N. end of the town, was built 1817–20 to the designs of the celebrated Regency architect, John Nash.

½ m. N., on the W. side of the Suir, are the neglected, but interesting, choir and tower of Cahir "Abbey", a priory of Canons Regular of St Augustine which was founded about 1220 by Geoffrey de Camville. ¾ m. NW. is Tobar Íosa, a holy well which still retains its ancient repute; there is an early cross-slab here.

3½ m. N., on the E. side of the Suir, in Knockgraffon, a very fine motte-and-bailey marks the site of a castle erected in 1192 – probably by Philip of Worcester – during the progress of an Anglo-Norman "drive" against Donal Mór O Brien's kingdom of Limerick. (The O Sullivans, ancient Eóghanacht stock of the district, were expelled and forced to carve out a new lordship for themselves in the mountainous coastlands of SW. Munster; see Bantry, Castletown Bearhaven, Glengarriff, et al.) To the N. of the motte are remains of a medieval nave-and-chancel church, further N. the ruins of a 16th cent. Butler castle. The church is said to have been that in which Seathrún Céitinn (see Tubbrid, below) delivered the sermon which infuriated the English Lord President of Munster.

3½ m. NNE. are the ruins of Outeragh church and castle. Seathrún Céitinn was parish priest of Outeragh in 1610.

4½ m. E., in Derrynagrath, are the ruins of an early-13th cent. church (with Transitional chancel arch). 2½ m. W. is Loughlohery (below).

2¼ m. SE. are the remains of Loughlohery castle; NW. are the ruins of a diminutive church or oratory. 1½ m. SW. of the castle are the remains of Ballymacadam church (used as a barn).

1 m. S., in Grangemore, is St Patrick's Stone, a roadside boulder with "the imprint of the saint's knees".

5 m. SSW., at Tubbrid, are the ruins of a mortuary chapel, burial place of the vicar, Father Eóghan Ó Dubhthaigh (1550), and of Seathrún Céitinn (Geoffrey Keating; about 1570–1650), who erected it in 1644. Ó Dubhthaigh was the author of a metrical satire on the notorious Miler Mac Grath (see Cashel). Keating, poet, historian, and religious writer, is celebrated as the master of classical Modern Irish prose (Foras feasa ar Éirinn, Trí biorghaoithe an bháis, Eochair-sgiath an Aifrinn). He was born in Burgess, 1 m. W. of Tubbrid. In middle life he was parish priest of Outeragh (above), and later of Tullaghorton (see Castle Grace under Clogheen). A sermon against vice in high places enraged the Earl of Thomond, and the priest-scholar had to seek safety in flight. Among his places of refuge was Rehill Castle (belonging to the Butlers of Cahir), and it was probably there that he died (1650 ?). A short distance NNW. of the mortuary chapel is St Kieran's Well. – 2¼ m. ENE. are the ruins of Ballydrinan church. – 2¼ m. S. is Castle

Grace (see under Clogheen). – 2¾ m. NW., in an ancient, circular enclosure, are the ruins of White Church.

8½ m. SW. is Burncourt (see Ballyporeen).

4 m. NW., in the ancient churchyard of Killardry, is part of a fine, medieval, tomb-effigy.

4½ m. WNW. (1 m. SW. of Killardry), at the foot of the Galty Mountains in Toureen, is the ancient monastic site of Peakaun, named after the celebrated anchorite Béagán (Beccanus). The remains (Nat. Mons.) include a small church with a simple W. door and Romanesque E. and S. windows (insertions), four stone crosses, some thirty early gravestones (mostly fragmentary), a holy well, and two bullauns. The great E. cross (shaft only in situ) was composite in character (of the same crutched form as St Patrick's Cross, Cashel), and formed part of an elaborate construction; it bears a long inscription in Irish and rudimentary incised ornament. The best-preserved gravestones are inscribed CUMMENE–LADCEN, SOADBAR, DOMNIC, SOERLECH, FLAND, DONGUS.

10 m. WNW. (5½ m. W. of Peakaun), in Ardane, is St Berrahert's Kyle (see Galbally).

CALEDON, Co. Tyrone (Map 3, A5), formerly Kennard, is a village on the Armagh (8 m.)–Aughnacloy (7 m.) road. The village was laid out in the English manner in 1816 by Lord Caledon, who also changed its name.

1¼ m. SSW. is Caledon House, seat of the Earl of Caledon whose younger brother, Field Marshal Earl Alexander of Tunis, was born here in 1891. The house is a splendid Georgian and Regency mansion. The main building was erected in 1779, to the designs of Thomas Cooley; the wings, colonnades, and circular drawing-room in 1812, to the designs of John Nash; the upper storey is an addition of 1835. The dining-room, drawing-room, and boudoir, are fine apartments with noteworthy marble and stucco embellishments. The house occupies the site of the castle of Sir Felim O Neill, last Gaelic lord of the district and leader of the Ulster Rising in 1641. The column with a statue of the 2nd Earl of Caledon (1777–1839) is by Thomas Kirk (1777–1845). – ¼ m. NE., at Lady Jane's Well, are the head and shaft of a High Cross (Nat. Mon.) brought thither in 1872 from Glenarb, 3 m. to the north. Glenarb (Cluain Oirb), site of an early monastery, had seven stone crosses. Two of them are now in Tynan Abbey demesne (see under Middletown, Co. Armagh).

CALLAN, Co. Kilkenny (Map 6, A5), is a market town where the Kilkenny (10 m.)–Clonmel (22 m.) road crosses the little Owenree, alias King's River.

At the Anglo-Norman invasion William the Marshal (see New Ross) established a manor at Callan and founded the town (1217). In 1391 the manor was sold to James Butler, 3rd Earl of Ormond. On 14 Sept. 1407, Lord Deputy le Scrope and James Butler, 4th, or "White", Earl of Ormond, routed Walter de Burgo and Tadhg O Carroll of Éile (Ely) at Callan. O Carroll, who was Butler's brother-in-law, was a noted patron of poetry and music; he and 800 of his followers fell in the battle. In 1650 the town was attacked by Col. Reynolds with the larger part of Cromwell's army. Captain Mark Mac Geoghegan heroically defended one of the town gates to the last man, but the Ormondist governor of the strong castle (*see* West Court, *below*), Sir Robert Talbot, surrendered without firing a shot.

Amhlaoibh (Humphrey) Ó Súiliobháin (about 1780–1837), Kerry-born schoolmaster, diarist, and collector of Irish MSS., lived in Callan.

In the town are the ruins of the 15th cent. parish church and of the "Abbey", a friary of Augustinian Observants. The former, dedicated to the Assumption of the Blessed Virgin Mary, is a very interesting, aisled, nave-and-chancel edifice with square W. tower (13th cent. ?; upper part 17th ?). The chancel has been adapted for use as the Protestant parish church, but the nave and aisles (Nat. Mon.) have long been roofless. In the chancel are preserved a large medieval font and fragments of several 16th cent. tombs. In the nave are fragments of 15th–17th cent. monuments, including that of John Tobin (1541) by Rory O Tunney.

The friary was founded about 1462 by Émonn mac Risderd Butler of Pottlerath (*below*) and was colonized from Connacht. The buildings were erected (1467–70) by Émonn's son, James (father of Sir Piaras Rúa Butler, Earl of Ossory and Ormond). In 1462 the friary was affiliated to Santa Maria del Popolo, Rome. The conventual buildings have long since disappeared, but substantial remains of the church survive. In the chancel are fine sedilia.

In Main St is a Peter Grant statue of Edmund Ignatius Rice (*see* West Court, *below*).

In West St are remains of Skerry's Castle, which some claim to be the gatehouse heroically defended by Mark Mac Geoghegan in 1650.

NW. of the town, in West Court demesne, are the great motte (Nat. Mon.) – a modified hillock – and traces of the bailey of William the Marshal's castle of Callan. Some remains of the later Butler castle may be seen at West Court, a Georgian mansion built about 1793, for Lord Callan. In West Court North is the farmhouse in which was born Edmund Ignatius Rice (1762–1844), founder of the Irish Christian Brothers.

4 m. E. is Newtown (*see under* Kells).

3 m. SE., in Ballytobin, are the ruins of a medieval parish church (Nativity of the Blessed Virgin Mary).

3 m. S., in Coolaghmore, are remains of Coolagh medieval parish church; the site of the nave was re-used as a Catholic church, 1818–96. In the churchyard are two medieval gravestones.

2½ m. SW., in Kilbride churchyard, is the grave of Amhlaoibh Ó Súiliobháin's parents, brothers, and three young children. The Irish epitaph was composed by Amhlaoibh. 3 m. S. is Garryrickin House, built about 1818 by the 18th Earl of Ormond, in place of one erected about 1660 by Walter Butler of Kilcash. Walter was a protector of the Catholic bishop of Ossory, Dr James Phelan (1669–95), who repeatedly held ordinations at Garryrickin. Walter's son, Christopher, was Catholic archbishop of Cashel, 1711–57; his grandson, Walter of Garryrickin (1703–83), succeeded to both the Kilcash and the Ormond estates in 1766; his great-grandson John (1740–95), conformed to the State church in 1764, and in 1791 recovered the title of (17th) Earl of Ormond, which the Irish House of Lords held not to have been extinguished by the attainder of the 2nd Duke in 1715. In Butlerswood, the adjacent townland to the S., is the small roadside tumulus called Leacht na Méar. – 2½ m. SW. of Garryrickin House is Killamery, where St Gobán Fionn (alias Mo-Ghobóg) founded a monastery in the 6th cent. The only relics of the monastery are a fine 8th cent. High Cross (Nat. Mon.), an early

Killamery High Cross, Callan (east face)

gravestone, Tobar Naoimh Niocláis (St Nicholas's Well), and a bullaun (250 yds S. of the graveyard). The cross is believed to stand early in the celebrated series of Irish figured crosses. Most of the carving consists of interlaces, frets, and other abstract ornament. The weathered figure subjects include: N. arm: *Jacob wrestles with the Angel; Temptation of St Anthony; SS Paul and Anthony in the Desert;* W. face: *Hunting scene; Procession with chariot; Crucifixion.* The W. side of the base is said to bear the inscription: OR[ÕIT] DO MAEL-SECHNAILL ("A prayer for Mael-Sechnaill"). Nearby to the S. is the early gravestone. It has the (repeated) inscription: OR[ÕIT] AR ANMAINN AEDAIN – OR[ÕIT] AR AN-MIN AEDAEN ("A prayer for the soul of Aedán"). 250 yds S. of the graveyard is a bullaun.

6 m. SW. is Killenaule, home of Charles Joseph Kickham (1828–92), Young Irelander, Fenian, and novelist (*Knocknagow*, etc). His epitaph, in the local graveyard, is by the celebrated Fenian, John O Leary.

3 m. NNW. is Killaloe. It takes its name from an early monastery founded by one of the saints Mo-Lúa, alias Do-Lúa (probably the Do-Lúa Lebdeic who figures in the *Life* of St Cainneach of Clonbroney and Aghaboe. The site is thought to be marked by surface traces, etc., at Ardawns, alias Páirc Philib). Nearby, E. of the road, is Tobermolua, Mo-Lúa's Well.

6 m. NNW. is Kilmanagh, site of an early monastery founded by St Nadál, master of St Seanán of Inis Chathaigh (*see under* Kilrush). The only relic here is Tobar Nadán, St Nadán's (Nadál's) Well. A medieval wooden figure of St Nadán, preserved at Kilmanagh till about 1875, is now in St Kieran's College, Kilkenny. – 1 m. SW. is Pottlerath (Ráth an Photaire, potter's ringfort). Near Pottlerath House was the castle of Émonn mac Risderd Butler (d. 1464), grandson of James, 3rd Earl of Ormond, and grandfather of Sir Piers Rúa Butler, Earl of Ossory and Ormond. Émonn was a noted patron of Irish literature, and in his castle Seán Buidhe O Clery wrote (about 1454) the celebrated Bodleian MS. Laud Misc. 610 (*Saltair Émuinn mhic Risderd*). Religious poems by Émonn's father (Risderd Butler of Polestown), including the lovely *Is áille Ísa iná 'n chruinne* composed on the day of the poet's death, are also in the manuscript. *Leabhar na Carraige* (*see* Carrick-on-Suir), now in the British Museum, seems also to have been written for Émonn. The two MSS. were given to the Earl of Desmond as ransom for Émonn after the battle of Piltown (*q.v.*), 1462. Near the site of Émonn's castle are the ruins of Teampall na Rátha, a small nave-and-chancel church with good E. window. – 4 m. NNW. of Kilmanagh is Tullaroan (*see under* Freshford).

CAMPILE, Co. Wexford (Map 6, B6), is a village on the New Ross (8 m.)–Ramsgrange (3 m.) road E. of the River Barrow.

2 m. NNE. is Ballykeerog castle built by the Suttons, followers of Hervey de Montmorency (*below*). The remains comprise keep and bawn with flankers.

2 m. E. are the ruins of the de Montmorency castle of Killesk. Some 3 m. further E. are the defaced remains (Nat. Mon.) of the 13th–14th cent., hall-type, Prendergast castle of Rathumney.

4 m. SSW. are the twin fishing villages of Arthurstown and Ballyhack, on the E. shore of Waterford Harbour. Adjoining Arthurstown on the SE. is Dunbrody Park, seat of Lord Templemore. At Ballyhack there is a ferryboat service to Passage East on the opposite side of the estuary. Ballyhack castle originated as a preceptory of the Knights Templar, subject to the preceptory at Kilcloghan (*see under* Fethard, Co. Wexford). It was wrecked by Cromwell in 1649. The chapel recalls that at Ferns (*q.v.*).

1 m. WSW. is Dunbrody Abbey (Nat. Mon.), the finest medieval ruin in Co. Wexford. The abbey was built about 1210 onwards by the English Cistercians of St Mary's Abbey, Dublin, at that time a dependency of Buildwas (Shropshire) to which Hervey de Montmorency (*see* Great Island, *below*) – Strongbow's uncle and seneschal – had granted lands here about 1178. (The abbot of Buildwas, influenced, perhaps, by reports of "the waste of the place, the sterility of the lands, and the wildness and ferocity of the local barbarians", had transferred the property to St Mary's Abbey in 1182.) From a clause in de Montmorency's charter, granting asylum to malefactors who should take refuge there, the abbey became known as the Abbey of St Mary of Refuge, though its formal dedication was to SS Peter and Paul. The remains comprise cruciform church with five-bay aisled nave, six transept chapels, and low central tower; also a cloister garth with some remains of the sacristy, six-bay groin-vaulted chapter-house, and undercroft of the dormitory, etc., on the E. side, and of the refectory on the S. side. The work is, in the main, early 13th cent., but the tower is a 15th cent. insertion; the living-rooms over the S. transept chapels are additions of about the same period. The architectural details, in the austere Cistercian tradition, are good, but the foundations of the church and the construction in general are poor. (In places the walls were bonded merely with tough clay.) And so the church had to be buttressed at an early stage of its history.

3 m. WNW., at the N. end of Great Island (formerly Hervey's Island, after Hervey de Montmorency, who had the *caput* of his barony on the island), which is no longer insulated, are the remains of the large circular earthwork of Kilmokea. Surviving only in isolated sectors, they consist of two banks of earth and stones with intervening ditch. The enclosure is some 1,000 ft in diameter from N. to S., and 900 ft from E. to W. It is bisected by the road to Ballinlaw ferry. In the SW. quadrant are the graveyard and site of the ancient church of Kil-

Dunbrody Abbey, Campile, from the north-east

mokea; in the NW. are traces of a square earthwork. There is a bullaun in the W. ditch to the S. of the ferry road. On the N. periphery are remains of a circular annexe with internal structures. There is a second bullaun at the lowest part of the ditch here. The whole possibly represents a fortified Anglo-Norman village. of the 13th–14th cent., something otherwise unknown among Irish monuments. It is said to have been held by insurgents in 1798 against troops advancing from the E. To the E. is a large rectangular earthwork (254 ft); this is probably the site of a medieval manor-house. Towards the S. end of the island are the remains of two castles.

3 m. NNW., to the S. of Whitechurch, are three pillarstones, perhaps the remnant of a stone circle.

5 m. NNW., near Killowen House, is a ringfort with internal sub-enclosures: bullaun.

CAPPOQUIN, Co. Waterford (Map 5, D5), is a small market town on the Dungarvan (11 m.)–Lismore (4 m.) road. It is set in beautifully timbered country where the Glenshelan River joins the Blackwater at the foot of the Knockmealdown Mountains, and is a convenient base for touring the lovely Blackwater valley, as well as – by minor roads – the Knockmealdowns. Fishing and boating may be had on the Blackwater.

In the graveyard at the Catholic church is buried the poet Patrick Denn.

3 m. N. is Boola bridge. The road leading N., up Glenafallia to Newcastle, Co. Tipperary, passes Mount Melleray Cistercian abbey, founded in 1832 in what was then a barren wilderness by Irish monks expelled from France in 1822. The new abbey church (built of the stones of George ·Richard Pain's "castle" for Lord Kingston at Mitchelstown) is a disappointing essay in the Gothic manner. The abbey guest-house dispenses hospitality gratis, but offerings from the guests never come amiss. At the abbey are five ogham stones from the ancient cemetery of Kilgrovan. – At the head of Glenafallia the Newcastle road crosses the Knockmealdowns between Knocknafallia (2,189 ft) and Knocknanask (1,500 ft). The road leading NW. from Boola bridge joins the spectacular Lismore–Clogheen road 1 m. SSE. of The Gap (*see* Clogheen).

3 m. NNE., close to the summit of Cluttahina Hill (625 ft) is a ringfort with an interesting souterrain.

8 m. NE., by the Clonmel road, in the old churchyard 1 m. S. of Ballynamult village, are fragments of an ancient stone cross with fret and interlace patterns.

8 m. ENE., via Millstreet, are the ruins of Sleady Castle, a fortified house built in 1628 by Pilib an tSíoda MacGrath.

2½ m. SSE. is Affane, scene of a celebrated battle, 1 Feb. 1565, between the Earls of Ormond and Desmond. Affane House occupies the site of Affane Castle, birthplace of Valentine Greatraks (1629–83), "The Stroaker", who cured scrofula and other diseases by stroking with his hands and by hypnotism and faith-healing; Charles II of England was numbered among his patients.

5½ m. S. is Dromana House (*see* Aglish).

5 m. SSW., to the W. of the Blackwater, are the ruins of Okyle church (14th/15th cent.). The river scenery hereabouts (Blackwater and Bride) is very lovely. 2 m. S. are the remains of Strancally castle, a Desmond stronghold destroyed by Ormond in 1579; a trap from the dungeon opens on to the Blackwater. The house called Strancally Castle was designed by George Richard Pain (*see* Cork).

CARLINGFORD, Co. Louth (Map 3, C6), is a small resort and seaport charmingly situated on the Newry (12 m.)–Greenore (3 m.) road, at the foot of Slieve Foye (splendid views) which rises 1,935 ft above the S. shore of Carlingford Lough. The lough, a beautiful estuary (noted for its oysters) between the Mourne Mountains and the Cooley peninsula, acquired its modern name (its ancient name was Snámh Aighnech) from the Vikings who resorted there. In 926 Muirchertach of the Skin Cloaks, King of Cenél nEógain, defeated a Viking force there and beheaded 200 of the pirates.

In the Middle Ages an English town grew up here under the shadow of the castle, first built in the 12th cent. by Hugh de Lacy. King John stayed at the castle for three days on his way to attack de Lacy at Carrickfergus. Later on the place came to be an important border fortress of the English Pale. In 1596 a force of Hugh O Neill's made an unsuccessful attempt to surprise the castle. In 1642 part of the town was burnt by the insurgent Ulstermen. That same year the town was seized for the English Parliament by Sir Henry Tichborne. In 1649 it was retaken by Inchiquin (belatedly turned Royalist), only to be lost to Parliamentarian Sir Charles Coote the following year. In 1689 the place was fired by Berwick's retreating Jacobites; Schomberg subsequently used it as a hospital station.

The only considerable fortification surviving today is the shattered King John's Castle (Nat. Mon.), strikingly sited on a rock commanding the landing-place. The D-shaped plan is unusual, while the gateway (on the W. side) is noteworthy as having been designed to admit only a single horseman at a time. Only the W. wall, SW. tower, and the remains of the gatehouse belong to the earliest phase (late 12th or early 13th cent.). The E. part, originally three storeys high with the courtyard doorway on the first floor, dates from 1262.

The Mint (Nat. Mon.), situated just off the Square, is a fortified town house of the 15th/16th cent. It is said to occupy the site of a mint erected in 1467. It has curious window-carvings ("revived" pre-Norman motifs, etc.).

Taafe's Castle, opposite the railway station, is a fortified 16th cent. town house. The Taafes were a leading family of the Pale (*see* Smarmore Castle *under* Ardee).

The Tholsel, originally one of the town gates, is so called because it served for a time as the meeting place of the Sovereign and twelve Burgesses of Carlingford. In the 18th cent. it also served as the town gaol.

The tower of the Protestant church was originally one of the towers of the town wall, other portions of which also survive.

Radharc an tSléibhe, in Dundalk St, behind the Protestant church, was the birthplace of Thomas D'Arcy Magee (1825–88), poet and Canadian statesman.

The Rectory and Ghan House are interesting Georgian houses.

To the S. of the Protestant church are the ruins of a Dominican friary founded in 1305 by Richard de Burgo (?) and rebuilt in the 16th cent. They comprise the nave, choir, and tower, of the church, and some traces of the conventual buildings.

3 m. SE. is Greenore, a beautifully situated small seaside resort and decayed port. There is a 3-m. (shingle) beach. Boating and sea fishing can be had here.

¾ m. S., in Roosky, is the "Priory", where considerable traces of a medieval monastery can be recognized; the church was pre-Romanesque. ¾ m. SW., alt. 550 ft, in Carlingford townland (South Commons), is a double-court cairn; in neighbouring Irish Grange are a much disturbed cairn (with megalithic chambers) and a ruinous segmented chamber tomb.

4 m. S., near the coast, is Ballug castle, a 15th cent. stronghold of the Bagnalls. 1 m. SE., in Templetown, are the remains of Kilwirra (Cill Mhuire, St Mary's Church), a small, simple structure with plain Romanesque S. door and window. – 5½ m. W., at Rockmarshall House, is a court cairn.

5 m. N., in Cooley, is Omeath, a small resort near the head of beautiful Carlingford Lough. There is a ferry to Warrenpoint (*q.v.*). The Omeath district was the last area in Leinster where Irish survived as a living language. (The Cooley peninsula preserves the name of the Cúailnge of early Irish literature and history.) Good views of the lough and the Mourne Mountains may be had from Flagstaff Cairn and the Long Woman's Grave on the road from Carlingford.

CARLOW, Co. Carlow (Map 6, B4), pleasantly sited on the E. bank of the Barrow, 12 m. S. of Athy and 9 m. N. of Bagenalstown, is capital of its county, cathedral town of the Catholic diocese of Kildare and Leighlin, an important road and marketing centre, and a manufacturing town of some consequence (sugar, footwear, milling, malting).

Its strategic position made Carlow an important Anglo-Norman and English stronghold in the Middle Ages. About 1180 Hugh de Lacy built a (motte-and-bailey ?) castle to command the river crossing. This first castle was succeeded by a strong stone fortress (*below*), built (probably by William the Marshal) between

1207 and 1213 at the confluence of the Burren
and Barrow. William was Strongbow's successor in the Lordship of Leinster (see New
Ross). After him Carlow passed, through his
daughter, Maud, to Roger le Bigod, Earl of
Norfolk. Subsequently the castle fell to the
Crown and was granted to the Howards who
held it until the reign of Henry VIII, though
after 1327 much of the modern County Carlow
was recovered by the Irish of Leinster. The town
was walled in 1361 by Lionel, Duke of Clarence, son of Edward III and his Lieutenant in
Ireland. In 1405 it was captured and burned
by the great Art Óg Mac Murrough Kavanagh,
King of Leinster; in 1577 by Rory Óg O More
of Laois. In the Eleven Years' War it was
taken and held by the Confederate Catholics, but
in 1650 was surrendered to Ireton. In 1798 the
Insurgents made a determined assault on the
town, but were thrown back with heavy loss.
Four hundred and seventeen of their dead were
buried in quicklime at the Graiguecullen gravel
pits W. of the river, where a monument marks
their graves.

The once great castle is now represented by
only a fragment (Nat. Mon.) of the keep, or innermost citadel. This was of that peculiarly Norman-
Irish type represented also at Enniscorthy (q.v.),
Ferns (q.v.), Lea, Co. Offaly (see under Portarlington) and Quin, Co. Clare (q.v.), viz. a rectangle with drum towers at the angles.

The Court House (1830) is a typical Classical
building by Sir Richard Morrison (1767–1849).

Commissioners of Public Works in Ireland
Romanesque doorway at Killeshin, Carlow

The Cathedral of the Assumption of the
Blessed Virgin Mary (1828–33) is a Gothick
essay by Thomas A. Cobden, who took over
from Joseph Lynch in 1829. It contains a fine
monument (1839) by John Hogan to Bishop
James Doyle (1786–1834) who, as J.K.L.
(James, Kildare and Leighlin), was a prominent
champion of Catholic emancipation.

The Protestant parish church (St Mary's) is
partly 18th cent., partly early-19th cent. Gothick.

2 m. NE. is Oak Park, a good early-19th cent.
house with Ionic portico; now an agricultural
research centre.

3½ m. NE. is Ballaghmoon (Bealach Mugh-
na), Co. Kildare, where, in 908, Cormac mac
Cuilenáin, celebrated bishop-king of Munster
(see Cashel), who had invaded the Uí Néill–
Leinster borderlands (see Monasterevin) at the
head of the forces of Munster and Ossory, was
routed and slain by the armies of the King of
Tara (Flann Sinna), Leinster, and Connacht.
According to a local tradition, Cormac's corpse
was borne in a wagon drawn by seven unguided
oxen to the ancient burial place at Killeen
Cormac (see Colbinstown, under Dunlavin),
where it was interred and a little church erected.
A rival tale says Cormac was buried at Castledermot.

1½ m. ENE. is Pollerton House, a Georgian
mansion built by the Burton family. 4 m. ENE.
is Burton Hall, another 18th cent. Burton
mansion, this time of brick.

2 m. E., in Kernanstown (Ballykernan), in
the demesne of Browne's Hill House, is the
Mount Browne Dolmen, a very fine portal
dolmen whose capstone, the largest in Ireland,
weighs over 100 tons; nearby were two smaller
tombs. Browne's Hill House was built about
1763 to the design of Peters.

4 m. S., near Ballybannon, is a motte.

1 m. SW., by the road to the W. of the
Barrow, is a fine ringfort. 2 m. further SW.,
serving as a gateway, is the Butler castle of
Cloghrenan, which Sir Peter Carew claimed
under his fabricated title to Idrone (see Leighlinbridge), so driving Sir Edmund Butler into
fruitless rebellion, 1588. The Royalist forces
mustered here before the Battle of Rathmines
(Baggotrath) in 1649. At the end of the 17th
cent. the castle passed to the Rochforts. 1 m.
SW. are the remains of ancient St Brigid's
Church.

3 m. WNW., at the foot of Slieve Margy, is
Killeshin (Gleann Uisean), Co. Laois. St
Comghán founded a monastery here before the
close of the 5th cent. Among those associated
with the monastery were St Aodhán (d. 843)
and St Díarmait, alias Mo-Dímmóc, who was
abbot until 847. It was a lector of this monastery, Dubhlitir Úa hÚathgaile, who made the
Irish adaptation of the treatise De sex aetatibus
mundi. The church was destroyed in 1041, the
monastery burned in 1077. The monastery

disappears from history after 1082. The lofty Round Tower was wantonly demolished in 1703, and all that now survive are the W. gable and fragments of the N. and S. nave walls of a Romanesque church together with fragments of a 15th cent. chancel (Nat. Mons.). The richly carved Romanesque W. doorway (four orders) is particularly fine; there are traces of a mutilated inscription on the jambs and imposts. Above is a simple, Romanesque window. In the N. wall one Romanesque window survives. Inside the ruin is the basin of a font of about the same mid-12th cent. date. In a field to the S. is a fine motte-and-bailey.

1 m. NNW., near the W. bank of the Barrow, are the remains of Sleaty (Sléibhte) church (partly 12th cent.) and two plain early crosses (Nat. Mons.). The earliest church here is said to have been founded by Bishop Fíacc Finn, disciple of the famous *file*, Dubthach moccu Lugáir, and a convert of St Patrick's. From Sleaty appears to have come the 8th cent. poem, *Génair Pátraicc* (Fiacc's Hymn), a metrical biography of St Patrick. Muirchú's celebrated 7th cent. *Life of St Patrick*, the basis of all subsequent Patrician biography, was written "at the dictation" of Bishop Áed of Sleaty (d. 700).

CARNA, Co. Galway (Map 1, B6), is a small village and quiet holiday and fishing resort on Ard Bay, Connemara, 36 m. W. of Galway and 22 m. SE. of Clifden.

1½ m. E. is Lough Skannive. One of the islands is a well-walled crannóg.

6 m. E. is Kilkieran, which takes its name from a church (scant remains) dedicated to St Ciarán of Clonmacnois. Ciarán's day (9 Sept.) is celebrated at the holy well.

3 m. SSW., on Mweenish Island (road bridge), is Tobar na Seacht nInghean, Well of the Seven Daughters (of a king of Leinster; *see* Rinvyle, Bunowen *under* Ballyconneely, *and* Inisheer *under* Aran Islands).

3½ m. WSW. is An Más (Mace), convenient starting point for the crossing (1½ m.) to Crúanacára (Cruach Mhac Dhara), alias St Mac Dara's Island, one of the most venerated holy places of the West. (Local boats dip their sails three times when passing it.) Pilgrimages take place here on 16 July (regatta afterwards) and 25 Sept. St (Síonnach) Mac Dara founded an eremitical monastery here. The remains (Nat. Mons.) comprise the ruins of a small, stone-roofed church of unusual interest (timber, elbow-cruck construction translated into stone), its carved gable-finial, the saint's *leaba*, a holy well, and three pilgrimage "stations" with early crosses, cross-slabs, etc.

2 m. NW. is Crúanacaola, Croaghnakeela, with remains of a church and a well dedicated to St Keelan.

3 m. NW., by the seashore, are the ruins of St Mac Dara's parish church, Moyrus (defaced Transitional features). 1 m. N. is Tobar Síonnach, a holy well; pilgrimage, 16 July.

CARNDONAGH, Co. Donegal (Map 2, D1), is a market and manufacturing village on the Derry (20 m.)–Malin (3 m.) road.

The Catholic parish church (1945) is an Italianate-Romanesque structure by Ralph Byrne (*see* Mullingar *and* Cavan). The statues and such details as columna and capitals are good, but the Stations of the Cross are bad.

½ m. W. is Donagh (Domhnach Glinne Tochair, alias Domhnach Mór Maighe Tochair), site of an early bishopric, possibly Patrician. (At any rate, St Patrick is the patron.) The church was presumably monastic in the age of primitive Irish monasticism, but it later became a parish church of the diocese of Derry. From the early period there survive four remarkable monuments: St Patrick's Cross with its two flanking stelae (Nat. Mon.), by the roadside opposite the Protestant church, and a tall cross-pillar in the graveyard. Some would date St Patrick's Cross to the 7th cent., and regard it therefore as one of the most important monuments of early Christian art in the British Isles. At the top of the E. face is a cross of two broad, interlaced ribbons, with birds beneath the arms; in the middle is a grotesque *Crucifixion*; at the foot are the figures of three ecclesiastics. The W. face is covered by an interlacing of broad ribbons. The S. side bears the outlines of three figures, one above the other; the N. side has traces of an interlaced pattern. The stelae have human figures, spirals, etc., carved in the same shallow manner. The graveyard cross-pillar has on the E. face a *Crucifixion* above an interlaced cross which stands on a fret-pattern base; on the W. face a "marigold" cross, with fret-pattern shaft flanked by two ecclesiastics, stands above "an incircled star or cross of four rays on a fretwork base". The Protestant church has some medieval frag-

St Patrick's Cross (west face), Donagh

ments; 150 yds S. is Labbypatrick, a prehistoric chamber tomb.

½ m. SSW., at the ancient church site of Kilbride, Ballyloskey, is a pillar stone with incised, grotesque, human figure.

3 m. NE., near Gortnacool, Drumaville, is a cairn; 400 yds N. is Cuill Carn, a chamber tomb. 2 m. SE. is Carrowmore (below).

3½ m. E., in Carrowmore, two stone crosses and a rock with a bullaun and an incised cross mark an ancient church site; the W. face of the East Cross has traces of an incised figure. 1 m. NE. is Clonca (see under Culdaff). – 2 m. NW. is Cuill Carn (above).

2 m. S., in Glentogher, is Cashel chamber tomb. 3 m. further S., in Carrowmore, is another.

4½ m. SW., on the W. side of Glentogher, rises Slieve Snaght (2,019 ft). On the summit is Tobar na Súl, blessed, it is said, by St Patrick; there was formerly a Lughnasa assembly here on Heatherberry Sunday.

2½ m. NW., at Collin, Carndoagh, is a rock-cut souterrain of three chambers. ¾ m. W., in Straths, is a chamber tomb; 1 m. S., in Glenmakee, is another.

CARNEW, Co. Wicklow (Map 6, C5), is a village on the Gorey (9 m.)–Tullow (13½ m.) road. The 17th cent. O Toole castle, modernized and incorporated in the Rectory, was a British garrison post in 1798. It was captured by the Insurgents, who fired the village. Thirty-six of them were afterwards executed at the castle, where there is now a monument to them.

CARNLOUGH, Co. Antrim (Map 3, C3), is an Antrim Coast Road resort and fishing village on a sandy bay at the foot of Glencloy, between Glenarm (3 m.) and Cushendall (11 m.). There are pretty falls on the little Glencloy River.

George Shiels (1884–1949), author of *The New Gossoon* and other popular Abbey Theatre plays, lived at Carnlough.

CARRAN, Co. Clare (Map 1, D7), is 10 m. S. of Corcomroe Abbey and 11 m. N. of Corrofin, near the edge of a large *polje* in the limestone, The surrounding country is rich in megalithic, early historic, and medieval remains. To the W. lie some of the finest of the Burren karsts. The road E. to Glencolumbkille (3 m.) affords fine views of the Burren hills.

1 m. NE., in Termon, are the ruins of Templecronan (Nat. Mon.), a small 12th cent. church: trabeate W. door ornamented with Romanesque animal masks; angle mouldings; carved heads in the W., N., and S. walls; in the N. wall a Late Gothic door. SE. of the church is St Cronan's Bed (Nat. Mon.), a gabled, stone tomb recalling St Manchán's Shrine in Boher church, Clara; NE. of the church (in the next field) is a second tomb. Two fields S. of the church are St Cronan's Well and a pilgrims' "station". Nearby is Eye Well.

1 m. S., is Castletown. 1½ m. due E., in Cappaghkennedy, is Cromlech, a well-preserved gallery grave; 400 yds NE. is a hill-top cairn. 1 m. SSW. of Castletown, on a roadside rock-pinnacle in Tullycommon, is Cashlaungarr (Nat. Mon.), a stone ringfort. ½ m. ENE. is Cahercommaun, a trivallate cliff-fort of A.D. c. 800 (Nat. Mon.). The outer enclosures may have been for livestock. Traces of twelve stone huts, including a guard-house and sentry post, survive. A souterrain in the largest hut led to an escape down the cliff face. The fort was excavated by Harvard archaeologists in 1934. – 400 yds SSW. of Cashlaungarr, and ¼ m. N. of Creevagh crossroads, is Dermot and Grania's Bed, a wedge-shaped gallery grave. 4 m. ESE. of Creevagh crossroads, in Gortlecka, is Cromlech, a wedge-shaped gallery grave.

3 m. SW., is Fanygalvan (see under Ballyvaghan).

4½ m. W. is St Cronan's Church, Poulacarran (see under Ballyvaghan).

CARRICK, Co. Donegal (Map 2, A3), is a small village on the Killybegs (11 m.)–Glencolumbkille (6 m.) road, near where the Owenwee and Glen rivers meet at the foot of Slieve League (below). It is a good angling centre, as well as a base for exploring a beautiful part of Donegal.

2 m. S., on the W. shore of the estuary, is the little village of Teelin, a convenient place for obtaining boats for sea fishing or for exploring the majestic coast between Slieve League and Slievetooey (see under Ardara).

Teelin is also a convenient place from which to climb Slieve League (1,972 ft). The spectacular route is via Carrigan Head and Lough O Mulligan to the head of Bunglass cliffs (1,024 ft). At Amharc Mór (The Great View), on the Bunglass cliffs, the climber is rewarded with a prospect of the stupendous cliffs of Slieve League rising nearly 2,000 ft from the Atlantic. From Amharc Mór the somewhat precarious One Man's Pass leads on to easier ground, and so to the summit. (Climbers ascending by this route are advised to take a guide. An easier ascent, omitting Amharc Mór and One Man's Pass, is via Lergadaghtan Mountain.) The summit itself affords one of the most remarkable panoramas in Europe. Nearby the remains of St Aodh mac Bric's Oratory and holy wells mark the site of a hermitage associated with SS Assicus (see Racoon under Ballintra) and Aodh mac Bric (see Rahugh under Tullamore, Killare under Ballymore, Co. Westmeath, and Rathlin O Birne under Glencolumbkille).

1½ m. SW. of Teelin, in Croaghlin, is Dermot and Grania's Bed, a chamber tomb; 400 yds SW. is Uaghneenderg, another chamber tomb.

CARRICKFERGUS, Co. Antrim (Map 3, D4), is a small Belfast Lough port, resort, and market town on the Belfast (11 m.)–Larne (14 m.) coast road. Its name, Carraig Fhearghus, is thought by some to commemorate the

The Castle, Carrickfergus   *D. W. Gardner*

death by drowning of Fergus, son of Erc, the Dál Ríada (North Antrim) kinglet who brought the Irish settlements in Scotland under his rule and from whom the Royal House of Scotland claimed descent. The name properly applies to the peninsular rock on which stands the remarkable castle.

When William de Burgh, "Brown" Earl of Ulster, was killed (1333) near Carrickfergus by rival kinsfolk, the Norman Earldom of Ulster soon collapsed, leaving Carrickfergus an isolated stronghold of the English Crown. The Irish never had sufficient intelligence to destroy the place utterly, although the Clannaboy O Neills had been quick to seize the opportunity of swarming across the Bann from Co. Derry, so that by the 16th cent. they were masters of all S. Antrim (save Carrickfergus) and much of Co. Down.

Carrickfergus Castle (Nat. Mon.) is believed to have been begun by either John de Courcy or his supplanter as Earl of Ulster, Hugh de Lacy, between 1180 and 1205. In 1210 it was taken from de Lacy by King John after a nine-day siege. In 1315–16 it held out for over a year against Edward Bruce. In 1384 it was destroyed by Niall Mór O Neill of Tír Eoghain, "King of Ulster". In 1597 the Governor was ambushed and beheaded by James, son of Somhairle Buidhe, Mac Donnell (*see under* Antrim, Glens of). In 1690 the castle was taken from the Jacobites by Schomberg, and on 14 June in that year William of Orange landed beneath its walls at the spot now marked by a commemorative stone. In 1760 the French naval commander Thurot (whose grandfather was an O Farrell), took the castle and town after a gallant defence. On 24 April 1778, the first action in European waters by an American ship took place offshore, when Paul Jones (a Scotsman by birth), in the *Ranger*, defeated the British *Drake*. In the 18th cent. the castle served as both a county and a state prison. Among those confined there in 1796 were the United

Irishmen, Luke Teeling and William Orr. The castle comprises three late-12th to mid-13th cent. wards. The entrance is between massive, D-shaped (originally circular) towers reduced in height at a Tudor-period adaptation for artillery. In the outer ward are Tudor gun platforms, that on the left having storerooms beneath. The curtain between outer and middle wards survives only in fragmentary form. At the S. end of the middle ward is a water gate. The curtain of the inner ward (entrance modern) marks the limits of the first stone castle, the nucleus of the fortress; the lower part dates from the 1180's. In the NW. corner of this ward is the great, four-storey, Norman keep, with its entrance (as normally) at first-floor level (cf. Maynooth castle *and* King John's Castle, Athenry). The ground floor has two barrel-vaulted chambers (cf. Rindoon castle *under* Lecarrow), one with a well shaft. On the second floor is the Great Hall (restored); the arch is 16th cent. The original Great Hall seemingly stood against the E. curtain of the inner ward. Open to the public: 1 April to 30 Sept.: Mon. to Sat., 10 a.m.–1 p.m., 2 p.m.–6 p.m.; Sun., 2 p.m.–6 p.m.; 1 Oct. to 31 March: Mon. to Sat., 10 a.m.–1 p.m., 2 p.m.–4 p.m.; Sun., 2 p.m.–4 p.m. Admission 6d. (children 3d.). *Son et lumière* (July to Oct.) commenced 1963.

The Town Hall, High Street, retains the charming, 1779 façade of the County Court House where Luke Teeling and William Orr were "tried" for administering the oath of the United Irishmen, 1797. Behind it is part of an ogee-capped turret of the gatehouse of Joymount, Sir Arthur Chichester's 17th cent., Tudor house on the site of the medieval Franciscan friary.

St Nicholas's Church was commenced in 1185. It owes its aisleless, cruciform shape to a rebuilding for Protestant use in 1614, but had previously had both N. and S. aisles, the latter double. In the truncated nave are to be seen fragments of the original arcades. The N. transept (Donegall Chapel) was rebuilt in 1614 by Sir Arthur Chichester, the ground floor as a mausoleum, the upper storey as a family pew (Jacobean woodwork); at the N. end is an elaborate Renaissance memorial with effigies of Sir Arthur (d. 1625), his wife, infant son (d. 1597), and brother, Sir John Chichester (d.1597); the *St John the Beloved* window (1929) is by Ethel Rhind, the *St Andrew* window (1929) by Catherine O Brien. The chancel is 14th/15th cent. The three-light *Good Shepherd, Good Samaritan, Prodigal Son* window is by Lady Glenavy (1912); the three-light *SS Columba, Patrick, Aidan* is by Ethel Rhind (1912). The tower dates from 1778.

Much of the 17th cent. town wall survives, including the North (or Spittal) Gate (Larne road) and N. corner bastion. There is no trace of St Mary's Abbey (Premonstratensian) founded by John de Courcy and his wife, Affrica, daughter of the King of Man.

Andrew Jackson (1767–1845), 7th President of the United States of America, came from a Carrickfergus family.

3 m. NE., in Ballyhill (Bellahill), is Dalway's Bawn (Nat. Mon.), probably built in 1609 by John Dallowaye. Though the original dwelling house has disappeared, this is the best preserved of Ulster's Plantation "bawn and flanker towers". The rectangular bawn has circular towers at three angles. The ring over the gate-way is said to have served as a gallows. 1½m. NNE. is Ballycarry (*see* Whitehead).

2 m. ENE. is Kilroot, where Dean Swift held his first living (1694–6). There was an early monastery here (Cill Rúaidh) founded by St Colmán, disciple of Ailbhe of Emly (*see under* Tipperary).

2 m. W., on Knockagh (917 ft), is the County Antrim 1914–18 War Memorial.

2 m. NW., in Duncrue, are the largest of the Carrickfergus salt mines (mining ceased in 1938).

CARRICKMACROSS, Co. Monaghan (Map 3, B6), is a market town on the Ardee (12 m.)–Monaghan (26 m.) road, famous for the hand-made lace industry established in 1820. In Elizabethan times the Earl of Essex built a castle here, on the site of the present Convent of St Louis. The steepled Protestant church dates from 1779.

The Catholic church has ten two-light windows by Harry Clarke (1925): *Blessed Oliver Plunkett; St Rita; St Laurence O Toole; St Dabhac* (sic); *Death of Our Lady; Entombment of Christ; St Kieran; Death of St Joseph; Death of St Patrick; St Damhnat.*

2 m. SW. of the town are Lough Fea demesne and House. (Admission by applying to the Agent, Main St.)

3½ m. N., in Donaghmoyne, is Mannan Castle (Nat. Mon.), a great, hill-top motte-and-bailey constructed, *c.* 1193, by Peter Pipard, brother and heir of Gilbert Pipard (*see*

Ardee). In 1244 Sir Ralph Pipard encased it with stone.

7 m. NE. is Inishkeen (*see under* Louth).

8 m. NW., in Lisnadarragh, is roadside Cromlech, a prehistoric chamber tomb.

CARRICKMORE, alias **TERMON ROCK,** Co. Tyrone (Map 2, E3), is a village on the Pomeroy (7 m.)–Omagh (11 m.) road. Remnants of the medieval parish church may be seen in the graveyard beside the Catholic church. ½ m. SW. is Relicknaman, Relig na mBan, The Women's Cemetery (Nat. Mon.). It is said that women sinners were sometimes buried here, and that no woman would enter the place. St Columcille's Well and Grave, the latter seemingly a natural rock-hollow, suggest that it is the site of an early monastery.

2½ m. N., in Mullanmore, alt. 500 ft, is Carnanbane, a round cairn. Nearby are traces of a stone circle. 1¼ m. NW., and ⅔ m. E. of Loughmacrory House alt. 300 ft in Mullanmore, is Labby Dermot (Nat. Mon.), a gallery grave. – ½ m. NW. of Loughmacrory House, alt. 700 ft, is Loughmacrory court cairn (Nat. Mon.). – ¼ m. N. is Dermot and Grania's Bed (Nat. Mon.). – About ½ m. W. (300 yds S. of Lough Fingrean) is Loughmacrory Giants Grave, a low, chambered cairn. 150 yds E. of Lough Fingrean is Loughmacrory Carnanbane, seemingly a court cairn. ½ m. E. of Lough Fingrean is Loughmacrory stone circle. – ½ m. W. of Loughmacrory House and ¼ m. ENE. of Lough Dorpin, in Altdrumman, is Cloghogle (Nat. Mon.), a portal dolmen with enormous capstone.

3 m. E. is Tremoge (*see under* Pomeroy).

1½ m. SE., 300 yds E. of Termon House in Athenry, is Druids Altar, a collapsed chamber tomb.

2 m. NW., in Clare, alt. 500 ft, are The White Stones (Nat. Mon.), a court cairn.

2 m. NNW., midway between Crockdun and Legnashammer, is Aghnagreggan chamber tomb (Nat. Mon.), seemingly a court cairn.

CARRICK-ON-SHANNON, Co. Leitrim (Map 2, B6), the small county town of Co. Leitrim, is situated by the River Shannon, on the Longford (23 m.)–Drumshanbo (9 m.) road. The town was incorporated by James I and acquired a reputation for its strong Protestant-ism. It is a good coarse-angling centre.

There is a good 18th cent. court-house, and a good Protestant church built in 1827.

2 m. SE. is the village of Jamestown, called after James I. In the Middle Ages there was a Franciscan friary here. In 1650 the Catholic hierarchy met in the friary to try and devise means of saving the Catholic cause from the victorious Cromwellians. Sir Charles Coote I founded the town in 1622 to command the Shannon crossing. In 1645 it was captured by a royalist force under Lord Carlingford; in 1689 by the Enniskillen Williamites (subsequently driven off to Sligo by Sarsfield). Of the 17th

cent. town fortifications only one gateway survives.

The road from Jamestown to Drumsna passes close to The Dún (*see under* Drumsna).

3 m. NW., at Tumna (Co. Roscommon), on the S. bank of the Boyle, are the remains of Tumna Church; nearby is St Eidin's Grave, a prehistoric chamber tomb.

CARRICK-ON-SUIR, Co. Tipperary (Map 6, A6), formerly Carrickmacgriffin, is a beautifully sited market town on the Suir, 15 m. NW. of Waterford, 24 m. NE. of Dungarvan, 13 m. E. of Clonmel, and 16 m. S. of Callan. The town is a convenient centre for exploring the beautiful Suir valley, as well as Slievenamon (*see under* Fethard) and the Comeragh Mountains (Fauscoum, 2,597 ft; Coumshingaun, a lake-filled corrie high up on the mountain is well known to rock-climbers) some 8 m. SW.

Although the manor of Carrickmacgriffin belonged to the Anglo-Norman le Brets in the 13th cent., the town was really the creation of the Butlers, Earls of Carrick and Ormond, who acquired the property in the 14th cent. By the river, at the E. end of Castle St, are the unusually interesting remains of the latest castle (Nat. Mon.). The first Butler castle here was erected in 1309, on the site, we are told, of a Poor Clares convent; but the oldest part of the existing buildings – two towers, etc., on the S. side – was built by Émonn mac Risderd Butler (*see* Pottlerath *under* Callan), a famous warrior and a noted patron of Irish letters. (*Leabhar na Carraige*, alias the *Book of the O Mulconrys*, now British Museum Add. MS. 30512, was written for him in this castle *c*. 1450 by William Mac an Legha; *see* Pottlerath *under* Callan; *also* Piltown; *and* Hoare Abbey, Cashel.) It has been claimed that Anne Boleyn, mother of Elizabeth I of England, was born in the castle;

she was a grand-daughter of Thomas, 7th Earl of Ormond (d. 1555). To Émonn mac Risderd's castle the 10th Earl of Ormond (Black Tom, d. 1614) added the good Elizabethan manor house which forms the N. side of the castle court; the Long Gallery, recently repaired and partly restored, is the sole surviving Irish example of its period. A splendid view towards the S. may be had from the castle parapet.

The parish church of St Nicholas of Myra, William St, is a Romanesque essay (1880) by George C. Ashlin, a pupil of Pugin's.

On the S. side of the river is the suburb of Carrickbeg (Abbeyside). St Molleran's parish church (1827) incorporates the tower and part of the N. wall of the church of St Michael's Franciscan friary, founded 1336/47 by James, 1st Earl of Ormond; John Clyn, the annalist, was the first Guardian; in 1447 the friary was re-founded by Émonn mac Risderd. When the parishioners were constructing the present edifice Catholic Emancipation had not yet been won, and the Protestant rector threatened to seize the building. On the advice of O Connell his threats were ignored.

3½ m. N. is Newtown (Newtown Lennan, Newtown Lingawn). All Saints' parish church (1885) is another Romanesque essay by Ashlin. Not far from Scogh bridge are remains (Nat. Mon.) of a medieval church which incorporates 12th cent. fragments; the carvings include a rude sandstone figure (a bust). – 1 m. N., in Ahenny, is the ancient monastic site, Kilclispeen (St Crispin's Church). The remains here include two splendid 8th (?) cent. High Crosses (Nat. Mons.) and the base of a third. The crosses are decorated with carved bosses, interlaces, spirals, frets, and other abstract motifs. The bases have figured panels. The panels of the S. cross are very weathered; they include figurations of horsemen and of Daniel

Manor house and castle, Carrick-on-Suir

Commissioners of Public Works in Ireland
North Cross, Kilclispeen, Carrick-on-Suir (east face of base)

in the Lions' Den. Those on the N. Cross are in better condition. The subjects include: W. face: seven ecclesiastics; N. face: two monks on horseback followed by two others in a two-horse chariot; E. face: miscellaneous animals and a palm tree under which stands a human figure; S. face: procession of monks with a horse carrying a headless corpse. The missing cross, "the most beautiful of the three", is said to have been stolen (*c.* 1800) and lost in a shipwreck off Passage East. – 1¼ m. NE. of New-town, at the foot of Knockandrowla in Castle-town, is the ancient monastic site, Kilkieran. The remains (Nat. Mons.) include three stone crosses – two of them High Crosses of Kilclis-peen type – and fragments of at least one other carved cross. The W. Cross is covered on all faces with interlaces, frets, spirals, etc. On the E. face of the base is a procession of horsemen. The E. Cross is not decorated. In 1858 these two crosses, then prostrate and broken, were

"restored in an admirable manner by a blind mechanic". The tall, slender, N. Cross bears some faint traces of superficial ornament. The derelict Osborne mausoleum stands on or near the site of the ancient church. A portion of a 9th (?) cent. carved cross which served as lintel of the doorway has recently been cement-ed to a jamb fragment to form a pillar. E. of the churchyard are Tobar Chill Chiaráin and a bullaun. – Knockandrowla, alias Baunfree Hill, alias Kilmacoliver Hill (814 ft), commands far-flung prospects. NW. of the summit, in the Church Field, is Lawe's Churchyard, formerly Ráth Chiaráin. Here, in a small, circular en-closure are remains of a chambered cairn. – 3 m. S. of Kilkieran is Whitechurch (*see under* Pil-town). – 2½ m. NW. of Newtown, in Rath-clarish, is a great univallate ringfort.

1½ m. NE., at Tinvane House, is a fragment of a stone cross from Kilcreggane, Co. Water-ford; it bears the Leonard arms.

Commissioners of Public Works in Ireland
North Cross, Kilclispeen, Carrick-on-Suir (west face of base)

Commissioners of Public Works in Ireland
South Cross, Kilclispeen, Carrick-on-Suir
(*east face*)

3½ m. NE. is Castletown House (*see* White-church *under* Piltown).

2¼ m. E. is Tibberaghny (*see under* Piltown).

2¼ m. SE., in Rath, Co. Waterford, is a pre-historic chamber tomb. 1¾ m. S., in Ballyquin, the ancient church-site of Kilquan; some 150 yds N. are two chamber tombs, one a portal dolmen.

3½ m. SE. are the fragmentary remains of Mothel "Abbey" (Nat. Mon.), a priory of Canons Regular of St Augustine which suc-ceeded an early monastery founded by St Broccán (Brogan). In a farmyard S. of the "Abbey" is Cloch na Coimirce (Stone of Pro-tection), an early cross-pillar. 3 m. SE., in Whitestown East, is a prehistoric chamber tomb. – 1½ m. SSW., in Clonea, are the ruins of a small nave-and-chancel church with plain Romanesque chancel arch and S. window and an inserted S. door. The Gothic Revival church (860) is by J. J. McCarthy, "the Irish Pugin"; the bronze crucifix over the high altar is said to have been dug up near the ruins of Rathgor-muck church (*below*).

5 m. SW., in Rathgormuck, are the remnants of a medieval church with small, castle-like tower; to the N. are the remains of Rathgor-muck castle. At Millvale is a small chamber tomb.

6½ m. NW., on the slope of Slievenamon, is Kilcash. The remains of a small church with battered, Romanesque S. doorway mark the site of an ancient monastic foundation which had associations with St Colmán úa hEirc. In the Middle Ages the church passed into the possession of the Knights Hospitaller. In the churchyard is the tomb of Archbishop Chris-topher Butler (1673–1757; *see* Garryrickin House *under* Callan); at the time of the 1848 Rising the mitre and other leaden ornaments were stolen to make bullets. A rudely carved font from the church may be seen at the mod-ern Catholic church. To the E. of the ancient church are the ruins of Kilcash castle, where Lord Castlehaven, noted Confederate Catholic commander in the 1641–52 war, wrote his *Memoirs*. The haunting, early-18th cent. song, *Cill Chais* (English rendering by "Frank O'Con-nor"), mourns the death of Margaret Butler, Viscountess Iveagh ("Lady Veagh"). Her first husband, the attainted Jacobite, Brian Maginnis (Mac Guinness), having died in the Austrian service, she married Colonel Thomas Butler of Kilcash Castle, a nominal Protestant who connived at her sheltering of Catholic bishops and priests. She was buried in Archbishop Butler's tomb in the nearby churchyard. 5½ m. SW. is Kilsheelan (*see* Clonmel).

CARRIGAHOLT, Co. Clare (Map 4, C2), is a seaside village at the mouth of the Shannon, 8¼ m. SSW. of Kilkee. In 1588 seven Armada ships found refuge from storm for four days off Carrigaholt.

SE., by the pier, are the turreted bawn and tower (Nat. Mon.) of a Mac Mahon castle taken after a four-day siege in 1599 by the renegade 4th Earl of Thomond, who hanged the defenders (in breach of the surrender terms) and gave the place to his brother Donal. The latter's grandson, another Donal, was the cele-brated 3rd Viscount Clare who raised Clare's Dragoons and two regiments of infantry for James II. When the Williamites confiscated Lord Clare's 57,000-acre estate, the castle and part of the estate passed (via the Earl of Albe-marle) into the hands of the Burtons, who retained it until the present century. The 6th Viscount Clare (d. 1761), who refused to turn Protestant for the sake of his ancestral lands and titles, became a Marshal of France and fought against England at Dettingen (1743), Fontenoy (1745), and Rocroy (1746). With the death (1764) of his son, Charles, 7th Viscount Clare and titular Earl of Thomond, the senior line of the ancient royal stock of Thomond was extinguished.

The Atlantic and Shannon Estuary shores be-tween Carrigaholt and Loop Head (10 m.; *below*) offer some beautiful cliff scenery.

3 m. NE. are the ruins of Kilcrony, a small oratory; nearby is Tobercrony, a holy well.

3½ m. ENE. is Doonaha, birthplace of the noted scholar, Eoghan Ó Comhraidhe (Eugene O Curry, 1796–1862).

1½ m. S., in Kilcredaun, are remains of two small churches. The larger, Kilcredaun proper, has a decorated Romanesque E. window and remnants of a plain Romanesque W. door. The smaller, ruder, church, Teampall an Áird, is on a ridge to the S.: beautiful view across the mouth of the Shannon estuary; to the E. are Tobercredaun and a 19th cent. coastal battery.

3 m. W. is Cross. ½ m. W. are the ruins of Killballyowen parish church. – 1½ m. NW. is Doondoillroe, a promontory fort. – 5 m. W., via Kilbaha, is Moneen church. In a side chapel is preserved the "(Little) Ark", relic of the worst days of landlordism. The only place where the local tyrant was powerless in law to prevent the celebration of Mass was on the foreshore between high and low water. In 1852, Fr. Michael Meehan devised the movable "Ark" so as to provide the celebrant with shelter from wind and rain. – ½ m. N. of Moneen road junction is the Bridge of Ross, a splendid example of sea-erosion. – The minor road SW. from Moneen leads (3 m.) to Loop (properly *Leap*) Head, which takes its name (Irish *Ceann Léime* from *Léim Chon Chulainn* ("Cú Chulainn's Leap"), the chasm sundering Dermot and Grania's Rock from the mainland. The headland offers splendid views.

4 m. NNW. is Knocknagarhoon (410 ft), with great sea caves and arches which should be viewed from the sea.

CARRIGALINE, Co. Cork (Map 5, C6), is a village on the Cork (8 m.)–Crosshaven (5 m.) road, at the head of the Owenboy estuary. There is a noted pottery here. The South Union Hunt has its headquarters at the village. The road ESE. to Crosshaven clings to the delightfully wooded S. shore of the estuary. The Protestant church is by George R. Pain (*see* Cork).

The Owenboy figures in Denny Lane's well-known ballad, *Carrigdhoun*. In the estuary below the village is Drake's Pool, where Sir Francis Drake is reputed to have taken shelter from pursuing Spaniards in 1587.

¾ m. ENE., on the N. side of the estuary, are remains of Carrigaline castle, a Cogan stronghold which passed to the Desmond Geraldines. The Mac Carthys of Muskerry demolished it in revenge, it is said, for the maltreatment of a Mac Carthy heiress. This was the birthplace of James Fitzmaurice (killed in 1579), leader of the great Munster revolt against Elizabeth I.

3 m. ENE., at Castle Warren to the SW. of Ring(askiddy) village, are remains of Barnahely castle (de Cogans). 1¼ m. further ENE. is an early-19th cent. redoubt, part of the defences of Cork Harbour. Offshore is Spike Island (*see under* Cobh).

4 m. S. is Tracton, site of the Cistercian abbey of Albus Tractus, founded in 1224/5 by Maurice Mac Carthy and colonized from Whitland, Carmarthenshire; only a few ornamental details survive. 1¼ m. NE. are the ruins of Kilpatrick, a medieval parish church.

2 m. WNW., on a steep rock over the Owen-

boy, is 17th cent. Ballea Castle, one of the few Co. Cork castles still occupied. The earliest castle here was a Cogan stronghold. In 1439 Robert de Cogan acknowledged the Earl of Desmond as his mean lord. Subsequently the castle was acquired by the Mac Carthys of Muskerry, who are found in possession in the 16th cent. In 1604, following on the English victory in the Nine Years' War, the castle was granted to Sir George Carew, who sold it to Richard Boyle (*see* Bandon, Youghal, Lismore). The latter sold it to Edward Marteel, from whom it was purchased back by Tadhg Mac Carthy. The Mac Carthys lost it for ever at the Cromwellian confiscation. 4½ m. SW., in Heathburn Hall townland, is a stone alignment. – 1 m. WSW. of the castle is a fine, bivallate ringfort of two acres. – 2 m. NW. of the castle, at the head of a small glen in Kilnahone, is a univallate ringfort of three acres; it has a souterrain.

CARRIGART, alias **CARRICKART**, Co. Donegal (Map 2, C2), is a village resort on the coast road from Milford (10 m.) to Creeslough (8 m.). It lies at the neck of beautiful Rosguill, the peninsula between Milford Bay and Sheephaven.

Immediately W., on Sheephaven, three square miles of dunes flank a two-mile beach.

The circuit of Rosguill, with its splendid views and lovely beaches is delightful. The following mileages are from Carrigart:

1¾ m. NW. is Rosapenna with its fine strand and well-known golf links.

3 m. NW. is the little resort, The Downies alias Downings: good curving beach and lovely views across Sheephaven.

3 m. N., by the roadside at Clontallagh post office, is part of a small crude cross. A bohereen leads to Mevagh Old Church on Mulroy Bay: fragmentary remains of a small Transitional (?) church and a tall ancient stone cross. On the hill SW. of the churchyard, in Mevagh townland, is a large series of rock scribings.

5 m. N. is the beautiful lonely beach, Tranarossan. 1 m. E., on Mulroy Bay, is another quiet beach (small).

CARRIGTOHILL, Co. Cork (Map 5, C6), a village on the Cork (10 m.)–Middleton (6 m. road. There are remains of a medieval church.

1 m. N. is Annegrove, a 17th cent. house rebuilt in the 18th cent.; very fine gardens.

1 m. NE., at The Rock, is a series of limestone caves discovered in 1933.

½ m. SE. are the ruins of Barryscourt, alias Claidhe Dubh Castle, rebuilt in 1585; the chapel is interesting.

1 m. SW., in Cork Harbour (road causeways), is Foaty, alias Fota, Island. Formerly part of Barryscourt, the island is celebrated for its beautiful demesne (gardens, tropical and other trees, etc.). Fota House, home of the Lords Barrymore (now of the Hon. Mr Bertram Bell, heiress of the last Lord Barr

more), is a good early-Georgian house (with 19th–20th cent. additions) whose windows have been mutilated. It has some good apartments and excellent stairways. The collection of portraits and other paintings includes works by Titian, Innocenza da Imola, and Carvalho. 3 m. SW., on the S. side of Foaty Island, is Belvelly bridge, giving access to Great Island (*see* Cobh).

CASHEL, Co. Tipperary (Map 5, D4), is a small market town at the junction of roads from Thurles (13 m.), Urlingford (20 m.), Fethard (10 m.), Clonmel (15 m.), Cahir (11 m.), and Tipperary (12 m.). In medieval times the ecclesiastical capital of Munster, it is noted for the variety of its historic monuments.

Secular and ecclesiastical history combine to make Cashel one of the most celebrated places in Munster. In the 4th/5th cent., Eóghanacht dynasts led by Conall Corc conquered the rich countryside and set up a fortress on St Patrick's Rock, which dominates the town from the N. They had probably come over from Wales, where the Irish colonies were succumbing to Welsh pressure. At any rate, previous contact with the Roman Empire is reflected in the Latin name, *caiseal*, cashel (= *castellum*), of their fortress; no other Irish royal seat had a Latin name. The Eóghanacht quickly spread to other fertile regions of Munster, and down to 944 their principal ruler was unchallenged Over-king of Munster. Since the first of such over-kings had been kings of Cashel, the title King of Cashel remained synonymous with that of King of Munster, even when, as frequently happened, the superior crown passed to a branch of the Eóghanacht which had severed its connection with Cashel itself. In Munster law and tradition the King of Cashel knew no superior, and it was not until 859 that Munster acknowledged the overlordship of the King of Tara. Throughout the centuries the Eóghanacht rulers had intimate associations with the Church, and at least four of the kings of Cashel were ecclesiastics as well as secular rulers: Olchobar, scribe, anchorite, and king (d. 796); Feidlimid, scribe, anchorite, bishop, and king (d. 847); Cormac mac Cuilenáin, Latin and Irish scholar, bishop, and king (d. 908); Flaithbertach, abbot and king (d. 944). After the latter's death a period of anarchy left Munster an easy prey to the Scandinavians, from whom it had to be rescued by the usurpation of kings of the heretofore obscure Dál Chais (*see* Killaloe), viz. Mahon and his brother, Brian Boru, who led their forces to Cashel in 963 and crushed the Norse at Solohead (*see under* Tipperary) in 976. When Mahon was murdered by the resentful Eóghanacht of Desmond (Cos. Cork and Kerry), in 976, Brian took up the challenge, and within two years had made himself undisputed King of Cashel. Though his descendants (the O Briens of Thomond) dominated all Munster until 1119, and North Munster (Thomond)

until the Anglo-Norman conquest, their capital naturally remained by the Shannon. This fact combined with their effective hegemony of much of Tipperary to deprive Cashel of any lingering political significance, though King Muirchertach O Brien had a residence or fortress there as late as 1091. Hence it was no great sacrifice when, in 1101, the year he had made good his claim to the high-kingship, Muirchertach handed over the Rock to be the see of the projected archbishopric of Munster. Closely connected with these developments was the abandonment of the Cashel district by the Eóghanacht dynasty which is known to subsequent history by the surname Mac Carthy, and which found compensation by carving out a new kingdom, the Kingdom of Cork, in Desmond. Perhaps the last great act by an Eóghanacht ruler at Cashel was the erection (1127–34) of a lovely little Romanesque cathedral ("Cormac's Chapel") by Cormac Mac Carthy, King of Desmond.

Muirchertach O Brien's gift of the Rock of Cashel to the Church was but one of the acts of a reforming synod which had assembled under his presidency. Five years later another important decision of the synod was given effect, the archdiocese of Cashel was formally constituted, and Máel Ísa ("Malchus") Úa hAinmire, Bishop of Waterford, became its first ruler. (The Catholic archdiocese still exists, but since Penal times has had its see at Thurles, *q.v.*; the Protestant archbishopric was abolished in 1839, and the diocese is today united to those of Waterford and Lismore.) In 1169, Cormac Mac Carthy's cathedral proving too small, Donal Mór O Brien, King of Thomond, commenced the building of a new cathedral. It can scarcely have been completed when the most momentous event in the history of Cashel took place. This was the meeting, in the winter of 1171–2, of a national synod summoned by Henry II of England, which rounded off a century of ecclesiastical reform by hopefully acknowledging the English king's claim to the lordship of Ireland.

In the following century Donal O Brien's cathedral was swept away to make room for the church whose ruins still dominate the Rock. The builders were three successive archbishops: Máirín O Brien (1224–37), David, son of Ceallach Ó Gilla Phátraic (1239–52), and David Mac Cearbhaill (1255–89). In 1495 this church was set on fire by Gearóid Mór Fitzgerald, Great Earl of Kildare, because, as he explained to Henry VII of England, he "thought the archbishop was inside". It was fired a second time, 13 Sept. 1647, when the infamous renegade, Murrough (Murchadh) the Burner O Brien, Earl of Inchiquin, attacked Cashel with a Parliamentarian force. The small garrison and large numbers of the townsfolk withdrew to the Rock and refused to surrender. O Brien's men, setting fire to the buildings, gained a speedy entrance and butchered all and sundry. The sacred vessels were seized as loot, paintings of the saints used as horsecloths, and statues

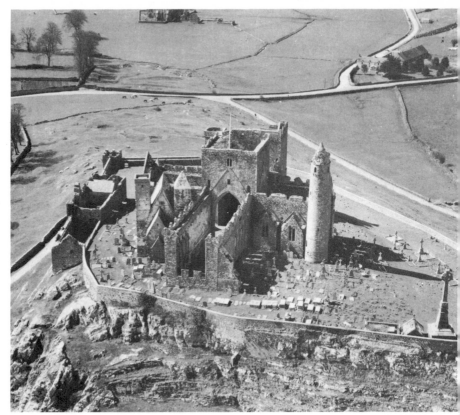

Aerial view (from the east) of St Patrick's Rock, Cashel.

profaned. Thereafter the buildings remained derelict until 1686, when the cathedral was repaired for Protestant use. In 1729 it was again re-edified, only to be abandoned in 1749 at the instance of Archbishop Arthur Price, who callously stripped the roof and left the venerable pile to the mercies of wind, weather, and vandals. In 1874 the ruins were handed over to the State, to be preserved as a national monument.

St Patrick's Rock, Cashel (alt. 200 ft), is a large limestone outcrop rising above the rolling farmlands. An easy approach from Rock Lane, on the S. side (reached via Ladyswell St or Camus Rd), leads to the gateway of the churchyard.

Adjoining the gateway is the Hall of the Vicars Choral (15th cent., with some 17th cent. features).

Between this and the S. porch of the cathedral is St Patrick's Cross, a much-weathered, figured, stone cross of rare, crutched, design (cf. Peakaun *under* Cahir). On the W. face of the shaft is a *Crucifixion*; on the E. face the figure of a bishop. On the E. face of the pedestal is an Urnes-style interlacement, enmeshing ribbon-beasts and birds, which dates the cross to about 1150; the N. face has a Romanesque lion ringed by pellets and concentric circles. (The sugges-

tion that the pedestal was the inauguration stone of the kings of Cashel is manifestly ridiculous.)

In the angle between the S. transept and the choir of the 13th cent. cathedral, is Cormac's Chapel, properly Cormac's Cathedral. It was commenced in 1127 and consecrated in 1134. This richly decorated little Romanesque church is one of the gems of 12th cent. Irish art, and its details repay close inspection. Its solid construction and superb double roof of stone preserved it from the worst effects of the disasters which wrecked the adjoining Gothic cathedral. It is cruciform in plan; but this is due to the unequal square towers which flank the junction of nave and chancel. (The S. tower has lost its original pyramidal roof and acquired a parapet.) The exterior wall faces are decorated with blind arcading, varied capitals and corbels, etc. – The entrance is now through a doorway of three richly decorated orders in the S. wall; but originally this doorway was subordinate to the great gabled N. porch of six orders, which is obstructed by the 13th cent. cathedral. Both doorways have carved tympana, features very rare in Irish Romanesque that of the S. door has a grotesque beast with trefoil tail, that of the N. door a centaur shooting with bow and arrow at a great trefoil-tailed lion which has struck down two smaller beasts. – Despite the gaping holes hacked through the S. wall a century or so ago by Archdeacon Cotton, the interior is today dark and gloomy. This is partly the result of the blocking up of two of the three windows in the W. gable and of the shading of the third by the later cathedral, partly the result of the loss of the polychrome painting which covered roofs and walls. The nave is roofed by a ribbed barrel vault, the chancel by a groined sexpartite vault. The side walls are arcaded in two storeys. The arcading was filled with painted figure subjects, diaper patterns, etc., while capitals, columns, mouldings, and the like, were picked out in colours. The principal feature of the interior is the grand chancel arch of four orders; here again we have to visualize polychrome enrichment. The chancel, which is dimly lit by a small window in each side wall, is closed by a shallow, rectangular, altar recess. The latter was lit by a curious slanting ope in each side wall. A doorway of three orders gives access to the fourstorey N. tower; the upper storeys were presumably reached by ladders; an external doorway in the E. wall has been closed up. The smaller S. tower, a belfry, contains the stairs leading to the crofts under the outer roof of stone; these may have been divided into two storeys by a timber floor. At the W. end of the nave (not *in situ*), is a great stone tomb-chest with a superb carving of the Urnes combattheme. Originally polychrome, the tomb is contemporary with the church.

The Cloigtheach (belfry), or Round Tower (92 ft), at the NE. angle of the N. transept of the 13th cent. cathédral, is doubtless somewhat earlier than Cormac's church, for the decoration of the Romanesque doorway cónsists simply of a low, flat architrave. This doorway faces in the general direction of the N. porch of Cormac's church, and may indicate the existence of an earlier church on the site of the latter, a church connected with Muirchertach O Brien's donation of 1101.

The 13th cent. Cathedral occupies the site of Donal Mór O Brien's cathedral of 1169. It is an aisleless, cruciform building with disproportionately long choir, excessively short nave, two E. chapels in each transept, and a great tower over the crossing. W. of the crossing was a rood screen (note responds). The nave had N. and S. porch arches half-way along its projected length; but only the S. porch was completed, for, early in the 15th cent., Archbishop O Hedian built a massive castle on the site of the W. end of the nave; he provided the castle with a Great Hall by inserting a floor over the nave. About the middle of the 14th cent. the central tower was raised in height and the church walls were crowned with battlements. At some unknown date a chantry chapel or a sacristy (disappeared) was added to the N. side of the choir. Turrets in the angles between nave and transepts give access to a wall passage encircling nave and transepts at triforium level; the S. turret also gives access to the central tower (view of lovely countryside).

In nave, transepts, and choir are the remains of altars, tombs, and other monuments, including the following: N. Transept: figures of apostles and saints (*Michael*, *John the Baptist* and *Thomas à Becket*), etc., from a HacketButler tomb; coat of arms and symbols of the Evangelists from the tomb of Archbishop Edmund Butler (d. 1533); figures of apostles, etc., from a 15th cent. tomb; Choir: S. side: tomb of the notorious renegade and pluralist, Miler Mac Grath (d. about 1622), for whom it was made in 1621 by Patrick Kerin. Mac Grath was consecrated bishop of Down and Connor by the Pope in 1567. Two years later

Cormac's Chapel, Cashel, 12th cent. tomb chest

Weepers from a medieval tomb chest, north transept of cathedral, Cashel

he conformed to the Protestant state church and was rewarded by Elizabeth I with the bishopric of his native Clogher in 1570, and this without incurring papal censure, which was not passed on him until 1580. In 1571 he had himself promoted to the Protestant archbishopric of Cashel, to which he contrived to add the bishoprics of Lismore (*q.v.*) and Waterford in 1581. In 1608 he exchanged Lismore and Waterford for Killala and Achonry. In addition to his bishoprics he accumulated no fewer than seventy-seven other benefices. In the meantime the Pope's archbishop of Cashel, Dermot O Hurley, was being hunted, captured, savagely tortured by order of Elizabeth, and (1584) put to death – by her warrant – without trial.

½ m. W. of the Rock, off the Mount Judkin road, are the ruins (Nat. Mon.) of Hore Abbey, last daughter of Mellifont. A priory-hospital was established here – probably before 1150 – by the Irish Benedictines of St James's Abbey, Ratisbon. In 1272 Archbishop Mac Cearbhaill replaced the Benedictines by Cistercians. He had dreamed, it is said, that the Benedictines were plotting to behead him. The remains, typically Cistercian (save that the claustral buildings were N. of the church), comprise fragments of the E. cloister range – including chapter-house and sacristy – as well as the ruins of a cruciform church with aisled nave, and with two chapels in each transept. The central tower and the screens shutting off the aisles and choir, etc., from the nave are 15th cent. features, as are the several storeys of living-room windows inserted in the embrasure of the

W. window. In the last century an Irish MS., now British Museum Add. MS. 11809, was found concealed in one of the abbey walls. It was written by the well-known 15th cent. scribe, Uilliam Mac An Leagha (Lee, Mac Kinley; *see* Carrick-on-Suir castle).

Off the N. side of Main St is Cashel Palace Hotel, formerly palace of the Protestant archbishops. This charming brick house was built by Sir Edward Lovett Pearce, architect of the Dublin Parliament House, for Archbishop Bolton (1730–44).

On the S. side of Main St is Quirke's Castle, a 15th cent. tower.

In Moor Lane, off the E. end of Main St (N. side), are the ruins (Nat. Mon.) of the fine church of the Dominican friary founded in 1243 by Archbishop David Ó Gilla Phátraic. Destroyed by fire, it was restored by Archbishop Cantwell about 1480.

On the Dublin road, at the N. edge of the town, is Alla Aileen, home of Michael Doheny (1805–63), prominent Young Irelander. His memoirs, *The Felon's Track*, are well known to students of the period.

The parish church of St John the Baptist, Friar St, was a decent, early-19th cent. Classical edifice until subjected to 20th cent. "embellishment". The churchyard occupies the site of Hacket's Abbey, a Franciscan friary founded by Archbishop Hacket about 1265; it replaced Cork as head of one of the four custodies of the Franciscan province in Ireland. The sole relics of the friary are a portion of a fine 14th cent. knightly effigy which lies forsaken in the churchyard and a stone tomb-chest which serves as a holy water font in the church porch. From the garden of the adjacent Presentation Convent a very fine view may be had of the Rock and its ruins.

In John St is the Protestant cathedral and parochial church of St John the Baptist (1750–83; spire, 1812), a good, small, Classical building; it occupies the site of a medieval church. The nearby Diocesan Library, re-edified 1965, is noteworthy for its collection of rare printings. Built into the churchyard wall is a fine series of medieval tomb effigies from the old cathedral and some of the town churches; among them is the 14th cent. effigy of an armoured knight said to be the cover of the tomb-chest now in the porch of the Catholic church.

2¼ m. NE. are the ruins of Gortmakellis castle, with a good 15th/16th cent. tower.

9 m. NE., near Killenaule, is Derrynavlan (see under Thurles).

3¼ m. ESE. is Knickeenagow, Mocklershill, birthplace of Charles Kickham, Fenian and novelist, 1828–82 (see Killenaule under Callan).

2¼ m. SE. is Knockbrit (see under Fethard, Co. Tipperary).

4¾ m. SE., in Rosegreen townland, is Shanacashlaun, a motte. 3 m. E. of this, close to Tullamain Castle (1835; by William Tinsley), are a motte and the remains of a medieval church. 2 m. S. of Rosegreen village is the 15th/16th cent. tower of Ballydoyle castle.

2 m. S., in Lalorslot, is Rathnadrinna, a quadrivallate ringfort with a smaller enclosure on the N. side of the entrance.

4¼ m. S. is Rockwell College, a boarding school for boys conducted by the Holy Ghost Fathers. In the entrance hall is a stained glass window by William Dowling; the subjects are the various activities of the school. The school also has three Evie Hone decorative windows (1941, 1942). The nucleus of the school is a house built c. 1830–40 to the designs of William Tinsley. There is a small, pretty lake, Loch Ceann, in the grounds. 2½ m. WNW., in Boytonrath, are the ruins of a castle set in a large, bivallate bailey; to the NE. are remains of a church; the district is rich in ringforts and ancient church sites.

4 m. SW., beside the Suir, is Golden (q.v.).

3 m. NNW., beside the Suir, is Ardmayle village. At the Anglo-Norman invasion Walter de Lacy built a castle nearly, whose motte remains. There are also remains of a medieval church and of a 17th cent. embattled house of the Butlers.

CASTLEBAR, Co. Mayo (Map 1, D4), the county town of Mayo and a market town with some small-scale industries (bacon-curing, hat-making), is at the junction of roads from Westport (11 m. SW.), Claremorris (18 m. SE.), Foxford (15 m. NE.), Newport, (11½ m. WNW.), Bangor Erris (37½ m. NW.), and Ballina (20 m. NNE.). The local lakes are being developed as angling attractions.

The town was founded at the beginning of the 17th cent. (incorporated 1613) by John Bingham, ancestor of the Earls of Lucan. On 27 Aug. 1798, Gen. Humbert (see Kilcummin under Killala), outwitting 1,200 British troops who barred his way at Foxford, advanced on Castlebar with 700 French troops and 1,000 untrained peasants. The town was held by Gen. Lake with 1,800 Highlanders, English Fencibles, militia, yeomanry, and two guns. The British broke at the fourth assault, leaving their stores, guns, and 1,200 prisoners in Humbert's hands. From the precipitate flight of the British cavalry to Hollymount and Tuam – some even to Athlone – the event has ever since been known as the "Castlebar Races". Humbert set up a provisional government in the town, with John Moore (d. 1799) of Moore Hall (see under Ballintober, Co. Mayo) as President of the Republic of Connaught. Moore died in prison after the French surrender at Ballinamuck (q.v.).

The Art Centre and Tourist Office (corner of the Mall) occupy a chapel whose foundation stone was laid by John Wesley in 1785. Michael Davitt founded the epoch-making Land League in the nearby Imperial Hotel, 16 Aug. 1879.

3 m. NE., at Turlough on the Foxford road, a Round Tower and the ruins of a 17th cent. church mark the site of an early monastery (traditionally Patrician). In the S. transept is a defaced capital, relic of a vanished Late Romanesque or Transitional church. Nearby Tobar Phádraig was a Lughnasa (Garland Sunday) station.

6½ m. SE., via the Ballyglass road, in Carrowjames, is a cemetery of ten inconspicuous flat tumuli with two pillarstones. The tumuli vary considerably in size. They are enclosed by ditches; two of them have external banks. Excavation showed six of them to cover cremated burials in pits (forty-two in all); these dated from the Bronze Age (urn-and-razor and other burials) to the close of the Iron Age.

CASTLEBELLINGHAM, Co. Louth (Map 3, B7), is a village on the Drogheda (14 m.)–Dundalk (8 m.) road. It takes its name from the Bellinghams, who displaced the long-established Gernons in Cromwellian times.

The castellated gateway at the S. end of the village is the entrance to Castle Bellingham, an early-18th cent. mansion with castellated additions. It occupies the site of a castle burnt by Jacobite troops in 1689, the then owner, Col. Thomas Bellingham, serving as guide to William of Orange throughout his campaign in Ireland. The demesne is very beautiful.

In the churchyard is buried Dr Thomas Guither, the 17th cent. physician who introduced frogs into Ireland.

¾ m. S. is Kilsaran, site of a preceptory of the Knights Templar. The Catholic church has some interesting monuments. ½ m. S. is the Greenmount (Nat. Mon.), a prehistoric tumulus. It has suffered much at the hands of amateur archaeologists.

2½ m. SE., on the joint estuary of the Dee and Glyde rivers, is the fishing village of Annagassan. The monastery of Linn Duachaill, founded by St Colmán son of Lúachán (d. 699), is believed to have stood in Linns townland. Caemhán, the last recorded abbot, was slain in 842 by the Vikings who had a fortress here 840–927. Near the mouth of the river is a promontory fort.

2¾ m. W., in Mansfieldstown, are remains (Nat. Mon.) of a late-17th cent. church incorporating fragments (15th cent. E. window, etc.) of a pre-Reformation church. A medieval font from this church is now in Ardee Protestant church. In nearby Braganstown is a 1624 monument to those commemorated by the O Conor Sligo monument in the Dominican friary, Sligo.

CASTLEBLAYNEY, Co. Monaghan (Map 3, B6), is a "Border" market town beside pretty Lough Muckno, on the Dundalk (18 m.)–Monaghan (15 m.) road. It takes its name from Sir Edward Blayney, who built a castle here and was Governor of the county under James I. By the lake is Hope Castle, formerly Blayney Castle and now a guest-house conducted by the Franciscan nuns. Permission to visit the demesne and to fish the lake may be had from the Agent, Hope Estate.

6 m. NE., in Knocknaneen, is a chambered cairn.

4½ m. SW., in Lattonfasky, is Cromlech, a chamber tomb. 4 m. NW., in Carrickanare, is Giants Grave, another chamber tomb.

4¼ m. NW., in Corlealackagh, is Giants Grave, an overgrown court cairn.

CASTLECOMER, Co. Kilkenny (Map 6, B5), is a small market town where the Athy (14 m.)–Kilkenny (12 m.) road crosses the pretty valley of the little Dinin Rua.

The town takes its name from a castle erected at the Anglo-Norman invasion (probably by William the Marshal). The invaders' first (motte) castle was destroyed by the O Brennans in 1200, but was soon replaced. Despite the castle, the O Brennans retained their hold hereabouts until 1635, when their lands were awarded to Sir Christopher Wandsford. The new proprietor planted English colonists, exploited the local anthracite mines, introduced hay-making to the district, and laid out "an elegant town exactly on the model of a famous one in Italy, viz. Alsinore". The buildings he erected included a castle on Colliery Hill and a Protestant church. In November 1641, the town was captured by Confederate Catholics under Capts. O Brennan and Bryan, but the castle held out until the following March. In 1798 the town was attacked and partly burnt by the Insurgents, who were driven off only after a sharp struggle. The Catholic church has a three-light memorial window (1920) by Michael Healy.

On the E. side of the town, in the grounds of derelict Castlecomer House, is The Garrison,

mutilated motte of the first Anglo-Norman castle.

2½ m. S., to the S. of the Dysart bridge–Smithstown road in Knockanaddoge townland, is Rathcally, a bivallate ringfort. ¾ m. NE. is the pretty little Rock of Foyle waterfall; beside it is a large ringfort; nearby is Clais an Aifrinn, a hollow where Mass was said in Penal times.

CASTLECONNELL village, Co. Limerick (Map 5, B4), is an angling resort – it gave its name to the two-piece, spliced, salmon rod – and decayed spa beside the Shannon, 8 m. NE. of Limerick and 7 m. SSW. of Killaloe. The famous salmon fishing here was severely affected by the Shannon hydro-electric scheme, but is recovering. The Shannon scheme also spoiled the famous fall and rapids on the river. On a rock over the river are remains of a Burke castle destroyed by the Williamite general, Ginckel, in 1691. Before the Burkes, the Ó Conaings were lords of the place; whence the name Castleconnell – Caisléan Úi Chonaing, Ó Conaing's castle (see Carrigogunnell under Limerick).

In the 18th cent. its medicinal well made Castleconnell a popular resort of Limerick folk. Relics of that era are to be seen in the small, decayed pump house and the many attractive old villas of the neighbourhood.

On Cloon Island are remains of a church; built with the W. wall are two early gravestones.

The derelict demesnes of the neighbourhood include Hermitage (Lord Massey), 1¼ m. S., and Mount Shannon, 2 m. further S. The fine Classical house in the latter, enlarged by the notorious "Black Jack" Fitzgibbon, Earl of Clare, about 1790, was burned down in 1922.

6 m. SE. is Clonkeen (see under Barringtonsbridge).

CASTLEDERG, Co. Tyrone (Map 2, D3), is a woollen-manufacturing village where the Strabane (12 m.)–Pettigoe (16 m.) road crosses the River Derg. There are remains (Nat. Mon.) of a Plantation bawn built by Sir John Davies about 1610; it had square flankers at the angles and a house against the N. curtain. The moat suggests that a castle had stood on the site.

1 m. NNE., alt. 300 ft, in Churchtown, is Todd's Den, a small, chambered cairn (Nat. Mon.). 300 yds SSW. is Druid's Altar, a ruined chamber tomb.

4 m. E. is Crew, Lower (see Meaghy under Newtownstewart).

4½ m. SW., beside Aghnahoo school, is Aghnahoo souterrain (Nat. Mon.). 600 yds S., on the E. slope of Leitrim Hill, alt. 400 ft, is Leitrim Druid's Altar (Nat. Mon.), a portal dolmen with enormous, cup-marked capstone. On the summit of the hill (687 ft) are the remains of a stone ringfort. – 3 m. SW. of Aghnahoo school, ⅔ m. SSW. of Killeter village, alt. 600 ft, is Killeter Giants Grave, a ruined, chambered, long cairn.

7½ m. NW. is Scraghy road-junction. N. of

and The Swearing Stone, an early, granite cross-slab with a circular perforation at the centre of the cross. The Round Tower (66 ft) was built in 919; the battlemented parapet is medieval, and the tower has doubtless lost something of its original height. The subjects carved on the High Crosses include *SS Paul and Anthony, The Apostles, The Crucifixion, The Fall, The Sacrifice of Isaac,* and *Daniel in the Lions' Den.* – At the Norman conquest Walter de Riddlesford built a motte-and-bailey castle at Castledermot (1181). About 1295 the town was enclosed by walls, of which fragments survive, notably between Barrack St and Main St. At the E. end of Abbey St are the ruins of a fine, Franciscan, friary church (Nat. Mon.).

Commissioners of Public Works in Ireland
North Cross, Castledermot (west face)

he Pettigoe road and 2 m. E. of Cushey's Bridge, is a low stone circle (Nat. Mon.). SE. of Scraghy school (Ederry road) are small standing stones (remains of circle ?). 1¼ m. E. of the school are remains of a chamber tomb Nat. Mon.).

CASTLEDERMOT, Co. Kildare (Map 6, C4), on the Kilcullen (17 m.)–Carlow (7 m.) road, was once a walled town, but is now a mere village.

St Díarmaid (d. 823), grandson of Áed Róin, King of Ulaid (*see* Faughart), had a hermitage (Dísert Díarmada, Tristledermot, Castledermot) here, which became the nucleus of an important monastery (*see* Tihelly *under* Tullamore, *and* Killeigh). Of the latter there survive (Church Lane) a Round Tower (Nat. Mon.), two 9th/10th cent. High Crosses (Nat. Mons.), the Romanesque W. doorway (innermost order missing; Nat. Mon.) of a church

Commissioners of Public Works in Ireland
South Cross, Castledermot (west face)

The friary is first mentioned in 1247. Enlarged by Thomas, Lord Ossory, in 1302, it was destroyed by Edward Bruce in 1317, but was rebuilt. The remains are those of a 13th cent. nave-and-chancel, preaching church enlarged in the 14th cent. by extending the choir and adding a short N. nave aisle and an elaborate, aisled N. transept with three E. chapels. The transept is probably that "Chapel of St Mary" built in 1328 by Thomas, 2nd Earl of Kildare, and in which he was buried. The tower on the N. side of the chancel is probably a 15th cent. addition. At the N. end of the village is St John's Tower alias The Pigeons' Tower (Nat. Mon.), sole remnant of St John the Baptist's Hospital (Augustinian Cruciferi) built in the 13th cent. by Walter de Riddlesford.

3½ m. N. are remains of Belan House and its demesne ornaments. The house was built in 1743 for the 1st Lord Aldborough by Richard Cassels and Francis Bindon. The house was dismantled from 1821 onwards, and only an ornamental temple, two of three obelisks, and the original stables survive in fair condition.

5 m. NNE. is Moone (see under Ballytore).

3 m. NW. is Kilkea Castle, 1849 "restoration" (an extra storey added all around, etc.) of an already much altered Fitzgerald castle wrecked in 1798. Garret Óg, 11th (Wizard) Earl of Kildare (d. 1585) is supposed to come from Mullaghmast (see under Ballitore) and the Curragh to the "haunted room" every seventh year mounted on a silver-shod, white charger. In 1634 Elizabeth Nugént, widow of the 14th Earl of Kildare, gave the castle to the Jesuits, who remained until 1646. That year they entertained (for twenty days) Rinuccini, papal nuncio to the Confederation of Kilkenny. In 1650 the castle was taken by the Cromwellian, Col. Hewson. Near the castle are the ruins of Kilkea, a small, simple, manorial church with later chancel and sacristy. In a 16th/17th cent. Fitzgerald chantry are panels (Crucifixion, etc.) of the tomb of William Fitzgerald of Castleroe and his wives (d. 1623, 1630); other fragments in W. wall of nave. Close to the River Greese is the motte of a castle erected in 1180 for Walter de Riddlesford, Strongbow's grantee of the manor (which passed in the 13th cent. to Maurice Fitzgerald, 3rd Baron O ffaly).

CASTLEGREGORY, Co. Kerry (Map 4, C3), is a small village and quiet seaside resort very beautifully situated at the head of the sandy Rough Point peninsula, 1 m. N. of the Tralee (15 m.)–Dingle (23 m.) road through Connor Pass. To the SW. rise the twin summits of Beenoshee (2,713 ft; see Anascaul) and Stradbally Mountain (2,627 ft), with little Lough Acumeen in the corrie between them. (Most readily climbed from Stradbally, 3 m. WSW. of Castlegregory, they afford magnificent views.) NW. of the village is Lough Gill (trout, fowling). The road SW. to Stradbally and Connor Pass commands splendid views of Brandon Bay and Mountain. The minor road

from Stradbally round Brandon Bay to Ballyquin is also noted for its scenery.

The village takes its name from a castle built by Gregory Hoare in the 16th cent. There is a tale to the effect that Lord Deputy Grey, accompanied by Sir Walter Ralegh and Edmund Spenser, stopped here in 1580 on his way to attack Dún an Óir near Smerwick (see Ballyferriter). The wife of the then owner, Hugh Hoare, disliked having to entertain the enemy and opened the wine kegs so that all the wine ran away. In his rage Hoare slew her, but himself dropped dead next morning. The castle was besieged and demolished by the Cromwellians, and no trace of it remains.

4 m. N., on the E. side of little Scraggan Bay, is the ruined church of Kilshannig, with a tall early cross-pillar (chi-rho, etc.). 2½ m. WSW. is the little village of Fahamore, point of departure for the Maharee Islands. The largest of these, Ilauntannig, lies 1 m. N. of Rough Point. Like Kilshannig, it takes its name (Oiléan tSeanaigh) from St Seanach, "brother" of St Seanán of Scattery Island (see under Kilrush), who founded an anchoritic monastery here in the 6th/7th cent. The remains of the monastery (Nat. Mon.) are enclosed by a massive dry-masonry cashel and include a tiny church (also a fragment of a second), three clocháns, three leachtaí or burial monuments, and a rude stone cross. About 100 yds away, near the cliff, is a rock with bullaun and incised cross. 1 m. NW. on Illaunimmil, are a prehistoric chamber tomb and a stone circle.

10 m. SW. is Connor Pass (1,300 ft; see under Dingle).

10 m. W., in the W. of two ancient graveyards on the slope of Brandon Mountain, in Faha townland, are a cross-slab and a cross-inscribed boulder. 3 m. NE., in Ballyquin, close to Caher Point, is Dermot and Grania's Bed, a prehistoric chamber tomb.

CASTLEISLAND, Co. Kerry (Map 4, D3), is a small market town where the Limerick (47 m.)–Killarney (14¾ m.) road crosses the little Shanowen. To the N. are the Glanaruddery Mountains (Knight's Mountain, 1,097 ft); to the E., Mount Eagle (1,417 ft), Knockanefune (1,441 ft), and Knockfeha (1,391 ft). There are remains of a Desmond castle, successor of one built in 1220 by the English Justiciar, Geoffrey de Marisco. The Herberts were granted confiscated Desmond lands here by James I, and took their title from Castleisland.

The Market House dates from 1747.

CASTLEKNOCK, Co. Dublin (Map 6, D7) is a village on the Dublin (6 m.)–Navan (24 m.) road, at the edge of the Phoenix Park. To the SW., in the grounds of Castleknock College (founded 1834 to become the ecclesiastical seminary of the archdiocese, now a well-known boarding school for boys conducted by the Vincentian Fathers), are remains of the castle from which the village takes its name. These consist of a ditched and ramparted oval motte, at one end of which is a secondary mound with remains of an octagonal keep. The first castle was constructed by Hugh Tyrel, who got lands here from Hugh de Lacy at the Anglo-Norman invasion. When the High-king, Rory O Conor, invested Dublin in 1171, in a major effort to expel the invaders, he set up his headquarters at Castleknock. After a two-month blockade his forces were dispersed by a surprise sortie. In 1317 Edward Bruce captured the castle. In 1642 it was taken by the Parliamentarian, Monk, who butchered the Confederate Catholic garrison.

The Protestant church has a three-light window (*SS Luke, George, Hubert*) by Harry Clarke (1928).

CASTLEMAINE, Co. Kerry (Map 4, C4), is a small market town where the Tralee (10 m.)–Killorglin (6¼ m.) road crosses the Maine. It takes its name from a Desmond castle (commanding the river crossing) which was destroyed by the Cromwellian, Ludlow. Various families and notabilities have taken titles from the place, among them the notorious Roger Palmer, Viscount Castlemaine (1634–1705) and husband of the Duchess of Cleveland (1641–1709).

2¼ m. SW., in the NW. corner of the demesne of Kilcolman Abbey (formerly home of the Godfreys), is the ruined nave-and-chancel church of Killaha "Abbey", properly the priory De Bello Loco. Dedicated to Our Lady, this house of Canons Regular of St Augustine was founded in 1215/16 by the Anglo-Norman Justiciar, Geoffrey de Marisco, as successor to the ancient Cill Cholmáin (Kilcolman). Restored and enlarged in 1445, it survived the Dissolution until 1576; the reticulated E. window is very late. The site of Cill Cholmáin is probably marked by the ruins of the White Church, a medieval parish church not far to the ESE. ½ m. WSW. of the nearby village of Milltown is Poll na Rátha, said to have been the quarry which provided the stones for Killagha priory. It cuts into a large bivallate ringfort (Fort Agnes) with a souterrain extending under the inner rampart.

1½ m. W., at an old burial ground in Ardcanaght, are two doubtful ogham stones (Nat. Mons.). Also in Ardcanaght is a Bronze Age cup-and-ring stone (Nat. Mon.).

CASTLEMARTYR, Co. Cork (Map 5, C6), is a small market town on the Midleton (6 m.)–Youghal (11 m.) road (which is noted for its scenery). In the demesne on the W. side of the village are Castlemartyr House (now a Carmelite priory) and the ruins of the castle of the Earl of Desmond's seneschal for the barony of Imokilly (*see* Cloyne). In 1569 the castle was attacked and taken by Sir Henry Sidney. In 1581, the Earl of Desmond being then in revolt against Elizabeth I, it was attacked by the Earl of Ormond, who hanged the seneschal's mother in sight of the walls. At the Desmond confiscation the castle and estate were granted to Sir Walter Raleigh (*see* Youghal), who sold them to the notorious Richard Boyle. Boyle restored and improved the buildings. In 1645 the castle was recovered by Edward Fitzgerald, only to be taken by the Parliamentarian, Murrough the Burner O Brien, shortly afterwards. At the Cromwellian victory it passed to Boyle's son, Roger, Lord Broghil, later Earl of Orrery (1621–79), who repaired and enlarged it. It was besieged and wrecked by the Jacobites in 1688. The remains comprise a 15th cent. bawn (with angle towers) and keep (incorporated in the curtain), as well as 17th cent. domestic quarters, etc. ½ m. SSW. are the remains of Ballyoughtera church.

3½ m. NE., on the little Dissour River, is Killeagh village. The beautiful woods of Glenbower, ½ m. NW., are a favourite resort for picnics. Formerly part of the Aghadoe estate, for 700 years the property of the Cappells, they are now a State forest. – 1½ m. S., in Castle Richard, is ruined, 15th cent. Inchicrenagh Castle (alias Castle Richard). The Fitzgeralds who lived here were hereditary keepers of Cloch ómrach Úa Mac Coille, alias the Imokilly Amulet, which was used to cure hydrophobia and murrain in cattle. – 2 m. SE. of Killeagh are the remains of Inchiquin castle (*see under* Youghal).

3 m. ESE. is Ightermurragh Castle, an embattled house built in 1641 by Edmund Supple and his wife "whom love binds one". 3¾ m. ESE. is Ballymacoda (*below*). – 2¾ m. SE. is Kilcredan (*below*). 1½ m. SW. of Kilcredan is Garryvoe (*below*).

6 m. ESE. is Ballymacoda village. 1 m. E. of the village is Ballykinealy, birthplace of the poet, Piaras Mac Gearailt (1702–95). – 3½ m. ESE. is Knockadoon Head, which takes its name from a promontory fort. – 2½ m. SW., near the E. end of Ballycotton Bay, is Ballycrenane castle, built by the Tyntes, who in the 17th cent. acquired lands here which had been forfeited by John fitz Edmund Fitzgerald in 1584. – The Ballymacoda district is the last Irish-speaking district in eastern Cork.

4¼ m. SE. are the ruins of Kilcredan Protestant Church, built in 1636 by Sir Robert Tynte of Ballycrenane castle, and callously unroofed by the church authorities in the 19th cent., thereby wrecking and exposing two fine Renaissance monuments, one of them the tomb of Sir Robert Tynte himself; one of the "weepers" was an effigy of Sir Robert's second wife, Elizabeth Boyle, widow of Edmund Spenser.

4 m. SSE. are the remains of the church and "pocket castle" of Garryvoe.

4¾ m. S. is Shanagarry (*see under* Ballycotton).

CASTLEPOLLARD, Co Westmeath (Map 2, D7), is a market village on the Mullingar (16 m.)–Granard (16 m.) road. It is a convenient centre for fishing Loughs Derravaragh (*below*), Lene, and Sheelin.

3 m. N. is Rathcreevagh motte-and-bailey.

2½ m. E. is Fore, a village which takes its name, Fobhar Féichín, St Féichín's Spring, probably from that "wonder" which flows underground from Lough Lene and springs up in the valley beside the ancient church.

Fore was the site of an important early monastery, of a medieval Benedictine priory, and of a small walled town which was one of the fortresses of the English marches.

The early monastery was founded by St Féichín, alias Mo Fhéca, Mo Éca (*see* Ballysadare, Cong, Omey Island, *and* Ard Oiléan). Féichín, noted even in childhood for his singular asceticism, was born 580/90 at Bile Féichín, which is generally supposed to have been in Co. Sligo. He was trained principally by St Nath-Í at Achonry. He died of the Yellow Plague, 20 Jan. 664/5. In his lifetime Fore is said to have had 300 monks. Between 771 and 1169 either the monastery or its satellite town, or both, were pillaged or burned down no fewer than twelve times. At the 12th cent. reformation the monastery appears to have adopted the Rule of the Canons Regular of St Augustine. Of this ancient monastery only the church (9th/10th cent.?) and some miscellaneous fragments remain. The ruins of the church (Nat. Mon.) stand in the W. graveyard. The original building was a simple rectangular structure with *antae* and high pitched gables. The most notable feature is the trabeate W. doorway with its massive (2½ tons), cross-inscribed lintel which has been thought to reveal Levantine influence. The chancel is an addition of about 1200, as the chancel arch (re-erected 1934) shows. The 15th cent. E. window replaces a twin-lancet original; underneath it is a fragment of the altar table. In the chancel are also preserved two early gravestones, fragments of stone crosses, etc. In the nave is a medieval font. In the graveyard is a stone ring-cross (Nat. Mon.). Nearby are the remains of St Féichín's Mill and of the Anchorite's Cell, a 15th cent. tower altered in the 17th cent. and adapted as the Greville-Nugent mausoleum in the 19th.

The Benedictine priory of SS Taurin and Fechin was founded about 1200 by one of the de Lacys. (Hugh de Lacy had seized the place about 1180; *see* Clonard *under* Kinnegad, *and* Durrow *under* Tullamore. A motte with rectangular bailey on the slope of the Ben of Fore to the E. of the village probably represents the first de Lacy stronghold. King John's campaign against the de Lacys brought him to Fore, 11 Aug. 1210.) The priory was a dependency of the abbey of St Taurin at Évreux in Normandy, to which de Lacy had granted the churches and tithes of Fore and St Féichín's Mill. It consequently suffered from the Anglo-French wars of the 14th cent. The decay was, however, arrested in the 15th cent. After the Dissolution the priory was granted to Christopher Nugent, baron of Delvin.

The remains of the priory (Nat. Mon.), the only certain Benedictine remains in Ireland, comprise those of the claustral buildings and of the church. The latter is an austere nave-and-chancel structure with castle-like W. and SW. towers which recall the priory's role of advanced fortress of the English Pale. It dates from 1200/1210, but the towers are 15th cent. additions. To the N. of the nave are the foundations of a chapel added at some unknown date, the arches leading to it blocked up since about 1870. To the W. of the chapel and the W. tower are traces of other buildings later than the tower. The surviving claustral buildings, like the towers, are of 15th cent. date, but incorporate 13th cent. fragments on the ground floor. The fragments of the beautiful cloister arcade (re-erected 1912) exemplify a type peculiar to 15th cent. Ireland. In the cloister are two 13th/14th cent., Anglo-Norman tombstones. The buildings around the cloister were apparently disposed as follows. E. Range: Ground floor: sacristy (under SE. tower), chapter-house, and dwelling apartment; Upper floor: prior's apartments. S. Range: Ground floor: stores; Upper floor: refectory. W. Range: Ground floor: residential apartment; Upper floor: dormitory. The original 13th cent. S. Range lay just outside the extant one, in line with the projecting kitchen at the SW. corner of the priory. Immediately to the SW. of the kitchen, and just inside the fragmentary SW. gateway of the monastery, are remains of the priory mill. To the SE. of the monastery is an old building, now used for farm purposes. To the NE., on Knocknamonaster, are remains of the priory pigeon-house; to the NW., remains of a rectangular building and a gateway.

In the E. graveyard, near St Mary's Church, are the remains of the medieval church of St Mary.

Of the medieval town defences only the ruined N. and S. gateways survive. Fragments of the priory cloister have been built into the masonry, showing that the gateways have been repaired since the Dissolution.

In the village street stand the head and upper part of a stone cross with a carving of the Crucifixion; they formerly lay in the E. graveyard. In front of the school are a plain stone cross and the socket of another. Within 2 m. of Fore are the remains of no less than fourteen wayside crosses, most of them small and plain. One, which is ½ m. N. in Clounageeragh, has a rude *Crucifixion*.

4½ m. S., overlooking lovely Lough Derravaragh, is Knockeyon (710 ft). The summit affords wide and beautiful views. Half-way up the steep slope over the lake are St Eyen's (Ion's) ruined chapel and holy well, formerly a place of pilgrimage on the first Sunday of harvest, *i.e.* a Lughnasa station.

7 m. S. is Taughmon (Teach Munnu, *see* Taghmon, Co. Wexford), called after a 6th cent. monastery founded by St Munnu (alias Finnu, alias Fintán). The ruins (Nat. Mon.)

are those of a 15th cent. semi-fortified manorial church dedicated to St Patrick. It was a rectangular, stone-roofed building with battlemented walls and castle-like W. tower (the latter an addition). In it is the tomb of Sir Christopher Nugent of Moyrath and Farrow (d. 1619). There is a similar church at Kilpatrick (*see under* Rathconrath).

3 m. SSW., in Faughalstown, on the E. shore of Loch Derravaragh, are the remains of a church; ½ m. NW. those of Mortimer's Court, a castle.

1½ m. NW. is Tullynally (from *c.* 1730 to 1961 called Pakenham Hall), until 1961 seat of the Earls of Longford, now home of Mr. Thomas Pakenham. The nucleus of the house was a 17th cent. stronghouse. About 1740, and again in 1780, this was enlarged and Georgianized. Between 1801 and 1806 it was castellated and embellished in the Gothick manner by Francis Johnston. James Shiel designed the octagonal dining room, as well as a Gothick gate lodge. In 1839 Sir Richard Morrison added the office and stable court and gave the Great Hall a new ceiling. The late Earl of Longford was a well-known Dublin figure: poet, playwright, and theatrical manager. The present Earl is a well-known author and British Labour politician.

CASTLEREA[GH] Co. Roscommon (Map 2, B6), is a small market town on the Roscommon (19 m.)–Claremorris (24 m.) road.

Castlerea was the birthplace of Sir William Wilde (1815–76), noted antiquary and oculist, husband of Lady Wilde (Speranza), and father of Oscar Wilde. His father, Dr Thomas Wilde, was a physician in practice here.

2 m. SE., near the railway, in Emlagh, are the base and shaft of a High Cross (Nat. Mon.) with interlaced and other ornament.

½ m. NW. is Clonalis House, seat of O Conor Don, representative of the once proud dynasty of the O Conors of Connacht, which gave two high-kings to Ireland in the 12th cent. (*see also* Ballintober, Co. Mayo; Ballintober, Co. Roscommon; Bellanagare; Cong; Roscommon; Tuam; Tulsk).

4 m. NW. is Lough Glinn, which has given its name to the local village and to a convent in the former seat of the Viscounts Dillon; the convent is noted for its cheeses. The Fitzgeralds of Desmond had a castle (of which one circular corner tower remains) here for a time during the Middle Ages. They were patrons of Urlaur friary, Co. Mayo (*see under* Ballyhaunis).

CASTLETOWN BEARHAVEN, Co. Cork (Map 4, C5), is a small port and seaside resort on the N. side of Bantry Bay, 9 m. WSW. of Ardrigole and 15 m. SW. of Lauragh, Co. Kerry. Boating, bathing, and sea fishing are available. Offshore lies Dinish Island. Bear Island, to the S. and SE., shelters deep Bear Haven, formerly a fortified anchorage of the

British Atlantic fleet (*see* Bantry). To the NW., N., and NE., rises Slieve Miskish, haunt of botanists and climbers. The coastal scenery NE. to Adrigole, and SW. to Knockoura (2 m.), and again further SW. between Dursey Sound (14 m.) and Ballydonegan (11 m.), is very fine.

6 m. N., overlooking Ballycrovane Bay in Faunkill and the Woods townland, is a 17½-ft ogham stone (Nat. Mon.).

1 m. SSW. is a fragment of the O Sullivan Beare castle of Dunboy, last Irish stronghold in the SW. to be taken by Elizabethan forces in the Nine Years' War. It was heroically defended against an English force under Sir George Carew in 1602 by an Irish-Spanish garrison commanded by Richard Mac Geoghegan. The assailants forced their way into the cellar just as the mortally wounded Mac Geoghegan was about to blow up the castle. The few survivors were butchered.

15 m. SSW. is Dursey Island, birthplace (1590) of Don Philip O Sullivan, author of *Historiae Catholicae Iberniae Compendium* (Lisbon, 1621).

11 m. W. is Allihies, where old copper mines are once more being exploited. They figure in Daphne du Maurier's *Hungry Hill* (*see under* Adrigole).

Bear Island holds little of note, save scattered 19th cent. redoubts and batteries. Near the sea in Ardaragh East, at the E. end of the island, is a wedge-shaped gallery grave (wrecked).

CASTLETOWN GEOGHEGAN, Co. Westmeath (Map 6, A2), is a village on the Ballymahon (14 m.)–Kilbeggan (5 m.) road, to the SW. of Lough Ennell (*see* Mullingar). There is a large Anglo-Norman motte-and-bailey here, but the place takes its name from a castle of the Mac Eochagáins (*below*) who held lands here until Cromwellian times. On the W. side of the village are remains of a medieval priory. There are many ringforts in the area, particularly in the country to the S. and SW.

1½ m. NE. is Monaghanstown pillarstone.

1 m. E., at the SW. corner of Lough Ennell, is Malachy's Fort, which some would identify with Dún na Scíath, seat of Melaghlin II, King of Meath and of Tara (949–1002, 1014–22). He died on Cró Inis (Cormorant Island, alias Hut Island) nearby, on 2 Sept. 1022.

1 m. SE. is Middleton House, a good Classical mansion (Boyd Rochfort family). A chair-shaped stone nearby is said to have been the inauguration stone of Mac Eochagáin.

3 m. W., in Garhy, is the Grave of the Warrior, remnant of a prehistoric chamber tomb.

4 m. NW. is Carn (Carn Fhiachach), where Fiachu, son of Niall Nine Hostager and King of Meath, had his residence. One of his sons, so the story goes, slew some of St Patrick's company at Uisneach, and the outraged saint's curse excluded his descendants from the succession. An alternative version of the tale recounts that Patrick visited Fiachu at Carn, but Fiachu refused to accept his teaching. From the

13th cent. onwards Cenél Fhiachach, the territory of Fiachu's descendants, was commonly called Mac Eochagáin's (alias Mageoghegan's) Country. The Mac Eochagáins (Mageoghegans, Geoghegans, Gahagans) maintained their lordship until the close of Elizabeth I's reign, and some of their branches retained their estates until Cromwellian times. The surname is still common in the adjoining parts of Cos. Westmeath and Offaly.

CASTLETOWNROCHE, Co. Cork (Map 5, C5), is a village where the Fermoy (9 m.)–Mallow (8 m.) road crosses the little Awbeg. Castle Widenham demesne has superb gardens. The house incorporates the remains of the Roche castle from which the village takes its name. The castle was attacked by Sir Walter Raleigh in the course of the Elizabethan wars. In 1649, the then Lord Roche having fled as an attainted royalist outlaw, it was defended against the Cromwellians by his wife. At the Restoration Lord Roche's loyalty failed to receive due recognition from Charles II. The title is now extinct, the last lord having been a mere stableboy, but too proud to accept wages.

The Protestant church, with curious windows in the steeple, dates from 1825.

Below the village the Awbeg flows through a limestone gorge. In the E. bank of the river, between Castle Widenham and Rock Savage, are eight small caves which have yielded remains of mammoth, reindeer, and "Irish elk".

2 m. N., on the W. side of the Awbeg, is Annes Grove with its wonderful gardens.

4 m. SE., on a lovely reach of the Blackwater, is Ballyhooly village. The Roche castle here, wrecked in the 1641–52 war, was restored as a residence by Lady Listowel in 1862; lovely view from tower. The church (1870) is by George C. Ashlin, a pupil of Pugin's. The Protestant church (1881) is by W. H. Hill.

1¾ m. S., close to the beautiful junction of the Awbeg and Blackwater, are the remains of Bridgetown (Ballindroghid) "Abbey", a 13th cent. Augustinian (Congregation of St Victor) priory which took the place of the ancient Cell Laisre. The remains include a church with long, Augustinian choir and fragments of the cloister and claustral buildings.

3 m. SW., on the N. bank of the Blackwater, is Monanimmy castle, associated with the Knights of St John. Edmund Burke (1729–97), who spent his early childhood with his maternal grandmother in Ballyduff, got his earliest schooling at a "hedge-school" held in the castle ruins. There he learned "all that the village schoolmaster could teach". On the opposite side of the river is the little village of Killawillin, alias Killavullen. Ballymacmoy House, to the W. of the bridge, was the home of a branch of the Hennessy family, famed for its brandy. In the river bank is a cave (Nat. Mon.) where remains of extinct arctic fauna have been found. 1 m. E., on the S. side of the river, is the tower of Carrigacunna (Carrigna-

conny), alias Rockwood, castle, a 15th cent. Nagle stronghold. The castle was the home of Sir Richard Nagle, Speaker of James II's Patriot Parliament. – 4½ m. ESE., alt. 1,124 ft in Ballydague, is Seehaunnamnafinna (Suidheachán na Mná Finne), a cairn. – 1½ m. SSE., alt. 872 ft, in Cloghvoolia North, is a cairn. – 3 m. SSE., alt. 1,345 ft, at Corran in Cloghvoolia North, is a cairn.

CASTLETOWNSHEND, Co. Cork (Map 4, E6), is a village on the W. side of beautiful Castlehaven, 5 m. SE. of Skibbereen and 14 m. SW. of Glandore. There is a ferry to the E. side of the haven. The road SW. to Toe Head Bay (6 m.) and Bawnlahan (5 m.) is noted for its scenery.

ENE. of the village, overlooking the landing place, are the ruins of "Bryans' Fort", a small star fort erected by the English planter, Col. Richard Townsend, about 1650. It was attacked by Jacobites in Nov. 1689 and taken by them the following year, only to be recovered shortly afterwards by the local Williamites.

At the SW. end of the village is Drishane House, life-long home of Edith Oenone Somerville (1858–1949), joint author with "Martin Ross" of *Some Experiences of an Irish R.M.*, *The Real Charlotte*, etc.

¾ m. NW., alt. 420 ft on Knockdrum, is The Fort (Nat. Mon.), a fine stone ringfort (restored). It has a guard-chamber in the rampart, remains of a central clochán, and three souterrains. An early cross-pillar has been set up inside the entrance. Outside the entrance is a stone with thirty-nine cup marks. Some 300 yds NNW., in Gurrane, are the Three Fingers, an alignment of pillarstones.

1½ m. SE. (via ferry), at Reen Point, is a promontory fort.

1 m. S., in Glenbarrahane, are Toberbarrahane, remains of St Barrahane's Church, and the ruins of the O Driscoll castle which gives to Castle Haven its name. On 1 Dec. 1601, six Spanish ships, mostly merchantmen, commanded by Pedro de Jubiaur, arrived in the haven with some 700 troops, food, stores, and five guns, for the expeditionary force at Kinsale (*q.v.*). On 5 Dec. the Spanish vessels were attacked by the English admiral, Sir Richard Leveson, with four warships, a merchantman, and a caravel. After a sharp encounter, in which the Spaniards lost two vessels and the English one, Leveson was driven off. The Spaniards then garrisoned the O Driscoll castles covering the entrance to Baltimore Bay, as well as Dunboy castle (*see under* Castletown Bearhaven), retaining Castle Haven as their base or magazine. The garrisons were included in the Kinsale capitulation and laid down their arms. Only that at Dunboy held out, to perish with glory. – 1¾ m. SW. of the castle, on an 80-ft cliff in Scobaun, is Portadoona promontory fort; it has a terraced rampart. Excavation yielded no finds, but the fort may be of the Early Iron Age. 2 m. further SW., in Toe Head

townland, to the W. of Toe Head, is Tón Dúinín, alias Dooneendermotmore, an eroded promontory fort defended by a fosse. Refortified in late medieval times, the site was occupied until the later 17th cent.

CASTLEWELLAN, Co. Down (Map 3, C5), is a town on the Downpatrick (11 m.)–Newry (19 m.) road. The principal feature is the demesne of the Annesleys of Newry.

3 m. SE. is Maghera (see under Newcastle, Co. Down).

3 m. S. is Tollymore Forest Park (see under Newcastle, Co. Down).

2½ m. SW., alt. 500 ft in Drumena, are a stone ringfort and a souterrain (Nat. Mons.). Also in Drumena, alt. 700 ft, is Carnbane, a whingrown cairn with central cist.

7½ m. NNW., alt. 850 ft on the S. slope of Cratlieve and commanding a splendid prospect, is Legananny Dolmen (Nat. Mon.), a noteworthy tripod chamber tomb. In the ancient churchyard 1¾ m. ESE. is an early crosspillar.

CAVAN, Co. Cavan (Map 2, D6), is the county town of Cavan and the cathedral town of the Catholic diocese of Kilmore. It lies on the main Dublin (71 m.)–Enniskillen (42 m.) road. The town grew up around a Franciscan friary founded about 1300 by Giolla Íosa Rúa O Reilly, Lord of East Breany (Bréifne, an ancient tribal name; see Dromahaire). Among the illustrious dead buried in the friary, besides the founder himself, were Myles the Slasher O Reilly, slain in the heroic defence of Finea bridge in 1644 (see under Granard); Primate Hugh O Reilly (1653); and the able Catholic Confederate soldier, Gen. Eóghan Rúa O Neill (1649). Nothing now remains of the friary, which was burnt by the English in 1451, 1468, and 1576, nor indeed of any other antiquity in the town, which was destroyed in 1690 after the defeat of Berwick's Jacobite force by the Enniskillen men under Gen. Wolsey. (The square tower by the friary belonged to an 18th cent. Protestant church.)

St Patrick's Cathedral (1942) is a disappointing sham-Renaissance structure by Ralph Byrne; it has sculptures by Albert Power.

The Protestant parish church (1810) and the Court House (c. 1828) are by John Bowden.

There are many ringforts in the vicinity of the town, as indeed throughout the county in general.

3½ m. NE. is Shantemon Hill, inauguration place of the O Reilly lords of East Breany. "Finn Mac Cool's Fingers", a row of pillarstones on the N. slope, may mark the spot. The "Pattern of Shantemon", a Lughnasa assembly, was held here.

3¼ m. SW., on the road to Crossdoney, is Kilmore (Cell Mór, the "great church" founded by St Feidhlimidh), which gives its name to the diocese. Here are St Fethlimidh's Cathedral (Church of Ireland); also a good motte-and-bailey. The cathedral is a modern Gothic edifice, but incorporates a fine, Late-Romanesque doorway from the early monastery (afterwards Premonstratensian) on Trinity Island, 3 m. W. in Lough Oughter. (The stones of the doorway have not all been correctly reset.) In the churchyard is the tomb of the Englishman, William Bedell, Protestant bishop of Kilmore from 1639 to 1642, compiler of an Irish grammar, and (in collaboration with Murtagh King, James Nangle, and Denis Sheridan) first translator of the Old Testament into Irish; he was buried with full honours by the Confederate Catholics. The motte-and-bailey was constructed by Walter de Lacy on the occasion of the abortive Anglo-Norman attempt (1211) to penetrate the North. It was dismantled by Cathal O Reilly in 1224.

2¼ m. NW. are the fine Farnham demesne and house, seat of the Maxwells (Lords Farnham). The Maxwells, of Scottish origin, have figured prominently in the Church of Ireland since the reign of Elizabeth I, and have given bishops to both Kilmore and Meath. The Farnham property was purchased in the 17th cent. by Robert Maxwell, Bishop of Kilmore. About 1700 his son built a house at Farnham, for which James Wyatt (see Ardbraccan House under Navan) designed a new library. From 1802 onwards the house was greatly enlarged by Francis Johnston. About 1839 it was further extended. In 1963 most of the house was swept away, and the residence now represents but the lesser of the Johnston wings (Johnston's Doric portico has been taken from the part demolished in 1963).

6 m. NW., on an island in Lough Oughter, are the ruins of Cloghoughter Castle (Nat.Mon.). The best preserved example of the native Irish type of circular tower-castle of the 13th–14th centuries, it was built by the O Reillys on the site of a crannóg and was probably their principal seat prior to the building of Tullymongan castle. In 1641–2 Bishop Bedell was imprisoned here by the Confederate Catholics, whose great general, Eóghan Rúa O Neill, died here in 1649, a grievous loss to the Irish cause.

7 m. NW. is Inishmore (see under Killeshandra).

CELBRIDGE, Co. Kildare (Map 6, C3), until the 18th cent. Kildrohid, Kildrought (Cill droichid, "church of the bridge"), is a Liffeyside village on the Leixlip (4 m.)–Clane (9 m.) road. It takes its name from a monastery founded by St Mo-Chúa of Clondalkin, whose well, Tobar Mo-Chúa, is near the mill. In the 18th and 19th centuries the village was the seat of a considerable woollen manufactory.

Oakley (Park), formerly Celbridge Hall, was built (by the architect of Castletown?) about 1724 for Arthur Price, who, when Vicar of Celbridge, proposed to Swift's "Vanessa", when Bishop of Meath began Ardbraccan House (see under Navan), and when Archbishop of Cashel wrecked the cathedral there. Oakley became the home of the Napier family to which belonged: Emily,

Duchess of Leinster and mother of Lord Edward Fitzgerald of 1798 fame; Caroline, Lady Holland and mother of Charles James Fox; and Gen. Sir William Napier (1785–1860), military historian. 300 yds W. of the house are the ruins of the Protestant parish church destroyed in 1798. The Conolly mausoleum has a splendid monument (by Thomas Carter; d. 1756) to William Conolly (1662–1729) of Castletown (*below*); the effigies are of Conolly and his wife, Catherine Conyngham; the wrought iron is noteworthy.

Celbridge Abbey was built by Dr Marley, bishop of Clonfert. Later it was the home of Esther Vanhomrigh (1690–1723), Swift's "Vanessa". A seat beneath the rocks by the river is alleged to have been the lovers' favourite retreat.

1 m. NNE. is Castletown, built about 1722 for William Conolly, Speaker of the Irish House of Commons, 1715–29. (Conolly had purchased the estate forfeited by its Jacobite owner, Sir William Dongan, Viscount Dongan of Clane and Earl of Limerick.) Until 1966 the home of Conolly's descendants, and reputedly the largest private house in Ireland, Castletown is an accomplished Early Georgian mansion, perhaps the most important, architecturally, of its period. The famous Bishop Berkeley of Cloyne asserts that "the plan is chiefly Mr Conolly's invention", that he himself was consulted on some points, and that designs for the elevation were made "by several hands". Maurice Craig attributes the design adopted to the youthful Edward Lovett Pearce, architect of the Dublin Parliament House. The mural and other decorative paintings include works by Giambattista Cipriani, Charles Reuben Ryley, and Thomas Ryder. 1¾ m. NW. of the house (2½ m. NNW. of the village) is Conolly's Folly, a large, obelisk-crowned triumphal arch erected in 1740 (to the design of Richard Cassels?) by William Conolly's widow. ¾ m. N. is Donoughmore (*see under* Maynooth).

½ m. NE., on the E. side of the Liffey, are the ruins of the medieval parish church of Donaghcumper. About ½ m. further NE. is St Wolstans, built by J. Allen, builder of Jigginstown (*see under* Naas); much altered. In the demesne are the remains (two gateways, tower, etc.) of a priory founded in 1202 in honour of the recently canonized St Wulfstan, bishop of Worcester. At the Dissolution the priory was granted to John Alen of Coteshall, Norfolk. The last Alen of St Wolstan's, a Jacobite, left Ireland with the Wild Geese.

3 m. S., to the E. of the Liffey, in Lyons Demesne (since 1962 seat of the Faculty of Agriculture of University College, Dublin), is Lyons Hill (Liamhuin), one of the early royal seats and public assembly places of the kingdom of Leinster, and later chief seat of the Mac Giolla Mo-Cholmógs of Uí Dúnlainge (*see* Newcastle, Co. Dublin). The hill (657 ft) affords a beautiful prospect of mountain and rich lowland. It is one of the places claimed as the scene

of Daniel O Connell's celebrated duel with D'Esterre (1815). Slight traces of earthworks are discernible on the summits and slopes. The ruins of a fortified house (*see* Newcastle Lyons, Co. Dublin) in the demesne mark the site of a village destroyed in 1642 by English troops from Dublin. The nearby church of the Blessed Virgin Mary has been much altered, and the chancel converted into a Lawless mausoleum. The 1548 memorial to Richard Aylmer bears the arms of the Flemings of Slane and the Tyrells. The Tyrells got possession of Lyons in the Middle Ages. From them it passed, seemingly by marriage, to the Aylmer family. The Aylmers sold it to the first Lord Cloncurry. Lyons House is a large stone mansion with colonnaded wings. The central block was built in 1797 by Oliver Grace for Michael Aylmer, the wings added in 1810 by Valentine Lawless, 2nd Lord Cloncurry (1773–1853), who is said to have spent £200,000 on the house. The interior has some good stucco ceilings; also charming tempera mural paintings (after Claude, ornaments found at Herculaneum, etc.), the remains of an extensive series by Gaspare Gabrielli, whom Cloncurry brought over from Rome in 1805. Lord Cloncurry was a member of the United Irishmen and an active opponent of the Union. He was imprisoned in the Tower of London, 1799–1801. For tactical reasons he opposed O Connell's campaign for Catholic Emancipation and refused to join his Repeal movement. For similar reasons he disapproved of Young Ireland, though sympathizing with John Mitchel. He was a generous landlord and lover of the arts. (John Hogan's admirable *Hibernia and Cloncurry* is a reminder of his patronage of that neglected sculptor.) The Hon. Emily Lawless (1845–1913), poet and author, lived in Lyons House. – 1¾ m. SW. of Lyons church is Oughterard (*see under* Kill, Co. Kildare).

1¼ m. SSW., on the W. bank of the Liffey, is Killadoon, a good house built about 1790 for the Clements family. ¾ m. SW. of the entrance gate, in Ardrass Lower, is St Patrick's Chapel, a stone-roofed, 15th cent. chapel (restored); nearby is St Patrick's Well; on the adjoining hill is St Patrick's Bed, a natural hollow. 1¼ m. SW. of the Chapel is Lodge Park, Straffan, built in 1773–5 for Hugh Henry, banker; it is now the residence of Mr R. S. Guinness. 2¼ m. ESE. of Straffan, a small graveyard marks the ancient eremitical site, Castledillon (properly Díseart Iollathan, corrupted to Tristledelan, and so to Castledillon). There is a broken gravestone here, with the engraved effigy of an ecclesiastic on one face and a fleur-de-lys cross on the other; the inscription is in Norman French. 2 m. S. of Straffan, in Whitechurch, are remains of a manorial castle and church, with Lady Well nearby; ¼ m. NE., in Clownings, is the site of a medieval moated house.

3½ m. W. is Taghdoe; *see under* Maynooth.

CHAPELIZOD, Co. Dublin (Map 6, D7), is a suburban Liffeyside village on the Dublin

(3 m.)–Lucan (10 m.) road. The adjacent reaches of the Liffey are notable for their beautiful parklands. The Protestant parish church has a late medieval tower.

Edward Tingham, 17th cent. statuary, lived at Chapelizod.

Alfred Harmsworth (1865–1922), first Lord Northcliffe, celebrated British press lord and propagandist, was born in Chapelizod.

A good secondary road to Lucan follows the winding N. bank of the Liffey.

1 m. NW., on the S. side of the river, is Palmerston House (now incorporated in the Stewart Institution for Imbecile Children). This great mansion was erected by John Hely Hutchinson, Prime Serjeant-at-Law and later Provost of Trinity College, who purchased the property in 1763. ¼ m. NE. are the remains of a small, early, nave-and-chancel church with trabeate W. door and plain, round-headed chancel arch and E. window. In it is a monument to Grace Keating (previously Lady Shruckburgh; d. 1677).

CHARLEMONT, Co. Armagh (Map 3, B5), is a village by the Blackwater on the Armagh (7 m.)–Dungannon (5½ m.) road. Commanding the river-crossing are the remains (Nat. Mon.) of a fort erected during Mountjoy's 1602 campaign against Great Hugh O Neill and subsequently enlarged. The main star fort was completed by 1624, the massive earthworks added in 1673. The surviving gateway (with the Caulfeild arms), beside the filled-in moat, was probably erected in the late 18th cent. The outer earthworks, with pointed bastions covering every part of the perimeter, are the finest example of 17th cent. artillery fortification in Ulster. In 1641 the fort was taken by Sir Felim O Neill, and was not recovered by the English (Cromwellians under Venables) until 1650. Held by the Jacobites in 1689–90, it was stormed by Schomberg's Williamites in the latter year. From then until 1858 it remained a British garrison post. The fine 17th-cent. governor's house – sometime home of the Caulfeilds, a Planter family – and the later barracks were burnt down by guerrillas in 1922 and subsequently demolished. When the Caulfeilds were raised to the peerage they took their title from Charlemont. The most distinguished bearer of the title was the Volunteer Earl, patriot and patron of the arts. (*See* Dublin City, Main Axis; Charlemont House, Parnell Sq.)

On the opposite side of the Blackwater, in Co. Tyrone, is Moy, a village laid out after the plan of Marengo in Lombardy for the Volunteer Earl; George Ensor designed some of the buildings. The great tree-lined "square" is spoilt by a bus shelter.

5 m. E. is Ardress House (Nat. Trust), a 17th cent. farmhouse charmingly remodelled by George Ensor, the Dublin architect, who came to live in it in about 1775. It has lovely stucco by Michael Stapleton of Dublin, including *Cupid Bound* (based on a Bartolozzi print after a painting by Angelica Kaufmann). The stucco has recently been restored in accordance with Stapleton's designs. In the dining room are paintings lent by Lord Castlestewart. Open to the public: April to Sept., Wed., Thur., Sat., 2–6 p.m.; July, Aug., Sept., Sun. 2.30–5.30 p.m.; admission 2/–, children 1/–.

CLANE, Co. Kildare (Map 6, C3), is a Liffeyside village on the Kilcock (10 m.)–Naas (7 m.) road.

There was an early monastery at Clane, of which Sinchell the Elder (*see* Killeigh) is said to have been first abbot; the only relic is the Wartstone, a bullaun by the Butterstream (opposite friary, *below*). In 1162 a national synod assembled at the monastery. It decreed that the masters of studies of all monastic schools should henceforth be alumni of Armagh. To implement the decree, High-king Rory O Conor assigned (1169) an annual stipend to the head of the Armagh school "to give lectures to students from Ireland and Scotland".

SE. of the village are remains of a Franciscan friary founded in 1258 by Sir Gerald fitz Maurice Fitzgerald, 4th baron O ffaly (d. 1287), whose mutilated effigy is still there; to the S., overlooking the Liffey, is a de Hereford motte to which the name Queen Buan's Grave has been given in recent times; nearby is Sunday's Well.

2 m. NE. is beautifully situated Clongowes Wood College (1814), the well-known Jesuit boarding school. The nucleus of the school buildings is Castle Browne, a much altered (1718 and 1788) FitzEustace castle which was a border fort of the English Pale. Forfeited for participation in the Catholic Confederation (p. 43), it was purchased in 1667 by the Brownes, who intermarried with the Wogans. In 1813 Gen. Michael Wogan-Browne, A.D.C. to the King of Saxony, sold the castle to the Society of Jesus. The interior of the old school chapel, now a public church, is an interesting example of inexpensive, early-19th cent. work in the Classical manner. The new chapel, an uninspired Gothic edifice, has Stations of the Cross by Séan Keating and a series of beautiful windows by Michael Healy (1873–1941) and Evie Hone (1894–1955). The Healy windows began with a remarkable three-light *St Joseph* in the choir (1916), continued with his two-light *St Patrick and St Brigid* (1920), and ended with the first three of a *Seven Dolours* series of two-light windows in the nave (1936–41): *Prophecy of Simeon, Flight into Egypt*, and *Search for the Holy Child*. Healy's work was cut short by death, and ended with the base and top of the fourth window, *Christ meets His Mother*, which was completed by Evie Hone. Evie Hone continued the series with *The Crucifixion* and *The Taking Down from the Cross* (1941). Her design for the last window of the series, *The Entombment of Christ*, exists only as a cartoon. Also in the chapel are two other Hone windows: a cir-

cular *Head of Christ Crucified* (1949) and a two-light *SS Ignatius and Francis Xavier* (1955). The great artist died before she had quite completed the latter. In a dark corridor near the chapel is hung Evie Hone's *The Taking Down from the Cross.* In the school museum is The Prosperous Crozier, a 10th cent. bachall-shrine found in a bog in Prosperous. N. and S. of the college are sectors of the Pale. To the N. of the main gate is Mainham, where there is an old churchyard with the ruins of a church and the 1743 mausoleum (note inscription over entrance; the Rev. John Daniel was the Protestant rector) of the Wogan-Brownes. Nearby is a motte, relic of the castle of the first Anglo-Norman proprietor, John de Hereford. 2½ m. NE. of Mainham church is the gatehouse (Nat. Mon.) of Rathcoffey Castle, chief seat of the Wogans descended from Sir John de Wogan, English Justiciar, 1295–1300. Nicholas Wogan of Rathcoffey (d. 1660) was one of the leading Confederate Catholics. To a branch of the family which lived at Richardstown belonged the celebrated Jacobite soldier, Sir Charles Wogan (1698?–1752?), who rescued the Princess Clementine Sobieska from Innsbruck and escorted her to Bologna to marry the Old Pretender. In later life he was for some years Corregidor, or chief magistrate, of La Mancha, and ended his life as Governor of Barcelona. In the 19th cent. the castle was purchased by Archibald Hamilton Rowan, member of the United Irishmen, who demolished it to make room for a new residence.

1 m. S. is Blackhall House, birthplace of the Rev. Charles Wolfe (1791–1823), poet ("The Burial of Sir John Moore"). He was curate at Donaghmore, Co. Tyrone, and died at Cobh, Co. Cork, where he is buried. The family was related to the Wolfes of Castlewarden, after whom Wolfe Tone was named. Tone is buried in Bodenstown churchyard, 2 m. SSE. of Clane (*see under* Kill).

4 m. SW., across the Grand Canal, is Landenstown House, an interesting Queen Anne house.

3½ m. WSW. (to the SE. of Prosperous) are the good Georgian houses of Killybegs (red brick, *c.* 1750) and Longtown.

7 m. NW. is Donadea Castle (*see under* Maynooth).

CLARA, Co. Offaly (Map 5, E1), is a market town and manufacturing centre (jute, flour-milling) where the Moate (4 m.)–Tullamore (15 m.) road crosses the Brosna river. It originated as a Quaker settlement. The Protestant parish church dates from 1770.

5 m. W., beyond Ballycumber, is Boher Catholic church. Here is preserved the large, portable, tomb-shaped shrine or reliquary made in the 12th cent. to contain the bones of St Manchán of Lemanaghan (*see under* Ferbane). Though much defaced, this reliquary is one of the most important products of the post-Viking Irish revival. It appears to have been made in the same atelier (Clonmacnois?) as the superb,

contemporary Cross of Cong, now in the National Museum. The 12th cent. bronze figurines formed no part of the original shrine.

CLARECASTLE, Co. Clare (Map 5, A3), formerly Clare, a village where the Ennis (3 m.)–Limerick (19 m.) road crosses the estuary of the Fergus, takes its name from a castle (incorporated in the derelict military barracks) commanding the river-crossing.

The Catholic church has a window by Michael Healy: *Veronica's Towel, Christ meets his Mother, Ecce Homo* (1927).

1 m. N. are the ruins (Nat. Mon.) of Clare "Abbey", a priory of Canons Regular of St Augustine, dedicated to SS Peter and Paul, which was founded in 1189 by Donal Mór O Brien, King of Limerick. The remains are largely of 15th cent. date, but include some late-12th–early-13th cent. work; the cloister has disappeared. At the Dissolution the monastery and its possessions were among the properties granted to Donnchadh O Brien, Baron of Ibracken, on condition he gave up the name of O Brien and undertook to use English manners, language, dress, etc.

1½ m. SE. is Carnelly House, a good early-18th cent. Stamer house (noteworthy saloon).

2 m. W. is Killone (*see* Newhall House *under* Ennis).

CLAREGALWAY, Co. Galway (Map 1, D6), is a hamlet where the Galway (6 m.)–Tuam (14 m.) road crosses the Claregalway River. The crossing is dominated by the massive tower of a 15th cent. Clanrickard Burke castle. In 1538 Lord Deputy Grey took the castle with the aid of artillery. In 1643 it was seized by local Burkes for the Confederate Catholic cause: In 1651 it was taken by the Cromwellian, Sir Charles Coote II. West of the castle are the ruins (Nat. Mon.) of a fine Franciscan friary founded by John de Cogan about 1240/50. The slender bell-tower, N. transept, and E. window are 15th cent.; the cloister has disappeared. There are some interesting 18th cent. tombstones with occupational symbols (ploughs, etc.).

5 m. NNE., to the W. of the Tuam road, in Caheravoley, is Cregboyne Fort (Nat. Mon.), a 17th cent. bawn with two angle turrets and rectangular traces of a house. There are several ringforts in the area, including Caheravoley itself, ½ m. ESE.

5 m. NE. is Knockdoe (216 ft), where, in 1504, Gearóid Mór, Earl of Kildare and English Lord Deputy, with the aid of O Donnell, routed Ulick III (Fionn), 3rd Mac William Úachtair of Clanrickard, and his O Brien, O Carroll, and O Kennedy allies.

6 m. NE. (1 m. E. of the Tuam road) are the remains of the tower and square bawn of Anbally castle (Burkes). The site being below winter flood level, the castle was erected on a built platform.

CLARE ISLAND, Co. Mayo (Map 1, B4), is a mountainous island (Croaghmore, alias Knockmore, 1,520 ft) at the mouth of Clew Bay. It is most conveniently reached from Roonah Quay (*see under* Louisburgh). Overlooking the harbour is the defaced Grania Wael's Castle (Nat. Mon.), a 15th/16th-cent. O Malley castle tower modernized in 1831 to serve as a coastguard station. Popular legend names it after Gráinne Ní Mháille, Grace O Malley, though she never held it. Gráinne (about 1530–1600) was the daughter of Dubh-Dara O Malley, lord of Upper Umhall. Her freebooting exploits on land and sea have passed – with the inevitable romantic exaggerations – into legend. She married first, Donal O Flaherty, lord of Ballynahinch, and second, Richard an Iarainn Burke, lord of Carra and Burrishoole. In 1574 she beat off an English seaborne expedition against Carraig an Chabhlaigh castle (*see under* Newport, Co. Mayo). In 1577 she was captured by the Earl of Desmond and imprisoned in Limerick and Dublin. In 1580 she helped the English against her rebel husband. After his death, in 1583, she took up her residence at Carraig an Chabhlaigh. In 1586 she was arrested for complicity in the Burkes' rebellion. Seven years later she appeared before Elizabeth I to petition for maintenance and a licence to harry the Queen's enemies with fire and sword. According to some, she was buried in Clare "Abbey" (*below*); according to others, in Burrishoole friary (*see* Newport). The well-known story about Gráinne and the heir of Howth, Co. Dublin (*q.v.*), is apocryphal. The earliest version is told of Richard O Cuairsci Burke (d. 1479).

From the harbour: ½ m. NE. is Toberfelabride, a lintel-roofed holy well of once wide repute. SW. of the well is a much rebuilt cashel enclosing Leaba Bhrighde (St Brigid's Bed – a beehive hut) and a shapeless altar of stone slabs. "Stations" are made here on 15 Aug.

1½ m. WSW. are the remains of Clare "Abbey" (Nat. Mon.), thought to have been a cell of Knockmoy Abbey (*see* Abbeyknockmoy). The ruins are those of a small, late-15th cent. nave-and-chancel church with two-storey N. annexe; over the chancel is a dwelling tower. The noteworthy feature is the sadly decayed, 15th and 17th cent. painting on the founder's tomb, E. wall, and chancel vault. In the churchyard is a tall cross-pillar. To the NNW. is decayed Toberfelamurry, with remains of a shapeless "altar" to the E. ¼ m. SW. of the "abbey" are remains of Doonagappul, a promontory fort.

3 m. WSW., on the W. side of Ooghaniska, is a spectacularly sited promontory fort. The cliff scenery hereabouts is good.

2 m. NW., in Ballytoohymore townland, is Doonallia promontory fort.

CLAREMORRIS, Co. Mayo (Map 1, D4), is a small market town and railway junction on the Ballyhaunis (11 m.)–Castlebar (16 m.) road.

2 m. NE. are the remains of Ballinasmalla "Abbey", a Carmelite friary said to have been founded by the Prendergasts.

7 m. NE., on the Kilkelly road, is Knock (Cnoc Mhuire), a place of pilgrimage ever since the apparitions claimed to have been seen at the gable of the church, 21 Aug. 1879.

8 m. SE. (2½ m. ESE. of Ballindine village), in Lisduff townland, is a wedge-shaped gallery grave. Between it and the road is a defaced ringfort with a souterrain. At the corner of a bohereen to the SE., and on the S. side of the Ballindine–Dunmore road, is a fragment of a chamber tomb.

CLARINBRIDGE, Co. Galway (Map 1, D6), is a small village on the Galway (10 m.)–Gort (14 m.) road, near the head of Dunbulcaun Bay, most easterly inlet of Galway Bay. The locality is noted for its oysters and scallops.

Adjoining the village on the SE. is the demesne of Kilcornan House. The house, now a school and training centre for the mentally handicapped, incorporates the tower of a 15th/16th cent. castle. Beside the avenue are the ruins of a small, simple, medieval church.

¼ m. E., by the N. side of the little Clarinbridge River, is an unusual earthwork (? medieval fortification).

2 m. S. is Kilcolgan (*q.v.*).

1¾ m. SW., by the seashore SW. of Ballynamanagh bridge, is Dunbulcaun, an unusual, multivallate ringfort with steep, motte-like, central mound.

2¼ m. W., by the roadside in Cottage townland, is Rathgurreen, a bivallate ringfort whose inner defences are later than the outer. The site is a commanding one.

2 m. NW., beside the Galway road, is Caheradrine(en), an early ecclesiastical site enclosed by remains of a strong cashel.

CLASHMORE, Co. Waterford (Map 5, D6), is a village where the Cappoquin (12 m.)–Ardmore (7 m.) road crosses the little Creagagh River, 2 m. E. of the Blackwater estuary.

The roofless Protestant church occupies the site of a monastery founded by St Mo-Chúa, alias Crónán, disciple of Cárthach of Lismore.

W. of the village is St Mo-Chúa's Well.

CLAUDY, Co. Derry (Map 2, E2), is a village on the Dungiven (11 m.)–Derry (10 m.) road.

1 m. NW., near the Derry road in Cregg, is the "White Stone" (Nat. Mon.), a fine prehistoric pillarstone of white quartz.

5 m. NE., (¾ m. SSW. of Loughermore bridge), alt. 800 ft on the E. and W. sides of Ballyholly Hill, are three stone circles with alignments (Nat. Mons.); also other megalithic structures. ¼ m. N. of Loughermore bridge, is the Clady Stone (cup-and-ring marks).

3 m. ESE., in Clagan, are three tall pillarstones (Nat. Mons.) overthrown in 1770. One has been re-erected.

4 m. SSW., in Althahoney, a stone cross (Nat. Mon.) marks an ancient church site.

2½ m. NW., on the Derry road in Crossalt, are the ruins of Brackfield Castle, a fortified bawn. It was built by the Skinners Company of London at the Ulster Plantation. 4¼ m. NNE., in Ballygroll, on a long hill ¾ m. E. of Slieve Buck, is a series of stone circles and cairns (Nat. Mons.). – 4½ m. N., in Mullaboy churchyard on the E. side of Slievebuck, is an ancient stone cross (Nat. Mon.).

CLEAR ISLAND, Co. Cork (Map 4, D6),

lies 6 m. SW. of Baltimore, from which it may be reached by mail-carrying motor-boat (four services weekly). Fastnet Rock, 4 m. SW., is the most southerly point in Ireland.

The population is still Irish-speaking and preserves many traditional customs. The cliffs and headlands offer many good walks and striking views of the mainland.

The rocky island, 3 m. by 1½ m., has been almost cut in two by the inlets, Ineer, or South Harbour, and Trawkieran, or North Harbour. Trawkieran (Tráigh Chiaráin) is called after St Ciarán of Seir Kieran (see under Birr), who was a native of the island. Near the NW. corner of the inlet are the remains of Teampall Chiaráin and Gallán Chiaráin, an early cross-pillar (Nat. Mons.); "rounds" are made at the pillar on the vigils of 15 March (St Kieran's day) and 25 March. Nearby is Tobar Chiaráin, a hollow in the shingle where water is procured for blessing the islanders' homes and sick. Teampall Chiaráin was a simple, 12th–13th cent. church with a small, two-light E. window and plain, Romanesque–Transitional S. door.

The following mileages are reckoned from Trawkieran:

¾ m. ENE., in Lissnamona, at the early church site called An Cillíneach, is an early cross-pillar. The site commands a fine view. ¾ m. E. is Knockcarntheen, highest point of the island (532 ft); it takes its name from a small cairn. – 1½ m. NE., in Comillane, is an alignment of four stones (two prostrate); the N. stone is holed.

1 m. ESE. is Croha West pillarstone.

1 m. SSE., in Glen West, overlooking South Harbour, is Gallán na mBánóg, an alignment of low stones; also on the hill is a pillarstone. A destroyed cairn here produced a stone slab decorated in the passage-grave style with spiral and serpentiform devices.

¾ m. SSW., to the SE. of Lough Errol in Ballyieragh South, is an early cross-pillar.

1½ m. SSW., in Ballyieragh South, is Dún Thomáis, a promontory fort with remains of a stone hut.

½ m. W., in Ballyieragh North, on the site of a promontory fort, are remains of the O Driscoll castle of Dún an Óir.

CLEGGAN, Co. Galway (Map 1, B5), is a

hamlet with a small fishing harbour on Cleggan Bay, 7 m. NW. of Clifden and 7 m. W. of Letterfrack.

¾ m. W., on the E. side of Sellerna Bay, in Knockbrack, is Labbadermot, a chamber tomb.

1½ m. NE., on a low cliff NW. of Cleggan House, is Druid's Altar, chamber tomb of a court cairn.

1¾ m. ENE., on the S. side of the road in Ballynew, is a partly wrecked court cairn.

3 m. E., in Clooncree, fragments of a small ornamented cross and St Ceannanach's Stone mark the spot where, says legend, the decapitated martyr placed his head while resting before returning to Aran. His blood left its mark on the stone. The whole aetiological legend was, of course, suggested by the saint's name, Ceannanach, from ceann, head. (In its Latinized-Anglicized form, Gregorius – Gregory, the saint's name is preserved by Gregory's Sound between Inishmore and Inishmaan, Aran Islands.) – ½ m. E. is St Ceannanach's Well (resorted to on 12 March).

6 m. SW. is Omey Island, which may be reached on foot at low tide. There are fine sands here, where pony racing takes place in August. In the sandhills near the N. shore the ruins of Templefeheen, a small medieval church, preserve the memory of a monastery founded by St Féichín of Cong (q.v.), Fore (see Castlepollard), and Ardoiléan (below). By the W. shore is Toberfeheen, Féichín's well. – 2 m. SW. of the Omey Island crossing, in Leagaun, is a pillarstone.

7 m. W. is Ardoileán, alias High Island, where St Féichín had another eremitical settlement. The remains (Nat. Mons.) include a diminutive church, two clocháns, several early cross-slabs, and fragments of three enclosing cashels. Near the highest point of the island is a holy well said to cure colic and kindred ailments; there is an early cross-slab here.

6 m. NW. is Inishbofin, a pleasant place for a simple holiday. When he was defeated at the Synod of Whitby (p. 25), Bishop Colman of Lindisfarne withdrew from the English mission. He came with his adherents – who included thirty English monks – to Inishbofin and set up a monastery. Disputes having arisen between the English and Irish brethren, he founded a new monastery for the English monks at Mayo (see under Balla) and ruled both houses until his death (674/6). The Inishbofin monastery disappears from history after 900. The island was captured from the O Flahertys by the O Malleys about 1380. In the 16th cent. the celebrated Gráinne Ní Mháille (see Clare Island) is said to have fortified the island for her fleet. In 1652 the island was surrendered to the Cromwellians, and it remained a garrison post until about 1700. The Cromwellians used the island as a "concentration camp" for priests and monks. At the harbour entrance is Cromwell's Barrack, embodying Bosco's Castle. Bosco is said to have been a pirate – Dane or Spaniard – allied with Gráinne Ní Mháille. The sadly defaced Barrack was a 24-gun star fort erected about 1652–7. 1 m. NE., close to a fine beach, is the site of St Colmán's monastery, with a featureless church and a bullaun. St Colmán's Well

has been forgotten, but St Flannán's Well remains. In the sandhills are remains of clocháns. – On the W. shore of the harbour is Doon Grannia, a cliff-top fort. – At the SE. end of the island, on a bold cliff, is Doonmore (alias Doonkeen) promontory fort. There are hut-sites to the E.

CLIFDEN, Co. Galway (Map 1, B5), "capital of Connemara", is a small market town and fishing port beautifully sited at the head of the N. arm of Clifden Bay, 50 m. NW. of Galway (via Oughterard) and 44 m. SW. of Westport (21 m. SW. of Leenaun). It was founded about 1812 by John Darcy of Killtullagh (*see under* Athenry), whose derelict "castle" (1815) is 1½ m. W. It is a noted angling centre and a convenient base for exploring some of the loveliest regions of the W. There are several good bathing beaches within reach of the town, of which the finest is the Coral Strand on Mannin Bay (3 m. SW.). The Connemara Pony Show, held at Clifden in mid-August, is worth visiting. Clifden Marconi Wireless Station, destroyed during the last Anglo-Irish war, was the first transatlantic wireless-telegraph station in Europe.

Some delightful walks and short tours may be had in the vicinity, one of the finest being NW. by the upper road, overlooking Clifden Bay, to Belleek and beyond. Longer tours, taking in some of the most celebrated beauty-spots of the W., include: Clifden–Letterfrack–Kylemore–Lough Inagh–Glendollagh–Clifden; Clifden – Letterfrack – Tully Cross – Gowlaun – Lough Fee, returning to Clifden via Kylemore or Lough Inagh; Clifden–Kylemore–Leenaun–Aasleigh–Delphi–Doo Lough (*see* Leenaun *and* Westport). The town is also a convenient base for exploring the Twelve Bens (*see* Ballynahinch), which offer special rewards to the climber.

2½ m. N., to the W. of the Cleggan–Letterfrack road, in Streamstown (alias Barratrough), is Clochalegaun, three pillarstones; to the W. is a ringfort. Also in Streamstown is a court cairn.

1 m. S., in Ardbear House demesne, is Toberbeggan, a holy well.

5 m. SSW. (1 m. NE. of Ballyconneely) is Derrygimlagh bog, where John Alcock and Arthur Whitten Brown crash-landed at the end of the first W.–E. flight across the Atlantic, 15 June 1919. A cairn has been erected at the edge of the bog close to the landing-place, and a monument (1959) at a viewing place on high ground 1½ m. away.

5 m. SW., by the N. shore of Loughnakilla, on Errislannan (Iorrus Fhlannáin, Flannan's peninsula), are Kilflannan – a ruined medieval church – Tobar Fhlannáin, and St Flannan's Bed; they are dedicated to St Flannán of Killaloe.

12 m. NW. is Ardoileán, alias High Island (*see under* Cleggan).

CLIFFONEY, Co. Sligo (Map 2, B4), is village on the Bundoran (8 m.)–Sligo (13 m.) road. It was formerly part of an estate belonging to Viscount Palmerston (1784–1865), British statesman and Prime Minister, some of whose property, including Classiebawn Castle 2½ m. to the NNW., descended to the late Countess Mountbatten. Lord Palmerston carried out many improvements on the estate, including the building of Ahamlish Protestant parish church (1815) and the construction of the harbour at Mullaghmore, a little resort overlooking Bunduff Strand 2½ m. N. of Cliffoney. In Bunduff is a well-preserved court cairn.

Less than ¼ m. W. is St Brigid's Well. There is an early cross-slab here.

1 m. NE., slightly to the E. of the Bundoran road and the hamlet of Creevykeel, is Creevykeel Giants' Graves (Nat. Mon.). This magnificent full-court cairn resembles those in Deerpark, Sligo (*q.v.*), Malin More, Co. Donegal (*see under* Glencolumbkille), and Ballyglass, Co. Mayo. An entrance passage through the E. end of the wedge-shaped cairn leads to a sub-rectangular ritual court, off whose W. end opens a two-chamber gallery grave. To the W. of the latter were two other tombs, opening off the N. and S. sides of the cairn respectively. Towards the W. end of the court are the remains of a small circular structure of the early historic period. The cairn was excavated in 1935 by the Harvard archaeological expedition. Four cremated burials were discovered, as well as Western Neolithic pottery, polished stone axes, flints, etc. 650 yds WSW. are the remains of another chamber tomb, while between the Bundoran road and Bunduff Lough are the ruins of three small stone ringforts.

½ m. S., in Cartonplank, is Tombannavor, alias Giant's Grave, an overgrown court cairn in a long mound.

CLOGHAN, Co. Offaly (Map 5, D2), is a village on the Banagher (6 m.)–Clara (15 m.) road.

Commissioners of Public Works in Ireland
Clononey castle, Cloghan

2 m. NW., on the road to Shannonbridge, are the well-preserved tower (modernized) and 17th cent. bawn of Clononey castle. It was occupied down to the 19th cent. In the bawn is a noteworthy slab commemorating two members of the Bullen (Boleyn) family exiled to Ireland after the execution of Anne Boleyn by Henry VIII. 1½ m. W. of the castle, in Moystown Demesne, remains of a church and an early gravestone mark the site of Tisaran, an early monastery founded by St Sárán; the stone is inscribed OR[ÓIT] DO BRAN ("A prayer for Bran").

CLOGHEEN, Co. Tipperary (Map 5, D5), is a village on the Clonmel (14 m.)–Mitchelstown (13 m.) road, at the N. foot of Knockshanahullion (2,150 ft) and Sugarloaf Hill (2,144 ft), two of the highest of the Knockmealdown mountains. The road S. to Lismore (*q.v.*). climbs Sugarloaf Hill by the well-known V-road, a series of hairpin bends affording superb panoramas of mountain and plain.

The Catholic parish church (1862–4), is by J. J. McCarthy.

2 m. E., on the N. side of the River Tar at Castle Grace, are remains of a de Bermingham (?) castle of about 1250; rectangular, with angle towers (three round, one square). ½ m. NE. are the ruins of the medieval parish church of Tullaghorton.

1 m. W. are the remnants of Shanrahan church and castle. In the churchyard is buried Father Nicholas Sheehy, who was hanged at Clonmel, 15 March 1766, after a trial on trumped-up charges brought against him (in gross breach of faith) by the bigoted gentry of S. Tipperary. His cousin, too, was hanged, for daring to give evidence in his defence. In 1867 the Lord Lismore of the day invoked military aid to prevent a memorial being erected over Father Sheehy's grave.

4 m. NW. is gutted (1958) Shanbally Castle, built for Viscount Lismore to the design of John Nash. 1½ m. NW., are the remains of Shanbally church. 1 m. NW. of the latter is Burncourt village (*see under* Ballyporeen).

CLOGHER, Co. Tyrone (Map 2, E4), which gives its name to the diocese, is now a mere village on the Enniskillen (23 m.)–Dungannon (21 m.) road, at the head of the pleasant Clogher valley. The country round about it is rich in ancient remains.

St Mac Cairthinn, according to legend St Patrick's "strong man" or bodyguard, was the first bishop at Clogher, which appears to have been the seat of a pagan oracle before he built a monastery, as instructed by Patrick, near the royal seat of Airgíalla. Of the early monastery the only relics are: a 7th (?) cent. cross-pillar (S. of the cathedral) with conventionalized *Crucifixus* (head defaced) and ribbon interlacing; two 9th/10th cent. High Crosses (reconstructed) found in the cathedral graveyard about 1912; and the lintel of a trabeate church

doorway (now in cathedral porch). In the 12th cent. Clogher became the see of a diocese for the kingdom of Airgíalla (*see* Louth). Nothing survives of the pre-Reformation cathedral, and the see of the Catholic diocese is now at Monaghan (*q.v.*). St Mac Carten's Cathedral is a small, 1818, Classical rebuilding of Bishop Stearne's 1744 church "in the ancient style of English architecture"; there is a second Church of Ireland cathedral at Enniskillen (*q.v.*).

The first Protestant bishop (1570) of Clogher was the notorious pluralist, Myler Mac Grath (*see* Cashel); the most distinguished probably John Stearne (1660–1745), scholar and collector of Irish manuscripts.

Park House, alias Old Palace, was erected about 1799 by Bishop Lord John Beresford. It is a rather gaunt block set on an arcaded podium and has not been improved by its accretions. The Deanery is another interesting house. In Clogher Demesne is a series of earthworks comprising a hill-fort (?; the royal seat of Airgíalla ?), a motte-and-bailey (?), and a saucer barrow (?).

5½ m. SE., on top of "Spink-ana-gaev" in Altadaven (*Alt a' Deamhain*, "The Demon's Cliff"), are St Patrick's Chair (cup marks), St Patrick's (alias Brigid's) Well (a bullaun), and the Mass Rock (alias Altar). Lughnasa celebrations were held here until recently; ½ m. S. is little Lough Beg, into which Patrick banished the demons of Alt a' Deamhain. 3 m. W., and ¼ m. NE. of Crockancrin, alt. 600 ft, are Derrydrummond Giants Graves (Nat. Mon.), the remains of a long chambered cairn. On the NW. slope of Culla More, alt. 800 ft, is Cullamore Giants Grave (Nat. Mon.), a court cairn. On the S. slope of the mountain, alt. 800 ft, is a cist grave with large, cup-marked capstone. SSW. of Culla More, in Ballywholan, are: alt. 400 ft, Carnfadrig (Nat. Mon.), a long, chambered cairn, and 200 yds. NE. of Greaghnasanna bridge over the Fury River, alt. 600 ft, Carnagat (Nat. Mon.), a double-court cairn.

3 m. SW. is Fardross House, an attractive small 18th cent. house with later additions.

2½ m. W., in Daisy Hill demesne, is Findermore Abbey Stone (Nat. Mon.), a low, cross-inscribed pillarstone. Here also is one of the two stone "chairs" found on Ashban Mountain (*see* Favour Royal *under* Aughnacloy). Some 2 m. further W. is Aghintain Castle (Nat. Mon.), a Plantation castle built in 1618 by Sir William Stewart.

6½ m. WNW., in Lislane, are: on the S. side of the Glenamuck River and 1¼ m. N. of Glenbane bridge, alt. 500 ft, the Giants Grave, a gallery grave with porthole entrance; ½ m. SE. of Glenbane bridge, alt. 700 ft, a ruined gallery grave.

2¾ m. NW. is Prolusk, birthplace of the novelist, William Carleton (1794–1869).

CLONAKILTY, Co. Cork (Map 5, A7), is a small market town on the Bandon (13 m.)–Skibbereen (19 m.) road, at the head of the land-locked Clonakilty Bay. The town was founded in 1614 by Richard Boyle, afterwards "Great" Earl of Cork (*see* Bandon).

1½ m. N. is the ancient church site of Temple-bryan, a large enclosure with remains of a primitive church, a souterrain, a well (Toberna-killa), and an 11-ft pillarstone; low down on the W. face of the stone is a cross *pattée*; on the adjoining angle is a faint ogham inscription. To the SE. is a circle of five (nine in 1743) large stones enclosing a white central stone.

1½ m. S. (via causeway) is Inchdoney, an island across the mouth of the bay. Sandhills, a good sandy beach, and excellent bathing are the principal attractions. ¾ m. S. of the causeway is a pillarstone; some 300 yds SE. of this are the remains of Inchdoney church. On the S. side of the island projects the Virgin Mary's Rock whose legend is the theme of Jeremiah Callanan's ballad.

6 m. SSW. is little Duneen Bay. A pictur-esque, winding, minor road leads SW. to Donoure (4¾ m.).

4¼ m. WSW., at Sam's Cross[roads], is a memorial, by Séamus Murphy, to Michael Collins (1890–1922), the great guerrilla organ-izer against the British, who was born in nearby Woodfield. It was unveiled, Easter 1965, by Gen. Tom Barry, who fought against Collins in the tragic Civil War of 1922–3.

6 m. W. is Dirk Bay, with Dunowen Head on the E. and Dundeady Island–Galley Head on the SW. At the head of the bay is the Red Strand. On the E. side of Dunowen Head are remains of Dunowen castle. On the neck of the Dundeady Island peninsula are the remains of Dundeady castle. 2 m. WNW. of the Red Strand, in Castlefreke Warren, are sandhills and the Long Strand (1 m.). At the NW. end of the strand is Cloghna Head, beyond which is Inch Strand (*see under* Ross Carbery).

3½ m. NW., in Letter, is Cromlech, a chamber tomb.

CLONASLEE, Co. Laois (Map 5, E2), is a village on the fine Mountmellick (11 m.)–Birr (17 m.) road round the N. and W. slopes of Slieve Bloom.

2½ m. W. are the ruins of Castle Cuffe built in the 17th cent. by Sir Charles Coote.

CLONDALKIN, Co. Dublin (Map 6, D7), once a walled town of the English Pale, is now a rapidly growing, unattractive, industrial vil-lage, or rather suburb, to the N. of the Dublin (6¼ m.)–Naas (14¾ m.) road. The principal industries are paper-making and tile-making.

The main road of the village cuts through the site of a monastery founded in the 7th cent. by Bishop St Mo-Chúa (alias Crónán) moccu Lugaedón, but which first appears in Irish records under the year 776. For a time in the later 8th cent. the abbacy seems to have been confined to the founder's kin, the Lugaedón sept. The "translation" of St Mo-Chúa's relics took place in 789. In 833 the monastery was

pillaged by the Vikings, who made a settlement nearby. They were defeated, and their fortress burned, by the king of Laois in 867. After the Anglo-Norman conquest the church was annex-ed to the deanery of St Patrick's Cathedral, Dublin. Of the monastery there survive the Round Tower (Nat. Mon.) and, in the Protest-ant churchyard, a large granite cross (Nat. Mon.), a small granite cross, and a rude granite basin (*see* St Maol-Ruain's Losset, Tallaght). An antiphonary belonging to the monastery is preserved in Trinity College library. In Carls-ruhe is a fragment of an ancient missal which may have come from the monastery.

SE. of the Protestant church is Clondalkin Castle, alias Tully's Castle (Nat. Mon.), a small, 16th cent. tower with 17th (?) cent. lean-to.

1¾ m. SE. is the gate-tower of Ballymount castle.

½ m. S., beside Brideswell Lane, is Bride's (alias St Brigid's) Well.

1 m. S. is Newlands House, home of Lord Chief Justice Kilwarden, who was assassinated on the occasion of Robert Emmet's rebellion, 1803; now Newlands Golf Club.

1½ m. S., on the Tallaght road, is the Georg-ian house, Belgard Castle. It incorporates a fragment of a castle of the Talbots (*see* Mala-hide) which was an important border fortress of the English Pale. Richard Talbot, James II's Earl of Tyrconnel, is said by some to have been born in the castle.

1 m. SW. is Baldonnell (renamed Casement) military aerodrome. It was from this aerodrome that the German fliers, Kohl and von Huenfeld, with the Irish airman, James Fitzmaurice, took off on the first successful E.–W. Atlantic flight, 1932.

3 m. SW. are the remains of the castle and tiny church, or chapel, of Kilbride.

1 m. NW., near the fragments of Deansrath castle, are the ruins of Kilmacudrick (alias Kilmahuddrick) church, a small, plain, medi-eval, nave-and-chancel parish church dedicated to St Cuthbert of Lindisfarne.

CLONEGALL, Co. Carlow (Map 6, C5), is an attractive village where the Tullow (7 m.)–Enniscorthy (14 m.) road crosses the little River Derry near its junction with the Slaney.

Beside the village is the demesne of Hunting-ton Castle, a fortified house of the 17th cent. which has been considerably modernized.

5 m. N., is Moylisha (*see* Aghowle *under* Shillelagh).

CLONES, Co. Monaghan (Map 2, D5), is a market and Border town on the Dundalk (41 m.)–Enniskillen (24 m.) road.

The history of Clones commences with a monastery founded by St Tighearnach, previ-ously bishop at Clogher (*q.v.*), who died here 549/50. He was a Leinsterman, but his mother was of Airgíalla (Uriel), and Clones became one of the principal monasteries of that king-dom. In the 12th cent. the monks became

Romanesque doorway, St Brendan's Cathedral, Clonfert

Canons Regular of St Augustine (SS Peter and Paul Abbey). There survive: in Abbey St, a fragment of a small 12th cent. church; in the ancient graveyard nearby, an imperfect Round Tower and St Tighearnach's Grave, the latter a 12th (?) cent., church-shaped tomb; in the Diamond (market place), a High Cross (Nat. Mon.) made up of the head and shaft of separate 10th

(?) cent. crosses. The weathered figurations on the cross include: South Face: *Fall of Adam and Eve, Sacrifice of Abraham, Daniel in the den of lions*; *Crucifixion*; North Face: *Adoration of the Magi, Miracle of Cana, Multiplication of the loaves and fishes*.

W. of the Diamond is a conspicuous motte-and-bailey (Clones Fort).

7 m. E., beyond Killeevan, is Carran (*see under* Monaghan).

CLONFERT, Co. Galway (Map 5, C2), is a townland 1 m. N. of the Ballinasloe (12 m.)–Banagher (5 m.) road and 5 m. NE. of Eyrecourt. In 558/64 Brénaind moccu Altai, alias Bréanainn son of Fionnlugh (Brendan the Navigator), whose legend made its own contribution to medieval literature and to the story of Atlantic discovery, founded a monastery here (*see also* Cnoc Bréanainn *under* Dingle). Among the famous names associated with the monastery are those of Cummine Fota and Cú-Chonnacht na Scoile (of the School) O Daly. Cummíne, who died about 662, was the author of a Penitential. He lived in intimate converse with Comgán moccu Cherda, "the fool of the Déise", who sang of Cnoc Raffand (Knockraffon) and Heaven. Cú-Chonnacht, a native of Bunbrosna, Co. Westmeath, died at Clonfert in 1139. His grandson, Aengus, was ancestor of the celebrated O Daly dynasty of poets. The monastery was ravaged by the Vikings in 844 and 845; it was destroyed by fire in 749, 1016, 1164, and 1179. At the 12th cent. reformation it was transformed into a priory (St Mary's *de Porto Puro*) of Augustinian Canons Regular. The same reformation saw Clonfert become the see of the newly founded diocese to which it has given its name. The skeleton of the small cathedral ascribed to Conor Maenmoy O Kelly, King of Uí Maine, 1140–80, survives substantially (caretaker's house is ¼ m. SW.); its superb W. doorway is one of the glories of Irish Romanesque. In its original form, the cathedral was a single-chamber church with *antae* at each gable. The chancel is an early-13th cent. addition; its two-light Transitional E. window is worth examination within and without. In the 15th cent. the friary-type bell-tower (the incorrect parapet is a modern "restoration") and the transepts (N. transept now missing) were added, the Transitional (presumably) chancel arch was replaced by the existing Gothic arch, Gothic windows were inserted in the chancel walls, and the inner (limestone) order was inserted in the Romanesque doorway. The cathedral was wrecked in the 16th cent. and partly re-edified for Protestant use in the 17th. It suffered again from restorers in the 18th and 19th centuries. (The uncouth treatment of the interior wall-faces dates from 1882.) In the nave is an interesting 15th cent. font; affixed to the adjacent wall are some early gravestones (the two inscriptions read: OR[ÓIT] DO BACLAT ("A prayer for Baclat"), and BECGÁN). The Jacobean woodwork stacked nearby came from

the 17th cent. bishop's palace. In the roofless S. transept is another early gravestone. (The Catholic cathedral is now at Loughrea, *q.v.* The Church of Ireland diocese is united with that of Killaloe, *q.v.*) From the 12th cent. to the Reformation, Clonfert also had a convent (in Nun's Acre, S. of the cathedral) of Canonesses Regular of St Augustine; it was a dependency of Kilcreevanty, Tuam.

1 m. SW., in Clonfert Catholic church, is an interesting 14th cent. wooden statue of the Virgin and Child.

5 m. SW., on the Killimor–Banagher, Co. Offaly road, is Eyrecourt (*q.v.*).

CLONMACNOIS, Co. Offaly (Map 5, D2), site of one of Ireland's foremost early monasteries, lies on the E. bank of the Shannon, 4 m. N. of Shannonbridge (*q.v.*), 13 m. (9 m. by boat) S. of Athlone (*q.v.*), and 14 m. SW. of Moate (*q.v.*). The ideal approach is by boat from Athlone. The remains (comprising eight churches, two Round Towers, three High Crosses, over 400 early gravestones, and two holy wells, Nat. Mons.) are of exceptional interest to the student of early Irish art and architecture.

As an ecclesiastical centre Clonmacnois (Cluain moccu Nóis, meadow of the race of Nós) had only one rival, Armagh. As a centre of Irish art and literature it had none. Many Kings of Tara and kings of Connacht, to say nothing of rulers of lesser degree and other eminent folk, were buried there.

The monastery was founded by St Cíarán, Son of the Wright and disciple of St Finnian of Clonard (*q.v.*), who came down-river from Inis Ainghin (*see* Lough Ree. with eight companions on 25 Jan. 545. Seven months later (9 Sept.), Cíarán died. His father, a chariot-builder, was a native of the North-East who had settled not far from Fuerty, Co. Roscommon, in the homeland of the Uí Briúin dynasty. Cíarán was thus a Connacht man by birth, and this doubtless contributed to the intimate relations between his great monastery and various Connacht dynasties which made Clonmacnois, in effect, the chief monastery of Connacht. In fact, Clonmacnois lay just over the frontier of Connacht, in territory which the Southern Uí Néill had conquered from Leinster as recently as 517, and with the Uí Néill, too, the monastery maintained a close and cordial friendship, particularly from the time of Melaghlin I (846–62). (Legend has it that Diarmait I, King of Tara, helped Ciarán with his own hands to erect his first wooden church at Clonmacnois.) When Díarmait was murdered in Dál Araide, 565, (*see* Rathmore *under* Antrim *and* Connor *under* Ballymena), his head was brought all the way to Clonmacnois for burial.

The significance of Clonmacnois for the development of Early Irish vernacular literature and historical records is made clear by the surviving products of its scriptorium: *Lebor na hUidre* (*Book of the Dun Cow*), the Bodleian

Library MS., Rawlinson B.502 – these are the
two oldest of the great Irish literary codices –
Chronicon Scotorum, the *Annals of Clonmacnois*, and the *Annals of Tigernach*. Its importance as a centre and repository of early Irish art
is indicated by the nature and quality of the
works which have come down to us, though
these can represent but a fraction of the output
of its workshops: the High Crosses, the unpar-
alleled series of early gravestones, St Kieran's
Crozier, the Crozier of the Abbots of Clonmacnois, the Cross of Cong (Nat. Museum),
and St Manchán's Shrine (*see* Boher *under*
Clara).

Clonmacnois had more than its share of misfortunes. It was ravaged by fire thirteen times
between 722 and 1205, and plundered by the
Vikings eight times between 832 and 1163. (In
844 the notorious Thorgestr (Turgesius) burned
down the monastery, and his wife, Aud (Ota),
gave oracles from the principal altar.) Irish
enemies assailed it no less than twenty-seven
times between 832 and 1163, English foes six
times between 1178 and 1204. It was finally reduced to complete ruin by the English garrison
of Athlone in 1552, when "not a bell, large or
small, or an image, or an altar, or a book, or a
gem, or even glass in a window, was left which
was not carried away".

In 1955 the Church of Ireland presented the
site to the State, which up to then had owned
only the masonry of the ruins. Since then the
treatment and maintenance of the monuments
has signally improved. A tragic blunder, has
however, been committed in allowing the cemetery to be extended without an investigation,
and new graves are constantly being dug through
archaeological deposits.

In its heyday Clonmacnois was more than
just a monastery. It was rather a monastic city
(in 1179 no fewer than 105 houses were burned
down), with workshops, and dwellings of workers and armed retainers as well as of the monks,
and some twelve or thirteen small churches and
oratories. Today there survive no workshops or
dwellings at all, while of the churches we have
the fragments of no more than eight. Some of
these churches are of architectural interest. In
addition, the group as a whole exemplifies the
incoherent character of early Irish monasteries
– with their multiplication of scattered, small-
scale, simple churches–which contrasts so markedly with the Continental coherent monasteries
dominated by a single, complex, great church.

The tour of Clonmacnois may conveniently
commence with the series of early gravestones
and fragments of two High Crosses admirably
displayed to the left of the Shannonbridge gate
of the cemetery. Next may be taken the South
Cross, a 9th/10th cent. High Cross, for the
most part covered with panels of interlacing
vine-scrolls and other ornaments, but having
a *Crucifixion* on the W. face of the shaft
(Christ's ankles are bound).

Immediately NE. is a small early church
called Temple Dowling because re-edified in

Commissioners of Public Works in Ireland

Gravestone inscribed OR[ŌIT] DO THUATHAL SAER
Clonmacnois

1689 by Edmund Dowling of Clondalare as a
family chantry or mausoleum. Built on to the
E. end is a later church, to which the name
Temple Hurpain has been attached, seemingly
with little justification. This building, which
may be Edmund Dowling's work, has a late-
Gothic S. door and a crude E. window.

NE. of these two churches is Temple Melaghlin, alias Temple Rí, a late-12th cent., rectangular structure. Two of the gable brackets
for barge-boards survive. The E. window is a
Western Transitional, two-light window with
plain mouldings. In the S. wall are an Early
Gothic lancet and a Late Gothic doorway.
There was a timber gallery over the W. half of
the church.

N. of Temple Melaghlin is diminutive Temple
Kieran, alias Eaglais Bheag. The fragmentary
masonry is a patchwork of different dates, but
includes remains of three *antae*. This is traditionally the burial place of St Cíarán, and
devotees still collect the sacred earth in the NE.
corner. In the late 17th cent. the local peasantry
kept "St Cíarán's Hand" here as a sacred relic.
The 11th cent. "Crozier of the Abbots of
Clonmacnois", now in the National Museum,
is said to have been found here early in the last
cent. along with a chalice and other objects.
Against the E. wall stands a 12th cent. gravestone.

NW. of Temple Kieran are the foundations
of Temple Kelly, thought to be the church

erected in 1167 by Conor O Kelly and the Uí
Maine. Near the SW. corner is a bullaun.

SW. of Temple Kelly is the Cathedral, alias
Daimhliag Mór, alias Mac Dermot's Church,
alias Mac Coghlan's Church. The first "great
stone church" of Clonmacnois was that built
in 900 by Flann Sinna, King of Tara, and
Abbot Colmán, son of Ailill. It was burned in
985, 1020, and 1077. A new church was begun
in 1080 by Conn na mBocht (father of Máel-
Muire, principal scribe of *Lebor na hUidre*, and
eponymous ancestor of the "family of Conn na
mBocht") and completed about 1100 by Flaithbertach Ó Loingsigh. Extensive restoration was
carried out in 1336 by Tomaltach Mac Dermot
(whence the name Mac Dermot's Church).
Interesting alterations and additions were made
by Dean Aodh Úa Máel-Eóin (Malone) in
1460. In 1647 the ruin was repaired for use by
Vicar Charles Mac Coghlan (whence the name
Mac Coghlan's Church). The remains are those
of a rectangular church with *antae* at each gable
and an early-13th cent. sacristy on the S. side.
In the W. gable are fragments of a fine Romanesque doorway inserted in the late 12th cent.
and reconstructed in the 15th. The E. gable has
disappeared. There are remnants of an unusual
Gothic chancel inserted into the E. end about
1460. It consisted of three low, groin-vaulted
aisles or chapels. The groins rested on eight
engaged half-columns and four octagonal columns. Above it would have been a loft, or rood-
gallery, approached from the chamber over the
sacristy. Turloch Mór O Conor (d. 1156), King
of Connacht and High King, was buried to the
S. of the high-altar; his son Rúairí (d. 1198),
last of the High Kings, was buried to the N. of
the altar. Beside Turloch's grave was that of his
grandson, Dermot; to the W. of Rúairí's grave,
that of his son, Conor Maenmagh (d. 1189).
By the N. wall of the nave are two weathered,
12th/13th cent. gravestones. At the NW. corner
is an interesting Perpendicular doorway with
figures of SS Patrick, Francis, and Dominic
above; the inscription reads: DOM[INU]S
ODO DECANUS . . . ME FIERI FECIT
("The Lord Aodh [Úa Máel-Eóin] Dean [of
Clonmacnois] had me made"). A Gothic door
in the S. wall leads to the stone-vaulted sacristy,
in which are stored miscellaneous carved fragments.

W. of the cathedral is Cros na Screaptra, The
Cross of the Scriptures, alias King Flann's
Cross. A partly defaced inscription at the base
of the shaft is said to record that Abbot Colmán
erected it in memory of Flann Sinna (d. 916)
King of Tara. The subjects figured include:
Base: *Horsemen, charioteers*; Shaft: W. face:
Arrest of Christ (?), *Soldiers guarding the tomb
of Christ, Crucifixion*; E. face: *The Last Judgement, Díarmait I and St Cíarán erecting the
cornerpost of a church* (?).

NE. of Cros na Screaptra is the shaft of the
North Cross; a seated figure with crossed legs
and antler head-dress is discernible.

W. of the North Cross is the Clogás Mór or

Commissioners of Public Works in Ireland

Cross of the Scriptures, Clonmacnois

Great Belfry, alias O Rourke's Tower, an
imperfect Round Tower some 62 ft high which
has been attributed to Fergal O Rourke, King
of Breany, who was killed in 964. Actually, the
completion of the belfry by Abbot-bishop
Gilla-Críst Úa Máel-Eóin in 1120/24 is recorded in some of the Annals. The top was struck
off by lightning in 1135, and it has been estim-
ated that nearly half of the tower is missing,
although it continued in use until the sack of
1552. The doorway is plain Romanesque.

NE. of the belfry is 12th cent. Temple Conor.
It was in ruins in 1735, but has been restored
to serve as the Protestant parish church. The
W. door and the smallest of the S. windows are
old features. On the N. side of the church are
modern mausolea of the Malone (Úa Máel-
Eóin) family.

At the N. edge of the cemetery is fragmentary
Teampall Finghin, alias Mac Carthy's Church,
a small nave-and-chancel church of unusual
interest. The fragments of the nave include the
remains of a Romanesque S. door and W. window. The handsome chancel arch is rather
mutilated; the innermost order is an insertion.
In the stone-roofed chancel a doorway gives
access to the Clógas Beag, or Little Belfry, a
fine, small Round Tower which is an integral
part of the church. (*See* St Kevin's Church *and*
Trinity Church, Glendalough; Kilmacnessan
under Howth; *and* the Augustinian monastery,
Ferns.) The rhomboidal stones of the roof are

Commissioners of Public Works in Ireland

Doorway of the Nuns' Church, Clonmacnois

set so as to produce a herring-bone effect. Near the Shannon, to the N. of the church, is St Finghin's Well, where the anchorite, Gormán, is said to have lived on bread and water for a year before his death (615/617); he was ancestor of the "family of Conn na mBocht" (*above*). NE. of the church formerly stood Temple O Kyllin.

A paved way (1070 ?) leads, via a gate in the E. wall of the cemetery, towards the fragmentary remains of the secluded Nuns' Church, a beautiful, small, nave-and-chancel Romanesque church built by Dervorgilla, wife of Tiernan O Rourke of Breany (*see* Mellifont Abbey). It was completed in 1167. The W. doorway and fine chancel arch (on which is a sheila-na-gig) were re-erected in 1865. Unfortunately, the restorers swept away most of the ancient cashel which had surrounded the church. To the N. the Pilgrims Road marks an ancient highway to the monastery.

W. of the cemetery, on a motte beside the Shannon, are the shattered remains of a strong castle with gatehouse on the NW. and keep on the N. This is possibly the castle erected in 1220 by the English Justiciar, John Gray.

¼ m. W. of the cemetery, beside the Shannon-bridge road, is St Ciarán's Well. There is a crude late Crucifixion slab here.

3 m. E., near Clonfinlough church, is the Clonfinlough Stone (Nat. Mon.), a large boulder covered with prehistoric scribings whose affinities are to be sought in the Iberian peninsula. According to Macalister they depict a battle.

CLONMANY, Co. Donegal (Map 2, D1), is a beautifully sited village 1¾ m. SSW. of Bally-

liffin (*q.v.*). The Clonmany River makes a pretty fall in Glanevin.

E. of the village are the Cloghbane pillar-stones.

1¼ m. N., at an ancient church site in Binnion, is a stone cross.

2¾ m. ESE. is Cloontagh (*see under* Bally-liffin).

2½ m. SE., in Meendoran, is a chamber tomb.

1¼ m. S., in Clonmany Glebe, is Cloghtogle, a chamber tomb. In the Middle Ages the O Morrisons of Clonmany Glebe were hereditary keepers of the Miasach, a book shrine now in St Columba's College, Rathfarnham.

1½ m. SSW., in Adderville, is a chamber tomb.

2 m. SSW. is Raghtinmore, where – says a local tale – Fionn mac Cumhaill dispensed his laws. On it is a cairn, and the plateau is littered with ancient hut sites.

5 m. SW., between Mamore Hill (1,381 ft) and Croaghcarragh (Urris Hills, 1,379 ft), is the steep, difficult pass of Mamore, noted for its splendid views.

6 m. WNW., at the mouth of Lough Swilly, is Dunaff Hill (690 ft), with magnificent views.

2 m. NNW. is little Tullagh Bay with a good beach.

CLONMEL, Co. Tipperary (Map 5, D5), county town of the South Riding of Tipperary, is an important market town and small-scale manufacturing centre (cider, footwear, perambulators) in the beautiful Suir valley, 13 m. W. of Carrick-on-Suir, 22 m. N. of Dungarvan, 11 m. E. of Cahir, and 15 m. SE. of Cashel. To the S. and SE. rise the Comeragh Mountains (Knockanaffrin, 2,478 ft). 7 m. NE. is Slievenamon (*see under* Fethard). The Suir valley, downstream to Carrick and upstream to Cahir, is noted for its scenery. The high ground N. of the town affords splendid views of the Comeragh, Knockmealdown, and Galty mountains. The circuit Clonmel–Gurteen–Glenpatrick–Nier valley–Knocklofty–Clonmel (35 m.) will be found rewarding, the views in the Gurteen–Glenpatrick area being particularly fine; much of this circuit is, however, by minor roads, and it includes several hairpin bends.

At the Norman conquest the de Burgos acquired a manor at Clonmel, and Richard (d. 1243) probably founded the town. The manor belonged to the de Grandisons from 1267 to 1338, when it was purchased by the Earl of Desmond. Since it lay within the Palatinate of Ormond, created in 1328 (*see* Nenagh), conflicting interests soon occasioned feuds between the earls of Ormond and Desmond, conflicts which ceased only with the final overthrow of the latter in 1583. Like so many other Anglo-Norman towns, Clonmel remained loyal to the English Crown throughout the Middle Ages, but was ultimately driven to seek safety in the national camp and, in December 1641, admitted a Confederate Catholic garrison. The Supreme Council of the Confederation (*see* Kilkenny) assembled there in June 1647. On 27 April 1650, Cromwell appeared before the town, which was garrisoned by the gallant, able Hugh Dubh O Neill with 1,250 ill-supplied Ulster troops. Having breached the N. wall, the Cromwellians made their grand assault on the morning of 9 May, only to be thrown back with bloody loss – "the heaviest we ever endured either in England or here". O Neill's ammunition, however, was by then exhausted, and that night he and his men stole away. Skilfully concealing their defenceless condition, the townsfolk capitulated next day on a guarantee of life and estate, but the capitulation marked the ruin of the ancient burgher families, and for the next two hundred years Clonmel was controlled by a new oligarchy.

Like Waterford, Clonmel produced several notable Catholic leaders and scholars in the 16th and 17th centuries, among them the brothers Thomas and Stephen White and the brothers Geoffrey and Bartholomew Baron. It was for Thomas White, S.J. (1556/8–1622), that Philip II of Spain founded the celebrated Irish College of Salamanca (closed 1951). Stephen White (1574–1650), also a Jesuit, was a remarkable scholar – "Polyhistor", "first theologian of the century", "the wonder of Germany". Having been professor of theology at the universities of Ingolstadt (1608–9) and Dillingen (1609–22), he was recalled to Ireland in 1629 to teach at the abortive Back Lane college in Dublin (see Dublin, South-West). He collaborated with the Protestant primate, Ussher, and with continental scholars, as well as with his famous countrymen, John Colgan, Hugh Ward, and Patrick Fleming, in exploiting the rich mine of Irish ecclesiastical literature on the Continent. Geoffrey Baron (1607–51), a nephew of the celebrated Luke Wadding of Waterford, was one of the leaders of the Catholic opposition in Strafford's notorious "Graces" parliament of 1634. He took a very prominent part in the affairs of the Catholic Confederation and was hanged by Ireton when Limerick capitulated in 1651. His brother, Bartholomew, better known as Father Bonaventure Baron (1610–96), was famous as orator, philosopher, theologian, historian and Latin poet.

Laurence Sterne (1713–68), author of *A Sentimental Journey*, was born in Clonmel, his mother's native place. George Borrow (1803–81) attended school in the town during the few months his father was stationed there (1815). Father Abram Ryan, army chaplain and song-writer of the Confederate States (*The Sword of Robert Lee, Re-united, Erin's Flag*), was the son of Matt and Mary Ryan of Clonmel.

The Court House, Nelson St, is by Sir Richard Morrison (1800). It was the scene of the state trial of William Smith O Brien, Thomas Francis Meagher, Terence Bellew Mac Manus, and Patrick O Donohue, after the abortive Young Ireland insurrection of 1848.

The Municipal Library, Parnell St, houses the Clonmel Museum and Art Gallery.

In Mitchell St is the Mainguard, built as the seat of the courts of the Palatinate of Ormond, whose coat of arms, together with those of the municipality, still adorn it. Said to have been copied from a design of Sir Christopher Wren's, it was completed in 1674. James II was received by the Corporation here, 21 March 1689. After the extinction of the palatinate jurisdiction (1715), the building served as Tholsel and seat of the royal assizes, and the infamous trial of Father Nicholas Sheehy (see Shanrahan *under* Clogheen) took place there in 1766. About 1810 the building was adapted to private use and the ground floor, a loggia of open arches, was converted into shops.

At the Town Hall are preserved the civic regalia and municipal muniments; these may be inspected on application to the Town Clerk.

The Franciscan friary (1891–2), in nearby Abbey St, is by W. G. Doolin. The church, also by Doolin (1884–6), incorporates the 15th cent. tower and 13th cent. N. choir wall of the church of a friary founded in 1269. The friary was converted into a citadel after the Cromwellian conquest. In 1826 the friars managed to lease the remnants of their church and incorporated them (1828) in a nondescript structure. Doolin copied the details of his E. window from the E. window of the 13th cent. choir. In the church may be seen the basin of a font from medieval St Mary's (*below*); also the ,tomb (about 1533) of the Butlers of Cahir (see Cahir). The latter has effigies of an armoured knight and his lady; the polychrome colouring has altogether disappeared.

Mary St takes its name from the medieval parish church of the Assumption of the Blessed Virgin Mary, otherwise "Our Ladye of Clonmell" (13th cent., rebuilt in 15th). St Mary's parish church (Church of Ireland), erected in 1857 to the design of Welland, occupies the site, and incorporates interesting 15th cent. fragments (fine E. window, chancel arch, basement of tower, vestry, aisle walls, W. window, W. window of porch). Some 16th and 17th cent. tombstones of burgher families are preserved in the church. The N. and W. sides of the churchyard are bounded by portions of the medieval town wall, including the NW. angle tower and two flankers.

West Gate (1831), which closes the W. end of O Connell St, occupies the site of the medieval town gate whose name it bears. Nearby is the grammar school attended by George Borrow and described in *Lavengro*.

The present parish church of the Assumption (St Mary's), Irishtown (on the site of a Penal-times Mass house outside the town), is a Classical building of 1837–50; steeple and portico 1875–90. It has a good stucco ceiling; the expensive high altar (1867) was designed by the English architect, George Goldie. In the church may be seen the monument (1615) of John fitz Geoffrey White, first Mayor of Clonmel; it came from the old Franciscan church.

The Medical Missionaries convent has a

Madonna and Child (enamels) by Brother Benedict Tutty, O.S.B.

On the S. side of the river are the remains of St Nicholas' Church, alias Teampall na Pláighe. 4½ m. N., in Lisronagh, is the site of an Anglo-Norman manor, with remains of a castle and burgh. In the neighbourhood are several ringforts and other earthworks. 1½ m. NE. of the castle are the neglected remains of Baptist Grange church and castle and the site of an old village. The church had a three-bay chancel arch; in it is a medieval font. – 1¼ m. W. of Lisronagh castle is Donaghmore church (*below*).

2¼ m. NE., in Moortown, are the remains of a medieval nave-and-chancel church with central tower.

2 m. E. is Two-mile Bridge, alias Sir Thomas' Bridge, built in 1690 by Sir Thomas Osborne. Some 200 yds N. of the bridge, in Anner House, is "The Falconry", with a collection of birds of prey; demonstrations of falconry. Some 250 yds SE. of the bridge, in Co. Waterford, are the ruins of Tickincor, alias Kincor, a Tudor-style house built by Alexander Power in the reign of James I. 1 m. further E. are the ruins of the Butler castle of Derrinlaur.

5 m. E., on the S. side of the Suir, is Gurteen (-le-Poer) with its beautiful demesne and woods. At the W. end of the demesne is a prehistoric chamber tomb (capstone fallen).

5½ m. E., on the N. side of the Suir, is Kilsheelan. There are ruins of a nave-and-chancel church with Romanesque–Transitional N. doorway (mutilated) and a plain Romanesque chancel arch; both added in the 12th/13th cent. A motte marks the site of a castle erected by William de Burgo (?) at the Anglo-Norman conquest. 5½ m. NE. is Kilcash (*see under* Carrick-on-Suir).

4¾ m. SW., in Glebe (Co. Waterford), are the remains of Kilronan, a 12th (?) cent. church with 14th and 15th cent. features; it appears to have had a double roof of stone in the Irish manner.

2¼ m. WSW., in Marlfield, the Protestant church of Inishlounaght marks the site and incorporates some fragments (Transitional door-head of three orders, E. window, tomb fragments, etc.) of the Cistercian abbey De Surio, founded before 1148 by Melaghlin O Phelan of the Déise and colonized from Monasternenagh (*see under* Croom) in 1151; it was re-endowed by Donal Mór O Brien of Thomond in 1187. The abbeys of Fermoy, Corcomroe (*see* Kinvarra), and Glanragh, were daughters of Inishlounaght. In 1227 the abbey was affiliated to Furness Abbey, Lancashire, but the general chapter of 1278 restored it to Monasternenagh. The celebrated *Life* of St Máel M'Áedhóg ("Malachy") of Armagh by St Bernard of Clairvaux was written at the instance of "his dear friend", Abbot Comgán of Inishlounaght. – 1¼ m. NNW. is St Patrick's Well (*below*).

5 m. WSW., in a fine demesne, is Knocklofty

House, Georgian residence of the Hely-Hutchinsons, Earls of Donoughmore, who take their title from Donaghmore, Co. Cork (*see under* Coachford).

2¼ m. W., romantically sited in Patrickswell are the ruins of a 17th cent. church, a stone cross, and St Patrick's Well. The well, which figures in the *Life* of St Déaglán of Ardmore, was reputed to cure scrofula, sore eyes, etc. The church incorporates Romanesque and other fragments of an older structure. In it are stacked the remains of the altar tomb of Nicholas White of Clonmel (d. 1622). The tomb was erected in 1623 in a chantry chapel attached to the SW. corner of old St Mary's, Clonmel; when the chapel was thrown down (1805) the tomb-fragments were removed to St Patrick's Well. The figure subjects include *Crucifixion*, *Resurrection*, and *Virgin and Child*.

3 m. NW., in Giantsgrave, is the Giant's Broad Stone, alias Giant's Headstone, a 9-ft pillarstone with crosses on two faces.

4¾ m. NNW., in Donaghmore, Domhnach Mór Maighe Feimhin, the site of an early monastery founded by St Forannán is marked by the ruins (Nat. Mon.) of St Forannán's Church, a small, 12th cent., nave-and-chancel structure with the mutilated remnants of a fine Romanesque W. doorway and of a Romanesque chancel arch. The doorway had a pedimented porch and a tympanum with the figure of a two-tailed lion; the chancel had a double roof of stone. To the SE. are remains of a smaller church. 1¼ m. E. is Lisronagh (*above*).

CLOUGH, Co. Antrim (Map 3, C3), is a village on the road from Ballymena (7 m.) to Ballycastle (16½ m.). On a high basalt outcrop are some remains of a castle (Nat. Mon.) of various dates. It began as a motte-and-bailey and ended as a Plantation castle of 1600. The original castle was apparently constructed by the de Mandevilles (Mac Quillans), who were eventually ousted by the Mac Donnells. In 1641 the castle was besieged by the insurgent Irish. It was finally destroyed by Cromwellians. ¼ m. SW. are remains of the ancient church of Dunaghy.

1 m. SSE. is Doonbought (Nat. Mon.), a prehistoric fort reoccupied in medieval times.

2 m. WSW. is Dundermot (Nat. Mon.), a fine motte whose bailey has been destroyed.

CLOUGH, Co. Down (Map 3, D5), is a village at the intersection of the Castlewellan (5 m.)–Downpatrick (6 m.) and Newcastle (7 m.)–Ballynahinch (9 m.) roads. Close to the village is a motte-and-bailey with fragments of a stone castle.

1 m. N. are Seaforde village and demesne (Seaforde House, 18th cent.). 3 m. NNE. is Loughinisland. On an island (causeway approach) off the W. shore of the lake ruins of three churches (Nat. Mons.) mark an ancient monastic site. The featureless middle church

may be 13th cent., the north church 15th/16th cent. The date of the south church ("Felim Mac Cartan's Chapel") is quite unknown. The north church continued in use until 1720, when its roof was transferred to Seaforde Protestant church. 150 yds NE. of the lake is Annadorn Cromlech (Nat. Mon.), remnant of a chambered cairn. Annadorn Castle Hill takes its name from a former seat of the Mac Cartans. 2½ m. S. is Dundrum (q.v.).

CLOYNE, Co. Cork (Map 5, C6), is a village on the Middleton (6 m.)–Ballycotton (7 m.) road. There are limestone caves here.

The celebrated St Colmán mac Lénéne (d. 604), who had been a professional poet before becoming a monk, founded his principal monastery at Cloyne (see Kilmaclenine under Buttevant). He is the earliest known Irish poet making use of Latin rhymes whose work (fragments only) has survived. The monastery was plundered five times by the Norse between 822 and 916. At the 12th cent. reformation it was made the see of the newly organized diocese of Cloyne. The Catholic cathedral has been in Cobh (q.v.) since the passing of Penal times. The Protestant diocese has long been united with those of Cork and Ross.

Bishop John O Brien (d. 1768), was the author of the first Irish-English dictionary (published in Paris in 1768), as well as of works pirated by the notorious Gen. Vallancey. The celebrated philosopher, George Berkeley, was Protestant Bishop 1734–53. Dean Swift's "Vanessa" had bequeathed her entire estate to Berkeley and Robert Marshall of Clonmel near Cobh. Berkeley decided to use the money "for converting the savage Americans to Christianity" by founding St Paul's College, Bermuda (1725).

Of the ancient monastery the only relics are the 100-ft Round Tower and a remnant of the Fire House. The tower was struck by lightning in 1748/9 and the conical roof wrecked; the "restorers" reduced the height of the tower and added the battlements. On the opposite side of the street is much altered St Colman's Cathedral (Protestant), a cruciform church of c. 1270–80 with aisled nave of five bays and with a sacristy (chapter-house) projecting from the N. side of the choir. It was extensively repaired in 1642, and again in 1673/4. In 1705 the building was subjected to considerable "improvements": the demolition of the battlemented parapets, the carrying of the transept roofs into that of the nave, the addition of an Ionic doorcase to the Transitional W. doorway, etc. In 1705 the chancel arch was swept away and the E. bay of the nave taken into the choir; at the same time the choir was blocked off from the rest of the church. In 1856 the cathedral was "restored" (aisles widened, etc.). In the N. aisle are the monuments of Bishop Bennet (d. 1820), by J. Heffernan of Cloyne, and of Bishop John Brinkley (1826–35), celebrated astronomer; the latter is by the noted Tallow sculptor, John Hogan. In the long roofless N. transept (Fitzgerald Aisle), are the monuments of Bishop Woodward (d. 1794), an advocate of Catholic Emancipation, and George Berkeley (by Bruce Joy, 1890); also the 1611 tomb of the Fitzgeralds, seneschals of Imokilly (see Rostellan below, and Castlemartyr). The tomb was converted to his own use by the 3rd Earl of Inchiquin, whose great-grandfather had married into the Fitzgeralds of Cloyne; only fragments of the Fitzgerald effigies remain. In the S. transept (Poor's Aisle) is the 1677 tomb of Captain Bent (d. 1680); the monument of the Longfield family blocks the fine, five-light S. window. In the NE. corner of the churchyard are the scant remains of the Fire House (see Kildare and Inishmurray), of which nothing is known; it seems to have been an early church or oratory.

5 m. SE. is Shanagarry castle (see under Ballycotton).

2½ m. SW. are the interesting limestone caves of Carrigcrump.

1½ m. W., to the NW. of the mansion in Castle Mary demesne, is a prehistoric chamber tomb (much damaged) called Carraig a' Chotta.

3 m. W., on Cork Harbour, is pleasant East Ferry.

3 m. WSW. is Rostellan Castle, formerly seat of the Marquess of Thomond. The first castle here was built at the Anglo-Norman invasion by Robert de Marisco. Later the Fitzgeralds, seneschals of Imokilly, had a castle here. By the seashore (below high-water mark), is a prehistoric chamber tomb called Carraig a' Mhaistín. Rostellan, Aghada (4 m. W.), and Whitegate (6 m. SW.), are all pleasant little resorts on Cork Harbour.

9 m. SSW., and ½ m. E. of Power Head, is Dunpower, a promontory fort.

COACHFORD, Co. Cork (Map 5, B6), is a village and angling resort on the beautiful Cork (15 m.)–Macroom (9 m.) road. Fine views may be had hereabouts of the lovely Lee valley. The mountains to the NW., N., and NE., are particularly rich in ancient remains.

7 m. NNE. is Donaghmore, where St Laichtín (d. 622; see Freshford, Co. Kilkenny) founded a monastery. The early-12th cent. Shrine of St Laichtín's Arm, now in the National Museum, belonged to this monastery. The well-known poet, Eóghan Rúa Ó Súilleabháin (d. 1784), kept a school at Donaghmore for a time. – 3½ m. N., near the summit of Reanthesure (808 ft), in Beenalaght, is An Seisear, a six-stone alignment (one prostrate). – 4½ m. NE., in Pluckanes North, is a chamber tomb (roofless); 1½ m. SE. of this, in Garryadeen, is Tobar Laichtín, St Laichtín's Well; SW., in Garraun North, is a bivallate ringfort. ½ m. SW. of the fort (1½ m. SSE. of the Pluckanes North tomb) is Cromlech, another chamber tomb. 3 m. N. of Tobar Laichtin, in Lyradane, is a group of standing stones; 500 yds NE. of this, in Knockatota North, is a stone circle. 2¾ m. SE. of the Lyradane stones,

in Grenagh South, is a stone circle. – 1½ m. WNW. of Donaghmore, in Coolicka, is the Druid's Altar, remnant of a portal dolmen. 2 m. W. of the latter, in Kilmartin Lower, is a bivallate ringfort with a two-chamber souterrain whose innermost lintel is an ogham stone; two fields to the SW. is a stone circle. ¾ m. NNW. of this, in Barrahaurin, is a five-stone alignment (three stones prostrate). – 1½ m. NW. of Donaghmore, in Meenahony, are four standing stones. – 3 m. NNW. of Donaghmore, in Gowlane North, is a recumbent-stone circle with four stones set radially outside it.

3 m. S., in Roovesmore, is a large ringfort; three ogham stones, now in the British Museum, came from the souterrain. Also in Roovesmore is a fine stone alignment.

3¾ m. WSW., on the Lee, is Carrigadrohid. On a rock beside the bridge are the ruins of a late Mac Carthy castle. Legend would ascribe the choice of so obvious a site to the caprice of Dermot Mac Carthy's beloved, Una O Carroll. In 1650 the castle was attacked by Cromwellians commanded by Roger Boyle, Lord Broghill, who hanged Baothghalach ("Boetius") Mac Egan, Bishop of Ross, in sight of the walls for refusing to exhort the garrison to surrender. In the end Boyle took the castle by a ruse. The entrance from the bridge is supposed to have been constructed by order of Cromwell himself. 2¼ m. SE. of the bridge, in Knockavullig, is Cromlech, a chamber tomb; 400 yds SW. is a second tomb. – 1¾ m. SW. of the bridge, in Bawnatemple, is an early monastic site; less than ½ m. NE. is a chamber tomb; some 400 yds NE. of the latter is St Bartholomew's Well. – 2¼ m. SSW. of the bridge, in Shandangan, is Cromlech. – 4½ m. NW. of the bridge is Knockglass (see Kilberrihert under Macroom).

4¼ m. NW. via Peak, in Coolineagh, is the ruined ancient church of Aghabulloge, founded by St Eólang (Ólann), teacher of St Finn Bárr of Cork. Twenty-two yds SE. of the church ruin is an ogham pillarstone crowned by Caipín Ólainn (St Ólann's Cap), a lump of quartzite. In 1831 the caipín consisted of two superimposed stones. People swore by it and also used it to cure female complaints, headaches, etc. The phallic character of the monument caused the local priest to remove the caipín, but it was promptly replaced by the existing one. 150 yds N. is St Ólann's Stone, a boulder with the "imprint of the Saint's feet". Some 440 yds NNE. of the church is St Ólann's Well, covered by a clochán. Close by to the S. is an ogham stone set up here in 1851. It had been discovered in the foundations of Muilleann Rúa (Mullenroe), an old mill on the site of an erased ringfort a short distance to the N. of the well. Pilgrims make their "rounds" at the Caipín, Stone, and Well, on St Ólann's Day (5 Sept.) and at other times. – ½ m. NW. of the church is a standing stone. – 2½ m. E. of the churchyard, in Oldcastle, is a cairn (Nat. Mon.). – 2 m. NW. of St Ólann's Well is Sheskinny

crossroads. The following mileages are reckoned from this crossroads: 2 m. N., in Knocknagoun, is Cromlech. 1 m. E., in Rylane, is a stone circle; two fields E. is a large pillarstone; 1 m. E. of the circle, in Kilcullen South, is a cillín, or ancient cemetery with two pillarstones (one with an ogham inscription) and a souterrain (closed). – ¾ m SW., in Knockrour, is Kill, an ancient church site with two pillarstones (one with an ogham inscription) flanking the entrance. – ½ m. W (by road), in Oughtihery, is a stone circle. – 3 m NW., on the slope of Loughatooma, are two stone circles. – 6 m. NW., on the slope of Knockcraugh, are Dallaunayarra stone circles Some 3½ m. SW. (by road) of these, in Carrigagulla, is Browra stone circle.

COBH, Co. Cork (Map 5, C6), from 1849 to 1922 called Queenstown, is a port and yachting centre beautifully sited on the S. side of Great Island, 14 m. SE. of Cork. It is noted for its mild climate.

Great Island, between lovely Lough Mahon (estuary of the Lee) and splendid, land-locked Cork Harbour, is linked with lovely Foaty Island (see under Carrigtohill) by a road-bridge at Belvelly, 2¾ m. N. of Cobh. Near the bridge are the 15th/16th cent. tower of Belvelly castle and early-19th cent. martello towers. The main road from the bridge to Cobh passes down the W. side of the island via Rushbrooke (formerly a British naval dockyard); Lake Road, which turns E. at Rushbrooke, affords a splendid view of Cork Harbour. The longer road from Belvelly to Cobh, along the N. and S. sides of the island, is very picturesque.

During the French and American wars of the 18th cent. British Atlantic convoys assembled in Cork Harbour, which remained a British naval station until 1937; it was the principal base of American naval forces in European waters during the First World War. The Cork ship *Sirius*, first steamer to cross the Atlantic, sailed from Cobh, 1 April 1838, and Cork Harbour is still the principal Irish port-of-call for translatic liners.

The Royal Cork Yacht Club, oldest in the world (1720), has its headquarters at Cobh. Racing takes place each Wednesday and Saturday during the summer. Boats (sailing, rowing, motor) may be hired. There are facilities for sea bathing near the town. Good sea fishing may be had in Cork Harbour.

Cobh is the cathedral town of the Catholic diocese of Cloyne, St Colman's Cathedral (1868–1949) dominating the harbour. This is a large Gothic-Revival church by Edward Welby Pugin and George C. Ashlin; the interior is good of its kind; the carillon (forty-two bells) is the largest in the British Isles. The adjacent Diocesan Museum has a small collection of ecclesiastical antiquities.

The Protestant parish church has monuments by John Lawlor (1820–1901).

On the Quay – a good promenade – is

Plate 5. Glendalough, Co. Wicklow

an incomplete *Lusitania* memorial by Jerome Conor, the cost of which was subscribed in the United States.

¾ m. N. is the ruined church of Clonmel. The Rev. Charles Wolfe (1791–1823), author of "The Burial of Sir John Moore", and John Tobin (1769–1804), the dramatist, are buried here; so are many of the *Lusitania* victims; Tobin's grave is unmarked.

2 m. E., in Ballymore, was Reddington's Academy, first Catholic boarding school in Ireland since the enactment of the Penal Laws. Daniel O Connell, the Liberator, received his earliest schooling there.

¾ m. SW. is Haulbowline Island, headquarters of the Irish Naval Service. There are large steel mills and a dockyard here.

1 m. S. is Spike Island, with a large 19th cent. fort and former British base. From 1847 to 1885 the island was the principal penal depot in Ireland, the convicts being employed on the fortifications, dockyards, and other harbour works. Previously political prisoners (among them the celebrated John Mitchell) and other convicts had been detained in hulks anchored off the island pending transportation to Botany Bay and other penal settlements.

On the E. and SE. sides of Cork Harbour are the pleasant little resorts, East Ferry, Rosellan, Aghada, and Whitegate, all accessible by ferry.

2 m. W. (by ferry), is Monkstown (*q.v.*).

COLERAINE, Co. Derry (Map 3, B3), is a seaport and manufacturing town on the River Bann (4 m. from its mouth) and on the Ballycastle (19 m.)–Limavady (14 m.) road. (Northern Ireland's second university is to be established here.) While the place was of strategic significance from the earliest times, the town proper dates only from the end of the 16th cent., when it was planned by Sir John Perrot, the Lord Deputy, who had the oaken frames for the houses prefabricated in London. In 1613 town and countryside (previously O Cahan) were granted by James I to The Honourable Irish Society and planted with settlers from Britain. All traces of the pre-Reformation Dominican friary, which survived into the 17th cent., and of the O Cahan castle, have vanished. The Protestant parish church dates from 1611, but has been repeatedly rebuilt and modified.

· Gen. Sir Henry Lawrence (1806–57), of Indian Mutiny fame, came of a Coleraine family.

1 m. S. is Mount Sandel Fort (Nat. Mon.), a motte (?) standing 150 ft above the Bann.

2 m. SE., in Loughan, is a motte-and-bailey believed to be the remnant of a de Courcy castle. Nearby are the ruins of a castle and of Kilsantel church.

3 m. SSE., in the grounds of Camus House on the W. bank of the Bann, are a much weathered High Cross (Nat. Mon.) and a bullaun, all that survive of a monastery founded by St Comgall of Bangor (*q.v.*). Camus is also

Irish Tourist Board
Mussenden Temple, Downhill, Coleraine

the reputed site of the Cistercian abbey of Macosquin (De Claro Fonte), founded by the O Cahans (O Kanes) about 1218.

6¼ m. S., near Blackhill, is Crevolea Dolmen (Nat. Mon.), with a massive, basalt capstone weighing nearly forty tons; two of the four supporting stones were removed in the 18th cent.

3½ m. WSW., near the W. boundary of the Waterworks, is the three-chambered souterrain of Dunalis. On one of the roof-stones of the second chamber is Co. Derry's only ogham inscription.

1½ m. NNW., on the W. bank of the Bann, is Ballycairn motte-and-bailey, one of a chain of early Anglo-Norman strong points on either side of the river.

4½ m. NW., alt. 800 ft in Sconce townland, are remnants (Nat. Mon.) of the (Giant's) Sconce, a stone ringfort formerly called Dún Oisín. It has been unjustifiably identified with the Dún Ceithern (Adomnán's *munitio Cethirni*) of early history.

6½ m. NW., beyond the little resort of Castlerock (two Michael Healy windows in the Protestant church), is the Lions Gate of Downhill Castle, the great house built in 1780 by John Adam for the eccentric traveller and bishop of Derry, Lord Bristol (1730–1803). The treasures of its library and art collections were famous, but many were destroyed by fire in 1803. Only fragments of the house survive, but to the N. is cliff-top Mussenden Temple, built *c.* 1783 (by Michael Shanahan ?) as a sort of summerhouse library and called after the bishop's cousin, Mrs. Frideswide Mussenden. Now the property of the National Trust, it is open to the public at all times. The cliff commands splendid views, including Magilligan strand. S. of the demesne gate are some remains of Dunbo church (Nat. Mon.), abandoned in 1691. At the S. end of the townland is Dungannon, a ring-fort.

2½ m. W. is magnificent, 6-m. Magilligan Strand. Near Magilligan Point is one of the first Ordnance Survey base-line towers. At the Point an old battery and a martello tower guard the entrance to Lough Foyle. The road W. and S. (past Benyevenagh, 1,260 ft) to Limavady traverses a geologically interesting district.

COLLON, Co. Louth (Map 6, C1), is a village on the Slane (6 m.)–Ardee (7 m.) road.

Adjoining the village, in the demesne of Oriel Temple, alias Mount Oriel (built for John Foster, 1740–1829, Speaker of the Dublin House of Commons), is the Cistercian abbey of New Mellifont (1938); the lands belonged to medieval Mellifont Abbey (*q.v.*).

4 m. E. is Monasterboice (*q.v.*).

5 m. WSW. is Slieve Beagh, alias Slieve Brach, Buc Ré, etc. Along the crest (753 ft) and W. slope are thirty-two ring-works of varying kind and size: ring-barrows, ringforts, etc. In nearby Hoardstown is the Stuck Stone (Cloch Stocach), a 3½-ft standing stone which crowned a small mound. SE. of the hill is Mountfortescue with the Cup-and-Saucer, a small hill-fort with a small tumulus off-centre.

8 m. W., beyond Slieve Beagh, in Lobinstown, is the early monastic site, Killary. There are remains of two High Crosses and of a church (Nat. Mons.). The West Cross figurations include *The Fall, Noah's Ark, The Baptism of Christ, The Presentation in the Temple*. 3 m. SSW., in Knock, alias Lisknock, is an early monastic site: ring enclosure with portion of a small, early, decorated cross.

1½ m. NW. is Mount Oriel, eastern summit (810 ft; ringfort) of Sliabh Breagh; it commands a fine view.

COLLOONEY, Co. Sligo (Map 2, B5), is a village pleasantly sited 7 m. S. of Sligo, where the Owenmore and Unshin (which drains Lough Arrow) combine to force their way N. through the Collooney Gap between the E. spurs of Slieve Gamh and Slieve Daeane. The country round about is altogether delightful (*see* Ballintogher, Ballysadare, Beltra) and excellent fishing is available in local waters.

Collooney Gap was of major strategic importance in former times, and a strong castle to command it was built at Collooney in the Middle Ages. By the 15th cent. this castle was firmly in O Conor Sligo's hands, and in the 16th was his chief seat and stronghold. It was the siege of the castle by the great Red Hugh O Donnell which brought about the Battle of Curlieu in 1599 (*see under* Boyle), after which the castle surrendered to O Donnell. On 5 Sept. 1798 a mixed force of militia and dragoons under Col. Vereker attempted to hold the Gap against Humbert's tiny French force marching from Castlebar (*q.v.*) but was thrown back on Sligo with the loss of its guns. A rustic monu-

ment near the former Midland Great Western railway station commemorates the gallantry of Humbert's Irish aide, Capt. Bartholomew Teeling. (Vereker subsequently made a triumphal entry into Limerick and took "Collooney" for his motto.)

The Church of the Assumption (*c.* 1843) is a Gothic-Revival essay by Sir John Benson who also (1837) enlarged and remodelled the 1720 Protestant church (Cooper memorial by Gibson).

3 m. NE., NNW. of Ballygawley, at the ancient church site, Killeran, is Cloch an Easpuig ("the Bishop's Stone"), a pillarstone. SW. of the summit of Slieve Daeane (903 ft) is Cailleach Bhéarra's House, a chamber tomb.

2½ m. SE., overlooking the Unshin, is Markree Castle (Lieut.-Commander Cooper), a fine Georgian mansion castellated and otherwise modified by Francis Johnston in 1801.

2¼ m. SW., beside the Owenmore, is lovely Annaghmore demesne with many rare shrubs and trees. O Haras, one of the ancient noble stocks of the region, have lived here since the Middle Ages; Cormac O Hara of Annaghmore was a patron of the celebrated poet, Tadhg Dall Ó Huiginn (1550–91).

COMBER, Co. Down (Map 3, D5), is a small linen town on the Belfast (9 m.)–Downpatrick (18 m.) road, to the W. of Strangford Lough. In the 12th cent. the Whites founded a Cistercian abbey here; the Protestant church (1610 but much altered) stands on the site.

2½ m. SE. is Ballygraffan Dolmen (Nat. Mon.), a single-chamber prehistoric tomb half hidden in a fence.

7 m. SE., via Ringneill, is Mahee Island (causeway to mainland). W. of the golf course are remains (Nat. Mon.) of Nendrum Abbey, which was founded in the 5th cent. by St Mo Chaoi (after whom the island is called), and which disappears from history after 974. In 1178 Malachy, bishop of Down, joined with John de Courcy in introducing English Benedictines. The new foundation seems to have died by the end of the 13th cent. The remains include three or four concentric enclosing ramparts of dry masonry, church (12th cent.), the stump of a Round Tower, the ruins of huts and houses, the monks' cemetery, early grave-slabs, etc. These comprise one of the best surviving examples of the layout of a primitive Irish monastery (*see* Kiltiernan *under* Kilcolgan, Co. Galway, and Inishmurray, Co. Sligo). A charming anecdote about St Mo-Chaoi relates that a bird from heaven lulled him to sleep for 150 years. Nendrum Castle (Nat. Mon.) was probably built in the 15th cent.; it was altered in 1570 by an English settler named Browne. 6½ m. S. Sketrick Island (*below*).

2 m. S., in Ballynichol, are the Five Sisters, five orthostats which may be part of the façade of a court cairn.

7 m. SE., via Ardmillan, is Sketrick Island (causeway to mainland). Here are remains

(Nat. Mon.) of the tower and bawn (with subterranean, corbel-vaulted well) of a Mac
Quillan castle seized by Clannaboy O Neills,
but restored to Mac Quillan by Henry O Neill
of Tyrone, 1470.

CONG, Co. Mayo (Map 1, D5), is a village in
a beautiful setting near the NE. corner of Lough
Corrib, 9 m. SSW. of Ballinrobe, 23 m. NW. of
Tuam, and 28 m. N. of Galway. It is a convenient centre for fishing Loughs Mask and Corrib.
It is also a convenient centre for touring the
"Joyce Country". Adjoining the village on the
S. and SW. is the beautiful demesne of Ashford
Castle. Now a hotel, the magnificent mock
castle was built for Sir Arthur Edward Guinness, member of the famous Dublin brewing
family, who was created Baron Ardilaun in
1880. Loughs Mask and Corrib are connected
and fed by rivers which often flow underground;
in the vicinity of Cong village these have formed
a number of caves in the soluble limestone; the
most interesting of such caves are Poll na
gColm and Kelly's Cave (below). The cairns,
stone circles, and ringforts of the neighbourhood have led to its identification with the
setting of the first battle of Magh Tuireadh,
subject of a well-known Irish mythological tale.
Through the influence of Sir William Wilde's
"identifications" of monuments mentioned in
the story, bogus literary names have been
attached by the Ordnance Survey and others
to several of the local monuments. The real
Magh Tuireadh is in Co. Sligo (see under
Kilmactranny).
   Cong is known in Irish history as the site of
a monastery founded by St Féichín of Fore
(see under Castlepollard) in the 6th cent., and
rebuilt as an abbey of Augustinian Canons
Regular by King Turloch Mór O Conor early
in the 12th cent. Turloch's son, Rory, King of
Connacht and last High-king of Ireland, retired
to the monastery in 1183 and died there in 1198;
he was buried at Clonmacnois (q.v.). His son,
Maurice, was a canon of Cong, where he died
and was buried in 1224. Rory's daughter,
Nuala, Queen of Ulster (d. 1226), was also
buried in the monastery; likewise, perhaps, her
sister Finola (d. 1247).
   Of the ancient monastery of Cong the only
relic – apart from the superb Cross of Cong in
the National Museum – is Leac na bPoll, a five-
basin bullaun behind a cottage at the SE. end
of the village. The Augustinian monastery is
represented by the base of a medieval cross in
the village street, and by beautiful fragments of
an early-13th cent. abbey (Nat. Mon.) to the
SW. of the village. The cross-base is inscribed
OR[ÓIT] DO NICHOL AGUS DO GILLI-
BERD O DUBTHAICH RAB I NABAID-
DEACHT CUNGA ("A prayer for Nicholas
and Gilbert O Duffy who were abbots of
Cong"); the inscribed shaft is modern.
   Cong Abbey: of the abbey church only the
chancel survives; of the conventual buildings
only part of the E. range and a tiny fragment of

the cloister arcade. The beautiful N. door in
the chancel was put together in 1860 with
stones said to have been taken from a doorway
further W. in the N. wall; it seems likely that
it was originally a processional door in the S.
wall, opening into the cloister. (The top of the
central light of the E. window is also a 19th
cent. restoration.) The outstanding features of
the ruins are the three exquisite doorways of the
E. range. The central door opened into the
chapter-house, the N. door into the bookstore
(?), and the S. door into the slype, or cemetery
passage. The delicate, Romanesque–Early-
Gothic details of these doorways are among the
finest products of Irish medieval stone carving.
They are typical of a school or lodge of masons
active in the West (see Boyle, Inishmaine,
Knockmoy, and Corcomroe abbeys) at the
opening of the 13th cent. Some of the stones,
however, are the work of Peter Foy, a local
stone-carver employed by Sir Benjamin Lee
Guinness, 1860. Foy was also responsible for
most of the cloister arcade, of which the only
original parts are the first arch and its coupled
columns, at the N. end. – To the S. of the
abbey is a detached ruin of the 16th cent.; to
the W., on an island in the crystalline Cong
River, is the small Monks' Fishing House (Nat.
Mon.).
   1 m. NNW. are the ruins (Nat. Mon.) of the
15th cent., MacDonnell castle of Aghalahard.
The MacDonnells were galloglas in the service
of MacWilliam (Burke) Íochtair.
   ½ m. NE. in Nymphsfield is partly artificial
Kelly's Cave (Nat. Mon.).
   1¼ m. ENE., to the N. of the Cross–Headford
road in Cooslughoga, is a ringfort with a three-
chambered souterrain called Cuas Luchóige;
some of the uprights have cup marks. Nearby
was a cairn called Calliaghdoo.
   1 m. E., to the S. of the Cross–Headford
road, is Lackafinna ringfort with souterrain.
   1¼ m. NE., in Glebe and Tonaleeaun townlands, are four adjacent stone circles (Nat.
Mons.) of different kinds. The old rectory nearby occupies the site of a great stone ringfort.
2¾ m. N. of the rectory, in Caherrobert townland, is Caherrobert, a square fort with a
souterrain; about ¼ m. N. is Eochy's Cairn
(see Carn under Ballinrobe).–800 yds ENE. of
the stone circles, in Knock North, is Meeneen
Uisge, a deep well in a limestone chasm.
Nearby is Carn Meeneen Uisge, from which
Sir William Wilde extracted a Bronze Age
Food Vessel, and to which he attached the
bogus name Carn-an-Aoinfhir. 400 yds N. of
this, in Caherduff, are the ruins (Nat. Mon.) of
Caisleán na Coille, a strong 15th cent. castle
formerly renowned for its fairy revels. – 2 m.
NE. of the stone circles, at the junction of the
Cong–Ballinrobe and Headford–Cross–Ballinrobe roads, is the Long Stone of The Neale, a
short pillarstone. In the derelict demesne of
Neale House, to the NE. of The Neale village,
mounted in front of an "ancient cave" are medieval tomb fragments (Nat. Mon.). 1¼ m. S. of

the village, and close to the crossroads in Kildun, is a stone ringfort with a souterrain.

2 m. E., ½ m. S. of the road, is Moytura House, built by Sir William Wilde in 1865. Nearby is Caher Gerrode, a stone ringfort in which Wilde erected a tower commanding magnificent views. ½ m. further E., also to the S. of the road, is Caher Faeter (Pewter Fort) with souterrains. To the N. of the road is the great passage-grave-type cairn (Nat. Mon.) of Ballymacgibbon North.

3¾ m. E. is the hamlet of Cross. To the N., in Dowagh East, are Toberfraughaun and remains of Kilfraughaun, alias Kill-ard-creevena-Neeve, a small early church with trabeate W. door; it had an upper floor. – 1½ m. E., via the Kilmaine road, are the remains of the Castle of Cross, an early Gothic church with W. tower. – 1 m. SE. are the remains of Caher Mayo, a great stone ringfort.

4¾ m. SW. is the little island of Inchagoill, one of the beauty-spots of Lough Corrib. Here are (Nat. Mons.) the ancient St Patrick's Church, a cross-pillar inscribed LIE LUGUAEDON MACCI MENUEH ("the stone of Luguaedon, son of Menb"), Templenaneeve, an early cross-slab, a cross-pillar and three bullauns. St Patrick's Church was a nave-and-chancel structure; the Luguaedon stone is near the trabeate W. door; the inscription is the oldest surviving Irish inscription in Latin characters. Templenaneeve is a Romanesque nave-and-chancel church with a notable W. doorway. This is not only much weathered, but was incorrectly reassembled in 1860. The early cross-slab has been built into the S. wall.

¾ m. W. is Poll na gColm, alias The Pigeonhole, a limestone river cave. (It may be reached by road or along the W. bank of the Cong River in Ashford Castle demesne.)

4½ m. WNW. are the overgrown remains of Temple Brendan, alias Rosshill Abbey. They include traces of an enclosing cashel, an ancient church, a small cross-pillar, and a fragment of

an early gravestone inscribed OR[ÕIT] DO MAEL BRE[N]DAIN ("A prayer for MáelBréannain").

5½ m. WNW., on the shore of Lough Mask in Cappaghnagappul, are remains of Ballindonagh castle. Offshore is Oiléan Rúa, alias Red Island, sometime seat of a branch of the O Flahertys. Lame David Duignan wrote part of the Royal Irish Academy MS., 24 P 9, in the house of Rúairí, son of Tadhg Óg O Flaherty, on Red Island, April 1651.

3 m. NW., by Lough Mask, are remains of the unusual little castle of Ballykine.

6 m. WSW. is Cornamona, a good fishing station on Lough Corrib. Delightful views may be had from the adjacent Dooros peninsula.

4 m. N. is Lough Mask Castle (*see under* Ballinrobe).

CONNEMARA, Co. Galway (Map 1, B5–D6) – in older Irish Conmhaicne Mara – is, properly speaking, more or less identical with the barony of Ballynahinch. In more recent times, however, the name is often taken to include parts of the barony of Moycullen (Iar-Chonnacht) and of the half barony of Ross ("Joyce's Country") as well, and it is in this convenient, if inaccurate, sense that it is used in this *Guide*.

The region is one of the most romantically beautiful in Ireland and is deservedly popular with tourist and angler, as well as with the lover of quiet, restful holidays.

The landscape is dominated by two fine mountain groups, the Twelve Bens (Beanna Beóla) and the Maumturk range, whose peaks reward the climber with superb panoramas of lake, moorland, and sea. The Twelve Bens (Benbaun, 2,395 ft) may conveniently be explored from Clifden (*q.v.*) or Ballynahinch (*q.v.*); a delightful circuit of them is Clifden–Letterfrack – Kylemore – Glendollagh – Clifden. The Maumturk range (Leckavrea, 2,012 ft) may be explored from Maum or Ballynahinch; the

Cottages near Rossaveel, Connemara

circuit is simple: Maum Cross – Maum – Leenaun – Glendollagh – Recess – Maum Cross.

The countless lakes of Connemara include several of great beauty, notably Ballynahinch Lake, Derryclare, and Lough Inagh (*see under* Ballynahinch), Kylemore Lough (*see* Kylemore), Lough Fee (*see under* Leenaun), Lough Nafooey (*see under* Maum); many of them, together with their rivers, afford excellent fishing.

The varied coastline has a number of excellent, uncrowded beaches, such as those of Mannin Bay (*see under* Ballyconneely) and Dog's Bay (*see under* Roundstone). It also, of course, offers opportunities for sea fishing.

As might be expected of so barren a countryside, antiquities are relatively few, but include some monuments of real interest (*see* Carna, Cleggan, *and* Rinvyle).

The population is, for the most part, concentrated round the periphery of the moors and mountains. It is particularly dense along the low shores W. from Galway to Bertraghboy Bay, where the harvest of the sea (fish and seaweed) makes a vital contribution to the economy of the crofters and farmers of an ungrateful land. This concentration has helped to save the Irish language, and so this coastal fringe includes one of the largest of the few surviving regions of Irish speech. With the ancient language goes something of the ancient way of life, and the traditional story-telling and singing of the S. Connemara coast are famous in folklore circles, just as its homespun tweeds enjoy high repute among discriminating judges. Of recent years the government has fostered tomato-growing, doll-making, afforestation, and peat-production as useful aids to the economy of a "depressed" area. Much has been done by local effort to improve the strain of the versatile and sought-after Connemara pony.

COOKSTOWN, Co. Tyrone (Map 3, B4), is
a market and linen-manufacturing town 10 m. W. of Lough Neagh on the Dungannon (11 m.)–Maghera (17 m.) road. The town is a convenient base for exploring the SE. Sperrin Mountains, rich in megalithic remains (*below*).

A noteworthy feature of the town is the straight, 1¼-m. High St, laid out in 1609 by Alan Cook, the founding Planter after whom the town is called.

The Convent of Mercy has a noteworthy Chapel (1966) by Lawrence Mc Conville. The exterior bronze symbols of the Trinity and the Evangelists are by Patrick Mc Elroy, who also did the altar Crucifix. The altar is by Michael Biggs, the Stations of the Cross by Bro. Benedict Tutty, the stained glass (*Virgin and Child*, etc.) by Patrick Pye.

SE. of the town is Killymoon Castle, formerly home of the Stewarts, now the Killymoon Golf Club. The house is essentially the work of the celebrated English architect, John Nash (1752–1835), who enlarged and remodelled a house of the Earls of Tyrone for Col. William Stewart (1780–1850) at a cost of £80,000. This

Northern Ireland Tourist Board
Killymoon Castle, Cookstown

was Nash's first great Irish house. The E. front, with its large circular tower over the entrance, recalls Kilwaughter Castle (*see under* Larne).

2 m. NNE. is Lissan Rectory, an Italianate villa by John Nash. Lissan (*Lios Áine*), like a local hill and well, preserves the name of the goddess, Áine (*see also* Annia's Cove *under* Augher *and* Knockainey *under* Hospital). According to folk belief, the O Corras (Corrs) are descended from her and she wails at their approaching deaths.

6 m. NE., ¾ m. W. of Moneymore, is Ballymully long cairn (Nat. Mon.), a long parabolic chambered cairn.

6 m. E., by the roadside ½ m. W. of Coagh village, is Tamlaght, Co. Derry (*see under* Moneymore).

13 m. E. (via Coagh), at Arboe Point on the W. shore of Lough Neagh, are the ruins of a 16th (?) cent. church, a very tall High Cross (Nat. Mon.), and Arboe "Abbey" (remnants of a small, ancient church; Nat. Mon.). These mark the site of a monastery founded in the 6th cent. by St Colmán mac Aidhe. The cross, 10th (?) cent., bears representations of Scriptural subjects, including: E. face: *Adam and Eve, Sacrifice of Isaac, Daniel in the Lions' Den, The Children in the Fiery Furnace*, and *Last Judgement*; W. face: *Nativity, Adoration of the Magi, Christ's Entry into Jerusalem*, and *Crucifixion*; N. side: *Baptism of Christ, Slaughter of the Innocents*, and *Judgement of Solomon*; S. side: *Cain and Abel, David and the Lion*, and *The Raven brings Bread to the Hermits, Paul and Anthony*. Arboe was formerly a place of Lughnasa celebrations (at Lammastide) which included prayers at the cross and washing in the lake. In the NW. corner of the churchyard is a hollow beech into which suppliants stick pins to record their wishing. 3 m. S., at Aghacolumb, is Arboe New Church (Protestant), erected in 1709 by Stewart Blacker and W. Latham. The E. window (16th/17th cent.), inner W. door, and font are said to have come from Arboe.

2 m. S. (1 m. NW. of Tullaghoge village) is

Loughry House, now an agricultural school. The house was built by the Lindsays in 1632 and rebuilt in 1671. It has recently in part been reconstructed. To the S. is a summerhouse where Dean Swift wrote several of his works. Some 600 yds N. of the house is Loughry Giants Grave (Nat. Mon.), a gallery grave. ½ m. E. of the main gate, in Ballymully Glebe to the N. of Tullaghoge village, is Tullaghoge Fort (Nat. Mon.), a hill-top ringfort, site of the house of O Hagan, who inaugurated each new O Neill of Tír Eóghain by installing him in a stone chair on the slope below. The last inauguration was that of Great Hugh O Neill (1593). In 1602 Lord Mountjoy destroyed the inauguration chair.

½ m. SW. are the ruins of Derryloran church (Nat. Mon.).

A good secondary road to the WNW. up the Ballinderry valley via Dunnamore bridge (7 m.) leads to the heart of the S. Sperrin moors and foothills with their remarkable wealth of prehistoric remains. (It joins the mountain road from Omagh to Draperstown at Broughderg crossroads, 15 m. from Cookstown, 18 m. from Omagh, and 10 m. from Draperstown.) 7 m. from Cookstown is Dunnamore bridge. In Tulnacross, close to the bridge, is a pair of pillarstones. 1¼ m. WNW. of Dunnamore bridge, alt. 500 ft, in Killucan, are the remains of two long cairns. Also in Killucan, alt. 700 ft, are: ½ m. S. of Lough Doo, Loadgarranbane (Nat. Mon.), a collapsed chamber tomb, and, ⅓ m. NE. of Loughtoornakeeragh, Carnanbane, a court cairn with circular chamber. – ¼ m. W. of Dunnamore Catholic church, alt. 500 ft, is Dunnamore Dermot and Grania's Bed (Nat. Mon.), a gallery grave. – 1¾ m. NW. of the church, in Beleevna Beg, to the S. of Black Rock, are a pillarstone and stone circle; ¼ m. SE., on the W. slope of Evishbrack, alt. 700 ft, are three pillarstones and considerable remains of a double stone circle. Just beyond Black Rock, in Beaghmore, the road cuts through a remarkable series of prehistoric monuments (Nat. Mons.) which are being exposed by turf-cutting. These include stone circles, alignments, avenues, pillarstones (more than 1,200), small cairns, and other structures, The circles sometimes occur in pairs with tangential alignments and associated cairns, etc. The countryside for miles around is littered with the wreckage of monuments uncovered in the past. – ¾ m. NE. of Black Rock and ⅓ m. SE. of Broughderg bridge, alt. 600 ft, are two round cairns. – 1¾ m. NE. of Broughderg bridge is Davagh bridge. ⅔ m. NE. of the latter, alt. 600 ft, is The Big Man's Grave (Nat. Mon.), a long, chambered cairn. On the Davagh Water ½ m. E. of the bridge, alt. 600 ft, in Davagh Lower, are a collapsed chamber tomb, a double stone circle with a double tangential alignment, part of a single circle, and three pillarstones (Nat. Mons.). – 2 m. NW. of Broughderg bridge are Broughderg crossroads (*above*). To the W. of the junction are: (*a*) by the roadside in Broughderg (⅓ m. SE. of Crocknaboley, alt. 700 ft), Carnanagarranebane (Nat. Mon.), a much ruined court cairn said to have contained seven graves; (*b*) 200 yds SW. of Broughderg post office, Crocknaboley, alt. 800 ft, Keerin Cromlech (Nat. Mon.), a ruined chamber tomb. – 5 m. SW. of Broughderg crossroads is Aghnascrebagh (*see under* Omagh).

The Cookstown–Lissan–Draperstown road crosses the SE. Sperrins by the lonely Lough Fea valley between Slieve Gallion (1,735 ft) and Fir Mountain (1,193 ft). 6 m. NNW. of Cookstown the road branches. The E. branch leads (4 m.) to a rewarding mountain track through the Windy Gap between Slieve Gallion and Crocknamohill (1,200 ft) to Desertmartin, Co. Derry. The main road ascends the valley to Black Water bridge (3 m.). ⅔ m. S. of the bridge is the Ballybriest group of monuments (*see under* Draperstown). – The by-road on the W. side of Lough Fea crosses the mountain to Ballynascreen (*see under* Draperstown). W. of this road, ¾ m. W. of the N. end of the lake and ¼ m. E. of Deeveg bridge, alt. 700 ft, are Slaghtfreeden Giants Grave (a chamber tomb) and four small, round cairns.

COOLANEY, Co. Sligo (Map 2, A5), is a village on the Owenboy, alias Owenbeg, 5½ m. W. of Coolooney and 10 m. NE. of Tobercurry.

¾ m. S., to the E. of the Ballymote road in Rathbarran, is a cairn. 1 m. S. of this, on the W. side of the road in Rathbarran Glebe, is a lofty mound with two concentric banks. A Bronze Age cist is said to have been found at the summit.

3 m. SSW., to the SE. of Killoran Lough, are the remains of Killoran church, which has given its name to the lake and the parish. 1¾ m. SW., in Knockatotaun, is the Leac, alias Druid's Altar, a ruined gallery grave.

2 m. SW., in Knockadoo, is a cairn.

2½ m. W., to the S. of the road in Gortakeeran, is the Giants Grave, a ruined chamber tomb; higher up the mountain is a wedge-shaped gallery grave. In Cabragh, which adjoins Gortakeeran on the W., are two further tombs: to the N. of the road a wedge-shaped gallery grave, to the S. of the road a denuded chambered cairn (Giants Grave).

COOTEHILL, Co. Cavan (Map 2, E5), is a market town on the S. road from Cavan (16 m.) to Monaghan (14 m.). It takes its name from the Cootes, English planters, whose notoriously brutal ancestor, Sir Charles Coote, acquired confiscated O Reilly lands here in the 17th cent. Just N. of the town is Bellamont Forest, a Palladian villa in brick attributed to Sir Edward Lovett Pearce (d. 1733) and built most probably for Thomas E. Coote, who was a lawyer. From Bellamont the Cootes took the title, Earl of Bellamont. The house is now the home of Major-Gen. Eric Dorman O Gowan

Cootehill was the birthplace of the distin-

Irish Tourist Board

Bellamont Forest, Cootehill

guished Austrian Field-Marshal, Thomas Brady (1752–1827), member of an ancient East Breany family.

3 m. NE., in Dartry demesne, is a derelict 1770 monument by Joseph Wolton (1722–1803) to Lady Anne Dawson (1733–69).

4½ m. NE., in Edergoole, Co. Monaghan, is roadside Giants Grave, a gallery grave.

3 m. SE., a short distance N. of the Shercock road, near Drumgoon, is Cohaw Giants Grave, a double-court cairn with five chambers. Just S. of the road there formerly stood another court cairn. About ½ m. NE. is the double-court cairn of Aghagashlan; ½ m. NNW. are remains of Mayo court cairn, beyond which, near the summit of Mayo Hill (fine view) is a pillarstone. About ¾ m. SW. of the first Cohaw cairn, also in Cohaw, is yet another. 1½ m. SE., to the NW. of the bridge over the Annalee, is a pillarstone, while ¼ m. SE. of the bridge is a fifth court cairn.

3½ m. SW. is Tullyvin, a Plantation village, which still retains its 17th cent. layout and circular green.

CORCOMROE ABBEY, Co. Clare (Map 1, D6), is a ruined Cistercian abbey (Nat. Mon.) on the S. side of Abbey Hill, 5 m. W. of Kinvara and 6 m. E. of Ballyvaghan. The abbey (de Petra Fertili) was founded in 1180 by Donal Mór O Brien, King of Limerick, and was colonized from Inishlounaght (*see under* Clonmel) about 1195. In 1249 it was temporarily affiliated to Furness Abbey, Lancashire, in consequence of the indiscipline, etc., of the Mellifont group of abbeys (the "Mellifont revolt"). A short-lived daughter house was established at Kilshane, Ballingarry, in 1198.

The remains include a church with interesting Transitional features, fragments of the claustral buildings, infirmary–guesthouse (to the S.), and gatehouse (to the W.). The church was a cruciform building with aisled nave (N. aisle never built ?) and a single E. chapel in each transept. There was no tower at the crossing, and the S. aisle was shorter than the rest of the nave. In the 15th cent. parts of the nave arcade were blocked up, a stone screen supporting a skimpy, friary-type tower was inserted between choir and nave (lay-brothers' choir), and an altar tomb and sedilia were inserted in the N. wall of the presbytery (chancel). The tomb, traditionally that of King Conor na Siudaine O Brien (d. 1267/8), has a crude royal effigy. In the wall above it is a slab with a rude, late, abbatial figure. In a Transitional recess of the S. presbytery wall is a medieval tomb cover of wood. Traces of polychrome painting can be discerned here and there on the plasterwork of the church.

2½ m. SE. of the abbey, via the bohereen joining the Corker Hill road at Shanvally, is Oughtmama, site of an early monastery associated with St Colmán (mac Duach ?). The largest of three churches (Nat. Mons.), in its later days parochial, has a pre-Romanesque nave and a plain Romanesque chancel. In it are a carved stoup and defaced early gravestones. ½ m. ENE. is Tobercolman. To the S., on the summit of Turlough Hill (945 ft) is a cairn.

3½ m. N. is New Quay. ¾ m. W. is Mount Vernon Lodge, seaside resort of the Gregorys of Coole (*see under* Gort), where Lady Gregory was visited by her literary friends, including W. B. Yeats and George Bernard Shaw (*see*

Effigy of an abbot, Corcomroe Abbey

Martyn, Guy de Maupassant, Paul Bourget, and George Bernard Shaw, for 1¼ m. SW. of New Quay (½ m. W. of Mortyclough, alias Burren, village), between the shore and the road in Parkmore, is Donoughmore O Daly's Monument, a plain pillar. The local branch of the O Dalys provided hereditary poets to the O Loughlins, lords of Burren, from the close of the 14th cent. onwards. The site of Donnchadh Mór's house and "college" in Parkmore were still being pointed out as late as 1839.

CORK, Co. Cork (Map 5, B6), third largest city in Ireland, is charmingly situated at the mouth of the beautiful Lee valley, 161 m. SW. of Dublin, 61 m. S. of Limerick, and 54 m. SE. of Killarney. It is an important seaport and a commercial and manufacturing (brewing, distilling, woollens, motor-cars, rubber, etc.) centre of note. It is also the cathedral city of the Catholic diocese of Cork and of the united Protestant dioceses of Cork, Cloyne, and Ross, as well as the seat of a constituent college of the National University of Ireland. It is a convenient centre for exploring the lovely valleys and coasts of Co. Cork, in particular the Lee valley, Lough Mahon (lower estuary of the Lee), and Cork Harbour.

also Doorus House *under* Kinvara). Yeats set his verse play, *The Dreaming of the Bones*, in the hills about Corcomroe Abbey. Shaw, impressed by the naked limestone of Burren – his "region of stone-capped hills and granite fields"– set Part IV, Act 1, of *Back to Methuselah* at "Burrin Pier", i.e. New Quay, which remains pretty much as he described it. But the literary associations of the district are much older than the time of Lady Gregory, W. B. Yeats, Edward

The history of Cork commences in the 6th/7th cent. with the foundation of a monastery by St Finnbárr, an obscure bishop-abbot of Connacht stock (d. about 630; *see* Lisnacaheragh *under* Crookstown), on the hill slope SW. of the present city. St Fin Barre's Cathedral may be on the site, as the stump of a Round Tower survived until the foundations were laid and there are Romanesque fragments preserved in the chapter house. Though it probably commenced as a hermitage, the monastery came in time to be the head of an important confederation of South Munster monastic churches. It was the setting of the 12th cent.

Effigy of Conor na Siudaine O Brien, Corcomroe Abbey

Visio Tnugdali, or *Vision of Tundale*, one of the most popular of Irish contributions to medieval vision literature. (German, French, Italian, Anglo-Norman, Middle English, and Norse translations.) It was also the subject of the celebrated 12th cent. satire, *Aisling Meic Conglinne, The Vision of Mac Conglinne*. Like so many Irish monasteries of the time, it suffered from the raids of the Vikings (820, 838, 845, 863), and again from the Norse pirate-traders who erected a short-lived fortress on one of the islands in the marsh (*corcach*) by the river in 846. In 917 these dangerous neighbours returned and founded a settlement on an island in the marsh, a settlement which marks the true beginning of the city. This Norse (Ostman) settlement, like others, was gradually absorbed into the Gaelic polity, though continuing to be ruled by its own mór-máer or jarl. When Turloch O Conor of Connacht shattered the unity of Munster in 1118, Cork soon became the capital of the Mac Carthy *Regnum Corcagiense*, or Kingdom of South Munster (i.e. Desmond in its old, true sense). At the Anglo-Norman invasion King Dermot Mac Carthy submitted to Henry II of England (1172), but failed thereby to save his kingdom, for it was attacked the following year by Raymond le Gros (*see* Lismore), and in 1177 was granted by Henry to Robert Fitzstephen and Milo de Cogan. The grant reserved to the English Crown the city of Cork and the surrounding "cantred of the Ostmen". The grantees vigorously set about realizing their opportunity, and soon much of the best land in South Munster was in the hands of the Barrys, the Courceys, Fitzgeralds of Imokilly, and other Anglo-Norman families, whose names thenceforth loom large in the history of medieval Munster. Cork city itself, though garrisoned with Anglo-Normans as early as November 1177, was left for the time being in King Dermot Mac Carthy's hands. As soon, however, as he had been slain in battle with the invaders (1185), the town was declared a dependency of the English Crown. The principal dates in the later history of the city are:

1188. Charter from Prince John of England in his capacity of "Lord of Ireland".
1195. Besieged and recaptured by the Mac Carthys.
1199. Grant of the liberties of Bristol.
1214. Franciscan friary (North Mall).
1229. Dominican friary (St Marie's of the Isle).
1241. Charter from Henry III.
1284. New city walls.
c. 1300. Augustinian friary.
1378. City burned by the Irish.
1495. Arrival of Perkin Warbeck, Yorkist pretender to English throne.
1642. English Lord President of Munster is besieged in the city by insurgent Irish.
1644. Murrough "the Burner" O Brien

captures the city for the Parliamentarians, and expels the Irish inhabitants.
1649. Captured by Cromwell; Irish once more expelled.
1690. Besieged and captured for William of Orange by John Churchill, later Duke of Marlborough.
1691. Patrick Sarsfield and the Jacobite army sail away to France.
1845. Queen's College, now University College.
1920. Assassination of Lord Mayor, Thomas Mac Curtain, by British forces. Death of Mac Curtain's successor, Terence Mac Swiney, after seventy-four days of hunger-strike in an English prison. Patrick St, City Hall, Public Library, and other buildings, are burned down by British forces.
1922. British garrison evacuates the city. Anti-treaty Republican guerrillas occupy it, but withdraw when Free State troops land at Passage West.
1938. British naval defences in Cork Harbour handed over to the Irish government.

In the 18th and early 19th centuries Cork silverware and glass enjoyed a high repute, and good pieces are much sought after. About the middle of the 19th cent. crochet-work and lace-making began to flourish in the city as cottage crafts. Representative examples of all four crafts may be seen in the Public Museum, Fitzgerald Park.

The roll of Cork artists and writers is not over-long, but the city can, perhaps, claim more painters of quality than any other in Ireland.

Painters

James Barry (1741–1806), son of a sea-captain turned tavern-keeper. He was a pupil of West's.

Robert Fagan (1745–1816).

Nathaniel Grogan (d. 1807), a pupil of the Cork painter, John Butts.

Samuel Forde (1805–28). Thomas Davis exaggeratedly classed him with Barry as a "creative painter of the highest order". He did much work for the architect, George Richard Pain. His unfinished *Fall of the Rebel Angels* may be seen at the School of Art, Emmet Place.

Daniel Maclise (1806–70), son of a shoemaker.

William McGrath (1838–1918), Member of the New York Academy.

Sculptors

Thomas Kirk (1777–1845), son of a Scotsman and father of Joseph Robinson Kirk (1821–94), also a sculptor.

John Hogan (1800–1858), the noted Classical sculptor, though a native of Tallow, has claims to be listed as a Cork artist. It was in Cork that he was brought up, and it was when employed as a draughtsman in the office of the brothers Deane that be taught himself the sculptor's art. It was in Cork, too, that he received his earliest commissions (see St Mary's Pro-Cathedral, below).

Architects

Sir Thomas Deane I (1792–1871) and his brother, Kearns Deane.

Sir Thomas Deane II (1828–99).

Benjamin Woodward (1815–61), who seems to have been responsible for much of the best work attributed to his partner, Sir Thomas Deane I.

Writers

Richard Millikin (1767–1815), poet.

William Maginn (1793–1842), author of *Homeric Ballads*, etc.

Thomas Crofton Croker (1798–1854), antiquary and folk-lorist.

Francis Mahony, "Father Prout" (1804–66), humourous poet.

Daniel Corkery, author of *The Threshold of Quiet*, etc.

Seán O Faoláin, novelist (*Bird Alone*, etc.) and biographer.

Michael O Donovan ("Frank O'Connor"; 1903–66), poet, playwright, novelist (*The Saint and Mary Kate*, etc.), and master-craftsman of the short story.

Scarcely a fragment is left of medieval Cork – nothing at all of the 16th and 17th cent. town. While the 18th cent. town had its quota of charming private houses, some of which survive in decay, there were very few buildings of any architectural pretensions prior to the advent of the brothers, James and George Richard Pain, about the year 1818. They had been pupils of John Nash and had been sent over to Ireland to superintend the erection of some of Nash's country houses (see Lough Cutra Castle *under* Gort). James (1779–1877) soon removed to Limerick, but George Richard remained in Cork. The best period of Cork building is that of the Pains and their disciples. Later, the Gothic Revival contributed one or two noteworthy buildings. Most of the more recent building, particularly the ecclesiastical, is bad. In the following list of the more notable buildings, etc., the three major, natural, divisions of the city are covered in the order: (a) North City: the city N. of the North Channel of the River Lee; (b) Central City: the older, central part of the city between the main branches of the river; (c) South City: the city S. of the South Channel of the Lee.

NORTH CITY

Our tour commences at Griffith Bridge (head of North Main St).

½ m. W., at Sunday's Well, is St Vincent's Church, a large Gothic-Revival work by Si John Benson; the presbytery was added b Goldie. St Vincent's Orphanage, Wellingto Rd, is also by Goldie; the chapel is by th Cork architect, Samuel Hynes.

400 yds E., on Pope's Quay, is St Mary' Church (Dominican), a good, if prosaic, Clas sical building (1832–9), by Kearns Deane. O the Lady Altar is displayed the worn ivor figurine of *Our Lady of Graces*. Flemish wor of the 14th cent., it originally belonged to th Dominican friary at Youghal.

¼ m. N. of St Mary's, Pope's Quay, is S Anne's Church, Shandon, a Protestant paris church erected 1722–6 on the site of medieva St Mary's Church, which had been destroye in the siege of 1690. Its principal title to fame i the well-known doggerel by "Father Prout about

> ". . . the bells of Shandon
> That sound so grand on
> The pleasant waters
> Of the River Lee."

150 yds N. of St Anne's, in Cathedral Rd, St Mary's Pro-Cathedral, popularly known a the North Chapel. The building was con menced in 1808, and the architecture reflec the condition of the Catholic Church in Irelan in the period immediately before and aft Emancipation. Having been damaged by fi in 1820, the interior was remodelled in 182 by George Richard Pain (further remodellir commenced 1965). The tower, etc., date fro 1862–7. The twenty-seven figures of apostl and saints, and the bas-relief *Last Suppe* are all youthful works, after engravings, b self-taught John Hogan; they were done f Bishop Murphy about 1818–19. The Bish Murphy mural monument (1857) is one Hogan's last works. The bust (1818) of Bishc Moylan is by Belfast-born Turnerelli. T statue (1889) of Bishop Delaney in front of t church is by John Lawlor.

½ m. N. of St Mary's is the Church of t Assumption, Blackpool. It was designed by t contemporary Cork sculptor, Séamus Murph who also carved the statues.

¾ m. E. of St Mary's, in Old Youghal Roa is Collins Barracks. The chapel has a thre light window (*St Michael, Christ in Glory, Patrick*) by Evie Hone (1939); the base w painted by Michael Healy when Evie Hor was ill.

¾ m. S. of the barracks and close to the jun tion of Lower Glanmire Rd and Mac Curta St, is St Patrick's Church (1836), a Classic edifice by George Richard Pain. One of t finest of Cork's Catholic churches, it has be marred by extension (1894). In the baptistry a small stained glass panel (*The Baptism Christ*) by Hubert Mc Goldrick. Further E., the high ground overlooking the lower L are the residential suburbs of Tivoli and Mo tenotte.

¾ m. S. of St Patrick's Church is the Custo House (see Central City, below).

CENTRAL CITY

Patrick St, principal shopping street of the city, curves from Grand Parade in the W. to St Patrick's Bridge in the N. At the N. end of the street is a dull statue of Father Theobald Mathew (1790–1861), celebrated apostle of Temperance, by John Henry Foley. "The Statue" is the focal point of the city bus services.

500 yds E. of St Patrick's Bridge, at the junction of the North and South Channels, is the Custom House – now the Harbour Board office – a good Classical essay (1814–18) by William Hargrave.

300 yds W. of St Patrick's Bridge, in Cornmarket St, is the Old Market. The lower portion of the façade is "Cork's only example of the Grand Style of the early 18th century"; it is attributed to an Italian. Nearby, at the junction of Lavitt's Quay and Emmet Pl., is the Opera House (1963–5); by Michael Scott and Associates.

In Emmet Pl. is the Crawford Municipal School of Art and Art Gallery. The buildings (by Arthur Hill) have been added to the 18th cent. Custom House (altered). The collections include (a) two Rodin bronzes, (b) casts, from antique sculptures in Rome, prepared under the supervision of Canova and presented by Pius VII to the Prince Regent, who gave them to Cork in 1818; through these John Hogan made his first acquaintance with Classical sculpture; (c) a *Minerva* (1822) done by Hogan for an insurance office in the South Mall; (d) thirteen casts from Hogan's works; (e) paintings by recent and contemporary Irish artists, including a collection presented by Sir John Lavery.

300 yds SW. of the Art School, off Paul St, is St Paul's Protestant Church, a Classical edifice of 1723 with a good interior; it is now a factory. Nearby, in a narrow lane linking Paul St and Patrick St, is SS Peter and Paul's Church, an excellent Gothic-Revival building by Edward Welby Pugin. The tower and spire were, unfortunately, never completed. The high altar was designed by Pugin's pupil and partner, George C. Ashlin of Dublin.

500 yds NW. of SS Peter and Paul's, on the W. side of North Main St, is St Peter's Protestant Church (1783–8). This church, which has lost its spire, occupies the site of one of the medieval city's two parish churches. Some memorials from its predecessors survive, including a Deane memorial of 1710 in the N. porch.

300 yds W., at the W. end of Peter's St, is the Mercy Hospital, which incorporates the Mansion House built in 1767 to the design of Davis Ducart. It has some good stucco ceilings.

¼ m. SE. of the Hospital, in Washington St, is the Court House erected in 1835 to the design of the brothers Pain. The splendid portico happily survived a fire in 1891 which destroyed the interior.

SE. of the Court House, on the E. side of South Main St, is the Protestant Church of the Holy Trinity, alias Christ Church. It occupies the site of the city's second medieval parish church, burial place of the leading families of the town, and probable scene of Edmund Spenser's marriage to Elizabeth Boyle (*see* Youghal). Having suffered severely in the 1690 siege, the old church was demolished in 1717, the aisled crypt alone surviving. The new church was erected, about 1720, to the design of Coltsman; it had a tower and spire, since removed. In 1825 the interior was remodelled and the W. front erected by George Richard Pain. The apse is a much later addition, by W. H. Hill (senior). The relics of old Christ Church include the interesting tombstone of Mayor Thomas Ronan (d. 1554) and his wife, Johanna Tyrry (d. 1569).

300 yds SE. of Christ Church, at the S. end of Grand Parade, is South Mall, financial centre of the city. The Cork and County Club is by George Richard Pain. The Cork Savings Bank (1841–2), at the corner of Parnell Place, is by the brothers Kearns and (Sir) Thomas Deane; in the public office is a statue (1840) of William Crawford by John Hogan. Some 300 yds ENE., at the junction of the North and South Channels, is the Custom House (*above*).

To the S. of South Mall, on Father Mathew Quay (Charlotte Quay), is the Capuchin Church of the Holy Trinity (1825), an interesting Gothick essay (1825) by George Richard Pain for Father Theobald Mathew. Pain's design for a lofty lantern and spire was never carried out, unfortunately, and the existing unsuccessful lantern and spire are 1880 additions by Coakley.

SOUTH CITY

¼ m. SW. of Holy Trinity Church, off Abbey St, is St Nicholas's Protestant Church (1850). The Traction monument is by John Bacon, R.A., sculptor of the Pitt memorial in Westminster Abbey and of the Dr Johnson and Howard memorials in St Paul's Cathedral, London. A short way E. is the tower of Red Abbey, sole relic of the monasteries of medieval Cork. Red Abbey was an Augustinian priory founded *c.* 1300. During the siege of 1690 Churchill placed a battery in the priory garden and, it is said, watched the bombardment from the tower.

Nearby, in Dunbar St, is St Finbar's, South, alias, the South Chapel, a Georgian church of 1766 (transepts later). The altar-piece is a later, less successful, version of John Hogan's *Dead Christ* (*see* Carmelite church, Clarendon St, *under* Dublin, Main Axis). The *Crucifixion* is by the Fermoy painter, John O Keeffe (*c.* 1797–1838). The monument in the S. transept to Bishop Florence MacCarthy (1761–1810) is by the Derry-born Cork sculptor, James Heffernan (1785–1845).

1¼ m. SE. of St Nicholas's Church, at Turner's Cross, is the Church of Christ the King,

St Fin Barre's Cathedral, Cork, from the north-east

an essay in a modern idiom by Barry Byrne of Chicago; the great doorway figure, *Christ the King*, was designed by the American sculptor, John Storrs; the opus sectile *Crucifixion* is by Hubert McGoldrick (1936).

Some 300 yds W. of St Nicholas's Church, in Fort St (off Barrack St), is Elizabeth Fort. The first fort here was built on the site of "Temple Croghenigh" in the reigh of Elizabeth I. In 1603 the citizens, refusing to proclaim James I, demolished it, but were promptly compelled by Lord Deputy Mountjoy to rebuild it. In 1649 Cromwell had the walls strengthened. In Sept. 1690, the fort was fiercely assailed by John Churchill's Williamites. In 1835 it was converted into a prison. Later it became an artillery barracks. In 1920–21 a detachment of the notorious Black and Tans was quartered in the barracks. After the British evacuation Anti-Treaty Republicans occupied the place. These burned down the barracks when Free State troops arrived in 1922. The curtain wall of the 17th cent. fort survives.

A short distance W. of the fort is St Fin Barre's Protestant Cathedral (1867–79), an imposing and costly building in the then fashionable French Gothic style, by "brilliant, playacting" William Burges of London; the ornamental details are often clumsy and ponderous,

the figure carvings insipid. This cathedral replaces the small Georgian successor of the medieval cathedral, itself on or near the site of St Finnbárr's monastery. The tombstone in the churchyard inscribed "Henry Murrough" marks the grave of the Cork painter, Samuel Forde (1805–28).

½ m. SW. of the cathedral, in Lough Rd, is the Church of the Immaculate Conception (alias St Finbar's, West), a Romanesque piece (1881) by George C. Ashlin; extensions of 1929 by James F. McMullen.

½ m. W. of St Fin Barre's Cathedral, in Fernhurst Ave., is the Honan Hostel for university students. St Finn Barr's chapel (1915) is one of the sights of Cork. This is an essay in the Irish Romanesque style by James F. Mc Mullen. The exterior is not at all successful (W. front a feeble echo of St Cronan's Church, Roscrea) but the interior and its appointments repay examination. The Tabernacle has good enamels by Oswald P. Reeves. The antependium and other embroideries are by the Dun Emer Guild, Dublin. There are good *opus sectile* Stations of the Cross. Eight of the windows are by Sarah Purser, eleven by Harry Clarke. The window subjects are as follows. Chancel: E. window, *Our Lord* (Purser), N. window, *St John* (Purser), S. windows, *Our Lady* (Clarke), *St*

Joseph (Clarke); Nave: S. wall (commencing at E. end), *St Ita* (Clarke), *St Colman* (Purser), *St Brendan* (Clarke), *St Gobnet* (Clarke), *St Flannan* (Purser), *St Cárthach* (Purser); W. wall, *SS Brigid, Patrick,* and *Colmcille* (Clarke; the *St Patrick* is one of the artist's best windows in Ireland); N. Wall (commencing at the W. end), *St Munchin* (Purser), *St Fachtna* (Purser), *St Ailbhe* (Purser), *St Déaglán* (Clarke), *St Albert* (Clarke), *St Finbar* (Clarke). The pavement illustrates the Canticle of the Three Children in the Fiery Furnace. The statue of St Finnbárr in the gable of the W. doorway is by Oliver Sheppard.

Adjoining the Honan Hostel is University College (main entrance in Western Road), the most successful example of 19th cent. university architecture in the country. The college was founded in 1845 as one of the hotly disputed Queen's Colleges. It is now a constituent college of the National University of Ireland. The original buildings, unfortunately never completed, are by the firm of Sir Thomas Deane I. The quality of the design suggests the hand of Deane's gifted partner, Benjamin Woodward (*see* Museum Buildings, Trinity College, *under* Dublin, Main Axis). The W. wing was rebuilt after destruction by fire in 1862. The Science Laboratories are additions by Arthur Hill. Recent expansion has spread the college over the site of the former County Gaol, but the excellent Classical gaol gate (1818), by James and George Richard Pain, has been happily preserved. The college has a fine library and an important collection of ogham stones.

A short distance N. of the college is Fitzgerald Park. The Public Museum has small collections illustrating the story of Cork and Munster from prehistoric times to the present day.

Places and monuments within easy reach of the city

2¼ m. N. is Glennamought Bridge. ¾ m. N. of the bridge are the remains of Kilcully church. 2¼ m. NW. of the church, in Ballinvarrig, are standing stones (The Long Stone). 1½ m. further N. is Whitechurch, celebrated for its early-18th cent. Court of Poetry – successor of the ancient bardic school of Blarney (*q.v.*). The Court was initiated by Liam an Dúna Mac Cairteáin (1688–1717), and continued by Liam Rúa Mac Coitir (1680–1738) and Seán na Raithíneach O Murchadha (1700–1762).

6 m. N., in Dunbulloge, are remains of an ancient church. In the graveyard is buried the Cork scribe, Donnchadh Ó Floinn. In a field on the opposite side of the road is an ogham stone. 1 m. E., in a circular enclosure, is the ancient church site, Temple Michael. 5 m. SE. of the latter is Riverstown House (*below*).

7 m. N. is the village of Carrignavar. When the Mac Carthys of Muskerry lost Blarney (*q.v.*) they settled at Carrignavar, where they retained a last remnant of their ancestral dom-

ain until 1924. There are remains of their castle near their later residence (now the Sacred Heart Missionary College). In the village is a 1962 memorial to the Bardic School of Blarney, of which the Mac Carthys were patrons. ¼ m. E., opposite the Protestant church, is a tall pillarstone. – ½ m. S., in Ballyhesty, are two pillarstones; a third has been buried. – 2 m. N. of the village, in Gormlee, is a pillarstone, 9 ft 10 in. high. – 2 m. NE., in Ballynabortagh, is Killeagh Rath, an ancient church site; 1 m. E. is Tubbereenmurry, birthplace of Mícheál Óg Ó Longáin (1766–1837), scribe, schoolmaster, organizer of the United Irishmen, and Ireland's first Republican poet, to whom is attributed the well-known *Maidin Luan Cingcíse*; nearby are Cromlech, a standing stone, and a square earthwork.

4½ m. NE. is Riverstown House. In the wing built in 1745 by Jemmet Brown, Protestant Bishop of Cloyne, is the dining-room with a splendid figured ceiling (after Poussin's *Time Rescuing Truth from Discord and Envy*) and eight bas-relief wall-panels of Classical subjects, all the work of Paul and Philip Francini; reconditioned by the Irish Georgian Society, 1965, and now open to the public May to Sept., 10 a.m. – 6 p.m.; 2/6d.

3½ m. E., on the S. side of the Lee estuary, is the beautifully sited suburb of Blackrock. Blackrock Castle, by the water's edge, was built in 1830 to the design of James and George Richard Pain. It occupies the site of an early-17th cent. fort built for Lord Deputy Mountjoy. Dundanion Castle, Blackrock Rd, sometime home of Sir Thomas Deane, architect, preserves the name of the castle from which William Penn set out for America in 1669.

5½ m. SE., in Rochestown Capuchin church, are four Michael Healy windows (1906): *St Kevin, St Columcille, St Enda, St Finnbar.*

3 m. W., on the Macroom road, is Carrigrohane bridge. 1 m. WNW. are the remains of Carrigrohane church. Nearby, incorporated in a modern residence, are remains of Carrigrohane castle. The castle was erected on a precipitous crag overlooking the Lee. Tradition avers that it was a Mac Carthy stronghold, but it certainly belonged to the Barretts in its later days. The remains are of two periods, 14th/15th and 16th/17th cent. Great Hugh O Neill lodged at the castle in the course of his 1599 Munster campaign. There is a cave at the foot of the rock. 1½ m. WSW. is Ballincollig (*q.v.*).

3 m. NW., in St Catherine's graveyard, Killeens, are remains of Templenakilleeny, a small, early church.

CORROFIN, Co. Clare (Map 1, D7), is a small market village on the Kilfenora (8 m.)–Ennis (16¾ m.) road, SE. of pretty little Lake Inchiquin, on the edge of which are the ruins of two O Brien castles.

Sir Frederick Burton (1816–1900), painter and Director of the National Gallery, London, was born at Corrofin House.

2¼ m. NNW. is Killinaboy. Remains of a church, with 11th (?) and 12th cent. and later work, mark an early monastic site named after St Inghean Bhaoth (*see also* Crossinneenboy *under* Kilfenora); over the S. door is a perfect sheila-na-gig. W. of the church, beside the Fergus, is De Clare's House, a bawn with ivied turret. – 1 m. NW. of the church is Rooghaun road junction. ¾ m. (via steep hill) NNE. of the junction and 300 yds W. of the road, in Parknabinnia, is Giant's Grave, a wedge-shaped gallery grave set in remains of a cairn. 1 m. NW. of the road-junction (500 yds NE. of Giant's Grave) and close to the W. side of the road, in Parknabinnia, is "Cromlech and Cairn", another wedge-shaped gallery grave in a ruinous cairn. 500 yds. N. is Cromlech, another gallery grave. About ½ m. E. of this, in Commons North, is Cromlech, yet another gallery grave (incorporated in field fences). To the SE., in Leana, is a hill-top cairn with a wedge-shaped gallery grave; wide views.

3 m. S. is Dysert O Dea (*q.v.*).

COURTMACSHERRY, Co. Cork (Map 5, B7), is an attractive fishing village and little seaside resort on the Argideen estuary near the NW. corner of Courtmacsherry Bay. It is 11 m. S. of Bandon, 9 m. E. of Clonakilty and 19 m. SW. of Kinsale.

1¼ m. W., by the seashore in Abbeymahon (better: Abbeymaune=Mainistear Úa mBadhamhna), are remains of a castle. Nearby are featureless fragments of the Cistercian abbey De Fonte Vivo, alias Maune (Úa mBadhamhna; sometimes misread Maure) Abbey. Dedicated to St Mary, it was founded in 1172 by Dermot Mac Carthy, King of Desmond, and was colonized from Baltinglass. It appears to have been restored or refounded in the 16th cent. by Lord Barry of Barryroe. The buildings were sacked by Parliamentarians in 1642 (*see* Timoleague, *below*). Abbeystrowry (*see under* Skibbereen) is thought to have been a cell of Maune.

3 m. WNW., at the mouth of the Argideen, is the village of Timoleague. It takes its name, Tigh Mo-Laga, from an early monastic foundation of St Mo-Laga's (*see* Labbamolaga *under* Mitchelstown). Attractively sited by the sea are the ruins (Nat. Mon.) of a large Franciscan friary founded in 1312 by Donal Glas Mac Carthy. It was the burial place of the Mac Carthys Riabhach. Dispersed by the Reformation, the friars returned in 1604 and repaired the friary, making many alterations to the buildings. In 1629 the *Book of Lismore* (*see* Kilbrittain, *below*) was in the custody of the friars and was consulted by Brother Michael O Clery, chief of the Four Masters. In 1642 the Friary was burned, "with all the towne", by an English force led by Lord Forbes. The remains comprise church and claustral buildings. As befits a house of the Strict Observance, the architectural details are severely plain. The church consists of choir, bell-tower, nave with S. aisle, and S. transept with W. aisle and one E. chapel. The

lofty, arcaded recesses of the choir are unusua[l] The bell-tower is an addition by Edmund d[e] Courcy, Franciscan Bishop of Ross (d. 1518) who also built a dormitory, a library and a[n] infirmary. The nave has been lengthened wes[t]wards by three bays, but the E. end of the ori[g]inal nave aisle has been cut off by the transep[t] which is a manifest afterthought. Only a fra[g]ment of the cloister remains, but the claustr[al] buildings are relatively well preserved. The[y] comprise: W. Range: kitchen with dormito[ry] above; N. Range: store with library above; [E.] Range: store with cellars below and chapt[er] room above; N. Wing of E. Range: refecto[ry] with dormitory above and a later building (d[e] Courcy's infirmary ?) added on the N. – Th[e] parish church (a Romanesque essay by th[e] Limerick brothers, M. and S. Hennessy) ha[s] one of Harry Clarke's last windows (three-ligh[t] 1929–30): *Holy Family* and *Flight into Egyp[t] Assumption, Coronation of the Virgin*, an[d] *Christ meets his Mother*; *Miracle of Cana* an[d] *Death of St Joseph*. – To the N. of the villag[e] are the ruins of a Mac Carthy Riabhach cast[le.] In 1642 it was defended by Roger O Shaug[h]nessy. – 5½ m. E., in Kilbrittain, was one of t[he] principal castles of Mac Carthy Riabhach. [It] stood on the site of a de Courcy strongho[ld] captured when the Mac Carthy's recovered th[is] part of their ancestral kingdom. The last Ma[c] Carthy castle here was built in 1596. On 1 Ju[ne] 1642 it was captured by the English (*see* Ba[n]don) under Lord Kinalmeaky, son of Richar[d] Boyle, Earl of Cork. In the castle Kinalmeak[y] found an Irish MS., perhaps the *Book of Lismor[e]* (written for Finghin Mac Carthy Riabhach, [d.] 1505; *see* Lismore). – 2¾ m. NW. of Timoleagu[e] on Mullaghseefin, Monteen, are megalith[ic] remains.

CRAUGHWELL, Co. Galway (Map 5, B2[)] is a small village on the Galway (16 m.)–Loug[h]rea (7 m.) road. Nearby are the Galway Blazer[s'] kennels.

1¾ m. E. is St Cleran's, home of John Husto[n,] film director. The good early-19th cent. hou[se] (re-edified by Michael Scott) was the birthplac[e] of Australian explorer, Robert O'Hara Burk[e] (1820–61). There are remains of a castle and [of] a manorial church (on an early site ?).

3¾ m. SE., in Toorclogher, is Dermot an[d] Grania's Bed, a wedge-shaped gallery grav[e.] 2¾ m. S. (via Mannin crossroads), on the [N.] side of the road in Aggardbeg, is a ring-barro[w.] ¾ m. ESE., on the S. side of the road in Ball[i]namannin, is Lisheen, alias The Lios, a rin[g] barrow. ¾ m. E. of the latter, in Kilquain, is [a] pillarstone (Gallaun); to the N., in the sam[e] townland, is Leaba Nóra, a small, chambere[d] tumulus. ½ m. SE. of Lisheen is Ballylin pilla[r] stone (Gallaun). 2 m. S. of Lisheen is Monk[s]field ring-barrow (*see under* Adrahan).

3 m. W., in the neglected graveyard of Kil[l]eeneen, is the neglected grave of Antoine [Ó] Reachtabhra, "Blind Raftery" (1784–1834[)] whose songs are still popular.

CREESLOUGH, Co. Donegal (Map 2, C2), is a village and tourist centre on the Letterkenny (16 m.)–Dunfanaghy (6 m.) road, near the head of Sheephaven.

½ m. E. are a picturesque bridge and waterfall on the Duntally River.

2½ m. N., in Doocashel Glebe, is Dermot and Grania's Bed, a chambered cairn.

2 m. NE., enclosed by the sea and a rock-cut fosse, are the bawn and keep (Nat. Mon.) of Castle Doe, Caisleán na dTúath. Modernized c. 1800 and occupied until c. 1900, this was originally the stronghold of Mac Suibhne na dTúath (Mac Sweeney na Doe), Mac Sweeny of the Túatha. The celebrated Red Hugh O Donnell was fostered here. Sir Cahir O Doherty set up his headquarters at the castle in 1608 before attacking the English fortress at Derry. At the Plantation the castle was assigned to one, Sandford, but was recovered by the Mac Sweenys at the start of the Eleven Years War. It was at the castle that Eoghan Rúa O Neill landed from Flanders in 1642 to take his place in the great Ulster effort to undo the Plantation. In 1650 the castle fell to the Cromwellian commander, Coote. The detaching by Col. Myles MacSweeny of some 1,400 men from the Irish army for the purpose of recapturing the place contributed largely to the disastrous defeat at Scarrifhollis in 1650 (see under Letterkenny). Under Charles II the castle served as an English military post. At the Williamite rebellion it was seized for James II by the Mac Sweenys. The adjacent graveyard is said to mark the site of a Franciscan friary founded by the Mac Sweenys. A late-medieval Mac Sweeny tombstone resembles the Mac Sweeny tombstone at Killybegs (q.v.).

4 m. NNE. are the very beautiful peninsula and demesne of Ards. Ards House, formerly residence of the Stewart family, is now the Capuchin friary of Árd Mhuire. Admission to the grounds may be had on application.

4½ m. SE., and 2½ m. S. of lovely Glen Lough, is the wild pass of Barnesbeg between Crockmore (1,160 ft) and Stragaddy (946 ft). ¾ m. S. of the bridge over the Owencarrow, and to the N. of the railway line, is St Glasny's Grave.

Creeslough is a convenient place for climbing Muckish (see under Gortahork), 4 m. SW.

5½ m. SW. (via rough, untarred, minor road), between the Muckish–Errigal range and the Derryveagh Mts, is the wild and empty Calabber valley. 6 m. SW. of Calabber bridge the road improves and descends the Dunlewy Gap (see under Gweedore) to Dunlewy and Creeslough.

8 m. SSW. is Glenveagh (see Kilmacrenan).

3 m. NNW., in Ballymore Upper, is Dermot and Grania's Bed, a court cairn.

CROOKHAVEN, Co. Cork (Map 4, C6), is a delightful inlet 8¾ m. SW. of Skull and 5 m. ENE. of Mizen Head. Its safe anchorage is a favourite resort of yachtsmen. The haven has given its name to a fishing village and quiet little resort, part of which lies on the N. shore, part

on the S. shore. The scenery to the SW., W., and N. is very fine. There is a beautiful sandy beach at Barley Cove, 1¾ m. W.

For the antiquities of the district see Goleen and Mizen Head under Skull.

CROOKSTOWN, Co. Cork (Map 5, B6), is a village on the southern road from Cork (18 m.) to Macroom (9 m.), near the head of the Bride valley. There are several Mac Swiney and other castles in the area; also numerous megalithic monuments.

5 m. NNE. is Roovesmore (see under Coachford).

1¼ m. NE., on Carraig an Dúna, are the ruins of Castlemore, alias Dundrinane castle. At the Norman invasion the de Cogans built a castle here, seemingly on the site of a fort. The place was later recovered by the Mac Carthys of Muskerry. In the later 16th–earlier 17th cent. the castle was held for Mac Carthy by Mac Swiney galloglas.

2½ m. ENE., in Knockshanawee, alt. 690 ft, is a trivallate ringfort. A souterrain in the fort was roofed in part with six ogham stones; it has been demolished and the stones removed to University College, Cork. The site commands a splendid view. 5¾ m. ENE. is Kilcrea (see Ovens under Ballincollig).

4 m. SE., in Garranes, is Lisnacaheragh (Nat. Mon.), a large, trivallate ringfort. It has been claimed that this fort is the Ráth Ráithlenn of early Irish legend, a seat of the Eóghanacht kings of Uí Echach, and the birthplace of St Finbar of Cork. Excavation yielded no evidence of either military or ordinary domestic occupation, but showed that metal-workers and allied craftsmen had been very active in the fort during the period round about A.D. 500. (St Finbar's father was a craftsman in metal.) The interior was contained a number of timber-post houses. 4¾ m. NE. is Kilcrea (see Ovens under Ballincollig). – 1¼ m. SW., in Moskeagh, is a pillarstone which formerly had a "surrounding mound".

1¼ m. S., in Bellmount Upper, is Cromlech; two fields to the WSW. is a stone circle.

2 m. SSW., in Laghtneill, is Niall's Grave, a roofless gallery grave giving its name (Leacht Néill) to the townland.

2 m. SW., is Bealnabla where Michael Collins was ambushed and killed, August 1922. An unworthy memorial marks the spot. Less than ½ m. N. of the crossroads is Currabeha stone circle.

CROOM, Co. Limerick (Map 5, B4), is a small market town where the Limerick (12 m.)–Charleville (12 m.) road crosses the Maigue. About 1197/1200 Hamo de Valognes granted a manor here to Gerald fitz Maurice, brother of Thomas of Shanid (see Shanagolden), lord O ffaly, and ancestor of the Kildare Geraldines. It was this manor, which remained with the Kildare Fitzgeralds until Silken Thomas's rebellion (p. 40), that suggested the celebrated Fitzgerald motto and war-cry, "Crom Abu". The castle, built before 1216, was repaired by John Darcy in 1334; it had a circular bawn; a fragment of a 15th/16th cent. tower is all that survives. The town itself was walled in 1310.

The poet, Seán Ó Tuama an ghrinn (1706–75), in his palmy days kept a hostelry at Mungret Gate, near the Fair Green. On the death of Seán Clárach Mac Domhnaill, 1754, he summoned the local poets to a Court of Poetry which continued to meet at intervals. Aindrias Mac Craith and Father Liam Inglis were among the active members of the Court. Ó Tuama is buried in Croom churchyard, Mac Craith at Kilmallock.

2 m. N. and 400 yds E. of the Limerick road, on the NE. slope of a ridge in Killonahan, is one of the best stone ringforts in the county.

2 m. NE., via Tory Hill, formerly Druim Assail (572 ft). On the occasion of the second battle of An Aonach (*below*), Gerald, 14th (Rebel) Earl of Desmond, took up his position on the hill, so as to join the Catholic insurgents at the first sign of victory. His courage failed, however, and leaving his brave brother in the lurch, he withdrew to Askeaton (*q.v.*). The hill commands a splendid view; below the summit are remains of a hillfort.

4 m. NE. is Glenogra castle, a Desmond stronghold of 1400–1420, with an octagonal keep set in a rectangular bawn. Nearby are the remains of St Nicholas's Church (Transitional).

2½ m. E., to the S. of Monaster, are remains of Monasternenagh, Mainistear an Aonaigh, alias Mainistear na Maighe, otherwise the Cistercian Abbey of Magium, founded in 1148 by Turloch O Brien, King of Thomond, in thanksgiving for his victory over the Norse at Rathmore (*below*), and colonized from Mellifont. The abbey was the parent of the abbeys of Inishlounaght (*see under* Clonmel), Abbeydorney (*q.v.*), Holy Cross (*see under* Thurles), and Monasterore (*see under* Midleton). In 1209 the abbey of Abbeyfeale was annexed to it as a cell. In 1227 it was itself affiliated to Margam in Glamorganshire. The fragmentary remains (Nat. Mon.), which date largely from the later 12th cent., have some interesting Late Romanesque and Transitional features. The cruciform church (*c.* 1185–1205) had an aisled nave, a barrel-vaulted chancel, and three E. chapels in each transept. Only the E. half of the nave was arcaded. In the 15th (?) cent. the two E. bays of the nave and the transept arches were blocked up; at the same time the S. transept was given a barrel-vault roof. Only fragments survive of the claustral buildings. Nearby, on the Camoge, are remains of the abbey mill and bridge. The abbey takes its name from Aonach Cairbre, alias An Aonach, Nenagh, meeting-place of a public assembly and great fair, the site of which may be marked by the remains of "two conjoined cairns" on the N. side of the river. 700 yds E. of the cairns are two ring barrows. Two battles took place at An Aonach, the first on

19 July 1370, the second on 3 April 1580. In the first battle, King Brian of Thomond routed his deposed uncle, Turloch, and Gearoid *file*, 3rd Earl of Desmond, "with incredible slaughter". Desmond and his men took refuge in the abbey, but Brian violated the sanctuary and took them prisoner. In the second battle, Sir Nicholas Malby, Elizabethan Governor of Connacht, with 600 foot, 450 horse, and artillery, routed Sir John of Desmond and Papal Legate Saunders, who had Spanish officers and 2,000 men, but few firearms and no artillery. The defeated sought refuge in the abbey, but the English, turning their guns on it, battered the cloister and refectory. They then carried the place by storm, beheaded the abbot (who had been present at the battle) on the altar steps, put forty of the monks to the sword, and wrecked the abbey.

4 m. E. is Rathmore, scene of Turloch O Brien's victory over the Norse, 1148. There are remains of a late-15th cent. Desmond castle here. It was held by Irish and Spanish troops in 1579–80, but fell to Malby after the battle of Monasternenagh.

2 m. NW., in Carrigeen, an imperfect Round Tower (65½ ft; Romanesque doorway) and a ruined church (Nat. Mons.), formerly enclosed by a square cashel, mark the site of Dísert Oéngusso, Aonghus's Hermitage, called after Oéngus céle Dé (*see* Clonenagh *under* Mountrath, Dysertenos *under* Stradbally, *and* Tallaght).

2 m. NNW., via the Limerick road, is Caherass Court, sometime home of the Roches.

3 m. NNW., via the Limerick road, is Fanningstown castle.

CROSSHAVEN, Co. Cork (Map 5, C7), a popular small resort on a little sheltered cove at the mouth of the beautiful Owenboy estuary, 13 m. SE. of Cork, is a noted yachting centre (Royal Munster Yacht Club). It is also a good centre for fishing on Cork Harbour.

Poulnacallee Bay (Church Bay) to the SE., Myrtleville Bay to the S., and Weaver's Point are popular bathing places. On the N. side of the estuary is Curraghbinny, with the Giant's Grave, a cairn on the summit (266 ft); the cairn originally had a dry-wall kerb.

1¼ m. NE., on Rams Head, at the mouth of Cork Harbour, is Camden Fort, one of the 19th cent. fortifications of Cork Harbour. The cliffs hereabouts afford fine views.

CROSSMAGLEN, Co. Armagh (Map 3, B6), is a village on the Dundalk (13 m.)–Castleblayney (4 m.) road.

½ m. NNW., in Carran, are two pillarstones, one prostrate (Nat. Mon.).

2 m. N., in Annaghmare, is the Black Castle (Nat. Mon.), a wedge-shaped cairn with a court grave at the broad end and two lateral chambers near the narrow end. The façade of the deep forecourt is a "post-and-panel" construction of orthostats and dry walling. Ex-

Plate 6. The Office of Arms and Bedford Tower, Dublin Castle

cavations (1963, 1964) revealed both cremated and unburnt human remains, Western and other neolithic pottery, hollow scrapers, a javelin of flint, and bones of ox (?) and pig. 2 m. further N., in Kiltybane, alias Lisleitrim, is Lisleitrim Fort (Nat. Mon.), a trivallate ring-fort with deep ditches and a souterrain. In Lisleitrim Lough is a large crannóg.

4 m. NE., in Dorsey, Ummercam (Johnston), and Tullynavall, is The Dorsey (Nat. Mon.), a 300-acre enclosure bounded by an earthen rampart set between two ditches; where it crosses boggy ground the rampart is carried on piles. The Dorsey was presumably constructed to close the highway to the North and the royal seat of prehistoric Ulster at Navan near Armagh (q.v.).

2½ m. W., in Lough Ross, is a crannóg where the leaders of the 1641 insurrection are supposed to have conferred.

1¼ m. S., in Lissaraw, is a ringfort with an open souterrain in the rampart.

2 m. NW., in Corliss, is the Beech Fort (Nat. Mon.), a fine ringfort with an open souterrain.

CROSSMOLINA, Co. Mayo (Map 1, D3),

is a small market town where the Ballina (8 m.)–Belmullet (39 m.) road crosses the River Deal close to the NW. corner of Lough Conn. It is a convenient centre for fishing Loughs Conn and Cullen, as well as the Deel, Moy, and other rivers of W. Mayo. The country round about is rich in ringforts and other ancient remains.

¾ m. N. are remains of Abbeytown "Abbey", thought to have been founded in the 10th cent.

4½ m. ENE., in the grounds of Castle Gore, are the ruins of 16th cent. Deel castle. Castle Gore was built for the Earl of Arran about 1790.

3 m. SE., on Castle Island, Lough Conn, are remains of an O Conor castle.

6¼ m. SE., near the N. tip of a peninsula in Lough Conn, are remains of little Errew Abbey (Nat. Mon.): a plain, nave-and-chancel church (late 13th cent. ?) on the S. side of a garth which had ambulatories on S., E., and N. sides. These are remains of a house of Augustinian Canons, successor of an early monastery founded by St Tighearnán. Nearby Templenagalliaghdoo (Nat. Mon.) is a fragment of a nunnery.

3¾ m. W., close to a farmhouse 100 yds S. of the Bangor Erris road, is a remarkable long cairn with three court graves.

CRUMLIN, Co. Antrim (Map 3, C4), is a

village on the road from Lisburn (12 m.) to Antrim (9 m.).

¾ m. ENE. are the ruins of Crumlin Church, with eight remarkable sedilia at the E. end (four each in the N. and S. walls). Across the river is a well-preserved motte, The Mound.

CRUSHEEN, Co. Clare (Map 5, B3), is a

village on the Gort (11 m.)–Ennis (9 m.) road.

½ m. SW., in Caheraphuca, is Giant's Grave (Nat. Mon.), a wedge-shaped gallery grave.

¾ m. S. is Inchicronan, a lake peninsula. At the neck of the peninsula are remains of a 15th cent. O Brien castle where, in 1651, the Cromwellian, Ludlow, defeated a royalist force. Conor O Brien of Leamaneh (see under Kilfenora) was killed in the engagement. ¾ m. SSW. of the castle are the ruins (Nat. Mon.) of an Augustinian priory founded c. 1400 on a site whose history goes back to St Crónán of Tuamgraney (see under Scarriff). There are remains of a Transitional, nave-and-chancel church of c. 1200 to which a sacristy (on the N.) and a transept and residence, etc. (on the S.) were added in the 15th cent. In 1615 the church was adapted for Protestant parochial use by Donogh O Brien, Earl of Thomond.

6 m. W. are the remains (Nat. Mon.) of Ruan parish church; 15th cent.

CULDAFF, Co. Donegal (Map 2, E1), is a

village on the main road from Moville (9 m.) to Carndonagh (6 m.). There is a good, small beach at the mouth of the Culdaff River. In the river is St Bodan's Boat, a stone on which the saint crossed over from Scotland, as witness the marks of his fingers.

1¾ m. NNE., beyond Bunnagee pier, is Doonowen, a double promontory cut off from the mainland by a wall of dry masonry. On the N. promontory can be traced the outline of various structures which may represent the castle of Donowen held in 1601 by Gartell, son of Seán Buidhe O Doherty. On an islet to the E., the site commanding splendid views, are remains of a chamber tomb.

4 m. N. is Glengad Head, to the NW. of which are four miles of fine cliffs up to 800 ft high.

2½ m. SE., in Knockergrana, is a court cairn.

2 m. S., in Clonca, are the ruins of a church mainly of the Plantation period; but the lintel of the W. doorway belongs to a pre-Romanesque church. On the lintel are traces of a cross and other carving. Inside the church is the 16th cent. gravestone of Magnus Mac Orristin; the symbols include sword, hurley (golf club ?), and ball; the inscriptions read FERGUS MAK ALLAN DO RINI IN CLACH SA ("Fergus Mac Allan made this stone") and MAGNUS MEC ORRISTIN IAE (?) FOTRL SEO ("Magnus Mac Orristin . . ."). In the outer face of the W. wall is a fragment of a gravestone with an Irish inscription. In the field to the W. of the church is the 12-ft shaft of St Buadan's (Bodan's) Cross, an elaborately carved High Cross (Nat. Mon.). The figured panels include *Miracle of the loaves and fishes* (top of E. face). Near the cross-shaft lies the head of a second High Cross. St Buadan's Bell is preserved in Bogan church, 1 m. NE. ¼ m. SE. of the latter, on Mass Hill, Glackadrumman, is a stone circle. ½ m. SW. of this, on the top of Black Hill, alias Deen Hill (255 ft), in Larraghirril, is Druid's Altar, a court cairn.

1 m. SW. of Clonca church is Carrowmore (see under Carndonagh).

CUSHENDALL, Co. Antrim (Map 3, C3), is a quiet little resort (good small beach) delightfully situated at the N. end of the famous Antrim Coast Road (*see under* Larne), in the mouth of Glenballyemon and Glenaan. It takes its name ("Dall-side") from the little Dall River. It is 23 m. NW. of Larne, 15 m. SE. of Ballycastle, 20 m. NNE. of Ballymena, and is a convenient base for exploring Glenariff (*below*).

1 m. NE. are the ruins of Layd Church (Nat. Mon.), a burial place of the Mac Donnells of Antrim (*see* Antrim, Glens of); the vaulted tower is a 15th cent. addition. From 1696 to 1790 the church served the Protestant parish. The 1832 Protestant church has a Michael Healy window, *The Light of the World* (1917).

1½ m. S., at the foot of Glenariff, loveliest of the Glens of Antrim, is beautiful Red Bay with its good beach. On a promontory overhanging the road are scant remains of a Biset motte-and-bailey castle (1242 ?) crowned by fragments of a castle built by Sir James Mac Donnell in 1561, destroyed by Seaán the Proud O Neill of Tír Eóghain in 1565, and rebuilt, probably by Somhairle Buidhe Mac Donnell, in 1568. Dismantled by Somhairle's son, James, in 1597, it was restored by another son, Randall, 1st Earl of Antrim, in 1604. It was finally slighted by Cromwellians in 1652. The beauty spot of 5-mile Glenariff is the so-called Fairy Glen (property of the Ulster Transport Authority; admission free) in the upper valley: streams, waterfalls (Eas na Larach "The Mare's Waterfall", Eas na gCrúb "The Fall of the Hooves"), etc.

2 m. WNW. (via lane from the Ballymoney road), alt. 450 ft, in Lubatavish on the slope of Tievebulliagh (1,346 ft), is Cloghbrack, alias Ossian's Grave, a two-chamber court cairn (Nat. Mon.) overlooking the junction of Glenaan and Glencorp. In Neolithic times the fine-grained stone of Tievebulliagh was exploited at an "axe factory" whose products have been found as far away as SE. England.

CUSHENDUN, Co. Antrim (Map 3, C3), is an attractive small summer resort charmingly sited by the little River Dun (whence its name, "Dun-side"), at the foot of Glendun and Glencorp, 4½ m. N. of Cushendall and 12 m. SE. of Ballycastle. The Dun holds brown trout; also occasional salmon and sea trout. The good beach is backed by a sandy green. The local coast, moors, and valleys are noted for their varying scenery.

Most of the village was built for Ronald Mac Neill (Lord Cushendun, 1861–1934) by Clough William Ellis. Village, green, and beach now belong to the National Trust.

Moira O Neill (Mrs Agnes Skryne, d. 1958), author of *Songs of the Glens of Antrim*, lived in Rockport Lodge, near the N. end of the beach. Castle Carra, close by, is a fragment of a Mac Donnell castle (*see* Antrim, Glens of); local legend asserts that it was here the Mac Donnells murdered Seaán the Proud O Neill of

Tír Eóghain (1567); a nearby cairn is said mark Seaán's grave (he was actually buried Glenarm); the neighbouring monument con memorates Sir Roger Casement (1864–191 and other Antrim men who died for Irish fre dom. Above the old sea cliff in Ballycleagh a three pillarstones (one prostrate in road fence

The earliest known Irish artefacts are "Lar ian" flints found at the base of the gravels c the N. side of the Dun.

1¼ m. WSW., in Ballure, Inispollan, are Mass-enclosure and altar of Penal times.

6 m. NW. – 1¼ m. WSW. of Loughaveem alias Carey Lough – in Glenmakeerin (alt. 800 on Carneighaneigh), is a double–court cair

The steep, winding road N. to Torr Hea (7 m.; nearest point to Scotland, 13 m.) offe splendid views, especially at Green Hill (5 m but is not recommended for cars or cyclists. T constant sight of Ailsa Craig and the Mull Kintyre from all the higher ground reminds that throughout the Gaelic centuries the narro seas hereabouts were a highway linking t motherland with its Scottish daughters. (speech and culture, Ireland and Gaelic Scc land were one world.) Torr Head itself affor rewarding prospects. 1½ m. SW., on the summ (1,253 ft) of the mountain which now bea its name, is Carnanmore, alias Carnlea (Na Mon.), one of the most northerly of Iri passage graves: scribings on one roofstone.

DAINGEAN, Co. Offaly (Map 6, A3), form erly Philipstown, is a village on the Tullamo (12 m.)–Edenderry (11 m.) road, beside t Grand Canal. It takes its name (*daingea* fortress) from the medieval island fortress of Conor Faly. When the region was Plant under Mary Tudor the capital of the new constituted King's County was set up here a named Philipstown after Mary's husban Philip II of Spain. The place never prospere In 1833 it was supplanted as county seat Tullamore (*q.v.*). The rather spoilt small Cou House has been attributed to James Gando At the S. end of the village is Fort Castle, 18 cent. successor of the fort erected in the 16 cent. by Sir William Brabazon, English Lo Justice, to hold down the conquered O Con Faly territory.

5 m. N. Croghan Hill (769 ft) rises above t Bog of Allen. On the hill – referred to in Spe ser's *Faerie Queene* – are a prehistoric char bered cairn, several holy wells, the ruins of tv churches, and the remains of O Conor Faly Castle, alias Croghan Castle. The summ affords a splendid view.

4 m. NW., at Kilclonfert, are the ruins of castle and a church. SW. is St Clavin's Well.

DALKEY, Co. Dublin (Map 6, E7), coastal suburb and resort between Dalke Sound and Dalkey Hill, 8 m. SE. of Dubl city. Boating, bathing, and fishing facilities a available at various places along the shor From Sorrento Park (to the SE.) and Dalke

Hill (see Killiney Hill, below) views may be had of some of the loveliest stretches of the Irish coast. The earliest surviving antiquities are the ruined church (Nat. Mon.) and an early gravestone in the churchyard in Main St. The church is a pre-Romanesque structure altered and enlarged in the Middle Ages. The gravestone has an incised ringed cross and concentric circles (see Rathmichael under Loughlinstown). In the Middle Ages Dalkey was an important landing-place for cross-channel passenger traffic, and three fortified houses of the 15th–16th centuries still survive. Of these one is incorporated in the Town Hall. Another, Archbold's Castle (Nat. Mon.), stands on the opposite side of the street. The third, Bullock Castle, overlooks Bullock Harbour about 1 m. N. beside the main Dún Laoghaire road.

George Bernard Shaw lived in Torca Cottage on Dalkey Hill from 1866 to 1874. He has paid his own tribute to the inspiring beauty of this boyhood home.

300 yds offshore to the SE. (boats obtainable at Coliemore Harbour) is Dalkey Island, from which the suburb takes its name (Norse for Thorn Island). The crossing is amply rewarded by the beauty of the coastline as seen from sea-level at the S. end of the sound. On the island are the ruins of St Begnet's Church (Nat. Mon.), a small, early structure with massively lintelled W. doorway, bold antae at either gable, and living quarters over the W. end. The bell cote is an addition. In front of the door is a rock with a ringed cross carved in relief. The E. end of the church was altered by the builders of the nearby martello tower and battery, who set up their living quarters in it. Nearby, on the brink of the sound, is a holy well, formerly resorted to by sufferers from sore eyes.

The beautiful coast road S. of Dalkey (Vico Road) skirts Dalkey Hill and then Killiney Hill, passing in succession on the left a men's bathing place and the popular bathing place of White Rock. A large part of Killiney Hill is now preserved as a public park (Victoria Park). The summit (480 ft) affords a magnificent panorama of sea, mountain, valley and plain. At the foot of the hill is popular Killiney Strand, one of the finest, as it is the most beautifully situated, of the Dublin suburban beaches. About ¼ m. W. of the beach are the ruins (Nat. Mon.) of an early nave-and-chancel church with later N. aisle. It takes its name (Cill Inghean Léinín, Killiney) from the saintly Daughters of Léinín (see Cloyne). On the soffit of the trabeate W. doorway a Greek cross is carved in relief. ¾ m. to the SSW., and close to the Ballybrack–Shankill road, is Ballybrack (Shanganagh) Dolmen, a portal dolmen.

DELGANY, Co. Wicklow (Map 6, D3), is a prettily situated village on the Bray (6 m.)–Wicklow (12 m.) road, 1½ m. SW. of Greystones.

In the Protestant parish church is the splendid 1790 monument of David Digges La Touche of Bellvue (below). It is the work of the Dublin sculptor, John Hickey (1756–95): figures of La Touche, his wife, and sons, David, John, Peter; repaired by Harrison, 1895.

A fragment of a church, St Crispin's Cell, and the shaft of a granite High Cross (Nat. Mons.) mark the site of a 6th/7th cent. foundation attributed to St Chuaróg, royal Welsh disciple of St Kevin, to whom he is said to have given the deathbed viaticum. The cross-shaft is inscribed OR[ÓIT] DO ANLUA[N] OCUS DU CONBRAN SAIR ("A prayer for Anluan and for Conbran the wright").

In 1021 King Ughaine of Leinster routed Sigtryggr, Norse king of Dublin, with heavy loss at Delgany.

W. and NW. of the village is Delgany State Forest, formerly Bellvue Demesne. Bellvue was called Ballydonough until 1753, when David Digges La Touche (d. 1785) built the house.

¾ m. N. are remains of the Archbold castle of Kindelestown (Nat. Mon.).

3 m. ESE. are remains of Ballynerrin church.

3 m. SE. is the quiet little resort of Kilcoole (Cell Chomgaill) with remains (Nat. Mon.) of St Mary's Church, a small, plain, nave-and-chancel structure of c. 1200 on the site of St Comgall's 6th cent. foundation. At the beach 1 m. E. Sir Thomas Myles and James Creed Meredith landed 600 rifles for the Irish Volunteers in August 1914 (see Howth).

1 m. W. is the Glen of the Downs, a wooded defile on the Dublin–Wicklow road.

DELVIN, Co. Westmeath (Map 6, B2), is a village on the Castlepollard (12 m.)–Athboy (9 m.) road.

The scrub-covered motte near the S. end of the village is a relic of the castle built in 1181 by Hugh de Lacy for his brother-in-law, Gilbert de Nangle (de Angulo), to whom he granted the barony of Delvin. (From Gilbert descends the noble family of Nugent, which has held estates in the barony down to our times. A famous member of the family was Father Francis Nugent, "Laulinus Nugentius", son of Edward Nugent of Ballybranagh, alias Walshestown, and his wife, Margaret O Conor Faly. "One of the four most learned men in Europe", he became a Capuchin in 1591 and founded the Irish province of the order. He became professor at Louvain University, and died at Charleville on the Meuse in 1634.) Close to the motte are the ruins of a 13th cent. keep of the distinctively Norman-Irish variety found at Carlow (q.v.) and a few other places. The derelict Protestant church nearby incorporates the 15th cent. tower and other fragments of the medieval manorial church. The Church of the Assumption at the N. end of the village is by George Ashlin. Nugents helped to build and decorate it.

3 m. NE. is Ballinlough Castle, home of Sir Hugh Nugent. Nearby are the remains of an O Reilly castle.

4 m. SW. is Reynella House, built in 1793.

1¾ m. NW. is Ballinvalley, birthplace of Brinsley Mac Namara, the playwright, whose novel, *The Valley of the Squinting Windows*, and Heffernan series of plays are set in this countryside.

DERRY, Co. Derry (Map 2, D2), officially Londonderry from its association with the City of London, is the fourth largest city in Ireland and the second largest in Ulster. It stands on the W. bank of the River Foyle, a short distance above Lough Foyle, and is a seaport and a British naval and air base, as well as an important manufacturing centre.

The history of Derry begins with a monastery founded by St Columcille (Columba) in 546 in Calgach's oak-wood (Doire Calgaich). The monastery suffered repeatedly at the hands of the Vikings, but came through the Viking period with enhanced importance, and in the 12th cent. replaced Kells (Co. Meath, *q.v.*) as the metropolis of the Columban monasteries. In 1110/11 the synod of Ráth Breasail instituted a diocese to serve the kingdom of Tír Eóghain. Until 1246 the see was at Maghera, Co. Derry (*q.v.*), but in that year was transferred to Derry. In 1600 an English force under Sir Henry Docwra came round by sea to Culmore and seized Derry, so turning the defences of Gaelic Ulster, which had so long thrown back every frontal assault. Docwra completely demolished the monastery and churches, save for the Round Tower, to get materials for his fortifications. In 1608 Sir Cahir O Doherty attacked and destroyed the English garrison in the course of a short-lived rebellion. In 1613 James I granted Derry, together with enormous estates, to the citizens of London, who laid out the city, surrounded it with stout walls, and planted it with Protestant settlers. In 1648 and 1649 the town was held by Parliamentarians under Sir Charles Coote against Royalist besiegers; and was relieved by Eoghan Rúa O Neill, commander of the Catholic army of Ulster! But the greatest event in its modern history was the epic 1688–9 Siege, when the citizens and garrison, inspired by the Rev. George Walker, rector of Donaghmore, expelled vacillating Governor Lundy and refused to admit a Jacobite garrison. The city was thereupon unsuccessfully blockaded from 18 Dec. 1688 to 28 July 1689 by Jacobite forces (which were actually outnumbered by the defenders). Boom Hall, on the Foyle, recalls that it was there the blockaders had thrown a boom across the river to halt relieving ships.

The kernel of the modern city is the little Plantation town encompassed by the wall (Nat. Mon.) completed in 1618 to the design of Sir Edward Doddington. Most of the wall survives, through it has lost its 30-ft ditch and three bulwarks, or bastions, and has been pierced by three modern "gates". Within the wall the layout of the Plantation town is well preserved: a central market square (the Diamond) at the intersection of four main streets leading from the four original gates, Shipquay Gate, Fer (quay) Gate, Bishop's Gate, and Butcher Gate (one in each side of the fortifications). T Town Wall affords an interesting promenad A convenient place of access is at Shipqu Gate, Foyle St (facing the 1908 Gothic Guil hall; collection of local antiquities), whence t circuit best proceeds via Coward's Bastion the N. angle; reputedly the safest place durii the siege), Gunner's Bastion, and Butcher Gate, to the Royal Bastion with its 18 George Walker column (statue by Edwa Smyth's son, John). Further S., at the SV angle of the wall, is the Double Bastion, wi Roaring Meg, a great gun which made its noi contribution to the defence. To the E. Bishop's Gate, a 1789 triumphal arch (I James Gandon) commemorating William Orange; keystones and panels are by the Mea sculptor, Edward Smyth, noted for his work the Custom House and Four Courts, Dubli Beyond Bishop's Gate the wall continues pa Church Bastion (at S. angle; flanked by tv 1627 sentry posts) to Ferry(quay) Gate, and to Shipquay; but Bishop's Gate is a convenie place for descending.

Near Bishop's Gate (via Bishop's St ar Columb's Court), on the highest ground with the walls, is St Columb's Cathedral, built (162 33) for the Protestant settlers by the City London. On plan this interesting example 17th cent. Gothic is an English parish churc aisled nave and W. tower. In 1778 Bishop t Earl of Bristol had the tower raised 21 ft ai surmounted by a spire (rebuilt 1823). The cha cel (1887; on 1633 foundations), chapter hou (1910), and S. chapel (1910) are the most rece additions. In the porch is a Rogan monume signed by Cork-born Joseph Robinson Ki (1821–94). The aisles have some interestii monuments, including (N. aisle) one to Joh Elvin (1674; mutilated) and (S. aisle) one Bishop Knox (by Behnes, 1834). The windo glass is bad. In the Chapter House are relics the siege; also watercolours of the cathedi in its original form. – Nearby, in Bishop St, the Court House (1813–17), by John Bowde the portico (like that of Bowden's 1824 chur in Mount St Crescent, Dublin, SE.) is modell on the Erechtheum; the statues of *Justice* ai *Peace* on the wings are by Edward Smyth (1812). The nearby Society House and Deane are good, well maintained, Georgian house The Freemasons' Hall, facing the Court Hous scarcely suggests that here was the Bishop Palace largely rebuilt (*c.* 1716) by eccentric Lo Bristol; house and garden occupy the site Derry's medieval house of Canons Regular St Augustine.

SW. of Bishop's Gate is Long (=Roun Tower St. St Columba's Church and churc yard occupy part of the site of Columcille monastery; built into the base of a churchyai Calvary is "St Colum's Stone", a double bu laun brought here in 1897 from St Colum Well (now a pump) in a neighbouring stree

From Bishop's Gate, Bishop St leads N. to the Diamond (1914–18 War Memorial on the site of the 1622 Town House), Shipquay St (where George Farquhar, playwright, was born of English parents, 1678), and Foyle St. ½ m. WNW. of the Guildhall, in Infirmary Rd, is St Eugene's Cathedral (1873), dedicated to the patron (properly St Eoghan) of Ardstraw (*see under* Newtown Stewart). This Gothic-Revival church has an excellent tower and spire, but the interior is ruined by horrid glass and other "art". ½ m. NNE. is the site of the former Foyle College (1814), lineal descendant of the Free School founded in 1617 for the Planters; in the grounds is a statue (formerly in Lahore; by Sir Joseph Edgar Boehm, R.A., sculptor-in-ordinary to Queen Victoria) of Sir John Lawrence, governor-general of India. Like his brother Henry, he went to school at Foyle College, as did John Bagenal Bury (1861–1927), the historian. Nearby to the N. is Magee University College (1865).

On the E. side of the Foyle is the suburb of Waterside. N. of Eglinton Barracks are remains (Nat. Mon.) of St Brecan's Church ("St Colum's Chapel"). On the Dungiven road, in Altnagelvin, the unlovely mass of the North West General Hospital (1961; by Yorke, Rosenberg, and Marshall of London) dominates the countryside; near the main entrance is a bronze *Princess* (sic) *Macha* by F. E. McWilliams.

3¼ m. NE., via the coast road to Coleraine is Lough Enagh: Rough Island is a crannóg whose history began in neolithic times.

2 m. N., via the Culmore road, is Belmont House. In the garden is "St Colum's Stone" alias "St Patrick's Stone" (Nat. Mon.), a large block with two central footprints; it may have been the inauguration stone of a Gaelic ruler. Close by is the 16th cent. tomb-effigy of an armoured knight found in the city.

5 m. NNE., beyond Boom Hall (*c.* 1770), is Culmore. A 19th cent. fort (Nat. Mon.), successor to one built in the 17th cent. by the London Companies, guards the mouth of the Foyle. 1 m. W., beside the Protestant church, is a fragment of a church built by the London Companies about 1686 and used as a hospital by the besieging Jacobites. Amelia Earhart, American aviator and first woman to fly the Atlantic, landed at Culmore in 1932.

5 m. WNW., on Greenan Mountain (803 ft), are the ruins (Nat. Mon.) of the celebrated hill-fort of Grianán Oiligh, alias Greenan Elly, "The Grianán of Ailech (Oileach)". It gave its name to the early Northern Uí Néill (descendants of Niall Nine Hostager) over-kingdom of Ailech (roughly the modern county of Donegal), whose most famous components were Cenél Conaill (their territory Tír Chonaill, whence "Tyrconnell") and Cenél Eóghain (their territory Tír Eóghain, whence "Tyrone"). The fort was originally the royal seat of Tír Eóghain, whose stocks in the course of the Middle Ages spread E. and SE. over so much of the modern counties, Tyrone, Derry, Armagh, and whose ruling

family after 1241 was the illustrious House of O Neill, descended from Niall "Black-knee", King of Ailech (916–19). In 676 the fort was destroyed by the Southern Uí Néill led by Fínechta "the Festive" of Brega (East Meath). In 1101, though by then it presumably had merely a symbolical significance, it was wrecked by Muriertach O Brien, King of Munster, in revenge for the destruction of Kincora (*see under* Killaloe) in 1088 by Donal Mac Lochlainn, King of Ailech. (According to the story, each of O Brien's men carried away a stone of the northern fortress.) The remains comprise three rings of defences surrounding an inner citadel, or massive ringfort of dry masonry 77 ft in internal diameter and now 17½ ft high. The inner face of the latter is built in three terraces approached by stairways. (Unfortunately, it has suffered at the hands of "restorers", and the upper terraces and stairways are 19th cent. work; prior to the "restoration" the wall was only about 6 ft high.) There are two galleries in the thickness of the wall. At the centre of the enclosure were formerly the remains of a rectangular structure. – 150 yds NW. is a pillarstone. 3 m. SSW. is Portlough (*see under* Newtown Cunningham).

DINGLE, Co. Kerry (Map 4, B4), is a small market town and fishing port on the S. side of the Corcaguiney peninsula ("Dingle Peninsula") 30 m. WSW. of Tralee. To the N. rises the Bandon Mountain range, the lower slopes of Ballysitteragh (2,050 ft) affording fine views across Dingle Bay. The town is a convenient base for exploring W. Corcaguiney, with its inspiring mountain and coastal scenery and its extraordinary wealth of prehistoric and early historic remains.

In the Protestant churchyard is a Desmond tomb of 1540. The Catholic presbytery stands near the site of the house of Count Rice, an officer of the Irish Brigade in the French service, who planned to bring Marie Antoinette there for safety. At the upper end of Main St is a boulder with cup marks, etc.; it is said to have come from the Milltown group (*below*).

The secondary road to Tralee, via Stradbally and Castlegregory (*q.v.*), climbs 6 m. NE. to Connor Pass (1,300 ft) between Beenabrack (1,961 ft)–Beenduff (1,579 ft) on the W., and Knockmoylemore (1,598 ft)–Slieveanea (2,026 ft) on the E.; splendid views of Dingle Bay and mountainous Iveragh may be had enroute; in the mountains E. and W. of the pass are romantic little lakes and tarns. The road beyond the pass to Stradbally affords magnificent views of Brandon Mountain (*below*) and Brandon Bay. 3½ m. NE. of the Pass (¾ m. S. of Kilmore bridge), on the NW. slope of Slievenagower (1,603 ft) in Ballyhoneen, are the Giants Grave and three pillarstones.

2¼ m. N., in the Commons of Dingle, are several clocháns. (The whole W. slope of Ballysitteragh is littered with clocháns and other ancient remains; see Ballyheabought, *below*.)

2 m. E., in Ballineetig, is Gallán Mór, a pillarstone (Nat. Mon.).

4½ m. E. is Lispole village. In the mountains to the N. are many fine cirques. In Churchfield, NW. of the bridge, is St Martin's Church (Nat. Mon.), a small, early church with architraved trabeate W. door; it stands in a large, oval earthwork. 2 m. S. of the village, in Aghacarrible, is a ringfort with L-shaped souterrain; in the latter are three ogham stones and an early cross-slab. There are many ringforts and pillarstones in the area. ¾ m. SW. of the Aghacarrible fort, on the slopes of Sea Hill in Doonties West and Doonties Commons, are remains of many clocháns.

2 m. SE., in the ancient, oval graveyard of Ballintaggart, are nine ogham stones (Nat. Mons.). 1¼ m. E., in Emlagh East, are a ringfort and Cloch an tSagairt, a cross-inscribed ogham stone (Nat. Mons.). The stone, on Trabeg strand, was the first ogham stone to be noticed by a modern antiquarian (Edward Lhuyd). – 1½ m. SE., in Doonsheane, are a good beach and Doonmore, a promontory fort (Nat. Mon.) commanding fine views.

1¼ m. W., in Milltown (beyond the village), is a low cairn with a prostrate stone having cup-and-circle and other prehistoric scribings. W. of these are remains of a chamber tomb. To the N. are Geataí na Glóire, The Gates of Glory, a pair of pillarstones. By the roadside in the next field is Gallán Chille Breice, alias the Milestone, an 8-ft pillarstone. In a field on the opposite side of the road is a fourth pillarstone.

2½ m. SW., on the W. side of Dingle Harbour, is Burnham, formerly home of the de Moleyns family (Lords Ventry), descendants of John Mullins, a Cromwellian trooper who acquired estates here in 1666. 1½ m. SE., on the impressive cliffs of Ballymacadoyle, is the Doon, one of the finest of Kerry promontory forts. The multivallate defences divide the fort into three wards. The site commands magnificent views, and is itself worth viewing by boat.

6 m. WSW. is Ventry (q.v.).

12 m. W. (via Ventry and Slea Head) is Dunquin (q.v.).

3½ m. WNW., in Ballymorereagh, ruined Teampall Geal (alias St Manchan's Oratory; Nat. Mon.), St Manchan's Grave (with an early cross-slab), two small cross-inscribed stones, Tobar Mancháin, and a partly defaced ogham stone (with two incised crosses and an inscription in half uncials), mark the site of an early anchoritic establishment. The half-uncial inscription, FECT QUENILOC SON, is thought to be an 18th cent. forgery. 1 m. E. as the crow flies is Kilfountain (below).

2½ m. NW. is Kilfountain, St Fiontán's Church, or Cell. In the disused burial ground are the foundations of a small church, remains of clocháns, a bullaun, and an early cross-pillar with chi-rho and inscriptions in both ogham (EQODDT) and half-uncials (S[AN]C[T]I FINTEN). On the hill slope to the NE. is a

pillarstone. – 1 m. W. as the crow flies is Teampall Geal, Ballymorereagh (above).

2 m. NNW., in Ballyheabought, are remains of a great, bivallate ringfort; the inner rampart is stone-faced and terraced; in the enclosure are remains of clocháns. Also in the townland are remains of twenty-five clocháns (see also Glin North, below).

4 m. NNW., at the ancient burial ground of Reenconnell, is a stone cross (Nat. Mon.). 1 m NE. of Reenconnell crossroads, in Glin North are a ringfort and a clochán (Nat. Mons.). The whole mountain slope in Glin North, Glin South, Ballyheabought, and Commons of Dingle is littered with the remains of clocháns and other monuments.

4¾ m. NNW. is Ballinloghig. A splendid mountain walk, with magnificent views, may be made E. and NE. to the knife-ridge between the cirques of Brandon Peak, to the summit (2,764 ft), and thence NNW. above the tremendous cirques of Brandon Hill (see Ballybrack below). – ¾ m. WSW., at the ancient burial ground of Currauly, is an early cross-pillar (broken); 1¼ m. NE., via the Saints' Road, is Ballybrack (below).

5½ m. NNW. is Ballybrack. In the townland is a clochán with a covered chamber (Nat. Mon.). The Saints' Road from Currauly (above), still used by pilgrims (29 June) and marked by Stations of the Cross, climbs NE from Ballybrack "village" to the summit of Cnoc Bhréanainn (Brandon Mountain; 3,127 ft), second highest mountain in Ireland. The spectacular cirques of the mountain command fine views. Just below the summit are St Brendan's Well, remains of St Brendan's Oratory (Nat. Mon.), and ruins of several clocháns (Nat. Mons.) enclosed by traces of cashel. These mark the site of an early anchoritic settlement associated with the celebrated St Bréanainn, alias Brendan the Navigator, 484 577 (see Clonfert, Co. Galway). The aluminium cross on the oratory has been made from spars of a German bomber which crashed on the mountain during the Second World War. A walk N. and NNW. along the mountain ridge will lead the pilgrim-tourist to Brandon Monument (Nat. Mon.) in Arraglen on the slope of Masatiompán (2,509 ft). This is a prostrate ogham stone with incised Maltese crosses (one with chi-rho); the ogham inscription reads: "The priest Ronann son of Comogann". Beyond Masatiompán are the fine cliffs of Brandon Head.

7 m. NNW., in Ballynavenooragh, are: stone ringfort with ruins of two clocháns, stone fort with ruins of three clocháns, a roofless clochán, the Baker's Clochán and enclosure, and two double clocháns (Nat. Mons.). 1 m. NNW., in Ballyknockane, is Doonrec promontory fort; to the NE. commence the great cliffs of Brandon Head. Also in Ballyknockane are: a stone ringfort with remains of a clochán, a stone fort with two double clocháns, and an ancient church site with a broken cross-inscribed stone (Nat. Mons.).

DONABATE, Co. Dublin (Map 6, D2), is a village and small holiday resort to the E. of the Dublin (11¼ m.)–Balbriggan (7½ m.) road and within convenient reach of the excellent 1½ m. sandy beach (backed by dunes; Malahide Island Golf Club) which extends from Portraine in the NE. to the Malahide (*q.v.*) estuary in the S. The parish church has a two-light window by Harry Clarke: *Suffer little children to come unto me* (1925). The Protestant parish church (1758) has gallery stucco (by Robert West ?; see Newbridge House, *below*).

1 m. NE. is Portraine (Portrane), a small seaside resort with remains of a 15th cent. church and castle. The former has a small, square W. tower. ½ m. NW., in Burrow, is St Mo-Chuda's Well. Portraine House was the home of Swift's Stella; there is now a large mental hospital in the demesne, close to the excellent beach. The Round Tower to the E. of the hospital is modern.

1 m. SW. are remains of Kilcrea castle.

1½ m. SW. is Seafield (Hall), erected by the Seavers family about 1720–30. The interior mural decorations include twelve monochrome panels of niched Classical figures by an unknown painter of the period.

1¼ m. WSW., in the demesne of Newbridge House, are the ruins of Lanestown castle. Newbridge House was enlarged (by Richard Cassels ?), 1736–43, for Charles Cobbe, Protestant Archbishop of Dublin. Cobbe's son made additions which include a drawing-room with fine ceiling by Robert West. John Wesley stayed at Newbridge House in 1767.

1 m. WNW. is Turvey House, Georgian successor of one built in 1565 by Sir Christopher Barnewall with materials from the Augustinian nunnery of Grace Dieu (*see under* Ballyboghill).

DONAGHADEE, Co. Down (Map 3, D4), is a small port and quiet resort, 4¾ m. ESE. of Bangor (7 m. by coast road). It is a convenient base for exploring the Ards (E. side of Strangford Lough).

The most notable thing in Donaghadee is the harbour (1821–37), prior to 1865 a packet station on the short route to Scotland (Portpatrick). Together with its handsome lighthouse (lantern altered), the harbour is the work of Sir John Rennie, who was assisted by his son, John, and by David Logan of Eddystone Lighthouse fame. A triumphal arch proposed as gateway to the S. pier was not erected.

Overlooking the harbour is The Moat, a motte crowned by a 19th cent. folly.

The Protestant parish church occupies a pre-Reformation site. Built in 1636 for Hugh, Viscount Montgomery, it has been greatly altered. There are 17th cent. gravestones.

3 m. S. (1 m. W. of Millside), in Ballycopeland, is a carefully restored tower-windmill (Nat. Mon.). Open: 1 April to 30 Sept.: weekdays, 9.30 a.m.–1 p.m.; Suns., 2–5.30 p.m.; 1 Oct. to 31 March: Sats., 10 a.m.–1 p.m.; Suns., 2–4 p.m.

DONAGHPATRICK, Co. Meath (Map 6, C2), is on the N. side of the Blackwater between Navan (6 m.) and Kells (6 m.). It takes its name from the "great church" (*domnach*), 60 ft long, which St Patrick built on a site given to him by Conall Cremthainne, son of Niall Nine Hostager. An early monastery here had been reduced to parochial status by the Middle Ages. The site is marked by the graveyard (originally circular) of St Patrick's Church (C. of I.; 1886), which incorporates the 15th cent. residential tower (a human mask high up in the N. face; windows and parapet modern) of the medieval parish church. A plain polygonal font, a plain cross (?) shaft, and one gable of an early tomb (?) of Slane type have been grouped together NE. of the church; the tomb gable formerly stood to the S. of the church. On the opposite side of the road are the scrub-covered motte (quadrivallate) and bailey of a de Lacy (?) castle. On the S. side of the Blackwater, in Castlemartin, a 17th cent. stronghouse (ruinous) commands the river crossing; fine old bridge.

1½ m. W. of Donaghpatrick church, in Teltown, is Rá Doo (Ráth Dubh, "Black Ring Fort"; Nat. Mon.); it has lost a rampart. In Teltown (Old Irish *Tailtiu* "the well formed"), the celebrated Aonach Tailteann – (pre-Gaelic ?) Lughnasa festival and principal public assembly and fair of the Uí Néill confederation – was held each year at the beginning of August. The place was a prehistoric cemetery, and games in honour of the dead were a primary purpose of the gathering. To preside at the aonach was a prerogative of the King of Tara. The assembly was in abeyance for most of the 10th and 11th centuries. It was revived in 1120 by Turloch O Conor of Connacht, aspirant to the high-kingship, and again (for the last time) in 1168, after the landing of the first Anglo-Normans, by his son, Rory. – In St Patrick's time, so runs the tale, Coirpre, son of Niall Nine Hostager, had his seat at Teltown. Unlike his brother, Conall of Donaghpatrick, he was hostile to the saint, whose household he scourged into the river. A memory of the ancient aonach survived in the tradition of Teltown Marriages, chance espousals for a year and a day. On the expiry of that term, a couple desiring to separate should come to the centre of Ráth Dubh, there stand back to back, one facing N., the other facing S., and walk away from one another out of the fort. – ¼ m. NE. of Ráth Dubh are two parallel, linear earthworks (Nat. Mon.; remnant of a great fort ?). The hill top (292 ft) offers wide prospects over the rich lands of Meath. Adjoining the earthworks is Lag an Aonaigh ("site of the aonach"). The adjacent laneway running S. from St Catherine's Church is Cromwell's Road; it is the successor of an ancient paved way. Near its junction with the Donaghpatrick–Oristown road is a hollow claimed to be the site of an artificial lake on which sham aquatic fights were staged as part of the aonach. S. of the main road the lane (now

Cromwell's Pass) continues on, past remains of the little church called Cill Tailteann, to a ford across the Blackwater. The church was ravaged by the Dublin Norse in 1156, and by Díarmait Mac Murrough and his Norman hirelings in 1170.

DONARD, Co. Wicklow (Map 6, C4), is a village 1 m. E. of the Baltinglass (7½ m.)–Ballymore Eustace (10 m.) road. It has been claimed that Bishop Palladius, St Patrick's predecessor, founded a church here for his disciple, St Sylvester, brother of Solinus. At the village are the featureless ruins of a medieval church; inside, at the W. end, is a recumbent medieval gravestone; a dubious tradition says it marks the grave of St Sylvester. Close to the church, on the SSW., is Ball Moat, a 20-ft mound with a low bank around the summit. In the garden of the former Civic Guard station is preserved an ogham stone which originally stood close to an uninscribed stone on Old Mills farm, Whitestone, 3 m. SW.

½ m. N., at Box Bridge, is a stone with nineteen bullauns. A second bullaun stone has been broken up. On the adjacent eminence are two ruined mounds.

2 m. N., in Kilbaylet Upper, is the King's Stone with the "print of St Kevin's foot"; the saint once stepped from the top of Slieve Gad (*see under* Hollywood) on to the stone, and thence to Mullica, the next ridge to the W.; the nearby pillarstone is held to be natural. On the border of Kilbaylet Upper and Blackmoor are three small ringforts close together.

1 m. E., in Donard Demesne East, is Raheen's Mound.

1 m. SE. is Muldarragh Rath, survivor of a pair of ringforts set side by side.

A fine walk of 4 m. SE. leads to the remains of fortified Leitrim Barracks in the Glen of Imail. Above the glen rise Table Mountain (2,308 ft), Lugnaquilla (3,039 ft), and Keadeen Mountain (2,145 ft). Michael Dwyer, celebrated 1798 leader, was born in the glen in 1771, and it was one of his retreats when "on the run". Hence the erection of Leitrim Barracks. In plantation ⅛ m. NE. of the barracks is Knickeen Long Stone, a pillarstone with an ogham inscription. In Derrynamuck (5½ m. SE. of Donard in the SE. corner of the glen) is Michael Dwyer's Cottage (Nat. Mon.). In 1799 Dwyer and his companions were trapped here by British troops. Samuel MacAllister gave his life by drawing their fire so as to enable Dwyer and the rest to escape. The NE. slopes of the Glen of Imail are used as an artillery range. Lugnaquilla can be climbed from Coan by following a stream beside the boundary of the range.

2½ m. SW. is Castleruddery Lower stone circle (*see under* Baltinglass).

1½ m. NW., on Blackmoor Hill in Broomfield townland, is the Druid's Altar, a massive chamber tomb (wrecked). 1½ m. NW. is Merginstown motte-and-bailey.

DONEGAL, Co. Donegal (Map 2, B3), which gives its name to the county, is a market town and small seaport where the road from Ballyshannon (14 m.) to Ballybofey (17 m.) crosses the River Eske at the NE. corner of Donegal Bay.

While the place was occupied in Viking times (Dún na nGall, Fort of the Foreigners), its real significance dates from the time when, in the later Middle Ages, it became the chief seat of the O Donnells, kings of Tír Chonaill. After

Michael Dwyer's Cottage, Derrynamuck, Glen of Imail

the "Flight of the Earls" (p. 42), the town was "Planted" by Sir Basil Brooke, to whom it owes its Plantation layout (including the Diamond, or market-place).

The ruins of Donegal Castle (Nat. Mon.), near the Diamond, include the great square tower of the castle erected by Red Hugh II O Donnell in 1505 and altered by Sir Basil Brooke, who inserted the 17th cent. features and added the fine Jacobean fortified house in 1610. The banqueting hall has a splendid Jacobean fireplace.

¼ m. S., beside the estuary of the Eske, are the remnants (Nat. Mon.) of Donegal "Abbey", a Franciscan friary founded by Red Hugh I O Donnell and his wife, Nuala O Brien, in 1474. The founders and their son, Young Hugh, who took the habit, are buried there. In 1591 the English seized the friary and fortified it, but were expelled in 1592, by Great Red Hugh O Donnell. In 1601 the English (aided by renegade Niall Garbh O Donnell) seized it once more, and it was attacked a second time by Red Hugh. On this occasion the English magazine blew up and wrecked the buildings. In 1607 the friary was granted to Sir Basil Brooke. The fragments include parts of the church and of the cloister arcade, etc. After the English conquest of Tír Chonaill the Franciscan community of Donegal remained in being for many years, moving about from one place of refuge to another. In the convent, then settled at Bundrowes, the Four Masters, Michael O Clery (see Kilbarron under Ballyshannon), Peregrine O Clery, Peregrine Duignan (see Castlefore under Ballinamore, Co. Leitrim), and Fearfeasa O Mulconry, compiled their celebrated Annals between the years 1630 and 1636.

There are two recent memorials to the Four Masters in the town, an obelisk in the Diamond and disappointing St Patrick's Church (1931–5).

6 m. N., between the Bluestacks and Banagher Hill, is Eglish Glen, a local beauty spot.

5 m. NE., in a beautiful setting at the foot of the Bluestack Mountains (Mullaghnadreasruhan 2,219 ft, Banagher Hill 1,268 ft, and Croaghnageer 1,793 ft) is well-stocked Lough Eske. At the SW. and NW. corners respectively are the wooded demesne of Lough Eske Castle (with ruins of an O Donnell castle) and Ardnamona. On an island at the S. end of the lake are the keep and bawn of an O Donnell castle which figured in the 16th cent. wars. The road circling the lake offers a succession of delightful views. 2 m. beyond the N. end of the lake is Eas Dúnan, a pretty waterfall on the Corraber River which flows down from lonely, cliff-ringed Lough Belshade between the Bluestacks and Croaghbarnes (1,431 ft).

8 m. NE. is Barnesmore (see under Ballybofey).

1 m. S., on the Eske estuary, are remnants of Magherabeg "Abbey", a small, 15th cent. Franciscan Tertiary friary.

4 m. W., at Mount Charles, is a Georgian house built by Lord Conyngham.

8 m. W. is Inver, with a sandy beach at the head of Inver Bay. The ruins of a small church mark an early monastic site.

8 m. NW., in the Bluestacks, is Sruell Glen with the Grey Mare's Tail, a waterfall on the Sruell River.

DONERAILE, Co. Cork (Map 5, B5), is a village on the Buttevant (3 m.)–Mitchelstown (14 m.) road, beside the pretty Awbeg.

The town was part of Edmund Spenser's estate (see Kilcolman Castle, below). His son sold it to Warham St Leger, English Lord President of Munster and ancestor of Viscount Doneraile, in 1627. Doneraile Court is a fine brick house erected in 1725 to the design of Rothery. It was here that Mary Barry, wife of the 1st Viscount Doneraile and afterwards Mrs Aldworth, hid herself in a clock to spy on a meeting of Freemasons. Discovered, she was admitted to membership for secrecy's sake, so becoming the first woman Mason.

Tadhg Ó Duinnín, last hereditary poet to the Mac Carthys and last official head of the Blarney bardic school, died parish priest of Doneraile in 1726. He had become a priest after the death of his wife and child.

Canon Sheehan, author of Luke Delmege, My New Curate, and other novels, was parish priest of Doneraile from 1895 to 1913. His memorial is a statue (1925; by Francis Doyle-Jones) in front of his church.

1¼ m. E., by the Awbeg, are the remains of Creagh castle.

2 m. E. in Carker Beg, alias Carker Lodge or Lissa, 200 yds from Labbavacken (Labbavuchan) bridge, is a chamber tomb.

4½ m. E., on the S. bank of the Awbeg, are the ruins of Wallstown church and castle.

3½ m. SE. are the ruins of Castle Kevin (Roches).

1½ m. NW., on Oldcourt Hill, is a trivallate ringfort with a souterrain. Nearby is a tumulus said to have been covered with a white deposit. Bones and pottery were found in it.

3¼ m. NNW. are remains of Kilcolman castle, a Desmond stronghold granted, together with 3,028 acres of land, to Edmund Spenser after the Desmond Rebellion. Spenser had come to Ireland in 1580 as secretary to Lord Deputy Grey of Wilton. In 1587 he took up residence at Kilcolman, where he was visited by Sir Walter Raleigh in 1589. After settling there he became Clerk to the English Council of Munster. His barbarous views on the treatment of the Irish provoked his ostracism by Maurice, Viscount Roche of Fermoy, who proclaimed that "none of his people should have trade or commerce with Mr Spenser", who thus was the precursor of Captain Boycott (see Lough Mask House under Ballinrobe). At Kilcolman Spenser wrote, not only his notorious View of the Present State of Ireland, but also the first three books of the Faerie Queene, Colin Clout's Come Home Again, the lovely Amoretti sonnets, and Epithalamium, the last two for Elizabeth Boyle of Kilcoran (see under Youghal), whom he mar-

Irish Tourist Board

Doonagore castle, Doolin

ried in 1594. Apart from a visit to London in 1590–91, Spenser resided continuously at Kilcolman from 1587 until the insurgent Irish burned the castle in October 1598. His infant son is said to have perished in the flames, Spenser and his wife to have escaped with difficulty. The following year the poet died in London. His family subsequently returned to the Cork estate, whence one Catholic grandson of Spenser's was transplanted to Connacht (*see* Ballinasloe) by the Cromwellians as an "Irish Papist". A second Catholic grandson managed to retain some property in Co. Cork until the Williamite rebellion, when it was granted to a rebel cousin.

DOOLIN, alias **FISHERSTREET**, Co. Clare (Map 1, C7), is a fishing village on a small sandy bay 5 m. SW. of Lisdoonvarna. It is the nearest port to Inisheer, Aran Islands.

1 m. NE. are the ruins of Killilagh parish church (*c.* 1500). Nearby is St Lonán's Well. 3 m. NE. is Ballynalackan (*see under* Lisdoonvarna).

The road S. to Liscannor (7 m.) passes Doonagore castle, an unusual, circular tower inside a small (very decayed) bawn.

DOWNPATRICK, Co. Down (Map 3, D5), from which the diocese and county of Down take their name, is a cathedral and market town near the SW. corner of Strangford Lough, 21 m. S. of Belfast and 32 m. NE. of Newry.

Previously Dún-dá-leth-glas, or simply An Dún, the place acquired the name Dún Pádraig, "Patrick's Dún", at the time of the "discovery" (*below*) of the relics of SS Patrick, Columcille, and Brigid.

About 1 Feb. 1177, John de Courcy (p. 34) took the place, then the seat of Rory Mac Donlevy, King of Ulster (=Co. Down), by surprise. Rory's attempt to recover it was crushed with heavy loss, and de Courcy established his principal castle there. Eighty-three years later, as the first step in a concerted effort to rid the country of foreign power, Brian O Neill, King of Tír Eóghain, who had been acknowledged

King of Ireland by Connacht and Thomond, marched against the northern citadel of the foreigners. The desperate Battle of Down (1260) was decided by the archers and armoured cavalry of the invader. Brian himself (thenceforth Brian Chatha an Dún, "Brian of the Battle of Down"), perished, and with him eight Connacht lords and fifteen of the principal Ó Catháins (*see* Limavady).

The most important feature of Downpatrick is the Protestant cathedral. According to legend, St Patrick founded a church inside Ráth Celtchair, a hill-fort, part of whose rampart is traceable SW. of the cathedral. There certainly was an early monastery there. Repeated Viking attacks contributed to the decay of the monastery, which was only revitalized when St Máel-M'Áedhóg ("Malachy") Úa Morgair (*see* Bangor) introduced Canons Regular of St Augustine in 1137. Six years after seizing Down, de Courcy grasped the opportunity offered by the "discovery" of the relics of SS Patrick, Brigid, and Columcille to transfer the see of the diocese from Bangor to his capital. He replaced the Irish Augustinians by English Benedictines from Chester, and changed the dedication of their church from the Holy Trinity to St Patrick. In 1184 the Benedictines began to build a new cathedral, which may never have been completed. Cathedral and Benedictine priory were destroyed by earthquake in 1245 and burnt by Edward Bruce in 1316. Repaired more than once, the whole complex was destroyed by an English force in 1538, after which the ruins lay derelict until 1790. Between 1790 and 1826 Charles Lilly of Dublin drastically "restored" the E. end of the cathedral to serve as second cathedral of the Protestant diocese of Down and Dromore (*see* Dromore, Lisburn, *and* Hillsborough). In the course of the "restoration" all traces of the early and medieval monasteries were swept away, the Round Tower serving as a quarry for the 1826 tower of the cathedral.

Lilly's Holy Trinity Cathedral (dedication restored 1609) represents merely the aisled choir and chancel of the Benedictine cathedral, more or less as re-edified in the 15th cent. (It is doubtful if nave or transepts were ever built at all.) Of the medieval fragments incorporated in the fabric the most interesting are the capitals and responds of the arcades. Relics of the pre-Norman age are two fragments set into the E. wall of the Chapter Room (S. "transept"): (*a*) a small wheel cross with defaced figure of an abbot (or bishop) bearing bachall and book (?); (*b*) a fragment of a smaller figured cross. The nearby font basin was probably a cross base. The choir stalls and pews are good 18th/19th cent. work.

Outside the E. end of the cathedral is a 9th/10th cent. High Cross which formerly stood at the centre of the town. The fragments were re-erected here in 1897; the weathered figurations include a *Crucifixion*. S. of the cathedral a monolith inscribed PATRIC marks the alleged grave of St Patrick. This is a bogus antiquity commissioned (1900) by Francis Joseph Biggar. Patrick died at Saul (*below*), and knowledge of his burial place had been lost by the 9th cent.

E. of the cathedral is the attractive South-well School (Bluecoat School), 1733.

The Protestant Parish Church, Church Ave., dates from 1560; much altered; tower 18th cent. In the churchyard is buried Thomas Russell of the United Irishmen ("The man from God knows where"; *see* Belfast). He was hanged in Downpatrick for complicity in Emmet's Rebellion (1803).

1½ m. N. (via English St) is a remarkable motte-and-bailey (Nat. Mon.), relic of John de Courcy's castle. It was formerly enclosed on three sides by tidal waters.

2 m. NE. is Saul (Sabhal Pádraic, "Patrick's Barn"), legendarily the place of Patrick's first church, a barn (close to his landing place) given him by Díchú, the local lord. Later there was an important monastery (Augustinian after 1130) on the site, which is occupied today by St Patrick's Churchyard (300 yds W. of village). By the S. gate of the churchyard are a medieval tombstone and a carved fragment. In the grave-yard are two ancient, stone-roofed mortuary houses (*see* Carrowdaff *under* Moville), one of them appropriated as a mausoleum. In the 1933 Protestant church is part of an interesting early gravestone; the 13th cent. font-basin is from Burnchurch (*see under* Kells, Co. Kilkenny); the *St Patrick* window is by Catherine O Brien. 200 yds W. of the churchyard are the Mearing Well (holy well) and a bullaun in the native rock. – The monument (statue of St Patrick by Francis Doyle-Jones) on the hill overlooking Strangford Lough commemorates the supposed fifteenth centenary (1932) of Patrick's landing. – 2 m. NE. of Saul is Raholp (*see under* Strangford).

1¾ m. E., in Struel, are St Patrick's Wells (Nat. Mons.) and the ruins of an 18th cent. church. There are four wells here, fed from a common source (below St Patrick's Chair, formed of four rocks on the nearby slope). The N. well is traditionally for drinking; the next one is for the eyes; the others are for bathing body or limbs. The larger, stone-roofed men's bath house is attributed to Lady Betty Cromwell (late-17th cent.). The roofless bath house was for women. Still visited for cures, especially on St John's Eve, the wells were formerly visited on Cromm Dubh's Friday (the Friday before Lammas) also. – 1 m. E., beside the road, is Ballyalton Druidical Ring (Nat. Mon.): an elliptical court cairn with a pillar-stone 40 ft out from the portal. The tomb proper comprises two connecting chambers to the E. of a cremation pit in the body of the cairn. Excavations (1933) yielded neolithic flints, celts, and sherds. ½ m. N., on Slievena-griddle (414 ft), are the prostrate remains of a chambered cairn.

3 m. S., in Ballynoe (¼ m. – by lane – from the former railway station), is Ballynoe Stone Circle (Nat. Mon.): a ring of stones 108 ft in diameter; two external pillarstones to the W.; opposite these, but inside the circle, an arc of five stones; in the E. half of the circle, a kerbed, oval cairn; outlying pillarstones to the N., S., SW., and NW. Excavation (1937–38) showed that a cremated cist-burial had been set into either end of the cairn; between cairn and circle were pockets of cremated bone with occasional sherds of passage-grave pottery. – 1½ m. W. of Ballynoe village is Castleskreen (Nat. Mon.), a 13th cent. motte inside a univallate ringfort. ½ m. W. is a later Castleskreen (Nat. Mon.): motte with fragments of a stone castle. In Erenagh, the townland adjoining Castleskreen townland on the N., was the site of Carrick Abbey, the earliest recorded abbey of a Continental order in Ireland, pre-dating Mellifont Abbey (*q.v.*) by fifteen years. In 1127 Niall Mac Donlevy founded the abbey for monks of the reformed Benedictines of Savigny (Normandy). After the Congregation of Savigny had united (1147) with the Cistercians, Carrick became affiliated to Furness Abbey, Lancashire. When John de Courcy invaded Ulster, the monastery was turned into a fortress by the Irish, and was destroyed in the course of the fighting. About 1180 de Courcy gave the monks a new home at the ancient monastery of Inis Cumscraidh (*below*), which a King of Ulster had – so it seems – previously bestowed on either the Savignians or the Cistercians.

1 m. SW., in Demesne townland, is Magnus's Grave, a low, tree-grown mound alleged to mark the grave of Magnus Barefoot, King of Norway, who was slain (1103) on a foray into Ulster when on his way home from a visit to High-king Muirchertach O Brien at Kincora (*see under* Killaloe).

2½ m. NW., on the left bank of the Quoile, in Inch (Inis Cumscraigh), are the beautifully sited remains (Nat. Mon.) of St Mary's Abbey De Insula. About 1180 de Courcy established the homeless monks of Carrick (*above*) here. At the time the place (site of an early monastery) belonged to the Cistercians of Combe Abbey in England, having been previously given either to them or to Savignians by the King of Ulster. Little more than the E. end of the abbey church survives, but the foundations of the whole complex have been uncovered. The E. wall of the chancel has three Transitional lancets (*c.* 1200). The transepts each had two E. chapels (cf. Grey Abbey). In the 15th cent. the nave was abandoned, and the choir enclosed by walls which cut off the transepts as well. To the SW. are the foundations of a 15th cent. well and bakery; to the NW., some traces of the infirmary (?). The church of the early monastery had stood in the graveyard N. of the abbey; a rude *Crucifixion* from the W. doorway is preserved in the Protestant parish church.

DOWRA, Co. Cavan (Map 2, C5), is a Shannon-side village on the Drumshanbo (10 m.)–Belcoo (10 m.) road, about 2 m. N. of mountain-ringed Lough Allen. Between the E. bank of the river and the foot of Slievenakilla (1,787 ft) a 3-m. stretch of the Worm Ditch, or Black Pig's Race, an ancient frontier earthwork, runs S. and SW. from the village to the head of the lake. According to one legend this earthwork was made by a great serpent; according to another by a monstrous black pig. Its date is unknown, but it is generally supposed to mark a prehistoric or protohistoric frontier of Ulaid (Ulster). For further stretches *see* Garrison (Co. Fermanagh), Belcoo (Co. Fermanagh), Clones (Co. Monaghan) *and* Granard (Co. Longford).

At the head of Lough Allen is Inishmagrath, a small island with the remains of a church ascribed to St Bé-óg.

6 m. WSW., on a small hill N. of Lough Allen, in Kilnagarns Lower, is a ruinous court cairn; excavation yielded neolithic sherds and flints. Close by are remains of a chambered cairn which yielded a Beaker sherd.

DRAPERSTOWN, Co. Derry (Map 3, A4), locally known as The Cross of Ballynascreen, is a village at the SE. edge of the Sperrin Mountains (near the head of Glenconkeine), on the road from Derry (28 m.) to Cookstown (16 m.). It was built and given its official name in 1818 by the proprietors, the London Company of Drapers. There is a small collection of local antiquities and bygones in the Town Hall.

6 m. SSE., via Iniscarn, on the NE. summit of Slieve Gallion (1,623 ft), is a cairn; 200 yds SW. is a chambered cairn. The mountain was a Lughnasa station.

4 m. SSW. is Black Water bridge. Some 1,200 yds SE. of the bridge, alt. 700 ft, in Corick, are three stone circles, two with tangent alignments; NW. are the remains of a chamber tomb; NNW. is a large pillarstone in a small circle (Nat. Mons.). – ⅔ m. S. of the bridge, alt. 800–850 ft in Ballybriest, are: Carnanbane (Nat. Mon.), a double-court cairn which yielded neolithic sherds, arrows, etc. ; 100 yds S., a single-chamber tomb (Nat. Mon.); 200 yds E., a chambered round cairn. There are stone circles in the neighbourhood. – ¾ m. W. of the bridge, alt. 800 ft in Tullybrick, is the Giants Grave, a small cairn with a gallery grave.

4 m. SW. is Ballynascreen, which takes its name from the ancient church-site, Scrín Cholaim Chille (Columcille's Shrine).

10 m. SW. are Broughderg crossroads (*see under* Cookstown).

1¼ m. WNW., in Strawmore, are the Slaght Illeraů pillarstones; four have been removed, nine remain. 1½ m. further WNW., alt. 400 ft, in Drumderg, is "Dergmore's Grave" (Nat. Mon.), a chamber tomb.

DRIMOLEAGUE, Co. Cork (Map 4, D5), formerly Dromdaleague, is a village on the Dunmanway (18 m.)–Bantry (12 m.) road, 8 m. N. of Skibbereen. The new Church of All Saints (by Frank Murphy) is one of the few recent churches of interest in Ireland.

3 m. NW., near Leitry bridge, are the ruins Castle Donovan (15th/16th cent.). 3½ m. N of the castle, in Cullenagh, are four standi stones; ¾ m. NE. of these is a single standi stone; ¾ m. NW. (¼ m. W. of Cullenagh Lak is Dermot and Grania's Bed, a prehistor chamber tomb.

DRIPSEY, Co. Cork (Map 5, B6), is woollen-manufacturing village to the E. of t Dripsey river, on the picturesque Cork (13 m. Macroom (12 m.) road to Killarney (41 m.).

The by-roads N. and NW. towards the Bo geragh Mountains are worth exploring. T foothills, as well as the higher slopes, are ve rich in ancient remains, the chief of which a listed under Coachford (2 m. W.).

1½ m. NNW., in the demesne of Drips Castle, are the ruins of the moated rock cas of Carrignamuck, built in the 15th cent. Cormac Láidir Mac Carthy (*see* Blarney; *al* Kilcrea *under* Ballincollig).

DROGHEDA, Co. Louth (Map 6, D1), is historic town on the Dublin (30 m.)–Dunda (21 m.) road. In recent years it has ma appreciable progress as a manufacturing cent and seaport. The principal industries are c ment, linen, brewing, and iron-founding. T town is a convenient base for exploring t lovely Boyne countryside, and for visiting t famous prehistoric cemetery of Brugh Bóinne (*see* Newgrange).

Like so many Irish seaports, Drogheda trac its origin to the Norse, who established then selves here under Thorgestr (Turgesius) in 91 The Anglo-Norman invaders were quick appreciate the strategic significance of the plac and had built a motte castle (Hugh de Lacy and a bridge across the Boyne before the clc of the 12th cent. Down to 1412 there were t municipalities here, one on either side of t river. Both were walled in the 13th cent.

During the Middle Ages Drogheda was o of the most important English towns in Irelar In 1395 Richard II received the submissions Niall Óg O Neill, Prince of the Irish of Ulst and other Gaelic rulers in the Dominican fria (*below*), where he held his court. Several pa liaments met here in the later Middle Ages, most notable being those of 1465, which pass an Act setting up a university at Droghe "where may be made bachelors, masters a doctors in all sciences and faculties as at C ford"; of 1467–8, which attainted and behead Thomas, 7th Earl of Desmond; and of 149 which enacted the notorious Poynings' La extending to Ireland "all statutes concerni the public weal, made within the realm England".

In 1641 Sir Henry Tichborne and Lo Moore successfully held the town with 1,0 men for the English Parliament against Felim O Neill, but it subsequently fell to t Royalists. In 1649 Sir Arthur Aston held it f King Charles with a garrison of 3,000 me mostly English, against Cromwell. On 10 Sept. Cromwell stormed the town, which fell at the third assault. Some 2,000 of the defenders, including Aston, were butchered by express command of Cromwell, and many of the survivors transported to the Barbadoes. In 1689–90 Lord Magennis of Iveagh held the place for King James, but surrendered to the Williamites on the day after the Battle of the Boyne (*below*).

At the corner of Shop St and West St is the attractive little 18th cent. Tholsel, now a bank. Nearby, in West St, is Peter's Church (Oliver Plunkett Memorial Church), Gothic-Revival successor to a church by Francis Johnston. At the W. door is a small, 15th cent. font (figures of angels, symbols of the Passion). On a side altar is displayed the embalmed head of Blessed Oliver Plunkett (1629–81), Archbishop of Armagh, who was hanged, drawn, and quartered at Tyburn.

In Old Abbey Lane (off the W. end of West St) are some remains of the church of the Augustinian Crucifers' Priory and Hospital of St Mary d'Urso, founded in 1206 by Ursus de Swemole, perhaps on the site of an early monastery.

Near the N. edge of the town, in Upper Magdalene St, is 14th cent. Magdalene Steeple, central bell-tower of the church of the Dominican friary of St Mary Magdalene, founded in 1224 by Lucas de Netterville, Archbishop of Armagh, who was buried in the church in 1227. It was in this friary that, on 16 March 1395, Niall Óg O Neill of Tír Eóghain made formal submission to Richard II of England.

A short distance SE., in William St, is Protestant St Peter's Church, second (1748–92; tower and spire added by Francis Johnston) successor of the church in whose steeple 100 men held out against Cromwell until he burned it about their ears. It occupies the site of medieval, collegiate St Peter's. In the porch, as well as medieval fragments, is an early gravestone inscribed TNUDACH COCMAN F; it is said to have come from Marley churchyard. In the church is a medieval font with *Baptism of Christ* and *The Twelve Apostles*. The churchyard has some interesting tombstones, including a double-cadaver stone (17th cent.; cf. Beaulieu, *below*). Isaac Goldsmith (d. 1769), uncle of Oliver, and John Van Homrigh (d. 1785), father of Swift's "Vanessa", are buried there.

Not far away, to the SE., at the junction of King St and St Lawrence St, is "St Lawrence's Gate", a splendid 13th cent. barbican (two lofty, battlemented, circular towers linked by a loop-holed curtain) which stood on the outer edge of the moat in front of the vanished gate whose name it bears. Nearby are the good 18th cent. houses of Drogheda Grammar School, one of them originally the residence of Lord Chief Justice Singleton.

The town S. of the river is dominated by the cross-crowned Mill Mount (Barrack St), motte of the Norman castle built in the 12th cent. to

Irish Tourist Board
Barbican of St Lawrence's Gate, Drogheda

command the bridge; the bailey is covered by the military barracks. SE., in Mary St, is St Mary's Church, which incorporates something of the church of a Carmelite friary founded in the 13th/14th cent. Fragments from the friary were built into the graveyard wall, etc.

E. of the town is the Boyne Viaduct, an excellent piece of mid-19th cent. railway engineering by Sir John McNeill, noted Scottish engineer.

The civic insignia of Drogheda include a fine mace and sword of state that were presented by William III.

For a historic town of its size, Drogheda can claim relatively few notable citizens. Among such may be included the harpist, Eachmharcach O Kàne (1720–90), and the actress, Eliza O Neill (1791–1872), daughter of the actor, John O Neill, and wife of Sir William Beecher, M.P. for Mallow.

3¾ m. N. (via the Annagassan road), in Ballymakenny, is an original and graceful Protestant church designed by Francis Johnston for Primate Robinson (*see* Rokeby Hall *under* Dunleer) and completed in 1793. It was Johnston's first essay in the Gothick manner. The primate's arms are carved over the door. The interior still retains its pristine character, for the clear windows (cf. St Catherine's, Tullamore) and high pews have all survived. The glebe house is also by Johnston.

2 m. ENE. is Beaulieu House (Mrs Waddington). From the Anglo-Norman invasion until the Cromwellian conquest Beaulieu, alias Bewley, was the property and seat of the illustrious Plunkett family, from which have sprung the noble houses of Louth, Fingal, and Dunsany,

and to which belonged the Blessed Oliver Plunkett. The Cromwellian regime granted the property to Sir Henry Tichborne, afterwards 1st Baron Ferrard of Beaulieu (line extinct), from whom it passed to the Montgomerys. Beaulieu House is a beautiful brick mansion attributed to Sir Christopher Wren; it was built for Tichborne about 1660–66. At the nearby Protestant church are a medieval coffin slab with floriated cross and a typical 17th cent. cadaver tombstone. They are said to have been found in the river.

4 m. E. is Baltray, a small seaside and golfing resort: 2-m. sandy beach.

5 m. E., on the S. side of the Boyne estuary, is Mornington (properly Mariners' Town). The Maiden Tower originated as an Elizabethan shipping beacon. An excellent, 6-m., sandy beach extends S. to Gormanston (see under Balbriggan). On it are the little resorts of Bettystown (6 m. SE. of Drogheda) and (1 m. S.) Laytown; 18-hole golf links; on the N. side of the Nanny River is a tumulus.

4 m. SE., in the grounds of Pilltown House, is an ogham stone from Painestown.

3½ m. SW., near Donore, is Platin (see under Duleek).

4 m. W., on the N. side of the Boyne in Co. Louth, is Townley Hall, a large, rather gaunt, Georgian-style mansion by Francis Johnston. In 1956 house and demesne were acquired by Trinity College, Dublin, to be its first School of Agriculture (Kells Ingram Farm). ½ m. SW. of the house are remains of a mound with a de-volved passage grave. It had been erected on top of a Neolithic habitation site. – At the E. side of the demesne is King William's Glen, leading down from the height of Tullyallen where William of Orange's army encamped before the Battle of the Boyne. On the day of the battle (1 July 1690), the Williamite right flank rested here, and the left flank in a similar ravine 1 m. to the E., the centre and artillery being drawn up on the high ground in between. The greatly inferior Jacobite army was drawn up S. of the river in front of Donore Hill. Wil-liam's superior numbers enabled him to turn the Jacobite position by sending some 15,000 men upstream to cross the river at Rosnaree and Slane, wheel towards Duleek, and thus imperil the Jacobite lines of communication. In the meantime William's main force crossed the river by the fords and shallows at and below Oldbridge. Outflanked, outnumbered, and out-gunned, the Jacobites had to retreat, but their rearguards put up a spirited resistance. – Old-bridge House is by Francis Johnston (?).

5½ m. WNW. is Mellifont Abbey (q.v.).

5½ m. NNW. is Monasterboice (q.v.).

DROICHEAD NUA, alias NEWBRIDGE,

Co. Kildare (Map 6, C3), is a small manu-facturing and market town of no antiquity, where the Naas (8 m.)–Kildare (5 m.) road crosses the River Liffey. In British days it was a garrison town, but the barracks are now occu-pied by a rope-works, a cutlery factory, and the headquarters of Bórd na Móna, the Turf Board responsible for the large-scale exploitation of Ireland's peat resources.

N. of the town is Newbridge Dominican College, a boarding-school for boys. Nearby, on the E. bank of the Liffey, in Oldconnell, is a fine motte.

1½ m. SE., in Great Connell, are the remains of the Augustinian Priory of Our Lady and St David, founded in 1202 by Myler fitz Henry as a cell of Llanthony Prima in Wales. In the Middle Ages this was one of the most import-ant of Anglo-Irish monasteries, and the prior was a Lord Spiritual of Parliament. In the graveyard is the excellent effigy from the altar-tomb of Walter Wellesly, Prior of Great Connell, Bishop of Kildare, and Master of the Rolls (d. 1539); built into the graveyard wall are panels (Crucifixion, Ecce Homo, St John, St Patrick) from the tomb chest. In the Reilgín, or cemetery, at the nearby Protestant church is a fragment of a second episcopal effigy. Also in Great Connell, at Coonachah, is a prehistoric granite Longstone (see Punchestown under Naas).

DROMAHAIRE, Co. Leitrim (Map 2, B5),

is a pleasantly sited village on the Sligo (12 m.)–Drumshanbo (21 m.) road, not far from where the pretty Bonet flows into Lough Gill.

Dromahaire was the chief seat of the Ó Ruairc (O Rourke) kings of Bréifne (anglice Breany, Brennie, see Cavan) who played a conspicuous rôle in pre-Norman Ireland. It was later the seat of their descendants, the O Rourke lords of West Breany. It is from Drom-ahaire that Dervorgilla (founder of the Nuns' Church at Clonmacnois, q.v., and benefactress of Mellifont Abbey) is alleged to have eloped from her husband, Tigernán Ó Ruairc, king of Bréifne. The banishment (1167) of her para-mour, Díarmait Mac Murrough, king of Lein-ster, provided Henry II of England with the wished-for pretext to undertake the conquest of Ireland.

½ m. W., on the left bank of the Bonet, are the ruins of Creevelea "Abbey" (Nat. Mon.), a Franciscan friary founded in 1508 – and thus the last of the pre-Reformation Irish friaries – by Margaret O Brien, wife of Eóghan O Rourke. Accidentally burned down in 1536, its restoration was undertaken by Brian O Rourke. The 17th cent. English conquest of Breany led to the banishment of the friars, but they re-turned about 1642, repaired the church, and reoccupied the friary for a time. At a later date the Protestant lessee of the buildings allowed them to return, and to roof part of the church with thatch, in return for an exorbitant rent. The well-preserved remains are those of a typical Irish friary, but the details are often curious and degenerate rather than beautiful. The tower, which is coeval with the church, has been much modified since the Dissolution. Among those buried here are Sir Tadhg O Rourke, Lord of West Breany (d. 1605); his widow, Máire O Donnell, presented a chalice (now at Butlersbridge, Co. Cavan) to the friary in his memory, in 1619. Nearby is a ruined church said to occupy the site of the Patrician church of Drumlease.

3 m. N. is O Rourke's Table, a flat-topped height affording beautiful views of Lough Gill (*see under* Sligo) and the Dromahaire valley.

4 m. NE, in Lisgorman, is Cromlech, alias Grania's Bed, an unusual chamber tomb built against an overhanging rock (alt. 790 ft). Close to Mullaghduff school is Lisgorman Giants Grave, another chamber tomb.

6½ m. NE. is Gortermone Giants Grave, a ruined court cairn (alt. 690 ft).

1 m. E., adjoining the fragmentary remains of O Rourke's Castle on the left bank of the Bonet, is Old Hall, which incorporates portions of a castle and bawn built in 1626 by Sir Edward Villiers, brother of the Duke of Buckingham and grantee of escheated O Rourke lands.

5 m. ESE. is Belhavel Lough. 1 m. N. the ruins of Killarga church and a holy well mark the site of an early monastery of which the O Trevors became erenaghs. In 1588 Charles Trevor carried Brian Óg Ó Ruairc away from Oxford, where he was being "de-Gaelicized". 2½ m. E., in Mullaghmore, is a court cairn.

5 m. SW. is Ballintogher, Co. Sligo (*q.v.*).

4 m. NW. in Kilmore, on the NE. shore of Lough Gill, is Parkes Castle (Nat. Mon.), a Plantation castle with large bawn defended by a gatehouse and two flanking towers. It figured prominently in the war of 1641–52.

DROMARD, Co. Sligo (Map 2, A5), is a village on the Sligo (15 m.)–Ballina (24 m.) road. There are ruins of a Mac Donagh castle. To the S. and SW. rises Slieve Gamh, alias the Ox Mountains (Knockalongy 1,786 ft, and Knockachree 1,766 ft).

3½ m. SW., on the lower slope of Knockachree, 1¼ m. S. of Red Hill (*below*), is Loch Achree, "Ireland's youngest lake". It was formed by an earthquake in 1490. The mountains above it offer splendid panoramas of mountain, plain and sea.

1¼ m. WNW., near the road to Skreen, is a chamber tomb.

2¼ m. W. is the village of Skreen. An old churchyard and overgrown fragments of a medieval church mark the site of an early Columban monastery which acquired the name Scrín Adhamhnáin because St Adhamhnán (locally pronounced Awnawn), biographer of Columcille, deposited there a reliquary (Latin *scrinium*, whence Irish *scrín* = Skreen) containing a collection of miscellaneous relics. E. of the churchyard is roadside St Adhamhnán's Well, with a pillar erected in 1591 by Eóghan Mac Domhnaill, Vicar; but there is no trace of the memorial to him erected in 1599 over "the great well of Scrín" by his widow, Bean-Mhumhan Óg Duignan. – S. of the village rises Mullach (alias Cnoc) Rúadha, alias Red Hill (555 ft). On the summit is a large stone ringfort.

On the NE. slope, in Mullaghroe, is a chambered cairn. To the W. of the hill is Doonflin, where An Dubhaltach Óg Mac Fhirbhisigh (*see* Lacken *under* Inishcrone) was murdered (1671) in an inn by Thomas Crofton. 2 m. WSW. is Grangebeg Giants Grave, a chamber tomb.

2½ m. NW., in Ardabrone, are the remnants of the great castle of Ardnaglass, one of the chief strongholds of the O Dowds of Tireragh; later of their Mac Swiney galloglas.

DROMISKIN, Co. Louth (Map 3, B7), is a hamlet 1 m. W. of the Dundalk (7 m.)–Castlebellingham (1¾ m.) road.

St Patrick founded a church here, which he confided to Da-Lua, alias Mo-Lua, alias Lugaid, son of King Aengus of Cashel (d. 515/16). It was succeeded by a monastery whose most celebrated abbot was St Rónán (d. 664), son of Bearrach of Kilbarry. His relics, enshrined in 796, were long venerated here. St Rónán is associated with the story of Suibne Geilt and the battle of Mag Roth. Áed Finnliath, King of Tara, was buried in the monastery A.D. 879. The monastery was occupied by Vikings for some years in the late 10th cent., and thereafter disappeared from history. The only certain relic of it is the stump of a Round Tower (Nat. Mon.), the roof of which is modern. The head of a figured High Cross (Nat. Mon.), which stands on a modern shaft, is said to have come from Baltray. The E. gable of a small 13th cent. church marks the position of the monastic church. Nearby is St Ronan's Well. In the Middle Ages the Archbishop of Armagh had a manor at Dromiskin.

3½ m. W. is modernized Darver Castle, a 16th cent. square keep with corner turrets. 1 m. N., adjoining a modern house, is the well-preserved tower of Killincoole castle.

1 m. NW. is the tower of Milltown castle.

DROMORE, Co. Down (Map 3, C5), is a cathedral and market town where the Banbridge (8 m.)–Hillsborough (5 m.) road (main Dublin–Belfast road) crosses the Lagan. It gives its name to the diocese of Dromore, the Catholic cathedral of which is at Newry. The Protestant diocese is united with that of Down.

The ecclesiastical importance of Dromore may be traced to a monastery founded about A.D. 600 by St Colmán, alias Mo-Cholmóg, moccu Arti. The Protestant Cathedral of Christ the Redeemer and its churchyard occupy the site of the monastery. The nucleus of the cathedral dates from Bishop Thomas Percy's transformation (1808) of the church built by Jeremy Taylor soon after 1661 to take the place of medieval St Colmán's Cathedral, burned down in 1641. Taylor was administrator of Dromore, as well as Bishop of Down and Connor, and it is at Dromore that he was buried. The only ancient relic in the cathedral is an early gravestone ("St Colmán's Pillow"). The altar plate includes a chalice inscribed *Deo dedit humillima Domini ancilla D. Joanne Taylor.*

Bishop Percy, 1729–1811 (see Lisburn and Ballinderry), rebuilder of the cathedral and author of the celebrated *Reliques of Ancient English Poetry*, is buried in the transept.

By the Lagan bridge is a 9th/10th cent. High Cross of granite (Nat. Mon.), which at one time stood in the market-place, but which was demolished during the religious upheaval of the 17th cent. It was put together again and set up in its present position in 1887. The base, the lower part of the shaft, and most of the head are original.

S. of the bridge are the very dilapidated remains of a castle built in 1610.

In Mount St, beside the Lagan, is the Mount, alias the English Mound (Nat. Mon.), perhaps the best preserved motte-and-bailey in Northern Ireland.

¾ m. NW. is Dromore House, formerly the Bishop's Palace. It was begun in 1781 by Bishop the Hon. William Beresford, and completed by his successor, Bishop Percy, who embellished the grounds and demesne after the model of "Shenstone's celebrated seat at Leasowes". In the grounds is St Colman's Well.

3½ m. E., in Lappoges, are the Giants Graves, a short court cairn very much overgrown.

DROMORE, Co. Tyrone (Map 2, D4), is a village on the Omagh (25 m.)–Enniskillen (17 m.) road. St Patrick is reputed to have founded a nunnery here for the first woman to take the veil at his hands. WSW., via John St, are the ruins of a Protestant church erected in 1694 and later enlarged.

4 m. SSW., in Castlemervyn Demesne townland, are the ruins of Trillick Castle, thought to have been built by Lord Castlehaven about 1630. About 270 yds SE. are six pillarstones, perhaps the remains of a stone circle with central pillarstone.

4½ m. NW., alt. 300 ft. in Dullaghan, is Druid's Altar, a small, roofless chamber tomb.

4½ m. N. is Dooish (see under Drumquin).

DROMORE WEST, Co. Sligo (Map 1, E3), is a village charmingly situated where the Sligo (22 m.)–Ballina (18 m.) road crosses the little Dunneill River near a pretty waterfall. In the village are the ruins of the medieval parish church of Kilmacshalgan, re-edified for Protestant use in 1616, and abandoned in 1812.

2¼ m. S., near the W. bank of the Dunneill River in Belville, are Na Clocha Breaca, alias the Bracked Stones, a ruined chamber tomb.

5 m. SW., in Tawnatruffaun, close to the confluence of the Easky and Fiddengarrode, is the Giant's Griddle, a portal dolmen; on two stones of the adjacent fence are two cup-and-ring marks; near by is a ruined tomb. 1½ m. WSW., close to the Owenykeevan in Caltragh, are Greadall Mhór na bhFian and Greadall Bheag na bhFian (the Great Griddle of the Fiana and the Small Griddle of the Fiana), two gallery graves sited on a hillock in a large bog.

2 m. NW. (¼ m. N. of Ballymeen), on the borders of Doonaltan and Alternan Park (Alt Fharannáin "Farannán's cliff, gully"), is the "Saint's Grave", alias "St Farannán's Bed", a recess in the cliff over a stream. W. of the stream is Dabhach Fharannáin, alias St Ernan's (Farannán's) Well. St Farannán, a contemporary of Columcille and Mo-Laise of Inishmurray, was celebrated for his austerities, and Alternan was for centuries a place of pilgrimage where man and beast were cured. (The place figures in the celebrated 12th cent. tale, *Buile Shuibhne*.)

DRUMCLIFF, Co. Sligo (Map 2, B4), is a hamlet where the Sligo (4½ m.)–Bundoran (18 m.) road crosses the Cowney or Drumcliff River at the head of Drumcliff Bay, to the SW. of Ben Bulben and Slievemore and to the W. of lovely Glencar.

SE. of the Cowney bridge the main road cuts through the site of a monastery which was founded, tradition asserts, by Columcille himself. Be this as it may, all the higher offices in the monastery were for centuries reserved for members of Cenél Conaill, the royal Donegal sept to which Columcille himself belonged. Of the monastery there survive (Nat. Mons.) the stump of a Round Tower (on the W. side of the road) and, in the Catholic graveyard, the shaft of a tall, plain, stone cross, as well as a figured High Cross (11th cent.?). The sculptures of the latter include subjects from the Old and New Testaments (*The Fall of Adam and Eve, The Crucifixion*, etc.). In the Protestant churchyard is the grave of the poet, William Butler Yeats (1865–1939), at his own request buried here (where his grandfather had been vicar, 1811–46), in the heart of a countryside he knew and loved so well and of which he sang in some of his loveliest lyrics. He died at Roquebrune, but his remains were brought home by naval vessel in 1948. The epitaph is his own composition. – 200 yds W. of the bridge, on the N. bank of the Cowney, is Giants Grave, a wedge-shaped gallery grave (overgrown).

2 m. NE. rise the precipitous slopes of flat-topped Ben Bulben (1,750 ft) and Slievemore, alias King's Mountain (1,527 ft), whose summits reward the climber with splendid prospects. The flora include *Arenaria ciliata* and *Saxifraga nivalis*. Ben Bulben figures prominently in Irish literature and legend. It was on the slope of the mountain that Díarmait Ó Duibhne, lover of Gráinne, was supposed to have met his tragic fate at the hands of the vengeful Fionn Mac Cumhail.

4 m. E., lovely, cliff-walled Glencar lies between Slievemore and Truskmore (2,113 ft) on the N. and Crockauns (1,527 ft) on the S. In the valley are a small lake and the cascades of Sruth-i-naghaidh-an-áird – which fling themselves over the cliffs of Tormore in three wind-tossed leaps – and (1 m. further E.) Corglass. The aerial ropeway on the side of the valley brings down the high-grade barytes mined on the plateau above.

Irish Tourist Board

High Cross, Drumcliff, west face

2¼–4 m. SE., in Drum East, Drumkilsellagh, Kilsellagh, and Cashelgal, are the ruins of four chamber tombs and of a cemetery cairn (Kilsellagh); the Cashelgal tomb is a full-court cairn, the Kilsellagh tomb is a gallery grave in a well-preserved cairn.

DRUMCOLLIHER, Co. Limerick (Map 5, A5), is a village on the Newcastle (9 m.)– Mallow (17 m.) road.

3 m. SW., at Tullylease, Co. Cork, are remains (Nat. Mon.) of an early monastery and its Augustinian successor. The monastery was founded by the 7th cent. Anglo-Saxon saint, Beretchert, alias Berichter, Beiricheart, etc., who is said to have come to Ireland with his brother, St Gerald (*see* Mayo). The remains comprise: Tobar Beiricheart and Tigh Beiricheart (Beiricheart's Well and House); Cloch na hEilte, a bullaun where a doe (*eilit*) allowed herself to be milked; a nave-and-chancel church with 12th and 15th–16th cent. work; and a number of early gravestones. Fragments of gravestones removed to the National Museum are represented by cement casts. The most important gravestone has an excellently incised cross and other patterns and bears the inscription: QUICUMQUÆ HUNC TITULU[M] LEG-

ERIT ORAT PRO BERECHTUINE. The cross resembles remarkably closely that on a well-known page of the early-8th cent. *Book of Lindisfarne*, and the stone may possibly be the monument of the founder of the monastery rather than, as is generally supposed, of a namesake who died in 839. St Beiricheart's name is still popular in the area under the guise of Benjamin. The saint is also honoured at Kilberrihert in the adjoining parish, at Kilberrihert in Trughanacmy, Co. Kerry, and at St Berrihert's Kyle, Ardane, in the Glen of Aherlow (*see under* Galbally).

4 m. WSW. via Broadford, in Lacka Lower, are the remains (Nat. Mon.) of Killaliathan, alias Killagholehane, a church of various dates.

DRUMQUIN, Co. Tyrone (Map 2, D3), is a small village on the Castlederg (8 m.)–Dromore (10 m.) road.

4 m. SSW., near the summit of Dooish, alt. 1,000 ft, are the ruins of two round cairns, a small stone circle, and a low alignment.

6 m. SSW. is Dullaghan (*see under* Dromore, Co. Tyrone).

1¼ m. W. are the ruins of Lackagh Church, a rectangular structure with Jacobean windows (Nat. Mon.). 300 yds NW. is Lackagh Holy Well.

5½ m. W., alt. 700 ft in Ally, is Giants Grave, a court cairn (Nat. Mon.).

1½ m. NW., in Kirlisk, are remains of Castle Curlieus, a Plantation castle erected by Sir John Davies.

3 m. NW., on a field fence in Killoan ½ m. WNW. of Barravey House, is the Head Stone (Nat. Mon.), base of a stone cross. There are four panels of rude spirals on the front.

DRUMSHANBO, Co. Leitrim (Map 2, C5), is a village and angling centre at the S. end of Lough Allen, 11 m. N. of Carrick-on-Shannon.

5½ m. NNE., in Cleighran More, is Cromlech, a court cairn.

5 m. NNW., on a promontory projecting from the W. shore of Lough Allen, are remains of an old church. 1 m. further, to the S. of Tarmon (Corglass), are remains of St Patrick's Church, an early structure.

6 m. NW., on either side of the Arigna valley, Co. Roscommon, are coal-pits where small-scale mining is carried on. They supply, among other things, a small power station.

DRUMSNA, Co. Leitrim (Map 2, C6), is a village where the Longford (17 m.)–Carrick-on-Shannon (3 m.) road crosses the Shannon. The Dún, a remarkable, and possibly prehistoric, earthwork, ½ m. long, cuts off the great loop in the Shannon between Drumsna and Jamestown. The main work consists of a great ditch and bank and had but a single entrance.

1 m. S., near the 19th cent. Protestant church, are the fragmentary ruins of Annaduff "Abbey". The original foundation dates from the 8th cent.

DUBLIN, Co. Dublin (Map 6, D3, 7), at the mouth of the River Liffey, is the capital of Ireland and the seat of government of the Republic. It is a cathedral and university city and, after Belfast, the second largest port and manufacturing centre in the island. Sited at the head of a lovely bay, where the fertile Central Lowland meets the sea by the foot of the Dublin–Wicklow mountain massif, it lies within easy reach of many delightful beauty spots, excellent beaches, and lonely mountain moors. From the point of view of architecture and lay-out it is one of Europe's beautiful capitals. As befits a city with a distinguished tradition in letters, the sciences, and the arts, it has good libraries, theatres, museums, and art galleries. Few cities of its size offer so many and so varied opportunities for outdoor enjoyment: fourteen golf-courses, three race-courses, sailing, bathing, fishing, hunting, and sporting clubs of every kind.

HISTORY

Though human settlement on and about the site of the city goes back to remote prehistoric times, and though there were several churches and monasteries in the area in the early historic period, the story of Dublin as a city does not commence until A.D. 841, when Norse Vikings constructed a defended shipstead by the Black Pool (Duibhlinn, Norse Dyfflin, whence English Divelin, Dublin) below a hurdled ford (áth cliath, whence the Gaelic name of the town, Baile Átha Cliath) which carried an ancient highway across the Liffey. In 852/3 the settlement was reinforced by fresh Norse arrivals led by Olaf the White, who constructed a small fortified town on the steep ridge where Christchurch and Dublin Castle now stand. Olaf was joined by Ivarr the Boneless, a Danish Viking who played a conspicuous rôle in the Danish conquest of England, and who succeeded Olaf as king of Dublin in 871. Within a century the town overlooking the Liffey had become the capital of a little Norse pirate and trading kingdom (Dyfflinarskiri, Dublinshire) which never reached westwards further than Leixlip and Clondalkin, but which at its maximum extended northwards to include most of the modern Co. Dublin and stretched southwards as far as a narrow coastal fringe as far as Wicklow or Arklow. Down to 1042 Dublinshire was ruled, with few interruptions, by descendants of Ivarr, who made it their base for piratical, commercial, and dynastic enterprises in the Scottish islands, Man and northern England. (In 873 there began a long-drawn-out, intermittent struggle between Dublin and York, whose Danish rulers belonged to the same family as Dublin's.) The last Irish effort to expel the Norse from Dublin ended in the disastrous "Battle of Dublin" fought at Cell Mo-Shámhóg (Islandbridge) by the Liffey, where Niall Black-knee, King of Tara, was slain, A.D. 919. Thereafter Dublin assumed more and more the character of a

useful trading centre, became more and more susceptible to Gaelicization, and gradually found an accepted place in the Gaelic polity. In the course of the 10th cent. the town was captured more than once by Irish kings, but these were content to exact recognition of their supremacy. In 999 it joined in a Leinster revolt against Brian Boru, but the rebel army was routed at Glenn Máma near Saggart. Fourteen years later Leinster and Dublin revolted again. The issue was decided on Good Friday of the following year in the celebrated Battle of Clontarf, where the Leinster–Dublin army, strongly reinforced from overseas, was destroyed. Norse Dublinshire lived on, however, under its half-Irish, half-Danish ruler, Sigtryggr Silkbeard (who reigned until 1036), and it was probably only after Clontarf that it entered on its most prosperous phase (Sigtryggr was the first ruler in Ireland to issue a coinage, which was modelled on that of Æthelræd II of England). It was now, too, that the inhabitants finally abandoned heathenism, and that Sigtryggr founded Dublin's first cathedral, Christchurch (probably after a pilgrimage to Rome in 1028). The first bishop, Dunan, was an Irishman, but Sigtryggr sent him for consecration to England, where the Danish king Cnut was then reigning.

By this date the little walled town had, doubtless, attained to the size and form it was to keep until the 14th cent.: about 700 yds from E. to W. (i.e. from Cork Hill to Cornmarket) and less than 300 yds from N. to S. (i.e. from about the line of Cook St and West Essex St to that of Little Ship St and the S. side of Dublin Castle). Outside the walls, to the W. and SW., lay the great Green of Dublin with its cemeteries. On the E. side of the town lay the flat ground later known as Hoggen Green and represented, in part, today by College Green. Here were the Thingmote, or Public Assembly mound, the burial mounds of the kings, and the now forsaken sanctuary of their gods, the latter probably on the site later occupied by the first church of St Andrew. At the NW. end of the town a solitary bridge led to the N. suburbs and the country beyond.

After Sigtryggr's death his dynasty died out, and the power and status of Dublin's Scandinavian rulers declined. From 1052 to 1071 the town appears to have been one of the seats of Dermot I of Leinster, whose sway extended even to the Isle of Man. (It was in Dublin that the exiled Harold Godwinson, later to be England's last Saxon king, spent the winter of 1051 as Dermot's guest.) After 1071 Dublin and Man seem to have formed a sort of joint Scandinavian kingdom. From 1071 to 1114 Dublinshire was dependent on Turloch Mór O Brien of Munster and his successor, Muirchertach. At the opening of the 12th cent. the immediate rulers of Dublin are found to be new Norse dynasts, who rank merely as earls and who remain subject to one or other of the Irish over-kingdoms until the coming of the Anglo-Normans. Thus the authority of the infamous

Dermot III (Mac Murrough) of Leinster in Dublinshire was such that he was able (1163) to found a nunnery (later known as St Mary de Hogge) and an Augustinian priory (All Hallows) just outside the E. wall of the city. Shortly before that High-king Muirchertach Mac Lochlainn had confirmed Dermot's claim to Dublin, and had helped in elevating his brother-in-law, St Lorcán ("Laurence") O Toole, to the archbishopric. (Dublin had been made one of the four archbishoprics of Ireland in the ecclesiastical reorganization of 1152.) In 1166 Dublin acknowledged the high-kingship of Rory O Conor of Connacht, and joined with him the next year in driving Dermot Mac Murrough overseas. When Dermot had secured the help of Anglo-Norman adventurers, Dublin was one of the first places against which he turned, and on 21 Sept. 1170 he and his hirelings seized the town by treachery. When, on Dermot's death, his Anglo-Norman lieutenant and son-in-law, Richard Strongbow, set himself up as heir to Leinster (including Dublin) in defiance of Irish law, high-king and Norse earl collected powerful forces for his expulsion from the city. The unfortunate earl was routed in a premature assault, captured, and – defiant to the last – beheaded in his own hall. The high-king, nevertheless, proceeded with his blockade, and by autumn had reduced the Anglo-Norman and Leinster garrison to dire straits. Strongbow's terms for submission having been summarily rejected, the garrison made a despairing sortie on 1 Sept. 1171, took the Irish army completely by surprise, and dispersed it. Incapable of appreciating either the contemporary European situation or the strategic significance of Dublin, the Irish made no further attempt to drive out the newcomers. A year later Henry II of England gathered a great army to prevent Strongbow from setting up an independent kingdom in Ireland. One of his first steps was to force Strongbow to surrender Dublinshire and the maritime towns of Leinster to the English Crown. From that date until 1922 Dublin was to remain the citadel and key base of England's fluctuating power in Ireland. Henry spent the winter of 1171–2 in the town, where he received the formal submission of several trusting Irish princes. Before his departure he granted the town to "his men of Bristol", with the free customs and liberties of their native city. About the same time the surviving Norse, by now fairly thoroughly Gaelicized, removed themselves (or were removed) to the neighbourhood of St Michan's parish church and St Mary's Abbey on the N. side of the Liffey, where Oxmantown, formerly Austmannabyr, Ostmaneby, still recalls their later name for themselves. By the 14th cent. they had ceased to be a distinct element in the population.

Apart from a 1312 extension N. to the river, the walled town of Dublin hardly grew at all during the Middle Ages. Within the walls the principal buildings were the castle, Christ-

church, and the parish churches of St Audoen (originally St Columcille's), St Michael, St Nicholas, St Werburgh, St John the Evangelist, and St Mary le Dam. In the suburbs were: West Suburbs: the hospital and priory of the Knights of St John, St Lawrence's Leper House, the Augustinian abbey of St Thomas the Martyr, the Crutched friary and hospital of St John the Baptist; South Suburbs: the Franciscan friary, St Bride's (Brigid's) parish church, the church and almshouse of St Michael le Pole, St Patrick's Cathedral, the archiepiscopal palace of St Sepulchre, the Carmelite friary, St Stephen's leper hospital, and the parish churches of St Peter de Hulle and St Stephen; East Suburbs: the Augustinian friary, the Augustinian nunnery of St Mary de Hogge, the Augustinian priory of All Hallows, and St Andrew's parish church; North Suburbs: the Dominican friary, the parish church of St Michan, and the Cistercian abbey of St Mary.

The Reformation, the wars of the 17th cent., and neglect dealt hardly with Dublin's medieval heritage. At the close of the Cromwellian period the town wall, with its eight gates and nine towers, was in poor repair; the castle was "the worst in Christendom"; the cathedrals and parish churches were ruinous; the abbeys and friaries were gone. The population, too, had decayed, city and suburbs between them mustering no more than 9,000 souls. The next 140 years were to witness a remarkable transformation. By 1800 the population was climbing to 200,000, and the city had spread in all directions; notably to the NE. and SE., where a splendidly planned series of noble squares and thoroughfares provided the worthy setting for superb public buildings and magnificent private houses embellished by the skill of stucco workers, stone-carvers, wood-carvers, painters, glassmakers, silversmiths, and other craftsmen. These spectacular developments were the outward expression of the sense of security of the new Protestant ascendancy, supplanters of the ancient Catholic aristocracy, Gaelic and Old English, destroyed by the conquests of the 17th cent. Their culmination coincided with the assertion of that ascendancy's legislative independence of England. When that independence was sold in 1800 for cash, titles, and the prospect of enduring ascendancy, Dublin's brief glory dimmed and a long, slow decline set in.

The splendour of 18th cent. Dublin has, of course, to be viewed against a lurid background: a large majority deprived of civil and religious rights, a majority consisting for the most part of downtrodden, poverty-stricken peasants whose crushing rents supported the extravagant magnificence of their landlords. When the Union caused the great landowners to abandon Dublin, and brought about the decay of Irish industry and commerce, the lot of the masses went from bad to worse. Then came the famines and land clearances of the 19th cent. to pile horror on horror. Ever-renewed hordes of the homeless and penniless crowded into Dublin, where one splendid street after another degenerated into slum. Only in our own time, and as a result of social and political revolutions, has the process of decay been stopped, the wheel turned back. In the interval Dublin had lost much of her treasure to poverty, war, and the philistines. Though the philistines continue to rage unchecked, enough of greatness survives to make the city even yet a capital of uncommon beauty.

By far the largest part of Dublin's 18th cent. building was devoted to secular purposes, for the state Church had money only for its prelates, and the law confined the Catholic Church to humble back-lane retreats. Not until the lapsing of the Penal Laws did Catholic churches of architectural quality again become possible. Dublin's sixty or seventy Catholic churches, are, therefore, all buildings of the 19th and 20th centuries. At first the Classical tradition still prevailed, and gave the city several churches of merit. In due course the Gothic Revival killed that tradition, but itself gave Dublin a couple of good churches. Since then the standard of ecclesiastical architecture in the capital, as throughout the country generally, has fallen, and most of the recent suburban churches are deplorable.

The tale of 19th and 20th cent. secular building (and street planning) follows a more or less parallel course, good work continuing to be done until as late as the 1860s or 70s. The decline which set in thereafter has not yet run its course, and most of Dublin's recent suburban development, municipal or private, does little credit to the city's taste. It may be that the worst is now over, at least in the industrial and commercial spheres, where occasional buildings like the Central Bus Station, Dublin Airport, and some of the suburban factories, raise hopes of a future not unworthy of the past. If these hopes are to be realized, the Dublin craftsmen will need to resume their discarded skills.

Outstanding dates in Dublin's history

837. Norse arrive with fleet of sixty ships at the Liffey and make a settlement by the river.
841. Norse found a harbour-fort.
852/3. Foundation of fortified Norse town.
871. Ivarr the Boneless founds Dublin's Danish dynasty.
919. Battle of Dublin; Niall Glúndubh, King of Tara, routed and slain by Norse.
921. Sigtryggr of Dublin becomes ruler of York also.
937. Dublin burned by Donnchad Donn, King of Tara. Norse power begins to decline.
1014. Battle of Clontarf.
1029. Crushing defeat of Dublin Norse by king of South Brega.
c. 1030. Dunan first bishop of Dublin; foundation of first Christchurch.

1052–72. Dermot I of Leinster master of Dublin.
1072–1114. Dublin a dependency of the O Brien kings of Munster.
1096. Bishop Samuel O Hanly founds St Michan's Church to the N. of the Liffey.
1147. St Mary's Abbey, hitherto Savignian, becomes Cistercian.
1152. Dublin becomes one of Ireland's four archbishoprics.
1161/2. St Lorcán O Toole becomes archbishop.
1163. Dermot Mac Murrough of Leinster founds All Hallows and St Mary de Hogge.
1170. Dermot Mac Murrough recovers Dublin with help of Strongbow's Anglo-Normans.
1171. High-king Rory O Conor fails to expel Normans; last Norse earl slain.
1171/2. Henry II of England appropriates Dublin and grants town to Bristol men.
1173. Rebuilding of Christchurch commences.
c. 1188. Foundation of Priory and Hospital of St John the Baptist (Augustinian Canons Hospitaller).
1213. St Patrick's collegiate church becomes Dublin's second cathedral.
1213–28. Castle built.
1229. Henry III grants a new charter and the right to elect a mayor.
1312. City walls extended to river.
1317. Edward and Robert Bruce march on Dublin; the citizens set fire to the suburbs.
1348. The Black Death; 14,000 die in Dublin between August and Christmas.
1394–5. Richard II winters in Dublin and knights O Neill, O Brien, O Conor, and Mac Murrough in Christchurch, 25 March 1395.
1487. Lambert Simnel crowned as Edward VI of England in Christchurch.
1534. Silken Thomas Fitzgerald rebels, seizes city, but fails to capture castle.
1536. Anglo-Irish parliament acknowledges Henry VIII of England as King of Ireland and Head of the Church of Ireland.
1591. Foundation of Trinity College.
1641. Failure of Irish plot to seize city and castle.
1647. Royalist Ormonde surrenders Dublin to Parliamentarians to prevent it falling into Confederate Catholic hands.
1649. Battle of Rathmines: Parliamentarians defeat Ormonde's attempt to recover the city. Landing of Cromwell.
1662. Ormonde returns as representative of Charles II; beginnings of modern Dublin.
1665. The Mayor of Dublin becomes Lord Mayor.
1667. Royal College of Physicians founded.
1680–1701. Royal Hospital, Kilmainham.
1689. The Patriot Parliament summoned by James II: "the last legislative assembly

of the older Irish race up to 1922, and the last in which the Roman Catholic faith was represented".

1690. Dublin falls to William of Orange.

1714. The North Wall commenced; beginnings of the modern port of Dublin.

c. 1720. Luke Gardiner commences development of the Henrietta St–Gardiner St area as a fashionable quarter.

1729. New Parliament House begun.

1745. Leinster House begun.

c. 1750. Development of Merrion Square region begun.

1751–7. Rotunda Hospital.

1752–9. Parliament Square, Trinity College.

1757. Wide Streets Commissioners set up.

1774. Royal Exchange (later the City Hall).

1781–91. Custom House.

1782–3. England acknowledges independence of the Dublin Parliament.

1785. Royal Irish Academy founded.

1786–1800. The Four Courts built.

1800. Union of Ireland and Great Britain.

1802. Parliament House converted into Bank of Ireland.

1803. Robert Emmet's rebellion.

1814–18. General Post Office.

1815. Dublin's first post-Reformation Catholic church: St Michael's and St John's, on the Blind Quay.

1816. St Mary's "Metropolitan Catholic Chapel", alias the Pro-Cathedral, Marlborough St.

1834. The Dublin and Kingstown Railway opened.

1840. Reform of Dublin Corporation, with consequent election (1841) of Daniel O Connell as first Catholic Lord Mayor.

1851. Catholic University of Ireland founded; John Henry Newman, Rector, 1853–8.

1865. International Exhibition, Earlsfort Terrace.

1881. Catholic University transformed into University College.

1908. National University of Ireland founded; University College granted a charter as a constituent college.

1913. Eight-month lock-out commences in August. Labour Movement founds the Citizen Army; Irish Republican Brotherhood and Eoin Mac Neill found the Irish Volunteers.

1916. Easter Week Rising of the Irish Volunteers and Citizen Army. Proclamation of the Irish Republic. General Post Office, together with Lower O Connell St and neighbouring streets, destroyed; Four Courts damaged by shell-fire.

1919. First Dáil Éireann meets in Mansion House.

1919–21. Armed struggle for independence; Dublin the scene of constant guerrilla activities; Custom House destroyed (1921).

1922. Dáil Éireann ratifies Anglo-Irish Treaty of 6 Dec. 1921, setting up Irish Free State. British garrison withdraws. Civil War. Four Courts and Upper O Connell St destroyed.

EMINENT DUBLINERS

The roll of illustrious Dubliners includes the names of:

Letters

Richard Stanyhurst (1547–1618), historian and Catholic theologian.

Sir James Ware (1594–1666), historian and antiquary.

Jonathan Swift (1667–1745), patriot, pamphleteer, satirist (Gulliver's Travels, etc.).

Sir Richard Steele (1672–1729), essayist, dramatist, and founder of the London Tatler.

Edmund Burke (1729–97), orator and political philosopher, champion of American liberties.

Edmund Malone (1741–1812), Shakespearean scholar.

Richard Brinsley Sheridan (1751–1816), actor and dramatist (The School for Scandal, The Rivals, The Duenna, etc.).

Thomas Moore (1779–1852), poet and adapter of traditional Irish airs (Lallah Rookh, Moore's Melodies).

Charles Robert Maturin (1782–1824), whose "novels of terror" won the regard of Baudelaire and Balzac.

Samuel Lover (1797–1868), poet and novelist (Handy Andy, Rory O Moore, etc.).

Charles James Lever (1806–72), novelist (Harry Lorrequer, Charles O Malley).

Joseph Sheridan Le Fanu (1814–73), novelist (The House by the Churchyard, In a Glass Darkly, etc.).

William E. H. Lecky (1838–1903), historian.

Oscar Wilde (1854–1900), poet, wit, dramatist (The Importance of Being Earnest, The Ballad of Reading Gaol, etc.).

John Millington Synge (1871–1909), dramatist (The Playboy of the Western World, Deirdre of the Sorrows, etc.).

George Bernard Shaw (1856–1950), wit, dramatist, Nobel Prize winner.

William Butler Yeats (1865–1939), poet, dramatist, Nobel Prize winner.

James Joyce (1882–1941), poet and writer (Dubliners, A Portrait of the Artist as a Young Man, Ulysses, Finnegan's Wake, etc.).

James Stephens (1882–1950), poet, author (The Crock of Gold).

Sean O Casey (1884–1964), dramatist (The Plough and the Stars, Juno and the Paycock, etc.).

Music

John Field (1782–1837), pianist and composer whose nocturnes inspired Chopin; he taught Glinka, founder of the Russian school.

Michael William Balfe (1808–70), conductor and composer of operas (The Bohemian Girl, Il Talismano).

National Gallery of Ireland, Dublin

Portrait of James Joyce by Jacques Émile Blanche

Sir Charles Villiers Stanford (1852–1924), composer of opera, songs, chamber music and symphonies.

Painting

Edward Luttrell (1650–1710), painter and one of the earliest mezzotint engravers.

Nathaniel Hone I (1718–84), portrait painter and a founder member of the Royal Academy, London.

George Barret (1732–84), landscape painter and a founder member of the Royal Academy.

Robert Carver (1750–91), landscape painter.

Sir Martin Archer Shee (1769–1850), portrait painter.

William Sadler (1782–1839), landscape painter.

James Arthur O Connor (1791–1841), landscape painter.

Nathaniel Hone II (1831–1917), landscape and seascape painter, member of the celebrated Barbizon Group, and founder of the modern school of Irish painting.

Patrick Vincent Duffy (1836–1909), landscape painter.

John Butler Yeats (1839–1922), portrait painter; father of Jack Yeats and William Butler Yeats.

Walter Frederick Osborne (1859–1903), painter of field and street life.

Sir William Orpen (1870–1931), portrait painter.
Jack Butler Yeats (1871–1957), brother of William Butler Yeats.

Sculpture
Thomas Kirk (1777–1845).
John Henry Foley (1818–74).

Stained Glass
Michael Healy (1873–1941).
Harry Clarke (1889–1931).
Evie Hone (1894–1955), latest representative of the remarkable Hone dynasty of artists, and perhaps greatest of the trio whose work has spread the fame of Dublin glass.

Medicine
Abraham Colles (1773–1843), remembered for "Colles's Law", Colles's Fracture", and "Colles's Fuchsia".
Sir Philip Crampton (1777–1858), surgeon. Co-author with Robert Graves of the bedside teaching which made the Dublin medical schools famous.
Robert Graves (1796–1853), who introduced bedside teaching into medical education. His *Clinical Lectures* was an international textbook.
Francis Rynd (1801–61), inventor of the hypodermic syringe.
Sir Dominic Corrigan (1802–80), specialist in diseases of the aorta; gave his name to "Corrigan's Disease", "Corrigan's Pulse"; inventor of "Corrigan's Button".
William Stokes (1804–78), author of *Diseases of the Chest* and *Diseases of the Heart and Aorta.* Also remembered for "Stokes-Adams's Syndrome." and "Cheyne-Stokes's Respiration".
Sir William Wilde (1815–76), noted ophthalmologist, otologist, and archaeologist; father of Oscar Wilde. In medicine remembered for "Wilde's Incision" and "Wilde's Cord".

Science
Sir William Rowan Hamilton (1805–65), discoverer of quaternions, whose work foreshadowed the quantum theory and recent discoveries in nuclear physics.
George Salmon (1819–1904), mathematician.
Sir Robert Stawell Ball (1840–1913), astronomer and mathematician.
George Francis Fitzgerald (1851–1901), mathematician.

STREET GUIDE

Explanation
For the convenience of the visitor the city is here divided into four quarters: NW., NE., SW., and SE., the River Liffey being taken as the E.–W. axis, and the principal N.–S. traffic artery, from Parnell Sq. in the N. via O Connell St, College Green, Grafton St, and St Stephen's Green to Harcourt St station in the S., being taken as the N.–S. axis. Streets, etc., lying along the main N.–S. axis are taken separately and given first place. The Index of Principal Buildings and Places of Interest indicates their location.

Index of Principal Buildings and Places of Interest
Abbey Theatre, Marlborough St: NE.
Aldborough House, Seán Mac Dermott St: NE.
Art Galleries: see Charlemont House *and* National Gallery.
Árus an Uachtaráin, Phoenix Park: NW.
Bank of Ireland, College Green: N.–S. axis.
Belvedere House, Great Denmark St: NE.
Botanic Gardens, Glasnevin: NE.
Casino, Marino: NE.
Castle: SW.
Charlemont House, Parnell Sq.: N.–S. axis.
Chester Beatty Library, Ballsbridge: SE.
Christchurch Cathedral, Christchurch Pl.: SW.
City Hall; Cork Hill: SW.
Civic Museum, William St: SW.
Clanwilliam House, St Stephen's Green: N.–S. axis.
Custom House, Beresford Pl.: NE.
Department of Defence, Phoenix Park: NW.
Dublin Institute for Advanced Studies, Merrion Sq.: SE.
Folk Museum: see Royal Hospital.
Four Courts, Inns Quay: NW.
Government Buildings, Merrion St: SE.
Guinness Brewery, James's St: SW.
King's Hospital, Blackhall Pl.: NW.
King's Inns, Henrietta St: NW.
Leinster House, Kildare St: SE.
Marino Casino, Marino: NE.
Marsh's Library, off Patrick St: SW.
Merrion Sq.: SE.
Mornington House, Merrion St: SE.
Municipal Gallery: see Charlemont House.
Museum, Civic, William St: SW.
Museum, Folk: see Royal Hospital.
Museum, National: see National Museum
National Gallery, Merrion Sq.: SE.
National Library, Kildare St: SE.
National Museum, Kildare St *and* Merrion Sq.: SE.
Northland House: see Royal Irish Academy.
Park of Remembrance (1914–18 War Memorial), Kilmainham: SW.
Parnell Sq.: N.–S. axis.
Phoenix Park: NW.
Powerscourt House, William St: SW.
Pro-Cathedral, Marlborough St: NE.
Rotunda Hospital, Parnell Sq.: N.–S. axis.
Royal Dublin Society, Ballsbridge: SE.
Royal Hospital, Kilmainham: SW.
Royal Irish Academy, Dawson St: SE.
Royal Irish Academy of Music, Westland Row: SE.
St Audoen's Church, High St: SW.
St George's Church, Hardwicke Pl.: NE.
St Mary's Church, Mary St: NW.
St Michan's Church, Church St: NW.
St Patrick's Cathedral, Patrick St: SW.

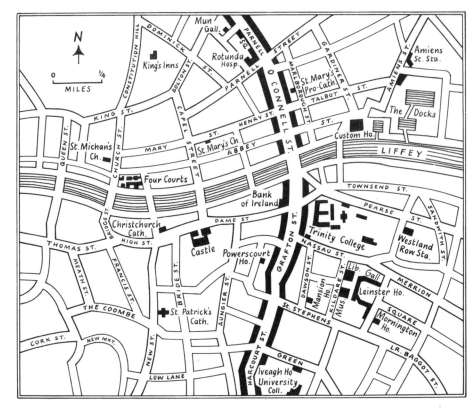

Sketch map of central Dublin

St Stephen's Green: N.-S. axis.
Trinity College: N.-S. axis.
Tyrone House, Marlborough St: NE.
University College (*a*) Earlsfort Terrace: SE.
                    (*b*) St Stephen's Green, N.-
                    S. axis.
                    (*c*) Merrion St: SE.
                    (*d*) Donnybrook: SE.
Zoological Gardens, Phoenix Park: NW.

Main North–South Axis

Parnell Square, originally Rutland Square, is the second earliest of Dublin's great Georgian squares. It was begun about the middle of the 18th cent. By 1792 the residents included twelve members of the Irish House of Lords, twelve members of the Commons, and two Protestant bishops. It is now largely given over to offices and institutions of various kinds.

On the N. side, Palace Row, is mutilated Charlemont House, since 1930 the Municipal Gallery of Modern Art. In its day one of the finest of Dublin's mansions, it was built (1761–3) by Sir William Chambers for James Caulfeild, Earl of Charlemont (*see* Marino *under* Dublin NE.), Commander-in-Chief of the Irish Volunteers who helped secure the independence of the Dublin legislature. The chaste façade has been marred by the uncalled-for 1933 doorway. All that survive of the 18th-cent. interior

are the oval staircase and the small, front drawing room.

The nucleus of the collection of paintings in the Municipal Gallery was due to the talent and

J. Bambury, Dublin
Charlemont House, Parnell Square

Municipal Gallery of Modern Art, Dublin

In the Omnibus *by Honoré Daumier*

generosity of Sir Hugh Lane. Lane was drowned in the *Lusitania* on 7 May 1915, shortly after making a codicil to his will, leaving the famous "Lane Pictures" to Dublin. Unfortunately, the codicil was unwitnessed, and therefore invalid. A protracted battle went on for many years between the British and the Irish – individuals, public bodies, and State authorities – until 1959, when an agreement was reached that the collection would be divided into two parts to be shown alternately in Dublin and London in five-year cycles, starting in 1960. By this arrangement half of the collection is always to be seen in Dublin. The thirty-nine pictures of the Impressionist period include:

E. Boudin (1824–98). *The Beach at Tourge-ville-les-Sablons.*

J-B. Corot (1796–1875). *The Palace of the Popes of Avignon; Summer Morning.*

G. Courbet (1819–77). *Snow Scene; The Pool.*

C. Daubigny (1817–78). *Honoré Daumier.*

H. Daumier (1808–79). *Don Quixote and Sancho Panza.*

E. Degas (1834–1917). *On the Beach.*

J. Forain (1852–1931). *Legal Aid.*

J. Jongkind (1819–91). *Skating in Holland.*

E. Manet (1832–83). *A Concert in the Tuileries; Madame Eva Gonzales.*

C. Monet (1840–1926). *Vétheuil: Sunshine and Snow.*

B. Morisot (1841–95). *A Summer Day.*

C. Pissarro (1831–1903). *View from Louveciennes.*

A. Renoir (1841–1919). *Umbrellas.*

Theodore Rousseau (1844–1910). *Moonlight.*

E. Vuillard (1868–1940). *The Mantlepiece.*

Besides the pictures mentioned there are many important works by 19th and 20th cent. masters, including Boudin, Chinnery, Constable, Corot, Daubigny, Degas, Fantin-Latour, Géricault, Harpignies, Ingres, Augustus John, Gwen John, Mancini, Millet, Monet, John Nash, Segantini, Sargent, Wilson Steer, Turner, and Whistler.

The Irish school is represented by John Butler Yeats, Sir William Orpen, Walter Osborne, Evie Hone, Nathaniel Hone, Jack B. Yeats, Louis Le Brocquy, Patrick Scott, Patrick Collins, Norah Mc Guinness, George Campbell, Gerald Dillon, Derek Hill, and Patrick Hennessy.

Contemporary European painting is represented by the following:

Bonnard. *Boulevard de Clichy.*

Bores. *Still Life.*

Ciry. *The Virgin of Pity.*

Clave. *Girl with Cockerel.*

Coignard. *Labours.*

Municipal Gallery of Modern Art, Dublin

Sir Hugh Lane, *portrait by John S. Sargent*

218   DUBLIN

Cortot. *Reflets.*
De Segonzac. *Environs de St Tropez.*
Guttuso. *Red Roofs.*
Lhote. *Landscape.*
Lhurcat. *Coq Guerrier* and *Decorative Land-scape.*
Picasso. *Les Orchidées.*
Piper. *Cavesby Cross with Hollyhocks.*
Rouault. *Christ and the Soldier.*
Reybeyrolle. *Fish.*
Smith, Matthew. *Cornish Landscape.*
Souter. *Calabria.*
Souverbie. *Composition.*
Utrillo. *La Rue Marcadet.*
Vlaminck. *Opium.*
The stained glass collection includes work by Evie Hone and Harry Clarke. The latter's *Geneva Window* (1928–30) of subjects from the works of modern Irish writers, is particularly noteworthy.

The small sculpture collection includes works by Carpeaux, Barye, Dalou, Degas, Epstein, Henry Moore, Rodin, Jerome Connor, and Andrew O Connor. Admission: Tue., 10.30 a.m.–9 p.m.; Wed. to Sat., 10.30 a.m.–6 p.m.; Sun. 11 a.m.–2 p.m.; lecture: Sun. 12 noon.

No. 14 (Palace Row) still has some good interior decoration, notably a coved ceiling with lunettes (1760) by Jacob Ennis, drawing master in the Royal Dublin Society's Art School.

"Findlater's Church" (Presbyterian; by Andrew Heiton of Perth), at the NE. corner of the square, figures in Joyce's *Ulysses.*

The 1916–22 Garden of Remembrance (1966) was designed by Daithí P. Hanley. The oval pool is to have a symbolic sculpture by Oisín Kelly.

The E. side of the square (and its southerly prolongation, Cavendish Row) contain some of the most palatial of Dublin's Georgian houses, the exteriors too often mutilated. No. 11, the Sheriff's Court, was the town house of the Earl of Ormond. No. 9, erected 1756/7 by Frederick Darley and John Ensor for Dr Bartholomew Mosse, has fine stucco, as well as superb carved doors by John Kelly. No. 6 was the house of Richard Kirwan (1733–1812), noted Co. Galway scientist. No. 5 was the birthplace of James Joyce's "Buck Mulligan" (Oliver St John Gogarty; *see* Ely Place *under* Dublin SE.). No. 4 was the town house of the Earl of Wicklow. (For the W. side of Cavendish Row *see* Rotunda Hospital, *below.*)

On the S. side of the square, but facing Parnell St, is the (Rotunda) Lying-in Hospital, celebrated in the annals of obstetrics. Designed for the philanthropist, Dr Bartholomew Mosse, by Richard Cassels, it was erected after Cassels's death by his assistant, John Ensor. Typical of Cassels is the combination of central block and curved flanking colonnades with end pavilions. (While never one of Dublin's best buildings, the hospital has been altogether spoiled by horrid 19th–20th cent. additions on the W. side.) The tower cupola was originally surmounted by a gilt cradle, crown, and ball. The staircase has fine stucco by William Lee. But the glory of the hospital is the exotic, almost baroque, chapel designed and executed

J. Bambury, Dublin

The Rotunda Lying-in Hospital

by Barthélemy Cramillion, a little-known French stucco worker. The projected gilding, and the chiaroscuro paintings by Giambattista Cipriani (for the ceiling compartments), were never carried out. The gardens (now largely built over) at the rear of the hospital were laid out by Mosse as a revenue-raising pleasure ground for the world of fashion, complete with walks, amphitheatre, "orchestra" for music, temples for refreshment, and assembly rooms for balls, routs, and concerts. At the E. end of the hospital is the Rotunda after which it is now named. Today the Ambassador Cinema, the Rotunda was erected in 1764 as an assembly room, to the designs of John Ensor, and improved by James Gandon in 1786, when the frieze and Coade stone plaques by Edward Smyth were added. In the course of its chequered history this fine hall witnessed many memorable events: the first public appearances of John Field and of Michael O Kelly, Mozart's friend; a concert by Franz Liszt; Newman's University Discourses; the 1783 Volunteer Convention. About 1910 the building was savagely adapted for use as a cinema; it has recently been subjected to further abuse. Adjoining it on the NE., i.e. on the W. side of Cavendish Row, are the New Assembly Rooms (1784-6). The plan was by Frederick Trench, the elevations by Richard Johnston, elder brother of the more famous Francis. The Supper Room was for many years the well-known Dublin Gate Theatre, the Ballroom a palais de danse! In general, the 20th cent. treatment of these attractive buildings has been on a par with that of the Hospital, the Rotunda, and the Gardens. In 1961 the Pillar Room (now the Town and Country Club) was redecorated.

West side: Vaughan's Hotel was one of Michael Collins's rendezvous during the 1919-21 struggle for independence. No. 33 has good stucco decorations.

O Connell St has been in turn Drogheda St and Sackville St. Once the home and haunt of fashion, it is today a vulgar commercial thoroughfare "resplendent with cinemas and ice-cream parlours" (Maurice Craig). In the late 1740s banker Luke Gardiner replanned the then narrow N. half as an "elongated residential square", with tree-planted Gardiner's Mall forming a fashionable promenade down the middle. From 1784 onwards the Wide Streets Commissioners laid out the S. half on the same great scale, so spoiling Gardiner's concept. In the 19th cent. the thoroughfare was gradually invaded by commercial interests. Nevertheless, it still retained something of its 18th cent. dignity until the bombardments of 1916 and 1922. The only noteworthy feature today is the Classical façade of the General Post Office, all that survives of Francis Johnston's work (1814-18); the statues over the portico, Fidelity, Hibernia, and Mercury, are by John Smyth, eldest son of Edward Smyth (see Custom House and Four Courts). The Post

Office was the headquarters of the 1916 insurgents, who here proclaimed the Irish Republic. Destroyed by gunfire, it was rebuilt in 1929 by uninspired architects of the Office of Public Works. In the public office is a 1916 memorial, Death of Cuchulainn by Oliver Sheppard.

In the C.I.E. Passenger Bureau (No. 59 Lower O Connell St) may be seen, to some disadvantage, Evie Hone's My Four Green Fields window (designed for the Irish Pavilion, New York World Fair, 1939).

The centre of the street is lined by statues, mostly of indifferent quality. They are (from N. to S.):

Charles Stewart Parnell (1846-91), Home Rule leader, by the Dublin-born American sculptor, Augustus St Gaudens (1911).

Father Theobald Matthew (1790-1861), Temperance reformer, "by Miss Redmond".

Sir John Gray (1816-75), proprietor of The Freeman's Journal, by Sir Thomas Farrell.

William Smith O Brien (1803-64), Young Ireland leader, by Sir John Farrell.

Daniel O Connell (1775-1847) by John Henry Foley. The base, with Éire Casting Off Her Fetters, and the winged figures of Patriotism, Fidelity, Eloquence, and Courage are by Thomas Brock, who completed the monument in 1882, eight years after Foley's death.

O Connell Bridge, originally Carlisle Bridge, was built in 1791 to the design of James Gandon. In 1880 it was rebuilt to its present width, the slopes flattened, and Edward Smyth's sculptured keystones removed.

Westmoreland St (together with the adjoining D'Olier St) was laid out about 1800 by the Wide Streets Commissioners as a street of shops with uniform, pilastered ground floors (perhaps by James Gandon). The statue (1857) of Thomas Moore (1779-1852), at the junction with College St, is by Christopher Moore.

College Green, at the junction of Westmoreland St, Dame St (see Dublin SW.), and Grafton St, is the last relic of the wide Hoggen Green which lay outside the E. wall of the medieval town.

On the E. side is Trinity College – "The College of the Holy and Undivided Trinity near Dublin", founded in 1592 by Elizabeth I, at the instance of the Protestant establishment, so as to reduce the numbers seeking higher education in France, Italy, and Spain, "whereby they have been infected by popery". The college occupies the site of the Augustinian priory of All Hallows, founded by Dermot Mac Murrough of Leinster. Catholics were excluded from degrees until 1793; from scholarships, fellowships, and other offices until 1873. The only Catholic provost in the history of the college was the Rev. Michael Moore, appointed by James II in 1689. He saved the library from destruction by Jacobite troops quartered in the college. Forced to flee from Williamite Ireland, he became professor of Greek and Latin philosophy in the Collège de France, Principal of the Collège de Navarre, and Rector of the University of Paris. Until our own day Trinity remained essentially Protestant and English in spirit. In point of student numbers it is the third largest university establishment in Ireland, but recruits a substantial proportion of its students in Britain. The roll of famous Trinity men includes the names of William Congreve (1670–1729; English-born of English parents), George Farquhar (1678–1707; Derry-born of English parents), Oscar Wilde (1854–1900), and John Millington Synge (1871–1909), dramatists; Jonathan Swift (1667–1745; Dublin-born of English parents), satirist, patriot, and political pamphleteer, Theobald Wolfe Tone (1763–98), Henry Grattan (1746–1820), Robert Emmet (1778–1803), Thomas Davis (1814–45), John Mitchel (1815–75), James Clarke Luby (1821–1901), and Isaac Butt (1813–79), patriots; George Berkeley (1685–1753), philosopher; Oliver Goldsmith (1728–74), poet; Edmund Burke (1729–97), orator and political philosopher; Sir William Rowan Hamilton (1805–65), mathematician; George Francis Fitzgerald (1851–1901) and Ernest Thomas Sinton Walton, physicists; John Joly (1857–1933), geologist

and inventor; Dr Patrick Duigenan (1737–1816), notorious anti-Catholic; Lord Clare (1749–1802), one of the architects of the Union; Lord Carson (1854–1935), leader of the Protestant, Unionist resistance to Home Rule.

The college buildings were reconstructed on a grand scale in the 18th cent., and extended in the 19th, so that practically nothing survives of earlier date than 1700.

The Palladian façade, College Green, is attributed to Henry Keane and John Sanderson of London; the excellent stone carving is by David Sheehan. The statues of Edmund Burke and Oliver Goldsmith, like the statue of Henry Grattan at the centre of College Green, are by John Henry Foley.

The W. court (1752–9) is called Parliament Sq. because the Dublin parliament defrayed most of the cost. Its wings terminate in externally identical buildings by Sir William Chambers and Graham Meyers. That on the S. side (1781) is the Theatre (examination hall), that on the N. (1779–90) the Chapel. The Theatre has one of the best interiors in the college, with stucco by Michael Stapleton (d. 1801). It contains an organ case captured from the Spaniards in 1702; also a fine monument to Provost Baldwin, carved in Rome about 1771–

Trinity College Library

Detail from the Book of Kells

82 by Christopher Hewetson of Kilkenny (1739?–98). The gilt oak chandelier came from the House of Commons on the north side of College Green. The Chapel too has good stucco (by Michael Stapleton) and woodwork; unfortunately also dreadful 19th cent. stained glass. The 17th cent. plate survives. NE. of the Chapel is the Dining Hall erected to the design of Richard Cassels in 1745–9, but shortly afterwards rebuilt by other hands. In it are displayed portraits of George III as Prince of Wales (by Hudson), Adam Loftus, first Provost of the college, Henry Grattan, and members of the college who attained to high office under the British regime.

The belfry (1853) is alleged to mark the position of the crossing of the medieval priory church of All Hallows. Flanking it are statues of William Hartpole Lecky (1838–1903; historian), by Sir William Goscombe John, and of Provost George Salmon (1819–1904; Protestant theologian), by John Hughes (1911).

On the E. side of Library Sq. are the Rubrics, a range of brick apartments dating from 1700. On the S. side is the great Library (1712–32) by Thomas Burgh. The ground floor, designed as an open loggia to insulate the library above from the marshy ground below, was unfortunately walled up in 1892 to provide increased storage space. The roof-line, too, has been altered; it was originally masked by the parapet balustrade. The entrance hall has rococo plaster by Edward Semple; the staircase (1750) is by Cassels. The splendid Long Room on the first floor was altered in 1857 by Benjamin Woodward, who threw the first and second floors into one under a timber barrel-vault. The 17th cent.

stairs to the galleries are said to have come from the old library. The busts which adorn the room include *Swift* by Roubilliac, *Dr Patrick Delany* by Van Nost, *Thomas Parnell* and *Dr Clements* by Edward Smyth.

The Library houses Ireland's greatest collection of books, MSS., and historical papers. The more remarkable treasures include:

Codex Primus Usserianus, a mutilated 7th cent. Irish gospel book ("Old Latin" text).

The *Book of Durrow*, an important 7th cent. illuminated gospel book from the Columban monastery of Durrow, Co. Offaly (*see under* Tullamore).

The *Book of Kells*, most famous of insular illuminated gospel books. This wonderful codex dates from the later 8th century. It was for long the chief treasure of the Columban monastery of Kells, Co. Meath (*q.v.*)., but may have been written and painted in the celebrated Columban monastery of Iona, in Scotland.

The *Book of Dimma*, an 8th/9th cent. illuminated gospel book from the ancient monastery of Roscrea (*q.v.*). Its silver-plated bronze case was made c. 1150 for Tadg O Carroll of Éile.

The *Book of Mulling*, a 7th cent. illuminated gospel book (9th cent. additions) from the ancient monastery of St Mullins, Co. Carlow (*q.v.*).

The *Garland of Howth*, an 8th–9th cent. illuminated gospel book from Ireland's Eye, Howth (*q.v.*).

The *Book of Armagh*, a 9th cent. gospel book which contains the only surviving early Irish copy of the complete New Testament. It also has an important collection of Patrician documents, including a copy of the saint's famous

Confessio, perhaps transcribed from the original draft. (Down to 1680 the codex was in the custody of hereditary keepers who derived their surname, Mac Maoir, Wyre, from their office. The last keeper pledged it for £5 to go to London to give perjured evidence which helped bring Oliver Plunkett, Catholic Archbishop of Armagh, to the scaffold.)

The so-called *Book of Leinster*, an important Irish literary codex compiled in the monastery of Terryglass (*see under* Portumna) some time between 1151 and 1224, and long preserved in the monastery of Núachongbháil, Co. Laois (*see under* Stradbally).

Also worthy of notice is the Library's small collection of antiquities, including a fine, medieval, Irish harp ("Brian Boru's Harp").

Between Burgh's Library and the Museum Buildings (*below*) new library buildings are in course of erection (commenced 1964) to the design of Paul G. Koralek, who won the premium in an international competition.

E. of the Rubrics is New Sq., bounded on the N. and E. by mechanical 1843 essays in the 18th cent. manner. At the NW. corner is the Printing House, a little Doric temple built in 1734 by Richard Cassels for John Stearne, Bishop of Clogher, who left his collections of books and MSS. to the college. On the S. side are the interesting Museum Buildings (1853-5), by Benjamin Woodward (1815-61) of the firm of (Sir Thomas) Deane and Woodward (architects also of the Kildare Street Club on the opposite side of College Park). This, "the finest secular building the Gothic Revival ever produced", houses the engineering and geological departments. The delightful carvings are the work of the brothers John and James Shea. The interior has been recently remodelled, but the excellent domed entrance-and-staircase hall survives. Ruskin was so pleased with this building that he commissioned Woodward and his stonecarvers for the ill-fated Oxford Museum.

S. of Parliament Sq. and facing the N. end of Grafton St is the Provost's House (1759), the only one of Dublin's great Georgian houses still serving its original purpose. The design is an adaptation by John Smith of Lord Cork's design for Gen. Wade's London house. (Lord Cork is, of course, the Lord Burlington of English architectural history.) The principal features of the interior (recently happily restored) are the entrance hall, octagonal staircase, and splendid saloon – "the finest private reception room in Dublin" (Craig). The pictures include an excellent Gainsborough portrait of the Duke of Bedford, Chancellor of the University in 1765.

On the N. side of College Green is the Bank of Ireland, a post-Union transformation of the beautiful Parliament House built between 1729 and 1739 to the design of Sir Edward Lovett Pearce (1699?-1733) and enlarged between 1785 and 1794 by James Gandon and Robert Parke. Of Pearce's work there survive the superb Ionic "piazza" and projecting gallery-pavilions facing College Green, the Commons' division lobbies, the House of Lords, and the Lords' conference and robing rooms. The central door (blocked up) from the "piazza" gave on to the Court of Requests, the latter in turn on to the main lobby of the House of Commons. The W. door led into the Commons' entrance hall, off which opened the division lobbies around three sides of the House. The N. door led into the Lords' entrance hall, which in turn opened on to the lobby of the House of Lords and the Lords' robing rooms. The central portico and the pavilions were to have been crowned by three statues each; but these were never erected, the only external sculpture here in Parliament's time being the royal arms of the central pediment (by John Houghton, who also carved the capitals of the colonnade). The side elevations of Pearce's building were quite plain, being masked by huddles of houses. Between 1785 and 1789, following on the opening up of Westmoreland St, the building was extended eastwards by James Gandon, who erected the E. front, with its magnificent Corinthian portico, and joined it to Pearce's work by an austere, niched, quadrant screen devoid of columns or balustrade. Gandon's great portico, designed as a new, major entrance to the House of Lords, opens on to a vestibule, which in turn gives on to a delightfully chaste little rotunda, and thence on to a corridor skirting the N. side of the House of Lords. The delicate ox-head frieze of the rotunda is by Edward Smyth, who also carved the now eroded statues of *Minerva* (*Wisdom*), *Justice*, and *Liberty* over the portico. (In 1946 the insignia of these fine statues were restored by Smyth's great-great-grandson.) Before Gandon's work was completed, the Commons' accommodation was extended westwards to Foster Place. This task, carried out between 1787 and 1794, was entrusted to Robert Parke, who balanced Gandon's work by a new W. front (with Ionic portico), which he linked to Pearce's front by an open quadrant "piazza" of balustraded, free-standing columns set in advance of a niched screen. The W. vestibule was designed as a waiting room for sedan chairmen and others. – Pearce's House of Commons was a noble, octagonal, domed chamber. In 1792 it was destroyed by fire, and replaced by an inferior, circular chamber with waggon-head roof, designed by Vincent Waldré, a Vicenzan architect who had come to Dublin in 1787. – The last session of Parliament held in College Green ended 2 Aug. 1800, and in 1802 the British Government sold the buildings to the Bank of Ireland, with the secret stipulations that both Houses should be so altered as to preclude "their being again used upon any contingency whatever as public debating rooms", and that the exterior of the building should be so altered as to reconcile the populace to the loss of their Parliament. Francis Johnston (1761-1829) was chosen to make the transformation. Johnston blocked up the windows and central doorway of Pearce's "piazza" and added the statues of *Commerce, Hibernia,* and *Fidelity* to the portico. (These were designed by Flaxman, but carved by Edward Smyth and his son, John.) He replaced the Commons' and Lords' entrance halls by the present W. and E. halls; the stucco, which blends with that of Pearce's lobbies, is by Charles Thorp. He replaced the Court of Requests and the Commons' vestibule by the fine Cash Office, where all the carving is by Edward Smyth's pupil, Thomas Kirk, who also did the fireplace in Johnston's E. entrance hall. Johnston replaced Waldré's House of Commons by the Bank Board Room, Governor's Office, and Accountant General's Office. (The stucco of the Board Room ceiling is by Thorp.) The House of Lords and the Lords' robing and conference rooms he left substantially unchanged. The former now serves as meeting place of the Court of Proprietors, the others as Transfer Office, Cashier's Office, and Dividend Office. Externally, Johnston's most significant alterations were to the quadrant screens: he abolished Parke's "piazza" by bringing the screen forward and re-erecting it between the columns, and he replaced Gandon's screen by the existing balustraded-and-niched screen with engaged columns. Johnston also added the monumental guardhouse gateways in Foster Place. (The gateway closing the W. end of Foster Place has recently been blocked up in adapting the structure for the Central Bank of Ireland. It is crowned by a superb trophy, the work of Thomas Kirk.) Since Johnston's time the only significant addition to the building has been the great gateway (1860) in Westmoreland St. – The principal showpiece of the building today is Pearce's House of Lords (closed to public March, April, Sept., and Oct.). It contains a magnificent Dublin glass chandelier (1,233 pieces) of 1788 and two tapestries (1733) by John van Beaver, probably to the design of Johann van der Hagen; also the original mantelpiece (1748/9), a fine example of Dublin work of its period, and the House of Commons Mace (London-made, 1765). An inferior statue of George III by John Bacon, Jr, occupies the position of the Lord Lieutenant's Throne. (The Throne itself, and many of the Lords' benches, have been in the Royal Irish Academy for over a century, as have been some brass candelabra from the Court of Requests. The Lords' Mace, made in Dublin in 1766, is in the National Museum. The Commons' benches are in Swift's Hospital, James's St, Dublin SW.) In the Directors' Luncheon Room is a very fine rococo ceiling from La Touche's Bank in Castle St. Dating from before 1735, it is the earliest known Irish stucco ceiling with full human figures. The subject is *Venus Wounded by Love,* the artist unknown.

The College Green memorial (1966) to Thomas Davis, Young Ireland leader, is by Edward Delaney.

The entire College Green block between Foster Pl. and Anglesea St was formerly filled by Francis Johnston's first (1790) Dublin building, Daly's Club. The club was founded in 1750 by Patrick Daly, and soon became the principal gaming house of the Ascendancy. The blackballing of the Hon. William Conyngham in 1752 resulted in the founding of the rival Kildare Street Club (*see* Kildare St, Dublin SE.), which supplanted Daly's and caused it to close down in 1823. Johnston's clubhouse, "the most superb gambling house in the world", consisted of a lofty, pilastered, central block with plain, slightly lower, side wings. The central block survives in a mutilated form: Johnston's circular attic windows squared off and (quite recently) a new storey superposed; the interior chopped up for offices; the ceiling of the great card room covered over.

Grafton St, linking College Green and St Stephen's Green, originated as a country lane. It became a residential street in the 18th cent., but has long since succumbed to increasingly vulgar commercialization. Percy Bysshe Shelley lodged at No. 17 in 1812. No. 60 was the birthplace of Samuel Lover (1797–1868), novelist. No. 79 occupies the site of Whyte's Academy, whose pupils included Richard Brinsley Sheridan, Thomas Moore, and Robert Emmet, as well as the future Duke of Wellington. About the middle of the W. side is Johnston's Court, giving convenient access to St Teresa's Church (Discalced Carmelites) where, under the high altar, is a *Dead Christ* in marble by John Hogan (1829). The church was long the second largest Catholic church in Dublin. Its obscure, withdrawn situation was typical of early post-Penal times.

St Stephen's Green, earliest and largest of Dublin's great squares, was originally a common outside the town wall. In 1664–5 the periphery was laid out in building plots and the central part enclosed. The following year the enclosed green was levelled to serve as a military exercise ground. In the course of the 18th cent. the older houses about the Green were replaced by lordly mansions which still survive. Many of these came through mortgages into the hands of the La Touche family of bankers.

North Side: No. 8, now the United Services Club, and No. 9, now the Stephen's Green Club, date from 1754 and 1756 respectively. Both have suffered from refronting, but contain good 18th cent. stucco. No. 16, now the Presbyterian Association, was built (1776) for Gustavus Hume of Castle Hume, Co. Fermanagh. It was later the palace of the Protestant Archbishop of Dublin. The stucco is by Michael Stapleton. No. 17 (1776–8), since 1850 the Dublin University Club, was originally Milltown House (Leeson family); it too has fine ceilings and other stucco by Michael Stapleton. The Shelbourne Hotel occupies the site of Kerry House, alias Shelburne House. In 1798 Kerry House was one of Dublin's "torturing barracks", where insurgents and suspects were

J. Bambury, Dublin

The Royal College of Surgeons, Ireland

ill-treated. Among the many famous guests of
the Shelbourne Hotel were Amanda McGet-
trick Ross, Thackeray (it figures in his *Irish
Sketch Book*), and George Moore (it figures in
A Drama in Muslin). Nos. 32 (Shelbourne
Rooms), 33, and 34 date from 1770 and contain much good plasterwork by Michael Stapleton; two floors have been added to No. 32.

East Side: The Bank of Ireland office at the
corner of Merrion Row occupies the site of
Tracton House whose splendid Apollo room
has been re-erected in Dublin Castle. No.
41 (1745) is by Benjamin Rudd. No. 44 has
stucco by Stapleton, Robbins, and Richardson.
Nos. 52 and 53 are a Michael Stapleton pair of
1771. The former, now seat of the Representative Church Body (Church of Ireland), was the
residence of the Rt Hon. David La Touche. Besides stucco by Stapleton, it has monochrome
wall paintings by Peter de Gree, a Flemish
chiaroscuro painter who worked in Ireland
1786–9 (*see* Mount Kennedy House *and* Woodstock *under* Newtown Mountkennedy). Nos.
54, 55 and 56 have been St Vincent's Hospital
since 1834. No. 56 was built by the brothers
West in 1760 for Usher St George, later Lord
Hume. All three have "brilliantly disordered"
stucco.

South Side: Iveagh House, now the Department of External Affairs, incorporates Nos. 80
and 81. (No. 80 was built in 1730 by Richard
Cassels for Bishop Clayton of Killala.) Some
of the 18th cent. interior work has survived.
Cecil Young of London remodelled and extended the houses for the Guinness family in
the 1860's, but the principal apartments are

no better than might be expected of Young's
time. In the entrance hall may be seen John
Hogan's *Shepherd Boy* (1850). Nos. 82–87
formed the main buildings of the Catholic
University (the Medical School was in Cecilia
St, St Mary's House at No. 6 Harcourt St);
with the exception of No. 87, they now form
part of University College (*see* Earlsfort Terrace, Dublin, SE.). No. 82 had been the residence of Francis Higgins (1746–1802), the
"Sham Squire", editor of *The Freeman's
Journal*, British spy, and underworld boss; it
now houses the internationally celebrated Irish
Folklore Commission. No. 84 was rebuilt in
1878 as the Aula Maxima of the then University College; it has recently been remodelled
as a theatre and ballroom. No. 85, Clanwilliam
House, was built about 1740 by Richard
Cassels; the beautiful saloon has a splendid
coved ceiling with stucco figure-subjects and
arabesques by the Francini brothers. No. 86,
Newman House, is one of the finest of Dublin's
great houses. It was built, 1760–65, probably by
Robert West (*see* Dominick St, Dublin NW.),
for Richard Chapell ("Burn Chapel") Whaley,
execrated priest-hunter and father of the notorious rake, "Buck" Whaley. The interior has
notable stucco, probably by West. The lead lion
on the portico is by John Van Nost, Jr. Tradition ascribes the scale of Whaley's house to a
vulgar desire to outdo No. 85. In 1853 both
houses were purchased by Cardinal Cullen and
thrown together to form the headquarters and
St Patrick's House of the Catholic University
of Ireland, which opened its doors the following
year with John Henry Newman as first Rector

(1853–8; it was in preparation for this that Newman had delivered his celebrated *Discourses on the Scope and Nature of University Education* at the Rotunda, Parnell Sq., 1852.) After Newman's, the most distinguished names connected with the University were probably those of: Eugene O Curry (1796–1862), whom Newman appointed Professor of Archaeology and Irish History, thereby founding University College's fine tradition in Celtic Studies; Thomas William Allies (1813–1903), one of the most learned members of the Oxford Movement, Professor of Modern History; John Hungerford Pollen (1820–1902), member of the Oxford Movement, Professor of Fine Arts; Denis Florence McCarthy (1817–82), poet and translator of Calderon, Professor of English Literature; John Casey (1820–91), Professor of Mathematics; Henry Hennessey (1826–1901), Professor of Physics; and George Sigerson (1838–1925), physician, scientist, poet, and historian, Lecturer in Botany. Failing to secure British recognition, the schools of the University – other than the Medical School – declined. The Faculties of Arts and Science were therefore transformed into University College in 1881 in order to prepare students for the degrees of the non-teaching Royal University of Ireland (1882–1909). The following year the college was entrusted to the Jesuits. This Jesuit college, seated in Nos. 84–6, was the University College where Gerard Manley Hopkins (1844–89) was professor, and Patrick H. Pearse (1879–1916), Eamonn de Valera (b. 1882), Thomas M. Kettle (1880–1916), and James Joyce (1882–1941) were students. (In the students' magazine, *St Stephen's*, Joyce's first writing appeared; references in the magazine to "the Hatter" are to Joyce.) In 1909 the college was reunited with the medical school and transformed into a college of the new, undenominational, National University of Ireland. In due course the lecture halls and library were transferred to Earlsfort Terrace, and Nos. 85 and 86 now provide clubrooms and society rooms for the students. In these are hung some interesting portraits and pictures. Adjoining No. 86 is the neo-Byzantine University Church (1855–6) by John Hungerford Pollen. It was erected by Newman as chapel and place of ceremonial assembly of the Catholic University, but now serves parochial purposes. In the nave is a bust of Newman by Farrell. The nearby Wesleyan Centenary Church (1843) is by Isaac Farrell.

West Side: The Unitarian Church has windows by Ethel Rhind (two-light *Good Samaritan*, 1937) and A. E. Child (five-light *Discovery, Truth, Inspiration, Love, Work*; 1918). Nos. 119 and 120 were formally designed as a pair in 1761; the elevation is said to be after Cassels. The Royal College of Surgeons at the corner of York St was built in 1806 to the design of Edward Parke. In 1827 it was extended N., and recentred, by William Murray, losing in the process. Interiors by both architects survive. The statues of *Aesculapius, Minerva* and *Hygieia*

are by John Smyth, eldest son and collaborator of the great Edward Smyth. In 1916 the college was the headquarters of a contingent of the Citizen Army under the command of Michael Mallin and the Countess Markievicz (Constance Gore-Booth). Nos. 124–5 (then one house) were the home of Dr Robert Emmet, whose patriot sons, Robert and Thomas, were born there.

St Stephen's Green Park owes its beauty to the munificence of Sir Arthur Guinness (Lord Ardilaun), at whose expense it was laid out in 1880. In 1916 it was occupied for a time by Michael Mallin's contingent of the Citizen Army. The triumphal arch at the NW. corner is a Boer War memorial to the Dublin Fusiliers. Close by is a memorial, by Séamus Murphy, to Jeremiah O Donovan Rossa (1831–1915), the Fenian leader. Other monuments in the park are: a statue of Lord Ardilaun by John Henry Foley; a *Three Fates* fountain by Josef Wackerle, gift of the German people in thanksgiving for Ireland's share in relieving distress after the Second World War; excellent busts of James Clarence Mangan (1803–49), poet, by Oliver Sheppard; Thomas M. Kettle (1880–1916), patriot and orator, by Francis Doyle; and the Countess Markievicz (*see* Lisadell *under* Raghly), by Séamus Murphy.

Harcourt St (1778) leads from the SW. corner of St Stephen's Green to the S. Circular Rd. This once fashionable residential street is now given over almost entirely to hotels and commerce. Thanks to its pleasant curve and the scale of its houses, it is still one of the best of Dublin's great Georgian streets, the efforts of insurance companies and other philistines notwithstanding. No. 4 was the birthplace of Edward Carson (Lord Carson, 1854–1935), organizer of Orange resistance to Home Rule. No. 6 was in its time St Mary's House of the Catholic University (Newman resided there with some of the students). At a later date it was the headquarters of the Sinn Féin Bank, where Michael Collins conducted the Department of Finance of the proscribed first Dáil Éireann (1919). No. 9 is a Michael Stapleton house. No. 14 was the home of Sir Jonah Barrington, rascally patriot and author of *Historic Anecdotes and Secret Memoirs of the Union*. No. 17 was the central block of Clonmell House, built (? by Stapleton) about 1777–8 for "Copperfaced Jack" Scott, Earl of Clonmell, who amassed a fortune by swindling Catholics out of lands held in trust. The house has lost its low side wings, but still retains some good ceilings and other features. In 1830 it was divided into two parts, the larger of which later served as Sir Hugh Lane's Municipal Gallery of Modern Art. No. 76 was the headquarters of Dáil Éireann's loan organization, 1919–20, with a secret hideout for documents and a way of escape over the roofs for Michael Collins. No. 40, best preserved of Harcourt Street's fine houses, is now the High School for

Protestant boys, endowed from a trust established by Erasmus Smith (1611–91), who had acquired great Irish estates at the Cromwellian confiscations. W. B. Yeats went to school here. At the S. end of the street is Harcourt St Station (1859) by George Wilkinson, an exceptionally good piece of early railway architecture.

Dublin South-West of the River Liffey and Westmoreland St–Grafton St–Harcourt St

Aungier St leads from South Great George's St to Redmond's Hill. No. 12 occupies the site of the house where Thomas Moore (1779–1852) was born. The Calced Carmelite priory occupies part of the site of the medieval Carmelite priory. The early-19th cent. church by George Papworth had one of the finest neo-Classical interiors in Dublin and a noble high altar. It has been replaced by a vast unworthy successor in which the only feature of note is the 15th cent, wooden statue of *Our Lady of Dublin*. Said to have come from St Mary's Abbey, this fine statue is displayed in a vulgar and utterly incongruous setting. Ugly St Peter's Church (1863–7) is by Lord Carson's father, who lived for a time in nearby York St; the opus sectile *Charity* is by Ethel Rhind (1928).

Back Lane runs from Cornmarket to Nicholas

St. The Earls of Kildare had a house (Kildare Hall) here in the 16th and 17th centuries. In 1628 the Jesuits opened a house in the Lane with the help of the Countess of Kildare. It had a school and chapel with "all things most fair and graceful like the Banqueting House at Whitehall". The school had a Faculty of Theology and Scripture. In 1630 Trinity College denounced it to the authorities with the complaint that "His Holiness [the Pope] hath erected a New University at Dublin to confront His Majesty's College there". The Jesuits were evicted, and the buildings annexed to Trinity under the name Kildare Hall. The derelict Tailors' Hall (1704–8; by Robert Mills?) is the sole survivor of Dublin's guild halls. Condemned to demolition by Dublin Corporation, it is being purchased for private restoration. In 1792 the hall was the meeting place of the "Back Lane Parliament", i.e. the Catholic Committee (p. 46), whose secretary at the time was none other than the Protestant "inventor" of Irish republicanism, Theobald Wolfe Tone. The original entrance seems to have been the central doorway in what is now a basement. The simple interior has a good wooden screen and staircase.

Bridge St runs from Cornmarket to Whitworth (alias Father Matthew) Bridge. Early in the

Shrine of Our Lady of Dublin, Calced Carmelite priory

reign of Charles I the Capuchins established a friary in Bridge St. It was closed, together with sixteen other "public houses of massing priests", in 1630 and made over to Trinity College as St Stephen's Hall. No. 9 was the house of Oliver Bond (1762–98), United Irishman. The Brazen Head Hotel, Dublin's oldest tavern (founded 1688), was a meeting place of the United Irishmen.

Castle St parallels Lord Edward St from Cork Hill to Christchurch Pl. Sir James Ware (1594–1666), noted Anglo-Irish antiquary, lived and died in Castle St. An Dubhaltach Mac Firbhisigh, last of an illustrious line of hereditary Gaelic scholars (*see* Lacken *under* Inishcrone), worked for a time in his house. Castle St was the birthplace of Thomas Doggett (d. 1721), the actor who became joint manager of Drury Lane Theatre, London, and initiated the annual "coat and badge" race of the Thames Watermen. At the E. end of the street are the Municipal Buildings, originally Newcomen's Bank. The oldest part, by Thomas Ivory, contains an elliptical room with fine painted ceiling. In 1856–8 the building was doubled in size by duplication of the E. elevation. The porched entrance was added at the same time. On the opposite side of the street are the remains of the ground floor of La Touche's Bank, built before 1735; a lovely stucco ceiling which graced the principal room has been re-erected in the Bank of Ireland. A dingy passage through Bristol Buildings is the present entrance to St Werburgh's Church, Werburgh St (open weekdays, 10 a.m.–4 p.m.). In its day one of the most attractive of Dublin's Protestant churches, this unfortunate building was erected in 1715, to the design of Thomas Burgh, on the site of the medieval successor to pre-Norman St Werburgh's. In 1754 Burgh's church was destroyed by fire. Restored, probably by John Smith (Smyth), it was reopened in 1759. Nine years later a graceful tower and spire of 160 ft, probably also by Smith, were added to the two-storey, gabled W. front. Spire and tower were taken down (1810 and 1836) at the instance of fearful Dublin Castle authorities. Since then the facade has been further mutilated by the removal of its pilastered and pedimented upper storey. The interior was restored in the early 1960s. As the parish church of the castle, St Werburgh's served as Chapel Royal down to 1790. Hence the Lord Lieutenant's pew in the gallery, with Royal Arms inserted by Smith in 1767 when adding the upper, school-children's, gallery and the organ case. The curious, but attractive, wooden pulpit was carved for the Chapel Royal of the castle by Richard Stewart to the designs of Francis Johnston. In the porch is preserved a 16th cent. Fitzgerald tomb with effigies of an armoured knight and his lady and niched figures of the *Twelve Apostles*, etc. It is said to have been removed at the Dissolution from All Hallows Augustinian Priory to the now vanished church of St Mary le Dam, and thence to St Werburgh's. In the church vaults are buried Sir James Ware and Lord Edward Fitzgerald; (p. 46); in the churchyard, Lord Edward's captor, Town Major Sirr.

Christchurch Pl., formerly Skinners Row, at the intersection of Lord Edward St., High St, Nicholas St and Winetavern St, was the heart of the Norse and medieval cities. It is dominated by Christchurch Cathedral, cathedral church of the Protestant archdiocese of Dublin and Glendalough. The first cathedral (aisled) here was built about 1038 by Sigtryggr Silkbeard, king of Norse Dublin, for Dublinshire's first bishop, the Irishman, Dunan. The second bishop, Giolla-Pádraig ("Patrick"; 1074–89), also an Irishman, seems to have introduced Benedictines from Winchcombe and Worcester as a monastic chapter. The fourth bishop, Samuel O Hanly (1095–1121), dissolved the monastic chapter. In 1152 the diocese was raised to metropolitan rank, and the fifth bishop, Grene ("Gregory"; 1121–62), Dublin's only Norse bishop, became first archbishop. In 1163/4 his successor, St Lorcán ("Laurence") O Toole (1162–80), re-introduced a monastic chapter, this time Augustinian canons of the Congregation of Arrouaise. About 1173, shortly after the Anglo-Norman conquest of the city, Dunan's cathedral was swept away and the crypt, choir, and transepts of a new, greater, church begun, in accordance with an agreement between St Lorcán and Strongbow, Robert FitzStephen, and Raymond le Gros. An aisled five-bay nave was begun about 1212, and lengthened westwards by an additional bay about 1234. About the same period a new priory for the cathedral canons was erected on the S. side of the church. The timber belfry of the cathedral was blown down in 1316, and replaced by one of stone in 1330. In the second half of the 14th cent. the choir was extended E. so as almost to equal the nave in length. At the same time the Chapel of Great St Mary, on the N. side of the choir, was rebuilt. In 1539 the Augustinian priory was dissolved and replaced by a secular Dean and Chapter. On Easter Sunday, 1551, the English Protestant liturgy was read for the first time. By 1588 the tower had become unsafe and was taken down. In 1562 the nave vaulting collapsed, bringing down the S. wall, which was only crudely replaced. Neglect and decay during the 17th and 18th centuries had reduced the church to a dangerous condition by 1829, when it had to be closed for repairs and alterations. These included the transference of the Norman door from the W. wall of the N. transept to its present position in the S. transept. Finally, between 1871 and 1878, the entire church was savagely "restored" by George Edmund Street, one of the best English Gothic Revivalists, at the expense of Henry Roe, a wealthy Dublin distiller. Street swept away the great 14th cent. choir and built a new E. arm on the plan of the

13th/14th cent. tomb effigies, Christchurch Cathedral

12th cent. crypt. He also pulled down the Chapel of Great St Mary (replacing it by the present Chapter House), rebuilt the tower, rebuilt the S. nave arcade, put in new vaulting, rebuilt the W. front to his own design, refaced most of the exterior, removed the N. porch, and added the flying buttresses and the baptistry. Street also built the adjacent Synod Hall (on the site of the parish church of St Michael and all Angels, whose much-altered 17th cent. bell-tower it incorporates) and linked it to the cathedral by the attractive covered footbridge spanning the roadway of St Michael's Hill. The great complex is, therefore, as it stands today, in large part a Gothic-Revival work. It has, none the less, real architectural merit, perhaps best appreciated from the nearby quays, whence it masses dramatically on the hill.

As the principal church of the old English colony in Ireland, intimately associated with the viceregal court and the civic life of Dublin, Christchurch was the scene of many stirring events. Down to the 16th cent. it was here that the Lord Deputies took the oath of office. It was here, too, that Lambert Simnel was crowned Edward VI of England, 24 May 1487, his crown a golden circlet from the statue of the Blessed Virgin Mary in St Mary's Abbey (*see* Carmelite priory, Aungier St, *above*). From 1177 onwards the principal treasure of the cathedral was Bachall Íosa, St Patrick's enshrined crozier captured from the Archbishop of Armagh by John de Courcy. In 1538 it was burned at the order of Henry VIII's archbishop, the Englishman, George Browne. In 1608 the semi-ruined priory buildings were turned into law-courts. In 1695 the first Four Courts were erected by Sir William Robertson on the St Michael's Hill side of the ruins; later dwelling houses and shops came to cover the rest of the site. These structures were all swept away in

1821 to open up the S. side of the cathedral to view for the first time in its history. In 1886 removal of the last of the debris on the site of the priory brought to light the remains of the beautiful 13th cent. Chapter House, sole relic of the Augustinian claustral buildings.

Of the surviving medieval portions of the cathedral, the most remarkable is the groin-vaulted crypt, the only one of its age (12th/13th cent.) in these islands to extend under an entire church. In it are mouldering the altar-tabernacle and candlesticks used when the cathedral was restored to Catholic use in the time of James II. Here too are many medieval mouldings, gravestones, etc.; likewise statues (1684), by William de Keyser, of Charles II and James II, which adorned the Tholsel, or City Council House and Exchange, erected nearby in 1676–82 and pulled down in 1806. (These are the oldest secular statues in Dublin.) Here, too, lie dismembered the monument of Lord Chancellor Bowes (d. 1767), and the monument to Nathaniel Sneyd (d. 1833) by Thomas Kirk, R.H.A. The most interesting features of the cathedral itself are the late-12th to early-13th century Transitional transepts (which retain their original choir-aisle arches and chapels), the W. arches of the choir, and the arcade capitals and upper parts of the N. nave wall. (For all its originality of detail, the nave was very much a West English building, the work of imported masons and carvers.) The monuments include: W. Wall of Nave: Sir Samuel Auchmuty (d. 1822) by Thomas Kirk, R.H.A.; S. Nave Arcade: the armoured tomb effigies of "Strongbow's Son" (late-13th cent.) and of "Strongbow" (1340); the former, a demi-figure, was doubtless a visceral monument, and may commemorate the burial of Strongbow's bowels in Dublin; the latter may have been brought from Drogheda in the 16th cent.;

Chapel of St Laud: medieval effigy; St Laurence O Toole Chapel: a slab with the effigy of a lady ("Strongbow's Wife"), found in the Chapter House, and a slab with the effigy of a 12th/13th cent. archbishop; S. Transept: very fine monument of Robert, 19th Earl of Kildare (1674–1743), by Henry Cheere (1703–81); a Renaissance mural monument with kneeling effigies of Francis Agard of Newcastle, Co. Wicklow, and his daughter, Lady Cecilie Harrington; SE. apsidal chapel: a medieval effigy; S. Porch: a 1751–6 Prior monument by John Van Nost, Jr.

Cork Hill is the short street linking Castle St with the junction of Dame St and Parliament St. It takes its name from the Earl of Cork's house, which stood beside Lucas's Coffee House on the site of the present City Hall.

The City Hall (1769–79) was erected as the Royal Exchange by Thomas Cooley (1740–84; of London ?), whose design was chosen in open competition with the architects of Great Britain and Ireland. (The rest of Cooley's life was spent in Dublin, the only place where work of his is known.) The principal feature of his Exchange was a noble, domed and colonnaded rotunda designed as the meeting place of Dublin's merchants. The ambulatory is now partitioned off as offices, and Cooley's conception further marred by the use of the rotunda as a gallery for monumental statuary. (In 1867 the doorcases of the porticoes were injudiciously remodelled. Later on the windows were spoiled by turning them into great plate-glass voids. The ponderous balustrade in front of the entrance steps is an 1814 replacement of the original iron railings.) All the ornamental carving in the building was done by Simon Vierpyl. The statues displayed in the rotunda include: an excellent baroque *Charles Lucas* by Edward Smyth, who, at the age of 23, was awarded the premium in competition with Vierpyl, his master; and John Van Nost; *Henry Grattan*, by Sir Francis Chantrey; *Daniel O Connell*, *Thomas Davis* and *Thomas Drummond* by John Hogan. In the Muniment Room are stored municipal archives going back to the 12th cent.; also the civic regalia. The latter include the Lord Mayor's great gold S-collar presented by William III.

Besides Cork House and Lucas's Coffee House, old Cork Hill was also the site of the Eagle Tavern, meeting place of the notorious Hell Fire Club founded in 1735 by the first Earl of Rosse and others. One of the members' exploits was to set fire to their place of carousal so as to savour the sensations of the damned! Behind the City Hall is Dublin Castle (*q.v.*).

Crampton Quay extends from Aston's Quay to Wellington Quay. Noonan's shirt factory, facing the Metal Bridge, was built by Frederick Darley in 1821 as the Merchant's Hall.

Crow St, between Dame St and Temple Bar, was famous in its day for the Theatre Royal of which "Buck" Jones (*see* Newman House, St Stephen's Green S. *under* Dublin, Main Axis) was a patentee. In 1822 an "Orange" audience pelted Lord Lieutenant the Marquess of Wellesley with whiskey bottles for banning the dressing-up of William III's statue on 12 July. Among the stars who appeared on the theatre's boards was Peg Woffington.

Dame St, Dublin's principal commercial and insurance street, runs from College Green to Cork Hill. The street was widened in 1785–6 by the Commissioners for Making Wide and Convenient Streets, the enlightened planning authority (1757–1840) to which Dublin owes so much. The best building in the street today is Edward Parke's Commercial Buildings (1796–9; windows mutilated). These occupy the site of the Old Rose and Bottle inn, and are intimately associated with one of the romantic episodes of Dublin's mercantile history. In 1695 the *Ouzel*, a merchantman belonging to the firm of Ferris, Twigg, and Cash, sailed for the Levant under the command of Captain Eoghan Massey. Remaining long overdue, she was given up for lost, and the underwriters paid the owners' claim in full. In 1700 she suddenly reappeared, more richly laden than when she had sailed away. She had been seized by Algerian pirates, but the captain and his Irish crew had eventually recovered her, and with her rich Algerian booty. The underwriters and shipowners fell out over the ownership of the spoil. Their dispute was eventually composed by the arbitration of a committee of merchants. The happy outcome gave such widespread satisfaction that the committee transformed itself, in 1705, into the Ouzel Galley Society, a convivial association for settling mercantile disputes. The officers of the society were captain, lieutenants, purser, boatswain (complete with silver whistle), gunner, carpenter, and so on; the ordinary members formed the crew. The "ship's company" met in various taverns, including the Rose and Bottle. New members had to drain a bumper of claret at a single draught from a bowl of Irish glass. When the Commercial Buildings were erected, the serious business of the society was conducted there, and the annual November meeting was held in the courtyard, where a carved panel of the *Ouzel* may still be seen. The Society was wound up in 1888, and today some of its functions are discharged by the Dublin Chamber of Commerce (founded 1783), which had its seat in the Buildings from 1799 to 1965. – The Munster and Leinster Bank, at the corner of Palace St., is by Sir Thomas Deane; enlarged some years ago.

Donore Ave. leads from the S. Circular Rd to Cork St. St Victor's Protestant Church has a three-light window (*Hope, St Catherine, St Victor*) by Michael Healy.

Drimnagh is an unprepossessing new suburb on the Dublin–Crumlin–Clondalkin road. Drimnagh Castle, now a house of the Irish Christian Brothers, was a stronghold of the Barnewalls, with whom it remained until 1606. During the 1641–52 war it was an outpost of Dublin, held in turn by the Royalists and the Parliamentarians. All that remains of the Barnewall castle are the modified 16th cent. gate-tower and some fragments incorporated in the later house; but its original extent is indicated by the moat enclosing an area 200 by 150 ft.

Dublin Castle is situated at the rear of the City Hall. It may be entered from Palace St (off the W. end of Dame St) or by way of the principal gate, at the junction of Cork Hill and Castle St. The period of its first building cannot be determined precisely, but lay between 1204 and 1268. Until 1922 it was the citadel of English authority in Ireland, the official residence of Lords Deputy and Lords Lieutenant, the seat of State Councils and, from time to time, of Parliament and the Law Courts. Very few English kings ever stayed in it; Richard II (probably) in 1384, 1394, and 1399; James II and William III (perhaps) in 1690; George V in 1911. Notable prisoners incarcerated in it were; Donal Mac Murrough, King of Leinster (1327–30); Dermot O Hurley, Archbishop of Cashel, barbarously tortured (1584) on the orders of the Protestant Archbishop of Dublin, Adam Loftus, and Sir Henry Wallop; Red Hugh II O Donnell and Art O Neill (1587–91); Richard Nugent, Lord Delvin (1607); Peter Talbot, Catholic Archbishop of Dublin (1678); Ernie O Malley, Dick McKee, Peader Clancy, and other guerrillas (1920; McKee, Clancy, and Conor Clune were murdered after torture). The castle was never called on to withstand a major siege or assault. In 1534 it was unsuccessfully besieged by Silken Thomas Fitzgerald. The plan of Rory O More and Conor Maguire to seize it, 23 Oct. 1641, was betrayed. A project to seize it by *coup de main* in 1916 was abandoned, when, as it happened, it was manned only by a corporal's guard.

The history of the structure is one of recurring decay, disaster, and reconstruction, culminating in the wholesale rebuilding of 1730–1800, which gave it in all essentials the form it has today, when but few indications of the medieval structure survive. The Upper Castle Yard coincides, more or less, with the layout of the medieval fortress. At the NW., NE., and SE. angles stood great drum towers. At the SW. angle the castle impinged on the town wall, and here the tower was rectangular. A little to the E. of this a fourth drum tower (Bermingham Tower) was added in the 14th cent. Midway between it and the SE. angle was a smaller, projecting tower. The twin-towered gateway stood at the centre of the N. curtain, between the present main gate and the Bedford Tower. The curtain, apart from a masked fragment on the S. side (and fragments of the E. and N. walls uncovered in 1961), was removed long ago. Of the towers only the SE.

tower (Record Tower) and fragments of the Bermingham Tower, of the NE. tower (uncovered 1961), and of the small S. curtain tower now survive. The SE. tower was "restored" by Francis Johnston; the others are hidden by 18th–19th cent. work.

The complacent, intimate, 18th cent. Castle is Dublin's last great building in brick. Edward Lovett Pearce, George Ensor, Joseph Jarratt, and perhaps Thomas Ivory, all appear to have had a hand in it. In its original form the main entrance to the state and viceregal apartments was an open, pillared hall, and the ground floor of the S. range was an open arcade. Hall and arcade were, unfortunately, blocked up in the 19th cent., and an ugly iron-and-glass awning prefixed to the entrance. In the same century the high roof with dormer windows was removed, so as to permit the addition of the attic storey all around the yard, so spoiling the elevations.

Since 1961 the E. range (completed 1800) and part of the S. range have been demolished and are being rebuilt with further modifications. Fortunately, the new work will restore the play of light and shade by reopening the arcades of the S. range.

The best architectural feature of the Upper Yard is the elevation of the N. side: two great, triumphal-arch gateways flanking the Office of Arms (now the Genealogical Office and Heraldic Museum) with its pillared Musicians' Gallery and charming Bedford Tower. The latter is raised on the remains of the W. tower of the medieval gateway. The lead statues crowning the gateways are the work of Van Nost. *Note*: the Heraldic Museum is open to the public, 9 a.m.–1 p.m. and 2.15–4.30 p.m., Monday to Friday; 10 a.m.–12.30 p.m. on Saturday.

The State Apartments in the S. range (closed during rebuilding) are normally open to the public, 10 a.m., 12 noon, 3 p.m. (admission 6d). They are approached from the main entrance by the Grand Staircase. A lobby to the left of the landing leads to St Patrick's Hall (1783), on the site of the aisled Great Hall begun in the reign of Henry III and later used as the parliament house. St Patrick's Hall was the State Ballroom and (after the disestablishment of the Church of Ireland, 1869) the place of investiture of the Knights of St Patrick. It is now the place of inauguration of the Presidents of the Republic. (It was here that President John Fitzgerald Kennedy of the United States received the Freedom of Dublin and honorary doctorates of the National University and of Dublin University, 1963.) At one end is a Musicians' Gallery, at the other a gallery for spectators. The paintings at either end of the ceiling depict St Patrick lighting his first Paschal Fire and Henry II receiving the submission of the Irish kings. The centre-piece is an allegory of George III (with Liberty and Justice!). All are the work of Vincent Waldré of Vicenza, who rebuilt the House of Commons in College Green. (The paintings were restored in 1957 by Alastair

Stewart.) On the walls are displayed the banners and armorial achievements of the Knights of St Patrick. A curving passage leads to the circular Supper Room in the Bermingham Tower; a doorway in the N. wall leads to the panelled State Drawing Room, alias the Picture Gallery, and the ornate Presence Chamber, or Throne Room. These rooms, in their present form, represent a remodelling by Francis Johnston. (The central part of the Drawing Room was originally the State Dining Room.) The oval painted panels in the Presence Chamber are by an unknown (Venetian ?) painter. The 18th cent. Presence Chamber, in the E. wing, a finer apartment than Johnston's, was turned into a drawing room *en suite* in the last cent. In 1941 it was destroyed by fire, and is now (1966) being rebuilt. The Apollo Room from Tracton House (St Stephen's Green) and the *Hibernia* and *Arts and Sciences* ceilings from Mespil House (Mespil Rd) are to be re-erected in this wing.

An archway (widened, 1962) in the middle of the E. range leads to the Lower Castle Yard. Here is the great Record Tower (now the State Paper Office), refaced and re-battlemented by Francis Johnston (1811–19). At its foot is the Chapel Royal (1807–14), an interesting example of Johnston's work in the Gothick manner. All the exterior carvings are by Edward Smyth and his son, John, who also did all the interior stucco, apart from George Stapleton's ceiling. The woodcarving is by Richard Stewart. (His pulpit is now in St Werburgh's; *see* Castle St.) The coats of arms along the galleries and in the gallery windows are those of the successive representatives of the English Crown. The last available space took those of the last Lord Lieutenant, Lord Fitz-Alan (1922). The E. window contains some old Continental glass depicting scenes from the Passion. In 1943 the chapel was re-consecrated as a Catholic church dedicated to the Most Holy Trinity. (Open to visitors 9 a.m.–6 p.m. on weekdays; closed on Sundays except for 10 a.m. Mass.)

Essex Quay extends from Wellington Quay to Wood Quay. William Mossop (1751–1804), the celebrated medallist, whose designs were from the hand of Edward Smyth, lived here in 1784. St Michael's and St John's Church (1815; Thomas Betagh monument by Turnerelli), whose bell was the first Catholic church-bell to toll (1828) in Dublin after the Reformation, was until recently hidden away behind the tall houses fronting the quay. Strictly speaking, the church, a pseudo-Gothic effort of J. Taylor's, stands in Lower Exchange St, formerly Smock Alley. It occupies the site of the celebrated Smock Alley Theatre (1662–1815), successor to the Werburgh St theatre of 1637–41, which had been closed by the Puritans. Among the famous names associated with the theatre are those of George Farquhar (1678–1707, author of *The Beaux' Stratagem*), Thomas

Doggett (d. 1721; *see* Castle St *above*), Peg Woffington (1716–60), Charles Macklin (1697–1797), and Henry Mossop (1729–74), father of William Mossop. Farquhar's departure for London was due to the accidental wounding of a fellow actor.

Eustace St runs from Dame St to Wellington Quay. Brindley's Printing Works preserves the very English façade of Dublin's earliest Presbyterian meeting-house (1717).

Fishamble St runs from Christchurch Pl. to the junction of Essex and Wood Quays. Henry Grattan was born here in 1746. James Clarence Mangan was born in a house which stood on the site of Archbishop Ussher's 17th cent. house. Kennan's Ironworks incorporates the entrance of the Charitable Musical Society's Music Hall, erected to the design of Richard Cassels in 1741. This was for a long time Dublin's largest public hall, and was used for lectures, balls, and public debates as well as for concerts. Handel conducted the first performance of *Messiah* there, 13 April 1742. He also conducted *Acis and Galatea* there. In 1748 his *Judas Maccabaeus* was given its first performance there.

Francis St leads from Cornmarket to the Coombe and Dean St. It takes its name from the medieval Franciscan friary, the site of which is occupied in part by the Church of St Nicholas of Myra (1829; portico and tower, 1860). The architect, John Leeson, intended this Classical church to have a short spire, but substituted a dome for it in response to the criticism of the purists. The cost of the church was largely defrayed by the parish priest, Fr Flanagan, an amateur sculptor, some of whose work may be seen there. Fr Flanagan also commissioned the fine plaster *Pietá*, by John Hogan, which fills the reredos of the high altar. Hogan also did the two kneeling angels which flank the altar. Their wings are said to have been added by a later parish priest!

Harold's Cross, once a rural village with some pleasant houses, is now a built-up suburb to the S. of the Grand Canal, between Rathmines and Kimmage. Mount Jerome Cemetery includes Dublin's largest Protestant burial ground, in which are buried Thomas Davis (1814–45), Young Ireland leader; Thomas Kirk (1777–1845), sculptor; George Petrie (1789–1866), antiquary, painter, and collector of Irish folk-music; and Edmund Dowden (1843–1913), poet and literary critic. The O Shaughnessy memorial has a *Resurrection* panel (1915) by Michael Healy. The cemetery office was the house of John Keogh (1740–1817), sometime leader of the Catholic Committee founded in 1756 to strive for amelioration of the Penal Laws. No. 142 Harold's Cross Road, a small, late-Victorian house, was for many years the home of John Butler Yeats (1839–1922), painter

National Gallery of Ireland, Dublin
Portrait of George Moore by John Butler Yeats

and father of the gifted brothers, William Butler Yeats the poet, and Jack Butler Yeats, the painter.

High St, between Christchurch Pl. and Cornmarket, was the principal street of medieval Dublin, and here stood two of the Norse town's parish churches. St Michael's Church is represented by the bell tower incorporated in the Synod Hall, Christchurch Pl. (*q.v.*), St Columcille's by its medieval successor, St Audoen's. (The change in dedication from an Irish to a foreign saint was due to Henry II's "men of Bristol".) The tower of St Audoen's (probably 1670; restored 1826 and later) has the three oldest (1423) bells in Ireland. In the porch are: a pre-Norman gravestone, relic of St Columcille's Church; the double-effigy mensa of a tomb-cenotaph commemorating Roland Fitz-Eustace (Lord Portlester; d. 1496) and his wife, Margaret Jennico (*see* New Abbey *under* Kilcullen, Co. Kildare); a very weathered tomb effigy; a good, medieval tomb slab callously used as a paving stone; and some medieval floor-tiles (set in the window ledges). The nave, tastelessly re-pointed, serves as the Protestant parish church: the Transitional doorway is about 1190; the four W. bays of the blocked-up arcade are late-13th cent., the fifth bay later; the font is medieval; in the N. wall are two Renaissance monuments (originally polychrome ?) with kneeling effigies. The 14th cent. chancel and the S. nave aisle (widened in 1431 as St Anne's Chapel), together with its E. chapel (Chapel of the Blessed Virgin Mary, alias Portlester Chapel), are roofless ruins (Nat. Mon.). The Chapel of the Blessed Virgin, where stood the FitzEustace (Portlester) cenotaph, was erected about 1455 by Roland FitzEustace. Like St Anne's Chapel, it served one of the

guilds (*below*) which held their Halls in the tower (vanished) of nearby St Audoen's Arch. Close to the N. side of the church is a fragment of the medieval town wall, including St Audoen's Arch (1240; upper part 19th cent.), sole survivor of the town gates (it gave access to a Liffey strand). Here the guilds of the Butchers (Virgin Mary), Bakers (St Anne's), Smiths (St Loy's), Bricklayers (St Bartholomew's), and Feltmakers at one time held their Halls.

St Audoen's Catholic Church, High St, one of the last of Dublin's Classical churches, was erected 1841–7, to the design of Patrick Byrne. The great Famine prevented the completion of the work in the architect's lifetime, and the inferior portico (1898) is by Ashlin and W. H. Byrne. The masterly interior lost the dome over the crossing in 1884. The statue of the *Madonna and Child* is by John Hogan's Italian friend, Benzoni.

James's St, leading from Thomas St to Mount Brown and Kilmainham, was the start of the ancient highway to the West. The site of St James's Gate is incorporated in the world-famous Guinness Brewery, successor of Rainford's Brewery purchased by Arthur Guinness in 1759. The vast complex includes some pleasant late-18th and early-19th cent. features, as well as imposing examples of 19th–20th cent. industrial architecture. There are conducted tours of the brewery. St James's Church is an example of Patrick Byrne's Gothic; decent interior. The Protestant church (also St James's; usually closed), on the opposite side of the street, has a two-light window (*Truth, Justice*) by Michael Healy (1916). No. 174 was the birthplace of William Thomas Cosgrave, Arthur Griffith's successor as President of the Executive Council of the Irish Free State (1922–32). – In Bow Lane, which runs from the junction of James's St and Steevens Lane to Kilmainham Lane, is St Patrick's Hospital, better known as Swift's Hospital. It was founded by Dean Swift:

> "He gave the little wealth he had
> To build a house for fools and mad;
> To show by one satiric touch,
> No nation wanted it so much."

Dr Robert Emmet, father of the patriot, was visiting State physician from 1770 to 1803. – The attractive building was erected 1749–57 to the design of George Semple, and enlarged in 1778 by Thomas Cooley, who added the low side wings and extended the rear wings. (The windows and one of Cooley's wings have since been spoiled.) The hospital, an up-to-date psychiatric centre, has an interesting collection of Swiftiana and other 18th cent. relics, including benches from the College Green House of Commons.

Kilmainham, an urban district at the W. end of the S. Circular Rd, between James's St and Inchicore, takes its name from the ancient church, Cell Maighnenn. "Strongbow" founded a priory and hospital of the Knights of St John of Jerusalem here before 1176. It survived until the Reformation. In the 17th cent. the priory lands on both sides of the Liffey were turned into a royal deer park, later the Phoenix Park (*q.v.*). In 1679 a portion of the park to the S. of the river, including the site of the priory, was assigned to a Royal Hospital for old and disabled soldiers. The hospital (entrances from the S. Circular Rd and Military Rd) was erected between 1680 and 1687 to the design of Sir William Robinson, Surveyor-General of Ireland, but the fine tower and spire (136 ft) were only built – "as it was first intended" – in 1701. The site chosen was an admirable one, commanding the spaces of the Phoenix Park. The hospital, not unworthy of it, was laid out on a courtyard-and-piazza plan with open, ground-floor loggia on three sides and on parts of the fourth. The doorways at the centre of each range have excellent tympana of carved wood, now smothered in paint. Over the main door are the arms of the 1st Duke of Ormonde, in whose Lord Lieutanancy the building was erected. In the N. range are, from W. to E., the Master's Lodging, the Great Hall with grand portico and tower, and the Chapel. In front of the chapel door is a pair of beautiful wrought-iron gates (arms of Queen Anne). The chapel ceiling is a papier-mâché facsimile (1902) of the excellent stucco original. The very fine wood-carving at the corners of the sanctuary is the work of James Tabary, a Huguenot craftsman. The canopied pew in the gallery was that of the Master, who was always the British Commander-in-Chief in Ireland. The great E. window (sill lowered in 1850) is alleged to contain tracery and glass from the medieval priory. The wooden tracery of the other large windows is a 19th cent. replacement of the original Classical work. (It should be noted that, in their original state, the external wall-faces of the hospital were of uncoursed limestone. The drab plaster coating is 19th cent. work, as is

also, of course, the blocking of the loggia on the N. side of the courtyard.) The former Deputy Adjutant-General's house, at the E. end of the terrace, dates from 1800. The former Adjutant-General's Office (1808) is by Francis Johnston. The Hospital survived the establishment of the Irish Free State by only five years. Subsequently the buildings served as headquarters of the Civic Guard. In 1949 they were vacated as unsafe, and are still (1966) being restored and adapted for use as a Folk Museum. The castle-like gate-tower on the S. Circular Rd is also by Johnston; it originally stood on the Liffey quay at Bloody Bridge. Nearby, on the N. side of the avenue, is an ancient graveyard with a weathered High Cross (Nat. Mon.), sole relic of Cell Maighnenn.

At the junction of the S. Circular Rd and Inchicore Rd is Kilmainham Courthouse, said to be by George Papworth. Derelict Kilmainham Gaol (1800, architect unknown), now being restored as a memorial, figured prominently in 18th–20th cent. history; open Suns., 3–5 p.m. Among the patriots held here at one time or another were: Henry Joy Mac Cracken (1797; *see* Belfast); Sam Neilson (1798; *see* Rathfryland); Robert Emmet (1803); Thomas Russell (1803); William Smith O Brien, whose son was baptised in the prison chapel (1848); John O Leary, Fenian (1865); Charles Stewart Parnell (1881); twenty-six Invincibles (1883); Patrick Pearse and other 1916 men. A short distance W., in Colbert Road, is the entrance to Islandbridge Park of Remembrance, memorial to the Irishmen who fell in the First World War. It was designed by Sir Edwin Lutyens. When clearing the site several Viking graves were found.

Kingsbridge Station, beside the Liffey at the junction of Victoria Quay and Steevens' Lane, was erected 1845–61 as terminus of the Cork and Limerick railways. It is a good "Renaissance palazzo" by Sancton Woods.

Merchant's Quay lies between Wood Quay and Usher's Quay. St Francis's Church (1834) was by Patrick Byrne, whose design was never completed. Of recent years the church has been enlarged and altered for the worse. The mural paintings are by Muriel Brandt. (The popular name of the church, "Adam and Eve's", recalls the fact that its Penal-times predecessor was hidden away in nearby Cook St behind a tavern with the sign *Adam and Eve*.) Bro. Michael O Clery, chief of the Four Masters, transcribed the Lives of SS Finian and Benignus in the Cook St convent. On St Stephen's Day, 1629, convent, school, and chapel were demolished, and the friars arrested, at the behest of the Protestant archbishop, Bulkeley. The friars repeatedly returned, to be as repeatedly arrested and dispersed. Today their church is noted for its large weekday congregations. The gilt bronze *Our Lady* (1955), on the Winetavern St corner of the convent, is by Gabriel Hayes.

Irish Tourist Board

Detail of entrance, Kilmainham Gaol

Parliament St runs from Grattan (formerly Essex) Bridge to Cork Hill. It was the first (1762) street opened by the Wide Streets Commissioners. James Clarence Mangan (1803–49), gifted lyric poet, lived at No. 3.

Patrick St connects the junction of New St, Upper Kevin St, and Dean St, with Nicholas St, and so with Christchurch Pl. Here, in the valley of the little River Poddle (now covered over), was one of the early suburbs outside the walled town, a suburb with its own pre-Norman parish church. From the Middle Ages until 1860 much of the district was the Archbishop's Liberty. By the close of the 19th cent. it had become one of Dublin's worst slums. Most of the decayed tenements were cleared away by the first Earl of Iveagh, who replaced them by sanitary, if barrack-like, blocks of flats, etc., and St Patrick's Park. On the S. side of the park is:

St Patrick's Cathedral is the largest church (300 ft long) ever built in Ireland. It occupies the site of the pre-Norman parish church of St Patrick, a site which legend would associate with the saint himself. In 1191 the church was rebuilt as a collegiate church by Archbishop Comyn. Comyn's successor, Henry de Londres, having quarrelled with the dean and chapter of Christchurch, advanced St Patrick's to cathedral status in 1213, his choice being guided by the fact that St Patrick's stood outside the city in the Archbishop's Liberty, and was therefore in his exclusive jurisdiction. The rivalry between the new and the old cathedrals was ended in 1300 by a papal decree recognizing the precedence of Christchurch. At the Reformation Christchurch wholly ousted its rival, and St Patrick's was reduced to the status of a parish church; but the short-lived Catholic restoration under Philip and Mary gave it back its cathedral status.

In 1320 Archbishop Alexander de Bykenore instituted the University of Dublin at St Patrick's, a papal charter having been obtained in 1312. The university languished from the start for lack of endowment, and finally petered out somewhere after 1494. In 1568 Parliament made an abortive effort to revive it. In 1584 Lord Deputy Perrot proposed to abolish the cathedral, convert the fabric into law courts, and devote the cathedral revenues to the foundation of "two universities with a couple of colleges". He was thwarted by Archbishop Loftus, a few years later one of the sponsors of Trinity College. And so the cathedral survived, retaining its diocesan status until the disestablishment of the Church of Ireland in 1869, when it was set apart as "national cathedral" of that Church. The immortal Jonathan Swift was Dean of the cathedral chapter, 1713–45.

The cruciform church has aisled nave (eight-bay), transepts, and choir (four-bay), and a four-bay, square-ended, eastern Lady Chapel recalling that of Salisbury. It is thought that the westernmost bay of the S. aisle, now the baptistry, is a relic of Comyn's collegiate church; but the rest of the building derives from the 13th–14th cent. cathedral. The Lady Chapel was built in 1270. In 1315 the spire was blown down, and the following year the church was damaged by fire on the occasion of Edward Bruce's threat to the city. In 1362 another fire damaged the NW. part of the nave, so that Archbishop Minot had to rebuild the four W. bays of the N. aisle. About the same time he built the great NW. tower (147 ft), curiously out of alignment with the church. In 1544 the piers and vaulting of the nave collapsed; at the rebuilding the piers were replaced by granite shafts. In 1749–50 the 100-ft granite spire (architect, George Semple) was added to Minot's tower. (Swift had prevented the erection of a brick one in 1714.) In the 17th, 18th, and early 19th centuries the fabric suffered severely from neglect and abuse, so that the N. transept and Lady Chapel became altogether ruined. The latter was rebuilt 1845–50 (architect, Richard Carpenter). A general restoration of the cathedral was undertaken in 1864–9 (architect, Sir Thomas Drew), the cost being borne by Sir Benjamin Lee Guinness. Drew found it necessary to rebuild much of the structure from the ground up. Most of the exterior facing is his work, as are also the piers of the nave arcade, and all the vaulting (stone only over the choir). The N. and S. porches, the W. door and window, and the nave buttresses are altogether new features. In 1901 the organ chamber was added by Drew, Lord Iveagh defraying the cost.

The usual entrance is by the S. porch. Nearby is a statue of Sir Benjamin Lee Guinness by John Henry Foley (1818–74).

The Choir is the best preserved part of the medieval fabric. It served as the chapel of the now moribund Order of St Patrick, which was instituted in 1783 by George III. The knights' banners hang above the stalls. After the disestablishment of the Church of Ireland the installation ceremony was transferred to Dublin Castle.

The principal monuments, etc., of the cathedral are as follows.

South aisle: at the foot of the second pier are the graves of Jonathan Swift (1667–1745) and his "Stella" (Esther Johnson, 1681–1728). The nearby door of the robing-room is flanked by Swift's monument to "Stella" and Patrick Cunningham's bust (1775) of Swift, the latter the gift of Swift's publisher. The immortal epitaph above the door was composed by Swift himself.

South transept: this transept was walled off for centuries to serve as the chapter-house. (The old chapter-house door with a hole cut through it recalls an armed quarrel in 1492 between the Earls of Kildare and Ormond. The latter took refuge in the chapter-house. When the quarrel was patched up the hole was cut in the door so that Ormond might safely shake hands with Kildare.) On a bracket stands a medieval statue of St Patrick. In the SW. corner is the tomb of Swift's servant, McGee. The adjacent monument to Lady Doneraile is by Simon Vierpyl.

South choir aisle: in the wall are interesting brasses in memory of Dean Sutton (d. 1528), Dean Fyche (d. 1537), Sir Edward Fitton (d. 1579), and Sir Henry Wallop (d. 1608); the Fyche brass has silver inlay. In a small recess is the tomb effigy of an unidentified archbishop. St Stephen's Chapel: by the S. wall is the tomb of Archbishop Tregury (d. 1471).

North choir aisle: here are the mutilated effigy of an archbishop, and the tablet with which Swift marked the grave of the Duke of Schomberg (1615–90), William III's general, who fell at the Boyne.

North transept: for much of the 18th cent. this transept was partitioned off to serve as parish church of St Nicholas Without [the Walls]. It has been rebuilt twice since 1830. In the NW. corner may be seen Swift's simple wooden pulpit.

North aisle: the monuments here include: the Renaissance monument of Archbishop Thomas Jones (d. 1619), with effigies of the prelate and his son, Lord Ranelagh; a statue (intended for O Connell St) of the Marquess of Buckingham by Edward Smyth (1788); a bust of John Philpot Curran (1750–1817); Lady Morgan's memorial to Turloch O Carolan (1670–1738), celebrated harpist and writer of Gaelic songs; and a memorial to Samuel Lover (1797–1868), novelist (*Handy Andy*, etc.). The Boardman tablet by John Smyth makes use of an allegory of Charity designed by his father, Edward Smyth, for William Mossop, the noted medallist. In the NW. corner may be seen a pre-Norman gravestone, relic of the ancient church of St Patrick. It was found at the site of St Patrick's Well, close to Minot's tower.

Nave: built against the westernmost bay of the S. arcade is that "very famous, sumptuous, glorious tombe" (by Edward Tingham of Chapelizod) which was erected in the choir by Richard Boyle, "Great" Earl of Cork (1566–1643), to the memory of his wife. Its removal in 1633 by Lord Deputy Strafford to its present, more appropriate, position fomented a feud which contributed to Strafford's downfall and execution in 1641.

SE. of the cathedral, in Guinness St (cut through the Deanery grounds at the 1864–9 restoration), is Marsh's Library, oldest public library in Ireland. It was founded by Archbishop Narcissus Marsh, and the building was begun about 1702 by Sir William Robinson. The exterior was refaced and altered in details at the Guinness restoration, but Robinson's altogether charming interior happily survives. The library has an interesting collection of MSS. and early printed books. (Hours of admission: Thur., 11 a.m.–12.30 p.m.; 3 p.m.–4.30 p.m.; Sat., 11 a.m.–1 p.m.; other weekdays, 11 a.m.–1.30 p.m.; 3 p.m.–4.30 p.m.; closed during July.)

Adjoining the library on the SE. (entrance Upper Kevin St) is a police station which incorporates fragments (vault, window, etc.) of the medieval archiepiscopal palace of St Sepulchre and its 16th and 17th cent. successors. St Patrick's Deanery (entrance now from Upper Kevin St) is the 1781 successor of Swift's Deanery. It has a fine staircase hall, some woodcarving by John Houghton, and a few relics of Swift.

Rathfarnham: *see* p. 410.

Rathmines is a 19th cent. suburb to the S. of the Grand Canal. In 1649 the Parliamentarian garrison of Dublin decisively routed Ormonde's besieging Royalist army here.

Portobello Barracks chapel (most convenient entrance by the Canal gate) has a three-light window (*Good Shepherd, St Patrick, St Joseph*) by Evie Hone (1937).

The Church of Our Lady of Refuge (1850), Rathmines Rd, was by Patrick Byrne. It was destroyed by fire in 1921, since when the original saucer-dome and good interior have been succeeded by the present inferior works. The Protestant parish church, Belgrave Rd, is by John Semple (1833). It originally had a vault similar to that of the "Black Church", Mary Pl. (Dublin, NW.). It has an early (1909) Michael Healy, four-light window (*SS Philip, Peter, Paul, Andrew*).

St Andrew St leads off Suffolk St. St Andrew's Protestant Church, a good Gothic-Revival essay by Lanyon, Lynn, and Lanyon, is the successor of one (1793–1807) by John Hartwell, completed by Francis Johnston, which had over the entrance a statue of St Andrew by the great Edward Smyth. This the gentlemen of Daly's Club, College Green, found an admirable target for pistol practice. Badly corroded, it stands in the churchyard.

Michael Collins had an office in No. 3, 1920–21. It had a specially contrived hiding place for Dáil Éireann's gold.

Steevens Lane, which runs from the junction of Bow Lane and James's St to Kingsbridge, takes its name from Dr Richard Steevens (d. 1710), son of a Cromwellian immigrant. Steevens left his large estate in trust for his sister Grizel (1654–1747), better known as Madam Steevens, and for the founding of a general hospital after her death. Madam Steevens decided to found the hospital in her own lifetime. Plans were drawn up by Thomas Burgh as early as 1713, but the building was not commenced until about 1720, and was not opened until 1733. Nevertheless, it is the oldest public hospital in Ireland, and one of the oldest in the British Isles. The simple building, whose completion was supervised after Burgh's death by Edward Lovett Pearce, has been called "the last kick of the seventeenth century" (Craig). Despite its dull modern paint, it is a quaint and rather charming building, reproducing on a smaller scale the plan of the Royal Hospital, and has some excellent wrought-iron. The clock tower is an addition of 1735–6. The semi-mansard roofs and the squinch arches at the angles of the courtyard are also additions. Burgh's chapel at the SE. corner was swept away in 1909. The hospital has a valuable library, bequeathed by Edward Worth (d. 1733), one of the early trustees; it is housed in the Board Room, which still retains its original fittings. Madam Steevens had her residence in the rooms on the left-hand side of the main doorway. She always wore a veil when visiting the sick poor. In this way originated the legend that she had the face of a pig, result of a beggarwoman's curse on her mother. Despite her hopeful habit of sitting unveiled at an open window, the legend persisted until the day of her death, and long after. Dean Swift was one of the early trustees of the hospital, and when he died the hospital gave the site for nearby Swift's Hospital (*see* James's St). – A short distance N. is Kingsbridge Station, (Dublin, SW.).

Suffolk St: *see* **St Andrew St.**

Synge St leads from Grantham St to Lennox St across Harrington St (South Circular Rd). George Bernard Shaw was born in No. 33 (then No. 3) in 1856.

Templeogue is a growing suburb on the Terenure (1½ m.)–Tallaght (2 m.) road. Spawell House, a curious building near the Dodder bridge, recalls a short-lived 18th cent. spa. Cypress Grove, opposite the bridge, was, after 1761, the home of the Countess of Clanbrassil, and later of the Earl of Roden. The gardens were then delightfully laid out. Charles Lever (1806–72), novelist, lived for a time in Templeogue House, early-19th cent. successor of a Queen Anne house belonging to the Domvilles. It incorporates fragments of a Talbot castle. In the 18th cent. the grounds were splendidly laid out and adorned, but in 1780 everything moveable, including a beautiful garden temple, was moved to the grounds of Santry Court (*see* Santry, Dublin, NE.). In 1950 the temple was removed to Luggela (*see under* Roundwood).

Terenure (formerly Roundtown), a village on the Harold's Cross–Rathfarnham road, has been engulfed by 19th–20th cent. suburbs. St Joseph's Church has one of Harry Clarke's best windows, *The Adoration of the Cross* (three light; 1920). Bushy Park was the home of the Shaws, the family of which George Bernard Shaw was a collateral. Terenure College (1860; Carmelite) incorporates Terenure House, originally seat of the Deane family. Fortfield Rd nearby recalls Fortfield, Barry Yelverton's country house (*c.* 1785; recently demolished). The Holy Ghost Missionary College, Whitehall Rd E., has a *St Columcille* window (chapel) by Hubert McGoldrick (1940) and an *Abstract Panel* (staircase) by Evie Hone (1937).

Thomas St, linking Cornmarket with James's St, takes its name from the abbey of St Thomas the Martyr (founded in 1177 by Henry II for Augustinian Canons of St Victor), which stood to the S. of the present St Catherine's Church. At the E. end of the street is the great Gothic-Revival Church of SS Augustine and John (1860–72), by Edward Welby Pugin and George C. Ashlin. (The vault is a timber sham.) It has a very fine four-light window (*St Augustine*) by Michael Healy (1934), set up opposite the position for which it was designed and further obscured by a wire screen; it is best viewed by bright morning light. The other art is hardly worthy of the building. Nearby John St and John's Lane preserve the memory of the Hospital of St John, first Irish house of Augustinian Cruciferi; it was founded, by Aildred the Palmer and his wife, outside the city's west gate (New Gate). No. 152 Thomas St is the successor of the house in which Lord Edward Fitzgerald was arrested, 18 May 1798. At the W. end of the street is St Catherine's Church (1760–69) by John Smyth. The tower never received its spire, but the façade is a good composition and the sadly decaying galleried interior (good chancel) is interesting. Robert Emmet was executed in front of the church in 1803.

Usher's Quay lies between Merchant's Quay and Usher's Island. No. 15, the home of his aunts, was the setting of James Joyce's short story *The Dead*. Queen's Bridge (1764–8), oldest and most beautiful of Dublin's bridges, is attributed to Gen. Vallancey, army engineer and crackpot antiquary.

Werburgh St runs from the junction of Castle St, Lord Edward St, and Christchurch Pl., to Bride St. (For St Werburgh's Church *see* Castle St.) Dublin's first theatre was opened in Werburgh St in 1636 by John Ogilby, Master of the Revels. The same year saw the production of the first Anglo-Irish play, James Shirley's *Saint Patrick for Ireland*. The theatre was closed by the Puritans in 1641. (At the Restoration Ogilby opened its successor in Smock Alley; *see* Essex Quay.)

William St connects St Andrew St with Johnston's Pl. (junction of Lower Mercer St and South King St).

Powerscourt House (1771–4), now Ferrier, Pollock, & Co., was built for Viscount Powerscourt by Robert Mack. In 1807 it was sold to the Commissioners of Stamp Duties, who filled the sides of the courtyard with brick buildings. In 1835 it was purchased by the present owners, who afford courteous facilities to the rare, interested visitor. The house is one of the most imposing of Dublin's private palaces (ground floor windows spoilt). The massive blind attic is said to have been intended for an observatory. The rather overwhelming façade, with its coarse details, offers a striking contrast to the delicately decorated interior. Hall and staircase

re by James McCullagh (the carving by Igna-
ius McDonagh); the reception rooms by Michel Stapleton.

No. 58, the Civic Museum, was built (1765–
'1) for the Society of Artists, the octagonal
oom being for the Society's exhibitions. From
791 to 1852 this room served as Municipal
Council Chamber, whence the former name,
City Assembly House. (In 1799 the Irish Bar
net here and voted against the proposed Union
of Ireland with Britain.) It was later the Court
of Conscience, presided over by the Lord
Mayor until 1924. From 1920 to 1922 the out-
awed Supreme Court of the Irish Republic held
ts sessions here. The collection of Dublin relics
s in the custody of the Old Dublin Society.

*Dublin South-East of the River Liffey and
Westmoreland St–Grafton St–Harcourt St*

Baggot St, Lower (1791), the ancient Baggot-
ath Lane, alias Gallows Lane, leads from
Merrion Row to Upper Baggot St and Mespil
Rd. It takes its name from the Baggots, remains
of whose castle of Baggotrath stood at the
orner of Herbert St until the last cent. The
reat Baggot estates and the castle passed to
he Fitzwilliams in the 15th cent. In 1649 the
astle was wrecked by the Parliamentarian
arrison of Dublin to prevent its use by the
esieging Royalists. On 2 Aug. of that year a
trong Royalist detachment was routed at the
astle in the opening phase of the Battle of
Rathmines. No. 67 Lower Baggot St was the
ome of Thomas Davis (1814–45), Young
Ireland leader; No. 128 the home of the patriot
rothers, John and Henry Sheares, executed in
798. The Bórd Fáilte–Córas Tráchtala offices
1962), at the bridge, are by Michael Scott and
Associates.

Ballsbridge, Dublin's diplomatic quarter and
ne of the city's finest suburbs, takes its name
rom the bridge spanning the Dodder on the
Dublin–Merrion road. Formerly the township
of Pembroke, the district is notable for its
xcellently planned streets and terraces of good
ouses. These date, for the most part, from
bout 1830 to 1860, but retain the spacious
ignity of the preceding age. The finest are
robably Ailesbury Rd, Lansdowne Rd, Mespil
Rd, Morehampton Rd, Pembroke Rd, Welling-
on Rd, and Upper Baggot St. On the W. side
of the main Merrion road are the show-grounds
nd the headquarters of the Royal Dublin
Society. The Society was founded in 1731 to
romote the application of practical economics.
ts first home was in Mecklenburgh St. In 1756
t moved to Shaw's Court; in 1766 to Grafton
t; in 1815 to Leinster House, Kildare St (*q.v.*).
ts more important activities today include the
ublication of Scientific Proceedings, a world-
amous Horse Show (Aug.), a Spring Show
agricultural and industrial; May), and a
inter series of chamber music recitals. On
he opposite side of the street is the head-

quarters of the Hospitals Trust, organizers
of a well-known series of great sweepstakes.
Nearby, in Pembroke Rd, is the Veterinary
College of Ireland, shared by the University
College and Trinity College Faculties of
Veterinary Science. At the junction of Merrion
Rd and Simmonscourt Rd is the Masonic
Girls' School. There is a Patrick Pollen window
here, *The Good Shepherd* (1957). In Lansdowne
Rd are the Botanic Gardens of Trinity College;
also the headquarters stadium of the Irish
Rugby Football Union, venue for international
and other major matches.

The Intercontinéntal Hotel (1963), at the
corner of Lansdowne Rd and Pembroke Rd,
is by the American architect, William B.
Tabler.

The American Embassy (1963–4), at the
junction of Pembroke Rd, and Clyde Rd, is by
the American architect, John McL. Johansen.

St Bartholomew's Church, Clyde Rd, has a
Catherine O Brien window, *Emmaus* (1941).

In Shrewsbury Rd is the Chester Beatty
Library, with collections of Oriental and Western MSS., bindings, etc., housed in two galleries, one of which was opened in the summer of
1953 and the other in the summer of 1957. The
library is a personal one, reflecting the tastes
and interests of its owner, who has been for
more than forty years collecting books and
manuscripts of all kinds and of many countries,
notably those of the East and more particularly
the Islamic East. The original building contains
a Chinese Library, an exhibition of Japanese
MSS., colour prints and colour-print books,
and a very fine collection of European bindings
and Western MSS. These range in date from
the 8th to the 16th centuries and cover a wide
field, including Bibles, Psalters and Gospels,
and medieval and Renaissance texts and clas-
sics. The earliest Biblical MS. is the Gospels
from Stavelot Abbey, executed in Flanders
about A.D. 1000; but Bede's Commentary on
the Epistles and the Apocalypse, written probably in Nonantola (Italy), is earlier by about
two hundred years. The Walsingham Bible of
the 12th cent. and that made for Cardinal
Albergati in 1428 are other notable exhibits.
Outstanding for the beauty of the miniatures
and the sumptuousness of the illumination are
the French and Spanish Books of Hours of
the 14th and 15th centuries. – In the show-cases
of the hall of the 1957 gallery are about 600
Chinese snuff bottles of various precious and
semi-precious stones, the most prized being
those of sapphire, garnet, aquamarine, tur-
quoise and jade. Also in this gallery are a few
of the Biblical papyri, perhaps the best-known
of the Library's many treasures. These famous
papyri include the oldest known MSS. of the
New Testament (A.D. 200–250), and of the
Septuagint version of the Old Testament. Here
one can also see a fraction of the celebrated
collections of Korans and Indian and Persian
MSS. and miniatures, as well as Chinese scrolls
and jade books, Siamese MSS., rhinoceros-

horn cups, and Chinese Imperial robes. A particularly interesting exhibit is the 1259–60 MS. of Omar Khayyam, which is just two hundred years older than that on which Fitzgerald based his famous version. Times of opening: Wed., May to Oct., 2.30–5.30 p.m.; Nov. to April, 2.0–5.0 p.m.

Burgh Quay extends from O Connell Bridge to Butt Bridge. The Corn Exchange (about 1815), by G. Halpin, had an interesting interior with a rectangular lantern carried on cast iron columns; it has been obscured by crude partitions. The printing works of the *Irish Press*, next door, was originally Conciliation Hall, Daniel O Connell's party headquarters, and later the Tivoli Theatre.

Clare St joins Leinster St and Merrion Sq. N. It was laid out in 1762, and some of the houses have fine interiors, particularly No. 29, formerly the Leinster Club. No. 5 was the residence of the Rev. Thomas Leland, D.D., historian and antiquary (1722–85).

Dawson St (about 1705) links Nassau St and St Stephen's Green, N. In its heyday it was a fashionable residential street. The Mansion House (1705), official residence of the Lord Mayor since 1715, is a good Queen Anne house of brick, spoiled by stucco, balustrade (replacing figure-subject panels), windows and other Victoriana. There are some good portraits here, including the 1st Duke of Northumberland (1742–86), by Reynolds. The Round Room was run up in 1821 by John Semple (architect of the "Black Church", Mary Pl.) for a ball and banquet in honour of George IV, and has served ever since as a public hall. It was here that the first Dáil Éireann assembled, 21 Jan. 1919, to adopt Ireland's Declaration of Independence and ratify the proclamation of the Irish Republic by the insurgents of 1916. Of the 73 Republican deputies elected, 14 Dec. 1918, no fewer than 36 were in British prisons. (The 26 Unionists and 6 Nationalists did not attend.) The Mansion House remained the seat of Dáil Éireann's public sessions until the British banning of the assembly, 10 Sept. 1919. The negotiations between the Irish leaders and the British Commander-in-Chief, preliminary to the Truce of 1921, were conducted here.

No. 19, Academy House, originally Northland House, was built in 1770 for the Knox family of Dungannon, probably by John Ensor, architect of the Rotunda, Parnell Sq. (Dublin N.–S. axis). The interior contains some notable plasterwork reflecting Chinese influence. Wolfe Tone was a frequent visitor to Northland House, as a close friend of the Hon. George Knox, Lord Northland's anti-Union son. In 1852 the house was acquired by the Royal Irish Academy. Founded in 1783 and granted a royal charter in 1785, the Academy is Ireland's foremost learned society, still recruiting its membership from the whole island. Its *Trans-*

actions, Proceedings, and other publication include notable contributions to Science and Mathematics as well as to "Polite Literature and Antiquities". Its magnificent collection of Irish antiquities now forms the nucleus of the National Museum's collection, but the Academy's library, with a remarkable collection of Irish MSS., still remains in Academy House The more important treasures include: the *Cathach,* 6th/7th cent. MS. of the Psalter possibly written by St Columcille (*see* Ballymagrorty *under* Ballintra); *Lebor na hUidre* Book of the Dun Cow, an 11th–12th cent literary codex compiled at Clonmacnois (*q.v.*) the *Stowe Missal,* an 8th–9th cent. Mass-book which belonged to the monastery of Lorrha (*q.v.*); the *Leabhar Breac,* Speckled Book, an early 15th cent. liturgical codex (*see* Duniry) the *Book of Ballymote* (*see* Ballymote), *Leabhar Úa Maine,* and the *Book of Lecan* (*see* Lackeen *under* Inishcrone), 14th–15th cent. literary codices; a holograph text of the *Annals of the Four Masters* (1632–6). Hours of admission to library: Mon. to Fri. 9.30 a.m.–5.30 p.m. Sat. 9.30 a.m.–1 p.m.; closed Aug. – The chair of the President of the Academy was originally the throne in the College Green House of Lords The members' benches also came from the House of Lords. Other relics of the old Parliament House include some brass chandeliers.

St Anne's Church (Protestant), despite its 1868 "Romanesque" façade by Sir Thomas Deane, remains essentially the 1720–21 church of unusual quality by Isaac Wills. The curved shelves on either side of the chancel were provided to hold the bread distributed weekly under the bequest of Lord Newtown (d. 1723). The Elizabeth Phibbs memorial (S. gallery) is by Edward Smyth, of Custom House and Four Courts fame. The *Charity* (1911), *St Christopher* (1914), and *Michael* windows are by Wilhelmina Geddes, one of the first of the Dublin stained glass artists; she worked in London for many years.

D'Olier St (about 1800) leads from O Connell Bridge to the junction of College St and Pearse St, where the flower bed is said to occupy the site of the Steyne, or Long Stone, a Norse pillarstone which survived until about 1700. No 9 was the residence of Samuel Lover (1797–1868), novelist.

Donnybrook is a residential suburb on the main Dublin (2½ m.)–Bray (10½ m.) road. The old village was the scene of a famous fair founded in 1204. Having become notorious for disorder, it was suppressed in 1855. The Sacred Heart Church has a two-light window (*SS Patrick, Ethne, Fedelm*) by Michael Healy (1914–15). In the grounds of Montrose, Stillorgan Rd, are the studios of Telefís Éireann (Irish Television); by Michael Scott and Associates (1961–62). Nearby is the 300-acre site of the new University College. The Physics Chemistry, and Bio-chemistry buildings (1962–

4) are by Downes & Meehan. *See also* Earls-rt Terrace, Dublin SE. At the SE. angle of the University College grounds, Foster Ave. joins tillorgan Rd. St Thomas's Church has a porch window, *St George* (1941), by Evie Hone. On the opposite side of Stillorgan Rd is the en-rance to St Helen's (1750), one of the first ountry houses erected on the Fitzwilliam state. It is now one of the provincial head-uarters of the Irish Christian Brothers.

Duke St connects Grafton St with Dawson St. The Smoking Room (remodelled) on the first oor of the Bailey Restaurant was the meeting lace of Parnell and his closest associates, and ter of Arthur Griffith and his friends (in-luding James Montgomery, noted wit, and Oliver St John Gogarty, surgeon and poet). Davy Byrne's public house, on the opposite ide of the street, had associations with James oyce and other writers. The character of the lace has been completely altered.

Earlsfort Terrace links Adelaide Rd with the unction of Lower Leeson St and St Stephen's Green. On the W. side is University College Administration, Library, Faculties of Arts, Philosophy, Celtic Studies, Law, and Depart-nents of Anatomy, Pathology, and Architect-re. A new college is in course of erection at Donnybrook (*q.v.*). The Engineering Depart-nent is in Merrion St (*q.v.*), the Faculty of Agriculture at Lyons (*see under* Celbridge), the aculty of Veterinary Science at Ballsbridge. *See also* St Stephen's Green, South, *under* Dublin, N.–S. axis.) The Earlsfort Terrace buildings occupy the site and part of the build-ngs erected for the Great Exhibition of 1865, nd extended in 1888 to provide examination alls for the non-teaching Royal University of Ireland (1882–1909). The site was the E. end f Coburg Gardens (1817–65), previously the ardens of Clonmell House (Harcourt St), and rom 1865 to 1941 the Iveagh Gardens attached o Iveagh House, St Stephen's Green. Only a raction of Rudolph M. Butler's projected ollege buildings were erected (1914–19). The ollege has been a constituent college of the National University of Ireland since 1909, but races its origin to the Catholic University of 851 (*see* St Stephen's Green, S. *under* Dublin, N.–S. axis). In point of numbers (9,000 full-ime students) it is the largest university institu-ion in the country. It has played a leading part n creating the new Ireland, and the roll of its nembers includes such names as those of Eóin MacNéill (1867–1945), historian, founder of the he Gaelic League, founder of the Irish Volun-eers, Minister of Education in the first Irish Free State Government; Douglas Hyde (1866–1949), co-founder of the Gaelic League, Pro-essor of Modern Irish, and President of Ire-and; Thomas MacDonagh (1878–1916), Lect-rer in English Literature, poet, a founder of Edward Martyn's Irish Theatre (1914), and Commandant of the Dublin Brigade in the 1916

Rising; Kevin O Higgins (1892–1927), Minister for Justice in the first Irish Free State Cabinet; Patrick McGilligan, Minister for Industry and Commerce in the first Irish Free State Cabinet; Osborn J. Bergin (1873–1950), eminent Celtic scholar; Hugh Ryan (1873–1931), chemist; Arthur Conway (1875–1950), mathematical physicist; and E. J. Conway, biochemist, a pioneer of the micro-diffusion technique and inventor of the Conway Unit. The historic Dáil Éireann Treaty Debate (14 Dec. 1921–10 Jan. 1922) took place in the Council Chamber, now the History Library. In the School of Archi-tecture is a collection of fine Greek funeral stelae; also a collection of architectural and sculptural casts, including John Hogan's plaster models of the *Drunken Faun*.

Ely Pl. is a cul-de-sac continuing the line of Merrion St to the S. of Merrion Row. It con-tains several fine late-18th cent. houses, some with good ironwork, and admirable interiors. No. 8, Ely House, was built by Michael Staple-ton in 1770 for the extravagant Henry Loftus, later Earl of Ely (*see* Rathfarnham); it was after-wards the residence of Sir Thornley Stoker, surgeon, and is now the headquarters of the Knights of Columbanus; it has some particu-larly fine stucco and other decorations. Palatial No. 6 also has an excellent Stapleton interior; it was the home of execrated "Black Jack" Fitzgibbon, Earl of Clare (1749–1802), whose promotion of the Union so aroused the fury of the Dublin mob. No. 3 was the home of the celebrated orator, Barry Yelverton, Lord Avon-more (1736–1805), whose beautiful country house, Fortfield, Kimmage, was recently de-molished. No. 4 was the town house of John Philpot Curran (1750–1817), famous forensic orator and father of Robert Emmet's sweet-heart; later it was the residence of George Moore (1852–1933). The small plot on the opposite side of the street was Moore's garden. House and garden (and Ely House too) figure prominently in his great Dublin trilogy, *Ave, Salve atque Vale*. No. 5, another Stapleton house, was the home of Chief Justice Kendal Bushe (1767–1843). No. 15 is also a Stapleton house. No. 25 was the home of James Joyce's sometime boon companion, Oliver St John Gogarty, surgeon, poet, wit, and author. It is now the seat of the Royal Hibernian Academy.

Fitzwilliam Sq., between Pembroke St and Fitzwilliam St, is the smallest, latest (1820), and perhaps best preserved of Dublin's Georgian squares. Like Fitzwilliam St and Fitzwilliam Pl., it is now for the most part given over to the consulting rooms of physicians and surgeons. No. 2 was the town house of William Dargan (1799–1867; *see* the National Gallery, Merrion Sq., *below*).

Fitzwilliam St, Lower and Upper, extends from Merrion Sq. to Fitzwilliam Pl. Until the 1965 demolition of the block between Baggot St and

Upper Mount St, it combined with Merrion Sq. E. (begun about 1780), Fitzwilliam Sq. E., and Fitzwilliam Pl. (about 1830–40) to provide Dublin's longest Georgian street. The vista is closed at the S. end by a distant glimpse of the Dublin mountains; at the N. end (since 1934) by the pseudo-Georgian National Maternity Hospital and the unfortunately sited gasholder on Sir John Rogerson's Quay. – No. 28 Fitzwilliam Pl. is that Dublin rarity, a Gothic-Revival dwelling. Queen Victoria is said to have commissioned it (and never paid) for her "whipping girl".

Grand Canal St leads from Fenian St to Shelbourne Rd. Sir Patrick Dun's Hospital is named after its founder, a Scottish doctor (1642–1713), who was a favourite of William III and a pioneer of Dublin medicine. The uninspired building (1799–1808) is by Henry Aaron Baker, apprentice of James Gandon, later the pupil and partner of James Gandon, and in due course Master of the Royal Dublin Society's architectural school. George Papworth is also said to have had a hand in it.

Grand Parade, on the S. bank of the Grand Canal, leads W. from Leeson St Bridge to Charlemont St Bridge. In the foyer of the new office-warehouse of Carroll Group Distributors Ltd. is a noteworthy Aubusson tapestry designed by the contemporary Irish painter, Louis le Brocquy: *Legend of St Brendan the Navigator and Tobacco.* Some of the motifs were suggested by early and medieval Irish art, e.g. the procession on the N. cross at Kilclispeen, Ahenny, and the hunting scene of the transept mural at Holy Cross abbey.

Hatch St (1810 onwards) leads from Lower Leeson St to Harcourt St. University Hall is a Jesuit hall of residence for university students. The chapel has five single-light symbolical windows by Evie Hone (1947).

Herbert St (about 1830) leads from Lower Baggot St to Mount St Crescent. Sir Charles Villiers Stanford (1852–1924), composer, was born and grew up in No. 2.

Holles St leads from Merrion Square E. to the junction of Fenian St and Hogan Pl. Archibald Hamilton Rowan, United Irishman, died (1834) in No. 1.

Kildare St (1745 onwards) runs from St Stephen's Green N., to Leinster St.
At the NE. corner, overlooking College Park, is the Kildare Street Club, a distinguished, Venetian-style, brick palazzo (1860–61) by Thomas Deane I and Benjamin Woodward; it is now largely given over to the Phoenix Assurance Company; the noteworthy stonecarving is the work of John and James O Shea and Charles W. Harrison; it was Harrison who carved the engaging monkeys, birds and other

beasts. Nos. 4 (refronted) and 5 were built in 1748 by Edward Nicholson. No. 6, the Royal College of Physicians of Ireland, is a decadent effort (1860–64) in the Classical manner by William G. Murray; re-fronted 1966. It occupies the site of the first Kildare Street Club (destroyed by fire, 1860). The College was founded by the Duke of Ormond in 1667. In 1692 a charter of William and Mary made it a Protestant preserve. Today it is once more nonsectarian. The statues of Sir Dominic Corrigan (1802–80), Sir Henry Marsh (1790–1860), and William Stokes (1804–78) are by John Henry Foley.

Facing Molesworth St is Leinster House, present seat of Parliament. It is flanked on the N. by the National Library and the National College of Art, on the S. by the National Museum.

Leinster House (*see also* Carton, *under* Maynooth, *and* Frescati, Blackrock, *under* Dún Laoghaire), by Richard Cassels, was begun for the Earl of Kildare in 1745, the first of Dublin's great 18th cent. houses to be built S. of the Liffey. Having two formal fronts, and a central corridor on the long axis, it is a country rather than a town house. This is hardly to be wondered at, as it was built on the SE. edge of the city, with open country to the E. The entrance hall and principal rooms are noble apartments. They were redecorated towards the end of the 18th cent., James Wyatt participating in the work. The house has been claimed as the prototype for the White House, Washington, U.S.A., built on a suggestively similar plan by Carlowborn James Hoban (1762–1832). The house was sold in 1815 to the Royal Dublin Society, whose additions included an octagonal lecture theatre on the S. side. In 1922 it was purchased by the first Irish Free State Government to serve as a parliament house. The Senate meets in the 18th cent. saloon, Dáil Éireann in the remodelled lecture theatre. The public is admitted to the debates of both Houses. (Admission tickets may be obtained from deputies or senators, or from the Superintendent.) The principal apartments may be seen only when Parliament is not sitting. (Applications should be made to the Superintendent.) – On Leinster Lawn, at the E. front of Leinster House, is a memorial by Raymond McGrath and F. du Berry to the founders of the Irish State, Arthur Griffith, Michael Collins, and Kevin O Higgins; the bronze portrait medallions are by Laurence Campbell. Nearby is a statue of Prince Albert by John Henry Foley.

As the headquarters of the Royal Dublin Society, Leinster House became the focus of some of the Society's most important activities and institutions. From these developed the National College of Art, the National Library, and the National Museum. The College of Art occupies an obscure, inadequate structure in a corner between the N. end of Leinster House and the Library; Dublin's major art exhibitions are held there.

Plate 7. Lough Nafooey, Co. Galway

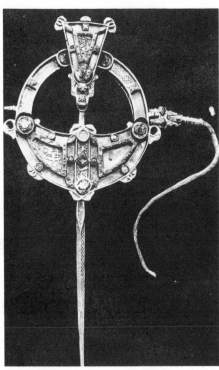

National Museum, Dublin

The "Tara" Brooch

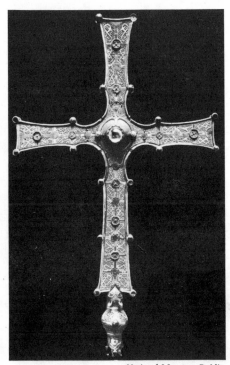

National Museum, Dublin

The Cross of Cong

The National Library and National Museum are matching buildings (1885–90) of pedestrian design by Sir Thomas Deane II; the elevations have been significantly altered by the removal of corroded statuary and the replacement of corroded details in Mount Charles stone by plainer work in limestone and granite. The Library has important collections of books, MSS., prints, drawings and historical archives (including the Ormond Archives from Kilkenny Castle and collections of designs by 18th–19th cent. architects and stucco decorators). A valuable new feature is the collection of microfilm copies of Irish MSS. and documents in foreign archives and libraries. Hours of admission: Weekdays, 10 a.m.–10 p.m.; Sat. 10 a.m.–1 p.m. The Library is closed during Aug. A reader's ticket is required for the Reading Room.

The National Museum houses overcrowded collections of various kinds, some of them of outstanding importance and world-wide fame. The Irish Antiquities, Irish Folk-Life, Irish Military History, Ethnographical, Art & Industrial, and Botanical collections are housed in the Kildare St building; the main Natural History collections in Merrion St. Hours of Admission: Tue. to Sat., 10 a.m.–5 p.m.; Sundays 2–5 p.m. The Museum is closed on Mondays.

Irish Antiquities Division: The kernel of the collection of Irish antiquities is provided by the Royal Irish Academy's superb collection. Particularly noteworthy are:

Bronze Age: The splendid series of gold lunulae, torques, gorgets, fibulae, etc.; the bronze buckets and cauldrons, and the bronze, leather, and wooden shields.

Iron Age: The magnificent gold collar with Celtic repoussé ornament from Broighter, Co. Derry, the repoussé bronze dishes, the Petrie "Crown", and the bronze horse trappings.

Early Historic Period: Such masterpieces as the Moylough Belt Reliquary (8th cent.); "Tara" Brooch (8th cent.) and other splendid penannular brooches; Ardagh Chalice (8th cent.); Shrine of St Patrick's Bell (12th cent.); Cross of Cong (12th cent.); and the series of 10th–12th cent. enshrined staffs, including the Lismore Crozier (12th cent.).

The overcrowded Ethnographical Collection includes unique and now irreplaceable material, some of it collected by Dr James Patten, surgeon in H.M.S. *Resolution* during Captain Cook's second voyage (1772–5) to the South Seas.

Art and Industrial Division: Here the outstanding exhibits are to be found among the excellent collections of 18th cent. Irish glass and silver.

On the W. side of the street is the Department of Industry and Commerce (1939–42) by J. R. Boyd Barrett. The stone carvings are by Gabriel Hayes.

No. 39 was the home (1821–39) of Sydney Owenson, Lady Morgan, whose literary salon

Irish Tourist Board

Early Iron Age bronze disc, National Museum, Dublin

Irish Tourist Board

Gold torque, National Museum, Dublin

was one of the few bright spots in post-Union Dublin. No. 45, Doneraile House, has some good features (including doorway, staircase, etc.).

Leinster St (about 1760) leads from Nassau St to Clare St. No. 5 was the residence of Lord Kilwarden, "the justest judge in Ireland", killed by a mob on the occasion of Robert Emmet's rebellion, 1803. It was later occupied by Archibald Hamilton Rowan, a member of the United Irishmen.

Lincoln Place, formerly Park St, leads from Leinster St to Westland Row. Sir William Wilde had an eye hospital here. Fanning's public house (now Lincoln's Inn) figures in Oliver St John Gogarty's *As I was Going down Sackville Street*. Kennedy's, at the corner of Westland Row, is another public house with literary associations.

Merrion Sq., second largest of Dublin's great squares, lies to the NE. of St Stephen's Green. It was laid out in 1762 by John Ensor for the Fitz-

National Museum, Dublin

Early 19th cent. decanters, made in Cork

The Shrine of the Cathach, National Museum, Dublin

william Estate, but was not completed until the end of the century. The great brick houses preserve their Georgian elevations in varying degree, and combine to offer splendid vistas, particularly along the E. and N. sides. Many of them have excellent stucco interiors. The Rutland Memorial (1791), on the W. side of the park, is by Henry Aaron Baker; it has lost its fountain and most of its Coade stone ornaments.

Many of the great names in modern Dublin history are associated with Merrion Sq.: No. 1, Sir William and Lady Wilde ("Speranza" of *The Nation*) and their son Oscar; No. 5, Sir William Stokes, physician; No. 14, Sir Philip Crampton (1777–1858), surgeon; No. 42, Sir Jonah Barrington (1760–1834), diarist; No. 58, Daniel O Connell (1775–1847); No. 70, now the Arts Council's headquarters, Joseph Sheridan Le Fanu (1814–73); No. 82, William Butler Yeats (1865–1939).

No. 5 is now the School of Cosmic Physics of the Dublin Institute for Advanced Studies; No. 8, the Royal Institute of the Architects of Ireland; No. 49, the offices of the National University; No. 63, the Royal Society of Antiquaries of Ireland; Nos. 64 and 65, the School of Theoretical Physics (where Schroedinger was Senior Professor) of the Dublin Institute for Advanced Studies; No. 84, Plunkett House, the headquarters of the Irish Agricultural Organization Society. Plunkett House preserves the memory of Sir Horace Plunkett (1854–1932), founder of the Irish co-operative movement. The poet-painter, George William Russell (AE.; 1867–1935) worked here for many years as editor of the *Irish Homestead* (merged with the *Irish Statesman* in 1923).

On the W. side of the square is Leinster Lawn, garden of Leinster House, Kildare St (*q.v.*). It is flanked on the N. by Sir Charles Lanyon's National Gallery, 1859–60 (extensions, including the long Leinster Lawn façade, by Sir Thomas Deane II, 1884). Deane's work is repeated on the S. side of the lawn by the National History Division of the National Museum.

The National Gallery was erected by subscriptions to a testimonial to William Dargan (1799–1867), railway entrepreneur and "arch improver of his time", whose statue (by Thomas Farrell, R.H.A.) stands on the lawn. George Bernard Shaw, whose favourite statue (by Troubetsky) also stands on the lawn, left a third of his estate to the Gallery. The collections of over 6,000 paintings, of which about 700 are on view (the extension due for completion in 1967 will provide exhibition space

Merrion Square, north side

for a further 400), are of very high quality and include a number of celebrated works. The excellence is largely due to Sir Hugh Lane (*see* Municipal Gallery).

Times of admission: Mon. to Wed. 10 a.m.– 6 p.m.; Thur., 10 a.m.–9 p.m.; Sat., 10 a.m.– 6 p.m.; Sun., 2 p.m.–5 p.m.; closed Fridays. Guide-lectures on Suns. and Weds.

The principal pictures (in alphabetical order of the schools represented) are:

Doorway, Merrion Square

Part of the façade of the National Gallery

AUSTRIAN

W. Huber (1490–1553). *Portrait of Anthony Hundertpfundt.*

Salzburg School. *The Crucifixion.*

J. Seisenegger (1505–67). *A presumed daughter of Charles V.*

Unknown: *The Apostles setting forth*; on reverse, *St Veronica.*

BRITISH

J. Crome (1769–1821). *Heath Scene after a Storm.*

T. Gainsborough (1727–88). *Mrs Horton, later Duchess of Cumberland; Mrs King; Landscape with Cattle.*

W. Hogarth (1697–1764). *George II and Members of his Family*; *The Mackinnon Family.*

J. Hoppner (1758–1810). *Portrait of the Artist.*

Sir Godfrey Kneller (1646–1723). *De Ginkel, Earl of Athlone.*

Sir Thomas Lawrence (1769–1830). *John Philpot Curran*; *The Duchess of Devonshire; The 5th Lord Inchiquin.*

Sir Peter Lely (1618–80). *James I; Duke of Ormonde; Oliver Cromwell.*

Sir Joshua Reynolds (1723–92). *George, 2nd Earl Temple, with his Wife and Son; Robert, 2nd Earl of Northington, K.P.; Mrs Frances Fortescue; Caricatures of Englishmen in Rome, c. 1751; Charles, Earl of Bellamont.*

G. Stubbs (1724–1806). *Sportsmen Resting.*

Turner de Lond (*fl.* 1820). *George IV's Entry into Dublin.*

F. Wheatley (1747–1801). *Portrait of Mr and Mrs Richardson.*

Also a fine collection of English watercolours (Cozens, Constable, Turner, Cotman, *et al.*).

DUTCH

H. Avercamp (1585–1664). *A Winter Scene.*

F. Bol (1611–81). *A Lady.*

P. Claesz (1590–1661). *Still Life.*

P. Codde (*c.* 1600–1678). *Interior with Figures.*

A. Cuyp (1620–91). *Milking Cows.*

D. van Delen (1605–71). *Interior of a Dutch Room.*

C. Dusart (1660–1704). *A Dutch merrymaking.*

W. C. Duyster (1599–1635). *Interior with Soldiers.*

G. van den Eeckhout (1621–74). *Christ Teaching in the Temple.*

J. van Goyen (1596–1656). *View of a Town in Holland.*

Franz Hals (*c.* 1580–1666). *A Young Fisherman of Scheveningen.*

W. K. Heda (1594–1678). *Still Life.*

B. van der Helst (*c.* 1612–70). *Portrait of an Old Lady.*

M. Hobbema (1638–1709). *The Ferry Boat.*

P. de Hooch (*c.* 1630–77). *Players at Tric Trac.*

W. Knijf (*fl. c.* 1650–77). *The Windmill.*

P. Lastman (1562–1649). *Joseph Selling Corn in Egypt.*

J. Lievens (1607–74). *Rembrandt's Father.*

J. Lis (1570–1629). *The Vision of St Jerome.*

N. Maes (1632–93). *Vertumnus and Pomona.*

A. van der Neer (*c.* 1603–77). *A Riverside Town on Fire.*

F. Post (*c.* 1612–80). *View in Brazil.*

Rembrandt (1606–69). *Shepherds Resting at Night; Portrait of a Young Man; Young Woman; Dutch Interior; Head of an Old Man; La Main Chaude.*

J. van Rossum (*fl.* 1650). *Portrait of Adriaan van Ostade.*

J. van Ruysdael (*c.* 1629–82). *A Wooded Landscape; A Stormy Sea.*

S. van Ruysdael (1600–1670). *The Halt.*

J. Steen (*c.* 1626–79). *The Village School.*

M. Stomer (1600–1650). *The Betrayal of Christ.*

G. Ter Borch (1617–81). *Four Spanish Monks.*

J. B. Weenix (1621–60). *The Sleeping Shepherdess.*

D. van Wijnen (1661–?). *A Fantasy; The Temptation of St Anthony.*

E. de Witte (1617–92). *Interior of Antwerp Cathedral.*

FLEMISH

Antwerp School. *The Descent of the Holy Spirit.*

A. Benson (1521–50). *The Taking of Christ.*

C. Bleeker (*fl.* 1625–55). *A Raid on a Village.*

Bosch. *Flagellation of Christ.*

Dirk Bouts (*c.* 1420–75). *St Nicholas.*

Brueghel the Younger (1564–1638). *A Peasant Wedding.*

J. de Cock (d. 1529). *Flight into Egypt.*

Colin de Coter. *Enthronement of St Romuald.*

G. David (*c.* 1450–1523). *Christ bidding Farewell to His Mother.*

A. van Dyck (1599–1641). *Portrait of Frederick Marselar; A Boy Standing on a Terrace.*

J. Jordaens (1593–1678). *Supper at Emmaus.*

"The Master of the Magdalene Legend". *Departure of St Romuald.*

"The Master of the Silver Window" (*fl. c.* 1500). *Scene from the Life of St Augustine.*

F. Pourbus (*c.* 1570–1622). *Portrait of a Lady.*

M. van Rogmerswaele (1497–1567). *The Calling of St Matthew.*

P. P. Rubens (1577–1640). *St Francis of Assisi; Christ at the house of Martha and Mary; St Dominic.*

F. Snyders (1597–1657). *A Breakfast.*

D. Teniers (1610–90). *Peasants' Merrymaking.*

R. van der Weyden (*c.* 1400–1464). *St Luke Painting the Virgin.*

A. van Ysenbrandt (*fl.* 1550). *Madonna and Child.*

FRENCH

J. B. S. Chardin (1699–1779). *Card Tricks.*

F. Clouet (*c.* 1516–73). *Portrait of Margaret Fitzgerald.*

T. Couture (*c.* 1815–79). *The Judge Asleep.*

A Peasant Wedding *by Pieter Brueghel the Younger*

C. F. Daubigny (1817–78). *Landscape.*
E. Delacroix (1798–1863). *Demosthenes by the Sea Shore.*
J. L. Forain (1852–1931). *Court Room Scene.*
J. L. A. T. Géricault (1791–1824). *A Horse.*
Claude Lorraine (1600–1682). *Juno and Io.*
C. Monet (1840–1927). *River Scene.*
B. Morisot (1841–95). *The Black Bodice.*
F. Nicolas (1400–1465). *St Jerome translating the Bible.*
J. B. Pater (1696–1736). *A Rural Scene.*
J. B. Perronneau (1731–96). *Portrait of a Man.*
N. Poussin (1594–1665). *The Entombment; The Marriage of Thetis and Peleus.*
School of Avignon, *c.* 1420. *Annunciation.*

GERMAN
L. Cranach the Elder (1472–1553). *Judith with the Head of Holofernes.*
C. Faber (*c.* 1500–1553). *Portrait of Heinrich Knoblauch.*
G. Pencz (*c.* 1500–1550). *Portrait of a Man.*

IRISH
G. Barret (1732–84). *Powerscourt Waterfall.*
J. Barry (1741–1806). *Adam and Eve; Portrait of Edmund Burke; Portrait of a Harper.*
M. G. Brennan (1839–71). *Church Interior at Capri.*
G. Chinnery (1774–1852). *Portrait of a Mandarin; Portrait of Mrs Coyningham.*
P. V. Duffy (1836–1909). *A County Wicklow Farm.*

R. Fagan (1745–1816). *Sarah and Jeffrey Amherst.*
J. Fisher (*fl.* 1770–1809). *Landscape.*
J. P. Haverty (1794–1864). *First Confession.*
T. Hickey (1741–1824). *An Actor between the Muses of Tragedy and Comedy.*
N. Hone the Elder (1718–84). *Piping Boy.*
N. Hone the Younger (1831–1917). *Ardmore.*
J. M. Kavanagh (*c.* 1860–1918). *Old Convent Gate, Dinan.*
M. J. Lawless (1836–64). *The Sick Call.*
W. Mulready (1786–1863). *Bathers Alarmed.*
E. H. Murphy (1796–1841). *Paroquets.*
Sir William Orpen (1870–1931). *The Knacker's Yard; The Dead Ptarmigan.*
James Arthur O Connor (1792–1841). *The Poachers.*
W. F. Osborne (1859–1903). *Orchard at Quimperlé; View of St Patrick's Close.*
R. Rothwell (1800–1868). *The Young Mother's Pastime.*
S. Slaughter (d. 1765). *A Lady and Child.*
P. Tuohy (1894–1930). *James Stephens.*
J. B. Yeats, senior (1839–1922). *The Artist's Wife; John O Leary; W. B. Yeats.*

ITALIAN
Bologna
G. M. Crespi (1664–1747). *The Massacre of the Innocents.*

Brescia
G. B. Moroni (*c.* 1520–78). *Portrait of a Gentleman and his two Children.*

Ferrara
L. Mazzolino (*c.* 1480–1530). *Pharaoh and his hosts overwhelmed in the Red Sea.*
C. Tura (1420–95). *Portrait of a Musician.*

Florence
Fra Angelico (1387–1455). *The Attempted Martyrdom of SS Cosmas and Damian.*
Fra Bartolomeo (1471–1517). *The Holy Family.*
G. del Biondo (*fl.* 1356–92). *Madonna and Child with Angels.*
G. M. Butteri (*c.* 1540–1606). *The Return from the Palio.*
A. di Giusto (1440–98). *The Assumption.*
Michelangelo Buonarroti (1475–1564). *The Holy Family with St John in a landscape.*

Genoa
B. Castiglione (1616–70). *Shepherdess finding the Infant.*
A. Magnasco (1681–1747). *Landscape with figures.*
B. Strozzi (1581–1641). *Summer and Autumn; Portrait of a Gentleman.*

Milan
A. da Solario (*c.* 1460–*c.* 1515). *An Italian Gentleman.*

Padua
A. Mantegna (1431–1506). *Judith with the Head of Holofernes.*

Parma
A. da Correggio (1494–1534). *Head of St Catherine the Martyr.*

National Gallery of Ireland, Dublin
Portrait of W. B. Yeats by his father,
J. B. Yeats

Rimini
G. Baronzio (d. *c.* 1362). *The Crucifixion; Christ appearing to St Mary Magdalene.*

Rome
D. Feti (1589–1624). *The Parable of the Lord of the Vineyard.*
G. P. Panini (1695–1768). *The Piazza Navona, Rome, 30 Nov. 1729.*
G. F. Penni (*c.* 1488–*c.* 1528). *Portrait of the Artist.*

National Gallery of Ireland, Dublin
Portrait of James Stephens by Patrick Tuohy

National Gallery of Ireland, Dublin
The Knackers' Yard *by Sir William Orpen*

Siena
A. da Bartolo (*c.* 1398–1428). *St John Preaching.*
Giovanni di Paolo (1403?–1483). *Painted Crucifix.*

Tuscany
O. Gentileschi (1562–1647). *David and Goliath.*
P. Uccello (1397–1475). *Madonna and Child; The Battle of Anghiari.*

Umbria
P. Perugino (1446–1523). *Pietà.*

Venice
J. Bassano (1510–92). *The Holy Family.*
G. Bellini (1426–1507). *Portrait of a Senator.*
B. Bellotto (1720–80). *Views of Dresden.*
A. Canaletto (1697–1768). *View of the Piazza San Marco, Venice.*
F. Guardi (1712–93). *The Doge Wedding the Adriatic.*
P. Longhi (1702–85). *The Artist painting a Lady's Portrait.*
L. Lotto (1480–1556). *Portrait of a Nobleman.*
A. Oliverio (*c.* 1500–1539). *Portrait of a Man.*
G. B. Piazzetta (1682–1754). *Decorative Group.*
S. del Piombo (1485–1547). *Portrait of Cardinal Antonio Ciocchi del Monte Sansovino.*
G. B. Tiepolo (1692–1769). *An Allegory of the Incarnation.*
J. Tintoretto (1519–94). *Portrait of a Venetian Gentleman; A Venetian Senator; Venice as Queen of the Adriatic.*
Tiziano Vecelli (Titian; *c.* 1489–1576). *Portrait of Baldassare Castiglione; Supper at Emmaus.*

SPANISH
J. Carena (1614–85). *The Infante Philip.*
F. Goya (1746–1828). *Conde del Tajo; Spanish Woman.*
El Greco (1545–1614). *St Francis in Ecstasy.*
Juan Gris (1887–1927). *Still Life.*
L. de Morales (1509–86). *St Jerome in the Wilderness.*
El Mudo (1526–79). *Abraham and the Three Angels.*
B. E. Murillo (1618–82). *Portrait of Joshua van Belle; The Holy Family; Mary Magdalen.*
J. Ribera (1588–1652). *St Procopius.*
F. Zurbaran (1598–1662). *St Justa.*

In 1950 the National Gallery received a large and important gift of pictures from Sir Chester Beatty. It includes a representative collection of works of the Barbizon Group.

Merrion St, Upper, leads from Merrion Sq. West to Merrion Row. The great building (1911–15) on the W. side (by Sir Aston Webb and Sir Thomas Deane II) was built to house the College of Science (extinguished) and government offices. In the W. range is the Engin-

National Gallery of Ireland, Dublin
St Francis in Ecstacy *by El Greco*

eering School of University College. No. 24, on the E. side of the street, now the Land Commission, was originally Antrim House. In 1765 it was purchased by Lord Mornington; hence the later name, Mornington House. Mornington's son, the future Duke of Wellington, was born here in 1769. The house has lost its cornice, but the good interior stucco (by Robert West ?) survives.

Mespil Rd, beside the tree-lined Grand Canal from Leeson St Bridge to Baggot St Bridge, was a street of pleasant, mid-19th cent. terraces. Laid out as part of a projected S. circular road, it acquired its name from Mespil House, a country house built near Leeson St Bridge in 1751 by Dr Barry. (The house, which had three of Dublin's very finest ceilings, has been replaced by blocks of flats. The *Jupiter and the Elements* ceiling has been re-erected in Árus an Uachtaráin, Phoenix Park; the *Hibernia* and the *Arts and Sciences* ceilings in Dublin Castle.) In its last days Mespil House was the home of Sarah Purser (d. 1943), painter, stained-glass artist and patron of the arts, to whom the Irish art revival owes so much. Her weekly "At Homes" were assemblies of the artistic and intellectual talent of Dublin, assemblies she dominated by her personality and acid tongue. The Irish Life Building (1961–2), by Downes and Meehan, is one of the most sensitive of Dublin's new buildings; the fountain is by Ian Stuart.

Milltown: *see under* **Sandford Rd,** *below.*

Molesworth St (1727 onwards) leads from the middle of Dawson St to the middle of Kildare St. It contains some of Dublin's earliest 18th cent. houses, a few (e.g. Nos. 15, 16) being of the "Dutch Billy" type normally associated with the weaving or other trades. The interiors of several are worth inspection. No. 5 (1735) is by Thomas Quin. Nos. 20–21 (1730) are by Ralph Spring. No. 20 has a particularly beautiful doorway. No. 33, Lisle House, has a fine interior.

Mount St, Lower (about 1820) continues the line of Merrion Sq., North, SE. to Northumberland Rd. John Millington Synge died at No. 130 in 1909. A garage occupies the site of Clanwilliam House, an outpost of Éamonn de Valéra's command (Boland's Bakery) during the 1916 Rising. It was held by four Volunteers armed with single-shot rifles. Four others were stationed in the nearby Parochial Hall, and two in No. 25, Northumberland Rd. On 26 April a British column of 800 men marching on Dublin from Dún Laoghaire reached the vicinity of the canal bridge. The Volunteers put up a fierce resistance for nearly eight hours, and only abandoned their posts when Clanwilliam House had been set on fire by bombs. Six of the ten Volunteers were by then dead or wounded, but they had cost the British column 234 casualties.

Mount St, Upper (about 1820) continues the line of Merrion Sq., South, to Mount St Crescent. The vista along the street and square is very fine, closed on the W. by Leinster House, on the E. by St Stephen's Church. This admirably sited building is the last (1824) of Dublin's neo-Grec Protestant churches. It was designed by John Bowden and completed by John Welland. The portico is modelled on the Erechtheum, the clocktower belfry on the Tower of the Winds and the Monument of Lysicrates. The *Christ among the Doctors* window is by Lady Glenavy (1907). E. of the church is Huband Bridge (1791), one of the most attractive of Dublin's unaltered canal bridges.

Northbrook Rd connects Leeson Park (off Upper Leeson St) with Ranelagh Rd. Over the door of St Anne's Hospital is an excellent stained-glass medallion (*St Anne Teaching the Virgin*) by Evie Hone (about 1944).

Pearse St (about 1810), formerly Great Brunswick St, parallels the Liffey from the junction of D'Olier St and College St to Ringsend Rd. Patrick H. Pearse, commander of the 1916 insurgents, was born in No. 27. The New Academy Cinema was originally (1824) the Dublin Oil Gas Station, and later the Antient Concert Rooms which figure in Joyce's *Ulysses*. The first (1902) production by the National Theatre Society was given here; it led to the founding of the Abbey Theatre.

Pembroke St, Upper and Lower (about 1820) connects Lower Baggot St with Lower Leeson St. Between Nos. 25 and 26 Upper Pembroke St is An Túr Gloine, the Tower of Glass, co-operative studio for ecclesiastical art founded in 1903 by Sarah Purser (d. 1943), who con-

tributed so signally to the creation of the Dublin school of stained glass. Besides Sarah Purser herself, Wilhelmina Geddes, Michael Healy (1873–1941), Catherine O Brien (d. 1963) and Evie Hone (1894–1955) were all members of the studio for greater or lesser periods. The studio is now conducted by Patrick Pollen.

Sandford Rd leads from Ranelagh to the junction of Eglinton Rd and Milltown Rd. The Protestant church has a 1927 Harry Clarke window (*SS Peter and Paul*). Milltown Park is a Jesuit house of studies and retreats. In the refectory are four Evie Hone windows (symbols of the Evangelists; 1953). Nearby Gonzaga College, a Jesuit school, has an interesting 1964–5 chapel, triangular on plan, by Andrew J. Devane. Milltown Protestant church has a three-light War Memorial window (*Sacrifice, Victory, Peace*) by A. E. Child.

Sandymount is a seaside suburb to the E. of Ballsbridge (*q.v.*), with many attractive, early-19th cent. villas. The Methodist church has windows by A. E. Child (*St Paul*, 1922), Ethel Rhind (*Dorcas Seated*, 1933) and Evie Hone (heraldic window, 1943; *Rock of Ages*, 1945). William Butler Yeats (1865–1939) was born at No. 2, Georgeville, Sandymount Ave.

Shrewsbury Rd: *see under* **Ballsbridge.**

South Wall, The (1708–62), is the longer of the two great 18th cent. works designed (by Capt. Bligh of the *Bounty*) to improve the navigation of the Liffey. It stretches from Butt Bridge to the Poolbeg Lighthouse (1762), a distance of more than 4 m. The construction of the wall also made possible the reclamation of the sloblands on which so much of SE. Dublin now stands. On the Wall, to the E. of Ringsend, is the Pigeon House, where the E.S.B. coal-fired power station occupies the Pigeon House Fort, begun in 1748, enlarged and modified at different dates, and manned well into the last century. The fort was named after an innkeeper named Pigeon, whose hostelry, on the site of the fort, was frequented by packet-boat passengers. The walk (or cycle run) to the end of the Wall is most rewarding. From the lighthouse, set right in the middle of the beautiful bay, a delightful panorama can be enjoyed. There is a men's bathing-place at the old Half Moon battery.

Westland Row connects Pearse St with Lincoln Pl. Oscar Wilde (1854–1900) was born in No. 21. The Royal Irish Academy of Music (founded 1856) occupies the old town-house of Lord Conyngham; the façade was freed of a plaster blanketing in 1963; the interior has good ceilings and wall plaques and noteworthy door cases. St Andrew's Catholic Church (1832–7), by James Boulger, is one of the largest of Dublin's post-Emancipation, neo-Grec, churches. The tabernacle of the Blessed Sacrament altar has an excellent small *Transfiguration* group by

John Hogan (1800–1858; completed by his son, John Valentine Hogan). Hogan also carved the lovely Elizabeth Farrell monument (recently cleaned with abrasives). The names on the monuments in the church read like the roll of the medieval Pale, in striking contrast to the newly-come names which predominate in Dublin's Protestant churches.

Dublin North-East of the River Liffey and O Connell St–Dorset St

Beresford Pl., at the junction of Eden Quay, Lower Abbey St, Gardiner St, Store St, and Custom House Quay, was laid out as a quadrant of matching houses to provide a setting for the Custom House. The achievement was successfully undone by the 1889 "Loop Line" overhead railway. The place is now dominated by the 1962–4 Liberty Hall, which was the first of the city-centre breaches in Dublin's Georgian skyline.

The magnificent Custom House (1781–91) is by James Gandon, London-born son of a Huguenot father and a Welsh mother, and pupil of Sir William Chambers. Gandon's masterpieces, the Custom House and Four Courts, remain even yet – time, war, and the Office of Public Works notwithstanding – the glories of Dublin's architecture. In 1921 the Custom House was the seat of key departments of British government in Ireland. Accordingly, on 25 May it was raided by 120 men of the Dublin Brigade of the I.R.A. They set it on fire, destroyed the records, and thereby reduced the British civil administration to virtual impotence. The great building blazed for five days, until little more than the shell remained. After the establishment of the Irish Free State it was reconstructed by the Office of Public Works, which radically altered the interior plan and made several significant changes in the exterior. The more important of these were the substitution of Ardbraccan limestone for the Portland stone of the dome peristyle; the omission of the "visual abutment" of the base of the dome by failing to restore the chimney stacks and high roof of the central north–south block; the erection of an obtrusive, boiler-house chimney; and the replacing by windows of the six niches which had alternated with the eight original windows over the arcades of the river front. (The unfortunate blocking up of the ground-floor arcades of the E. and W. fronts was an older offence.)

The sculptures of the Custom House are, for the most part, of remarkable quality. Until the great fire the pediment of the S. portico was crowned by allegorical statues of *Neptune*, *Mercury*, *Plenty*, and *Industry*, the two former by Agostino Carlini, the two latter by Edward Smyth. (Their loss, too, contributes to the weakening of the "visual abutment" of the dome.) Smyth also did the colossal statue of *Commerce* which crowns the dome; the heads about the base of the dome; the allegorical

Barnaby's Picture Library

Detail of the Custom House

sculpture (designed by Carlini) in the tympanum of the S. front (*Union of Britain and Ireland* – seated on a marine chariot drawn by sea-horses, with Neptune banishing Famine and Despair); the admirable keystones (symbolizing the Atlantic Ocean and the thirteen principal rivers of Ireland) of the basement storey (on these he was assisted by Benjamin Schrowder from Winchelsea); the superb Arms of the Kingdom of Ireland on the end pavilions; and the ox-head frieze on the N. front. The mediocre statues of the N. front are by Joseph Banks of London; they represent the Quarters of the Globe. The Dublin Brigade memorial at the W. front is by the Breton sculptor, Yann Renard-Goullet.

The nearby Bus Station is by Michael Scott and Associates (1953).

Clontarf–Dollymount is a seaside suburb on the Dublin (2 m.)–Howth (7 m.) road. In 550 a church was founded here by St Comgall of Bangor; nothing is known of its history. Clontarf is celebrated as the place of Brian Boru's great victory over Leinster and Norse Dublin, Good Friday, 1014. St Anthony's Church has a three-light window, *King of Kings* (1933), by Hubert McGoldrick. The Church of St John the Baptist (C. of I.) has a Catherine O Brien window, *Our Lord with Children* (1950). Clontarf Castle (19th cent.; now an hotel) stands on the site of a medieval commandery of the Knights Templar (later of the Knights Hospitaller of St John of Jerusalem). St Anne's was the residence of Lord Ardilaun; the demesne is now being developed by the Dublin Corporation. The "Bull Wall", a breakwater running out to the North Bull, is a popular bathing place. The North Bull is a large island of sand heaped up by the tides; it is a Bird Sanctuary and popular bathing-place. Nearby, in St Gabriel's Rd, is St Gabriel's Church (1953) by Louis C. Peppard and Hugo Duffy. One of Dublin's few recent churches of any interest, it has a good interior. (For Clontarf Presbyterian Church, *see* Marino.)

Drumcondra is a 19th–20th cent. suburb on the main Belfast road beyond the Royal Canal. St John the Baptist Church (Protestant; 1743) contains a splendid monument to Marmaduke Coghill (1673–1738) by Scheemakers, teacher of Simon Vierpyl. The life-size figures represent Coghill (robed as Chancellor of the Irish Exchequer), Religion and Minerva. The long, uncouth inscription concludes by informing the reader that Coghill "died of gout in the stomach". In the churchyard are buried Thomas Furlong (d. 1827), one of the principal translators employed by James Hardiman for his *Irish Minstrelsy*, and, in one grave, Francis Grose (1731–91), antiquarian and artist, and James Gandon (1743–1823).

The nearby Missionary College of All Hallows (Gothic Revival building by J. J. McCarthy) incorporates Drumcondra House, erected about 1720 by Sir Edward Lovett Pearce (architect of the Parliament House) for Marmaduke Coghill, and perhaps the best-preserved early Georgian mansion in Dublin. The S. front is severe, the (later?) E. front highly ornamented. There are some good, early-Georgian interiors. In the grounds is a charming, 18th cent. temple (a fake ruin), introduced probably by the Earl of Charleville, who succeeded to the property in 1755. (Charleville's widow married again, this time by moonlight in an arbour within the temple.) The name of the college recalls the medieval priory of All Hallows by Hoggen Green. These Drumcondra lands had belonged to the priory. The college chapel has a rose window (*Assumption* and symbols) by Evie Hone, 1953.

St Patrick's Training College incorporates Belvedere House, a late-17th cent. house with 18th–19th cent. additions. It passed through a succession of owners (including the Coghills and Primate Lord Rokeby). The drawing-room is a fine, mid-18th cent. apartment. The new chapel, students' lodgings, etc. (1963 onwards), are by Devane of Robinson, Devane, and O Keefe.

Corpus Christi Church, Home Farm Rd, is by John J. Robinson.

Beaumont Convalescent Home (Sisters of Mercy), Beaumont Rd, beyond Whitehall, was the residence of Arthur Guinness, who founded the world-famous Guinness brewery.

Eccles St (*c.* 1750–*c.* 1820) connects Dorset St with Berkeley Rd. As planned, it was to have had an elliptical circus at the W. end. No. 7 was the home of James Joyce's *Ulysses* character, Bloom. Nos. 18–19 were originally Tyrawley House. No. 59 was the residence of Cardinal Cullen (1803–78); No. 63 the residence of Sir Boyle Roche (*c.* 1750–1807). No. 64 was the home of the celebrated architect, Francis Johnston (1761–1829). Johnston doubled the width of the house by adding the portion (later increased in height) adorned with plaques emblematic of the arts. (The garden front is adorned with busts of George III and Queen Charlotte.) Johnston also erected a belfry in the garden. The frequent ringing of the bells annoyed his neighbours, and Johnston gave the bells to St George's Church, Hardwicke Pl. (*q.v.*). The house was afterwards occupied by Isaac Butt (1813–79), founder of the Parliamentary Home Rule Party. His parties in Johnston's Octagon Room were famous, and the bailiffs were frequent callers. At the W. end of the street· is the Mater Misericordiae Hospital (1860). The façades of the adjacent brick houses (Mater Private Nursing Home), like those of the Dominican convent and school, have been treated in barbarous fashion. The convent chapel has a window by Lady Glenavy, *St Patrick* (1909).

Gardiner St (Lower, Middle,.and Upper) leads down from Lower Dorset St to Beresford Pl. It was laid out about 1787, Middle Gardiner St, which has some splendid houses, being the oldest part. In its heyday this was one of the very finest of Dublin's Georgian residential streets, with a magnificent, ¾-m., downhill vista closed by the Custom House, a vista long since ruined by the infamous "Loop Line" railway. By the present century the street had been largely given over to badly decayed tenements. Many of these have been reconditioned as working-class flats by Dublin Corporation, but the fine interiors are gone. (A very objectionable feature of the reconditioning is the concrete replacement of the area railings.) The Labour Exchange at the S. end of the street was originally Trinity Church (Protestant), by Frederick Darley, 1838. At the N. end is the Jesuit church of St Francis Xavier (1829–32), by Joseph B. Keane; the interior has recently been happily redecorated under the direction of Michael Scott; the *St Aloysius* figure in wood is by Oisín Kelly. The houses opposite (1810) may be by Francis Johnston.

Glasnevin is a suburb beyond the Royal Canal, to the W. of Drumcondra. St Berchán Clárainech (Flat-face), better known by his pet-name, Mo-Bhí (d. 545), founded a monastery on the banks of the Tolka, of which no trace at all survives. Among his disciples here were SS Comgall of Bangor and Columcille of Derry and Iona, in whose time the monastery church was on the E. bank of the river, the monks' huts on the W. bank.

The Botanic Gardens (founded 1795 by the

Royal Dublin Society and taken over by the State in 1878) are particularly beautiful. They occupy the demesne of the house where the poet, Tickell, lived, 1725–40. The poet's house (altered) is now the residence of the Director. The beautiful yew-walk beside the Tolka, despite its name, has no connection with Addison. Some of the conservatories are by Frederick Darley. Of particular interest are the cycads, orchids, herbaceous borders, and conifers. Open: Weekdays: 9 a.m.–6 p.m., summer; 10 a.m.–dusk, winter. Sundays: 11 a.m.–6 p.m., summer; 11 a.m.–dusk, winter. The nearby Bon Secours Nursing Home occupies the site of Delville, residence of Swift's celebrated friends, Dr and Mrs Delaney. – Sir Richard Steele lived in Elmhurst, Glasnevin. – Prospect Cemetery, Finglas Rd, Dublin's principal burial ground, dates from 1831. Here are buried: Daniel O Connell (1775–1847), the Liberator; John Philpot Curran (1750–1817); Barry Sullivan, celebrated actor (1821–91); Charles Stewart Parnell (1846–91); O Donovan Rossa (1831–1915); Sir Roger Casement (1864–1916); Arthur Griffith (1872–1922); and Michael Collins (1890–1922).

Great Charles St (about 1800) leads from the SE. corner of Mountjoy Sq. to Richmond Pl. No. 12 was the house of George Petrie (1789–1866), antiquary, painter, and collector of Irish folk-music.

Great Denmark St, begun as Gardiner's Row (about 1775–80), leads from Frederick St and Parnell Sq. to Gardiner's Pl. and Mountjoy Sq. Belvedere House was built in 1786 by Michael Stapleton, "the Dublin Adam", for William Rochfort, 2nd Earl of Belvedere. Splendidly sited at the head of superb North Great George's St, it is still one of Dublin's finest mansions, though the excellent façade has been spoilt by the usual 20th cent. plate-glass voids. A fluted frieze and cornice take the place of the customary flat coping. The interior is lavishly decorated with excellent Stapleton stucco. The principal apartments are the Venus Room, Apollo Room and Diana Room. The ceiling centrepiece of the former has been mutilated, but the decoration of the other rooms survives intact. The Diana Room (Library) also has its original mahogany organ and bookcases. Since 1841 the house has been part of a Jesuit school (Belvedere College) which also incorporates No. 5, Great Denmark St (Killeen House), likewise by Stapleton. James Joyce went to school there (1893–8), and the school figures in his *A Portrait of the Artist as a Young Man*.

Hardwicke Pl., at the intersection of Temple St and Hardwicke St, is the setting – a crescent in front (now spoilt by municipal flats) and a step-shaped, vista-yielding blind alley behind, devised by Francis Johnston for his Great St George's Church (1802–13), perhaps the finest of Dublin's later Protestant churches. The 200-ft spire is a highly individual adaptation of the spire of Gibbs's St Martin-in-the-Fields, London, but the interior (marred by bad, 19th cent. glass) is wholly Johnston. Galleries on three sides are cantilevered on an inner wall. The chancel is at the middle of a long side. Until 1880 there was a three-decker gallery (entered by the E. door, now closed) behind the Communion Table. The very wide, flat ceiling was a fine constructional feat. The Johnstonian decorations – woodcarving and the rest – are by Richard Stewart and others. The whole has recently been admirably redecorated to the designs of Denis O'D. Hanna. – The memorials include some by Edward Smyth's son, John; Sir Charles Metzler Giesecke, F.R.S. (1761–1833), Ephraim Mc Donnell (d. 1835). The *Faith, Hope,* and *Charity* keystones under the portico are by Edward Smyth. Edward Bunting (1773–1843), pioneer collector of Irish folk music, was organist to the church.

Jones's Rd connects the N. Circular Rd with Clonliffe Rd. Here is situated Croke Park, headquarters stadium of the Gaelic Athletic Association and venue each Aug.–Sept. of the final matches for the All-Ireland Hurling and Gaelic Football championships. Hurling is Ireland's only native outdoor game. Like shinty (Scotland), bandy (Wales), and golf, it derives from a very ancient game of the insular Celts, a game which figures in Irish heroic literature (where scores are made by holing the ball). A first-class match is a memorable exhibition of speed and skill.

Killester is a new suburb to the N. of Clontarf. There are remains of a medieval church; also a good Vocational School by Brian P. Hooper and R. J. Mayne.

Marino, a new suburb to the W. of the Howth road beyond Fairview, preserves the name of Marino House, seaside retreat of the "Volunteer Earl" of Charlemont (*see* Parnell Sq., Dublin, N.–S. Axis). In the grounds of the O Brien Institute, Malahide Rd, is the delightful Casino (Nat. Mon.) designed for Charlemont's garden by Sir William Chambers and erected 1762 by Simon Vierpyl, sculptor and builder, whom Charlemont had brought from Rome in 1750. Vierpyl worked from models and instructions supplied from London. Edward Smyth (1749–1812), great architectural sculptor and stuccoer, was at that time an apprentice of Vierpyl's, and may have had a hand in the decorations. The elevations derive from the end pavilions of Chambers's rejected design for Harewood House, Yorkshire, a design he later adapted – with no greater success – for a palace for the Queen Mother of Sweden. In the basement are kitchen, scullery, pantry, butler's pantry, wine cellar, servants' hall, and ale cellar. On the principal floor are vestibule, saloon, study, and a bedroom. The upper floor has bedrooms and dressing closets. Though for

Irish Tourist Board

Hurling

many years callously abandoned to neglect and decay, this architectural gem still retains interesting interior features. The parapet offers a delightful view. In 1919–21 the extensive underground out-offices were used as a soundproof small-arms school by the Resistance.

No. 3, Marino Terrace, was the home of William Carleton (1794–1869), novelist and folklorist. No. 8, Inverness Rd, was the home of James Joyce in 1890.

Clontarf Presbyterian Church (1889–90), at the corner of Howth Rd and Fairview, is by Sir Thomas Drew. It has an unusual Harry Clarke window, *Resurrection and Deposition* (1914–18 War Memorial).

The Church of the Visitation (1855), Fairview Avenue, is by Patrick Byrne.

Marlborough St (*c.* 1740–60) runs from Eden Quay to Parnell St. Near the S. end is the Abbey Theatre, founded in 1904 by Lady Gregory and W. B. Yeats (with the financial assistance of Miss Annie Elizabeth Fredericka Horniman of Manchester). The dramatists and players who made the theatre world-famous include William Butler Yeats, John Millington Synge, Seán O Casey, Máire O Neill, Sara Allgood, Barry Fitzgerald (William Shields), Maureen Delaney, F. J. McCormick (Peter C. Judge), Eileen Crowe, Siobhán McKenna, and Cyril Cusack. In 1951 the theatre was destroyed by fire, with the loss of many precious relics. The new theatre, by Michael Scott and Associates, opened in 1966.

Just N. of the Earl St–Talbot St intersection is Tyrone House, built in 1740 by Richard Cassels

for Marcus Beresford, Viscount (later Earl of) Tyrone. In 1798 John Claudius Beresford used the house as a torture barracks. His barbarous pitch-capping and flogging of rebels and suspects in the riding school are not yet forgotten. The house, which has some good ceilings and a fine staircase, is today the secretariat of the Department of Education. In 1835 the Board of Education, as it then was, defaced the house by substituting the building-blocks porch, etc., for Cassels's elegant doorway and by removing the Venetian window which formed the centrepiece above it. The domed, central building to the E. is the Central Model School which George Bernard Shaw attended as a child; today Irish is the sole medium of instruction. The white marble *Pietà* is by the Italian sculptor, Luppi. It was the Italian Government's thank-offering for Irish post-war relief.

On the opposite side of the street is St Mary's Catholic Pro-Cathedral (1815), by the amateur architect, John Sweetman, whose only work it is. The church was intended for O Connell St, but the opposition of the Protestant oligarchy consigned to it this less conspicuous and less suitable site. Prior to the introduction of the dome and a new window system, the interior revealed the inspiration of Chalgrin's St Philippe du Roule, Paris (1769–94). Extensions of the aisles have spoiled the interior vistas and proportions. The high altar is by Belfast-born, Dublin-taught Peter Turnerelli (1774–1839); above it is a good stucco *Ascension*. The monuments in the church include statues (1855 and 1882) of Archbishop Murray (1768–1852) and Cardinal Cullen (1803–78) by Sir Thomas

Farrell (who was preferred to John Hogan by the sponsors of the Murray monument). In the SW. porch is a Purcell monument by Hogan. In the E. lunette gallery may be seen a large model of the church as designed by Sweetman. The Pro-Cathedral's Palestrina Choir was endowed by Edward Martyn of Tullira, Co. Galway (*see under* Ardrahan). The celebrated tenor, John, Count McCormack (1884–1945), was for a time a member.

Mountjoy Pl. (*c.* 1791) is a cul-de-sac at the SE. corner of Mountjoy Sq. No. 1 was built and decorated by Michael Stapleton for himself in 1791; he died there in 1801. The three adjoining houses are also by him.

Mountjoy Sq. (1792–1808) was laid out for Luke Gardiner, Lord Mountjoy. It is now badly decayed, especially on the S. and SW. Nos. 7, 8, 39–44, and 58 were fine houses by Michael Stapleton; they have very good interiors. Other houses were by Charles Thorp; No. 61, Annesley House, has a very fine doorway. The original intention was to have St George's Church (*see* Hardwicke Pl.) at the centre of the square.

North Great George's St (*c.* 1775 onwards) runs downhill from Great Denmark St to Parnell St. It is one of the finest of Dublin's 18th cent. streets, with a splendid vista from either end. No. 2 was the Dublin residence of John Dillon (1851–1927), son of the Young Ireland leader, John Blake Dillon, and himself leader of the Irish Nationalist Party at Westminster. No. 20 was the home of Sir Samuel Fergusson (1810–86), poet and antiquary. Nos. 34 and 35 (Kenmare House) are by Michael Stapleton. No. 38, by Charles Thorp, Sen., was the home of Sir John Pentland Mahaffy (1839–1918), Provost of Trinity College and noted "character". No. 45 was the home of Charles Thorp, Sen., builder and stuccoer.

Seán MacDermott St, originally Gloucester St, joins Cathal Brugha St to the intersection of Amiens St, Portland Row, and North Strand. It was laid out about 1772 and had many fine, large houses. By the present cent. it had become, like the rest of this quarter, one of Dublin's foulest slums. The houses are now in process of renovation as working-class flats (with the Corporation's customary concrete eyesores). About half-way down the street is an unfinished Regency terrace and, facing it, a good neo-Grec Presbyterian church (1835), now a corn-store.

At the E. end of the street is gaunt Aldborough House (1792–98), latest of Dublin's great Georgian mansions. It was built by Edward Stratford, 2nd Earl of Aldborough, for his wife, on the then edge of the city – whence RUS IN URBE on the portico. The design has been doubtfully attributed to Sir William Chambers. The house has lost one wing-

pavilion, its balustraded parapet, and half of the curved double perron giving on to the garden. It has an "astonishing top-lit" staircase hall "like a well-shaft or a mine or one of Mr Howard's model penitentiaries" (Craig). The surviving wing may have contained a theatre. Between 1813 and 1830 the house was the Feinaglian Institution, a school employing advanced methods of education. During that time a chapel, hall, and other additions were made. For the past seventy years the place has been the Post Office Stores, and the once beautiful gardens have long been built over.

Dublin North-West of the River Liffey and O Connell St–Dorset St

Arran Quay, laid out about 1680, lies between Inns Quay and Ellis Quay. No. 12 was the birthplace of Edmund Burke (1729–97).

St Paul's Church (1835–42) is a good building erected, with very slender resources, to the design of Patrick Byrne (1783–1864). The erection of a Catholic church of such quality on a main thoroughfare evoked resentment in obdurate Protestant breasts. (Its modest predecessor of 1785 may still be seen hidden away behind the backs of the houses on the Quay.) The classical portico, surmounted by bell-tower and cupola, is a feature of Dublin's riverside architecture. The high altar, dramatically lit from above by concealed lighting, is set before a curved end-wall screened behind a pair of Ionic columns. The wall-painting was a good copy of Rubens's *Conversion of St Paul* until, relatively recently, some "itinerant dauber was permitted to introduce an incongruous figure into the centre". Recently a vulgar, concrete "Lourdes Grotto" has been heaped against one of the outer walls of the church.

Aughrim St runs from Manor St (continuation of Stoneybatter) to the N. Circular Rd. In the mortuary chapel of the Church of the Holy Family is a *Resurrection* window by Hubert McGoldrick.

Blackhall Pl. extends from Stoneybatter to Hendrick St. On the W. side is beautiful King's Hospital, alias the Bluecoat School. It was built (1773 onwards) to the design of Thomas Ivory (1720–86), one of the best Irish architects of his day. (King's Hospital was founded in 1672 by Charles II for aged men and poor boys, but soon became exclusively a boys' charitable school.) Ivory's magnificent project was never completed, as Parliament failed to vote the necessary funds. In 1779 Ivory had to abandon the arcaded quadrangle he had proposed for the rear of the building; the lofty central tower and lantern never got any higher than the colonnade of the main order; the chapel never received its intended furnishings. (Ivory resigned in disgust as soon as the façade and boardroom were finished, 1780.) The ornamental carving is by Simon Vierpyl (who was in charge of the stonework); the plasterwork by Charles Thorp, Sen. The building was "completed" by John Wilson. In 1894 the unfinished central tower was taken down, and the stunted cupola erected in its stead. The chapel (1777) is very good; the *Resurrection* painting is by Waldré (*see* Dublin Castle: State Apartments), the *Resurrection* window (1935) by Evie Hone. In the boardroom (damaged by fire some years ago; Thorp's ceiling since reproduced in facsimile) may be seen a painting, by Trotter, showing Ivory and Vierpyl receiving instructions to cut down the scheme for the school.

Blackhall Pl. and Blackhall St (down which King's Hospital faces) were laid out by Ivory as the setting for his great design. In this way disappeared almost the last trace of Oxmanstown Green. (Oxmanstown, formerly Ostmaneby, Austmannabyr, so called after the Scandinavian settlers there; *see* p. 211.) Blackhall St is today a quiet, decaying Georgian backwater, while the Place has been ruined by unworthy 19th–20th cent. erections.

Church St leads from Inns Quay to North King St. St Michan's Church (C. of I.) occupies the site of the first suburban church (1096) of Norse Dublin. The present building dates from 1685–86, but was drastically restored in 1828. The only ancient relic is a recumbent episcopal effigy in the chancel, most likely the effigy of Bishop Samuel O Hanly (1096–1121), presumed founder of the first church here. Handel is said to have used the Renatus Harris organ during his Dublin visit. The 17th cent. vaults happen to be constructed of magnesium limestone, which absorbs moisture. The resultant dryness of the atmosphere tends to "mummify" corpses buried there. Viewing them is one of Dublin's macabre entertainments for tourists.

Constitution Hill leads from Church St to Dominick St. On the E. side are the King's Inns, whose neglected lawns afford a welcome open space for the dwellers of nearby tenements. (For the King's Inns *see* Henrietta St.) Just off the Hill, to the NW., is Broadstone Station (1841–50), an unusually fine example of early railway architecture; by John Skipton Mulvany. The noteworthy E. colonnade was added in 1861. The building is now used as a road freight depot.

Dominick St, Lower and Upper (1755 onwards), leads from Parnell St to Constitution Hill. In the last couple of years it has lost most of its 18th cent. houses. The first house here was No. 20, Lower Dominick St (five doors S. of the church), built for himself by Robert West, a master-builder and brilliant stuccoer. It is now St Saviour's Orphanage, but the interior is still one of the sights of Dublin, with magnificent staircase hall, Venus Room (now a dormitory), and other notable apartments, including the room now used as a chapel. St Saviour's Dominican Priory and Church (1858)

are by J. J. Mc Carthy. The church has a *Dead Christ* by John Hogan (completed by his son, John Valentine Hogan, d. 1920). No. 36, opposite the church, was the birthplace of Archibald Hamilton Rowan (1751–1834), United Irishman. Arthur Griffith (1872–1922), founder of Sinn Féin and President of the Provisional Government of the Irish Free State, was also born in Dominick St. Joseph Sheridan Le Fanu (1814–73), novelist, lived at No. 45 Lower Dominick St.

Dorset St, connecting Bolton St (Municipal College of Technology) with Drumcondra Rd, follows the ancient highway to the North. It contains some large houses of 1750–60. Richard Brinsley Sheridan was born at No. 12 Upper Dorset St. The Hibernian Bank occupies the site of the house where Seán O Casey, playwright, was born (1884).

Grangegorman Rd leads from Brunswick St to the N. Circular Rd. The great complex of Grangegorman Mental Hospital includes the former Richmond General Penitentiary (1812) and the former Richmond Lunatic Asylum (1814–17), typical examples of Francis Johnston's institutional architecture.

Green St leads from North King St to Boot Lane. The Central Criminal Court sits in the dull court-house (1792–97) by Richard Johnston. Newgate Gaol (by Thomas Cooley, 1773) stood next door until 1877. The court-house was the place of trial of the brothers Sheares (1798); Robert Emmet (1803); John Mitchel, Charles Gavan Duffy, and William Smith O Brien (1848); and the Fenian leaders of 1867. Lord Edward Fitzgerald died of wounds in the prison, 1798, and the 1848 Young Irelanders were incarcerated there while awaiting trial.

Henrietta St (about 1720 onwards) leads from Bolton St to the entrance of the King's Inns. It was the earliest of N. Dublin's great 18th cent. residential streets, and remained the most fashionable until the Union. Thereafter it declined, and early in the present cent. many of the magnificent houses fell into the clutches of an Alderman of Dublin Corporation. This City Father ripped out the fine staircases, mantelpieces, etc., for sale in London, and converted the houses into slum tenements. No. 3 was the Earl of Kingston's house; No. 4 the Earl of Thomond's; No. 5 (now 5 and 6) the Rt Hon. John Ponsonby's. Nos. 8, 9, 10 are now a convent of the Sisters of Charity of St Vincent de Paul. Nos. 9 and 10 were built in 1730 by Richard Cassels, the latter (Mountjoy House) for Luke Gardiner, Lord Mountjoy, the banker-landlord who laid out this and so many other great N. Dublin streets. Despite 19th–20th cent. ill-treatment, both houses still retain good, original features, e.g. the salon (now a chapel) and very fine staircase hall of No. 9. Frederick Darley's bleak King's Inns Library

(1827) occupies the site of the three earliest houses in the street. – The King's Inns (1795–1817), at the head of the street, is the Irish Inns of Court, headquarters of the ruling body (The Benchers of the Honourable Society of the King's Inns) of the Irish legal profession. The Society traces its origin to the reign of Edward I. In 1541 it was granted the possessions of Dublin's Dominican friary by Henry VIII, and, giving its headquarters the new name, the King's Inns, transferred them to the site of the friary (*see* Inns Quay). In 1795 the Inns were moved to their present site, and James Gandon was commissioned to design the buildings. Associated with him in the work was his pupil and partner, Henry Aaron Baker. A curved, triumphal arch (royal arms by Edward Smyth) gives access to a narrow court set at an angle to the axis of the street. On the N. side of the court is the Benchers' Dining Hall (first part to be completed); on the S., the Prerogative Court (now the Registry of Deeds). At the W. end a second triumphal arch pierces the central block to give access to the principal front, facing Constitution Hill. Here are the ceremonial entrances to the Dining Hall and Prerogative Court. The Caryatids and Persae flanking these (*Security* and *Law* guarding the Prerogative Court; *Ceres* and a *Bacchante* guarding the Dining Hall) are by Edward Smyth. Smyth also did the rather unsuccessful bas-reliefs of the upper storey (*Prudence, Justice and Wisdom at a Blazing Altar; Restoration of the Society of the King's Inns, 1607; Ceres and Companions offering the Fruits of the Earth*). In 1808, annoyed by ignorant interference, Gandon resigned his commission, and handed over all his drawings for the completion of the work to Baker. The building was not completed until 1816–17, when Francis Johnston finished the Prerogative Court and built the cupola and its colonnade in accordance with the Gandon–Baker design.

Since then a wing has been added to each side of the W. front, throwing it out of scale. However, the Dining Hall (recently restored), with Edward Smyth's stucco figures of *Justice, Prudence, Fortitude,* and *Temperance*, remains pretty much as Gandon left it, the least abused and altered of all the great architect's works. Facing the W. front is a statue of *Themis* from the rotunda of the Four Courts, where it held aloft a gas-jet.

Henry St leads W. from O Connell St to Mary St. When danger forced him to abandon No. 76 Harcourt St, Michael Collins had his National Loan offices in No. 21. His principal office was next door, in No. 22, until the Black and Tans discovered it shortly before the Anglo-Irish Truce of 1921.

Inns Quay lies between Upper Ormond Quay and Arran Quay. The name recalls the fact that the site of the medieval Dominican friary here was occupied by the King's Inns from 1541 to 1775. In 1776 the erection of the Public Record Offices on the W. end of the site was commenced, the architect being Thomas Cooley. Cooley's plans were for a quadrangle entered through an open screen on the S. side. The pedimented N. range was intended to have an open arcade on the ground floor. Cooley died in 1784, when only the S. and W. sides had been completed. The following year it was decided to transfer the Four Courts from St Michael's Hill (*see* Christchurch Pl., Dublin, SW.) to Inns Quay, and to integrate the necessary building with Cooley's work. The task was entrusted to James Gandon, who thus gave Dublin his second masterpiece. Now mutilated, it is the seat of both the Supreme Court and the High Court of the Republic.

Gandon's Four Courts (1786–1802) was controlled by the cramped site and the existing

The King's Inns, west front, the wings are additions

Plate 8. Leinster House, Dublin, west front

Cooley work. The architect was also constantly hampered by lack of funds and by carping criticism. He reduced the size of Cooley's quadrangle, modified the W. and N. ranges, substituted the great, domed, central block for Cooley's E. range, and replaced the S. side by a longer, more monumental screen with triumphal-arch centre-piece. The new quadrangle thus obtained he duplicated on the E. side of the central block.

The dominant feature of the building is the great, domed, central mass. (Gandon proposed to have the portico project out over the footpath.) The excellent statues (1792) on the pediment are by Edward Smyth; *Moses* flanked by *Justice* and *Mercy*, with *Wisdom* and *Authority* seated on the corners; the *Moses* is a masterpiece of architectural sculpture. Behind the portico a curved porch gave access to an apsidal vestibule opening on to the admirable rotunda beneath the double dome. From this the four courts (King's Bench, Chancery, Exchequer, and Common Pleas) radiated towards the corners of the enclosing square; a fifth court, the Rolls Court, lay on the main N.–S. axis. The four axial entrances to the rotunda and the four open entrances to the courts were flanked by pairs of great Corinthian columns standing in depth. The wall niches between the entrances were left empty, but later received statues of eminent 19th cent. lawyers. In the attic pedestal of the inner dome were eight sunk panels; the four over the court doorways contained scenes (stucco) from legal history. Above them, on consoles between the windows, were eight colossal stucco figures of *Punishment, Eloquence, Mercy, Prudence, Law, Wisdom, Justice,* and *Liberty*. From the tops of their heads an acanthus arabesque encircled the dome, enclosing medallions of ancient lawgivers (*Moses, Lycurgus, Solon, Numa, Confucius, Alfred the Great, Manco Capax,* and *Ollamh Fodhla*) above the windows. This magnificent decorative scheme was executed by Edward Smyth.

In the 19th and 20th centuries inferior structures (Law Library, Public Record Office, Land Registry, etc.) were crowded in behind Gandon's building. In 1916 the whole complex was occupied by Volunteers under the command of Edward Daly, but suffered only minor damage from British gunfire. In April 1922, the buildings were seized by Anti-Treaty forces. The following June, Free State troops attacked them. Some major breaches were made in the walls of the Four Courts by shellfire, but the real disaster was caused by the explosives with which the defenders had mined the buildings. The double dome and the interior of the central block were destroyed; the SE. and SW. wings, and the SW. part of the arcaded screen, were badly damaged. The Law Library too, and the Public Record Office with its irreplaceable archives, were completely destroyed. In the work of reconstruction (completed 1932) the Office of Public Works found another

opportunity for its talents. The open arcades of Gandon's quadrangles were blocked up; the E. and W. wings, shorn of the panelled blocks at the centre of the blocking courses, were pushed back 10 ft; their roof-lines were radically altered; four of the nine first-floor niches of the central block were converted into windows; the outline of the dome was altered; cement was used in place of stone when renewing the entablature and stepped blocking course of the dome; the crowns on Edward Smyth's fine trophies of Arms over the triumphal-arch gateways of the screens were replaced by spheres; and the site of the Rolls Court, and most of the rest of the interior, were replanned on new lines.

The Law Library is the focal centre of the Irish legal profession. Irish barristers, unlike their English brethren, do not have chambers. Instead, they wait for business in the Library, and the loud calling of their names when solicitors arrive with briefs is a local phenomenon. The Solicitors' Building is the headquarters of the Incorporated Law Society, governing body of the solicitors' profession. It has an armorial window by Michael Healy (1936).

Mary's Abbey, linking the intersection of Upper Abbey St and Capel St with the junction of Boot Lane and Arran St, preserves the name of the Cistercian abbey of St Mary. The early history of the abbey is obscure. It may have been an early-12th cent. foundation (by the Leinster dynast, Donal Mac Giolla Mo-Cholmóg?). It was affiliated to Savigny in Normandy (*see* Carrick Abbey *under* Downpatrick). Savigny joined the Cistercians in 1147, and in 1156 transferred its Dublin daughter to Buildwas Abbey, Shropshire. The Dublin monks clung to their independence until 1174, when Henry II forced them to submit to Buildwas. The only portions of the abbey surviving today are the chapter-house (Nat. Mon.) and adjacent slype of about 1190. (They form the basement of a warehouse in Meeting-house Lane.) In the Middle Ages the abbey was frequently used as a meeting-place of the English Council, and it was in the chapter-house that Silken Thomas Fitzgerald dramatically threw off his allegiance to Henry VIII in 1534, by flinging down his Lord Deputy's Sword of State in the presence of the Council. A 15th cent. statue of the Blessed Virgin, which belonged to the abbey, is now enshrined in the Carmelite Church, Aungier St (p. 226).

Mary Pl. joins Dorset St with Mountjoy St. Here is St Mary's Chapel-of-Ease (1830), by John Semple; handed over to the Irish Red Cross Society by the Church of Ireland in 1966. Best known as the "Black Church", this classic example of Semple's highly individual Gothick (*see* Rathmines, Dublin SW., *and* Monkstown *under* Dún Laoghaire) is remarkable for its parabolic, corbelled vault. (In effect the building has neither walls nor ceiling, but is, structurally speaking, all vault.) The W. gallery is a timber-and-plaster simulation of stonework.

Mary St (*c.* 1675) continues the line of Henry St to Capel St. At No. 29 Michael Collins had (1920–21) one of his hidden offices as Minister for Finance and Director of Intelligence of the proscribed first Dáil Éireann. It had a secret room for his papers. Shabby St Mary's Church (1700) is the oldest unaltered Protestant church in Dublin, and the first to be built with galleries. In it Theobald Wolfe Tone (born nearby in Wolfe Tone St) and the "Volunteer Earl" of Charlemont were baptized, and John Wesley preached his first sermon in Ireland. Archibald Hamilton Rowan, United Irishman, is buried in the churchyard. The interior is of great interest. All the cornices are of richly carved wood. Most of the fittings are original, and the organ-case is magnificent, with a hollow-relief frieze of figures in early-18th cent. costume. The William Watson memorial tablet is by Edward Smyth. The churchyard has been laid out as a Wolfe Tone memorial park and presented to the city (1966) by the church authorities.

North Brunswick St links Stoneybatter with Church St. Hidden away off the N. side is Brunswick Villa, a curious little 18th cent. model village complete with green. The Morning Star Hostel is the headquarters of the Legion of Mary, a voluntary lay organization for good works, now spread throughout most of the Catholic world.

North Circular Rd runs from the Phoenix Park to Portland Row. At the junction with Cabra Rd is St Peter's Church (Vincentian), a large, Gothic-Revival essay by George Goldie of London. In the S. aisle is a three-light *Sacred Heart* window (1919) by Harry Clarke. The door light and four two-light windows of the adjacent Mortuary Chapel are also by Clarke (1921): Symbols of the Passion, etc. Nearby is Dalymount Park, Dublin's principal Soccer stadium.

Phoenix Park, The, on the NW. side of the city (principal city entrances from Parkgate St, the N. Circular Rd and Conyngham Rd, Islandbridge), covers 1,752 acres, and is one of the largest and most magnificent city parks in Europe. Its history goes back to the seizure by the Crown of the lands of the priory of Kilmainham (*see* Dublin, SW.). On the priory lands N. of the Liffey there was erected early in the 17th cent. a viceregal country residence, The Phoenix. In 1662 further lands were acquired for the purpose of creating a royal deer park of over 2,000 acres around The Phoenix. In 1679 the priory lands to the S. of the river were set aside for the Royal Hospital, Kilmainham, and the park thus reduced more or less to its present limits. The supervision of the park was confided to a ranger and two keepers, chosen from persons of the proper station and politics. In the Lord Lieutenancy of the Earl of Chesterfield (1744–47) the park received the essentials of its existing layout.

Just inside the Main Gate (Parkgate St) are the beautiful People's Gardens. To the E. is the Department of Defence, designed as the Royal Military Infirmary by James Gandon, but erected (1787 onwards) by W. Gibson, who

Commissioners of Public Works in Ireland

Earth, *detail of a ceiling from Mespil House, now in Áras an Uachtaráin, Phoenix Park*

designed the cupola. Beyond the People's Gardens are the Zoological Gardens (1830), noted for the breeding of lions.

On the S. side of the main road are hundreds of acres of playing fields for hurling, football, cricket, etc. Here, too, is the colossal Wellington Testimonial (205 ft) by Sir Robert Smirke (1817 onwards). The bronze *Emancipation* panel designed by John Hogan was executed by his Italian friend, Benzoni, from Hogan's model. A projected equestrian statue of Wellington was never executed. Further W., to the N. of the main road, is the Polo Ground.

Close to the main road-junction of the park is the beautiful Phoenix Column, erected by Lord Chesterfield in 1747. Nearby is Áras an Uachtaráin, residence of the President of the Republic. The house originated as a small park ranger's lodge *c.* 1751–2. In 1782 it was purchased for the Lord Lieutenant's use, and later enlarged to make it his chief official residence. Michael Stapleton did work there in 1787, possibly the *Aesop* ceiling. The Doric porch of the N. front was added in 1808. In 1815–16 Francis Johnston added the Ionic portico of the S. front; also dining and other rooms (on the site of the present ballroom and its counterpart on the W.). In 1840 the formal garden was laid out by the celebrated Decimus Burton. The E. and W. wings of the garden front were added, seemingly, for Queen Victoria's 1849 visit; the W. wing was reconstructed 1946–47, the E. wing 1954–57. In 1952 the lovely *Jupiter and the Elements* ceiling from Mespil House (Mespil Rd, Dublin, SE.) was erected in the President's Reception Room. The house also has good 18th cent. mantelpieces from Mountjoy Sq. On 6 May 1882, Lord Frederick Cavendish, newly arrived Chief Secretary for Ireland, and T. H. Burke, the Under-Secretary, were stabbed to death in sight of the house. These Phoenix Park Murders did much to embitter Anglo-Irish relations.

NW. of Áras an Uachtaráin is the Papal Nunciature (the Under-Secretary's lodge of British days); SW. is the residence of the United States Ambassador (originally the Chief Secretary's Lodge). The latter is an 18th cent. house enlarged in 1775 and subsequently modified; it has stucco by Michael Stapleton.

On the S. side of the park, sited on the steep terrace of the Liffey, is St Mary's Chest Hospital, built in 1766 as the Royal Hibernian Military School. Joseph Sheridan Le Fanu (1814–73) was born here; his father was chaplain to the Military School. The Protestant chapel is by Thomas Cooley (1771). The main building was enlarged by Francis Johnston (1808–13); it has recently been mutilated.

DULEEK, Co. Meath (Map 6, C2), now bypassed by the Drogheda (5 m.)–Ashbourne (11 m.)–Dublin (23 m.) road, is a place with a long history. It takes its name from a *daimh liag*, house of stones, i.e. an early stone-built church. Its history begins about A.D. 450 with

the setting up of a bishopric by St Patrick, who confided it to the care of St Cíanán (d. 24 Nov. 489). The subsequent history of the foundation is obscure. It would seem in time to have acquired a predominantly monastic character. It was sacked several times by the Norse between 830 and 1149, and was pillaged by the Anglo-Normans in 1171. The bodies of Brian Boru and his son lay in state there in April 1014, on their way to Armagh. In the 12th cent., seemingly, the monastery was reconstituted as St Mary's Abbey of Canons Regular of St Augustine by one of the O Kellys of Brega. About 1174 Bishop Echtigern Mac Maíl-Chíaráin of Clonard merged the bishopric of Clonard (*see under* Kinnegad) with those of Duleek, Trim, Ardbraccan (*see under* Navan), Kells, and Slane, to form the diocese of Meath, the see of which was transferred to Newtown Trim (*see* Trim) by his successor, the first Anglo-Norman bishop, Simon de Rupefort, alias Rochefort.

Hugh de Lacy established a manor at Duleek and constructed a motte-castle. About 1180 he granted St Cíanán's Church (by then parochial), together with certain lands, to the Augustinian priory of Llanthony Secunda outside Gloucester, and the Llanthony canons built a grange, or farmhouse, as the headquarters of their estate. Medieval Duleek also had a hospital (Le Magdelyns) and a frank house.

The churchyard at the Protestant church occupies part of the site of the early monastery and its Irish Augustinian successor. The oldest surviving relics (Nat. Mons.) are three early gravestones, two 10th (?) cent. High Crosses, a Romanesque fragment, and the remnant of St Cíanán's Church. The latter is outside the churchyard to the NW.; St Cíanán's grave was at the N. side of the chancel; built into the N. wall is an early gravestone inscribed OR[ÓIT] DO SCANLAN ("A prayer for Scanlán"); in the Middle Ages a church dedicated to St Patrick stood on the N. Inside the churchyard, to the N. of the modern church, stands the North Cross: the figure subjects include a *Holy Family* (?) and a *Crucifixion*.

The remains (Nat. Mon.) of St Mary's Abbey are SW. of the modern church, viz. the S. aisle and arcade of a 15th cent. church and a massive tower erected in the 16th cent. at the W. end of the nave. – This tower had been built against the Round Tower of the early monastery (cf. Lusk), as is shown by the "matrix" of the Round Tower in its N. face. Other pre-Norman relics at the tower are an early gravestone and a Romanesque pilaster-capital. – Under the arcade have been placed miscellaneous fragments, including an early gravestone and the base and head (with *Crucifixion*) of the South Cross. – In the aisle are some 16th–17th cent. monuments, including the effigial tomb (defaced) of Dr James Cusack, Bishop of Meath (1679–88), and the rich tomb of John, Lord Bellew, "shot in the belly in Oughrim 1691". Besides the arms of Bellew, Plunkett, Preston, and St Lawrence, the

North Cross, Duleek

latter has figure carvings (*Crucifixion; SS Michael, Peter, Patrick, Cíanán* (?), *Catherine of Alexandria*). Noteworthy is the "first draft" on the under side of the mensa. – The E. window of the aisle (arms of Sir John Bellew and Dame Ismay Nugent beneath it) is a 1587, post-Gothic replacement suggestive of a re-edification of the church after a period of decay. (The abbey had been granted to Edward Moore – *see* Mellifont Abbey – at the Dissolution.)

S. of the churchyard, in the village market-place, is part of the shaft (Nat. Mon.) of a rudely figured wayside cross erected in 1601 by Jennet Dowdall in memory of herself and her husband, William Bathe (d. 1599) of Athcarne (*below*): Bathe–Dowdall arms and figures of SS Cíanán, Patrick, James, Thomas, James the Less, and Catherine of Alexandria, as well as an *Ecce Homo*. (There are other Jennet Dowdall–William Bathe crosses in Lunderstown (*below*) and Reask–Gaulstown (*below*); *see also* Louth Hall *under* Ardee, *and* Baronstown *under* Slane.)

An inscription on the bridge (of St Mary Magdalen) over the old bed of the Nanny Water

records that it was [re]built in 1587 by William and Genet Bathe of Athcarne.

In Duleek House demesne (sometime property of the Marquesses of Thomond), between the Nanny Water and the road, are slight traces of the Llanthony grange, which had a domestic chapel dedicated to St Michael.

3 m. N. is Donore, a village on the southern Navan (13 m.)–Drogheda (4 m.) road. At the Battle of the Boyne, 1 July 1690 (*see under* Drogheda), the Jacobite camp stretched along the slopes of Donore Hill (402 ft), and James II's command-post was near the ruined hill-top church. When their left flank was turned, the Jacobites retired in tolerable order towards Duleek, and halted for the night on the S. side of the Nanny. In Donore church are the remains of a Synnott altar-tomb.

2½ m. NNE., in Platin, is the ruined, 16th cent. family chapel of the D'Arcys whose home was recently demolished. The Darcys of Platin descended from Sir John Darcy, an Englishman who was several times Justiciar in the 14th cent., and whose son, William, married the widow of the 2nd Earl of Kildare.

3 m. E., beside the Julianstown road, are the ruins of Kilsharvan (Kilkarvan), alias the Chapel of Ralph de Nugent. This was a 13th cent. nave-and-chancel structure with sandstone details; a S. chapel has disappeared. This was one of the properties in dispute between Llanthony Prima and Llanthony Secunda early in the 13th cent.

2 m. SE. is the 4-m. ridge of Bellewstown Hill (530 ft), which affords fine prospects of mountain, river, plain, and sea. Bellewstown Racecourse is on the hill-top.

1¾ m. S., beside the Dublin road in Lunderstown, and near the entrance gate to Annesbrook, alias Loughanmore Demesne, is a second Jennet Dowdall–William Bathe wayside cross (1600). Annesbrook is a good small house with Ionic portico. – ¼ m. NNW. of the house is St Cíanán's Well.

4 m. SSE., in Ardcath, are the remains of a large, late-13th cent. parish church with 14th cent. E. window. One of the Meath possessions of Llanthony, it may have been built by one of the de Russeburys. 4 m. ESE. is Fourknocks (*see* The Naul *under* Balbriggan).

2¼ m. SW., by the roadside on the border of Reask and Gaulstown, is the White Cross (1600; Nat. Mon.), finest of the Jennet Dowdall–William Bathe crosses (Renaissance details); the figure carvings include a *Crucifixion* and *Virgin and Child*. About ½ m. SE. is Athcarne Castle, an Elizabethan stronghouse (with additions) built in 1590 by William Bathe. 1¾ m. W. of the White Cross, on the W. side of the Slane road and to the N. of Balrath crossroads, is the Aylmer Cross (Nat. Mon.), a late-medieval wayside cross "beautified" in 1727 by Sir Andrew Aylmer and his lady, Catherine; on one face is a *Crucifixion*, on the other a *pièta*.

6 m. WSW. is Kentstown (*see under* Navan).

DUNCANNON, Co. Wexford (Map 6, B6), is a pleasant little village and resort on the E. shore of Waterford Harbour, 5 m. S. of Campile and 8 m. N. of Hook Head. There is a good sandy beach here.

On a rocky promontory W. of the village is Duncannon Fort. A pre-Norman fort here gave its name to the place. In the 12th/13th cent. an Anglo-Norman castle took the place of this dún. In 1588 Elizabeth I's government replaced the castle by a strong fort, which in 1645 was taken by the Confederate Catholics after a two-month siege. It was successfully held by them against the Cromwellian general, Ireton, in 1649, but surrendered after the capitulation of Waterford. Thereafter the fort was rebuilt several times, and the latest works date from the last century. In 1690 the defeated James II took ship at Duncannon for Kinsale, en route for France, and shortly afterwards John Churchill, later 1st Duke of Marlborough, captured the fort. From Duncannon he advanced into S. Munster to take Cork and Kinsale for William of Orange, who himself sailed from Duncannon for England that same year.

DUNDALK, Co. Louth (Map 3, B6), county town of Louth, is a prosperous manufacturing town, seaport and market centre. It stands at the head of Dundalk Bay, on the main Dublin (52 m.)–Belfast (51 m.) road, within convenient distance of lovely Carlingford Lough. The principal industries are engineering, shoemaking, tobacco, brewing, and book printing.

In 929 Muirchertach of the Skin Cloaks, King of Aileach, captured a Norse fleet in the bay. Later in the same cent. King Cellachán of Munster is said to have been rescued from Viking captors after a fierce naval engagement there.

The town traces its origin to the grant by Prince John of the surrounding country to Bertram de Verdon in 1185. Under the protection of de Verdon's castle (*see* Castletown, *below*) a settlement sprang up which grew in time into a walled town. The town has taken its English name from Dún Dealgan, a prehistoric fort in the neighbourhood, which early Irish literature treats as the home of the mythical hero, Cú Chulainn. The Irish name of the town was Sráidbhaile (Dhúin Dealgan) as distinguished from Trághbhaile, or Baile na Trágha (the present suburb of Seatown), and Dún Dealgan (the townland of Castletown). In the later Middle Ages the town was an important border-fortress of the English Pale and a base for English attacks on Ulster. As such it figures prominently in the various wars. In 1223 Brian O Neill of the Battle of Down burned the place, as did Edward Bruce in 1315. In 1316 Bruce was crowned King of Ireland in the presence of his Irish allies on neighbouring Knocknamelan. In 1430 Eóghan O Neill destroyed the fortress of Trághbhaile; in 1444 he plundered the place. In 1483 Red Hugh I O Donnell plundered and burned the town. Pursued by

the English Justiciar, he turned and routed him between Dundalk and Louth. Between 1560 and 1650 the town was attacked or besieged six times. It figured prominently in the Eleven Years' War, and in 1689 was held for a time by the Jacobites. The town walls were thrown down in 1724.

In the Market Sq. is the Court House (1813–18) by Edward Park (John Bowden supervising architect). The design and measurements of the Doric portico were taken from the Temple of Theseus as given in Stuart's *Antiquities of Athens*.

At the N. end of Clanbrassil St is the Protestant parish church of St Nicholas. It incorporates the remains of the 13th cent. parish church; the tower dates from the 14th cent., but was drastically remodelled in 1685. Early in the 19th cent. considerable alterations and additions were carried out by Francis Johnston. In the churchyard are some interesting monuments: the cenotaph chancel-slab erected by Sir John Bellew and his wife, Ismay Nugent, who died in 1588 and were buried at Duleek (*q.v.*); the memorial of Thomas Field and his wife, Margaret Hollywood (both died in 1536), which originally stood in a chantry chapel erected by Field; a memorial erected in 1859 to Robert Burns, whose sister, Agnes Galt, is buried in the churchyard.

Some slight remnants of St Leonard's Hospital of the Augustinian Crutched Friars (founded by Bertram de Verdon) may be seen at the rear of the Municipal Library, Chapel St. In the library is housed the Co. Louth Archaeological Society's collection of local antiquities.

St Patrick's Church, Francis Pl., is a Gothic essay (1835–47) by Thomas John Duff of Newry (*see* St Colman's Cathedral, Newry, *and* St Patrick's Cathedral, Armagh). The high altar and reredos were designed by J. J. McCarthy. The side-altar sculptures, *Agony in the Garden* and *The Dead Christ* are by Sir Thomas Farrell (1827–1900). The churchyard screen (1850) is by Thomas Turner, the great tower (1903) by Ashlin and Coleman.

The Dominican church, Anne St, has a Michael Healy window (*St Dominic receiving the Rosary; Sacred Heart;* 1913).

Seatown "Castle", at the corner of Castle St and Mill St, is actually the 15th cent. tower of a Franciscan friary founded about 1244 by John de Verdon. Admiral Sir F. Leopold M'Clintock, K.C.B., F.R.S. (1819–1907), Arctic explorer (*The Voyage of the "Fox" in Arctic Seas*), was born at Kincora House, Seatown Pl.

4 m. N. is Faughart (Fáchard, Fóchard), supposed birthplace of St Brigid (*see* Kildare). There are remains of an old church (Teampall Bhríde na hÁirde Móire, alias Teampall Áird) on the site of a monastery attributed to her. In 735 a battle was fought nearby in which the King of Tara, Áed IV (Allán), defeated Áed Róin, King of Ulaid. The latter had violated an Uriel church, and after the battle he was be-

Commissioners of Public Works in Ireland

The Giant's Load, Proleek, Dundalk

headed on a stone at the door of Faughart church. Near the W. corner of the church is the Grave of King Edward Bruce. Also in the churchyard are Tobar Bhríde, the rough base of a High Cross. WNW. of the churchyard is a fine Anglo-Norman motte erected on an earlier dwelling-site (there are souterrains here). 2 m. E is Aghnaskeagh (*below*). – 4 m. SE. is Proleek (*below*).

4–4½ m. N., to the W. of the Newry road, in Aghnaskeagh, are two prehistoric cairns and a ringfort. Cairn A (Nat. Mon.) is less than 1 m. N. of the reservoir. It was found on excavation to be an oval cairn with a roofless portal dolmen at the centre, and to have six secondary cist graves. The grave goods found here were Neolithic and Bronze Age. At the N. end of the cairn was an ironworkers' furnace of the early Christian centuries. Cairn B (Nat. Mon.) 50 yds to the S., is a round cairn with four separate chamber tombs of Neolithic age; to the NE. is an earthen fort. ½ m. SSE. of Cairn B, and ½ m. N. of the reservoir, in Drumnasillagh, is a court cairn. 1¾ m. S. of the reservoir, in Proleek, are the Giant's Load (Nat. Mon.) – a fine portal dolmen – and a wedge-shaped gallery grave ("the grave of Para Buí Mór Mhac Seóidín, a Scottish giant who came here to challenge Finn mac Cool"). – 1½ m. E. of the reservoir is Ravensdale village; 2 m. NNE. (via Anaverna), on the summit (1,674 ft) of Clermont, is a round cairn with a passage grave and a secondary tomb, both disturbed.

10 m. N. is Kilnasaggart (*see under* Newry).

4 m. SE. is the small seaside resort of Blackrock. 3 m. W., on the road to Louth, are Heynestown motte and castle, the latter a tower with round angle turrets. Nearby is Dunmahon castle, where 200 persons are said to have been slaughtered in 1641 while hearing Mass. On the River Fane, to the S., are remains of Rosmakea Franciscan friary.

3½ m. SW., in Rathiddy, is Clochafarmore (*see under* Louth).

5 m. SW. is Stephenstoun House (*see under* Louth).

1½ m. WNW., in Castletown, is Móta Dhúin Dealgain, motte-and-bailey (Nat. Mon.) of Bertram de Verdon's castle. In modern times it has been identified with the Dún Dealgan of early Irish literature, and may well be an adaptation of an earlier esker ringfort. Castlefolly, whose ruins crown the summit, was built in 1780 by a Capt. Byrne whose rhyming epitaph may be seen in the nearby churchyard. The summit affords a fine panorama. – To the N. is Dealg Fhinn, a pillarstone. SE. is Bellews Castle, built (1472–79) by Richard Bellew and modified in the 16th and 17th centuries; it has beautifully crenellated parapets. Beside it, on the site of an older church, are the ruins of a 15th–16th cent. manorial church; there are two 17th cent. tombs in the chancel. 1¾ m. N. is Kilcurry Catholic church with two windows designed by Sarah Purser (1908): *Episodes from the lives of SS Patrick, Columcille, Brigid* (painted by Catherine O Brien), *Episodes from the lives of SS Fainche and Brendan* (painted by H. Bardon).

3 m. NW., in the Catholic church, Bridgeacrin, is a single-light window (*Agony in the Garden, St Thomas, Judith*) by Michael Healy (1923).

4½ m. NW., affording beautiful views, is Castle Roche, or Roche Castle, alias Dún Gal (Nat. Mon.), a strong rock-castle built early in the 13th cent. by Rohesia Verdon (Róis Mhór Ní Ghairbhe). For a long period it was Bellew property. The remains include a fine, twin-towered gatehouse and a battlemented curtain, as well as fragments of a great hall and a keep (?). A window in the W. end was popularly known as Fuinneóg an Mhurdair, because Róis Mhór was said to have had the builder thrown from it. The larger rock surface E. of the castle seems also to have been enclosed by a wall.

DUNDRUM, Co. Down (Map 3, D6), is a village and small port on Dundrum Bay, 2½ m. S. of Clough and 4 m. NNE. of Newcastle. On a hill-top are the beautifully maintained remains (Nat. Mon.) of a great castle which was an important fortress of the abortive Norman Earldom of Ulster. The earliest castle, of motte-and-bailey type, was taken from de Lacy in 1210 by King John of England. The exact date of the stone castle is unknown, but the great donjon probably dates from 1230–40, the fragmentary gatehouse from *c*. 1300. Some time after 1333 the castle fell to the Magennises, who held it until 1601, when Felim Magennis surrendered it to the Crown. It passed to Lord Cromwell and, in 1636, to Sir Francis Blundell. In 1641 the Magennises seized it; Cromwellians slighted it in 1652.

The remains comprise three distinct parts: (*a*) a 13th cent., polygonal, upper ward with, in places, a great rock-cut ditch; it was entered by a gatehouse with one D-tower and one rectangular tower; the circular donjon has a deep well in the basement; the ramparts afford delightful views; (*b*) a 15th cent. lower ward; (*c*) remains of a 17th cent. Blundell house.

DUNDRUM, Co. Dublin (Map 6, E7), is a village and suburb on the Milltown (10 m.)–Enniskerry (9 m.) road. In St Nathi's Church (C. of I.) may be seen Evie Hone's earliest (1933) work in stained glass, three small panels of the *Annunciation* and abstract subjects, also one by Ethel Rhind, *Psalm 18* (*c*. 1914) and five by Catherine O Brien: *Jesus meets Martha* (1917), *Emmaus* (1919), *Jesus at the Sea of Tiberias* (1919), *After the Transfiguration* (1936), *Like a tree planted by a riverside* (1947). The Catholic church has a three-light window (*Our Lady Queen of the Rosary with SS Catherine and Dominic*) by Michael Healy (1919). There are ruins of a medieval castle in the grounds of Dundrum Castle. Mount Anville, now a Sacred Heart convent and boarding school for girls, was the home of William Dargan (1779–1867), engineer, railway promoter, organizer of the Great Exhibition of 1865, and founder of the National Gallery. Roebuck Lodge, near Clonskeagh, was the home of Maud Gonne Mac-Bride (1866–1953). A woman of remarkable beauty, she inspired some of Yeats's loveliest poems and devoted her life to the struggle for Irish freedom in all its phases. Her husband, Major John MacBride, was executed for his part in the 1916 Rising.

DUNFANAGHY, Co. Donegal (Map 2, C2), is a village and holiday resort with an excellent, sandy beach on the W. shore of Sheep Haven, 28 m. NW. of Letterkenny and 8 m. NE. of Falcarragh.

¾ m. S., in Kill, is Altar, a prehistoric chamber tomb. ½ m. WSW., in Rinclevan, is Labby, another chamber tomb.

4 m. N. are the lofty cliffs of Croaghnamaddy (835 ft) and Horn Head, celebrated haunts of sea-fowl. They afford splendid panoramas. Indeed, the whole promontory rewards the explorer (on foot) with a rich variety of splendid sea and mountain scenery.

2 m. E., N. of the road to Creeslough, is Port na Blagh, where there is also an excellent beach. 1 m. further E. is the beautiful and secluded beach of Marble Hill.

5 m. SE. is the beautiful Ards Peninsula (*see under* Creeslough).

2 m. W. is Trawmore, a 1½-m. sandy beach backed by extensive sandhills; less than ½ m. N. is MacSwiny's Gun, a marine tunnel where the air booms during heavy storms. N. of the latter is the sea-eroded Templebreaga Arch, alias Marble Arch.

2½ m. NNW., in Cleggan, is Dermot and Grania's Bed, a ruined court cairn.

DUNGANNON, Co. Tyrone (Map 3, B5), is a linen town on the Strabane (50 m.)–Portadown (17 m.) road. It is a convenient centre for fishing the Blackwater and its tributaries, the Torrent and Oona: trout, salmon, perch, bream.

In late medieval and early modern times Dungannon was one of the principal seats of the O Neills of Tír Eoghain. In 1602, following the Irish defeat at Kinsale (*q.v.*), the castle and town were burned to prevent them falling into English hands. At the Plantation the place was granted to Sir Arthur Chichester. In more recent history it is celebrated for the meeting, 15 Feb. 1782, of the representatives of 143 corps of (Protestant) Volunteers of the Province of Ulster, who asserted Ireland's claim to parliamentary independence and untramelled trade, and welcomed the relaxation of the Penal laws against the Catholic majority.

Nothing survives of the O Neill castle, or of the new house built by Great Hugh O Neill and whose roofing lead he converted into bullets for his long and gallant struggle against Elizabeth I. Nor does anything remain of Chichester's Plantation castle. The structure at the head of the town, called O'Neill's Castle, was erected in 1790 by Hannynton on the site of Chichester's stronghold.

The Royal School, Northland Row, dates from 1628, but the present buildings were erected in 1786 by the Protestant primate, Richard Robinson (Lord Rokeby). John Nicholson of the Indian Mutiny went to school here. A bronze statue of him (by Brock), no longer acceptable in Delhi, has been erected at the school gate. Northland Row is a good Georgian terrace.

At the W. edge of the town is a fine old coaching inn (semi-derelict; part used as a technical school).

Adjoining the town on the SE. is Northland House, formerly seat of the Knoxes, Earls of Ranfurly, whose ancestor was granted lands here at the Plantation (*see also* Academy House, Dawson St, Dublin, SE.).

5 m. SE. is Moy (*see under* Charlemont, Co. Armagh).

2 m. SW. is Castlecaulfeild. The Protestant parish church, built by Lord Charlemont in 1685 and enlarged in 1838, is an interesting structure with noteworthy S. and W. doorways. In the W. porch is a 17th cent. font. The E. window and the N. and S. windows of the transepts incorporate 15th/16th cent. label stops etc. from Donaghmore church (*below*). In the S. transept is buried the Rev. George Walker of Derry fame, who was rector here for a time. The Rev. Charles Wolfe, author of "The Burial of Sir John Moore", was curate here from 1818 to 1823. S. of the village are the ruins (Nat. Mon.) of Castle Caulfeild erected 1611–19 by Sir Toby Caulfeild (ancestor of the Earls of Charlemont) on the site of a stronghold of the O Donnellys. In 1642 it was burned down by Patrick O Donnelly, but was repaired and

re-occupied by the Caulfeilds. In 1670 the 1st Viscount Charlemont permitted the Catholic primate, Oliver Plunkett, to use the courtyard for ordinations. John Wesley preached at the gate in 1767. The remains are those of a U-shaped manor house of late Elizabethan type. At the NE. angle is an earlier (O Donnelly?) gatehouse, but the rest of the enclosing curtain has vanished.

2½ m. NW. is Donaghmore (*domhnach mór*, great church). St Patrick is said to have founded a church here, over which he placed Cruimther Colum (Colum the Priest). Subsequently a monastery arose on the site. In the 13th cent. its successor was noted for its costly shrines. From the ruins of the medieval church some fragments were removed to Castlecaulfeild church (*above*) in 1685. All that remains today at Donaghmore itself is the 9th/10th cent. figured High Cross (Nat. Mon.) in the village street, where it was re-erected in 1776. The cross is imperfect, and may in fact comprise portions of two different crosses. The figure subjects include: W. face: *Fall of Adam and Eve, Cain and Abel, Sacrifice of Isaac*; E. face: *Announcement of Christ's birth to the Shepherds, Pilate washing his hands, Baptism of Christ, The Crucifixion*. The N. and S. sides have interlace and other patterns.

DUNGARVAN, Co. Waterford (Map 5, D6), administrative centre of Waterford county, is a market town and small seaport on the W. shore of the Colligan estuary (Dungarvan Harbour), 27 m. SW. of Waterford, 11 m. ESE. of Cappoquin, and 18 m. NE. of Youghal. The town is a convenient base for exploring the Monavulliagh–Comeragh Mountains (*see under* Carrick-on-Suir) and the S. Waterford coast. The Drum Hills region to the S. and SW. is the last area of Irish speech in E. Munster.

The town grew up in the shelter of an Anglo-Norman castle, of which substantial remains are incorporated in the ruins of the British military barracks destroyed in 1921. The castle figured in the Eleven Years' War, surrendering to Cromwell in 1649, when it and the parish church were wrecked by the conqueror.

The Church of the Assumption is a renovation (*c.* 1890) by George Ashlin of a plain structure erected in 1828 to the design of George Richard Pain of Cork.

St Augustine's Church, Abbeyside, incorporates the tower of a small Augustinian friary founded about 1290. A fragment of the choir also survives. Nearby is St Catherine's Well. To the N. are remains of a MacGrath castle.

3 m. N., at Kilgobnet, are remains of a small Romanesque church despoiled by 19th cent. church builders. The parish church (1826) was remodelled in 1883 by W. Doolin.

8 m. NNE. are remains of Kilrossanty church.

9 m. NNE., via the Carrick-on-Suir road, in a moorland field near the ancient church site of Garranmillon, are two ogham stones.

6 m. NE., in Ballykeroge, are the ruins of a Walsh castle. Nearby is Cloch Labhrais, a boulder which was said to speak from time to time.

10 m. NE. is the "Ogham Cave" of Drumlohan (*see under* Stradbally).

4 m. ENE. is Clonea (*see under* Carrick-on-Suir).

6 m. SSE., in the Déise Gaeltacht, is An Rinn, alias Ring. Nearby are good small beaches. 1 m. E. is the old fishing village of Ballynagaul, to the E. of which is Helvick Head (230 ft) commanding very fine views. 4 m. S. of Ring, near the coast in Ballynamona Lower, is Cailleach Bhéarra's House, alias Dolmen, one of the few court cairns in Munster; ½ m. S., at Carraig Philip, is a defaced cliff-fort. 6 m. S. of Ring, in Ballynaharda, is Rinanillaun promontory fort. In Ballykilmurry, between Rinanillaun and Mine Head, is another promontory fort.

3 m. NW., at Ballymacmague crossroads, where the road bifurcates to Cappoquin and Clonmel, is a memorial to Master McGrath, the greyhound which won the Waterloo Cup in 1868, 1869, and 1871, and was defeated only once in thirty-seven courses. Both the Cappoquin and Clonmel roads are noted for their scenery. The latter traverses charming Colligan Glen to climb the slopes between the Knockmealdown and Monavulliagh (Seefin, 2,387 ft) Mountains, and then descends to the wild and picturesque Nier valley (*see under* Clonmel). The descent offers fine views of the Galtee Mountains. 7 m. N. of Ballymacmague crossroads and 1½ m. E. of the Clonmel road, in Knockboy, are the ruins of St Seskinan's Church (15th cent.); six ogham stones have been built into the fabric; a seventh lies inside the church. Also in Knockboy are Lisatorny, a ringfort, and the little Fort of the Three Stones. 6½ m. further N., and 600 yds E. of the Clonmel road, alt. 800 ft on Drumgorey Hill, is "Torreagh Hill", a fine circular earthwork.

6½ m. NW. are the limestone caves of Kilgreany, Ballynamintra, and Carrigmurrish. Prehistoric remains found in Kilgreany cave included two human skeletons of *c.* 9000 B.C., the oldest known evidence for the presence of man in Ireland. In Whitechurch demesne nearby are further caves.

DUNGIVEN, Co. Derry (Map 3, A3), is a village where the Maghera (14 m.)–Derry (21 m.) road crosses the head of attractive Glengiven (Roe Valley) 9½ m. S. of Limavady. To the S. rises the main Sperrin range (Mullaghaneany, 2,070 ft; Sawel, 2,240 ft) with several pretty glens. The Roe holds salmon and brown trout; Banagher Reservoir holds brown trout (permits from Derry Corporation).

John Mitchel of Young Ireland fame was born at Camnish, near Dungiven, where his father was Unitarian minister.

The 1839 "castle" incorporates parts of the fortified Plantation bawn (Nat. Mon.) built by the Crown in 1617 and granted to the Skinners' Company of London.

¾ m. S., on a 200-ft cliff above the River Roe, is the ruined church (Nat. Mon.) of an Augustinian priory founded in 1100 by one of the O Cahans. The remains comprise a mainly 12th cent., undecorated, Romanesque chancel and an earlier nave with 14th/15th, 16th and 17th cent. features. A Round Tower which stood at the SW. corner fell in 1784. The most remarkable feature is the 14th/15th cent. O Cahan tomb in the S. wall of the chancel. It has a beautiful, flamboyant canopy, a noteworthy effigy in contemporary Irish armour, and, in arcaded panels below, six gallogla "weepers". According to tradition the effigy is that of Cooeyna-Gall O Cahan (d. 1385). N. of the church is a bullaun still visited by pilgrims. N. of the Dungiven end of the paved footpath leading to the priory is a fine pillarstone.

4 m. NNW. are Bovevagh church and Saint's Tomb (Nat. Mons.). According to local tradition a church was founded here by St Ringán, but the existing remains can hardly be older than the 13th/14th cent. The tomb is SW. of the church. Like the O Heney tomb at Banagher Church (below), it is in the form of a stone-roofed church.

3 m. ESE., in Boviel, is Cloghnagalla, a neolithic gallery grave. 1 m. SW., in Cashel, built against a prehistoric cairn, is the White Fort (Nat. Mon.), a polygonal, stone ringfort; the rampart incorporates two burial cists belonging to the cairn.

2½ m. SSW., in Magheramore, is the ruined church of Banagher (Nat. Mon.), held to have been founded in the 11th cent. by an obscure local saint, Muiredach O Heney. The W. door is square-headed without, round-arched within. The chancel, later than the nave, has Late Romanesque and Transitional details. In the churchyard is a tomb (Nat. Mon.), traditionally that of the founder; it is built in the form of a stone-roofed church (cf. Bovevagh, above, Clones, and Tamlaghtard under Limavady) and is contemporary with the chancel. At the W. end is a weathered figure; Banagher sand from beneath it is believed to give success to an O Heney in contests of every sort, and has even been thrown at racehorses to help them win! Also in the churchyard is a rude cross. 100 yds W. of the church is another. These are said to be the survivors of five crosses which marked the limits of the monastic land. ½ m. S. is ruined Carnanbane court cairn.

DUNGLOW, alias **DUNGLOE**, Co. Donegal (Map 2, B2), is a small fishing port and angling resort on the Lettermacaward (10 m.)–Burtonport (5 m.) road.

It is a convenient base for exploring the indented coast and its islands, as well as for fishing the Rosses – 60,000 rock-strewn acres with many small lakes – which lie to the N. The local roads are not for fast driving.

The Lough Anure area (4 m. NE.) is geologically interesting, as well as very beautiful.

5 m. SW. is Maghery, where there is a good beach. On the peninsula to the N. are remains of the ancient church of Teampall Crone. To the SW. is Crohy Head with its cliffs and marine caves (accessible by boat).

5½ m. NW., off Burtonport, is Rutland Island. In 1785 the Duke of Rutland tried to establish a port here, traces of which remain. As a counter-move the Marquess of Conyngham developed Burtonport, which is now an important herring-fishing station.

7 m. NW. is Aran, alias Arranmore, Island (reached by motor-boat from Burtonport). On the W. side of the island are fine cliffs and interesting marine caves.

DUNIRY, Co. Galway (Map 5, C2), is a small village on the Loughrea (8 m.)–Portumna (7 m.) road. It takes its name from a fort, Dún Daighre. In the later Middle Ages a branch of the celebrated Mac Egan family of hereditary scholars had its home at Muileann Dúna Daighre, the Mill of Duniry (see Park under Dunmore). In the 16th cent. these Mac Egans possessed the celebrated Leabhar Breac, an early-15th cent. codex of religious literature compiled by the Mac Egans of Múscraighe Thíre in N. Tipperary; hence the alternative name of the codex, Leabhar Mór Dúna Daighre, The Great Book of Duniry. At the same period the Duniry Mac Egans owned the 13th/14th cent. Trinity College, Dublin, codex, H.2.152, the oldest surviving "brehon law" MS.

1½ m. ESE. are the unusually well-preserved ruins (Nat. Mon.) of Pallas castle, a Burke stronghold which, together with its estate, was confiscated by the Cromwellian regime and assigned to the transplanted Earl of Westmeath, in whose family (Nugent) it remained until recently. The remains comprise a large, unusually well-preserved bawn (gate house rebuilt), a 16th cent. tower, fragments of a large 17th cent. house, and an 18th cent. malthouse. 3 m. E., in Kilcorban, are the ruins of St Corban's Church, burial place of the Nugents of Pallas. A Dominican friary was founded here in 1466. In Loughrea Museum are several wooden figures which probably came from this friary. 4½ m. NE., in the loop of a small stream, is Kilmore Fort, a large ring-fort (border of Pollfeeneen and Cloonacusha).

DUNKINEELY, Co. Donegal (Map 2, B3), is a fishing village on the Donegal (12 m.)–Killybegs (5 m.) road.

1 m. SW. are the fragmentary remains of Killachtee church (Transitional); in the graveyard is a fine, early cross-slab. ¾ m. S., on the shore of Mac Swyne's Bay, are remains of the 15th cent. castle of Mac Swyne of Banagh (see Killybegs).

2½ m. NW., and ½ m. N. of Bruckless village, is the Reilig, where "stations" are held during the nine days following 23 June. The remains here include St Conall's Bed, a holy well, and early cross-slabs.

DÚN LAOGHAIRE, Co. Dublin (Map 6, E7), 8 m. SE. of Dublin, with which it forms a single conurbation, is the terminus of the principal Ireland–England passenger shipping service (car ferry inaugurated 1965). It is a major seaside resort and Dublin's largest dormitory suburb. Dún Laoghaire is the headquarters of Irish yachting (Royal Irish Yacht Club, National Yacht Club, Royal St George Yacht Club, and others) and the base of the Irish Lights Service, which maintains the lighthouses, lightships, etc., around the Irish coasts. The great harbour (1817–21), by Rennie, was a major work of 19th cent. marine engineering. The East Pier is a popular promenade where band recitals are given during the summer. Boats may be hired at the harbour. Bathing facilities are available at Dún Laoghaire Baths, Blackrock, Salthill (*q.v.*), Sandycove, Seapoint, and other places along the seafront. From 1821 to 1920 Dún Laoghaire was called Kingstown, in commemoration of George IV's departure from the harbour after his state visit to Dublin. A dull monument near the Mail Boat Pier records the royal occasion.

1¼ m. E. of the Town Hall are Sandycove Baths and the "Forty Foot" (men's bathing place). The martello tower figures in Joyce's *Ulysses* and is now a Joyce Museum.

1 m. SW. of the Town Hall, York Rd Presbyterian Church has three Ethel M. Rhind twolight windows: *Prudent Virgin* and *Faithful Servant* (1909), *The Kingdom of Heaven is like unto a net* (1922), *The Good Samaritan* and *The Lost Coin* (1925).

1 m. W. of the Town Hall is Monkstown Protestant Church, a highly individual, Gothick structure (*c.* 1830) by John Semple (*see* Mary Place, Dublin, NW.): noteworthy plaster vault; chancel memorial to Richard Browne (d. 1838) by Thomas Kirk. ½ m. S. is 15th cent. Monkstown Castle (Nat. Mon.): small keep, gatehouse, and part of curtain.

2 m. W., on the Dublin road, is Blackrock, in the 18th cent. a fashionable watering place and seaside retreat. St John's Church was Patrick Byrne's first (1842) essay in the Gothic manner. It was based on Pugin's drawings of the church of Stanton St John, Oxfordshire. The exterior does less than justice to the interior, with its unusual, lofty chancel. In the new aisle is a three-light window (*Our Lady, St Brigid, St Patrick*) by Evie Hone, one of the artist's last works (1954–55). Nearby Maretimo was the 18th cent. seaside house of Lord Cloncurry. Its elaborate gardens were ruined by the railway line. – All Saints Church (Church of Ireland) has two windows (1918) by Wilhelmina Geddes: *Michael, Raphael.* – "Leoville", 23 Carysfort Ave., was the home (1892–3) of James Joyce and his parents. – "Frescati", at the foot of Mount Merrion Ave., is a remnant of the seaside house of the Fitzgeralds of Kildare; Lord Edward Fitzgerald of the United Irishmen and his wife, Pamela, lived there in 1793. Further W. in Williamstown, is Blackrock

College (1860: Holy Ghost Fathers), the well-known boys' school. Éamon de Valera was a pupil and, later, mathematics master here. The buildings (nucleus Castledawson House) are devoid of merit, but have three armorial and decorative windows (1936–37) and a lunette (*Our Lady*, 1940), by Evie Hone. The school chapel has two pairs of single-light windows (1938) by Michael Healy: *Annunciation, Visitation*. The Senior House ("Castle") chapel has a three-light *Pentecost* (1940–41) by Evie Hone. – 1¾ m. S. of St John's Church, on the Cabinteely road, is Deansgrange. In Kill Ave. is St Fintan's Church, alias Kill o' the Grange (Nat. Mon.), a small, pre-Romanesque church with chancel of *c.* 1200; N. of the church is a simple, early cross.

DUNLAVIN, Co. Wicklow (Map 6, C4), a village 11 m. N. of Baltinglass and 6½ m. SE. of Kilcullen, was founded by the Bulkeleys, 17th cent. grantees. In 1702 it passed to the Worth-Tyntes. The "baroque" stone-domed Market House was erected by the first Worth-Tyne proprietor. In accordance with the usual, bad, Irish practice, the arches were blocked up in 1835.

2 m. NE., in Friar Hill, is a tumulus with a cist grave. On the S. side of the same valley, in two adjacent fields of Forristeen townland, are the Piper's Stones, two large granite boulders. The larger has a cross. Cremation burials and pottery have been found near the smaller.

3 m. ENE., in "Crushlow Churchyard", Crehelp, is a granite pillarstone with a subrectangular perforation. It is said locally to mark the grave of Norse "Prince Harold". Marriages used to be solemnized at it. In the Churchyard Field, Crehelp, is a bullaun.

3 m. SE. is Merginstown motte-and-bailey (*see under* Donard).

2 m. S., in Tornant Lower, is Tornant Moat, a platform ringfort with external bank. On a ridge to the SE. (beyond St Nicholas's Graveyard) is the remnant of a tumulus in which was found a stone with passage-grave scribings, now in the National Museum. At the E. end of the ridge, in Tornant Upper, is a raised, circular platform ringed by twelve granite and white quartz boulders, one of which (broken) bears a small circle and a large, channelled semicircle. These are the remnants of a circle of great stones shattered by splitting and blasting. At the centre of the platform is a hollow from which a large boulder has been extracted. In the next field to the E. is a small, circular earthwork. 100 yds N. of the latter are the stump and broken head of a shattered granite pillarstone. ¼ m. NNE. of Tornant Moat is St Nicholas's Well.

4½ m. ESE. is Broomfield (*see under* Donard).

2½ m. SW., on the summit of Brewel Hill (Co. Kildare), are the Piper's Stones, four large boulders ringed by a wide, double entrenchment now largely defaced. One of the stones (the Piper's Chair) is of white quartz.

3½ m. SW., in Colbinstown (Co. Kildare), is the ancient cemetery of Killeen Cormac, so called, it is said, after "King Cormac of Munster". According to local legend a dispute arose about the king's place of burial, so the corpse was placed on a car drawn by unguided oxen. These drew it to the neighbourhood of Killeen Cormac, whereupon a hound leaped from a neighbouring hill to a stone in the cemetery, leaving the imprint of a paw on the stone to indicate the position of the king's grave. The remains in the cemetery comprise: King Cormac's Grave, marked by a pair of pillarstones, one of which bears two lines and the "imprint of the hound's paw"; seven other pillarstones – two with grooves; four early cross-slabs; two cross-shafts; a unique slab with incised figure of Christ Crucifer (retouched in the last cent.); and one complete and four fragmentary ogham stones. There were formerly two more ogham stones here; one has been destroyed, the other (bilingual) taken to the National Museum.

2½ m. SW. is Knockdoo hill-top pillarstone. One version of the Killeen Cormac legend represents the hound as leaping from this hill.

4 m. SW., on a commanding site, is Ballycore Long Stone. The field was formerly the venue for local wrestling matches.

DUNLEER, Co. Louth (Map 3, B7), is a village on the Drogheda (9 m.)–Dundalk (13 m.) road. There was an early monastery (Lann Léire) here, associated with St Brigid, who is said to have lost and regained her sight at the local holy well. The W. tower of the 19th cent. Protestant church incorporates Transitional fragments which, with three early gravestones in the adjacent hall, are the sole relics of Lann Léire. Near the church is a ruinous motte.

2¾ m. SE. is Rokeby Hall, designed by Francis Johnston for Archbishop Robinson (Lord Rokeby) of Armagh and completed in 1793/94. Johnston also designed for the same primate thirty farmhouses on the estate, as well as the Protestant churches of Clonmore (ruined; to the NE. near Barmeath Castle, seat of the Bellews) and Ballymakenny (see under Drogheda). Rokeby Hall is still a private residence, but the demesne is very decayed. 1½ m. E. of the main gate is the fine ringfort of Rathdrummin.

1¼ m. S. is Athclare castle (16th cent.), still inhabited. It has good Jacobean carvings.

2 m. NW., on the Ardee Rd, Dromin medieval church marks the site of a monastery founded by St Finnian of Moville (see under Newtownards). Nearby is Móta Dhruim Fhinn, an Anglo-Norman motte.

DUNMANWAY, Co. Cork (Map 4, E5), is a small market town where the Bandon (18 m.)–Bantry (20 m.) road crosses the little Dirty River a short distance above its junction with the Bandon. The by-road to Bantry through the Shehy Mountains via Togher Bridge, Cousane Gap (762 ft), and Kealkil is rewarding; cyclists and walkers only.

5½ m. ESE., via Manch bridge, are the ruins of Ballinacarriga castle, a 15th cent. O Hurley stronghold.

6¼ m. NW., on the N. side of the Bandon, is the unusual tower of Togher Castle, built probably by Tadhg an Fhórsa Mac Carthy of Gleann an Chroim, about 1590 (?). At the Cromwellian confiscation it was granted to two brothers named Hoare. It was re-roofed and restored in the late 19th cent. by a local priest.

6 m. NNW., is Farranahineeny (see under Inchigeelagh).

DUNMORE, Co. Galway (Map 1, E5), is a market village on the Tuam (10 m.)–Ballyhaunis (11 m.) road. It takes its name from a great fort belonging to Turloch Mór O Conor, King of Connacht and High-king (1106–56). At the Anglo-Norman conquest the manor was granted by de Burgo to one of the de Berminghams, whose descendants, becoming Gaelicized, changed their name to Mac Fheorais. The ruined "abbey" (Nat. Mon.) was the church of a small Augustinian friary founded about 1423 (?) by Walter Mór de Bermingham, Baron Athenry (d. 1428). It has a Perpendicular W. doorway with Bermingham arms above. The mutilation of the building is largely explained by the long utilization of the chancel as the Protestant parish church.

The country about Dunmore is very rich in ringforts of various kinds.

½ m. NW., beside the little Sinking River in Castlefarm, are the remains (Nat. Mon.) of the strong, 13th cent., Bermingham castle of Dunmore, thought to occupy the site of King Turloch O Conor's fort. The modern road cuts off the upper ward and keep from the lower ward or bailey; the whole work was enclosed by a curtain wall. The first castle here was clearly of the motte kind. To the W. is Rathcoll, alias Knockmannanan, carved out of an esker; the central mound is the traditional grave of King Turloch.

7 m. SE. (6 m. SW. of Glenamaddy), in Park West, are remnants of Park castle, for centuries the home of a branch of the Mac Egans (see Duniry). The Mac Egans of Park were hereditary brehons to the O Conors of Connacht, their reward being twenty-four townlands in this district. They were still at Park in 1627, but later in the cent. were involved in the general Irish ruin and lost their estates. Manuscripts from their Park law-school are preserved in the British Museum and in Trinity College, Dublin.

2 m. S., in Carrowpadeen East, is a prehistoric chamber tomb.

3½ m. W., in Addergoole, is the head of a granite cross with an unfinished Crucifixion.

DUNMORE EAST, Co. Waterford (Map 6, B7), is a small resort and sea-fishing port at the W. side of the entrance to Waterford Harbour, 11 m. SE. of Waterford. The harbour was constructed as a mail-packet terminus from 1814 onwards to the design of Nimmo, whose admirable pier stores, harmonizing with the Doric lighthouse, have recently been mutilated by the Office of Public Works. – There are cliffs and pleasant coves nearby. At Black Knob signal tower, S. of the harbour, is the Shanooan, a promontory fort; a cave in the cliff has acquired the silly name of Merlin's Cave. On the coast SW. to Brownstown Head (7 m.) are five promontory forts.

2 m. N., commanding a very fine view, is Carrick a Dhirra, alias Knockadirragh (430 ft). Near the summit at the S. end, in Harristown, is a V-passage grave set in a round cairn. The primary grave-goods included a stone axe-amulet. Secondary deposits included three Bronze Age urn burials. At the foot of the hill are remains of Kilmacomb, a church called after St Mo-Chumma.

DUNNAMANAGH, Co. Tyrone (Map 2, D3), is a village on the Strabane (8 m.)–Claudy, Co. Derry (8 m.) road.

4¾ m. ESE., in Loughash, alt. 500 ft, is Cashelbane, a chambered, round cairn. 1 m. SW., 150 yds SW. of Loughash school, alt. 600 ft, is Loughash Giants Grave (Nat. Mon.), a wedge-shaped gallery grave with double entrance (a Beaker feature ?). There are twelve cup marks on the central jamb of the portal. Excavation has yielded cremated burials, Beakers, and Bronze Age relics.

2½ m. W., alt. 400 ft, is Windy Hill Giants Grave, a ruinous overgrown chamber tomb. To the NW., in Ballylaw, are remains of White Fort, a stone ringfort.

3½ m. WSW. is Killynaght (*see under* Strabane).

3½ m. NNW., ⅓ m. E. of Kildorragh, alt. 600 ft, in Gortmellan, is the Grey Stone, a chambered round cairn.

DUNQUIN, Co. Kerry (Map 4, B4), 3½ m. SW. of Ballyferriter and 5 m. (8 m. via the coast and Slea Head) W. of Ventry, is well known to students of the Irish language. It is a pleasant place for a quiet holiday and is the "port" for the crossing to the Blasket Islands (*q.v.*). SE. of the village rises Sliabh an Iolair, alias Mount Eagle (1,695 ft); the summit affords fine views.

440 yds SSW. of the "village" is Dún Binne, a promontory fort (very fine views).

½ m. E., in Baile an Bhiocáire, alias Vicarstown, is Tigh Mhóire, an ancient burial ground with an early cross-pillar, a fragment of an early cross-slab, and Uaigh an Spáinnigh, "the grave of a Spanish nobleman lost off the Blaskets" in 1588.

1¼ m. SSW. a slight earthwork cuts off the 80-acre promontory fort of Doonmore. At the summit of the fort is Gallán an tSagairt, an ogham stone re-erected in 1839; the site commands impressive views. The road SE. and S. traverses the lower slopes of Been, or Gable, Hill (1,395 ft) and Sliabh an Iolair (1,695 ft) via

Slea Head to Kilvickadownig and Ventry. The view E. from Slea Head is particularly fine. The lower slopes are strewn with ancient remains. (The more important of those in Coumeenole South are listed in the following paragraph. For those further E. *see* Kilvickadownig–Fahan–Glanfahan *under* Ventry.)

1¾ m. S. is Coumeenole "village". 400 yds E. is a small, perfect clochán. 180 yds S. is an ancient burial ground; there are two cross-slabs here. A short distance SE. is Púicín Mháire Ní Sháirséal, a ruined clochán largely below ground level. SSW. of this is Clochán O Lee, a complex of three clocháns with a "yard". On the summit of the hill are four clocháns (Nat. Mons.).

DUNSHAUGHLIN, Co. Meath (Map 6, C2), is a village on the Dublin (20 m.)–Navan (12 m.) road. It takes its name (Domhnach Seachnaill) from a church founded by Bishop Secundinus (Seachnall), who came to Ireland, probably from Gaul, with Auxilius and Iserninus about 438/9, and who died in 447/8. To Secundinus has been attributed a celebrated hymn in honour of Patrick, *Ymnum sancti Patrici magister Scotorum*. From his name was formed the Irish personal name Máel-Sheachnaill, later euphonized Máel-Sheachlainn, a favourite name with the Southern Uí Néill (witness their surname Ó Máel-Sheachlainn, O Melaghlin). Secundinus's church was on or near the site of the Protestant parish church, where the lintel (Nat. Mon.) of the W. door of a pre-Romanesque church is preserved; on it is carved a primitive *Crucifixion*. A fragment of the nave arcade of a medieval church also survives.

The small Classical court-house is by Francis Johnston.

2 m. N. is Trevet, site of an early monastery founded by St Lonán. Sir Thomas Cusack, Lord Chancellor under Henry ·VIII and Mary Tudor, was buried here with his wife, Matilda D'Arcy, in a double-effigy tomb (*see* Skreen *under* Tara).

2 m. E. is Lagore, where a bog represents the silted-up lake (Loch Gabhair) which gives the place its name. In the lake was a crannóg, seat of the kings of Brega. It was excavated (1934–36) by the Harvard Archaeological Mission, and yielded much interesting material and information.

2½ m. NW., on the Kilmessan road, is Killeen Castle, until recently seat of the Plunkets, Earls of Fingal (*see* Beaulieu *under* Drogheda). The mansion is an 1801 remodelling by Francis Johnston of a medieval castle. The original castle here was built, it has been alleged, about 1180 by Hugh I de Lacy, who enfeoffed the ancestor of the Cusacks (de Kensac) in the manors of Killeen and Dunsany (*below*). In 1403 Sir Christopher Plunket (d. 1445) acquired the manors by marrying the Cusack heiress. It may have been he who (about 1425/50) built the two manorial churches, interesting examples of a Pale type of parish church; aisleless nave and chancel with intervening rood loft (lord's gallery?); angle turret; priest's dwelling over sacristy (cf. Rathmore *under* Athboy). In the Killeen church are remains of three 15th cent. Plunket tombs: a fragment of a slab carved in sunk relief with the heads of an armoured knight and his lady; a double effigial slab in similar technique; the effigy of an armoured knight in very flat (incised) technique.

1½ m. NW. of Killeen, on the Kilmessan road, is Dunsany Castle, seat of the Plunket Barons Dunsany. Like Killeen, Dunsany came to the Plunkets by Sir Christopher's 1403 marriage to the Cusack heiress. The castle, which has very fine 18th cent. features, interesting porcelain, pictures, armour, MSS., relics of Blessed Oliver Plunket, etc., is open only to Córas Iompair Éireann coach parties (enquire at C.I.E. Passenger Services, 59 Upper O Connell St, Dublin). The late Lord Dunsany (1878–1960), friend and patron of Francis Ledwidge (*see* Slane), was a poet and novelist of distinction. E. of the castle are the ruins of St Nicholas's Church, also built about 1425/50, on the site of an older church, by Sir Christopher Plunket. It is of the same type, as the Killeen church. (The E. window is modern, the tracery copied from Killeen church.) In the chancel are five sedilia, an interesting, 15th cent. baptismal font, and a 15th cent. double-effigy tomb. The carvings on the font include a *Crucifixion*, as well as figures of the Apostles. The tomb effigies are those of Sir Thomas Plunket (armoured) and his first wife, Anne Fitzgerald; the figure-carvings on the ends of the tomb include a *Scourging of Christ*. (Sir Thomas is probably buried with his second wife, Joan Preston, at Killeen.) At the demesne gate is a 16th/17th cent. roadside cross with a rude *Crucifixion*. 2¼ m. N. is Rath Maeve (*see under* Tara).

DURROW, Co. Laois (Map 6, A4), is a Noreside village at the intersection of the Abbeyleix (6 m.)–Urlingford (13 m.) and Borris-in-Ossory (14 m.)–Ballyragget (5 m.) roads.

Castle Durrow, now a convent, is a fine house overlooking the Nore. It was built in 1716 for the first Lord Castle Durrow.

2 m. NE., on the Abbeyleix road, is the small, early-Georgian house of Dunmore.

6½ m. SW., to the W. of Cullahill, is Aghmacart, formerly a seat of the Mac Gillapatricks (Fitzpatricks) of Ossory. There are remains of an Augustinian priory founded by the Mac Gillapatricks before 1168 on the site of an earlier monastery.

8 m. SW. is Cross of the Beggar (*see under* Urlingford).

DYSERT O DEA, Co. Clare (Map 1, D7), formerly Díseart Tola, lies to the S. of the Corrofin (4 m.)–Ennis (22 m.) road.

A hermitage or anchoritic establishment

Commissioners of Public Works in Ireland

High Cross, Dysert O Dea, east face

(díse[a]rt=*desertum*) was founded here by St Tola (d. 737), a bishop of Clonard. There are remains (Nat. Mon.) of a nave-and-chancel Romanesque church with interesting door and window (incorrectly re-assembled). Close to the NW. angle are remains of a Round Tower. E. of the church is the White Cross of Tola (Nat. Mon.), a fine, 12th cent. High Cross. On the E. face are a Crucifixus and the figure of a bishop, on the W. face zoomorphic (including Urnes) and other abstract patterns. The base is made up from Romanesque fragments taken from the church. To the N. is O Dea's Castle, with a fine bawn.

In 1318 Dysert O Dea was the scene of one of the decisive battles of Munster history. Here Muirchertach O Brien and his allies routed Richard de Clare (see Bunratty) and put a halt to the Anglo-Norman conquest of Thomond.

5¼ m. WSW. via Mauricemills (Drehidna-multia), in Drumanure, is Cromlech, a wedge-shaped gallery grave.

1 m. NNW., in Rath, is Rathblamack, called after St Blathmac ("Blawfugh"), founder of a church about ½ m. to the SW., where are remains of a nave-and-chancel church of various dates (interesting Romanesque fragments with Urnes ornament, sheila-na-gig, etc.).

EASKY, Co. Sligo (Map 1, D2), is a village and small seaside resort on the coast road from Sligo (25 m.) to Ballina (17 m.).

¾ m. N., on the shore, is the ruined tower of the Mac Donnell castle of Roslee. The Mac Donnells were by origin Hebridean galloglas in the service of the O Dowds (see Skreen and Ardnaglass under Dromard, Co. Sligo).

By the roadside to the E. of the village is Fionn Mac Cool's Fingerstone, alias the Split Rock. Fionn, the story runs, tried to hurl the stone into the ocean, but it fell short. Enraged, he struck it with a second stone and split it.

¾ m. S., in Fortland, is Cromlech, remnant of a massive court cairn. ½ m. SSW., in Bookaun, are remains of a gallery grave. About ½ m. SE. of Fortland Cromlech, near the river, is a second court cairn.

EDENDERRY, Co. Offaly (Map 6, B3), is a market and shoe-making town on the Innfield, alias Enfield (12 m.)-Tullamore (22 m.) road at the edge of the Bog of Allen.

Immediately S. of the town are the remnants of hill-top Blundell's Castle. The second Marquess of Downshire (1753–1801; see Hillsborough) married a Blundell, and so acquired the Edenderry property. The Downshires built most of the town, including the handsome, 1826 Corn Market cum Court House (later spoiled by the blocking up of the ground-floor loggia). Only the shell survived a recent fire. It has since been cheaply reconstructed as the Father Paul Murphy Memorial Hall.

Edenderry stands near the edge of the English Pale, and there are many border castles in the vicinity.

3 m. N., on Carrick Hill (387 ft), are the remains of the medieval church and castle of Carrickoris (Carraig Fheorais, Bermingham's Rock, cf, Carbury Hill, below). In 1305 Muirchertach O Conor, king of Uí Fáilghe, and thirty-one other leaders of the O Conors Faly were murdered after a banquet in the castle by "the treacherous Baron", Sir Pierce Bermingham, and Jordan Cumin. The English king failed to punish the murderers, and the crime was one of the complaints cited by the Irish princes in their Remonstrance of 1317 to Pope John XXII. It was Sir Pierce's son, John, who defeated Edward Bruce (see Faughart under Drogheda). – At the N. end of the hill, above a great limestone quarry, is the Witch's Stone, cast, says legend, from Croghan Hill (see Daingean) by a witch at an early saint. Near the summit is the Mule's Leap, eight holes said to be the footprints of a mule which ran off with a saint from Carrickoris church. At the S. foot of the hill, in the angle of the Edenderry and Carbury roads, is Tober Crogh Neeve, alias Tobercro, the Well of the Holy Cross, formerly greatly venerated.

4½ m. N., in Glyn, is Lady Well, where a fair and *pátrún* used to be held on 15 Aug.

5 m. N., in Ballyboggan on the W. bank of the Boyne in Co. Meath, are the ruins of a large, plain, cruciform, 13th cent. church, all that survives of the once wealthy English priory De Laude Dei, founded for Canons Regular of St Augustine by Jordan Cumin. In 1538 the Protestant reformers publicly burned the venerated crucifix belonging to the priory.

4 m. ENE. the road to Innfield (Enfield) crosses the shoulder of Carbury Hill (470 ft), which commands wide prospects over the Central Plain. On the summit of the hill is a small, low tumulus raised over a cremated burial. NE. is a low, earthen ring which enclosed two Iron Age cremations. Further NE. is a larger, similar ring which enclosed four Iron Age cremations and fifteen inhumations. On the NE. shoulder of the hill is a motte, probably constructed by the first Anglo-Norman proprietor, Meiler fitz Henry, who had been granted the district by Strongbow. In the 14th cent., castle and district (thenceforth "Bermingham's Country") were acquired by the Berminghams, but the castle was in the English king's hands for most of the century. In 1447 the castle was re-edified by the Deputy, Sir John Talbot ("Scourge of France"). Twenty years later it was in the possession of O Conor Faly, who imprisoned the Earl of Desmond and other Anglo-Irish notables in it. In 1475 it was destroyed by O Donnell. Rebuilt once more, it was burned down by the O Kellys, O Maddens, and O Conors Faly in 1546. In 1562 it was granted to the Cowleys (Colleys), later Wellesleys, ancestors of the celebrated Duke of Wellington, and it was they who built the Tudor–Jacobean stronghouse. SE. of the castle are scant remains of Teampall Do-Ath; Colley mausoleum in churchyard. On the SE. slope of the hill is Newbury Hall (Mrs Smith), an attractive house built c. 1760 for Arthur Pomeroy, Viscount Harberton, perhaps by the architect of Lodge Park, Straffan. Trinity Well in the demesne is the source of the Boyne.

2 m. W. is Monasteroris (Mainistear Fheorais, Bermingham's monastery), where Sir John Bermingham, Earl of Louth, founded a Franciscan friary in 1325. The remains here include a small parish church, a dovecot on a tumulus or motte, and the overgrown ruins of

the friary. The latter was fortified by the O Mores in the 16th cent., and endured a long siege by the Earl of Surrey, Lord Deputy. It served as the Protestant parish church until 1777. A modern cross commemorates Fr Mogue Kearns and Anthony Perry, who were hanged at Edenderry for their part in the 1798 Insurrection.

4 m. W. are the ruins of Ballybryan church. 1½ m. SW. are those of Ballybrittan castle. 3½ m. NW. are remains of the strong Bermingham castle of Kinnafad, commanding a ford of the Boyne. 1½ m. further NW. is Grange castle, a Tyrrell stronghold, part of which was still occupied in the 19th cent.

EDGEWORTHSTOWN, alias **MOS-TRIM**, Co. Longford (Map 2, D7), is a market village on the Mullingar (17¾ m.)–Longford (8¼ m.) road. It takes its modern name from the Edgeworth family. Edgeworthstown House, now a nursing home, is a greatly altered Georgian house. It was built by much-married Richard Lovell Edgeworth (1744–1817), author and inventor and father of the celebrated novelist, Maria Edgeworth (1767–1849). The Edgeworth family vault is at the Protestant church, where there is also a tablet to the memory of Richard Lovell Edgeworth.

3 m. N. is Firmount. Essex Edgeworth, Protestant Rector of Edgeworthstown and father of the Abbé Edgeworth de Firmont who attended Louis XVI on the scaffold, inherited the place and, removing to France, took the appellation "de Firmont".

6 m. N. is Ballinalee, native place of Gen. Seán Mac Eóin ("the Blacksmith of Ballinalee"), famous guerrilla leader in the struggle for Irish independence, later a general officer in the Irish army and a cabinet minister in three governments. Just S. of Ballinalee is Currygrane, birthplace of Sir Henry Wilson (1864-1922), Chief of the Imperial General Staff, who was assassinated in London for his part in the British effort to crush the Irish independence movement.

5 m. S., beside the Caldragh Stone in Caldragh, Killeen, is an early cross-slab.

3 m. SW. is Ardagh, which has given its name to the diocese. St Patrick is said to have founded a church here, over which he set St Mel as first bishop. The ancient ecclesiastical foundation is represented today by the ruins of St Mel's Church, alias the "Cathedral", a small, primitive, stone church in which St Mel is reputed to be buried. The saint's enshrined bachall, or staff, is preserved in St Mel's College, Longford (q.v.). Ardagh Hill (650 ft), formerly Slieve Golry, is the Brí Léith, alias Sliabh gCállraighe, of Irish mythology and literature and the setting of much of the charming tale of Midir, Étaín, and Eochu. It was an important local Lughnasa station until recent times. Ardagh House, now a convent, is the house which Goldsmith once mistook for an inn, an episode recalled in She Stoops to Conquer. E. of

the hill, in Breany, is a ringfort set in a fourteen-stone circle.

2 m. N.W. is Moatfarrell, where the O Farrell Lords of Annaly are said to have been inaugurated. There are remains of a motte-and-bailey and of a medieval church.

4½ m. NW. is Lissardowlan (see under Longford).

ELPHIN, Co. Roscommon (Map 2, B6), is now only a market village on the Roscommon (18 m.)–Boyle (16 m.) road, but it had an important place in the ecclesiastical history of Connacht and has given its name to a diocese. St Patrick established a bishopric here, over which he placed Bishop Assicus (see Racoon under Ballintra) and later, Bishop Betheus, the nephew of Assicus. They were assisted by Betheus's mother, the holy matron Cipia. To these Patrician bishops the modern diocese of Elphin ultimately traces its origin. In the Middle Ages there were houses of Augustinian canons and Franciscan friars, and also a collegiate church, at Elphin. The pre-Norman cathedral was burned by de Burgo's invading forces in 1235. Of the medieval churches and religious houses nothing remains, and Sligo is now the cathedral town.

Elphin has been claimed as the birthplace of Oliver Goldsmith, whose grandfather, the Rev. Oliver Jones, was a curate here and lived at Smith Hill, 1 m. to the NW. Goldsmith was actually born at Pallas, Co. Longford (see under Ballymahon), but he was educated at Elphin Diocesan School, as was later the distinguished oculist and antiquary, Sir William Wilde. Dr Charles Dodgson, great-grandfather of Lewis Carroll, was C. of I. bishop of Elphin (1775–95).

5 m. N., in Runnaboll, W. of Mantua House, is St Patrick's Bed, a former Lughnasa (Garland Sunday) station.

6 m. NE., in the parish of Kilmore, is Hill Street. Hereabouts there was a priory of Augustinian canons, founded in 1232. Some old ruins in Kilbride are said to mark the site.

1 m. WSW. is the Co. Roscommon Old I.R.A. memorial (1962–63). To the W. is the ancient church site, Shankill.

ENNIS, Co. Clare (Map 5, A3), on the Galway (42 m.)–Limerick (23 m.) road, is the capital of the county and the cathedral town of the Catholic diocese of Killaloe. It has some small industries, and is a convenient centre for exploring the principal antiquities of the county. The only modern building of note is the (1852) County Court House, which has a good, Ionic portico. In the bleak vestibule is an 1850 statue of Sir Michael O Loghlen (1789–1842), Master of the Rolls, by Joseph Robinson Kirk.

Close to the bridge over the River Fergus are the ruins (Nat. Mon.) of a Franciscan friary founded about 1250 by one of the O Briens of Thomond. The magnificently tall five-light E. window, which held blue painted glass, dates

St Francis with the stigmata, Ennis friary

from the restoration by Turlough Mór O Brien (1287–1306), while the vaulted sacristy dates from the early 14th cent., and the transept, cloister, and tower (pinnacles modern) from the 15th. The church has interesting figure-carvings, notably a series of panels (*Christ's Passion and Death* etc.) from a Mac Mahon tomb of *c.* 1470. Part of the cloister arcade has recently been re-erected.

The column at the centre of the town commemorates Daniel O Connell (1775–1847), who was M.P. for.Clare 1828–31. Clare (the "Banner County"), with Ennis as its capital, has been very much to the fore in 19th and 20th cent. politics. (Éamon de Valera represented the county from 1917 to 1959.)

In O Connell St is a small County Museum (1964).

At the Limerick end of the town is the little

Cathedral of SS Peter and Paul, commenced (1831) shortly after Catholic Emancipation, to the design of Dominic Madden (*see* St Jarlath's Cathedral, Tuam), and consecrated in 1843; belfry 1871. The interior is an interesting example of "carpenter's Gothick".

There are some good Georgian houses near the Protestant church.

William Mulready (1786–1863), the painter, was a native of Ennis, where his father was a breeches-maker, while Thomas Dermody (1775-1802), poet, author of *The Harp of Erin*, rake, and soldier, was the son of an Ennis school-master. Harriet Smithson (1800–1854), the actress, was the adopted daughter of the Rev. Dr James Barrett, Rector of Ennis. (Her father was an actor-manager.) Although not so much appreciated in London, she took the Continent by storm and was much admired by Gautier. In 1833 she married Hector Berlioz, the composer, who described her as "La Belle Smithson, dont tout Paris délirait". She died of a stroke, and is buried at Montmartre.

1 m. E., on the left bank of the Fergus, is the ancient church of Doora, with Transitional windows (insertions ?).

4 m. SW., via the Kildysart road, in the grounds of Newhall House, are the ruins (Nat. Mon.) of Killone (Cill Eóin, "St John's Church"), an Augustinian nunnery dedicated to St John. The foundation is attributed to King Donal Mór O Brien. The church has interesting Transitional features of *c.* 1225. Under the E. end is a crypt (unusual). The claustral buildings are 15th cent. Newhall House is a fine brick house built in 1764 for Charles Mac Donnell of Kilkee. It was locally believed that the nearby lake turned red whenever a Mac Donnell was to die. This belief was explained by the legend of the slaying of a mermaid from the lake by the Newhall butler, who had found her robbing the cellar; her blood turned the lake red. – Nearby Edenvale House, formerly home of the Stac-pooles, is now the County Sanatorium. There are caves in the Killone–Edenvale limestone.

2 m. NW., off the road to Corrofin, in Drum-cliff, are the remains (Nat. Mons.) of a Round Tower and of a much altered 12th/13th cent. church. St Conall founded an early monastery here. 2 m. further N. are the ruins of the 15th cent. castle of Ballygriffy. 3 m. NNE. of the latter is the very ruinous, 15th cent., parish church (Nat. Mon.) of Ruan (Portlecka). *See also* Clarecastle *and* Quin.

ENNISCORTHY, Co. Wexford (Map 6, C6), an important market town and distributing centre, picturesquely sited where the road from Ferns (7 m.) to Wexford (15 m.) crosses the Slaney at the head of the navigable tidal waters, is also the cathedral town of the Catholic diocese of Ferns. The valley of the Slaney below the town to Wexford and the sea is very beautiful, the lowermost reaches of the river passing through the barony of Shelmalier, fam-ous in song and story for its fowling and fishing.

The Entombment of Christ, from the Mac Mahon tomb, Ennis friary

The town grew up around the castle built on a rock at the head of the tideway, probably by Philip Prendergast, who had married the heiress of Strongbow's son-in-law, Robert de Quency. With the Gaelic resurgence it came into the possession of the Mac Murroughs Kavanagh, and Donal Riabhach Mac Murrough, King of Leinster (1440–76), had his seat there. In 1586 the castle was repaired by Sir Henry Wallop. Edmund Spenser had a lease of it for a time. It was attacked and captured by Cromwell in 1649. In 1798, during the occupation of the town by the insurgents, it served as a prison. In the 19th cent. it was restored for residential use by the Earl of Portsmouth, descendant of Sir Henry Wallop, but fell into disrepair again and was modernized a second time about 1900. Now the property of the local Athenaeum Club, it houses a collection of Co. Wexford bygones, etc. The remains are those of the peculiarly Norman-Irish type of rectangular keep (*see* Carlow *and* Ferns) with drum towers at the angles. The place of the SE. tower is taken by a turret.

St Aidan's Cathedral (1843–48), by Augustus Welby Pugin, is a Gothic-Revival building of high quality within and without. The spire-crowned tower at the crossing was built largely of stones taken from the ruins of a Franciscan friary (between the castle and the river) founded by King Donal Riabhach Mac Murrough Kavanagh. After the Dissolution the lands of the friary were held for a time by Edmund Spenser (*see* Black Castle *below, and* Kilcolman *under* Doneraile).

At the N. end of the town are remains of the ancient church of Templeshannon.

In the Market Sq. is a 1798 memorial by Oliver Sheppard, with bronze figures of Fr John Murphy of Boleyvogue (*below*) and a Wexford pikeman. The insurgents stormed the town on 28 May 1798, and set up their principal encampment on Vinegar Hill (391 ft) to the E. There, on 21 June, a large force of them was almost completely surrounded by Generals Lake and Johnson with 20,000 troops. The ill-armed insurgents stood up to overwhelming fire for several hours, before making their escape through the last remaining gap in the enemy lines. The windmill (stump; Nat. Mon.) on the hill was the insurgent command-post.

4 m. NE. is the motte (Nat. Mon.) of Ballymoty More; erected by Gilbert de Borlart (Boisrohard), a follower of Strongbow.

8 m. NE. is Boleyvogue. It was the burning by British soldiery of the Catholic chapel, Fr John Murphy's dwelling, and some twenty farmhouses, on the night of Sat. 26 May 1798, which precipitated the great Wexford insurrection.

7 m. E. is Oulart Hill (500 ft), where, on 27 May 1798, Fr John Murphy's small insurgent force defeated the British troops sent against them. Next day the insurgents went N. and took Camolin, where they found some arms. They then marched via Ferns to Scarawalsh bridge where they recrossed the Slaney. On 28 May, their numbers swollen to 7,000, they stormed Enniscorthy, and their victory there caused the revolt to spread through the entire county.

8 m. SE., in the home of the Curran family, Crossabeg, is preserved a 14th/15th cent. oak figure of St Maol-Rúáin of Tallaght. It was found in 1760 at St Maol-Rúáin's Well, Ballinaleck, site of a monastery dedicated to the saint.

4 m. S., near Edermine, is a private chapel by Augustus Welby Pugin.

6 m. SW., in Ballybrennan, are the ruins of Kilcowanmore (Church of Cúán Mór) and St Cowan's Well. Less than ½ m. SW. of the well, adjoining the site of Ballybrennan castle, are pillarstones; one has cup marks and grooves. 1 m. ESE. of the well is Ballybrittas Cromlech, a portal dolmen. 4 m. S. of the latter, in Barmoney, is Druid's Altar, another portal dolmen.

ENNISKERRY, Co. Wicklow (Map 6, D3), is a village very beautifully situated in the Dargle valley, 12 m. S. of Dublin (via Dundrum–Stepaside–The Scalp) and 3½ m. SW. of Bray. The Catholic church (about 1843), by Patrick Byrne, was one of the first Gothic Revival churches in Ireland. Adjoining the village on the SW. is magnificent Powerscourt Demesne, formerly the property of Viscount Powerscourt, now of the Powerscourt Estates Company. It is noted for its exotic and other trees and offers a series of delightful walks and drives, including one of 4 m. up the Dargle to Powerscourt Waterfall (Deerpark townland), where the stream comes slipping down 398 ft from the shoulders of Djouce Mt (2,384 ft), War Hill (2,250 ft), and Tonduff (2,107 ft). Superbly sited Powerscourt House (Mr and Mrs Slazenger) was built by Richard Cassels *c.* 1730, but was enlarged, and the garden front altered, in the 19th cent. The beautiful terraces (1843–75) were designed by Daniel Robertson. The Japanese Garden dates from 1908. The Demesne and Gardens (entrance, Eagle Gate) are open to the public, Easter to Oct., 11 a.m.–5.30 p.m.; adults 2/6, children 1/6 (parties of twenty or more, 2/– and 1/– respectively). The Waterfall (entrance, Waterfall Gate) is accessible all the year round; adults 1/–, children 6d; cars and motor cycles, 6d. Driving from Eagle Gate through the demesne to the waterfall involves payment of both fees.

2 m. N., to the W. of the Dublin road, are the fragmentary remains of Killegar, a medieval nave-and-chancel church. There are two early gravestones of Ballyman (*see under* Bray) type, and a fragment (with *Crucifixion*) of a granite cross of Cornish type. Traces of a circular enclosing wall or bank survive. Nearby is a holy well. The site affords magnificent prospects of a beautiful countryside. 2 m. N. is the Scalp (*see under* Golden Ball).

1 m. E., to the N. of the Bray road, at the house called St Valery, Fassaroe, is a granite cross (Nat. Mon.) of Cornish type with a rude, weathered *Crucifixion*. Nearby is a stone "font". Neither is *in situ.*

2 m. ESE., via the Bray road, are remains of Kilcroney church (Nat. Mon.) with fine trabeate W. door. 60 yds E. was St Croney's Well.

½ m. SE. is "The (Glen of the) Dargle" (Powerscourt Demesne; pedestrians only), where the little river tumbles its way through a deep, wooded defile. View Rock is so called from the prospect it affords of Powerscourt and the mountains beyond (Kippure, 2,475 ft). Lover's Leap, a great rock nearby, has engendered the inevitable tales of romantic doom.

1 m. SSW., on the S. bank of the Dargle, is Tinnehinch House (Grattan Bellew family). This plain house, originally an inn, was presented to Henry Grattan by a grateful Dublin Parliament in 1782. Tinnehinch bridge crosses the Dargle at one of the loveliest spots in a very lovely district. 1 m. further SSW. is Charleville House, built *c.* 1810 for the 2nd Viscount Monck; the elevation echoes that of Lucan House (*see* Lucan). The demesne has some splendid trees.

4 m. W. of Enniskerry is Glencree, with Kippure (2,475 ft) and Tonduff (2,107 ft) on the SW. and S., and Glendoo Mt. (1,829 ft) and Prince William's Seat (1,825 ft) on the N. Kippure, Tonduff, War Hill, and Djouce Mt afford wonderful views in clear weather. A circuit of Glencree can be made from Enniskerry by following the road W. past the N. side of Powerscourt Demesne and on to Glencree Reformatory at the head of the valley; thence S. for a short distance along the Military Road before turning SE. along the S. side of the valley to Valeclusa (a house) and Tinnehinch. Glencree Reformatory (disused) was originally a barracks guarding the 1798 Military Road from Rathfarnham through the solitudes of the Wicklow mountains (*see* Aghavannagh). Nearby is a small German cemetery of the Second World War. 1 m. S. of the Reformatory, in deep basins under Kippure, are Lower and Upper Loughs Bray. 3 m. S. of the latter, via the Military Road, is the Sally Gap (*see under* Roundwood). The Military Road offers a rewarding upland drive to Glenmacnass (*see under* Laragh).

6 m. W. (alt. 500 ft), in Glaskenny, Glencree, is Donnchadh Dearg, a portal dolmen (capstone fallen). 400 yds S., in Onagh, is a granite slab with a shallow basin and five cup marks.

1¼ m. W., in Powerscourt Demesne, is St Mo-Ling's Well.

¾ m. WNW., close to a lane on the N. side of the Glencree road, is Parknasilloge Cromlech, a megalithic cist (remnant of a multiple-cist cairn ?).

ENNISKILLEN, Co. Fermanagh (Map 2, C4), on the Omagh (27 m.)–Sligo (40 m.) road, is the county town of Co. Fermanagh and a cathedral town of the Protestant diocese of Clogher (*see* Clogher). It is charmingly situated on an island in the River Erne, between Upper and Lower Loughs Erne, and is an ideal centre from which to explore the beautiful lakes (*see* Lough Erne, Upper) as well as a lovely countryside rich in prehistoric, historic, and architectural monuments.

Enniskillen's strategic situation in the difficult Erne valley early marked it out as a place of military importance, and in the later Middle Ages it was a key stronghold of the Maguires. When the English at last conquered the North, James I granted the place, together with considerable estates, to Capt. (later Sir) William Cole, and Enniskillen thereafter became an important stronghold of the Protestant settlers. It served them as a rallying point during the Irish uprising of 1641, and in 1689 rallied to the cause of William of Orange, in whose name the inhabitants repelled an attack (1690) by Tyrconnell, James II's Lord Lieutenant.

Fort Hill takes its name from the 1689 star fort in whose remains is set the column (excellent view) to Gen. Sir Galbraith Lowry Cole (1772–1842), who fought in the Peninsular War and became Governor of Cape Colony. He was the second son of the first Earl of Enniskillen (created 1789) and a direct descendant of William Cole, the Planter.

St Macartan's Cathedral, Church St, second cathedral of the Protestant diocese of Clogher, was built in 1840, but incorporates a 17th cent. tower and N. porch. The font dates from 1666. The old colours of the Royal Inniskilling Dragoon Guards and of the Royal Inniskilling Fusiliers are laid up here.

In Wellington St is Enniskillen Castle (Nat. Mon.), long used as a barracks. A Maguire castle which stood here at least from the 15th cent. figured prominently in the 16th cent. wars. In 1594 it was captured and garrisoned by the English, but was retaken by Maguire the following summer. Seized once more by the English, it was eventually restored by them to Maguire. In 1602 Niall Garbh O Donnell and the English came up the lake and destroyed Enniskillen, but it was not until 1607 that Maguire was finally dispossessed. In 1612 command of the castle was given to Capt. William Cole. The lower storey of the original keep is incorporated in a later building. A fine water-gate of c. 1580/90 also survives. The Sconce, ¼ m. SE. in Broad Meadow, is a later earthwork constructed for the defence of the town

The Convent of Mercy has seven windows by Michael Healy (1905 and 1906): four windows of Irish saints, an *Annunciation*, a *St Benedict Joseph Labre*, and a *St Anthony*; also two windows by Sarah Purser: *St Michael* (1905), *St Elizabeth* (1906); and six by Lady Glenavy: *The Presentation* (1905; two windows), *St Margaret Mary* (1905), *Sacred Heart* (1905), *Immaculate Conception* (1906), *St Macartan* (1906).

¾ m. NW. is beautifully situated Portora Royal School, founded in 1628 by James I; the buildings are largely 18th cent. Oscar Wilde and Samuel Beckett went to school at Portora. In the grounds are the remains of a Plantation castle built by William Cole on the site of 15th cent. Maguire castle. It has suffered from schoolboy experiments with explosives as well as from time and the elements.

5 m. N., via the road to Irvinestown, are the limestone caves known as the Daughters.

5½ m. ENE. is Mullyknock (*see under* Tempo).

1½ m. SE. is Castle Coole, seat of the Earl of Belmore, now the property of the Nat. Trust. Held to be the finest Classical mansion in Ireland, this noble house was built, 1789–98, for the 1st Earl. The exterior is by Richard Johnston, elder brother of Francis, but James Wyatt, Jun., who designed the interior, may have Grecianized Johnston's design. The house has excellent stucco by Joseph Rose, and carvings by David Sheehan and John Houghton. The joinery is excellent and the joiners made much of the furniture on the spot. Open: 1 April to 30 Sept.: Tue., Wed., Fri., Sat., and Bank Holidays, 2–6 p.m.; 1 July to 30 Sept.: Sun. also 2.30–5.30 p.m. Admission: adults 2/-, children and parties 1/-. Lough Coole has Ireland's only breeding colony of grey-lag geese (introduced c. 1700). Also in the demesne is Gortgonnell Standing Stone, a boulder with four bullauns.

9 m. SE., in Upper Lough Erne, is Bellisle, formerly Seanadh, where, in the 15th cent., Cathal Maguire compiled the celebrated *Annals of Ulster*.

3 m. S. are the ruins of Lisgoole "Abbey". There was an early monastery here, which in time adopted the Augustinian Rule. In 1580 it passed to the Franciscans. Bro. Michael O Clery completed his redaction of the *Book of Invasions* at Lisgoole Franciscan Convent, 20 Dec. 1631.

11 m. S., via the road to Belturbet, is Knockninny (St Ninnidh's hill, 630 ft; cf. Inishmacsaint *under* Lough Erne, Upper). On the summit, in Shehinny, is a ruinous round cairn; 200 yds NW. is another; a third has disappeared. ¼ m. S., in Corratrasna, is Giants Grave, a ruinous chamber tomb (Nat. Mon.). There were formerly two chamber tombs on the E. side of the hill. On the SW. slope, alt. 300 ft in Shehinny, is a cave inhabited, and also used as a burial place, in prehistoric times. Also on the hill is St Ninnidh's Well. At Knockninny was the seat of a branch of the Maguires. After the Williamite triumph Brian, son of Conor Modarra Maguire, was a noble supporter of impoverished Gaelic scholars and scribes, maintaining them in his house here and employing them to copy the principal historical MSS. of Ireland. "And so he gave relief and great encouragement to noble fathers' sons who had never been brought up to do the work of serfs or manual labourers."

11 m. SSW. are some remains of Kinawley parish church (Nat. Mon.) on the site of an early abbey or church founded by St Náile (successor of St Rabharnóg), from whom the place takes its name. In the graveyard is Tobar Náile, which cured jaundice. On the nearby hill was Cloch na dTuras, a great boulder which was a Lughnasa station. 5 m. NW. of Kinawley, to the W. of the road to Swanlinbar and on the E. slope of Benaughlin, alt. 550 ft, is Doohatty

Glebe Giants Grave (Nat. Mon.), a much altered court grave. Benaughlin (1,221 ft) was an important Lughnasa station. 5 m. N. is Florence Court (*below*).

8½ m. SW. is Florence Court (Nat. Trust), magnificent seat of the Earls of Enniskillen (descendants of William Cole). The pre-Palladian house was built in 1764 (by Davis Ducart ?) for Lord Mount Florence (created Earl of Enniskillen in 1784). The excellent rococo plasterwork is of the Dublin school (by Robert West ?). Badly damaged by fire in 1955, the house has been restored under the supervision of Sir Albert Richardson. 4½ m. W. is the Marble Arch, where the Cladagh River emerges from a complex system of underground chambers and galleries which draw their waters from surface streams rising on Cuilcagh Mt (2,188 ft), Co. Cavan; some of the caves are accessible by boat. ½ m. W. of the bridge across the Cladagh, in Killesher, is "St Lasair's Cell" (Nat. Mon.), a three-chamber souterrain in a mound. The nearby church site, Killesher, is named after St Lasair; the remains here are those of a medieval church re-edified for Protestant use in the 17th cent. – 1¼ m. W. of Marble Arch school, in Kilnameel, is the Dumbies, an overgrown court grave. – 4 m. NW. of Killesher is Belcoo (*q.v.*).

6½ m. WSW. is Belmore Mt (fine views; W. peak 1,105 ft; E. peak 1,316 ft.). On the E. edge of the mountain (alt. 900 ft), best approached via Letterbreen creamery on the road to Belcoo, is Moylehid Giants Grave, a wrecked chamber tomb. On the Eagle's Knoll (alt. 1,150 ft) is Moylehid Cairn (Nat. Mon.), a round cairn with the ruins of a cruciform passage grave. Not far away (alt. 1,161 ft) are remains of Moylehid Cashel (Nat. Mon.). – On the S. slope of the mountain (¾ m. NW. of Mullaghdun Protestant church) is Carrickmacsparrow Giants Grave (Nat. Mon.), a ruined court grave.

8 m. W., near Boho, is a series of labyrinthine caves with a subterranean stream. 1 m. SW. of Boho crossroads is Coolarkan Cave, which has a large chamber and engulfs a surface stream. The moorland NW. of Boho has many swallow-holes and pot-holes, including Noon's Hole, the deepest in Ireland. A plain Gothic doorway (from a medieval church ¾ m. NW.) has been re-erected as the W. doorway of Boho Protestant church. In Toneel churchyard are the base, shaft, and a fragment of the head of a 9th/10th cent. High Cross (Nat. Mon.). The figure sculptures include *The Fall of Adam and Eve*, *Baptism of Christ*, etc. The cross derives from an early monastery which stood here. 1 m. NW., in Killydrum, is St Feber's Holy Well, with an ancient font close by. ⅓ m. W. of Toneel church are the Reyfad Stones (Nat. Mon.), six large stones, five of which have "cup-and-ring" marks. 3½ m. W. of the church, on the shore of Loughnacloyduff (2½ m. NE. of Black Bridge on the Belcoo–Garrison road), alt. 900 ft, is Clogherbog "inscribed" cave, a partly artificial

cave with scribings like those found in some passage graves. – 1½ m. NW. of Boho crossroads is Aghanaglack "Standing Stone" (Nat. Mon.), the base and shaft of a plain, stone cross; a portion of the head lies beside it. Nearby is Aghanaglack Cave (Nat. Mon.), artificially modified. Further W., 1 m. N. of the "Devil's S" on the Boho–Belcoo road (alt. 700 ft), is Aghanaglack Giants Grave (Nat. Mon.), a fine double-court cairn.

4 m. NW., by the lake, was Castle Hume, Richard Cassels's first (*c.* 1727) Irish house; he was brought to Ireland by Sir Gustavus Hume to build it; only the dovecot and part of the stable block survive. 2¼ m. further N. is Ely Lodge, originally seat of the Loftus family (which inter-married with the Humes, whence Ely Place and Hume St, Dublin). 3 m. W. of Castle Hume, in Castletown Monea demesne, are remains (Nat. Mon.) of a Plantation castle with Scottish features. It was built (1618–19) by the Rev. Malcolm Hamilton, Rector of Devenish. In 1688 the castle was the residence of Gustavus Hamilton, Governor of Enniskillen. Monea Protestant church has a good, 15th cent. window from St Mary's Abbey, Devenish (*see under* Lough Erne, Upper). There is a Wilhelmina Geddes window (1913) here. ¾ m. SW. of the church are the ruins of Tullykelter castle, a 17th cent. Scottish-style strong-house built by James Somerville (d. 1642), a Planter from Cambusnethan, Ayrshire. 1¼ m. WSW. of Monea church is Tullycreevy Cairn (Nat. Mon.). 3¼ m. NW. of Monea church are the ruins of Derrygonnelly church, built in the 17th cent. by Sir John Dunbar. Knockmore Mt (919 ft), to the W. of Derrygonnelly, has many caves. 3 m. NW. of Derrygonnelly, on the shore of Carrick Lough, are the ruins of Aghamore, or Carrick, church (Nat. Mon.), built by Gilbert O Flanagan and his wife, Margaret Maguire (d. 1498). 4½ m. N. of Derrygonnelly, on the W. shore of Lough Erne, are the ruins of Tully castle (Nat. Mon.), a Plantation bawn with Scottish-style stronghouse built by Sir John Hume, a Planter from Manderston, Berwickshire, and destroyed by Capt. Rory Maguire on Christmas Day, 1641, when most of the garrison were slaughtered (*see* Castle Archdale *and* Crevenish castle *under* Irvinestown).

1½ m. (by boat) NNW. is Devenish (*see under* Lough Erne, Upper).

12½ m. NNW. is Killadeas (*see under* Lough Erne, Upper).

ENNISTIMON, Co. Clare (Map 1, D7), a small market town by a picturesque fall on the River Cullenagh (Ennistimon River), is 3 m. from Lehinch, 40 m. from Limerick, and 17 m. from Ennis. It grew up around a castle built by Turlough O Brien in 1588.

Trout fishing is to be had on the Cullenagh and Daleagh rivers.

The Catholic parish church (1953), by W. H. D. McCormick, is one of the better recent churches in Ireland. The mural Stations of the

Cross (1955) are by Fr Aengus Buckley, O.P.

3½ m. N. is Kilshanny, with ruins of a church, Cill tSeanaigh (Kiltheana), of about 1200; N. door and S. window are Transitional, the rest later. The original foundation here was by St Seanach (whose bell is preserved in the British Museum), but the remains are those of an Augustinian monastery founded c. 1194 by King Donal Mór O Brien.

2 m. W. is Lehinch (q.v.).

3 m. NNW., in Ballydeely, is Carn Connachtach, a large cairn.

EYRECOURT, Co. Galway (Map 5, C2), is a village on the Killimor (7 m.)–Banagher, Co. Offaly (6 m.) road. It is called after the Eyres, a Cromwellian family which had an estate here. George Eyre, master of the Galway Blazers and M.P. at the end of the 18th cent., has been immortalized as Charles Lever's "Charles O Malley".

3 m. NW. at Belview (formerly Lissareaghaun), Lawrencetown, is a fine gateway (urn and pediment missing) erected by Walter Lawrence (1729–96) to commemorate the achievement of Grattan's Volunteers. (The Lawrences descended from a Lancashire follower of Sir John Perrot, the Elizabethan Lord Deputy, who married the daughter of O Madden of Longford (5½ m. SW. of Eyrecourt) towards the close of the 16th cent.)

2½ m. E., in Lismore, are remains of one of the principal castles of the O Maddens. It passed by marriage to the Burkes, and eventually to the Dalys of Dunsandle. The remains include the tower and parts of the bawn of a 15th–16th cent. castle, as well as a 17th cent. house.

3 m. SE. is Meelick, a Shannonside hamlet. In 1203 William de Burgo, accompanied by the sons of Conor Maenmagh O Conor, invaded Connacht and erected a motte castle here. "And the spot where the castle was erected was around the great church of the place, which was filled round about with earth and stones up to the gable." From this base de Burgo devastated the country far and wide until called off by the English Justiciar. About 1229 his son, Richard, built a stone castle at Meelick. This was destroyed in 1316 by Felim O Conor (see Athenry). Close to the site of the castle is the parish church (tomb of Fergus Madden of Lismore, 1671), re-roofed church of a Franciscan friary founded in 1414 by an O Madden. Dispersed at the Reformation, the friars returned in 1630. John Colgan, celebrated historian, was Guardian in 1635. The friary lay derelict from the Cromwellian victory until 1686. The Williamite rebellion dispersed the friars for the third time.

3 m. S., at Fahy on the Portumna road, are remains of a medieval church.

FEAKLE, Co. Clare (Map 5, B3), lies in the remote heart of the East Clare hills, on the north road from Gort (15 m.) to Scarriff (6 m.).

The poet, Brian Mac Giolla-Meidhre, alias Merriman (1757–1805), is buried in the old churchyard, but no monument marks his grave. His celebrated satire *Cúirt an Mheadhon Oidhche* has been translated into English by the late Lord Longford, Arland Ussher, and Frank O Connor. Merriman was born at Clondegad, and was schoolmaster at Kilclenin near Feakle.

3¾ m. NW., in Ballycroum, are Tobergrania, Altóir Ultach, and Dermot and Grania's Bed, three gallery graves. Tobergrania, which has a "porthole" slab, was formerly regarded as a well whose water had curative virtues.

FENIT, Co. Kerry (Map 4, C3), is a village 8 m. W. of Tralee, of which it is the outer port.

St Bréanainn moccu Altai, Brendan the Navigator (484–577; *see* Clonfert, Co. Galway, *and* Cnoc Bréanainn *under* Dingle) was born in the vicinity.

5 m. N., on a rocky promontory near the NW. entrance to Barrow Harbour, is Round Castle. The site affords a beautiful prospect of the Dingle Peninsula and the NW. Kerry coast.

3 m. NE. is Lissodigue cave.

FERBANE, Co. Offaly (Map 5, D2), is a village on the Clara (10 m.)–Cloghan (4 m.) road.

½ m. S., on the E. bank of the Brosna, is Gallen Priory, a Georgian house (Gothicized and smothered in cement; now a convent). The house derives its name from Gailinne na mBretan, Gallen of the Britons (Welsh), a monastery said to have been founded by St Canoc, or Mo-Chonóg, in the 5th cent., and which was situated between the house and the river. Little is known of the monastery, which is first mentioned in the Irish annals in the 9th cent. In the Middle Ages it had become an Augustinian priory. No traces of the monastic buildings survive above ground; but beneath a Holy Tree is part of the shaft of an elaborately carved, early stone cross, while a large number of fragmentary 7th/8th–11th cent. gravestones have been recovered by excavation. A short distance S. are the ruins of a 15th cent. parish church (Nat. Mon.); the early gravestones are displayed here.

6 m. N. are remnants of Doon castle, an O Mooney stronghold with a sheila-na-gig.

5 m. NE., on the Ballycumber road, is Lemanaghan (Liath Mancháin, originally Tuaim nEirc), where fragments of a Romanesque church and six early gravestones mark the site of a monastery founded by St Manchán (d. 665). One gravestone is inscribed: BENDACHT FOR A[NMA]IN AILBERTIG ("A prayer for the soul of Ailbertach"). N. of the church are traces of St Manchán's House. E. of the church is St Manchán's Well, from which an ancient causeway leads to the "abbey". The latter is an enclosure with a diminutive pre-Romanesque oratory, traditionally the cell of St Manchán's mother, St Mella. Between well and "abbey"

Milled peat electricity station (1957), Lumcloon, Ferbane

is the stone where, legend asserts, mother and son met each day without conversing. St Manchán's shrine, a splendid, 12th cent., tomb-shaped reliquary containing bones of the saint, has never left the district, and is now preserved at Boher church (*see under* Clara). Lemanaghan castle belonged to the O Molloys.

FERMOY, Co. Cork (Map 5, C5), is a market town, important road junction, and noted angling centre on the lovely Blackwater, 23 m. NE. of Cork, 10m. S. of Mitchelstown, 16 m. W. of Lismore, and 18 m. E. of Mallow. To the N. rise the Kilworth Mountains (W. end of Knockmealdown); to the SW., the Nagles Mountains. Boats are available for exploring the beauties of the river. Delightful walks may be had in the valleys of the Blackwater, Funshion, and Araglin rivers.

As a town, Fermoy is the creation of John Anderson, a Scots merchant settled in Cork, who purchased the Fermoy estate in 1791. He offered the British Government sites for large barracks, and built the town to meet the needs of the garrison. From 1797 to 1922 the town was one of the principal British military centres in Ireland, with training grounds at Kilworth Camp and Moore Park (*see* Kilworth, *below*).

In the Middle Ages the Cistercian abbey of Castrum Dei (Mainistear Fhear Maighe) stood on the S. bank of the river. Like Holy Cross Abbey (*see under* Thurles), this abbey too had begun in the 12th cent. as a house of Benedictines of the Order of Tiron and had numbered Donal Mór O Brien among its patrons. Becoming Cistercian before the close of the century, it was colonized from Inishlounaght (*see under* Clonmel). It was dissolved in 1560, and not a trace survives.

There are a few small Georgian houses opposite the unusual Protestant church (1802)

on the N. side of the river. In the church is a medieval stoup, or mortar, with grotesque masks; its history is unknown. The bridge across the Blackwater dates from 1689; it was widened by Anderson.

3¼ m. NE. is Kilworth. ¾ m. SW. of the village, above the Funshion River (trout), in the grounds of Moore Park, is the Condon castle of Cloghleagh. Forfeited in 1581, it was recovered by the Condons in 1641, but fell to the Parliamentarian commander, Sir Charles Vavasour, two years later. – 3 m. E. is the wild and lovely Araglin valley (*see under* Lismore); the ruined castle in Castle Cooke townland was another Condon stronghold. – 2 m. SE., to the N. of the Araglin, are the ruins of Ballyderown castle. 3½ m. NW., in the Kilworth Mountains, is Kilworth Camp.

2½ m. ENE., on the N. side of the Black-water, is Mount Rivers. The 18th cent. town stocks of Fermoy are preserved here. SW. of the house are remains of the Condon castle of Licklash.

1½ m. E., on the S. side of the Blackwater, are the remains of the Condon castle of Carrig-brick.

3 m. E., on the Tallow road, is Carysville, formerly Baile Mhic Phádraig (Duchess of Westminster). It occupies the site of a Condon castle. The Carysville fishery is one of the best on the Blackwater.

4½ m. SE., in the grounds of Coole Abbey, the remains of two early churches with *antae* (Nat. Mons.) mark the site of an early monastery. The larger church has had a Gothic chancel and SW. porch added in the 13th cent.; it was used as a Protestant church until the 18th cent. St Patrick's tooth is said to have been preserved here in the Middle Ages. 2¼ m. SW. is Castlelyons (*below*).

5 m. SSE. is the village of Castlelyons. St

Nicholas's Protestant Church, SW. of the village, was built in 1776 by Lord Barrymore within the nave of a medieval church whose E. window it incorporates. E. of the church are the Barrymore mausoleum, with wrought-ironwork of local make, and a monument (1753) to James Barry, Viscount Barry and Buttevant (1676–1747). The monument is by David Sheehan (d. 1756), the angels of the entablature by John Houghton (d. 1775?). On the E. side of the village are the remains (aisleless nave, tower, chancel, E. and W. cloister ranges; Nat. Mon.) of the Carmelite friary of the Virgin Mary, founded in 1307 by John de Barri; there are some medieval gravestones here (Nat. Mons.). At the S. end of the village are remains of Barrymore Castle, alias Castle Lyons, a Tudor stronghouse with later additions. This was the chief seat of the Lords Barrymore until its destruction by fire in 1771. SSE. of the castle are remains of Barrymore Stables and Barrymore Barn. – 4 m. E. of Castlelyons, on the Bride, are remains of the Geraldine castle of Aghern. – 4½ m. SE. of Castlelyons are the ruins of the early church of Britway; NW. is St Brigid's Well. In nearby Curraghdermot was born the poet, Liam Rúa Mac Coitir (1680–1738); he lived for a time at Mountbell (Cnoc an Loiscreáin) on the Castlemartyr road.

2 m. S., on Knockaunacorrin (731 ft), are remains of Carn Thiernagh, a large chambered cairn, and of a later hill-fort.

5¼ m. WSW., to the S. of the Blackwater in Ballymaclawrence, is a ringfort-type burial-ground (cillín) with a souterrain.

2½ m. W., on the N. bank of the Blackwater, is Castle Hyde demesne. On a rock behind the house are remains of Castle Hyde, originally an O Mahony stronghold. The first Hydes here were Cromwellian Planters; a descendant, Douglas Hyde (1860–1949), was co-founder of the Gaelic League, Professor of Modern Irish in University College, Dublin, and President of Ireland (1938–45).

5 m. W., on the N. bank of the Blackwater, is Ballyhooley (see under Castletownroche).

6 m. NW. is Glanworth (q.v.).

FERNS, Co. Wexford (Map 6, C5), now a quiet village on the Gorey (11 m.)–Enniscorthy (8 m.) road, gives its name to one of the principal dioceses of the ancient kingdom of Leinster, and was also for a time the royal seat of that kingdom. Its history commences with the foundation of a monastery by St M'Aodhóg (Mogue), alias Aidan (d. 626), on land given to him by a newly converted Hy Kinsella ruler. M'Aodhóg is generally assumed to be the Breany saint of that name (see Drumlane under Belturbet). His monastery here was the principal of several foundations in the region, and after his death he was buried in it. His relics were subsequently enshrined in a casket which, together with its satchel, is now preserved in the National Museum. At an early date the church of Ferns supplanted St Abban's founda-

tion in Magh Arnaidhe (see Kilabban under Athy) as the principal church of southern Leinster. It survived repeated ravaging by the Norsemen, and at the 12th cent. reformation became the see of a diocese corresponding to Hy Kinsella. Somewhat earlier the notorious Díarmait na nGall Mac Murrough had fixed his residence near by. He was a generous patron of the Church (see Baltinglass) and, presumably as a contribution towards the revitalizing of St M'Aodhóg's foundation, he founded St Mary's Abbey for Canons Regular of St Augustine. It was burned down in 1154, but he rebuilt it in 1160, and there he died in 1171. After Díarmait's death Ferns passed (by Anglo-Norman law) to his son-in-law, Strongbow, and subsequently to Strongbow's heirs, but was recovered by the Mac Murroughs in the 14th cent. The see of the Catholic diocese is now at Enniscorthy (q.v.). The Protestant diocese is united with those of Leighlin (see under Leighlinbridge) and Ossory (see Kilkenny).

The principal relics of the past at Ferns are fragments of a great castle, of the cathedral, and of the Augustinian monastery.

The castle (Nat. Mon.), at the NW. end of the village, is thought to occupy the site of King Díarmait's residence. It exemplifies a Norman-Irish type: rectangular keep with drum-towers at the angles (see Enniscorthy and Carlow); in the SE. tower is a chapel. The castle was presumably built (about 1226) by some member of the Earl Marshal's family (see Carlow and New Ross), but was for long the residence of the bishop. In the 14th cent. it fell to the resurgent Mac Murrough kings of Leinster. It was dismantled in 1641 by the Parliamentarian, Sir Charles Coote, who slaughtered the inhabitants of the town.

Burnt down in 1577, the early-13th cent. cathedral is represented only by its chancel, shorn of its aisles and incorporated in little (1817) St Edan's (sic) Cathedral (C.I.). There is a 13th cent. episcopal tombstone here. E. of the cathedral is a beautiful fragment of an early-13th cent. church (Nat. Mon.). In the graveyard is a portion of the shaft (Nat. Mon.) of a High Cross, alleged to mark the grave of King Díarmait. Portions of two plain High Crosses (Nat. Mons.) are built into the N. wall of the graveyard, and fragments of two similar crosses may be seen near the gate. Outside the graveyard is St Mogue's Well; the 1847 well house has carved heads from Clone church (2 m. S.).

S. of the cathedral is St Mary's Abbey (Nat. Mon.), which is usually assumed to have occupied the site of M'Aodhóg's monastery and is represented today merely by the vaulted sacristy, NW. bell-tower, and N. wall of a nave-and-chancel church 64 ft long; but the foundations of a cloister garth, 72 × 66 ft, lie buried on the S. side. The most interesting feature is the ruined belfry, square on plan as far as the level of the church roof, where it turns into a Round Tower.

NE. of the cathedral, near the rectory, are fragmentary remains of St Peter's Church (Nat. Mon.), a modest, nave-and-chancel structure with a Late Romanesque window in the S. wall of the chancel and two Gothic lancets in the E. gable. It has been suggested that this is a post-Reformation building, and that the S. window derives from Clone church (2 m. S.), and the Gothic windows from the cathedral.

7 m. NNE., on the SE. slope of Slieveboy (1,387 ft), are remains of Kilbride church; not far off is a prehistoric chamber tomb. This hill, and indeed most of the high ground N. of Ferns, affords magnificent prospects of the Slaney valley and the Blackstairs Mountains.

5 m. SE. is Boleyvogue (*see under* Enniscorthy).

2 m. S. are remains of Clone church, from which fragments were taken to Ferns.

FETHARD, Co. Tipperary (Map 5, D4), is a small, decayed market town where the Callan (14 m.)–Cashel (10 m.) road crosses the little Clashawley River 7 m. N. of Clonmel.

The town came into being in the 14th cent., and in 1376 Edward III of England gave permission to the townsfolk to enclose it with walls. Fragments of the towered wall and of one of its four gates survive; likewise four "castles", i.e. tower houses and a number of houses with the armorial bearings of their builders. Of these last the principal is Everard's Mansion, incorporated in a British military barracks. The Protestant parish church of the Holy Trinity incorporates some windows, the W. tower, etc. of the late-15th cent. parish church. E. of the church is a castle, or tower house; S. of this are two others. At the E. end of the town are the ruins (refectory, dormitories, kitchen, etc.) of an Augustinian friary founded outside the walls, c. 1303–6, by Walter de Mulcote; built into a wall near the E. end of the church is a sheila-na-gig. Early in the 19th cent. the friars returned to Fethard and re-edified the remains of their church.

¾ m. S. are the ruins of Templemartin, a small church.

4½ m. N. (3¼ m. S. of Killenaule), on the borders of Cooleagh and Grangebarry, is a crossroads. The neighbouring townlands are exceptionally rich in ringforts, earthworks of various kinds, and other ancient remains. In the NE. angle of the crossroads (Cooleagh townland) is a quadrivallate ringfort. N. of this, on the W. side of the road in Lismortagh, is a trivallate, rectilinear earthwork. – 600 yds W. of the crossroads, in Grangebarry, are two bivallate ringforts. – ½ m. SE. of the crossroads, in Cooleagh, are remains of a church. Some 300 yds S. of this is a curious ring-work with adjoining enclosures. To the NE. are a diamond fort and other earthworks. – Some 2 m. NE. of the crossroads is an old village-site. – 1 m. E. of the crossroads are remains of St Johnstown church. 1¾ m. NE. of the latter, in Shanakyle, is a great polygonal earthwork, 700×500 yds (an

early monastic site?). 2 m. W. of this is Peppardstown ringfort (*below*). – 1½ m. W. of the crossroads is Templemacduagh, an ancient church-site.

2½ m. NNE. are the ruins of Slainstown castle; to the N. are a univallate ringfort and Lady's Well.

¾ m. NE., overlooking the Mullinahone road, are the ruins of Cramp's Castle. 2½ m. E., in Friarsgrange, is Shanaclogh, a bivallate castle-site (?).

2½ m. NE. are the ruins of Knockkelly castle, a 16th cent. castle with large bawn and angle turrets. 1 m. NNE., at the E. side of the road in Rathkenny, is a bivallate ringfort; ¼ m. further N., in Peppardstown, is another. Between the two were St James's Church and St James's Well. About ½ m. W. of the Peppardstown fort, in Higginstown, and further W. in Milltown St John, is a system of ancient roads and earthworks, including Ballynascullogge, a large, sub-rectangular enclosure (a village site ?). Some 700 yds W. of these are the Cooleagh forts and church-site (*above*).

3 m. SE., above the River Clashawley, are the remains of Kiltinan castle. This was a fine rock-fortress with a fortified well; three of the angle towers survive (two of them incorporated in a modern house). From the base of the rock gushes the Roaring Spring. In 1649 the castle was taken by Cromwell after a sharp defence. W. of the castle are the ruins of a medieval church which, from c. 1195 to the Dissolution, belonged to St Mary's Abbey, Osney, Oxfordshire; there is a sheila-na-gig in the church. N. of the castle and church is the site of an extensive medieval village.

5 m. SE. rises Slievenamon (2,368 ft), renowned in song and Fiana story; it is the Síd ar Femin of Irish mythology. Delightful views of the Suir valley may be had from the slopes. There is a cairn on the summit.

4 m. S. is Lisronagh (*see under* Clonmel).

1¾ m. W. is the 15th/16th cent. tower of Barretstown castle (Nat. Mon.).

4½ m. W. is Tullamain Castle (*see* Rosegreen *under* Cashel).

4¾ m. NW. is Knockbrit, birthplace of the authoress, Marguerite Power (1789–1849), who became Countess of Blessington. She was a celebrated beauty and a friend of Lord Byron. There are a number of very fine ringforts in this area, notably in the townlands of Mobarnan (Moandoolish Fort), Woodhouse, Foulkstown (Magorban Glebe Fort), and Anne's Gift.

FETHARD, Co. Wexford (Map 6, C7), is a village on the E. coast of the Hook Peninsula (Rinn an Dubháin) which separates Waterford Harbour from Bannow Bay. There is a good sandy beach nearby.

1½ m. SSE. is rocky Baginbun Head. At the E. corner of the headland is Dún Domhnaill, a small promontory fort. Some thirty acres of the main headland are cut off on the landward side by the remains of a great ditch flanked by ramparts. These are believed to represent the fortifications "of earth and boughs" constructed by Raymond le Gros, who landed here with the vanguard of Strongbow's army at the beginning of May, 1170. The tiny force was joined by Hervey de Monte Marisco with a few more men, and the whole party sat down to await Strongbow. Their camp was attacked by a combined force of Waterford Norse and Déise and other Irish, some 3,000 strong. The attackers were thrown back with great slaughter after their ranks had been broken by stampeding a herd of cattle. After their victory the Anglo-Normans broke the limbs of their prisoners, seventy of the leading citizens of Waterford, and hurled them into the sea.

The country round about is rich in church and castle ruins. One of the best of the castles is that (Nat. Mon.) by the pier at Slade, 6 m. SW. of Fethard. The remains here comprise a gracefully tapered tower of perhaps the late 15th cent. and, attached to it, a slightly later fortified house. The castle was the home of the Laffans, a Gaelic family which survived here until the Cromwellian confiscation, when the property was unjustly assigned to the neighbouring Loftus family, ancestors of the Earls (later Marquesses) of Ely. In 1641 the castle was occupied by Confederate Catholic forces, but appears not to have been involved in actual hostilities. The annexes at the E. and W. ends may have been added by the builders of the 18th cent. salt works adjoining the pier.

4½ m. N. the house called Tintern Abbey stands inside the remains of the church of Tintern (Minor) Abbey, a daughter of Tintern Major in Monmouthshire. The abbey was founded in 1200 by William the Marshal, Earl of Pembroke, in fulfilment of a vow made when imperilled by a storm at sea. The remains comprise nave (aisles gone), crossing with tower (upper part 15th cent.), presbytery (inserted Tudor windows), and S. transept (pseudo-Gothic reconstruction) with three chapels. Some of the presbytery details derive from Tintern Major (1269–88). After the Dissolution the lay grantee built a residence inside the church; parts (e.g. the Tudor windows of the presbytery) survive. The nearby parish church and bridge were built of stones from the monastery.

FINGLAS, Co. Dublin (Map 6, D7), is a village and growing industrial suburb on the Dublin (4 m.)–Ashbourne (10 m.) road. It takes its name, Fionn-Ghlais, Fair Rill, from a holy well (chalybeate) formerly resorted to by sufferers from eye diseases. (The 18th cent. quack, Dr Achmet Borumborad, né Patrick Lynch, who contrived to extract an annual grant from the Dublin Parliament to provide the citizens with sea-water baths, built a pump-room over the well, and Finglas had its brief day as a fashionable watering place.)

About 560 a monastery was founded at Finglas by St Cainneach (Canice), whose disciples helped to evangelize the district. The history of the monastery is obscure, save for a period in the 8th and 9th centuries when, as one of the "Two Eyes of Ireland", it was intimately associated with Tallaght (q.v.) in the Céle Dé movement. In 780 Abbot St Dub-litir (d. 796) presided at the "congress" of Tara. Proximity to Dublin exposed the monastery to the full fury of the Viking storm, and so contributed to its decline. The last recorded abbot died in Rome in 1038. Thereafter the monastery disappeared from history and the church became a parochial one.

The ruins of the medieval parish church of St Canice, in Protestant use until 1843, are those of a nave-and-chancel building with later S. aisle and vaulted N. porch. In the SE. corner of the churchyard is a High Cross with badly weathered interlacing and other ornament. It stood on the old abbey land of Finglas until Cromwellian times, when it was buried for safety. It was recovered, and set up in its present position, in 1816. In the Protestant church are 17th cent. monuments, removed from the old church in 1843.

William of Orange camped at Finglas 5 July 1690, after his victory at the Boyne. King William's Rampart, a stone-revetted earthwork to the N. and S. of the Ratoath road on the W. side of the village, is alleged to mark the site of his camp.

2¼ m. W. is Dunsink (see under Blanchardstown).

3½ m. NNW. is Dunsoghly Castle (Nat. Mon.), a fine residential tower with traces of extensive outbuildings (and a courtyard ?) on the N. and the ruins of a 16th cent. chapel on the S. To the W., SW., S., and E. are remains of 17th cent. hornworks with three bastions. To the NW. and N., beyond the Castle Orchard, was formerly a long reach of stout earthworks. The three-storey tower has rectangular corner turrets. A stairway in the NE. turret gives access to the upper floors and roof-walk. The roof is still supported by the original timbers. The top room of the SW. turret can be entered only by an opening in the beehive vaulting, and presumably served as a prison. From the turret parapet-walks splendid prospects may be had of the rich Dublin–Meath lowland, the Dublin Mountains, and the heights of Howth and Lambay. The castle was built by Thomas Plunkett, Chief Justice of the King's Bench and a cadet of the Plunketts of Killeen (see under Dunshaughlin), who purchased the property early in the 15th cent. The chapel was erected in 1573 by Sir John Plunkett (d. 1582), Chief Justice of the Queen's Bench. A tablet over the doorway bears the symbols of the Passion and the initials of Plunkett and his third wife, Genet Sarsfield. Sir John also built a chapel at St Margarets (below), where he likewise enclosed St Margaret's Well to make a bath for pilgrims. During the 1641–53 war the castle served as an important English outpost, and to that period may be ascribed the outer bastions and earthworks. 1 m. ENE., near the Catholic church, is St Margaret's (originally St Brigid's) Well, "a tepid medicinal spring which never freezes"; it was formerly much frequented. ¼ m. NE. of the well are the ruins of the medieval parish church of St Margaret, which has given its name to the village, townland, and parish; it is the successor of an early church called Domhnach Mór. Attached to the church at the SE. are the ruins of the chapel built by Sir John Plunkett of Dunsoghly (d. 1582) for his place of burial. 3¼ m. NNW. is Kilsallaghan church, where there is a Michael Healy window: *Christ the King* (1917).

FINTONA, Co. Tyrone (Map 2, D4), is a village on the Omagh (9 m.)–Fivemiletown (8 m.) road. The E. window and other carved stones of the ruined Protestant church came from Donacavey (*below*).

1½ m. N., at Donacavey, are the remnants of a medieval church; also of St Patrick's Cross (Nat. Mon.): the shaft of a stone cross with interlace and other ornament.

5 m. S., on the W. slope of Ballyness Mt, alt. 800 ft, is Carnagat, a small, round cairn with a horseshoe-shaped chamber.

FOXFORD, Co. Mayo (Map 1, D3), is a village on the main Castlebar (12 m.)–Ballina (10½ m.) road, 1¾ m. E. of Lough Cullin. Its woollen manufactures enjoy a high repute. The industry is conducted by the Irish Sisters of Charity, who (1891) introduced it to provide work in one of the most poverty-stricken regions in Ireland.

Admiral William Brown (1777–1857) and the poet, Frederick Robert Higgins (1896–1941), were natives of Foxford. Admiral Brown was "father" of the Argentine navy. He is commemorated by a bronze bust, the work of the Argentinian sculptor, Vergottini (1957).

3¼ m. NE. are the ruins of Templemoyle church.

3¼ m. S., beyond Ballylahan bridge, are the ruins of a keepless castle with twin-towered gate house. It was built by Jordan d'Exeter (ancestor of the Mac Jordans) late in the 13th cent.

5 m. SSW. is Strade (*see under* Bellavary).

4¾ m. W. is Pontoon, one of the angling centres for Loughs Conn and Cullin.

FOYNES, Co. Limerick (Map 4, E2), is a Shannon-estuary village and port on the Limerick (24 m.)–Tarbert (17 m.) road. For some years there was a transatlantic seaplane base here, but it has been superseded by Shannon Airport, further up the estuary on the N. shore. The scenery along the Shannon SW. to Tarbert is beautiful.

Sir Stephen de Vere (1812–1904), brother of Aubrey de Vere (*see* Currah Chase *under* Askeaton), is buried in Foynes churchyard. He and Charlotte O Brien (1845–1909), daughter of William Smith O Brien (*see* Cahermoyle House *under* Ardagh, Co. Limerick), were prominent social workers. They led the campaign against the notorious "coffin ships" used to transport poverty-stricken emigrants to America. Charlotte O Brien is buried in Knockpatrick graveyard (*below*).

On a hill overlooking the village is a cross to the memory of Edmond Spring-Rice (1814–65), son of the 1st and father of the 2nd Lord Monteagle. The Spring-Rices' home is Mount Trenchard, 2 m. W. by the Shannon; they were a famous Liberal family (*see* Limerick).

1 m. S., on the commanding height of Knockpatrick (572 ft), are the remnants of a medieval church. A ruined small cist on the hill acquired the name Suidheachán Pádraig, "Patrick's Seat". In Knockpatrick townland is a ringfort terraced on to the hill-slope; nearby is Croaghane, a large, oval ringfort. There are many interesting earthworks on the high ground S. past Shanagolder.

FRENCHPARK, Co. Roscommon (Map 2, B6), is a hamlet on the Castlerea (9 m.)–Boyle (10 m.) road. Douglas Hyde, co-founder of the Gaelic League and first professor of Modern Irish in University College, Dublin, was born at the Rectory. When he retired he came to live at Ratra House, which had been purchased for him by public subscription; but he was soon recalled by unanimous agreement of all political parties to be first President of Ireland under the Constitution of 1937.

In the demesne is a five-chambered souterrain.

1 m. E., in Cloonshanville, a badly wrecked, small-towered church (very good E. window) is all that remains of Holy Cross Dominican friary, founded in 1385 by Mac Dermot Gall. 400 yds SW. is a rough, stone cross having a raised circle on the W. face. In early times Cloonshanville was the site of a church associated with Bishop Comitius, disciple of St Patrick.

2½ m. SE. is Bellanagare (*q.v.*).

FRESHFORD, Co. Kilkenny (Map 6, A5), is a village on the Kilkenny (9 m.)–Urlingford (9 m.) road, 6 m. SW. of Ballyragget. Its name is a misinterpretation of Irish *achadh úr*, "fresh (green) field". The Protestant parish church (1730) incorporates the W. gable and fine, unusual, Late-Romanesque porch of a monastic church, successor of one founded by Bishop St Laichtín (Lachtán), alias Mo-Lachtóg (d. 622), a disciple of St Comgall of Bangor (*see* Donoughmore *under* Coachford, Co. Cork). The porch has a small, shallow, figured frieze above the impost of each outer pilaster; on the return face of one jamb is a figured panel. The plain innermost arch and the S. jamb carry the inscriptions: OR[ÓIT] DO GILLA MO-CHOLMOC U CE[NN]-CUCAIN DO RIGNE and OR[ÓIT] DO NEIM INGIN CUIRC ACUS DO MATH-

Irish Tourist Board
Romanesque doorway, Freshford

GAMAIN U CHIARMEIC LASDERNAD IN TEMPUL SA ("A prayer for Gilla Mo-Cholmóc Ó Cenncucáin, who made [this]". "A prayer for Niam, daughter of Corc (Ó Cuirc?), and for Mathgamain Ó Ciarmeic, for whom this church was made"). Nothing is known of the persons named. The small round window above the porch may be a restoration. E. of the church, beside the Kilkenny road, is Tubberlochteen (Laichtín's Well).

1¾ m. N., in Clontubrid, at the ancient well-house (defaced) of Toberadrugh, alias Tubbera(d)roo, alias the Saint's Well, may be seen the figured gable-finial of an ancient church.

3½ m. ESE., in Three Castles Demesne, are the ruins of the Church of Three Castles, a parish church with castellated residence at the W. end. 1½ m. ESE., beside the Nore, is a motte – relic of Strongbow's (?) Castledough – built to command the principal road from Kilkenny. Three Castles bridge across the Dinin was a place of Lughnasa celebrations (*Pátrún* of the Dinin, last Sunday of July).

1½ m. SE., beside Wellbrook House, are the ruins of the small 13th-14th cent. parish church of Clashacrow, with residential W. tower. To the NE. is a medieval dovecot.

2¼ m. SSW., in Rathealy, is the Moat (Nat. Mon.), a two-acre, bivallate (formerly trivallate) ringfort with souterrain and traces of rectangular houses. A few hundred yds SE. is Stooic Rawhaeola, a pillarstone.

5½ m. SSW. is Tullaroan, formerly also known as Courtstown or Corstown. From the 13th cent. to the Williamite rebellion, the Graces (of Anglo-Norman origin) had their chief seat nearby, a great castle swept away about 1800. (The well-known group of Irish poems, including "Marbhna Oiliféir Ghrás", on the Graces and the Grace country, long thought to be by Seán (mac Bháitéir) Breathnach (1580–1660) of Inishcarran (*see under* Mullinavat), are now known to be 19th cent. forgeries.) SE. of the village are the remains of a small medieval parish church dedicated to the Assumption of the Blessed Virgin Mary. To the original nave-and-chancel church Sir John Grace added, in 1543, a S. chapel, or transept, with richly decorated, Perpendicular doorway. In the ruins are several medieval gravestones. Graves are decked on 14 Aug., eve of the annual *pátrún* at nearby Tobar Mhuire, alias Lady Well. 150 yds W. of the churchyard is the Moat, 20 ft high, the "Tulach" from which the place takes its name (?). The neighbourhood is rich in ringforts and other earthworks. – 4 m. SSE. is Kilmanagh (*see under* Callan).

1¾ m. SW. are the ruins of Ballylarkin "Abbey" (Nat. Mon.), a small 13th cent. parish church with good, late-14th cent. sedilia. 50 yds NW., on the W. side of the road, is a tumulus. 2¼ m. SW., in Upper Tubbrid (-britain), are remains of a nave-and-chancel church and of a Grace castle; 2½ m. SW. are the ruins of Kildrinagh parish church. There are many earthworks of various kinds in the area.

4 m. WSW., is Clomantagh Lower (*see under* Urlingford).

3 m. NW., via the Fertagh road, are the remains of Balleen church and hill-top castle. The latter was the principal seat of the Mountgarret Butlers in the early 17th cent.; the latest part dates from 1640. It was dismantled by the Cromwellians in 1650.

GALBALLY, Co. Limerick (Map 5, C5), is a small village near the head of the beautiful Glen of Aherlow, 9 m. SW. of Tipperary, 5 m. S. of Emly, and 11 m. N. of Mitchelstown. The main road to Tipperary skirts the NW. flank of the Slievenamuck (1,216 ft) range (Tipperary Hills), but a minor road down the N. side of the valley sends a branch (at Newtown, 5 m. NE.) across the hills, which affords fine panoramas at various points.

At the village are remains of a narrow, 15th cent., parish church.

½ m. E., in Co. Tipperary, is the ruined church (Nat. Mon.) of Moor "Abbey", a Franciscan friary founded (by O Brien of Aherlow ?) in 1471, only to be destroyed by fire the following year. During the Elizabethan

T. Edmondson

Stacking turf near Freshford

wars the friary frequently served as a strong point; it was burned by English troops in 1569. The following year it was again attacked by English troops, who mutilated and murdered three of the friars. During the recent Anglo-Irish war the local Royal Irish Constabulary made several attempts to blow up the ruins because of the cover they afforded to the Resistance. The visible remains are those of a simple, friary-type church of 1470, with a Franciscan-type belfry of somewhat later date.

1 m. NE., in Corderry, is Dermot and Grania's Bed, a wedge-shaped gallery grave.

4½ m. NE., at the summit of Slievenamuck (1,215 ft), in Shrough, is Dermot and Grania's Bed a roofless chamber tomb.

9 m. E., in Ardane on the S. side of the Glen of Aherlow, is St Berrahert's Kyle (Nat. Mon.), an oval enclosure with over fifty early gravestones, fragments of two early crosses (one figured), and a bullaun; to the E. is St Berrahert's Well. This early church site is called after the 7th cent. Anglo-Saxon saint, Berechert of Tullylease (*see under* Drumcolliher). 5½ m. E. is Peakaun (*see under* Cahir).

3¼ m. SW. is Ballylanders village. ½ m. N. is an ancient church site. A *pátrún* is held at the ruins and at Lady Well, 15 Aug.: devotional exercises, parades, games, and dancing. – 2¼ m. NW., in a by-road fence in Ballyfroota, is Cromlech, remains of a chamber tomb; to creep under the roof-stone is said to cure backache.

2 m. WSW., in Ballingarry, is Ballingarry Down, a platform ringfort with a fine view of Slievereagh and the Galtees. On the summit were remains of a rectangular medieval house, latest of a succession of houses, those at lower levels being of different type as well as of pre-12th cent. date.

1½ m. W. is Duntryleague Hill (822 ft), commanding magnificent views. W. of the summit is Leaba Dhiarmada agus Ghráinne, a ruined passage grave (Nat. Mon.). A stone circle is probably the kerb of a vanished cairn. Nearby ring-barrows yielded no evidence of their date.

4 m. W. is Doonglaura (Dún gCláire), alias Glenbrohane Mote, a bivallate, oval hillfort on the slope of Slievereagh; it affords beautiful prospects to NE. and E. The summit of Slievereagh (1, 531 ft) affords superb prospects (*see* Kilfinnane).

GALWAY, Co. Galway (Map 1, D6), is situated at the mouth of the short Galway River, near the NE. corner of beautiful Galway Bay, 132 m. W. of Dublin and 64 m. NW. of Limerick. It is the principal town of Connacht as well as of its county, and is a small seaport and a small-scale manufacturing centre (woollens, iron, fertilizers, milling, chemicals, hats, cotton-printing, china, etc.); it is also an important market centre, a university town and the cathedral town of the diocese to which it has given its name. As the gateway to Connemara, a popular seaside resort (*see* Salthill, *below*), and a convenient centre for boating and fishing on Lough Corrib (*q.v.*), it is one of the best-known holiday and tourist centres in the country. Galway Races (on the Tuesday, Wednesday, and Thursday preceding the first Monday of August) are an all-Ireland occasion at which many Grand National winners have made their appearance.

John Lynch (about 1599–1673), author of *Cambrensis Eversus*; Roderick O Flaherty (1629–1718; *see* Park *under* Spiddal); An Dubhaltach Óg Mac Fhirbhisigh (1585–1670; *see* Castle Forbes *under* Inishcrone); Richard Kirwan of Cregg (1733–1812), "great chymist of Ireland"; John Wilson Croker (1780–1857), journalist and founder of London's Athenaeum Club; Joseph Patrick Haverty (1794–1864), painter; his brother, Martin Haverty (1809–87), essayist and historian; were all either natives of Galway or intimately associated with it.

The town, like its clear river (Abha na Gaillmhe, Galway River), takes its name, Cathair na Gaillmhe, City of Galway, from the locality (Gaillimh) in which it is set. It originated with the permanent seizure (1232–43) of parts of the O Flaherty–O Halloran territories by Richard de Burgo and his fellow Anglo-Normans. De Burgo built a castle by the river in place of an O Flaherty stronghold. The town as such seems to have begun as a seignorial borough of the de Burgo manor of Loughrea (charter from Walter de Burgo, Earl of Ulster, who died in 1271) and had native Irish as well as "English" burgesses. By an obscure process it attained to the status of a royal borough (1396 letters patent from Roger Mortimer, Earl of March and Ulster, in his capacity as Lieutenant of Richard II of England). This helped to detach it from the local de Burgo – by now Mac William *Úachtair* – interest and to make it a firm bulwark of the English Crown in the West, and an island of English speech and culture. At the same time its isolation from the seat of English power, combined with its ever-increasing prosperity – based on security and the expansion of trade with France, Flanders, the Baltic, and Spain – fostered a spirit of independence. In effect, the town developed into a sort of tiny city-state, ruled by a merchant oligarchy (chief officer accorded the rank of mayor by 1484 letters patent). A disastrous fire in 1473 cleared the way for a well laid-out 16th–17th cent. town of tower and courtyard houses (a 1651 picture-map may be seen at University College), many of which survived into the 18th and 19th centuries.

The ruling oligarchy of medieval Galway was drawn from a group of aristocratic merchant families, almost all of Anglo-Norman or English extraction. The most celebrated of these were the fourteen "Tribes": Athy, Blake, Bodkin, Browne, Darcy, Deane, Font, French, Joyce, Kirwan, Lynch, Martin, Morris, and Skerret. Foremost of the Tribes were the Lynches, who supplied the town with no fewer than eighty·four mayors between 1485 and 1654.

Some of these Tribes, we are told, had their hereditary traits: the Joyces were "merry", the Blakes "positive", and so on; not all the traits were complimentary. Traits common to all were the gift of making money, and unswerving loyalty to the English Crown and to the Catholic Church.

Second only to the Burkes – if even to them – as traditional foes of the townsfolk were the despoiled O Flaherties, and a celebrated 1549 inscription over the West Gate read:

"This gate was erected to protect us
    from the ferocious O Flaherties."

(In 1951 and 1964 a "ferocious O Flaherty" was elected mayor of the town!)

In 1580, Mayor Dominick Lynch founded, near the quay, a Free School which developed into an important centre of Catholic culture and nationalist activity, drawing its pupils from far and near. It was suppressed by James I in 1615, but revived early in the following reign. Its most famous headmasters were Alexander Lynch – under whom the school is said to have had 1,200 students! – and Dr John Lynch, author of *Cambrensis Eversus*. Both John Lynch and Roderick O Flaherty acquired their polished Latinity at the school. In 1627 the number of scholars flocking to Galway was so great that the Corporation ordered all "forreigne beggars and poor schollers" to be whipped out of the town. The school disappeared amid the universal ruin which followed the Cromwellian victory in 1652.

Galway's loyalty to the English Crown survived all religious and other injustices until 1642. Only then, too late, did the townsfolk join their fate with that of the nation. The outcome was a nine-month land-and-sea blockade by the Cromwellian, Sir Charles Coote II, which ended with the surrender of the town, 5 April 1652.

The Williamite rebellion was another disaster, one from which the town but slowly recovered. A century and a half later came the great Famine of 1846–7, which seemed to mark the end. In the present century, however, and notably since the re-establishment of the Irish state, the town has gradually recovered, and today the population is greater than ever before.

The focal centre of the town is Eyre Sq., originally an open space in front of the main gate. The John Fitzgerald Kennedy Memorial Garden (1965–6) was designed by Wilfrid Cantwell and James Fehily. The doorway (with oriel above) from a Browne mansion in Lower Abbeygate St stands forlorn on the W. side. Near by are remains of a 1936 memorial to Pádraic Ó Conaire (1882–1923), Galway-born Irish writer, is by Albert Power, R.H.A. Opening off the NE. corner of the square is Foster St: the chapel of the Magdalen Asylum has a window (*Sacred Heart, Blessed Virgin Mary, St Joseph, St Mary Magdalen*) by Evie Hone (1952).

T. H. Mason

Reader's desk, church of St Nicholas of Myra, Galway

T. H. Mason

Gravestone from the north transept of the church of St Nicholas of Myra, Galway

From the head of the square the principal shopping street winds its way westwards to the river and William O Brien Bridge. In its short length it has four different names: Williamsgate, William's St, Shop St (formerly High Middle St), Mainguard St. Its continuation beyond the bridge, to the SW. in the direction of Salthill, is called Dominick St, Upper and Lower.

At the junction of Shop St and Upper Abbeygate St (formerly Littlegate) is Lynch's Castle, now occupied by the Munster and Leinster Bank. This much-altered, early-16th cent. towerhouse (ruthlessly scoured in 1966) preserves some interesting features: arms of Henry VII of England, of the Lynch family (both in Shop St), and of the Kildare Fitzgeralds (Abbeygate St); also gargoyles, rare in Ireland. In its original form the house had a high, pyramidal roof and stepped battlements. Nearby houses, and others further W. and S., preserve sorry fragments of the limestone houses for which 16th and 17th cent. Galway was famous. Scattered here and there throughout the old town are many other fragments.

NE. of William O Brien Bridge, in Market St, is the Protestant parish church of St Nicholas of Myra. It preserves the shell of the medieval town parish church, which began as a dependency of the Cistercian abbey of Knockmoy (*see* Abbeyknockmoy). The burgesses had many complaints about the abbey's provision of priests to serve the church and, at their request, Pope Urban VI reorganized the vicarage about 1385, only to cause a century of quarrelling

about the right of presentation. The quarrel was resolved in 1484, when Archbishop Donatus O Murray of Tuam, quondam vicar of the parish, secured a bull from Innocent VIII transforming the vicarage into a college (community) of priests (cf. St Mary's, Athenry) elected by the mayor, bailiffs, and equals of the town, to serve the church; the Warden, or head of the college, was elected annually by the same municipal authorities. Resistance of the townsfolk also delayed the introduction of the Reformation; but in 1568 the Mass was at last prohibited and the Protestant service was introduced into their church. Thereafter the townsfolk were burdened with a Protestant college (official) as well as a Catholic college (unofficial). At the time of the Confederation of Kilkenny the Catholics recovered possession of both the church and the college house. At that time, too, Galway became a centre of unprecedented Irish cultural activity, and we find An Dubhaltach Óg Mac Fhirbhisigh compiling part of his celebrated *Book of Genealogies* in the college house. – The church occupies the site of an earlier chapel, fragmentary traces of which may be discerned in the chancel S. wall. At first it had no tower, and the nave aisles were low and narrow. The tower (recently smothered in cement) seems to have been added about 1500; the pyramidal spire dates from 1683; the parapet is an 1883 restoration. Between 1486 and 1535 the S. aisle was enlarged to its present size by Dominick Dubh Lynch and his son, Stephen. In 1561 the S. transept was lengthened and galleried by

Nicholas Lynch to provide for a family chantry; the S. window is 15th cent. work from the older transept. Between 1538 and 1583 the N. aisle was enlarged to its present size as a French family chantry; the Blessed Sacrament Chapel (recently re-roofed) dates from about 1538. The W. door of the nave is an insertion of the late 15th cent.; it has been mutilated by the 17th/18th cent. Gothick window above it. The S. porch apparently dates from the 15th cent., but the doorway is a 16th cent. insertion. The gargoyles of the S. aisle are closely akin to those of Lynch's Castle. Noteworthy features inside the church are: the fine, 16th cent., Joyce wall-tomb in the S. transept (it has lost its polychrome colouring); the 16th cent. font; the 15th cent. stoup; the 15th cent. reader's desk (the "Confessional") from some monastic or similar refectory, which has been stupidly erected at the entrance of the Blessed Sacrament Chapel; and the gravestones (set in the floor) with symbols of crafts and callings. The church and its monuments were savagely mutilated by the Cromwellians; they continue to suffer from "restorers". – At the NE. corner of the churchyard, in Market St, are fragments of two 16th/17th cent. houses. 19th cent. fantasy has inserted in one of them a tablet which declares that James fitz Stephen Lynch, Mayor in 1493, executed his son "on this spot". It is doubtful if any Lynch ever executed his son; even if he did, there is no reason for selecting "this spot" as the scene of horror.

Parallel to Shop St, on the S., is Middle St. The pro-cathedral of St Nicholas of Myra (1816; closed 1965) exemplifies Catholic church architecture towards the close of Penal times. The nearby Augustinian church exemplifies the change that had taken place by 1855. Taibhdhearc na Gaillimhe, "The Galway Theatre", produces plays in the Irish language only. The foremost names connected with it are those of Mícheál Mac Liammóir, Hilton Edwards, Siobhán McKenna, and Walter Macken.

At the SW. corner of the old town, by the river mouth and the site of the medieval quay, is the old Fish Market. On the N. side is a fragment of a 16th cent. tower-house. On the S. side is a fragment of the town wall, with twin-arched gateway. One of the arches being blocked up, the gateway was long known as An Póirse Caoch, or The Blind Arch. To it and to an adjacent portion of the Fish Market modern fantasy has given the names Spanish Arch and Spanish Parade.

To the N. of Williamsgate, in Francis St, is the Franciscan church, an 1849, neo-Grec essay by James Cusack; the original altars are pleasantly rustic pieces. The church occupies a portion of the site of the friary which was founded in 1296, by Sir William Liath de Burgh, just outside the town wall and which became the principal burial-place of the leading families of the town. In an area to the N. of the portico may be seen fragments of "Sir Peter French's tomb gilt with gold . . .", the

making of which cost £500 in the 16th cent.; the "weepers" are carved in the Gothic tradition of the high Middle Ages, but the ornamental details reflect Renaissance influence. In a small enclosure on the S. side of the church (entrance through the friary) are fragments of a 17th cent. *Holy Trinity* resembling those in the pro-cathedral. These, and a few miscellaneous scraps, are all that have survived the Cromwellian fury of 1652. In the ancient cemetery behind the church are some pathetically crude Poor Clare and sacerdotal gravestones by an unpractised 17th cent. hand.

N. of the Franciscan church is the skinny-columned Court House, a dull, neo-Grec piece (1812–15) by Sir Richard Morrison. The English royal arms which crowned the pediment (and further overweighted the portico) are preserved at University College.

Behind the Court House is the Upper Bridge, which affords one of Galway's popular sights: shoals of salmon ascending the crystal-clear river. The Cathedral of Our Lady Assumed into Heaven and St Nicholas (1957–65) occupies the site of the County Gaol of British days where generations of patriots were imprisoned; Wilfred Scawen Blunt was gaoled there in 1887 for championing the cause of Lord Clanricarde's oppressed tenants (*see* Woodford). The cathedral, by J. J. Robinson, is a sad disappointment. The plaques of the main (north) doors (*Prodigal Son, Mary Magdalen, Woman of Samaria at the well, Christ calms the storm, Christ cures the paralytic, Christ cures the blind man, Christ and St Thomas, Conversion of St Paul, Martyrdom of St Stephen*) and the bronze *Virgin and Child* over the central door are by Imogen Stuart. The tympana sculptures (*Baptism, Marriage, Confirmation*) are by Murphy. The chief features of the spacious interior are the mosaics (*Crucifixion*, angels of the dome pendentives) and windows (*Temptation of Christ, Multiplication of the loaves and fishes, Transfiguration, Mission of the Apostles*; W. aisle) by Patrick Pollen and the rose windows (*Mysteries of the Rosary*) designed by George Campbell; Pollen also did the *St Joseph the Worker* mosaic for the shrine in the nave. The Stations of the Cross are by Gabriel Hayes. There are also windows by John Murphy (*Melchisedech, Isaac, Jacob, Joseph*; N. transept), Laurence Walsh (*Samuel anoints David, David with Goliath's head, King David, Judgement of Solomon*; W. transept), and Gillian Deeney (*Adoration of the Magi, Christ teaches the multitudes from the ship, Thou art Peter*, and *Christ heals the paralytic*; E. aisle). In the Chapel of St Nicholas three limestone panels (*God the Father, God the Son, Blessed Virgin*) from a *Coronation of the Virgin* group have been re-assembled (*Holy Ghost* modern) as the altar reredos. Long preserved separately in the pro-cathedral, they are said to have come from medieval St Nicholas's and date from some 17th cent. phase of Catholic recovery. The Mortuary Chapel has a Patrick H. Pearse–John

Fitzgerald Kennedy memorial mosaic (*Resurrection* with portrait roundels) by Patrick Pollen.

SW. of the bridge is the Poor Clares' convent, Nuns Island. Here are preserved a 13th cent. *Enthroned Madonna* and 17th cent. figures of St Clare and the Infant Jesus.

A short distance NW. of the cathedral is rapidly-growing University College, founded in 1845 as one of the unacceptable Queen's Colleges, since 1908 a constituent college of the National University of Ireland. As befits a university so close to large areas of Irish speech, many of the courses are given through the medium of Irish as well as of English. The original building (1846–50), by Joseph B. Keane, is an interesting, Tudor-style period piece suggested by the Oxford–Cambridge type of college. The new Botany and Zoology building is by Michael Scott and Associates. In the library may be seen the 1485–1818 municipal records and a large pictorial map of the town as it was in 1651. In the grounds are preserved miscellaneous fragments from old houses in the town; also the English (Hanoverian) royal arms from the Court House, an amusing example of rustic architectural sculpture.

SW. of University College is its teaching hospital, the Regional Hospital. Further W., in St Mary's Rd, is St Mary's College, junior seminary of the diocese. The original building (1910–12), by Prof. William A. Scott, has been sadly mutilated.

The Dominican Convent, Taylor's Hill, has an Italian Baroque (17th cent.) statue of the Blessed Virgin Mary; also a 17th/18th cent. (Penal-times) Irish copy of another continental statue of Our Lady.

The Claddagh, on the SW. side of the town, beyond the river, preserves no more than the name of the Irish-speaking fisher quarter. The once large fleet of púcáns and gleótógs has dwindled away; the great huddle of thatched cottages has been replaced (1937) by arrays of unsightly concrete houses; the distinctive Claddagh costume has disappeared; the King of the Claddagh no longer reigns; few of the inhabitants now speak the ancient tongue. The so-called Claddagh Ring, once handmade by Galway goldsmiths, was the traditional wedding-ring of a wide area (including the Aran Islands, Connemara, Iar-Chonnacht, Joyce's Country, etc.) served by Galway; the oldest datable examples were made in 1784. The Dominican friary and church occupy part of the site of the friary founded in 1488 and razed *c.* 1651. In the church are windows by Michael Healy (*St Dominic receiving the Rosary*; 1935) and Hubert McGoldrick (*St Dominic leading Nuns to the Convent of San Sisto*; 1939); also a 17th cent. Italian Baroque statue of the Blessed Virgin Mary. Nearby is a badly sited statue (by Kavanagh) of Fr Tom Burke (1830–83), noted preacher and controversialist, who was born in Galway.

The Jesuit church, Sea Rd, has a small Lady Chapel by Michael Scott; the feature is a lovely mosaic, *Our Lady of the Wayside*, designed by Louis Le Brocquy (1957).

Salthill, suburb to the SW., is a popular seaside resort, with promenade, bathing-places, championship golf links, tennis courts, and dance halls. The tawdry Church of Christ the King has a *Crucifixion* in wood by Claire Sheridan, figures of the Sacred Heart and the Blessed Virgin by Oisín Kelly, and three altars by Michael Scott.

4 m. W. is Trawbaun, alias the Silver Strand, a popular small beach.

E. side of the Galway River:

1 m. N., beside the river, are the remnants of Terryland Castle, a 17th cent. house of the Earls of Clanricarde.

5 m. N. is Annaghdown (*q.v.*).

3 m. NE., via the Tuam or Monivea roads, in Ballybrit, is Galway racecourse.

11 m. NE., via the Headford road, is Cregg Castle, ancestral home of Richard Kirwan (1733–1812), eminent scientist and Fellow of the Royal Society. The Queen Anne house (much restored in 1949) incorporates the tower of a 15th/16th cent. castle.

2¾ m. E. is Merlin Park Regional Sanatorium, a good example of modern hospital planning. In the grounds is the tower of the Lynch castle of Doughiske.

4 m. E., to the S. of the Oranmore road, is Roscam, site of an early monastery. The remains comprise ruined Round Tower, fragments of a medieval church (Nat. Mons.), two bullaun stones, and a massive, semi-circular cashel enclosing the site. 500 yds NE. is Cloch an Liagáin, alias Gallaun, alias the Long Stone, a pillarstone.

W. side of the Galway River:

2 m. NNW., on the E. side of the Oughterard road in Dangan Lower, is a tree-crowned tumulus.

GARRISON, Co. Fermanagh (Map 2, C4), a village at the head of Lough Melvin, on the Belleek (5 m.)–Manorhamilton (10 m.) road, is a good angling centre.

4 m. NE. (2¾ m. NNW. of Tullylaughdaugh fork roads), in Killybeg, are three pairs of pillarstones, two wedge-shaped gallery graves (Giants Graves, Nat. Mons.), and other megalithic remains.

4½ m. SE. (1 m. NE. of Kiltyclogher) are the remains of Kilcoo monastery (Nat. Mon.), founded by or dedicated to St Patrick. They comprise some slight trace of a building, an early, cross-inscribed gravestone with the inscription OR[ÓIT] DO MAELCLUCHI ("A prayer for Máel-Cluchi"), and a cross-shaft standing on a small, stone-ringed mound.

5 m. SE., in Kiltyclogher village (Co. Leitrim), is a statue (by Albert Power) of Seán Mac Dermot, the 1916 leader. 2 m. SE. and 1 m. W. of Upper Lough Macnean, on a hill-slope to the W. of the linear earthwork known as the Black Pig's Race (*see below*), is Corracloona

Plate 9. The Gap of Dunloe, Co. Kerry

(Co. Leitrim) gallery grave (Nat. Mon.); the portal slab has a "kennel hole". Cornacully (Co. Fermanagh) court cairn is 2½ m. NE.

7 m. SE. (1 m. NE. of Tullyrossmearn post office) is Cornacully Giants Grave (Nat. Mon.), a ruined court cairn (?).

3 m. S. is the N. end of a long sector of the Black Pig's Race (*see under* Dowra, Co. Cavan), which extends along the W. side of the valley nearly the whole way to Upper Lough Macnean.

4 m. SSW. is Glenaniff (*see under* Manorhamilton).

GARVAGH, Co. Derry (Map 3, B3), is a small town where the Coleraine (11 m.)–Maghera (10 m.) road crosses the Agivey (salmon, trout, etc.). Immediately W. of the town is Garvagh Forest. Garvagh House (Lord Garvagh) has been the property of the Cannings since the early 17th cent.; George Canning (1770–1827), British statesman and Prime Minister, father of Earl Canning, was born here, and Denis O Hempsey (1695–1807), the Garvagh-born harpist, died here at the age of 112.

3 m. E., at Moneydig crossroads, is the Daff, alias the Daff Stone (Nat. Mon.), a chamber tomb in a round cairn.

3 m. S., in Ballydullaghan, is Cornaclery Round Cairn, with a large cist which held a Beaker burial. About 1 m. further S., in Tamnyrankin (⅜ m. NW. of the village), is a mutilated court cairn, the largest cairn in Co. Derry.

3 m. SSW., alt. 650 ft, in Cuilbane, is a circle of fifteen pillarstones (Nat. Mon.). In Slaghtaverty (the next townland to the W.), 600 yds ENE. of Dunavenny bridge, is a denuded cairn (Nat. Mon.).

6½ m. SSW., in Knockoneill, is a court cairn. 3 m. S. is Slaghtneill (*see under* Maghera).

3 m. W., in Ballintemple, is a six-chambered, rock-cut souterrain. ¾ m. W., in Gortnamoyagh, is a basaltic rock (Nat. Mon.) with two footprints called "St Adamnan's Footprints" and the "Giant's Track". It may have been the inauguration stone of a Gaelic ruler. A similar pair of footprints may be seen in the garden of Belmont House, Shantallow, Derry City.

GEASHILL, Co. Offaly (Map 6, A3), is a neat village on the Tullamore (9 m.)–Portarlington (9 m.) road. A motte points to early Anglo-Norman penetration of the district, but in the later Middle Ages the district was held by the O Dempseys. After them it was held by the Fitzgerald Lords O ffaley. Near the Protestant church are some remains of the castle (originally O Dempsey) which was held in 1642 by Lettice Fitzgerald (daughter of Lord O ffaley, widow of Sir Robert Digby, and ancestress of the Barons Digby) against two attacks by Confederate Catholics under her cousin, Lord Clanmaliere (O Dempsey).

3 m. ESE., in Ballykean, to the E. of the remains of O Dempsey's Castle, is the Sconce, a rectangular earthwork said to have defended O Dempsey's "frame house".

6 m. E., on Walsh Island in Clonsast Bog, are the remains of Ballintemple church. Among the monuments here is the tombstone of "Eveline, daughter of Dermot, wife of Lewis fitz Maurice", who died in 1603.

GLANDORE, Co. Cork (Map 4, E6), is a fishing village and quiet, small resort beautifully situated on Glandore Harbour, 6 m. WSW. of Ross Carbery and 9 m. E. of Skibbereen. The roads SE. to Tralong Bay, NW. to Leap, and W.–SW. (via Union Hall) to Carrigillihy Harbour, Blind Harbour, and Castle Haven, are noted for their scenery.

W. of the village are remains of a medieval church. Nearby, incorporated in a modern residence, are remains of Cloch an Trághbhaile, alias Glandore Castle. The Barrets built a castle here in 1215, which was wrecked by Finghin of Rinn Róin (*see* Ringrone *under* Kinsale) Mac Carthy. The later castle belonged to the O Donovans.

¾ m. SE. is Kilfinnan Castle, sometime home of the Townsends, more recently a hotel; it incorporates remains of a medieval castle.

3½ m. NE. is Commonagh village. 3¾ m. N. of the village, in Carrigagrenane, is a circle of low stones.

1¾ m. E., in Dromberg, commanding a beautiful view, is a recumbent-stone circle (Nat. Mon.). At the centre was a dedicatory burial in an urn; the recumbent stone has cup and other markings on the upper surface. To the W. is an ancient hut-site with an open-air cooking-place.

On the opposite side of Glandore Harbour (road bridge) is the little village of Union Hall. 650 yds NW. is Rock Cottage, where Swift wrote *Carberiae Rupes* in the summer of 1723. Union Hall is the main gateway to Myross, the promontory between Glandore Harbour and Castle Haven. "Myross is one of the most secret places in Ireland, without traffic, almost without pulse of life" (Daniel Corkery), but its byways reward the questing tourist. Here Seán Ó Coileáin (1754–1817; *see* Timoleague), the roystering "Silver Tongue of Munster" and author of the lovely Jacobite song, "An buachaill bán", conducted a "hedge school". – 1¾ m. SE. of Union Hall, close to the sea, in Carrigillihy, are the remains of a small, oval, stone "ringfort", dated by pottery to the Early Bronze Age. It had enclosed a little oval house of dry masonry and timber posts. In the early historic or the medieval period a small, quadrangular house of dry masonry and timber posts was erected in the ruins. Some 760 yds N., just inside the entrance of Glandore Harbour, is a bivallate promontory fort. Excavations here produced neither finds nor traces of internal structures. – 2½ m. S. of Union Hall are the remains of Myross church. – 3 m. SW. of Union Hall, by a beautiful byroad, is Castle

Drombeg stone circle, Glandore

Haven; there is a ferry to Castletownshend (*q.v.*); ½ m. N. of the ferry are the ruins of Raheen castle. In the Protestant parish church is an E. O. E. Somerville Memorial window (1918) by Harry Clarke.

1¾ m. NW. is the village of Leap, so called from its proximity to the wide ravine (the "leap" proper) at the head of Glandore Harbour. "Beyond the Leap, beyond the law" was an old saying.

2½ m. NW., in Carrigdownane Lower, are the remains of a small, simple, medieval church.

GLANWORTH, Co. Cork (Map 5, C5), is a pleasant, woollen-manufacturing village on the Fermoy (6 m.)–Kilmallock (18 m.) road, beside the pretty little Funshion River. There are fragmentary remains of a Roche castle destroyed by Ireton's artillery in 1649. There are also ruins of the church of a Dominican friary founded by the Roches in 1475; nearby is St Dominic's Well. At the S. end of the village are remains of the church, Teampall Lobhair.

1 m. E., in a quarry S. of the road in Manning, is Tigh Alluis, a souterrain with beehive chambers. 130 yds SSE. is a wrecked chamber tomb. – ¼ m. NE., in Cuppoge, is a circle of eighteen stones, 70 ft in diameter. ¾ m. NNW. of this, in Dunmahon, are standing stones; 440 yds WNW. are remains of a castle; 440 yds NNE. remains of a church. 1 m. N. of the latter, to the E. of the Ballindangan road in Killeeneemer, is a standing stone in a field-fence; N. of this is a bullaun. 600 yds further N. the remains (Nat. Mon.) of a cashel and of

Killeeneemer itself, a small, early church with *antae* and trabeate, architraved, W. doorway, mark the site of an early monastery.

1¼ m. SE., in Labbacallee townland, is Labbacallee (Nat. Mon.), largest and finest of Irish wedge-shaped gallery graves. The covering cairn had a straight-sided, wedge-shaped kerb with in-curved termination at the E. end. The tomb proper is higher as well as wider on the W. At the E. end is a small, inner chamber shut off by an upright slab with one of the upper corners broken away. Remains of at least five persons had been buried in the tomb with Neolithic/Early Bronze Age pottery, animal bones, etc. The primary burial, in the closed E. chamber, was that of a woman whose skull was deposited in the large, outer chamber. 800 yds NE., on the Funshion, is Manning's Ford, where a Parliamentarian force under Sir Charles Vavasour was routed by Lord Castlehaven immediately after the massacre at Cooleigh, June 1643.

1 m. SW. in Glanworth townland, to the E. of the road, are remains of a cairn with a roofless chamber tomb. 300 yds SW., on the opposite side of the road, in Moneen, is a low cairn. This had a four-phase history. Phase I, Neolithic: a low ring-barrow covering pits, stakeholes, charcoal spreads, fragments of a human skull, and Neolithic sherds. Phase II, Early Bronze Age: within the original fosse a four-cist cairn, central cist megalithic; unburned burials, all buried at the same time; the pottery was Food Vessel and Beaker (?). Phase III, Middle Bronze Age: a cremated burial with two

Food Vessels interred just outside the fosse. Phase IV, Late Bronze Age: a cremation covered by an Encrusted Urn and accompanied by a second vessel; this burial was brought within the consecrated cairn-enclosure by means of an arc-like extension of the fosse to the SW. Three fields W., in Páirc na hAltóra, is Cromlech, alias Druids Altar, remnant of another chambered cairn.

1½ m. NNW., in Laght, is a pillarstone; ½ m. E., in Ballynamona, is another.

GLENAMOY, Co. Mayo (Map 1, C3), is a hamlet and road junction on the Belderg (7½ m.)–Belmullet (12½ m.) road.

7 m. N. is the little cove of Porturlin. ½ m. NW., at Altnapastia, begins a very fine range of cliffs. A splendid view is to be had from the summit (761 ft) of the hill ¾ m. W. of Altnapastia.

8 m. NNW. is Portacloy, a delightful little cliff-ringed cove with a small beach. The cliff scenery to the E. and W. is very fine. ¾ m. NNW. is Doonvinalla, a great promontory fort whose defences have, for the most part, been carried away by collapse of the cliffs. 1¼ m. offshore are the Stags of Broadhaven, four sheer rocks up to 300 ft high. – 1½ m. W. is Benwee Head (829 ft), with a stupendous cliff and magnificent views.

9 m. NW., in the sandhills, is the ancient churchyard of Kilgalligan, which includes a large cairn.

6 m. NW., SSW. of Ross Port, in Rosdoagh, is Druids Circles, a ritual monument comprising two concentric circles of thirty-three and sixteen stones respectively; nearby are remains of a small chamber tomb (Nat. Mons.).

5 m. WNW., on the W. side of Sruwaddacon Bay, is the little village of Pollatomish. 2½ m. NW. is the cliff fort, Dooncarton. In the late 16th cent. there was a Burke castle here. The site commands a very fine view.

GLENARM village, Co. Antrim (Map 3, C3), at the foot of the lovely valley from which it takes its name, is a seaside resort on the Antrim Coast Road, 12 m. NW. of Larne and 14 m. SE. of Cushendall. The Glenarm River holds brown trout, salmon, and sea trout.

Glenarm was the birthplace of Professor Eóin Mac Néill (1867–1945), distinguished historian and Celtic scholar, founder of the Gaelic League, co-founder and Commander-in-Chief of the Irish Volunteers (1914), friend of Roger Casement, and Irish Free State Minister of Education, 1923–6; also of his brother, James McNeill (1869–1938), first Irish High Commissioner in London and second Governor-General of the Irish Free State.

In the cemetery of the Protestant parish church are scant remains of a Franciscan Tertiary friary founded in 1465 by Robert Biset. Seaán the Proud O Neill was buried there in 1567.

Glenarm Castle has been the seat of the Mac Donnells of Antrim (Earls of Antrim; *see* Antrim, Glens of) since 1636, but the house was greatly altered in the last century. The demesne (waterfall, delightful walks, etc.), encloses most of the glen.

GLENAVY, Co. Antrim (Map 3, C4), is a small village on the road from Lisburn (10 m.) to Antrim (11 m.).

1½ m. ESE., in Ballynacoy, is the Green Mound (Nat. Mon.), a small, oval motte with two ditches and intervening rampart.

3 m. E., in Tullynewbane and Ballymoneymore, is Forescore Fort, an unusual earthwork: oval ringfort with a crescentic annexe.

5 m. W. (via Sandy Bay), in Lough Neagh, is Ram's Island (bird sanctuary), where a ruined Round Tower marks an early monastic site.

GLENBEIGH, Co. Kerry (Map 4, C4), is a small seaside resort and noted tourist, angling, and golfing centre on the Killorglin (8 m.)–Cahirsiveen (17 m.) road, at the mouth of the beautiful valley from which it takes its name. Close to the village are the ruins of Winn's Folly (Winn Castle, alias Glenbeigh Towers), a castellated mansion erected in 1867 for the 4th Lord Headley of Aghadoe, a notorious landlord, who aspired to set up here as a feudal baron. The 5th Lord Headly turned Muslim and, having made the pilgrimage to Mecca, assumed the title "Al Hadji". The house was burned down in 1922.

SE. of the village rises Seefin (1,621 ft), from which a splendid mountain walk of some 20 m. leads SW., W., and N. around the valley, past Meenteog (2,350 ft), Coomacarrea (2,541 ft), Teermoyle Mt (2,442 ft), Mullaghnarakill (2,182 ft), and Beenmore (2,199 ft), with their lake-filled cirques and corries, to Drung Hill (2,104 ft). A minor road leads SE. from the village via Windy Gap (1,061 ft) to lovely Glencar (*below*), affording fine views of the Dingle peninsula en route.

3 m. NE., beyond the River Caragh, are the sandhills of Dooks. 2 m. E. of Caragh bridge is Lough Caragh, which fills the lower part of beautiful Glencar. 3 m. E. of Glencar is Lough Acoose, a convenient starting-point for the ascent of Macgillicuddy's Reeks (Carrauntuohil, 3,414 ft, highest mountain in Ireland); the ridge walk, Skregmore (2,790 ft) – Beenkeeragh (3,134 ft) – Caher (3,200 ft) – Carrauntuohil, is very fine; the cliffs offer many opportunities for rock-climbing.

1½ m. W., at Ross Behy, are sandhills and an excellent, 2-m. beach.

The road SW. from Glenbeigh to Cahirsiveen, clinging to the steep N. slope of Drung Hill, affords a spectacular view of the Dingle Peninsula and the Blasket Islands. Beside the old road over the brow of Drung Hill (5½ m. SW.) is Leacht Fhíonáin, alias Leacht an Daimh (Laghtfinnan Penitential Station), a cairn with an ogham stone. Nearby is Tobar Fhíonáin. The cairn, says local tradition, is the grave of St Fíonán, patron of the parish (Killinane; *see also* Killemlagh *under* Ballinskelligs). The place was formerly an important Lughnasa station with which was associated a cattle fair.

3½ m. SW., in Coolnakarragill Upper, is a stone with concentric circles and other scribings.

GLENCOLUMBKILLE village, Co. Donegal (Map 2, A3), takes its name from its valley, set remotely amid splendid mountain and coastal scenery at the SW. corner of Co. Donegal, 7 m. NW. of Carrick and 16 m. (via Glengesh; *see under* Ardara) WSW. of Ardara. Its inhospitable soil long made the district one of the poorest in Ireland, but a successful cooperative movement organized by the curate, Fr MacDyer, has made life better for everybody. The neighbourhood is rich in antiquarian remains.

The valley is called after the great saint of Derry and Iona who, says a medieval legend still current among the inhabitants (Irish-speaking), had a successful contest there with demons for whom St Patrick was no match. There was an early monastery – seemingly Columban – in the valley; the Mac Niallusaighs (Mac Eneilis) were hereditary coarbs. There seem also to have been foundations connected with SS Fanad and Conall (Caol ?; *see* Inishkeel *under* Naran-and-Portnoo). On Columcille's Day (9 June) a three-mile *turas* (pilgrimage) brings the devout to fifteen "stations" round and about the village. Most of the stations are marked by early cross-slabs and pillars (Nat. Mons.).

The first station is the remnant of a court grave (Nat. Mon.) in the W. wall of the ancient churchyard at the Protestant church; nearby is a souterrain. The second station is a very fine cross-pillar W. of the churchyard. Nearby are remains of a prehistoric chamber tomb (a court grave ?; Nat. Mon.). The third station is Áit na nGlún ("place of the knees"), a cairn ¾ m. NW. in Garveross. ¼ m. N. of this, on Mullach na Croise in Beefan, is the fourth station: a ring-enclosure with cairn and small cross-slab. NE. is the fifth station: a ring-enclosure (Nat. Mon.) with ruinous dry-masonry Columcille's Chapel and three cairns with cross slabs; in the NE. corner of the chapel is Columcille's Bed. Outside the enclosure, on the E., is the sixth station: cross-inscribed Leac na mBonn ("stone of the footsoles"), alias Leac na hAthchuingne ("stone of the request"). Further up the slope (half-way to the next station) is Columcille's Chair; natural. N. of that is the seventh station, Columcille's Well; there was a cross or cross-pillar to the W. ¼ m. NW. is rocky Screig na nDeamhan where Columcille overcame the demons; beyond Ceann Glinne (Glen Head) the coast rises to 700 ft. ¼ m. SSE. of Columcille's Well is the eighth station, Garraidhe an Turais ("pilgrimage garden"), alias Lios Cháigh ("holy enclosure"), having three cairns, each with a cross-slab or fragment. The ninth station – a

cairn – is ¾ m. SE., in Farranmacbride. En route is Aimir Ghlinne ("stone trough of the valley"). The Farranmacbride cairn has a fine, perforate, cross-pillar called Clo'n Aoineach. ¼ m. NW. of it is Munnernamortee (Nat. Mon.), a large, much-disturbed, central-court cairn with two-segment galleries and remains of four (?) subsidiary chambers. 400 yds SE. of Clo'n Aoineach, in Faugher, is the tenth station, a roadside cairn with cross-slab. The eleventh station (a cairn) is a short distance E. The twelfth station is across the road in Drumroe: cairn with very fine cross-pillar. Some 400 yds N. of the eleventh station, in the roadway in Drum, is a cross-pillar; further up the slope, in Cloghan, is ruinous Cill an Spáinnigh ("the Spaniard's Church"); also in Cloghan are St Conall's Well and, not far away, a cross-slab; on the hill-top above Cill an Spáinnigh, in Drum, is another cross-slab; there is yet another in Bun na nDrungán between Drum and Ceann na Caoilleadh (Kinnahillew); these were all stations of Turas Conaill ("St Conall's Pilgrimage"). The thirteenth station of Columcille's *turas* is in Gannew, near the police station: cairn with cross-pillar. ¼ m. SW. across the Murlin River (pilgrims cross by the stepping stones), in Cashel, is the fourteenth station: cairn with cross-pillar. The fifteenth, and last, station is at a pair of cross-slabs (parts of the same cross-pillar ?) in the churchyard where the *turas* started.

¾ m. SW. of the churchyard, in Kilaned (Cill Fhánaid "Fánad's Church"), are St Fánad's Well, a bullaun, St Fánad's Cell (remnant of a diminutive oratory), and St Conall's Well. (Turas Fánaid is no longer regularly carried out.) 1 m. W. of these, near the shore in Doonalt, is a cross-slab with complex design. ¾ m. further W. is Doon Point with remains of the fort which gives it its name.

3 m. SW. of Glencolumbkille village is Malin More village. ½ m. S. of the crossroads is Dermot and Grania's Bed, a portal-dolmen complex (Nat. Mon.) – ½ m. ENE. of the crossroads is another Dermot and Grania's Bed. ¾ m. ESE. of this is a third chamber tomb with the same name; nearby is Cloghacorra, a standing stone. Less than ½ m. SSE. of this is Cloghanmore (Nat. Mon.), a full-court cairn (largely reconstructed) with twin two-segment galleries at the W. end of the court; also a subsidiary chamber to either side of the court entrance (each with lozenge, curvilinear, and other devices on a jamb stone). ½ m. further SE. is another court cairn.

2 m. S. of Malin More village is Malin Beg village with beautiful, sheltered, little Trawbane strand to the SE. SW. of the village, overlooking Ougue Port cove, is Pollnamona, a natural bridge; 300 yds. W. are remains of Teampall Caomháin, "Caomhán's Church" (Nat. Mon.). There is another Teampall Caomháin on Rathline O Birne, 2 m. W. of Ougue Port; nearby are penitential stations and a holy well. The island also has associations with St Aodh mac

Bricc (*see* Slieve League *under* Carrick, Rahugh *under* Tullamore, *and* Uisneach *under* Bally-more, Co. Westmeath). The roadway to the lighthouse crosses a natural bridge.

GLENDALOUGH, Co. Wicklow (Map 6, D4), "Valley of the Two Lakes", famous for its beauty and its remarkable early monastic re-mains (Nat. Mons.), is a short, deeply incised valley 1 m. W. of Laragh. The usual approach from Dublin is via Bray and Roundwood, but the longer route via Blessington (*q.v.*), Holly-wood (*q.v.*), and the Wicklow Gap is more re-warding. Another rewarding approach is Dublin – Rathfarnham – Loughs Bray (*see under* Enniskerry) – Sally Gap (*see under* Round-wood) – Glenmacnass – Laragh.

The W. end of the valley is closed by Cona-valla (2,421 ft), down which flows the little Glenealo stream, to pond up in the Upper Lake beneath the steep, wooded slopes of Camaderry (2,296 ft) on the N. and Lugduff (2,154 ft) and Mullacor (2,179 ft) on the S. In ancient, more or less roadless, times, the valley was doubtless the most isolated spot in a wilderness of moun-tain and forest; and it was this which led St Cóemgen (Kevin; d. 619 ?) to establish a hermitage to the S. of the Upper Lake, after the completion of his monastic training at Kilna-managh near Tallaght (*see also* Hollywood, Co. Wicklow).

Despite his wishes, disciples gathered round St Kevin until his hermitage had become a small monastery by the lake shore. The ever increas-ing numbers of the monks eventually led to the establishment of a larger monastery to the E. of the lake, where the principal group of monu-ments is today; but this eastward spread of the monastery probably did not take place until well after Kevin's death.

Kevin's reputation for sanctity early made the monastery a notable place of pilgrimage, and such it remained until the *pátrún* was suppressed by Cardinal Cullen of Dublin in 1862. It also soon became the burial-place of the local rulers and the most important eccle-siastical centre in the whole of Wicklow. Its early history is much like that of other early monastic centres. It was destroyed by fire no less than nine times between 775 and 1071, pillaged at least four times by the Vikings in the 9th and 10th centuries, and in 1174 devastated by a great flood. Bishops of Glendalough are recorded from 1107 onwards, but the greatest name in the history of the place, after St Kevin's, is that of St Lorcán O Toole, who was abbot from 1153 to 1162, when he became Archbishop of Dublin. In 1214 King John united the diocese to that of Dublin. In 1398 the monastic settlement was destroyed by the English of Dublin. It recovered, however, though with diminished resources. In 1450 the diocese was reconstituted, but it survived only until 1497. The monastery, on the other hand, endured until the 16th–17th cent. English con-quest of Wicklow. Thereafter the buildings gradually fell into decay. Their present condi-tion is due to works of conservation and

Commissioners of Public Works in Ireland

Glendalough, showing Cathedral, Round Tower and St Kevin's Church

restoration carried out by the Office of Public Works since 1873.

The earliest monastic sites are on the S. side of the Upper Lake, and two of them (Templenaskellig, alias Dysartkevin, and St Kevin's Bed) can be approached only by boat. Together these probably represent the original Dísert Caéimgin (Kevin's Hermitage).

Templenaskellig stands on a shelf above the lake. The remains are thought to occupy the site of Kevin's first church, or at any rate of his first monastery, in the valley. The remains of the church – a small, rectangular structure with round-headed, two-light E. window – are largely a Board of Works reconstruction. In the church are some early gravestones. Outside the E. end are several others, as well as a stone cross with concentric squares and circles. W. of the church is an upper, walled-in, sub-rectangular enclosure thought to be the site of the monks' huts. The site as a whole would thus represent a tiny, primitive monastery, the church being the latest of a successive series. To the E. is St Kevin's Bed, a small cave in the sheer rock 30 ft above the water. (The ascent calls for caution.) It seems to be artificial, at least in part. According to tradition St Kevin lived in it. Presumably he retired there periodically for penitential exercises, as did his illustrious successor, St Lorcán O Toole. (The boatmen's silly tale of Kevin and the persistent Kathleen is a modern concoction.) Further to the E., best approached from Reefert (*below*), is St Kevin's Cell.

Near the SE. corner of the Upper Lake, and on the S. bank of the Poulanass, alias Lugduff, River, is tiny Reefert Church. Here, says tradition, was the burial-place of the local rulers.

The chancel, Reefert Church, Glendalough

Church and cemetery were formerly enclosed by a dry-built cashel. (The existing enclosing walls and terraces are modern.) The church is a small, nave-and-chancel structure with trabeate W. doorway (re-assembled) and plain, Romanesque windows and chancel arch, the latter a reconstruction of the original stones. At the external angles of the nave are gable-brackets, or corbels, which took the verges of the roof. (These brackets have been re-set at different levels.) In the cemetery are a number of stone crosses and early gravestones. One of the latter is inscribed OROIT [AR] DIARMAIT ("A prayer for Diarmait"); a second, OR[ŌIT] DO ... DO ... OGG. SW. of Reefert, high up on a cliff above the mouth of the Poulanass River, are remains of St Kevin's Cell, a beehive hut. Nearby are platforms levelled out of the mountain slope.

To the N. of the Poulanass River are the foundations of a small, rectangular structure (a church ?). The two rude crosses in the W. wall may be post-monastic grave marks.

Further N. are the dilapidated remains of a small, stone ringfort with traces of round huts inside. Nearby (to the SE., E., and NE.) are three stone crosses. Still further N., near the roadside and to the E. of the bridge over the Glenealo River, is a broken stone cross. Further E., at the car park, is a stone cross. Near the NW. corner of the Royal Hotel is the site of the Market Cross preserved in St Kevin's Church (*below*). To the NW. are the Seven Fonts, a series of bullauns. Further NW., close to the bridge over the Glendasan River, is St Kevin's Keave, a holy well.

Immediately SW. of the Royal Hotel, on the S. side of the Glendasan River, is the old Gatehouse of the later monastic "city". (This is the only surviving example of an early Irish monastery gatehouse.) The enclosing wall of the "city" has disappeared, as has also the upper storey of the gatehouse itself. The passage from the gatehouse is flanked by ancient masonry, and its causeway paved with ancient paving. In the W. wall is set an early cross-slab.

SW. of the gatehouse is a fine Round Tower (103 ft). The roof has been reconstructed with the original stones.

In a square, raised enclosure 150 yds SW. of the tower is St Mary's Church, alias Our Lady's Church, supposedly the oldest in the lower part of the valley. It may have belonged to a convent of nuns situated outside the monastery. The Romanesque chancel and N. door are 12th cent. additions. On the soffit of the fine, trabeate W. doorway is incised a saltire cross. There seems to have been a timber screen, or a rood-beam, towards the E. end of the nave. Traces of burning are noticeable here and there in the nave walls, and the masonry suggests a rebuilding. In the outer face of the S. wall are marks of a lean-to roof. In the chancel are two early gravestones; in the cemetery three others and a stone cross.

SE. of the Round Tower is SS Peter's and

Early cross-slab, Glendalough

Romanesque details from Glendalough

Paul's Cathedral, consisting of 10th cent., pre-Romanesque nave (48 × 30 ft) and 12th cent. chancel and sacristy. (There may have been an earlier chancel.) The nave masonry indicates three phases of building and rebuilding. At the external angles of the nave are *antae*, or projections of the side walls, which carried the roof verges. The W. doorway is trabeate. In the N. wall are remains of an inserted, Late Romanesque doorway contemporary with the chancel arch. The latter is an 1875–79 reconstruction, largely with the original stones. Fixed to the inner face of the N. wall are three early gravestones. The least damaged of these is inscribed OR[ŌIT] DO DIARMAIT and OR[ŌIT] DO MACC CAIS ("A prayer for Diarmait" and "A prayer for Mac Cais"). The fragment with foliated ornament formerly bore the inscription OR[ŌIT] DO MUIRCHER[TAC]H U CHA-THALA[IN] OCUS DO GUTNODAR A Ω .I. DO THIGERNA U FOG[ARTAIG] ("A prayer for Muirchertach Ó Cathaláin and for Gutnodar A Ω, i.e. for the lord of Uí Fógartaigh"); Muirchertach was slain in the battle of Móín Mór, A.D. 1151.

SW. of the cathedral is the monastic cemetery, at the centre of which stands the Priest's House, a curious, small, Late Romanesque building of 1170. The name is modern, and refers to its use as a burial-place for some of the local clergy. Originally it may have been a mortuary chapel, or have housed the shrine of St Kevin. The remains are largely a Board of Works reconstruction. The sculptured tympanum over the S. doorway was perfect in 1845. Petrie's drawing

of that year shows a seated king or bishop flanked by two kneeling figures, that on the left bearing a crozier or a bachall, that on the right carrying a bell. (This stone may not belong to the building at all; it looks earlier.) In the external face of the E. wall is an unusual arched recess with fine Romanesque details. The Board of Works walling which fills it may not accurately represent the original construction.

St Kevin's Cross, to the E. of the cemetery, is a plain, granite monolith, 11 ft high.

SE. of the cemetery is the remarkable little St Kevin's Church. This is a steep-pitched, stone-roofed structure (22 ft 8 ins × 14 ft 7 ins) to which a stone-roofed chancel (disappeared) and sacristy were added. From the W. gable rises a small belfry of the standard, early Irish (Round Tower) kind. The W. doorway is trabeate, but there is a relieving arch above it. The door itself was hung on the outside. The walls are "battered" inwards in traditional Irish fashion. The interior of the nave was divided by a flat ceiling into two storeys. The nave was originally lit by only two tiny windows, one in the S., the other in the E. wall. Subsequently the latter was blocked up, the chancel arch opened in the E. wall, and the chancel (still standing in 1772) and sacristy added. The ruin served as the local Catholic church from 1810 to 1850; it now serves as a store for crosses, early gravestones, and carvings collected from various sites in the valley. These include the 12th cent. granite Market Cross which formerly stood to the NW. of the Royal Hotel. On the E. face of the cross proper is a *Crucifixion*, with the figure of an

ecclesiastic below; on the base are two small
figures in high relief; the W. face and the sides
bear zoomorphic interlaces, etc. There is also
a gravestone from Reefert inscribed OR[ÕIT]
DO BRESAL A Ω IHS XPS ("A prayer for
Bresal A Ω Jhesus Christus").

St Kieran's Church, to the E. of St Kevin's
Church, survives only in very fragmentary form.
It is the smallest known nave-and-chancel
church (nave 19 × 14½ ft, chancel 9 × 9 ft) in the
country.

A path leading S. from the cemetery crosses
the Glenealo River to the Deer Stone, a bullaun
into which, says legend, a doe permitted herself
to be milked when St Kevin had no cow. Less
than 400 yds E. is St Kevin's Well. Less than
780 yds E. of the well, on the S. bank of the
Glendasan River, is St Saviour's Priory. It is
said to have been founded by St Lorcán O
Toole in 1162 for Canons Regular of St
Augustine. The remains are those of a small,
Romanesque, nave-and-chancel church with a
plain rectangular structure (the conventual
building ?) on the N. side. The walls of the
latter, the N. and S. walls of the nave, the
chancel arch, and the E. window have all been
re-erected by the Board of Works. The charming details (not always correctly reassembled)
of arch and window repay examination.

At the road junction to the E. of the Royal
Hotel is a slab with two crosses on the S. side.
180 yds further E. are the ruins of Trinity

Church, a small, nave-and-chancel structure
with a square annexe at the W. end. The latter
was corbel-roofed in stone, and supported a
60-ft belfry of Round Tower type (*see* St Kevin's
Church) which collapsed in a storm in 1818. The
pre-belfry church was entered by the trabeate
W. doorway, which is contemporary with the
plain Romanesque chancel-arch and windows.
The round-headed S. door is an insertion
necessitated by the addition of the belfry.

GLENGARRIFF, Co. Cork (Map 4, D5), a
craggy wooded glen of the Caha Mountains
(*see under* Adrigole), opening on to a delightful
inlet of Bantry Bay, is one of the loveliest of the
many lovely places in SW. Ireland. The village
to which it gives its name is 17 m. S. of Kenmare, 10 m. NW. of Bantry, 20 m. ENE. of
Castletown Bearhaven, and 35 m. WSW. of
Macroom. The mild climate and sheltered
location of the glen favour a luxuriant, Mediterranean flora (arbutus, fuchsia, etc.). Boating,
bathing, freshwater and sea fishing, rough
shooting, hill climbing, and a wide choice of
delightful walks and tours, are all to be had
hereabouts.

Close to the village is beautiful Poll Gorm.
½ m. further W., at Cromwell's Bridge, is
another well-known beauty spot; the (ruined)
bridge is said to have been thrown across the
river at an hour's notice. Offshore lies justly
celebrated Garnish, alias Ilnacullin, with ex-

J. Allan Cash

Garnish Gardens, Glengarriff

quisite gardens (noted particularly for magnolias, camellias, rhododendrons, and rare conifers) laid out and planted (1910–13) by Harold Peto for John Annan Bryce, whose son, Rowland, bequeathed the island to the nation. It was here George Bernard Shaw wrote *St Joan*. Open to the public 10 a.m.–5.30 p.m. daily; adults 2/6, children 1/–.

¾ m. W., on the NE. slope of Shrone Hill, is a chamber tomb.

2 m. NE., in Camrooska, is a chamber tomb.

10 m. NE., under the W. slope of Priest's Leap (1,896 ft) and Knockboy (2,321 ft), is a romantic pass on the old Bantry–Kenmare road.

7½ m. SW., via Furkeal bridge, is Sugarloaf Mt (1,887 ft), noted for its views.

GLENMALURE, Co. Wicklow (Map 6, D4), is a wild, 8-m. valley 2¾ m. W. of Rathdrum. It may also be entered by the Military Road from Laragh (*q.v.*). From Arklow (via Avoca) and Aughrim the most direct approach is via Ballinaclash. On the N. side of the valley rise Kirikee (1,559 ft), Carriglinneen (1,507 ft), and Mullacor (2,179 ft); at the head of the valley Conavalla (2,421 ft), Table Mt (2,308) ft, and Cannow Mt (2,611 ft); on the S. side, Lugnaquilla (3,039 ft), Cloghernagh (2,623 ft), Carrawaysticks (2,218 ft), Croaghanmoira (2,187 ft), and Ballinacor Mt (1,724 ft). The little Avonbeg descends from the slopes of Conavalla to cut its way through impressive moraines. The road up the valley is good as far as Barravore ford. Thereafter a track leads up to the divide (2,283 ft) between Glenmalure and the Glen of Imaal (*see* Donard).

The remote situation of the valley made it a stronghold of the local resistance to English rule at various periods, and it was the scene of several English defeats in the 13th, 14th, and 16th centuries. The most celebrated of these was in 1580, when Fiach O Byrne routed Lord Deputy Grey de Wilton with heavy loss. It was to Fiach's house in Ballinacor – traditionally near Ballinacor House – that Red Hugh O Donnell of Tirconnell fled for shelter when he escaped from Dublin Castle in 1592. Betrayed to the English, Fiach was captured in a cave in the valley, and was beheaded, 8 May 1597. On Christmas Eve, 1600, Lord Deputy Mountjoy's troops burned Ballinacor. After the 1798 rising the valley was one of the refuges of Michael Dwyer and his followers. It was to suppress such obdurate resistance that the Military Road and its strong posts, including Drumgoff Barracks at the Avonbeg crossing, were constructed. (Dwyer destroyed Drumgoff Barracks, but they were rebuilt.)

GLENTIES, Co. Donegal (Map 2, B3), is a village at the SW. corner of the Donegal Highlands, on the Ardara (14 m.)–Ballybofey (22 m.) road. The Owenea and Stracashel rivers, good angling rivers, meet here, and there is also good fishing in some of the local lakes.

There is a State fish-hatchery here, as well as thriving knitting and homespun industries.

3½ m. NE., between Loughs Finn and Muck, is Crocam Giants Grave, a ruined, prehistoric chamber tomb.

3½ m. NW. (¾ m. SW. of Letterilly House), in Lackaghatermon, is Dermot and Grania's Bed, a prehistoric chamber tomb.

5 m. NW., to the NW. of Gweebara bridge and Lettermacward, is the 2-m. sandy beach of Dooey. In the dunes is Cloch an Stucáin, a pillarstone marking a settlement and burial-place of the early centuries A.D.

GLIN, Co. Limerick (Map 4, D2), is a village on the Foynes (9 m.)–Tarbert (4 m.) road by the S. shore of the Shannon estuary. The glen to the S. (Glencorby), from which it takes its name, provides the title of the Fitzgeralds, Knights of Glin, whose home is at Glin Castle (about 1770; castellated in 19th cent.; noteworthy outer and inner halls) to the W. of the village. The Knights of Glin descend from John, grandson of Thomas of Shanid (*see under* Shanagolden), ancestor of the Geraldines of Munster; they have resided in or near Glin for some 700 years. A fragment of their old castle (Cloch Ghleanna) may be seen in the village. It was attacked from land and sea in 1600 by Sir George Carew, Elizabeth I's President of Munster; the Knight was killed in the hand-to-hand fighting and the castle was destroyed.

The tower overlooking the harbour is a 19th cent. "folly", built by a Dr Hamilton.

3 m. SE., via Flean Beg, in Tinnakilla, is Cromlech, a prehistoric chamber tomb. 200 yds S. is Cloch Liosliagáin, a pillarstone.

GOLDEN, Co. Tipperary (Map 5, D4), is a Suirside village 4 m. WSW. of Cashel and 8 m. ENE. of Tipperary. There are remains of a round castle on a rock in the river.

1¼ m. S., on the W. bank of the Suir in Athassel, are the neglected, 4-acre ruins (Nat. Mon.) of St Edmund's Priory (Canons Regular of St Augustine). This magnificent monastery is said to have been founded by William de Burgh (d. 1205), who had been granted lands about Kilfeakle (*see under* Tipperary) at the Norman invasion of the Kingdom of Limerick. Its wealth made it one of the most important Norman monasteries in Ireland, and the prior was a lord of parliament. A town which grew up about the priory was burned by adherents of the Earl of Desmond in 1319 and by Brian O Brien in 1330; no remains are visible. Much of the priory itself was destroyed in 1447. At the Dissolution it was acquired by the Earl of Ormond. – The entrance to the precincts is by a portcullis gateway and a gatehouse with porter's lodge. Long reaches of the enclosing wall survive on W., S., and E. The fine, 4/5-period church, on the N. side of the cloister garth, is basically Cistercian on plan: cruciform with aisled nave (six bays; arcades gone) and with chapels (two) in each transept; but the great NW. tower (foundations only) is an Augustinian feature. Choir, crossing, and transepts are early-13th cent., the nave late-13th cent. The large NE. chapel (Lady Chapel?) is an addition. Noteworthy details include: (a) the arch or doorway (c. 1260) in the rood (?) screen ("rood-loft" blocked up) between nave and choir; (b) the tomb effigy placed upright against the church wall; (c) the fragment of a tomb panel with five miniature figures of knights. This last (? from the tomb of Walter de Burgh, Earl of Ulster, d. 1271) is thought to have been imported ready-made from Dundry near Bristol. – After the 1447 disaster the nave was left roofless, and the central tower replaced by a loftier one with living quarters (hence the blocking of the "rood loft" and the transept arches). – The cloister ambulatories are 14th/15th cent. (post 1447?) work. The E. cloister range comprised sacristy, slype to cemetery, much altered chapter house, sub-vaults, and dormitory (upper floor); latrines projected on the S. In the S. range was the refectory (fine doorway of c. 1260) with sub-vaults beneath. – SW. of the priory proper were the farm buildings. – 1¾ m. W. is the ancient church site, Templegobban. – 5 m. SE. is Boytonrath (see Rockwell College under Cashel).

2 m. W. are the ruins of Thomastown Castle, sometime seat of the Matthews, Earls of Llandaff. Fr Theobald Mathew (1790–1861), Capuchin apostle of Temperance, was born here; the memorial statue (1939) was unveiled by his great-nephew, Archbishop David Matthew, historian.

4 m. NW., on the Limerick road, are the ruins of the O Dwyer castle of Killenure; early-17th cent. The central block had six gables terminating in tall chimney stacks. The four angle turrets finished in gabled dormers, and had each a single tall chimney.

GOLDEN BALL, Co. Dublin (Map 6, E7), is a hamlet on the Dublin (8 m.)–Enniskerry (4 m.) road, 1¼ m. SW. of Carrickmines.

2½ m. ESE. is Rathmichael (see under Loughlinstown).

1½ m. SE. the Enniskerry road makes its way through The Scalp, a picturesque, boulder-strewn gorge carved by Ice Age meltwaters.

3 m. SE. is Killegar (see under Enniskerry).

¾ m. SW., beyond Kiltiernan Lodge, are the remains (Nat. Mon.) of Cill Tighearnáin, an early monastery: cashel enclosing a souterrain and an early, single-chamber church with trabeate W. door; the S. door and E. window are insertions. Inside the church is preserved a small granite bullaun. Nearby is St Tiernan's Well.

½ m. W., in Kiltiernan Domain, is Giants Grave (Nat. Mon.), a magnificent portal dolmen with enormous, granite capstone. Finds here included neolithic sherds and flints.

½ m. NW., by the side of the Dublin road, is St Patrick's Well.

½ m. N., to the NE. of Jamestown House, is St James's Well, partly roofed with two early gravestones. Above it stands an early cross-slab with a rude figure on the SW. face.

GORESBRIDGE, Co. Kilkenny (Map 6, B5), a village on the Gowran (4 m.)–Borris (5 m.) road, is pleasantly situated beside the River Barrow.

5 m. NE., is Ballyloughan, Co. Carlow (see under Muine Bheag).

2 m. S. are the ruins of Ballyellin (Co. Carlow) castle.

2 m. SE., in the fine demesne of Mount Loftus, are the ruins of Drumroe castle. The road on the S. side of the demesne bisects Raheennamaghil ringfort; a couple of fields SE. of the ringfort is Cloghvickree, a pillar-stone. – 4 m. SE. is Ullard (see under Graiguenamanagh).

3 m. SW., in Powerstown East, is a motte.

1 m. W. are remains of Lord Galmoy's Castle.

GOREY, Co. Wexford (Map 6, D5), is a market town on the Arklow (12 m.)–Enniscorthy (19 m.) road, below the SE. slopes of the Wicklow Mountains.

Like Enniscorthy, Wexford, and New Ross, Gorey figured prominently in the 1798 insurrection. To maintain their cause the insurgents had to break out into the surrounding counties. On 3 June, therefore, they stormed Gorey in an effort to reach the coast road to Dublin via Arklow, but did not know how to exploit their victory. Their camp was on Gorey Hill (418 ft), just SW. of the town.

The Loreto convent is by Augustus Welby Pugin, who may also have been architect of the adjacent church. The Protestant parish church has windows by Michael Healy (St John, 1904), Harry Clarke (St Stephen, 1922), and Catherine O Brien (Angel, 1910; Christ and Peter on the Water, 1957).

1 m. N. is Ramsfort House, built to the designs of George Semple in 1751. Here is preserved a stone from the bishop's palace built at Ferns by the aged Bishop Thomas Ram in 1630. The inscription reads:

"This house Ram built for his
　　succeeding brothers:
Thus sheep bear wool, not for
　　themselves, but others."

5 m. N. are the ruins of the Esmonde castle of Limerick, with, nearby, the remains of a church. 2½ m. NW. is Pallis (see below).

2¼ m. NE. is cairn-crowned Tara Hill (833 ft); nearby to the SE. is Ballymoney strand.

4 m. SE. is Courtown Harbour, a small sea-side resort with a good 2-m. beach. 1 m. S., at Ardamine, are a fine cairn and a sculptured stone cross. 4½ m. S. of Ardamine, beside the sea, are the scanty ruins of Glascarrig Abbey, founded in 1190 by Condons and others for Benedictines of the Tironian reform, and colonized from St Dogmaels in Pembrokeshire.

Nearby is a motte constructed by a Cantitune nephew of Raymond le Gros. 3 m. further S. (SE. of Ballygarrett) is Cahore beach.

8 m. NNW., in Pallis, is a motte. A branch of the O Dalys, most celebrated of Irish bardic families, settled in Pallis. About 1600 Cearbhall O Daly persuaded Eleanor Kavanagh to elope with him by singing for her the lovely song she had inspired, "Eibhlín a Rúin" (Eileen Aroon), the oldest Irish harp tune whose original words survive.

GORT, Co. Galway (Map 5, B2), is a small, well laid-out, market town on the Galway (23 m.)–Ennis (19 m.) road. The pleasant countryside is rich in prehistoric and historic remains and in literary associations. The town takes its name, Gort Inse Guaire, from Guaire Aidhne, celebrated 6th cent. King of Connacht and patron of St Colmán mac Duach. In the Middle Ages the O Shaughnessys had their principal stronghold here. In the 17th cent. the confiscated O Shaughnessy lands were granted to the Verekers (later Viscounts Gort; *see* Lough Cutra Castle, *below*).

To the E. and NE. rise the Slieve Aughty Mountains (Cashlaundrumlahan, 1,207 ft).

2 m. N. is the entrance to Coole Park (demolished), home of Augusta, Lady Gregory (1852–1932; *see also* New Quay *under* Corcomroe Abbey), who took an eminent part in the 19th–20th cent. literary and dramatic revival. Coole Park was the resort of most of the leading writers of the revival; its woods and lake were sung by Yeats. The callous demolition of the house in 1941 came more swiftly than even Yeats's melancholy prophecy of 1927 can have envisaged:

"Here, traveller, scholar, poet, take your stand
When all these rooms and passages are gone,
When nettles wave upon a shapeless mound
And saplings root among the broken stone.
And dedicate – eyes bent upon the ground,
Back turned upon the brightness of the sun
And all the sensuality of the shade –
A moment's memory to that laurelled head."

Apart from the shapeless mound and broken stone, the sole relics of the great days are a lovely avenue of cedars and an immense copper beech tree, on which Lady Gregory's guests carved their initials. Many of these are now illegible, but *G*(eorge) *B*(ernard) *S*(haw), *S*(eán) *O C*(asey), *W*(illiam) *B*(utler) *Y*(eats), *J*(ack) *B*(utler) *Y*(eats), *V*(iolet) *M*(artin) – the "Martin Ross" of "Somerville and Ross" fame – *A.E.* (George Russell), and *K*(atherine) *T*(ynan) *H*(inkson) can still be read. – ½ m. NNW. of the N. gate of Coole Park, on the Kinvara road, are the ruins of Kiltartan church, a simple structure incorporating primitive, Transitional, and Late Gothic features; in the chancel is an altar-tomb (no figures). – Opposite the N. gate of Coole Park a side road to the SW. passes

Commissioners of Public Works in Ireland
Ballylee castle, Gort

the shattered, but imposing, remains of Ballinamantain (alias Kiltartan) castle, a 13th cent. de Burgh castle with strong, towered bawn (Nat. Mon.). The nearby river flows underground.

5 m. NE. is the 16th cent. tower of Ballylee castle, the "Thoor Ballylee" of Yeats's poems. The poet had it, and the adjoining cottages, repaired and made his home in them in the 1920s, and it was here that his volume of poems, *The Tower*, was written. His "Meditations in Time of Civil War" (1923) describe the tower and the life about it. A tablet commemorates his sojourn:

"I, the poet William Yeats,
With old mill boards and sea-green slates
And smithy work from the Gort forge,
Restored this tower for my wife George;
And may these characters remain
When all is ruin once again."

Yeats abandoned Ballylee in 1929, and all too soon everything was "ruin once again". The place was restored as a Yeats Museum for the centenary (1965) of the poet's birth. – Ballylee has older, Gaelic, literary associations too, for close to the castle was the home of sweet Mary Hynes, the miller's daughter loved and sung by Blind Raftery (*see* Killora *under* Craughwell).

6 m. NE. is Peterswell, called after a well dedicated to St Peter. In the church is a single-light window, *Our Lady of the Rosary*, by Evie Hone (1950).

Lough Cutra Castle, Gort

4 m. E., in Kilcrimple, to the E. of Ballyturin Lough, is Dermot and Grania's Bed, a prehistoric chamber tomb.

1½ m. SSE. is the Punchbowl, an 80-ft chasm where the underground river from Lough Cutra is visible.

3 m. SSE., on the W. side of the small, pretty lake after which it is called, is Lough Cutra Castle, built (1810) for the 1st Viscount Gort, by the brothers Pain of Cork to the design of John Nash. It bears a strong likeness to East Cowes Castle, Isle of Wight. In the mid-19th cent. it was sold to the Goughs. It was recently purchased by the present Viscount Gort. On two of the islands in the lough are the ruins of churches; on a third are the ruins of a castle.

5 m. S. are the ruins of Ardamullivan castle (Nat. Mon.), a 16th cent. O Shaughnessy stronghold with interesting windows. 1 m. E., in Derrycallan North, to the S. of Ballynakill Lough, is Dermot and Grania's Bed, a prehistoric chamber tomb.

2 m. SSW., in Ballybaun, is Caher Mugachane, a stone ringfort; the site affords a fine view.

5 m. SSW., between Lough Aslaun and Lough Do, is the well-preserved 16th cent. O Shaughnessy castle of Fiddaun (Nat. Mon.); the fine bawn is of unusual plan. There was also an outer bawn, of which the little gatehouse remains. The nearby village of Tubber (Tubberreendoney) takes its name from the holy well, Tobar Rí an Domhnaigh, The King-of-Sunday's Well.

3 m. SW. is Kilmacduagh (*q.v.*).

2 m. W. is St Colman's Church, Tirneevin; the single-light *The Sower Sowing his Seed* (1963) was designed by George Campbell, R.H.A., the painter. 3 m. NNE., to the E. of the road in Ballynastaig, is Nastaig Fort, a ringfort with a fine souterrain (now the local spring well) and a chamber in the rampart. 500 yds E., on the limestone in Crannagh townland, is Dermot and Grania's Bed, a tall chamber tomb. Some 800 yds S. of the fort (via the bohereen) and also in Ballynastaig, is a wedge-shaped gallery grave. – W. of Ballynastaig is Caherglassaun Lake, alias Lough Deehan. It is drained by underground channels to the sea (3 m.) and rises and falls with the tides. – 2 m. NE. of Ballynastaig is the 15th/16th cent. tower of the O Hynes castle of Lydacan (Nat. Mon.).

GORTAHORK, Co. Donegal (Map 2, B2), is a village and resort at the head of Ballyness Bay, on the Dunfanaghy (10 m.)–Gweedore (9 m.) road, to the N. of the Errigal–Muckish range of mountains. It is in the heart of the Donegal Gaeltacht, and together with Falcarragh, 2 m. NE., provides convenient quarters for students of the Cloghaneely summer school for Irish (Coláiste Uladh). Gortahork and Falcarragh are the best centres from which to climb Muckish (2,197 ft). The stiff ascent is best made via Muckish Gap, 6 m. SE. of Falcarragh. The summit affords one of the most magnificent panoramas in Ireland. On the W. peak is Meskan Mave (*see also* Knocknarea *under* Sligo), a prehistoric cairn.

3–4 m. N., off the coast, are Inishbofin, Inishdooey, and Inishbeg. On Inishdooey are Doonmore promontory fort and the remains of an ancient church.

2½ m. NE., in the grounds of Ballyconnell House, is Cloch Cheannfaoladh (Ceannfaoladh's Stone), which gives its name to the village and parish of Cloghaneely. This is a large boulder with a red crystalline vein. The latter is explained as the petrified blood of Faoladh, whose head (*ceann*) was cut off here by Balor of the Baleful Eye, alias Balor of the Mighty Blows, legendary giant of Tory Island. 2 m. NE., in Ray, the ruins of a medieval church and a great monolithic cross (Nat. Mons.) mark the early monastic site of Moyra, alias Myrath. Legend asserts that the cross was hewn on Muckish by St Columcille himself. 1¾ m. NNE. of the church, in Ballyboe, is Altar, a chamber tomb; less than ½ m. WNW. is Cloghacorr, a central-court cairn; in Errarooey Beg, the next townland to the N., is a cairn.– 1½ m. S. of Cloghaneely, in Ballintemple, is the ruined church of Tullaghobegly.

5 m. S. of Falcarragh, between Errigal (2,466 ft) and Aghla More (1,916 ft), is lonely Altan Lough.

GORUMNA ISLAND, Co. Galway (Map 1, C6), lies to the S. of Lettermore Island (with which it is linked by a road bridge) on the E. side of Kilkieran Bay, some 30 m. W. of Galway. To the SW. lies Lettermullen Island, with which it is also linked by a road bridge. The landscape of both islands is wild and picturesque.

4½ m. S. of Lettermore bridge, at Trawbaun on the E. shore of the island, are remains of an ancient church.

5 m. SSW. of Lettermore bridge (1 m. SE. of Lettermullen bridge), in Maumeen, are the remains of a small, simple church with trabeate W. door.

GOWRAN, Co. Kilkenny (Map 6, B5), is a village at the intersection of the Kilkenny (9 m.)–Goresbridge (4 m.) and Leighlinbridge (9 m.)–Thomastown (8 m.) roads. In early and medieval times the place was of considerable strategic importance, as it commanded Bealach Gabhráin, ancient route through the bogs and forests of the Leinster–Ossory marches. At the Anglo-Norman invasion it fell to Strongbow, whose heir, William the Marshal, granted the manor to Theobald fitz Walter, ancestor of the Butlers. The manor remained Butler property until the 17th cent., and the castle was the principal seat of the Butlers in the interval between the loss of Nenagh (*q.v.*) and the acquisition of Kilkenny (1391). The town itself was founded by Theobald fitz Walter. In 1317 the town was captured by Edward Bruce, and in 1414 was destroyed by the local Irish. In 1608 James I made it a parliamentary borough. In 1650 it was held for a short time by Lord Ormonde's regiment against the Cromwellians, Sankey and Hewson. When the Ormondists capitulated, the Cromwellians slaughtered their English colonel and other officers, as well as their Franciscan chaplain, and burnt the castle.

The principal feature of the village is the medieval parish (collegiate) church of the Assumption of the Blessed Virgin Mary, burial place of the 1st and 3rd Earls of Ormond as well as of branches of the Butler family. It occupies the site of a much more ancient foundation. In its original, late-13th cent. form, the church consisted of an aisled nave and a long chancel. In the 14th cent. a massive, square tower was inserted between nave and chancel; in the 17th, a Keally mortuary chapel was erected adjoining the W. end of the S. nave aisle. The site of the chancel is now occupied by a 19th cent. Protestant church which incorporates the medieval tower; the nave and aisles (Nat. Mon.) are roofless and the S. arcade has gone, but many of the details are beautiful or otherwise interesting: foliage carving of Somersetshire type, early plate tracery, etc. The quatrefoil columns of the N. arcade recall St Canice's Cathedral, Kilkenny, as do windows in the aisles. The monuments include:

N. aisle: a niche tomb with low-relief, 14th cent. effigy of a knight believed to be the 1st Earl of Ormond; a niche tomb with low-relief, 14th cent. effigy of a lady believed to be the 1st Countess of Ormond; Renaissance monument (1646) of James Keally and his two wives, Ellen Nashe and Mary White.

"Both wifves at once alive he could not have,
  Both to inioy at once he made this grave."

Nave: an early cross-pillar.

Keally Chapel: Renaissance monument of Piers Keally and his wife, Alison Hackett.

Protestant church: an early cross-pillar; a

Commissioners of Public Works in Ireland
14th cent. effigy, Gowran parish church

cross-inscribed ogham stone discovered in the foundations of the medieval chancel; a tombstone with effigy of Ralph "Julianus" (d. 1252/53), parish priest; a tombstone with effigy of a lady (about 1500); a medieval font; a 16th cent. Butler tomb with effigies of two armoured knights; a 16th cent. Butler tomb, by Rory O Tunney, with effigy of an armoured knight.

Beside the town is the demesne of Gowran Castle, formerly seat of Lord Clifden. In the Pigeon Park is the tower of the Butler castle of Ballyshawnmore, captured by the Cromwellians in 1650; also a large, defaced motte.

3 m. NE. is Paulstown, alias Polestown. There are remains of a castle belonging to a branch of the Butlers descended from Richard, a younger son of James, 3rd Earl of Ormond. Richard's son, Émonn mac Risderd Butler, was celebrated as a warrior and a patron of Irish literature (*see* Carrick-on-Suir; *also* Piltown, *and* Pottelrath *under* Callan).

3 m. SE., in Powerstown East, is a motte.

3½ m. SSE. are the ruins of the Butler castle of Neigham.

3 m. SW., in the old churchyard at Dungarvan, is a fragment from the 1581 tomb of Donal fitz Piers Archdekin, alias MacCoda, of Cloghala, and his wife, Catherine Blancheuld (Blanchville, Blanchfield). It is signed by the maker, Walter Kerin. The carvings include miniature effigies of an armoured knight and his lady; the only other miniature effigy surviving in Ireland is on the monument of Edmund Purcell in St Canice's Cathedral, Kilkenny.

5 m. SW., at Tullaherin (more correctly Tullaherim), is an early monastic site marked by a 73-ft, imperfect Round Tower (Nat. Mon.) and the ruins of a nave-and-chancel church of various dates. Near the base of the tower is a fragment of an ogham stone. 2 m. SSW. is Kilfane (*see under* Thomastown).

1½ m. W. is roadside Rathcusack, a fine ringfort.

3 m. W. are the ruins of the Church of Kylebeg, ancient nave-and-chancel parish church of Blanchvilleskill. It was dedicated to St Nicholas of Myra.

5 m. NW., are Freestone Hill and Clarabricken (*see under* Kilkenny).

5 m. NNW., in Freneystown, are an ancient churchyard and the tower of a castle built by Oliver Cantwell, Bishop of Ossory, 1487–1527. Adjoining the churchyard is a ringfort-type enclosure with the gravestones of the Seven Bishops. The enclosure is the ancient church site, Teach Scuithín, Tiscoffin, which gives its name to the parish; here, too, is Scoheen's (= Scuithín's) Well.

GRAIGUENAMANAGH, Co. Kilkenny

(Map 6, B5), a small market and woollen-manufacturing town on a beautiful reach of the Barrow at the foot of Brandon Hill (*below*), is at the junction of roads from Goresbridge (7 m.), Borris (8 m.), New Ross (11 m.), Inistioge (6 m.), and Thomastown (9 m.). The road SW. across the hills to Inistioge (*q.v.*) affords lovely views. The Barrow southwards to New Ross (*q.v.*) is well worth exploring by boat or on foot.

The town takes its name from the monks of the Cistercian abbey of Vallis Sancti Salvatoris, founded about 1207 by William the Marshal (*see* New Ross), and colonized from Stanley in Wiltshire. The monks, who had been invited to Ireland by Ó Ríain of Idrone, settled in turn at Loughmeran, near Kilkenny, and Annamult (*see under* Kells, Co. Kilkenny) before settling down beside the little Dubh Uisge River which gave their monastery its best known name, Duiske Abbey. At the Dissolution the abbey was acquired by the Earl of Ormond, and so passed to the Butler Viscounts Galmoy, who held it until the Williamite rebellion. In 1813, after standing long in ruins, the chancel, crossing, transepts, and part of the nave of the church were re-roofed, in poverty-stricken, untutored manner, to serve as parish church of Graiguenamanagh. The W. end was re-edified in 1886. (Expert restoration is now projected.) The plan of the abbey church (largest of Irish Cistercian

churches), which was built about 1212–40, is identical with that of Strata Florida, Cardiganshire. It had an aisled nave of seven bays, three E. chapels in each transept, and a tower (square below, octagonal above) over the crossing. The chancel had a ribbed vault of three bays, and the chapels had barrel vaults. The transepts had an unusual clerestory of round, multi-cusped windows. A beautiful processional doorway opened from the S. aisle on to the cloister; it is now the entrance to the 1916 baptistery. The Transitional features are strongly reminiscent of those at Kilkenny cathedral, and may be the work of the same masons. The surviving details are worth examination, but it should be remembered that many of the carvings have been "restored" by a modern hand (John O'Leary). The monumental remains include the effigy of a knight (about 1310) armed in transverse banded mail. The fragmentary remains of the claustral buildings have to be sought out in backyards and gardens S. of the church. Noteworthy in the E. (dormitory) range is the large chapter-house (?) of later date than the rest. In the S. range is the refectory with elevated recess for reader's desk. In the modern graveyard are two granite High Crosses. The North Cross is from an early monastic site in Ballyogan (*below*). The figure subjects include: E. face: *Crucifixion, Fall, Sacrifice of Isaac, King David;* W. face: *Massacre of the Innocents.* The South Cross is from the early monastic site, Aghailten (Achadh Chailltin; associated with St Báirrfhionn mac Aodha) near Ullard (*below*). It has a rude *Crucifixion* and panels of interlacings.

½ m. SSE., overlooking the E. bank of the Barrow in Co. Carlow, are the ruins of the small Butler rock-castle of Tinnahinch. Near by are the ruins of St Michael's Church and St Michael's Well.

2 m. NE., on the W. bank of the Barrow in Cloghasty South, are remains of a 15th cent. castle commanding the river crossing.

3 m. NE. is Ullard, site of a monastery founded by St Fiachra, who died, A.D. 670, near Meaux, where his hermit's cell became the nucleus of the great abbey of Breuil. (As St Fiacre, he enjoyed high repute in medieval France.) The remains (Nat. Mons.) at Ullard include a 9th/10th cent. High Cross (upper part modern) and a ruined church with altered Romanesque chancel arch and doorway. (There is also Romanesque carving on a chamfered impost of the original chancel arch.) The figure subjects on the cross include: E. face: *Crucifixion, King David with Harp, Sacrifice of Isaac.*

2¼ m. SSE., in Ballyogan, are the remains of Galmoy Castle, called after the Butler Viscounts Galmoy. ½ m. W., by the roadside, is Páirc an Teampaill, alias the Chapel Field, site in turn of an early monastery (High Cross now at Graiguenamanagh) and a manorial church,

4½ m. SSE., on the E. side of the Barrow, is St Mullins, Co. Carlow (*q.v.*).

4½ m. SSW. (via Sackinstown), on the summit of Brandon Hill (1,694 ft) and commanding delightful views, are a prehistoric cairn and a stone circle.

GRANARD, Co. Longford (Map 2, D6), is a small market town on the Cavan (20 m.)–Athlone (30 m.) road, from which the Earl of Granard (*see* Newtown Forbes) takes his title. The place was sacked by Edward Bruce in 1315. In 1798 a party of insurgents retreating from Ballinamuck (*q.v.*) was routed here, and most of those taken prisoner were slain.

There is a good motte-and-bailey (Nat. Mon.) here, relic of Hugh de Lacy's transient lordship of Meath and of the abortive Anglo-Norman attempt to penetrate into Breany (*see* Cavan). It was constructed in 1199 by Richard de Tuit, who was enfeoffed in Granard by de Lacy.

1½ m. NE. the road to Bellanagh passes across a 3-m. sector of the Dúnchaladh, or Black Pig's Dyke (*see under* Belcoo, Clones, Dowra *and* Garrison), which blocked the gap between Loughs Kinale and Gowna.

2½ m. SE., near Abbeylara, are remains of Laragh Cistercian abbey, founded by Richard de Tuit (killed 1211) and colonized from St Mary's Abbey, Dublin, in 1214. A semi-circular earthwork N. of Abbeylara is locally believed to be the site of a church founded by St Patrick.

5 m. NW., in pretty Lough Gowna, is Inchmore, where the remnants of Teampall Cholaim

Irish Tourist Board

Cottage by Lough Gowna, Granard

Chille mark the site of a Columban (later Augustinian) monastery. The slight remains include a fragmentary church with three Late Romanesque windows. A bronze bell from the monastery is preserved at Aughnacliff church on the mainland, 2 m. to the NW. There is a ruined prehistoric chamber tomb in Aughnacliff.

GRANGE, Co. Sligo (Map 2, B4), is a village on the Sligo (9 m.)–Bundoran (14 m.) road, between the foot of Ben Bulben (*see* Drumcliff) and Streedagh strand. Boats can be hired here for the crossing to Inishmurray (*q.v.*).

3 m. ESE., in Cloghragh, on the NW. slope of Ben Bulben, are remains of a prehistoric chamber tomb.

2¼ m. W., by the seashore in Agharrow, the ruins of Staad "Abbey" mark the site of a monastery founded by St Mo-Laisse (*see* Inishmurray), whose name is recalled by Poll-molasha (Poll Mo-Laisse), 1½ m. SW., and by St Mo-Laisse's Well in Cloonagh, 5 m. SW. of Raghly (*q.v.*). ½ m. N. of the "abbey", in Streedagh, are Giants Grave – a ruined court cairn – and Na Clocha Breaca, a wedge-shaped gallery grave in a round cairn.

The coast hereabouts saw the wreck of several ships of the Spanish Armada, whose fate is recalled by Carricknaspania (Carraig na Spáinneach, "Rock of the Spaniards"). It was of this district that Sir Geoffrey Fenton reported to Lord Burleigh: "I numbered in one strand less than five miles in length eleven hundred dead corpses."

GREY ABBEY, Co. Down (Map 3, D5), a village of the Ards Peninsula to the E. of Strangford Lough, on the Newtownards (7 m.)–Portaferry (10 m.) road, takes its name from the small Cistercian abbey founded here in 1193, for monks from Holm Cultram in Cumberland, by Affrica, wife of John de Courcy and daughter (by his Irish wife) of Godred, King of Man. The abbey was dissolved *c.* 1541–43. In 1572 the buildings were burned by Sir Brian O Neill of Clannaboy to obstruct the English colonization of the Ards.

The beautifully conserved ruins (Nat. Mon.) are typically Cistercian in plan, and the earlier work typically Cistercian in the restrained use of ornament. The remains comprise those of an aisleless, cruciform church with two chapels in each transept, tower over the crossing, night stairs to church from dormitory, and fragments of the chapter-house, day-room, refectory (on S. side of cloister garth), etc. Most of the surviving work can be assigned to the end of the 12th cent., but the rather elaborate W. doorway of the church is *c.* 1220, while the N. and S. windows of the chancel have Perpendicular tracery of the late 15th cent. A recumbent tomb-effigy in the N. wall of the choir is thought to represent the foundress, while the mutilated figure of an armoured knight in a chapel of the N. transept is said to be the effigy of her husband. The church was re-roofed to serve as Protestant parish church in the 17th cent. To this period of re-use the bell-cote and small window of the W. gable belong. Open to the public: 1 April to 30 Sept., weekdays 10 a.m.– 1 p.m., 2–6 p.m.; Suns., 2–6 p.m.; 1 Oct. to 31 March, Sats., 10 a.m.–1 p.m., 2–4 p.m.; Suns., 2–4 p.m. (Closed on Christmas Day.) Admission 6d. – The picturesque demesne of Grey Abbey House, in which the ruins are situated, is the property of the Montgomery family.

On Chapel Island, 1½ m. WSW. in Strangford Lough, are some remains of a small early church with clay-bonded walls. The small enclosure to the E. was probably a cemetery.

2 m. NW. is Mount Stewart House (seat of the Marquess of Londonderry), an 18th cent. Classical building. The splendid 80-acre gardens (Nat. Trust) are noted for their rare plants, shrubs, and trees. (Open to the public: 1 April to 30 Sept., Weds., Sats., Suns., and Bank Holidays 2–6 p.m.; 2–9 p.m. in May and June; adults 2/6, children and parties 1/6.) Close to the private aerodrome are two cists from a multiple-cist Bronze Age cairn removed in 1786. On Moat Hill is an imposing motte; ¼ m. SE. are the last remnants of Templecran, a small church.

GREYSTONES, Co. Wicklow (Map 6, D3), is a seaside resort on the Bray (5 m.)–Wicklow (10 m.) road. There are good beaches to the N. (shingle) and S. of the town. The Catholic parish church has two single-light windows (*The Good Shepherd, Our Lady of the Rosary– Battle of Lepanto*) by Evie Hone (1948).

GWEEDORE, Co. Donegal (Map 2, B2), is a hamlet on the Gortahork (8½ m.)–Dungloe (10¼ m.) road.

The country round about is extremely beautiful, and there is excellent fishing to be had in the Clady River and the local lakes and streams.

From Gweedore a fair road leads E. and SE. past Lough Nacung and Dunlewy Lough to the Dunlewy Gap (6 m.) between the Derryveagh Mountains (Slieve Snaght, 2,240 ft; Dooish, 2,147 ft) and the heights of Errigal (2,466 ft), Aghla More (1,916 ft), and Muckish (2,197 ft). Errigal, between Dunlewy Lough and lonely Altan Lough, is the highest mountain in Donegal. A beautiful cone with white quartzite facings, it rewards the climber (much loose scree) with one of the finest panoramas in Ireland.

Dunlewy Lough and Lough Nacung lie in the valley between Errigal and Tievealehid (1,413 ft) on the N., and Crocknafarragh (1,707 ft) and Slieve Snaght (2,240 ft) on the S. They are fed by the Devlin River and Cronanly Burn, which flow into Dunlewy Lough close to the hamlet of Dunlewy, a noted centre of homespun tweed-making. The Cronanly Burn flows down through Gleann Nimhe, the Poisoned Glen (a cliff-sided corrie of stark beauty under Slieve

Snaght), whose name is attributed to the abundance of spurge.

Beyond Dunlewy Gap is the Calabber valley (*see under* Creeslough).

¼ m. S. of Dunlewy is the ancient church site of Trian na Cille, where there is an early cross-slab.

HACKETSTOWN, Co. Carlow (Map 6, C4), is a village on the Baltinglass (9 m.)– Tinahely (7 m.) road, in the foothills of the Wicklow Mountains. It was the scene of two battles in 1798.

3 m. S. is Clonmore, the ancient Cluain Mór M'Áedóc, where, in the 6th cent., St M'Áedóc úa Dúnlainge (?) founded a monastery. The site of the monastery is divided by the roadway. In the graveyard S. of the road are the head and shaft of an unfigured High Cross; also early gravestones, etc. In the churchyard N. of the road is an ancient stone trough. W. of the churchyard is St Mogue's Cross, another granite High Cross. Further W. is St Mogue's Well. 120 yds. W. of this and S. of the road is a triple bullaun. 200 yds. WNW. of the bullaun are remains of a large, 13th cent., English royal castle (keepless type) which, with the manor, was acquired by the Earl of Kildare in the 15th cent. – 300 yds E. of Clonmore crossroads, in Minvaud Upper, is a motte-and-bailey, relic of Raymond le Gros's 1181 castle of Fotheret O Nolan.

HEADFORD, Co. Galway (Map 1, D5), is a market village and angling resort on the Galway (17 m.)–Ballinrobe (15 m.) road, 4 m. E. of Lough Corrib. The country round about – the O Flaherty homeland prior to the Anglo-Norman invasion – is rich in ancient remains, most notably ringforts of varying kinds. (Many Bronze Age cairns and other prehistoric monuments have been swept away in the last hundred years or so.) The poet "Eva of the *Nation*" (Mary Kelly, 1826–1910), who married the Young Irelander, Kevin O Doherty, was born near Headford.

2½ m. N., in Moyne, Co. Mayo, is an ancient oval church-site enclosed by a cashel; near the W. end of the church are two pillar-stones between which coffins are carried. Not far away are the ruins of Moyne castle.

1¾ m. NNE., on the E. side of the Ballinrobe road in Largan, is Doon, a fine ringfort. ½ m. NNW., to the W. of the road, are Lissacromlech (a ringfort) and a pillarstone. ½ m. further N. is roadside Doonlaur, a fine univallate ringfort; ½ m. NE. is Cahernaman, a trivallate ringfort.

6½ m. ENE. are Castle Hacket demesne and Knockmaa. In the demesne are the bawn and tower of a Hacket – later Burke – castle which was inhabited until 1703. Knockmaa (552 ft), which dominates the countryside, is called after Meadhbh (Maeve), mythological "Queen of Connacht", and is celebrated in oral tradition as the Otherworld seat of Finnbhearra, "King

Plate 10. The Giant's Causeway, Co. Antrim

of the Connacht Fairies". On the summit, which commands a beautiful panorama, is a prehistoric cairn (the Carn Ceasarach of medieval legend). Close by is Finnbhearra's Castle, an 18th/19th cent. folly which may incorporate another cairn. The summits of the foothills were also crowned by cairns. On the SE. slope is Calliagh Cave, a three-chamber souterrain in a ringfort.

4½ m. SE., at the ancient church-site of Kilcoona, is the stump of a Round Tower.

6½ m. SE. is Cahermorris ringfort.

4 m. SW., just offshore in Lough Corrib, is Illauncarbry, with a massive stone ringfort (overgrown). On the lake shore are remains of the late 13th cent. Gaynard – later Burke – hall-type castle of Cargin. Clydagh House, to the W., is a late Georgian house. 1½ m. NW. is Annaghkeen (below).

4½ m. WSW., in Annaghkeen, 500 yds NE. of the remains of the Burke castle, is a disturbed Bronze Age cairn with central cist; it was covered by a mound of earth. 200 yds. N. is Carn Mór ("Annaghkeen Cairn"), a large Bronze Age cairn (disturbed 1907). S. of the castle, near the lake, is Carn Beag, a small cairn.

2 m. W., by the Annaghkeen road, are the ruins of Killursa, Cill Fhursa, "Church of Fursa" (Nat. Mon.), an ancient structure (trabeate W. doorway) enlarged in medieval times. The dedication implies that a monastery was founded here by St Fursa ("Fursey", 584–652), a disciple of St Brendan of Clonfert (q.v.; also Annaghdown and Cnoc Bréanainn under Dingle). Fursa afterwards settled for a time at Burgh Castle in Suffolk, and ultimately at Péronne in France, where his enshrined remains became the object of pilgrimage and whence his cult spread to the Low Countries and to Germany. The story of his visions of Hell and Heaven was celebrated in medieval Europe. (He has been called the "precursor of Dante".) 4 m. W., in Lough Corrib, is Inchiquin, a well-known angling station. The ancient burial ground of Rathmath marks the site of a monastery founded by St Brendan the Navigator. St Fursa is said to have been born there (his parents having sought refuge with Brendan).

1½ m. NW. (½ m. N. of the Annaghkeen road) are the exceptionally well-preserved remains (Nat. Mon.) of Ross "Abbey", a Franciscan Observantine friary founded by a Gaynard in 1498. At the Dissolution the friary was granted to the Earls of Clanricarde, who protected the friars, so that they returned seven times between 1538 and 1753. In 1596 the buildings were occupied as an English strong point; in 1656 they were pillaged by Cromwellian troops. The remains comprise church and conventual buildings. The church consists of chancel, central tower with rood-loft, nave with S. aisle and S. transept (double); as at Kilconnell, the transept has three E. chapels; opening off the W. end of the aisle is a 17th cent. Jennings chantry-chapel. The tiny cloister is exceptionally well preserved. As at Rathfran Dominican friary (see under Killala), there is a second court N. of the cloister garth. The conventual buildings give an excellent idea of the character and arrangements of a medieval Franciscan house. On the E. side of the N. court is the refectory, with reader's desk at the NE. window; overhead was the principal dormitory. At the NW. angle of the N. court is the kitchen with interesting fish-tank and fireplace; adjoining it on the N. is the mill, on the E. the bakery (with a second dormitory above). The tall, late building ("Burke's Castle") adjoining the church on the NE. may have been the lodging of the Guardian.

HILLSBOROUGH, Co. Down (Map 3, C5), is a small linen town on the Dromore (4¾ m.)–Lisburn (4 m.) road. Like Hilltown, it takes its name from the descendants of Sir Moyses Hill, an English army officer who, at the Plantation, obtained confiscated Magennis lands to which, in 1611, he added 5,000 Magennis acres in the Hillsborough–Lisburn area and, in 1616, the Upper Clannaboy castle and lands of Castlereagh (Belfast) – and who had married a sister of the redoubtable Somhairle Buidhe Mac Donnell, cousin and son-in-law of Great Hugh O Neill. About 1630 Peter Hill (son of Moyses) began the erection of a village and of a fort commanding the pass on the main highway from Belfast to the South. The place was destroyed by the resurgent Irish in 1641. In the 1650s Peter's uncle and heir, Col. Arthur Hill, who ran with both the Cromwellian hare and the Restoration hounds, built an artillery fort in the pass "for the incouragement of an English Plantation". In 1660 the fort was made a royal garrison, with Hill and his heirs hereditary Constables. Two years later Hill obtained a charter for his new town (to be called Hillsborough), for which he built a Protestant church the same year. William of Orange stayed at the fort, 19–23 June 1690, en route to the Boyne, and there he granted the famous *Regium Donum*, or state stipend, to the clergy of the Presbyterian Church.

The most famous of the Hills was Wills Hill (1718–93), 1st Marquess of Downshire, sponsor of Goldsmith's *Deserted Village*, and George III's stupidly implacable Secretary of State for the American Colonies. ("His character is conceit, wrongheadedness, obstinacy, and passion" – Benjamin Franklin.) The 2nd Marquess (1753–1801) was an advocate of religious toleration. His strenuous opposition to the Union cost him dear.

At the centre of the Market Sq. is the attractive Court and Market House (Nat. Mon.) commenced for Wills Hill, and completed for his son in 1797, by Robert Furze Brettingham (1750?–1806).

On the SW. side of the square is Government House (formerly Hillsborough Castle), seat of the Governor of Northern Ireland. The splendid wrought-iron gates came (1936) from Rich-

Government House, Hillsborough

hill Castle, Co. Armagh; they may be the work of the Thornberry brothers from Falmouth, who had settled in Co. Armagh. The house was commenced for Wills Hill *c.* 1760, was enlarged for the 2nd Marquess of Downshire *c.* 1797 by Brettingham (who added most of the S. wing, portico excluded), and was further enlarged and modified at various subsequent dates. (Between 1840 and 1856 the architect was William Sandys, who added the E. and S. porticos, etc.)

At the N. end of Main St, facing the gate of St Malachi's Church, is a statue (by W. H. Lynn) of the 4th Marquess of Downshire (1812–68).

St Malachi's Church (completed 1772) is an interesting, Gothick period piece with most of its original furnishings intact. Thought to incorporate much of the fabric of its 1662 predecessor, it was built for Wills Hill, who aspired to have it made the cathedral of the Protestant diocese of Down. The architect is unknown (George Richardson?), but Hill himself closely supervised the work. In 1898 the chancel was re-arranged by Sir Thomas Drew, who set the prayer desk and the pulpit back against the side walls and aligned the pews (which had been behind the desk and pulpit) along the walls. That year, too, the screens shutting off the baptistry and the vestry from the W. end of the nave were removed. In 1951–65 Denis O'D. Hanna screened off the transept towers and removed the old vestry at the W. end of the nave; Sir Albert Richardson, P.R.A., designed the new electric lights. Noteworthy features are: the 18th cent. prayer desk, pulpit, and box pews; the E. window, by Francis Elgington of Bermingham to the design of Sir Joshua Reynolds (1723–92); the N. transept memorial, by Forsythe, to the 5th Marquess of Downshire (1844–74); the State Chair from the

Chapel Royal, Dublin Castle (lent by the Dean and Chapter of Christ Church, Dublin, "that it may be used in the Church . . . wherein the Representative of the Queen of England is wont to worship"); the S. transept organ (from Hillsborough Castle) of 1795, by G. P. England; the nave monument (1774), by Nollekens, to Henry and Peter Leslie; and the W. gallery organ (1772), by John Snetzler (several times rebuilt). The flags at the chancel arch are those of the East Down Regt. of the Ulster Volunteers. – William Harty (1879–41), father of Sir Hamilton Harty, composer and conductor, was organist to the church 1878–1918. Near the W. door is a birdbath memorial to Sir Hamilton.

The nearby Fort (Nat. Mon.) is Col. Arthur Hill's 17th cent., star-shaped, artillery fort: stone-faced earthen rampart with simple parapet, spear-shaped corner bastions. A 1758 Gothick tower house occupies the site of the original gate-tower. A contemporary, Strawberry-Hill gazebo crowns the 1758 cart entrance. The lawn gates in front of the tower house are late 18th cent., as are those at the Hillsborough Sq entrance.

At the S. end of the town are the 1829 Shambles, now the setting of an annual art exhibition. Further S. is the fine 1792 Rectory, now a school; recently mutilated.

The 1848 hill-top column S. of the town commemorates the 3rd Marquess of Downshire (1788–1845).

HILLTOWN, Co. Down (Map 3, C6), is a village at the N. foot of the Mourne Mountains, at the intersection of the Newry (8 m.)–Newcastle (11 m.) and Rathfryland (3 m.)–Rostrevor (8 m.) roads.

2 m. NE., in Goward, is Pat Kearney's Big Stone, alias Cloughmore, a portal dolmen with granite capstone of fifty tons.

$1\frac{3}{4}$ m. ENE., also in Goward, is a court cairn (Nat. Mon.). Here were found (1932) ox bones and the first Neolithic pottery ever recovered from an Irish chamber tomb; the tomb was occupied, probably as a dwelling, in the early Iron Age. 100 yds NW. is "Castle Commogue", remnant of a second tomb (?); to the E. is a segmented gallery grave. NE. of the summit of Goward Hill is a round cairn.

1 m. E. are some traces of Clonduff church, burial-place of the Magennises of Iveagh (*see* Rathfryland).

1 m. ESE. is Ballymaghery motte-and-bailey (Nat. Mon.) with three concentric ditches.

3 m. SW. is Carmeen Hill (*see* Crown Bridge *under* Newry).

HOLLYWOOD, Co. Wicklow (Map 6, C4), is a village E. of the Ballymore Eustace ($12\frac{3}{4}$ m.) –Baltinglass (4 m.) road. Its name recalls a holy wood which figures in the *Life* of St Kevin of Glendalough (*q.v.*), whose first hermitage was hereabouts. The hermitage is commemorated by St Kevin's Bed SSW. of the Protestant church. (Nearby formerly were St Kevin's Chair, St Kevin's Cave, and St Kevin's Well. They are still remembered in local tradition.) The Protestant church has a 17th cent. vaulted stone roof. On a rock W. of the church is a motte site.

$1\frac{3}{4}$ m. NNE. is Poll an Phúca (*see under* Blessington).

$1\frac{1}{4}$ m. NNE., $\frac{3}{4}$ m. beyond Horsepass bridge at "Killerk Graveyard" (an oval mound), is the Bishop's Grave, marked by a broken granite cross with a cross in a circle inscribed on the E. face.

A good road leads S. and SE. from Hollywood up the valley of the King's River to the Wicklow Gap, and thence down Glendasan to Glendalough. In places this road follows the ancient pilgrims' road (St Kevin's Road) from populous W. Wicklow across the mountain wilderness to St Kevin's famous sanctuary. The moorland scenery is very fine.

$3\frac{1}{2}$ m. SE. is Lockstown Upper road junction. The "Hollywood Stone", a labyrinth boulder in the National Museum, came from an old roadway a short distance N. 5 m. ESE. of the junction are the remnants of Tampleteenawn, an ancient nave-and-chancel church. $2\frac{1}{2}$ m. WNW. of the church, at Wooden Cross on the top (1,200 ft) of Togher ridge, is a roadside cross-inscribed boulder. 1 m. WSW. of this, beside an old road in Granabeg Upper, is an early cross-pillar. Boulder, cross-pillar, and the "Hollywood Stone" were probably route markers on an ancient pilgrims' way from Hollywood to Tampleteenawn and so to Glendalough. $2\frac{1}{2}$ m. SE. of Tampleteenawn, in a lonely wilderness delightful in clear weather, is the summit of the Wicklow Gap (1,469 ft). To the N. rises Tonlegee (2,684 ft), easily climbed and offering magnificent panoramas. SW. and S. rise Table Mt (2,302 ft) and Camaderry (2,296 ft). In a corrie beneath Camaderry is Lough Nahanagan (1,382 ft). Between the lough and the modern road the overgrown course of granite-paved St Kevin's Road is visible. From the Gap the road leads quickly down Glendasan, with its tumbling stream and abandoned lead workings, to Glendalough (*q.v.*) and Laragh (*q.v.*). Between road and stream St Kevin's Road is discernible in places.

From Hollywood two roads lead S. through Hollywood Glen ($1\frac{1}{2}$ m.), an Ice Age "overflow valley" 3 m. long and 150 ft deep. At the head of the Glen, $1\frac{1}{2}$ m. S. of Hollywood via the E. road (old road) to Donard, are remains of St Kevin's Church, Dunboyke, a primitive nave-and-chancel structure. In the nave is an early gravestone; near the SE. angle of the chancel is another. $\frac{1}{2}$ m. SW. of the church, close to the Baltinglass road in Athgreany, are the Piper's Stones (Nat. Mon.), a circle of fourteen granite boulders with an outlier (the Piper). Forty-one yds NE. (twenty-one yds NW. of the Piper) are two smaller stones. Some of the stones have grooves and/or cup marks. Legend has it that circle and outlier are a piper and dancers petrified for violating the Sabbath (*see* Kilgowan *under* Kilcullen, Co. Kildare).

$3\frac{1}{2}$ m. S., on the E. side of the Glen, is Slieve Gad, or Church Mt (1,789 ft). On the summit, which affords extensive views, are the shapeless remains of a dry-stone ringfort or a cairn; also a few moulded stones of a church traditionally associated with St Kevin.

$4\frac{1}{2}$ m. S., via the same road, is Kilbaylet Upper (*see under* Donard).

$1\frac{1}{2}$ m. SW., near the road at the E. boundary of Kinsellastown, is Crithanacauytheen, a low, oval mound.

3 m. SW., in Lemonstown, is the Moat (Nat. Mon.), a Bronze Age tumulus enclosed by a ditch and bank; a Food Vessel was found in it.

HOLYWOOD, Co. Down (Map 3, D4), cradle of Irish golf, is a holiday resort and dormitory suburb on the E. shore of Belfast Lough, $5\frac{1}{2}$ m. NE. of Belfast and $6\frac{1}{2}$ m. WSW. of Bangor.

St Laisrén founded a monastery here in the 7th cent.

In High St is Ireland's only permanent maypole. The Unitarian (First Presbyterian) Church, High St (1849), is a good Classical building. Across the street is ***Johnny the Jig***, bronze of a small boy playing an accordeon; it is by Rosamund Praeger (1867–1954), "who loved children and delighted in their ways".

Near the junction of High St and Bangor Rd the patchwork remains of a small church of various dates (good tombstone with foliate cross and shears) mark the site of a friary of Franciscan Tertiaries destroyed by Sir Thomas O Neill of Clannaboy in 1572 to prevent its becoming an English strongpoint. Nearby to the S., and close to Brook St Telephone Exchange, is a Norman motte. A short distance away, on Bangor Rd, is lovely little Ballymenoch Park with splendid trees.

St Columkille's Church, Belfast Rd, erected 1872–74, is by T. Hevey.

2 m. NE. is Cultra Manor, where the excellent 200-acre Ulster Folk Museum was inaugurated in 1964.

HORSELEAP, Co. Westmeath (Map 5, E1), is a hamlet on the Kilbeggan (5 m.)–Moate (6 m.) road.

½ m. N. are the remains of the motte-and-bailey castle of Ardnurcher, erected by Hugh de Lacy in 1192. They consist of a double trench cutting off the end of an esker, and of a flat, rectangular motte with a small, raised bailey to one side. The castle was burned by Felim O Conor of Connacht in 1234. A modern legend derives the name Horseleap from Hugh de Lacy's horse, on which he is said to have jumped across the fosse on to the motte when pursued by the Mageoghegans.

2 m. E. is the Mageoghegan castle of Donore. In 1650, towards the close of the Cromwellian war, James, son of Niall Mageoghegan, held it for Connla Mageoghegan against Commissary-General John Reynolds. The castle was taken and James, together with forty or fifty men, women, and children, put to the sword.

There are some fine houses in the area, notably Rosemount (1773) at the SW. foot of Knockastia (*see under* Moate).

HOSPITAL, Co. Limerick (Map 5, C4), a village on the Limerick (17 m.)–Mitchelstown (16 m.) road, takes its name from the Ainy (*see* Knockainy, *below*) Preceptory of the Knights Hospitaller of St John of Jerusalem, founded before 1215 by the English Justiciar, Geoffrey de Marisco, then lord of the manor of Ainy (Anya). After Kilmainham (Dublin, South-West), this was the most important house of the Hospitallers in Ireland. Remains of the "Hospital Church" (Nat. Mon.) survive. In it are remnants of three interesting tombs: a de Marisco tomb of 1260, with high-relief effigy of a mailed knight; a much battered de Marisco tomb of the later 13th cent., with effigies of a mailed knight and his lady; a 14th cent. slab with the effigy, in very low relief, of a mailed knight. These, like all such monuments, were originally painted in bright colours.

1½ m. NNW., in Ballynamona is an embanked stone circle cut by a roadway.

3 m. NE., commanding a noble view, is Cromwell (properly Cromaill) Hill (586 ft). Here are Dermot and Grania's Bed, Suidhe Finn, Suidheachán na Féinne, a stone ringfort, a small earthen ringfort (Cromwell's Fort), and other remains. Dermot and Grania's Bed is a ruinous wedge-shaped gallery grave on the W. spur. Suidhe Finn (Fionn's Seat) is a small, stone-kerbed tumulus on the summit. Suidheachán na Féinne (Seat of the Fiana), on the E. slope, is a large, oval, enfossed and terraced mound with a causeway on the S.; E. of the centre is a smaller mound. The stone ringfort is

on the S. slope. The S. spur of the hill was called Caisleán Chruim Dhuibh, Crom Dubh's Castle (Crom Dubh was an ancient harvest deity). In the glen below is the cave, Dermot and Grania's Bed; another cave is the Fairy Piper's Cave.

3 m. S. is Knocklong; S. of the village are remnants of a 16th cent. O Hurley castle and a hillside cairn. – 2 m. SE. is Scarteen, headquarters of the well-known Scarteen Foxhounds, the original "Black and Tans" whose name suggested the nickname of a notorious British force employed in Ireland, 1920–21.

1½ m. W., at the SE. foot of Cnoc Áine, the 537-ft hill from which it takes its name, is Knockainy village. In Irish mythology Cnoc Áine is the Otherworld seat of the sun-goddess, Áine (*see also* Lissan *under* Cookstown *and* Ania's Cove *under* Augher; cf. Pallas Green, *also* Tuamgraney *under* Scarriff). Down to 1879 men used to bring flaming *cliara* (bunches of hay and stray on poles) to the summit, there make a *deiseal* circuit of Mullach an Triúir (*below*), and then visit village, fields, and herds to bring them good luck. Formerly also a great fair (Aonach Áine) was held here at the beginning of harvest. (Later legend makes Áine one of the *mná sidhe* who bewail the deaths of the Desmond Fitzgeralds.) On the summit of the hill is damaged Áine's Cairn; to the W. is Mullach an Triúir, three small, conjoined ring-barrows; N. of these are remains of a circular enclosure with a small central cairn.

HOWTH, Co. Dublin (Map 6, E7), is a fishing port and popular suburban resort on the N. side of Howth Head, 9½ m. NE. of Dublin. The name (Norse *höfuth*, head) is properly that of the great hilly promontory (Irish *Beann Eadair*; 563 ft), well known for its cliff and moorland scenery and its prospects of the coast from the Mourne Mountains in the NE. to the Wicklow Mountains in the S.

The Protestant parish church has a two-light window (*St Peter; The Calling of St Andrew*) by Evie Hone (1943) and a three-light *Faith, Hope, and Charity* by Sarah Purser (1905).

Howth Harbour was built at the beginning of the 19th cent. for the Holyhead–Dublin packet-boat service, but speedily silted up and was replaced by Dún Laoghaire. George IV landed there in 1821. On 26 July 1914, the harbour was the scene of the Howth Gunrunning, when the Irish Volunteers, emulating the Ulster opponents of Home Rule (*see* Larne), landed 900 rifles from Erskine Childers' yacht, *Asgard* (*see also* Kilcoole, *under* Delgany).

Overlooking the harbour are the ruins (Nat. Mon.) of the collegiate parish church of the Blessed Virgin Mary ("St Mary's Abbey"). The first church on the site is said to have been erected by Sigtryggr (Sitric), king of Norse Dublin, as early as 1042. A parish church was certainly built here in 1235 (*see* Ireland's Eye, *below*). The twin-aisled remains, however, are for the most part those of a 14th cent. building with 15th/16th cent. modifications and additions. In the 15th cent. the E. part of the S. aisle was remodelled by the St Lawrences (*see* Howth Castle, *below*) to serve as a family chantry. In it stands the tomb of Sir Christopher St Lawrence, 13th Baron of Howth (d. 1462), and his wife, Anna Plunket of Ratoath. The knight's effigy is armoured in the fashion of the contemporary Dublin school of monumental stone-carvers. The ends of the tomb are divided into panels with figures of *The Crucifixion, Angels with Censers, St Peter, St Catherine, St Patrick*, and *St Brigid*. Beneath the tomb is the entrance to the St Lawrence burial crypt. S. of the church are the ruins of the 15th/16th cent. college, or residence of the community of priests attached to the church. The bells of the church are preserved at Howth Castle (*below*).

A short distance W. of the harbour is the gateway to Howth Castle and Demesne. The great castle has been the seat of the St Lawrence family since the 16th cent., but the first St Lawrence, Almeric I, had settled at Howth 400 years earlier, when he was granted the manor by Henry II. His motte-castle stood on the site of the martello tower at the head of the E. pier. The present castle dates from 1564. It was rebuilt in 1738, modernized and enlarged in the first half of the 19th cent. to the designs of Sir Richard and Vitruvius Morrison, and again in the 20th cent., when the architect was Sir Edwin Lutyens. The 16th cent. castle is represented by the keep (at the SW. corner of the existing complex) and by the disused NE. gate-tower. The male line of the St Lawrence family became extinct in 1909 on the death of William, 4th Earl and 30th Baron of Howth, and the estates passed to his nephew, Julian Gaisford. Legend associates the castle and the St Lawrences with the celebrated Gráinne Ní Mháille (*see* Clare Island, *and* Rockfleet *under* Newport, Co. Mayo). The sea-queen is said to have found the castle gate closed one day at dinner time. In revenge she carried off the young heir to Rockfleet, and released him only on the promise that Howth Castle would never again be closed against the hungry traveller. To this day a place is always set at the St Lawrence table in readiness for the unexpected guest. The demesne and gardens are justly renowned for their beauty, particularly when the rhododendrons and azaleas are in bloom. (Only the gardens are open to the public: 22 April to 17 Aug., 2.30–6.30 p.m.; a small charge for admission.) – ½ m. SW. of the castle, at the foot of Carrigmor, alias Muck Rock, is Finn Mac Cool's Quoits, alias Aideen's Grave, a prehistoric chamber tomb.

¾ m. E. of the harbour are Puck's Rocks, where St Nessan struggled with the Devil.

The hill to the S. of the town is traversed by a network of roadways and footpaths which afford a variety of easy beautiful walks.

2 m. SSE. of the harbour is the Bailey lighthouse (1814). It occupies the site of the innermost citadel of a great promontory fort whose wards, the Great Bailey and the Little Bailey, were defended by ramparts and ditches across the necks of the promontory. The view from the slopes above is exceptionally beautiful, especially towards sunset. The cliff scenery to the W. is particularly fine.

1 m. W. of the harbour and ½ m. E. of Sutton crossroads is Corr Castle (Nat. Mon.), a small, granite tower. ½ m. NW. of Sutton crossroads and on the W. side of the Baldoyle road is the Knock of Howth, a small tumulus. 1¼ m. SE. of Sutton crossroads is St Fintan's Church (Nat. Mon.), a tiny structure incorporating remains of at least two periods, early and medieval. It seems to have been repaired in the 19th cent. Traces of an enclosing vallum are discernible. 300 yds SE. is St Fintan's Well. Further SE., near the summit (550 ft) of Shelmartin, is a much rebuilt burial cairn. On Dung Hill (554 ft), to the NE., is a small, rebuilt cairn with traces of a dry-wall revetment. 800 yds SSE. is Cross Cairn, alias St Patrick's Cross, a small heap of stones. The views hereabouts are very fine.

1¼ m. N. of the harbour is Ireland's Eye, a rocky islet with an excellent little beach. Towards the E. side of the island is St Nessan's Church, more correctly Kilmacnessan (Church of Nessan's Sons), sole remnant of a monastery founded in the 6th/7th cent. by the brothers Diuchaill, Mo-Nissu, and Neslug, whose festival falls on 15 March. About 702 the island was pillaged by Welsh marauders. Towards the close of the following cent. the Vikings made an encampment there, which was besieged by Irish forces in 897. In 960 a Viking fleet plundered the island. After the Anglo-Norman invasion the church was reduced to parochial status, and was replaced in 1235 by the more convenient one at Howth. The remains of the church have been excessively restored. It was a small nave-and-chancel structure which had a Round Tower rising from the chancel vault (cf. St Kevin's Church and Trinity Church, Glendalough). The original W. gable and doorway were removed early in the 19th cent. by the builders of a Catholic chapel in Howth. The only other relic of the ancient monastery is the *Garland of Howth*, an 8th–9th cent. illuminated gospel-book now in Trinity College, Dublin.

INCHIGEELAGH, Co. Cork (Map 4, E5), is a village on the N. shore of Lough Allua, a beautiful expansion of the Lee, 10 m. SW. of Macroom and 24 m. NE. of Bantry. A favourite resort of painters, it is a convenient base for exploring the Sheehy Mountains to the SW. (Akinkeen, 2,280 ft; Conigar, 1,886 ft).

1½ m. E., on the S. side of the Lee, are the ruins of the O Leary castle of Carrignacurra (Castle Masters).

3¾ m. SSE., in Carrigdangan, is Bealick, alias Tuama-na-vranna, alias Bórd an Rí, alias Na Leaca Cruacha, a wedge-shaped gallery grave.

4 m. SSW., to the W. of the road in Lacka-

baun, are Mearogafin, standing stones which give their name to Mearogafin Mt. 2 m. SE., on the slope of Carrigarierk in Clogher, is Labbadermot, a chamber tomb. 1¼ m. SE. of the latter, in Farranahineeny, is five-stone alignment (Nat. Mon.).

5½ m. SW. via the old Bantry road, in Cornery, is a group of standing stones. ½ m. NW. of this, in Carrignamuck, close to Carrignamuck Lough, is Giants Grave, a chamber tomb; 150 yds ENE. is a second; ¾ m. W., in Derrynagree, is a four-stone alignment. – ½ m. SW. of the Cornery standing stones is Lackanargid ("flagstone of the silver"). 300 yds W. of this, in Cloghboola, is a third Giants Grave. ½ m. SW. of the latter is Cromlech, another tomb. 1 m. WNW. of this last, on the slope of Douce Mt, in Derryriordane South, is Bórd an Rí ("the king's table"), a chamber tomb; 1 m. NE. is Kealvaughmore ogham stone (*below*).

5½ m. W. is Ballingeary, formerly a noted resort of students of Irish. 2½ m. NW., in Bawnatemple, is a 19-ft-9-in. pillarstone, the tallest in Ireland – 1½ m. NW., to the N. of the Gougane Barra road in Keamcorravooly, is a chamber tomb (wrecked); 200 yds N. is Uaigh an Fhathaigh ("the giant's grave"), a wedge-shaped gallery grave. – 2½ m. WNW., in Derreenlunnig, is Stockanscrahin, a pillarstone. – 2¼ m. WSW., to the N. of the Gougane Barra road in Gortafludig, is Tuama an Mhinistre, a wedge-shaped gallery grave (ruined); nearer to Gougane Barra lake are three standing stones. –1½m. S., on Kealvaughmore hill, is an ogham stone. – 2½ m. S. (1 m. SW. of the preceding), in Derryvacorneen, is Bórd an Rí, a wedge-shaped gallery grave (ruined). – 3¼ m. SW. is the precipitous, romantic defile of Keamaneigh, where the Macroom–Bantry road pierces the Shehy Mountains between Foilastookeen (1,693 ft) and Doughill Mt (1,553 ft). 2¼ m. S. of the pass (to the W. of the road in Cappaboy Beg) are a stone circle and – to the W. and SW. – several standing stones.

4½ m. WSW. of Ballingeary (1¼ m. NW. of Keamaneigh), under the frowning cirques of Bealick (1,764 ft), Conigar (1,886 ft) and Foilastookeen (1,698 ft), is romantic Gougane Barra, where St Finbar of Cork had an island hermitage (pilgrimage, 25 Sept.). The memorial church is by Samuel F. Hynes. The beautiful forest park was opened in 1966.

INISHCRONE, Co. Sligo (Map 1, D3), is a small seaside resort with a good beach on the E. shore of Killala Bay, 10 m. N. of Ballina. Both Ballina (*q.v.*) and Easky (*q.v.*) are within convenient reach of the trout and salmon angler.

¼ m. NE. are the ruins of a 17th cent. Plantation castle. Between the castle and the shore are the remnants of a prehistoric chamber tomb.

2¾ m. N. is Lacken, alias Lecan (Leacán Mhic Fhirbhisigh). Scarcely a stone remains of the castle erected in 1560 by the Mac Fhirbhisigh (Ma Cribhsigh) family which supplied hereditary poets and historiographers to the O Dowds of Tireragh from the 14th to the 17th cent. The head of the family conducted a school of historical lore at Lacken, and also filled a leading role at the inauguration of each O Dowd. Three celebrated codices were compiled by, or under the direction of, members of this family (two of them taking their names from the place), the *Great Book of Lecan*, the *Yellow Book of Lecan*, and An Dubhaltach Óg Mac Fhirbhisigh's *Book of the Genealogies of Ireland*. The first-named was compiled about 1416–18 under the direction of Giolla-Íosa Mór Mac Fhirbhisigh, and is now in the Royal Irish Academy; the second was compiled about 1391 by Giolla-Íosa (son of Donnchadh Mór) Mac Fhirbhisigh, and is now in Trinity College, Dublin. The third was compiled at various places over many years by An Dubhaltach Óg (1585–1671), who was murdered at Doonflin, near Skreen, by the English planter, Thomas Crofton. It is now in the library of University College, Dublin.

1½ m. S., in Muckduff, is the Grave of the Black Pig, a tumulus.

1¾ m. SSW., not far from the sea in Scurmore, is Cruckancornia, a tumulus on whose NE. side are seven pillarstones known as the Children of the Mermaid. One of the O Dowds possessed himself of a mermaid's mantle, and thereby changed her into a woman. They wed and had seven children. The wife recovered her mantle and was able to resume her true nature. She changed the children into the pillarstones and returned to the sea. There was an Augustinian friary in Scurmore, founded in 1454 by Tadhg O Dowd.

INISHMURRAY, Co. Sligo (Map 2, A4), a small, recently abandoned island, lies 4 m. off the mainland. It is approached from Streedagh (*see under* Grange) or from Rosses Point (*q.v.*).

The island (named after St Muireadhach of Killala?) is famous for its relics of the early monastic age. The monastery was founded by St Laisrén, alias Mo-Laisse, son of Déaglán, who seems to have been trained at Candida Casa in Galloway. Next to nothing is known of the history of the place, which vanishes from Irish records after a Viking raid of 807.

The monastery remains (Nat. Mon.) comprise a massive dry-stone rampart pierced by four openings, the main gateway facing NE. (The S. entrance is the creation of the Office of Public Works' "restorers", 1880.) Beside the main entrance is a pilgrims' "altar" with a cross-pillar from Teampall Mo-Laisse cemetery (*below*). In the thickness of the rampart are several chambers. (The niches in the inner face are the creation of the "restorers", who wantonly transferred several early gravestones to them.) Flights of steps give access to the parapet.

The pear-shaped enclosure is subdivided into four parts; the dividing walls have traces of chambers.

In the N. sub-enclosure is Tráthán an Charghais (the Lenten Praying Place), a sub-rectangular clochán.

In the largest sub-enclosure is Teach Mo-Laisse ("Mo-Laisse's House") a diminutive oratory with trabeate W. doorway and stone roof (reconstructed); a century ago it served the islanders as their Sunday church, and was therefore sometimes called An Séipéal, "the Chapel". By the S. wall runs Leaba an Naoimh ("The Saint's Bed"), a stone bench. On the altar are fragments of early gravestones, one of them inscribed OR[ŌIT] DO MUREDACH HÚ CHOMOCÁIN HIC DORMIT ("A prayer for Muredach Úa Comocáin. He sleeps here"). Another stone in the oratory is inscribed OR[ŌIT] DO MURCHAD ("A prayer for Murchad"). A third reads CRUX CRUX . . . Outside the door is an early cross-slab; to the SE. is a second. Towards the centre of the sub-enclosure is Teampall Mo-Laisse, "Mo-Laisse's Church", alias Teampall na bhFear, "the Men's Church", seemingly the monastic church proper; in recent times only men were buried here. In the cemetery are a bullaun and eight early cross-slabs or gravestones, one of them inscribed OR[ŌIT] DO COINMURSCE ("A prayer for Cú-Mhursce"). S. of the church is a perforate cross-pillar; expectant mothers used to place their fingers in the holes in the N. and S. faces and their thumbs in those in the E. face, and so raise themselves from their knees. Beside this is a plain pillarstone. E. of the church is a platform of dry masonry, SW. of the church, on the larger of two "altars", are the celebrated Clocha Breaca (" Speckled Stones "). The Clocha Breaca, five in number, have inscribed cross-patterns and other devices. They were used to bring down maledictions on one's enemies. (An Englishwoman is said to have journeyed to Inishmurray to "turn" them against Hitler.) Facing the S. entrance is Altóir Bheag ("Small Altar"), with a fine cross-pillar and several plain pebbles.

In the W. sub-enclosure are: Túr Uí Bhréan-aill, "O Brenall's Tower", alias the Schoolhouse, a clochán which served for a time as the islanders' school; and Teach (alias Teampall) na Teine "the Fire House", a small medieval building. The lintel of the Teach na Teine door-way is inscribed with a cross of much earlier date. A stone hearth in the floor, traditionally the site of a perpetual fire, was broken up by the Board of Works restorers.

Outside the cashel, on the N., is Teach an Aluis, "the Sweat House", a rectangular, corbel-roofed bath house.

SE. of the monastery are Teampall Mhuire, "St Mary's Church", alias Teampall na mBan, "the Women's Church", and Reilig na mBan, "the Women's Cemetery". There is a bullaun here; also two early gravestones, one of them inscribed [ORŌIT AR] ——AILAD OCUS AR MAEL BR[IGTE ?] Ó RÓRC OCUS AR ÉILEISE ("A prayer for . . . ailad and for Mael-Brigte (?) Ó Ruairc and for Éileise").

Nearby is a perforate cross-pillar greatly venerated by women.

Spaced out round the shore of the island is a series of *leachtaí* ("memorials") and *tráthái* ("praying stations"), usually having cross-slabs or cross-pillars at which pilgrims performed traditional exercises. The exercises usually began at Teach Mo-Laisse, whence the pilgrim proceeded *deiseal* around the island to the following: (*a*) Ula Mhuire ("St Mary's Station"), at the head of Clashymore Harbour. (*b*) ¼ m. W. of the harbour: Tráthán na Ríghfhear (?), "Station of the Royal Men" (?), with remains of a clochán. A short distance N. is "weird and awful" Poll na Sean-Tuinne, "Cavern of the Old Wave". (*c*) 600 yds NE. of this: Crois Mhór, a magnificently sited *leachta*. (*d*) 600 yds E. of the third station: Tráthán Aodha, "Aodh's Station". Nearby are an altar and Leachta na Sagart, "Memorial of the Priests", a few bleached stones. N. of Tráthán Aodha is Tobar na Cabhrach, "Well of Assistance", which Mo-Laisse may have blessed. Attached to the corbel-roofed well-house is an open-air " bath". Stormy seas may be stilled by draining the well into the ocean and reciting certain prayers. 300 yds E. is a nameless "altar". (*e*) 500 yds SE. of this, at Rú, the easternmost point of the island: Leachta Phádraig, "Patrick's Memorial", with a beautiful view of the mainland. (*f*) ¼ m. WSW. of Rú: An Trínóid Mhór, "The Great Trinity"; the cross-pillars here and at the next *leachta* are among the most interesting on the island. (*g*) Nearby, to the SW.: An Trínóid Bheag, "The Little Trinity". (*h*) Nearby, close to Teampall Mhuire: Tráthán Mhuire, "St Mary's Station", with an early cross-pillar. (*i*) W. of Teampall Mhuire: Leachta Cholaim-chille, "Columcille's Memorial"; the cross-slab here has three crosses on one face and a single cross on the other. (*j*) SE. of the last: Cros an Teampaill, "Church Cross". (*k*) 150 yds W.: Reilig Odhráin, "Odhrán's Cemetery". There are two early crosses on the "altar" here, and in the cemetery is a cross-pillar having five crosses on one face.

INISHTURK, Co. Mayo (Map 1, B4), is a beautiful, rarely visited island 8 m. SW. of Roonah Quay (*see under* Louisburgh) and 10 m. NNW. of Cleggan. There is a lovely little harbour with a beach at Portadoon, on the S. coast.

INISTIOGE, Co. Kilkenny (Map 6, B6), is an attractive village in a beautiful setting where the Kilkenny (16 m.)–New Ross (10 m.) road crosses the Nore by a fine 18th cent. bridge of ten arches. It is a convenient centre for exploring the beauties of the Nore and Barrow valleys. The road NE. to Graiguenamanagh (6 m.) crosses the saddle between Coppanagh (1,202 ft) and Brandon Hill (1,694 ft) and affords delightful views. On the summit of Brandon Hill are a prehistoric cairn and a stone circle; the views are very beautiful.

In 962 the king of Ossory routed the Norse of Dublin, under Olaf, son of Sigtryggr, at Inistioge. About 1206–10 Thomas fitz Anthony, Anglo-Norman seneschal of Leinster, founded the Priory of SS Mary and Columba (Columcille) for Canons Regular of St Augustine. Around the priory a small town grew up. At the Dissolution the priory and its possessions were granted to the Butlers, who conveyed them to Stephen Street in 1703. In 1778 they passed to the Tighes (*below*). In 1649 the town was captured by Col. Abbott's Cromwellians, who put the defenders to flight by firing the town gates.

In the tree-lined market square is a portion of a cross to the memory of David FitzGerald (d. 1621) of Brownsford (*below*) and his wife, Johanna Morres. The carvings include the symbols of the Passion and the arms of Fitz-Gerald of Brownsford impaled with those of Morris.

The Protestant parish church occupies the site of the chancel of the medieval priory church, whose 15th cent. central tower it incorporates. In its original form the church was a Transitional building with short, aisleless nave. The central tower, Lady Chapel, and N. transept with tower, were added at various dates. The Lady Chapel served as the Protestant church until 1824; in its ruins are two 16th cent. tombstones. The N. tower ("Black Castle"), square below and octagonal above, was converted (1874) into a Tighe mausoleum; it contains an effigy by Flaxman of Mrs Mary Tighe (1772–1810), daughter of the Rev. William Blatchford of Rosanna and author of *Psyche*. In the ruined nave is a tombstone with the effigy of one of the medieval priors (the first, Alured?). In the Protestant church is a 12th cent. font from the medieval parish church of Kells; only one of the corners was carved originally. In the churchyard are three early-17th cent. tombstones.

On a rock over the river is the motte-and-bailey of a castle erected by Thomas fitz Anthony.

S. of the village, at the foot of Mt Alto (919 ft), is the demesne of Woodstock (formerly Kilclondowne), now a State forest. Woodstock House was the most magnificent 18th cent. house in Co. Kilkenny. It was built about 1735 to the design of Francis Bindon for Sir William Fownes, ancestor of the Woodstock Tighes, and remained the seat of the Tighes until 1922, when, together with its splendid library, it fell victim to the Civil War.

2½ m. SE., on the E. side of the Nore in Clo(o)namery, alias Cloone, are remains of an ancient ecclesiastical foundation dedicated to St Bronndán (Broondawn): a 12th (?) cent. nave-and-chancel church (Nat. Mon.), an early cross-pillar, a granite basin, and, W. of the churchyard, the foundations of two beehive huts. The church still has its W. *antae* and lintelled and architraved W. doorway with a cross in relief on the lintel. The chancel is an addition; its Romanesque E. window may have come from the original E. gable of the nave. Between the church and the river are the remains of a castle; the motte is a relic of the castle erected by Milo, son of Bishop David of St David's, Pembrokeshire; the later stone castle belonged to the FitzGeralds.

3 m. SSE., on the W. side of the Nore, is the tower of the FitzGerald castle of Brownsford.

5 m. SSE., in Glenballyvalley, is the early church site of Teampall an Chillín. There is an early cross-slab here.

5½ m. SSE. is Ballyneale (*see under* New Ross).

4½ m. S. are the remains of Mullennakill church. 1 m. NW., on Coolnahau Hill, is Tigh Mo-Ling, alias St Mo-Ling's Cave (*lit.* house), a rock-shelter where the saint is said to have lived before settling at St Mullins (*q.v.*; *see* Listerlin, *below*). ¾ m. SE. of the cave, in Mullennakill, are: Tobar Chrann Mo-Ling (Well of Mo-Ling's Tree), alias St Mullin's Well; Crann Mo-Ling (Mo-Ling's Tree); the Altóir (a rough stone bench); and the Iomar (an ancient font from Mullennakill church). A "pattern" is held here on 20 Aug. or the Sun. following. – 3 m. SSE. of Mullennakill church, in Listerlin, is the hill-top motte of a castle erected by Milo, son of Bishop David of St David's. The nearby Protestant church occupies the site of medieval St David's Church. A few hundred yds S. is Tobar Naoimh Mo-Ling, St Mo-Ling's Well, where the saint is said to have lived before removing to the cave near Coolnahau; there are three venerated stones here, one of them a bullaun. The neighbourhood is rich in ringforts.

INNFIELD, alias **ENFIELD**, Co. Meath (Map 6, C2), is a village on the Dublin (27 m.)–Mullingar (24 m.) road. For some reason which was probably unknown even to itself, the old Midland Great Western Railway Company named its station here "Enfield".

1¾ m. E., in Cloncurry, Co. Kildare, are a tree-crowned motte and remains of a medieval church. Cornelius, Bishop of Kildare, was buried here in 1223. In the churchyard is the grave of Teresa Brayton (1868–1943), author of the popular song, "The old bog road". She was a native of Cloncurry. In 1347 John Roche founded a Carmelite friary in Cloncurry; not a trace survives.

2½ m. S., via Johnstown and Fear English Bridge, in Dunfierth churchyard, Co. Kildare, built into a Hamilton vault, are fragments of the altar-tomb of Sir William Bermingham, 1st Baron Carbury (*see* Carbury Hill *under* Edenderry), who died in 1548. They include the effigy of Sir William in "white" armour.

IRVINESTOWN, Co. Fermanagh (Map 2, D4), is a small town on the Enniskillen (9½ m.)–Strabane (32 m.) road.

2¾ m. N. is Keeran Giants Grave (Nat. Mon.), a wedge-shaped gallery grave.

4 m. W. is Castle Archdale, a fine Georgian house of 1773. Requisitioned by Coastal Command, R.A.F., in the Second World War, it has

been derelict since 1959, but is to be converted into a hotel. In the demesne are fragments (Nat. Mon.) of a Plantation bawn built in 1615 by John Archdale of Darsham, Suffolk, who obtained confiscated lands here. It was destroyed in 1641 by Capt. Rory Maguire, who butchered the Archdale children, but was rebuilt and re-occupied until its final destruction in 1689. In Castle Archdale Bay are White Island and Davy's Island (*see* Lough Erne).

$3\frac{1}{2}$ m. NNW., in Kiltierney Deerpark, are cairns and a stone circle (Nat. Mons.). The former comprise a central cairn and twenty-two smaller surrounding cairns. On the central cairn are six large stones, two bearing Bronze Age scribings. The circle (incomplete) stands on a raised platform; one of the eight stones is isolated from the rest and contains a bullaun. Also in Kiltierney Deerpark are traces of "Abbey", a grange which belonged to the abbey of Assaroe (*see under* Ballyshannon). Near by is a cross-inscribed slab.

$4\frac{1}{2}$ m. SE., at the ancient church site of Kilskeery, Co. Tyrone, are two stone crosses.

ISLAND MAGEE, Co. Antrim (Map 3, D3–4), is a peninsula forming the S. and E. sides of Larne (2 m.) Lough, and is reached from Belfast ($22\frac{3}{4}$ m.) via Whitehead.

On 8 Jan. 1642, the garrison of Carrickfergus butchered the Catholic inhabitants as a reprisal for a falsely rumoured massacre of Protestant Planters. The victims are said to have been hurled over the tall Gobbins Cliffs (240 ft) on the E. side of the peninsula. These cliffs, noted for the seabirds which breed there, are accessible by footpaths.

At the N. end of the peninsula, in the garden of a house in Ballylumford, $\frac{3}{4}$ m. SSW. of Brown's Bay, is Druid's Altar, alias Ballylumford Dolmen, a small, single-chamber, prehistoric tomb (Nat. Mon.). Brown's Bay is a good sandy cove.

JULIANSTOWN, Co. Meath (Map 6, D2), is a village on the Drogheda (4 m.)–Balbriggan (6 m.) road. The Protestant church has a War Memorial window (1918) by Michael Healy.

$1\frac{3}{4}$ m. SE., in Sarsfieldstown, are fragments of a 15th cent. cross commemorating Sir Christopher Barnwall, 2nd Baron Trimleston, and his wife, Elizabeth Plunket. Near the old Keenogue chapel site is a fragment of another cross: *Crucifixion, Virgin and Child, St Laurence*, etc.

$1\frac{1}{2}$ m. WSW. is Dardistown Castle, an 18th cent. house built on to the remains of a 16th cent. castle. 2 m. WNW., on the N. side of the Boyne, is Kilsharvan (*see under* Duleek).

KANTURK, Co. Cork (Map 5, B5), is a small market town on the Mallow (13 m.)–Newmarket (6 m.) road, at the confluence of the Dalua and Allow rivers. The rivers figure in Spenser's *Faerie Queene* (*see* Doneraile). The Gothic Revival parish church, convent, and schools (1860–65) are by John Hurley of Cork.

1 m. S., in Paal East, are the ruins (Nat. Mon.) of Mac Donagh's (i.e. Mac Donagh Mac Carthy's) Court, alias Kanturk Castle, a large fortified house of about 1609. (The Mac Donagh Mac Carthys were lords of Duhallow.) The walls stop short at the corbels intended to bear the parapets; presumably they would have been crowned by many gables. Jealous English settlers complained to the Privy Council that the house was "much too large for a subject", and the Council forbade the completion of the work. The enraged Mac Carthy is said to have thrown away the glass tiles he had had made for the roof.

$5\frac{3}{4}$ m. NE. are the ruins of Castle Cor (Barrys).

4 m. E. is Knocknanuss (448 ft), where, 13 Nov. 1647, Murrough O Brien "of the Burnings", Earl of Inchiquin and, at that stage of his career, Parliamentarian Lord President of Munster, destroyed Lord Taafe's Confederate Catholic army. One of Taafe's wings, the Mac Donnells of Antrim, swept all before it, only to become involved in the general rout, surrounded, and cut to pieces. Among the fallen was the gallant Alasdar Colkitto Mac Donnell, the comrade of Montrose.

5 m. ESE. are the ruins of Castle Magner. In 1649 Richard Magner went to Clonmel to pay court to the conquering Cromwell. Cromwell gave him a letter for Col. Phaire, governor of Cork. The letter contained instructions to execute the bearer. Magner, however, read the letter and passed it on to his enemy, the Cromwellian governor of Mallow, who, ignorant of the contents, conveyed it to Phaire, with the hoped-for result. $2\frac{3}{4}$ m. ESE. is Lohort Castle (*below*).

6 m. ESE. is Cecilstown village. $3\frac{1}{4}$ m. NE. is Kilmaclenine (*see under* Buttevant) – $1\frac{1}{2}$ m. ESE., in Ballyclogh, are remains of a castle and a church; $\frac{3}{4}$ m. SE. is Rathnee, a trivallate ringfort. – $\frac{3}{4}$ m. SW. is Lohort Castle, incorporating the 15th cent. tower of a Mac Donagh Mac Carthy stronghold. The castle was reduced with artillery in May 1650 by the Cromwellian, Sir Hardress Waller. In 1750 the tower was repaired by the Earl of Egmont, and was continuously occupied thereafter. In 1876 it was refurbished once more.

$5\frac{3}{4}$ m. SW., in Dromagh, are remains of an O Keefe castle and of a medieval parish church. 3 m. WNW. of the castle, in Drominagh South, is Keel Aodh, alias Drominagh Fort, a very large (but defaced), univallate ring-enclosure containing a long, sub-rectangular sub-enclosure. Near the NW. angle of the latter is a low cairn of quartz. In the SE. angle is an oval grave.

$5\frac{3}{4}$ m. NNW., in Bawnmore North, is Kilmacoo, an ancient church site at the centre of a trivallate, hill-top ringfort. The place takes its name from a St Mo-Chuda, perhaps the Mo-Chuda of Lismore.

KEADY, Co. Armagh (Map 3, B6), is a market village and angling centre (River Callan and

Aughnagurgan Lake), on the Armagh (8 m.)–Castleblayney (10 m.) road.

4½ m. ENE,, in Corran, is the Grey Stone (Nat. Mon.), a pillarstone reputed to mark the grave of the bull which is said to have driven St Patrick from his first Armagh church.

4½ m. SSE. and ½ m. E. of Tullynawood Lake, alt. 800 ft, is Dolmen, a ruinous chamber tomb (Nat. Mon.). In the next field is Giant's Grave, a ruinous chambered cairn (Nat. Mon.).

KELLS, Co. Kilkenny (Map 6, B5), is a village on the Kilkenny (8 m.)–Kilmaganny (7 m.) road, to the S. of the Owenree crossing.

About 1192 Strongbow's seneschal of Leinster, Geoffrey fitz Robert de Monte Marisco, erected a motte-and-bailey castle here and founded a town. He also founded (c. 1193) a priory (below) for Canons Regular of St Augustine from Bodmin in Cornwall; this in place of an ancient monastery founded by St Ciarán of Seir. In 1252 the town was burned by William de Bermingham; in 1316 it fell to Edward Bruce. Early in the 14th cent. the manor passed to Arnold le Poer. A sneer by the new proprietor at Maurice, 1st Earl of Desmond, for being an Irish poet, provoked a war in the course of which Kells was burned (1327) by Desmond's men and adherents (including de Berminghams). In 1346 the manor was granted to Walter de Bermingham. In the 16th cent. it passed to the Mountgarret Butlers, who held it until the Cromwellian confiscations.

Adjoining the Catholic church are the Moat (motte of Geoffrey fitz Robert's castle) and remains of the heptagonal bawn of a stone castle. There are fragmentary remains of the medieval parish church: it served as a Protestant church until about 1850.

½ m. E. of the village are the impressive ruins (Nat. Mon.) of the five-acre, fortified, Augustinian Priory of St Mary, founded by Geoffrey de Monte Marisco. They are enclosed by a wall and divided into two courts by a branch of the river and a high wall with central gateway. In the North Court are the ruins of the claustral buildings and cruciform church. The church, like that at Athassel (see under Golden) had a NW. bell tower and a NE. Lady Chapel. The nave had no S. aisle, while the N. transept had a W. aisle. In the 15th cent. a low tower was inserted over the crossing. In the N. transept is a slab with two portrait heads in high relief. There are six dwelling-towers of 15th cent. type: one (Pilib na mBonn's Castle, so called after an 18th–19th cent. recluse cobbler whose life suggested Banim's *Peter of the Castle*) at the S. side of the chancel; one (with dovecot) flanking the inner gateway; four at the curtain of the South Court, alias the Burgess, which seems never to have had buildings of stone. The fortified outer gateway of the priory was in the E. curtain.

3½ m. NNW., at Burnchurch, are the ruins (Nat. Mon.) of the 15th–16th cent. castle of the Fitzgeralds, barons of Burnchurch. Cromwell camped here in 1650. In the 18th cent. the castle

and estate passed to the Floods (below). The five-storey castle tower was occupied until 1817, and so is well preserved; it has an unusual number of passages and chambers in the walls. The great hall, which was attached to the tower, and the bawn wall – apart from the ruined NE. turret – have disappeared. The Protestant church occupies the site of medieval St Dallán's Church. (A 13th cent. font from the latter is now at Saul; see under Downpatrick.) In the churchyard are some 16th cent. tombstones, including that of . . . fitz Thomas Fitzgerald (1586), by Walter Kerin. 2 m. N., in Ballybur, is a 16th cent. castle tower with bartisans.

6 m. NNE. (via Stonyford), in Danesfort, are the ruins of the medieval parish church of St Michael. At Danesfort crossroads is a large ringfort with traces of buildings; nearby are a smaller ringfort and remains of a medieval dovecot. The whole looks like an ancient site adapted by Anglo-Norman conquerers to their purposes. 2 m. ENE., in Annamult, are remains of the early church of Béal Bárr. Some 400 yds away are the ruins of the Friars' Castle and Friars' Barn and the site of the Friars' Chapel, relics of the grange of Annamult which belonged to the Cistercians of Duiske Abbey (see under Graiguenamanagh). The monks lived at Annamult and at Loughmerans NNW. of Kilkenny before settling at Duiske.

1½ m. S. is Kilree, site of an early Brigidine monastery which is represented today by an ancient church, a Round Tower belfry, a monolithic High Cross (Nat. Mons.), and Gloonbride (below). The ruined nave-and-chancel church has *antae* and a trabeate W. doorway; it was remodelled in the Middle Ages. The Round Tower (96 ft) has lost its top storey. The High Cross (8th cent. ?) is decorated with spirals, frets, and carved bosses, and also has figure subjects. These include: E. face, arms: *Hunting Scene and Procession of Horses;* W. face: *A Figure flanked by two Horsemen;* S. arm, end of: *Jacob and the Angel; Temptation of St Anthony; SS Paul and Anthony in the Desert.* 200 yds NNE. of the church is Gloonbride (Glún Brighde, St Brigid's Knee), a stone with the "imprint of the saint's knees". 200 yds further N. is Tobar Brighde, "Brigid's Well".

3½ m. SSW., in Dunnamaggan, are remains of an ancient church. In the churchyard is an unusual High Cross with a *Crucifixion* on the W. face and a niched figure on each of the four faces. At the S. end of the churchyard is the Ráth, a diminutive circular enclosure with bank and fosse. Between the churchyard and the Catholic church is St Leonard's Well; an alabaster figure found here is now at St Kieran's College, Kilkenny. In the Catholic church is a medieval font from the ancient church.

2½ m. W., in Newtown, is the tower of a Swe(e)tman castle. To the NW. are remains of All Saints' Church; in the churchyard (Reilig Naomh an Domhain) are 16th–17th cent. Swetman tombstones, including that of John Swetman and his wife, Elenna Faning; by

Walter Kerin, 1600. In adjoining fields are
scant traces of New Town, alias Earley's Town
(Nova Villa d'Erley). The road SW. from New-
town bridge to Mallardstown cuts through a
four-acre ringfort in Rathculbin. Less than 1 m.
W. of the bridge, but to the N. of the little
King's River, are remains of Castle Eve, a
Swetman stronghold; the latest wing was
Elizabethan.

KELLS, Co. Meath (Map 6, B1), officially
Ceanannus Mór, is a market town near the
River Blackwater, on the Navan (11 m.)–
Virginia (13 m.) road.

The name Kells is an English corruption of
Anglo-Norman *Kenlis*, itself a corruption of
Irish *Ceanannus*. The place is celebrated by
reason of the important Columban monastery
which has left us such remarkable artistic
treasures as the *Book of Kells* (now in Trinity
College, Dublin), the Crozier of Kells (now in
the British Museum), and the fine High Crosses
described below. The date of the foundation of
the monastery is unknown, but in 804 "Kells
was given without battle to Columcille the
Musical". In 807, Iona having been thrice
pillaged by the Vikings (who butchered sixty-
eight of the monks in 806), Abbot Cellach
transferred the headquarters of the league of
Columban monasteries to Kells. But Kells
itself was plundered by Norsemen that very
year, and its church destroyed. The new church
was not completed until 814. Between 920 and
1019 the monastery was plundered four times
by Norsemen. In the 12th cent. the Rule of the
Canons Regular of St Augustine was either
adopted by the Columban monks or introduced
by the monks of a new foundation. At all
events, from the 12th cent. on there was at Kells
an Augustinian priory dedicated to the Blessed
Virgin Mary. It seems to have lain to the W. of
the town, but has disappeared without trace;
as has also the Augustinian Crucifers' Hospice of
St John the Baptist, which lay to the E. of the
town. In March 1152, Kells was the meeting
place of a national synod under the joint
presidency of Cardinal Paparo, papal legate, and
Christian, Bishop of Lismore (previously first
abbot of Mellifont). The purpose of the synod
was to crown the work of ecclesiastical reform
by suppressing a number of petty bishoprics
(including Kells itself) and instituting the four
metropolitan provinces of Armagh, Cashel,
Dublin, and Tuam. In 1170 the place was
burned by Diarmait Mac Murrough and his
Anglo-Norman allies, as a stroke against
Tiernan O Rourke of Breany (*see* Dromahaire).
In 1176 Hugh I de Lacy, who is supposed to
have re-edified the abbey, set about erecting a
castle, but on learning of the loss of Slane (*q.v.*),
razed it to the ground, so that Kells seems to
have had no castle in early medieval times. In
1315 Edward Bruce routed a large Anglo-
Norman army under Roger Mortimer and the
de Lacys outside the town, which he then
burned down.

Commissioners of Public Works in Ireland
Tomb mensa and cross-slab, Kells

Of the Columban monastery there still sur-
vive, in whole or in part, five 10th cent. High
Crosses, a Round Tower, St Columcille's
House, and some other fragments.

The Market Cross, which was presumably a
boundary cross, stands at the centre of the
town. For many years it lay prostrate and
dismembered, and is said to have been re-
erected by Dean Swift. According to tradition,
it was used as a gallows by the local British
authority in 1798. The figure subjects include:
E. face: *Procession of Horsemen; Guards at the
Tomb of Christ; Fall of Adam and Eve; Cain
and Abel; Sacrifice of Isaac;* W. face: *The
Crucifixion;* N. side: *Jacob wrestles with the
Angel.*

The remains of the other four crosses are in
the graveyard of the Protestant parish church,
which occupies the site of the Columban
monastery. Here the E. Cross (on the S. side of
the church) has the unusual interest of having
remained unfinished, so that it reveals something of the method of fashioning these remarkable monuments; on the E. face are a *Crucifixion*

and a panel of four figures. The N. Cross is represented merely by a small conical base with interlaced ornament. Of the W. Cross there survive the base and part of the panelled shaft. The subjects represented include: E. face: *The Baptism of Christ, The Fall,* etc.; W. face: *Noah and the Ark,* etc. Nearby is the S. Cross, or Cross of Patrick and Columcille. On the E. face of the base is the almost illegible inscription, PATRICI ET COLUMBAE CRUX, to which it owes its name. The subjects include: E. face: *A Hunting Scene; The Fall; The Three Children in the Fiery Furnace; Daniel in the Lions' Den,* etc.; W. face: *A Procession of Horsemen with Dog and Chariot; The Crucifixion; The Last Judgement.* At the S. gate of the graveyard is the roofless Round Tower (90 ft; Nat. Mon.). N. of the church now stands detached the square bell-tower of a medieval church; the 15th cent. windows are good; the spire was added in 1783 by Thomas Cooley, architect of the City Hall, Dublin; the battlements are more recent still. Set into the S. face of the tower are miscellaneous fragments, including two gravestones from the early monastery and the figured lid of a 13th cent. tomb. The latter displays the effigies of a man and his wife, with, above them, a *Crucifixion.*

NW. of the churchyard is Teach Colaim Chille, alias St Columcille's House (Nat. Mon.), a stone-roofed structure – thought to have been a church – of essentially the same constructional type as St Kevin's Church, Glendalough (*q.v.*), St Flannan's, Killaloe (*q.v.*), and other Irish Romanesque churches. The original (west) doorway has been blocked up and the ground level lowered about five feet.

The simple court house is by Francis Johnston.

Robert Barker (1739–1806), portrait painter and inventor of the panorama, was a native of Kells.

1½ m. N. are the remains of Dulane church, a pre-Romanesque structure with *antae* and a massive door lintel. The founder of Dulane (Tulén) was the somewhat nebulous St Cairneach ("Cornishman"), traditionally a disciple of St Patrick. Some would identify him with the Welsh saint, Carantoc.

5 m. NNE., in Kilbeg, is a motte.

7 m. NE. is Robertstown (*see under* Nobber).

2 m. ENE., on the ridge between the Moynalty River and the Blackwater, is Headfort House, ancestral seat of the Marquess of Headfort, who is a descendant of Thomas Taylor, a Cromwellian who came to Ireland to assist Sir William Petty in making the profitable Down Survey, and who purchased the Headfort estate in 1660. His descendant, the 2nd Earl of Bective, was created Marquess of Headfort in 1800. Headfort House, now a school, was designed by Robert Adam, but his design was simplified by Lord Bective and the actual work was carried out under Irish supervision. The façade, of Ardbraccan limestone, is plain and austere. Not so the state apartments. The salon is typical Adams; the paintings are by Antonio Zucchi. The Chinese drawing-room has a fine Bossi mantelpiece. The magnificent demesne slopes down to the Blackwater, and was laid out so as to include a series of islands and ponds or small lakes. The superb gardens enjoy international fame as a "vast and varied horticultural museum".

2½ m. NW., near Moat House, is Derver motte-and-bailey.

1½ m. WNW., on the Hill of Lloyd (Mullach Aide, Mullaghloid; 428 ft), is a tower (100 ft), with lighthouse-type lantern, erected (1791; to the design of Henry Aaron Baker) by Thomas Taylor, 1st Earl of Bective (born 1724) in memory of his father, Sir Thomas Taylor, whose monument may be seen in Kells Protestant church. 2¼ m. WNW., between the railway and the road to the S. of the Blackwater, is Keim churchyard, Castlekeeran, originally Bealach Dúin, later Díseart Chíaráin whence Tristlekeeran, Castlekeeran. Here three High Crosses (Nat. Mons.) with some interlacing are disposed around the churchyard. The base of a fourth may be seen in a ford of the little tributary of the Blackwater. The crosses were presumably termon, or boundary, crosses of the monastery founded here by St Ciarán (d. 775), reputed author of a *Life* of St Patrick. An ogham stone serves as marker of a modern grave. There are also traces of a 14th cent. church (Nat. Mon.). St Ciarán's Well is still a place of pilgrimage (first Sunday in August).

6 m. WSW., in Diamor, are a motte-and-bailey and a good ringfort. The latter is one of seven or eight sited on the hills of the locality.

3 m. SW. is Balrath, one of the many fine "big houses" of the Kells countryside. It was built in 1761 for the Nicholson family. Kilskeer, 4 m. WSW. of Balrath crossroads, takes its name (Cill Scíre) from a nunnery founded by St Scíre, great-great-grandniece of Niall Nine Hostager. There was a Round Tower here.

KENMARE, Co. Kerry (Map 4, D5), is a small market town and angling resort, charmingly sited where the Killarney (20 m.)–Glengarriff (17 m.) road crosses the head of the magnificent sea-inlet called Kenmare River. It is noted for its hand-made lace (Poor Clare Convent).

Kenmare is a convenient base for exploring the Beare and Iveragh peninsulas, well known for their mountain and coastal scenery.

In 1645 Archbishop Rinuccini, papal nuncio to the Confederation of Kilkenny, landed at the head of the estuary and was received by the Mac Finghin Mac Carthys at Ardtully castle near Kilgarvan (*below*).

The town was founded by Sir William Petty (*see* Lauragh) in 1670.

Near the bridge is Cromwell's Fort, a 17th cent. castle. 600 yds SW., in Parknagullane (ground of The Shrubberies), Reenagoppul, is a small chamber tomb at the centre of a circle of fourteen stones.

Pilgrims still resort to Our Lady's Well, NW. of the town.

7 m. E., in a beautiful setting, is Kilgarvan. In 1261 Finghin of Rinn Róin (*see under* Kinsale) Mac Carthy halted the Anglo-Norman tide in Desmond at the famous battle of Callan near the junction of the Roughty and Slaheny rivers. The road S. from Kilgarvan to Bantry Bay is difficult and (in places) dangerous, but rewarding. – 1½ m. W. of Kilgarvan, at the junction of the Roughty and Owbeg, in Ardtully, is the site of Abbey Oriel, an early monastery. – 3 m. SSW., in Gurteen near Glanlough, is a stone circle.

1½ m. SE., in Kenmare Old, close to Sheen bridge, are a holy well and remains of a church dedicated to St Fíonán.

8 m. SE. (via Dromagorteen bridge and the valley of the Sheen River), on the N. side of the lovely Coumeen Shroule valley ¾ m. NW. of Drehidoughteragh (bridge), in Garranes, is the ancient church site of Teampall Fhiachna. Pilgrims resort to the ruined church, St Fiachna's Well, and a bullaun, on Good Friday, Easter Saturday, and Easter Sunday.

1½ m. W. is Dunkerron castle, O Sullivan Mór's chief stronghold.

5 m. WSW. are the ruins of the MacCraith O Sullivan castle of Cappanacushy.

6¼ m. WSW. are the ruins of the O Mahony castle of Dromore. 1 m. further the beautiful Blackwater valley debouches on Kenmare River.

7 m. SW., on the S. side of Kenmare River, is Lohart "stone circle", remnant of a chamber tomb; part of the chamber survives.

9 m. W., in Drumlusk, is a pair of pillarstones, one with ogham inscription and incised circle and curve.

KERRY, RING OF, is the name given to the superb 109-m. circuit of the Iveragh peninsula: Killarney – Parknasilla – Sneem – Darrynane – Waterville – Cahersiveen – Glenbeigh – Killorglin (*qq.v.*).

KESH, Co. Fermanagh (Map 2, C4), is a village on the Irvinestown (5½ m.)–Pettigoe (5½ m.) road.

3½ m. N., in Montiaghroe, is a megalithic group: (*a*) opposite the church: three pillarstones; (*b*) 200 yds SE. of the church: a stone circle with tangent alignment (Nat. Mon.); adjacent remains of two circles; (*c*) ¼ m. SE. of the church: three pillarstones; (*d*) ¼ m. SW. of the church: six stones (of a circle ?). 1 m. further N., in Drumskinny, is a Neolithic (?) stone circle with tangent alignment and small cairn (Nat. Mon.).

2 m. SW., on the shore of Lough Erne in Crevenish, are the ruins (Nat. Mon.) of a Plantation castle built before 1618 by Thomas Blennerhasset (*see* Castle Caldwell *under* Belleek). In 1641 it was held by Deborah, Lady Blennerhasset, and her second husband, Capt. Rory Maguire, destroyer of Castle Archdale (*see under* Irvinestown) and of Tully castle (*see under* Enniskillen). It was here that Sir William Cole of Enniskillen and other leading Planters were apprised of the imminent Irish rising.

3 m. W. (via road bridge) is Boa Island (*see under* Pettigoe).

4 m. NW. (1½ m. NE. of Clonelly bridge), in Formil, are remains of four stone circles (one with two converging alignments).

KILBEGGAN, Co. Westmeath (Map 6, A3), is a market village where the Kinnegad (19 m.)–Athlone (20 m.) road crosses the Brosna.

The village lies near the S. edge of Mageoghegan's Country (*see* Carn *under* Castletown Geoghegan). It takes its name from a monastic church founded in the 7th (?) cent. by St Béagán (Beccanus). According to some, the site of the church is marked by a mound at the Church of the Relic, ½ m. S. on the Tullamore road. About 1150 St Béagán's decayed, or defunct, monastery was succeeded by a Cistercian abbey (Benedictio Dei), founded by the Mac Coghlans (?) and colonized from Mellifont. At the Dissolution the abbey and its great possessions were granted to Ross Mageoghegan, a notorious adherent of the English. Nothing of its buildings survives.

3 m. SSW. is Durrow (*see under* Tullamore).

KILCOLGAN, Co. Galway (Map 1, D6), is a hamlet on the Galway (11 m.)–Gort (11 m.) road, 2 m. S. of Clarinbridge. Nearby is the little Dunkellin River, a salmon river. The countryside round about is very rich in ancient remains, especially ringforts of earth and stone. (The barony of Dunkellin, about 120 sq. m., has some 400 surviving forts.)

½ m. E. a by-road cuts through the early monastic site of Killeely, with ruins of an ancient church (medieval modifications), traces of enclosing earthworks, and a bullaun.

1½ m. SE., to the E. of the road in Caherpeak East, is a stone ringfort with remains of seven or eight rectangular, dry-stone houses. Nearby to the NNE. is a hut site (the "Cist Grave" of the Ordnance Survey).

2 m. SE., in Kiltiernan East, is Kiltiernan (Nat. Mon.), an early monastic site. The circular enclosure of some four acres is surrounded by remains of a cashel, and is sub-divided by radiating and other walls. At the centre is the cemetery with the ruins of an early church (fine trabeate W. door); the chancel was an addition; no arch. To the W. are remains of a souterrain. In some of the sub-enclosures are remains of rectangular houses of dry masonry. Excavation of the church nave and four of the houses yielded no closely dating evidence. 1½ m. W., in Carraghadoo, are the ruins of Caherrory, a stone ringfort with house sites and a souterrain (blocked up). Nearby, to the WSW., is a hut site (the "Cist Grave" of the Ordnance Survey).

1 m. SW., on the N. side of the Kinvara road, in Killeenmunterlane townland, is Killeenmunterlane, alias Knockanakilleen, a diminutive,

circular, anchoritic enclosure with fragmentary remains of a diminutive oratory.

2 m. SW. (½ m. NW. of the Kinvara road), is Drumacoo, an early monastic site (Nat. Mon.). Here are the remains of a small church, St Sorney's Well, St Sorney's Bed (ruined), and a simple early cross-slab. The original church had a trabeate W. door. Early in the 13th cent. it was lengthened and widened, Transitional lancets etc. were inserted at the E. end, and a new entrance was made in the S. wall. Collapse of the new S. wall caused the church to be narrowed again. The beautiful S. door is one of the minor masterpieces of the Connacht Transitional style, and seems, like the E. windows, to be the work of the Boyle–Cong–Knockmoy–Corcomroe school of masons. In the Middle Ages the coarb of Drumacoo maintained a leper-house and a guest-house.

2¾ m. SW., ½ m. SE. of Ballinderreen hamlet, in Muggaunagh, is a cemetery of long cist graves.

KILCONNELL, Co. Galway (Map 5, C1), is a village on the N., or Athenry, road from Ballinasloe (6 m.) to Galway (34 m.). It takes its name from an early monastery founded by St Conall, of which nothing remains though the site continues to be used as a cemetery. Beside the village are the fine ruins (Nat. Mon.) of the Franciscan friary founded c. 1414 by William Mór O Kelly of Uí Maine. In 1464, at the instance of Melaghlin O Kelly, the friars adopted the Observantine reform. In 1512 Tully O Donnellan erected the chapel still called Chapel Tully. In 1596 the friary was occupied for nine months by an English garrison which, however, spared both the friars and the buildings. In 1651 the friary was stubbornly and success-

Commissioners of Public Works in Ireland
Franciscan friary, Kilconnell

fully defended against Cromwellians by Major Dermot O Daly. The church is a typical friary church, with central tower, S. nave aisle, and aisled S. transept of c. 1450–75; the latter has three E. chapels, the central one of which is Chapel Tully. At the SE. corner of the chancel is a late chapel or sacristy. In the N. wall of the nave are two fine 15th/16th cent. canopy tombs; they have, of course, lost all their polychrome colouring. The W. tomb has as "weepers" SS John, Louis, Mary, James, and Denis. Its finial has figures of a bishop and an abbot. The E. tomb, an O Daly monument, has good tracery. A portion of the monument of the celebrated Boetius Mac Egan, O.F.M., Bishop of Elphin (d. 1650), has been appropriated for the 1752 Dalton of Raara tomb in the transept. Only portions of the claustral buildings and the small cloister survive; they are crude and late. In the Guardian's lodging at the SE. corner is the pathetic rustic monument of Mathew Barnewall, 12th Lord Trimleston, who was transplanted to Connacht "by orders of the usurper Cromwell". Tradition alleges that St Ruth was buried in the friary after the battle of Aughrim, but Loughrea is the more credible place of his burial.

At the W. end of the village is a Donnellan memorial cross of 1682 (Nat. Mon.).

KILCORMAC, alias **FRANKFORD**, Co. Offaly (Map 5, D2), is a village on the Birr (10 m.)–Tullamore (13 m.) road, at the foot of Slieve Bloom. The parish church stands on part of the site of a Carmelite friary founded in 1406 by Aodh O Molloy. A missal which belonged to the friary is preserved in the library of Trinity College, Dublin. The important Irish MSS., Trinity College H.2. 152 and Royal Irish Academy Stowe D.4. 2, were written in Kilcormac in 1300. The parish church has a good, 16th cent., wooden *Pietà*, reputed to have come from the pre-Reformation church of Ballyboy.

5½ m. NE., near Mountbolus, are the ruins of Rathlikeen castle and church.

¾ m. SW. is Temora House, formerly the home of Count Magawley-Cerrati of Parma, a member of the Empress Maria Theresa's household.

2 m. NW., on the N. bank of the Silver River, is Broughal castle, an O Molloy stronghold reduced by Lord Deputy Grey in 1538.

KILCULLEN, Co. Kildare (Map 6, C3), is a village where the Naas (8 m.)–Athy (18 m.) and Naas–Carlow (32 m.) roads cross the Liffey. The Church of the Sacred Heart and St Brigid (1869–75) is by J. J. McCarthy.

1 m. E., beside the Liffey, New Abbey graveyard marks the site of a Franciscan Observantine friary founded in 1486 by Sir Roland Fitz Eustace of Harristown (*below; see also* Ballymore Eustace, Clongowes Wood *under* Clane, *and* Castlemartin, *below*), 1st Baron Portlester. The friary ruins were used as a quarry for a nearby Penal-times (c. 1786) "Mass house". Fragments survive of the tomb of Sir

Roland (d. 1496) and his wife, Margaret Jennico (*see* St Audoen's Church, High St, *under* Dublin, South-West) : mensa with effigies, panels with *Virgin and Child, St Michael, St Francis*, and the arms of Fitz Eustace and Dartas (?); these panels were built into a wall of the "Mass house". Another Fitz Eustace effigy from Old Abbey is now in the Protestant church, Ballymore Eustace.

2 m. ENE. is Carnalway church, where there is a Harry Clarke window: *St Hubert* (1922). In Harristown, next townland to the east, is another of the Co. Kildare Long Stones of granite (*see* Furness, Punchestown, *and* Craddockstown, *under* Naas, Longstone *under* Ballymore Eustace, *and* Kilgowan *below*). Harristown House (Mrs Beaumont) is a good 18th cent. house. Harristown castle was a Fitz Eustace stronghold.

2 m. SSW. is Old Kilcullen, where St Patrick is said to have founded a bishopric over which he placed Bishop Mac Táil (d. 549). There was an early monastery here, of which there survive the base of a Round Tower, traces of a Romanesque nave-and-chancel church, and portions of three stone crosses (Nat. Mons.). The West Cross has some panels of figure carving.

¾ m. NW. is Knockaulin (600 ft), crowned by a circular (20-acre) hillfort which is ringed by a massive earthen bank with internal ditch. Traces of ringforts can be seen in the enclosure. Ancient embanked roadways lead up to it. The place has been identified with Dún Ailinne, an early seat of the Kings of Leinster.

4½ m. SSE., in Kilgowan, are a Long Stone of granite and the Piper's Stones. At the latter a circular ditch and bank demarcate a ritual enclosure with a central ring of stones enclosed by an earthen bank.

1 m. NW. is Castlemartin (1730), a fine house belonging to the Blacker family. It occupies the site of a castle which was one of the chief seats of the Fitz Eustaces from the 14th cent. onwards. The last of the Castlemartin Fitz Eustaces left Ireland with the Wild Geese. Near the house are the shamefully neglected remains of the manorial Church of the Virgin Mary, a small, simple, 15th cent. structure with castle-like dwelling tower; there are fragments of a good, 15th/16th cent., Fitz Eustace tomb: weepers, broken effigy (armoured), etc.

KILDARE, Co. Kildare (Map 6, B3), is a small cathedral, garrison, and market town on the Newbridge (6 m.)–Monasterevin (8 m.) road.

While the town traces its origin to the Anglo-Normans, the place has a much more ancient and distinguished history. In the 5th/6th cent. St Brigid, "the prophetess of Christ, the Queen of the South, the Mary of the Gael" (who was born of a Fotharta sept in Uí Fáilghe), founded a monastery here which became the principal church of the Kingdom of Leinster. This was remarkable in Ireland for being a double monastery (i.e. one part for nuns and the other

for monks) ruled by an abbess and an abbot-bishop. A 7th cent. description of the church tells of an unusually large edifice having a screen, covered with paintings and hangings, cutting off the E. end. Another screen down the centre separated the nuns from the monks. To either side of the altar were the costly metal shrines of the first abbess, St Brigid, and of the first abbot-bishop, St Conlaed. The monastery may have been the successor of a pagan sanctuary, some of whose ritual it inherited. At any rate, a perpetual fire was kept burning there until the Dissolution (*see also* Cloyne *and* Inishmurray). A 12th cent. account describes the fire as burning in a circular-fenced enclosure, forbidden to men, where it was tended by nineteen nuns. Among the great names associated with the abbey are those of Abbot Lochéne Sapiens (d. 696) and Sedulius Scotus, 9th cent. Latin poet and scholar. The monastery suffered much from the Vikings (who in 835 carried off the shrines of the two saints). In 1132 Dermot Mac Murrough, King of Leinster, sacked the town and abbey and had the abbess shamefully maltreated. For all its disasters, however, the abbey still possessed in the late 12th cent. an illuminated gospel-book whose beauty won the admiration of Giraldus Cambrensis. – In 868 the church was rebuilt by the wife of Aed Finnliath, King of Tara. It was burned in 1050, and again in 1067. In 1110 or 1111 the Synod of Ráth Breasail made Kildare the see of a new diocese. (The Catholic diocese is united with that of Leighlin; cathedral at Carlow since the close of Penal times. The Protestant diocese is united with Dublin and Glendalough.) By 1223 the cathedral was ruined, and the first Anglo-Norman bishop, Ralph of Bristol, set about building the prototype of the existing St Brigid's Cathedral (C.I.). In 1484 the cathedral was repaired and decorated. By 1615 it was altogether in ruins. In 1641 the tower, used as a fortress, was bombarded by Lord Castlehaven, the Confederate Catholic general. In 1686 the choir was re-edified in the Classical style to serve as Protestant cathedral of the diocese, the remainder of the ruin being left to disintegrate until little more was left than one wall of the tower, the walls of the S. transept, and the N. and S. walls of the nave. In 1875–96 the remnants were "restored" by George Edmund Street, who was also responsible for the disastrous remodelling of Christchurch in Dublin. The interior contains a few medieval relics: the effigy of a bishop supposed to be John of Taunton (1233–58); a tomb mensa with effigy (Renaissance armour) of Sir Maurice Fitzgerald of Lackagh (d. 1575), signed by the artist, Walter Brennagh (Breathnach=Walsh); some fragments of 15th/16th cent. sculptures, including three small *Crucifixions* and an indulgenced *Ecce Homo*. The modern features include a Harry Clarke window (*St Hubert*). SW. of the cathedral is the fine Round Tower (106 ft), which has a Romanesque porch originally crowned by a gabled pediment; the original conical roof was replaced by the battlemented parapet in modern times. S. of the tower are the remains of a tall granite High Cross; to the E. the remains of St Brigid's Fire House.

Off the E. side of the Market Place is a 15th cent. tower of Kildare Castle. For some years Lord Edward FitzGerald, Commander-in-Chief of the United Irishmen, and his wife, Pamela, had their home in adjacent Kildare Lodge. The first castle at Kildare was erected by William Marshal, Strongbow's son-in-law and successor as Lord of Leinster. Before 1253 the manor had passed to the de Vescis. In 1316 it was granted to John FitzGerald, 6th Baron O ffaley and 1st Earl of Kildare. In the Elizabethan wars the castle was destroyed and the town depopulated. In 1641 the town was captured by the Confederate Catholics; in 1647 by the Parliamentarian, Col. Jones; in 1649 by the Royalist Lord Lieutenant, Ormonde.

E. of the town is the entrance to Tully House, seat of the National Stud founded in 1916 by Lord Wavertree. The interesting gardens were laid out in 1906 by the celebrated Japanese gardener, Eito. They are open to the public: 16 March to 16 Oct., 2.30–6 p.m. daily.

¼ m. SSW. of the 'town are fragmentary remains of the church of Grey Abbey, the Franciscan friary of the Blessed Virgin Mary, built by the de Vescis. A Lady Chapel was added by Thomas, 2nd Earl of Kildare (d. 1328); eight Earls of Kildare were buried there.

1 m. SSE. of the Market Place, in Tully, is a fragment of a preceptory of the Knights Hospitaller, founded by the de Vescis. In 1566 the place passed to Sir William Sarsfield, Mayor of Dublin and great-great-grandfather of the celebrated Jacobite, Patrick Sarsfield, Viscount Tully and Earl of Lucan (*see* Lucan).

5 m. N., on Grange Hill (745 ft), which affords splendid prospects of the Wicklow Mountains and the Central Lowland, is the Chair of Kildare, a limestone outcrop.

8 m. NE. is the Hill of Allen (Allmhuin; 676 ft), famous in legend as the Otherworld seat of mythological Fionn mac Cumhail (Fionn son of Cumhal, Finn Mac Cool). The tower on the summit is a folly erected 1859/63 by Sir Gerald Aylmer of Donadea. It is said to occupy the site of a prehistoric tumulus.

1¼ m. E. (via the Newbridge road) is the nearest point of The Curragh, the largest unfenced area of arable land in the country (5,000 acres). In the E. third is the Curragh Camp, an army training-centre; St Brigid's Church (by G. McNicholl, T. J. Ryan and M. J. Curran, 1958–59) is one of the few recent Irish churches of any merit; the *St Brigid* over the main door is by Oisín Kelly, the altar crucifix by Patrick Pye (a pupil of Kelly's), the tabernacle and altar furnishings by Brother Benedict of Glenstal Abbey. – The Curragh is the headquarters of Irish horse racing, with several training stables nearby and a racecourse on the N. side. Scattered over the grasslands

are a number of prehistoric ritual earthworks, ring-barrows, etc. The principal ones are as follows: 1¼ m. N. of Kildare is an irregular enclosure; 250 yds E. of this, a ring-work (defaced by golf greens, etc.); 200 yds ESE. of this, another mutilated ring-work; ¼ m. N. of this last, a small barrow, 200 yds ESE. of which is Raheenairy, a ring-barrow. 100 yds NE. of Raheenairy is a ring-work which contained a ritual victim (buried alive); 200 yds further NE. is another ring-work. 550 yds S. of this, close to the railway, is a small barrow; to the E. of the railway is a ring-work. Hereabouts, N. and S. of the railway, are traces of the Race of the Black Pig, an ancient cattleway (?). – Less than 1¼ m. NE. of Kildare (to the N. of the racecourse road) is a multiple ring-work which contained fifteen secondary burials (medieval); less than 1 m. E. is Walsh's Rath, a defaced ring-work; ½ m. ENE. of this is Flat Rath. – 1½ m. E. of Kildare, to the S. of the Dublin road, is a ringfort; ½ m. E. (to the W. of the Curragh Camp) is Gibbet Rath, where 350 United Irishmen were massacred in 1798 after laying down their arms. E. and SE. of Gibbet Rath are barrows. – 4 m. ESE. of Kildare, and ¾ m. S. of the Curragh Camp, on the rifle range, is a barrow; SE. are two others;

12th cent. "Doorty" Cross, Kilfenora

Commissioners of Public Works in Ireland

Grotesque tomb effigy, Kilfenora

Commissioners of Public Works in Ireland

Episcopal effigy, Kilfenora

¾ m. E. of these, and also on the rifle range, are five or six barrows. ¾ m. E. of the Camp, on Racehorse Hill, are three barrows; at the foot of the hill is Donnelly's Hollow, where Dan Donnelly defeated the English champion, George Cooper, in a celebrated prize fight, 13 Dec. 1815.

7 m. SW. is the ruined FitzGerald castle of Nurney.

5 m. W., at Lackagh, are a motte and the ruins of a FitzGerald castle (*see* Kildare cathedral) and of a medieval church.

KILDORRERY, Co. Cork (Map 5, C5), is a village on the Mitchelstown (7 m.)–Mallow (14 m.) road.

2¼ m. NNE., on the N. side of the Funshion in Aghacross, are St Molaga's Well and Temple Molaga, an ancient sandstone church with trabeate W. door and some later, Gothic, features. The church and well are called after St Mo-Laga (*see* Labbamolaga *under* Mitchelstown). In the churchyard is a holy well. A *pátrún* used to be held here on Easter Sunday, the devotional exercises being followed by athletic contests and dancing.

1½ m. W., to the NW. of Farahy village, is Bowens Court (built 1765–75; by the younger Rothery (?); top floor removed 1961), until recently the home of Elizabeth Bowen, the well-known novelist, whose ancestor, Col. Henry Bowen, acquired Roche lands here at the Cromwellian confiscation.

KILFENORA, Co. Clare (Map 1, D7), is a village in the heart of Co. Clare, on the Lisdoonvarna (5 m.)–Corrofin (8 m.) road. In the 12th cent. the ancient church (Cill Fhionna-

bhrach) from which it takes its name was made the see of a little diocese now administered by the Bishop of Galway. (The Protestant diocese is united with those of Killaloe, Kilmacduagh, and Clonfert.)

Of little St Fachtnan's Cathedral there survive: (*a*) the Transitional chancel (*c.* 1200) and the N. wing, both roofless (Nat. Mons.); (*b*) incorporated in the ugly Protestant church, the W. gable and the five-bay Gothic arcades of the nave. The three-light E. window of the chancel may be by the master mason of Killaloe cathedral. Noteworthy also is the unique, sedilialike, 15th cent. tomb in the N. wall. The door and S. window are 15th cent. The carved fragments in the chancel include two crude effigies. In the graveyard are three stone crosses (Nat. Mons.) of the 12th cent.; one (South Cross) is a mere fragment; the second (North Cross) has panels of interlacing; the third ("Doorty" Cross) has curious figure-carvings and Urnes ornament. W. of the churchyard stands a very fine 12th cent. High Cross (Nat. Mon.), with a *Crucifixion* on the E. face. Another Kilfenora High Cross is now in Killaloe cathedral.

2 m. NE., in Ballykinvarga, is Caherballykinvarga, a ruinous bivallate stone ringfort with remains of huts, chevaux-de-frise, etc. 1¾ m. NNE., at Noughaval, Tobermogua (holy well) and the remains of a church and crosses mark an ancient monastic site; the church has inserted Transitional and Gothic features; in the churchyard is an 18th cent. O Davoren chapel. Also in Noughaval townland are the remnants of Carntemple, a massive, diminutive oratory of the early anchoritic site, Cill Bhreacáin.

Capital, east window, Kilfenora

The ridge SE. of Noughaval church has ruinous forts and chamber tombs, including (1 m. SE. of the church, in Ballyganner North) Caheranedan fort and a nearby court cairn ("Ballyganner Cromlech").

3 m. ENE., in Ballyganner South, is Cromlech, a wedge-shaped gallery grave; ¾ m. NE. is another. ⅔ m. E., in Clooneen, is Dermot and Grania's Bed, also a gallery grave.

3½ m. ESE., on the road to Corrofin, are the interesting ruins of the O Brien castle of Leamaneh (Nat. Mon.). They comprise a residential tower of 1480 (at the E. end) and an early-17th cent. fortified house. The surrounding bawn can still be traced; also some demesne walls. The ornamental gateway to the bawn and a great stone fireplace from the house were removed in the last cent. to Dromoland (*see under* Newmarket-on-Fergus). (Leamaneh was the home of Conor O Brien, who was killed by the Cromwellians at the battle of Inchicronan, 1651 (*see under* Crusheen), and of the celebrated Máire Rúa Mac Mahon, his wife. The story has it that when her husband's corpse was brought home, she told the bearers to take it away, as there was no place for a dead man in her house. To save her son's estate from sequestration, she then offered to marry any Cromwellian officer selected by Gen. Ludlow. Cornet Cooper of the Limerick garrison was the unlucky man.) The surrounding country contains many O Brien and MacNamara castles, as well as stone forts and chamber tombs; 1½ m. SE. of Leamaneh castle is Crossinneenboy, a T-shaped stone (12th cent. ?) set in a boulder. At each end of the transom is a human mask. It is named after St Inghean Bhaoith of nearby Killinaboy (*q.v.*). 600 yds W., in Ballycasheen, is Dermot and Grania's Bed, a portal dolmen. – 1½ m. NE. of Leamaneh castle, in Deerpark, is Cromlech, a wedge-shaped gallery grave. It is 1¾ m. SSE. of Poulacarran church (*see under* Ballyvaghan).

KILFINNANE, Co. Limerick (Map 5, C5), is a village on the Kilmallock (6 m.)–Mitchels-town (12 m.) road, at the foot of the Ballyhoura Mountains. The valleys through the mountains to Mitchelstown and to Kildorrery are worth exploring.

The principal feature of the village is the great trivallate mound; it may be an Anglo-Norman adaptation of a ringfort.

3 m. NE., on the W. end of Slieve Reagh, alt. 700–800 ft in the townland of Cush, is an interesting series of ringforts and tumuli. The S. group of ringforts consists of six conjoined forts with a large rectangular enclosure on the W.; excavations here revealed Bronze Age urn and other burials, rectangular and other houses, souterrains, etc. NW. of these monuments are three Late Bronze Age tumuli. To the N. of these is another ringfort; further N. are remains of three conjoined ringforts; NE. of these is a ringfort with rectangular N. annexe.

3½ m. NNE., in Balline, is the ancient church-site, Emlygrennan. St Mo-Lua's Well, 250 yds E., is perhaps the best-known holy well in the county. "Rounds" are still made, particularly on 3–4 Aug., at the well and in the churchyard, where two ancient slabs serve as marking stones of the "Rounds" path.

8 m. NE. is Duntryleague (*see under* Galbally).

1½ m. E. is Palatines Rock, said to have been the meeting-place of Palatines settled hereabouts in 1740 from the Rathkeale (*q.v.*) area.

3 m. SW. is Ardpatrick (*q.v.*).

KILFREE, Co. Sligo (Map 2, B6), was an ancient church which gave its name to a townland and a parish, and also, in more recent times, to a railway junction to the N. of the Boyle (8 m.)–Tobercurry (15 m.) road.

7 m. WNW. of Kilfree junction, to the S. of the Tobercurry road near Mt Irvine, are some remains of the Carmelite cell of Knockmore, founded by the O Garas.

3 m. SW., overlooking the NW. corner of Lough Gara, are the ruins of Moygara castle, chief seat of the O Garas. A castle appears to have been built here in the 13th cent. by the Anglo-Norman Cuisins, but it had fallen to the O Garas by 1338. The remains are probably 16th cent., and comprise a large square tower and a rectangular bawn with square corner towers. There is a sheila-na-gig over the entrance. Nearby is a prehistoric chamber tomb.

KILKEE, Co. Clare (Map 4, D2), a seaside resort since early Victorian days, is built along the ¾-m. sandy beach at the head of little horseshoe-shaped Moore Bay, 35 m. SW. of Ennis, 20 m. SSW. of Milltown Malbay, and 8 m. WNW. of Kilrush. Duggerna Rock at the W. side of the bay has several attractive rock pools (watch out for rising tides). Not far away is a puffing hole. The long ranges of cliffs to N. and SW. are best viewed and explored by boat, but they also afford a variety of rewarding walks. The Creagh and Cooraclare, alias Doön-beg, rivers (trout) are within convenient reach.

The parish church (1963–64) is by J. Thompson.

NNW., between Moore Bay and Lackglass Bay, is George's Head (Ceann Foirchigh). Here are a sea-tunnel, remains of a promontory fort, and a ring-barrow.

2 m. N. is Corbally Hill (328 ft); very fine view.

The cliffs beyond Duggerna Rock offer many vantage points. Gloomy Intrinsic Bay recalls the 1836 wreck of the *Intrinsic*.

2¼ m. SW. is Foohagh Point (185 ft), with traces of Doonaunroe, a promontory fort. There is a sea-tunnel here. ¼ m. NE. is a splendid sea cave. The cliff scenery S. of the Point is very beautiful. 2 m. SW. of the Point is Castle Point (151 ft) with remnants of a MacMahon – later MacSwiney (gallogla) – castle and of Doonlicka, a promontory fort.

4 m. NE. is Bealaha. 3 m. NW. overlooking Farrihy Bay, is Doonegall Point, with remains of the largest and strongest of Clare's promontory forts. There was also a fort on Farrihy Point.

7 m. NE. is Doonbeg. An Armada ship ran aground near the river mouth. The local beaches are noted for their beautiful shells. By the bridge are remains of a 15th/16th cent. MacMahon castle. (The MacMahons descended from Mahon O Brien, great-great-grandson of Brian Boru.) 2 m. N. is 2-m. Tráigh Bhán (White Strand) with its dunes. 1 m. NW. are remains of the MacGorman sea-shore castle of Doonmore. 1 m. NW. are remnants of Killard, a small 12th cent. and later church; NW. is Tobar Chruithneóir an Domhan, "Well of the Creator of the World".

16 m. ENE. (9 m. E. of Doonbeg), in Caher-murphy, are remains of a MacGorman castle: fragment of tower and complex earthworks. At the N. end of the valley is the stone ringfort which gives Cahermurphy townland its name.

KILKEEL, Co. Down (Map 3, C6), is a seaside resort and fishing port at the mouth of the Kilkeel River and at the foot of the Mourne Mountains, 18 m. SE. of Newry and 13 m. S. of Newcastle. The Kilkeel River rises in the Silent Valley (6 m. N., between Slievenagore, 1,102 ft, and Slieve Binnian, 2,449 ft), where it has been dammed to form great reservoirs for the city of Belfast; the valley is well worth a visit. – Behind Bridge St and Newcastle St are the ruins of a medieval church, altered at various dates and dismantled in 1818. It stood inside a ringfort-type enclosure. To the W. is a small stone cross.

¼ m. NE. is the Crawtree Stone (Nat. Mon.), a portal dolmen.

2¾ m. SW., in Ballynahatten townland, is Loughananka, a roofless portal dolmen with traces of a cairn.

4½ m. SW., on the shore of Carlingford Lough, are the 14th (?) cent. great keep and fragmentary gatehouse and curtain of the English royal fortress of Green Castle (Nat. Mon.). The first castle (1261) may be represented by the artificial mound close to the ruins. The castle was entrusted to the de Burgo earls of Ulster. It was besieged and taken by the Irish in 1343, but was soon recovered. In 1399 the constableship was given to Janico Dartas, but later passed to the earls of Kildare. With the overthrow of the Kildare Fitzgeralds in 1535, the castle reverted to the Crown. Subsequently it was granted (together with the "kingdom of Mourne" and the lordship of Newry and Carlingford) to the Bagnals. It seems to have been wrecked by Cromwellian artillery in 1652. Nearby are the ruins of a medieval church. The peninsula affords a beautiful view of Carlingford Lough and the Mourne Mountains.

1 m. WNW., at Massfort, is Dunnaman Giants Grave (Nat. Mon.), a prehistoric gallery grave with the remains of four or five chambers.

2 m. WNW. is Ballyrogan, alias Mourne Park, the fine demesne and seat of the Earl of Kilmorey. In the demesne is Mourne Park Giants Grave, a ruined court cairn. 3 m. W. of the main gate is Kilfeaghan Cromlech (*see under* Rostrevor).

KILKENNY, Co. Kilkenny (Map 6, B5), capital of its county and cathedral town of the diocese of Ossory, is an important market centre and the seat of several small-scale manufactures, such as brewing, clothing, footwear. It is pleasantly situated in fertile country where the Dublin (73 m.)–Clonmel (32 m.) road crosses the Nore, 24 m. SW. of Carlow, 30 m. N. of Waterford, and 21 m. SSW. of Abbeyleix. Though, in typical Irish fashion, it turns its back on its river, it is one of the most attractive, as it is one of the most interesting, of Ireland's inland towns; with rows of Georgian houses as well as its castle, churches, and other memorials of a storied past, and with pleasant walks by the Nore and its canal. It is also a convenient centre for touring the beautiful valleys of the Nore and Barrow, and for visiting the many fine monuments of a historic countryside.

The nucleus of the town was the monastery (Cill Chainnigh) founded by St Cainneach ("Canice") moccu Dalann of Aghaboe (*q.v.*). At the Anglo-Norman invasion most of the modern County Kilkenny fell to Strongbow, as pretended heir to the Kingdom of Leinster, and about 1172 he built a castle to command the crossing of the Nore. On his death Leinster passed, by English law, to his son-in-law, William the Marshal, who replaced Strongbow's castle by a stone fortress – where he had his chief seat – and incorporated the town (1204). In 1245 the Marshal Liberty of Kilkenny passed to the de Clares, and from them, in 1314, to the absentee Despensers and Straffords. In 1391 James Butler, 3rd Earl of Ormond, purchased the manor and castle of Kilkenny and other Despenser fiefs. The following year he acquired the Strafford share of the Liberty. Thereafter Kilkenny castle was the principal seat of the Earls of Ormond, and Kilkenny town the centre of an Anglo-Irish lordship which was never recovered by the Old Irish or their culture.

By reason of its strategic importance and of the power of its lords, the town played a conspicuous rôle in Anglo-Irish affairs throughout the Middle Ages, and was one of the principal meeting-places of Anglo-Irish parliaments. The parliament of 1366 enacted the notorious Statutes of Kilkenny, in an effort to stem the gaelicization of the Anglo-Norman colony in Ireland. (These enactments forbade the colonists, and the Irish living among them, to intermarry with the Irish; to use the Irish language, or Irish dress, or Irish surnames; to play hurling; or to admit Irish clerics and monks to cathedrals, benefices, or monasteries, in territories under Anglo-Norman control.) In the winter of 1348–49 the town was ravaged by the Black Death. In 1568 it was besieged by Sir James Fitzmaurice. In 1575 the cathedral was the scene of the formal submission of Rory O More of Laois to Elizabeth I. In 1609 James I conferred on the town the rank and dignity of a city. In 1619 the Jesuits opened their first Irish college in the city. From 1642 to 1648 the city was the seat of the Supreme Council and the General Assembly of the Catholic Confederation ("Confederation of Kilkenny"). In the event, the choice of a capital in the heart of the Butler territory was to prove disastrous to the Catholic cause, for it exposed the Confederation unduly to the influence and machinations of the Marquess of Ormonde, Charles I's representative. In 1648 the town admitted Ormonde, who dissolved the Confederation and installed a royalist garrison under the command of Sir Walter Butler and Edward Walsh. On 22 March 1650, Cromwell laid siege to the place. Five days later, after the fourth assault, Butler and Walsh surrendered with military honours.

Father James Archer, s.j. (1550–1605), one of the most effective agents of the Counter-Reformation in Ireland, was a native of Kilkenny; from 1596 to 1602 he laboured to convert Hugh O Neill's war into a national struggle for independence and the saving of Catholicism. Other celebrated citizens of Kilkenny were: John Banim (1798–1842), novelist and dramatist and co-author with his brother, Michael Banim (1797–1847), of the *O Hara Tales*; and Kitty Clive (1711–85), daughter of William Rafter of Kilkenny, who acted with Colley Cibber at Drury Lane and also in David Garrick's company. She died at Strawberry Hill and is buried in Twickenham churchyard; her friend, Horace Walpole, erected a memorial to her and wrote:

"Ye smiles and jests, still hover round
This much consecrated ground.
Here lies the laughter-loving dame,
A matchless actress, Clive her name;
The comic muse with her retired,
'And shed a tear when she expired."

The Castle, from 1391 until recently chief seat of the Butler earls, dukes, and marquesses of Ormonde, stands on an eminence over the Nore at the SE. corner of the old town. It has been the scene of many stirring events, including the reception, 20 Nov. 1645, of the Papal Nuncio by the President and Supreme Council of the Catholic Confederation, which had set up its headquarters in the castle. – William the Marshal's 13th cent. fortress, which has imposed its form on all subsequent buildings on the site, was a trapezoid enclosure with a massive drum tower at each angle. It survived, substantially intact, until the 17th cent. After the Restoration (1660) it was Frenchified by the first Duke of Ormonde, but fell into decay in consequence of the attainder (1715) of the second duke, so that by 1780 only two of the four sides remained standing. Some rebuilding was undertaken towards the close of the 18th cent., and large-scale restoration at various periods in the 19th cent. The latest work included the great picture gallery designed by Benjamin Woodward of Cork. Three of the great angle towers and the main N. wall of the medieval castle survive, though in greatly altered form. The Classical gateway in the W. wall was one of the first duke's alterations (1684). All the rest of the structure is 18th–20th cent. work. (The great art collection was dispersed some thirty years ago; the invaluable collection of medieval muniments has been acquired by the National Library, Dublin.)

Facing the castle, on the opposite side of the Parade, are the Castle Stables, now the Kilkenny Design Workshops (silver, textiles, ceramics, wood-turning, etc.). The nearby offices of the Revenue Commissioners occupy the premises of the famous Kilkenny Private Theatre. Tom Moore played in the theatre in 1808, 1809, and 1810, and it was there that he met and fell in love with his wife, the sixteen-year-old actress, Bessy Dyke.

The wall of the medieval English town ran SW. from the SE. angle of the castle to a point near the intersection of Ormonde Rd and Lower New St, where it turned N. to parallel the Nore for half a mile to Abbey St, where it turned E., and then N., to the little Bregagh River, which it followed to the Nore. (A fragment may be seen behind the Vocational School in Lower New St; Talbot's Tower may be seen from the garden of the Club House Hotel.) The main axis of the small parallelogram enclosed between the wall and the two rivers is represented by the line of High St and Parliament St.

Off the E. side of High St is St Mary's Lane with St Mary's Church (since 1963 a Protestant parish hall), which incorporates the ill-used nave (aisles gone), transepts, and part of the chancel of the 13th cent. parish church of Blessed Mary. (The steeple is an 1819–20 replacement of one erected in 1343.) In the church is a 13th cent. font found at St Kieran's Well near the Old Market. Church and churchyard contain some thirty medieval and early modern monuments. Of these the most important are: Roofed portion of chancel: Nicholas Knaresborough (1629); N. Transept: Richard Rothe (1637); John (d. 1590) and Letitia Rothe (d. 1602), parents of Bishop David Rothe who, in consequence of the Cromwellian victory, was buried in their grave instead of in St Canice's Cathedral (*q.v.*); Churchyard: tomb mensa with effigies of William and Margaret Goer; tomb mensa with effigy of Heleyn, wife of William de Armayl (now in the Shee burial place); Renaissance tombs of Sir Richard Shee (about 1608), Elias Shee (d. 1613) whom Holinshed mentions, and John Rothe (d. 1620) and his wife, Rose Archer. The Rothe–Archer tomb (made in 1612) formerly stood in the N. transept. Sir Richard Shee's tomb has Late Gothic panels, with figures of Apostles, etc. – Also in St Mary's Lane may be seen the rear gable of Shee's Hospital or Almshouse (alias St Mary's Poorhouse); the front gable is in Rose Inn St. The almshouse was founded in 1581 by Sir Richard Shee and his wife. During Penal times a passage in the upper storey served as chapel for the Catholics of Kilkenny; it was compulsorily closed in 1740. The building was remodelled and put to new uses in 1871.

The most conspicuous building in High St is the arcaded Tholsel, erected in 1761 as the Exchange and Town Hall; the civic regalia and muniments are worth inspection. Here and there in the street the observant eye can recognize details of 16th and 17th cent. houses; e.g. Woolworth's premises mask a 16th–17th cent. Shee house. Behind No. 15 is the ruined "Hole in the Wall", a once-famous courtyard tavern. No. 77 has a good Georgian shop front. Between High St and St Kieran St are the Slips, old stepped lanes whose houses have been much altered. St Kieran St is a narrow lane once full of old coaching inns, among them Kyteler's Inn (No. 27). A celebrated Kyteler was Dame Alice, who, in 1324, was charged by the deranged bishop, Richard Leatherhead, with witchcraft, heresy, and murderous assaults on her four husbands. She escaped to England, but her maid, Petronilla, was burned at the stake.

Parliament St, formerly Coal Market, is so called in memory of the General Assembly of the Catholic Confederation. The Assembly met in a house belonging to Robert Shee that survived until 1862, when it was pulled down to make place for the gate of the New Market. On the same side of the street is the County Court House, a good Classical building of 1794; the ground-floor loggia was unfortunately blocked up in the last cent., when the upper floor was remodelled and the external stairways were added by William Robertson. On the opposite side of the street is the Rothe House (Nat. Mon.), a fine double-court house built in 1594 for John Rothe. Restored 1965-6, it houses the museum and library of the Kilkenny Archaeological Society, the local Tourist Office, etc. A Catholic Confederation banner was found concealed in the house about 1850.

At the (Bull) Ring, ENE. of Parliament St, are the ruined choir (*c.* 1232; extended about 1324) and central tower (*c.* 1350) of the Franciscan Friary (Nat. Mon.) founded by Richard the Marshal. Messrs Smithwick, with commendable enterprise, have recently freed other remnants from their brewery buildings. The 13th cent. font was brought here from St Kieran's Well outside the Old Market. Friar John Clyn, noted 14th cent. annalist, was a member of the community.

In Abbey St, W. of Parliament St, is Black Abbey Dominican church. This is a crude 18th–19th cent. re-edification of the church of the Dominican friary of the Most Holy Trinity, founded outside the NW. angle of the town by William the Marshal in 1225. Apart from a brief spell in 1603-4 and the period of the Catholic Confederation, the church was used as a courthouse from the Dissolution until about 1700. Thereafter it fell into ruin, and about 1780 the Dominicans themselves demolished the choir to make way for a new convent. About 1788-93 the surviving portion of the church was re-roofed, but it was not re-opened for regular public worship until 1840. The medieval remains comprise: 13th cent. aisled nave, 14th cent. S. transept (good windows), early-16th cent. central tower, and the lower part of the W. tower. Preserved in the adjoining convent are a 15th cent. alabaster carving of the Blessed Trinity, a fine 16th cent. Flemish statuette of the Virgin (smothered in modern paint), and a crude Penal-times oak figure of St Dominic. E. and NE. of the church are fragments of the town wall, including Blackfriars, alias Trinity, Gate. A few hundred yds SW. (Kenny's Well Rd), enclosed in an ancient well-house, is St Kenny's (Cainneach's) Well.

A short distance S. of Black Abbey, in James's St, is the Cathedral of the Assumption (1843-57), a dull building in a hard, Gothic style by "Mr Butler, architect, of Dublin". The baptistry and chapter-house-cum-sacristy are late-19th cent. additions by William Hague, who also designed the font, baptistry, iron screens, high altar reredos, and pulpit. (The works themselves were produced in Dublin, London, and Munich factories and, like the other decorations of the cathedral, are typical examples of the dead "art" of their time.) The statue of the Blessed Virgin is by John Hogan's Italian friend, Benzoni. The mural decorations of chancel, Lady Chapel, and St Joseph's Chapel, are by W. J. Westlake of London. The Sacred Heart altar was erected by the father of Patrick and William Pearse of 1916 fame.

In Irishtown, on the N. side of the Bregagh River, St Canice's Cathedral and a Round Tower mark the site of the ancient monastery from which Kilkenny derives its name. They may be conveniently reached from Parliament St via St Canice's Steps (1614), whose walls contain fragments of medieval carvings.

The Round Tower (101 ft) is practically the

sole surviving relic of the monastery. It lost its original roof and acquired its stepped battlements in the Middle Ages. The view from the parapet is rewarding.

St Canice's Cathedral is the second successor of the abbey church to which the see was transferred from Aghaboe (*q.v.*) by the Synod of Ráth Breasail (1111). Its immediate predecessor, a small, typically Irish, Romanesque, nave-and-chancel structure, was swept away early in the 13th cent., but some of the carved capitals and voussoirs were recovered in modern times. It stood immediately E. of the existing N. choir-aisle/chapel and on practically the same axis. The much larger, Gothic church – it is the second largest of Ireland's medieval cathedrals – may have been begun by Hugh de Rous, first Anglo-Norman bishop, and continued by his two immediate successors; but the major portion of the work was due to Bishop Hugh de Mapilton (1251–56), and its completion to Bishop Geoffrey St Leger (1260–86). In 1332 the lofty central bell tower collapsed, bringing down much of the choir and of the transept chapels. The reconstruction was commenced by Bishop Richard de Ledrede (1316–61), but was not finished until the time of Bishop Hacket (1460–78). Bishop de Ledrede also installed the celebrated stained glass E. windows of the chancel depicting the Life, Passion, Resurrection, and Ascension of Our Lord. These survived the iconoclasm of the first Protestant bishop, the Englishman, John Bale (1553) – who destroyed the statues, paintings, and other ornaments of the cathedral – but fell victim to the Cromwellians, who wrecked the church (which had been recovered by the Catholics in 1642). In 1661 Bishop Griffith Williams repaired the choir for Protestant use. Further repairs, etc., were carried out between that date and 1750; but in 1759 Bishop Pococke (1756–65) found the building in a state of decay. Pococke, "the dullest man that ever travelled", enlisted the aid of Sanderson Miller of Radway, a master of pseudo-Gothic, who prepared a model for his proposed restoration without ever having laid eyes on the cathedral! Pococke in person supervised the work, which included the shifting of many of the monuments and the erection of a Classical gallery, etc., in the choir. In 1843 Dean Vignoles began a long series of improvements. Then in 1866 a general restoration was undertaken, the architect being Sir Thomas Newenham Deane, to whom the cathedral owes its present appearance. (Deane was responsible for the absurd treatment of the interior wall faces; for removing the screen which had carried the medieval rood-loft; and for the good, but un-Irish, hammer-beam roof.) Charles W. Harrison of Dublin (*see* Kildare St Club, Kildare St, Dublin SE.) did the stone carving.

The cathedral (224 × 128 ft overall) is unusually consistent in style and unusually symmetrical in plan: a cruciform church with aisled nave of five bays, choir-cum-chancel flanked on either side by two E. chapels projecting in echelon from the aisleless transepts, low central tower, and S. porch.

The oldest part is the chancel, which may be of Bishop de Rous's time; the remainder of the E. arm, including the transepts, is probably the work of Bishop de Mapilton. All the dressings and ornamental features are of sandstone, whereas in the nave they are of limestone. The outstanding feature of the chancel is the three-light E. window, which contained Bishop de Ledrede's famous glass. The clerestory windows in the side walls are the work of Sir Thomas Deane, who, presumably, based them on traces of the originals. The sedilia and the arches between the choir and choir aisles are also Deane's. In the N. wall is a tomb with a fine 13th cent. episcopal effigy.

The transepts preserve their original features little altered, but the doorway in the N. transept seems to be a restoration. To one side of this doorway is a good 13th cent. tomb niche; to the other has been placed St Kieran's Chair, a 13th cent. seat which probably came from the choir. The small E. chapel of the N. transept is said to have served as a medieval parish church, but the 17th cent. Catholic bishop, John Rothe, says it was the Lady Chapel. The elaborate details of the N. choir aisle suggest it had a special dedication. Down to Deane's time it was entered, not by the existing arch, but by an ogee-headed doorway of 15th cent. type. The S. choir aisle, now a vestry, served as the chapter house until 1866. In the early part of the 19th cent. the arches from this aisle into the choir were blocked up, and the W. third of the aisle was an open yard with a 15th (?) cent. stair turret giving access to Bishop Pococke's Classical gallery; the E. two-thirds were vaulted. The adjoining chapel was entirely reconstructed by Deane, on the original plan and largely with original materials. "More glass than wall", it represents a late-13th cent. enlargement of the original chapel. Despite Bishop Rothe (*above*), it is thought to have served as Lady Chapel in pre-Reformation times; it is now used as the chapter-house.

The NW. pier of the crossing seems to be 13th cent.; the other three date from the 14th cent. reconstruction. The two E. piers seem to have been designed to carry an extra inner ring to the chancel arch. The elaborate star-vaulting is part of Bishop Hacket's work; the 13th cent. crossing may have been crowned by an open lantern under the lofty belfry storey which was not replaced by the 14th cent. restorers.

The nave arcades are carried on quatrefoil columns with mid- and late-13th cent. details. The clerestory windows, somewhat over-large, are likewise quatrefoil. Beneath the centre light of the W. window is a unique gallery with trefoil arches. Its function has not been satisfactorily explained. The mullions of some of the aisle windows are made up of stones of later date, intended for some other purpose. The outer arch of the late-13th cent. S. porch had detached nook-shafts of marble flanked by double roll mouldings. The W. doorway is (by Irish standards) elaborate. The adoring angels of the lateral roundels indicate that the central roundel had a figure of Christ or of the Virgin and Child. The stepped parapets of the cathedral, and of the Round Tower, are 14th/15th cent. additions. Such parapets are a standard feature of later Irish Gothic.

Upwards of a hundred funerary and other monuments have survived the cathedral's misfortunes. Some are fragmentary; some have been incorrectly assembled; all have lost their polychrome colouring, etc. The most important are:

N. nave arcade: (*a*) monument of . . . , son of Henry de Ponto de Lyra, 1285. (*b*) James Schortals, Lord of Ballylarkin and Ballykeefe, and his wife, Katherine Whyte, 1507; armoured effigy in high relief, probably by Rory O Tunney; the side slab with Apostles, also by O Tunney, belongs to another tomb. (*c*) Edmund Purcell, captain of Ormond's kerns (d. 1549), and his wife, Elena Grace; fragmentary; symbols of Passion, etc.; mutilated miniature effigy of armoured knight in low relief; the only other Irish effigy of this kind is at Dungarvan (*see under* Gowran). (*d*) Sir John Grace, Baron of Courtstown, and his wife, Onorina Brenach (=Walsh), 1552; effigy of armoured knight, "weepers" (Apostles), etc.; by Rory O Tunney (?).

N. transept: (*e*) canopied tomb; the three W. figures (from another tomb) are probably by Rory O Tunney.

N. choir wall: (*f*) effigy of Bishop de Ledrede.

S. choir aisle: (*g*) Bishop David Rothe; erected by Rothe in the Lady Chapel when the Catholics recovered the cathedral in 1642; the Cromwellian victory prevented his burial in the cathedral (*see* St Mary's Church, *above*); the monument was taken down, its carvings of the Crucifixion, Blessed Virgin, etc., destroyed, and its inscription defaced by the Protestant bishop, Parry (1678).

S. transept: (*h*) Piers *Rúa*, 8th Earl of Ormond (d. 1539), and Margaret Fitzgerald (d. 1542), his countess; effigies in high relief; the "weepers" on the N. side and the Butler-Cantwell arms, etc., on the S. side may be by Rory O Tunney, but do not belong to the mensa. (*i*) James, 9th Earl of Ormond (d. 1546); armoured effigy; the "weepers" on the front may be by Rory O Tunney. (What is said to have been the finest of the Ormond tombs was that of Thomas, 7th Earl, which stood to the right of the high altar; it was destroyed by the Cromwellians.)

S. nave arcade : (*j*) baptismal font ; .13th cent.

S. nave aisle: (*k*) Richard Butler, 1st Viscount Mountgarret (d. 1571); effigy in "white" armour. (*l*) Honorina Shortall (*née* Grace, d. 1596); effigy; the front panel of the tomb is from another monument (by Rory O Tunney ?).

(*m*) Unknown widow; effigy; the "weepers" by Rory O Tunney (?).

North of the cathedral are the 18th cent. Bishop's Palace and St Canice's Library. The library has some interesting MSS., including the *Red Book of Ossory*, and about 3,000 printed books of the 16th and 17th centuries. SW. of the cathedral is the 18th cent. Deanery. In the 17th cent. the houses of the bishop, dean, precentor, treasurer, and archdeacon stood within an enclosure called Paradise. Also within the cathedral precincts was a college (i.e. a community) of eight vicars choral founded by Bishop Geoffrey St Leger; to it was attached a school for "noble and distinguished youths". On the opposite side of the cemetery was a public school room founded by Piers *Rúa* (d. 1539), 8th Earl of Ormond, and his countess, for the training of youth in the higher branches of learning. Stanihurst, who was a pupil there, has left a glowing account of the school as conducted (about 1555–66) by Peter White, "that famous lettered man".

St Patrick's Graveyard, off Lower Patrick St, at the S. end of the town, marks the site of Domhnach Mór, an early church, and of its successor, a medieval parish church; in it are some medieval and 16th and 17th cent. tombstones. St Patrick's Church (1896–99) has a medieval wooden figure of St Patrick. To the SW., in College Rd, is St Kieran's College (1836–39), Catholic seminary of the diocese of Ossory. Thomas Mac Donagh, poet and patriot, and Francis Sheehy Skeffington, pacifist, were students of the college; both were killed by the British during the 1916 Rising, the former after court martial, the latter without trial. The college museum has an interesting collection of medieval and other ecclesiastical antiquities, including a monstrance, vestments, etc., belonging to David Rothe, Bishop of Ossory, 1618–50. Rothe was for a time the only Catholic bishop in Ireland, and was later one of the outstanding personalities of the Catholic Confederation, which was, in large measure, due to him. A scholar of distinction, he collaborated in the researches of Messingham, Ussher (the Protestant primate), and the immortal Brother Michael O Clery. His own writings include the celebrated *Analecta de Rebus Catholicorum in Hibernia* (Cologne, 1616–19) and *Hiberniae sive Antiquioris Scotiae Vindiciae* (Antwerp, 1621). He founded the *Congregatio Pacifica* for the promotion of peace and charity.

Greene's Bridge at Irishtown is a good – if rustic – Palladian essay of *c*. 1765 (parapets 1835); it has been attributed to George Smith.

On the E. side of Lower John St, not far from John's Bridge, is Kilkenny College, otherwise the Grammar School, a Protestant boarding school founded here in 1666 by the first Duke of Ormond. The school has been called the lineal descendant of Piers *Rúa* Butler's and Margaret Fitzgerald's foundation of 1539 at St Canice's Cathedral (*above*), but that school died in consequence of the Reformation. Accordingly, in 1642, the General Assembly of the Catholic Confederation founded a new "free school or colledge" in Rose Inn St, but the Cromwellian victory ended that. The accession of James II, in 1685, saw a relaxation of the Penal Laws against the Catholic majority, and the Bishop of Ossory seized the opportunity to found a new college for boys. In 1689 the Protestants abandoned the Duke of Ormond's college, whereupon King James erected it into the Royal College of St Canice, "consisting of a Rector, eight professors, and two scholars *nomine plurium*", and handed it over to the majority. The Williamite victory restored the minority to power and privilege, and the school returned to Protestant ownership. For a time the school enjoyed a high repute, and its roll includes the illustrious names of William Congreve, George Farquhar, Jonathan Swift, George Berkeley, and William Magee. The oldest surviving buildings date from 1782.

On the W. side of Lower John St is St John's Church (C. of I.), an 1817 rebuilding of the Lady Chapel (*c.* 1290; E. window *c.* 1300) of the church belonging to the New Priory and Hospital (for the poor and needy) of St John the Evangelist, founded *c.* 1211 by William the Marshal, Jun., for Canons Regular of St Augustine whose previous house had been at the E. end of John's Bridge. From the multitude of its windows the chapel was known as the "Lantern of Ireland". At the Dissolution the priory was granted to the mayor and citizens. In 1645 the titular prior granted it to the Jesuits for a novitiate and college, but the Cromwellians expelled them five years later. In 1780 most of the priory and the church was demolished to make room for military barracks. All that survive are the roofless chancel (beautiful seven-light E. window of *c.* 1250) and fragments of the nave and of the claustral buildings (Nat. Mons.). The chancel monuments include the tomb of ". . . Purcell and Joan, his Wife", 1500, with mutilated effigies of an armoured knight and his lady.

6½ m. N., near the graveyard in Mohil, is a large ringfort, traditional site of Teampall Mhaothail. A short distance away is the famous Cave of Dunmore (Nat. Mon.; strangers are recommended not to explore the caves without guides).

4½ m. NE., in Sandfordscourt, formerly Cantwellscourt, is the tower of a 15th cent. Cantwell castle; a wall chamber in the fourth storey was called Leaba chaol chruaidh an Chantualaigh, "Cantwell's narrow, hard bed". There are some interesting ringforts and a number of ancient church sites in the neighbourhood.

2 m. E., in Leggetsrath East "churchfield", is an ancient church site with an early cross-pillar.

5½ m. E., in Church Clara, are remains of St Colmán's medieval parish church. Built into the E. gable is an ogham stone. In the ruins are fragments of a Shortal tomb, etc. 100 yds N. is a bullaun (not *in situ*); nearby is St Colmán's Well. About 500 yds N. of the church are remains of the Archer castle of Clarabricken. There are interesting ringforts and other earthworks in the area, including Knockanteemeave, by the roadside ½ m. NNW. of the castle. Further NNW., in Clara Upper, is Clara Castle (Nat. Mon.). This small 16th cent. Shortal castle is unusually well preserved, and is a very attractive example of a fortified dwelling of its period. The second floor probably formed the private suite of the owner; the uppermost chamber, the family living room. – 2¼ m. (by road) E. of Clara church is Freestone Hill (464 ft). On the summit is a Bronze Age cemetery cairn. It has been considerably disturbed by an oval Iron Age hill-fort with a central enclosure. The fort was defended by a terrace bank. Now crumbled, this had an outer facing of dry masonry supported by spaced timber posts. Both inside and outside the fort are traces of iron workings.

3½ m. SE., beautifully situated on the W. bank of the Nore in Kilferagh, is Fiachra's Churchyard with "St Fiachra's Statue", a mutilated, rudely carved, episcopal effigy. To the S. is St Fiachra's Well. W. of the churchyard is a nameless, circular church site with the foundations of a small, ancient church; the enclosing vallum has a plain Romanesque entrance. Kilferagh House incorporates the tower of a Forstal castle. 500 yds downstream from Fiachra's Churchyard are the beautifully situated ruins of Kilferagh parish church, Sheastown, with *antae* at the E. chancel gable and plain, round-headed N. and S. doors. The monuments here include the tomb of Robert Forstal (d. 1585), his wife, Catherine (d. 1583), James Forstal and his wives, Elisia Shortal (d. 1597) and Ellen Comerford; it was made by James Conney, 1608.

5 m. SE. is Bennettsbridge, properly St Benet's Bridge. The medieval highway from Dublin to the South crossed the Nore here. This is a convenient starting-point for exploring the lovely lower reaches of the Nore by canoe or cot. 2 m. SE. is Kilbline castle, one of the longest occupied in the county.

5 m. S. is Danesfort (*see under* Kells).

1½ m. SW. is Castle Blunden (Sir William Blunden Bt), a good house of *c.* 1750.

5½ m. SW., at the ruins of St Nicholas's parish church, Grove (Tullaghanbrogue), are two medieval tombstones.

5 m. NW. is Three Castles Bridge (*see under* Freshford).

KILL, Co. Kildare (Map 6, C3), is a small village off the Dublin (16 m.)–Naas (5 m.) road. The motte of John de Hereford's invasion castle survives. John Devoy (1842–1928), the Fenian leader, was a native of Kill.

1 m. N., in Bodenstown, are the remains of a small, medieval, nave-and-chancel church. In the churchyard is the grave (vulgar memorial)

of Theobald Wolfe Tone (1763–98), Protestant father of Irish Republicanism. Not far from the crossroads is part of the farmhouse where Tone lived for some years with his parents, brothers, and sisters.

3½ m. NNE. is Castlewarden motte (Adam de Hereford).

3 m. NE., in Oughterard, are remains of a hill-top Round Tower and small church (1009 ?). The stone-roofed chancel of the church was used as a burial-place by the Ponsonbys of Bishopscourt House (a fine Georgian mansion, 1½ m. SW., built in 1788 by William, Lord Ponsonby, and afterwards seat of the Earl of Clonmell). A vault off the nave is the tomb of Arthur Guinness (d. 1803), the famous Dublin brewer. 1¾ m. NE. is Lyons (*see under* Celbridge).

2½ m. S. is Furness (*see under* Naas).

KILLADYSERT, alias Killdysertmurhull, Co. Clare (Map 4, E2), 14 m. SW. of Ennis and 20 m. E. Kilrush, is a village on the N. shore of the shannon estuary. It takes its name from a hermitage (*diseart*) of St Murthaile's. There are remains of a medieval parish church with dwelling-tower.

4 m. E., on Inis Gad, alias Canon Island, in the Fergus estuary, are the remains (Nat. Mon.) of St Mary's Priory (Abbey ?), a house of Canons Regular of St Augustine. They stand inside a cashel (site of an early monastery?). King Donal Mór O Brien of Thomond is claimed as the founder of the priory. The friary-type, nave-and-chancel church is early-13th cent.; W. porch, tower, and chapels, 15th cent. Parts (sacristy and part of the chapter house) of the E. claustral range are early-13th cent. The remainder, like the cloister ambulatories and the S. range (kitchen and refectory with dormitory over), is early-15th cent.

KILLALA, Co. Mayo (Map 1, D3), a village on the W. shore of Killala Bay, 6½ m. NW. of Ballina and 6 m. E. of Ballycastle, takes its name (Cill Alaidh) from a church founded by St Patrick and assigned to St Muireadhach. A somewhat dubious 7th cent. Bishop Cellach of Killala is the central figure of the romantic tale *Betha Cellaig*. When the Irish Church was re-organized in the 12th cent., Killala became the see of the diocese to which it has given its name. St. Patrick's Cathedral (Protestant; *c.* 1670/80) occupies the site and incorporates a few small fragments of the medieval church. Of the early monastery there survive only the 84-ft Round Tower (Nat. Mon.) and an elaborate souterrain. (The Protestant diocese is now united with Tuam. The Catholic cathedral is now at Ballina.)

1 m. ESE. are the well-preserved remains of Moyne "Abbey" (Nat. Mon.) a friary founded, *c.* 1455, by one of the Mac Williams (Burkes) for Franciscans of the Strict Observance and consecrated in 1462. In 1579 raiding English troops tortured one of the friars to death. In 1582 others slew a second friar. In 1590 the friary – like those of Rathfran (*below*) and Rosserk (*see under* Ballina) – was burned by Sir Richard Bingham, English Governor of Connacht. The church has a wide S. aisle, a two-chapel S. transept and a chapel S. of the chancel. The tower is an insertion. Graffiti of 16th cent. ships may be seen on the plaster of

Irish Tourist Board

Moyne, Killala; the Franciscan friary from the south-east

the W. nave wall and the respond of the aisle arcade. The Renaissance W. door appears to be an insertion. The view from the tower is very fine. In the E. claustral range are the vaulted chapter room and the part-vaulted sacristy. At the NE. angle is the refectory (with reader's desk at the projecting window); it opens off the kitchen. Over refectory, chapter room, and sacristy were the dormitories. Adjoining the friary on the E. are the ruins of an 18th cent. house whose builders used the friary as a quarry. 3¼ m. SSE. are the fine ruins of Rosserk friary (*see under* Ballina).

2 m. SE., close to the road in Crosspatrick, is St Patrick's Cross, a stone with rudely incised cross.

4½ m. W. are the ruins of Bally castle.

6 m. WNW., via Tonrehown bridge and Kincon, in Rooghan, is a ruined court cairn. About 1 m. N., in Ballybeg, are the Cloghabracka, a full-court cairn with frontal forecourt.

4 m. NNW., 1 m. NE. of Palmerstown bridge, is Carbad More dual full-court cairn, with a circular court at each end opening on to a gallery grave. On the E. side of the road, in Rathfranpark, are two ringforts. Further E. are remnants of Rathfran "Abbey" (Nat. Mon.), a Dominican friary founded in 1274 by Sir Richard de Exeter. Like Ross friary (*see under* Headford), it had two courts (cloister garth and "domestic" court). The S. chapel was 15th cent. E. of the friary is St Brendan's Well. 600 yds N. of the ringforts are remains of Rathfranpark wedge-shaped gallery grave. There was a stone circle close by. In the adjoining townland of Rathfran is a stone circle (Nat. Mon.). N. of Mullaghmore crossroads, in Breastagh, is a tall ogham stone re-erected in 1853. The damaged inscription reads L[E]GG . . . SD . . . LENGESCAD MAQ CORRBRI MAQ AMMLLONGITT. It probably commemorates the grandson of the 5th cent. local king, Amalngaid, whose name is embedded in that of the barony of Tyrawley (Tír Amalngaid). – 3½ m. NNE. of Palmerstown bridge, in Foghill, is a pillarstone, said to have been erected by St Patrick. 1¾ m. NE., in Ballinlena, are St Cummin's Well and the ruins of Kilcummin, a small, early church. N. of the church is St Cummin's Grave, marked by two pillarstones and an early gravestone with three "Patrick's" crosses. Up to 1840 Leac Chuimín, a flat stone which was "turned" against slanderers and other wrongdoers, was kept at the grave; it is said to have been taken away by the priest and used as a wall-stone in Ballina cathedral. In the graveyard is said to be an early gravestone inscribed OR[ÕIT] AR AN-MAIN M[AIC] ETICH ("A prayer for the soul of Mac Étich"). It was on the seashore nearby that Gen. Humbert's French force landed, Aug. 1798.

KILLALOE, Co. Clare (Map 5, C3), a small market town on the Limerick (13 m.)–Scarriff (11 m.) road, is beautifully situated on the W.

bank of the Shannon, where the noble river, emerging from Lough Derg, makes its way through the gap between Slieve Bernagh (Glenagallagh, 1,458 ft) and the Arra Mountains (Tountinna, 1,517 ft). It is the cathedral town of the Protestant diocese (united with Clonfert, Kilfenora, and Kilmacduagh) of Killaloe. (The Catholic cathedral is now at Ennis, *q.v.*) It is a convenient centre for fishing Lough Derg (*see also* Mountshannon; *also* Dromineer Bay *under* Nenagh) and for exploring its beauties, and is a station for the C.I.E. cruises on the Shannon. The roads to Mountshannon (via Scarriff) and Portroe are noted for their scenery.

Since the 12th cent. at least, the name of the place, Cill Da Lúa, has been taken to mean the Church of Do-Lúa, alias Mo-Lúa, and the saint in question is commonly identified with Mo-Lúa (Lugaid moccu Ochae; 554–609) of Drumsnat (Druim Sneachta; near Monaghan) and Clonfertmulloe (*see under* Borris-in-Ossory). However, the patron of Killaloe is St Flannán, an 8th (?) cent. prince of Dál gCais. The rise to power of Dál gCais in the persons of Brian Boru and his descendants (the O Briens), and the proximity of the monastery to the ancestral seat of the O Briens, combined to make Killaloe one of the leading ecclesiastical centres of Munster, and at the 12th cent. reformation it became the see of a diocese corresponding to the O Brien kingdom of Thomond. In 1185 Donal Mór O Brien burned the place to baffle the first Norman invaders. Four years later he routed the Normans at Killaloe.

The principal feature of the town is St Flannan's Cathedral (C. of I.; in its Catholic days, St Mary's Cathedral?), attributed to King Donal Mór O Brien (d. 1194). A simple, Late Transitional, aisleless, cruciform building, with tower (upper part *c.* 1800) over the crossing, it has been modified (N. transept remodelled, middle of nave reconstructed, etc.) at various dates. Noteworthy are: the rich Romanesque doorway (from an older church) which frames a window at the SE. angle of the nave; the early gravestone and cross-fragment in the pavement beneath this window; the nearby, 12th cent. High Cross (removed from Kilfenora in 1821) with *Crucifixion* and ornament of interlacings and frets; the cross-fragment with the ogham and Runic inscriptions: BENDACHT [AR] TOROQR[IM] ("A blessing on Toroqrim") and [TH]URGRIM RISTI [KR]US THINA ("Thurgrim carved this cross"); the "unfinished" medieval font; the Late Transitional E. window; the Transitional corbels of the tower and of the roof timbers of the choir; the Transitional window in the E. wall of the S. transept. In the churchyard is St Flannán's Church (Nat. Mon.), well-preserved, stone-roofed nave of a Romanesque nave-and-chancel church. In it are stored an early gravestone and some Romanesque fragments including a small figure.

Beside the Catholic parish church have been

re-erected the remains of St Mo-Lúa's Oratory (Nat. Mon.), removed in 1929 from Friars' Island (submerged in the course of the Shannon hydro-electric works). The stone-roofed chancel was an addition to the timber-roofed nave. The churchyard is alleged to occupy part of the site of Kincora, celebrated seat of the Kings of Dál gCais and of Thomond. In 1088 the fortress was demolished by Donal MacLochlainn, King of Oileach (*see* Greenaun Elly *under* Derry). In 1103 Magnus Barefoot, King of Norway, visited King Muirchertach O Brien at Kincora (*see* Demesne *under* Downpatrick).

1½ m. NNW., near the W. bank of the Shannon in Ballyvally, is tree-planted Béal Boru Fort, a massive earthen ring-work (an uncompleted motte, relic of an early Anglo-Norman raid into Thomond?). It has been heaped up over a derelict, palisaded ringfort of the 11th (–12th?) cent. Béal Boru and Brian Boru take their sobriquet from the place. 2 m. further N., on the SE. slope of Craglea, are the remains of Greenaunlaghna, a ringfort named after King Lachtna of Dál gCais, great-grandfather of Brian Boru. Craglea (1,010 ft) commands splendid prospects of beautiful Lough Derg and the Shannon. N. of the hilltop is Carrick-eeval, Aoibheal's Rock, traditionally the seat of Aoibheal, banshee and war-sprite of Dál gCais. Near the E. brow of the hill is Tobereevul (Aoibheal's Well).

KILLARNEY, Co. Kerry (Map 4, D4), most celebrated and commercialized of Ireland's tourist resorts, is a market town at the junction of the Limerick (67¾ m.)–Bantry (48¼ m.) and Cork (53 m.)–Tralee (20 m.) roads. It is the cathedral town of the Catholic diocese of Kerry. The romantic lake and mountain scenery of the region is world-renowned. The region is also noted for the wealth, variety, and profusion of its flora (including *Arbutus unedo* and the rare *Trichomanes radicans* fern). It also contains a number of interesting ancient monuments.

Among the many notabilities who have visited Killarney were Charles James Fox, William Makepeace Thackeray, Sir Walter Scott, Maria Edgeworth, and Alfred Austin.

In the town itself the only building of note is St Mary's Cathedral (1842–1912), by Augustus Welby Pugin (completed by Edward Welby Pugin and George C. Ashlin of Dublin); interior decoration designed by J. J. McCarthy ("the Irish Pugin"); this is one of the best Gothic Revival churches in the country, though the interior is perhaps too narrow and austere and is marred by the iron bracings of the crossing piers. The Town Hall houses a small collection of modern Irish art. The Presentation and Mercy Convents are noted for the making of fine lace. On Cnoc na Martra (Martyr's Hill, College St) is a monument (by Séamus Murphy) to the most celebrated of Kerry's Gaelic poets: Goffraidh Ó Donnchadha of the Glen (d. 1677); Aodhagán Ó Rathaille (*c.* 1670–1728); Eóghan Rúa Ó Súilleabháin (d. 1784); and Piaras Feiritéir (*see* Ballyferriter), who was treacherously hanged by the Cromwellian commander, Nelson, in 1653. Cnoc na Martra is so called because Fathers Cornelius McCarthy and Thaddaeus Moriarty were hanged on the hill (1651/52).

The Lakes of Killarney, to which the district

Irish Tourist Board

The Upper Lake, Killarney

primarily owes its fame, lie at the foot of MacGillycuddy's Reeks (*see* Lough Acoose *under* Glenbeigh) and the Mangerton Mts (Mangerton, 2,756 ft; Stoompa, 2,281 ft; Dromderalough, 2,139 ft). They are Lough Leane ("Lower Lake", 5,000 acres), Muckross Lake ("Middle Lake", 680 acres), and the Upper Lake (430 acres).

On the W. side of Lough Leane and Muckross Lake rise Tomies Mt (2,413 ft), Shehy Mt (1,827 ft), and Purple Mt (2,739 ft), cut off from the main range of MacGillycuddy's Reeks by the wild, 4-mile Gap of Dunloe. At the S. end rises Torc Mt (1,764 ft), down which tumbles picturesque Torc Cascade; the summit is one of the best viewpoints in the district. The Upper Lake is ringed by Purple Mt, Derrylooscanagh (1,675 ft), and the Mangerton range.

A stay of at least a week is suggested to those who wish really to sample the scenery. For the visitor who has to be content with a one-day visit, the following circuit is recommended: W. via the N. end of Lough Leane and Aghadoe to Beaufort bridge; thence S. to Kate Kearney's Cottage at the N. end of the wild Gap of Dunloe, where cars must stop; thence on foot or pony through the Gap to the Upper Lake (6 m.); thence by boat through the Long Range to Lough Leane. (For details of places on this circuit, see below.)

Between the town and Lough Leane is Kenmare demesne. Kenmare House, seat of the Brownes, Earls of Kenmare, was destroyed by fire in 1913. The site commands a superb view of Lough Leane. The greater part of the demesne was purchased in 1956 by an American syndicate, the last earl having died "unwed, undaughtered, and unsonned". The Brownes, though descended from that Sir Valentine, an English undertaker who, by sharp practices, acquired confiscated O Donoghue Mór lands here during the Plantation of Munster (p. 41), quickly found their way to the Catholic camp, but never to the hearts of Gaelic poets like Aodhagán Ó Rathaille. The circumstance that, through the most critical phase of Penal times, there was only one son in each of two successive generations, helped the family to retain its estates intact though remaining Catholic. (The law prescribed the subdivision of Catholic estates among all the sons of each generation.) In the demesne is the beautifully sited championship course of Killarney Golf Club. – On Ross Island, at the S. end of the demesne (2 m. SW. of the town by road), are the fine ruins of Ross Castle, chief seat of O Donoghue Mór. After the Desmond Rebellion it was acquired by Mac Carthy Mór, but soon fell into the clutches of Browne. In 1652 it was held by Lord Muskerry with 1,500 men against a Cromwellian force of 1,500 foot and 700 horse, commanded by Ludlow. The defenders held out until floating batteries were brought up overland to bombard the castle from the water as well as the land. The remains comprise a mas-

Irish Tourist Board

Avenue, Muckross demesne, Killarney

sive 15th cent. tower – with later additions – and a small bawn. A delightful view of Lough Leane may be had from the battlements. S. of the castle are ancient copper workings, last exploited in the 18th and early 19th centuries. Governor's Rock headland, noted for its native flora, is a Nature Reserve. 1 m. NW. (boats from the castle pier), commanding delightful views, is Inisfallen, a small island which, until the destruction of its trees and shrubs, was one of the gems of Killarney. A monastery was founded here in the 6th/7th cent., perhaps by Faithliu (whence Inis Faithlenn, "Faithliu's Island"), son of Áed Damán, King of West Munster, perhaps by St Fíonán Lobhar. In the 12th cent. the monks became Canons Regular of St Augustine. Later in the Middle Ages they conducted a hospital here. The remains (Nat. Mons.) comprise: (*a*) St Mary's Priory: small cloister garth, church with 12th cent. nave (*antae* and trabeate W. doorway) and 13th cent. chancel; (*b*) a small, plain Romanesque oratory; (*c*) a decorated Romanesque oratory. The celebrated *Annals of Inisfallen* are now in the Bodleian Library, Oxford.

1¾ m. S., on a promontory in Lough Leane, are the fragmentary remains of Castle Lough, a Mac Carthy Mór castle (*see* Pallis *under* Beaufort bridge, *below*).

2½ m. S. is Killegy, a small, early church with bell-tower restored in the 18th cent. Rudolf Ehrich Raspe (1737–94), Hanoverian scientist and embezzler, and author of *The Travels and Adventures of Baron Munchhausen*, is buried in the churchyard. He came to Killarney in 1793 as geological adviser to the Herberts, who were exploiting the copper lodes of Ross Island and the Muckross estate. – On the opposite side of the road is the magnificent, 10,000-acre Bourne–Vincent Memorial Park, formerly Muckross (Abbey) Demesne. It was presented to the nation in 1932 by Mr and Mrs Bowers Bourne of California, and their son-in-law, Senator Arthur Vincent. It is noted for its palms, bamboos, azaleas, magnolias, hydrangeas, New Zealand flax, rare ferns, etc. Since 1965 Park, gardens, and house (completed 1843) have been open to the public daily from April to Sept. Admission to gardens free, to the house and its Folk Museum 2/6 per person. At Carraig an Cheoil, in the demesne, are the well-preserved ruins (Nat. Mon.) of Muckross "Abbey", a friary founded in 1448 for Observantine Franciscans by (Donal) Mac Carthy Mór (d. 1468). After the Dissolution the friars clung to the place and, in 1589, two of them were murdered by English raiders. In 1596 the heiress of Mac Carthy Mór, in defiance of the English Government, eloped from her father's castle at Pallis (see Beaufort bridge, below) with Finghin Mac Carthy Riabhach, and married him at night in the ruined friary church. Finghin paid for his temerity with imprisonment in the Tower of London. Between 1616 and 1626 the friars re-edified the ruins, finally departing only after the Cromwellians had sacked the place in 1652. The remains date for the most part to the period 1448–1500. They comprise: a typical friary-type, nave-and-chancel church with later, Dominican-type, belfry and S. transept; a beautiful small cloister; and the usual conventual buildings. In the chancel are the tombs of the founder and of several ancient Kerry families (O Donoghue of the Glen – including the poet, Goffraidh, who died in 1677 – Mac Carthy Mór, O Sullivan Mór, Mac Gillycuddy, as well as of their upstart supplanters. The poets, Aodhagán Ó Rathaille (c. 1670–1728) and Eóghan Rúa Ó Súilleabháin (d. 1784), are also buried at the friary. – By the shore of Muckross Lake are the "Colleen Bawn Rock", the "Colleen Bawn Caves" and ruined "Danny Man's Cottage". These names, and the attendant tales, are all bogus, for the real Colleen Bawn had no connection with Killarney (see Kilrush; also Ballycahane House under Croom). When Boucicault wrote his melodrama, The Colleen Bawn, based on Gerald Griffin's novel, The Collegians, he transferred the setting to Killarney; Benedict inevitably followed suit in his opera, The Lily of Killarney. From the latter these Killarney sites acquire their names. – At Muckross village is the starting-point (signposted) for the easy ascent of Mangerton (2,756 ft). At 2,206 ft is the Devil's Punchbowl, one of the sights of Killarney. The 2-m. walk from Mangerton to Stoompa (2,281 ft), along the crest of the fine cirque of Gleann na gCapall (Loughs Erhugh, Managh, and Garogarry), is most rewarding. The descent can be made via Lough Guitane.

4½ m. S. is Torc Cascade, one of the best-known Killarney beauty-spots; there are other falls higher up the stream. The summit of Torc Mt (1,764 ft) affords a superb panorama.

2½ m. E., in Lissyviggeen, are the Seven Sisters (Nat. Mon.), a diminutive circle of six stones within an earthen bank, to the S. of which is a pair of outliers.

17 m. E. (3 m. S. of Knockacappal), in Gortnagane, is a chamber tomb. Nearby are Cahercrovdarrig ringfort and a holy well. To the SSW. rise the cairn-covered Paps of Dana (2,273 ft and 2,284 ft). The mountainous country to the N. is Sliabh Luachra, famous for its 17th–18th cent. school of poetry, of which Eóghan Rúa Ó Súilleabháin and Aodhagán Ó Ráthaille were the most celebrated members.

4 m. SE., in the Flesk valley, are the ruins of Killaha Castle, a late tower-house which belonged to O Donoghue of the Glen. It was here that the poet-chieftain, Goffraidh Ó Donnchadha (d. 1677), gave his famous feasts. Charles Lever's The O Donoghue is set in the district. 2 m. further SE., in the Demon's Cliff near Glenflesk, is Robber's Cave, alias Owen Mac Carthy's Cave, called after an outlaw.

5 m. SSE. is Lough Guitane, a wild mountain lake. Several fine walks and climbs can be made hereabouts (Bennaunmore, 1,490 ft; Crohane, 2,162 ft; Stoompa, 2,281 ft, etc.).

2¾ m. WNW., in Parkvonear, is Round Castle (Nat. Mon.), a circular tower set in rectangular earthworks, etc. To the N. is the site of Aghadoe Monastery, founded in the 6th/7th cent. by St Fíonán Lobhar. The remains (Nat. Mon.) include the stump of a Round Tower and the ruins of a small nave-and-chancel church ("Aghadoe Cathedral"). The oldest parts of the latter are the W. gable, with Romanesque doorway (incorrectly re-assembled), and the E. gable (two Transitional lights). These are relics of a church commenced in 1158 by Olaf Mór O Donoghue. In the chancel are an ogham stone and a tombstone of 1581. Near the tower are two figured slabs (The Crucifixion, Descent from the Cross). The site commands a delightful view of the lakes and mountains. Aghadoe House (1 m. W.) was the home of the Winns, Lords Headley – "the Headleys were mad from start to finish" (see Glenbeigh).

1 m. W., to the N. of the Killorglin road, in Fossa, is a pillarstone.

5½ m. W. is Beaufort bridge. The chief seat of Mac Carthy Mór, Pallis Castle, stood close to a ringfort a few hundred yds NNE. 1½ m. N., in Rosnacartan Beg, is Lismarnaun, a trivallate ringfort affording a magnificent view. – 1¼ m. S. in a beautiful 3,000-acre demesne with exotic trees, shrubs, and plants, is Dunloe Castle, a modernized O Sullivan Mór stronghold. Exquisite views of Lough Leane may be had hereabouts. In a field near the avenue, close to an ancient cemetery and Tobar Chríost, are seven ogham stones which had been used as building material by the makers of a souterrain. – 2 m. S. is the famous Gap of Dunloe, a narrow, 4-m. defile (impassable by cars) through Mac Gillycuddy's Reeks. Ponies may be hired at Kate Kearney's Cottage, a tavern called after a celebrated local beauty of the early 19th cent., who sold poteen to tourists. (The poteen doubtless inspired the inept, silly names inflicted by the tourists on so many of Killarney's beauty spots.) At the S. end of the Gap delightful views open up, of the Upper

Lake to the SE. and of Cummeenduff Glen ("Black Valley") to the SW. – 4½ m. SW. of Beaufort bridge, in Gortboy, is a boulder with concentric circles, cup-marks, "dumb-bells", and other prehistoric scribings. Gortboy school is the accepted starting-point for the ascent of Carrauntuohil (via Hag's Glen, Loughs Gouragh and Callee, and the Devil's Ladder). In clear weather the panorama from the summit is magnificent (*see* Lough Acoose *under* Glenbeigh). – 3¼ m. WSW. of Beaufort bridge is the ancient church-site of Kilgobnet; there is an early cross-slab here. 1¼ m. SE., in Shanacloon, is Lisnagullaun, a trivallate ringfort with a three-chamber souterrain. 2 m. SSW. of Kilgobnet, in Ballyledder, is Lispadrickmore, a bivallate ringfort with a four-chamber souterrain and commanding a fine view. – 2¾ m. W. of Beaufort bridge, in Churchtown, are the ruins of Knockane Church and the burial-place of the Mac Gillycuddys (Mac Giolla Mho-Chuda), an offshoot of the Mac Carthy Mór dynasty.

KILLEIGH, Co. Offaly (Map 6, A3), is a village on the Mountmellick (9 m.)–Tullamore (5 m.) road.

Killeigh takes its name from Cell Achid (Drommo Fota), a celebrated monastery founded by St Sinchell the Elder (d. 549). In the 9th cent. Cell Achid and Teach Theile (*see under* Tullamore) were ruled by the abbot of Castledermot (*q.v.*). In the 12th cent. Cell Achid became a Priory of Canons Regular of St Augustine. The fabric of the Protestant Chapel-of-Ease embodies obscured fragments – 1150 (?) and later – of the nave of the Augustinian church, whose choir and chancel are almost completely ruined. The adjacent house, "The Abbey", and its stable yard incorporate miscellaneous fragments and details of the priory, including a vaulted chamber (with staircase) on the N. side of the choir. Nothing survives of Killeigh's medieval Augustinian nunnery, or of the Franciscan friary founded in 1293 (?) by O'Conor Faly. Killeigh Holy Well ("The Seven Blessed Wells") still attracts devotees.

It was at Killeigh that, on St Sinchell's Day, 1433. Margaret, daughter of Tadhg O Carroll of Éile and wife of An Calbhach Mór O Conor Faly, gave one of her celebrated festivals to 2,700 exponents of the "arts of Dán or poetry, musick, and Antiquitie". (The other festival was at Rathangan, Co. Kildare, 15 Aug. 1433.)

KILLESHANDRA, Co. Cavan (Map 2, D5), is a small market town and angling centre to the W. of Lough Oughter, on the road from Longford (20 m.) to Belturbet (10 m.).

The Protestant church was built in 1688 by Lord Southwell. It originally consisted of a nave and a large S. transept. In the latter is a good Jacobean-type doorway, while in the nave is a font with an elaborate canopy. The churchyard is of ringfort type.

4 m. N., in Kildallen, on the way to Ballyconnell (8½ m.), was the home of the ancestors of Edgar Allan Poe (1809–49). Kildallan is named from an early church represented by the Relig, a small, circular, hill-top graveyard. ½ m. N. is Carndallan (*see under* Ballyconnell).

6 m. NE., in Inishmore, is Corrabrassan Fort, a great oval ringfort; ½ m. NE. is Granshagh Fort.

KILLORGLIN, Co. Kerry (Map 4, C4), a small market town and angling centre (River Laune) on the Tralee (16 m.)–Cahersiveen (25 m.) road, is best known for its annual Aonach an Phuic – Poc Fair (10–12 Aug. inclusive). The feature of the fair is the merrymaking connected with the Poc, a large, beribboned, white, male goat. On the evening of Gathering Day (10 Aug.; 11 Aug. is the Fair Day proper), the goat is escorted with triumphant revelry to the market-square where it is hoisted aloft to preside over the trafficking in cattle, sheep, and horses until the evening of Scattering Day (12 Aug.), when it is lowered from its perch and escorted away with much noisy merriment. The origin of the custom is uncertain. Similar fair symbols were formerly displayed at Mullinavat (also a *poc*), Cappawhite (a white horse), and Greencastle, Co. Down (a ram).

The town grew up around Castle Conway, alias Killorglin Castle, an advance post (1215) of the Anglo-Norman Fitzgeralds confided to the Knights Hospitaller.

A short distance S. of the bridge, in Farrantoreen, is a stone with an elaborate cross pattern. On the E. side of the river are the re-

Irish Tourist Board

Poc Fair, Killorglin

mains of Dromavally church, 400 yds S. of which is Foilnagower (Cliff of the Goats) ringfort with a souterrain.

1½ m. N. is Ballykissane Pier, where, in 1916, a car with Volunteers going to meet Sir Roger Casement (*see* Ardfert) and the German armsship, *Aud*, plunged into the sea, so wrecking the enterprise. A monument commemorates those who lost their lives.

3½ m. N., in Callanafersy West, is a ringfort (Nat. Mon.) with remains of at least two souterrains.

2¼ m. E., on the N. side of the Laune, is Lisnadreeclee, a fine, trivallate ringfort. 3 m. SE., close to the river, is the 16th cent. tower (Nat. Mon.) of the Murray castle of Ballymalis.

3½ m. ESE., on the S. side of the Laune, is the bivallate ringfort of Ardraw; it commands a very fine view.

7 m. ESE. is Gortboy (*see* Beaufort bridge *under* Killarney).

3 m. SE., in Kilcoolaght, is an ogham stone (Nat. Mon.).

4 m. SE. is Kilgobnet (*see* Beaufort bridge *under* Killarney).

6 m. SSW., in Ahane, is an early cross-slab.

KILLUCAN, Co. Westmeath (Map 6, B2), is a village on the Trim (16 m.)–Mullingar (8 m.) road. St Etchenn's Church (C. of I.) stands on an ancient site (overgrown medieval fragments in churchyard) and has a good medieval font basin. (*For* Etchenn, *see* Clonfad *under* Kinnegad.) The Regency rectory is now the modest residence of the Church of Ireland Bishop of Meath (*see* Ardbraccan *under* Navan).

300 yds S. of the church is the shaft of a roadside, 17th cent., John O Melaghlin memorial cross. 500 yds further S., in Rathwire (Ráth Ghúaire), is a motte-and-bailey, with considerable foundations of a stone castle in the bailey. The motte-and-bailey represents the castle Hugh de Lacy is said to have built here for his brother Robert. On 14 Aug. 1210, King John's campaign against the de Lacys brought him to Rathwire. Cathal Crovderg O Conor of Connacht met him there by appointment, but their negotiations produced no agreement, as Cathal had failed to bring his son, Aedh, to John as a hostage. In 1450 Rathwire was destroyed by Mageoghegan.

1 m. NE., on an esker in Joristown, is a ringfort with a bullaun at the centre. It presumably marks an ancient monastic site. There are many ringforts in the district.

6 m. SW. is Knockaville, which takes its name (Cnoc an bhile) from a venerated tree (*bile*) associated with St Féichín of Fore (*see under* Castlepollard).

3 m. NW., in Clonlost Demesne, are St Columcille's Well and remains of a medieval church. Clonlost House is a good Georgian house.

KILLYBEGS, Co. Donegal (Map 2, B3), is a village on the Donegal (17 m.)–Glencolumb-

Irish Tourist Board
Making a Donegal carpet, Killybegs

kille (13 m.) road. It is an important herringfishing station. The well-known hand-tufted Donegal carpets are made here.

In the Catholic church is preserved the interesting gravestone of Niall Mór MacSweeney. It was found near the MacSweeney of Banagh castle to the SW. of Dunkineely (*q.v.*). There is a similar MacSweeney gravestone at Creeslough (*q.v.*).

3 m. NNE., in Carricknamoghill, is Dermot and Grania's Bed, a court cairn.

Less than 1 m. WNW., in Cashelcummin, is a court cairn.

1½ m. S., on Farbreaga Hill, is a ruined prehistoric chamber tomb; ⅓ m. S. of this is a small stone ringfort.

4½ m. WSW., in Bavan, is Dermot and Grania's Bed, remnant of a court cairn. In Shalwy, next townland to the W., is Muinner Carn, a ruinous court cairn. In Croaghbeg, the townland W. of that again, is Portabane Carn, a (central ?) court cairn, partly overgrown (court cultivated).

1½ m. W. is Fintragh, an excellent beach at the foot of Crownarad (1,621 ft).

8 m. W., on the road to Glencolumbkille, is Kilcar, a centre of the tweed, embroidery, knitting and other cottage industries. There are remains of an old church. 2 m. SE. is Muckross Head, where there are marine caves. Between Muckross and Croaghmuckross (916 ft) is Traloar, a good small beach.

KILLYLEAGH, Co. Down (Map 3, D5), on the W. shore of Strangford Lough, 19 m. SE. of Belfast and 6 m. NE. of Downpatrick, is noteworthy for the interesting castle, belonging to the Hamilton Rowan family, which crowns the remains of an Anglo-Norman motte-and-bailey. In the 13th/14th cent. the early castle was replaced by one of stone, represented by the SW. tower and adjacent parts of the existing structure. John de Mandeville was warden of this castle in 1336. The de Mandevilles held the surrounding country (barony of Dufferin) until the 16th cent., when they were ousted by the Clannaboy O Neills. In 1561 Queen Elizabeth granted the country to one Whyte of Dublin, but Seaán the Proud O Neill of Tyrone captured the castle and town. After Seaán's death the Whytes obtained possession, and in 1610 sold the castle and lands to Sir James Hamilton, who in 1625 enclosed the bailey by the stone wall which still stands. The Hamiltons remained loyal to the Crown, and the castle was severely damaged when besieged and captured by Parliamentary forces under Monck in 1648. In 1666 Henry Hamilton, 2nd Earl of Clanbrassil, restored the castle and, extending it towards the E., built the SE. tower, his architect being James Robb (see Waringstown under Lurgan, and Ballynahinch). To this restoration belong also the parapet of the bailey walls, the square towers at either end of the S. bailey wall, and the subterranean dome and access-passage of the bailey draw-well. In 1850–62 the castle, having been derelict for many years, was restored and given its Rhenish aspect. Archibald Hamilton Rowan (1757–1834), a founder member of the Northern Whig Club, Belfast (1790), and Secretary of the Dublin Committee of the United Irishmen, was the son and heir of Gawin Hamilton of Killyleagh.

Sir Hans Sloane (1660–1753), a founder of the British Museum, was a native of Killyleagh.

5 m. NNE. are the remains of Ringhaddy castle and church (Nat. Mons); nearby is a motte. The castle, like Killyleagh castle, was owned in turn by de Mandevilles, Whytes, and Hamiltons.

8 m. NNE. is Sketrick (see under Comber).

KILMACDUAGH, Co. Galway (Map 5, B2), 3 m. SW. of Gort, was one of the greater early monasteries of Connacht. It takes its name from the 6th cent. founder, St Colmán mac Duach (see Keelhilla under Kinvara, Oughtmama under Corcomroe Abbey, and Templemacduagh under Kilmurvey, Inishmore, Aran Islands). According to legend, King Gúaire Aidhne miraculously discovered his kinsman saint in the Keelhilla hermitage. Impressed by his sanctity, he offered him the site for a monastery. The saint decided to leave the choice of site to Providence. One day, as he journeyed through a great wood, his girdle fell to the ground. This the saint took to be a sign from Heaven, and there he built his monastery, Kilmacduagh. (After his death his wonder-working girdle was enshrined. It survived, in the custody of the O Shaughnessys, until the 17th cent., if not later.) At the 12th cent. reformation Kilmacduagh became the see of a diocese cor-responding to the lordship of Uí Fiachrach Aidhne.

The remains (Nat. Mons.) at Kilmacduagh comprise Templemore mac Duagh (or Cathedral), Round Tower, site of Templebeg (mac Duagh), Labbamacduagh, Teampall Eóin Bhaiste, Templemurry, the Abbot's House (Seanchloch), and O Hyne's Monastery.

The W. part of the nave of the cathedral is a small 10th/11th cent. structure which was lengthened E. in the 12th cent., acquired a N. transept in the 14th/15th cent. and a S. transept (Lady Chapel), a new chancel, and a sacristy in the 15th. The original trabeate doorway can be discerned in the W. gable. In the 17th cent. the chancel arch was reconstructed, and the N. transept adapted for use as burial-place of the O Shaughnessys. In it are rude 17th cent. carvings, *Crucifixion* and *St Colman*.

The fine 11th/12th cent. belfry (112 ft), the Round Tower, inclines from the perpendicular. The site of Templebeg mac Duagh is to the SW. of the tower.

Labbamacduagh, the traditional burial place of St Colmán, was SW. of the cathedral; its position is marked by the grave of Bishop French (1852).

John the Baptist's Church (Teampall Eóin Bhaiste) is a small, featureless ruin NNE. of the cathedral; it was a simple nave-and-chancel structure.

Templemurry (Teampall Mhuire), St Mary's Church, is a small, early-13th cent. ruin ENE. of the cathedral.

Seanchloch, alias Glebe House or the Abbot's House, is a 14th/15th cent. tower-house N. of the cathedral.

O Hyne's Monastery (Mainistear Mhuintear Eidhin) lies NW. of Seanchloch. It was a small, late-12th cent. or early-13th cent. monastery of Augustinian canons, laid out on the orthodox European plan. The original Transitional features (grouped shafts and columns of chancel arch, E. window, etc.) are of the very high quality characteristic of Western Transitional work. The quoin shafts of the church recall those at Corcomroe (q.v.); the E. window recalls that of Clonfert (q.v.). The N. wall of the church collapsed at an early date and was replaced by one erected inside it, so stilting the chancel arch. Only the E. range of the (later) claustral buildings survives (as a mausoleum).

2¾ m. SW., by the roadside E. of Boston, Co. Clare, are the remains of Cloondooan castle, one of the strongest in Thomond. In 1586 it was held for seven days by Mahon O Brien against Sir Richard Bingham, English governor of Connacht. When it surrendered Bingham massacred the garrison and wrecked the castle.

KILMACRENAN, Co. Donegal (Map 2, C2), which gives its name to the parish, is now only a small village and angling centre on the Leannan River, at the junction of roads from Letterkenny (7 m.), Rathmelton (16 m.), Milford (5½ m.), and Creeslough (9 m.), but it has exceptionally interesting associations. It derives its name, Cill mhac nÉnáin, Church of the Sons of Énán, from an early ecclesiastical foundation of which the O Friels were hereditary erenachs. Earlier it was Doire Ethne, Ethne's Oakwood, and it was here that St Columcille was fostered by the priest, Cruithneachán. The saint later founded a monastery at the Termon of Kilmacrenan. On 3 May 1592, twenty-year-old Red Hugh O Donnell was elected successor to his father in the church: "The precise place where the nobles came together was at Kilmacrenan . . . the place where Columcille was fostered, and it was by him the church was first established; and in it O Donnell was inaugurated in the lordship of his territory; and it was the erenach of the same church who inaugurated him." In 1608 Sir Cahir O Doherty, who had rebelled against his English masters (see Derry), was defeated and slain nearby.

About 500 yds N. a roadway bisects an old graveyard believed to occupy the site of Columcille's monastery. To one side of the road is the site of a church; to the other, the ruins of a Franciscan Tertiary friary established, seemingly after 1536, by Manus O Donnell.

2¼ m. E., in Letter, is Giants Grave, a large court cairn. 300 yds SSE., in Gortnavern, is a pillarstone. – 1 m. NNE., in Ray, is a pillarstone.

2 m. W. Carraig an Dúin, Doon Rock, rises from the moorland. At its S. end is the stone where, according to tradition, each succeeding O Donnell was inaugurated by the O Friel erenach of Kilmacrenan. SE. of the Rock is Tobar an Dúin, Doon Well, since Penal times a place of pilgrimage reputed for its cures. 4¼ m. WNW. (300 yds S. of the Dunfanaghy road) is Ballybuninabber Druids Grave, alias Giants Grave, a chamber tomb.

6 m. SW., on a hill-slope 1 m. E. of beautiful Gartan Lough, is Church Hill, a small angling resort. Gartan was the birthplace of St Columcille (A.D. 521). A flagstone 2½ m. W. of Church Hill, in Lacknacoo on the W. side of the lake, is said to mark the precise spot. (Nearby is a modern commemorative cross.) About 1 m. N. of the stone, in Churchtown, are remains of St Columcille's Chapel and of the "Abbey"; also two stone crosses which mark the reputed site of Columcille's first foundation; this was one of the principal burial-places of the O Donnells of Tír Chonaill; the O Nahans were hereditary erenachs. The saint is reputed to have been baptized at Teampall Douglas, Drumbologe, 1½ m. SE. of Church Hill; the ruined church there has an interesting 16th cent. window.

5 m. NW., to the N. of the Dunfanaghy road, on the S. slope of Crockmore, are the Dane's Houses, two ruined chamber tombs.

A superb circular tour from Kilmacrenan goes via Church Hill – Gartan Lough – Glenveagh – Doochary to Fintown, returning via Breenagh–Fox Hall–Church Hill Station to Kilmacrenan. Beyond Church Hill the road skirts Gartan Lough, and then climbs the Bullaba

River valley to a pass in the Glendowan Mountains (Croaghacullin, 1,430 ft, and Moylenanav, 1,771 ft, on the S.; Leahanmore, 1,461 ft, and Farscollop, 1,388 ft, on the N.) which opens on deep, narrow Glenveagh. This pass affords one of the finest views in Donegal; to the SW. rises Slieve Snaght, 2,240 ft; to the N., Staghall Mt, 1,599 ft, and Dooish, 2,147 ft. In the valley below, the Owenbeagh runs down to Lough Beagh. (The great Glenveagh Deer Forest, on either side of the valley, is stocked with deer, and only the gardens and house grounds are open to the public: 2–5 p.m. on Weds., May to Aug.; prior application must be made in writing to the Agent, Milford.) It was to Lough Beagh that the aged and sorely wounded Godfrey O Donnell retired after hurling back the English invaders of his patrimony at Credan near Sligo in 1257. He lay helpless for a year, and Brian Chatha an Dúin O Neill (see Downpatrick) of Tír Eóghain seized the opportunity to invade Tír Chonaill. The dying O Donnell had himself borne on a bier at the head of his army and routed the enemy near the Swilly, only to die at Conwal (see under Letterkenny) immediately afterwards.

KILMACTHOMAS, Co. Waterford (Map 6, A7), is a village on the Waterford (16 m.)–Dungarvan (13 m.) road, a few m. E. of the Monavulliagh and Comeragh Mountains (see Carrick-on-Suir and Dungarvan).

Tyrone Power (1797–1841), actor and comedian, was a native of Kilmacthomas. The poets, Tadhg Gaelach Ó Súileabháin (1715–95) and Donnchadh Rúa Mac Conmara, lived in the village for some years.

2 m. NE. is Newtown churchyard, burial-place of Donnchadh Rúa Mac Conmara.

7 m. SE., at Kilbeg, alias Killbarrameaden, are remains of an ancient nave-and-chancel church. Nearby is Tobar Barra Mhéidín, alias St Ita's Well.

3 m. SSE. is Ballylaneen (see under Bunmahon).

9 m. NW., alt. 1,200 ft on Fauscoum, highest (2,597 ft) of the Comeragh Mountains, is Coumshingaun, a fine glacial cirque whose cliffs are well known to climbers. ½ m. N. are Crotty's Rock and Cave, called after an 18th cent. outlaw.

KILMACTRANNY, Co. Sligo (Map 2, B5), is a village between Loughs Arrow and Skean, on the road from Ballyfarnan (3 m.) to Boyle (8 m.).

Near the ancient churchyard is a stone cross (plain). SE. of the churchyard is Stuckera Mound, so-called because formerly crowned by a pillarstone (stocaire). About ½ m. N. is Carrickard gallery grave. To the W. of the main road, in the adjoining townland of Cloghmine, are remains of a chamber tomb and of a burial mound. ¼ m. N. of this, in Treanmore, is a ruined chamber tomb called Loinneach. ½ m. E. of this, in Carricknagrip, is Carraig na gCliopa, a large stone; the roadway on the S. has destroyed a chamber tomb called Cliopach Mór. 1¼ m. N. of Carraig na gCliopa, in Coolmurly, are the remains of a four-chamber court cairn (Giants Graves). 1¼ m. NNW. of this are the remains of Shancough, alias Shancoe, church. St Patrick founded a church here, over which he placed the priest, Oilbhe. In the later Middle Ages there was a branch of the Duignans (*see* Ballyfarnan *and* Ballinamore) seated here, and one of the sources of Mícheál Ó Cléirigh's recension of the *Book of Invasions* was *The Book of the Duignans of Shancoe.* Shancoe was the home of the eminent scribe, Lame David Duignan (d. 1696), who there wrote most of the important Royal Irish Academy codex, B. iv. 1, between 1671 and 1674 (*see* Aughnanure Castle *under* Oughterard). David's grave is at Ballindoon friary (*below*). 1½ m. NW. of Shancough church is Mounttown, formerly Knockmore. Charles O Conor of Bellanagare (1710–91; *see under* Frenchpark), noted Irish scholar and antiquary, was born here, where his father had settled after losing his patrimony for loyalty to James II.

1½ m. NW., in Highwood, are remains of a chamber tomb and of the Premonstratensian house of Athmoy, a cell of Trinity Abbey, Lough Key (*see under* Boyle). 1 m. N., in Moytirra East, is Leacht an Fhir Mhóir, alias Giants Grave, a double-court cairn (Nat. Mon.) with peculiar double entrance (a Beaker feature?). There was a second court cairn ¼ m. W.; ¼ m. N. of the site, in Moytirra West, are the remains of Cloch na dTrí bPosta, alias Druid's Altar, a tripod dolmen. Also in Moytirra West are remains of the round (?) cairn with wedge-shaped gallery grave which produced the first Bell Beaker pottery found in Ireland. The Moytirra townlands preserve the name of Magh Tuireadh, Plain of Pillars, celebrated in early Irish mythological and historical tradition as the scene of two battles in which the Túatha Dé Danann were victorious. The medieval literati shifted the scene of the second battle to the vicinity of Cong, Co. Mayo (*q.v.*).

4½ m. NW., on Inishmore in Lough Arrow, are the remains of a monastery.

5 m. NW. is Ballindoon Friary (*see under* Riverstown).

KILMAGANNY, Co. Kilkenny (Map 6, A6), is a village on the Kells (6 m.)–Carrick-on-Suir (10 m.) road, at the foot of the Walsh Mts.

In Rossenare Demesne, to the E. of the village, are fragmentary remnants of Castle Hale, chief seat of Walsh, Lord of the Mountain, down to Cromwellian times (*see also* Tullaroan *under* Freshford). Walter Walsh, alias Bháitéar Breathnach, of Castle Hale (d. 1619), was the subject of a well-known *caoine* by his poet son, Seán Breathnach (1580–1660; *see* Inchacarrin *under* Mullinavat *and* Lismatigue *under* Knocktopher).

2¾ m. E. is Aghaviller (*see under* Knocktopher).

2 m. SW., in the ancient churchyard of Lamoge, are two ogham stones.

6 m. W. is Killamery (*see under* Callan).

KILMAINE, Co. Mayo (Map 1, D5), is a poor hamlet on the Headford (9 m.)–Ballinrobe (5 m.) road via Shrule. The district is rich in small tumuli and in ringforts of earth and of stone.

¾ m. N., in Raunaskeera North, is a small ringfort, Raheenagooagh, with a souterrain. Raunaskeera is a corruption of Ráth Easa Caorach, the name of the ringfort where the last MacWilliam Íochtair was inaugurated, 1595.

KILMALLOCK, Co. Limerick (Map 5, B5), is a small market town on the E. road from Limerick (20 m.) to Ráthluirc, alias Charleville (6 m.).·

The place takes its name from a monastery founded by St Mo-Cheallóg (d. 639/656); the site is said to be that marked by remains of a hillside church, 1 m. NW. of the town.

The town itself was a creation of the Anglo-Normans, most notably of the White Knights and the Desmond Fitzgeralds. It was fortified in 1375. In 1570 it was sacked for three days by Sir James Fitzmaurice, the Sweenys, and the Sheehys, so that it "became a receptacle and abode of wolves". In 1583 the Earl of Desmond and his countess were surprised in the depths of winter by the English, and only escaped by spending the night up to their necks in the river. In 1645 Lord Castlehaven used the castle (King's Castle) as a Confederate Catholic arsenal; Cromwell used it as a hospital and depot in 1651. By the end of the war the town was utterly ruined and deserted. Its subsequent recovery was short-lived, for the Williamite war left it in decay once more. It has never really recovered.

The modern parish church of SS Peter and Paul is a good Gothic-Revival building (1879–89) by J. J. McCarthy.

Nearby, at the junction of Sheares St and Sarsfield St, is 15th cent. King's Castle (disfigured; Nat. Mon.).

In Orr St, on the N. side of the town, are the remains (Nat. Mon.) of the collegiate parish Church of SS Peter and Paul, a building of the 13th–15th cent. In 1600 this church was the scene both of the humiliating submission of Hugh O Neill's "Súgán" Earl of Desmond to Elizabeth I, and of the famous Protestant service which led to the rejection by the townsfolk of the unhappy 15th earl, an English puppet. The chancel (*c.* 1300) served until recent times as the Protestant parish church, but the aisled nave (arcades and aisles 15th cent.) and S. transept (*c.* 1300; much altered) have long been in ruins. The belfry at the W. end of the N. aisle has been claimed as the truncated Round Tower of a pre-Norman foundation. Inside the church are interesting 17th cent. monuments. Aindrias Mac Craith

(An Mangaire Súgach), fine 18th cent. poet, is buried in the grave of the Hawthorne family, at the W. side of the 15th cent. S. door (porch gone). Séamus Ó Cinnéide, another well-known 18th cent. poet, lived in the town.

The outstanding monument of Kilmallock is the Dominican Friary on the N. bank of the little Loobagh River. It was founded *c.* 1291 by one of the Fitzgeralds; it was restored and enlarged in the 14th and 15th centuries. The remains (Nat. Mon.) include portions of the claustral buildings as well as of the fine church (choir, bell tower, nave with S. aisle, and aisled S. transept). The choir has a splendid, 13th cent. five-light W. window, the transept a rich, reticulated window of the 15th cent. The monuments include that (broken) of Edmund Fitzgibbon (1552–1608), last of the White Knights and betrayer of the "Súgán" Earl of Desmond.

In Emmet St is ruined Blossom's Gate, alias the Bla Porte, sole survivor of the medieval town's four gates.

1 m. SE. is Mount Coote, birthplace of Sir Eyre Coote (1726–83), the conqueror of Hyder Ali.

1 m. SW. is Ash Hill Towers, an 18th cent. Coote house castellated in 1837. One handsome Georgian elevation survives; also some Adam-style stucco.

KILMESSAN, Co. Meath (Map 6, C2), is a village on the Dunshaughlin (7 m.)–Bective (6 m.) road. There are remains of a motte. In the church is a 1915 window by Michael Healy.

1½ m. SSW. is Kilcarty, a good 18th cent. house (by Thomas Ivory?).

2¼ m. SE. is Dunsany (*see under* Dunshaughlin).

KILMORE QUAY, Co. Wexford (Map 6, C7), is a seaside village near Crossfarnoge

Point at the E. end of Ballyteige Bay. It is noted for its lobsters and its deep-sea fishing. It is also the port of departure for the Saltee Islands (*q.v.*).

½ m. N. is Ballyteige castle (15th/16th cent.) with well-preserved, high-walled bawn and a tall tower (in partial use).

From Kilmore Quay a long beach and line of sandhills extends NW. as far as Cullenstown, a distance of 6 m. as the crow flies. There is a good sandy beach at Cullenstown, which is best approached from Wellington Bridge (*q.v.*) or Bridgetown (*q.v.*) and Duncormick.

KILREA, Co. Derry (Map 3, B3), is a small linen village and fishing centre on the river Bann, 5 m. SE. of Garvagh. The Mercers' Company of London, to which the place was granted at the Ulster Plantation, are responsible for the civic buildings.

KILRUSH, Co. Clare (Map 4, D2), is a small port and manufacturing town on the N. shore of the Shannon estuary, 27 m. SW. of Ennis. The ruins of a nave-and-chancel church (pre-Romanesque with later features) mark the site of a foundation of St Seanán's (*see* Scattery Island, *below*).

1½ m. offshore is Scattery Island (Inis Chathaigh). In the 6th cent. St Seanán founded a monastery here. It suffered much from Viking raiders and 10th cent. Viking settlers. At the 12th cent. reformation the monastery church was made the see of a short-lived diocese. About 1190 the monastery was reorganised as a college of secular canons attached to the diocese of Killaloe. The remains (Nat. Mons.) comprise: (*a*) in cemetery near landing place, 15th (?) cent. Cill na Marbh "The Church of the Dead"; 200 yds NW., the site of Seanán's monastery with: (*b*) remnants of the enclosing cashel, (*c*) the Collegiate Church of SS Mary and Seanán, alias the Cathedral (a much

Cottages, Kilmore Quay

altered, pre-Romanesque church), (d) a small
church which had a rich, Romanesque chancel
arch of c. 1180, (e) a Round Tower; (f) W. of
the monastery, Tobar Sheanáin, "Seanán's
Well"; (g) 150 yds N. of the monastery,
Teampall Sheanáin, "Seanán's Church" (a much
altered, fragmentary, little nave-and-chancel
church) and an early gravestone inscribed
OR[ÕIT] DO MOENACH AITE MOGROIN
and OR[ÕIT] DO MOINACH ("A prayer for
Moenach, tutor of Mogrón, a prayer for
Moinach"); (h) 250 yds SW. of the monastery
(500 yds WSW. of Cill na Marbh), fragments
of pre-Romanesque Teampall Áird na nAingeal,
"Church of the Hill of the Angels". Pebbles
from Scattery were believed to protect the
bearer against shipwreck, and new boats were
sailed *deiseal*, or sunwise, around the island.

3 m. to the E. is the large stone fort of Carrow-
donia.

5 m. E., in the graveyard of ruined Killimer
parish church, is the grave of the Colleen Bawn,
whose murdered body was washed ashore here.
On her tragic story Gerald Griffin based his
novel, *The Collegians*. Boucicault's play and
Benedict's opera, *The Lily of Killarney*, were
adapted from this story. Killimer preserves the
name of St Íomar, a contemporary of St
Seanán's. Her well and *leac* lie to the east.

KINGSCOURT, Co. Cavan (Map 3, A7), is
a village on the Navan (19 m.)–Shercock (8m.)
road.

St Mary's Parish Church has three two-light
windows (*Annunciation, Crucifixion*, and *Ascension*) and one three-light window (*Apparition at
Fatima*) by Evie Hone (1947–48). The *Ascension*
was one of the artist's favourite works, and is
an outstanding example of contemporary Irish
glass. The windows are best seen by good,
forenoon light.

¾ m. SE. is the ancient church site of Ennis-
keen (founder St Earnán?).

KINLOUGH, Co. Leitrim (Map 2, B4), is a
village on the Donegal–Leitrim border, 6 m.
SW. of Ballyshannon and ½ m. W. of Lough
Melvin.

2 m. SE., on an island near the lake shore,
are the ruins of Rosclogher castle (late 15th
cent.); on the lake shore itself the ruins of an
"abbey". On Inishtemple, in the middle of the
lake, there are the ruins of another early
church.

8 m. SE., at the S. end of the lake, near St
Mogue's (M'Aodhóg's) Well, are the last remnants of the medieval parish church of Rossinver, said by some to occupy the site of a
foundation of St Tighearnach's. But the
medieval monastic church of Rossinver claimed
St M'Aodhóg (*see* Drumlane *under* Belturbet)
as its founder. Near the churchyard gate is an
early gravestone of Clonmacnois type; to the
SE. (marking a modern grave) is a second.

4 m. S. is Glenade (*see under* Manorhamilton).

Part of The Ascension *by Evie Hone,
St Mary's Parish Church, Kingscourt*

KINNEGAD, Co. Westmeath (Map 6, B2), is a market village at the junction of the Dublin (39 m.)–Athlone (36 m.) and Dublin–Mullingar (11 m.) roads.

5 m. NE. is the Church of the Assumption, Killyon, a student essay (1954–57) by James Fehily. The interior has been quite spoilt with bad statuary, altar cloths, etc. 3 m. ENE. is Donore castle (*see* Inchamore bridge *under* Trim).

1¾ m. E. are the remains of Ardnamullan castle.

4 m. E. is Clonard. 600 yds NE. of the main road, on the E. side of the Trim road, the Protestant church marks the site of the celebrated monastery founded in 515, in what was then Leinster, not Meath, territory, by St Finnio (alias Finnian) moccu Telduib (d. 549), bishop and abbot. Later legend made St Finnian the "tutor of the saints of Ireland", and in particular of the "Twelve Apostles of Ireland", i.e. of the foremost monastic founders of the 6th cent. He may have been the author of the oldest Irish penitential, *The Penitential of Vinnianus*. In time Clonard came to head a league of Leinster monastic churches, and subsequently grew to be one of the pre-eminent monasteries of ancient Ireland, its school being among the first half-dozen. The celebrated Ailerán *Sapiens* (d. 665) is said to have been *fer légind*, or headmaster, of the school. He was the author of an adaptation of St Jerome's *Book of Hebrew Names*, and of a Latin verse concordance of the Gospels. He was also credited with a *Life of St Féichín* (*see* Fore *under* Castlepollard) and with treatises on the virtues and miracles of SS Patrick and Brigid. The monastery was pillaged five times by the Vikings, and suffered repeatedly by fire. In 1045 "the town of Clonard with its churches was wholly consumed, being thrice set on fire in one week". In 1136 the monastery was sacked by the men of Breany (*see* Cavan), who stole from the sacristy St Finnian's sword and stripped naked O Daly, chief poet of Ireland. In 1143 the library was destroyed by fire. In 1170 Díarmait Mac Murrough and his Anglo-Norman allies sacked and plundered the place. The episcopal monastery survived all these vicissitudes, and about 1174 became the see of the diocese of Meath, newly constituted by Bishop Echtighern Mac Maoil-Chiaráin from the ancient petty bishoprics of Clonard, Kells, Ardbraccan, Slane, Trim, and Duleek. (Máel-Muire Úa Dúnáin, who presided as papal legate over the synod of Cashel (1101) and who died at Clonard in 1117, styled himself Bishop of Meath.) In 1175 the monastery adopted the Rule of the Canons Regular of St Augustine. In the same century O Melaghlin, King of Meath, founded an important convent for Augustinian nuns at Clonard. In 1201, the first Anglo-Norman bishop transferred the see to Trim (*q.v.*) and the ancient abbey lost its Gaelic character; but as St Peter's Priory (Augustinian) it survived until the Dissolution. The ruins were swept away early in the 19th cent., and

the sole surviving relic of medieval Clonard is the excellent 15th cent., octagonal, sculptured font in the Protestant church. The figure subjects include *The Flight into Egypt*, *The Baptism of Christ*, *St Peter*, *St Finnian* (?), and other saints. In 1182 Hugh de Lacy built a castle near the monastery (cf. Durrow *under* Tullamore, *and* Fore *under* Castlepollard). It was destroyed by O Keary of Carbury in 1200, but the conspicuous motte survives (W. of the Trim road). – The countryside is rich in ringforts and earthworks of various kinds. – Near Leinster Bridge (1¼ m. SE. of the village), between the Ballyboggan road and the Boyne, is a neglected, small mound marking the grave of 150 Wexford and Wicklow insurgents who lost their lives, 11 July 1798, in an attack, led by Joseph Holt, on twenty-seven Yeomanry strongly posted nearby in a Tyrrell mansion. The defenders fought with desperate courage, as did also the insurgents who so greatly outnumbered them. After several hours the latter were driven off. – 3 m. SW. of Clonard, on the left bank of the Boyne, are the remains of Ticroghan Castle, alias Queen Mary's Castle, and its 17th cent., enclosing star fort. After Cromwell's sack of Drogheda in 1649, the Royalist commander in Ireland, Ormonde, retired to Ticroghan from Trim. The following year the castle was stubbornly defended by Lady Fitzgarret against the Parliamentarian colonels, Reynolds and Hewson. According to legend, the attackers were about to withdraw when they noticed that the defenders, short of ammunition, were firing silver bullets. The assault was renewed and the castle captured.

3 m. W., beside the old Galway road, is the small, ancient churchyard of Clonfad (Clúain fota Baítán Aba). It marks the site of a monastery founded by St Etchen, the bishop who is said to have ordained St Columcille. – St Colmán mac Lúacháin (*see* Lynn *under* Mullingar) was also ordained here. Abbot Óengus mac Tipraite (d. 746) composed a Latin hymn in honour of St Martin of Tours, which came in time to be credited with magical powers. In the churchyard are the upper part and socket of an unfigured High Cross and a fragment of a smaller cross. Between the two old roads is a fragment of another early cross. A new cross (1958) has been erected at the nearby Bishop's Grave to commemorate St Etchen. In the field E. of the churchyard is a large, low ringfort.

KINNITTY, Co. Offaly (Map 5, D2), is a village on the Birr (8 m.)–Mountmellick (16 m.) road. A road to Mountrath (14 m.) climbs Slieve Bloom (Arderin, 1,734 ft) by way of the pretty valley of the Camcor River, and descends by the valleys of the Delour and Mountrath rivers. It offers rewarding prospects.

1¼ m. NE. is 19th cent. Castle Bernard, now the property of the Department of Lands (Forestry Division). On the terrace is the shaft of a High Cross (Nat. Mon.) whose figure carvings include (W. face) *The Fall of Adam and Eve* and (E. face, mutilated) *The Crucifixion*. The stable-yard buildings incorporate fragments of medieval monastic buildings. In the Protestant churchyard are part of a granite cross and an early cross-pillar. All these are presumably relics of the monastery founded here in the 6th/7th cent. by St Fínán the Crooked, disciple of St Brendan of Clonfert.

1½ m. NNW., on the N. bank of the Camcor in Ballincur, are the remains of Drumcullen "Abbey", founded in the 6th cent. by St. Bárrind. There is a fragment of the head of a High Cross here, with a *Crucifixion* on one face. – N. of the church is a fine motte, doubtless the Motte of Kinnitty mentioned in medieval records. ¾m. N. (2 m. by roundabout road), on Knockbarron (437 ft), are St John's Well and St John's Rock (a natural boulder). A *pátrún* was held here on St John's Eve.

2 m. SE., between Knocknaman (1,113 ft) and Carroll's Hill (1,584 ft), is pretty Forelacka Glen.

4 m. SW. is Seir Kieran (*see under* Birr).

7 m. SW. is Leap Castle (*see under* Roscrea).

KINSALE, Co. Cork (Map 5, B7), is a charming, decayed, old seaport on the Bandon estuary, alias Kinsale Harbour, 16 m. SSW. of Cork and 12 m. SE. of Bandon. It is a pleasant place for a restful holiday, with good bathing at Summer Cove (*below*). The roads NW. to Inishannon (*see under* Bandon) and along the coast to the S. are noted for their scenery.

The town traces its origins to the Anglo-Normans. The surrounding country was part of Milo de Cogan's share of the Kingdom of Cork (*see* Cork). De Cogan's heiress, Margaret, married a de Courcy, and their son, Patrick de Courcy, was eponymous ancestor of the de Courcys of Kinsale, Ringrone, Crichcursi, etc., who adopted the Irish surname, Mac Pádraig. In 1334/5 the town received its first royal charter, the so-called Constitution of Kinsale, from Edward III.

During the Middle Ages Kinsale was a place of small consequence, and not until 1601 did it achieve its place in Irish history. In Sept. of that year a Spanish fleet, with 3,814 infantry on board, put into Kinsale. The town and the de Courcy castles of Ringrone and Castle Park were quickly seized, and the Spaniards sat down to await the arrival of Irish assistance from distant Ulster. The English Lord Deputy, Mountjoy, promptly blockaded the town and harbour, but the Spaniards held out stubbornly. Early in December O Neill and O Donnell arrived from Ulster and blockaded the English army in its turn, soon reducing it to sore straits. Pressed by the Spanish commander, Don Juan de Aguila, and by O Donnell, O Neill consented to a surprise attack at dawn on Christmas Eve. The plan was betrayed; part of the Irish army lost its way; de Aguila did nothing. Instead of attacking, the Irish army was itself attacked. Vacillation at the top threw away the one

remaining opportunity of success, and the anticipated triumph turned into an overwhelming disaster. Hugh O Neill's heroic nine-year struggle was, in effect, at an end. On 2 Jan. 1602, Kinsale was once more in English hands.

In 1649 Prince Rupert's Royalist flotilla was blockaded in the harbour by a Parliamentarian fleet. James II landed at Kinsale, 12 March 1689, to commence his abortive campaign for the recovery of his throne. From Kinsale, too, he sailed to lasting exile after the Battle of the Boyne, the following year. After the fall of Cork, John Churchill took the town for William of Orange.

In the 17th and 18th centuries Kinsale was an important British naval base. For centuries, too, it was a stronghold of the English, Protestant colony in W. Cork. (No Irish, no Catholics, were allowed to settle within the walls until the close of the 18th cent., and the first post-Reformation Catholic church was not erected until 1809.) Though the rapid advances in ship-building and in armaments began to draw shipping away to Cork as early as the middle of the 17th cent., the well-fortified, land-locked harbour of Kinsale retained its naval significance to the close of the 18th cent.

The town is sited on the slope of Compass Hill (delightful views), its attractive Georgian houses terraced into the hillside. In Church St is the Protestant parish Church of St Multo, alias Multose (M'Eilte, M'Eiltín). This incorporates much of the fabric of an early-13th cent. church, successor of a Romanesque, monastic one, which itself was presumably the successor of an early foundation by St M'Eilte. The 13th cent. church consisted of chancel, aisled nave of four bays, short N. transept, and NW. tower. Medieval additions included the extension of the N. aisle and the addition of transepts on the N. (Southwell Aisle) and S. (Chapel of the Blessed Virgin; now roofless; built in 1550 by Geoffrey Galway, merchant) of the nave. The church suffered repeatedly from mutilation at the hands of the 17th cent. Protestant colonists and at those of their successors in the 18th and 19th centuries: blotting out the mural paintings with limewash; sweeping away the chancel arch, wall parapets, and E. window (1730); adding a stage to the tower (1759–60); replacing the N. arcade by timber posts; and spoiling the gables, aisle walls, etc., so as to squash the structure under a single roof (1835). Round the turn of the cent. the church was "restored"; it has since been extended. In the N. face of the tower is a fragment of a Transitional window. In the porch are preserved the town stocks (18th cent.); also a wooden tablet commemorating Thomas Chudleigh of Kinsale, who made the prefabricated gunboats or floating batteries for the bombardment of Ross Castle, Killarney, 1650. Inside the church may be seen a 17th (?) cent. font and some late-medieval monuments, including a 16th cent. *Crucifixion* panel from the Chapel of the Blessed Virgin Mary. The N. transept has a good five-light window (by Sarah Purser ?).

To the E. of St Multo's, in the tiny Market Square, is the New Tholsel or Courthouse, an interesting decayed structure of 1706; it has recently been repaired to serve as a local museum. Abbey Lane, NW. of the church, preserves the memory of the medieval Carmelite friary which stood just outside the town wall.

In Cork St is a 16th cent. tower house (Nat. Mon.) called Desmond Castle or the French Prison. (The latter name recalls that French prisoners-of-war were incarcerated here in Napoleonic times.)

3 m. NE., in Pallacetown Demesne, Mitchelstown, is Druid's Altar, a chamber tomb.

7½ m. NE., in Piercetown, is an alignment of five stones.

5 m. E. (via Ringnanean), on the E. shore of Oyster Haven, is Mount Long Castle, a fortified house built in 1631 by John Long (Ó Longaidh). It figures in the 1641–52 war. The cornice of the principal room had figures of Scriptural subjects and field sports.

1¼ m. ESE., via Scilly (the fishermen's quarter of Kinsale), is Summer Cove, a popular bathing resort. A short distance S., on Rinncurran, are the massive ruins of Charles Fort, principal fortification of the harbour. The fort was built about 1677 (on the sites of a Barry Óg castle and of the medieval parish church of the Holy Trinity) to the design of Sir William Robinson, architect of the Royal Hospital, Kilmainham (see Dublin, SW.). Many alterations and additions were made in the course of the 18th and 19th centuries, and the barracks were occupied continuously down to the British evacuation in 1922. The fort was then burned down by Republican Irregulars. 2¼ m. SE. of the fort, in Ballymacus, is a prehistoric chamber tomb (wrecked).

A ferry connects the town with Ringrone (Rinn Róin), a promontory projecting from the S. side of the harbour. In 1261 (Finghin) Mac Carthy Mór, victor at the battle of Callann near Kenmare, was routed and slain at Rinn Róin by Milo de Courcy; he was thereafter known as Finghin of Rinn Róin. On the promontory are the sadly dilapidated ruins of Old Fort, alias James's Fort, named after James I. It was built (1601–3) to the design of the celebrated English engineer, Paul Ive (Ivy). Later in the cent. it was remodelled by Sir William Robinson (see Charles Fort, above). From time to time thereafter further modifications were made. At the centre of the fort, surrounded by traces of a primitive, bastioned enceinte, are remains of Castle Park (de Courcys), which was stormed by John Churchill's Williamites, 3 Oct. 1689. A covered way leads NE. from the castle to a ruined blockhouse battery at the tip of the promontory. The remains of the battery, now incorporated in a factory, include 15th and 16th cent., as well as later, work. William Penn of Pennsylvania was

Clerk of the Admiralty at James's Fort, his father being Governor of the town and fortress, and Victualler of the Royal Navy. ¾ m. SW. of the fort, in Castlelands, are remains of Ringrone castle (de Courcys) and church.

10 m. S. is Old Head of Kinsale (Srubh Chearmna). At the neck of the peninsula are the remains of a 15th cent. de Courcy (Mac Pádraig) castle. The last de Courcy to reside here was Gerald (d. 1759), 24th Baron Kingsale. Nearby, on the highest point of the head (259 ft), are remains of a signal station erected during the Napoleonic wars; it commands a magnificent view of the coast. The *Lusitania* was torpedoed 10 m. S. of the Head in 1915, with the loss of more than 1,500 lives. The sinking helped to bring the United States into the war against the Kaiser's Germany.

7 m. SW. is Ballinspittle. Less than ½ m. W. of the village, in Ballycatteen, is a fine trivallate ringfort. Excavation showed that a palisade had stood inside the innermost rampart; that the entrance had been closed by a series of gateways; and that the interior (only one quadrant excavated) had contained timberpost houses and souterrains. Finds, including sub-Roman pottery from the Frankish area, dated the occupation to the period around A.D. 600. – 1¾ m. S. of the village, at the E. end of Courtmacsherry Bay, is Garrettstown Strand, a popular little resort with excellent bathing and good cliff scenery. – 4¾ m. SW. of Ballinspittle is Coolmain Castle, for a time residence of Donn Byrne (d. 1928), the Ulster novelist.

2 m. NW. is White Castle. 1½ m. WNW., by the water's edge in Doonderron, is the Doon, a steep platform ringfort (a motte?).

5½ m. NW., where the Bandon bends in great beauty, are the ruins of Poll na Long, alias Shippool, castle, an interesting Roche castle of 1543 with ground-level gunports which commanded the approach by water and "impeached a landing". 2 m. NW. is Inishannon (see under Bandon).

KINVARA, Co. Galway (Map 1, D6), is a market and sea-fishing village at the SE. corner of Galway Bay, 6 m. SW. of Kilcolgan, 5 m. WSW. of Ardrahan, and 13 m. E. of Ballyvaghan. It is a convenient centre for exploring the E. side of Burren.

At the centre of the village are remains of a medieval parish church.

Francis A. Fahy (1854–1935), ballad writer, was a native of Kinvara. His popular *Ould Plaid Shawl* is set

"Not far from old Kinvara in the merry month of May."

½ m. ENE., on an almost isolated rock, is Dungory Castle, a small 16th cent. O Hynes castle with six-sided bawn (wall a 1642 rebuilding); it was for a time a residence of the Martins of Tullira (see Laban under Ardrahan), and has recently been refurbished by Christabel, Lady Ampthill; admission, 2/6d. The castle is the setting for the opening of *The Irish Chief-*

J. Allan Cash

Dungory Castle, Kinvara

tains and their Struggle for the Crown, a well-known historical novel by Charles Froud Blake-Forster (1851–74). The original Dungory, Dún Ghúaire, was a seat of 6th cent. King Gúaire Aidhneach of Connacht, and figures in the legend of the king's Easter dishes (*see* Keelhilla *below*). NE. of the castle, on a low promontory defended by a fosse and bank, is a small, boulder-strewn ringfort. ¼ m. NE. of the castle, to the W. of the Galway road, is Tobermacduagh (holy well).

7 m. SSE. is Kilmacduagh (*q.v.*).

8½ m. SW. (via Funshinmore and Cappaghmore crossroads), under the cliffs of Slievecarrin in Keelhilla, is the site of St Colmán mac Duach's hermitage. Here, according to medieval legend, he spent seven years, attended only by one mass-server. At the end of that time, when Easter came, he had food for neither himself nor his attendant. He placed his trust in Providence, however, and all was well. Just at that moment the Easter banquet was being served to Colmán's kinsman, King Gúaire, in his fortress near Kinvara. The dishes were miraculously borne aloft and carried away through the air. The king and his retinue followed them, and so discovered the saint. Impressed by his sanctity, Gúaire offered him the site for a monastery (*see* Kilmacduagh). In proof of the story, the "tracks" of the royal cavalcade across the limestone survive today as *Bóthar na Mias*, the Road of the Dishes (weatherings in the limestone exposures). The remains at Keelhilla comprise: St Mac Duach's Bed, a "cave" (formed by fallen blocks of limestone) on the scree below the mountain cliff; St Mac Duach's Church, Tobermacduagh, and a Penitential Station, all together to the N. of the Bed; ¼ m. SE., the Grave of St Mac Duach's Servant; leading NE. from the church site, *Bóthar na Mias*. Keelhilla in its isolation well exemplifies the character of the ancient Irish hermitages. The view from the Bed is inspiring, and helps to explain the contribution of the hermits to early Irish nature poetry.

5½ m. SW. is Corcomroe Abbey (*q.v.*).

2¼ m. NW. is Durras House, now an An Óige youth hostel. It was for a time the property of Count Florimond de Basterot (1836–1904), friend of Lady Gregory and W. B. Yeats. It was here that the Gregory–Yeats project for a national theatre was born, and here too that de Basterot introduced his cousin, Edward Martyn of Tulira (*see under* Ardrahan), to Guy de Maupassant, Maurice Barrès, and Paul Bourget.

KNOCKTOPHER, Co. Kilkenny (Map 6, B6), is a village on the Thomastown (5 m.)–Waterford (20 m.) road.

Matthew fitz Griffin, seneschal of Leinster, built a castle here at the Anglo-Norman conquest. In 1312 the place passed to the Butlers, who made it one of their principal seats. In 1650 the castle was wrecked by Cromwellian artillery.

The medieval parish church of St David served as the Protestant church until about 1870, when it was demolished and only the W. tower (Nat. Mon.) and a few fragments were left standing. SE. of the churchyard is Knocktopher Moat, alias Garrison Castle, motte of fitz Griffin's castle; the masonry fragments are all that survive of the Butler castle. Knocktopher House, on the opposite side of the road, incorporates the tower, kitchen, etc., of the important Carmelite friary of St Saviour; it was founded in 1356 by James Butler, 2nd Earl of Ormond.

1¼ m. SSE. is Ballyhale. The parish church of St Martin of Tours incorporates the "Castle of Ballyhale", actually the W. tower of the medieval church of Kiltorcan; two medieval fonts serve as holy-water stoups.

1½ m. SSW. is well-preserved Kilcurl castle, a Purcell stronghold in the 16th and 17th centuries. 2½ m. S., in Kilkeasy, are the ruins of a church with remains of a fine Romanesque doorway.

1 m. SW., in Ballyboodan, is an ogham stone.

5½ m. SW., in Lismatigue, is Móta Lios 'ac Thaidg, the Moat of Lismatigue (a tumulus ?). Nearby are remains of a medieval church and of the castle where the poet, Sean mac Bhaitéir Breathnach, died in 1660 (see Inchacarrin *under* Mullinavat). 2 m. SW. is Leac an Scáil (see *under* Mullinavat).

1¼ m. W., in Sheepstown, are the ruins of a 12th cent. church (Nat. Mon.) with angle-rolls and a plain Romanesque doorway as well as later features. 2 m. SW., in Aghaviller, the stump of a Round Tower, ruins of a church (Nat. Mons.), and Tobar Bhréanaill (holy well), mark the site of an ancient monastic (later parochial) foundation, dedicated to St Brendan of Birr (*q.v.*). The medieval residential tower of the church appears to be imposed on a stone-roofed chancel of earlier date.

KYLEMORE, Co. Galway (Map 1, B5), one of the best-known beauty spots of Connemara, and a good angling centre, is the pass between Doughruagh (1,756 ft), Altnagaighera (1,791 ft), and Garraun (1,975 ft), on the N., and the Twelve Bens (Bengooria, 1,460 ft, Knockbrack, 1,460 ft, Benbaun, 1,577 ft), on the S. From Kylemore Lough the Dawros River flows W. through the pass to Ballynakill Harbour. The valley is at its best when rhododendron and fuchsia are in bloom.

At the foot of steep Doughruagh, on the N. shore of little Pollacappul Lough, is Kylemore Abbey, a convent (with school) of Benedictine nuns (Irish Dames of Ypres) who settled here after the First World War. The nuns treasure a captured British flag entrusted to their keeping by the Irish Brigade after the battle of Fontenoy (1745). The abbey is a great Victorian "castle" built at enormous expense by a wealthy Liverpool merchant, Mitchell Henry, M.P. (1826–1910). To the E. is a costly Gothic church which he also erected; to the W. is Taghaillia, site of a prehistoric chamber tomb.

LAMBAY ISLAND, Co. Dublin (Map 6, D2), 4 m. SE. of Rush, is a well-known bird sanctuary. Its Irish name is Reachrainn, whence Portraine (Port Reachrainne) on the mainland. There is a boat service three times each week from Rogerstown near Rush (*q.v.*); but, since the island is the private property of Lord Revelstoke, permission to land must be sought from the Steward (postal address: Lambay Island, Rush, Co. Dublin).

St Columcille founded a monastery on the island, and entrusted it to the deacon, Colmán. It suffered severely from the Vikings, and no trace of it survives, unless it be Trinity Well, situated towards the centre of the island on the SSW. slope of Knockbane (418 ft). After the battle of Aughrim the island was used as a place of internment for Jacobite prisoners-of-war.

Lambay Castle, Lord Revelstoke's house, which was designed by Sir Edwin Lutyens, incorporates remains of a small 15th cent.

castle where Archbishop James Ussher (1581–1656) wrote several of his works.

500 yds NE. of the harbour, on Gouge Point, is the Garden Fort, a promontory fort.

LARAGH, Co. Wicklow (Map 6, D4), at the junction of Glendalough, Glendasan, Glenmacnass, the Annamoe valley, and the Clara valley, is the meeting-place of roads which traverse some of the most beautiful parts of the Wicklow Mountains.

NE. of the bridge over the Glenmacnass River is Laragh Barracks, one of the posts which guarded the old Military Road from Rathfarnham. The road NE. follows the pretty Annamoe valley to Lough Dan and Roundwood (*q.v.*). That NNW. leads up Glenmacnass, along the line of the Military Road, to the Sally Gap (see *under* Roundwood); 4½ m. from the bridge is the waterfall which gives the valley its name.

SE. is the beautifully wooded Clara valley, down which the lovely Avonmore tumbles its way. Two roads run down the valley to Rathdrum (*q.v.*). The main road follows the W. bank of the river; but the parallel road E. of the river, along Trooperstown Hill (1,419 ft), is also good, and is more rewarding. Splendid views may be had from Trooperstown Hill, notably in Ballard on the NW. shoulder. ¾ m. S. of Laragh (½ m. S. of Derrybawn bridge), the old Military Road branches from the main Rathdrum road and climbs its way to Glenmalure. (It is suitable for cars, but care is recommended.) 2½ m. S. of Derrybawn bridge are the remains of the O Byrne castle of Knockrath.

1 m. W. are Glendalough (*q.v.*) and Glendasan. The road up Glendasan leads to the Wicklow Gap (see *under* Hollywood).

LARNE, Co. Antrim (Map 3, D4), is a manufacturing town and seaport (car-ferry service to Stranraer) 21 m. NE. of Belfast. As the S. terminus of the famous Antrim Coast Road, it is a popular tourist centre and holiday resort, with yachting, bathing (sand and shingle beaches), golf, tennis, and other amenities. It is a good centre for exploring Islandmagee (*q.v.*; ferry) and the Glens of Antrim (*q.v.*).

Edward Bruce landed at Larne, 25 May 1315. In 1914 Carson's "loyal" Ulster Volunteers, organized to resist the Irish Home Rule Act, ran a cargo of German guns into Larne, so setting off the chain of events which led to the Irish Republican insurrection of 1916, the War of Independence (1919–21), and the partition of Ulster. The Round Tower at the harbour commemorates James Chaine, a former proprietor, to whom Larne is indebted for the Stranraer steamer service.

James MacHenry (1785–1845), Irish-American writer, was born and died at Larne.

The Curran (*corrán*, a sickle, referring to the shape of the tongue of land), just S. of the town, is one of the most remarkable prehistoric stations in these islands. From the quantity of flint artefacts embedded in the ancient beach here, the name "Larnian" has been given to the Mesolithic culture of Ireland. Fragmentary Curran Castle (Nat. Mon.), a small 16th (?) cent. tower, is popularly mistaken for long vanished Olderfleete (Ollarbha) Castle, which stood at the mouth of the Larne River.

Inver (SW. part of the town) Church (C. of I.) has two two-light windows by Wilhelmina Geddes: *SS Patrick and Columcille* (1923) and *Christ meets Mary and Martha* (1927).

4 m. N. is Ballygalley Head (300 ft), which offers a magnificent prospect towards Gorse Craig. On a precipitous, insulated rock N. of the head are scant remains of Carncastle, alias O Halloran's Castle. ½ m. W., incorporated in a hotel, is Ballygalley Castle (Nat. Mon.), Ireland's best preserved "Scottish baronial" castle; it was built by James Shaw of Greenock in 1625. About 1 m. W. of the castle, in Ballyhackett, is a motte. Sallagh Braes, W. of Carncastle village, are a magnificent amphitheatre of basalt with a safe, cliff-top path; Knockdhu, at the N. end, offers magnificent views of sea and land. – 6 m. WNW. of Carncastle village is Dunteigue bridge, ¼ m. ENE. of which is Dunteigue Giants Grave (Nat. Mon.), a wedge-shaped gallery grave. ¼ m. N. of this, on the S. slope of Craigy Hill, is a long cairn with a ruinous chamber tomb (Neolithic).

6 m. SSE. is Ballycarry (*see under* Whitehead).

2 m. S., on the road to Whitehead, is Glynn, an attractive village in picturesque Glenoe. W. of the village are the ruins of a church said to occupy the site of a Patrician foundation.

3½ m. WSW. is Kilwaughter Castle; by John Nash.

LAURAGH, Co. Kerry (Map 4, C5), is a small village on Kilmakilloge Bay, Kenmare River, at the junction of the Glantrasna and Glanmore valleys, 14 m. SW. of Kenmare, 6 m. NE. of Ardgroom, and 3½ m. N. of Healy Pass (*see* Adrigole, Co. Cork). The coast roads SE. to Eyeriesbegga and NW. to Kenmare, and the Healy Pass road to Adrigole, are noted for the beauty and variety of their scenery. One of the delightful local walks is that up Glanmore to the foot (6 m.) of Hungry Hill (2,251 ft; *see* Adrigole, Co. Cork). To the NW. is the beautiful demesne of Derreen House, property of Viscountess Mersey, descendant of Sir William Petty (the noted English adventurer who amassed vast estates in Ireland at the Cromwellian confiscations) and of the Kerry Fitzmaurices.

4 m. NE., on the N. slope of Knockanouganish, is a stone circle.

6 m. NE. is the pretty Cloonee–Inchiquin chain of lakes. Inchiquin Lough and the cirques of Cummeenanimma, Cummeenaloughaun, etc., are well worth visiting.

5½ m. SW., in Ardgroom townland, is Canfea stone circle (with outlier).

¾ m. W. is the Knockacappul pair of pillarstones.

2½ m. W., in Cashelkeelty, is a second pair of pillarstones.

2½ m. NW., overlooking the harbour to which it gives its name, is Kilmakilloge, an ancient church-site with remains of a two-period (Romanesque and earlier) church. The monuments here include that of the last Mac Finghin Dubh O Sullivan (d. 1809). 400 yds NE. is the holy lake, Lough Mackeenlaun, long famous for its floating tussocks. It is called after St Mo-Chíonlán, and a *pátrún* is held here on 7 and 8 July. By the E. shore are the remains of the primitive Church of St Cilian (martyred at Würzburg in 697).

LECARROW, Co. Roscommon (Map 2, C7), is a hamlet on the Athlone (11 m.)–Roscommon (10 m.) road.

A short distance SSW., on the W. side of the road, are the ruins of a large prehistoric chamber tomb.

2½ m. E., at the NW. corner of Rinndown (Rinn Dúin) peninsula, Lough Ree, a graveyard and remains of little St John's Church preserve the memory of the medieval Hospital of St John the Baptist (Augustinian Crucifers). Seán Mór Ó Dubhagáin, *ollamh* of Uí Maine, died there in 1372. A short distance S. a towered wall (564 ft), with central gateway, crosses the peninsula from shore to shore. 800 yds S. of the wall an embanked ditch cuts off the tip of the peninsula. Near the W. end of this ditch are remnants of a nave-and-chancel church. Well, ditch, and church are the sole visible relics of a town (fortified in 1251) which had grown up in the shelter of a strong English royal castle at the E. end of the ditch. The first castle here was erected *c.* 1227 by the English Justiciar, Geoffrey de Marisco, in preparation for the invasion of Connacht. The remains of the castle – in a dense thicket and scandalously neglected – seem to represent three main phases: (*a*) a motte castle (on the site of a promontory (?) fort, the *dún* of *Rinn Dúin*) with embanked ditch cutting off the tip of the peninsula; (*b*): an early-13th cent. polygonal castle of stone with rectangular keep incorporated in the curtain; the keep had a twin-vaulted basement as at Athenry, Adare, Carrickfergus, and elsewhere; (*c*): 16th–17th cent. modifications (adaptations for musketry, etc.). In front of the gate are remains of a bridge across the ditch. The inner gate (with portcullis) is late.

2½ m. SSE., on a limestone exposure in Carnagh West, is a stone ring-enclosure (Nat. Mon.) with remains of a rectangular house. It may have been a Neolithic–Early Bronze Age homestead of Knockadoon, Lough Gur, type.

LEENAUN, alias **LEENANE,** Co. Galway (Map 1, C5), is a hamlet at the SE. corner of beautiful Killary (Harbour), 20 m. NE. of Clifden, 9 m. NW. of Maum and 18 m. SSE. of Louisburgh. It is a very convenient centre for exploring some of the finest regions of the West.

Fjord-like Killary (Harbour), 8 m. long (sometime station of the British Atlantic fleet), is the drowned lower valley of the Erriff River. The Mweelrea Mts (Mweelrea, 2,688 ft; Bengorm, 2,303 ft) rise steeply from the N. shore. At the E. end is the Devil's Mother (2,131 ft). On the S. shore rise the lower summits of Maumturk (1,822 ft).

8½ m. NW., is Doo Lough (*see* Louisburgh).

3 m. NE., on the Erriff River, is Aasleagh, a waterfall.

5 m. WSW., at the foot of Garraun (1,975 ft), is lovely Lough Fee with its rhododendron-smothered island. 1 m. NNW. of the lake is Salrock (*q.v.*). The road along the N. shore of little Lough Muck leads to the coast NE. of Gowlaun; there are some good small beaches hereabouts; the coastal scenery is very fine.

LEHINCH, Co. Clare (Map 1, C7), is a small seaside and golfing resort on Liscannor Bay, 19 m. NW. of Ennis. It has a good beach with sand dunes.

At the N. end of the links are the remains of Dough Castle, the property of Daniel O Brien in the mid-17th cent. The sand holes here are reputed to be the haunts of Donn, the Fairy King.

For other features of the area, *see under* Liscannor *and* Ennistimon.

LEIGHLINBRIDGE, Co. Carlow (Map 6, B5), is a small village where the Carlow (9 m.)–Muine Bheag (5 m.) road (the old highway from Dublin to the South) crosses the Barrow.

In 1181, John de Claville, a follower of Hugh de Lacy, built a castle (*below*) to command the river-crossing. About 1270 the Carews, the Anglo-Norman proprietors of the day, founded a Carmelite friary – the first in Ireland. In 1320 a stone bridge was built by Maurice Jakis, canon of Kildare cathedral, who also built bridges over the Liffey at Kilcullen and Newbridge. The 14th cent. Gaelic recovery delivered the neighbouring territory (Idrone) to the Mac Murroughs Kavanagh, but the English Crown managed to keep control of the river crossing, and in 1547 the Lord Deputy combined the then castle and the friary into a fortress to secure it against the O Mores and O Conors. In 1567 Sir Peter Carew of Devon fabricated a hereditary claim to Idrone and obtained the constableship of the fortress, which he made the chief seat of his family in Ireland. In 1577 it was seized and wrecked by Rory Óg O More. Rebuilt once more, it was finally demolished by the Cromwellian, Col. Hewson. The remains, a 14th cent. tower (Nat. Mon.), are now known as the Black Castle.

¼ m. S., beside the Barrow, in Burgage demesne, is Ballyknockan Moat, motte of de Claville's "castle of Leighlin".

3 m. NE., at Nurney, a granite cross (Nat. Mon.) with simple ornament marks the site of an early monastery.

3 m. E. (1¼ m. SSW. of Nurney), in Agha, the remains of a church with *antae*, trabeate door, and later features mark the site of the early monastery of Achadh Urghlais.

2 m. W. is (Old) Leighlin, where a monastic church was founded in the 5th or 6th cent. The name of its founder is unknown (Gobán Fionn of Killamery?), but under abbot Laisrén moccu Imde (alias Mo-Laisse, Do-Laisse, d. 639), "apostolic delegate" and champion of the Roman method of computing the date of Easter (*see* Taghmon, Co. Wexford), it became one of the foremost monastic churches of Leinster. And so, at the 12th cent. Reformation, it became the see of the diocese to which it has given its name. (The Catholic diocese is now united with Kildare, the Protestant with Ossory and Ferns.) The only relics of the older, monastic church are St Laserian's Cross (an imperforate High Cross), St Laserian's Well (in a field W. of the cathedral), and the pedestal of a cross in the churchyard. St Lazerian's Cathedral (C. of I.) is one of the smaller medieval Irish cathedrals. The remains are substantially those of a late-13th cent. church with additions. At first the church consisted only of a nave and long chancel. N. and S. transepts were very soon added. In the 15th cent. the N. chapel was added and the bell tower inserted. The building has suffered much from the iconoclasm of the Reformation and from neglect; the N. transept is roofless; the S. transept has been swept away. The few surviving features of interest include a font which probably derives from a 12th cent. cathedral (attributed to Bishop Donat, about 1185), some good late-13th and 15th cent. details, the tombstone of Bishop Sanders (with indent of a brass effigy now lost), and a 16th cent. altar-tomb which reproduces as an ornament the elaborate ribbing of the crossing vault, itself resembling that of St Canice's Cathedral, Kilkenny.

Somewhere in the country round Old Leighlin–Leighlinbridge was the Wood of Leighlin, Art Óg Mac Murrough's "greatest fortress", in which lay that principal house of his which was burned down by Richard II of England, 28 Oct. 1394.

LEITRIM, Co. Leitrim (Map 2, C6), which gives its name to the county, is a small Shannonside village on the Carrick-on-Shannon (4 m.)–Drumshanbo (15 m.) road. Some traces remain of a medieval O Rourke castle.

2 m. SE. are the ruins of the medieval parish church of Kiltoghert.

LEIXLIP, Co. Kildare (Map 6, D7), is a village on the Dublin (10 m.)–Maynooth (5 m.) road, at the confluence of the Liffey and the Rye Water. (The latter is here the historic boundary of the kingdoms of Leinster and Brega.) It takes its name – Salmon-leap, a relic of Norse Dublinshire – from the fall on the Liffey which is now harnessed by a power station.

The Protestant parish church has a medieval W. tower.

Leixlip Castle (the Hon. Desmond Guinness), overlooking the confluence of the Rye Water and the Liffey, is an early-18th cent. house which incorporates two much altered towers etc. of a medieval castle. The first castle here was erected in the 12th cent. by Adam de Hereford, who had been granted "the cantred of O ffelan nearest to Dublin" by Strongbow.

St Catherine's, on the N. side of the Liffey, was designed by Francis Johnston in 1798. The kitchen was placed on the far side of the yard and communicated with the residence by an underground passage. Nearby are St Catherine's Wells.

1¼ m. SW. is the Wonderful Barn, a five-storey, bottle-shaped structure with external stairway, built in 1743 by Lady Connolly of Castletown (see Celbridge; see also Connolly's Folly, alias Carton Obelisk, under Maynooth).

LETTERFRACK, Co. Galway (Map 1, B5), is a small village beautifully situated on the Clifden (6½ m.)–Leenaun (9 m.) road, near the SE. corner of beautiful Barnaderg Bay (Ballynakill Harbour). The village was founded by a 19th cent. Quaker named Ellis, as one of a series of mission settlements along the N. Connemara coast. (There is still a relatively strong Protestant community in the area.)

Good bathing may be had on Barnaderg Bay and elsewhere. The Dawros River, which flows down from Kylemore (q.v.) to Ballynakill Harbour, offers excellent fishing. To the SE. rises Bengooria, alias Diamond Hill (1,460 ft); it affords magnificent views. Letterfrack is also a convenient centre for visiting such noted beauty spots as Kylemore (q.v.), Rinvyle (q.v.) and Lough Fee (see under Leenaun).

1 m. W., on the highest point (162 ft) in Rosleague (to the W. of Barnaderg Bay), is a pillarstone; ½ m. SW. is a second hill-top pillarstone; beyond the Traheen River, in Roscrea, is a third; S. of the road, in Moyard, is a small pillarstone.

LETTERKENNY, Co. Donegal (Map 2, C2), cathedral town of the diocese of Raphoe (q.v.), is situated near the head of Lough Swilly, on the Derry (20 m.)–Glenties (27 m.) road. It is one of the two administrative centres of Co. Donegal (the other being Lifford).

The only building of note is St Eunan's (=Adhamhnáin's) Cathedral (1890–1901). This is a mediocre, late Gothic Revival structure (by Hague and Mac Namara) tricked out with pseudo Irish-Romanesque details. The clerestory windows (1928–29) are by Harry Clarke. In the transepts are three Michael Healy windows: *Convention of Druim Ceat* (five-light, 1910), *Dallán and Conán Maol* (two-light, 1910), and *St Helena* (two-light, 1911). The carvings which smother the arch of the crossing depict episodes from the lives of SS Adhamhnán and Columcille. The bronze statue (1929), in the churchyard, of Cardinal O Donnell is by Francis Doyle.

S. of the town (E. of Old Town bridge) is a pillarstone. ¾ m. ESE. of the bridge, in Leck, is another.

3 m. E. is Farsetmore, the Fearsad Mór, or great sandspit at the mouth of the Swilly, where the O Donnells routed Seán the Proud O Neill in 1567.

2 m. W., on the Glenties road, is Conwal, site of an ancient monastery, one of whose 6th/7th cent. abbots, Fíachra, is said also to have been abbot of Clonard, Co. Meath (see under Kinnegad). The remains comprise a very ruinous medieval parish church, a holy well, and two early cross-pillars with spiral, fret, swastika, and other patterns. Godfrey O Donnell, King of Tír Chonaill, died and was buried at Conwal in 1258 (see Kilmacrenan). Conwal Dún is believed to have been a stronghold of the ancestors of the O Cannons; the inauguration place of the O Cannons, Kings of Tír Chonaill, was nearby.

3 m. SW., below New Mills, is Scarriffhollis, a ford over the Swilly where, on 21 June 1650, Sir Charles Coote's Parliamentarian army destroyed the last Royalist-Catholic army in Ulster. The latter was commanded by Heber Mac Mahon, Bishop of Clogher, who had been commissioned general in April and had driven the Parliamentarians out of Counties Derry and Armagh. Coote had retired behind the Foyle and had sought to dispute its passage at Strabane, but had been outflanked by Mac Mahon, who had also beaten off an attack by Coote's cavalry near Lifford. The bishop, however, proceeded to disperse his forces (see Castledoe under Creeslough), while allowing the Parliamentarians to bring up reinforcements. Undeterred by Coote's superiority and strong position, he resolved, against the advice of his officers, to accept battle at Scarriffhollis. 1,500 of his men, including Major-Gen. O Cahan and most of the principal officers, fell on the field, and large numbers were slain in the rout that followed. Those officers who surrendered on promise of quarter were butchered by Coote, including Col. Henry O Neill, son of Eóghan Rúa, who was clubbed to death outside Coote's tent. Bishop Mac Mahon escaped, but was wounded and captured two days later, and taken to Enniskillen, where, six months afterwards, Coote hanged him "with all the circumstances of contumely, reproach, and cruelty he could devise".

LETTERMULLAN, Co. Galway (Map 1, B6), is a small island to the W. of Gorumna Island (q.v.), with which it is linked by a road bridge. Close to the bridge are traces of a castle which was the residence of Murchadh Mac Hugh in 1584.

Off the SW. corner of the island is isolated Golam Head (95 ft), with a martello tower.

LIFFORD, Co. Donegal (Map 2, D3), one of the two administrative centres of Donegal, is situated on the west bank of the Foyle opposite

Strabane (*q.v.*), 16 m. SSW. of Derry and 17 m. SE. of Letterkenny.

1½ m. WNW., at Murlough, is a noteworthy church by Corr and McCormick of Derry. The stained glass is by Patrick Pollen, the Stations of the Cross by his wife.

LIMAVADY, Co. Derry (Map 3, A3), a market town, is situated where the Derry (17 m.)–Coleraine (14 m.) road crosses the River Roe at the mouth of lovely Glengiven. It takes its name (properly Newtown Limavady, previously Drumachose), from Léim a' Mhadaidh, "Dog's Leap", site of the principal O Cahan castle, 2½ m. S. near Largy bridge. The Roe holds salmon and brown trout.

Thackeray's "Sweet Peg of Limavady" lived in Ballyclose St. William Massey (1856–1925), Prime Minister of New Zealand, was a native of the town.

6½ m. N., in Tamlaghtard (Magilligan), is the site of an early monastery with remains of a church and St Aodhán's Grave (Nat. Mons.). Nearby is Tobar Easpuig Aodháin, "Bishop Aodhán's Well". The "Grave" is a 12th cent. mortuary-house. 1 m. NNE., on Church Hill Duncrun, is a cross-inscribed stone (Nat. Mon.), sole relic of an early monastery attributed to St Patrick.

10 m. N. is Magilligan Strand (*see* Castlerock *under* Coleraine).

5½ m. NE. (via the main Coleraine road and Bolea), near the Waterworks in Largantea, is Well Glass Spring Cairn, with a double-chamber tomb; it was excavated in 1936, the finds including Beakers.

6 m. NE., on the "B" road to Coleraine, is Largantea bridge. 800 yds NE. is a low, round cairn; 300 yds WNW. is a second cairn, with a third 90 yds SW. 450 yds SSW. of this last are three others and a pillarstone. West of these, in Grange Park, are four small cairns and six hut-sites. 1 m. W. of the bridge, alt. 1,000 ft in Grange Park, is a round cairn.

1½ m. E., in Fruithill (Drenagh), are the remains of Drumchose church, probably built in the 13th cent. St Cainneach of Aghaboe (*q.v.*), a native of this country – Ciannachta – had his principal northern foundation here.

4¼ m. SE., in Carrick East, is a chambered cairn (Nat. Mon.). 3 m. ESE., in Kilhoyle, alt. 700 ft at the foot of Donald's Hill, is another (Nat. Mon.). Near the summit of Donald's Hill (1,318 ft) is an overgrown cairn.

1 m. S., in Roepark Demesne, is the Mullach (Mullach na gCros), alias "Daisy Hill", a natural grassy height thought to be the meeting place of the celebrated "Convention of Druim Ceatt" summoned in 576 by King Áed son of Ainmire, at which St Columcille championed the cause of the *filid*, or Gaelic literati, and saved them from banishment. The real purpose of the meeting was to concert the defensive measures of the Northern Uí Néill and Dál Riatai against the menacing power of Baetán mac Cairill, King of Ulaid.

2 m. SW. is the early monastic site, Tamlaght Finlagan, called after St Fionnlugh, brother of St Fiontán of Dún Blesci (Co. Limerick) and disciple of Columcille. There are fragments of a medieval church here.

1 m. W., in Moneyrannell, is the Rough Fort (Nat. Trust), a large ringfort.

3 m. W., in Ballykelly, is Walworth Church (Nat. Mon.), built beside their castle in 1629 by the Fishmongers' Company of London; the chancel was added in 1719.

LIMERICK, Co. Limerick (Map 5, B4), capital of its county and cathedral town of the diocese of Limerick, is the fourth largest city in Ireland. Situated at the head of the Shannon estuary, 13 m. ESE. of Shannon Airport, 121 m. SW. of Dublin, 64 m. N. of Cork, and 64 m. SSE. of Galway, it is a seaport and manufacturing centre (bacon, milling, clothing, butter, condensed milk, tobacco, etc.) as well as an important market and communications centre. Limerick lace (guipure), made at the Good Shepherd Convent, is much sought after. The town is a convenient base for touring the Lough Derg country (*see* Killaloe) and some of the more interesting parts of Counties Limerick, Clare, and Tipperary.

The older city falls into three principal parts: English Town, on King's Island (Inis Ubhdain, alias Sibtonn) in the Shannon (the sub-river is called Abbey River); Irish Town, on the mainland to the SE.; and Newtown Pery, to the SW. of Irish Town.

The city had its origin in a Norse settlement which was established on Inis Ubhdain in A.D. 922, and rapidly became a menace to the whole of Munster. In 967 King Mahon of Thomond (E. Co. Clare; later, for a time, all Clare and Limerick and parts of Tipperary and Kerry) and his celebrated brother, Brian Boru (*see* Béal Boru *under* Killaloe), broke the power of the Limerick Norse at the battle of Solohead, near Tipperary. The pursuit raged all the way to Limerick, where the citadel was sacked and "the good town reduced to ashes". Thereafter the Norse town survived only by the grace of the Thomond kings, who valued it as a trading centre. (Hrafn, friend and informant of Ari who made voyages from Iceland to America, was a merchant of Limerick.) Muirchertach Mór O Brien, King of Munster (1086–1118) and High-king of Ireland (1101–18) as well as King of Thomond, actually made Limerick his principal seat. His grandson, Donal Mór O Brien, King of Thomond (1168–94), made the town his undoubted capital (he was *Rex Limricensis*, his kingdom – Clare, Limerick, Tipperary, and N. Kerry – *Regnum Limricense*). The family connection with the town was maintained – despite the Anglo-Norman settlement – down to the reign of Donnchadh Cairbreach O Brien (1210–42). – The first recorded bishop of Limerick, Giolla Íosa, alias "Gilbert" (1106/7–40), took a prominent part in the 12th cent. Reformation, and was

Papal Legate at the National Synod of Ráth Breasail (1111). He was an Irishman, but his immediate successors down to 1190 seem to have been Hiberno-Norse. – Limerick was an early objective of the Anglo-Normans, and in Oct., 1175, was stormed by Raymond le Gros. The following spring he had to depart, whereupon Donal Mór O Brien razed the place to the ground. Thereafter Donal was able to keep the invaders at bay, and the town was rebuilt, Donal himself founding a new cathedral. The disputed Thomond succession which followed his death gave the Anglo-Normans their opportunity, and the town was soon firmly in their hands, receiving its first charter from Prince John in 1197. In 1201 John reserved to the English Crown the city and the Cantred of the Ostmen (Norse) outside the walls. The Norse living within the walls were driven out into the Cantred, where they long survived. (The still surviving Harold family is believed to be of Norse ancestry.) Throughout the rest of the Middle Ages Limerick remained an English trading colony directly dependent on the Crown – to which it remained inflexibly loyal – but ruled by its own freemen. In 1315 it was occupied for a spell by Edward Bruce. In 1369, following on the battle of Monasternenagh (*see under* Croom), the Mac Namaras, King Brian O Brien's allies, sacked the town and installed an Irish governor. The townsfolk slew the governor, and expelled the Irish. But the Irish menace remained, and in 1466 King Tadgh of Thomond was able to impose an

annual tribute, which the town had to pay until the following cent. For all that, it continued to prosper, and by the coming of the Reformation had no fewer than fifteen parochial, monastic, and other churches. In 1642 the town was captured after a siege by a Confederate Catholic force, and remained in Confederate hands until Oct. 1651. Then, after a three-month siege by Cromwell's son-in-law, Ireton, the valour of the townsfolk, and of the garrison commanded by Hugh O Neill, was betrayed by the Ormondist faction. The victors executed, among others, Major-Gen. Purcell, ex-Mayors Fanning and Stritch, Geoffrey Baron, Sir Geoffrey Galwey, and Bishop Turloch Oilbhe O Brien of Emly. After the battle of the Boyne William of Orange attacked the town with 26,000 men. Once more the old walls witnessed gallant deeds. Features of the defence were Patrick Sarsfield's daring cavalry raid to Ballyneety behind the Williamite lines, to destroy the approaching siege train, and the heroic defence of a great breach in the town wall (where the Williamites lost 2,000 men). After three weeks William withdrew discomfited. On 4 Sept. of the following year his troops reappeared before the walls. The inferior garrison held out for a month. Then, the Williamites having taken the Thomond bridgehead by storm and butchered the defenders, the Jacobites capitulated, 3 Oct. 1691, on terms guaranteeing minimal civil rights to the Catholic majority and permitting the fighting men to join the French service. Two weeks later a great

Irish Tourist Board

Choir stalls with carved misericords, St Mary's Cathedral, Limerick

French fleet arrived in the estuary with strong reinforcements and abundant supplies. The Jacobites stood by their bond. Not so the victors; with the Jacobite forces (the "Wild Geese") – who included almost the entire surviving native aristocracy and leadership – out of the way, the civil articles of the Treaty of Limerick were soon violated. In the course of the following century the city gradually recovered from its wounds, a notable development being the laying out of Newtown Pery with its well-planned streets of Georgian brick houses. During this same century the town was the birthplace or resort of several well-known Gaelic poets: Father Liam Inglis, O.S.A. (d. 1778) was born in Limerick; Brian Mac Giolla-Meidhre (*see* Feakle) died in the town, 1805; Aindrias Mac Mathghamhna kept a tan-yard in the city; Seán Lloyd was living in the city in 1775. Notable Limerick names in Anglo-Irish literature are those of Gerald Griffin (1803–40), playwright and novelist (*The Collegians, The Colleen Bawn*), and Kate O Brien, distinguished contemporary novelist. Francis Bindon (1690?–1765) of Clooney, Co. Clare, painter, architect, and associate of Richard Cassels, was born in Limerick.

The more important relics of medieval Limerick are in English Town. In Nicholas St, to the E. of Mathew Bridge, is St Mary's Cathedral (C. of I.). The church was founded by Donal Mór O Brien after the fire of 1176. The original (about 1180–95?) Romanesque–Transitional church was cruciform (aisleless chancel and transepts, aisled nave of four bays), plan and certain details reflecting the influence of the Cistercian architecture (Burgundian variety) current in the Ireland of that time. To this simple, austere building a bell-tower, at least nine chantry chapels, battlements, and a S. porch were added in the course of the 13th, 14th, and 15th–16th centuries. Thereafter the Reformation, the Cromwellians, war, and 17th, 18th, and 19th cent. restorers – including the Englishmen, James Pain, William Bardwell, William Slater (and George Edmund Street ?), the Kerryman, James Franklin Fuller, and the Limerick men, Joseph Fogerty and William Sidney Cox – all left their marks on the cathedral which, nonetheless, has its interesting features. In the chancel (lengthened early in the 13th cent., restored in the 17th, and again by Pain, 1831, and by Slater, 1860–61) are: (*a*) the alleged tombstone of King Donal Mór O Brien; (*b*) a 15th (?) cent. slab inscribed DONOH and alleged to commemorate Bishop Donnchadh O Brien (d. 1207; said to have completed the transepts and lengthened the chancel); (*c*) the monument erected 1678 to Donnchadh O Brien, "Great" Earl of Thomond, in place of one wrecked by the Cromwellians (it includes the remains of the effigies of the earl and his countess from the original, 1621, monument, which Donnchadh had ordered to be like that of Sir Francis Vere in Westminster Abbey); (*d*) a fragment of the 1421 tomb of Bishop

Conor O Dea (*see* St John's Cathedral, *below*), whose 15th cent. effigy was spared by the Cromwellians only to be destroyed by 19th cent. "restorers". In the choir (and nave) are late 15th cent. stalls whose misericords are the only carved examples surviving in Ireland. In the S. transept (remodelled by Slater, 1862; Westropp monument by Poole of Bath) is an excellent 15th cent. Galwey–Bultingfort tomb originally polychrome; restored by Slater, it now incorporates the mensa (episcopal effigy erased) of an older tomb. The choir room E. of the transept occupies the site of the chantry chapels of SS Mary Magdalen and James (14th cent.; restored about 1420?). The S. aisle is flanked by four chantries, the three eastern of uncertain dedications, the western (about 1480) dedicated to St George; the Lord Glentworth (d. 1844) monument in the latter is by E. M. Bailly, R.A. The aisle pier second from the west has a slab with carvings of the Crucifixion, Christ and Satan, and St Michael and Satan. The N. aisle is flanked by three chantries, the latest now serving as baptistry. The largest, St Nicholas's Chapel, possibly dating from the 14th cent., was restored about 1490 (and by Fuller, 1869); the 1836 Bishop Jebb statue is by Bailly. The nave piers have Transitional capitals. The bell-tower was erected over the W. bay in the 13th cent.; the bell-chamber is 15th–16th cent.; the parapet affords a fine panorama. The Romanesque W. doorway was wantonly "restored" by Fuller in 1895, only the hood and the innermost of its four orders being left. In the churchyard, at the S. side of the cathedral, is the Sexten vault with medieval *Pelican in her piety* (symbolic of Christ the Redeemer) and *Seven-headed dragon* (symbolic of Antichrist).

Close to the cathedral, on the SW., is the riverside County Court House, a Classical building of 1809 by the Limerick architects, Nicholas and William Hannan (interior reconstructed, 1957).

Commanding Thomond Bridge, a short distance NW. of the cathedral, are the remains of King John's Castle (Nat. Mon.), a once splendid fortress of 1200 which was an integral part of the town defences. The magnificent twin-towered gatehouse, N. curtain, NW. and SW. angle towers, and S. curtain, survive in part; at the SE. angle is a fragment of a 1611 bastion which replaced the medieval angle tower there. The medieval works show various alterations: the gate towers have lost their rectangular projections towards the court; the angle towers have been reduced in height and reinforced with strong vaultings, to bear heavy guns. The interior was altogether spoilt by 18th–19th cent. barracks and 20th cent. municipal dwelling-houses. Fragments of the town wall survive nearby at St Munchin's Church (C. of I.), Church St.

E. of the castle, in the grounds of the Convent of Mercy, Convent St, are remains of the Dominican Friary of St Saviour (1227), founded by Donnchadh Cairbreach O Brien, King of

Irish Tourist Board
17th cent. statue of Our Lady, Dominican
church, Limerick

Thomond (buried here, 1241), and rebuilt by
James, 6th Earl of Desmond who was buried
there in 1462; carvings of the 15th cent. and
later have been placed at two grottoes. In
1644 Pope Innocent X erected the friary into
a university for the Catholic Confederation (of
Kilkenny).

At the W. end of Thomond Bridge, mounted
on a pedestal, is the "Treaty Stone", on which,
according to tradition, the articles of capitulation were signed in 1691.

In the grounds of St Anne's Vocational
School, W. of Mary St, are the remains (Nat.
Mon.) of Fanning's Castle, a late-15th cent.
house.

Irish Town is connected to English Town
by two bridges across the Abbey River. Beyond
the SE. bridge (Ball's Bridge), Broad St and
John St lead SE. towards St John's Cathedral
(*below*). At the S. end of the W. bridge (Mathew
Bridge) is the Custom House, an attractive
building (1769; by Davis Ducart) which is
unworthily maintained. (The principal front is
to the river.) Rutland St leads from the bridge

to Patrick St and O Connell St, main axis of
Newtown Pery, the handsome Georgian town
(now in decline) laid out on Pery lands outside
the municipal boundary by Davis Ducart for
Edmond Sexton Pery (1719–1806; Speaker of
the Dublin House of Commons, 1771–85;
Viscount Pery, 1785) and the Independent
Citizens – heirs of the old Merchants' Guild –
so as to free the city merchants and tradesmen
from the shackles of the corrupt Vereker–
Smyth–Prendergast clique which had secured
control of the old municipality. At the foot of
Rutland St is the Town Hall, an attractive
brick house built in 1805 by the Independent
Citizens as the Commercial (alias Mercantile)
Buildings. Some of the city muniments and
regalia may be seen here; others are in the City
Library, Pery Sq. (*below*). O Connell St
terminates in the Crescent (1857 statue of O
Connell by John Hogan). Further W., in Upper
Henry St, is St Alphonsus's Church (Redemp-
torist), a Gothic Revival essay (1858–62) by
P. C. Hardwick of London, for whom William
Edward Corbett of Limerick superintended the
building. The high altar, reredos and altar rails
are by George Goldie of London. The "decorations" and additions are deplorable.

SE. of O Connell St, in Pery Sq., is the
People's Park with Rice Memorial Column
(by the famous engineer, Alexander Nimmo)
commemorating the achievements of Thomas
Spring-Rice (1790–1866), 1st Baron Monteagle
of Brandon (*see* Foynes). Spring-Rice was a
Protestant liberal lawyer who devoted himself
to civic reform and justice for Catholics; he was
Chancellor of the United Kingdom Exchequer,
1835–39. Also in the park is the Public Library,
Art Gallery, and Museum: small collections
of local antiquities and modern Irish paintings.
Nearby, to the N., is St Saviour's Church
(Dominican), a remodelling, 1860 onwards, of
an 1815–16 building. Chancel, high altar, and
Lady Chapel are by J. J. McCarthy. The high
altar tabernacle and reredos and the aisled
nave are by George Goldie. (From 1870 onwards Maurice Hennessy of Limerick supervised the work for Goldie.) Above the Lady
Altar is a 17th cent. statue of Our Lady brought
from Flanders in 1640 and presented to the
Dominicans by Patrick Sarsfield, a city merchant, in atonement for the sentencing to
death of Sir John Burke of Brittas by the
donor's uncle. (Sir John was arrested for
preventing the seizure of the priest secretly
saying Mass in his house on the Feast of the
Holy Rosary, 1607.) The Savings Bank nearby
in Glentworth St, a little Doric temple, is by
W. H. Owen, a Welsh architect who settled in
Limerick.

In Henry St (N. of O Connell St) are the
Franciscan church (1876 onwards; by William
Edward Corbett), the 1784 Protestant Bishop's
Palace (now Messrs. Rank Ltd; windows
spoilt), and the former town house (also 1784)
of the Perys, later Earls of Limerick.

On the S. side of the city, near the site of

*Mitre of Conor O Dea, St John's Cathedral,
Limerick*

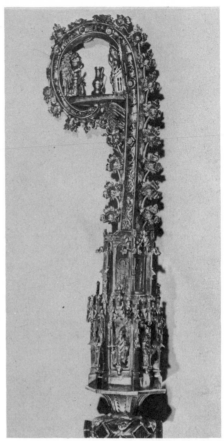

*Crozier of Conor O Dea, St John's Cathedral,
Limerick*

Irish Town's John Gate, is St John's Sq, with
three sides of stone-fronted houses by Davis
Ducart. Nearby is St John's Cathedral, a good
Gothic-Revival building (1856–61) by P. C.
Hardwick. The fine tower and spire are by M.
and S. Hennessy of Limerick. The statue of
the Virgin and Child is by John Hogan's friend,
Benzoni. In the cathedral treasury may be seen
the beautiful mitre and superb silver-gilt crozier
made by Thomas O Carryd in 1418 for Conor
O Dea, Bishop of Limerick (1400–1426). These
are the only great pieces of Irish ecclesiastical
art of the High Middle Ages still remaining
in their historic custody. The crozier is the only
medieval Irish crozier to survive at all; its
quality gives an idea of the artistic losses which
resulted from the Reformation and from the
English conquests of the 16th and 17th centuries. In the cathedral treasury may also be
seen the interesting Arthur Cross, an altar-
cross reliquary made for Bishop Richard
Arthur in 1625 by Philip Leyles (Lawless?);
the figured plating of the stem comes from a
cross of about 1400. In the presbytery garden
is a Patrick Sarsfield memorial statue (1881)
by John Lawlor of Dublin.

N. of the cathedral, at and near St John's
Hospital, are fragments of the city walls,
including a sallyport and part of the "Black
Battery" blown up, along with many of King
William's English and German troops, on the
occasion of the abortive grand assault of 1690
(the "Battle of the Breach"), which took place
in and about the hospital grounds.

Sarsfield St leads NW. from O Connell St to
Ennis Rd. On Sarsfield Bridge is a 1916–22
memorial by Albert Power (completed by his
son). It takes the place of a statue (1857; by
Patrick Mac Dowell, R.A.) of Viscount Fitzgibbon erected in memory of the Limerick men
who fell at Balaclava, and which patriotic
fervour had consigned to the waters below.

Sarsfield Bridge leads to the Ennis Rd, where
is the Church of Our Lady of the Rosary
(1949–50). This temporary wooden church, by
F. M. Corr and W. H. D. Mc Cormick (*see*
Ennistimon), is one of the more significant of
recent contributions to Irish ecclesiastical
architecture and art. The teak statue on the
tower (*Our Lady of Fatima*) is by Oisín Kelly,
the nearby *Annunciation* by Imogen Stuart.
Over the entrance (inside) is a *Deposition from*

the Cross by Andrew O Connor; this is the plaster model for the bronze now in the Tate Gallery, London. The Sanctuary figures of the *Sacred Heart* and *Our Lady* are by Yvonne Jammet. The *St Anne* is by Éamonn Costello. In the baptistry is a single-light *Baptism of Christ* by Evie Hone (1950); the font is by T. Quinn.

On the right bank of the Shannon (via the N. Circular Rd), in the grounds of Old Church near Barrington's Pier, is ruined St Mainchín's (Munchin's) Church, better known as Kilrush (Nat. Mon.): an early church with trabeate W. door. The curious window in the S. wall was brought here from a Franciscan (Tertiary?) church in Mary's Lane.

3½ m. N., at Ardnacrusha, is the power station of the Shannon hydro-electric scheme (1925), first step in the development of native power resources by the new Irish state. Permission to view the plant should be sought from the Electricity Supply Board, Dublin.

1¼ m. E. (via Clare St), in Singland, St Patrick's Well marks the site of an early monastery whose Round Tower and church were levelled in 1766. According to legend, St Patrick baptized Cairthenn, King of Dál gCais, at the well, which is still a place of pilgrimage on 17 March.

7 m. E. is Barringtonsbridge (*q.v.*).

2 m. SE. are the remains of the early church of Donaghmore.

3 m. SW. is Mungret, site of a monastery founded by the deacon, Neassán (d. 551), who, according to some, was a disciple of St Patrick. The monastery was one of the greatest of the early monasteries of Ireland, and the learning of its monks was proverbial. It survived every disaster, including repeated devastation by the Norse, and in the 12th cent. may have adopted the Rule of the Canons Regular of St Augustine. In its heyday it had six churches; but all that now survive are: (*a*) a 12th cent. church with trabeate W. door; (*b*) the "Abbey", a 13th–15th cent. nave-and-chancel church with dwelling tower at the W. end; (*c*) a small 13th (?) cent. chapel (all Nat. Mons.). In the churchyard is the grave of Séamus O Dála(igh) of Loughmore (1750–1810), one of the Maigue poets. – 2 m. NW. of Mungret are the shattered remains of the great rock castle of Carrigogunnel (Carraig Ó gConaing). The first castle here was built *c.* 1201 by William de Burgo, son-in-law of Donal Mór O Brien. About 1336 the O Briens built a new castle which was later acquired by the Earls of Desmond. In the following century the 6th Earl enfeoffed his foster-brother, Brian, son of King Conor of Thomond, in the castle and the extensive territory thereafter known as Pobal Briain (Pubblebrien). In 1536 the castle surrendered to Lord Deputy Grey, who had attacked it for two days with artillery; he hanged the garrison. In 1655 Donnchadh O Brien sold Carrigogunnel to Michael Boyle, brother of the Earl of Cork and Protestant Archbishop of Dublin. In Aug.

1691, it was surrendered to the Williamites, who blew up the defences in 1698. The lower ward had a gate on the SE., a postern to the W., and a great hall at the NE. angle. In the small, paved upper ward are the remains of a great keep, a circular bastion, a long range of buildings, and a 16th cent. house. Nearby are remains of St Margaret's Church. 2 m. ENE. of the castle is Tervoe House, a Monsell house of 1785 enlarged in 1830; late Adam-style decoration. 1½ m. NW. is Cooperhill House (1791).

LISBURN, Co. Antrim (Map 3, C5), on the River Lagan, is a cathedral and manufacturing town (linen, ropes, etc.) on the main road from Belfast (8 m.) to the South. Formerly known as Lisnagarvey, the place was granted in 1609 by James I to Sir Fulke (later Viscount) Conway, who planted it with English, Welsh, and Scottish settlers and built a castle in 1627. In 1641 town and castle suffered at the hands of the insurgent Irish. In 1707 they were destroyed by fire. The prosperity of Lisburn dates from 1699, when William III granted a patent to Samuel Louis Crommelin (1652–1727), a Huguenot refugee from Picardy, who introduced Dutch looms and reorganized the linen industry. Descendants of some of Crommelin's Huguenots still live in the town.

In the Castle Gardens, Castle St, is a gateway (Nat. Mon.) bearing the date 1677, all that survives of Conway's castle.

The Technical School, Castle St, occupies the home of Sir Richard Wallace (1818–90), a local landlord whose London residence, Hertford House, is now the Wallace Museum. Sir Richard's collection of paintings, the Wallace Collection, was presented by his widow to the British nation.

Christ Church, cathedral of the Church of Ireland diocese of Connor, was built by the Planters in 1623 as a parish church, and was raised to cathedral status in 1662; spire added in 1807. Among the memorials are: one (1827) to the celebrated Jeremy Taylor, author of a *Discourse on Friendship* ("I believe some wives have been the best friends in the world") and of *Ductor Dubitantium*, etc., who was bishop of Down and Connor 1661–67 and who is buried at Dromore (*q.v.*); one to Lieut. William Smith Dobbs (1780; by Edward Smyth, the Meath sculptor), killed in the encounter with Paul Jones off Carrickfergus (*q.v.*) in 1778. In the churchyard are several Huguenot tombs.

In the triangular market-place is a handsome Assembly Room (formerly also the town Market House). Nearby is a statue (by John Henry Foley) to John Nicholson (1821–57), hero of the Siege of Delhi, who was born in Dublin, but whose family hailed from Lisburn. Native-born Lisburnmen were Henry Munro, linen merchant (who led the 1798 insurgents to victory at Saintsfield, Co. Down, but was defeated at Ballynahinch, taken prisoner, and hanged in front of his own door), and

Bartholomew Teeling of the United Irishmen, who was also hanged in 1798. Teeling's mother was Mary Taafe of Smarmore, Co. Louth (*see* Ardee).

Lambeg Church (C. of I.) occupies the site of a 15th cent. Franciscan Tertiary friary.

3 m. NNW., beside the fragment of the Jacobean house called Castle Robin, is the motte (also a remnant of the bailey) of a 12th cent. Norman castle. 2 m. NNE. is Collin Mountain (1,085 ft). On the summit is a round cairn which may cover a passage grave.

5 m. E. is Drumbo (*see* Newtownbreda *under* Belfast).

2½ m. SSE., at Todd's Grove, Duneight, is a large, bivallate ringfort. Less than 1 m. S., by the little Ravernet, is a motte-and-bailey (Nat. Mon.) on the site of an earlier stronghold.

6½ m. WSW. is the early monastic site of Trummery: roughly circular churchyard, fragments of a medieval church, the site of a Round Tower.

LISCANNOR, Co. Clare (Map 1, C7), is a small fishing village at the N. end of Liscannor Bay, 22 m. NW. of Ennis. The bay was of strategic interest as offering an easy landing-place for invading forces in Armada times, when the place was held by Sir Turlough O Brien, and again during both the Napoleonic and Second World Wars. John P. Holland (1841–1914), patriot and inventor of the submarine, was a native of Liscannor. His great invention was inspired by the hope of smashing British naval power, and so freeing his native land.

The castle W. of the village was an O Brien stronghold.

1 m. NE. of the village, on the seashore, is Kilmacreehy, Mac Creiche's Church, a medieval nave-and-chancel parish church. Nearby is St Mac Creiche's Well. Two tide-covered rocks are St Mac Creiche's Bed (or Grave). According to legend the "city" of Cill Stuihín lies submerged in the bay. Hugh Mac Curtin (1680–1755), the antiquarian, was born and died near here.

2½ m. NW. is a 19th cent. monument to Cornelius O Brien, M.P., of nearby Birchfield. O Brien compelled his tenants to pay for it. Nearby is Daigh (alias Dabhach) Bhrighde, St Brigid's Well. Here, at nightfall on Sathærn Chranndubh (Chromdubh), the Saturday preceding the last Sunday of July, crowds used to assemble, from the Aran Islands as well as the mainland, for the first part of a Lughnasa celebration which continued next day at Lehinch. The celebrations included merrymaking and a singing vigil through the night, as well as "rounds" of prayers at the well.

Edwin Smith

The Cliffs of Moher, Liscannor

3 m. NW. are the Cliffs of Moher (highest point 668 ft), which rise sheer from the Atlantic. The usual viewpoint for visitors is (Cornelius) O Brien's Tower (a disused tea house erected in 1835), 587 ft above the sea. Here a magnificent view may be had across the mouth of Galway Bay and the Aran Islands towards Connemara. The cliffs take their name from an ancient promontory fort, Mothair, which stood on Hag's Head until removed in the last cent. to make way for a signal tower.

LISCARROLL, Co. Cork (Map 5, B5), is a village on the Buttevant (7 m.)–Drumcolliher (7 m.) road.

There are remains (Nat. Mon.) of the third largest 13th cent. castle in Ireland: a quadrangular court with cylindrical angle-towers, a strong rectangular gatehouse (upper storey 15th cent.) in the S. curtain, and a rectangular tower in the N. curtain. Towers and curtain have lost their battlements, and the SE. tower, which contains the castle well, has been reduced to a fragment. There appear to have been buildings against the curtain all around the courtyard. The castle was probably built by the Anglo-Norman Barrys. On 20 Aug. 1642 it was attacked by Garret Barry, general of the Confederate Catholic army of Munster. The small garrison surrendered on 2 Sept. Next day Murrough the Burner O Brien and Sir Charles Vavasour arrived with an English army and dispersed the Confederates after an obstinate resistance. The victors were quickly obliged to retire.

LISDOONVARNA, Co. Clare (Map 1, D7), is a "spa" (sulphur and chalybeate springs) and popular holiday resort set 400 ft above sea level in the bleak uplands of West Clare, 8 m. N. of Ennistimon and 10 m. SW. of Ballyvaghan. It is a convenient centre for exploring the wild beauties of Burren, and of N. Clare in general, so rich in prehistoric chamber tombs and other antiquities.

A rewarding tour is the circuit, Lisdoonvarna –Doolin–Ballynalackan–Ailladie–Black Head– Ballyvaghan – Corkscrew Hill – Lisdoonvarna (36 m.).

3½ m. N., in Slieve Elva, is Pollnagollum, entrance to one of the longest (4½ m.) caves in the country.

6 m. NE. is Corkscrew Hill (*see under* Ballyvaghan).

5 m. SW. is Doolin (*q.v.*).

7 m. SW. are the Cliffs of Moher (*see under* Liscannor).

3 m. NW. is the interesting rock castle of Ballynalackan, a 15th cent. O Brien stronghold: tower and well-preserved bawn.

LISMORE, Co. Waterford (Map 5, D5), a market town beautifully sited in the celebrated Blackwater valley, at the S. foot of the Knockmealdown Mountains, is a noted angling centre and a convenient base for touring some of the loveliest regions in E. Munster. It is 13 m. S. of Clogheen, 4 m. W. of Cappoquin, 18 m. NNW. of Youghal, and 16 m. E. of Fermoy.

Lismore is famous in Irish history as the site of a double monastery founded towards the close of his life by St Cárthach, alias Mo-Chuda (*anglice* Carthage, d. 637/8) of Rahan (*see under* Tullamore). The famous Welsh saint, Cadoc of Llan Carvan, and St Cathaldus, 7th cent. Bishop of Tarentum in S. Italy, are said to have been trained there. The monastery was sacked five or six times by the Vikings, but never lost its pre-eminence in the kingdom of the Déise (Decies), and was one of the strongholds of the 8th–9th cent. céle Dé movement (*see* Tallaght). In the 12th cent. it was one of the leading monasteries of Munster, figured prominently in the reform movement, and, *c.* 1120, became the see of a diocese for the Déise. Almost immediately after his landing in Ireland (1171), Henry II paid a two-day visit to the Papal Legate, Bishop Gilla Críst Úa Con-Doirche of Lismore, in furtherance of his pretensions. He took advantage of the occasion "and the bishop's benevolence" to pick the site for an English castle. Two years later Lismore was pillaged by Anglo-Normans led by Raymond le Gros. Díarmait Mac Carthy, King of Desmond, came up to drive off the "teachers of respect for churches and ecclesiastics", only to meet with a sharp reverse. In 1185 Prince John of England, as Lord of Ireland, erected a castle (*below*) beside the river. In 1363 the diocese was united by Pope Urban V with that of Waterford, but it retained its own cathedral until the Reformation. (The Church of Ireland diocese is united with those of Waterford and Cashel and Emly.) In 1589 the bishop's castle was presented to Sir Walter Raleigh by the notorious pluralist, Meyler Mac Grath (*see* Cashel). Raleigh sold it to Richard Boyle, "Great" Earl of Cork (*see* Youghal), in 1602. In 1641 and 1643 the castle was held against the Confederate Catholics by Roger Boyle, Earl of Orrery; but in 1645 it was taken by Lord Castlehaven, and a Catholic garrison held it until the arrival of Cromwell. In 1753 the castle passed, with the Boyle estates, to the 4th Duke of Devonshire on his marriage to Lady Charlotte Boyle.

In its heyday Lismore had, it is said, no fewer than twenty churches. In the 17th cent. the ruins of eight still survived. Today only a few scraps remain to recall ancient greatness. Greatly altered St Carthage's Cathedral (C. of I.) dates from 1633, when it was erected by the notorious Richard Boyle on the site of the ruined pre-Reformation cathedral, some fragments of which (chancel arch, S. transept windows, etc.) it incorporates. In it may be seen an elaborate Mac Grath tomb of 1557, with figures of *The Crucifixion, Ecce Homo, Apostles, SS Gregory the Great, Cárthach, Catherine of Alexandria, Patrick*, etc. There are early-19th cent. stained glass windows by George Mc Allister of Dublin. Built into the W. wall are

The Castle, Lismore

a Romanesque figured corbel, five early grave-stones, and other fragments, found when erecting the 1827 bell-tower, whose spire "called forth Thackeray's rapturous admiration".

The imposing "Castle", superbly sited above the Blackwater, was built by Joseph Paxton, of Crystal Palace fame, for the 6th Duke of Devonshire, but it incorporates fragments of the medieval episcopal castle. The Romanesque gateway has been purloined from a 12th cent. church, which probably stood nearby at Reilig Mhuire, alias Reilig na nEasbog, burial-place of St Cárthach, of Archbishop Ceallach ("Celsus") of Armagh (d. 1129; *see* Ardpatrick), and of other illustrious dead. The site of the traditional Tobar Chárthaigh, St Cárthach's Well, is occupied by the castle gate lodge. (What passes now as Cárthach's Well – *patrún* on 14 May – is properly Tobar na Ceárdchan, "The Forge Well".) In 1814 the "Lismore Crozier" (National Museum) and the so-called *Book of Lismore* were discovered hidden in one of the castle walls. The *Book of Lismore*, an important collection of Irish saints' Lives and much secular material, was compiled in the 15th cent. by Aonghus Ó Callanáin, Friar Ó Buagácháin, and other scribes, for Finghin Mac Carthy Riabhach and his wife, Catherine Fitzgerald, daughter of the 8th Earl of Desmond. In 1629 it was at Timoleague friary, where the celebrated Brother Michael O Clery, chief of the Four Masters, made use of it. When and how it found its way to Lismore remains a mystery. (*See* Kilbrittain *under* Courtmacsherry.) Richard Boyle's sons, Robert (1627–91), the chemist (formulator of "Boyle's Law"), and Roger (1621–79), later Earl of Orrery, were born in old Lismore Castle. Adele

Astaire, the dancer, who married the late Lord Charles Cavendish, lived in the existing castle for some years.

St Carthage's Church (1881–84) is a Lombardo-Romanesque structure by W. G. Doolin.

1 m. E., on the S. side of the Blackwater, is Lismore, alias Round Hill, motte-and-bailey of the castle erected by Prince John in 1185 and destroyed by the Irish.

5 m. SE. is Okyle (*see under* Cappoquin).

6 m. W. is Ballyduff Castle, an interesting fortified house erected in 1628 by the "Great" Earl of Cork. 2 m. W. are the ruins of Mocollop castle, with circular keep and square flankers. James, 6th Earl of Desmond and son of Gearóid *file* (Earl Gerald, the Gaelic poet), died here in 1462. In 1642 the castle was taken by Confederate Catholics from Richard Boyle's representative, but was abandoned by them shortly afterwards. In July 1645 it was re-occupied by Lord Castlehaven. On 15 Feb. 1647 Lord Inchiquin captured it for the Parliamentarians. In Jan. 1650 it was gallantly defended by Richard Maunsell against Cromwell, whose artillery battered it. Portraits of Maunsell and his wife, and a store of arms, etc., were discovered in the castle in 1826. 3 m. N. of Mocollop is Labbanacallee, a chamber tomb giving its name to the townland.

LISNASKEA, Co. Fermanagh (Map 2, D5), is a village on the Clones (11 m.)–Enniskillen (11 m.) road. The townland, Lisoneill, takes its name from the *lios* where O Neill of Tyrone used to inaugurate Maguire. By the close of Elizabeth I's reign this was already "a deserted old fort . . . of small stones, surrounded by a fosse, covered with tall trees at the edge".

The cross in the Cornmarket incorporates the base and part of the shaft of a High Cross from an early monastery; on one face is a weathered *Fall of Adam and Eve*, on another are thirty-two bosses.

In the Protestant churchyard, S. of the village, are the ruins of Castle Balfour (Nat. Mon.), a Plantation castle built by Sir James Balfour about 1618, refortified by the Cromwellian, Ludlow, in 1652, and partly dismantled in 1689.

½ m. NNE., in Cornashee, is the Moat (Nat. Mon.), a cairn-topped (?) mound.

5 m. NE. is Brookeborough, ancestral home of Field Marshal Lord Alanbrooke.

1¾ m. S., in Aghalurcher, on the site of an early foundation of St Rónán's, are some remains (Nat. Mon.) of a medieval parish church. In the vaulted chapel or sacristy is the effigy of a bishop holding a book and crozier. A short distance N. is St Ronan's Stone.

LISTOWEL, Co. Kerry (Map 4, D3), is a market town on the Tarbert (11 m.)–Tralee (16 m.) road.

Bryan Mac Mahon, writer of distinction, is a schoolmaster here, while John B. Keane, the dramatist, runs a pub.

There are remains (Nat. Mon.) of a castle of the Fitzmaurices, Lords of Kerry, the last fortress to be held against Elizabethan forces in the Desmond wars. In 1600 the castle surrendered to the Elizabethan commander, Sir Charles Wilmot, who put the garrison to the sword. The Fitzmaurice estates were thereafter confiscated, but were restored by James I.

5¾ m. ENE. is Knockanure. Corpus Christi Church (1963–64) is by Michael Scott and Associates. It has three works by Oisín Kelly: *Last Supper* (porch screen), *Virgin and Child*, and *Crucifix*. The tapestry Stations of the Cross were designed by Leslie Mc Weeney.

4 m. NW. is Gunsborough, birthplace of Lord Kitchener of Khartoum (1850–1916).

LIXNAW, Co. Kerry (Map 4, D3), is a village 6 m. SW. of Listowel. There are remains of The Court, a castle of the Knights of Kerry which surrendered to the Elizabethan commander, Sir Charles Wilmot, in 1602. It was considerably enlarged in the 18th cent., but fell into ruin 150 years ago. E. of the village is a monument to John, 3rd Knight of Kerry.

1 m. SW., near Gortaneare, are the ruins of two churches.

3¼ m. SW., in Tonaknock, close to the ancient church-site of Killahan, is a plain, sandstone cross (defective; Nat. Mon.).

LONGFORD, Co. Longford (Map 2, C6), on the Edgeworthstown (8¼ m.)–Strokestown (12 m.) road, is the county town of Co. Longford and the cathedral town of the Catholic diocese of Ardagh and Clonmacnois. In the Middle Ages the O Farrells of Annaly had a castle here, and in 1400 built a Dominican friary. No trace of either survives. The fragments of a castle incorporated in the old military barracks belong to one built in 1627 by the first Aungier Earl of Longford, and unsuccessfully besieged by Eóghan Rúa O Neill.

St Mel's Cathedral, a Classical church which Pugin denounced as "a bad copy of that wretched compound of pagan and Protestant architecture, St Pancras New Church in London", is one of the better post-Emancipation churches in Ireland. The original architect was Joseph B. Keane. Building began in 1840, but was broken off during the Famine years and not completed until 1893; the final form of the belfry (about 1860) being due to John Burke, that of the portico (1889–93) to George C. Ashlin. In the adjacent diocesan college (St Mel's) is a small collection of local antiquities, including the remains of St Mel's enshrined bachall.

3½ m. SE. is the fine motte-and-bailey of Lissardowlan, relic of the Anglo-Norman invasion. The motte-castle was destroyed by Áedh O Conor of Connacht in 1224. Later in the 13th cent. the district was recovered from the invaders by the O Farrells, and it was they who built the stone castle.

8 m. SW. (2¾ m. NW. of Killashee), in Ballynakill graveyard, are a number of early grave-slabs (Nat. Mon.) of the Clonmacnois type, indicating that this is the site of an early monastery (perhaps Cluain Deochra founded by the 6th cent. bishop, Earnán); also a Bishop's Grave, perhaps that of William Mac Carmaic, Bishop of Ardagh (d. 1373).

LORRHA, Co. Tipperary (Map 5, C2), is a small village 6 m. N. of Borrisokane, 5 m. E. of Portumna, and 8 m. W. of Birr.

St Rúán, alias Rúadhán (d. 584), disciple of Finnian of Clonard (*see under* Kinnegad), founded a monastery here. The tale of his cursing of Tara (*q.v.*) is among the best-known fictions of early Irish history. His monastery became one of the foremost monasteries of Munster. One of its "wonders" was a food-giving tree, perhaps a sacred tree in heathen times. In the 12th cent. Lorrha adopted the Rule of the Canons Regular of St Augustine. The celebrated 9th cent. Stowe Missal (Royal Irish Academy) belonged to the old monastery of Lorrha, where it was probably written. Its metal shrine (National Museum) was made at Clonfert, or at Clonfertmulloe, for Brian Boru's son, Donnchadh, and for Mac Cráith Úa Donnchadha, King of Cashel; it was refurbished by Philip O Kennedy, Lord of Ormond (d. 1381). During some period of persecution the Missal was secreted in a wall of the O Kennedy castle of Lackeen (*below*), to be discovered about 1735, when the place was being remodelled. No local scholar could read it, so Aindrias Mac Cruitín (*see* Kilfarboy *under* Milltown Malbay), the West Clare poet and *seanchaí*, was brought over for the purpose (having been first provided with a new suit, a horse, and ample "expense" money). St Rúán's Bell, now in the British Museum, was preserved at or near Lorrha until the 19th cent.

The Protestant church and churchyard, at the E. end of the village, occupy the site of St Rúán's monastery. In the churchyard are the stumps and bases of two 8th/9th cent. High Crosses. Of Kilclispeen (see under Carrick-on-Suir) type, they were demolished by the Cromwellians. The church has a two-light window (*The Holy Women at the Tomb of Christ*) by Michael Healy (1918); the roofless nave has a 13th (?) cent. S. doorway, inset in which is a smaller, 15th cent. doorway with interesting details. In a cottage garden at the churchyard gate may be seen other medieval carvings. NE. of the church is a defaced motte.

NW. of the Protestant church is "St Rodan's Abbey" (Nat. Mon.), ruined church of the Augustinian priory Beatae Mariae Fontis Vivi; it has an interesting, small, Perpendicular doorway.

SW. of the village is the ruined church (Nat. Mon.) of a Dominican friary founded in 1269 by Walter de Burgo. The adjacent parish church occupies the site of the conventual buildings; in the gable may be seen some medieval fragments.

4 m. NE., in Lisheen and Lisballyard, are St Kieran's Well and St Kieran's Stone.

2¾ m. E. is the 16th cent. O Kennedy castle of Lackeen: tower and large bawn; Nat. Mon. S. of the castle, in Gort an Phíobaire, is the site of the vanished village of Piperstown. 2¼ m. NE. of the castle are Lisheen and Lisballyard (*above*).

LOUGH CORRIB, Co. Galway (Map 1, C5–D6), second largest lake (27,000 acres) in Ireland, is a beautiful, island-studded sheet of clear water, some 27 m. long from near Galway in the S. to the Galway–Mayo border in the N. It is famous for its large trout (Mayfly "dapping" is a speciality).

The S. and E. shores are, for the most part, low; but on the W. and N. the foothills and outliers of the Iar-Chonnacht and Joyce's Country mountains (see Connemara) crowd close to the waters. Their great variety, induced by the ever-changing light, presents a delightful scene.

The shores and islands abound in monuments of all periods. Sir William Wilde (1815–76), father of Oscar Wilde, and a leading antiquarian of his time, devoted an excellent Victorian book to them (*Lough Corrib, its Shores and Islands*, new edition available). In this Guide they are referred to under Annaghdown, Cong, Galway, Headford, Maum, Moycullen, and Oughterard (*q.v.*).

LOUGH DERG, Co. Donegal (Map 2, C3), is a small, lonely lake in the mountains of S. Donegal. It is most readily reached from Pettigoe (*q.v.*), 5 m. to the S.

Lough Derg was internationally celebrated in the later Middle Ages as the place of St Patrick's Purgatory, a cave where Patrick was said to have fasted for forty days and to have had a vision of the Otherworld. It was believed that any properly disposed pilgrim entering the cave might, by St Patrick's help, himself behold the horrors of purgatory and hell. Pilgrims came to Lough Derg for this purpose even from distant lands. Excesses caused the pilgrimage to be banned by Popes Alexander VI and Pius III, but the place continued to attract pilgrims, even after the Cromwellians had desecrated and blocked up the cave. Although the latter has disappeared, and the practices connected with it have long since ceased, the lake is still the most important place of pilgrimage in Ireland. Every year thousands come to Station Island (½ m. offshore in the S. part of the lake) between 1 June and 15 Aug. They travel from and to their homes fasting, and spend two nights on the island, one of them keeping vigil in the basilica. By day they perform the "stations", or traditional exercises, their only food being a single meal each day of dry bread and black tea. The penitential exercises include a barefoot circuit of the basilica, the Crosses of St Patrick and St Brigid, and six other "stations" ("beds") marked by remains of ancient monastic huts. The basilica is a fine octagonal building by William A. Scott. It has a notable series of windows (1927–28), *Apostles and Saints holding Stations of the Cross*, by Harry Clarke.

¾ m. NW. of Station Island is Oileán na Naomh (Saint's Island), alias St Da-Bhé-óg's Island, site of St Patrick's Purgatory. There are ruins of a medieval church and other remains of a small Augustinian priory, as well as of its predecessor, an early monastery founded by St Áed, alias Da-Bhé-óg, who was presumably also the founder or patron of the monastery represented by the "beds" on Station Island. The early foundations appear to have been derelict by the first half of the 12th cent., when the Canons Regular of St Augustine came to Lough Derg.

LOUGH DERG (Map 5, B3–C2), largest and loveliest of the Shannon lakes, is the meeting-place of Counties Galway, Tipperary, and Clare. Some twenty-five miles long, it reaches from Portumna in the N. almost to Killaloe in the S. It is served by C.I.E. cruises from both these towns, and is noted for its trout and coarse fishing. *See further under* Killaloe, Mountshannon, Nenagh, Portumna, Scariff.

LOUGH ERNE, LOWER, Co. Fermanagh (Map 2, C4), is a beautiful sheet of water stretching for 18 m. from Enniskillen to Belleek. It is well-known to anglers for its grilse, sea trout, and brown trout, and acquires added interest from the early historic and medieval antiquities on its islands and shores.

3 m. NNW. of Enniskillen is Devenish

(Daimh-inis, "Ox Island"), with its early and medieval ecclesiastical remains (Nat. Mons.) on and near the site of a monastery founded in the 6th cent. by St Mo-Laisse. The remains comprise: St Mo-Laisse's House, St Mo-Laisse's Bed, the Teampall Mór, St Mary's Priory, and a Round Tower, as well as stone crosses and early gravestones. – Fragmentary St Mo-Laisse's House was a small, stone-roofed, 12th cent. oratory with architraved trabeate doorway and moulded angle pilasters. What is probably the carved capital of one pilaster is built into the W. gable. The Teampall Mór or Great Church, also called St Mo-Laisse's Church, was the church of a "culdee" priory (which survived until the 17th cent. English conquest of the region), but also served as the parish church. It was a Transitional structure of the early 13th cent. In the cemetery are two early gravestones. – The 12th cent. Round Tower, 81 ft high, is one of the finest in Ireland. It has a sculptured cornice (human heads and other devices). Built into the tower is a sculptured cross from a crannóg in Drumgay Lough. – St Mary's Priory was a house of Canons Regular of St Augustine. The church appears to be 15th cent. (see the 1449 slab from the E. wall, now at entrance to tower stair); the sacristy has a Perpendicular doorway. The E. window was removed to the Protestant parish church at Monea (see under Enniskillen) in 1804. In the choir is an early gravestone. In the cemetery are a small cross with a *Crucifixion* on the E. face; an early gravestone; and a tomb effigy. – It was to Devenish that the early-11th cent. reliquary, Soiscél Mo-Laisse, now in the National Museum, originally belonged. Admission to Round Tower and Museum : 1 April to 30 Sept., Mon. to Sat., 10 a.m. – 6 p.m.; Sun., 2–6 p.m.; 1 Oct. to 31 March, Sat. and Sun., 10 a.m.–sunset; nominal charge.

7 m. N. of Devenish (12½ m. NNW. of Enniskillen), in Killadeas graveyard on the E. shore of the lake, are three early Christian carved stones. The most important has on the S. face the crudely delineated figure of an abbot bearing a bell and a bachall; also traces of an Irish inscription. On the W. face is a human face and an interlaced pattern (7th cent.?). A second stone has a cross and traces of an Irish inscription on the face, and cup marks on the back. The third stone bears a small inscribed Greek cross.

9 m. N. of Devenish, in Castle Archdale (see under Irvinestown) Bay, is White Island, with the ruins of a church with a Romanesque S. door (Nat. Mon.). Into the N. wall have been built a human mask and eight fantastic sculptures possibly of 9th/10th cent. date. Their significance is uncertain (one represents an abbot, others armed warriors), but they throw light on early Irish costume. Also in Castle Archdale Bay is Davy's Island, alias Inishmore, where there is a fragment of a church (Nat. Mon.). The island once belonged to the Augustinians of Lisgoole (see under Enniskillen).

5½ m. NW. of Devenish (2½ m. W. of Killadeas), close to the W. shore near Blaney, is Inishmacsaint, site of an island-monastery founded in the 6th cent. by St Ninnidh (see Knockninny under Enniskillen). Apart from a crude, ancient cross (Nat. Mon.), 13 ft high, the only remains are those of a small, 12th cent. church.

At the N. end of the lake lies Boa Island (see under Pettigoe).

LOUGH GUR, Co. Limerick (Map 5, B4), is a small lake 2½ m. NNE. of Bruff and 12 m. SSE. of Limerick. Gearóid *file* (Gerald the Rhymer), Earl of Desmond, who disappeared in 1398, is said to sleep beneath its waters. Every seventh year he emerges to ride the moonlit ripples of the lake. Though Gearóid was long famous in Irish literary history, most of his surviving poems had to wait until 1963 for their first printing; his wife, Eleanor Butler, was famous in poetic tradition for her gallantries.

The light limestone soil of the district attracted Neolithic cultivators, and they and their successors have left many monuments in the area. For convenience of listing these, Holycross crossroads on the main Limerick (12¼ m.)–Bruff (2¼ m.) road is here taken as the starting-point of a circuit of the lake (proceeding *deiseal*, i.e. sunwise, in the traditional manner).

½ m. N. of the crossroads, to the E. of the Limerick road, in Grange, is the Lios (Nat. Mon.), largest stone circle in Ireland. A ring of contiguous standing stones, backed by an earthen bank 30 ft wide, encloses a level, circular enclosure 150 ft in diameter. A paved passage flanked by standing stones pierces the bank on the E. side. N. of the entrance is Rannach Chruim Dhuibh, largest stone of the circle. Excavations showed that the interior of the circle had been artificially raised above its natural level, and dated the structure to the local Neolithic–Bronze Age transition (ritual deposits of Neolithic ware, Beaker, and Food Vessel). Across the field fence to the SE. is Cloch a' Bhile, a pillarstone. In the next field to the N. a circle of fifteen stones within a slight bank encloses a low mound (Nat. Mon.). To the SW. are nine surviving stones of a circle of sixty-nine stones (Nat. Mon.). On the opposite side of the Limerick road are remains (Nat. Mon.) of a chamber tomb. The adjacent hollow to the NW. is said to have been the site of a stone circle.

In the fields between the Lios and the lake shore are traces of Cladh na Leac, an ancient roadway.

400 yds NE. of the Lios, at the foot of Ardaghlooda Hill, is a pillarstone (Nat. Mon.). On the hill are ancient field walls and a circular enclosure (summit). 300 yds N., in swampy ground, is Crock Island, a crannóg. By the lake shore, 300 yds SE. of Loughgur House, is a stone circle (Nat. Mon.). E. of this is a platform ringfort with attached enclosures, 300 yds N. of which, on Knockfennell, is a stone ring-

fort. On the summit of Knockfennell (531 ft) is a small cairn; in the valley below, to the E., are Red Cellar Cave and ancient cultivation terraces. Some 400 yds ESE. of these is a group of ancient house and hut sites with their fields, etc. (Nat. Mons.). 440 yds E. of these is Leagaun, a pillarstone; 200 yds N. of this is a hill-top pillarstone; some 200 yds SE. of the first pillarstone is a third (also Leagaun). 400 yds SE. of this last is an undateable stone circle which had an internal fosse; nearby, to the SE., is a flat, kerbed cairn which contained Urn burials. On Carraig Aille, the ridge to the S., are two stone ringforts, as well as ancient fields and stone enclosures (all Nat. Mons.). Excavation has dated the occupation of the forts to the 8th–10th centuries. During its later history the lower of the forts lost its warlike character, and undefended houses were built outside of and on top of the defences.

At Loughgur crossroads, SE. of Carraig Aille, is a large, slab-like standing stone (Nat. Mon.). The road to the SW. leads back to Holycross crossroads (1½ m.). ¾ m. WSW., on the S. side of this road, in Loughgur townland, is a wedge-shaped gallery grave (Nat. Mon.) in which were buried more than twelve individuals. The grave-goods included decorated Neolithic ware, as well as Beaker and Early Bronze Age pottery. 400 yds N., at the foot of Knockadoon, are the ruins of 15th cent. Killalough Castle, alias Black Castle. Some 400 yds WNW. of the castle, on Knockadoon, is a circular Neolithic cemetery (Nat. Mon.) surrounded by a double-kerbed bank; further NW. is a similar enclosure (Nat. Mon.); SW. of this is an irregular enclosure of similar construction. On the S. and W. slopes of the hill were found many Neolithic and Bronze Age habitation sites (including a rectangular, aisled, Neolithic house-site). Less than 400 yds N. of Black Castle is a double-kerbed enclosure; NNE. are remains of a hill-top cairn (Nat. Mon.). At the NE. foot of the hill is the fine 15th cent. tower of Lough Gur Castle, alias Bourchier's Castle, alias Castle Doon. This castle and Black Castle (above) closed the approaches to Knockfennel, then an island. They were one of the chief seats of the Earls of Desmond. After the Desmond rebellion Lough Gur Castle was granted to Sir George Bourchier, ancestor of the Earls of Bath, who continued to reside there till 1641. Close to the castle is a pillarstone; 150 yds E. is a bullaun; 440 yds WNW. is a small cave. To the NE., in a corner of the lake, is Bolin Island, a crannóg. Some 400 yds SSW. of the cave is an irregular enclosure with double-kerbed bank.

¼ m. SW. of Loughgur gallery grave are the ruins of Teampall Nua, a simple, 15th cent. church. 300 yds SE. is Carriganaffrin, a rock where Mass was said in Penal times. 440 yds SW., to the S. of the road in Ballynagallagh, is Leaba na Muice, a ruined chamber tomb (Nat. Mon.). Some 400 yds S. of the latter are the last remnants of Mainister na Galliagh, a medieval nunnery. NW. of the nunnery is the Hero's Grave, a cairn, to the W. of which is a second stretch of Cladh na Leac.

On Garret Island in the lake are the dubious ruins of Desmond's Castle, so-called.

2 m. NNE. of Holycross crossroads, in Grange, is the Mote, a small ringfort with hut-sites. In the next field to the S. is a rectangular platform with ring-barrows. Also in Grange is Dromin, a ringfort 400 ft in diameter. In the adjacent townland of Ballingoola are further ring-barrows; also housemounds with ring-ditches (Iron Age?).

2 m. WNW. of Holycross crossroads is Caherguillamore (see under Bruff).

LOUGHLINSTOWN, Co. Dublin (Map 6, E7), more correctly Laughanstown, is a suburban village on the Dublin (9 m.)–Bray (3 m.) road.

1 m. E. is Ballybrack, alias Shanganagh, portal dolmen (see Killiney under Dalkey).

1½ m. SE., near the E. side of the road, are the slight remains of Kiltuck church. Close by are two small granite crosses with crude representations of the Crucifixion.

1¼ m. SSW. are the fragmentary remains (Nat. Mon.) of the early monastery of Rathmichael; St Comgall of Bangor (q.v.) is said to have been the founder. The remains include part of the enclosing ring-wall of earth and stone; the stump of a Round Tower; fragments of a 12th/13th cent. nave-and-chancel church; a granite cross-base; several early gravestones with concentric-circle and/or herring-bone patterns (see Ballyman under Bray; Killegar under Enniskerry; and Tully under Cabinteely); a rock-cut bullaun NE. of the church; and, ½ m. SE., in the lane to the S. of Shankill House, a granite cross of Cornish type with a Crucifixion.

1½ m. SW. is Puck's Castle, a ruined 15th/16th cent. fortified house of the Dalkey type. Less than 200 yds SSE. (¼ m. SSW. of Rathmichael) is a hill-fort (prehistoric?).

LOUGH NEAGH, (Map 3, B4–C5), shared by the five counties of Antrim, Down, Armagh, Tyrone and Derry, is the largest lake in either Great Britain or Ireland, being 153 sq. m. in area. It receives the waters of the Upper Bann and is drained by the Lower Bann. It takes its name, Loch nEachach, from the horse-god, Eochu, Lord of the Otherworld beneath its waters.

In this Guide the principal antiquities of the lake shore are listed under the nearest town or village, e.g. Glenavy.

LOUGHREA, Co. Galway (Map 5, B2), a small cotton-spinning and market town on the S. or main road from Ballinasloe (19 m.) to Galway (22 m.), is pleasantly situated beside the small lake which gives it its name. In the Middle Ages it was the principal seat of the Mac William Uachtair Burkes (Earls of Clanricarde). Today it is the cathedral town of the

W. A. Green

Basket weaving, Lough Neagh

diocese of Clonfert. Seamus O Kelly (1880–1918), journalist, Abbey Theatre playwright, and author (*The Weaver's Grave, Wet Clay*, etc.), was born at Mob Hill.

To the S. and SW. rise the Slieve Aughty Mountains (Cashlaundrumlahan, 1,207 ft).

The principal medieval monument is the interesting church of the Carmelite friary founded *c*. 1300 by Richard de Burgo. The ruins are piously maintained, unhappily with little taste or judgement, as witness the "pointing" of the masonry.

The glory of Loughrea is St Brendan's Cathedral (1897–1903). The dull exterior of this insignificant, nuinspired, Gothic-Revival essay by William Byrne suggests nothing of the riches within. The interior, completed and furnished under the direction of Professor William A. Scott of University College, Dublin, epitomizes the development of the ecclesiastical arts and crafts in Ireland from 1903 to 1957. John Hughes was the sculptor of the excellent *Virgin and Child* in the Lady Chapel. A. E. Child (*see* Laban *under* Ardrahan), Sarah Purser, Hubert McGoldrick, Michael Healy, Evie Hone, and Patrick Pye did the windows, which admirably illustrate the beginnings and development of the Dublin school of stained glass. The windows, in order of date, are as follows. 1903: Child, *Annunciation, Agony in the Garden, Resurrection* (all two-light). 1904: Healy, *St Simeon*; Purser, *St Ita* (painted by Catherine A. O Brien). 1906: Child, *Baptism of Christ* (two-light). 1907: Healy, *Holy Family, Virgin and Child with SS Patrick, Brendan, Colman, Iarlaith, Columcille, Brigid* (in Lady Chapel). 1908: Healy, *St Anthony*. 1908–12: Purser, *Crucifixion, Nativity* (two three-light, in E. transept, painted by Child; Purser herself painted the little *St Brendan* of the porch, undated). 1925: McGoldrick, *Sacred Heart*. 1927: Healy, *St John the Evangelist*. 1929: Child, *SS Clare and Francesca* (two-

light). 1930: Healy, *Tu Rex Gloriae Christe*. 1932: Healy, *Regina Coeli*. 1934: Child, *Centurion*. 1935: Healy, *St Joseph*. 1936: Healy, *Ascension* (three-light). 1937: Child, *St Patrick*. 1936–40: Healy, *Last Judgement* (three-light, beside his *Ascension* in W. transept). 1942: Hone, *St Brigid* (features "sweetened" to order). 1950: Hone, *Creation* (rose). 1957: Pye, *St Brigid* (porch). Healy's *Ascension* and *Last Judgement* are among his finest works. The altar rails, font, and all the stone carvings are by Michael Shortall. Scott designed the sanctuary pavement and all the ironwork and wooden furnishings. The *opus sectile* Stations of the Cross are by Ethel Rhind. Jack B. Yeats was one of those who designed embroideries for the cathedral.

NE. of the cathedral is part of a 15th cent. town gate. It has been converted into a museum of ecclesiastical art (some noteworthy chalices, medieval figures, and vestments), etc., from the diocese.

There are several crannógs in the nearby lake.

4 m. NNE., in Turoe (NW. of Bullaun), is the Turoe Stone (Nat. Mon.), a remarkable phallic stone of the 1st cent. A.D., covered with three-plane, abstract, curvilinear ornament in the Celtic style. It formerly stood close to a nearby ringfort. Only four stones with comparable carving are known from these islands, three of them within the bounds of the ancient kingdom of Connacht (*see* Killycluggin *under* Ballyconnell *and* Castlestrange *under* Athleague).

7 m. NE. is the Hill of Finnure, that Cnoc Findabhrach in Maenmagh where lived Findabhair, daughter of Niall Nine-hostager and wife of the King of Connacht, who "died of shame and disgrace because the poet Findollán made a verse in praise of her and she found no gold for him for it".

1½ m. ESE., on the S. side of the Portumna

road in Moanmore East, is the Seven Monuments (Nat. Mon.), a stone circle set in an earthen bank. The neighbourhood is rich in ringforts, including Rathsonny (trivallate with berm and souterrain) and univallate Rahannagroagh, both Nat. Mons., 1 m. ESE., in Masonbrook townland.

7 m. ESE., at Drumgaroe, Streamstown, is a prehistoric chamber tomb.

3 m. S., in Killeenadeema, are remains of a church and castle; ½ m. N. is St Díoma's Well.

9½ m. SW. is Peterswell (see under Gort).

6 m. WSW. is Isertkelly (see under Ardrahan).

LOUGH REE, Cos. Roscommon–Westmeath–Longford (Map 2, C7; Map 5, D1), one of the great lakes of the Shannon, stretches for 16 m. above Athlone, from which it may easily be explored by motor-boat. Several of the islands contain interesting antiquities.

Close to the Westmeath shore, 4 m. NNE. of Athlone, is Hare Island, formerly Inis Ainghin. St Cíarán founded a monastery here before founding Clonmacnois (q.v.). Near the S. shore are some overgrown monastic ruins; the little church has been adapted for use as a mausoleum by the Dillons. Lord Castlemaine built a summer home on the island at the end of the 18th cent.

2 m. further N., on Inchmore, the ruins of a church mark the site of an early monastery founded by St Líobán.

2 m. NE. of Inchmore is Inchbofin (Inis Bó Finne). A monastery was founded here by St (Mo-)Rí-óg (d. 588), said to have been a brother of St Mel of Ardagh (q.v.). In the Middle Ages the monastery adopted the Rule of the Canons Regular of St Augustine. The remains (Nat. Mons.) include two small churches. The S. church is a small, nave-and-chancel structure with plain Transitional chancel arch and windows and a Gothic S. door. The N. church (Augustinian) consists of a nave with disproportionately large N. transept, to the W. of which is a two-storey sacristy wing. The NE. window of the nave is Romanesque. The S. door of the nave is Gothic, like the windows of the transept. There are remains of an enclosing cashel. There are also a few early gravestones of Clonmacnois type. Only three bear inscriptions: MAEL MARTAIN; [O]ROIT DO [CH]ORMACAN; OR[OIT] ... R. To the NE. of Inchbofin is Saints Island, a peninsula on the Longford shore.

2 m. NW. of Inchmore, on the Roscommon shore, is Rinndown (see under Lecarrow).

In the N. half of the lake is Inchcleraun (Inis Clothrann), where St Díarmaid, teacher of Cíarán of Clonmacnois (q.v.), founded a monastery in the 6th cent. In 719 St Sionach died there. In 1141 Giolla-na-Naomh O Farrell, King of Annaly, was buried there. Giolla-na-Naomh Ó Duinn, lector of the monastery and a celebrated poet and historian, died in 1160. In the 12th cent. the monks adopted the Augustinian Rule and, as a small priory of Canons

Regular, the monastery survived until the Dissolution. The remains (Nat. Mon.) comprise: (a) remnants of an enclosing cashel which had a Romanesque gateway (voussoirs in Teampall Mór, below); (b) diminutive, once stone-roofed, Teampall Dhíarmada, "Dermot's Church", with gable antae and trabeate doorway; (c) Teampall Mór, "Great Church" (with Transitional and later features), and the E. cloister range of the priory; (d) Teampall Mhuire, "St Mary's Church", a nave-and-chancel structure; (e) Teampall na Marbh, "Church of the Dead". The few early gravestones include one inscribed OR[ÕIT] DO LAITHB[ER]TACH ("A prayer for Flaithbertach"). NW. of the enclosure, on the highest point of the island, is Clogás an Oileáin, "Bell-tower of the Island", a church (Nat. Mon.) with W. bell tower. SE. of this are remnants of Grianán Meidhbhe, "Maeve's Solar", a circular structure.

LOUISBURGH, Co. Mayo (Map 1, B4), is a village on the Westport (14 m.)–Leenaun (18 m.) road.

2½ m. E., at Old Head, is a pleasant little beach dominated by Croagh Patrick.

1 m. E. are the remains of Kilgeever Church and Tobar Rí an Domhnaigh where some Croagh Patrick (see under Murrisk) pilgrims complete their penitential exercises. The site affords a delightful view.

6 m. S., in Srahwee, to the NE. of Lough Nahaltora, is Tobernahaltora, a wedge-shaped gallery grave regarded locally as a holy well.

7 m. S., via the Leenaun road, are the romantic solitudes of Glencullen and Doo Lough. At the S. end of the glen, by the little Owengar and Fin Lough, is a fishing lodge to which one of the Lords Sligo, overcome by the Grand Tour, gave the name Delphi!

7½ m. SW., in Cloonlaur, is the Killeen, an ancient churchyard with a great cross-pillar (incised "marigold" cross). At the head of a grave between this cross-pillar and the gate is an early cross-slab. 1½ m. WSW. is ¾-m. Bunlough strand. – 1½ m. NW. is 2-m. Sruhir Strand ("Carrownisky Strand"). Near the S. end, in Cross, is a pillarstone. N. of Sruhir Strand is White Strand. Not far from the junction of the two, in the Dooghmakeon sandhills, is a cross-pillar alleged to bear an ogham inscription. – 1½ m. SSE. of the Killeen is Aillemore Cromlech, a court cairn whose two-segment chamber had a high-pitched roof. – 2½ m. SSW. of the Killeen, at the foot of Mweelrea (2,688 ft), are the sandhills and beaches of Kinnadoohy.

4 m. W. is Roonah Quay, starting-point for Caher Island (q.v.), Clare Island (q.v.), and Inishturk (q.v.).

LOUTH, Co. Louth (Map 3, B7), which gives its name to the county, is a simple village 7 m. SW. of Dundalk and 5 m. N. of Ardee. It has, however, a long history, and was once of considerable importance.

St Mochta (d. 535), "a British pilgrim, a holy

Paul Kavanagh

Cloghfarmore, a pillarstone in Rathiddy,
Co. Louth

man, a disciple of the holy bishop Patrick", founded a church here, precursor of a flourishing monastery. The monastery suffered severely from Norse raiders in the 9th cent. About 1135/40 the king (Donnchadh O Carroll) and bishop of Uriel transferred the diocese from Clogher (*q.v.*) to St Mary's Church, Louth, where it remained for some sixty years. About 1148 Donnchadh and Bishop Aodh(án) O Kelly reorganised the monastery as St Peter and Paul's Abbey of Augustinian Canons, and transferred it to Cnoc na Seangán, "Pismire Hill" – thereafter Cnoc na nApstal, "Hill of the Apostles" – 3¼ m. SW. in Thomastown.

The sole relic of the early monastery is St Mochta's House (Nat. Mon.), a small, stone-roofed, 12th/13th cent. church; door and windows modern. Nearby are remains of Louth "Abbey", a long, 14th (?) cent. friary-type church.

W. of the village is Fairy Mount, motte of an 1185/90 English royal castle.

Ardpatrick, SE. of the village, was the loca-

tion of a Columban monastery. Ardpatrick House, given him by his kinsman, Lord Louth (*see* Louth Hall *under* Ardee), was for a time the residence of the Blessed Oliver Plunkett.

2½ m. N. is Castlering, alias Castlefranke, a motte-and-bailey. In nearby Ash Big and Ash Little are two mounds which give their names (*ais*) to the townlands.

2 m. NE., in Rathiddy, to the E. of the Dundalk road, is Cloghfarmore (Nat. Mon.), a fine pillarstone, in modern times identified as the pillar to which the mythical Cuchulainn was said to have bound himself in his last combat.

4 m. ENE., on the little River Fane, is Stephenstown House, a fine Georgian house built by the Fortescues in 1750. Open to public, mid-May to end of Sept., Thur. and Fri., 3–6 p.m.; admission 2/6d.

4¾ m. W., at Killanny, are the remains of a medieval church or monastery (Mainistear Chill Eannaidh); also a motte with traces of a bailey, relic of the Pipard settlement of the barony of Ardee (*q.v.*). The stone castle which succeeded the motte-and-bailey castle was destroyed by Mac Mahon in 1594.

4 m. NNW. is Inishkeen, which took its name, Inis Caín Dego, from St Daig mac Cairill (d. 587), disciple and artificer of Ciarán of Clonmacnois. The scant remains (Nat. Mon.) of the early monastery include the stump of a Round Tower. Nearby is a motte. Inishkeen is the native place of Patrick Kavanagh, poet and novelist, whose *The Great Hunger* and *Tarry Flynn* reflect aspects of local life.

LUCAN, Co. Dublin (Map 6, D7), a suburban village on the Dublin (8¾ m.)–Maynooth (8 m.) road, is situated on a beautiful reach of the Liffey where the latter is joined by the little Griffeen. In the 18th cent. it was a fashionable spa.

Adjoining the village on the W. is beautiful riverside Lucan Demesne. In the Middle Ages the manor of Lucan passed through various hands, including those of the Fitzgeralds. On the attainder of the 10th Earl of Kildare it was confiscated and leased (1554) to one Matthew King, on condition that he lived in the castle himself, or placed in it liege men who would use English speech and dress and hold no communication with the Irish. Shortly afterwards it was acquired by Sir William Sarsfield, Mayor of Dublin and great-great-grandfather of the celebrated Jacobite soldier, Patrick Sarsfield, Viscount Tully and Earl of Lucan. At the Cromwellian conquest the property was granted to Sir Theophilus Jones, but in the 1670s was restored to the great Patrick Sarsfield, who may have been born at Lucan. At the Williamite Revolution the property passed (by marriage) to Agmondisham I Vesey. In 1772 his son, Agmondisham II, designed Palladian Lucan House to replace the 16th cent. Sarsfield castle, whose ruins still stand to the SE. The house, which was later remodelled, has stucco by Michael Stapleton and medallions by

Angelica Kaufmann. Agmondisham II seems also to have built the *cottage orné*, ¾ m. W. of the house, and likewise the bath house with antechamber at St John's Well. The house (recently restored) is now the residence of the Italian Ambassador. Beside the castle ruins are those of the medieval parish church of the Blessed Virgin. The so-called Patrick Sarsfield Memorial in the demesne is an 18th cent. garden ornament.

2 m. NNE., to the N. of the Liffey, in the magnificent demesne of Woodlands, is Luttrelstown Castle, a 19th cent. castellated mansion incorporating portions of a medieval castle.

½ m. NE. is St Edmondsbury, now the convalescent home of Swift's Hospital, Dublin. The original house was built by Edmund Sexton Pery, Speaker of the Irish House of Commons, 1771–85, and afterwards Viscount Pery (*see* Limerick). He was an opponent of the Union. The house still has some fine rooms, but the windows of the entrance front have been spoilt. Nearby Woodville, also hospital property, is another good 18th cent. house, built for Henry Clements, Vice-Treasurer of Ireland.

¾ m. SE., at Esker, are the remains of St Finian's Church (parochial).

400 yds S., in Petty Canon, on the E. side of the Newcastle road, is a ringfort with a souterrain.

2 m. SW. are the remains of Adderig church (medieval).

LURGAN, Co. Armagh (Map 3, C5), is an important linen centre on the Portadown (5 m.)–Belfast (21 m.) road, 2½ m. SE. of Lough Neagh. It was founded by the Brownlows for English planters in the reign of James I. In 1654 the first "settled meeting" in Ireland of the Quakers (English settlers) was held in Lurgan. The broad main street was laid out towards the end of the 17th cent. The Linen Hall is the hub of the town, which has prospered since Samuel Waring introduced damask weaving in 1691. An exciting project envisages a new city called Craigavon, with 100,000–150,000 inhabitants, to be built (1966–76) closer to the lough and taking advantage of it for recreational amenities.

Lurgan is a good centre for fishing the middle Lagan and Lough Neagh. The 53-acre lake in the excellent town park is stocked with trout. Lurgan Castle (Brownlow House) formerly home of the Brownlows (Lords Lurgan), is now an Orange Hall.

George W. Russell (1867–1935), better known as "A.E.", journalist, poet and painter, was born in William St. James Logan (1674–1751), one of the founders of Pennsylvania, and Field Marshal Sir John Dill (1881–1947) were also natives of Lurgan.

3 m. E. is Magheralin (*see under* Moira).

2 m. SE., at Waringstown, are the charming house (1667) and the parish church (1681; chancel, aisle, and transept are additions; the Gothicization is 19th cent.) designed by James Robb (*see* Ballynahinch *and* Killyleagh) for William Waring. The interior presents perhaps the best surviving example of late-17th cent. Protestant ecclesiastical architecture in Ireland. The village still has a few late-17th cent. dwelling houses, originally thatched.

LUSK, Co. Dublin (Map 6, D2), is a village on the Dublin (14 m.)–Skerries (5 m.) road.

Bishop St Cuindid, alias Mac Cuilinn (d. 497), founded a monastery here. When he died he was buried in the cave (*lusca*) from which the place takes its name. The monastery suffered severely from the Vikings. The last recorded bishop (Ailill) died in 965; he was also bishop of Swords (*q.v.*). After the Anglo-Norman invasion the monastery and its possessions were granted to St Mary's Abbey, Dublin. There was also an Augustinian nunnery, which Archbishop Comyn transferred to Grace Dieu (*see under* Ballyboghill) in 1190.

The Protestant parish church (1847) and churchyard occupy portions of the site of St Mac Cuilinn's monastery, of which the only surviving relic is the Round Tower (Nat. Mon.; capping modern). To it has been attached the square tower (about 1500) of a large church demolished in the 19th cent. In the medieval tower are housed the effigy tombs of James Bermingham of Ballough (d. 1527) and of Sir Christopher Barnewall of Turvey (*see under* Donabate) and his wife, Marion Sharl. The Bermingham effigy is one of the few 16th cent. armoured effigies of the English Pale, and the only one with Irish-style harness. The Barnewall tomb, erected in 1589, is an elaborate Renaissance work of Italian (?) and Kilkenny marble. It was erected by Dame Marion Sharl and her second husband, Sir Lucas Dillon of Moymet. Also worthy of notice are the tombs of William Archdall of Dublin (d. 1751) and of Sir Robert Echlin of Rush (d. 1757). – In a garden at the

T. H. Mason
Medieval church tower and Round Tower, Lusk

S. end of the village is St Mac Cuilinn's Well with a double bullaun ("the imprints of the saint's knees").

St Maculind's Church at the other end of the village is an Irish Romanesque essay (c. 1924) by John J. Robinson. It has windows (1924) by Harry Clarke: *St Mac Cuilinn* and three three-light symbolic windows.

NW. of the village, to the W. of the road in Regles, is a small tumulus. At the E. end of the townland, N. of the road leading W. from the Protestant church, is the traditional site of an ancient monastery.

MACROOM, Co. Cork (Map 5, A6), is an unattractive market town in the picturesque Sullane valley, 23 m. W. of Cork, 31 m. SE. of Killarney, and 34 m. NE. of Bantry. The roads to Cork (Lee valley), Killarney (Derrynasaggart Mountains), and Bantry (Shehy Mountains) are noted for their scenery.

The town has some good late-Georgian houses, a Protestant church by George Richard Pain of Cork, and a pleasant, small, early-19th cent. Market House. The latter is the successor of the market house beside which Eileen Dubh O Connell of Darrynane met and loved the ill-fated Art O Leary in 1768 (*see* Kilcrea *under* Ballincollig).

Macroom Castle, a burnt-out mansion by the E. bank of the Sullane, incorporates the tower and other remains of a 15th cent. castle which was one of the principal seats of the Mac Carthys of Muskerry (the others being Blarney and Kilcrea). In 1649 David Roche, Sheriff of Kerry, and Baothghalach ("Boetius") Mac Egan, Bishop of Ross, were assembling forces here to relieve Clonmel, then under siege by Cromwell. They were unexpectedly attacked by Roger Boyle, Lord Broghill, and their troops dispersed. The bishop was captured, and brought to Carrigadrohid (*see under* Coachford), where he was murdered for refusing to exhort the garrison to surrender. Donagh Mac Carthy of Macroom (Viscount Muskerry) was the last Royalist commander to hold out against the Cromwellians in Munster (*see* Ross Castle, Killarney). In 1654 Cromwell granted his castle and manor at Macroom to Admiral Sir William Penn, father of William Penn of Pennsylvania. At the Restoration Lord Muskerry recovered Macroom, and Penn was compensated with the Power castle and lands of Shanagarry (*see under* Ballycotton) and the O Hea castle and lands of Aghamilla (near Clonakilty).

4 m. NE. is Rusheen crossroads. About 1 m. N., in Knockglass, are remains of a wedge-shaped gallery grave. – 2 m. NNW. (¾ m. NNW. of the Knockglass tomb), in Parknalicka, Kilberrihert, is another wedge-shaped gallery grave. – ½ m. NW. of Rusheen crossroads is the ancient church-site of Kilberrihert (*see* Tullylease *under* Dromcolliher). Also in Kilberrihert is a large souterrain, partly rock-cut. – 2 m. NW. of Rusheen crossroads, in a farmyard in Caherbaroul, are an early cross-pillar and a bullaun found ¼ m. N. of Parknalicka. ½ m. N., on Caherahaboom Hill, are a pillarstone and remains of a wedge-shaped gallery grave. 2½ m. NE. of these is Dooneens stone circle.

1¼ m. E., on the E. side of the Sullane (near its confluence with the Lany) in Bealick, is Laght, two large stones set on end (there were three here in 1794); 60 yds SE. is another standing stone. These may be remains of a chamber tomb. (The name, Laght Mahon, appears to be a 19th cent. invention.) 1½ m. NW. is The Bealick, a prehistoric chamber tomb.

2¾ m. SE., in Mashanaglass, are remains of a 16th cent. castle with two redans, or angular projections. It was the sole Mac Carthy Mór stronghold in the territory of Mac Carthy of Muskerry, and was confided to the keeping of the Mac Swineys, a family of professional mercenaries (galloglas). Eóghan Mac Swiney, last of his name to live here, was attainted for his part in the 1641–52 war.*

10 m. SW. is Inchigeelagh (*q.v.*).

3½ m. W., on the N. side of the Sullane, is the tower (Nat. Mon.) of the rock-castle of Carrigaphooca, an early-15th cent. stronghold of Mac Carthy of Drishane (*see under* Millstreet). It has no fireplaces; the living quarters were presumably in a vanished hall. The castle originally had a bivallate bawn, and was surrounded by the waters of the river. It was stormed by O Sullivan Beare and Cormac Mac Carthy of Muskerry in 1602. The rock, says tradition, was the haunt of a *púca* or malicious sprite; hence its name. Some 400 yds NE. is a small circle of five stones, remnant of a recumbent-stone circle (Nat. Mon.). – 1¼ m. N. of the castle, in Killaclug, is an oval chamber tomb (roofless). – 1 m. W. of the castle is a 9-ft pillarstone. 2½ m. SW. of this, in Cools, are two standing stones. ½ m. SE. of these, in Caherdaha, are a 7-ft pillarstone, etc., a stone ringfort, and a bivallate ringfort.

10 m. W. is Reananerree village. ¾ m. W., in Derryfineen, is a 10-ft pillarstone. 1½ m. N. of Reananerree, in Gortanimill, is a 25-ft, recumbent-stone circle with a large white stone at the centre.

4½ m. NNW., to the W. of the Carriganimmy road in Gortavranner, are two fine pillarstones. Some 600 yds N., to the E. of the road, in Caherbirrane, is a wedge-shaped gallery grave. 1¼ m. E. of the latter, in a field adjoining the Macroom road in Scrahanard, is a ruinous cairn with remains of a wedge-shaped gallery grave; on the inner face of the end upright is a curious series of scorings; nearby are another cairn and a ringfort with a souterrain. Further E., in Lackaduv, is The Bealick, a wedge-shaped gallery grave with single enormous capstone; in a nearby field is another tomb. 1 m. NW. of Scrahanard road junction, also in Lackaduv, is a small circle of five stones flanked by two alignments; in an adjoining field is a small cairn. ¼ m. NW. of these last are remains of the ancient church of Carrignaspirroge. A short distance N. of the latter, in Knockraheen, are several standing stones, including one 10 ft 4 in. high. 1¼ m. NW. of Carrignaspirroge is Carriganimmy village, birthplace (1839) of Canon Peadar Ó Laoghaire, noted Irish writer. It was at Carriganimmy that the unfortunate Art Ó Laoghaire (O Leary) was killed in 1773 (see Kilcrea under Ballincollig). 1 m. SW. of the village, near the summit of Carrigonirtane, is a wedge-shaped gallery grave. ¼ m. S. of this, in Cabragh, are five single standing stones; also an alignment of three stones, with two other stones at right angles to it. Some 800 yds S. of these is an alignment of six stones (two prostrate). 120 yds from these is a hill-top standing stone.

10 m. WNW., where the main Cork–Killarney road penetrates the Derrynasaggart Mts (Mullaghanish, 2,133 ft), is Ballyvourney village, formerly a noted resort of students of Irish. 1 m. SE. is the parish church. A much worn, 13th cent. wooden figure of St Gobnat is preserved here. It is displayed to pilgrims on the saint's day (11 Feb.) and on Whit Sunday. Some still make the traditional Tomhas Ghobnatan, a length of woollen thread, or of ribbon, measured against the statue and used for curative purposes. Down to 1843 the statue was in the custody of the O Herlihys, hereditary erenachs of Teampall Ghobnatan (below). ¾ m. W. of the church, in Glebe, is the site of a nunnery founded in the 6th/7th cent. by St Gobnat. The remains here comprise Tigh Ghobnatan (St Gobnat's House; Nat. Mon.), Teampall Ghobnatan (the shell of a late medieval church), St Gobnat's Grave (with other pilgrims' stations), and Tobar Ghobnatan (St Gobnat's Well), etc. Tigh Ghobnatan, alias An Ula Uachtarach, is outside the churchyard (Reilg Ghobnatan) gate. It was a small, circular, dry-masonry hut, with thatch (?) roof supported by a central post. Excavation has shown that the occupants were smelters of iron and workers in bronze. The house itself was the successor of a rectangular timber house (or houses) used for the same purposes. Outside the door is the house well. (The 1951 statue to the S. of the house is by the Cork sculptor, Séamus Murphy.) Inside the churchyard gate is St Gobnat's Grave, alias An Ula Láir, a small mound on which rest three bullauns, discarded crutches, etc. Teampall Ghobnatan incorporates some fragments of an earlier church, including An Gadaí Dubh, alias Gadaí Ghobnatan. This is a human-mask voussoir from a Romanesque arch. Its name arises from the legend that one of the masons of the church stole his fellows' tools; his likeness was carved in stone as a reminder of the crime. Over one of the church windows is a sheila-na-gig. Outside the SE. angle of the church is the Priest's Grave. The traditional pilgrims' rounds follow the order: An Ula Uachtarach, An Ula Láir, Ula Bhréanainn or An Tríu Ula (outside the

W. end of the church), Chancel, Priest's Grave, Holy Well. ¾ m. E. of the well are St Abbán's Grave and Tobar Abbáin. St Abbán is said to have given Gobnat the site for her nunnery. The grave is a small cairn with a short cist, and is set about by three ogham stones. On it lies a bullaun. Pilgrims make their rounds here also. – ½ m. NE. of Ballyvourney church, in Killeen, is St Gobnat's Stone, an interesting early cross-pillar. On each face is a Greek cross inscribed in a double circle. The cross on one face is surmounted by a small crozier-bearing figure, recalling a well-known portrait in the Book of Durrow. The stone was found at the site of a dried-up holy well nearby.

MAGHERA (originally Ráth Lúraigh), Co. Derry (Map 3, B4), is a small town on the Belfast (39 m.)–Derry (35 m.) road, at the E. foot of the Sperrin Mountains. The Moyola River, 2 m. SW., is a good trout stream.

Charles Thompson (1730–1824) who, as Secretary of the United States Congress, wrote the manuscript of the American Declaration of Independence, was born at Maghera.

At the SE. end of the town is the ruin of a 12th cent. nave-and-chancel church with a unique W. doorway, unfortunately obscured by a later tower. Like the plain doorway at Bovevagh (see under Dungiven), this is square-headed without, round-headed within, and has the traditional inclined jambs. Over the lintel is an elaborate Crucifixion in bas-relief. The architrave and jambs are beautifully decorated with plant, chequer, scroll, and other motifs. A few Romanesque fragments also survive. The nave seems to have had antae. The patron is obscure St Lúrach, after whom the place was formerly called and whose "grave" is a low knoll, marked with a plain 3-ft cross, 40 yds W. of the church. From the synod of Ráth Breasail (1110/11) until 1246 the see of the diocese of Ardstraw (Derry) was here, and this, no doubt, explains the special features of the church.

4 m. NE., 1 m. beyond Culnady, is the great trivallate ringfort, Dunglady (Nat. Mon.). The outer rings are densely overgrown.

1¾ m. NW., in Tirnony, is the ancient church-site of Killelagh. About 200 yds SE. is a portal dolmen (Nat. Mon.). 1¼ m. NW. of the church, to the W. of the N. end of Killelagh Lough in Tirkane, is a sweat house (Nat. Mon.). 2¼ m. N. of this, alt. 800 ft in Slaghtneill, is a much disturbed chambered cairn (Nat. Mon.).

MALAHIDE, Co. Dublin (Map 6, D2), is a small seaside resort at the mouth of the Broad Meadow Water, 9 m. NE. of Dublin and 3 m. ESE. of Swords. There are good sandy beaches, but they have danger spots to be avoided at certain stages of the tide.

SW. of the village are Malahide Demesne and Castle (not open to public). The castle is the seat of Lord Talbot de Malahide, whose family settled here at the Anglo-Norman conquest. The property was confiscated by the Cromwellians and granted to the regicide, Miles Corbet, but was recovered by the Talbots at the Restoration. The castle is for the most part post-medieval (it has good rococo plaster of the Robert West school), and has lost its outworks, though traces of the moat can be recognized. The 6th Lord Talbot was a great-great-grandson of James Boswell (1740–95), biographer of Dr Samuel Johnson. The castle treasures formerly included a great collection of Boswell's private papers. Despite its losses to American and English galleries, the castle still houses one of the largest family collections of paintings left in Ireland. E. of the castle (on the site of an earlier church) are the ruins of the "abbey", a 15th–16th cent. manorial church dedicated to St Sylvester, until 1873 the burial place of the Talbots. It was a nave-and-chancel structure with priest's dwelling over the sacristy. The carvings include two sheila-na-gigs. In the nave is the fine 15th cent. effigy tomb of Maud Plunket, heroine of Gerald Griffin's ballad *The Bride of Malahide*. Her first husband, Lord Galtrim, was slain in battle on their wedding day. She subsequently married the owner of Malahide.

1 m. SE., by the shore, is Robswalls Castle, a 15th cent. Bermingham castle which passed to the Barnewalls.

3 m. SW. is St Doolagh's Church (*see under* Portmarnock).

MALIN, Co. Donegal (Map 2, D1), is a village on Inishowen, 4 m. N. of Carndonagh. It still retains its 17th cent. (Plantation) layout and triangular village green.

N. of the village, in the grounds of Malin Hall (1758), is a prehistoric chamber tomb. In the same townland of Norrira is a rock-cut souterrain with five chambers.

¾ m. NNE., on the borders of Carrowmore and Balleeghan Upper, is Druids Altar, a chamber tomb.

In Drumcarbit, next townland to the E. of the village, is a chamber tomb. In Templemoyle, the townland ESE. of Drumcarbit, is another.

1¼ m. WNW. is Friar's Cell, a tiny primitive structure. 2 m. further NW. are the sandhills of Lag. 2 m. NW. of Lag church, in Culoort, is Dunargus (alias Five Fort), a promontory fort.

6 m. NNW., in Ballygorman, is Dungolgan, a promontory fort. 1 m. E. is Doherty's Dún, another. 6 m. offshore is deserted Inishtrahull, the northermost island of Ireland. There was an early monastery or hermitage here, to which belonged the early gravestone, with an incised "marigold" cross, now at Malin Hotel. Somebody has recently given this gravestone the absurd name of the "Cursing Stone".

8½ m. NW. (4 m. WNW. of Dungolgan) is Malin Head, most northerly point of Ireland.

MALLARANNY, alias **MULRANNY**, Co. Mayo (Map 1, B4), is a delightfully situated little resort, with sandy beaches, on the N. shore of Clew Bay, 11 m. WNW. of Newport, 8 m. SE. of Achill Sound, and 20 m. SSW. of Bangor Erris. It enjoys a very mild climate, and is a convenient centre for touring Achill and the lovely wilderness N. towards Ballycroy and Tullaghan Bay. To the W. rises Corraun Hill (1,715 ft); to the N., Claggan Mt (1,256 ft). Corraun Hill offers magnificent views; the 27-m. circuit of the peninsula is also rewarding.

7 m. N., in Drumgollagh, is Cromlech, a court cairn.

8 m. SSW. is Curraun. The new church has a 1924 *St Brendan* window designed by Wilhelmina Margaret Geddes (1888–1955), painted by Ethel Mary Rhind, and presented to the church in 1943 by Saiah Purser.

MALLOW, Co. Cork (Map 5, B5), a market and sugar-manufacturing town on the N. side of the beautiful Blackwater, is an important road and rail junction, 21 m. NNW. of Cork, 8 m. S. of Buttevant, and 17 m. W. of Fermoy.

At the Anglo-Norman conquest the O Keefe territory hereabouts was acquired by the Flemings, but soon passed to the Roches and, before the end of the 13th cent., to the Geraldines of Desmond, who were the real founders of the town. In 1584, following on the attainder of the 15th Earl of Desmond, the place was granted to Sir Thomas Norreys, English Lord President of Munster. Following Hugh O Neill's victory at the Yellow Ford (1598), Munster rose in arms and the English fled from Mallow after firing the town. Subsequently it passed by marriage to the Jephsons. Castle Garr (Short Castle), at the W. end of the town, was taken by Castlehaven's Confederate Catholics in 1642, the town itself in 1643, Mallow Castle (*below*) in 1645. In 1650 Cromwell captured the castle. Thereafter the town remained a typical "New English", Protestant, settlement. In the 18th and early 19th centuries it was a watering place of the Anglo-Irish gentry of Co. Cork, and the "Rakes of Mallow" acquired considerable notoriety.

Thomas Davis (1814–45), Young Ireland leader and a founder of the celebrated *Nation* newspaper, was born at 72 Thomas Davis St. P. A. (Canon) Sheehan (1852–1913), novelist, was born in O Brien St. William O Brien (1852–1928), Nationalist leader, was also a native of the town.

Both Anthony Trollope and Mrs Henry Wood lived for a time in Mallow.

Apart from the Court House, Market House, and some good dwelling houses, the only relics of Mallow's fashionable heyday are original little Spa House (now a private dwelling), the fine race-course, and the three gushing spouts of The Springs (Fermoy road).

At the SE. end of the town are the ruins (Nat. Mon.) of Mallow Castle, "a goodly, strong, and sumptuous house" built by Sir Thomas Norreys before 1598 on the site of a castle belonging to Sir John of Desmond. The

Plate 11. Glen Head, Glencolumbkille, Co. Donegal

house was burned by the Jacobites in 1689. After the Williamite victory the Jephsons converted the 17th cent. stables into a residence (altered and enlarged in 1837, completed 1954).

6½ m. ENE., on the N. side of the Lee, is Monanimmy (*see under* Castletownroche).

5¼ m. E., on the summit of Moynass Mountain (921 ft), is Laghtgal, a cairn.

1½ m. SE. is Bearforest House, a good, small "villa elegant" (1807–8) by Sir Richard Morrison, the Midleton-born architect.

3 m. SSE., near the summit of Knockaroura (857 ft), is a stone circle (wrecked); less than ½ m. ENE. is a cairn.

5 m. SSE. is Ballynamona Protestant church (1717).

5¾ m. SSE. are the extensive, but fragmentary, ruins (Nat. Mon.) of Mourne "Abbey", a preceptory of the Knights Hospitallers of St John of Jerusalem. It was founded before 1216, probably by Alexander de Sancta Helena. At the Dissolution it was granted to Tadhg Mac Carthy of Muskerry. The preceptory defences – a strong curtain with two towers and a keep – enclosed an area of several acres. The church was 180 ft long, its tower sited in unusual fashion over the W. end of the choir. (A Hospitaller tombstone is now in Kilshannig churchyard, 1½ m. SSE. of Rathcormack, *q.v.*) In 1520 a fierce battle took place near the preceptory, between the Earl of Desmond and Cormac Óg Mac Carthy of Muskerry (aided by Mac Carthy Riabhach and Sir Thomas of Desmond); the Earl and 1,000 of his followers were slain. Not far ESE., in Greenhill, alias Placus, is an ogham stone; some 40 yds away, by a fence, is a fragment of a second. – 2¾ m. NE., in Moneen East, is a standing stone. – 2 m. SE. is Ráth an Tóiteáin, alias Burn Fort, a ringfort which gives its name to the townland; in the souterrain was found an ogham stone. Also in the townland are a standing stone and remains of a prehistoric chamber tomb. 1 m. NE. of Burnfort village, in Island, are remains of a chamber tomb. 250 yds SW. are the remains (Nat. Mon.) of a wedge-shaped gallery grave set in a heel-shaped cairn delimited by a spaced-out "kerb". There was a cremation pit near the E. end of the chamber. The few finds included flint scrapers. Tomb and cairn were partly restored following excavation in 1957. A third tomb was removed in 1877. – 2 m. SSE. of the preceptory, close to the railway in Lissard, is a pair of standing stones. – 1¼ m. NW. of the preceptory are the ruins (Nat. Mon.) of Castlemore, alias Barrett's Castle. The first castle here was a 13th cent., de Cogan, motte castle (the fosse survives). The later castle was acquired by the Earl of Desmond in 1439. Early in the 17th cent. the Barretts obtained possession of it, and held it until the Williamite confiscations (1691). 1 m. W. of the castle, beside the Lyre in Dromore South, is Dooneen Rock. Here is Réim na Gaoithe, a recumbent-stone circle (nine stones with a large central stone).

6 m. SSW., W. of the Blarney road, in Ballybanaltra, alias Nursetown More, is a 10-ft pillarstone.

7½ m. SSW., in Carrigcleenamore, is Carraig Chlíodhna, Cleena's Rock. A great rock at the SE. end is traditionally the door to the Otherworld seat of the goddess Clíodhna (*see* Ross Carbery).

4½ m. W., on a lofty rock by the S. bank of the Blackwater, is Dromaneen Castle (Nat. Mon.), a large O Callaghan stronghouse of the 16th and 17th centuries, in a bawn of six acres. The SE. flanking tower (demolished) of the bawn served as a dovecot. The site commands a delightful view. 2¾ m. N. is Longueville (*below*).

4 m. W., to the N. of the Blackwater, is Longueville, formerly Garrymacony. O Callaghan lands here, confiscated by the Cromwellians, were purchased by the Longfields in 1698. They built the beautifully sited house, 1700–1740. (It was enlarged early in the 19th cent.) Richard Longfield was created Baron Longueville in 1795, whence the change of place name. For supporting the Union he was rewarded with a viscountcy. Arthur O Connor, the Republican leader (*see* Fort Robert *under* Ballineen–Enniskean), was his nephew, and might have been his heir but for refusing to forswear his principles. (Longueville is now once more O Callaghan property.)

6 m. NW. is Kilmaclenine (*see under* Buttevant).

8 m. NW. is Lohort (*see under* Kanturk).

MANOR CUNNINGHAM, Co. Donegal (Map 2, D2), is a village on the Derry (15 m.)–Letterkenny (6½ m.) road, close to the head of Lough Swilly.

W. of the village is a fine pillarstone.

½ m. S. is the ancient church site of Raymoghy, where St Columcille came to be instructed by Bishop Brugach. ¾ m. SSE., in Carrickballydooey, is a pillarstone with two incised crosses. ½ m. S. of Carrickballydooey bridge, in Labbadish, is the Giants Bed. – 1 m. ENE. of Carrickballydooey pillarstone, in Ballyboe, is a pair of pillarstones. – ¾ m. SW. of Raymoghy church-site, in Pluck, is a pillarstone (Nat. Mon.).

2½ m. NNE., on Lough Swilly, are the ruins of Balleeghan "Abbey", a 15th cent. Franciscan Tertiary church with inserted details of the Plantation period. 1 m. NNE., in Ballylawn, is a pillarstone.

1¼ m. NE., in Drean, is a pillarstone.

MANORHAMILTON, Co. Leitrim (Map 2, B4), is a strategically sited Border village in the beautiful Bonet River valley, near the head of lovely Glencar. It is the junction of roads from Dromahaire (10 m.), Bundoran (16 m.), Belcoo (14 m.), and Garrison (8 m.). The Bonet, which flows down from pretty Glenade Lough to Lough Gill (*see under* Sligo), holds salmon and sea trout.

The surrounding hills offer many pleasing

prospects and are rich in archaeological remains, including chamber tombs, most of them unrecorded.

A short distance N. are remains of a stronghouse built in 1638 by Sir Frederick Hamilton, grantee of confiscated Irish lands.

2½ m. SSE., in Tullyskeherny are the remains of two court cairns (Giants Graves). One has six or more subsidiary chambers, as well as a two-segment gallery grave.

2½ m. SSW. is Larkfield church. Not far away is Giants Grave, a ruined gallery grave.

8 m. WNW. is beautiful Glencar with its lake and waterfalls (see under Drumcliff).

3 m. NW. are Glenade and (5 m.) Glenade Lough. The lovely valley is flanked by steep, often cliff-like, limestone hills, notably on the S. and W. (Truskmore, 2,113 ft). These offer good rock-climbing. On the shoulder of the mountain above Leacanarainey, at the N. side of the mouth of the glen, is Altar, a prehistoric chamber tomb (passage grave?).

3 m. NW., on the N. side of Glenade in Barracashlaun, is a two-court cairn.

7 m. N. is Glenanniff. There are passage graves in the mountains on the N. side of the valley, but Dermot and Grania's Bed high up on the W. side is a natural cave.

8¾ m. N., in Mautiagh, is Giants Grave, a two-court cairn. ½ m. NE., in Shasgar overlooking Lough Melvin, is Giants Grave, a court cairn.

MARKETHILL, Co. Armagh (Map 3, B5), is a little market town on the Armagh (7 m.)–Newry (13 m.) road, in the famous Armagh apple country. The nearby Cusher River is a trout and dollaghan stream.

Gosford Castle, 1½ m. N., a great, Norman-style fantasy, was commenced by Thomas Hopper in 1819 for the 2nd Earl of Gosford; the "keep" is not by Hopper. Some of the carving is by Edward Smyth's son, John. Dean Swift was a frequent visitor to the earlier Acheson residence here; hence his "walk", "chair", etc. in the demesne.

4 m. W., alt. 827 ft in Carnavanaghan, is hill-top Vicar's Cairn (Nat. Mon.), a much reduced cairn some 20 ft high. In 1795 it was 132 ft in diameter and was enclosed by a circle of standing stones; in 1815 fifty-five standing stones still remained.

6 m. NNW. is Rich Hill (see under Armagh).

MAUM, alias **MAAM**, Co. Galway (Map 1, C5), is an angling (salmon, sea trout, brown trout) centre in the magnificent Maum valley which climbs for some 8 m. from the NW. arm of Lough Corrib to the saddle overlooking the head of Killary (Harbour). It is 14 m. NW. of Oughterard, 9 m. SE. of Leenaun, and 13 m. W. of Cong. Behind the hamlet rise Lugnabrick (1,628 ft) and Knocknagussy (1,494 ft); on the opposite side, Leckavrea (1,307 ft) and the rest of the Maumturk range. The Failmore, Bealanabrack, and Joyce's River (this is the heart of

Cecil W. Vanston

St Brendan *by Evie Hone, Kilmeelickin church,*
Maum

Joyce's Country) unite in the valley on their way down to Lough Corrib.

3 m. NW., in Kilmeelickin church, is a single-light window (St Brendan) by Evie Hone (1950). 3¾ m. NW., at Griggin's Bridge, a road to the right (NNE.) climbs the little valley between Rinavore (1,409 ft) and Bunnacunneen (1,902 ft) to beautiful, mountain-ringed Lough Nafooey. (The circuit, Maum–Lough Nafooey–Clonbur–Cornamona–Maum, is recommended; also circuit of the Partry Mountains via Lough Nafooey and Tourmakeady.)

3 m. SE., in Lough Corrib, are the 13th cent. keep and curtain (Nat. Mon.) of the O Conor island castle, Caisleán na Circe, Castlekirke.

2 m. WNW., at Cur, a footpath climbs SW. to Maumeen (3 m.), a mountain saddle associated with St Patrick, where Leaba Pháraic, "Patrick's Bed" (a rock recess) and Tobar Pháraic, "Patrick's Well" mark a place of pilgrimage and Lughnasa celebrations. Formerly of great repute, they are still visited on the last Sunday of July. The well was believed to cure murrain in cattle, as well as human ills. (See also Tullywee under Ballynahinch.)

MAYNOOTH, Co. Kildare (Map 6, C3), is a village beside the Royal Canal, on the main Dublin–Galway road, between Leixlip (5 m.) and Kilcock (4 m.).

At the W. end of the main street is St Patrick's College (*below*). Inside the gate is St Mary's Church (C. of I.), which incorporates the tower and fabric of a manorial church associated with the great castle of the Earls of Kildare, whose massive ruins (Nat. Mon.) are to the right of the gate. The earliest castle here was, doubtless, constructed for Gerald fitz Maurice (d. 1203), 1st Baron O ffaly and ancestor of the Fitz Geralds, Earls and Marquesses of Kildare and Dukes of Leinster. The ruins include fine gatehouse, massive keep, great hall, etc. The keep probably dates from the 13th cent.; the other works are of various dates. (The castle was enlarged in 1426 by the 6th Earl.) The 8th and 9th Earls of Kildare (Garrett Mór and Garret Óg) had a notable library (MSS. and printed books) of Irish, Latin, French, and English literature at the castle. Stronghold of the rebel Silken Thomas, the castle was taken after a week's siege in March 1535, by Henry VIII's deputy, Sir William Skeffington. Skeffington bombarded the castle with the first siege guns used in Ireland. His execution of the survivors of the garrison made the "Pardon of Maynooth" a byword in contemporary Ireland, and marked the beginning of a long tradition of brutality in Anglo-Irish wars. Re-edified in 1630, the castle was pillaged in 1641. In 1647 it was dismantled by order of Eóghan Rúa O Neill and was thereafter abandoned. The manorial church was reorganized on a collegiate basis in 1521 by Garret Óg, who stipulated that the community (St Mary's College: provost, vice-provost, five priests, two clerics, and three choristers) serving it should pray "for the prosperity of the Kings of England, for the good estate of the Earl of Kildare, his wife and kindred, while living, and for their souls after death". Henry VIII suppressed the foundation, 1538. In the church ("restored", 1770) is buried the noted German-born architect, Richard Cassels, who died in 1757 while working at Carton (*below*).

St Patrick's College is the greatest Catholic seminary in these islands, and has supplied priests and bishops to Great Britain, Australia, Canada, the U.S.A., Africa, China, the Philippines, and even France. It was founded in 1795 by the English authorities, who had become alarmed by the Revolution in France, where so many Irish priests had had till then to seek their education by reason of the Penal Laws. As an incidental consequence of the disestablishment of the Protestant state church in 1869, the seminary ceased to be a Royal College, and was given £369,040 by way of compensation for the loss of its annual Parliamentary grant. In 1896 it was accorded the status of a Pontifical university, with faculties of Philosophy, Theology, and Canon Law. In 1908 the Senate of the new National University of Ireland accorded it the status of a Recognized College of the University, with faculties of Arts, Celtic Studies, Philosophy, and Science.

The great complex consists primarily of two large courts or squares. The nucleus of it all was the stark Classical residence known as Stoyte House (central block of the E. range; on the site of the Earl of Kildare's medieval Council House), to which harmonizing N. and S. wings were added. Early-19th cent. additions included the N. and S. sides of St Joseph's Sq. and the Junior House. No architect appears to have been employed as such, but prominent among the builders were Michael (designer of the chapel about 1796) and Francis Stapleton, members of a Dublin family of distinguished architect-builders and stuccoers. Such men could hardly have failed, whatever the financial stringencies, to provide well-proportioned, dignified buildings. Their work has been appreciably modified of late.

In 1845 extensive additions were entrusted to the celebrated English Gothic-Revival architect, Augustus Welby Pugin. "The architect wanted one thing, the (college) authorities another, the builder had his own view, and the presiding genius, the Board of Works, wanted something else." The result was the great, and in many respects admirable, though still incomplete, Gothic quadrangle (1845–50) which contains St Mary's and St Patrick's Houses. The College Chapel (1875–1902), by Ireland's foremost Gothic Revivalist, J. J. Mc Carthy, architect also of the Senior Infirmary and its good chapel, is one of the major departures from Pugin's plan. Mc Carthy in his turn died before the completion of his design (the Chapel

Deegan Photographs

The Chapel, St Patrick's College, Maynooth

Deegan Photographs
The Saloon, Carton, Maynooth

being finished by his pupil, William Hague), and his white marble high-altar was replaced in 1911 by the existing, inferior, if more pretentious, work. Since Mc Carthy's time there have been many unfortunate departures from the architectural tradition of the college. By and large, the college mirrors the 19th–20th cent. rise and fall of the artistic standards of the resurgent Catholic Church in Ireland.

In the sacristy may be seen Viavicenzi's *Flight into Egypt* (formerly at Carton; presented by Hermione, Duchess of Leinster); in the library, a limestone head of St Patrick by the Cork sculptor, Séamus Murphy. The library has a large collection of late MSS. and early printed books in the Irish language.

The college museum contains a small, but interesting, collection of antiquities and works of art, mainly ecclesiastical. These include an *Ecce Homo* rescued by the Caddels of Harbourstown from Cromwell's sack of Drogheda and miscellaneous chalices, reliquaries, vestments, etc., of the 16th, 17th, 18th, and 19th centuries. Among the vestments are those of Geoffrey Keating (*see* Tubbrid *under* Cahir), as well as vestments presented to the Irish College of Salamanca by Queen Maria Barbara of Spain (1746–59), to the Irish College of Nantes by Queen Marie Antoinette, and to Maynooth College by the Empress Elizabeth of Austria. The museum also contains early electrical apparatus invented or used by the Rev. Nicholas Callan (1799–1864), who was Professor of Science at Maynooth, 1826–64. He rounded off Faraday's work on electro-magnetic induction, was responsible for the step-up transformer and for the induction coil (1836), and discovered the principles of the self-induced dynamo (1837).

At the E. end of the main street is the 1,000-acre demesne of Carton, where the Rye Water feeds an artificial lake. The mansion was remodelled (about 1739–47) by Richard Cassels

for the 19th Earl of Kildare. (The coat of arms in the pediment is by John Haughton and John Kelly, who also did "decorations of boys, cornucopias, etc.") The superb state apartments include a saloon with a coved stucco ceiling by Paul and Philip Francini; the organ (1839) is by Lord Gerald Fitzgerald. The dining room (1815) is by Sir Richard Morrison. In the grounds is the Shell Cottage made by the 3rd Duchess of Leinster. The present proprietor is Lord Brocket.

2 m. ESE., on the S. side of the canal, is Donaghmore, site of an early monastery. The remains here include an ancient field-system, as well as the ruins of a small nave-and-chancel church. An ogham stone found at the church is in the National Museum. ¾ m. S. is 140-ft Carton Obelisk, alias Conolly's Folly, erected in 1740 (to the design of Cassels?) by Speaker Conolly's widow to close a 2½-m. vista from the back of Castletown (*see under* Celbridge).

3 m. S. the ruins of Taghadoe (locally Taptoo) Round Tower (65 ft; Nat. Mon.) and church mark the site of a monastery founded by St Túa (whence the name Teach Túa, Taghadoe, Túa's house), alias Ultán the Silent. 3 m. SW. is Rathcoffey (*see* Mainham *under* Clane).

7 m. SW. is Donadea. In the Protestant church is a fine, Renaissance, canopied tomb (1626) with kneeling effigies of Sir Gerald Aylmer (d. 1634) and his wife, Dame Julia Nugent (d. 1617), as well as figured panels (*Crucifixion, Blessed Virgin, SS Jerome, Gregory, Ambrose, Augustine*); it was brought here from the pre-Reformation church. The Aylmers, who remained Catholics until the 18th cent., lived at Donadea from the 15th to the 20th cent. Their latest residence, a large "castle" by Sir Richard Morrison and his son, William Vitruvius, was sold (by the Department of Lands) for demolition in 1940.

MELLIFONT ABBEY, Co. Louth (Map 6, C1), 4½ m. WNW. of Drogheda, was the first Cistercian abbey in Ireland. The Cistercians of

Irish Tourist Board
The lavabo, Mellifont Abbey

Mellifont were among the first Irish representatives of a great European order; their monastery one of the first Irish representatives of the classic, integrated, monastic architecture of medieval Europe.

The abbey was founded in 1140 by Donchadh O Carroll, King of Uriel (*see* Louth), at the instance of the celebrated reformer, St Máel M'Áedhóg ("Malachy") Ó Morgair, Bishop of Down (he had resigned the archbishopric of Armagh in 1137). Impressed by his experience of St Bernard's rule at Clairvaux, Máel M'Áedhóg had had some Irish novices trained there. These, accompanied by a number of French Cistercians, came to Mellifont in 1142. Soon afterwards St Bernard sent a skilled master-mason, Robert by name, to aid them in the building of the new-style abbey. By 1148 four daughter houses had been founded: Bective, Co. Meath; Boyle, Co. Roscommon; Monasternenagh, Co. Limerick (*see under* Croom); and Baltinglass, Co. Wicklow. By 1272 these in turn had sent out twenty other offshoots, mostly in Munster and Leinster.

The first church of Mellifont was consecrated in 1157, on the occasion of a national synod presided over by Cardinal Paparo, the papal legate. The High-king, Muirchertach Mac Lochlainn, presented 160 cows and 60 oz. of gold to the abbey; other princes, too, made valuable gifts, while Dervorgilla, wife of Tiernan O Rourke of Breany, gave 60 oz. of gold, a gold chalice for the high-altar, and ornaments and furnishings for nine other altars. It was to Mellifont that she finally retired, and it was there that she died in 1193. That same year Máel M'Áedhóg's relics were brought from Clairvaux and deposited in the abbey.

The abbey was suppressed in 1539 (at which time it had only about twenty-seven choir monks), and in 1566 the buildings were granted to Edward Moore, ancestor of the Earls of Drogheda. Moore turned the abbey into a fortified residence, and it remained the seat of his family until the 18th cent. It was here, in the house of his friend Sir Garret Moore, that Great Hugh O'Neill, starved into surrender, submitted at last to the English Lord Deputy Mountjoy, in March 1603. In 1641 the place was captured by Sir Felim O Neill, on the occasion of his abortive attack on Drogheda.

The ruins (Nat. Mon.) are highly interesting, though very fragmentary, consisting for the most part of little more than foundations. The plan is the normal Cistercian one: on the N., a cruciform church; on the S., chapter-house, refectory, kitchen, dormitories, etc., ranged in integrated order round a cloister. The church had an aisled nave of eight bays, aisleless chancel, transepts with E. chapels (the N. transept had W. chapels also); noteworthy is the unique, recently unearthed, pseudo-crypt at the W. end. In the course of the 13th, 14th, and 15th centuries many alterations and extensions were carried out, some of which can be readily recognized. Thus, the first church was smaller

Commissioners of Public Works in Ireland
Carved head, Mellifont Abbey

than the second; instead of three square-ended E. chapels in each transept, it had one square-ended chapel flanked by two apsidal chapels – the only certain instances of the apse in medieval Ireland. Between the W. ambulatory of the cloister and the W. (cellar) claustral range was a processional way connecting the S. cloister ambulatory with the W. end of the church. Conspicuous among the ruins are: the fragments of the Romanesque (about 1157) cloister arcade; the remnant of the unique octagonal Transitional lavabo or washing-place (the miscalled Baptistry) on the S. side of the cloister, facing the door of the refectory; and the 14th cent. eastern extension (miscalled St Bernard's Chapel) of the chapter-house. In the floor of the latter have been set encaustic tiles from the church; the brickwork about the altered windows dates from the Moore occupation. N. of the abbey are the remains of the 15th cent. castle-like gatehouse. The small, plain church NE. of the precincts is probably post-Reformation.

MIDDLETOWN, Co. Armagh (Map 3, A5), is a market and Border town on the road from Monaghan (7 m.) to Armagh (8 m.).

½ m. SE. is Rathtrillick, a large, trivallate ringfort (Nat. Mon.).

3 m. N. is Tynan village, on the site of an early monastery, of which the only relic there is a 9th/10th cent. High Cross (Nat. Mon.) which formerly stood in the churchyard. The cross is decorated with bosses on the head and a *Fall of Adam and Eve* in a panel near the foot. A second cross (Nat. Mon.) in the churchyard was removed about 1844 to Tynan Abbey demesne, where it stands on the terrace close to the house. Also in the demesne are two High

Crosses from Glenarb (*see under* Caledon, Co. Tyrone); one (Nat. Mon.) is on an island in Corfehan, the other in Fairview (Mucklagh) ½ m. WSW. of the village. The Fairview cross has a very weathered *Crucifixion*.

1½ m. SW. are the ruins of Ardgonnell castle (Nat. Mon.), an O Neill castle which was remodelled towards the end of the 17th cent., probably by Sir Robert Hamilton.

MIDLETON, Co. Cork (Map 5, C6), is a market town where the Cork (14 m.)–Youghal (17 m.) road crosses the head of the Owenacurra estuary, near the NE. corner of Cork Harbour. It was founded by the Brodericks, later Earls of Midleton, about 1670.

Sir Richard Morrison, (1767–1849), architect, a pupil of Gandon's and father of William Vitruvius Morrison (1794–1838), was a native of Midleton.

The Protestant parish church was built in 1825 to the design of the brothers Pain, pupils of John Nash (*see* Cork). It occupies part of the site of the Cistercian abbey of Monasterore, alias Chore (Chorus Sancti Benedicti), named, like the Owenacurra and Ballynacorra, from a local weir (*cora*). The abbey was colonized from Monasternenagh (*see under* Croom) in 1180. The founder's name is unknown. At the Dissolution the abbey and its appurtenances were granted to the Fitzgeralds of Cloyne, who held them until the Cromwellian confiscation.

John Philpot Curran (1750–1817; *see* Newmarket) went to school at Midleton College, founded in 1696 as a free grammar school by Elizabeth Villiers (Countess of Orkney), mistress of William of Orange, in an effort to overcome the opposition to William's grant to her of the 95,649 acres in Ireland which James II had been given by Charles II at the Restoration. The building was remodelled on ponderous Georgian lines in 1829.

¼ m. NE., at Foxe's Quarry, Park North, are limestone caves.

10½ m. NNE. (via Clonmult), in Garryduff, is a small ringfort (originally bivallate), with stonefaced earthen rampart. Excavation revealed traces of hearths, furnaces, and timber-post houses. The finds included sub-Roman pottery of Rhenish types and a unique, small gold "wren", and date the two-phase occupation of the fort to the 7th and 8th centuries. The larger and stronger ringfort nearby yielded no evidence of occupation at all.

1¾ m. ENE. are the remains of Cahermone castle: part of moat, 15th cent. tower, remnants of later buildings. It was a Fitzgerald (Knights of Kerry) stronghold.

1½ m. S., on the E. shore of the estuary, are the ruins of Ballynacorra church. Also in Ballynacorra is a tumulus.

MILLFORD village, Co. Donegal (Map 2, C2), is an angling centre (Lough Fern and Leannan River) near the head of Mulroy Bay, on the Rathmelton (4 m.)–Carrigart (10 m.) road. It is convenient for exploring the lovely Fanad district (*see under* Portsalon). The circuit Millford – Kerrykeel (Carrowkeel) – Portsalon – Fanad Head – Kerrykeel – Millford is highly rewarding.

Local beauty spots are the Fairy Glen, and secluded Bunlin Glen (1 m. NW.) with its two waterfalls, the Grey Mare's Tail and Golan Loop.

St Peter's Church (1961), by McCormick and Corr, is a good, simple essay in the contemporary idiom. The stained glass is by Patrick Pollen (*SS Columcille, Adamnan, Comgall*), Patrick Pye (*SS Patrick, Brendan, Eunan* – sic!), Phyllis Burke (*SS Malachy, Brigid, Attracta*), and Imogen Stuart (*St Garvan*). The tapestry altar dorsal (*The miraculous draught of fishes*) was designed by Colin Midleton of Belfast. The ceramic Stations of the Cross are by Imogen Stuart. The *St Peter* over the door is by Oisín Kelly. The sacristy weathervane is by Iain Stuart.

3½ m. NNE. (1¼ m. S. of Carrowkeel village) is Gortnavern (Dermot and) Grania's Bed, a good portal dolmen.

2½ m. NE., in Tirhommin, is Ballyboe Altar, a prehistoric chamber tomb.

1½ m. E., on the N. shore of Columbkille Lough, is Columcille's (alias St Columb's) Chair, a natural rock.

1½ m. SSE., in Loughakey, is a chamber tomb. About ½ m. SSE., in Legmuckduff to the N. of Lough Aweel, is another.

1½ m. SW. and ½ m. W. of the Lough Fern road, smothered in a field fence in Gortmacallmore, is Cromlech, a portal dolmen (?).

3½ m. WSW. (via Bunlin bridge), in Carrownaganonach, is Doon More, a stone ringfort.

1¼ m. NW. (to the W. of the road 400 yds N. of Bunlin bridge), in Cratlagh, is Altar, a chamber tomb. 1¼ m. NW. of Bunlin bridge, on the E. slope of Crocknalaght in Cratlagh, is Dermot and Grania's Bed, another chamber tomb.

4¾ m. NNW., in Cranford, is Giants Grave, a chamber tomb.

MILLSTREET, Co. Cork (Map 4, E4), a village of the upper Blackwater valley, is attractively situated on the Macroom (13 m.)–Kanturk (12 m.) road, near the mouth of the pass between the Derrynasaggart (Caherbarnagh, 2,239 ft; Mullaghanish, 2,133 ft) and Boggeragh (Musheramore, 2,118 ft) Mountains. The Boggeraghs are rich in megalithic remains.

1¾ m. NNE., in Drishane, is the tower (Nat. Mon.) of a castle built in 1436 by Dermot Mac Carthy. The fireplaces and armorials were inserted by the Walls family in the 17th cent. Nearby are remains of a church.

3¾ m. SE., in Tullig, is a stone alignment; ¼ m. ENE., in Brook Park, is a stone circle with outlier.

5¾ m. SE., in Knocknakilla, on the upper slope of Musheramore, is a stone circle (Nat.

Drishane castle, Millstreet

Mon.) of Kealkil (*see* Bantry) type; not far away, to the N., of the Coachford road, are remains of a cairn (Nat. Mon.). 2½ m. NNE. is Tullig alignment (*above*).

5¼ m. SSE., in Glentane East, are remains of a chamber tomb; also a stone circle enclosed by a fosse, outside which is a standing stone.

6½ m. SSE. is Carriganimmy (*see under* Macroom).

MILLTOWN MALBAY, Co. Clare (Map 4, D1), is a small market town 20 m. W. of Ennis (via Inagh) and 7 m. SW. of Lehinch.

2 m. SW. is the little seaside resort of Spanish Point (bathing, sea fishing, golf) with its sandy beach. The headland takes its name from the Armada Spaniards ship-wrecked thereabouts in Sept. 1588, when Sir Turloch O Brien of Liscannor and Boetius Clancy, Sheriff of Clare, butchered the survivors at the command of Sir Richard Bingham, English governor of Connacht.

2 m. NW., in Freagh, are a good bathing-place ("Silver Strand") and remains of an O Brien castle.

2 m. NE. are remains of Kilfarboy, a late-15th cent. parish church on the site of a foundation (c. 740) attributed to St Laichtín. In the churchyard are buried Andrias Mac Cruitin (d. 1749) and Mícheál Ó Coimín (d. 1760), Gaelic poets, writers, and scholars. (Mac Cruitin was hereditary ollamh to the O Briens.) The holy well is dedicated to St Joseph.

5½ m. SE., alt. 700–800 ft, on the S. slope of Slieve Callan in Knockalassa, is Leaba Dhiarmada agus Ghráinne, a ruinous, wedge-shaped gallery grave. The summit (1,282 ft) of Slieve Callan is the highest point in West Clare. Booleynagreana (½ m. N. of the gallery grave) and

its little lough were the site of Lughnasa celebrations (Comthineól Chruim Duibh). N. of the lough was Leacht Chonáin, a cairn associated with the poltroon of Fiana literature; an ogham inscription was forged on its pillar-stone. – 3 m. SSE. of the Knockalassa tomb and 1¼ m. E. of Doo Lough, in Carncreagh, is Dermot and Grania's Bed, a ruinous, wedge-shaped gallery grave.

3½ m. SW. is Quilty, a fishing village. The ugly, 1909–11 church commemorates the valour of the twelve men who, in four currachs, tried to rescue the crew of the French ship, *Leon XIII*, wrecked offshore in the great storm of Oct. 1907. 1½ m. S. is Kilmurry, with remnants of the late-medieval parish church, Cill Mhuire Ó mBreasáin. – 1½ m. SW., in Tramore, are remains of an O Brien castle. – 2½ m. SW. (by currach) is Inis Chaorach, alias Mutton Island, with traces of an anchoritic settlement attributed to St Seanán (*see* Scattery Island *under* Kilrush).

MITCHELSTOWN, Co. Cork (Map 5, C5), a market and creamery town on the main Dublin (126½ m.)–Cork (32 m.) road, 7 m. N. of Fermoy, is beautifully situated in the valley between the Kilworth and Galty Mountains (Lyracappul, 2,712 ft; Galtymore, 3,018 ft).

Creation of the King family (Earls of Kingston), the town is a good example of early-19th cent. planning. At the N. end is College Sq., with Main St opening off the S. side. The vista at the S. end of the street is closed by the Protestant parish church erected in 1823 to the design of George Richard Pain, a pupil of John Nash, who settled in Cork (*q.v.*).

College Sq. takes its name from Kingston College, an asylum for decayed Protestant gentlefolk. (Beneath the college chapel is the Kingston family vault.) A statue of John Mandeville and three crosses in the pavement commemorate a Land League meeting held here in 1887, in the course of which three men were killed by the police. At the W. side of the square is the entrance to Mitchelstown Castle demesne, noted for its landscape gardening. The "castle", seat of the Earls of Kingston, was a large Tudor-style mansion erected in 1823 to the design of George Richard Pain. It was burnt down in 1922, and the stones were taken away to build the new abbey church at Mount Melleray (*see under* Cappoquin). The medieval castle here belonged to the Fitzgerald White Knights. Captured by Confederate Catholics in 1641, it was recovered by the English, only to be retaken by Castlehaven in 1645. It ultimately passed by marriage to Sir John King, who was created Baron Kingston by Charles II in 1660. In 1768 the castle was replaced by a fine Georgian house, pulled down to make room for Pain's "castle". An ancient grave-yard in the demesne marks the site of the hermitage or monastery of Brigown (Brí Ghabhann), whose founder, St Fionn-Chú(a), died of the Yellow Plague in 664. He was noted for his austerities. An aetiological legend asserts that, having surrendered his assured place in Heaven to a king of the Déise, he had seven smiths (*gabha*) make him seven sickles, on which he mortified his flesh for seven years, so as to win a new place for himself. The Round Tower of Brigown remained standing until 1720.

4 m. NE., in Co. Tipperary, is the ruined church of Kilbeheny. John O Mahony (d. 1877), co-founder with James Stephens of the Fenians, was born nearby.

10 m. NE., in Coolagarranroe, Co. Tipperary, are the celebrated "Mitchelstown" Caves (*see under* Ballyporeen).

4 m. SSW. is the ruined hill-top castle of Caheradriney, a stronghold of the Condons. It occupies the site of an ancient fort, which gave its name to the 695-ft hill. 2 m. WSW. is Killeeneemer (*see under* Glanworth).

4 m. SW., in Nutgrove (near Ballindangan level crosssing), is a 10 ft 9 in. pillarstone.

7 m. WSW. is Kildorrery (*q.v.*).

5 m. NW., in Labbamolaga Middle, is the ancient monastic site of Leaba Mo-Laga, alias the Teampaillín (Nat. Mon.). It takes its name from St Mo-Laga, disciple of St David of Wales and founder (?) of Lann Beachaire (*see* Bremore *under* Balbriggan; *also* Kildorrery *and* Timoleague). The remains here include ancient dry-masonry enclosing wall, scant fragments of a small Romanesque or Transitional church (it had quoin shafts), and remains of a diminutive oratory with *antae* and architraved, trabeate W. door. At the S. side of the oratory is Mo-Laga's *leaba* ("bed", "tomb"); to spend a night underneath the limestone slab cures rheumatism. In the enclosure are a small, early cross-slab and the Clocha Mallachta or Cursing Stones (*see* Inishmurray), six glacial pebbles. 80 yds S. of the churchyard, in Parkaleegawn, are four (formerly eight) orthostats, remnants of an oblong structure (a chamber tomb ?). Current legend explains them as petrified robbers of the monastery; but it has been claimed that these too were formerly called Leaba Mo-Laga.

MOATE, Co. Westmeath (Map 5, D1), a village on the Kilbeggan (9 m.)–Athlone (9½ m.) road, takes its name from the earthwork, Moatgrange, to the SW., which is reputedly called after Gráinne Óg, wife of one of the O Melaghlins, the ancient ruling stock of Meath.

1¾ m. N., in the grounds of Shurock House, is an early gravestone inscribed OR[ÓIT] DO MAELMAIRE ("A prayer for Máel-Maire"). It comes from Calry churchyard.

5 m. NE. is Knockastia, alias Knockast (659 ft), which commands wide prospects. On the summit is a low, Bronze Age cairn which covered forty-three (including urn-and-razor) burials (thirty-nine cremations).

3½ m. NW. is Mount Temple, alias Ballyloughloe. Nearby is an Anglo-Norman (de Lacy?) motte "fashioned out of an esker and apparently untouched since it bore its wooden tower and wooden palisades". In 1208 the "town of Ballyloughloe" was plundered and partly burned by the O Melaghlins. In 1234 it was burned by Felim O Conor of Connacht. 1 m. W. is the 16th cent. O Melaghlin castle of Carn.

MOIRA, Co. Down (Map 3, C5), is a linen and market village on the Belfast (12 m.)–Lurgan (5 m.) road. Hereabouts was fought, 24 June 637, the battle of Mag Roth (Moira), in which the King of Tara, Domnall II (of Cenél Conaill in Co. Donegal), defeated his rebel foster-son and quondam ally, Congal Clóen, son of the King of Dál Áraide (E. Derry, W. Down and most of Antrim), and the latter's allies, the Kings of Scottish Dál Ríada (Argyllshire) and of Ulster (the modern diocese of Down). The battle was one of the most celebrated in Gaelic literary legend. "These were the glories of the battle: the defeat of Congal Clóen in his falsehood, by Domnall in his truth; the madness of Suibne Geilt; and the taking of Cenn Fáelad's brain of forgetting out of his head. And it is not the fact of Suibne's madness which makes a glory of the battle, but the stories and poems he left in Ireland after him."

From Moira the Rawdon family, whose residence lay to the NW. of the village, takes its title (Earls of Moira). The Protestant parish church is a good example of early-18th cent. Gothick. It was erected by Lord Hillsborough and Sir John Rawdon. Berwick Hall, ½ m. E., is a 17th cent. Plantation farmhouse (altered). – ½ m. SW., in Aughnafosker, is Pretty Mary's Fort, a fine multivallate ringfort. A nearby ford is said to be that by which Slige Midluachra, the great roadway from Tara, crossed the Lagan.

1¾ m. SW. is Magheralin, *Machaire Lainne* (*Rónáin*), which took its distinguished name from Lann (Rónáin), an early monastery founded by 7th cent. St Rónán Fionn. The site of the monastery is marked (Nat. Mon.) by the remains of a 15th cent. parish church (residential tower, 17th cent.) which incorporates, as a side chapel, a much later church. Re-edified for Protestant use after the Restoration, the church served in the 18th cent. as the cathedral of the diocese of Dromore. It was dismantled in 1845. The 1845 Protestant church has two-light windows (1908) by A. E. Child (*SS Comgall and Finnian*), Lady Glenavy (*SS Gall and Columbanus*), and Michael Healy (*SS Patrick and Columcille*).

MONAGHAN, Co. Monaghan (Map 3, A6), on the Clogher (15 m.)–Castleblayney (15 m.) road, is the capital of the county to which it gives its name, and also the cathedral town of the Catholic diocese of Clogher. In 1462 Felim Mac Mahon, the local lord, founded a friary for Conventual Franciscans, some fragments of which survive near the Diamond. It was destroyed, and several of the friars beheaded, in 1540, in the course of an English compaign against O Neill of Tír Eóghain. In 1613 James I incorporated the small, English, Protestant settlement as a parliamentary borough.

The good Market House, built in 1792 for Gen. Robert Cuningham, afterwards 1st Baron Rossmore, is spoilt by tasteless fascia boards. The dull Court house is by John Bowden. St Mac Cartan's Cathedral (1861–92) is a very fine Gothic-Revival church by J. J. Mac Carthy. The exterior has been marred by incongruous Carrara marble statues, the interior by bad glass. A 12th/13th cent. bronze crucifix found at Donagh, Glaslough (*below*), has been adapted for use as a processional cross. In the bishop's house are two two-light windows (*SS Mac Cartan, Brigid; SS Patrick, Damhnat;* 1911–12) by Michael Healy.

Sir Charles Gavan Duffy (1816–1903), founder-editor of the epoch-making *Nation* newspaper and one of the leaders of the Young Ireland movement, who afterwards became Prime Minister of Victoria, was born in Dublin St. One of his sons was Mr Justice Gavan Duffy (d. 1951), an Irish signatory of the 1921 Anglo-Irish Treaty, and later President of the High Court.

1½ m. N. is St Mac Cartan's College, wheie is preserved an interesting 14th/15th cent. bronze altar cross, the so-called Cross of Clogher.

4 m. N. is Anketell Grove, a Georgian house.

6 m. NE., overlooking the lake of Glaslough, is Castle Leslie, home of Sir Shane Leslie, Bt, author. The house (1878) is by Lanyon, Lynn, and Lanyon; one gate-lodge is by John Nash. The house and its art and other treasures are open to the public on the afternoons of the first Sunday of each month. 1¼ m. WSW. is the ancient church site, Donagh (Domhnach Faoinir). The church was re-edified about 1508, later adapted for Protestant use by Planters, and finally abandoned in 1650. Close by are the base of a medieval stone cross, a small High Cross with a weathered, rude *Crucifixion*, and a fragment of a larger cross. The High Cross was found in Donagh Bog, and, in 1911, was erected here by Sir Shane Leslie and F. J. Bigger.

7 m. SE. is Clontibret, where, in 1595, Great Hugh O Neill sharply defeated Sir Henry Bagenal as he returned to Newry after revictualling the fort at Monaghan. It was O'Neill's first direct clash with the English in the Nine Years' War.

4½ m. SSW., in Leck, is the Mac Mahon's Stone. 4 m. SW. of this, in Calliagh, is Giants Grave, a chamber tomb. 3 m. WSW. of the latter, in Cairn, is Cromlech (*see under* Newbliss).

5 m. SW., in Carnbane, is a court cairn (Nat. Mon.). 3¼ m. S., in Carn, is Cromlech (*see under* Newbliss).

5 m. WSW., near Smithborough, is Drumsnat (Druim Sneachta). Mo-Lúa of Clonfertmulloe (*see under* Borris-in-Ossory) had a mon-

astery there. One of the earliest Irish literary codices was 8th cent. *Cín Dromma Snechta*, "the Book of Drumsnat".

4½ m. NW. is Tedavnet where, in the 6th cent., St Damhnat founded a monastery for women. Her name being Latinized as Dymphna, she has been unjustifiably identified with the saint of that name long venerated at Gheel in Flanders as patroness of the insane. St Damhnat's enshrined bachall, or staff, was sold by the last of the Ó Luain (O Loone, alias Lamb) hereditary custodians to George Petrie, and is now in the National Museum. St Damhnat is also commemorated at Caldavnet on the slope of Slieve Beagh, 3 m. NW. of Tedavnet.

MONASTERBOICE (Mainistear Bhuíthín), Co. Louth (Map 6, D1), in Newtown Monasterboice, to the W. of the Drogheda (5¾ m.)–Dunleer (5¼ m.) road, is an early monastic site celebrated for its High Crosses. The monastery is attributed to St Buíthe (later Buíthín, Buín, *anglice* Bween, Boyne), son of Brónach, who is said to have died 521, but of whom nothing is really known. The monastery figures in Irish records only between the years 759 and 1122. The most celebrated name in its history is that of Flann Mainistreach, Flann of Monasterboice (d. 1056). *Fer légind*, or Latin master, of the monastery, he was the reputed author of versified treatises on the Túatha Dé Danann, the Kings of Tara, etc. In 968 the place appears to have been occupied by Norse freebooters, for in that year Domnall, King of Tara, attacked it and slew 300 Vikings in one house alone. In 1097 the belfry (Round Tower) was destroyed by fire, and with it books and other treasures.

The remains (Nat. Mons.) at the site comprise two churches, a pre-Gothic sundial, two early grave-slabs, a Round Tower, and three High Crosses.

The churches are small, simple, rectangular

West Cross, Monasterboice, east face

Commissioners of Public Works in Ireland
Muiredach's Cross, Monasterboice, east face

Commissioners of Public Works in Ireland
Muiredach's Cross, Monasterboice, west face

structures of minor interest. The North Church is hardly older than the 13th cent. N. of it is an early gravestone inscribed OR[ŌIT] DU RUARCAN ("A prayer for Ruarcán"). The South Church is older, and appears to have had a chancel. In it is a bullaun.

The Round Tower, or *cloigtheach* (belfry of the monastery), though shorn of its uppermost part, is still about 100 ft high.

Towards the NE. corner of the graveyard is the imperfect North Cross, said to have been shattered by Cromwell. The head has simple panelling, a simple *Crucifixion*, and a fine spiral composition. The shaft is modern.

The West Cross, to the S. of the North Church, is traditionally *Cros Bhuíthin*, St Bween's Cross. It is exceptionally tall (21 ft 6 in.). The subjects figured are not all intelligible. They include: E. face: *David killing the lion and bear, Abraham's sacrifice of Isaac, David with the head of Goliath, David kneeling before Samuel, The Three Children in the Fiery Furnace, Christ in Majesty*; W. face: *Resurrection, Baptism of Christ* (?), *Crucifixion, Crowning with Thorns, Peter drawing his sword at Gethsemane, The Kiss of Judas.* Beside this cross is an early gravestone.

The South Cross, traditionally *Cros Phádraig* (St Patrick's Cross), is now commonly called Muiredach's Cross by scholars because of the inscription, at the bottom of the W. face of

the shaft, which Macalister reads: OR[ŌIT] DO MUIREDACH LASNDERNAD I[N] CHROS ("A prayer for Muiredach by whom the cross was made"): This Muiredach is conventionally identified with the abbot of that name who ruled 890–923. The cross (17 ft 8 in.), though not perfectly proportioned, is the finest of the remarkable Irish series of early figured crosses. (These were essentially "picture books" of Scriptural and other edifying stories for the unlettered. In their original condition they were almost certainly picked out with polychrome painting, and should be visualized as glowing with colour like contemporary metalwork and painted books.) The figure subjects on this splendid cross include: Base: *Animal figures* (the signs of the Zodiac ?), etc.; E. face: *The Fall, The Murder of Abel, David and Goliath* (?), *Moses smiting the Rock* (?), *Epiphany, Last Judgement, SS Anthony and Paul in the Desert*; W. face: *Arrest of Christ, Christ and Doubting Thomas* (?), *Christ presents a key to St Peter, a gospel to St Paul* (?), *The Crucifixion, Moses praying with his arms supported by Aaron and Hur.* The summit of the cross is fashioned (as frequently, e.g. the W. Cross) in the shape of a shingle-roofed church with gable-finials.

¾ m. NE., in Paddockstown, is Cailleach Bhéarra's House, a prehistoric gallery grave (Nat. Mon.). 400 yds NNE. is a boulder with prehistoric scribings.

MONASTEREVAN, Co. Kildare (Map 6, B3), is a village where the Kildare (7 m.)–Port Laoise (13 m.) road crosses the River Barrow and the Grand Canal. The cross in the Market Place commemorates Father Prendergast, who was hanged here for his part in the insurrection of 1798.

To the S. of the village is Moore Abbey, sometime seat of the Moores, earls of Drogheda (*see* Mellifont Abbey). It occupies the site of the early monastery from which the village takes its name, Mainistear Eimhín. The monastery, also called Ros Glas, alias Ros Glaise of the Munstermen, was founded by St Eimhíne, who was of royal Munster stock. It was Bishop-King Cormac mac Cuilenáin's claim to jurisdiction over it which brought about the battle of Ballaghmoon (908; *see under* Carlow). In the 12th cent. this monastery was refounded as a Cistercian abbey (Ros Glas, alias de Rosea Valle), dedicated to SS Mary and Benedict, by Dermot O Dempsey, King of Uí Fáilghe. In the 17th cent. the confiscated abbey was acquired by Sir Adam Loftus, 1st Viscount Ely. It passed to the Moores in the 18th cent. The mansion was remodelled in 1767 and Gothicized in 1846. For some years it was the residence of the celebrated singer, John McCormack, and is now a home for epileptics.

3 m. S. is Kildangan Castle, seat of the More O Ferrals.

MONEYMORE, Co. Derry (Map 3, B4), is a Plantation market and linen village on the Maghera (12 m.)–Cookstown (5 m.) road. It owes its origin to the Drapers' Company of London.

8 m. E., on the edge of Lough Neagh in Salterstown (2 m. S. of Ballyronan), is a 17th cent. Salters' Company of London bawn guarding the old lake-port of Moneymore.

1 m. SE. is Springhill, 17th–18th cent. home of the Lenox-Conynghams, now the property of the Nat. Trust. This charming, simple house was built after 1685 by "Good Will" Conyngham, of Scottish Planter stock. It was enlarged in 1765 and again about 1850. The staircase is good, the furniture, paintings, and Siege of Derry relics interesting. Admission to grounds and house: 1 April to 30 Sept., Tue. to Sat. (inclusive) and bank holidays, 2–6 p.m.; also Sundays, 1 July to 30 Sept., 2.30–5 p.m. Adults 2/–, children and parties 1/– each. 2¾ m. S., in Tamlaght (½ m. W. of Coagh), is Cloghogle (Nat. Mon.), a chamber tomb; the colossal capstone is of quartzite, whereas the supports are of basalt.

9 m. SE. is Arboe (*see under* Cookstown).

1 m. NW., in Ballymully, is a long, chambered cairn (Nat. Mon.).

MONKSTOWN, Co. Cork (Map 5, C6), is a small residential suburb and resort at the NW. corner of Cork Harbour, some 7 m. SW. of Cork city. There is a ferry service to and from Rushbrooke (*see under* Cobh).

Castle Mahon, alias Monkstown Castle, now Monkstown Golf Club, is a strong-house of 1636. It was built by Anastasia Archdeacon (Mac Coda), *née* Gould, for a net cost – so the tale asserts – of 4d.; i.e. after she had deducted the cost of the workmen's keep from their wages. And her husband was dissatisfied! In the main hall is a good fireplace of 1636; the upper part was added by Bernard Shaw, a collateral of George Bernard Shaw's ancestor, who held Castle Farm on lease early in the last cent.

The house, Carrigmahon, is by George Richard Pain, pupil of John Nash (*see* Cork Court House).

The Church of the Sacred Heart (1867–73) is by Edward Welby Pugin and George C. Ashlin.

MOUNTMELLICK, Co. Laois (Map 6, A3), is a market town where the Tullamore (15 m.)–Port Laoise (7 m.) road crosses the Owenass to the E. of Slieve Bloom. The town originated as a Quaker settlement (*see* Lurgan), and in 1677 the first Quaker school in Ireland was opened there. Later the town was a prosperous linen-spinning centre, shipping its goods by the Grand Canal. The principal streets are still essentially 18th cent. in character and have some good houses.

6 m. W., on the slope of Slieve Bloom (best approach is via Rosenallis), is Capard House, a Georgian house of the Piggotts. 1 m. S. is picturesque Cathole Glen, where the Owenass forms a series of cascades and trout pools.

2 m. WNW. is Summer Grove, a good, small, early Georgian house.

4 m. WNW. is the village of Rosenallis, which, like Mountmellick, was a Quaker colony and linen centre. The stump of a Round Tower and traces of a church are all that survive of an early monastery.

MOUNTRATH, Co. Laois (Map 6, A4), is a small, decayed market town on the Port Laoise (8 m.)–Roscrea (16 m.) road, to the SE. of Slieve Bloom. The highest point of the mountain, Arderin (alias Cruachán; 1,734 ft) affords wide prospects. It was until recently the site of attenuated Lughnasa celebrations on the last Sunday of July (Cruachán Sunday, Height Sunday, etc.).

There was an early monastery at Mountrath, associated with St Patrick, and a nunnery associated with St Brigid. No trace of either survives. In the early 17th cent. the place came into the possession of Sir Charles Coote. At the Restoration his son, a savage supporter of the Parliamentarian cause who made his peace betimes with Charles II, received large additional grants of land and was created Earl of Mountrath. In the 17th and 18th centuries the Cootes fostered the linen industry, and Mountrath was then a thriving place.

St. Fintan's Church is a Gothic-Revival essay by John S. Butler.

5 m. NNE., on the slope of Conlawn Hill (1,004 ft), is Ballyfin House, now a boarding school. The estate belonged originally to the O Mores. At the Elizabethan confiscation of the O More territories it was acquired by Sir Patrick Crosby (Mac Uí Chrossáin), ancestor of the Crosbies, Earls of Glandore. At the Restoration it was awarded to Periam Pole, ancestor of the Wellesley Poles, Earls of Mornington. The 3rd Earl of Mornington (d. 1845) sold it to Sir Charles Henry Coote, who built the house to the designs of Sir Richard Morrison (1767–1849), a pupil of Gandon's. Morrison was assisted by his son, William Virtruvius Morrison. The gardens were laid out by the late Sir Edwin Lutyens. The Tower of Ballyfin is said to command a view of seven counties.

1½ m. E. is Clonenagh, where St Fintán moccu Echdach (d. 603), patron of the O Mores, founded a famous monastery on the site of the hermitage of his master, St Colum moccu Cremthainn Áin (d. 549; Clonenagh was in Uí Cremthannáin territory; see also Terryglass under Portumna). Fintán was famous for his asceticism and manual labours. St Comgall of Bangor is said to have been his disciple. Óengus the Culdee (see Tallaght; also Dysert(enos) under Stradbally, Co. Laois, and Carrigeen under Croom) was a member of the community here before going to Tallaght. He is said to have commenced his celebrated Martyrology at Coolbanagher (see under Port Laoise), continued it at Clonenagh, and completed it at Tallaght. Only a few mounds mark the site of the monastery today.

2 m. SSW., on the River Nore, is the village of Castletown, noted for its home crafts.

3 m. NW., on the slope of the mountain, is Roundwood House, probably by Richard Cassels.

MOUNTSHANNON, Co. Clare (Map 5, C3), is a village and angling centre delightfully situated on the Clare side of Lough Derg, on the road from Portumna (16 m.) to Limerick (30 m.).

1 m. SE., beautifully situated in Lough Derg, is Inis Cealtra, alias Holy Island, with its notable early monastic remains. St Caimín (Caimmíne; d. 654), half brother of King Gúaire Aidhne of Connacht, sought to lead a solitary's life on the island, only to have disciples swarm about him. Other saints associated with the place are Colm of Terryglass (see under Portumna) and Caolán. The monastery suffered much from the Norse, but recovered, Brian Boru being credited with a hand in the recovery. (Marcán, his brother, who held the abbacies of Killaloe and Terryglass as well as of Inis Cealtra, died at the monastery in 1010.) In 1033 Conn Úa Sinnaig, "anchorite of Ireland", died there, and in 1111 Cathasach, "head of the piety of Ireland". – The circuit of the monuments (which are set in a complex of earthworks) may conveniently

begin at the ancient landing by the eastern shore. (a) NW. of the landing is a little ring enclosure with the ruin of the remarkable "Anchorite's Cell" encasing two pairs of rude orthostats. This is thought to have been the penitential cell of an anchorite (inclusus). At the pavement before the door is an early gravestone, SE. of which is a cross base. (b) Encroaching on the S. side of the ring enclosure is the Saints' Graveyard with remains of diminutive Teampall na bhFear nGonta, "Church of the Wounded Men", and many gravestones of the 8th, 9th, 10th, 12th, and later centuries. Near the SW. corner is a cross base inscribed ILAD I[N] DECHENBOIR ("The Grave of the Ten"). (c) W. of the graveyard are the ruins of St Caimín's Church, attributed to Brian Boru. The Romanesque doorway and chancel are 12th cent. work; in their present form door and chancel arch are 1879 Board of Works attempts at restoration. In the church are kept a High Cross, two other crosses, some early gravestones, etc. The High Cross, covered with interlacing, has a figured panel (one of them The Fall) at the end of each arm. The smaller of the other two bears the inscriptions: OR[ÓIT] DO ARDSENOIR HERENN .I. DO CATHASACH ("A prayer for the archsenior of Ireland", i.e. for Cathasach), and O[RÓIT] DO THORNOC DO RINGNI IN CROIS ("A prayer for Tornóg who made the cross"). The Cathasach in question is thought to be the Cathasach who died in 1111. Outside the church door is a bullaun. (d) SW. of St Caimín's is the Clogás ("Belfry"), a Round Tower which has lost its top storey; NW. is a cross base. (e) 100 yds NW. of this last, in sub-rectangular Garraidhe Mhícheáil, "Michael's Garden", are traces of diminutive St Michael's Oratory. (f) 150 yds SSE., in a small rectangular enclosure (Romanesque entrance rebuilt 1879), is little St Brigid's Church whose Romanesque doorway was also rebuilt in 1879. (g) 50 yds SE., again in a rectangular enclosure, is St Mary's Church, largest of the island. This is a plain, simple structure with a plain Transitional window in the S. wall. There are a few early gravestones here. The altar frontal and "reredos" have been constructed of pieces taken from the 17th cent. Mac Uí Bhriain Áradh monument in the S. wall. 50 yds E. is Lady Well, where the religious exercises of the pátrún formerly held on the Fri., Sat., Sun., and Mon. of Whitsuntide used to begin.

MOVILLE, Co. Donegal (Map 2, E2), is a seaside resort on the W. shore of Lough Foyle, 19 m. N. of Derry. Before the last war it was a port of call for transatlantic liners.

3½ m. N., in Carrowblagh, alias Leckemy, on the road to Culdaff, is a sweat house.

6 m. NNE. is pretty Glenagiveny, valley of a small river descending to the little bay W. of Balbane Head.

3 m. NE., opposite Magilligan Point, Co.

Irish Tourist Board
The "Skull House", Carrownaff, Moville

Derry, is Greencastle, a small resort with an excellent beach. Here are the fragmentary, overgrown ruins of the great castle (Nat. Mon.) of Northburg, alias Greencastle, built in 1305 by Richard de Burgo, "Red" Earl of Ulster. In 1316 it was captured by Edward Bruce and his Irish adherents, but was recovered by de Burgo in 1318. When the de Burgo power in Ulster collapsed in 1333, the castle fell into Irish hands. In 1555 An Calbhach O Donnell revolted against his father and, procuring a *gunna cam* from Scotland, wrecked the castle. In 1600, though ruinous, it was held for O Doherty. In 1608 it was captured by the English and, together with the whole of Inishowen, granted to Sir Arthur Chichester. Until the end of the 19th cent. the castle was included in the defences of Lough Foyle, and so was modified from time to time. The medieval remains include a 14th cent., twin-towered, residential gate house giving entry to a small yard, beyond which was the upper ward with large NE. tower and small SE. tower; the rectangular tower at the N. curtain was a 15th cent., O Doherty addition. East of the castle is a 19th cent. battery, now a hotel.

7 m. NE. is Inishowen Head (313 ft). It offers fine views of the Derry and Antrim coasts. A line of cliffs extends to the NW. Beneath the Head is Stroove Strand, a small bathing beach.

1 m. W., in Carrownaff, are the remains of an ancient church, a plain monolithic High Cross, and the "Skull House". The latter is a small, stone-roofed mortuary house. The first church here is attributed to St Patrick, but a St Finnian is said to have been buried here.

5 m. WNW., in Ballylawn, is hill-top (1,058 ft) Squire's Cairn.

4 m. W., in Tullyally, is a prehistoric chamber tomb.

MOYCULLEN, Co. Galway (Map 1, D6), is a hamlet on the Galway (7 m.)–Oughterard (10 m.) road.

4½ m. NNE., to the E. of Ross Lake (Lough Lonan), is St Annin's Well, ½ m. NW. are the featureless ruins of Killannin, a medieval parish church dedicated to St Annin; in the tomb of the Martins of Ross is buried Major Poppelton, Napoleon's esteemed custodian on St Helena, whose wife was a Martin of Ross House (*below*). ¼ m. NW. of Killannin are the ruins of Templebegnaneeve, a diminutive oratory with trabeate W. door; in the next field, to the SE., is a bullaun.

3¼ m. SE., in Cloonliff, near the E. shore of Ballycuirke Lough, are remains of Templebeg, a small nave-and-chancel church; to the N. is a bullaun called Glúna Phádraic, "St Patrick's Knees"; ½ m. N. is St Patrick's Well.

2½ m. S., in Killagoola townland, are remnants of Templeany, "Enda's Church", a small nave-and-chancel structure; to the W. is a double bullaun called Glúna Phádraic; to the N. is Tobereany, "Enda's Well".

3½ m. NW., on the W. side of the main road in Rosscahill, are the fragmentary remains of Temple Brecan, a small, early church; to the SW. is a double bullaun.

4 m. NNW., to the E. of the main road, is Ross House, former home of the Martins and birthplace of "Martin Ross" (Violet Martin, 1862–1915), who collaborated with her cousin, Dr Edith Oenone Somerville, in the celebrated "Somerville and Ross" series of novels and tales.

7 m. NW. (1½ m. SW. of the Oughterard road via Magherabeg), near the N. shore of little Buffy Lough, is Carna, a ruined cairn which local tradition makes the "grave of a chief called Buffy".

MUFF, Co. Donegal (Map 2, D2). is 6 m. NNE. of Derry, on the Moville (13 m.) road.

1½ m. NNE., in Ardmore, is a massive pillar-stone with cup-and-circle devices.

5 m. NE., on Lough Foyle, is Quigley's Point. ¼ m. N. is Carrowkeel Cromlech, a pre-historic chamber tomb. There are also chamber tombs in the adjacent townlands, Cabry and Tromaty. 5 m. N. of Quigley's Point, in Drung, is yet another.

2 m. NNW., at the foot of Eskaheen Mountain (1,377 ft), are the ancient monastic (Columban) site and holy well of Eskaheen (Iskaheen, *Uisge Chaoin*, "pure water"). Somewhere hereabouts is the grave of Eógan, son of Niall Nine Hostager and eponymous ancestor of Cenél Eóghain (Tír Eóghain, Tyrone, from whom the O'Neills have descended). W. of the hillside overlooking the church is An Chloch Mhór, alias the Giants Stone, alias "Morton God", a ruinous chamber tomb.

MUINE BHEAG, Co. Carlow (Map 6, B5), a small market town on the E. bank of the Barrow (salmon, trout, pike) 9¾ m. S. of Carlow and 16 m. NE. of Kilkenny, was founded towards the close of the 18th cent. by Walter Bagenal of Dunleckny Manor (*below*), who intended it "to be of considerable architectural

pretensions and to bear the name Versailles".
(The Bagenals had purchased this part of
Idrone from Sir George Carew in 1585; *see*
Leighlinsbridge.) Re-routing of the coach road
disappointed Walter's ambitions and left the
place with no prouder name than Bagenals-
town, which it kept until the present century.
The court house has a good Doric portico.

1½ m. NE. is Dunleckny motte. Dunleckny
Manor was the home of the Bagenals.

3 m. ENE., near Kildreenagh, are the head
and part of the shaft of a sculptured cross.

2¼ m. E. are the ruins of Ballymoon Castle
(Nat. Mon.), a castle of unique type, but of
whose history nothing whatever is known.
There is reason to doubt the legend that it was
never completed. It is a square enclosure without
angle towers, but having rectangular towers
projecting from the faces of three of the walls.
On the fourth side there was presumably a
barbican in front of the gateway. Inside there
were buildings against all four walls. A fine
double fireplace in the N. wall indicates the
position of the great hall.

3¾ m. SE., in Lorum, is a small granite cross
(Nat. Mon.). It is a relic of a monastery
founded by St Laisrén of Leighlin (*see under*
Leighlinbridge). 1½ m. ENE. is fragmentary
Ballyloughan Castle (Nat. Mon.), a keepless
castle (*c.* 1300) with twin-towered gatehouse,
towers at the SW. (hall-tower) and NE. angles,
and a turret at the NW. angle. From the 14th
to the later 17th cent. the castle was in the
possession of the Kavanagh Mac Murroughs. –
4½ m. SE. of the Lorum cross is Killoughternane (*see under* Borris).

1¼ m. W., on the W. bank of the Barrow, is
Malcolmville, a mid-Georgian house (Vigors
family).

MULLINAVAT, Co. Kilkenny (Map 6, B6),
is a village pleasantly situated in the Black
Water valley of the Walsh Mountain, 17 m.
SSW. of Thomastown and 8 m. NNW. of
Waterford.

SW. of the village, in the angle of the Black
Water and the Assy, stood the castle or "court"
of Inchacarrin, home of the poet, Seán mac
Bháitéir Breathnach (1580–1660; *see* Kilmaganny; *see also* Lismatigue *under* Knocktopher), on whom were fathered the forged
poems on the Graces (*see* Courtstown, *under*
Freshford).

2½ m. SE. is Tory Hill (966 ft), called after
the outlaw, Eamonn Denn (*fl. c.* 1688). Lughnasa was celebrated here on Fraochán Sunday,
alias Tory Hill Sunday (second Sunday of July).

2½ m. W., in Listrolin, is Cloch an tSaighdiúra, alias Cloch an Phalmaire, a pillarstone.

5 m. NW., alt. 450 ft in Kilmogue, is Leac
an Scáil (Nat. Mon.), a magnificent portal
dolmen. 4 m. WSW. is the Owning–Piltown
group of tombs (*see* Piltown).

MULLINGAR, Co. Westmeath (Map 6, A2),
county town of Westmeath and cathedral town

of the diocese of Meath (*see* Trim), is situated
on the Dublin (50 m.)–Longford (24 m.) road.
It is the market centre of Ireland's premier
cattle county, and is the junction of the
Dublin–Cavan, Dublin–Sligo, and Dublin–
Galway railways. (In pre-railway days it was
served by the now derelict Royal Canal.) It is
a convenient base for exploring the interesting,
and in places very attractive, Westmeath lake
country and for fishing Loughs Ennell, Owel,
Derryvaragh, and Lene (the two first-named are
noted Mayfly waters).

Mullingar was the chief manor of the barony
of Magheradernan, granted by Hugh I de Lacy
to William le Petit. The 19th cent. jail occupies
the site of the Petits' stone castle, successor to a
motte castle. In the Middle Ages there were
houses of Augustinian Canons (Domus Dei,
c. 1230) and of Dominicans (Holy Trinity,
1237) in the town, as well as a parish church
(All Saints), but no trace of any survives.

The town is dominated by the disappointing
Cathedral of Christ the King, erected in 1936 to
the design of Ralph Byrne. The only pleasing
features are the mosaics by the Russian artist,
Boris Anrep, in the chapels of SS Anne (*St
Anne presents the Virgin Mary in the Temple*;
1954) and Patrick (*St Patrick lights the Paschal
Fire at Slane*; 1949). The pediment sculpture
(*The Blessed Virgin presents the 1831–36 Cathedral of the Immaculate Conception to Christ
the King*) is by Albert Power. The cathedral
museum has vestments which belonged to
Blessed Oliver Plunkett (1629–81), Archbishop
of Armagh.

4 m. NNE., to the E. of the Castlepollard
road, is Knockdrin Castle, a large 19th cent.
Gothic mansion. On the opposite side of the
road is Ballynagall House, formerly Castle
Reybell, built 1807–16 to the designs of Francis
Johnston; it has stucco by Michael Stapleton.

6 m. NNE. is Taughmon; *see under* Castlepollard.

3 m. NE., on the Delvin road, is the Pass of
Rathconnell, alias "Pass if you can". In 1642
the English garrison and colonists withdrawing
from Athlone had to fight their way through
the pass.

5 m. SE. the Mass Bush memorial in Vilans-
town marks the site of a bush where Mass was
celebrated in churchless Penal times.

3 m. SSW. is pretty Lough Ennell. Near the
NE. corner of the lake the fragmentary ruins of
Lynn church mark the site of Lann meic
Lúacháin, a monastery founded by Colmán,
son of Lúachán, patron of the Clann Cholmáin
Uí Néill and a disciple of St Mo-Chuda of
Lismore (*q.v.*). His enshrined relics were preserved here from the 8th cent. until the time of
the notorious Viking, Thorgestr (Turgesius),
when they were buried for safety and thereby
lost. On Spy Wednesday, 1122, they were discovered in the cemetery, "a man's cubit in the
earth", and the shrine was restored by Gilla
Críst Ó Mocháin, goldsmith of Lynn. In 1394
monastery, church and shrine were destroyed

by Muirchertach Óg Mac Eochagáin. – 1 m. S. of Lynn is Belvedere, the good 18th cent. house from which Robert Rochfort (1708–72) took his title, Earl of Belvedere. The nearby Jealous Wall, a Gothick "ruin" by Barradotte, is supposed to have been erected so as to shut out the sight of the nearby home (Tuden Park) of the earl's brother, Arthur, whom his lordship accused of being the paramour of Lady Belvedere (see Gallstown House under Rochfortbridge).

4 m. WNW. is Slanemore Hill (499 ft). On the summit, enclosed by a ditch, are three tumuli, the central one having a terrace, or step, near the top. A splendid view is to be had from the top of the largest. Slanemore and adjoining Slanebeg are doubtless the Slemain Mide where the Ulster forces are described as camping in Táin Bó Cúalnge and where, in 494, Colmán Rímidh, King of Cenél Eóghain and of Tara, defeated Conall, son of Áed mac Ainmirech. 5½ m. NNW. of the hill, near the W. shore of Lough Iron, is Tristernagh House. It occupies the site of a priory of Canons Regular of St Augustine founded by the Anglo-Norman, Geoffrey de Costentin, about 1200, presumably as successor to the ancient monastery of Cell Bicsige (Kilbixy), Bicsech's (alias Bisceach's) Church (below). All that survives of the priory are two 14th cent. arcades embedded in post-Dissolution work. W. of the house is the ancient cemetery of Templecross, with a small, late 15th cent., parochial church with priest's residence at the W. end. 2 m. N. of Templecross is Baronstown House (Malones), built in 1755. Just inside the entrance gate are: to the E., the site of the medieval town of Kilbixy; to the WNW., remains of Brigid's Hospital, alias Leper House. NNW. of the latter, and beyond Baronstown church, is Kilbixy motte, erected by Geoffrey de Costentin in 1192. W. of the demesne gate is St Brigid's Well. ¼ m. SE. of the demesne gate is St Bisceagh's Well. Edmund Malone (1741–1812), Shakespearean scholar, was a member of the Barronstown family.

5 m. NW., near the W. shore of Lough Owel, are the ruins of Portloman castle. ¾ m. N., on the shore of the lake, are the remains of Portloman "Abbey", a medieval parish church. There is a decorated medieval gravestone in the cemetery. ½ m. SW., close to the S. side of the road, is Lack Loman. Portloman and Lack Loman preserve the memory of St Lommán, a disciple of St Patrick (see Trim), who founded a monastery at Portloman (where Colmán mac Lúacháin of Lynn was baptized) and a church on Inis Mór, alias Church Island, near the E. shore of the lake.

3 m. NNW. is Lough Owel. In 845 Melaghlin, King of Meath, drowned the notorious Viking, Thorgestr (Turgesius), in the lake.

MULTYFARNHAM, Co. Westmeath (Map 2, D7), is a village 2 m. to the NE. of the Mullingar (9 m.)–Edgeworthstown (12 m.) road.

The Franciscan church incorporates the remains (nave, inserted tower, added S. transept etc.) of the church of a Franciscan friary founded before 1272 by William Delamere (hibernicé Mac Herbert) and sacked by English troops in 1601. In 1641 a Provincial Chapter here endeavoured to compose the dispute arising from Tuileagna O Mulconry's criticisms of the works of Brother Michael O Clery, chief of the Four Masters. The friary was the family burial place of the Nugents.

1½ m. SW. is Wilson's Hospital, a school with good 18th cent. buildings. The United Irishmen of Westmeath, mustered to assist Humbert's Franco-Irish army, had their headquarters here 5–7 Sept. 1798. On 6/7 Sept. they were routed, despite their bravery, at Bunbrosna, 1 m. to the SW., by an English force of infantry, cavalry, and artillery, under the command of Lord Longford.

3 m. SW., on the ridge between Loughs Owel and Iron, in Rathbennet, is a small Bronze Age tumulus.

NAAS, Co. Kildare (Map 6, C3), county town of Kildare, is a small garrison town and marketing centre on the Dublin (21 m.)–Kildare (13 m.) road.

As its Irish name (Nás na Ríogh) denotes, the place was one of the royal seats of Leinster in early times. St Patrick is said to have come here in the course of his missionary journeyings, and the Protestant parish church is supposed to occupy the site of his camp. At the Anglo-Norman invasion Maurice fitz Gerald, ancestor of the Fitzgeralds, was granted the surrounding cantred of O ffelan by Strongbow, and it is he, presumably, who built the castle represented by the North Moat (W. of Main St). In the Middle Ages Naas was a prosperous town with an Augustinian priory-hospital (St John the Baptist's) as well as Augustinian, Dominican, and Franciscan friaries, of which nothing at all survives. In 1316 it was plundered and burned by the Bruces. In 1534 the castle was taken from Silken Thomas's garrison by Sir William Skeffington (see Maynooth). In 1577 the town was sacked by Rory Óg O More of Laois. In 1650 it was captured by the Cromwellian, Col. Hewson. It also figured in the 1798 insurrection.

The dull Court House is by Sir Richard Morrison.

St David's Church, Main St, incorporates the great W. tower (much altered, 1781) and two window embrasures of the medieval parish church, which had a S. aisle and chantries dedicated to the Holy Trinity, St Mary, and St Catherine. The baptismal font has a handsome medieval basin.

The parish church of SS Mary and David, Sallins Rd, is an 1827 "Carpenter's Perpendicular" structure by Thomas A. Cobden. The 1858 Gothic-Revival tower and spire were modelled on those of St Andrew's Church, Ewerby, Lincolnshire. The 1954 Mortuary Chapel is by A. D. Devane.

6 m. NE. is Oughterard (*see under* Kill).

3 m. E. is Furness (Forenaghts). Furness House (Mr P. Synnott) is a good small house of *c*. 1730–40. In Forenaghts Great (alt. 543 ft) is Longstone Rath (Nat. Mon.), a prehistoric ritual enclosure surrounded by a great earthen ring in which are two openings. At the centre is a 17-ft granite pillarstone. Excavation revealed a large, roofless cist at the W. side of the stone. It contained the cremated bones of at least two individuals, fragments of a bowman's wrist-bracer, a flint knife or arrow, and sherds of pottery. The site commands a beautiful view of the Wicklow Mts and the plains of Kildare, Meath, and Offaly. Behind Furness House are the ruins (Nat. Mon.) of a small nave-and-chancel manorial church with Romanesque doorway, windows, and chancel arch. 2 m. E. is Rathmore (*see* Kilteel *under* Rathcoole).

3 m. SE. is Punchestown, celebrated in horse-racing circles as the place of the annual three-day Kildare and National Hunt Race Meeting. On the E. side of the Woolpack Road (the medieval highway from Dublin to Kilkenny – via Rathcoole, Kilcullen, Athy) is the Long Stone of Punchestown Great (Nat. Mon.), a tapering granite monolith 19½ ft high. It fell in 1931, and was found to be 23 ft long and to weigh 9 tons. It was re-erected in 1934, on which occasion a small, irregular cist grave was found to abut against the SW. side of the socket. ½ m. SW., to the W. of the road, in Craddockstown West, is another Long Stone of Co. Wicklow granite. (For other Long Stones *see* Kilgowan *under* Kilcullen, Longstone *under* Ballymore Eustace, Mullaghmast *under* Ballintore, Tankardstown *and* Ardristan *under* Tullow.) 2½ m. SSE., in Sillagh, is The Ring, half of a great bivallate earthwork (an uncompleted hill fort ?); 600 yds S. is Donode motte.

2½ m. S. is Killashee, which takes its name (Cell Auxili, Cill Ausaile) from a church founded by Bishop Auxilius, a 5th cent. missionary bishop who, doubtless, fixed his see here because of the proximity of the royal seat at Naas (cf. Old Kilcullen near Dún Ailinne). The derelict Protestant church incorporates the unusual 15th/16th cent. tower (square below, circular above) of a medieval church. Nearby is St Patrick's Well. In the grounds of Killashee House there are interesting souterrains.

1 m. SW., beside the road to Kildare, are the massive, overgrown remains of Jigginstown House, a huge, palatial brick building begun, "and in a manner finished", by Lord Deputy Thomas Wentworth, Earl of Strafford, for the entertainment of Charles I and for use as a country residence for the English Lord Deputy. Had it been completed, it would have been the largest unfortified residence ever built in Ireland (390 by 120 ft). The designer/builder is said to have been John Allen "of great skill in architecture". Ancestor of the Viscounts Allen of Stillorgan (*q.v.*), he had come to Ireland towards the close of Elizabeth I's reign as a factor for the Dutch. In plan the house consists of a central block flanked by square projecting wings. The most remarkable feature is the groin-vaulted basement with its rows of panelled and moulded brick columns. (The house was one of the earliest brick buildings in Ireland.) On 15 Sept. 1643 the Confederate Catholics signed a "Cessation" with Charles I's Lord Deputy, Ormonde, at Jigginstown. Close by is the tower of Rag Castle.

NARAN and **PORTNOO**, Co. Donegal (Map 2, B3), are twin little resorts on Gweebarra Bay, 7 m. NNW. of Ardara and 7 m. WNW. of Glenties. The local countryside is beautiful.

Naran has a very good 1-m. beach (Trawmore) backed by dunes. Less than ½ m. offshore is Inishkeel, still a place of popular pilgrimage by reason of its associations with St Conall Caol (feast day, 2 May), who founded a monastic retreat here in the 6th cent. Dallán Forgaill, author of *Amra Choluim Chille*, the celebrated (A.D. 597) elegy on St Columcille, is buried here. There are remains of two churches, an early cross-slab with figure subjects, part of a cross with broad ribbon interlacing, etc.

2 m. SSE. of Naran, in Kilclooney More, are a court cairn and, nearby, twin portal dolmens (Dermot and Grania's Bed). 1 m. SSW., close to Kilclooney bridge, is a roadside Mass Rock of Penal times.

2 m. S. of Naran is Doon Lough, with a well-preserved stone ringfort on one of the islands. There is also a fort on an island in Lough Birroge, ¼ m. WNW. (¾ m. SW. of Portnoo).

3 m. SW. of Portnoo is Rosbeg, with a good beach on Dawros Bay. 1 m. SE., on Loughros More Bay, is Trawmore, a sandy beach backed by extensive dunes. ¼ m. N. of Trawmore is Kiltooris Lough (trout); on the SW. shore a low cross-pillar and remains of a church mark an ancient site; on O'Boyle's Island are remains of a castle.

¾ m. W. of Portnoo is Dunmore Head (418 ft) offering fine views of the spectacular coast to the SW.

NAVAN, Co. Meath (Map 6, C2), officially An Uaimh, the county town of Meath, is a prosperous, small-scale industrial centre (woollens, carpets, furniture, farming implements) and market town at the confluence of the Boyne and Blackwater, on the Dublin (28 m.)–Kells (11 m.) road.

The town is most attractively situated in a pleasant pastoral countryside, but has altogether failed to exploit the advantages of its setting, for it turns its back on a lovely river and provides none of the popular facilities for boating or bathing that one would expect. There are, however, some beautiful riverside walks in the immediate vicinity, while the loveliest reaches of the Boyne (*see* Slane) are within easy reach by bus, car, or bicycle. The

Plate 12. The Four Courts, Dublin

important antiquities of Tara (*q.v.*), as well as those of the Boyne and Blackwater valleys (*see* Bective, Kells, Slane *and* Trim) are also within easy reach.

Prior to the Anglo-Norman invasion there was a monastery dedicated to the Blessed Virgin Mary at Navan. It was re-edified by Jocelin de Angulo, to whom Hugh I de Lacy granted Navan and the lands of Ardbraccan (*below*). Only traces survive, as barracks and a school were in turn built on the site. De Angulo built a motte-castle on a lofty esker to the S. of the Blackwater, and the town subsequently grew up under the protection of his descendants. Though the castle site has been encroached on by a gravel pit, the motte is still to be seen near the railway on the W. side of the town.

With the waning of the Penal Laws, Bishop Patrick Joseph Plunkett (1779–1827) fixed his see at Navan, and until 1830 the local Mass-house was, in effect, the first post-Reformation cathedral of Meath. The successor (1836) of the Mass-house, a simple, tasteful, Classical edifice, was designed by the parish priest, Archdeacon O Reilly, who modelled the plan on that of Francis Johnston's St George's Church, Dublin: a rectangle with chancel opening off one long side and with galleries around the other three sides. Many years ago the building was ruthlessly transformed into a pseudo-Romanesque affair and furnished with vulgar marble altars. More recently the Classical reredos (with painted *Jerusalem* background) of the High Altar was veiled from sight and the excellent *Christ Crucified* designed specifically for it by the Co. Meath sculptor, Edward Smyth (of Four Courts, Dublin, fame), was mounted on a barbarous cross. (Earlier this century the *Christ*, Smyth's only religious work, had been supplied with a plaster beard!) The bust of Archdeacon O Reilly is by Terence Farrell.

4 m. N. are the remains of Kilberry church and motte-castle.

1½ m. NE., at Donaghmore on the W. bank of the Boyne, the fragments of a small 16th cent. church and a Round Tower (Nat. Mon.) mark the site of a "great church" built by St Patrick and entrusted to the care of Cassán, a priest. St Cassán's wonder-working relics were venerated here for centuries. The tower has a Romanesque doorway, with a *Crucifixion* above and a human mask on either side of the architrave. 1¼ m. E., near the river, are the ruins (Nat. Mon.) of the 16th cent. D'Arcy castle of Dunmore. It was burned down in 1799. There is a D'Arcy mausoleum in the adjacent chapel. 2½ m. NE. of the castle is Broad Boyne bridge. 450 yds below the bridge is Log an Rí (the King's Hole), where, on the first Sunday of Harvest, used to be held a *pátrún* at which people swam their cattle across the river to guard them against "the good people" as well as against certain diseases. Nearby, on the S. side of the Boyne, is Knockminawn tumulus.

3 m. NE., on the S. side of the Boyne, is Ardmulchan where, in 968, the Leinstermen

and the Norse of Dublin under Olaf Cuarán defeated the Southern Uí Néill. On a height overlooking the river are the remains of the medieval parish church of St Mary. It occupies the site of an early foundation, as witness the early cross-inscribed gravestone used as the lintel of one of the windows. N. of the church is a motte.

½ m. SE., beside the Duleek road, are the ruins of Athlumney Castle (Nat. Mon.), a 15th cent. Dowdall castle with 17th cent. house attached. Tradition asserts that the last occupier, Sir Launcelot Dowdall, set fire to it with his own hand rather than have it shelter the usurping William of Orange. W. of the road are the remains of a 14th cent. manorial church with triple belfry.

4¼ m. ESE., in Realtoge, is a large univallate ringfort (Nat. Mon.) with souterrain and traces of huts. 2¾ m. ESE., in Kentstown Protestant church (1797), is the mensa (with flat-relief effigy) of the tomb of Sir Thomas de Tuite (d. 1363) which stood in Danestown medieval church, ¼ m. S. beside a ringfort (Nat. Mon.). 4 m. SSW. of the latter is Skreen (*see under* Tara).

1¾ m. SSE. is Kilcarn bridge. ¾ m. ENE. is Johnstown church. Built into a face of the tower is a figure (archbishop with right hand raised in blessing) from Bective Abbey. Against an inner wall has been mounted a noteworthy 15th/16th cent. font basin (*Twelve Apostles, Coronation of the Virgin*) from the medieval church of Kilcarn (½ m. S.; fragments only).

2¾ m. S., in Ardsallagh, are the ruins (Nat. Mon.) of St Brigid's Church (parochial), a nave-and-chancel building erected by the de Angulos in the 12th/13th cent. and rebuilt in the 15th.; the Transitional chancel arch survives. There is a St Brigid's Well in the demesne of Ardsallagh House, a fine Georgian mansion built for Peter Ludlow, M.P. and 1st Earl of Ludlow (1730–1803). 2¼ m. S. of the church, on the S. side of the Boyne, is Ballinter House, one of the best of the "big houses" of Co. Meath. It was built by Richard Cassels for John Preston, M.P. (1700–1781) and grandfather of the 1st Baron Tara.

4½ m. S. is Bective Abbey (*see* Bective).

3 m. WNW. is Ardbraccan (alias Tibridultan), which takes its name from St Breacán, founder of a monastic church here in the 7th cent. St Ultán moccu Conchobair (d. 657/63), Bishop of Ardbraccan, was one of the first two men known to have concerned themselves with recording the acts of St Patrick (who had founded a church at nearby Domnach Tortáin). He may have been the author of a skilful and elaborate poem, *Brigit bé*, in honour of St Brigid. A *Life* of Brigid and a Latin hymn in her honour have also been attributed to him. Bishop Tírechán (*fl.* 670), author of a celebrated memoir of St Patrick, was a disciple of Ultán's. Ultán is also honoured as a patron of sick children; he is said to have set up a hospital at Ardbraccan for infants whose mothers

had been killed by a great plague. Cathal Crovderg O Conor of Connacht made formal submission to John of England at Ardbraccan in July 1210. The Protestant parish church (1777) has a medieval bell-tower; Bishop Pococke (1704–65), the historian, is buried in the churchyard. Nearby is St Ultán's Well (Tiobraid Ultáin). On the high ground is a small de Angulo motte. Ardbraccan House, formerly the seat of the Protestant bishops of Meath, was commenced by Arthur Price of Oakley, Celbridge (*q.v.*), when Bishop of Meath (1734–44). It is usually attributed to the famous English architect, James Wyatt (1746–1813); it occupies the site of a castle which figured prominently in the Eleven Years' War (1641–52). ¾ m. NW. of the house is the White Quarry, which has provided the Ardbraccan limestone for several of Dublin's great buildings. 2 m. W. of the house is Mullyfaughan, alias Faughan Hill (366 ft), scene of the famous battle of Ocha (Focha), A.D. 482/3, in which the usurping King of Tara, Ailill Molt of Connacht, was overthrown by the combined forces of the Southern Uí Néill, Cenél Eóghain, and their satellites. One consequence of the battle was the securing of Cenél Eóghain's participation in the succession to the kingship of Tara.

2½ m. NW., close to the Kells road and the W. bank of the Blackwater, are the ruins of Liscartan castle and manorial church. The castle is a massive 15th cent. structure of two towers linked by a hall; it was held by Sir William Talbot in 1633. The simple rectangular church has been disfigured by large 18th cent. windows in the side walls, but the excellent E. and W. windows survive. There was a screen at the junction of nave and chancel; the roodloft (lord's gallery ?) above was approached by a stair in the N. wall.

2 m. NW., in Nevinstown on the E. side of the Blackwater, is the shaft of a cross erected in 1588 by Michael de Cusack, Lord of Portraine and Rathaldron, and his wife, Margaret Dexter. ½ m. NW. is Rathaldron House, a 19th cent. castellated mansion which incorporates the 15th cent. square tower of Rathaldron castle.

5 m. NW. is Donaghpatrick (*q.v.*).

NENAGH, Co. Tipperary (Map 5, C3), is a market town and small-scale manufacturing centre (aluminium ware, textiles) on the Roscrea (20 m.)–Limerick (25 m.) road. It is a convenient centre for fishing Lough Derg (*see* Dromineer, *below*) and for touring the beautiful Lough Derg countryside (*see* Killaloe, Mountshannon, Portumna, *and* Scariff), rich in antiquarian remains.

The name of Nenagh (An Aonach; anciently Óenach Téite) recalls that this was the meeting-place of one of the principal public assemblies of Munster. At the Anglo-Norman invasion this part of Munster, Ormond, belonged to the O Brien Kingdom of Limerick, otherwise Thomond, and the N. portion was allotted by

Irish Tourist Board

The castle donjon, Nenagh

the invaders to Theobald Walter, "Butler of Ireland" and ancestor of the great house of Butler. Theobald came to Nenagh about 1200, fixed on it as the *caput* of his chief manor, and built (about 1217) the great castle whose fragmentary remains still dominate the town. The castle remained the chief seat of the Butlers until the second half of the 14th cent., when – the O Briens and O Kennedys having destroyed the local Anglo-Norman colony – the Earls of Ormond transferred to Gowran (*q.v.*). For nearly 150 years thereafter Nenagh remained in the possession of the O Briens (Mac Uí Bhriain) of Ára, but in 1533 it was recovered by Gaelicized Sir Piers Rúa Butler, Earl of Ossory (Earl of Ormond, 1537). In 1548 O Carroll of Éile burned the place. A hundred years later the castle was captured for the Catholic Confederation by a detachment of Eóghan Rúa O Neill's army, only to be retaken for the Earl of Ormond by Murrough "the Burner" O Brien. In 1650 the castle surrendered to Ireton after a brief siege. When the Williamite rebellion broke out, "Long" Anthony O Carroll seized it for King James, but it fell to Ginkel after a 24-hour siege in 1690. It was slighted by the Williamites. In 1703 the Butler connexion with Nenagh was severed by the sale of manor and town to pay the Duke of Ormond's debts.

The principal feature of the town is the Butler castle (Nat. Mon.). This was a pentagonal fortress with twin-towered gatehouse on the SW., strong towers at the NW. and SE. angles, and a mighty circular donjon (Nenagh Round) on the NE. The latter, the most remarkable structure of its kind in Ireland, is now 100 ft high; but the uppermost twenty-five feet date from about 1860, when the ruin was "castellated after the manner of Windsor" by the Catholic Bishop of Killaloe. Nearby is the parish church of St Mary of the Rosary, a large and costly Gothic-Revival edifice (1892–1906) by W. G. Doolin; details poor.

In Abbey St are remains (Nat. Mon.) of the church, etc., of a Franciscan friary founded about 1250 by Bishop Donal O Kennedy of Killaloe and his kinfolk. This was one of the most important Franciscan houses in the country. Towards the close of the 13th cent. the indecent enmity between the English and Irish elements in the Franciscan Order led to an effort to segregate the factions by concentrating the Irish friars in the "Custody of Nenagh", to which were assigned the friaries of Nenagh, Athlone, Claregalway, Galway, Armagh, Cavan, and Killeigh. The plan failed; the English friaries decayed; and Nenagh became the effective centre of the Order in Ireland. It is only in the Annals of Nenagh that we find reference to lectors, and it would seem as if the intellectual life had a special significance among the Irish friars. The final destruction of the friary was due to the Cromwellians.

4 m. ENE. is Rathurles, a remarkable trivallate ringfort whose noteworthy stone gateposts lie prostrate in the field on the NE. Inside the fort are the ruins of a plain 15th cent. church built probably by the O Kennedys Donn of Upper Ormond. ¼ m. S. are the ruins of a small, 16th cent., round castle (O Kennedy Donn). ½ m. SE. of the latter, in Rathfalla, is a large bivallate ringfort. Other good ringforts lie to the S. and SW.

8 m. E. is Toomyvara (*q.v.*).

1 m. SE. are the battered remains of Tyone (Teach, alias Tigh, Eóin), a priory and hospital of the Augustinian Crucifers, dedicated to St John (Eóin) the Baptist. A dependency of the Hospital of St John the Baptist, Dublin, it was founded about 1200 by Theobald Walter. In 1342 it was burnt by O Kennedy, who slew five of the canons. The 14th cent. Irish recovery placed it in Irish hands, and when Sir Piers Rúa Butler recovered Ormond in 1533 it was an O Meara (*see* Toomyvara) he installed as prior. The O Mearas retained control of the place until the Dissolution.

3 m. SE., in Ballynaclough, are remains of a church and of a 13th cent. castle (motte, fragment of great hall, etc.), relics of the manor of Weyperous (Gué Pierreux) granted to the de Mariscos by Theobald Walter.

4½ m. S. are the ruins of Kilboy House, built in the 18th cent. by William Leeson for Henry Prittie, 1st Baron Dunalley, and burnt down in 1922. ¼ m. SE. are the remains of Dolla church. 3 m. SE. of Dolla crossroads is Cooneen Hill (1,543 ft). On the summit, in Lisgarriff West, is Dermot and Grania's Bed, a small cairn. ½ m. SW. of this, in Foilnamuck on the W. slope, is another Dermot and Grania's Bed; this is a ruinous chamber tomb. Some 3 m. SSW. of the latter, in Curreeny Commons, are remains of a wedge-shaped gallery grave also called Dermot and Grania's Bed.

6½ m. SSW. (2 m. W. of Dolla crossroads, *above*) is Silvermines, a village at the foot of the Silvermine Mountains (1,609 ft). The silver, lead, and zinc ores hereabouts have been exploited from time to time throughout the centuries. 1 m. SW. of the village are remains of Dunalley castle, an O Kennedy stronghold from which the Cromwellian Pritties took their title. 2¼ m. S. of the village, on the N. side of the Mulkear River, in Bauraglanna, is a prehistoric chamber tomb. ¼ m. S. of this is Fir Bréaga stone circle. Less than ½ m. further S., on the slope of Slievekimalta (Keeper Hill, 2,279 ft), is Dermot and Grania's Bed.

3 m. SW., to the W. of the Limerick road, is Lissenhall House (Georgian).

7½ m. W., in the Ara Mountains (Tountinna, 1,517 ft), is the village of Portroe, best known for its proximity to the great "Killaloe" slate quarries. The by-road through the mountains to Killaloe offers excellent views of lower Lough Derg. 2½ m. S. of the village, in Lackamore, is the Giants Grave, a ruined gallery grave. – 3¼ m. SW., at The Gap, is Knockaunreelyon (Cnocán Rí Laighean, Hillock of the Kings of Leinster); ½ m. SW., on the slope of Tountinna in Coolbaun, are the remains of a prehistoric chamber tomb called the Graves of the Leinstermen; fine view. – 2 m. W. of Portroe, in the ruined church of Castletown Ara, is a tomb of the O Briens of Ara (Mac Uí Bhriain Áradh).

3½ m. NW. are the ruins of Monsea church, a 15th cent. rebuilding of a 13th cent. edifice.

5¾ m. NW. is pretty Dromineer Bay, one of the favourite fishing resorts on Lough Derg with angling, boating, and bathing. By the lake shore are the ruins of a medieval church (overgrown) with Romanesque fragments. The castle, an early-16th cent. structure, was built by the O Kennedys, who gave it and its manor to the Earl of Ormond in 1556 in exchange for other property. 1¼ m. W., close to the lake in Shannonvale, is a very large univallate ringfort.

3½ m. NNW., in Ballyanny, is a low, stone-kerbed tumulus with a concentric stone ring.

7 m. NNW., in Johnstown, are the ruins of Killodiernan, a Romanesque church whose W. door has been likened to that of Teampall Finghin at Clonmacnois.

NEWBLISS, Co. Monaghan (Map 2, E5), is a village on the Clones (5 m.)–Ballybay (11 m.) road.

Newbliss House is the home of Sir Tyrone Guthrie, theatre director.

2¾ m. NE., in Garran, is Giant's Grave, a prehistoric chamber tomb. ¾ m. N., in Lecklevera, is a court cairn; ¾ m. NE., in Tiredigan, is Giant's Grave, alias Cairnbane, also a court cairn. 1½ m. NW. of Lecklevera road-junction, in Cloghernagh, is Giant's Grave, a court cairn. 1¼ m. SE. of Lecklevera road-junction, in Carn, is Cromlech, a court cairn.

8 m. SE. (2 m. WNW. of Rockcorry), in Edergoole, is Giant's Grave, a court cairn.

NEWCASTLE, Co. Down (Map 3, D6), is a small port and well-known seaside and golfing resort delightfully situated on Dundrum Bay, at the NE. foot of the Mourne Mts, 31 m. S. of Belfast and 25 m. E. of Newry. It takes its name from a late-16th cent. castle of the Magennises, which was erected on an old fortsite at the mouth of the Shimna River. The excellent 3-m. sandy beach is backed by extensive sand dunes and one of the two golf courses is a championship course (Royal County Down). The town is a very good base for exploring the historic lowlands of E. County Down, as well as the lovely Mourne country.

Immediately S. and SW. of the town Slieve Donard (2,796 ft) rises from the sea, with Slieve Commedagh (2,312 ft) behind it. Slieve Donard (Sliabh Domhanghaird, anciently Slíab Slánga) offers splendid prospects, near and far. It is named after St Domangard of Ráth Murbhuilg (*below*), son of Echu (last pagan king of the region) and immortal guardian of the mountain, who died about 506 (?). On the summit is a much altered cairn with a passage grave. 270 yds NE. is a second cairn. Associated in popular legend with St Domhanghard, these cairns were formerly stations of a popular pilgrimage (originally a Lughnasa celebration) on Crom Dubh's Sunday (July).

3 m. N., in Carnacavill, is the circular (cashel) churchyard, Ráth Murbhuilg, with remains of a church, the stump of a Round Tower, and two early cross-slabs (Nat. Mons.); these are relics of an early monastery founded by Bishop Domhanghard. A 13th cent. tombstone marks a modern grave. It is from the ring-enclosure (*ráth*) that the district is named Maghera – Machaire Rátha (Murbhuilg).

2 m. SSE. is the sea-cave called Donard's (Domhanghard's) Cave.

1½ m. S. is Bloody Bridge, so called from a 1641 massacre of Planters. In Ballaghanery Upper are the scant, overgrown remains of the tiny nave-and-chancel church of St Mary. It was a dependency of the church of Kilkeel.

2 m. NW., to the W. of Priest's Bridge on the Bryansford road, is Barbican Gate, entrance to Tollymore Forest Park. The 1200-acre park is set in a delightful countryside and offers a variety of attractions: camping and caravan sites, excellent arboretum, plantations, lovely river scenery (including waterfalls), old demesne follies and ornaments. At the W. end, on the S. side of the Shimna, is the King's Grave, a Food Vessel cairn. Hours of admission: 10 a.m. to sunset daily; very modest charges for cars, caravans, motor cycles, and tents.

NEWCASTLE, alias **NEWCASTLE-LYONS,** Co. Dublin (Map 6, D7), is a small village on the Rathcoole (3 m.)–Celbridge (5 m.) road, 12 m. SW. of Dublin. It takes its name from an English royal castle and manor erected here, at the time of the Anglo-Norman invasion, in the territory of the Mac Giolla Mho-Cholmógs (*see* Lyons Demesne *and* Lyons Hill *under* Celbridge), who sided with the invaders. But long before that time one of the many SS Finnian had founded a monastery here. In 1641 Newcastle was the headquarters of the Catholic forces operating in Co. Dublin. When abandoned by them the following year it was pillaged by an English force, which returned to Dublin rich in plate and stuff and cattle. In the 16th cent. the place contained six "castles", i.e. fortified town houses like the "castles" at Dalkey (*q.v.*). Of these, remains of two survive, one in the rectory grounds, the other in a field among the houses of the village. Near the gate of St Finian's Church (C. of I.) is the motte-and-bailey of the 12th cent. royal castle. The church is an early-15th cent. nave-and-chancel structure with a dwelling tower added (as often in the Pale) at the W. end. The chancel was callously unroofed about 1724, the chancel arch blocked up, and the excellent curvilinear E. window re-erected in the blocking. The nave, relentlessly modernized, has some good wood-carving dating from 1724. The church has plate presented in 1696 by Archdeacon Williamson. In the graveyard, on the S. side of the church, is an early granite cross with traces of a raised cross-in-a-circle on the E. face and of a raised cross, or figure, on the W. face. At the end of the village, beside the Lyons road, are St Finian's Fields and St Finian's Well.

1½ m. NE., in Castle Bagot demesne, are the remains of Kilmactalway church.

1½ m. SSW., beside a small house of 1750, are the remains of Athgoe castle; ½ m. S., those of Colmanstown castle; both belonged to the Locke family.

2 m. W. is Lyons Demesne (*see under* Celbridge).

NEWCASTLE WEST, Co. Limerick (Map 4, E3), is a small market town on the Limerick (25 m.)–Abbeyfeale (13 m.) road.

The Gothic-Revival parish church is by J. J. McCarthy, whose efforts were cramped by the conditions obtaining at the time.

Partly incorporated in a modern residence are remains of a great castle of the Earls of Desmond, viz. water fosse, bastion, part of the curtain, rectangular tower, circular keep, and two 15th cent. halls. One of the latter, Desmond's Hall, is complete, and has a fine vaulted basement. Following on the Desmond rebellion the castle was granted (1591) to Sir William Courtenay, ancestor of the Earls of Devon. It fell into the hands of the Sugán Earl of Desmond in 1598, but was retaken the next year. Confederate Catholics besieged it from Dec. 1641 until the following Easter Monday, when it surrendered and was burnt.

Three well-known 17th–18th cent. poets have associations with Newcastle West or its vicinity: Dáibhidh Ó Bruadair, whose poems include one on Ballyneety, was born in the vicinity; Dáibhidh Ó Cléirigh lived in the town; Father Liam Inglis, O.S.A. (d. 1778), whose *Caiseal Mumhan* was translated by Sir Samuel Ferguson, is buried in St John's Church.

6 m. E., at the centre of a seven-acre, bivallate

ringfort (with water fosse) bisected by the modern road, are remnants of nave-and-chancel St M'Aodhóg's Church. To the SE. is St Patrick's Well; to the SW. is Sunday's Well. Some would identify this site with that of a monastery founded by St M'Aodhóg of Ferns (q.v.) in a ringfort granted to him by the local lord (see Mahoonagh Beg, below). 2 m. SW., in Ballynoe, are the remains of St Íde's Church, Cluain Eilte (Clonalty); less than ½ m. W. are the ruins of Ballynoe castle.

3½ m. SE., in Mahoonagh Beg, are remains of a church with simple, Romanesque S. window; the church was restored in 1410. Some claim that here or hereabouts, and not at Cloncagh (above), was the site of St M'Aodhóg's monastery. There are many ringforts in the area.

6 m. S., in Killeedy (Cill Íde) churchyard, the ancient Clúain Credail, St Ida's Well and fragmentary remains of a Romanesque nave-and-chancel church mark the site of a nunnery founded by St Íde (Ida, "Ita"), alias Déirdre ("White Sun of the Women of Munster", and "Fostermother of the Saints"; d. 570/77), who "succoured many grievous diseases" and is mentioned in one of Alcuin's poems. According to legend, she was privileged to suckle Jesus, who came to her in the form of an infant. The nunnery seems early to have been replaced by a monastery for men, which was several times plundered by the Norse. The Romanesque church served for a time as Protestant parish church, until burnt down by "Whiteboys" early in the last century, since when the W. doorway has disappeared. At the junction of nave and chancel (S. side) is St Íde's Grave; in summer pilgrims strew it with flowers. Also in Killeedy townland, on a motte, are the remains of a Desmond castle. – 1½ m. W. of Killeedy is the tower (repaired 1840; Nat. Mon.) of the Desmond castle of Glenquin. In Glenmore, nearby, is the Big Man's Grave, alias Giants Grave, a tumulus. – 4 m. SW. of Killeedy, on Seeconglass Hill, is Boolaveeda, an oval enclosure formerly ringed by a stone rampart. This, says local tradition, was St Íde's dairy.

NEWGRANGE, Co. Meath (Map 6, C2), 5 m. SE. of Slane and 7 m. SW. of Drogheda, is famous for its prehistoric monuments.

The outstanding monument (Nat. Mon.) is a great chambered mound of turves and stones about 280 ft in diameter and about 44 ft high. In its original state it was probably a hemispherical mound some 50 ft high and had a covering of gleaming white quartz pebbles. As late as the close of the 17th cent. the summit was still crowned by a pillarstone. The body of the mound is bounded by a retaining-kerb of stones 8–10 ft long, many with spirals, lozenges, zig-zags, and other splendidly wrought prehistoric motifs. (The vertical retaining wall on top of the kerb is modern.) A few yards outside the kerb are twelve pillarstones, some of enormous size, survivors of a free-standing ring

of about thirty-six stones (the sockets of some of the missing stones have been located). Towards the SE. the kerb dips slightly inwards to a superbly decorated kerbstone which marks the entrance to the tomb. (The prostrate slab behind it originally sealed the doorway.) A 62-ft passage leads to the chamber. The passage is lined by stone uprights, 5–8 ft tall, and is roofed with massive lintels borne on corbelling. Uprights on either side bear prehistoric scribings, viz. on the right-hand side, Nos. 3, 6, 12, 18, 19, 20, and 21 (counting from the doorway), and on the left-hand side, Nos. 12, 13, 15, 17, 19, 22. The chamber is roughly cruciform in plan, and measures 18 ft from front to rear by 21 ft from side to side. The walls here too are faced with tall uprights (prehistoric scribings on the three uprights of the left-hand recess, on two uprights of the rear recess, and on one upright of the right-hand recess). The funnel-shaped roof of large, corbelled stones rises to 19½ ft. Resting on the floor of the recesses or cells are great stone trays or basins, one each in the left-hand and rear recesses, two in the right-hand recess, where the upper basin has two marginal, cup-like depressions. Excavations in progress since 1962 are shedding new light on the construction of both mound and passage-grave, and have shown that Beaker Folk appeared on the scene well after the completion of the monument.

About 80 yds W. of the great cairn are the remains of a satellite (diameter 35 ft).

Some 500 yds SSE. of the great cairn is a tumulus, 220 ft in circumference and 20 ft high; the remains of an enclosing ring-bank have recently been ploughed out. In the next field to the SW., close to the weir, are the ploughed-out traces of an earthwork some 450 ft by 400 ft. About 450 yds SE. of the tumulus, by the river, is a mound 90 ft in diameter and 20 ft high. Some 450 yds NNE. of it, on the brow of a steep rise, is a massive pillarstone, 10 ft high; an intervening pillarstone has disappeared. In the next field to the NE. is another pillarstone. About ¼ m. NNW. is a stone-kerbed tumulus, 280 ft in circumference and 12 ft high. 600 yds ENE. are three despoiled mounds; two are circular, but the middle one (natural?) looks like a long barrow.

400 yds NE. of these (1¾ m. NE. of the great Newgrange cairn) is the great chambered cairn of Dowth (Nat. Mon.), which has suffered so severely from the attentions of antiquarians and the Office of Public Works, as well as of road-makers and treasure-seekers. The mound is 280 ft in diameter and 47 ft high. Some of the kerb-stones bear prehistoric scribings. At the W. perimeter is the entrance to the principal tomb. Passages to left and right lead to the chambers of a souterrain (below). Straight ahead is the tomb-passage, 27 ft long. It is lined with uprights which support the lintelled roof, and is segmented by three sill-stones. The right-hand upright immediately before the first sill is decorated with scribings of the Newgrange

type. Others bear minor markings. The chamber proper (roof not corbelled) is cruciform and is more shapely, if smaller, than that at Newgrange. At the centre is a large stone tray reassembled from scattered fragments, only one of which was found at this spot. Three of the uprights of the main chamber and one upright of the left-hand recess are decorated. A narrow opening at the SW. corner of the right-hand recess leads to a unique additional series of small chambers. The main compartment here is floored with a large flagstone in which is an oval hollow, seemingly artificial. The souterrain whose passage cuts across the tomb-passage inside the entrance dates from early historic times; the passage is some 70 ft long; at either end is a beehive chamber; about half-way between these there is a high step, or obstruction, in the floor. Just inside the tumulus kerb, on the SW., is the entrance to a second tomb. The right-hand jamb-stone has a deep, wide, vertical groove. A passage 11½ ft long leads to a circular chamber 15 ft in diameter. On the right-hand side of this is a side-chamber. Two or three uprights of the main chamber are decorated, as are also the right-hand side and the lintel (upper surface) of the side-chamber.

150 yds SE. of the great Dowth cairn is St Bernard's Well. NE. of the latter are the ruins of a small medieval church (there is a crude figure in the S. wall) and of a castle. NE. of the castle is a small ringfort. ¼ m. ENE. of the castle is Dowth House (built for Viscount Netterville about 1780), which has good ceilings. W. and SW. of the house are two small tumuli (Nat. Mons.). The SW. mound (in the overgrown garden) has been opened from the top to expose a small, corbel-roofed, hexagonal chamber with five peripheral cells. Less than ¼ m. E. of the house is a large, circular, ritual enclosure surrounded by a great earthen bank. 250 yds NE. are the roadside Cloghalea (*clocha liatha*, grey stones), remnants of a monument destroyed by quarrying. – John Boyle O Reilly (1844–90), poet and Fenian, was a native of Dowth.

1¾ m. NW. of the great Newgrange cairn is the great cairn (Nat. Mon.) of Knowth, 280 ft in diameter and 40–50 ft high. On the summit is a wrecked beehive souterrain of the early historic period. This was discovered in the course of 1943 excavations, as was also about half of the retaining-kerb (now covered up again) of huge blocks of stone set on edge, many of them bearing prehistoric devices. Recent excavations have shown that the mound was incorporated in a motte castle by the Anglo-Normans. On the N. side of the cairn are the roofless remains of a small chamber tomb; four of the uprights of the passage, and all three of the chamber, carry prehistoric scribings. There were at least six satellites in the immediate vicinity of the great mound. ¼ m. SSW. of it is a bivallate ring-work. ¼ m. NNE. of Knowth House is another. 1¾ m. NE. of the house, in Monknewtown churchyard, is a late cross with *Crucifixion*, etc.; 300 yds NW. is a tumulus (chambered ?); 150 yds WNW. of this is a ring-work.

2½ m. NW. of Knowth cairn is Slane (*q.v.*).

NEWMARKET, Co. Cork (Map 5, A5), a village on the Kanturk (5 m.)–Abbeyfeale (22 m.) road, was founded in former Mac Auliff territory by the Aldsworths in the time of James I. John Philpot Curran (1750–1817), celebrated advocate and father of Sarah Curran, Robert Emmet's betrothed, was a native of the place and resided for a time at The Priory. He treated Sarah very badly for her association with a rebel. She later married an English officer, but Thomas Moore's

"She's far from the land
Where her young hero sleeps"

has assured her an unmerited reputation for fidelity to Emmet's memory. She died young, and is buried in Newmarket churchyard, as is also Mrs Aldworth, the woman Mason (*see* Doneraile).

NEWMARKET-ON-FERGUS, Co. Clare (Map 5, B3), is a village on the Ennis (7½ m.)–Limerick (23 m.) road, near Shannon Airport.

¾ m. W., in Kilnasoolagh Protestant church, is the recumbent effigy of Sir Donough O Brien (1642–1717); it is the work of William Kidwell (d. 1736), the Dublin statuary.

3 m. N., in a well diversified demesne of 1,500 acres, is Dromoland Castle, until 1962 seat of Lord Inchiquin, but now a luxury hotel with golf course, etc. The Lemaneh (*see under* Kilfenora) O Briens moved to Dromoland at the end of the 17th cent., but the present house, a "baronial castle" by James Pain of Cork, dates from about 1826. In the garden are a gateway from Lemaneh and an 18th cent. temple. William Smith O Brien (1803–64), nephew of the 13th Baron Inchiquin and leader of the Young Irelanders, was born at Dromoland. 2 m. NNE., inside the SE. entrance to Dromoland Demesne, is Mooghaun, a trivallate, stone hill-fort of 27½ acres. Close to the SW. entrance of the middle rampart is a small ringfort; on the W. side of the outer enclosure is another. Less than ½ m. S., in Langough, are the remains of a 5½-acre, bivallate, stone fort with large annexes on the NW. and SE.

4 m. NE., in Finlough, is Tomfinlough, site of a monastic or anchoritic foundation (*c.* 550) by St Luchtighern moccu Tratho. The remains comprise a holy well, the W. gable of a tiny oratory with trabeate W. doorway beneath three Romanesque masks, and the ruins of a Western Transitional church Gothicized about 1300 and altered again in the 15th cent. Built into the S. wall of the church is the Plague Stone, an early cross-slab.

4½ m. SE., in Drumline, is a 15th/16th cent. castle tower.

1½ m. SSW., one of the Urlanmore castles has outline paintings of animals in an upper room.

NEWPORT, Co. Mayo (Map 1, C4), is a village near the NE. corner of Clew Bay, 8 m. N. of Westport and 12 m. W. of Castlebar, on the road to Achill (19 m.). It is an angling (Newport and Burrishoole rivers, Loughs Beltra and Feagh) and deep-sea fishing resort, and a convenient centre for touring the Nephin mountain region.

The parish church (1914) is an interesting essay in the Irish Romanesque style, by Rudolph M. Butler. Its E. window (*Last Judgement*) was designed by Harry Clarke and painted under his supervision the year he died (1930).

2 m. NW., to the S. of the Achill road, are the ruins of Burrishoole "Abbey" (Nat. Mon.), a Dominican friary founded by Richard Burke of Turlough, MacWilliam *Íochtair*, who retired to the friary in 1469 and died there in 1473. The beautiful De Burgo–O Malley Chalice (1494) in the National Museum belonged to the friary. Nearby are the remains of a Burke castle.

4 m. SW., in Rosbeg, is Dermot and Grania's Bed, a court cairn.

3 m. W., on the shore of Clew Bay, is the tower of Carrigahooley (Carraig an Chabhlaigh), alias Rockfleet, castle (Nat. Mon.), a Burke stronghold. The famous Gráinne Ní Mháille (*see* Clare Island) beat off an English attack in 1574. In 1583, after the death of her second husband, Richard *an Iarainn* Burke, she took up her residence in the castle, which is the only one that can be positively associated with her.

NEWPORT, Co. Tipperary (Map 5, C4), is a village on the Limerick (11 m.)–Thurles (29 m.) road through the Slieve Felim–Mauherslieve Mts.

In the parish church is a stoup from Kilcommenty (*below*).

3 m. NNW., in Ballyard, is the ancient church-site, Kilcommenty. St Cominad's Bed here is a boulder with bullauns and the "prints of the saint's ribs and hands". St Cominad's Well still attracts devotees. In the adjoining townland of Cragg are remains of the O Mulryan castle of Cragg Owhny.

7½ m. E. is Rear Cross (*q.v.*).

NEW ROSS, Co. Wexford (Map 6, B6), is a busy little port as well as a manufacturing, marketing, and communications centre on the E. bank of the tideway of the Barrow, where the Waterford (15 m.)–Enniscorthy (21 m.) road crosses that noble river. In the Middle Ages it was an important seaport, rivalling Waterford. (In 1265 no fewer than 600 seamen from the crews of the ships there participated in the walling of the town.) For the tourist it is a convenient centre for exploring, by land or water, the beautiful valleys of the Barrow and Nore to the N.

The town was the creation of William the Marshal, Earl of Pembroke, and his wife, Isabella, heiress of Strongbow and Díarmait Mac Murrough's daughter, Aoífe. Through William's daughter, Maud, it passed as part of the Lordship or Honour of Carlow (*q.v.*) to the Earls of Norfolk. In 1265 it was walled by the townsfolk; the work has been described in a 14th cent. poem by Maurice of Kildare.

In October 1394 Art Óg Mac Murrough, King of Leinster, attacked and destroyed the town, and then retired to his forest fastnesses when assailed by Richard II and the feudal might of England. He later made the town his own, and there in the end (1418) he died. Edmund Spenser visited the town in the 16th cent. In 1643, being then in Confederate Catholic hands, it was unsuccessfully besieged by Charles II's Lord Lieutenant, James, Marquess of Ormond, who, however, defeated a strong force under Preston, Confederate Catholic commander for Leinster, which came up and attacked him. In 1649 the Catholic garrison, overawed by the fate of Drogheda and Wexford, surrendered to Cromwell, who had crossed the Barrow by a bridge of boats (the permanent bridge having been destroyed in 1643). On 4 June 1798 a large Insurgent force (including two Kennedys from Dunganstown, *below*), led by Bagenal Harvey, made a desperate effort to seize the town and river-crossing, and so break out into Cos. Kilkenny and Waterford. After ten hours of fierce fighting the valour of the garrison under Gen. Johnson overcame the inept leadership and lack of discipline of the equally brave and far more numerous attackers, who left some 2,000 dead behind them. In the course of the fighting much of the town was destroyed by fire.

The principal monument in the town (Church Lane) is the roofless chancel and transepts (Nat. Mon.) of St Mary's, the parish church of the "new town of Ross" founded by William the Marshal and his wife, Isabella. Dating from about 1210–20, they are among the earliest examples of pure Gothic work in Ireland. The memorials include a fragment of a slab to the memory of Isabella (d. 1220). Since she was buried in Tintern Major, Monmouthshire, the slab may either have been a cenotaph or have marked a heart-burial. It bears a mask (or human face) and a cross in place of an effigy, and has the fragmentary inscription: ISABEL: LAEGN . . ., meaning something like "Isabella, heiress of Leinster". The site of the crossing and of the aisled nave is occupied by the early 19th cent. Protestant church, which contains some interesting tombs and memorials. In the churchyard is the 1577 tombstone of Denis Felan, by Walter Kerin.

Nothing survives of the medieval Augustinian Crucifers' hospital-priory, or of the Augustinian, Franciscan, and Dominican friaries. Of the walls of the town only a few fragments now remain.

The Tholsel, in Irishtown, is a good building of 1749, rebuilt in 1806. (As so often, the ground-floor loggia has been blocked up.) Here may be seen the civic insignia and muniments, including the maces and James II's charter.

The Church of SS Mary and Michael is an interesting Gothick-Classical period piece. It has a *Pietà* (about 1840) by John Hogan.

1 m. N. are remains of the 15th cent. castle of Mount Garret, which was called after its builder, Garrett Butler and gave their title to the Lords Mountgarrett.

4¾ m. NNE., in Ballynabanoge, is the great Kilfive Rath. 1½ m. N., on Ballyleigh Hill (540 ft) in the strategically important Pollmounty Gap between the Barrow and the Blackstairs Mountains, is the Rath of Tork (Torsk), a 1½-acre ringfort of dry-built granite boulders. The hill was a Lughnasa site (Fraughan Sunday, i.e. last Sunday of July). Pollmounty castle was a Kavanagh stronghold. According to tradition, it was to Eibhlín Kavanagh of Pollmounty that Cearbhall Ó Dálaigh sang his celebrated elopement song, *Eibhlín a Rúin* (*Eileen Aroon*) about 1600 (*see* Pallis *under* Gorey).

3 m. NE. is the ancient cemetery of Scark, alias Skeirk, associated with King Brandubh of Leinster and St M'Aodhóg of Ferns.

5 m. ENE. is Robinstown Giants Grave, a wrecked prehistoric chamber tomb.

4¾ m. E., at Old Ross, is a fine motte, perhaps constructed by Strongbow.

8 m. ESE. is Carrickbyrne Hill (769 ft), formerly a Lughnasa station, which offers widespread panoramas in all directions. Nearby, in Carrigadaggan, is a memorial to Sir Ralph Abercromby. Humane and honourable British commander in Ireland for a short period before the '98 Insurrection, his protests against the behaviour of the British troops cost him his command.

4½ m. S. is Slievecoilta (888 ft), where a Forest Park with arboretum is being laid out in memory of John Fitzgerald Kennedy, President of the United States.

4½ m. SSW., in Dunganstown, are remains of the family home of Patrick Kennedy, great-grandfather of President Kennedy. The farm is still the home of his kinsfolk and was twice visited by President Kennedy.

4 m. SW., on the Barrow, is the 15th–16th cent. tower of Annaghs (Co. Kilkenny) castle.

2½ m. W. is Glencloghlea (Co. Kilkenny) portal dolmen.

6 m. W. is Listerlin (*see under* Inistioge).

NEWRY, Co. Down (Map 3, C6), is a seaport and manufacturing town on the main Dublin (65 m.)–Belfast (38 m.) road, a few miles N. of the strategically important Gap of the North, of the Border, and of lovely Carlingford Lough. It is also the cathedral town of the Catholic diocese of Dromore. To the E. lie the Mourne Mountains; to the W., Camlough Mountain and storied Slieve Gullion (*q.v.*); to the S., the Carlingford Mountains (*see under* Dundalk). The town takes its name from a yew-tree (An Iubhar) said to have been planted by St Patrick beside a church he had founded. About 1144

the great St Máel M'Áedóg Úa Morgair and Donnchad Mac Cearbhaill, King of Uriel, founded an abbey on the site of the yew-tree. About 1153 this abbey was colonized by Cistercians from Mellifont. In 1156 the High-king, Muirchertach Mac Lochlainn (of Cenél Eóghain) took the abbey under his protection and endowed it, and so is usually reckoned as the founder. The celebrated bishop of Kildare, Finn Úa Gormáin (d. 1160), was abbot for a time. In 1543 the abbey was transformed into a collegiate church. In 1552 Sir Nicholas Bagenal of Staffordshire, marshal of the English forces in Ireland, was granted the Lordships of Newry, Greencastle, and Mourne, and converted the abbey into a residence. No trace of it survives.

Because of its strategic position, Newry suffered repeatedly in the wars for control of the North. Towards the close of the 12th cent. John de Courcy built a castle there. The successor of that castle was destroyed in 1315 by Edward Bruce, rebuilt after his defeat, and destroyed again by Seaán the Proud O Neill in 1566. About 1575 Sir Nicholas Bagenal built hill-top St Patrick's Church (the first Protestant church in Ireland built as such), probably on the site of the castle. In 1689 the retreating Jacobites under Berwick fired the town, and only the tower of Bagenal's church survived; in the porch is a 1578 tablet with Bagenal's arms.

St Colman's Cathedral, Hill St, is a dull 19th–20th cent. Perpendicular building; the original architect was John Duff of Newry (*see also* St Patrick's Church, Dundalk, *and* St Patrick's Cathedral, Armagh). At the N. end of the street the Town Hall is built across the little Clanrye River. The nearby Court House is a simple Classical building of 1843. The Bank of Ireland (1826) is attributed to Francis Johnston.

John Mitchel (1815–75), celebrated Republican, journalist, and author, is buried in the Unitarian (First Presbyterian) churchyard, Old Meetinghouse Green, High St. His father was Unitarian minister in Newry for some years. He himself died at Dromlane House, Newry. The 1962 memorial to him in St Colman's Park, Hill St, is by Donal Murphy. The present Unitarian Church (1853) was Ulster's first Gothic-Revival church; architect, 23-year-old W. J. Barre of Newry.

Newry's link with Lough Neagh was the first (1730–41) major canal in the British Isles. Richard Cassels was engineer until 1736, when the work was entrusted to Thomas Steers of Liverpool. Sir Edward Lovett Pearce and Davis Ducart, a Sardinian, are also said to have had a hand in it.

3 m. N., in Drummiller, is a motte overlooking the Clanrye River.

6 m. NNE., on the Banbridge (14 m.) road, the churchyard of Donaghmore marks the site of a 5th/6th cent. monastery founded by St Mac Erca, brother of Mo-Chaoi of Nendrum (*see under* Comber). The enclosing rampart of the monastery is still recognizable. Beneath the churchyard is a large souterrain (closed) with

Archaeological Survey of Northern Ireland
8th century cross-pillar, Kilnasaggart, Newry

beehive chambers. On one of the capstones of the roof stands a figured High Cross (Nat. Mon.) dating from the 9th/10th cent. The much weathered sculptures represent subjects from the Old and New Testaments (*The Fall, Noah's Ark, The Crucifixion, The Last Judgement*, etc.). The cross, which had long lain overthrown, was set up in its present position in 1891.

2 m. NE., on the old Rathfryland road, is Crown Bridge, an interesting structure whose three E. arches are said to have been built about 1635 by Alderman Hawkins, grantee of the Magennis lands (*see* Rathfryland). ¼ m. N. is Crown Mound (Nat. Mon.), an overgrown motte-and-bailey resembling that at Ballyroney (*see under* Rathfryland). 3 m. ESE. of Crown Bridge, in Edenmore, is Carrigakill, a court cairn (overgrown); also in Edenmore is a 10-ft pillarstone inscribed IHS JC. In Mayo, the next townland to the E., is the Long Stone, another 10-ft pillarstone (Nat. Mon.). ¾ m. ESE. of Mayo bridge, in Edentrumly, is Lisbane, a hill-top ringfort. To the SE., on the summit (1,190

ft) of Mullaghmore (alias Carmeen Hill), is Carnadranna, a hill-top cairn.

5½ m. S., near Killeen, Co. Armagh, is the King's Ring, Clontygora (Nat. Mon.), a two-chamber court cairn. Close by are remains of a second court cairn.

2 m. SW., on the SE. slope of Camlough Mountain (1,385 ft), alt. 650 ft in Ballymacdermot, is a court cairn (Nat. Mon.).

5 m. SW. is Killevy (*see under* Slieve Gullion).

6 m. SW. is The Dorsey (*see under* Crossmaglen).

8 m. SSW., in Edenappa, Co. Armagh, ¼ m. ESE. of Kilnasaggart railway bridge, is the Kilnasaggart Stone (Nat. Mon.), an early Christian pillarstone with ten cross-inscribed circles (claimed to be an allusion to the Multiplication of the Loaves) on the N. face, another on the E. angle of the head, and a Latin cross and a large cross-inscribed circle on the S. face. Between these last is the inscription IN LOC SO TANIMMAIRNI TERNOHC MAC CERAN BIC ER CUL PETER APSTAL (thus Macalister; some of his readings are doubtful): "This place did Ternóc son of Ciarán bequeath under the protection of Peter the Apostle". Ternóc died about 714/16, and the stone is the earliest securely dated Christian field-monument in Ireland. At the foot of the stone are four early cross-slabs. SE. is a cross-inscribed boulder. The place is an early monastic or eremitical site, and the early graves here were disposed in a double circle at the S. foot of the pillar. ¼ m. SW. of Kilnasaggart railway bridge, in Carrickbroad, is Moyry Castle (Nat. Mon.), built in 1601 by Lord Mountjoy to secure the Moyry Pass, gateway to the Fews and the heart of the still Gaelic North. It is a small, square, three-storey tower set towards one corner of a rectangular bawn. In the same townland, on the slope of Carrickbroad Mt, are remains of a round cairn with a large cist grave (Nat. Mon.).

2½ m. NW. is Derrymore House (Nat. Trust), an interesting thatched villa built by Isaac Corry, M.P. for Newry 1776–1806, and last Chancellor of the Irish Exchequer. In the drawing-room the Act of Union is said to have been drafted. Open to the public: 1 April to 30 Oct., Wed., Thur., Sat., and Bank Holidays, 2–6 p.m.; admission 1/–. 1 m. NNW. is Bessbrook, a model linen village founded in 1855 by a Quaker, John Richardson Grubb, who permitted neither pawnshop nor public house.

NEWTOWNARDS, Co. Down (Map 3, D4), is a neat and well-planned town near the head of Strangford Lough, 10 m. E. of Belfast and 5½ m. S. of Bangor. It was founded by Hugh Montgomery, laird of Braidstone in Scotland, who, with James Hamilton (*see* Bangor) and Sir Moyses Hill (*see* Hillsborough), between 1605 and 1616 contrived to get hold of the lands of Upper Clannaboy and Great Ardes at the expense of feckless, alcoholic Conn O Neill of Castlereagh.

In Castle Place are the remains of the prominent Market Cross (Nat. Mon.) designed by Sir James Montgomery and erected in 1635. In its original state it was crowned by a parapet and a 20-ft lion-surmounted column, and was enriched with gargoyles, coats-of-arms, and other devices. The interior served as a town prison.

At the E. end of Court St is the ruined church (Nat. Mon.) of a 13th cent. Dominican friary, founded probably by the Savage family. After the Dissolution the abandoned buildings were destroyed by O Neill of Clannaboy to prevent their use as an English fortress. In 1632–36 the church was re-edified for Protestant parochial use and provided with a square bell-tower by the 1st Viscount Montgomery. Of the medieval structure only the N. arcade and part of the nave survive, but these present some interesting features. The church was long the burial place of the Montgomery family, and there are handsome monuments to their successors, the Londonderry and Colville families. Close by to the SW. are some traces of a 17th cent. Colville mansion.

In the great Market Place is a fine Market House and Town Hall of about 1770. It has an interesting lock-up.

Viscount Castlereagh (1769–1822) is reputed to have been born at Newtownards.

1 m. E., on the Millisle road (entrance on Old Movilla Rd), is the site of the celebrated abbey of Movilla (Magh Bhile), founded about 540 by St Finnbarr, alias Finnén, moccu Fíatach ("Finnian the Younger"), patron of Ulaid, who introduced the Vulgate to Ireland. Several famous 6th cent. saints and scholars were trained at Movilla, among them Columcille, who was ordained deacon there. The monastery was an important centre of Gaelic scholarship, and seems to have been intimately connected with the origin and evolution of the celebrated *Lebor Gabála Érenn* or *Book of Invasions*. There are remnants (Nat. Mon.) of a 13th cent. church extended W. in the 15th cent. In the E. gable are an inserted 12th (?) cent. window and four human masks. On the N. side of the chancel are an early grave-slab inscribed OR[ÕIT] DO DERTREND and eight 13th cent. gravestones.

4½ m. SE. is Mount Stewart (*see under* Grey Abbey).

1 m. SW. is Scrabo Hill (307 ft), with traces of ancient hut-circles, earthworks, etc. (Nat. Mon.). Many others were destroyed in the making of the golf-course and of the memorial tower to the 3rd Marquess of Londonderry. In Killynether, on the S. side of the hill, are forty acres of woodland, etc., belonging to the Nat. Trust (open to the public at all times; residence not open to the public).

5 m. W. is Dundonald (*see* Stormont *under* Belfast).

NEWTOWN BUTLER, Co. Fermanagh (Map 2, D5), is a Border village on the Clones (6 m.)–Lisnaskeagh (8 m.) road.

In 1690 Newtown Butler was the scene of a costly defeat of a Jacobite force under Gen. Mac Carthy, at the hands of the Protestant settlers of Enniskillen, led by Col. Wolseley.

3¾ m. S., in Annaghmore Glebe, is the Druid's Temple (Nat. Mon.) a circle of enormous stones which surrounded a large mound removed in 1712, when several Bronze Age burial chambers or cists were found.

3¼ m. SW., in the churchyard on Galloon Island, Upper Lough Erne, are the remains of two High Crosses (Nat. Mons.) carved with scriptural and other subjects, and having traces of Irish inscriptions; the head of the East Cross is at the W. end of the graveyard. The figure subjects include: East Cross: *The Baptism of Christ, The Adoration of the Magi, The Sacrifice of Isaac*; West Cross: *The Fall of Adam and Eve, Daniel in the Lions' Den, The Three Children in the Fiery Furnace*.

4 m. WSW., by Upper Lough Erne, is Crom Castle, late 18th cent. seat of the Earls of Erne. On the lakeshore, ½ m. SSE. of the house, are the remains of Crom Old Castle (Nat. Mon.), a Plantation castle built in 1611 by Michael Balfour, Lord of Mountwhaney, who sold it to Sir Stephen Butler, whose successor sold it in turn (1665/66) to Abraham Crichton, ancestor of Lord Erne. In March 1689 it was besieged by Jacobites under Lord Galmoy; in July, by Jacobites under Gen. Mac Carthy. It remained the home of the Crichtons until its accidental destruction by fire in 1764. Only the outer bawn wall and two flankers survive. In the magnificent demesne is an enormous yew, reputedly the largest in Ireland.

NEWTOWN CUNNINGHAM, Co. Donegal (Map 2, D2), is a village on the Derry (9 m.)–Letterkenny (15 m.) road.

1½ m. ENE. is Castleforward, a house built shortly after 1738. It probably occupies the site of the O Doherty castle of Culmacatraine. 3 m. NNW. of Castleforward crossroads, on the summit of Castle Hill, are the battered ruins of Burt Castle, a late 16th cent. O Doherty fortress which sprang into local importance when the English seized Derry. It was taken by Docwra in 1601, but was restored to Sir Cahir O Doherty in 1603. The English failed in an attempt to seize it again in 1607, but were successful the following year. At the Plantation it was leased to Sir Arthur Chichester. In its day the castle was a place of very great strength, surrounded on three sides by Lough Swilly and defended on the fourth by a bog. It commands superb views. ½ m. NW., close to the railway and seashore, are the ruins of Burt Church.

5 m. NE. is Greenan Elly (*see under* Derry).

NEWTOWN FORBES, Co. Longford (Map 2, C6), is a village on the Longford (3 m.)–Carrick-on-Shannon (20 m.) road. Just W. of the village is 19th cent. Castle Forbes, seat of the Earl of Granard. The ancestor of the Forbes family was Sir Arthur Forbes, a descendant of Lord Forbes of Aberdeen, who became a Lord Justice of Ireland. He acquired lands in Longford at the time of the 17th cent. confiscations, and began the building of a castle in 1619. His widow held the castle for the Crown against the Parliamentarians, and after the Restoration the family was rewarded with the earldom of Granard. Permission to visit the demesne must be obtained in advance.

6½ m. NE. is Carn, or Carn Clonhugh, Hill (916 ft), highest point in Co. Longford. It is crowned by a prehistoric cairn, and offers extensive views of the Central Plain.

4½ m. NNW., in Co. Leitrim, is the ancient churchyard of Cloonmorris. Near the E. gable of the ruined church is an ogham stone.

NEWTOWN HAMILTON, Co. Armagh

(Map 3, B6), a village (dating from 1770) on the main Dundalk (16 m.)–Armagh (12 m.) road, lies in the heart of the picturesque Fews (*Na Feadha*, The Woods) of Armagh. Eighteenth cent. lead-smelting brought about the destruction of the historic woodlands, so long a shelter of the vanquished against the English. Niall Mackennan (*fl. c.* 1700), poet-harper and author of *Little Celia Connellan*, was a native of the Fews.

3½ m. NE., in Ballymoyer Demesne, are the remains of a church built in the time of Charles II. In the churchyard is buried Florence Mac Moyer (d. 1713), last hereditary keeper (*maor*, Moyer) of the *Book of Armagh*, one of the treasures of Trinity College Library, Dublin. Mac Moyer pledged the book to raise funds for a journey to London for the purpose of giving perjured evidence against Archbishop Oliver Plunket.

2¼ m. N. is Blackbank Castle, a former English garrison post. There are traces of 16th cent. O Neill encampments in the vicinity.

2½ m. S., in Johnston's Fews (Johnston), are other earthworks, probably also of Elizabethan date, but occupied by Cromwellian forces in the 17th cent.

6 m. S. is The Dorsey (*see under* Crossmaglen).

NEWTOWN MOUNTKENNEDY, Co.

Wicklow (Map 6, D3), is a village on the Bray (10½ m.)–Wicklow (8 m.) road.

½ m. N. is Mount Kennedy House, built about 1785–86 by Michael Stapleton (?; by Thomas Cooley after designs of James Wyatt ?) for Col. Cuningham, the basement being constructed as a fort. (Cuningham later became 1st Earl of Rossmore.) It has good stucco by Stapleton and nineteen chiaroscuro paintings by Peter de Gree. Of these, eight were painted for the dining-room of David La Touche's house, 52 St Stephen's Green, Dublin (*q.v.*), whence they were removed to Woodstock (*below*). Adjoining the house is a fine motte. Mount Kennedy, previously Ballygarney, is called after Sir Robert Kennedy, who was granted the property in 1671.

2 m. NE. is Woodstock House, a good 18th cent. mansion. 1 m. NE. is Kilcoole (*see under* Delgany).

2m. SE., 1 m. from the sea, is the quiet little resort of Newcastle. It derives its name from an English royal castle of about 1200. The castle was taken more than once by the O Byrnes, and finally destroyed by them in 1405, when they occupied the surrounding country. In 1542 they surrendered the manor – the first part of Wicklow to be recovered by the English – to the Crown, and a new royal castle was built. A fragment of the gatehouse of this castle remains on a circular mound. To the N. is a rectangular earthwork.

2½ m. S. are Dunran Demesne – with a pretty glen – and Kiltimon. The "castle" in Dunran Demesne is a fake of about 1770. In the 16th cent. the O Byrnes had one of their chief castles at Kiltimon.

NEWTOWN STEWART, Co. Tyrone

(Map 2, D3), a pretty little linen manufacturing and market town on the Strabane (10 m.)–Omagh (10 m.) road, is pleasantly sited at the foot of Bessy Bell (1,387 ft), near where the Strule and Glenelly–Owenkillew unite to form the Mourne River. A noted angling centre, it is also a convenient centre for exploring the Munterlony and Sperrin Mountains (*see* Plumb Bridge).

The town takes its name from Sir William Stewart (ancestor of Lord Mountjoy), who acquired the place, then called Lislas, by marriage (*c.* 1628) to a daughter of Sir Robert Newcomen, Plantation grantee. It was burnt down by Sir Felim O Neill (*see* Caledon) in 1641. In 1689, after the abortive Siege of Derry, James II had the castle dismantled and the town burnt down again. Thereafter the place lay derelict until 1722. The castle (fragmentary; Nat. Mon.) was erected about 1618 by Sir Robert Newcomen. Nearby is a bridge erected about 1727.

¾ m. SW. is Harry Avery's Castle (Nat. Mon.). Though very ruined, the remains are of interest as exemplifying the medieval military architecture of areas remote from the centres of English power: they stand on a flattened natural eminence which was enclosed by a polygonal, towered curtain and, perhaps, a ditch; at the NE. end is the keep, which masquerades as a twin-towered gatehouse. Tradition associates the castle with Énrí Aimhréidh O Neill (d. 1392), but it may be later than his time. According to the story, O Neill had a sister with the head of a pig. To be rid of her, he offered a large dowry with her, but stipulated that the suitor who refused to wed her after seeing her should hang. Nineteen suitors decided that hanging was the lesser evil!

2 m. NNE., alt. 300 ft in Glenknock, is Cloghogle, a chamber tomb (Nat. Mon.).

2 m. NE., at Curraghdoos in Crosh, is Cloghogle, a ruined gallery grave.

4½ m. NE., at the junction of the Owenkillew

Baronscourt, Newtown Stewart

and Glenelly rivers, are the ruins of Corick-more "Abbey" (Nat. Mon.), a 15th cent. Franciscan Tertiary friary.

4 m. SSE., between the E. bank of the Strule and the railway, alt. 100 ft in Carrigans, is Cloghogle (Nat. Mon.), a court cairn.

2¾ m. S., to the W. of the Mountjoy road, alt. 200 ft in Beltany, is Cloghogle, a court cairn; to the W. is the summit of Bessy Bell (*below*).

1½ m. W. is a five-road junction. 2¾ m. S., alt. 400 ft in Ballyrenan, is Cloghogle (Nat. Mon.), a long cairn with three chamber tombs; some capstones have cup marks; excavation yielded beads and Late Neolithic pottery. 2 m. SE., on the summit of Bessy Bell (properly Sliabh Truim, Slieve Trim), is Donal Gorm's Cairn. 1 m. SSW. of this, alt. 800 ft in Glasmullagh, is Dermot and Grania's Bed, a ruined chamber tomb; nearby are four stone circles, two with tangent alignments. 3 m. SW. of these is the Legland cairn (*below*). – 4 m. S. of the Ballyrenan cairn, alt. 400 ft. on the W. slope of Manus Hill in Legland, is a two-chamber court cairn. – 2 m. S. of the road junction, between Bessy Bell and Mullaghcroy, is Baronscourt, seat of the Hamiltons, Dukes of Abercorn. The house dates from 1741, but was much altered in 1791–92 by Sir John Soane, and again in the early 19th cent. The Agent's House dates from 1690–1700; nearby Derrywoone Castle is a good example of a 17th cent. Scottish Planter's stronghouse. In the beautifully landscaped demesne are the partly artificial Loughs Mary, Fanny, and Catherine. In Lough Catherine is Island Mac Hugh, a crannóg first constructed in neolithic times and on which a small castle was erected in late medieval times. Bessy Bell and Mary Gray hills (the latter is on the opposite side of the Strule)

were given their silly names (those of the heroines of a Scottish ballad) by the Hamiltons. In 1536 Síoghraidh O Mulconry wrote a book of saints' Lives for Rose O Donnell, wife of Niall Óg O Neill, in Baile an tSen-chaisléin beside Bessy Bell. – 4 m. WSW. of the road-junction, alt. 400 ft in Meaghy, is Giants Den, a chambered cairn (overgrown). 2 m. WNW., in Crew Lower, are two pillarstones.

3¾ m. WNW., at Ardstraw, are the remains of a medieval church and of a late 17th cent. Protestant church. St Patrick established an episcopal see at Ardstraw, which he confided to Bishop Mac Ercae. In the 6th cent. St Eóghan, abbot-bishop, founded a monastery here. He is claimed as a disciple of St Finnian of Clonard, but seems rather to have been an alumnus of Candida Casa (Whithorn) in Galloway. At the 12th cent. Reformation the see was transferred to Maghera, Co. Derry (*q.v.*), and no trace survives of the ancient monastic episcopal foundation. 1 m. NNW. of Ardstraw bridge, alt. 400 ft in Clady Halliday, is Carnmore (Nat. Mon.), a three-chamber court cairn. – 3 m. NNE. is Lisky (*see under* Strabane).

NOBBER, Co. Meath (Map 3, B7), is a small village on the Navan (13 m.)–Kingscourt (8 m.) road.

Before 1196 Gilbert de Angulo built a castle (An Obair?) here; the motte survives. In 1201 John de Courcy was treacherously trapped in the castle by Hugh II de Lacy for delivery to King John.

Nearby Spiddal was the birthplace of the celebrated blind song-writer and harper, Turloch O Carolan (1670–1738).

5 m. NE., at Drumcondra, alias Drumconrath, is a motte. In Woodtown, 2 m. S. of

Drumcondra, is a well-preserved section of the Pale (earthworks).

6 m. SE. is Killary (*see under* Collon).

2 m. SW., in Cruicetown, is an early monastic site with remains of a simple Romanesque church (Nat. Mon.) containing a 1633 double-effigy tomb and other Cruice memorials. The 1688 cross (Nat. Mon.) with *Crucifixion* and *Virgin and Child* is also a Cruice memorial. Nearby is Robertstown Castle (Nat. Mon.), a 17th cent. embattled house.

OBRIENSBRIDGE, Co. Clare (Map 5, B3), is a decayed village at the only crossing of the Shannon between Killaloe (5 m.) and Limerick (9 m.). It was here that Ireton's Cromwellians forced a crossing of the river in 1651.

The picturesque river has been much altered hereabouts by the Shannon Electricity scheme, the power station of which is at Ardnacrusha (*see under* Limerick).

7 m. NW. (2 m. SE. of Broadford), in Formoyle More, is Cromlech, a wedge-shaped gallery grave.

OLDCASTLE, Co. Meath (Map 2, D6), is a small market town on the Kells (16 m.)–Ballinagh (17 m.) road.

There is a motte W. of the town.

To the SE. rises the 4-m. ridge of Slieve na Caillighe (sometimes called the Loughcrew Hills), which commands splendid views of the hill-ringed Central Lowland. On the three main heights, Carnbane West (842 ft), Carnbane East (911 ft), and Patrickstown Hill, are the remains (Nat. Mons.) of thirty chambered cairns and tumuli, a ringfort, a rectangular earthwork, a pillarstone, a stone cross, and other ancient monuments. The cairns and related monuments are the survivors of a remarkable passage-grave cemetery, which is particularly noteworthy for the wealth of its hieratic "art". The tomb types themselves present a series of variations on the cruciform plan. The largest of the Carnbane West cairns are those dubbed respectively D and L by archaeologists. D is about 180 ft in diameter. It has been considerably pulled about. No chamber has been found, and it is regarded as a cenotaph. Cairn L and its satellites are NE. of D and its satellites. Cairn L is 135 ft in diameter and contains a passage grave with seven lateral compartments; two of these have shallow stone basins, or trays, such as are found at Newgrange (*q.v.*). The principal Carnbane East cairn is Cairn T. It is about 115 ft in diameter. The tomb here is probably the classic example of an Irish cruciform passage grave. Twenty-eight of the great cairn stones bear scribings. The most noteworthy of such stones is the Hag's Chair, a massive kerbstone on the N. periphery. It is very unfortunate that most of the excavations on Slieve na Caillighe were conducted by amateurs; even more unfortunate that the recording was altogether inadequate. The normal burial rite appears to have been cremation.

Each tomb contained the remains of a number of persons, the bones and ashes being deposited either on the floor of the tomb, or on flat stones, or on stone basins like those in Cairn L. With the remains were sherds of coarse, crudely ornamented pottery, bone pins, stone beads and pendants, etc. Some of the cairns, notably Cairn H (immediately W. of Cairn L), appear to have been adapted for burial or other purposes in the Iron Age; but there is no reason for claiming that any of them were the tombs of historic personages. On the S. side of the ridge is Patrickstown motte. Down to 1864 no fewer than twenty-one tumuli survived to the S. of it. – About 2 m. E. of Slieve na Caillighe, on King's Mountain, a large stone with Newgrange-type spirals has been set up as a rubbing stone for cattle. It is all that survives of a chambered tumulus which stood on the spot. – At the SW. foot of Slieve na Caillighe are the ruins of Loughcrew House. Recently destroyed by fire, this was a good Classical mansion by the English architect, Cockerell. Near the SE. edge of the demesne is Lough Creeve (Crew), which has given its name to the house and the townland. The Loughcrew estate belonged to a branch of the great Plunket family (*see* Beaulieu *under* Drogheda) until the Cromwellian conquest, and his father's home here was the birthplace of Blessed Oliver Plunket (1629–81), Archbishop of Armagh, who was unjustly executed at Tyburn. There are ruins of a medieval church WNW. of the house.

8 m. SW. is Fore (*see under* Castlepollard).

2¼ m. WNW., in Dungummin Lower, Co. Cavan, is a cross-inscribed pillarstone (and ogham inscription ?).

OMAGH, Co. Tyrone (Map 2, D3), the county town of Tyrone, is a manufacturing (milling, shirtmaking), garrison, and market town attractively situated on the Strabane (20 m.)–Monaghan (34 m.) road, where the Camowen unites with the Drumragh River to form the Strule. Apart from a good 18th cent. Classical court-house, the town itself contains little of interest, but it is a convenient base for fishing the Glenelly and Strule rivers and for exploring the beauties and antiquities of the Munterlony and South Sperrin Mountains (*see* Plumb Bridge). One well-known circuit (35 m.) is NE. via Gortin Gap between Curraghchosaly (1,372 ft) and Mullaghcarn (1,778 ft; the climber will be rewarded with splendid panoramas) to Gortin; thence E. and SE. via Drumlea bridge and the NE. side of the Owenreagh valley to Sheskinshule; thence S. to Creggan and W. to Mountfield; and so back to Omagh.

1 m. SE. of the town is Creevenagh House, home of the Auchinlecks, Field-Marshal Sir Claude Auchinleck's family.

4¾ m. N., in Dunmullan, are the ruins of Cappagh church (Nat. Mon.).

12½ m. NE. is Aghascrebagh townland. Here are: (*a*) N. of the Aghascrebagh–Cookstown road, an ogham stone (Nat. Mon.); (*b*) S. of the road, alt. 600 ft, several large standing stones and a double circle of small stones with central chamber tomb (Nat. Mon.); (c) ¼ m. E. of the ogham stone, alt. 600 ft, a low tumulus crowned by a small pillarstone (Nat. Mon.). In Crouck, the next townland to the E., ⅓ m. ENE. of the schoolhouse, alt. 600 ft, is Dún Ruadh (Doonroe; Nat. Mon.), a large cairn enclosed by a ditch and bank. It contains a ring of uprights with intervening dry walling, and is said to have covered thirteen cists. Excavation has yielded some Late Neolithic pottery. To the SE. are the remains of a chambered cairn. – In Carnanransy, the next townland N. of Aghascrebagh, to the S. of the Greencastle–Draperstown road, alt. 700 ft, is Cloghmore (Nat. Mon.), a small court cairn. – 6 m. SE. of Crouck bridge is Dunnamore bridge (see under Cookstown). – 6 m. NE. of Crouck bridge is Broughderg crossroads (see under Cookstown).

4½ m. E., in Cloghfin townland, is Cloghfin, a collapsed chamber tomb.

1½ m. W. (⅛ m. NW. of Cornabracken schoolhouse) is Cornabracken Giants Grave, a chamber tomb with collapsed roof. – ½ m. W. of Cornabracken school, in Deerpark, is Cloghanacorite (Nat. Mon.), a large sandstone boulder of unknown significance.

OOLA, Co. Limerick (Map 5, C4), is a village on the Tipperary (6 m.)–Limerick (20 m.) road. There are ruins of a 16th cent. gabled towerhouse; an O Brien residence, it was blown up by Patrick Sarsfield in 1690.

ORAN, Co. Roscommon (Map 2, B7), is on the Roscommon (9 m.)–Ballymoe (6 m.) road. There was an early monastery here, of which there remain the stump of a Round Tower, a scrap of a pre-Romanesque church, and a holy well. 200 yds ESE. of the church is a low motte with two baileys. 600 yds SW., in a marshy valley, is a large, rectangular, bivallate earthwork.

4 m. S., on the Suck, is Dunamon Castle, which resembles that at Bunratty; it is now the novitiate of the Society of the Divine Word for Foreign Missions. The old parish church was at one time the castle chapel. It contains Caulfeild monuments.

ORANMORE, Co. Galway (Map 1, D6), is a small village at the junction of the Galway–Dublin and Galway–Limerick roads, 5½ m. E. of Galway. By the shore of Galway Bay stands the massive tower of a 16th cent. Clanricard Burke castle. It has recently been re-edified for occupation by Anita Leslie, the author.

There are many ringforts in the neighbourhood, most of which have souterrains.

3 m. ENE., in Mountain West, is Lisroughan, a henge-type circular earthwork (i.e. with bank outside the ditch). The entrance is flanked by two large stones. In the interior are some modern graves (infants).

2 m. SW. is Renville, a late Georgian house. There are several ringforts in the vicinity.

5 m. SW. (via Kilcaimin), at the head of Lackaloy creek, is a chamber tomb (portal dolmen ?). ⅓ m. N. of the latter, on the high ground overlooking Mweeloon Bay, is Rathmore, a fine ringfort.

3 m. W. is Roscam (see under Galway).

OUGHTERARD, Co. Galway (Map 1, C5), is a market village and well-known angling centre where the main Galway (17 m.)–Clifden (33 m.) road crosses the little Owenriff near the beautiful upper end of Lough Corrib. It is a convenient base for touring beautiful, romantic Connemara (q.v.) and Joyces Country.

¾ m. SE. are the ruins of the small medieval church, Kilcummin; 200 yds W., to the W. of the road, is St Cummin's Well.

2 m. SE., to the E. of the Galway road, are the ruins (Nat. Mon.) of the once fine O Flaherty castle of Aughnanure (16th cent.). At the time of the Cromwellian blockade of Galway this was one of the outposts guarding the town from attack around the head of the lake. In the midst of the alarms Lame David Duignan was working on Royal Irish Academy MS., 24 P 9, in the castle (see also Oileán Rúa, Lough Mask, under Cong). The remains comprise fragments of two bawns (the inner with corbel-roofed angle turret), a fine tower, and one wall of a beautiful hall (note window embrasures); the rest of the hall has been destroyed by river-erosion.

7 m. NW., on the summit of Knockaunnageeragh (1,009 ft), is Carn Seefin, a prehistoric cairn; magnificent view.

8 m. NW., at Curraun, opposite the Hill of Doon, is one of Lough Corrib's beauty-spots.

PALLAS GREEN, NEW, Co. Limerick (Map 5, C4), is a village on the Tipperary (10 m.)–Limerick (13 m.) road.

1¾ m. SW. is Pallas Green (Old). The name preserves that of Grían, alias Áine (see Knockainey under Hospital), a sun-goddess whose Otherworld seat was in nearby Cnoc Gréine. There is a fine motte here; also remains of a manorial church. The Anglo-Norman manor here was established by Geoffrey fitz Robert. In 1223 it was granted to Maurice fitz Gerald, Baron O ffaly. 3 m. NW., in Longstone, is a ringfort with a 9 ft 6 in. pillarstone which gives its name to the townland.

3 m. NNE. is 19th cent. Castle Garde, formerly home of the O Gradys. It incorporates a medieval tower.

3 m. WNW. (1 m. SW. of Dromkeen station), in the ancient graveyard of Dromkeen, is an early cross-slab.

PALLASKENRY, alias **SHANPALLAS**, Co. Limerick (Map 5, B4), is a village 2 m. N. of the Limerick (12 m.)–Askeaton (7 m.) road. There are remains of a Desmond rock-castle and of a bawn.

2 m. N. is Shannongrove House, a fine shooting lodge built in 1709 for the Burys: noteworthy doorway and brick chimney stacks.

2¼ m. SE., on the road to Kildimo, are remains (Nat. Mon.) of Killulta (or Kellallatan), a rude, diminutive church reputed to be the oldest in the county (9th/10th cent?). 3 m. E., in Ballyculhane, are remains of a Purcell castle: large bawn with angle-turrets and detached tower.

5½ m. S. is Currah Chase (see under Askeaton).

3 m. SSW., in (Killeen) Cowpark, are the well-preserved remains of a small 15th cent. church.

2 m. W. is Castletown Manor, a Georgian house, formerly home of the Wallers.

PASSAGE EAST, Co. Waterford (Map 6, B6), is a village and small port on the W. side of Waterford Harbour, 7 m. ESE. of Waterford. There is a ferry to the twin villages of Ballyhack and Arthurstown (on the Wexford shore within convenient reach of Dunbrody Abbey; see under Campile).

Strongbow landed at Passage, 23 Aug. 1170, with 200 knights and 1,000 other men. Next day he was joined by Raymond le Gros with 40 knights, and on 25 Aug. took Waterford by storm. On 17 Oct. 1171, Henry II of England arrived at Passage with 4,000 men in 400 ships. In 1649 Cromwell's son-in-law took the fort by storm.

1 m. S., at Crooke, are remains of a nave-and-chancel church and of a castle of the Knights Templar.

2 m. S. are the ruins of Geneva Barracks, of 1798 ill-fame. Their name preserves the memory of an abortive 1782–84 project to found a city here for emigré intellectuals and watchmakers from Geneva. The city was to have had a university which, it was hoped, would attract scholars from all parts of Europe.

3 m. S. is pleasant Woodtown strand.

2 m. NW., at Faithlegg, are the ruins of a nave-and-chancel church with a medieval font. Nearby are the remains of successive Ailward castles, the earliest represented by a motte-and-bailey, the latest by stone ruins. Henry II granted Faithlegg to Ailward Juvenis, and Ailwards owned the place until the Williamite revolution. Cromwell captured the castle in 1649 and butchered the garrison. 1 m. NE. of the church is Cheekpoint Hill (430 ft). It overlooks the confluence of the Suir and Barrow, and offers a very fine panorama.

PETTIGOE, Cos. Donegal–Fermanagh (Map 2, C4), is a market village and angling centre on the Donegal (17 m.)–Enniskillen (20 m.) road, near the N. shore of beautiful Lower Lough Erne (q.v.).

The Border follows the little Termon River through the middle of the village, which thus lies not only in two counties, but in two states.

Pettigoe is the gateway to Lough Derg, Co. Donegal (q.v.).

3 m. N., in Templecarne, alias Carn, graveyard, is a well-preserved bothóg, or timber hut, used as a Mass-shelter in Penal times. John Kells Ingram (1823–1907), scholar and author of Who Fears to Speak of Ninety-Eight?, was born in Templecarne. 4 m. N. is Tawlaght, site of a prehistoric burial place. There survive remains of a court cairn; ½ m. SW. are a second chamber tomb and the remains of others.

4 m. E., via Clonelly, is Formil (see under Kesh).

2 m. SW., on Lough Erne, is Termon Mac Grath (originally Termonn Da-Bhé-óg) castle, seat of the Mac Graths, hereditary coarbs of St Da-Bhé-óg's (Davoge's) monastery, Lough Derg. A notorious member of this family was Myler Mac Grath, the Elizabethan pluralist (see Cashel, Co. Tipperary). 5 m. (by road bridge) SW. of the castle is Boa Island. In Dreenan (at the W. end of the island) is Caldragh, an ancient churchyard. Here is a stone (Nat. Mon.) with twin cross-armed figures set back to back. It bears some resemblance to Gaulish figures and may be pre-Christian. Another effigial stone (Nat. Mon.) has been brought here from nearby Lusty More island.

PILTOWN, Co. Kilkenny (Map 6, A6), is a village on the Waterford (12 m.)–Carrick-on-Suir (4 m.) road.

In 1462 took place the famous battle of Piltown between Thomas, Earl of Desmond, and the rebel Lancastrian Butlers led by John, 6th Earl of Ormond, and Émonn mac Risderd Butler, who was captured. The price of his ransom was two great Irish literary codices, one of which is now in Oxford, the other in the British Museum (see Pottlerath under Callan, and Paulstown under Gowran).

The village has a good, early 19th cent. Market House (now the police station) built by Lord Bessborough. The sham castle is the monument of a Ponsonby killed in the Napoleonic wars. Bessborough House, seat of the Ponsonbys, Earls of Bessborough, was a fine mansion of 1744 by Francis Bindon of Clooney, Co. Clare. Burned down in 1922, it is now the scholasticate of the Oblates of Mary Immaculate.

3 m. NE., in Raheen, is a prehistoric chamber tomb.

2 m. SSE., on a beautiful reach of the Suir, is Fiddown. At the Protestant parish church are some medieval tomb fragments, etc., from the ancient church site of Kilmodalla, alias Kildaton, destroyed in 1830 to make way for the stables in Bessborough Demesne, Piltown. The tomb fragments include some from the tomb (by Rory O Tunney; about 1550) of Redmond Daton, alias D'Autun, and his wife, Helen Butler. The ancient churchyard marks the site of a 6th cent. monastery founded by St Mo-Medóg, son of Midgna and great-nephew of Colm of Terryglass (see under Portumna), who laboured as a missionary in Scotland and

France. The sole early relic is a stone basin. The 1747 Ponsonby mausoleum is an adaption of the chancel of a 13th cent. church demolished about 1870; in the E. gable is the head of a *Blessed Virgin Mary* slab; the Mary, Countess of Bessborough (d. 1713) monument and the William Ponsonby, Viscount Duncannon (d. 1724) monument are by William Kidwell of Dublin (d. 1736); the monument to the 1st Earl of Bessborough (d. 1758) and his wife is by Sir William Atkinson. – 2 m. SE., in Clonmore, are the ruins of a plain church with Late Romanesque chancel; 200 yds E. is Tiobraid Chainnigh, alias Toberaghcanice (Cainneach's Well). 1 m. further SE. are the ruins of the medieval nave-and-chancel church of Pollrone, with a medieval stoup and remains of a 1599 Brennagh tomb, perhaps that of Pierce Brennagh (Walsh) of Grange Castle (d. 1575) and his wife. The tomb effigies are in Elizabethan costume; the other carvings include a *Crucifixion, Christ's Seamless Robe, Veronica's Towel*, etc. Beside the road SE. to Doornane is Clais an tSagairt (The Priest's Trench), where Mass was said in Penal times.

1¼ m. WSW., close to the Suir in Tibberaghny (Tiobra Fhachtna), is the site of an early monastery whose patron was St Mo-Dhomnóg of Lambecher (*see* Bremore *under* Balbriggan). The remains include part of a carved cross-shaft (?) removed from its socket about 1860, an early stone trough, and remains of a church with early chancel and 13th/14th cent. nave; the cross-shaft carvings include figures of hieratic beasts, spirals, etc. SW. of the churchyard is St Faghtna's Well, after which the place is called. Nearby is Tibberaghny Moat, motte (with traces of the bailey) of a castle erected by Prince John of England in 1185 to command the Suir crossing. Tibberaghny Castle incorporates the tower of a 15th/16th cent. castle which belonged to the Mountgarret Butlers in the 17th cent.

3 m. NW. the Protestant church of Whitechurch stands in a large, ancient, circular enclosure divided into three parts by the modern roads. Castletown House, to the NE., was built about 1767–70 for Michael Cox, Protestant Bishop of Ossory, to the design of Davis Ducart. In Ballyheneberry, SE. of Castletown demesne, is a portal dolmen; capstone collapsed. In Killonerry, SW. of Whitechurch, bullauns, etc., mark the ancient church-site from which the townland derives its name. A few fields away is densely overgrown Cloch Liath, a portal dolmen; according to local tradition the fallen capstone was overthrown by St Patrick.

3½ m. NNW., at the little village of Owning, are remains of a medieval parish church (Assumption of the Blessed Virgin Mary); the chancel, an addition to the simple nave, has a beautiful S. door. High on the S. slope of Moondeega Hill is Poll an Aifrinn, where Mass was celebrated in Penal times. – The district was rich in prehistoric chamber tombs, some

Commissioners of Public Works in Ireland
Cross-shaft at Tibberaghny, Piltown

of which survive (*see* Raheen, Tubbrid, Ballyheneberry, *and* Killonerry, *above*; *also* Leac an Scáil *under* Mullinavat): close to the village, on the NE., is Cloch Bhán, alias Druid's Altar, an overgrown rectangular chamber; on Corrignanaug, overlooking the village, is Cloch an Phúca, alias the Hawk's Stone; in Clocharnach, townland of Curraghmore (the next townland to the N.), are fragments of a roadside tomb; also in Curraghmore, not far from a well-preserved motte, is the Giants Grave (collapsed); alt. 950 ft, in Garryduff, the townland adjoining Curraghmore on the SE., was Leaba an Fhir Mhóir, alias Leaba na Con, a wedge-shaped gallery grave; near the border of the two townlands is An Chloch Bhréaga, a pillarstone; another pillarstone, Cloch Fhada, alias Long Stone, stands to the W. of the road in Garryduff, 1½ m. NE. of Owning (near Glenbower crossroads); ½ m. E. of Owning, in Kilmanahin, is Leaba an tSaighdiúra, which one local tale makes the grave of a Cromwellian soldier. – 2 m. WNW. of Owning is the ancient monastic site of Kilkieran (*see* Newtown *under* Carrick-on-Suir).

PLUMB BRIDGE, Co. Tyrone (Map 2, D3), is a little village at the foot of Glenelly, the beautiful valley between the Munterloney Mountains (Mullaghbolig, 1,400 ft; Carnanelly, 1,851 ft) and the Sperrin Mountains (Mullaghclogha, 2,088 ft; Sawel, 2,240 ft). It is the junction of roads from Dunnamanagh (10 m.), Draperstown (21 m.), Omagh (via Gortin; 14 m.), Newtown Stewart (6 m.), and Strabane

(11 m.). The Draperstown road climbs Glenelly via Sperrin, alias Mount Hamilton, at the foot of Sawel, to Glengomna and Labby. The country round about is very rich in chamber tombs, stone circles, and other prehistoric remains.

3 m. N., ¼ m. E. of the Dunnamanagh road, alt. 800 ft. in Clogherny, is Meenerrigal Rocks Giants Grave, a gallery grave at the centre of a ring of stones. In the same townland, close to Butterlope Glen, alt. 700 ft, are the remains of five stone circles. 1½ m. NNW., ⅛ m. W. of the by-road on the E. slope of Balix Hill, alt. 800 ft in Balix Middle, is "White Rocks" (Nat. Mon.), a court cairn with V-shaped forecourt. ½ m. NE., 100 yds W. of Doorat crossroads, alt. 500 ft in Doorat, are two low stone circles. S. of Doorat school, alt. 500 ft, are remains of a stone alignment 150 ft long.

4 m. NE., ⅛ m. NW. of the summit of Mullaghcarbatagh, alt. 1,500 ft in Doorat, is a round cairn.

3½ m. ENE., to the E. of Glensass Burn, alt. 800 ft in Castledamph, is part of a double stone circle with central cairn and cist and a double alignment; E. of this is a cairn; 100 yds N. are two contiguous stone circles and remains of another double circle.

4 m. E., on the N. side of Glenelly, just N. of St Patrick's Church, alt. 400 ft in Glenroan, is a large stone with a cup mark which local legend regards as the imprint of St Patrick's knee; it was the capstone of a chamber tomb. In the churchyard is a stone with four cup marks. 1 m. NE. and ½ m. N. of the road from Glenroan bridge to Ederlin bridge, alt. 700 ft, is Glenroan Dermot and Grania's Bed (Nat. Mon.), a ruined chamber tomb; to the E. is a second ruined tomb (Nat. Mon.).

3 m. SE., on the SE. slope of Slievebeg, alt. 700 ft in Culvacullion, are six stone circles and the remains of a chamber tomb (Nat. Mons.).

3½ m. SW. is Corickmore (see under Newtown Stewart).

1 m. W., alt. 500 ft, is Letterbrat chamber tomb. 1½ m. W., to the S. of the Strabane road, is Meenagorp chambered cairn. 3 m. N., to the W. of Ballykeery Burn, alt. 600 ft, is Ballykeery Fort, an oval ringfort bounded by large upright flagstones and traces of a ditch (cf. Dunowen, Inishowen under Ballinrobe).

POMEROY, Co. Tyrone (Map 3, A4), is a village at the junction of the Stewartstown (10 m.) and Cookstown (10 m.) roads to Omagh (19 m.). The surrounding country is particularly rich in chamber tombs, stone circles, and other megalithic remains (see also Carrickmore and Cookstown).

2 m. NNE., ¼ m. SE. of Lough Bracken, are Edentoit pillarstones. Not far away to the W., in Moymore, are remains of seven low stone circles (Nat. Mons.), six of them with tangential alignments; also the remnants of a chamber tomb. ½ m. E. of the Edentoit stones, in Keenaghan, is Shanrelik (Sean Reilig, "old

graveyard"), where an overgrown court cairn and another chamber tomb have round about them many small, unconsecrated, Christian graves.

2½ m. SSW., ⅓ m. E. of Sturgeon bridge, alt. 700 ft in Cornamaddy, are two small stone circles with traces of tangent alignments. 150 yds N., in Turnabarson, are a tumulus, a stone circle, and traces of an alignment, etc. – 1½ m. WNW. and ½ m. NW. of Altmore Lodge, alt. 600 ft in Altmore, are two long cairns (Nat. Mons.), one of them (Giants Graves) a court cairn. Altmore was the birthplace of the brilliant American general, James Shields (Ó Siaghail; 1806–79), the only man to defeat Stonewall Jackson; being a Catholic, he had to find his education in a local "hedge school". All his life he remained devoted to the Irish cause and, as Governor of Oregon, was responsible for Irish immigration to the American North West and for the many Ulster names given to towns and townships there.

2 m. SW., close to the railway and NE. of Altinagh School, alt. 600 ft, is Gortnagarn court cairn.

2¾ m. WNW., alt. 700 ft in Tremoge, are two stone circles, one with an alignment of massive stones, the other with three tall outliers. 2 m. NNW., alt. 700 ft on the W. side of Lough Mallon, is Creggandevesky long cairn. ½ m. W., and ¼ m. N. of Scalp summit, alt. 700 ft, are Creggandevesky "Standing Stones", a ruined chamber tomb. ⅓ m. S. of the summit (1½ m. W. of the Tremoge circles), alt. 700 ft in the same townland, are a low stone circle and two pillarstones. – N. of Lough Mallon and ½ m. SE. of Evishatrask school, alt. 700 ft, is Cregganconroe "Cashel" (Nat. Mon.), a court cairn. Beside it is an alignment of nine stones.

2½ m. NNW., 300 yds SE. of Craiganawork hill, alt. 700 ft in Murnells, is Dermot and Grania's Bed, alias Labby Jerny (Nat. Mon.), a gallery grave with two enormous capstones. Beside it are a ruined long cairn and two standing stones.

5 m. N. is Killucan (see under Cookstown).

PORTADOWN, Co. Armagh (Map 3, B5), is a linen and manufacturing centre on the Armagh (11 m.)–Belfast (26 m.) road. It is also the centre of an important fruit-growing region, and its nurseries are known internationally for their roses.

The town is a creation of the late 18th cent. Like those of Ballymena, the people are industrious and careful, earning the reputation of being the "Aberdonians of Ireland".

There is a small museum in the Carnegie Library.

3 m. SW., on the S. side of the avenue to Ballintaggart House, is Ballintaggart court cairn (Nat. Mon.).

6 m. SW. is Rich Hill (q.v.).

4½ m. WNW. is the Diamond, a village which claims to be the birthplace of the Orange Order, which was founded after the Battle of the

Diamond, a sectarian riot which took place on 21 Sept. 1795.

7 m. WNW. is Ardress House (*see under* Charlemont).

6 m. NW., The Birches, on the Dungannon road, was the home of Thomas Jackson, father of President Andrew Jackson of the U.S.A.

PORTAFERRY, Co. Down (Map 3, D5), is a small port and resort beautifully sited on the E. side of the entrance to Strangford Lough, opposite Strangford. It is 29 m. from Belfast. The Queen's University, Belfast, marine biology station is here.

In Meetinghouse Lane is the Presbyterian church, a good Doric building.

On the W. side of Church Street are some fragments of the ancient parish church (Temple Cranny). In Castle St are the ruins of a 15th cent. castle (Nat. Mon.).

Portaferry House is by William Farrell.

4 m. N., on Castle Hill, Ardkeen, a promontory projecting into Strangford Lough, is a motte-and-bailey erected about 1180 by John de Courcy. Nearby St Mary's is a much altered manorial church, probably founded by the Savages, for centuries lords of much of this country. It has two early lancet windows in the N. side and a simple medieval grave-slab. 3½ m. E., on Ardkeen golf links, is Kirkistown Moat, the remains of a motte-and-bailey castle. Kirkistown Castle, to the NE., built by one of the Savages in 1622, has a fine bawn.

7 m. N. is Kircubbin village, a popular sailing station. Holy Trinity Church has a good Doric elevation.

1½ m. NE., in Derry, are the ruins of two small, early churches whose masonry is bonded with clay. One or both was dedicated to the virgin, Cumain.

6½ m. NE., in Ballyspurge (to the SE. of Cloghy village), are the ruins of the White House, a 1½-storey, Plantation house (*c.* 1640–50) with pistol-loops; fragments of the bawn survive.

2¼ m. ESE. in Keentagh, by the shore of Millin Bay, is a unique Neolithic long cairn (Nat. Mon.). Erected on top of a (field?) wall, it is ringed by spaced-out orthostats and bounded by a close-set kerb (duplicated at the N. end). It covered a long cist with remains of at least fifteen uncremated (and one cremated) persons. Sixty-four stones bore passage-grave and other devices. Between the cairn and the outer setting were several short cists, four with cremations. The few finds included sherds of passage-grave type. ¼ m. N. is a pillarstone. – 1 m. S., in Tara, is a hill-top ringfort (Nat. Mon.).

PORTARLINGTON, Co. Laois (Map 6, B3), is an 18th cent. town on the Tullamore (17 m.)–Kildare (13 m.) road, beside the River Barrow and near the Grand Canal. It takes its name (previously Port na hInnse) from Sir Henry Bennet, afterwards Lord Arlington, an Englishman who was given confiscated O

Dempsey lands here after the Eleven Years' War, and who introduced Protestant French and German settlers, but himself returned in the end to Catholicism. After the defeat of the Jacobites, William III granted the estate to the Huguenot, Gen. Henri de Massue, Marquis de Ruvigny, Earl of Galway, who settled Huguenot refugees on the lands and in the town; among them Jean Cavalier, the Camisard leader from the Cevennes. St Paul's Church (C. of I.) is the 1851 successor of de Ruvigny's Calvinist, 1696, Église Française de St Paul. (De Ruvigny also built an English Church – St Michael's – for the Church of Ireland Protestants.) The Act of Resumption, 1699, terminated de Ruvigny's ownership of Portarlington, which was eventually acquired by Ephraim Dawson, ancestor of Lord Portarlington. The Dawsons did much to improve the town, which still has many good, 18th–19th cent. houses.

N. of the town is Ireland's first (1950) turf-fired power station.

2½ m. E., between the canal and the Barrow, are the remnants of the castle of Lea (Leghe), a stronghold of the FitzGerald barons of O ffaly. It had a fine, Carlow-type, keep (about 1250 ?) at the centre of an inner, oval ward. The later (?), much altered, outer ward runs down to the river. The twin-towered gatehouse of the outer ward suggests a date of about 1297 for the latter. The castle had a stormy history. In 1285 it was burnt by the O Conors of Uí Fáilghe, in 1307 by O More, in 1315 by Edward Bruce. In the 14th and 15th centuries it was repeatedly in O Dempsey hands. When Silken Thomas rebelled (1534) he stored his treasure there. At the outbreak of the Eleven Years' War the O Dempseys seized it, and it was in Confederate Catholic hands for most of the war. In 1650 the Cromwellian colonels, Hewson and Reynolds, captured it and wrecked it.

4 m. S. is Emo Court (*see under* Ballybrittas).

PORT LAOISE, Co. Laois (Map 6, A4), county town of Co. Laois, is situated on the main Dublin (53 m.)–Limerick (70 m.) road, between Monasterevin (14 m.) and Mountrath (8 m.). It traces its origin to the Plantation of Laoighis and Uí Fáilghe under Mary Tudor, whence its former name, Maryborough (*see* Daingean, Co. Offaly). The town itself is noteworthy merely as the location of the Republic's only male convict prison. The Court House is by Sir Richard Morrison (1767–1849), a pupil of Gandon's.

Dr Bartholomew Mosse (1712–59), philanthropist and founder of Dublin's celebrated Rotunda Hospital, was born here; his father was the rector.

5 m. NE. is Shaen Castle (restored). Close by are remnants of a castle and a manorial church. In the nearby Protestant church of Coolbanagher is an interesting, 15th cent., carved font from a church which stood in the demesne of Emo Court (*see under* Ballybrittas). Built into the outer face of the S. wall is a noteworthy

Portarlington mausoleum by Gandon. Cool-banagher is the Cúil Beannchair where St Lughaidh (mac Lucht?) founded a monastery and where Óengus Céle Dé commenced his famous *félire* (*see* Dysertenos *under* Stradbally, Co. Laois).

4 m. E. is Dunamase (*see under* Stradbally, Co. Laois).

4 m. SSE., near Ballyknocken Castle, is the Pass of the Plumes, where Eóghan, son of Rúairí O More, defeated Essex in 1599. The bog pass takes its name from the helmet-plumes which strewed the ground after the battle.

6 m. W. is Ballyfin House (*see under* Mount-rath).

PORTLAW, Co. Waterford (Map 6, A6), is a leather-tanning village in a lovely setting, where the S. road from Waterford (10 m.) to Carrick-on-Suir (7 m.) crosses the little Clodiagh River. The pioneer model village built by the Quaker Malcolmsons for the workers of their cotton-spinning mills (1825–1904) has been vulgarized out of recognition. The parish church (1859; tower completed 1910) is a characteristic piece by J. J. McCarthy, "the Irish Pugin". Adjoining the village on the W. is the beautiful demesne of Curraghmore. (Admission on the afternoons of Thursdays and Bank Holidays; apply to the Estate Office.) 1½ m. from the entrance gate is Curraghmore House, splendid 18th cent. seat of the Marquess of Waterford (Beresford). It incorporates a much altered castle of the le Poher de la Poer–Paor–Power family. (In 1717 Sir Marcus Beresford acquired the property by marrying Lady Catherine Power, Cáitlín Paor, heiress of the last Earl of Tyrone of the Power name.) The 18th cent. decorations include excellent stucco, wood-carving by John Houghton, and paintings by Peter de Gree and Antonio Zucchi (husband of Angelica Kaufmann). The family portraits include works by Sir Thomas Law-rence, Sir Joshua Reynolds, and Thomas Gainsborough. The courtyard is noteworthy. In the demesne is a Shell House made by Cáitlín Paor; it has a statue of her by J. van Nost, Jun.

3 m. N., in the neighbourhood of Mount Bolton and Fiddown bridge, the scenery is very beautiful.

1½ m. SE., at Kilbunny, called after St Munnu (of Taghmon), are remains of a church with rebuilt Romanesque doorway, fragments of a 17th cent. Power tomb, and a crude 17th cent. figure inscribed MONNINE EP[ISCOPUS].

1½ m. NW. is Clonagam Protestant church; the Beresford mausoleum has some interesting monuments. On the summit of Clonagam Hill (Tower Hill) is a bogus Round Tower (18th cent.). On the hill-side are the pieces of a large window from medieval Christchurch, Water-ford.

PORTMARNOCK, Co. Dublin (Map 6, D2), is a village and seaside resort 8 m. NE. of Dublin (via Marino and Coolock). There is an excellent 2-m. sandy beach (The Velvet Strand), backed by sand dunes in which is situated the 18-hole championship course of Portmarnock Golf Club.

The ruins of St Marnock's Church and St Marnock's Well preserve the memory of St Ernín, alias M'Earnóg, founder of an early church hereabouts. M'Earnóg was "famous and most renowned throughout all the churches of Scotland" (Adomnán, *Vita S. Columbae*), where his name is preserved in those of Kilmarnock and Inchmarnock (*see also* Rathnew *under* Ashford). In the Middle Ages the church and its property were acquired by St Mary's Abbey, Dublin, where the saint's relics were enshrined in a special altar.

3¼ m. SW. are St Doolagh's Church and Well (Nat. Mons.), St Catherine's Well, and an ancient granite cross. The stone-roofed church (about 1200) includes an anchorite's cell with St Doolagh's Tomb, a chapel, and a 15th cent., battlemented, square tower. There are living quarters over the cell and chapel, as also in the tower. The whole is thought to have been built to accommodate a small community (including a hermit), successors of the 6th/7th cent. hermit who gave his name to the church. The 19th cent. Protestant church (by Sloane) occupies the site of the medieval parish church. St Doolagh's Well (alias the Baptistry) is enclosed by a stone-roofed octagon; it is said to have been decor-ated with paintings, etc., put up by Peter Frayne of Feltrim and destroyed by Sir Richard Bulkeley of Old Bawn after the Battle of the Boyne. St Catherine's Well is a small sub-terranean chamber with a sunken bath. St Doolagh's Lodge nearby was long the home of Nathaniel Hone (1831–1917), friend of Corot (with whom he lived at Barbizon) and Ireland's greatest landscape and seascape painter.

PORTRUSH, Co. Antrim (Map 3, B2), is one of Ireland's popular seaside resorts. It is beautifully situated on Ramore Head promon-tory, 6 m. W. of Bushmills, 4 m. E. of Port-stewart, and 6 m. N. of Coleraine. It has two good beaches, 2-m. East Strand and 1-m. West Strand. One of its two golf courses, Royal Portrush, enjoys an international reputation. The town is within convenient reach of the Bann (grilse and sea trout) and the Giant's Causeway (*see under* Bushmills). Boating attractions include Skerries rocks, 1 m. off-shore, and the caves of White Rocks, 2 m. E.

3 m. E. is Dunluce castle (*see under* Bush-mills).

2 m. S., in Carnalbridge, is the White Wife (Nat. Mon.), a pillarstone.

1¼ m. SE., in Glebe, are remains (Nat. Mon.) of a church with Transitional and later features.

PORTSALON, Co. Donegal (Map 2, D1), is a little resort superbly situated at the N. end of Ballymastocker Bay on Lough Swilly, 10 m. NE. of Milford and 6 m. S. of Fanad Head. It is a convenient base for sampling the attractions (beaches, brown-trout lakes, etc.) of the Fanad peninsula to the N. and NW. All the high ground, notably Dargan Hill (570 ft), 1½ m. NW., and Murren Hill (754 ft), 1 m. further on, offer splendid views of Lough Swilly and the mountains of Inishowen to the E. and SE., and of Mulroy Bay, the N. Atlantic coast, and the Donegal Highlands to the W. and SW.

An excellent beach runs 2 m. SE. to Saldhanha Head (frigate *Saldanha* wrecked, 1811) where the Knockalla Mountains (1,203 ft) terminate in steep cliffs (19th cent. battery) opposite Dunree Head.

2 m. NNE. are the spectacular Seven Arches (sea tunnels).

5 m. N. are the cliffs and Great Arch of Doagh Beg.

6 m. NW. is Ballyhieran Bay with a 1-m. sandy beach.

8 m. WNW., on the E. side of lovely Mulroy Bay, are the beaches and dunes of Sessiagh, Gortnatraw, and Doagh More.

PORTSTEWART, Co. Derry (Map 3, B2), is a beautifully situated popular little seaside and golfing (two courses) resort 5 m. N. of Coleraine and 4 m. W. of Portrush. 1½ m. SW., beautiful Crossreagh beach (sandhills) runs 1½ m. W. to the mouth of the Bann.

Thackeray came to Portstewart in 1842 and visited Charles Lever (1806–72), the novelist, who practised as a physician there.

Sir George White, defender of Ladysmith and father of Capt. Jack White of the Irish Citizen Army, was born (1835) at Low Rock Castle.

PORTUMNA, Co. Galway (Map 5, C2), is a small market town at the head of Lough Derg, lowermost and loveliest of the River Shannon's great lakes. Córas Iompair Éireann launches provide lake and river tours during the summer.

Adjoining the town on the S. is the quondam demesne of Portumna Castle, sometime seat of the earls and marquesses of Clanricarde. The last marquess was a notorious miser and landlord. On his death the direct line of the ancient house of Mac William *Úachtair* Burke became extinct; the earldom passed to the Marquess of Sligo; the estates to the Earl of Harewood, who sold them. In the demesne

R. McGuffin

The harbour, Portstewart

are the ruins of the Clanricarde "castle" and of a Dominican friary (Nat. Mons.). The "castle", a semi-fortified house of 1609, was accidentally destroyed by fire in 1826. Its successor (at the opposite end of the park), built to the design of Sir Thomas Newenham Deane, was burned down in 1922. The Portumna estates originally belonged to the O Maddens, and passed to the Clanricarde Burkes only in the early 16th cent., when the heiress of Murchadh Óg O Madden married Richard Mór Mac William. In 1634 the notorious Earl of Strafford held an inquisition at the Burke castle to establish the title of the English Crown to the land of Connacht. In 1651 the castle was besieged by the Cromwellian, Ludlow; in 1690 the Jacobite garrison surrendered to Gen. Eppinger. To the SE. are the interesting ruins (c. 1426–1500) of the Dominican Observant friary (Ireland's first house of the Observance) founded c. 1425 by the O Maddens on the site of a chapel belonging to Dunbrody Abbey (*see under* Campile).

3½ m. NNE., to the E. of the Eyrecourt road, are the remains (tower and bawn) of the small castle of Derryhiveney (Nat. Mon.). Erected by Donal O Madden in 1643, it was one of the very last true castles built in Ireland. It has Jacobean and other interesting details; there was a residential hall along the side of the bawn opposite the great tower; small flanking towers stood at two opposite angles of the bawn.

5 m. WNW. is Kilcorban (*see under* Duniry).

7 m. WNW. is Pallas (*see under* Duniry).

6 m. E. is Lorrha, Co. Tipperary (*q.v.*).

7 m. SE., near the E. shore of Lough Derg, is Terryglass, Co. Tipperary, site of a celebrated Leinster monastery on Munster soil. Its founder was St Colm(án) moccu Cremthainn Áin (d. 549/552; *see* Clonenagh *under* Mountrath), who was of Leinster royal stock and one of the twelve principal disciples of Finnian of Clonard (*see under* Kinnegad). The monastery was intimately associated with Tallaght (*q.v.*) and Clonenagh in the céle Dé movement, and with Lorrha (*q.v.*). The celebrated Terryglass anchorite, Máel-Díthruib (d. 840), had been a member of Máel-Rúáin's community at Tallaght. A well-known 9th cent. tract on Tallaght was written at or near Terryglass. Terryglass also had important literary associations: Flann, son of Lonán (slain about 893), ollamh of Ireland and one of the three principal poets of Connacht, is said to have been buried with his father, mother, son, and three kings of Muskerry, in Tulach Mo-Chaíme in the middle of the monastery. He is the earliest Irish professional poet of whom any definite tradition survives. He was called "Devil's Son" because he was so satirical and burdensome", and it was believed he went to Hell for his avarice. Sometime between 1151 and 1224 Áed Úa Cremthainn, "lector of the High King of the Southern Half of Ireland", coarb of Colm moccu Cremthainn Áin and "prime historian of Leinster in wisdom, and knowledge, and book-lore,

and science, and learning", compiled and wrote the so-called *Book of Leinster* at the behest of Bishop Finn of Kildare. From Tallaght came some of the material used in this great codex, which "sums up all the learning of the monastic period of Irish writing". (The MS. was first called the *Book of Leinster* – which it is not – in 1743. From the 14th cent. to that date it had always been known as *Leabhar na Núachong-bhála*, Book of Noughaval; *see* Stradbally, Co. Laois.) The abbey of Terryglass disappears from history after 1164, and its church was parochial in the Middle Ages. Few remains have survived the wars and religious revolutions. (Such as they are, their neglected condition is no credit to a nation which can be inordinately proud of its past.) Beside the decaying Protestant church are two walls of a relatively large church with trabeate W. door; also some medieval fragments. There are also some fragments in the Catholic churchyard, ½ m. NE. – ½ m. NW., by the lake shore, are the truncated ruins of Old Court, keep of a 13th cent. castle of Irish type which was probably built (by John Marshall ?) at the time of the Anglo-Norman (Butler) conquest of Ormond. This, despite its quite insignificant history and its fragmentary condition, has been taken into State care, while illustrious Terryglass Abbey is consigned to oblivion!

8 m. W. is Abbey (*q.v.*).

POYNTZ PASS, Co. Armagh (Map 3, B5), is a village (dating from 1790) on the Portadown (11 m.) – Newry (9 m.) road. There is now no trace of the castle where Lieut. Sir Toby Poyntz fought desperately to prevent Hugh O Neill from entering Down (1598).

½ m. SE., in Killysavan, Co. Down, and 1 m. NE. in Loughadian, are portions of the Dane's Cast (Nat. Mon.), a great travelling earthwork defending the frontier of the kingdom of the Ulaid in protohistoric times (*see* Scarva; *also* Killyfaddy *under* Armagh).

2 m. S., in the demesne of Drumbanagher House, are Tyrone's Ditches, earthworks constructed by Great Hugh O Neill in the course of the Nine Years' War.

QUIN, Co. Clare (Map 5, B3), a village 3 m. E. of the Ennis (4 m.)–Limerick (11 m.) road, is noted for its Franciscan friary (Nat. Mon.), allegedly the first Observantine house in Ireland.

The ruins, on the E. side of the little River Rine, admirably illustrate the architecture and arrangements of the medieval friaries: church (nave, chancel, S. transept, and belfry) and the usual conventual buildings grouped round an attractive cloister. They occupy the site, and cleverly incorporate part of the fabric, of a great castle built by Thomas de Clare, Anglo-Norman invader of Thomond (*see* Bunratty), and destroyed by the Irish in 1286. The friary was founded by Mac-Con MacNamara about 1433 and completed about 1450. There are many interesting tombs, including that of "Odo" (=Aodh) MacNamara, about 1500.

On the W. side of the river is St Finghin's Church (Nat. Mon.), a plain, aisleless, parish church of the early 13th cent. The E. window is a triple lancet, while the S. window is richly moulded. The SW. turret is an addition.

¾ m. ENE., in Danganbrack, is a lofty, gabled, 16th cent. tower with angle machicolations and tall chimneys. There are many other ruined MacNamara castles in the area.

1½ m. NNE., in Ballyhickey (close to Hazelwood House), is Cromlech, a wedge-shaped gallery grave.

2½ m. NE., in Toonagh (N. of Hell Bridge), is Magh Adhair, inauguration place of the kings of Dál gCais and their descendants, the O Brien kings of Thomond. A flat-topped, ditched mound (Nat. Mon.) is probably the scene of the ceremony. A small tumulus and a pillarstone (W. of river; survivor of two) proclaim the pre-Christian sanctity of the place. 500 yds SSW. is Cahercalla, a great, trivallate, stone ringfort.

3 m. SSW. is Mooghaun (*see under* Newmarket-on-Fergus).

RAGHLY, Co. Sligo (Map 2, A4), is a hamlet at the neck of a low promontory of the same name, on the W. side of Drumcliff Bay, some 9 m. W. of Drumcliff. The promontory offers a superb view of the mountains ringing Sligo Bay. Near the hamlet are the Pigeon Holes, two open rock basins into which the tide rushes with great force through underground channels. To the N. is sandy Tráigh Bhuí, alias Yellow Strand.

2 m. NNE., in Ballintemple (Beoláin), the ruins of the little church of Teampall Beoláin lie almost smothered in the sands, which first encroached on this area in the 18th cent. Since then hundreds of acres of farmland and many homesteads have been engulfed. The Ó Beoláins (Bolands) were hereditary erenaghs of Drumcliff (*q.v.*).

¾ m. NE. are the ruins of Ballymuldorry, alias Ardtermon, Castle, a 17th cent. fortified house with flanking towers and traces of a bawn. It was built by Sir Nathaniel Gore, ancestor of the Gore-Booths of Lissadill (*below*). ¾ m. ENE., on the N. slope of Cloghcor hill, is Druid's Altar, a ruined chamber tomb. – 1 m. E. of the castle, to the S. of the road in Cloghcor, is another. – 2½ m. NE. of the castle, just off the road to Lissadill, are the ruins of Dunfore, a stone ringfort with four souterrains. Nearby are the battered remnants of Dunfore Bawn, alias The Bawn, a 17th cent. O Hart stronghold.

4½ m. NE., 300 yds apart in Breaghwy, are the remains of two chamber tombs. Not far away is Doonan, a cairn.

4½ m. ENE. is beautifully situated Lissadill Demesne (open to the public). Lissadill House, a good Classical house of the 1830s, was the birthplace of the Arctic explorer, Sir Henry Gore-Booth (1843–1900), and of his remarkable daughters, Eva Gore-Booth (1870–1926), poetess, and Constance Gore-Booth, Countess Markievicz (1884–1927), who was condemned to death for her part in the 1916 Rising, but was spared. In 1918 she was elected the first woman member of the British House of Commons, but took her seat in Dáil Éireann instead. – W. of the bohereen leading from the back gate of the demesne to Ballinphull Protestant church is a fine tumulus. – At the turn of the 12th/13th cent. Lissadill was the home of the celebrated poet, Muireadhach Albanach ("Scottish") O Daly, brother of the even greater poet, Donnchadh Mór O Daly (*see* Boyle Abbey), and ancestor of the Mac Vurich (Mac Mhuireadhaigh) family "who more than any other race of bards maintained the Irish tradition in Scotland". About 1213 a tax-gatherer of O Donnell's, Fionn Ó Brolacháin by name, came to Lissadill to levy taxes. He insulted the poet, who promptly hewed him down with an axe. Fearing O Donnell's justice, O Daly sought refuge in Thomond, but was pursued by O Donnell's vengeance there, and thence to Limerick, and even to Dublin. In the end the poet fled to Scotland, where his art found fruitful patronage and his devotion a wife. During his exile he seems to have gone with a Scottish contingent on the Fifth Crusade (1217), and poems written by him in the Adriatic survive. In one of them he still sighs for Lissadill:

"How peaceful would my slumbers be
   In kind O Conor's fair demesne,
   A poet in good company
   Couched upon Éire's rushes green."
                              (trans. Robin Flower)

1½ m. NW., overlooking the Yellow Strand, is Knocklane Hill (189 ft), which is reputed to be haunted by the Baintighearna Bhán or White Lady, i.e. the white-robed ghost of the wife of Sir Nathaniel Gore of Ardtermon, which rides in a chariot drawn by golden-shod horses. The coast hereabouts has been severely eroded, and the tides make their way with tremendous force into subterranean channels at Roskeeragh Point to the west.

RAHENY, Co. Dublin (Map 6, E7), is a suburban village on the Dublin (5 m.)–Howth (4 m.) road.

The Catholic church (1960–62), one of the few good recent Dublin churches, is by Louis Peppard and Hugo Duffy; the porch is an echo of the Romanesque pediment at Clonfert.

St Assam's Church (C. of I.) was Patrick Byrne's last work (1863–64); Lord Ardilaun paid for it.

Belcamp Hall is now the College of Mary Immaculate. The chapel has twelve windows by Harry Clarke (1925): *Medallion of the Blessed Virgin, Medallion of St Joseph, SS Columcille, Dúileach, Damhnait, Brigid, Brendan, Maol M'Aodhóg, Lorcán O Toole, Eithne and Fedhlim, Gobnait, Patrick.*

1¾ m. NE., by the seashore, are the scant remains of Kilbarrack church, originally a dependency of Ireland's Eye (*see under* Howth). Mariners imperilled by the treacherous sands of Dublin Bay used to make their votive offerings here. In the church are buried James McNeill (1869–1938), second Governor-General of the Irish Free State, and his brother, Eoin Mac Neill (1867–1945), founder of the Gaelic League, founder and Commander of the Irish Volunteers, first Free State Minister of Education, and an eminent historian.

RANDALSTOWN, Co. Antrim (Map 3, C4), a linen and market town N. of Lough Neagh, on the Belfast (22 m.)–Antrim (5 m.)–Derry (43 m.) road, is attractively sited by the River Main, which flows from N. of Ballymena into the lake.

South of the town is Shane's Castle Park. (Open to the public, Easter to 30 Sept.; entrance by the main gate; 5/- per car. Lord O Neill's 1964 house – by Arthur Jury – and its gardens are not open to the public.) A 2½-m. avenue leads through the decaying demesne (many splendid trees) to the lakeshore remains of Lower Clannaboy O Neill castles and of the mansion which succeeded them. In the demesne are also two motte-and-bailey earthworks, Dunmore, alias The Mount, and Mac Donnel's Fort.

4 m. SW. in Churchtown, by Lough Neagh, are the remains (Nat. Mon.) of the small 13th cent. church of Cranfield (Creamhchoill). Close by is St Colman's Well, which remained a popular place of pilgrimage until well into the nineteenth century. "Cranfield pebbles", crystals of gypsum from the well, were believed to save men from drowning, women from the perils of childbed.

RAPHOE, Co. Donegal (Map 2, D3), is a village on the Stranorlar (10 m.)–Derry (16 m.) road.

Raphoe's place in history is due to a monastery founded by the celebrated scholar and ecclesiastical statesman, St Adomnán (*c.* 624–704), ninth abbot of Iona and author of a famous *Life* of his kinsman, St Columcille. The monastery had a collection (still extant in 1627) of documents relating to Adomnán, including the celebrated *Cáin Adomnáin*. At the 12th cent. Reformation Raphoe became the see of the diocese (established for Tír Chonaill) which still bears its name. After the English conquest of Ulster, George Montgomery, a Scotsman who had been chaplain to James I, was installed as first (1605–10) Protestant bishop. In 1835 the Protestant diocese was united with Derry. The post-Penal Catholic cathedral is at Letterkenny (*q.v.*).

Nondescript St Eunan's (=Adomnán's) Cathedral (C. of I.), re-edified in 1892 by Sir Thomas Drew, occupies the site of the medieval cathedral and its predecessors. In the tower (1737) porch is a fragment of a lintel *Crucifixion* from a doorway of Maghera (Co. Derry) type; another fragment is built into the outer face of the N. wall of the church. In the S. wall of the chancel are 13th cent. sedilia. In the S. porch are some carved fragments.

SE. of the cathedral is the ruined bishop's palace, a stronghouse erected about 1640 by Bishop John Lesley (who demolished the ancient Round Tower for building material). Besieged by Confederate Catholics in 1641, by Cromwellians in 1650, and by Jacobites in 1688, it was rebuilt in 1695 and Georgianized in the following century. In 1839 it was destroyed by fire.

2 m. S., on the summit of Tops Hill, is Beltany (*sic*) Ring (Nat. Mon.). The sixty-four surviving stones (one with cup marks) of the ring encircle a low platform 145 ft in diameter. SE. is an outlying pillarstone.

RATHCONRATH, Co. Westmeath (Map 2, D7), is a small village on the Mullingar (7 m.)–Ballymahon (10 m.) road. It takes its name (*ráth chonartha*) from the adjacent, trivallate ringfort; souterrains. The neighbouring townlands (particularly Milltown, Ballyglass, Rathtrim, and Kilpatrick) to the NW., N., and NE.. are rich in ringforts and other ancient remains. (The monuments in Ballyglass include an Anglo-Norman motte, and Liagán – three large stones set together – and the King's Grave, remnant of a prehistoric chamber tomb.) In the graveyard of the ruined medieval parish church of Rathconrath is the burial-place of the D'Altons, an Anglo-Norman family which held estates in Co. Westmeath until modern times.

A short distance SW. of the village, in Ballinlug, is Mweeleen Moat, a tumulus.

1¾ m. NE., in Kilpatrick, is Crocaphuca, a tumulus. ¼ m. W. is Kilpatrick Fort. ¼ m. N. of the latter are the ruins of a 15th cent. fortified church of Taghmon (*see under* Castlepollard) type.

1½ m. SSW. is Mount Dalton, birthplace of Gen. James D'Alton and his brother, Count Richard D'Alton, Governor of the Austrian Netherlands (d. 1790). The general built a new house here in 1784, at the back of which he and his brother erected a pyramidal monument ("Loughan Spire") with marble profiles of the Empress Maria Theresa, the Emperor Joseph II, and George III. Near the site of the medieval D'Alton castle is a cave. W. of Mount Dalton demesne, near Clonaboy crossroads, is Farthingstown pillarstone.

4 m. SSW. is the Hill of Ushnagh (*see* Killare *under* Ballymore).

3 m. WSW., in Tobercormick, to the NW. of Hallstown House, is Cruachán na gCeann, an irregularly triangular mound which local tradition holds to be the burial place of the heads of those slain in a battle nearby at Washford.

2 m. WNW. is Skeaghmore Hill (426 ft). A body of the United Irishmen of Westmeath assembled here in Sept. 1798, with a view to assisting Gen. Humbert's Franco-Irish force.

Only some of them joined the active insurgents at Wilson's Hospital (*see under* Multyfarnham). On the summit is Carraig na Muice, an outcrop with "two marks on it made by the Black Pig" to which is attributed the Black Pig's Dyke (*see under* Granard). On the ridge of the hill is a pillarstone.

3 m. WNW. is Mearscourt, named after the Meares family; it incorporates a late Jacobean house.

10 m. NW., in Emper, is Rathduff, a ringfort with an elaborate souterrain. In the shorter of the two passages is a wallstone with a cup mark, a double concentric circle, and other Bronze Age scribings.

RATHCOOLE, Co. Dublin (Map 6, D7), is a village on the Dublin (11 m.)–Kildare (23 m.) road. At the W. end of the village, near the Newcastle Lyons road, is St Brigid's Well. In the old churchyard is an ancient granite cross with traces of carving.

Felix Rourke, who was a well-known member of the United Irishmen, was born here. He took part in the Rising of 1798, and again in Emmet's Rising of 1803. Captured after the latter, he was taken home to Rathcoole to be hanged.

4 m. SW. is Kilteel, Co. Kildare. Close to the S. side of the by-road leading SE. are scant remains (Nat. Mon.) of the early monastery, Cill tSiaghail, which names the place: remnants of a nave-and-chancel church with fragments of a Late Romanesque chancel arch (figurations of *The Fall, Samson and the Lion, David with Goliath's Head*, etc.); the nave is later medieval; outside the W. wall of the churchyard is the lintel of a trabeate doorway. N. of the churchyard is a fragment of a medieval gateway; to the W. is another medieval fragment. SW. of the road-junction, and close to the E. side of the Rathmore road, are fragments (Nat. Mon.) of a High Cross. SSE. is "Kilteel Castle" (Nat. Mon.): a gateway with flanking tower. This and the other medieval fragments are relics of a commandery of the Knights Hospitaller of St John of Jerusalem, an important border fortress of the English Pale, founded by Maurice fitz Gerald, 2nd Baron O ffaly (d. 1257). In 1541 Henry VIII granted the commandery to Norfolk-born Thomas Alen (*see* St Wolstans *under* Celbridge). 2 m. SW. are remains of Rathmore, a large multivallate motte on top of a prehistoric cemetery. It has been attributed to Gerald fitz Maurice, 1st Baron O ffaly. The manor was the property of his descendants until Silken Thomas's rebellion (1534).

3 m. W. is Athgoe (*see under* Newcastle Lyons).

RATHCORMACK, Co. Cork (Map 5, C6), is a village on the Fermoy (5 m.)–Cork (16 m.) road, 2 m. SW. of Castlelyons.

3 m. N. is Carn Thiernagh (*see under* Fermoy).

1½ m. SSE., in Kilshannig churchyard, Ballinterry, is the gravestone of a Knight Templar from Mourne "Abbey" (*see under* Mallow).

1½ m. S. is Kilshannig House, a good Georgian house.

2 m. SW., near Kildinan, are the remains of Shanaclogh, a castle of the Earls of Desmond.

RATHCROGHAN, Co. Roscommon (Map 2, B6), to the W. of the Bellanagare (4½ m.)–Tulsk (3 m.) road, preserves the name of Cruachain, in Heroic epic and other early tales the seat of Ailill mac Máta who was King of Connacht by virtue of his marriage to "Queen" Medb (Meadhbh, Maeve; cf. English "Queen Mab"). Medb had previously been "wife" of King Conor mac Nessa of Ulster and of Tinne and Eochaid Dála of Connacht. She had a double in Medb Red-side, "wife" in turn of a King of Leinster and of three kings of Tara (Feidlimid Rechtaid, his grandson, Art, and the latter's son, Cormac). Medb Red-side "would not allow a king in Tara without his having herself to wife; and by her was built the royal rath on the side of Tara, viz. Rath Maeve" (*see* Tara). Plainly there was only one Medb. Plainly, too, she was a goddess. Her name is cognate with words in Irish, Welsh, English, and other languages, which signify intoxication. The reign of each Irish pagan king was inaugurated by a mystic marriage to a goddess. The "marriage" may have taken the form of a ritual beer-banquet which induced a "divine" intoxication of the new king.

As the seat of "sacred" kings, Cruachain had a religious significance which is exemplified by ancient references to its royal cemetery and to its Otherworld entrance.

In early literature the name Cruachain can refer to the great limestone plain (Magh nAoí, Machaire Chonnacht) of the Roscommon–Elphin–Strokestown–Castlereagh area, seat in protohistoric and early historic times of the Uí Briúin kings of Connacht descended from Brión, allegedly a half-brother of Niall Ninehostager of Tara. The Uí Briúin still dominated the plain in the 12th–13th cent., the ruling family being the O Conors of Connacht, whose representative, O Conor Don(n), still has an estate at Clonalis, Castlereagh, 12 m. SW. of Rathcroghan.

The Rathcroghan countryside is still rich in field monuments, of which only a selection can be offered here. Rathcroghan crossroads provide a convenient focal point for the visitor.

½ m. SSE. of the crossroads, in Toberrory, to the W. of the Tulsk road, is Rathcroghan itself, a large mound crowned with a small, degraded ring-barrow. (There was another ring-barrow 80 yds E.) 120 yds NNE. is Misgaun Meva, "Medb's Lump", a prostrate pillarstone; 100 yds W., in the next field, is Milleen Meva, "Medb's Mill", a block of stone. The field fence S. of Rathcroghan follows the line of an ancient roadway.

½ m. ESE. of Rathcroghan a bohereen leads

S. from the Tulsk road. About 750 yds S. of the junction a field path leads W. for ¼ m. to Knockannagorp, "Hillock of the Corpses", alias Dathi's Grave, a partly artificial mound (non-burial) enclosed by a bank and surmounted by a pillarstone. Less than 300 yds W. are remnants of a stone ringfort with a souterrain. 240 yds N. of this is a ruinous circular enclosure identified as Reilig na Ríogh, "The Cemetery of the Kings", by Charles O Conor of Belanagare (*q.v.*), but shown by excavation not to be a burial-place. 300 yds NW. is Oweynagat, "Cave of the cats", a limestone fissure with souterrain "vestibule", two of whose lintels bear ogham inscriptions. This is generally taken to be the Otherworld entrance ("Cave of Rathcroghan") of mythological literature. 60 yds NW. is a ring-barrow and 600 yds NNW. is Rathnadarve (*below*). 400 yds SW. of Oweynagat are Mucklaghs, two bivallate linear earthworks, one of which continues 600 yds SW. to the remnants of Cashelmanannan, "Manannán's Fort", a stone ringfort with annexes on W. and E. 800 yds ESE. of the fort (about ½ m. S. of Oweynagat) is Cloghannagorp, remnant of a chamber tomb (?).

180 yds SSW. of Rathcroghan crossroads, on a roadside knoll, is Rathbeg, a bivallate ring-barrow. 600 yds SSW. is roadside Rathnadarve, a large univallate ringfort; an ancient roadway led E. past Rathcroghan.

300 yds NW. of Rathcroghan crossroads, in Toberrory, is roadside Rathmore, a univallate ringfort. 150 yds SW., in Moneylea, a low tumulus (ring-barrow ?) serves as a farmyard dump. Futher SW. are remains of linear earthworks, including a short stretch of roadway (?) between two banks.

1¼ m. NNE. of Rathcroghan crossroads, to the E. of the Elphin road, in Grallagh, is a small, high, univallate tumulus.

½ m. NE. of Rathcroghan crossroads, in Toberrory, to the S. of a bohereen leading E. from the Elphin road, is a small tumulus. 400 yds E., to the N. of the bohereen, is Caran Fort, a univallate "ringfort" with an annexe on the N. and remains of a complex of linear earthworks; in the annexe are a souterrain (closed) and a small round barrow 10 ft high; the linear earthwork on the W, side continues S. to join an "avenue" leading E. to Rathscreg (*below*). 400 yds SE. is Courtmoyle (the Ordnance Survey's "Rathscreg"), a subrectangular earthwork. 300 yds ESE. of this is Rathscreg, a knoll enclosed by a low bank and crowned by a small tumulus inside a ringwork; on the E. side is a small rectangular enclosure. Caran Fort, Courtmoyle, and Rathscreg are linked by a complex of "avenues" and other linear earthworks. 300 yds NE. of Rathscreg is the well, Toberrory; some 170 yds E. is a complex earthwork (medieval ?).

6 m. S. of Rathcroghan is Carnfree (*see under* Tulsk), inauguration place of the kings of Connacht.

RATHDOWNEY, Co. Laois (Map 5, E3), is a small market town, noted for its beer, on the Abbeyleix (12 m.)–Templemore (11 m.) road.

Ledwich, the noted 18th cent. antiquary, was curate here for a time (*see* Aghaboe).

2 m. E., in Middlemount (Ballyvoghlaun), is Laragh motte, relic of a castle of Adam de Hereford (?).

4½ m. W. is Errill, where the ruins of St Kieran's Church (Nat. Mon.) and a monastic site (Nat. Mon.) preserve the memory of a foundation by St Cíarán of Saighir (*see under* Birr; *also* Fertagh *under* Urlingford). At the nearby crossroads are portions of a cross (Nat. Mon.) erected in 1622 to the memory of Florence Mac Gillapatrick (Fitzpatrick), baron of Upper Ossory, and of Katherine O More, his wife. They had both died in 1613.

2 m. NW., in Donaghmore, are a motte and remains of a manorial church.

RATHDRUM, Co. Wicklow (Map 6, D4), is a village perched above the Avonmore, at the SE. end of the Vale of Clara. It is a convenient road centre, 6 m. SW. of Wicklow, 9 m. NW. of Arklow, 7½ m. NE. of Aughrim, 8 m. E. of Glenmalure, and 6 m. SE. of Laragh. The parish church of SS Mary and Michael (1856–60) is by J. J. Mc Carthy.

6 m. N. is Parkroe Giants Grave, two pillarstones 26 ft apart. 160 yds to the SE. are the remains of a small cairn with central chamber.

1½ m. S. is Avondale (1779), birthplace and home of Charles Stewart Parnell (1846–91), the great Home Rule leader; it is now a State forestry school. Noteworthy features are: the Parnell museum, the Professor Henry memorial grove, the arboretum, the trial plots, and the seed-extraction nurseries. ½ m. further S., in Kingston, is a 7-ft pillarstone.

3½ m. S. the Avonmore is joined by the Avonbeg in that "Meeting of the Waters" made famous by Thomas Moore's song. Beside the Meeting is the skeleton of a tree in whose shade the poet is said to have dreamed away many an hour. The valley here is still charming, despite the scars of the railway and the many copper pyrites mines. It is dominated from the E. bank by the beautifully timbered demesne of Castle Howard. Behind Castle Howard is Cronebane (816 ft), worth climbing for the view; on the summit is the Mottha Stone, legendarily the hurling stone of Finn Mac Cool. From the "Meeting of the Waters" to Arklow, the Avonmore nowadays goes by the name, Avoca (Ovoca), given it by a pedant who identified it with Ptolemy's 'Oβoxa.

8 m. S. is Woodenbridge (*see under* Arklow). 2¼ m. SW., near the mouth of Glenmalure (*q.v.*), is the small village of Ballinaclash. 1 m. S. is Whaley Abbey, whose name recalls the notorious "Burn Chapel" Whaley and his son, "Buck" Whaley (*see* 85 St Stephen's Green, Dublin, Main Axis). The "abbey" ruins nearby

are those of the monastery of All Hallows; a 9th/10th cent. gravestone found here in 1880 is in the National Museum. 1½ m. SW. of the "abbey", in Mongnacool Lower, is Labbanasigha, alias the Fairy's Bed or Fairy House, a wrecked gallery grave; 270 yds NNW. is a large granite erratic with five cup marks. To the W. is a second cup-marked stone; to the NW. of the latter is a stone with cup marks and grooves.

RATHFARNHAM, Co. Dublin (Map 6, D7), is a village and suburb at the foot of the Dublin mountains, 4 m. SW. of the city centre. The village is a convenient starting-place for delightful mountain walks and tours via Rockbrook (*below*) to Glencullen (*see under* Stepaside) and Kiltiernan (*see under* Golden Ball), or via Killakee (*below*) to Glencree (*see under* Enniskerry) or Sally Gap (*see under* Roundwood) and beyond.

Beside the village is Rathfarnham Castle. Since 1913 a Jesuit House of Studies, this massive Elizabethan castle was built about 1585 by Archbishop Loftus, who had acquired an estate here, forfeited to the Crown by the rebellion of James Eustace, Viscount Baltinglass. At the outbreak of the 1641 war it was garrisoned by the Royalists, who held it until Ormonde handed over Dublin to the Parliamentarians in 1647. In 1649, the Royalists retook it by storm the day before the battle of Rathmines. In the 18th cent. castle and lands passed through various hands (including those of Speaker Conolly of Castletown, Celbridge, *q.v.*). In 1767 they were bought by Nicholas Loftus, 2nd Earl of Ely, descendant of Archbishop Loftus. Henry Loftus, Earl of Ely and 4th Viscount Loftus, built the triumphal-arch gateway by the Dodder and Georgianized the castle on a splendid scale. Much of the interior decoration by Angelica Kaufmann and other artists still survives. The adjacent Retreat House incorporates Cromwell's Barn (a 16th/17th cent. fortified barn in which Cromwell is alleged to have held a Council); the chapel has eight windows (1928) by Harry Clarke: *Lamb of God; Wounds of Christ;* three-light *St Joseph, Sacred Heart, Virgin and Child; St Ignatius; St Patrick; St Brendan; St Peter; St Paul.*

½ m. SE. is Loreto "Abbey", which incorporates a good early Georgian house built for William Palliser. At the time of the Union it was occupied by George Grierson, the King's Printer. The convent chapel has sculptures by John Hogan (1800–1858). ¾ m. E. of the "abbey" is Hall's Barn, erected about 1742 by a Major Hall; this curious structure was probably modelled on the Wonderful Barn at Castletown, Celbridge. – ½ m. S. of the "abbey" are the meagre remains of Priory, home of John Philpot Curran. On the opposite side of the road is Hermitage, where Robert Emmet courted Sarah Curran; the place, then called Fields of Odin, was the home of Edward

Hudson, M.D., father of Henry Hudson (1798–1889) the collector of Irish folk music; in 1910 Patrick Pearse set up the famous Coláiste Éinne (St Enda's College) here. ½ m. ESE. of Hermitage is Marlay, sometime residence of David La Touche, the 18th cent. banker; it has stucco by Michael Stapleton. 1 m. S. of Marlay, in Glynsouthwell demesne, Taylor's Grange, is Brehon's Chair, remnant of a prehistoric chamber tomb. Adjoining Glynsouthwell demesne on the W. is St Columba's College, a Church of Ireland boarding school run on English public school lines; the nucleus of the school is Holly Park, built about 1780 by tobacco manufacturer, Lundy Foot.

1½ m. S., at Whitechurch, are the remains of a small, medieval, nave-and-chancel church. By the roadside is The Wartstone, base of an ancient cross.

4 m. SSE., via Whitechurch, is Larch Hill (Kilmashogue) chamber tomb (ruined).

5 m. S., via Ballyboden and Rockbrook, on the summit of Tibradden (1,441 ft), is a bogus passage grave (Nat. Mon.).

1½ m. SSW., in Ballyboden, is the Augustinian College of Our Lady of Good Counsel; this is an example (by F. J. Mc Cormack and David Keane) of monastic architecture in the current idiom.

3½ m. SSW., via Rockbrook, in Mount Venus demesne, Woodtown, is Mount Venus Cromlech (Nat. Mon.), a ruined chamber tomb with enormous granite capstone.

3¾ m. SSW., via Ballyboden and Woodtown, on the summit of Mountpelier (1,271 ft), are the ruins of a massive, 18th cent, sporting lodge, popularly, but erroneously, called Hell Fire Club; it is said to have been built – by Speaker Conolly – of the stones of a great cairn. The road to the S. via Killakee Mountain is the N. end of the Military Road constructed after 1798 to control the mountain fastnesses. Noted for its scenery, it leads via Glencree–Sally Gap–Cloghoge–Glenmacnass–Laragh–Glenmalure–Aghavanagh to within 4 m. of Tinahely, keeping for much of the way to a great height.

RATHFRYLAND, Co. Down (Map 3, C6), on the Newry (11 m.)–Downpatrick (21 m.) road, is a village set on a conspicuous hill (506 ft) dominating the plain anciently called Magh Cobha. It takes its name from the large, but defaced, *ráth* or ringfort which lies towards the E. This was for long a seat of the petty kings of Iveagh, whose descendant, Art Magennis, 1st Viscount Iveagh, built (about 1611) the castle represented by the scant remains on the hill top. After the War of 1641–52, the Magennis estates were confiscated and were granted to Alderman Hawkins of London.

The Rev. Henry Boyd (d. 1832), translator of Dante, was rector of Rathfryland.

The area is rich in legends of Finn mac Cool, with whom popular legend associates several of the local prehistoric tombs (*see also* Hilltown).

5½ m. NE. is Ballyroney motte, with three extensive baileys. ½ m. SSE., on a hillock on the opposite bank of the Bann, is Seafin castle, stone successor of the motte-and-bailey castle. It was built in 1252 by the English Justiciar, Maurice fitz Gerald. Captured and wrecked the following year by Brian "of the Battle of Down" O Neill, King of Tír Eóghain, it was not restored until 1260. Nothing is known of its subsequent history, but it presumably fell to the Magennises in the 14th cent. These two castles were obviously designed in turn to command the pass between Slieve Croob and the Mourne mountains to the plains of E. Down. Ballyroney was the birthplace of Mayne Reid (1818–83), author of *The Scalp Hunters* and *The Headless Horseman*.

1¾ m. SW., on Long Stone Hill, Barmeen, is the Long Stone, a prehistoric pillarstone 12 ft high.

5 m. NW. is Ballynaskeagh (*see under* Scarva).

3½ m. NNW., on the summit of Knockiveagh (788 ft), Edenagarry, is a plundered Neolithic round cairn. The site commands a very fine prospect.

RATHKEALE, Co. Limerick (Map 5, A4), is a small market town on the Limerick (18 m.)–Newcastle West (6½ m.) road.

The Desmond Fitzgeralds had a castle here, which was burned by Malby after the battle of Monasternenagh (*see under* Croom); only fragments survive. There are remains of St Mary's Augustinian priory founded in the 13th cent. by Gilbert Harvey. The Protestant church has a 1676 Southwell monument. The good Gothic Revival parish church is by J. J. Mc Carthy.

1 m. W. is Castlematrix (alias Matrascourt, Matrackscourt, etc.). The tower was repaired early in the 19th cent. James, 9th Earl of Desmond, was murdered here by his servants in 1487.

In 1709 the Rathkeale neighbourhood was settled by Lord Southwell with Calvinist refugees from the Rhenish Palatinate. Descendants of these Palatines are still to be found hereabouts, but they have been absorbed by the native population and most of them are now Catholics (*see* Kilfinnane). A very popular folksong is "Inghean an Phailitínigh" (The Palatine's Daughter).

3 m. NNE., in Cappagh, are the remains of Kilmacluana, a small, plain, Gothic church. ¾ m. WSW. are the remains of a late-15th cent. castle of the Knights of Glin; it had a double bawn (gatehouse and angle turret) and a lofty five-story tower. 2½ m. WNW. of Cappagh village, in Gorteennamrock, are remains of a fine stone ringfort.

4 m. ENE., at Croagh, are remains of a medieval church (cruciform; collegiate) and tower; in the neighbourhood are several ruined Geraldine castles.

2 m. S., in Rathnaseer, are remains of an ancient nave-and-chancel church.

5 m. S., via the Kilmeedy road, is Cloncagh (*see under* Newcastle West).

4 m. SW., in Ballyallinan, are remains of an O Hallinan, later Mac Sheehy (Desmond galloglas), castle, and of Beinid's Church.

RATHLIN ISLAND, Co. Antrim (Map 3, C2), lies 5 m. off the coast. It is most readily reached from Ballycastle (*q.v.*), from which there is a thrice-weekly motor-boat service to Church Bay, near the former manor house of the Viscounts Gage. The spectacular coast is for the most part cliff-bound, and is the haunt of great numbers of sea birds.

St Comgall is said to have visited the island; St Columcille to have founded a monastery there. Rathlin was the first place in Ireland to be attacked by the Vikings (A.D. 795). Robert Bruce, King of Scotland, found refuge there from the English in 1306. In 1597 the Antrim Mac Donnells placed their aged and infirm, their women and children, on the island for safety. English forces, however, sailed to the island and slaughtered the entire population. The island was deserted for years thereafter. In 1797 the islanders supported the United Irishmen almost unanimously.

Near the N. coast, 2 m. NW. of Church Bay, is Doonmore, a stone ringfort on a small, detached basalt outcrop.

1 m. NW. of Church Bay, near Knockans North, are an old sweat house and Kilvoruan, a dilapidated circular enclosure – probably ecclesiastical – having a subsidiary enclosure inside.

In Ballycarry, near the NE. corner of the island, is Bruce's Castle, a high promontory defended by a wall (crumbled) on the landward side. This is the setting of the story of Robert Bruce and the Spider. Nearby is Bruce's Cave, a fine, basalt cavern.

S. of Church Bay are some curious caves.

RÁTHLUIRC, Co. Cork (Map 5, B5), for long Charleville, previously Rathcogan, alias Rathgoggan, is a market town at the intersection of the Limerick (22 m.)–Mallow (18 m.) and Kilmallock (6 m.)–Drumcolliher (11 m.) roads. It was founded by Roger Boyle (1621–79), Lord Broghil, later Earl of Orrery (a son of Richard Boyle, "Great" Earl of Cork), who named the place after Charles II. Orrery's house, which stood in The Park, N. of the town, was burned down by the Jacobite Duke of Berwick in 1690.

¼ m. SSE., in the ruined church of Ballysallagh, is the grave (Latin epitaph) of Seán Clárach Mac Domhnaill (1691–1754), noted Gaelic poet; his works included a translation of Homer. His farm in Kiltoohig, to the W. of the town, was the meeting place of a "Court of Poetry" frequented by Liam Dall Ó Hiffearnáin, Seán Ó Tuama (1706–75), and Eóghan Rúa Ó Súilleabháin (d. 1784).

2½ m. SSE., in Ballyhay, are remains of a church with a gabled Romanesque doorway in the S. wall. The sole ornaments of the doorway are two "ox-head label-stop" masks.

4¼ m. SE. are fragments (Nat. Mon.) of the 12th cent. church of Ardskeagh. St Scíath is held to have founded a nunnery here in the 6th cent.

7½ m. WSW., in Kilbolane, are remains (Nat. Mon.) of a late 13th cent. Cogan – later Desmond – castle of Liscarroll type.

RATHMELTON, Co. Donegal (Map 2, C2), is a village of the Letterkenny (8 m.)–Milford (4 m.) road, where the Leannan River flows into Lough Swilly. It is well known as a centre for fishing the Leannan and the local lakes (including Lough Fern near Milford).

The ruined church has an interesting, degenerate, Perpendicular E. window (17th cent. ?); built into the wall above it is the head of a simply decorated, Romanesque window from Aughnish, an island in Lough Swilly, 4 m. (by road) NE.

3½ m. E. are remains of Fort Stewart, a Plantation castle.

2¾ m. SE. are the ruins of Killydonnell Franciscan Tertiary Friary, founded by the O Donnells in the 16th cent.

4¾ m. SW. is Carn Hill (797 ft); wide views.

RATHMULLAN, Co. Donegal (Map 2, D2), is a small port and holiday resort on the W. shore of beautiful Lough Swilly, 7 m. NE. of Rathmelton. There is a ferry service with Fahan (*see under* Buncrana) on the E. shore.

In 1587 the 15-year-old Red Hugh O Donnell was lured from Mac Sweeny of Fanad's castle, which stood by the beach, into an English merchantman and taken to Dublin Castle. This act of treachery towards a family friendly to the English was one of the causes of the great war (1595–1603) between the still Gaelic North and the English Crown. In 1591 Red Hugh contrived a daring escape and the following year succeeded to the lordship of Tír Chonaill (*see* Kilmacrenan). – On 14 Sept. 1607, the Earls of Tyrone (Great Hugh O Neill) and Tyrconnell (Rúairí O Donnell, Red Hugh's successor) sailed away to the Continent from Rathmullan. This tragic Flight of the Earls marked the final overthrow of the Gaelic order in its last great stronghold, and cleared the way for the Plantation of Ulster. – In 1798 Wolfe Tone and the other prisoners from the French warship, *Hoche*, crippled in a desperate fight with a superior English force off Lough Swilly, were landed near Rathmullan (*see* Buncrana).

At Rathmullan are remains of a Carmelite friary of the Blessed Virgin Mary, built by Eóghan Rúa Mac Sweeny in 1516. The church was adapted as a stronghouse (1617–18) by Bishop Knoxe, second Protestant bishop of Raphoe, who converted the choir into a domestic chapel. The friary had survived intact until 1595, when it was pillaged by English raiders

from Sligo, who also plundered Tory Island. In the ruins are fragments of a Mac Sweeny tomb.

Near the pier is a 19th cent. battery, one of the series built to defend Lough Swilly when it was a British naval station.

3½ m. NNW., in Drumhallagh Upper, is Giants Bed, the chambers of a court cairn. In Drumhallagh Lower is St Garvan's Grave, a small cairn with an 8th cent. cross-slab on which is carved a plaited cross with two angels (?) above and two ecclesiastics below the arms. Near the road, at the S. end of the adjacent townland of Killycolman, is a cross-inscribed pillarstone. 1 m. further NW. is Creeveoughter Giants Bed, while in Carrowreagh, the neighbouring townland to the NW. of Creevoughter, is Dermot and Grania's Bed: these are prehistoric chamber tombs.

2½ m. NW. is Croaghan Hill (1,008 ft), with Crockanaffrin (1,137 ft) beyond. They reward the climber with splendid views. On the NE. slope of Croaghan is the Druid's Altar, a prehistoric chamber tomb.

RATHVILLY, Co. Carlow (Map 6, C4), is a village beside the Slaney, on the Baltinglass (10 m.)–Tinahely (8 m.) road.

There is a large motte just beside the village; it commands a very fine prospect which takes in Lugnaquilla, Mount Leinster, Slievenamon, and Slieve Bloom. The pleasant little d'Israeli School is by Joseph Welland, Vice-President of the Royal Institute of the Architects of Ireland, 1849–50. It was built (1826) for Benjamin d'Israeli of nearby Beechy Park.

½ m. NNE. is St Patrick's Well, where, legend asserts, the saint baptized King Crimthann of Leinster.

1½ m. N., to the E. of the Baltinglass road, is Broughillstown grooved pillarstone.

4½ m. ESE. is Tombeagh grooved pillarstone.

2 m. SE. is Williamstown Gallán, alias The Six Fingers, a grooved pillarstone. Fionn Mac Cumhaill threw it, 'tis said, from Eagle Hill, Hacketstown. According to another story it rolls down to the nearby Derreen for a drink from time to time.

3½ m. SE., on the E. bank of the Derreen near Acaun bridge, is Haroldstown portal dolmen (Nat. Mon.), which was used as a dwelling house in modern times; the capstone appears to have been grooved artificially. In the vicinity are the remains of a church and a holy well. 5 m. W. is Straboe (*see under* Tullow).

RATOATH, Co. Meath (Map 6, C2), is a village between Ashbourne (4 m.) and Dunshaughlin (5 m.). Before 1186 Hugh I de Lacy built a castle here, now represented by a very fine motte-and-bailey. Hugh II de Lacy granted the church to St Thomas's Abbey, Dublin, about 1196.

Richard Pigott (1828–89), the notorious forger of the letters used by *The Times* to implicate Parnell in the Phoenix Park Murders, was born at Ratoath.

2 m. S. is Fairyhouse Race-course, where the Irish Grand National Steeplechase is run on Easter Monday.

REAR CROSS, Co. Tipperary (Map 5, C4), is a road-junction on the Limerick (18½ m.)–Thurles (21½ m.) road. There are numerous megalithic monuments in the hills hereabouts. 1½ m. NE., in the roadway in Baurnadomeeny, is Cloghfadda, a fine pillarstone (survivor of a pair). To the NE. is Pagan Burial Ground, a low Bronze Age cairn. 150 yds S. of the pillarstone is Dermot and Grania's Bed, a Late Neolithic/Bronze Age gallery grave.

1½ m. S., in Shanballyedmond, are a court cairn and a pillarstone. The cairn – heel-shaped – was edged by sixteen orthostats with dry walling in the intervals. 2½ yds out was a unique peristyle of thirty-four timber posts which linked up with the "horns" of the funnel-shaped (cf. Balix *under* Plumb Bridge), paved court in front of the two-segment gallery. There were six cremations in the tomb. The finds included "Western Neolithic" sherds, flint arrowheads, and Bann flakes.

3¾ m. E. (1½ m. SW. of Kilcommon village) is Anglesey Bridge. W. of the bridge, in a disused burial ground in Coonmore, is Giants Grave, a long, green mound. – 1½ m. SW. of the bridge, in Knockshanbrittas, is Cromlech, a ruined gallery grave; nearby to the N. is a second; there was formerly a third (Giants Grave), ¼ m. E. – 2 m. NE. of the bridge, in Loughbrack, is ruinous Dermot and Grania's Bed; this was much the largest chamber tomb in the whole area. ½ m. NE., high up on Knocknabansha, is Cromlech, remnant of another gallery grave; 1,000 yds NNE. of the latter is Reisk pillarstone (*below*). – 3 m. ENE. of Anglesey Bridge is Inch. ½ m. E., in Knockcurraghbola Crownlands, is Cromlech, remains of a gallery grave; 1½ m. NNE. is the Knockcurraghbola Commons tomb (*below*). – 3 m. E. of Inch is Shevry crossroads. 2 m. NW., in Knockcurraghbola Commons, is Cromlech, remains of a very fine wedge-shaped gallery grave. – 1½ m. NW. of Inch, on the E. side of the road, in Reisk, is a pillarstone; there was formerly a chamber tomb 450 yds SW. 5½ m. NW. of the pillarstone is Curreeny Commons (*see* Kilboy House *under* Nenagh).

RINVYLE, Co. Galway (Map 1, B5), is a promontory on the lovely N. coast of Connemara, 5 m. NNW. of Letterfrack and 16 m. W. of Leenaun. Grilse, sea-trout and brown trout may be had in local waters. The district offers a variety of rewarding tours and hill climbing. Rinvyle House Hotel, which stands close to a small beach, belonged for many years to Oliver St John Gogarty, surgeon, author, poet, and wit. On the E. shore of Rusheenduff Lough, in the hotel grounds, is Liagaun, a pillarstone.

1½ m. W. of the hotel are the ruins of the 14th cent. O Flaherty castle of Rinn Mhíl. To

the E. of the castle, in Ardnagreevagh, is a prehistoric chamber tomb; it appears to be set in the side of a small ringfort, now crowned by a cottage. 250 yds SW. of the castle, in Kanrawer, is the Well of the Seven Daughters, called after the saintly daughters of a British (=Welsh) king. SSW. of the well, in Cashleen, is the Church of the Seven Daughters. ¼ m. SE. of the well is Cashleen Giants Grave, a portal dolmen (?). ¾ m. W. of the church are the remains of the promontory fort, Caheradoona. ¼ m. SW. of the church, not far from the houses in Tonadooravaun, is Dermot and Grania's Bed, a fine gallery grave.

2 m. SSE. of Rinvyle House Hotel, in Derryinver (on the high ground SW. of Tully Lough), is an alignment of six pillarstones; to the SW. is a fragment of a chamber tomb (?). Tully Mountain offers splendid views.

¾ m. offshore, N. of Rinvyle House Hotel, is Crump Island, with remains of an early church. 2½ m. SE. is Tully Cross. The church has three windows by Harry Clarke (1926): *Sacred Heart, St Barbara, St Bernard*. 3½ m. ENE., in Lettergesh East, is a good beach (Gowlaun beach).

RIVERSTOWN, Co. Sligo (Map 2, B5), is a village on the Collooney (7 m.)–Kilmactranny (8 m.) road, to the N. of Lough Arrow.

2 m. E. are the remnants of Drumcolumb (Druim Choluimcille) church and the broken ring-head of a plain, stone cross. Columcille is said to have placed his disciple, Finnbárr, in charge of a monastery here. A stone figure ("St Columcille") survived in 1836.

3¼ m. SE., in Heapstown, is the great passage-grave-type cairn (Nat. Mon.) which has given its name to the townland. It is traditionally the grave of Ailill (son of Eochu Muigmedóin and brother of Niall Nine Hostager) who gave his name to Tirerrill (Tír Ailella, "Ailill's country"). 2 m. NE. is Lough Nasool ("of the eyes"), traditionally associated with Balor of the Baleful Eye (*see* Tory Island). It is reputed to dry up every 100 years, and last did so in 1933. – 1¼ m. SE. of the cairn is Kingsborough House. The planter Kings changed the name, Eanach Uí Bheathnacháin, Annagh Iveanaghan, to Kingsborough. Lame David Duignan (*see* Shancough *under* Kilmactranny) wrote part of the Royal Irish Academy MS., B. iv. I, in Mac Donagh's house in Annagh Iveanaghan, the storm on the lake disturbing his labours. 1¼ m. ENE. of Kingsborough House, in Ballindoon, are the ruins of a Dominican friary founded in 1507 by the Mac Donaghs, the site of whose castle is ½ m. SSE. of the friary. The church has a singular belfry cum rood screen (magnified) at the junction of nave and choir. In the cemetery lie buried Lame David Duignan (d. 1696) and, nearby, the celebrated Great Counsellor Terence Mac Donagh (d. 1717), patron of Roderick O Flaherty (*see* Park *under* Spiddal). SE. of the friary is Dominic's Well; N. of it is

St Dominic's Stone (with a bullaun). Also in Ballindoon, near the lake, are remains of a prehistoric chamber tomb. 1 m. NE. of the friary, in Carrickglass, is Leaba Dhiarmada agus Ghráinne, alias the Labby, a fine portal dolmen with 70-ton capstone.

1¾ m. SSW., the remains of Tawnagh church mark the site of a church attributed to St Patrick. ¼ m. N. is St Patrick's Well.

ROCHFORTBRIDGE, Co. Westmeath
(Map 6, A2), formerly An Droichead, alias Beggar's Bridge, is a hamlet on the Kinnegad (10 m.)–Tyrrelspass (4 m.) road. It is called after Dean Swift's friend, political renegade Robert Rochfort (1652–1727), M.P. for Westmeath and Speaker of the Dublin House of Commons. It was in Gallstown House, 1¾ m. NE., that Robert Rochfort (1708–72), 1st Earl of Belvedere, imprisoned his wife (see Belvedere under Mullingar). NE. of the ruined church is a fine motte.

1 m. NW., at Castlelost on the Mullingar road, a motte-and-bailey and a fragment of a stone castle mark the seat of the Anglo-Norman Tyrrels from the 13th cent. to the Cromwellian conquest. 400 yds N. are remains of a semi-fortified, manorial church. Here is the effigy of an armoured knight, probably Sir John Tyrrel (d. 1607).

ROSCOMMON, Co. Roscommon (Map 2, B7), capital of the county to which it gives its name, is a small town on the main Athlone (20 m.)–Sligo (53 m.) road.

The place takes its name from the abbot-bishop, St Commán, who founded a monastery here in the 6th cent. The monastery was plundered by the Vikings in 802, and burned by Munster forces in 1134. It was a fer légind of this monastery, Gilla Commáin Ó Conghaláin (d. 1135), who extracted from the famous Cín Drommo Snechta (see Drumsnat under Monaghan) the texts copied in 1564 into the British Museum manuscript, Egerton 88. In time the monastery became a house of Canons Regular of St Augustine, and as such survived down to the middle of the 16th cent. No trace of it survives. There are, however, remains (Nat. Mon.) of the church of the Dominican Friary of the Assumption founded in 1253 by Felim O Conor, King of Connacht, and consecrated in 1257 by Bishop Tomaltach O Conor. King Felim was buried in the friary in 1265. In 1308 the friary was destroyed by fire, but lived on. It was rebuilt in 1453 (N. transept, traceried windows, etc.), and the surviving fragments belong, in the main, to about that date. The most interesting feature is Felim O Conor's Tomb, in a canopied niche in the chancel. The effigy may be dated to the 13th cent., and is presumably that of King Felim; but the eight weepers (galloglas) are late 15th cent., and may belong to the tomb of Tadhg O Conor (d. 1464).

The Court House is by Sir Richard Morrison (1767–1849).

W. of the town, on the Tulsk road, are the ruins (Nat. Mon.) of the great castle built in 1269 by the English Justiciar, Robert d'Ufford, as a Crown fortress. It was wrecked by Aedh O Conor in 1272, but was rebuilt, and once more had an English garrison by 1280. By 1340, however, it had fallen into the hands of the O Conors, who held it, with brief inter-missions, until 1569, when the Lord Deputy, Sir Henry Sidney, took it from O Conor Don. In 1578 it was granted to Sir Nicholas Malbie, Elizabethan Governor of Connacht. In 1641 it was held for the Parliamentary faction, but was captured by Confederate Catholics under Preston in 1645. It remained in Irish hands until 1652, when it was surrendered to the Cromwellian Commissary, Reynolds, who dismantled the fortifications. The remains are those of a splendid, 13th cent. keepless castle which had an unusually fine twin-towered gate-house on the E., a subsidiary gate on the W., and four great D-shaped corner towers. About 1580 the interior was remodelled and large windows were inserted in the towers and in the curtain.

5 m. NE., in the grounds of Holywell House, are the remains of Kilbride (St Brigid's Church) and St Brigid's Well. The Gunning sisters, celebrated 18th cent. beauties, are said to have owed their complexions to the waters of this well.

4½ m. E. are the ruins of Kilteevan church. It has an unusual small E. window (15th/16th cent.). Nearby is a holy well.

12 m. ESE. is Rinndown (see under Le-carrow).

8 m. SE., in Scregg, is Leaba Dhiarmad's Ghráinne, alias the Clochogle Stone, a ruined wedge-shaped gallery grave.

3 m. S., in the old graveyard of Mote Park in Mote Demesne, are the base and shaft of a late stone cross with an inscription in raised letters.

4 m. WSW. is Fuerty, where an ancient churchyard and two early gravestones (S. of the church) mark the site of a Patrician foundation confided to Justus, baptizer and tutor of Cíarán of Clonmacnois (q.v.). The early monastery here was closely associated with Clonmacnois. One of the gravestones bears a fish symbol – rare in Ireland – and the inscription OR[ÕIT] AR ANMAIN AIDACAIN ("A prayer for the soul of Aidacán"). This may have marked the grave of the Áeducán, "tanist-abbot of Clon-macnois and abbot of many churches", who died in 865. The other has the inscription OR[ÕIT] AR MOR ("A prayer for Mór"). ½ m. NE., to the E. of the Ballymoe road, is Dermot and Grania's Bed, a ruined chamber tomb. – 1 m. W., on the River Suck, is Castle-coote, celebrated in the 18th cent. for its flour mills. Castlecoote was the home of John Gunning, father of the celebrated Gunning sisters. – 3½ m. NW. is Dunamon (see under Oran).

2½ m. NW. is Rathbrenan, two conjoined

ringforts with attached bailey. Nearby is a tumulus. 300 yds NW. are two rectangular earthworks with low banks; one has an irregular annexe on the N.

ROSCREA, Co. Tipperary (Map 5, D3), is a market town and manufacturing centre (bacon, meat-canning) where the Port Laoise (24 m.)– Nenagh (20½ m.) road, i.e. the main Dublin– Limerick road, crosses the gap between the Slieve Bloom and Devil's Bit mountains, 11 m. SE. of Birr. The Inland Fisheries Trust has a 20-acre fish farm nearby.

In the 6th/7th cent. St Crónán mac Odráin, patron of Éile (Ely), founded a monastery on a desert promontory (Ros Cré) of a nearby lake (Loch Cré). Before his death he founded a second monastery, on a site more convenient for travellers and the poor. (To this monastery belonged the so-called *Book of Dímma*, an 8th cent. illuminated gospel-book now in the library of Trinity College, Dublin.) Later a subsidiary foundation, on an island (Inchnameo *below*) in the lake, was prominent in the céle Dé movement (*see* Tallaght). Echtgus Úa Cuánáin, author of an 11th/12th cent. poem (in Irish) on the Real Presence, was a member of the Roscrea community. The monastery ceased to exist in the later 12th cent., and its church became parochial.

Commissioners of Public Works in Ireland
West door, St Crónán's Church, Roscrea

The strategic importance of Roscrea early attracted the attention of the Anglo-Normans, and about 1212 the English Justiciar erected a motte castle to command the pass. In 1280 this was replaced by a strong stone castle, which was granted the following year to Edmund Butler, father of the 1st Earl of Ormond, and which remained in the possession of the Ormonds until the Williamite conquest.

On the E. side of the town the Dublin road and Church St cut through the site of St Crónán's second monastery. The scant remains (Nat. Mons.) comprise a Round Tower (imperfect), figured High Cross (12th cent.), and the W. gable of a Romanesque church demolished by the Church of England and Ireland in 1812. The gable, which has projecting *antae*, was one of the more elaborate Irish Romanesque elevations: porch of two orders under a tangent gable and flanked by a blind arcade of four bays; in the pediment, the much-weathered figure of an ecclesiastic ("St Crónán"). To the S. of the gable stands the cross ("Shrine of St Crónán"); parts of the shaft and head are modern. The E. and W. faces of the shaft are decorated with interlaced vine patterns; on the W. face of the head is a *Crucifixion* in high relief; on the E. face of the head is the figure of an ecclesiastic; the N. and S. sides of the shaft each have a much-weathered figure in high relief. The imperfect Round Tower, on the opposite side of the street, has a simple Romanesque doorway.

The angle between Castle St and the Mall is occupied by the very fine, but shamefully neglected, castle of 1280, an irregular polygon whose curtain wall was flanked by two D-towers as well as the imposing, rectangular gate-tower. The gateway through the latter is now blocked up and the entrance is a 19th cent. gateway flanked by an uncouth wicket; the gables and chimney-stacks are 17th cent. additions. There were vaulted buildings within the curtain, where much of the space is now given over to derelict County Council stores and roadmakers' dumps. On the S. side of the courtyard is a good Queen Anne house built by the Damers, into whose possession the castle passed in the 18th cent. The derelict state of the house is deplorable.

On the S. side of the town, in Abbey St, are remains (E. and N. walls of chancel, belltower, part of N. nave arcade, etc.) of the church of a Franciscan friary founded before 1477. Maol-Rúanaigh na Féasóige O Carroll of Éile and his wife, Bébhinn O Dempsey, may have built a new church in 1490; O Carroll was buried in the church, 1523. The greater part of the ruins were demolished about 1800 by the builders of the adjacent parish church; some ornamental fragments are preserved at Birchgrove House (*below*). The surviving ruin serves as gateway to the parish church, a Gothic-Revival building commenced in 1844 to the design of Dane Butler, but not completed – because of the Great Famine – until after 1866, when the work was entrusted to J. J. Mc

Carthy. Facing the W. door is a block of stone with weathered figure- and other carvings. Thought by some to be the shaft of a High Cross, it was brought here from Timoney (Túaim Domnic) Park, i.e. from the church site of Garravaun, 5 m. SE.

3½ m. N., in Ballybritt, Co. Offaly, are the remains of an O Carroll of Éile castle. 1¾ m. NNW. is Leap Castle (Léim Uí Bhanáin, "O Bannon's leap"), burned down in 1922; the mansion incorporated an important O Carroll castle of various dates. From the Letterluna branch of the O Carrolls were descended the celebrated Carrolls of Carrollton, to whom James II assigned vast estates in Maryland, in recompense for lands lost in Éile at the Cromwellian settlement.

1¼ m. E., at Birchgrove House, are some Romanesque and Gothic fragments; the latter came from the Franciscan friary in Roscrea. 1½ m. SE. are Monahincha bog and a tiny lake, relics of historic Loch Cré, which was drained away about 1730. The bog is named after the former island (inis, "inch"), Inis na mBeó, Island of the Living, which was one of the Wonders of pre-Norman Ireland, the belief being that the dead could not decay there. There was a céle Dé (p. 27) community on the island, of which Hilary, the anchorite and scribe who died in 807, was a famous member. In time the community was joined by Arroasian Canons, the remains of whose little Priory of the Virgin Mary are known as Inchnameo Abbey (Nat. Mon.). They comprise a small stone cross, the ruins of a beautiful little Romanesque church (Urnes Style details), and a two-storey annexe of uncertain date. The W. door of the church is in three orders framed by pilasters; the S. pilaster had an inscription beginning OR[ÕIT] DO T . . . ("A prayer for T . . ."). Much of the original work of the jambs and of the third arch is missing or defaced. One original window survives in the S. wall of the nave, beside a pair of 13th cent. insertions; a 15th cent. cusped light has been inserted in the W. window. The fine chancel arch is also in three orders. The S. window of the chancel is original; the E. window is a 13th cent. replacement. The chancel has external coign shafts or pilasters. The stone cross (12th? cent.) bears traces of interlaced ornament, as well as a weathered figure of Christ Crucified (robed). The traditional patron of the place was an unknown St Colum, whose feast fell on 15 May; but the earliest saint associated with it of whom anything is known is St Cainneach of Aghaboe (q.v.), who used to resort to it for solitary penitential exercises and who there wrote a gospel book, Glas Cainnigh.

5¾ m. SE., in Timoney Hills and Cullaun, are nearly 300 standing stones (Nat. Mons.); one group of sixteen forms a circle; the rest are in no coherent order.

2½ m. WNW. is Mount St Joseph's Abbey (Cistercian). There is a silk farm here.

5 m. NW. is Mary Immaculate House, a Salesian convent and convalescent home. The nucleus is Gloster, an attractive early 18th cent. house (with good two-storey hall) facing a terraced garden with ornamental water. The house, visited by John Wesley in 1749, was built for John Lloyd.

ROSMUCK, Co. Galway (Map 1, C6), is a parish in the heart of the Connemara Gaeltacht, 36 m. W. of Galway (via Casla, alias "Costelloe", and Screeb). In Turlough is the cottage (Nat. Mon.; much restored) which was used as a summer home by Patrick H. Pearse (1879–1916), poet and author, who commanded the Dublin insurgents in 1916. His writings in Irish and English drew much of their inspiration from the Rosmuck country and its people.

ROSS CARBERY, Co. Cork (Map 4, E5), is a quiet, picturesquely sited, little resort at the head of a shallow, landlocked inlet of Ross Carbery Bay, 10 m. WSW. of Clonakilty and 9 m. ENE. of Skibbereen. There are good strands at Inch and Castlefreke (below). The tides rushing into the sea caves of the bay produce a peculiar, melancholy roar. Hence Tonn Chlíodhna (Cleena's Wave), one of the three magic waves of Irish mythology (see Carrigcleenamore under Mallow).

The place was anciently known as Ros Ailithir, the Pilgrim's Promontory, after a pilgrim named Colmán. In the 6th/7th cent. Bishop-Abbot St Fachtna mac Mongaigh of Dairinis (see under Youghal) founded a monastery here, which became the principal monastery of Corca Loígde and was famous for its school. Like so many other Irish monasteries, it was a victim of Norse raids, among them one in the year 991, when the Waterford Norse destroyed it and took prisoner its famous fer légind, Airbertach mac Coisse(-Dobráin). He was ransomed by Brian Boru. To him are attributed some religious poems and a versified compendium of geography compiled from late Classical sources; all in Irish. They were composed for his pupils in the monastery school. Some time before 1197 the Irish Benedictines of Würzburg established a priory at Ross. It survived until the 16th cent. At the Synod of Kells, 1152, thanks, no doubt, to the ancient fame of its monastery, Ros Ailithir was chosen to be the see of a diocese corresponding to the civil territory of Corcu Loígde. The little diocese maintained its separate jurisdiction until recently.

At the S. end of the village, St Cummin's Well and the scant remains of Ross "Abbey" mark the site of the Benedictine Priory of Our Lady. At the E. side of the village is little St Fachtna's Cathedral (C. of I.; diocese united to Cork and Cloyne since 1617). It incorporates fragments of the pre-Reformation, cruciform cathedral whose nave and tower were levelled in the 17th cent. The existing tower probably dates from 1696; the capping and spire date from 1806. The rest of the church is almost

Plate 13. The Ardagh Chalice

entirely 19th cent., but the N. transept is probably largely medieval. The inside of the E. window is cased with a re-set, 13th cent. arch (jambs partly restored). The W. window is 1517 work of a well-known, cheap kind.

1¼ m. NNE., in Tinneal, is a pair of standing stones, NW. of which is a recumbent stone; remnants of a chamber tomb (?). 3¼ m. N. of these is the ancient church-site of Castleventry: univallate ring-enclosure, traces of church, Trinity Well.

1½ m. E., in Burgatia, are the remains of diminutive Teampaillín Fháchtna (St Fáchtna's little church); SW. of this is Lisfaughtna, a small ringwork; ¼ m. E. of the church is Tober-faughtna, where pilgrims still make their rounds. ¼ m. ENE. of the latter, in Bohonagh, is a recumbent-stone circle: four out of thirteen stones missing, three re-erected; a shallow grave at the centre held a cremation. 27 ft S. was a rectangular, timber-post structure of unknown age. SE. of the circle is a displaced stone with seven cup marks. 20 yds ESE. of the circle is a low tomb whose capstone has seven or more cup marks. – 500 yds S. of the well is Callaheenacladdig, one of the finest chamber tombs in Co. Cork.

2 m. SE. is Inch Strand. At the SE. end is Cloghna Head, beyond which is the Long Strand (*see under* Clonakilty). Offshore is Carraig Chlíodhna, Cleena's Rock, said to be haunted (by the goddess; *see* Tonn Chlíodhna, *above*). Between the strands is Castlefreke Demesne, formerly seat of Lord Carbery. In the demesne are the ruins of Rathbarry castle (motte nearby) and church.

1½ m. S., on a rock formerly linked with the mainland, are the remains of Downeen castle.

2¼ m. SW. is Tralong Bay, a cove with a small beach.

2¼ m. WSW., in Ballyvireen, is Coppinger's Court (Nat. Mon.), a large 17th cent. strong-house.

3½ m. WSW. is Drombeg stone circle (*see under* Glandore).

2 m. W. are the remains of Benduff Castle, alias Castle Salem, an O Donovan stronghold.

1 m. NW., is Derry House, childhood home and property of Charlotte Payne-Townshend ("Plain Townshend"), wife of George Bernard Shaw.

4 m. NW., in Reanascreena South, is a recumbent-stone circle: thirteen stones inside a fosse with low external bank. A central pit yielded no finds. 10 ft NNW. of it was a pit burial (cremation; no grave goods). 1¾ m. NNW. of this circle, in Carrigagrenane, is another recumbent-stone circle. 1½ m. NNE. of the latter, in Maulatanvally, is a third (with a white quartz boulder inside it).

ROSSLARE, Co. Wexford (Map 6, D6), is a seaside village and resort (4-m. sandy beach) on Rosslare Bay, 11 m. SE. of Wexford.

3 m. SE. is Rosslare Harbour: passenger and car-ferry service to Fishguard.

Here, in the SE. corner of Ireland – the baronies of Forth and Bargy (*see* Bridgetown) – are many places of quiet beauty or historical interest. There are many monuments of a storied past, including castles, churches, promontory forts, and ringforts.

6 m. SE., near the coast, is Ballytrent House, birthplace of John Redmond (1856–1918), leader of the Irish Party in the British House of Commons. Beside the house is a large bivallate ringfort.

5 m. S., at the head of Lady's Island Lake – a saltwater lagoon – is Lady's Island. It takes its name from a dependency of St Mary's Abbey (Augustinian), Ferns. Also dedicated to St Mary, this, though ruined, has been for centuries a place of pilgrimage. Near the ruins are the remains of a granite castle of the same date (*c.* 1237) with, adjoining it, a leaning tower of limestone. The earliest castle here was built by Rudolf de Lamporte (Lambert), who was killed on the Third Crusade. 2 m. SSE., in Clougheast, is the 15th cent. tower of a Codd castle. 2 m. S. of this is sandy Carnsore Point: ¼ m. N. are remains of a primitive monastery with cashel, small church, holy well, and large cross-inscribed boulder. The patron is St Vogue, usually identified with St Véoc (Béóc) who died at Lanvéoc, in Brittany, in 585. 7 m. ENE. of the Point is the famous Tuskar Rock, with a lighthouse built in 1815 and improved in 1885.

4 m. SW., in Ballysampson, is the birthplace of Commodore James Barry (1745–1803), "father of the American navy".

7 m. SW., in Tacumshin, alias Tacumshane, is one of the last Irish windmills (Nat. Mon.). Tacumshin Lake, like Lady's Island Lake, is a salt pill, or lagoon, cut off from the open sea by a storm beach.

Commissioners of Public Works in Ireland
Windmill at Tacumshin, Rosslare

ROSTREVOR, Co. Down (Map 3, C6), is a beautifully situated, small seaside resort on Carlingford Lough. It lies at the foot of the Mourne Mountains, 2½ m. E. of Warrenpoint, on the delightful Newry (8½ m.)–Newcastle (22¼ m.) road.

St Brónach's Bell (*see* Kilbroney, *below*) is preserved at the Catholic church.

W. of the town is an obelisk commemorating General Ross (1766–1814), a former proprietor of the town. He died of wounds received in the British attack on Baltimore, U.S.A., after the capture of Washington and Bladensburg.

1 m. NE., on the Hilltown road, is Kilbroney (Brónach's Church), alias Baile na Cille. The church is called after its founder, the Virgin Brónach, but the remains are those of a much later parochial church. SE. of the ruins is a large cross (Nat. Mon.) with all-over ornament on the W. face. Between it and St Brónach's Well is a small cross (Nat. Mon.) with crude conventionalized *Crucifixion* (as at Clogher, Co. Tyrone) on the E. face. Together with St Brigid (*see* Faughart *under* Dundalk) and St Blinne of Killevy (*see under* Slieve Gullion), St Brónach was a patron of seafarers. Hence the traditional prayer:

A Bhrighid atá i bhFochairt,
A Bhrónaigh atá i mBaile na Cille,
A Bhlinne atá i gCill-Shléibhe
Go dtugaidh sibh mise go hÉirinn.

St Brónach's enshrined staff, now in the National Museum, was long venerated in the church.

3 m. SE., in Ballyedmond Park, is Ballyedmond Cairn (Nat. Mon.), an oval single-chamber tomb with paved rectangular forecourt; Neolithic sherds, etc., were found under the pavement. 1¾ m. NE., on the summit of Knockshee (1,144 ft; Ballintur townland), is a round cairn. – 1 m. E. of Ballyedmond Cairn, and to the NW. of Ballintur post office, are the remains of Ballintur court cairn.

1 m. SE., 300 yds W. of Causeway Water and 500 yds N. of the Kilkeel road, is Kilfeaghan Cromlech (Nat. Mon.), a portal dolmen with a 40-ton capstone and traces of a cairn.

ROUNDSTONE, Co. Galway (Map 1, B5), is a decayed fishing village (lobster, crayfish, etc.) at the foot of Errisbeg (987 ft), on the W. side of Roundstone Bay (an arm of Bertraghboy Bay), 7 m. SW. of Ballynahinch and 14 m. SE. of Clifden. The village was built in the 1820s by the Scottish engineer, Alexander Nimmo, and settled with Scottish fisherfolk. Today it is a quiet little holiday resort, beloved of artists and botanists, and best known for the beauty of its countryside (the ascent of Errisbeg is one of the most rewarding in Connemara), for its flora, and for its proximity to Dog's Bay (*below*). The name of the village is a curious English bungling of Cloch na Rón (Rock of the Seals). It was to Roundstone Court that Thackeray came with Richard Martin (son of "Humanity Dick") to hear him dispense justice.

Kate O Brien, the novelist, lived for some years at the Fort, overlooking the harbour.

1 m. N., in the grounds of Letterdife House, is a small tumulus (rifled).

4 m. NE. is Toombeola (*see under* Ballynahinch).

2 m. NE., at the N. end of Inishee, are St Brendan's Monument (a small heap of stones) and Well; the latter is regularly resorted to for cures. 2 m. SSE. are the remains of little St Mathias's Church; to the S. is a holy well.

2 m. offshore, to the S., is Inishlackan. There was a Franciscan friary here at one time.

2½ m. SW., at the foot of Errisbeg, are Dog's Bay and Gorteen Bay. (The name, Dog's Bay, like that of Roundstone, is an English bungling of the Irish: Port na bhFeadóg, Bay of the Plover.) Here the tides and winds have piled up great dunes of fine white sand between the mainland and a small island, ½ m. offshore. At their feet are spread two lovely beaches, one facing SE., and the other NW.

ROUNDWOOD, alias **TOGHER,** Co. Wicklow (Map 6, D4), is a small village beside the Vartry, at the junction of main roads from Bray (12½ m.), Glendalough (7 m.), and Ashford (7 m.), with lesser roads from Newtown Mountkennedy (6½ m.), Enniskerry (10 m.), and Glencree (11½ m.; *see* Enniskerry) via the Sally Gap. It is thus a convenient centre for touring some of the finest parts of the Wicklow Mountains.

2 m. SSW. is Annamoe bridge. It was here that Laurence Sterne fell into the mill race.

3 m. S., 1 m. SE. of Annamoe bridge, is Castlekevin, whose name is a corruption of Dísert Cóemgein, "Kevin's hermitage". A castle built about 1214 by Henry de Londres, English archbishop of Dublin, was destroyed more than once by the Irish. Towards the middle of the 14th cent. the whole country round about was recovered by the Irish, and the castle became an O Toole stronghold. In 1591 Red Hugh O Donnell sought refuge there with Felim O Toole, after escaping from Dublin Castle, and there he was recaptured. In 1597 the castle was seized by the Lord Deputy, and so finally passed into English control. By the early 17th cent. it had fallen into ruin. All that survive today are a square motte (formerly revetted with masonry) with a long bailey (on the E.) and scant remains of the gate tower and of the NE. angle tower. 400 yds NW. is a ringfort.

3 m. W., via Oldbridge, is Lough Dan, a lonely lake in the valley between Knocknacloghole and Slievebuckh. The 1798 leader, Joseph Holt of Mullinaveigue (1 m. N. of Roundwood), found refuge in the mountains here after the collapse of the Rising.

9¾ m. NW., in a deep, cliff-girt corrie, is romantic Luggala with its little lake (Luggala Lake, alias Lough Tay). The lodge by the shore was built for Sir Philip Crampton (1777–1858), the celebrated surgeon. In the grounds has been erected (1950) a garden temple originally at Templeogue House (Dublin, South-West)

and afterwards at Santry Court. 3 m. NW. is
Sally Gap (1,631 ft), the saddle between Djouce
Mountain (2,384 ft) and Gravale (2,352 ft),
where the passable Luggala–Kilbride (15 m.;
see Blessington) road crosses the old Military
Road from Dublin via Rathfarnham, Glencree,
and Glenmacnass to Laragh. The latter offers a
very fine drive (through some of the loveliest
solitudes of the Wicklow massif) to or from
Glendalough.

RUSH, Co. Dublin (Map 6, D2), is a fishing
village and small seaside resort on the Dublin
(18 m.)–Skerries (5 m.) road, 4 m. E. of Lusk.
There are two good, sandy beaches. At the E.
end of the S. beach is Tobercalleen (St Caillín's
Well). The light, sandy soil in the vicinity is
particularly favourable for market gardening
and bulb-growing, and the bulb farms are very
attractive in spring.

¾ m. N. is Kenure Park, a Classical house of
c. 1830 which was the home of the Palmers until
1964. At one time the property belonged to the
2nd Duke of Ormonde. NE. of the house are
St Catherine's Well and the ruins of St Catherine's Church.

1 m. NE., by the shore, are the remains of
Giants Hill, a cairn.

2 m. NE., in Drumanagh, to the SE. of
Loughshinny, is a very large promontory fort,
from which a cave leads down to the shore.

1½ m. WSW., in Whitestown, is St Maurus's
Well. To the SW. is Rogerstown, point of
departure for Lambay Island (*q.v.*).

SAGGART, Co. Dublin (Map 6, D7), is a
small paper-making village at the foot of Saggart Hill, 8¼ m. SW. of Dublin and 1 m. ESE. of
Rathcoole. It takes its name, Saggart, alias
Tasagart (Teach Sacru, Teach Tacru), from an
early monastery founded by St Sacru, alias Mo-
Shacra, To-Shacru. Of the monastery the sole
surviving relics are a cross-pillar, a cross fragment, and a cross socket (the Wart Stone) in the
old graveyard. In the Middle Ages Saggart was
an English border strongpoint against the
O Tooles and O Byrnes.

¾ m. SE., in Boherboy, is Patrick's Well.
Also SE. of the village, to the S. of the road
near the Embankment, are Adam and Eve, a
pair of pillarstones.

1 m. S. is the Slade of Saggart, a narrow defile
by which the Dublin–Blessington road penetrates the W. end of the Dublin mountains.
On the E. side rises Verschoyle's Hill (1,097 ft);
on the W. side, Saggart Hill (Crockaunadreen-
agh, alias Knockandinny, 1,025 ft; Knockaniller, 1,132 ft; and Slievethoul, 1,308 ft), from
which magnificent views may be had. On Verschoyle's Hill are, alt. 1,000 ft, a cairn and, alt.
1,097 ft, a ringfort; ¾ m. further S. is Raheen Bank,
a tumulus or cairn. On the NE. part of Saggart
Hill, in Lugg, alt. 1,000 ft, are a semi-denuded
small cairn and an Iron Age ritual monument
(Nat. Mon.) enclosed by two ramparts with intervening ditch and having at the centre a mound

with surrounding bank and ditch. Excavations
(1939) showed that this monument had had a
complex history: Phase I: a "sanctuary" represented by 160 post-holes, scanty remains of a
cairn, three fireplaces, a pit, etc.; Phase II: some
five Iron Age circular huts of posts, with a
single communal fireplace; these lay 25 ft E. of
the remains of Phase I; Phase III: a ritual
monument to which the visible earthworks belonged. Between the central mound and the
outer ditch-rampart complex were a number of
post-holes, some of them forming an avenue
on the N. side of the mound. The latter covered
two cremations. ¾ m. WSW., on Knockandinny, are a small cairn and a circular platform
with ditch and external bank. Less than ½ m. S.
of these, on Knockaniller, are a large chambered cairn, remains of a small passage grave,
and a circular ditched platform. ½ m. further
S., on Slievethoul, are a small chambered cairn
and a circular ditched platform. In Glenaran-
een, to the S. of the Slade, is the Hungry Hill, a
tumulus.

The road, Saggart–Kilbride–Sally Gap–Luggala–Roundwood, traverses beautiful mountain
moorlands (*see* Roundwood).

SAINTFIELD, Co. Down (Map 3, D5), is a
small linen town on the Belfast (11 m.)–Downpatrick (11 m.) road. Its name is an English
rendering of Tamnach na Naomh, "grassy field
of the saints".

In 1798 the Antrim insurgents under Henry
Monro routed a force of York Fencibles here.

1 m. S. is Rowallane (Nat. Trust) whose
50-acre gardens are noted for their landscaping
and for their rhododendrons, magnolias, cher-
ries, wall plants, Chinese and Chilean shrubs,
etc. The gardens are at their best in Spring and
Autumn. Open to the public: 1 April to 30
Sept., Sun., Wed., Sat., and Bank Holiday
Mon., 2–6 p.m.; admission 2/–.

4 m. NW. is Drumalig, birthplace of the
philosopher, Francis Hutcheson (1694–1746).

ST JOHNSTOWN, Co. Donegal (Map 2,
D2), is a small Border village on the Derry
(7 m.)–Raphoe (6 m.) road.

3 m. S., on the River Foyle, are the remains
of Mongavlin "castle", a Plantation stronghouse
built 1619–22 by Sir John Stuart; it was James
II's headquarters during the Siege of Derry.

ST MULLIN'S, Co. Carlow (Map 6, B6),
is a little village charmingly situated on the
Graiguenamanagh (7 m.)–New Ross (8¾ m.)
road through the lovely Barrow valley. To
the W. rises shapely Brandon Hill (1,694 ft);
to the E., Dho Bran (1,679 ft) and the Blackstairs range. The rewarding ascent of Brandon
Hill is best made from either Inistioge (*q.v.*) or
Graiguenamanagh (*q.v.*).

The place takes its name (an anglicization of
Teach Mo-Ling; *see also* Timolin *under* Ballitore *and* Mullenakill *under* Inistioge) from the
important monastery founded here by St Mo-

Ling (properly Dairchell, Tarchell), a patron of South Leinster. (He is said to have secured a remission of the notorious Bórama tribute for the Leinstermen.) Mo-Ling is reputed to have been a disciple of St M'Aodhóg, and to have succeeded him as bishop of Ferns (*q.v.*); he is also said to have been a bishop at Glendalough (*q.v.*). Teach Mo-Ling, Moling's House, was his principal foundation, and there he was buried about 697. It long remained an important place of pilgrimage: St Mo-Ling's Day (17 June), St James's Day (25 July), and "Sumalen's Sunday" (the Sunday before 25 July). It was also the burial-place of the South Leinster kings and of their medieval representatives, the Mac Murroughs Kavanagh (including the celebrated King Art, 1417). The Mac Murroughs, who had their chief seat at Poulmounty (a few miles SE.; *see also under* New Ross; cf. Borris), were long the custodians of the enshrined 7th cent. gospel book called the *Book of Mulling* (= Mo-Ling), now in Trinity College, Dublin. The remains (Nat. Mons.) of Teach Mo-Ling are close to the Protestant church, which impinges on the site of the monastery. They include remains of a small nave-and-chancel church and of a two-apartment building ("St Mullin's Abbey") attached to a Round Tower (stump only). Close to the SE. corner of the church ruin is a figured High Cross (*Crucifixion*, etc.); part of the shaft is missing. E. of this are remains of a diminutive oratory ("St James's Chapel"). NE. of the Protestant church are remnants of St Mo-Ling's Mill. 150 yds N. of the monastery are St Mo-Ling's Well and remains of a bath house (*antae*). WNW. of the monastery is the motte of a Norman-invasion castle built by Raymond le Gros or by his nephew, William de Carew. S. of the monastery are remains of Caisleán Maol, built *c.* 1581 to enable a Mac Murrough who had thrown in his lot with the English to keep his recalcitrant kinsfolk in check. Templenamoe Hill, NNW. of the village, preserves the name of Teampall na mBó (Church of the Cows; some remains) which figures in the legend of St Mo-Ling.

SALROCK, Co. Galway (Map 1, B5), is a small hamlet beautifully situated at the head of Little Killary Bay, 9 m. E. of Rinvyle and 8 m. W. of Leenaun. The view from the pass to the NW. of Lough Fee is very fine. Close to the hamlet is an ancient church-site, traditional burial place of St Roc (after whom the place is named). Coffins are borne three times round the graveyard before burial; it was formerly the custom here (as elsewhere in Connemara and Mayo) to deposit the tobacco pipes used at his wake on the grave of the deceased. There is a holy well in the graveyard, and another to the S. The road to the NW. leads to the mouth of Killary Harbour (1 m.) and a magnificent view of that fjord-like inlet (*see under* Leenaun).

SALTEE ISLANDS, Co. Wexford (Map 6, C7), lie 2–4½ m. off the coast, to the S. of Kilmore Quay (*q.v.*). The Great Saltee is Ireland's most important bird sanctuary.

After the defeat of the Wexford insurgents in 1798, their leaders, Bagenal Harvey (*see* Bridgetown) and John Colclough, sought temporary refuge here, but were tracked down, discovered in a cave, and taken to Wexford, where they were beheaded.

SANTRY, Co. Dublin (Map 6, E7), is a village and growing manufacturing suburb on the Dublin (4 m.)–Swords (5 m.) road. The "Swiss-style" village erected in 1840 by Lady Domville is rapidly being smothered. St Papan's Protestant Church (1709) occupies the site of the 13th cent. successor of a monastery founded in the 6th cent. by St Papán. In it are a hexagonal 14th cent. font, a handsome reredos of 1709, an interesting pulpit, and the Domville family pew. Near the churchyard gate is the tomb of Richard Barry, 2nd Lord Santry (d. 1694), and his wife (d. 1682); it was restored in 1847.

2 m. N. is Dublin Airport. The terminal passenger building (altered) is by Desmond Fitzgerald. The interesting church (1962–63) is by A. D. Devane.

1¾ m. NE. is Woodlands, a small Georgian house erected about 1720 by the Rev. Jack Jackson, Vicar of Santry, brother of the "Dan" Jackson who figures in Swift and cousin of Henry Grattan's father.

SCARRIFF, Co. Clare (Map 5, B3), is an angling and market village on the Clare side of Lough Derg, 10½ m. N. of Killaloe.

2 m. S. is the village of Tuamgraney, where the interesting Protestant parish church incorporates the remains of a pre-Romanesque church (with *antae* and trabeate W. door), to which a Transitional chancel was added in the later 12th cent. A monastery was founded here in the 6th cent. by St. Crónán of Inis Cealtra (*see under* Mountshannon). It suffered from the Vikings, and the nave of the present church is alleged to represent a rebuilding by Abbot Cormac O Killeen (d. 969). In the church is preserved an early gravestone inscribed DORCHIDE [? CORCHIDE]. There are some Romanesque fragments taken (like the chancel windows?) from Killaloe (*q.v.*). At the boundary of the rectory glebe is Cloch Liath, a broken pillar-stone.

SCARVA, Co. Down (Map 3, B5), is a 1756 village on the Newry canal, between Tanderagee (8 m.) and Loughbrickland (3 m.). It was the rallying-place of the Williamite forces on their advance to the South in 1689. The event is commemorated by the mimic battle enacted in front of Scarva House on 13 July. Formerly sponsored by the Orange Order, but nowadays by the Royal Black Institution, this is a major, popular, rural occasion for Unionist Protestants of all denominations. Scarva House (1717) has a strong 17th cent. flavour. A large Spanish chestnut tree is said to have shaded King William's tent.

The course of the Newry river southwards represents the line of the W. frontier of Ulster as it was at some undetermined date, usually thought to be the 4th cent. Considerable stretches of the frontier defences, popularly called the Dane's Cast (Nat. Mon.), survive. These consist of banks and ditches constructed wherever there was no natural obstacle to stay an enemy. One such stretch may be seen in the demesne of Scarva House, where it turns NE. away from the river and towards Lisnagade House. Another long stretch is to be seen to the E. of Poyntz Pass, 3 m. S. of Scarva (*see also* Killyfaddy *under* Armagh).

¾ m. NW., in Terryhoogan, Co. Armagh, is Relicarn, an ancient church site. The 9th/10th cent. "Bell of Armagh", now in the National Museum, was discovered here about 1725, near the grave of the celebrated 17th cent. outlaw, Redmond O Hanlon (*see* Tanderagee).

2 m. E. is Lisnagade, focal point of more than a dozen strong ringforts. Of these the most important is trivallate Lisnagade itself (Nat. Mon.), which has been described as "the largest and most strongly entrenched rath in Ireland". The remains comprise, in fact, two ringforts and other earthworks, much altered in modern times. 500 yds NW. is Lisnavarragh, an oval, bivallate ringfort.

3 m. SE. is Loughbrickland village, founded about 1585 for English Protestant settlers by Sir Marmaduke Whitechurch, purveyor of clothing to the Elizabethan army. It was destroyed by the insurgent Ulstermen in 1641 and the church was not rebuilt until 1688. 4 m. SE., at Emdale, Ballynaskeagh (off the Rathfryland road), a plaque marks the ruins of the cottage where the Rev. Patrick Brontë (Ó Pronntaigh), father of Emily, Anne, and Charlotte Brontë, was born (1771).

SHANAGOLDEN, Co. Limerick (Map 4, E2), is a village on the Foynes (3 m.)–Newcastle West (10 m.) road. The Protestant parish church incorporates the nave of an early 13th cent. church whose chancel (Transitional E. window) is a ruin; in the church are a curious medieval font and a 1585 gravestone. Near the village is St Senan's Well.

2 m. E., at Old Abbey House, are remains of Monasternagalliaghduff, the Augustinian nunnery called St Catherine's of Uí Conaill (S. Catherina de Oconyl). The 13th cent. church (some 15th cent. details) opens off the E. side of a cloister court which had the refectory and kitchen on the S. and domestic buildings (with undercrofts) on the W. Remains of gatehouses, fish pond, and columbarium also survive.

4½ m. SE., close to the ruined church of Kilbradran (Kilbraydron), is Lisbane, a large bivallate, hill-top ringfort which gives its name to its townland. It had stone-faced ramparts; also large annexes on the N. and E.

2 m. SSW. is Shanid, where the Norse were routed in a fierce battle, 839. There are fragmentary remains of Shanid castle, "Desmond's first and most ancient house", which suggested the famous Desmond warcry and motto: *Shanid aboo*. (After 1280 the principal seats of the Desmond Fitz Geralds were at Tralee, Askeaton, and Newcastle West.) The motte-and-bailey are relics of the first Geraldine castle here (built by Thomas fitz Maurice, to whom Hamo de Valognes granted the place, 1197/1200). The motte is crowned by curtain walls (a shell-keep?), within which are remains of a polygonal keep (a juliet?). The castle first figures in history in 1230. It was captured by Red Hugh O Donnell of Tyrconnell in 1600. SE. is a large bivallate ringfort with remains of internal structures.

SHANNONBRIDGE, Co. Offaly (Map 5, D2), is a village on the Cloghan (8 m.)–Ballinasloe (10 m.) road, 5 m. SW. of Clonmacnois (*q.v.*). Nearby is a power station fired by milled peat. On the W. bank of the Shannon is a small, well-preserved, early-19th cent. fort, built to secure the Connacht bridgehead.

SHERCOCK, Co. Cavan (Map 3, A6), is a village on the Bailieborough (7 m.)–Carrickmacross (9 m.) road. Lough Sillan offers coarse fishing (pike, etc.).

3 m. NNW., in Corgreagh, Co. Monaghan, is Labbyfirmore, a long (court?) cairn.

SHILLELAGH, Co. Wicklow (Map 6, C5), is a small village where the Carnew (4½ m.)–Tullow (10 m.) road crosses the wooded valley of the Shillelagh River. The local woods are the modern representatives of a once great oak forest which, it is claimed, supplied roof timbers in the Middle Ages for Westminster Hall, London, as well as for St Patrick's Cathedral, Dublin.

1½ m. E. is Coolattin Park, seat of the Earl of Fitzwilliam.

5 m. WNW. (1¾ m. SW. of Coolkenna crossroads), in Aghowle Lower, are the ruins of an early-12th cent. church (Nat. Mon.), St. Finden's (*sic*) Cross (Nat. Mon.), a bullaun, a stone basin, and (near the SW. angle of the church) an early cross-slab. The celebrated St Finnian of Clonard founded his first monastery here. The church has a noteworthy trabeate W. door with double-faced architrave, bosses, etc.; also two small Romanesque windows. 2 m. S. of the church, alt. 800–900 ft, in Moylisha, is Leaba na Saighe, a roofless, wedge-shaped gallery grave (Nat.Mon.). On the hill-slope to the N. is a stone ringfort. In Money Upper, the townland bordering Moylisha on the N. and Aghowle Lower on the W., is the Mote, a cairn of stones and earth. At Rockview, near the Money–Moylisha boundary, is a chambered cairn (wrecked).

3m. NW., in the second field E. of Kilquiggin churchyard, are the head and socket of an early cross.

SHRULE, Co. Mayo (Map 1, D5), is a village where the Ballinrobe (9 m.)–Headford (5 m.) road, via Kilmaine, crosses the Shrule or Black River.

Commanding the river crossing is the tower (Nat. Mon.) of a Burke castle. In 1570 the castle was besieged by the English President of Connacht and the Earl of Clanricard. Mac William (Burke) Íochtair came up to relieve the place, and after a fierce engagement dispersed the besiegers.

At the NW. end of the village a featureless, early-13th cent. church (Nat. Mon.) marks the site of a foundation attributed to St Patrick.

2 m. NW. are the ruins of Kill "Abbey" (Cillín Bhréanainn, Killeenbrenan, "St Brendan's little church"), first (before 1426) Irish house of the Third Order Regular of St Francis. By 1536 it had some forty-six dependencies.

There are good ringforts on the high ground S. to Headford.

SIXMILEBRIDGE, Co. Clare (Map 5, B3), is a village on the Tulla (9 m.)–Limerick (9 m.) road. Mount Ievers is a fine Georgian house, built about 1730 for the Ievers family by John and Isaac Rothery (?); noteworthy drawing-room.

2 m. N. are remains of Ballymulcashel (Mountcashel) castle, built by Conor na Sróna O Brien, King of Thomond (1466–96).

1¼ m. NNW., in Ballysheen, are remains of Kilfinaghta, a 12th cent. Western Traditional church.

5½ m. NW. is Tomfinlough (*see under* Newmarket-on-Fergus).

2 m. NNE., in Knopoge, is Cromlech, a gallery grave.

SKELLIGS, THE, Co. Kerry (Map 4, A5), are a group of rock islets – Little Skellig, Great Skellig, Washerwoman's Rock – 7 m. W. of Bolus Head. They can be reached, in calm weather, from Ballinskelligs or Waterville or Valencia Island.

The Little Skellig is the most southerly of the few breeding places of the gannet in these islands.

The Great Skellig (Sceilg Mhichíl, Skellig Michael) is a huge rock rising to twin peaks, 715 and 650 ft above the Atlantic. Haunt of seabirds and seals, it was one of Europe's many ancient lofty places associated with the cult of St Michael (as Mont St Michel in Brittany and St Michael's Mount in Cornwall), and is famous for the well-preserved remains (Nat. Mons.) of an austere anchoritic settlement attributed to one of the Saints Fíonán. The settlement was raided by the Vikings in 823, and disappears from history after 1044. (The monks are said to have removed to Ballinskelligs, *q.v.*, in the 12th cent.) From East Landing a flight of ruined steps marks one ancient ascent to the main settlement. The modern approach from this point is via the lighthouse road along the SE. cliffs. Some 500

Clocháns, Skellig Michael

yds. SW. of the landing, steps and a path climb towards the monastery. On the sheer slopes NE. of the path are an early cross-slab, a ruined structure, and a cross carved in the round from the natural rock. 200 yds from the road the path reaches Christ's Valley, a saddle with two rude stone crosses on the S. side. To the W. rises West Peak with Needles Eye, a rock-chimney (714 ft); half-way up the peak is another ruin; there are artificial terraces on the steep slopes to the NE. and W. On the N. side of Christ's Valley the path to the monastery is joined by a flight of steps from North Landing; near the junction is an early stone cross. A flight of steps and a path lead NE. to the remains of the settlement proper. These are a series of enclosures set on steep terraces 550–600 ft above the ocean.

In the main enclosure are six dry masonry, corbel-roofed, stone huts (clocháns), a small oratory of Gallarus (*see under* Ballyferriter) type, the remains of little St Michael's Church, and the cemetery. In the latter are twenty-two early gravestones. On a platform N. of the oratory are a stone cross and a cross-slab; S. of the oratory are two cross-slabs; by the path SW. of St Michael's Church are two more. To the N. of the clocháns is a small, isolated oratory. To the SE. of them is the "Monk's Garden", below which are a ruined structure and the ancient stairway from East Landing. SW. of the clocháns are two early cross-slabs and remains of a souterrain. NW. of the clocháns, near the crest of the ridge, is an isolated stone cross. Superb views are to be had from various vantage points.

SKERRIES, Co. Dublin (Map 6, D2), is a popular small seaside resort on the Rush (5 m.) –Balbriggan (5 m.) road.

1¼ m. ENE. is St Patrick's Island (Inis Phádraig), where Patrick is said to have landed on his way from Wicklow to Ulster. According to a legend (not so popular with Skerries folk), the mainlanders stole the saint's goat from Inis Phádraig and ate it. There was an early monastery on the island. It was plundered by the Vikings in 795, and the Shrine of St Do-Chonna was carried off. In 1148 a national reform synod assembled at the monastery to make formal application to the Pope for palls for the first Irish archbishops, and sent St Máel M'Áedhóg (see Bangor) to Rome as its spokes-man. (He died en route, at Clairvaux, 2 Nov. 1148.) In the 13th cent. the monastery, by then an Augustinian priory, was transferred to Holmpatrick (below), and all that remains on the island are fragments of a tufa-roofed nave-and-chancel church.

At the S. end of the town is Holmpatrick, where the Protestant church occupies part of the site of the Augustinian priory transferred from St Patrick's Island. In the churchyard are the tombstones of the last prior, Richard de la Hoyde of Loughshinny (d. 1587), and of Eliza-beth Finglas (d. 1577).

2 m. SSW. are the ruins of Baldongan castle, which has been supposed to have belonged to the Knights Templar. Of this there is no evidence. It passed through the Barnewalls and the Berminghams to the Lords of Howth (Amy de Bermingham married Sir Christopher St Lawrence who died in 1542). In 1642 it was held by the Confederate Catholics, but was reduced with artillery by the Parliamentarians, its garrison of 200 men butchered, and the fortifications demolished. SE. are the ruins (Nat. Mon.) of a nave-and-chancel church with massive W. tower. 1½ m. NNW., in Grange, are St Movee's (Mo-Bhí's) Well and (in the nearby graveyard) traces of a small oratory. ½ m. NW. are the Camps, where Cromwell is alleged to have camped in 1649. A mound near the road is "the grave of some of his soldiers". 1 m. NW., just S. of the road overlooking Barnageeragh strand, is a disturbed cairn. 290 yds SE. is the site of another.

SKIBBEREEN, Co. Cork (Map 4, D6), is a small market town and fishing port where the Clonakilty (20 m.)–Ballydehob (10 m.) road crosses the Ilen, 8 m. S. of Drimoleague and 7 m. NE. of Baltimore. It is a convenient base for exploring the interesting coast of SW. Cork.

5 m. SE. is Castletownshend (q.v.).

4 m. SW. is lovely, almost completely land-locked, Lough Hyne (Ine). On Castle Island are the remains of Cloghan Castle (O Driscolls). At the S. end of the lough are Toberbreedy and the remains of Templebreedy: a well and church dedicated to St Brigid. The Marine Biology station of University College, Cork, is on Lough Hyne.

1 m. W., on the N. side of the Ilen, are the remains of Abbeystrowry, a cell of the Cister-cian abbey of Maune (see under Courtmac-sherry).

3 m. W. is New Court, an 18th cent. house with Gothick towers and a water gate built for Lord Riversdale.

5 m. W. are the interesting ruins of Agha-down House (Becher family) and its gazebo.

6½ m. SW., in the church of Kilcoe, is a window by Sarah Purser (Crucifixion, SS Patrick and Brigid). 1 m. SW. are the remains of the medieval church of Kilcoe. Some 500 yds SW. of the latter, on an offshore islet of Roaring Water Bay, are the ruins of a 1495 Clann Diarmada Mac Carthy castle. After the 17th cent. English plantation it was held by the Coppingers.

SKULL, Co. Cork (Map 4, D6), is a fishing village on Skull Harbour, an inlet of Roaring Water Bay, 14 m. W. of Skibbereen and 8¾ m. NE. of Crookhaven. It takes its names (scoil) from a school founded by the monks of Ros Ailithir (see Ross Carbery). To the NE. rises Mount Gabriel (1,339 ft).

The disused Protestant church incorporates medieval fragments.

¾ m. N., in Meenvane, is a univallate ringfort with a souterrain.

3 m. NE. the road to Bantry makes its way through a wild pass on the E. side of Mount Gabriel. Magnificent views are to be had here-abouts, and the rough defiles are noted for their glaciated rocks. In the valley to the N. are old copper mines whose deposits are being explored again. 5 m. N. of the pass is Dun-beacon stone circle (see under Bantry).

3¾ m. W., in Carriganine, Aderawinny, is a chamber tomb. 1¼ m. SW., close to the E. shore of Toormore Bay in Altar townland, is another. – 2¾ m. SSW. of Carriganine, at Castle Point (Léim Chon), is Black Castle, a late-15th cent. castle of the O Mahonys. It was taken by the English in 1602, following on the capitulation of Kinsale.

5 m. W. is Toormore. 2¼ m. N., on Dun-manus harbour, are the remains of Dunmanus castle. Not far away, in a swampy, tide-covered field, is a chamber tomb. On the N. side of Dunmanus harbour is a bivallate earthwork, site of a later castle. – 1¼ m. E. of Dunmanus castle is a bivallate ringfort commanding fine views seawards. – 1½ m. SW. of the castle, in Dunkelly East, is a bivallate cliff-fort. The road to the SW. affords fine views of Dunmanus Bay and the Beare peninsula.

6¾ m. W. is Ballyrisode (see Goleen, below).

7½ m. SW. is Goleen, where there is a good small beach. The roads and by-roads to the W. and SW. and along the N. side of the peninsula offer many fine views. 1¼ m. NE. is Ballydivlin chamber tomb; 1¼ m. ENE. of the latter is Ballyrisode chamber tomb. – 1¾ m. S. is Crook-haven (q.v.). – 2 m. SSW., in Tooreen, is a chamber tomb; a short distance SW., in Arduslough, is another; ¼ m. S. of the latter, in Leenane, is a third. ½ m. WSW. of the Arduslough tomb, in Letter, is a small stone circle. – 2¼ m. WSW. of Goleen, in Ballyvoge Beg, is a chamber tomb.

13 m. SW. is Mizen Head; the hill (765 ft) offers extensive views. 5 m. N (7 m. WSW. of Goleen) is Three Castles Head. E. of the Head, between the SW. end of little Doo Lough and the low cliffs of Coosnaronety, are remains of Dún Locha, a promontory fort. In the Middle Ages the O Mahonys erected a tower on the highest knoll on the line of the rampart. Subsequently the rampart was demolished, and fosses and a mortar-built wall were constructed to close the gap between the sea-cliff and the lake. At the same time a gatehouse was built beside the lake, and a turret between this and the main tower.

SLANE, Co. Meath (Map 6, C1), is now the name of a small village on the Drogheda (9 m.)–Navan (8 m.) road, just NW. of the bridge which carries the old Dublin–Ashbourne–Collon–Ardee turnpike road across the Boyne. The village is a convenient base for fishing some of the best reaches of the Boyne, or for exploring some of its loveliest scenery as well as some of its most celebrated antiquities.

Francis Ledwidge (1887–1917), the gifted young poet killed in Flanders, was a native of Slane. The Rev. Mervyn Archdall (1723–91), antiquary, was Rector of Slane. At the Protestant parish church are a 15th cent. doorway and armorial panel recently extracted from Stackallen church (*below*).

N. of the village rises Slane Hill (529 ft). It was on this hill, legend asserts, that St Patrick kindled his first Paschal Fire in breach of King Loígaire's decree. In early historic times there was an episcopal-monastic church here, associated with the Patrician bishop, St Earc (d. 512/14), whom legend credits with great austerities. In 948 the belfry (Round Tower), together with "the best of bells" and St Earc's enshrined crozier, was destroyed by Norse raiders. The place was subsequently laid waste on several occasions. In 1170 it was ravaged by Diarmait Mac Murrough and Strongbow. To the monastery belonged the lost *Yellow Book of Slane*, a literary codex drawn on by the compilers of *Lebor na hUidre* (*see* Clonmacnois). In 1174 Bishop Echtighern Mac Maoil-Chíaráin of Clonard (*q.v.*), implementing a decision of the Synod of Kells (1152), merged the bishopric in the new diocese of Meath. Thereafter the history of the hill-top church is obscure. In 1512 Sir Christopher Fleming and his wife, Elizabeth Stuckley, founded a college of four priests, four clerks, and four choristers, to serve the church. At the Dissolution the college and its possessions were granted to Sir James Fleming, descendant of the founder. In 1631, the anti-Catholic laws being relaxed, the Flemings installed Capuchins in the college, but these were expelled by Cromwell. The church was finally abandoned in 1723. The remains (Nat. Mons.) comprise a church and, NE. of it,

the College, a courtyard residential building with 16th cent. windows and other details. The church ruins comprise nave, later S. aisle, and a fine W. tower of about 1500 which offers a magnificent prospect of the Boyne valley from Trim to the sea. S. of the church are the gable ends of an early tomb (St Earc's?). Such a tomb would suggest that the churchyard occupies the site of the early monastery. Coffins brought to the cemetery for burial used formerly to be set down for a brief space at this ancient tomb. On the N. side of the graveyard is Tobar Pádraig (St Patrick's Well), alleged to rise and fall with the level of the Boyne floods. 300–400 yds NE. of the churchyard is a mound which may be one of the *fearta Fear Féicc*, "graves of the Fir Féicc", mentioned in early records. At the W. end of the hill is the motte of a castle that was built in 1175 by Richard le Fleming and was destroyed the following year by Melaghlin of Cinéal Eóghain.

The Boyne bridge crosses the river near the place where, in 947, the King of Tara, Congalach of Brega, and his Norse ally, Olaf of Dublin, were routed by Rury O Cannon, King of Cinéal Conaill, and where Williamite infantry made their surprise crossing, 12 July 1690 (*see* Drogheda *and* Duleek). On the N. bank of the river, in a dense thicket to the W. of the bridge (Slane Castle demesne), are the tumble-down remains of late 15th–16th cent. Múr na mBráthair ("Friars' Castle", "Friars' Dwelling"), alias St Earc's Hermitage. They consist of a little church or chapel, with an earlier low tower and dwelling intervening between nave and chancel. Fragmentary sculptures surviving include figures of St Catherine and an angel. Two Franciscan friars are recorded as living here in 1512. In the chancel is a 1667 monument erected by Randall Fleming, baron of Slane. W. of the church is the Apostles' Stone, a medieval tomb-fragment with figures of the Crucifixion and the Twelve Apostles. Further W., by the river, is Lady Well, to which pilgrims resort on 15 Aug., "Lady Day in Harvest" (the only day the public is admitted to the hermitage).

1¼ m. W. is Slane Castle, seat of the Marquess of Conyngham. Francis Johnston was the architect of various early 19th cent. alterations. ½ m. SW. of the main gate is Baronstown Cross (*below*).

2½ m. ESE. is Knowth cairn (*see under* Newgrange).

3 m. SE., on the S. bank of the Boyne, is Rosnaree, traditionally the burial place of King Cormac, son of Art. Prehistoric burials have been found on the higher ground near the river. It was by surprise crossings at Rosnaree ford and Slane, on 12 July 1690, that the Williamites turned the Jacobites' left flank and made their positions in front of Donore untenable (*see* Drogheda *and* Duleek).

3½ m. SW., on the S. bank of the Boyne, is Beauparc House, a good Georgian mansion of 1750.

Commissioners of Public Works in Ireland
Spiral pattern, Newgrange tumulus, Slane

Commissioners of Public Works in Ireland
Decorated kerbstone, Newgrange tumulus, Slane

4 m. SW. is Broad Boyne Bridge (*see under* Navan).

2 m. WSW., by the roadside in Carrick-dexter, is Baronstown (alias Barristown) Cross, the shaft (with long inscription) of a cross erected about 1590 by Dame Janet Dowdall for herself and her deceased husband, Oliver Plunket, fourth Baron of Louth (*see* Duleek; *also* Lough Hall *under* Ardee); the figures represent SS Peter and Patrick. Not far away is disused Tobar Pádraig (St Patrick's Well). ½ m. SE. of the cross, near the N. bank of the Boyne, are the remains of Castle Dexter. Nothing is known of its history. – 2¼ m. W. of the cross, in Stackallen, are remains of a church erected by Sir Barnaby Barnewall (d. 1493) and his wife, Margaret Plunket. It suffered much from a 19th cent. "restoration". The doorway and the armorial panel above it have recently been extracted and taken to Slane Protestant church.

5½ m. NW., in Rathkenny, is a chamber tomb with one end of the capstone fast in the ground. There are many inscribed devices on the capstone. Some of these have been interpreted as Iron Age Celtic motifs, and an Iron Age dating rashly claimed for the monument. 2 m. NW. is Lisknock (*see under* Collon). – 5 m. NNW. is Lobinstown (*see under* Collon). – 4 m. NE. is Slieve Beagh (*see under* Collon).

SLIEVE GULLION (1,894 ft), Co. Arm-agh (Map 3, B6), to the W. of the Dundalk (8 m.)–Newry (7 m.) road, dominates the Gap of the North, gateway into Ulster from the South. It offers prospects of a beautiful country-side rich in prehistoric and historic remains (*see also under* Newry). In the 17th cent. the moun-tain was the fastness of outlaw Redmond O Hanlon and his followers (*see* Tanderagee). The best approach from Newry is probably via Camlough and Lislea or Milltown.

On the S. summit is Calliagh Birra's House (Nat. Mon.), a cruciform passage grave (with corbelled, polygonal central chamber) in a great round cairn. Excavation of the disturbed tomb yielded only a flint arrowhead, three stone trays of Newgrange type, some flint scrapers, etc. Hours of Admission: 1 April to 30 Sept., Sats. and Suns., 2–6 p.m. On the N. summit, ½ m. NNW., is a smaller cairn; two cists, one with a Food Vessel, were found here.

Near the NE. foot of the mountain, 1 m. N. of modern Killevy Castle, in Ballintemple, is Killevy (Cill Shléibhe Cuilinn, "the church of Slieve Gullion"; Nat. Mon.). The ruin com-prises two conjoint, but not inter-communicat-ing, plain, rectangular churches. The W. church is pre-Romanesque; the E. church (13th cent.?; 15th/16th cent. insertions) has a simple, pointed E. window. There was formerly a Round Tower to the S. of the W. church. Killevy was one of the most important early nunneries in Ireland. It was founded in the 5th (?) cent. by one of Ireland's traditional patrons of seafarers (*see* Killbroney *under* Rostrevor), St Darerca, alias Mo-Ninne, later Blinne (who came to be claimed as founder by the medieval English monastery of Burton-on-Trent). Mo-Ninne's own church was of timber, and the date of the earliest stone church here is unknown. The nunnery declined after a Viking raid in 923, but appears to have been restored in the following century. It survived until the Dissolution (1542). ¾ m. SSE. is Clonlum North Cairn (Nat. Mon.), a court cairn. ½ m. S. of this is Clonlum Cromlech, or South Cairn (Nat. Mon.), a Bronze Age chamber tomb (finds in Armagh museum). 1¼ m. E., in Aghayalloge, is the S. angle of a mile-long reach of the Dane's Cast (*see under* Poyntz Pass).

On the W. flank of the mountain, 2½ m. SSW. of Lislea road junction and 4 m. NNW. of Forkill, in Ballykeel (300 yds SE. of the bridge), is a tripod dolmen set in the end of a long cairn (Nat. Mon.).

SLIGO, Co. Sligo (Map 2, B5), second largest town in Connacht, is a seaport, manufacturing town, and important marketing centre, as well as capital of the county to which it gives its name; it is also the cathedral town of the Catholic diocese of Elphin (*see* Elphin, Co. Roscommon), and, since 1962, of the Protestant diocese of Elphin and Ardagh. It is one of the most beautifully sited of Irish towns, set, as it is, between Lough Gill and the sea. It lies 22 m. SW. of Bundoran, where the coastal highway from Connacht to Ulster crosses the Garavogue River, and it offers attractions to tourists and holiday-makers of widely varying interests: beaches (Strandhill), golf (Strandhill and Rosses Point), angling (the Garavogue and Lough Gill), etc. It is a convenient base for exploring the fascinating region of mountain and lake, hill and dale, which extends from Lough Arrow to Lough Erne.

Sligo first came into prominence with the de Burgo invasion of Connacht (1235), when, together with extensive territories, it was granted to Maurice FitzGerald, Lord of Naas and Baron of O ffaly, ancestor of the Earls of Kildare (*see* Maynooth). FitzGerald built a castle here in 1245 to secure his prize, and to serve as base for the projected conquest of Tír Chonaill. He also founded (1253) a Dominican friary close by. Between 1245 and 1295 the castle was destroyed four times by either O Conor or O Donnell. In 1310 a new castle was built, and a new town laid out, by Richard III de Burgo, Red Earl of Ulster. In 1315 this castle was demolished by O Donnell. Thereafter the effective control of Sligo passed to the Carbury branch (later known as O Conors Sligo) of the ancient royal house of Connacht. This branch usually acknowledged the overlordship of O Donnell, who always endeavoured to keep Sligo out of menacing hands. In 1414 town and friary were destroyed by fire. In 1470 Áedh Rúa (Red Hugh) I O Donnell took the castle from O Conor, and thereby recovered possession of *Lebor na hUidre* (*see* Clonmacnois) and a *Lebor Gerr* (another celebrated literary codex), which O Conor's ancestor had acquired in 1359 as the ransom of O Doherty and other Tír Chonaill notables. In 1595 English besiegers of the castle, under George Bingham, severely damaged the friary. In 1641 town and friary were sacked by the Parliamentarian, Sir Frederick Hamilton (*see* Manorhamilton). In 1645 the town was captured by the notorious Sir Charles Coote. In 1689 it was seized by Williamite rebels under Lord Kingston, but was retaken by Patrick Sarsfield for King James.

Of the castle nothing at all remains, but a substantial portion (Nat. Mon.) of the once beautiful Dominican Friary of the Holy Cross, popularly known as the "Abbey", survives. The friary had a chequered history, and suffered much from accident, as well as from the English Reformation and the wars of the 16th and 17th centuries. After the fire of 1414, it was largely rebuilt about 1416 by Friar Brian Mac

Commissioners of Public Works in Ireland
O Craian tomb in the Dominican friary, Sligo

Donagh, scion of the Mac Donaghs of Tirerrill. The Sligo O Conors made it their family burial place, and were thus able, for a time, to stave off its dissolution. Among the illustrious dead buried there were Tiernan O Rourke of Breany (1418), Brian Mac Donagh of Tirerrill (1484), and Sir Donnchadh O Conor Sligo (1609) whose fine monument (*below*) survives.

The remains of the friary comprise the choir (or chancel) and part of the nave of the original 13th cent. church, the 15th/16th cent. belltower, parts of the 15th/16th cent. S. aisle and S. transept, and of the 15th cent. cloister and claustral buildings. Among the features of interest are: the 15th cent. E. window: the well-preserved 15th/16th cent. high altar – the only sculptured example to survive in any medieval Irish monastic church; the fragments of the tasteful 14th/15th cent. rood screen; the remains of the simple, but beautiful, cloister arcade; the reader's desk in the refectory (on the upper floor on the N. side of the cloister); and the interesting series of 16th and 17th cent. tombs and monuments. Of these last the most important are the O Craian (Crean) tomb of 1506 in the N. wall of the nave, and the O Conor Sligo monument of 1624 in the S. wall of the chancel. (Both have lost their polychrome colouring.) – The O Craian tomb is surmounted by the remains of an excellent traceried canopy, while the front of the chest is divided into nine beautifully canopied niches with figures of the

Crucifixion, the Blessed Virgin Mary, SS Michael, Dominic, John, Peter, and Catherine, and an archbishop. The Latin inscription may be rendered: "Here lie Cormac O Craian and Gehonna Nic Aengusa (Magennis) his wife. A.D. 1506." – The O Conor Sligo monument is a Renaissance piece of remarkable quality, considering the remoteness of Sligo from the main Irish centres of Renaissance influence. Above a boldly moulded cornice are the arms of O Conor Sligo, flanked by figures of SS Peter and Paul and surmounted by a crucifix. Beneath the cornice is a frieze with a long, illegible, Latin inscription. Below the frieze are two arched recesses with kneeling effigies of Sir Donnchadh O Conor Sligo and his wife. The tympana carry short Latin inscriptions. Beneath the recesses is a second long inscription, which may be rendered "Here lies the most famous knight Donnchadh O Conor, Lord of the County Sligo, together with his wife, the most illustrious Lady Eleanor Butler, Countess of Desmond, who had me erected, in the year 1624 after the death of her husband, who died 11 Aug. 1609. Likewise a daughter of her and her first husband, the Earl of Desmond, Elizabeth by name, a truly virtuous lady, was buried in this tomb, 30 Nov. 1623."

The modern Dominican church (High St) is a poor Gothic-Revival piece (1845–48) by Sir John Benson. It has a two-light window (1911) by Michael Healy: *SS Raymundus, Antoninus*.

½ m. E. of the medieval friary, close to the Garavogue in the uninspired municipal housing of Abbeyquarter North, are the weed-covered

Commissioners of Public Works in Ireland
Detail of cloister arcade, Dominican friary, Sligo

kerb and other remains of a prehistoric cairn; a shoddy Calvary group was erected here in 1950.

St John's Cathedral (Temple St) is a dull Romanesque essay (1869–75) by George Goldie of London. Not far away (John St) is the cathedral (since 1962) of the Protestant dioceses of Elphin and Ardagh. This is an unfortunate 1812 Gothicization of the Church of St John the Baptist and St Mary the Virgin erected, to the design of Richard Cassels, on the site of Sligo's first (17th cent.) Protestant church. Built into the W. wall of the nave is the mensa (defective) of the tomb of Sir Roger Jones of Banada (d. 1637), English Governor of Sligo; it has low-relief effigies of Sir Roger and his wife. In the N. transept is a brass tablet to Susan Mary Yeats, mother of William Butler and Jack Butler Yeats. The reredos *Creation*, in the chancel, was painted by Percy Francis Gethin (1874–1916) in memory of his brother, Reginald Owen Gethin (d. 1899).

The Town Hall (Quay St; 1865) is by Hague.

Boats are available on the Garavogue, which offers the pleasantest and most beautiful approach to Lough Gill, 2½ m. SE. of the town. On the E. bank of the river is the derelict demesne of Hazelwood (*below*), in its day one of the finest demesnes in Ireland; on the W. bank are the demesnes of Cleeveragh and Belvoir. Lough Gill itself (5 m. by 1½ m.), in its ring of wooded hills, is one of the loveliest and most romantic of Irish lakes. Its shores and islands offer many delights to the holiday-maker, as well as to the antiquarian, while its waters (partly free) provide the angler with salmon, trout, and pike. The largest island is Inis Mór, alias Church Island. At the N. end of the island some remains (Nat. Mon.) of a medieval church mark the site of a 6th cent. foundation of St Lommán's. Near the door is Our Lady's Bed, a cavity in the rock; women who pray there are said not to die in childbirth. The illustrious family of Ó Cuirnín, hereditary poets and historiographers to O Rourke of Breany (*see* Dromahair), had its chief seat here in the Middle Ages. (The lineal representative of the family still lived here at the time of John O Donovan's visit in 1839.) A fire which destroyed the church in 1416 burned all Ó Cuirnín's books, including a *Lebor Gerr*. 1¼ m. SE. of Church Island is "the lake isle of Inisfree" sung by W. B. Yeats. – Towards the SW. end of the lake is Cottage Island, alias Gallagher's Island, with remains of an ancient church. S. of the island, in Aghamore Far on the S. shore, the heights of Dooney (Doonee) Rock offer an excellent vantage point; the name, of course, recalls Yeats's *Fiddler of Dooney*.

By road a delightful circular tour of the lake can be made by going SE. from Sligo to Aghamore (with Dooney Rock) and Lahanagh; thence between Slieve Daeane (*see under* Collooney) and Slish (970 ft) to Cashelore (*see under* Ballintogher), and on to Dromahair (*q.v.*); thence by the E. and N. shores of the lake back to Sligo. (A bohereen leading N. from Gort-loman crossroads reaches the lake shore opposite Yeats's Inisfree; *see under* Ballin-togher.)

4 m. NE., via the Glencar road, is Drum East (*see under* Drumcliff).

4½ m. ENE. (½ m. S. of the Manorhamilton road beyond Colgagh church), in Magheran-rush (Magheraconrish), alias Deerpark, are the remains (Nat. Mon.) of the central-court cairn named Leacht Chon (mhic) Ruis, "the monument of Cú (son) of Rus". (The personal name is also embedded in the townland name.) Here the ritual court is an oval, or sub-rectangle, with the entrance at the middle of the S. side. At the W. end is a roofless, seg-mented gallery grave; at the E. end, a pair of similar galleries side by side. The tomb crowns a hill (500 ft) which offers lovely panoramas. In the next field to the S. are remains of a stone ringfort (Nat. Mon.) with a small, L-shaped souterrain. In the field S. of this are remains of Druid's Altar (Nat. Mon.), a chamber tomb. Other National Monuments in Magheraconrish are a stone circle, a small cairn (ruined), and remains of a stone hut. – About 2 m. N. of Leacht Chon Ruis, in Formoyle, is Giants Grave, rem-nant of a court cairn.

2 m. SSE. is Cairns (alias Belvoir) Hill (404 ft), easily climbed and offering delightful views. On the hill are two stone ringforts, two prehistoric cairns, and a "stone circle" (the remains of a third cairn?). At the SE. foot of the hill, near the lakeshore, 2½ m. from Sligo, are Tobarnalt(ha), alias Tobar an Ailt, holy well and Penal-times altar, where "stations" are made on Garland Sunday, alias Tobernalt Sunday (last Sunday of July). Built into the altar is a stone with the coat of arms of the French family. It has been taken from the monument of A(ndrew ?) Crean and E. F(rench), his wife, in Sligo "Abbey".

3½ m. SE. (via the Manorhamilton road), on a peninsula between the Garavogue and Lough Gill, is Hazelwood House, formerly home of the Wynnes, for whom it was designed by Richard Cassels. It is one of the finest of the smaller 18th cent. country houses of Ireland. The once lovely demesne is now derelict.

2 m. WSW. are the outliers of the important, but shamefully neglected, "Carrowmore" Group (Nat. Mons.) of prehistoric chamber tombs and other monuments. The main concentration of these will be found in Tobernaveen, Carrow-more, Graigue, and Knocknashammer, alias Cloverhill. More than eighty-five tombs are said to have survived down to the 19th cent., when they were rifled by amateur antiquarians or demolished by "improving" landowners, to the great loss of science. Today only about twenty-five tombs survive. Several of them belong to the passage-grave family. One of the most interesting is a small, horse-shoe chamber, now roofless, in Cloverhill some 200 yds E. of Laghtareel Hill; four of the nine uprights bear curvilinear devices. In addition to chamber tombs and cairns, the Carrowmore area con-tains a number of pillarstones, ringforts, etc.

4 m. WSW. is conspicuous, isolated Knock-narea (1,083 ft), whose summit (easily reached via Grange North) rewards the climber with a superb view that includes the mountains of Donegal, to the N., and Croagh Patrick and Nephin, to the SW., as well as Sligo Bay and the hills beyond Lough Gill. It is crowned by Miosgán Meabha (Miosgán Meva; *see also* Rathcroghan, Tara, Knockma *under* Headford, *and* Muckish *under* Gortahork), "Maeve's Lump" (Nat. Mon.), a passage-grave-type cairn, 200 ft in diameter, and 34 ft high. Nearby are the remains of satellite tombs, one of them a cruci-form passage grave. In Grange North, on the E. slope of the mountain, are the remains of an-other chamber tomb. On the S. side of the mountain, close to the Grange North–Cullen-duff road, is Knocknarea Glen, a deep wooded chasm ¾ m. long. There are caves in the N., NW., and W. escarpment of the mountain.

2½ m. W., in Cummeen, are chamber tombs (including Giants' Graves – Nat. Mon. – two roofless, opposed, galleries of a court cairn in an earthen ring), cairns, and other antiquities. Cummeen Strand figures in Yeats's early poetry.

5 m. W., at the foot of Knocknarea, is the seaside village and resort of Strandhill, more properly Larass (two good beaches; nine-hole golf links). ½ m. NNW., in Killaspugbrone townland, is Giants' Graves, alias Labbyna-wark, remnant of a segmented gallery grave. ½ m. further NNW., near Killaspug Point, are the ruins of the church of Killaspugbrone which gives its name to the townland and parish. It is called after Bishop Brón (d. 510/11), whom St Patrick is said to have placed in charge of a church here. St Patrick, we are told, shed a tooth, which fell on the threshold of the church. The tooth was enshrined and kept here. The reliquary, known as the Fiachal Pádraig, was re-edified at the expense of Thomas Bermingham, Lord of Athenry, who died in 1376. (The Berminghams had acquired lands in W. Sligo in the 13th cent., and one of their castles was at Buninna, on Ballysadare Bay.) In the 17th cent. the tooth was the most venerated relic in Connacht. The last titular abbot of Cong (*q.v.*) seized it from its hereditary custodian, so as to stop abuses. It is now in the National Museum. Killaspugbrone was a simple, rectangular, small church with trabeate W. doorway and a small, plain, Romanesque E. window. It had a Roman-esque doorway (inserted) of two plain arches in the S. wall.

5 m. NW., in "the Green Lands" sung by Yeats, is beautifully situated Rosses Point, a noted golfing resort (championship links) with good sea bathing.

SNEEM, Co. Kerry (Map 4, C5), is a village where the Kenmare (16 m.)–Waterville (20 m.) road crosses the head of the Sneem estuary. Set in a beautiful valley, it is a favourite resort of artists and climbers (the mountains to the NE., N., NW., and W. contain a notable series of cirques and corrie lakes).

A 15-mile mountain drive "of staggering beauty" may be made NE. (crossing the Blackwater valley at Geara bridge) to Windy Gap on the beautiful Killarney–Kenmare road.

The Italianate parish church (1865) was the gift of the 3rd Earl of Dunraven (*see* Adare), an Oxford Movement convert to Catholicism; the parish priest at the time was Father Michael Walsh (1828–66), the "Father O Flynn" of Alfred Percival Graves's well-known ballad; the E. window is a memorial to the poet, Aubrey de Vere (1814–1902; also an Oxford Movement convert; *see* Currah Chase *under* Askeaton). The Protestant parish church dates from the 17th cent.; much altered.

6 m. N. (no road) is Cloon West (*see under* Waterville).

2 m. SSE., in Derryquin, is Parknasilla, noted alike for its genial winter climate and its beauty. The Great Southern Hotel is successor to the residence of Charles Graves (1812–99), Protestant Bishop of Limerick and distinguished scholar, father of Alfred Percival Graves (1846–1931), and grandfather of Robert Graves, poet and novelist. The lovely gardens and woods are a maze of salt-water channels. 2 m. E., SW. of Tahilla, is the hill-top fort of Dunkilla. On the W. side of the bay is beautiful Garinish (Mr G. R. Browne), with its gardens, woods, and sandy coves. Garden-lovers (*not* the general public) should apply for admission permits either to the caretaker at Oyster Bed pier or to the Great Southern Hotel.

10 m. WSW. is Staigue Fort (*see* Castlecove *under* Caherdaniel).

SPIDDAL, Co. Galway (Map 1, C6), is a small seaside resort and market village 12 m. W. of Galway city. Village and locality are the resort of students of Irish and of many who seek quiet holidays. There is a small bathing beach on the E. side of the village; another at the harbour to the W. of the village; further W. are some pleasant small coves.

In the village is St Éanna's Church (1904), an excellent little building by William A. Scott. It has four windows by Sarah Purser and *opus sectile* Stations of the Cross (1928) by Ethel M. Rhind. In the adjacent graveyard are fragmentary remains of the "abbey", a medieval parish church.

Adjoining the village is the demesne of Spiddal House (formerly the home of Lord Killanin). The house is a partial reconstruction of one by Prof. Scott (1910) which was burned down in 1922; the carvings are by Michael Shortall.

2 m. E., in Park, was the home of Rúaidhrí, alias Roderick, O Flaherty (1629–1718), a pupil of An Dubhaltach Óg Mac Fhirbhisigh (*see* Castle Forbes *under* Inishcrone), and himself an antiquary of note (*Ogygia* and *A chorographical description of West or Iar Connacht*) and a great collector of MSS. He ended his days in extreme poverty, bereft of all his literary treasures. His traditional grave and the traces of his house are pointed out.

8 m. W., in Tully, St Colmcille's Church (1963–64; by Daniel Kennedy) is noteworthy for the effective simplicity of the interior and for the works in copper and enamels by Bro. Benedict Tutty, O.S.B., of Glenstal Abbey: font cover, Stations of the Cross, altar crucifix, tabernacle, and sanctuary lamp. Bro. Benedict also designed and made the processional cross, beautiful chalice, and altar cruets.

STEPASIDE, Co. Dublin (Map 6, E7), is a mountainside hamlet on the Dublin (8 m.)–Enniskerry (5 m.) road.

½ m. NNW., close to the remains of the 18th cent. Protestant church of Kilgobbin, is a 12th cent., granite High Cross (Nat. Mon.) with *Crucifixion* in low relief. There was an early monastery, Cell Gobbán, here.

½ m. N. are the ruins of Kilgobbin castle.

2¼ m. SSW., 350 yds W. of the Glencullen road, alt. 1,100 ft on the SE. slope of Two Rock Mountain in Ballyedmunduff, is Giants Grave (Nat. Mon.), a three-chamber wedge-shaped gallery grave. ¾ m. SE., to the E. of the road near Glencullen House gate, is Cloch na gCon, alias the White Stone (Nat. Mon.), a pillar-stone.

STEWARTSTOWN, Co. Tyrone (Map 3, B4), is a village on the Cookstown (6 m.)–Portadown (19 m.) road.

2 m. N. is the early Protestant church of Bally(na)clog. The Rev. Charles Wolfe (1791–1823), poet, had his first curacy here (*see* Castlecaulfeild *under* Dungannon).

13 m. NE. (via Coagh) is Arboe (*see under* Cookstown).

3 m. ENE. is Stuart Hall, seat of Lord Castlestewart. It was built by John Stuart Moore about 1760.

1 m. E. is Drumcairne House, Georgian seat of the Earl of Charlemont.

4 m. ESE., in Magheralamfield, is Mountjoy Castle (Nat. Mon.), built inside a star-shaped campaign fort by a Dutch engineer for Lord Mountjoy's 1602 campaign against Great Hugh O Neill. Captured by Sir Felim O Neill of Kennard (Caledon) in 1641, it was burned down in 1643. The remains are those of a square stone-and-brick building with four projecting, rectangular, loop-holed towers. 2¼ m. WSW., in Killary Glebe, is Clonoe Church, a 15th (?) cent. building restored for Protestant use by William Delgarno and Thomas Morris in 1699. In the church and graveyard are interesting tombstones.

3 m. SW., in the grounds of Roughan House, are the ruins (Nat. Mon.) of a small Plantation castle with round angle-turrets. It was built by Sir Alexander Stewart, but was burnt by Sir Felim O Neill in 1641. In the adjacent lake is a crannóg where Sir Felim is said to have been captured in 1653 by William Caulfeild, brother

of Lord Caulfeild (*see* Charlemont). He was taken to Dublin and hanged.

8 m. SE., in Lough Neagh, is little Coney Island (Nat. Trust), a tranquil waterfowl sanctuary; there are remains of a tower. Open always; boat available from Mr George Forker, Milltown, Birches (telephone Annaghmore 221).

STILLORGAN, (Map 6, E7), is a village on the Dublin (5 m.)–Bray (7 m.) road, in process of engulfment by rapidly spreading suburbs. Stillorgan Castle is now a hospice of the Order of St John of God. Obelisk House takes its name from a mausoleum built by Sir Edward Lovett Pearce for the Allen family. Pearce also prepared designs for converting the house into a Palladian mansion. He died at Tighlorcain House (then The Grove on the Allen estate), 7 Dec. 1733. The 1st Viscount Allen of Stillorgan was a grandson of the builder of Jigginstown House (*see under* Naas). The 2nd was satirized by Swift. – Oriel was the birthplace of the celebrated painter, Sir William Orpen, Bt (1870–1931). – The Esso Petroleum Co's. office (by J. E. Collins, 1961) has a courtyard sculpture by Ian Stuart.

STRABANE, Co. Tyrone (Map 2, D3), is a shirt-manufacturing, market, and Border town on the Derry (14 m.)–Omagh (20 m.) road. It is also an important communications centre, and one of the principal gateways to the Donegal Highlands. It is 1 m. SE. of Lifford (*q.v.*), on the Mourne River near where it unites with the Finn to form the Foyle. The O Donnell castle of Port na dTrí Namhad (1527) was on the near side of the Finn. Manus O Donnell, "Lord of Tír Chonaill, Inis Eoghain, Cinéal Moen, Fermanagh, and Lower Connacht", died there, 9 Feb. 1563. Thirty years earlier he had written his well-known *Life of St Columcille* in the castle.

The town itself offers little of interest, but has associations with a number of eminent men. Captain John Dunlap (1747–1812), printer of the first copies of the American Declaration of Independence and a pioneer American newspaper publisher (the *Pennsylvania Packet*, 1771), served his apprenticeship in Grey's printing works, Main St. He subscribed £4,000 to Washington's army and was a member of the American commander's bodyguard. (James Wilson, grandfather of President Woodrow Wilson, also worked at Grey's prior to emigrating in 1807; *see* Dergalt, *below*.) Guy Carleton, Lord Dorchester (1724–1808), Governor of Quebec 1766–96, who defended Quebec against the United States, 1775–76, and defeated the invaders at Lake Champlain, was a native of the town. Dr George Sigerson (1838–1925), poet and Professor of Biology, University College, Dublin, was born in Hollyhill, 3 m. NE.

6 m. NNE., in a fence on the border of Sandville and Lisdivin, is a pair of standing stones, one with an artificial groove across the top. 4 m. ENE., alt. 600 ft, is Gortmellan (*see under* Dunnamanagh).

4¼ m. NE. is Killynaght Rocking Stone, a collapsed chamber tomb. 2 m. ENE. is Windy Hill Giants Grave (*see under* Dunnamanagh).

2 m. ESE., in Dergalt, is the house (Nat. Mon.) of James Wilson, grandfather of Woodrow Wilson, President of the United States. East of Dergalt, alt. 800 ft on the W. slope of Evish Hill, is Dermot and Grania's Bed, a much-overgrown chambered cairn.

3 m. S. is Sion Mills village. St Teresa's Church (1962–63; by Patrick Haughy) is worth a visit. The lovely *Last Supper* of the façade and the baptismal font (*Good Shepherd*, *The Wise Virgins*, *Noah's Ark*, *St Michael and Satan*) are by Oisín Kelly. The windows (*Our Lady Spinning*, etc.) are by Patrick Pollen.

5 m. S., on a scarp above the E. bank of the Mourne, is Lisky Giants Grave (Nat. Mon.), a wrecked chamber tomb. 3 m. SSW. is Ardstraw (*see under* Newtown Stewart).

3¾ m. SW. is Urney Presbyterian Church, said to be the oldest Presbyterian church in the Foyle valley (1654; reconstructed 1695). There was an early monastery at Urney; also a nunnery of which St Samthann (d. 739) of Clonbroney near Granard was sometime prioress.

STRADBALLY, Co. Laois (Map 6, B4), is a village on the Athy (9 m.)–Port Laoise (7 m.) road. It stands in the heart of the historic territory of the O Mores of Laois, one of whose principal seats was at Noughaval (*below*). The O Mores of Noughaval were for centuries the owners of the so-called *Book of Leinster* (*see* Terryglass *under* Portumna), which was known as *Leabhar na Núachongbhála* (Book of Noughaval) down to the 18th cent. In 1447 O More of Noughaval founded a Franciscan friary (Mainistear na Laoighse) at Stradbally to be the burial place of his family. In 1563 the friary was granted to Capt. Francis Cosby, one of those responsible for the 1577 Massacre of Mullaghmast (*see under* Ballitore). Cosby made a castle of the friary. In 1596 and 1598 the castle was stormed by the O Mores. (The site is now occupied by the Presentation Convent.) On 15 Dec. 1588 three of the Stradbally friars were martyred after torture.

Kevin O Higgins (1892–1927), revolutionary leader and Cabinet Minister, who contributed so much to the Statute of Westminster, was a native of Stradbally, where his father, Dr T. O Higgins, practised as physician.

¾ m. ENE. is Brockley Park, built in 1768 for the Earl of Roden by Davis Ducart.

½ m. SE., Oughaval (alias Ochmills, Oakvale, etc.) townland and church preserve the name of An Núachongbháil (Noughaval, "New Foundation"), a monastery founded by St Colmán moccu Loígse, who had been a disciple of Columcille at Iona.

5¾ m. NE., beyond Vicarstown, on the bank of the Barrow, is the great ringfort of Dunrally. Henry Grattan built a residence in the enclosure.

5 m. SSE., to the N. of the by-road to Bally-lynan, is Ballyadams (*see under* Athy).

2¼ m. SSW. Timogue Protestant church is an interesting 18th cent. re-edification of an earlier church; restored 1964; there is a medieval font. 3 m. SE., in Clopook, is the Dún, a small, stone hill-fort with hut-sites. 3¼ m. S. of the latter, in Manger, is the Ass's Manger, remains of a gallery grave. 1¼ m. SE. of the Ass's Manger, on Boley Hill, is the small, prehistoric hill-fort of Dundrum; in 1798 the Wicklow–Kildare insurgents encamped here. Not far away is Gracefield, a house designed by John Nash in 1817 for the Grace family (*see* Arless). There are many ringforts as well as church and castle ruins in the area. – 3 m. W. of the Ass's Manger, in Monamanry, is Druid's Altar, remnant of a small, chambered cairn.

2¾ m. WNW., to the N. of the Port Laoise road, is the great Rock of Dunamase (150 ft), crowned by the shattered remains of a large castle. Long before the Anglo-Normans came, there was a fort here. It was plundered by the Vikings in 844, when Áed, coarb of Colmán moccu Cremthainn Áin of Terryglass (*see under* Portumna) and of Fintán of Clonenagh (*see under* Mountrath), was slain. Díarmait Mac Murrough gave the place to Strongbow as part of Aoífe's dowry. William Marshall, heir of Strongbow, had a motte castle here, with a ditch and rampart dividing the slope into two or three baileys. About 1250 his son-in-law and heir, William de Braose, rebuilt and enlarged the castle. Through de Braose's daughter it passed to the Mortimers. Conall O More of Laois (d. 1497) wrested the castle from the English, and rebuilt it to be the chief stronghold of his house, which it remained until the Plantation of Laois. In 1641 the Parliamentarian, Sir Charles Coote I, took it from the insurgent O Mores. In 1646 Eóghan Rúa O Neill recovered it for the Catholic Confederates, who held it until 1650, when it was attacked and destroyed by Cromwellians under Hewson and Reynolds. The ruins are those of a complex fortress. On the SE. is a D-shaped outer bailey. Behind this is a triangular walled courtyard entered by a twin-towered drawbridge gateway. Beyond this again, on the summit of the rock, is the heart-shaped inner ward. It is entered by a badly wrecked central gateway, and enclosed by an irregular, towerless curtain. Inside it, on the highest point of the rock, are the remains of a rectangular 13th cent. keep, altered at various dates; it may have been cut off from the rest of the inner ward by a cross-wall. – ¼ m. E. are Cromwell's Lines (a bivallate ringfort); S. of and below the Lines, and above the road through the gap, is the Cromwellian gun platform. – 1½ m. SW. of the Rock, on the W. slope of Hewson's Hill, are the ruins of Dysert(enos) church. Dysertenos (*Dísert Óengusa*) takes its name from the 9th cent. eremitical retreat of Óengus the Culdee, son of Óengaba (*see* Tallaght, *and* Clonenagh *under* Mountrath).

STRADBALLY, Co. Waterford (Map 6, A7), is a village near the sea, on the Dungarvan (8 m.)–Bunmahon (4 m.) road. There are remains of a medieval nave-and-chancel church. In Woodhouse demesne (open to the public) is the pretty little Tay valley. Adjoining the demesne is a good beach, and there are pleasant coves among the cliffs.

NE. of the village, at Toberkillea (holy well), Ballinvoony, are two ogham stones.

2 m. N., in Drumlohan, is an early church site. In the enclosing rampart is a celebrated souterrain ("the ogham cave of Drumlohan"; Nat. Mon.) incorporating ten ogham stones. 1¼ m. SE., in Ballinvoony, is a promontory fort.

2 m. SW., in Old Island townland, is a fine ringfort-type enclosure (site of an early monastery?), formerly revetted with stone. The gateway, facing W., was of large blocks. Inside is a bullaun. There was formerly a broken, cross-inscribed, ogham stone here; it is now incorporated in a field fence.

3 m. SW., in Ballyvoyle, is a large chambered cairn. Near Ballyvoyle Head, in Island Hubbock townland, is Teach na hUamhain promontory fort.

STRANGFORD, Co. Down (Map 3, D5), is a small fishing port on the W. side of the entrance to Strangford Lough, 9 m. NE. of Downpatrick. The many ruined castles of the neighbourhood reflect the insecurity of life and land in this part of Ulster in medieval and early modern times. Several of these castles are said to owe their origin to John de Courcy or other of the earliest Anglo-Normans who seized lands in Ulster.

In the town itself is Strangford Castle (Nat. Mon.), a much altered late 16th (?) cent. fortified town house; perhaps the best example in Ulster (entrance a reconstruction).

3 m. S. is Kilclief castle (Nat. Mon.), attributed to John Cely, or Seely, Bishop of Down (1412–41). Some of the windows have elaborate details. In the early 18th cent. the roof was of thatch, possibly an original feature. This castle seems to have served as a model for several 15th and 16th cent. Co. Down castles.

3½ m. SW. is Raholp Church, alias Teampall Maol (Nat. Mon.). Legend asserts that the original church here was entrusted by St Patrick to his artificer, Bishop Tassach. The ruins, which stand inside an earthen ringwork or rath (whence Ráth Cholpa, Raholp), have suffered from over-restoration. The genuine remains were those of a simple rectangular structure of stone bonded with clay (*see* Derry *under* Portaferry). There are several genuine early gavestones, but the stone altar, holy well, and some other features are suspect. – About ½ m. ESE. of Raholp village is Giants Grave (Nat. Mon.), the remains of a long-chambered (court?) cairn. ½ m. SE. of the cairn, on Castlemahon Mountain, is a stone circle; Western Neolithic sherds were found in a peripheral pit; a central cist contained a child burial. – About ¾ m. SSE. of the village is Loughmoney Cromlech (Nat. Mon.), a ruined chamber tomb. 700 yds E. of this, in Carrownacaw, is the Long Stone, a 10-ft pillarstone.

2 m. W. is Castleward House, built about 1765 for Benjamin Ward, 1st Viscount Bangor; one front is strictly Palladian, the other Gothick. The interior has excellent stucco (Gothick as well as Rococo) and panelling. The house and 600 acres of the beautiful demesne have been given to the National Trust by Viscount Bangor, who has lent the period furniture. Open to the public: Grounds: during daylight every day; House: 1 April to 30 Sept., Wed. and Sat. 2–5 p.m. Admission 1/–. ⅓ m. NNW. of the house are two prehistoric pillarstones. ½ m. NNE. of the house, in Audleystown, is Castle Ward (Nat. Mon.), a small, well-preserved Plantation castle built about 1610 by Nicholas Ward. ½ m. further NNE., is Audley's Castle (Nat. Mon.; apply to caretaker at Green Cottage), a well preserved 15th/16th cent. stronghold of the Audleys. Seemingly modelled on Kilclief, it had a small bawn, and is thought to occupy the site of an early 13th cent. motte-castle erected by the first of the Audleys to seize lands in Ulster. Castle and estate were sold in 1646 to Bernard Ward. ¼ m. NW. is a round cairn. On a low hill ¾ m. W. of the castle is a second round cairn; it contains a large cist. To the N. are the remains of Templecormick, a small dry-masonry church set inside a dilapidated cashel. Nearby are Toberdoney (holy well) and a rock-cut souterrain with lintelled roof. ½ m. further W. is Audleystown double-court cairn (Nat. Mon.). Its eight chambers contained thirty-four burials, mostly uncremated, which were accompanied by Western Neolithic pottery, etc. 2 m. W. (by the main road) is 16th cent. Walshestown castle (Nat. Mon.).

STROKESTOWN, Co. Roscommon (Map 2, B6), is an 18th and early 19th cent. village on the Longford (15 m.)–Elphin (7 m.) road. It was laid out for Maurice Mahon (1738–1819), who was created Baron Hartland in 1800: two streets intersecting at right angles, the broader terminating on the E. at his lordship's gate, on the W. at an octagonal church. Strokestown Park House (previously Baune House), sometime seat of the Mahons, who acquired the property late in the 17th cent., is a great 18th cent. mansion with Ionic portico. The ruins of a nearby medieval church were turned into a Mahon mausoleum.

4 m. SE. is Slieve Baune (Sliabh Baghna; 846 ft), offering excellent views of the Central Plain and of the middle Shannon and its lakes.

6½ m. S., in Fairymount, is the modern parish church of Tibohine parish. There are three Michael Healy two-light windows (1908) here: *God the Father with SS John and Elizabeth; Ecce Homo and Mater Dolorosa, with Lamb and Host; SS Peter and Anna, with Lamb*; also a Hubert Mc Goldrick window (*St Brigid*, 1922). Tibohine takes its name, Tigh Bhaoithín, from St Baithín Mór, great-grandson of Niall Nine-hostager, who founded a monastery there.

SUMMERHILL, Co. Meath (Map 6, C2), is a small village on the Trim (6½ m.)–Kilcock (7 m.) road. It was a good example of an "improving" landlord's planning: a tree-lined mall leading to the principal avenue to Lord Langford's great mansion. Miscellaneous medieval fragments, including the richly carved shaft of a 1554 Peter Lynch (*see* Knock Castle *below*) memorial cross, have been placed on the green. (There was another Peter Lynch cross near Rathmolyon, 3¼ m. W.) Lord Langford's mansion, attributed rather doubtfully to Richard Cassels, was twice destroyed by fire, completely so during the Civil War (1922). For forty years the ruins provided a scene of splendid, melancholy, desolation, but were bulldozed away (1961–62) by the Land Commission and the masonry taken to build a college in Dowdstown and a church in Kells. Today little more remains than two monumental flanking gateways. The radiating avenues of trees too are gone, save only that (renewed) leading from the village.– NE. of the house-site is Knock (Linch). In a grove near the NW. foot of the hill are the ruins of a 16th/17th cent. Lynch stronghouse (Knock Castle), defended in June 1642 for five days and nights by Barnaby Geoghegan of Ballynagreine against Charles II's Lord Lieutenant, Ormonde. Their ammunition expended, the fifty defenders surrendered on promise of quarter but were butchered to a man.

4 m. NE., in Galtrim, is the motte of a castle constructed by Hugh de Hose, to whom Hugh de Lacy had granted (about 1172) "all the land of Deece which Mac Giolla Sheachlainn held". The castle here was one of the many abandoned by the Normans after the destruction of Slane in 1176.

3½ m. ESE., in Kilmore churchyard, is the 1575 gravestone of the scribe, Rughraidhe Buidhe Mhag Mhaghamhna of Kilmeague, Co. Kildare: *Crucifixion* and inscriptions in Irish and Latin.

2 m. SE. are remains of Drumlargan church. Drumlargan is the Dungan Hill where, 8 Aug. 1647, Jones and the Parliamentarian army of Dublin destroyed the Confederate Catholic field army of Leinster ineptly commanded by Thomas Preston (*see* Trim). Col. Glengarry's regiment of Scottish "Redshanks" made a heroic stand. After the battle some 3,000 – nearly half – of Preston's men were massacred.

3½ m. NW. are remains of Dangan Castle, sometime home of the Wellesleys (*see* Carbury *under* Edenderry): the house was built on to the ruins of a Wellesley castle (a border fort of the Pale). The Duke of Wellington (*see* Trim) is said to have spent much time there as a boy. Dangan was the birthplace of Don Ambrosio O Higgins (1720?–1801), Spanish Viceroy of Chile and Peru and father of Bernardo O

Plate 14. Glenariff, Co. Antrim

Higgins, Liberator of Chile. 1¾ m. NNW. is Bray Hill (see Laracor *under* Trim).

SWINEFORD, Co. Mayo (Map 1, D4), is a small market town on the Charlestown (7 m.)–Foxford (9 m.) road, 7 m. NE. of Kiltimagh.

8 m. N., in Cartronmacmanus, is a court cairn (ruinous) with a "transept" on the N. side of each of the two segments of the gallery.

3 m. SW., in Meelick, a Round Tower (Nat. Mon.) marks the site of an early monastery attributed to St Broccaidh. There is an early gravestone here, with a crudely interlaced cross and border. It is inscribed OR[ŌIT] DO GRIENI ("A prayer for Griene").

SWORDS, Co. Dublin (Map 6, D2), a village on the Dublin (8 m.)–Drogheda (22 m.) road, is threatened with early engulfment by the city. It takes its name, Sord Choluim Chille, from a pure well (*sord*) said to have been blessed by St Columcille, who is also said to have consecrated a stone cross and founded a monastery which he committed to St Fíonán Lobhar ("the Leper"), and in which he left a gospel book written with his own hand. But the monastery does not figure in Irish records prior to the 9th cent., and it may be that a 6th/7th cent. foundation of St Fíonán's was conveyed to the Columban monks about that time. Bishops of Swords are mentioned in the 10th, 11th, and 12th centuries. In 1014 the bodies of Brian Boru and his son, Murchad, rested overnight at the monastery on their way to solemn burial at Armagh. The monastery was burnt six times between 1020 and 1166. The fire of 1130 destroyed the churches and their relics. Before the Anglo-Norman invasion the monastery and its possessions had been transferred to the Archbishop of Dublin, and Swords subsequently became one of the principal archiepiscopal manors. In 1219 the church was made a prebend – the "Golden Prebend of Swords" – in St Patrick's Cathedral, Dublin. (In 1366 the prebend was held by no less a person than the celebrated William of Wykeham, Bishop of Winchester and Chancellor of England.) Today the only relic of the ancient monastery is the Round Tower; it has a pre-Romanesque doorway. Adjoining it is the 14th cent., square steeple of the medieval prebendal church. Nearby (to the E. of the Protestant church) is a small stone cross.

At the N. end of the main street are the ruins (Nat. Mon.) of the archbishop's manorial castle. It was begun about 1200, but was modified in the 13th and again in the 14th and 15th centuries. In plan it is an irregular, 1½-acre pentagon. (The stepped battlements are typical of 15th cent. Irish work.) In its heyday it included a chamber and cloister for friars; also a range of buildings, including a Great Hall, or residence along the E. side. The principal remaining building is the gatehouse, with warden's quarters, etc. (modified in modern times), on the W. side, and a chapel with 13th cent. W. tower (containing porter's lodge below and chaplain's rooms above) on the E. side. At the SW. angle of the curtain is a turret on squinch arches. Nearby in the W. wall is a small square flanker. At the N. angle is a square tower which commands the whole castle. This was doubtless the Constable's quarters: stairways give access to the roof and to the parapet walks of the curtain. In the E. curtain also is a square flanker. The castle ceased to be an archiepiscopal residence in the 15th cent. (see Tallaght), and the constableship ultimately became hereditary in the Barnewall family.

The Borough School was designed by Francis Johnston (1761–1829).

At the S. end of the village is St Colum's Well.

2¼ m. N. are the ruins of Bellinstown (Bellingstown) castle.

1 m. ENE. on the seashore are the remains of Seatown castle.

¾ m. SE. is St Werburgh's Well.

2 m. W., by the roadside to the N. of Knocksedan bridge, is Brazil Moat, a large tumulus. NE. are the remains of Brazil House, home of the Boltons from at least 1630 onwards; it was destroyed by fire in the 19th cent. Brackenstown House, in the adjoining demesne, was the home of Robert Molesworth, 1st Viscount Swords, to whom Swift addressed his *Drapier's Letters*. ¾ m. SW. of Brazil Moat are the remains of Killeek church. 3 m. W. of the latter are the remains of Chapel Midway, a medieval parish church.

1 m. WNW., in Mooretown, some fragmentary medieval ruins ("Glasmore Abbey") and St Cronan's Well mark the site of an early monastery founded by St Crónán.

4½ m. NW. are the remains of Killossery church which, like Killeek, was a dependency of the "Golden Prebend of Swords". 1½ m. SW., at Kilsallaghan, are ruins of a medieval church and castle. The castle was held against Ormonde by Confederate Catholics in 1641.

TAGHMON, Co. Wexford (Map 6, C6), is a village on the New Ross (13 m.)–Wexford (8 m.) road, to the W. of Forth Mountain (779 ft). It takes its name, Teach Munnu, Munnu's house (see Taghmon *under* Castlepollard *and* Tihelly *under* Tullamore), from a monastic church of some consequence founded by St Munnu (Mo-Fhinnu), alias Fintán moccu Moie, son of the druid Tailchán (Tulchán). Munnu went to Iona just after St Columcille's death, but returned to Ireland on the instructions of Abbot Baíthíne. At the synod of Magh Ailbhe (on the borders of Carlow and Kildare), which met about 630 to consider the problem of the date of Easter, Munnu was the spokesman of the recalcitrant traditionalists against St Laisrén of Leighlin (see Leighlinbridge). He died in 635 and was buried at Teach Munnu, which today is represented only by its name, by Tobermunna, and by the head and base of St Munna's Cross in the graveyard. The Talbots had a castle here, of which a tower survives.

H. F. Lyte (1793–1847), author of the well-known hymn "Abide With Me", was for a time Protestant curate of Taghmon.

5 m. W. is Foulkesmill, where (as at Clongeen, 1½ m. SW.) battles took place in 1798. Longgraigue House, to the SW., was the headquarters of Gen. Sir John Moore.

6 m. W. is Newcastle motte.

TALLAGHT, Co. Dublin (Map 6, D7), is a village at the foot of the Dublin mountains, on the Dublin (7½ m.)–Blessington (12½ m.) road.

The place is celebrated in Irish history as the seat of a monastery founded by St Máel-Rúáin (d. 792), leader of the anchoritic (*céle Dé* "culdee") movement (p.27). Máel-Rúáin appears to have been a disciple of Fer-dá-chrich (d. 747) of Dairinis (*see under* Youghal). Among his own disciples were Máel-Díthruib of Terryglass (*see under* Portumna), Óengus mac Óengobann of Clonenagh (*see under* Mountrath), and Dysertenos (*see* Dunamase *under* Stradbally, Co. Laois; *also* Coolbanaghar *under* Port Laoise *and* Carrigeen *under* Croom), author of the earliest Irish martyrology (*below*). Closely associated with Tallaght in the *céle Dé* movement were Terryglass and Finglas (*q.v.*). So high indeed stood the fame of Tallaght and Finglas in the 9th cent., that the *Triads of Ireland* call them "The Two Eyes of Ireland". The prestige of Tallaght itself was such that in 811 the monks were able to prevent the King of Tara, Áed, son of Niall, from holding the great Assembly of Teltown (Aonach Tailteann), because the sanctuary of their monastery had been violated by the Uí Néill. Máel-Rúáin himself has been credited with the authorship of a religious *Rule* and (with lesser reason) of a hymn and a penitential. From his monastery came two celebrated documents, the *Martyrology of Óengus* (about 800) and the *Martyrology of Tallaght* (early 10th cent.). Its proximity to Norse Dublin exposed Tallaght to the Vikings, and the monastery appears to have decayed relatively early. After the Anglo-Norman invasion the church became parochial, and the abbey lands became an archiepiscopal manor. About 1324–49 the archbishops of Dublin erected, on or close to the monastery site, a manorial castle which was a bulwark of the English Pale and which in the following century became the chief archiepiscopal residence outside Dublin (*see* Swords). Only a small tower survives in the grounds of the Dominican friary which now occupies the site.

St Maelruan's (C. of I.) Church stands on the site of the medieval parish church, which itself occupied part of the site of the ancient monastery. The bell-tower is that of the medieval church, but the parapet has been altered. In the churchyard are St Mulroon's Losset, a large, rude, granite basin, and St Mulroon's Stone, a small, plain, granite cross.

2 m. NE. are the remnants of small Tymon castle. Kilnamanagh townland, to the NW., preserves the name of *Cella Monachorum*, where St Kevin of Glendalough received his early training from Eógan (of Ardstraw?), Lochán, and Énna.

2 m. SE. is Mountpelier (*see under* Rathfarnham).

2½ m. S. is Glenasmole, where the Dodder has been dammed to form a reservoir. At the head of the valley, to the E. of the Dodder and the N. of Glenasmole Lodge, is The Shed Stone, a small prehistoric chamber tomb. In the grounds of Glenasmole Lodge is Finn Mac-Cool's Stone, remnant of another chamber tomb (?).

2 m. SW., in Ballynascorney townland, to the W. of a lane crossing the hill from Jobstown to the Ballynascorney Gap, are a stone circle (remains of a chambered cairn ?) and Raheen-dhu, a bivallate ringfort. ½ m. NW., on Knockanvinidee, are stone circles.

TALLOW, Co. Waterford (Map 5, D6), a village on the Lismore (5 m.)–Youghal (12 m.) road, was the birthplace of the sculptor, John Hogan (1800–1858), as also of his weaver-poet namesake, John Hogan (1780–1858), Bard of Dunclug. The Tallow district was planted with English Protestants in the early 17th cent. by Richard Boyle, "Great" Earl of Cork (*see* Youghal).

1 m. N., on the River Bride, is Tallowbridge. Tallow Hill (592 ft), to the NE., offers very fine views. Lisfinny House, ½ m. W., incorporates the tower of a Desmond castle. Castle and lands were granted to Sir Walter Ralegh in 1587 (*see* Youghal).

7 m. ESE. is Strancally (*see under* Cappoquin).

3 m. SE., at Kilwatermoy, are remains of a medieval church and Tobar na Croiche Naomhtha (Well of the Holy Cross), where "stations" are made on 14 Sept.

2¾ m. W., near the Bride in Co. Cork, are the ruins of Mogeely castle, favourite residence of Thomas, 11th Earl of Desmond, whose wife was the celebrated "Old Countess" of Desmond (*see* Dromana castle *under* Aglish). The castle was part of the loot acquired by Sir Walter Raleigh at the Plantation of Munster. From Raleigh it passed to Richard Boyle.

2½ m. further W., on a rock over the Bride, are the ruins of Conna castle (16th cent.; Nat Mon.), birthplace of the "Súgán", Earl of Desmond. Slighted by Essex about 1599, but repaired, the castle was stormed by Confederate Catholics under Lord Castlehaven in 1645, bombarded without success by Cromwell in 1650, burned in 1653, and in part restored in the last century. 2 m. E. of Conna is Mogeely church, in use until 1776.

TANDERAGEE, Co. Armagh (Map 3, B5), is a small linen town on the Portadown (6 m.)–Poyntz Pass (5 m.) road. The "castle" (now a factory) occupies the site of a castle of the O Hanlons, whose lands were confiscated at the Plantation. In 1641 the O Hanlons recaptured the castle and destroyed it. In the second half of the cent., outlawed Redmond O Hanlon (*see* Slieve Gullion), hero of popular song and story, terrorized the English of Armagh and neighbouring counties. He is buried in the ancient graveyard, Relicarn (*see* Terryhoogan *under* Scarva), 2 m. SE.

TARA, Co. Meath (Map 6, C2), a low hill 1 m. W. of the Dublin (23 m.)–Navan (6 m.) road, is one of the most famous places in Ireland. Its fame, however, may be due to the fantasies conjured up by Thomas Moore's ballad, rather than to appreciation of its ancient significance, or of its monuments (which are not spectacular), or of its delightful prospects over the rich, rolling Midlands – "Gentle Midhe of the corn measures".

At the dawn of Irish history Tara is found to be an important centre of paganism – associated particularly with the goddess Medb (Maeve; the Queen Mab of English fairy lore; *see also* Rathcroghan). It was the seat of priest-kings who, in addition to being Over-kings of Meath, were also heads of the Uí Néill federation, and thus the most powerful kings in Ireland. The apotheosis of each King of Tara was his symbolic mating (at a ritual banquet, *Feis Temrach*, attended by all the Uí Néill kings as well as by his vassals) with the local earth goddess.

The Uí Néill descended from Niall Nine Hostager, who seized Tara in the 5th century and whose sons partitioned the Midlands (*Midhe*, Meath) and most of the ancient Fifth of the Ulaid between them. The dispersal of Niall's descendants over so much of the North, as well as the Midlands, was to affect the future of Tara, for the law of succession favoured collaterals rather than sons. In the event, the title "King of Tara" passed to rulers whose seats were elsewhere, often, indeed, far off in the North-West, so that the political significance of Tara withered away. (After 727/8 it was only a titular royal seat, though occasionally the venue for important gatherings.) The final victory of Christianity also contributed to the decline of Tara by depriving it of its religious significance, and Díarmait mac Cerrbeóil (Adamnán's *totius Scotiae regnator*, *Deo auctore ordinatus*; *see* Rathbeg *under* Antrim) was the last King of Tara to celebrate the heathen Feis (560). Medieval Christian writers could hardly confess the true nature of the Christian impact on Tara. They therefore invented a legend to the effect that the hill was abandoned because Díarmait mac Cerrbeóil had been cursed by St Rúadhán of Lorrha and the "Twelve Apostles of Ireland" for slaying an outlaw who had sought ecclesiastical sanctuary.

The ancient remains (Nat. Mons.) at Tara, thought not spectacular, are very extensive. Their official names are not necessarily genuine. (They derive from medieval documents as interpreted by modern scholars.)

The circuit of the monuments may conveniently commence at the churchyard, which encroaches on the ancient site. (Built into the tower of the Protestant parish church is a 15th cent. window. In the church are an ancient font and a 1595 memorial to Sir Robert Dillon and his wife, Catherine Sarsfield. The two-light E. window (*Pentecost*; 1936) is by Evie Hone. W. of the church is Adamnán's Cross, a broken pillar with a much-weathered figure which some would interpret as the Celtic god, Cernunnos. Nearby is a prehistoric standing stone (?).

Adjoining the churchyard on the W. is the Fort of the Synods (Nat. Mon.), a trivallate earthwork savagely mutilated some sixty years ago by British Israelites in a quest for the Ark of the Covenant. On the W. a small, earlier, burial mound (the King's Chair) has been brought within the ambit of the outer bank. Recent excavations have shown that the fort proper had had four structural phases between the 1st and 3rd centuries A.D. At the centre had stood timber houses. The defences had included timber palisades.

S. of the Fort of the Synods is the Fort of the Kings (Nat. Mon.), an oval hill-top, 950 ft by 800 ft, enclosed by a ditch with remains of a bank on its outer margin. Excavation has shown the ditch to have been cut into the underlying rock to more than 11 ft below the present surface. Near the N. end of the enclosure is the Mound of the Hostages (Nat. Mon.), alleged site of Lia Fáil, the inauguaration stone of the Kings of Tara. Excavation has shown this to cover the stone cairn of a small passage grave dating from about 2100 B.C. Secondary Bronze Age burials included one with Mediterranean faience beads of about 1350 B.C. Towards the centre of the enclosure are two conjoint earthworks (Nat. Mon.): the Royal Seat on the E., Cormac's House on the W. The Royal Seat is a normal bivallate ringfort with a rectangular house-site near the centre. Cormac's House is a high, flat mound enclosed by two banks and ditches. On the N. the outer bank bends around a pre-existing burial mound. A shoddy modern statue commemorates St Patrick's legendary visit to the court of King Loígaire. A pillarstone close by marks the grave of insurgents killed in the battle of Tara, 1798. It is said formerly to have lain near the Mound of the Hostages, and so is now labelled Lia Fáil.

S. of the Fort of the Kings are the remains of Loígaire's Fort (Nat. Mon.), a large, univallate ringfort.

NW. of the Fort of the Kings, on the flank of the hill, are the Sloping Trenches, alias the Sloping Graves (Nat. Mon.), two unusual ring-earthworks. Between them are three small mounds.

E. of the Sloping Graves is Grainne's Fort (Nat. Mon.), a burial mound enclosed by a ditch and bank. Gráinne ("Ugliness"; often rendered "Grace" in English!), like Medb, was a goddess.

Further E. is the Banqueting Hall (Nat. Mon.), a rectangular earthwork some 750 ft by 90 ft. Medieval accounts describe the Banqueting Hall (Tech Midchuarta, "House of Mead-circling") of Tara as a great hall of five aisles. The central aisle was a circulation passage with hearths, cauldrons, lights, etc. The others were divided into booths, or cubicles, allocated according to the social precedence of those feasting with the King of Tara.

Near the SW. angle of the Banqueting Hall is a small burial mound; there is another to the SW.

½ m. S. of Tara, on the next hill-top, is Rath Maeve (Nat. Mon.), a univallate hill-fort 750 ft in diameter. 2¼ m. S. is Dunsany Cross (see under Dunshaughlin).

4 m. E. of Tara is the Hill of Skreen (507 ft; fine views), whose name preserves the memory of Scrín Choluim Chille, "Columcille's Shrine", a monastery to which the great saint's relics were brought in 875. In 1127 the Dublin Norse carried off the shrine, but it was restored to its house inside a month. In 1185/86 the new, Norman, proprietor, Adam de Feipo, bestowed the church on St Mary's Abbey, Dublin. In 1341 Francis de Feipo founded an Augustinian friary at Skreen, where there was also a medieval nunnery. Crowning the hill are the ruins (Nat. Mon.) of a manorial church of Rathmore (see under Athboy), Killeen, and Dunsany (see under Dunshaughlin) type. In the massive 14th/15th cent. tower are stored a font basin, a tomb slab, and other medieval fragments. NE. of the church is a stone cross (Nat. Mon.) with rude Crucifixus. Skryne Castle, on the SE. slope of the hill, incorporates medieval work (largely obscured). Nearby is the motte of a castle built by Hugh de Lacy for Adam de Feipo. 1¼ m. S. (via Obertstown crossroads), on the Drogheda road, is St Columcille's Church. In the churchyard (to which they were brought from Trevet church N. of Dunshaughlin), exposed to the elements, are interesting fragments from the 1571, Renaissance-style, tomb of Sir Thomas Cusack (Lord Chancellor of Ireland under Henry VIII and Mary Tudor) and his wife: Crucifixion panel, weepers (Sir Thomas's four sons and six daughters), etc. – 2½ m. SE. of Skreen is Corbalton Hall, a good Georgian house.

1⅔ m. NW., in Lismullin, is Rath Lugh, a circular earthwork with a large, irregular annexe. It is thought to be named after the god, Lugh the Many-skilled (alias the Long-armed). Alicia de Angulo founded an Augustinian nunnery in Lismullin in 1240. Not far away was the Augustinian nunnery of Odder, founded by the Barnewalls.

TARBERT, Co. Kerry (Map 4, D2), on the Glin (4 m.)–Ballylongford (5 m.) road, is a quiet village overlooking a beautiful reach of the Shannon estuary.

¾ m. N. is Tarbert House, a Georgian residence. On Massy's Hill, ½ m. N., is a 17th cent. star fort.

1½ m. N., on Tarbert Island (road-bridge), is an early 19th cent. battery, built to command Tarbert Race between the island and Kilkerin Point on the opposite shore (where there is also an early 19th cent. fort).

TEMPLEMORE, Co. Tipperary (Map 5, D3), a small market town on the Roscrea (12 m.)–Thurles (9 m.) road, lies at the E. foot of the Devil's Bit Mountain (1,577 ft).

The town takes its name from a "great church" whose remains may be seen in the Town Park. The latter was formerly the demesne of The Abbey, seat of the Carden family. George Borrow, whose father and brother were stationed at Templemore for some months in 1816, describes the district in Lavengro (see Clonmel).

8 m. NE. are the ruins of Clonbuogh castle; to the W. are the remains of St Anne's Church.

3¼ m. S. are the ruins of Loughmoe Court (Nat. Mon.). The S. end is the tower of a 15th cent. castle; it has 17th cent. windows; in the first-floor room is a fine 17th cent. fireplace. The remainder, known locally as The Court, is a 17th cent. embattled house. Home of the Purcells, Loughmoe Court gave his title to Nicholas Purcell, Baron Loughmo[r]e, one of the Jacobite signatories of the Treaty of Limerick, 1691. W. of the railway are the ruins of a church with Purcell monuments.

2½ m. SW., near the Borrisoleigh road, are the remains of the five-storey keep of Knockagh castle.

4 m. SW., in Drom, are remains of a church and, nearby, a ringfort. According to some, this was the meeting-place of the celebrated synod of Rath Bréasail, 1110.

TEMPLEPATRICK, Co. Antrim (Map 3, C4), one of the oldest Presbyterian settlements in Ireland, is a village on the Belfast (11 m.)–Antrim (6 m.) road.

"Jemmy the Weaver" (James Hope, 1764–1847) is the most celebrated native of the place. Son and grandson of Presbyterian refugees from Scotland, he was a member of "Grattan's" Volunteers, an organizer of the United Irishmen, and a lifelong Republican. In the daylong battle of Antrim, 1798, he was in the foremost rank of the valiant rebels. Like Samuel Neilson and Thomas Russell, he was also involved in Robert Emmet's rebellion, 1803. He is buried in the family grave at Mallusk on the old Belfast road.

Upton Park, alias Castle Upton, a Robert Adam house, is the 1788–89 successor (remodelled 1830) of Sir Humphrey Norton's 1619 castle, which incorporated remains of a monastery. The monastery refectory survives (upper storey 1832). The Upton mausoleum (1783) is also by Adam. The Uptons (Viscounts Templetown) descend from a captain in the Earl of Essex's army (1598).

4 m. NE., in Ballypalady and Ballyhartfield, are six ringforts (one trivallate?).

3 m. ESE., in Craigarogan, is Granny's Grave, alias Carngraney (the Ordnance Survey's Carn Greine; Nat. Mon.): a passage grave whose "passage" – which held cremations – is shut off from the "chamber". The tomb is said to have been ringed by one or two stone circles enclosed by "an earthen ditch".

2 m. SSE. is Lyle's Hill (753 ft), which has given its name to one variety of Irish "Western Neolithic" pottery. 12½ acres of the hill-top are enclosed by a degraded, boulder-revetted bank (an unfinished Iron Age hill-fort?). At the summit is a low round cairn. The sill-stone (Ulster Museum) of the sill-and-jambs "entrance" in the megalithic kerb bears chevrons and hatched triangles. The disturbed central grave (circular) contained a cremated burial (young person), neolithic and Food Vessel sherds, a flint arrowhead, and a hollow scraper. In and under the cairn were thousands of Neolithic sherds and flints; also an axe and axe fragments of porcellanite from Tievebulliagh (see under Cushendall). On and in the pre-cairn soil were abundant Neolithic sherds and flints. Pre-cairn pits also held Neolithic sherds. Three post-cairn cists held cremations (Food Vessels and an Encrusted Urn). 6 m. SE. are the remains of Ballyyutoag court cairn.

2½ m. W. (½ m. E. of Dunadry), in Kilmakee (Mo-Chaoi's Church), are remains of a round cairn with megalithic kerb ("Stone Circle"; Nat. Mon.).

3 m. NW. is Donegore (see under Antrim). It was to Donegore Hill that Henry Joy Mac Cracken withdrew after the Battle of Antrim to await reinforcements which never came.

TEMPO, Co. Fermanagh (Map 2, D4), is a village on the Enniskillen (7 m.)–Fintona (10½ m.) road.

5¾ m. NNE., alt. 650 ft on Knockennis, is a ruined court cairn (Giants Graves: Nat. Mon.).

4½ m. E. are the remains of Tullyweel castle, home of the Brian Maguire, who, in 1638, caused the Royal Irish Academy MS., C. vi. 1, to be compiled from "the books of O Clery, O Duignan, and O Mulconry".

3¼ m. SSW., and ¾ m. NE. of Coolbuck church, alt. 450 ft in Cloghtogle, is Druids Altar, a chamber tomb. In the same townland, alt. 700 ft, is a round cairn. – ¼ m. NW. of the church, alt. 650 ft, is Coolbuck Druids Altar and Giants Grave (Nat. Mon.), a wrecked gallery grave. ½ m. W. of the church, alt. 550 ft, are remains of another chamber tomb; nearby is a low, round cairn. ¾ m. SW. of the church, alt. 550 ft in Mountdrum, is Giants Grave (Nat. Mon.), a chambered cairn.

½ m. SW., alt. 300 ft in Doon, is the Gray Stone, remnant of a chamber tomb. ¼ m. SE. (to the E. of the Enniskillen road), alt. 300 ft in Doon, are the Grey Stones (Nat. Mon.), two stones, now superimposed, with Bronze Age cup marks and spirals as well as bullauns.

2 m. further SW. is Mullynock, alias Topped Mountain (910 ft), with a cairn (Nat. Mon.) on the summit. A secondary cist contained remains of an adult male skeleton accompanied by a gold-mounted bronze dagger, traces of a cremation, and a Food Vessel.

¾ m. NW., alt. 600 ft in Edenmore, is a stone with three bullauns. Tradition holds that the two bullauns on the top are the imprint of St Patrick's knees.

3½ m. NW., in Ballyreagh, is Giants Graves, a court cairn (Nat. Mon.).

TERMONFECKIN, Co. Louth (Map 6, D1), is a small village on the Drogheda (5 m.)–Clogherhead (2¾ m.) road.

It takes its name from the celebrated 6th cent. saint, Féichín of Cong, Co. Mayo, and Fore, Co. Westmeath, who founded a monastery here also.

In the 12th cent. Donnchad O Carroll, King of Uriel (see Louth), founded a monastery of Canons Regular of St Augustine, St Mary's Priory of Augustinian Canonesses (a dependency of Clonard abbey of canonesses), Tempoll Leptha Féichín (the Church of Féichín's Bed), and a "great church".

The Anglo-Norman conquest of SE. Uriel split the primatial diocese of Armagh into two parts: one – including the primatial see – "among the Irish", where the English king's writ did not run; the other (Co. Louth) "among the English". Since after 1346 the primates, approved by the English Crown, were nearly always of English speech and descent, if not indeed English born (Octavian del Palacio, 1479–1513, was an Italian), they resided of necessity "among the English", principally at Termonfeckin, and made St Peter's Church, Drogheda, their pro-cathedral. After the Reformation the Protestant primates continued to reside at Termonfeckin until 1613. The primatial manor was destroyed at the 1641 insurrection.

The Protestant churchyard occupies the site of the ancient abbey, whose only relics are: (a) an early gravestone (in the church porch) inscribed OROIT DO ULTAN ET DO DUBTHACH DO RIGNI IN CAISSEL ("A prayer for Ultán and Dubhtach who made the cashel"); (b) a High Cross (Nat. Mon.); (c) a fragmentary early Crucifixion slab; (d) the base of a small early cross. On the E. face of the High Cross is a carving of the Crucifixion: on the W. face, one of the Last Judgement (Christ in Majesty?). The base of the cross is modern.

Termonfeckin Castle (Nat. Mon.) is a small, 16th cent. tower (relic of a Dowdall castle?).

Grianán, formerly Newtown House, S. of the village, is a training centre of the Irish Countrywomen's Association, to which it was presented by the Kellogg Foundation, U.S.A.

2¾ m. NNE. is Clogherhead, a fishing village and small resort. It takes its name from the nearby headland, which is flanked by excellent sandy beaches. In the village are remains of a small nave-and-chancel church. In Clogher

Head is The Red Cave, so called from the fungus-covered rock. The country round about is very attractive, and has many associations with the Blessed Oliver Plunket. He is said to have ordained priests at Glaspistol Castle ($\frac{1}{2}$ m. S. of the village), sometime home of the Dowdalls; the square tower is well preserved. – By the shore, to the N. of the village, is St Dennis's Well. – 1$\frac{1}{2}$ m. NW. of the village, beside the remains of Mayne church (15th cent. residential tower), is a motte.

THOMASTOWN, Co. Kilkenny (Map 6, B5), formerly Grenan, is a small market town beautifully situated on the Nore, at the junction of the Kilkenny (11 m.)–New Ross (16 m.) and Carlow (24 m.)–Waterford (21 m.) roads.

The town takes both its present English name and its Irish name (Baile Mhic Anndáin) from Thomas fitz Anthony, Anglo-Norman seneschal of Leinster, the motte of whose castle survives. In the Middle Ages it was a walled town, but the only remains of the fortifications are Sweetman's Castle and Low St "Castle" by the bridge. The principal feature of the town is the remnants (chancel arch, N. arcaded wall, fragment of W. wall; Nat. Mon.), of the parish church of the Assumption of the Blessed Virgin Mary ("St Mary's"), founded by fitz Anthony late in the 13th cent. The church comprised sacristy, chancel, aisled nave, and SW. tower; S. of the chancel was a detached chapel. After the Reformation all fell into ruin, save only the chancel, which was used as the Protestant parish church until 1809. In that year most of

Commissioners of Public Works in Ireland

Cantwell effigy at Kilfane, Thomastown

the ruin was swept away to build the existing Protestant church. In the churchyard are the head of a High Cross, two badly weathered effigies of ecclesiastics, and some 16th and 17th cent. tombstones. The Convent of Mercy has a statue of the Blessed Virgin Mary brought from Spain in 1660 by Patrick Lincoln, wine merchant.

$\frac{1}{2}$ m. SE., on a bretasche, or rectangular earthwork, on the W. bank of the Nore, are the well-preserved remains of Grenan castle (Nat. Mon.), which was for centuries a stronghold of the Dens.

Immediately SE. of the town, on the E. bank of the Nore, is Dangan townland. A century ago a prehistoric chamber tomb and nearby groups of pillarstones were reported here; in the three neighbouring townlands were thirty-six large tumuli.

2$\frac{1}{4}$ m. NNE., at Kilfane (site of an early monastery), are the ruins and churchyard (Nat. Mons.) of an early 14th cent. church which served as the Protestant parish church until 1850. (Hence the altered windows and doors.) The sedilia show traces of polychrome painting. The tower on the N. side was the priest's residence. There is a magnificent, Cantwell, armoured effigy of about 1320, An Cantual Fada – Long Cantwell. 2 m. NNE. is Tullaherin (*see under* Gowran).

4 m. E., to the W. of Saddle Hill, in Blessington, is a trivallate ringfort one acre in extent. The outer rings are of earth, the inner one of stone. To the E., at the foot of Saddle Hill, is another large ringfort.

5 m. SE. is Inistioge (*q.v.*).

2 m. SSE., near the W. bank of the Nore in Dysart, are remains of a fortified church. Nearby to the S. was Dysart castle, home of the Berkeleys and alleged birthplace of the celebrated philosopher, George Berkeley (1685–1753), Bishop of Cloyne (*q.v.*). Not far away, in Coolmore House demesne, is the river-bank cave which was the hiding-place of James Freney, the 18th cent. highwayman.

1$\frac{1}{2}$ m. SW., on the little River Eoir, are the fine ruins (Nat. Mon.) of the Cistercian abbey of Jerpoint (Eoiripons, de Jeriponte). The abbey was founded – on the site of a Benedictine (?) monastery – by Donal, grandson of Donnchadh, Mac Gillapatrick, King of Ossory, and was colonized from Baltinglass (*q.v.*) in 1180. In 1184 it, in turn, sent colonies to Kilcooly (*see under* Urlingford) and Killenny. In 1227, like Baltinglass, it was affiliated to Fountains Abbey, Yorkshire, in accordance with the anglicizing policy of the Anglo-Norman colony, but 160 years later the abbot was fined for contravening the notorious Statutes of Kilkenny by accepting Irish monks. The abbey was largely rebuilt in the 15th cent. At the Dissolution it was leased by the Crown to the Earl of Ormond. The ruins are perhaps the most interesting Cistercian remains in Ireland, notwithstanding the 19th cent. maltreatment of the cloister and claustral buildings. The original

Cloister arcade, Jerpoint Abbey, Thomastown

*View across cloister garth from the south-west,
Jerpoint Abbey, Thomastown*

church (about 1180–1200) closely resembled that of Baltinglass, but had a barrel-vaulted presbytery and transept chapels. It followed the normal Cistercian plan: cruciform, with aisled nave (six bays) and E. chapels (two) in each transept. In the E. part of the nave the piers are alternately cylindrical and square, as at Baltinglass; and the capitals have Irish Romanesque details, again recalling Baltinglass. There was a low screen (perpyn) wall between the piers of the arcade. The crossing and the three E. bays of the nave were screened off, to form the choir, by a pulpitum with two recessed chapels on its W. face. These served the lay brothers' choir,

which occupied the W. part of the nave. The large E. window is a 14th cent. replacement of a 12th cent. triplet; the central tower dates from the 15th cent.; the N. wall of the nave is a 15th cent. rebuilding. The S. arcade of the nave was blocked up, seemingly in the 15th cent., and the S. aisle taken into the cloister. Despite its 13th cent. appearance, the cloister arcade is 15th cent. work; the carvings, of unusual interest, include an armoured knight and his lady (claimed to be Peter Butler, d. 1493, and Isabella Blanchfield). (Another fragment, with figures of two armoured knights, may be seen in Fiddown Protestant church.) In the E. cloister range are the sacristy, chapter-house, and day room; the monks' dormitory was above; the S. range contained the refectory. A number of interesting monuments survive: the effigy of Felix O Dulany, Bishop of Ossory, 1178–1202, in the E. niche on the N. side of the chancel; the tombstone (about 1275) with very fine engraved effigies of "The Brethren", two mailed knights; and the Robert Walsh (d. 1501)–Katerine Poher tomb, by Rory O Tunney. – ¼ m. NW., in Newtown Jerpoint, are the site of a medieval town and the ruins of its little parish church (St Nicholas's). The church dates from the 12th/13th cent.; the unusual, groin-vaulted, rood gallery, and the three-storey dwelling tower which partly masks it, are 15th cent.; some of the windows are also 15th cent. In the graveyard is a tomb mensa with the effigy of an ecclesiastic in low relief; nearby are the base and socket of the town market cross. The town was founded in 1200 by William the Marshal, and fell into complete ruin in the 17th cent. – 1 m. SW. of Jerpoint Abbey, in Ballylowra, are two portal dolmens (one ruinous).

4 m. W., on the W. bank of the Nore, is Mount Juliet, a fine house built in 1780 for the Earl of Carrick. It is now the home of Major

St Christopher, Jerpoint Abbey, Thomastown

Weepers from an altar tomb, Jerpoint Abbey, Thomastown

McCalmont, who has a well-known stud farm here.

3 m. WNW. are the ruins of Ballylinch Castle, a 15th cent. tower with early 17th cent. house attached; in the 16th and 17th centuries it belonged to the Graces.

2 m. NW., at Legan "Castle", is a cross-inscribed ogham stone.

THURLES, Co. Tipperary (Map 5, D4), is a market and sugar-manufacturing centre on the Suir, 9 m. S. of Templemore and 13 m. N. of Cashel. Since Penal times it has been the cathedral town of the archdiocese of Cashel and Emly.

The town was a creation of the Butlers, who conquered the district at the expense of the O Fogartys of Éile.

Between West Gate and Parnell St are remains of Black Castle (1493?).

At the W. end of the bridge across the Suir is Bridge Castle, a tower of 1453 (?).

Further E., on the site of a medieval friary, is the Cathedral of the Assumption. This is a pedestrian essay (1865–72) by J. J. Mc Carthy in an Italianate Romanesque style. The high altar tabernacle was designed by the celebrated Baroque architect and painter, Andrea Pozzo, S.J. (1642–1709), for the Gesù in Rome; the back has been modified for its Thurles setting and the cupola added. The interior decoration was designed by J. C. Ashlin. The side-altar statues of the Sacred Heart and Our Lady are by Benzoni.

Opposite the cathedral is the entrance to St Patrick's College. Founded in 1836 "for the liberal education of young gentlemen", this is now a college for the education of priests,

chiefly for dioceses overseas. The National Synod of 1850 which, among other things, condemned the Queen's Colleges, was held here. In the library is a small collection of ecclesiastical antiquities, including St Caillín's Shrine, a book reliquary made in 1436 for Brian O Ruairc and his wife, Margaret O Brien. E. of the cathedral, in St Mary's Avenue, is St Mary's Protestant Church. Here may be seen the tomb of Edmund Archer, a 1520 (?) monument with figures of saints and the effigies of an armoured knight and his lady; it has lost its polychrome painting.

2 m. N. is unfinished Brittas Castle. Projected as a large-scale copy of Warwick Castle, complete with water moat, the building of this 19th cent. extravagance came to a sudden stop when the proprietor was killed by a falling piece of masonry.

4½ m. E., at Twomileborris, are ruins of a castle and a church; also a motte or tumulus. 2 m. further E., to the E. of the Urlingford–Cashel road, in Leigh(more), alias Leamakevoge (Líath Mór Mo-Chaomhóg), a complex of house-sites and earthworks surrounding two small ruined churches (Nat. Mons.) marks the site of a monastery founded in the 7th cent. by St Mo-Chaomhóg, nephew of St Íde, which became one of the principal monasteries of Éile, numbering Brian Boru among its patrons. The larger church, which represents at least five phases of construction and alteration between the 11th/12th and the 15th cent., has a simple Romanesque N. door and chancel arch. The present chancel was the original church, a small, single-chamber edifice with *antae*. This was enlarged by adding a chancel at the E. end. Later this chancel was demolished, and a relatively large nave erected to the W. of the original structure, which thereby became the chancel. In the 15th cent. the existing, smaller, nave was erected inside the walls of the large nave, the chancel was vaulted, and the Gothic windows were inserted. The smaller church, to the N., is a simple, single-chamber structure with *antae* and trabeate W. doorway. 6 m. E. of Leigh is Kilcooly Abbey (*see under* Urlingford). 8 m. S. of Leigh is Derryvella (*see under* Urlingford).

6 m. SE., via Horse-and-Jockey, are the ruins of Grallagh castle (Nat. Mon.): 16th cent. tower and traces of the bawn. 2¼ m. NW. is Moycarkey castle (*see under* Holy Cross Abbey, *below*).

8½ m. SE., via Littleton, on a 20-acre island emerging from a bog in Lurgoe, is the ancient monastic site of Derrynavlan, founded by Rúadhán of Lorrha (*q.v.*). Here are the Gobaun Saer's Grave (a small mound), the "Abbey" (remnants of a 13th cent. nave-and-chancel church), and some medieval carved slabs (Nat. Mons.).

4¼ m. SW., beside the Suir, are the interesting ruins (Nat. Mon.) of Holy Cross Abbey. It was founded in the 12th cent. for the Order of Tiron, Donal Mór O Brien, King of Limerick (Thomond), being an important patron. Like Fermoy abbey, the only other Tironian house in Ireland, it passed to the Cistercians before the close of the century, but was colonized from Monasternenagh (*see under* Croom). It took its name from a relic of the True Cross. The relic made the abbey a noted place of pilgrimage, and about the 15th cent. the buildings were extensively remodelled. (The work of this phase includes outstanding examples of the distinctly Irish style of Gothic, as well as of 15th cent. craftsmanship.) The remains comprise a well-preserved church, remnants of the cloister and its ranges, and – to the SE. – ruins of the infirmary and guest-house (abbot's lodging?). The church is typically Cistercian: cruciform with E. chapels (two) in each transept, low central tower, and aisled nave. At the 15th cent. rebuilding, the N. aisle, choir (including the two E. bays of the nave), tower, transepts, and presbytery (chancel) acquired their existing form; but the S. aisle and the four W. bays of the nave (the lay brothers' choir) were left unaltered (windows and door excepted), and are substantially 13th cent. work. Noteworthy features of the church are: the absence of a clerestory; the vaulting of the E. arm; the varied 15th cent. windows; the excellent 15th cent. sedilia in the presbytery, with the arms of England (first escutcheon) and Butler (third and fourth escutcheons); the mural painting (a hunting scene) in the N. transept; the unique 15th cent. shrine (?) between the chapels of the S. transept; the Transitional doorway (rebuilt) from the S. aisle to the E. walk of the cloister; and the living quarters over the E. end of the church (cf. Knockmoy and Kilcooly abbeys and Hore Abbey, Cashel). The frag-

ments of the cloister arcade (*c.* 1450) have some interesting carvings, e.g., on the SE. pier, the arms of Abbot Donnchadh Ó Conghail (*c.* 1448–55) with inscription recording the erection of the arcading (*me fieri fecit*). – 4 m. E. of the abbey are the ruins of Moycarkey castle: a 16th cent. tower at the centre of a large bawn; to the E. are remains of a church. – 3½ m. SW. of the abbey, in Clogher, is Druid's Altar, a chamber tomb. ¾ m. SW. of the tomb are the Druidical Stones of Clonoulty; remains, perhaps, of a great, rectangular, megalithic enclosure. In the Middle Ages there were small houses of the Knights Templar and the Knights Hospitaller of St John of Jerusalem in Clonoulty. 4 m. N. of the Clogher tomb are the ruins of Moyaliff church.

3 m. WNW., in Ballynahow, is the circular tower (Nat. Mon.) of a Purcell castle.

TIMAHOE, Co. Laois (Map 6, B4), is a village 7½ m. SE. of Port Laoise and 5 m. SW. of Stradbally, on the hill roads to Abbeyleix and Castlecomer.

It takes its name, Teach Mo-Chúa, from the monastery founded here by St Mo-Chúa, son of Lonán (d. 657). Of this monastery there survive fragments of a church and a very fine 12th cent. Round Tower (Nat. Mons.). The tower has a beautiful Romanesque doorway with details recalling Rahan (*see under* Tullamore). The church, to the E. of the tower, was converted into a small castle in the 17th cent., when the roofless nave was adapted to serve as the bawn and a tower was erected over the chancel.

In the Catholic church are two single-light windows (*Immaculate Conception* and *Sacred Heart*) by Michael Healy (1922).

½ m. W. of the village is the Rath of Ballynaclogh, motte and bailey of a castle built in 1182 for Meiler fitz Henry by Hugh de Lacy.

4 m. E. is Clopook (*see under* Stradbally, Co. Laois).

TINAHELY, Co. Wicklow (Map 6, C5), is a village on the Aughrim (8 m.)–Shillelagh (6 m.) road. Rebuilt by Earl Fitzwilliam after destruction in the 1798 rebellion, it has a good Court/Market House. Nearby, in Coolruss, are Black Tom's Cellars, remains of a large house begun by Lord Deputy Strafford about 1639, and, like his great house at Jigginstown, Co. Kildare (*see under* Naas), never completed.

5¾ m. N. is Moyne, birthplace of Edward L. Godwin (1831–1902), founder of the New York *Nation* (1865).

TIPPERARY, Co. Tipperary (Map 5, C4), which gives its name to the county, is a market town and manufacturing centre (dairy products, linoleum, etc.) of the fertile Golden Vale (Golden Vein), 26 m. SE. of Limerick, 12 m. WSW. of Cashel, and 14 m. NW. of Cahir. 3 m. S. rise the Slievenamuck (1,216 ft) hills, N. boundary of the beautiful Glen of Aherlow (*see* Bansha *below*, Cahir, *and* Galbally). Some pleasant walks with excellent views may be had in these hills, notably by the road to Newtown across the saddle between Slievenamuck and Carrigeenina.

The town, an Anglo-Norman creation, figures little in Irish history. During the 19th cent. Land War it was the scene of the abortive New Plan of Campaign: the tenants of the Smith Barry estate abandoned their homes for a time and moved to New Tipperary, outside the town.

John O Leary (1830–1907), Fenian leader and admired friend of William Butler Yeats, was a native of the town. Liam Dall Ó hIfearnáin, 18th cent. poet, and the grandfather of William Hazlitt (1778–1830), essayist, were natives of Shronell, 3 m. W. James O Neill, father of Eugene O Neill, the American playwright, was born near Tipperary.

In Main St is a good statue (by John Hughes, 1898) of Charles T. Kickham (1826–82), novelist and Young Irelander (*see* Mocklershill *under* Cashel).

¾ m. N., in Tipperary Hill, is the Moat, motte-and-bailey relic of the Anglo-Norman invasion of the Kingdom of Limerick.

5½ m. N., in Moatquarter near Donohill, is another motte-and-bailey; to the E. are remains of a manorial church, N. of which is St James's Well.

4¼ m. ENE., in Moatquarter, is Kilfeakle Moat, remains of a motte-and-bailey castle built in 1192 by William de Burgo during a Norman attempt on Donal Mór O Brien's kingdom (*see* Limerick); there are traces of a later stone castle, *caput* of a de Burgo manor; to the N. is the site of the ancient church which gives Kilfeakle its name. ¾ m. N. are the remains of the latest medieval castle of Kilfeakle, ¼ m. W. of which are those of a medieval church.

5 m. SE., at the mouth of the beautiful Glen of Aherlow, is the village of Bansha. Darby Ryan (1770–1855), poet, is buried here. The circuit of the valley is a pleasant drive of 25 m. 4 m. S., in Ardane, is St Berrahert's Kyle. For this and other antiquities of the valley, *see under* Galbally *and* Cahir.

5 m. W., in Lattin, is a large tumulus.

8½ m. W. is the little village of Emly. St Ailbe (later Oilbhe; anglicized "Alby", "Albert"), that "other Patrick of the island of Ireland", who died in 527, founded a church here which was the principal church of Munster prior to the rise of Cashel, and which became the see of a diocese which survived until 1718. The parish church occupies the site of the medieval cathedral: in the churchyard are St Alby's Well (visited 12 Sept.) and a rude stone cross.

4 m. NNW. is Solloghodbeg (Soloheadbeg). The first ambush of the Anglo-Irish guerrilla war (1919–21) took place near the quarry, 21 Jan. 1919; a monument at Sollogod (Solohead) hamlet, 4 m. W. of Tipperary, commemorates the event. Solloghod is the Sulchóid where King Mahon of Thomond and

his brother, Brian Boru, routed the Limerick Norse in 967.

7 m. WNW., in Longstone, is a ringwork with central pillarstone.

TOBERCURRY, Co. Sligo (Map 1, E3), is a market village on the Sligo (23 m.)–Collooney (14 m.) road.

3 m. NE. (3½ m. S. of Abbey Court, *below*) is Achonry, where St Nath-Í, disciple of St Finnian of Clonard, founded, about 530, a monastery which in the 12th cent. became the see of the diocese to which it has given its name. The medieval cathedral is represented, however, only by some shapeless ruins. The Catholic cathedral is now at Ballaghaderreen.

5¼ m. NE. (3½ m. N. of Achonry), at the foot of Knocknashee ("Hill of the Fairies", 910 ft), and to the E. of the Coolaney road in Lavagh, are the tower and S. transept chapels of Abbey Court (Cúirt Rúaidhrí Bhallaigh), a friary built in the 15th cent. for Franciscan Tertiaries (brethren and sisters) by the O Haras.

1½ m. E., near Caltragh, are the remains of Wellmount chambered cairn.

3 m. E., in Chaffpool, are the remains of two chamber tombs.

5 m. WSW., on the road to Aclare and beautifully sited beside the River Moy in Banada, are the remnants of Corpus Christi Priory, first Irish house of Augustinian friars of the Regular Observance. It was founded by Donnchadh Dubh O Hara in 1423, but was still incomplete in 1460. The stones of seven Burke castles are said to have gone into the buildings. 2 m. WSW. of Banada bridge is Coolrecuill, where the celebrated poet, Tadhg Dall Ó Huiginn (1550–91), made his home. The family home of the O Huiginns in the 16th and 17th centuries was at Dougherane, a few miles away (in the Curry district). – 5 m. W. of Banada bridge (1¾ m. WSW. of Aclare) are the remains of the O Hara castle of Belclare. – 5 m. NW. of Banada bridge, by the Ballina road in the Ox Mountains, is picturesque Lough Talt. 2 m. ESE. of the lake, in Castlerock (Castlecarragh), is Leaba Dhíarmada agus Ghráinne, a ruined court cairn. Nearby to the W. is the site of Castle Carragh. Tadhg Dall Ó Huiginn satirized the O Haras of Castle Carragh and paid for it with his life.

7 m. WNW. (2½ m. SW. of Cloonecool), in Sessuecommon, is Giants Grave, remains of a full-court cairn.

TOOMYVARA, Co. Tipperary (Map 5, D3), is a small village on the Nenagh (8 m.)–Roscrea (13 m.) road. In the 7th cent. St Donnán founded a monastery (Túaim, alias Teampall, Donnáin) here, which later became an Augustinian priory (dedicated to the Blessed Virgin) dependent on Monaincha (*see under* Roscrea). In the 15th and 16th centuries the wardenship of the priory was held by the O Mearas, who made the priory their place of sepulture. Hence the change of the name, Túaim Donnáin, to

Túaim Uí Mheadhra (Toomyvara) "O Meara's Túaim". Near the Catholic church is the "Abbey", ruined church of the 15th cent. priory; close to the N. wall is a fragment of the 15th cent. tomb of Joannes O Meara, with the effigy of an ecclesiastic. Across the road, in an ancient graveyard (site of Donnán's monastery?), is a small ruin; until recently there was a 9th/10th cent. gravestone near the E. door. 2½ m. E. are the ruins of Aghnameadle church. SE. are the remains of a castle and of Aghnameadle Court, sometime homes of a branch of the celebrated Mac Egans, hereditary jurists to the O Kennedys of Ormond. 4½ m. ENE., on Benduff Hill, Cloncannon, is Dermot and Grania's Grave, a small cairn.

TORY ISLAND, Co. Donegal (Map 2, B1), lies 7½ m. NW. of Horn Head. It is best reached by boat from Magheraroarty, Gortahork.

The coast is bounded by high cliffs and isolated tors in many places; but the features of greatest interest are the remains of Dún Bhalair and of the monastery founded by St Columcille in the 6th cent., and raided in 1595 by the English garrison of Sligo, led by George Bingham and Ulick, son of Réamonn na Scúab Burke.

The scanty monastic remains (Nat. Mon.) are situated in West Town. They comprise the ruins of a Round Tower, portions of a sculptured High Cross, a number of carved fragments, a plain, T-shaped, stone cross, and two early grave-slabs. There are also "cursing stones" said to have been effectively used in 1884, when the gunboat *Wasp* endeavoured to land police and troops to collect rates from the islanders. (The *Wasp* was wrecked with loss of life.)

Dún Bhalair (Doon Valor), Balar's Fort, a quadrivallate promontory fort at the E. end of the island, contains numerous hut-sites. It takes its name from Balar of the Baleful Eye, the mythological Fomorian associated with the island (*see* Cloch Cheannfhaoladh *under* Gortahork).

TRALEE, Co. Kerry (Map 4, C3), county town, bacon-curing and marketing centre, and small seaport, is situated at the head of Tralee Bay and the NE. corner of the magnificent Corcaguiney peninsula ("Dingle Peninsula"), 16 m. SW. of Listowel, 20 m. NNW. of Killarney, and 31 m. ENE. of Dingle. To the NE. rise Stack's Mountains; to the S. and SW., Slieve Mish (Baurtregaun, 2,796 ft). The town is a convenient base for exploring the beauties and antiquities of the E. half of Corcaguiney.

The palatine earls of Desmond had their principal castle at Tralee. Town and castle suffered severely during the rebellion of the 15th earl, and were granted thereafter to Sir Edward Denny, an English newcomer. In 1641 they were captured after a siege by Confederate Catholics led by Sir Piaras Feitéir (*see* Ballyferriter), but fell two years later to the notor-

ious renegade, Murrough the Burner O Brien. In 1691 the Jacobites fired the town on the approach of superior Williamite forces.

St John's Church, Castle St, is a good Gothic Revival essay (1870) by J. J. Mc Carthy. It has two windows (1957) by Patrick Pollen: two-light *Four Evangelists* and rose *Trinity*.

The Court House, Ashe St, is by Sir Richard Morrison (1767–1849), a pupil of Gandon's. It has a good Ionic portico.

The 1798 memorial in Denny St is by Albert Power.

In Abbey St is the graveyard of the Dominican friary of the Holy Cross, founded in 1243 by John fitz Thomas, ancestor of the Earls of Desmond. Thirteen earls were buried in the friary, of which little remains but a few carved stones preserved at the modern Dominican priory. The priory church was built by George Ashlin to the design of his master (and partner), Edward Welby Pugin. In the sacristy are stained glass panels by Michael Healy (1912).

2 m. NNE., on the hill-slope in Garrane, is Liosnadreeglee, a fine trivallate ringfort; there are many ringforts in the district.

3 m. ENE., in the grounds of Chute Hall, are two ogham stones taken from Kilvickillane, Smerwick Harbour (*see under* Ballyferriter), in 1848.

1 m. E. are the ruins of Ratass church (Nat. Mon.), a nave-and-chancel structure with *antae*, trabeate W. door (architrave), and simple Romanesque E. window.

3 m. E. is Ballyseedy House, built in 1760 for the Blennerhassets, after whom Blennerville village, on the Dingle road, was named.

8 m. E. is Glounageentha, alias Glanageenty, a defile in the Glannaruddery Mountains (Knight's Mountain, 1,097 ft). The unfortunate 15th Earl of Desmond sought refuge from the English here with his last adherents in the winter of 1583. On the morning of Martinmas he was discovered and butchered by an O Moriarty and an O Kelly! (His followers had seized cattle of O Moriarty's.) The cuckoo called that winter's night at Ard-mhic-Ghráinne. Down to recent times the fitful wail of the sea winds was known locally as "Desmond's howl". A low, coffin-shaped mound near the head of the glen is the Desmond's Grave of local tradition.

3¼ m. S., in Glanaskagheen, alias "Scota's Glen", a bogus ogham inscription and a flag-stone mark "Scota's Grave". Scota, according to a pedantic fiction, was the widow of Míl (Milesius), whose people – the prehistoric Gaelic invaders of Ireland – waged a great battle with the mythological Túatha Dé Danann at the foot of Slieve Mish. Scota and another Milesian princess, Fais, were among the slain. Fais was buried in Gleann Fhaise (Glenash; *see* Killelton, *below*).

3 m. SW., in the ruined medieval church of Annagh (Nat. Mon.), is a 13th cent. carving (armed horseman). 200 yds W., at the side of a ruined stone ringfort in Trughanacmy, are remains of a chamber tomb.

8½ m. SW. is the ancient church of Killelton,
The kerbed mound on which it stands is traditionally the grave of Fais, who was slain in the
battle of Slieve Mish (*see* Glanaskagheen,
above). There is also a pillarstone here; to the
W. and NW. are remains of clocháns, etc. 400
yds NW. is Cloch na Croise, a cross-pillar.

10 m. SW. is Camp village. There is a good
sandy beach to the N. – Some 400 yds SE., on
the lower slopes of Caherconree Mountain, are
remains of a chamber tomb; also a great ogham
stone, to which a forger has added FECT
CONURI. – ½ m. S. is Naoise's Grave. – 1 m.
SE., in Curraduff, is a pillarstone; there are
others in the neighbouring townlands of Glandine and Kilteenbane. Also in Curraduff is
Lisparkeenrelig, an early church-site. – 4 m.
SE., via the Finglas valley, is Caherconree
Mountain (2,715 ft). It takes its name from
Cathair Chon-Raoí, a great promontory fort
whose remote remains (Nat. Mon.) lie at the
altitude of 2,050 ft. The fort itself is called after
the mythological Cú-Raoí mac Dáire. A legend
explains the name of the Finglas, "white
stream": Cú-Raoí's faithless wife turned its
waters white with milk to inform her husband's
enemies of his presence; they climbed the mountain, took him unawares, and slew him. – 1¾ m.
WSW., in Scrallaghbeg, is Tobernagalt. Nearby, in Foilatrisnig, are Clochnagalt (a pillarstone) and a ringfort; S. of the latter, in
Glannagalt, is another pillarstone; to the W. is a
third; ¾ m. SE., in Doonore South (500 yds W.
of the main road), is a second Tobernagalt.
Glannagalt, Tobernagalt, and Clochnagalt take
their names (Gleann na nGealt, etc.; "Valley
of the Lunatics", "Well of the Lunatics",
"Stone of the Lunatics"), from the insane who
allegedly went there in search of a cure. – 2 m.
SSW., in Maumnahaltora, are a prehistoric
chamber tomb and penitential stations.

TRAMORE, Co. Waterford (Map 6, B7), on
Tramore Bay, 7 m. SSW. of Waterford, is one
of Ireland's popular seaside resorts. Local
walks are: E. along the Cush sandspit to
Tramore Burrow (2½ m.); SSW., via Doneraile
Walk and the cliffs, to the Metal Man on Great
Newtown Head (2½ m.); via the Waterford road
to the Metal Bridge and thence NW. to Kilbride (3 m.; remains of church, castle, and
earthworks at Kilbride; Knockeen, Carriglong, and Munomahoge chamber tombs within
easy reach); W. to Fennor and Dunhill (6 m.;
Dunhill chamber tomb, church, and castle
ruins, and Ballynageeragh chamber tomb within reach).

The sculptor, John Edward Carey (*c.* 1785–
1868) was a native of Tramore.

The Church of the Exaltation of the Holy
Cross (1856–71) is a good Gothic Revival building by J. J. Mc Carthy.

2 m. NNE., in Drumcannon, is St Conan's
Stone. 1½ m. W. is Carricklong passage grave
(*below*). – 3 m. N. is Ballindud Cromlech (*see
under* Waterford).

4 m. NNE., on the Waterford road, is Grace
Dieu, a good Georgian house.

5 m. ENE. the dilapidated remains of Kil-
macleague church, a bullaun, and a medieval
font, mark the site of a monastery founded by
St Mac Líag, disciple of Déaghlán of Ardmore.
The Anglo-Normans changed the dedication
to St Michael, and a *pátrún* is still held at
nearby Clohernagh on the Sunday within the
octave of Michaelmas. 1 m. NNW. of Clohernagh bridge is Ballyganner Kill(eenagh), an
ancient bivallate church-site of one acre. The
enclosure is divided by a drystone wall. Excavation revealed the post-holes of a timber structure (church?). The only surviving monuments
are an early cross-slab and a small cross-pillar.
– 3 m. ENE. of Clohernagh bridge is Harristown (*see under* Dunmore East).

3 m. N., in Carricklong, is a V-shaped passage grave. 1 m. W. is Munmahoge Cromlech,
a ruinous V-shaped passage grave. 2½ m. WNW.
of Munmahoge are Gaulstown and Pembrokes-
town (*see under* Waterford).

2½ m. SSW., on Great Island head, West-
town, is The Port, a promontory fort.

3 m. SSW., on the W. side of Lady's Cove, is
Illaunacoltia promontory fort (greatly defaced).
Nearby to the W. is Garrarus strand.

4 m. WSW., in Islandkane South, are the
remains of a small, rude church. ½ m. due S.,
on the headland adjacent to Sheep Island, is a
promontory fort. There are also remains on the
island.

5 m. WSW. is the secluded strand of Kilfarrasy. Nearby is the Island of Kilfarrasy, a
defaced promontory fort.

6 m. WSW., at Annestown, is a good beach.
To the SE. of the river-mouth and beach is
Green Island head, with remains of a promontory fort. SW. of the village is Carrickadurrish
promontory fort. – 1¾ m. WSW. is Dunbrattin
promontory fort. – 1½ m. NNE. is Dunhill
(*below*).

10 m. WSW. is Bunmahon (*q.v.*).

3½ m. W. is Fennor. The Church of the
Immaculate Conception (1894) is by Doolin.
2 m. W., at Woodtown bridge, are the remains
of the rock castle of Dunhill, a Power stronghold. 1¼ m. N. of the castle is The Church of
the Sacred Heart (1884), also by Doolin. Not
far away is a chamber tomb with earth-fast
capstone. In the adjoining townland of Ballynageeragh is a portal dolmen (Nat. Mon.). 2 m.
WNW. is Savagetown portal dolmen. – 1½ m. N.
of Fennor church is Matthewstown Giants
Grave, alias Leaba Thomáis Mhic Chába, a
V-shaped passage grave (Nat. Mon.). ½ m. N.
is Ballyvellon (*see* Gaulstown *under* Waterford).

2 m. WNW. is Carrickavantry chambered
tumulus.

TRIM, Co. Meath (Map 6, C2), since 1955
the cathedral town of the Protestant diocese of
Meath, is a small market town where the
Dublin (28 m.)–Athboy (8 m.) road crosses the

Boyne. In the Middle Ages it was one of the principal strongholds of the English Pale, with a great castle, an Augustinian priory, Dominican and Franciscan friaries, a nunnery-cum-hospital, and a parish church. Nearby were the cathedral of the diocese of Meath and an Augustinian hospital-friary. Were its medieval remains properly maintained, it would be one of the show-places of Ireland.

According to ancient tradition, the Trim country was converted to Christianity by Bishop Lommán, a British disciple of St Patrick's (*Patricii hostiarius*). The lord of the district, Felim, son of King Loígaire of Tara, presented "his territory with all his goods and all his race" to Lommán and Patrick, and Patrick built a church. In time the church acquired a monastic character, and Lommán's successors came to combine the offices of bishop and abbot. For generations they were drawn exclusively from Felim's descendants. In 1152 the Synod of Kells decreed the amalgamation of the little diocese with those of Ardbraccan, Slane, Duleek, and Clonard (*see under* Kinnegad), to form the diocese of Meath. This was duly done in 1174 by Bishop Echtighern of Clonard. In 1206 Simon de Rochfort, first Anglo-Norman bishop of the new diocese, transferred the see from Clonard to Newtown Trim (*below*).

At the Norman invasion Hugh I de Lacy set up the chief manor and castle of his lordship of Meath at Trim. His motte-and-bailey castle was levelled in 1174 by Rury O Conor, but was promptly restored by the warden, Hugh Tyrell of Castleknock. In time a town grew up in the shelter of the castle; it was re-walled in 1393. Several Anglo-Norman parliaments met there in the 15th cent. Among the enactments of the parliament of 1447 was one to the effect that every man wishing to be accepted as English should abandon his Irish-style moustache and shave both lips. At the beginning of August 1647, Preston (*see* Gormanston *under* Balbriggan), Confederate Catholic commander for Leinster, laid siege to Trim. Michael Jones came up with the Parliamentarians of Dublin and, in an effort to make Preston join battle, laid siege to Tremblestown castle (*below*). Preston thereupon set off for defenceless Dublin, but Jones overtook him at Dangan Hill (*see under* Summerhill). In 1649 a Confederate Catholic force occupied the town, but was driven out by the Parliamentarian, Sir Charles Coote II, who lost his life in the fighting.

The town is dominated by the Castle (Nat. Mon.) on the S. bank of the Boyne. This is one of the finest surviving examples of medieval military architecture in Ireland. The square keep, 75 ft high, with a tower projecting from the middle of each face, dates from about 1200/1220. (The mound on which it stands is doubtless a remnant of the motte of Hugh I de Lacy's original fortress, 1172–73.) On the ground floor are the Great Hall and a small chamber; in the E. tower is a small chapel. Of the curtain wall, which enclosed about two acres, considerable stretches (of various dates) remain. These include the gatehouse and eight flanking towers, of which the most interesting are the circular tower with a barbican (on the S.) and the square tower with a sallyport (on the N.). SE. of the latter is a crypt. The moat was fed by the Boyne. – King John's expedition of 1210 against the de Lacys brought him to Trim in July of that year. He confiscated the castle, but gave it back in 1215. In 1399 Richard II of England left his cousins, Humphrey of Gloucester and Henry of Lancaster (afterwards Henry V), in ward in the castle. Richard of York, heir (through the Mortimers) to the de Lacys and to the de Burgo earls of Ulster, and Lieutenant of Ireland since 1447, spent the winter of 1449–50 at the castle, and may have been there repeatedly in 1450 and again in 1459–60. The castle was taken, together with the town, by Silken Thomas in 1537. In 1647 the castle was refortified by the Confederate Catholics, but was captured, after bombardment, by Sir Charles Coote II.

W. of the castle, between Castle St and Emmet St, and again W. of Emmet St, are fragments of the town wall. The Court House occupies the site of the medieval Franciscan friary. Arthur Wellesley, later Duke of Wellington, lived as a boy in Emmet St (*see also* Dangan Castle *under* Summerhill). At the S. end of the street is a column raised in his honour in 1817. Nearby St Patrick's Church (1902) is by Hague.

On the N. side of the Boyne (Abbey Lane off High St) are the remnants of St Mary's Priory of Canons Regular (Victorine Congregation) of St Augustine: (*a*) beneath Talbot Castle, the undercroft of the refectory; (*b*) a part incorporated in fragmentary Nangle Castle (a late stronghouse; Nat. Mon.); (*c*) E. of the latter, the Yellow Steeple (Nat. Mon.), a magnificent 14th cent. seven-storey (125 ft), bell-tower blown up by command of Ormonde in 1649. The priory is commonly held to have occupied the site of the ancient episcopal-monastic church of Trim. Its miraculous statue of the Blessed Virgin, "the Idol of Trim", was wantonly destroyed at the Reformation. Talbot Castle, a late stronghouse (modernized) with the arms of Talbot, served for a time as the Protestant diocesan school (Arthur Wellesley was a pupil). 150 yds SE. are the remains (Nat. Mon.) of little Sheep Gate, survivor of the town's five gates.

Towards the N. end of the town is St Patrick's Protestant Cathedral (until 1955 the parish church). Built in 1802, it incorporates the tower and maltreated parts of the nave walls of the medieval parish church. The 19th cent. W. window has 15th cent. human masks. High above the 19th cent. doorway of the tower are the arms (impaling Mortimer and de Burgo) of Richard of York. In the porch are miscellaneous tomb and cross fragments, etc. Built against the W. wall of the nave is a medieval font; the coats of arms retain traces of their colouring. E. of the church are remains of the medieval chancel: excellent three-light, 15th cent. S. window, one of whose human-mask label stops wears a ducal coronet (Richard of York ?).

N. of the town some low mounds mark the site of a Dominican friary founded in 1263 by Geoffrey de Geneville, who had acquired the Liberty of Trim, half of the de Lacy lordship, by marrying one of two de Lacy heiresses. His grand-daughter brought his de Lacy inheritance to the Mortimers by marrying Roger III, Earl of March and Ulster.

4¾ m. NE. is Bective (q.v.).

1 m. E., on the N. bank of the Boyne at Newtown Trim, originally Nova Midia, are the ruins (Nat. Mon.) of the beautiful Cathedral of SS Peter and Paul and its priory. The see was set up here in 1206 by Bishop Simon de Rochfort, who confided the services and fabric to a community of Augustinian canons of the Congregation of St Victor of Paris. (From this fact the ruins are commonly, but erroneously, called Newtown Abbey.) The cathedral was destroyed by fire in the Middle Ages, and the nave-aisle and the transepts were never rebuilt. The ruins therefore represent, in the main, the choir (which was vaulted) and a short portion of the nave of de Rochfort's church. In the S. wall of the chancel is a weathered Romanesque aumbry; in the N. wall, a weathered episcopal effigy. The fragments of the Victorine priory include the chapter house and the refectory (which stands on an undercroft). E. of the cathedral are the ruins of the medieval parish church. A tomb fragment with small *Coronation of the Virgin* has been mounted in the outer face of the S. wall. In the church is the excellent, if weathered, altar tomb of Sir Luke Dillon of Moymet and his wife, Jane Bathe; Sir Luke's effigy has Renaissance armour. Sir Luke, Chief Baron of the Exchequer at the time of Elizabeth I, was father of the first earl of Roscommon. His uncle, Thomas, was prior of the cathedral canons in 1511. His father obtained possession of the priory temporalities at the Dissolution. He himself got those of St. Mary's Priory. Nearby is St Peter's Bridge, partly ancient. On the S. side of the river are the overgrown and neglected remnants of the Friary and Hospital of St John the Baptist (Augustinian Crucifers); the E. end of the church is 13th cent.; the residential tower to the W. is 15th.

3¾ m. SE. is Galtrim motte (*see under* Summerhill).

1½ m. SSE., in Knightsbrook, are the remains of "Stella's House". It occupies the site of the house where Dean Swift's "Stella" (Esther Johnston) lived with Mrs. Dingley. Nearby is "Stella's Well". ¾ m. SSE. is Laracor (Lethercor) Protestant church, successor of the church to which Swift ran the race with Delaney and in which his "dearly loved Roger" officiated as clerk; the altar plate used by Swift survives. 140 yds NW. of the church, opposite Knightsbrook motte, is the site of Swift's residence (Glebe House) when incumbent of Laracor (1700–1714; he was often an absentee). ½ m. SE. of Laracor crossroads is Bray Hill, alias Breemount (325 ft). This is the Brí Maic Thaidg where Giolla-na-Naomh ("Gelasius"), Archbishop of Armagh, held a reform synod in 1158. One of the synod's decisions was to make Flaithbhertach Ó Brolcháin, "heir of Columcille", bishop of Derry (*see* Maghera, Co. Derry) with authority over all the Columban houses in Ireland. 1¾ m. SSE. is Dangan Castle (*see under* Summerhill).

8 m. SW. is Inchamore bridge. 1 m. SSE. Castlerickard motte commands the crossing of the little Blackwater. In the adjacent church-yard is a good Swifte mausoleum (pyramid). – ½ m. W. of Inchamore bridge is the tower (square with round angle-turret) of Donore castle (Nat. Mon.). 3 m. WSW. is Killyon (*see under* Kinnegad).

3 m. W., to the W. of the Boyne, are the ruins of Tremblestown castle, ancestral home of the Barnewalls, Barons Tremblestown (Trimleston). Refortified in the Eleven Years' War, it was attacked and captured by the Parliamentarian, Col. Jones, in 1647. The family mausoleum is in a nearby ruined chapel.

3 m. NW. is Moymet Castle. Sir Luke Dillon (*see* Newtown Trim, *above*) built this strong-house in the 16th cent. NW. are remains of a small, 15th cent. manorial church.

TUAM, Co. Galway (Map 1, E5), is a small market and manufacturing (beet sugar) centre at the intersection of the Galway (21 m.)–Dunmore (10 m.) and Athlone (42 m.)–Ballin-robe (21 m.) roads. It is the see of the arch-diocese to which it has given its name; also of a Protestant diocese united with Killala and Achonry. The surrounding countryside is very rich in prehistoric and historic remains, notably so in ringforts, many of which have souterrains.

The first and second Protestant archbishops, Nehemiah Donnellan (1595–1609) and William O Donnell (1609–28), were associated in the production of the first translation of the New Testament into Irish (1602).

Henry Mossop (1729–74), actor and founder of Dublin's Smock Alley Theatre, was the son of Prebendary John Mossop. John Bermingham (1816–74), the astronomer, lived at Millbrook House, 9 m. NW.

The story of Tuam commences in the 5th/6th cent. with the foundation of a monastery by St Íarlaith ("Jarlath"), disciple of St Benignus (*see* Kilbannon, *below*). In the 12th cent. the expanding power of the O Conor Kings of Connacht added the Tuam district to their territories, and Tuam itself became one of their principal seats. It is not surprising, therefore, that the 12th cent. reformers should have chosen Tuam as the metropolitan see of Connacht. By the time of the Anglo-Norman invasion the place was well on the way to becoming the capital of Connacht. Thereafter, however, its importance was primarily ecclesiastical. Prior to the Reformation it had three churches and two monasteries: the Cathedral, St Íarlaith's Church, Holy Trinity Abbey (Premonstratensian), St John's Abbey (Augustinian Canons Regular), and Teampall na Scríne (where St Íarlaith's relics were enshrined); also a nunnery-cum-hospital.

The Protestant cathedral, Galway road, is a dull Gothic Revival building (1861–63), by Sir Thomas Deane. It incorporates the barrel-vaulted chancel of a small nave-and-chancel cathedral of about 1170–80 and the chancel (choir) added to it about 1312 as the first stage of an ambitious building project never carried further. The 12th cent. nave was destroyed by fire in 1787. For nearly a hundred years thereafter the Romanesque chancel served as a porch, to the further detriment of its fire-damaged arch. Though they have been damaged and have lost their polychrome colouring, this splendid six-order arch and the triple E. window of the chancel are among the outstanding relics of the Irish Romanesque style. Like the Market Cross (*below*) they reflect the Scandinavian (Urnes-style) influence so marked in 12th cent. Connacht art. In the S. nave aisle is the shaft of a 12th cent. High Cross with interlaced and other ornament. It is inscribed OR[ÕIT] DON RIG DO THA[I]RDELBUCH Ú CHON-CHOBAIR OR[ÕIT] DON THAER DO GILLU C[H]R[ÍST] U THUATHAI[L] ("A prayer for the king, Turloch O Conor. A prayer for the craftsman, Giolla-Críst O Toole"); and OR[ÕIT] DO CHOMARBA IARLAITHE .I. DO AED U OSSIN [LAS]IN DERNAD AN CHROS-SA ("A prayer for the successor of Íarlaith, i.e. for Áedh O Hession for whom this cross was made"). (Turloch O Conor reigned 1106–56; Áedh O Hession was Abbot of Tuam 1126–51, Archbishop of Tuam 1152–61.) The factory windows of the aisles present some pathetically funny examples of late Victorian art. The ugly parapet of the 14th cent. chancel is a 19th cent. "restoration". This part of the church now serves as synod hall and library. Disintegrating in the damp is a good set of 17th cent. choir stalls from an Italian Dominican friary. In the windows are some curious early 19th cent. experiments in stained glass. (A 15th cent. friary-type tower, which stood over the junction of the Romanesque chancel and the 14th cent. choir, was wantonly swept away by Deane.)

NW. of the cathedral are the fragmentary remains of Temple Jarlath, with an interesting Transitional three-light E. window; also some Romanesque fragments. This was the church of Holy Trinity Premonstratensian abbey founded by one of the de Burgos (on the site of Íarlaith's monastery?).

At the centre of the town is the imperfect "Market Cross", assembled from scattered pieces, one of which came from the Protestant churchyard. It is not certain that head and shaft belong together; if they do, the complete cross would have been exceptionally tall. On the head are: W. face: a *Crucifixion*; E. face: five standing figures; N. and S. ends of arms: a single figure. On the base are: E. and W. faces: a pair of standing figures; N. and S. sides: bases (for free-standing figures?). The shaft and base have an elaborate, all-over, Urnes-style, interlaced ornament very lightly carved. On the base are the inscriptions: E. face: [ORÕIT] DO THAIRDELBUCH U CHONCHUBUIR DOND RÍG [OCUS DO ...] RAFLATH ... SIN ... DO RIGNE I[N] SAETHAR-[SA] ("A prayer for Turloch O Conor, for the king; and for . . . raflath O Hession (?) . . . who made this work"); W. face: [ORÕIT DO AED] Ū OSSIN DOND ABBAID ... ("A prayer for Áedh O Hession, for the abbot. . .").

The Cathedral of the Assumption, Bishop St, is an early post-Emancipation (1827–37) structure in the Gothick style by Dominic Madden. In a shelter near the W. door are housed some early and medieval fragments. The statue of Archbishop Mac Hale (1791–1881) is by John Henry Foley.

2 m. N. is Fairy Mill Bridge. Close by to the E. is Muileann an Liupracháin, alias the Fairy Mill, a limestone cave with subterranean water-course; an unbelieving generation no longer leaves corn to be ground by the leprechaun.

2½ m. N., to the W. side of the road, is the 1673 monument of James Lally of Tullinadaly, great-grandfather of Lally-Tollendal. 2 m. further N., near Castletown House, is the site of Tollendal (Tollindally, Tullynadaly) castle, ancestral home of the Lallys (O Mulallys). James Lally, last Baron Tollindally, was out-lawed by the Williamites and became a colonel in the French service, commanding Lally's battalion of Dillon's Regiment. He was uncle of the illustrious Marshal of France, Lally-Tollendal (Thomas Arthur Lally, Baron de Tollendal, Count de Lally, 1702–66), who very nearly drove the British from India, and whom an ungrateful Louis XV "murdered with the sword of justice". (His name is now inscribed along with those of France's greatest soldiers on the Arc de Triomphe.) Tollendal (Tullynadaly, Tulach na Dála) means "the Mount (Hill) of the Public Assembly", i.e. it was the meeting-place of one of the open-air "parliaments" and fairs of Gaelic Ireland. Biennial fairs were still held at Tullinadaly until the beginning of the Second World War.

2½ m. NE., in the adjoining townlands of Marley and Aghlisk, are nine ringforts; one of these (Aghlisk) has a very fine three-chamber souterrain known as Gurranes Cave. Gurranes turloch, to the SE., was for centuries the Tuam race-course.

6 m. SE. are the ruins of Barnaderg castle, a 16th cent. O Kelly stronghold.

7 m. SSE. is Abbeyknockmoy (*q.v.*).

4 m. S. is Ballinderry castle, well designed for defence against firearms. Nearby, in Rathmore

townland, is Rathmore, a ringfort-type enclosure used as a children's burial ground. Its fine three-chamber souterrain is one of the largest known.

6 m. WSW. is Knockma (*see under* Headford).

2½ m. W. is Cloonfush. Temple Jarlath marks the site of a monastery founded by St Íarlaith before he settled at Tuam. SS Brendan of Clonfert and Colmán mac Lénéne of Cloyne are said to have been members of the community.

5¼ m. W., at Killower, Labbapatrick and the remains of a church mark an early monastic site.

1¾ m. NW., in Ballygaddy, is St Patrick's Monument (Leaba Phádraig), a rude altar where, says the local tale, St Patrick knelt in prayer. Two spots bare of grass mark where his knees rested. ¾ m. NW., at Kilbennan in Pollacorragune, a ruined Round Tower and fragmentary church (Nat. Mons.) mark the site of a foundation by St Benignus (Beannán, alias Mionnán), disciple of St Patrick and his successor at Armagh. St Íarlaith of Tuam is said to have been a disciple of St Benignus here. NW. of the church is Tobar Bannon, alias St Benen's Well. A medieval tale recounts how Patrick and Benignus called forth the spring by lifting the sod. Here they baptized and healed nine lepers. A great *pátrún* was held at the well (on the last Sunday of July) until well into the 19th cent., when the parish priest, scenting pagan practices (he was of those who thought Round Towers were pagan fire-temples!), set about suppressing it. Also in Pollacorragune, on the highest point of the esker, is Carn(an)fanny, a small Bronze Age tumulus; it covered a Cordoned Urn cremation with a razor. 700 ft SE. is a lower mound which covered four Iron Age skeletons. – 2½ m. NNW. of Kilbennan (1 m. NW. of Pollacorragune bridge), in the townland to which it gives its name, is Kilcreevanty, site of an important medieval nunnery (originally Benedictine, later Augustinian).

5½ m. NW., in Castlegrove East, is F(e)artagar Castle (Nat. Mon.). In Lissananny, to the NW., is a ringfort with an unusual three-chamber souterrain. – 3¾ m. NNW. of the castle, to the E. of the Claremorris road in Belmont, is a ringfort-type cemetery of 3½ acres, presumably an early monastic site.

9 m. NW. (via Milltown) is Millbrook House, home of John Bermingham (1816–74), the astronomer. In Banagher (SW. of Milltown bridge) is a ringfort with a three-chamber souterrain; there is a second souterrain in the NW. annexe.

2¾ m. NNW., in Gardenfield, are several ringforts. NE. of Gardenfield House is a pair of conjoined ringforts.

TULLA, Co. Clare (Map 5, B3), is a small town picturesquely situated on high ground 9 m. E. of Ennis.

There are remains of a medieval parish church; also of a barrel-vaulted 17th cent. church. There are several O Brien and Mac Mahon castles in the area.

6 m. SW. is Magh Adhair (*see under* Quin).

1¼ m. W., in Milltown, is Dermot and Grania's Bed, a wedge-shaped gallery grave, sole survivor of the eleven prehistoric chamber tombs recorded for this townland. 1 m. WNW., in Ballyslattery, alias Nutgrove, is Leaba Dhiarmaid, alias Giants Grave, another wedge-shaped gallery grave; there is a bullaun in a stone at the E. end.

2¾ m. NW., to the NW. of Tyredagh House in Tyredagh Lower, is Cromlech, a wedge-shaped gallery grave. 150 yds E. is a ring-barrow; still further E. is a 9-ft pillarstone. In Tyredagh Upper is Dermot and Grania's Bed, a ruinous gallery grave.

TULLAMORE, Co. Offaly (Map 6, A3), county town of Offaly, is a prosperous market and manufacturing (distillery, spinning-mill) town at the junction of roads from Birr (23 m.), Mountmellick (15 m.), Portarlington (17 m.), and Clara (9 m.). It is a convenient centre for visiting many places of note in early historic times.

The town is the creation of the Burys, a Co. Limerick family which (*c.* 1750) succeeded the Moores, Earls of Tullamore, who had obtained the confiscated lands of the O Molloys in the 17th cent. In 1785, still a mere village, it was destroyed as a result of an accident to a great balloon. Rebuilt on a much more ambitious scale, it supplanted Daingean (*q.v.*) as the county seat in 1833.

The early 19th cent. Market House on the Square was a decent building until its arcade was blocked up. In this quarter of the town are several good Late Georgian houses. The Court House (*c.* 1840) has a good Ionic portico. The nearby gaol is now a factory.

The Presbytery, Canal Harbour, was built as a hotel by the Grand Canal Company (defunct).

On the E. side of the town is St Catherine's Church (C. of I.), a fine example (1818) of Francis Johnston's Gothick; several windows retain their original clear glass. (Intending visitors to Rahan should ask the Rector for the key of Rahan church.)

4½ m. N. (Kilbeggan road), in Durrow Abbey demesne, is the site of one of the earliest (551) and most important of St Columcille's monasteries. The site, previously Ros Grencha, was given to Columcille by Áed mac Bréanainn, King of Tethba. Of the ancient abbey the only certain surviving remains are: a fine 10th cent. High Cross (Nat. Mon.). a small stone cross, a fragment with interlacing, the head of a small Transitional (?) window, and five early gravestones of Clonmacnois type, all W. of the derelict, early-18th cent. Protestant church (which may incorporate something of the fabric of a pre-Norman church). The subjects on the High Cross include: W. face: *Crucifixion, Soldiers*

Plate 15. Remains of a chambered cairn, Slieve na Caillighe, Co. Meath

Plate 16. Desmond's Castle, Adare

guarding the tomb of Christ, etc.; E. face: *Last Judgement, Sacrifice of Abraham, King David*; N. side: *Jacob wrestling with the angel, Flight into Egypt* (?); S. side: *The Fall*, etc. One gravestone, probably the largest of its kind, has an illegible inscription. Two others are inscribed OR[ÓIT] DO AIGIDIU and OR[ÓIT] DO CHATHALAN respectively. No monuments survive to such illustrious dead known to be buried here as Donal, King of Tara (d. 758), or Murchadh, grandson of Brian Boru (d. 1068), or Farrel Óg Mac Geoghegan (d. 1454), or Díarmaid, son of Eóghan O Daly, ollamh of all Midhe (d. 1448). Close to the NE. angle of the church is the head (altered) of an 11th/12th cent. cross with a *Crucifixion* and the figure of an abbot or bishop. NE. of the churchyard is Columcille's Well, resorted to on the saint's festival, 9 June. SE. of the churchyard is the Headache Stone, the base of a stone cross. The celebrated *Book of Durrow*, now in the library of Trinity College, Dublin, belonged to the abbey. About 1140–48 the abbey was reorganised as a monastery of Augustinian canons and nuns. It was desecrated by Hugh de Lacy in 1186, for the purpose of building a castle, of which the motte survives SW. of the mansion. About 1190 (?) the abbey was reduced to priory status and the nuns were removed (to Killeigh?).

5 m. NE., on the Tyrrelspass road, is Rahugh, which takes its name from the 6th cent. St Aodh ("Hugh"), son of Brec, founder of a monastery here (*see also* Killare *under* Ballymore, Slieve League *under* Carrick, *and* Rathlin O Birne *under* Glencolumbkille). In 859 a royal convention at the monastery confirmed the alienation of Ossory from Munster to the Uí Néill confederation. Máel Gúalaí of Munster reaffirmed his submission the previous year to Máel-Sheachlainn I, King of Tara. These events marked the first effective assertion of the primacy of the Kings of Tara. 250 yds E. of the church is St Hugh's Well. 200 yds SW. of the churchyard is St Hugh's Stone, a boulder with weathered ring-cross. It is reputed to cure headaches. Rahugh was for a time the seat of a Cromwellian Anabaptist colony. ½ m. NNW. of the churchyard is Walsh's Mound, a fine motte.

2 m. SW. is Charleville Forest, sometime seat of the Burys, Earls of Charleville. This is a fine Gothick house by Francis Johnston (1801). ¾ m. NW. are Christ's Stone and Christ's Well.

4 m. WSW., beyond Charleville Forest demesne, is Lynally, site of Lann Elo, an important monastery founded about 580 by Bishop Colmán Elo (mac Beógnaí) moccu Sailne (d. 611), patron of churches in Scotland as well as second patron of Connor, Co. Antrim (*q.v.*), on land near the River Ela given him by the King of Meath. Apart from *antae* at the W. gable, the overgrown church is featureless. It seems to have been largely rebuilt for Protestant use in the 18th cent. On the S. are fragments of claustral buildings. Two 8th/9th cent. gravestones found nearby are in the National Museum.

¾ m. W., on the N. side of the canal, are the ruins of Srah Castle, built by the Elizabethan officer, John Briscoe, in 1588.

4 m. W., on the N. bank of the canal, are the ruins of Ballycowen castle. There was an O Melaghlin castle here in the Middle Ages. It was captured by Lord Deputy Sir Leonard Gray in 1586, and granted to Thomas Nonnes in 1589. The remains are largely those of a fortified house built in 1626 by Sir Jasper Herbert.

7 m. W., between the canal and the Clodiagh River, are the remains of the great monastery of Rahan, founded, it has been claimed, by the Patrician bishop, Camelacus, author of a Latin hymn in praise of St Patrick. The most famous name associated with Rahan is that of St Cárthách (Mo-Chuda). At Easter, 636, Mo-Chuda was expelled by King Bláthmac of Tara, at the instance of the monks of Durrow (possibly for abandoning the traditional Irish dating of the festival), and withdrew to Lismore, Co. Waterford (*q.v.*). Thereafter the history of Rahan is obscure. The remains comprise earthworks and three small churches. The largest of the churches (tastelessly cemented) serves as the Protestant parish church (nave rebuilt in the 18th cent.); the stone-roofed chancel was originally flanked by a pair of transept-like chambers; between the chancel and nave is a very fine and unusual Romanesque arch; in the chancel is a unique, circular, Romanesque E. window. The other two churches (Nat. Mons.) are roofless ruins. One of them was a plain, pre-Romanesque structure into which a beautiful Romanesque W. doorway was inserted, and which was substantially rebuilt in the 15th (?) cent. The other was a simple, primitive structure. ¾ m. N., in Tullabeg, is St Stanislaus College, a Jesuit house of retreat. The chapel has five Evie Hone windows (1946): *Nativity, The Beatitudes, Last Supper, Pentecost, Jesus with Jesuit Saints*. The three first named are superb.

3½ m. WNW., to the N. of the Tullabeg road, are the ruins of Ballykilmurry castle.

3½ m. NW. is Tihelly, which takes its name (Teach Theille) from St Teille, son of Seigín. St Munnu of Taghmon (*q.v.*) is said to have given the place to the virgin Cera (d. 670 ?). In the later 9th cent. the monastery, like Killeigh (*q.v.*), was subject to the abbot of Castledermot. It disappears from history after 936. Besides remnants of a church, there survive an early gravestone and a High Cross (Nat. Mons.). The unusual cross has figurations of the Fall and the Crucifixion, as well as panels of beautiful zoomorphs, etc.

TULLOW, Co. Carlow (Map 6, C5), is a pleasant, small market town set in attractive country where the Carlow (10 m.)–Shillelagh (10 m.) and Castledermot (17 m.)–Bunclody (15 m.) roads cross the Slaney. It is a convenient centre for visiting the beauty-spots of S. Wicklow, as well as those of the Barrow Valley.

It is also convenient for fishing the upper Slaney and its tributaries.

The Protestant parish church has a Clement Nevil memorial (1745) by David Sheehan.

The Butlers built a castle at Tullow to command the important river-crossing. The successor of that castle was stubbornly held against the Cromwellians in 1650. When it fell, the garrison was mercilessly butchered and the defences demolished. There was an early monastery at Tullow; also an Augustinian friary founded in 1314, Nothing survives of either, save a stone cross in the graveyard and the name of St Austin's Abbey.

It was in a field near Tullow that, on 7 Jan. 1395, Art Óg Mac Murrough, King of Leinster, made formal submission to Richard II's representative, and undertook to quit Leinster together with his subordinate lords.

3 m. NE., in Tankardstown, are three pillarstones. One, Gallán, is grooved, and stands SW. of the road. Of the two N. of the road, one has a cup mark. In adjacent Tobinstown is another grooved stone. ¼ m. E. of Tobinstown crossroads is Acaun bridge (see under Rathvilly).

4 m. E., on high ground beside the old Shillelagh road in Rath East, Co. Wicklow, is Rathgall (Nat. Mon.), a four-ring, stone hillfort about 18 acres in total area. At the centre is a citadel, or strong ringfort, of dry masonry, 150 ft in diameter; the enclosing rampart is 18 ft thick at the base. 200 yds N. is the ruin of an 8¼-acre fort; only one ring survives, but traces of a second are discernible. 200 yds E. is a stone circle; "where the kings of Leinster are buried", says one local legend.

1¾ m. SE., on a long, low mound in Rathglass, are two pillarstones; one has an ogham inscription.

3 m. SE., in Co. Wicklow, is Ardoyne motte.

3 m. SSW., in adjacent fields in Ardristan, are two pillarstones, one of them grooved. In Aghade, next townland to the S., is Cloch an Phoill, Cloghaphile (Nat. Mon.), a perforate pillarstone legendarily associated with Niall Nine Hostager. In Aghade fox covert is a prehistoric gallery grave. "Aghade" represents Áth Fhádhad, the ford over the Slaney which gave its name to the principal church of St Iserninus (d. 468), disciple of St Patrick (see Kilcullen). The ancient churchyard ½ m. NW. of Aghade bridge probably marks the site of Iserninus's church; ½ m. SW. is Castlegrace Moat, a motte. The country around Aghade bridge is very attractive. In Ballynoe, alias Newtown, on the E. bank of the Slaney, are a grooved pillarstone and a small portal dolmen. 2½ m. SSE. of Aghade bridge is Ballintemple House demesne, noted for its rhododendrons. 2½ m. SW. of Aghade bridge is Ballon Hill (427 ft), site of a large Bronze Age cemetery.

4 m. SW., in Rathtoe, is Rath Mahon, a large ringfort; ½ m. WSW. is Rathtoe itself, the ringfort which has given its name to the townland. 3 m. N. of Rathtoe, in Glenoge, is Cloghstuckagh, alias Cloghstodagh, alias the Five Fingers,

etc.; a Bronze Age burial was found at its foot. Nearby is Kellistown, site of an early monastery whose Round Tower survived until 1807. Muirchertach mac Erca, King of Tara, routed and slew Oengus mac Nat Fraích, King of Cashel, in Kellistown, A.D. 490/491, while O Byrne and Mac Davy there routed and slew Roger Mortimer, Earl of March, Lord of Carlow, Richard II's Lieutenant in Ireland, and heir to the English throne, 10 July 1394.

1½ m. WNW. is Castlemore Mote, motte of a castle erected by Raymond le Gros. The early cross-slab came from an adjoining field.

3½ m. NNW., in Straboe, is Moatabower, a motte. 100 yds SW. is a pillarstone. Also in Straboe are the remains of Templeboy, a church; there is an early gravestone (Nat. Mon.) here from nearby Killerig where, besides the early monastery, there was also a preceptory of the Knights Hospitaller of St John of Jerusalem.

TULSK, Co. Roscommon (Map 2, B6), is a village on the Roscommon (12 m.)–Frenchpark (10 m.) road. There is a motte with baileys here. On top of the motte are the foundations of a circular tower, all that remains of a castle which belonged to O Conor Roe in the 15th cent. Beside the Strokestown road is a fragment of a Dominican friary founded in 1448 by the Mac Dowells. The parish church has a fourlight window (1913) by A. E. Child: *Baptism of Christ, Ecce Homo, Resurrection, Ascension, The Four Evangelists.*

3 m. NW. is Rathcroghan (q.v.).

3 m. SSW., is Carnfree (alias the "Hill of Carns"), that Carn Fraoich mhic Fhiodaigh Fholtrúadh which was the inauguration place of the Kings of Connacht. 300 yds SE. of Carnfree is Dumha Shealga, a tumulus associated in heroic and early religious literature with the Connacht dynasts (Uí Briúin). 300 yds NW. of Carnfree is a small ring-barrow. 530 yds E. of Carnfree is a ring-barrow with a 12-ft pillarstone; 45 yds ESE. is a prostrate pillarstone.

TYRRELSPASS, Co. Westmeath (Map 6, A2), is a small village on the Rochfortbridge (5 m.)–Kilbeggan (6 m.) road. It takes its name from the strategically important way through the bogs where, in July 1597, Piers Lacy and Capt. Richard Tyrrel ambushed and cut to pieces an English force commanded by Christopher Barnewall, son of Lord Trimleston. The village was laid out as a crescent around the village green in the late 18th cent. by the Countess of Belvedere. At the W. end of the village is the tower of a 15th cent. Tyrell castle.

5½ m. SE. is Rahugh (see under Tullamore).

3m. S. is Durrow (see under Tullamore).

URLINGFORD, Co. Kilkenny (Map 5, E4), is a village on the Durrow, Co. Laois (20 m.)–Cashel (14 m.) road, close to the Tipperary border.

NNW. of the village are the ruins of a nave-

Commissioners of Public Works in Ireland

Tomb of Piers Butler, Kilcooly Abbey, Urlingford

and-chancel church, and of a castle which belonged to the Mountgarret Butlers (*see* Clomantagh, *below, and* Ballyragget) in the 16th cent.

2 m. NE. is Johnstown. In St Kieran's Church (1832) are a window and a richly carved baptismal font from Fertagh (*below*). Built into the churchyard wall is a superbly carved, highly stylized crucifix, also from Fertagh. The Protestant church (1799) incorporates the W. doorway and Perpendicular E. window from Fertagh church. 2 m. NW. is Foulkstown House, a Georgian house built for the Hely family. In the demesne are the ruins of a 15th cent. Purcell castle and of an ancient church; an early church bell found in the nearby Decoy Well is now in the National Museum. 2½ m. NW. of the castle, in Rathosheen, are two ring-forts, both called Ráth Oisín; one is trivallate and has traces of buildings; the other, 200 yds S., was allegedly the burial place of Oisín, whose "grave" was formerly marked by two pillarstones.

4½ m. NE. is Cross of (the) Beggar, a cross-roads called after the Beggar's Inn which stood there. Nearby to the W. are Fertagh Round Tower (Nat. Mon.) and fragmentary "Abbey". St Cíarán (alias Pírán) of Saighir (*see under* Birr; *also* Errill *under* Rathdowney) founded a monastery at Fertagh. In 861 it was attacked by a Viking raiding party, which was routed and driven off by Cerbhall of Ossory. In 1156 the monastery and its Round Tower were burnt. In the 13th cent. the monastery was re-founded by the Norman Blanchevilles (Blanch-fields) as a priory of Canons Regular of St Augustine. The ruined "abbey" was the priory – later parochial – church (*see* Johnstown, *above*). It is a structure of various dates, and was used as a Protestant church until 1780. On the N. side is the 15th/16th cent. "Kilpatrick" Chapel, built as their burial place by the Mac Giolla Phádraig (Mac Gillapatrick, Fitzpatrick) lords of Upper Ossory. In it is the tomb (1540) of John Mac Gillapatrick of Upper Ossory d. 1468), with whom are buried his son, Brian,

his wife (Kathleen Milroy), and Brian's wife Nori[na]; this has effigies of an armoured knight and his lady, and is probably the work of Rory O Tunney. – ½ m. W. is Móta na Féarta, motte-and-bailey of a Norman castle. – 3 m. N. is Aghmacart (*see under* Durrow, Co. Laois). – 1 m. NE. is Glashere castle, which in the 16th and 17th centuries belonged to the Ormond Butlers. – 1 m. NW. is Galmoy, from which the Butlers, Viscounts Galmoy, took their title.

3 m. E., in Upper Balief, are the ruins of a Shortall castle with a circular tower. To the NE., on the top of Clomantagh Hill (1,154 ft), was Suidhe Finn cairn, most of which was removed about 1810; two cists were found in it, one with two skeletons, the other with a crema-tion. 1¼ m. E. of Balief crossroads are Cloman-tagh church and castle. The church, a 13th–14th cent. structure, was dedicated to the Nativity of the Blessed Virgin Mary. The castle ruins comprise bawn (with angle turret) and tower (with a sheila-na-gig). The turret at the top of the tower is called Mairgréad Ní Ghea-róid's Chair, after the wife of Piers Rúa Butler (*see* Ballyragget). Piers Rúa settled the castle on his son, the first Viscount Mountgarret.

5 m. ESE. (via Balief) is Tubridbritain (*see under* Freshford).

4 m. S., in Co. Tipperary, are the very inter-esting remains of Kilcooly Abbey (Nat. Mon.), a small Cistercian abbey in honour of the Blessed Virgin Mary and St Benedict, which was founded for the monks of Magh Airbh (*below*) about 1182 by Donal Mór Ó Brien, King of Thomond, and was colonized from Jerpoint (*see under* Thomastown) about 1184. It was destroyed by armed men about 1445, and restored by Abbot Philip O Mulwardayn, alias O Brothe (Brophy). The church (*c.* 1200) was a variant of the normal Cistercian cruci-form plan, with aisled nave and E. chapels (two) in each transept. The 1445 disaster occasioned extensive reconstruction about 1445–70, in the course of which the E. window triplet was replaced by the existing large tracer-

Mermaid panel, Kilcooly Abbey, Urlingford

ied window; the chancel vaulted; the central tower built over the crossing; the transepts rebuilt and vaulted; the nave arcades blocked up; the S. aisle thrown into the cloister; rooms built over the chancel, crossing, and transepts (*see* Holy Cross Abbey *under* Thurles); and both nave and chancel propped with ungainly buttresses. The church has two unique features: the pair of stalls (for abbot and prior ?) in the responds of the W. tower-arch, and the sculptured screen between the S. transept and the sacristy. The figure subjects on the screen include the *Crucifixion* and *St Christopher*. Unfortunately the screen – like the tombs and other carvings in the abbey – has lost all its colours. The monuments, etc., in the church include: (*a*) in front of the altar, the tombstone of the restorer of the abbey, Abbot Philip (d. 1463), and his parents; (*b*) the tomb of Piers fitz James Óg Butler of Clonamicklon (d. 1526), his parents, and his son, James; it has the high-relief effigy of an armoured knight and panels of "weepers" (apostles, etc.), and is signed by the maker, Rory O Tunney (RORICUS OTUYNE SCRIPSIT); the effigy is the earliest dated example by O Tunney; (*c*) the tomb of William Cantwell of Ballintogher and Clogharaily, and his wife, Margaret Butler (d. 1528), also by Rory O Tunney; (*d*) the tombstone of John Cantwell (d. 1532) of Moylassain (alias "Millicent") and his wife, Elicia Stouc, also by Rory O Tunney; (*e*) the tombstone of James Stoc and Margaret Butler, his wife, by Patrick O Tunney,

1587; (*f*) the tombstone of Donal O Hedyan and his son, 1452; (*g*) the fragmentary tomb of Richard C[antwell of B]allafeen and . . . [G]raes (Grace), his wife, by Walter Kerin, 1608; (*h*) and (*i*) the remains of two effigies in low relief; (*j*) a carved font. The claustral buildings were considerably altered in the 15th and 16th centuries, and again in more recent times. To the SE. is a detached building (? Infirmary); to the NE. a corbel-vaulted, circular dovecot. – 1¾ m. S. of the abbey are the ruins of the Butler castle of Clonamicklon, a bawn with a large, embattled, 17th cent. house. – 7 m. SW. of the abbey, in Derryvella bog, is an ancient oval churchyard enclosed by an earthen vallum. This is probably the site of the monastery of Daire Mór, whose foundation is ascribed to St Colmán (son of King Nat Fraích of Cashel), which was later known as St Mary's of Magh Airbh (de Arvicampo), and which was ultimately replaced by Kilcooly Abbey. – 6 m. W. of Kilcooly Abbey is Leigh (*see under* Thurles).

VALENCIA ISLAND, Co. Kerry (Map 4, B4), close to the mainland, 3 m. SW. of Cahirsiveen, is a delightful place for a quiet holiday. Its Spanish-looking name is an English corruption of Béal Inse, the name of the adjacent sound; its proper name is Oileán Dairbhre. Two ferries connect the island to the mainland. Knightstown, at the E. end of the island, is the "capital" and the principal resort. It was the E.

terminal station of the first Transatlantic cable (cable station closed 1965). The basic mileages below are reckoned from Knightstown.

1 m. W. are remains of the medieval church of Kilmore. ¾ m. further W. is the beautiful demesne of Glanleam, formerly home of the Fitzgeralds, Knights of Kerry, now the property of Lord Mounteagle. ¾ m. N. of Glanleam, at Fort Point, are the remains of Cromwell's Fort; inside it is a pillarstone.

2½ m. WSW., in Feaghmaan West, are remains of an ancient anchoritic enclosure with ruins of an oratory, a clochán, etc. WSW., to the S. of the road, is Gallaun, a pillarstone. In the next townland to the W., Tinnies Upper, are a cairn, a stone circle, a pillarstone, and some early graves (Nat. Mons.). To the S. of Tinnies Upper, in Imlagh bog, Coarhamore, is a rude stone cross. At Kildreenagh, alias Killeenadreena, in Cool East (W. of Tinnies Upper), is an ancient anchoritic enclosure with remains of three clocháns and of three small-rectangular structures; also the overgrown remains of an ancient tomb and a cross-inscribed ogham stone. As at Kilnasaggart (see Edenappa under Newry) and St John's Point (see under Ardglass), the graves here are arranged radially about the pillarstone. S. of the road, in Cool "village", is another ogham stone. Also in Cool East, to the N. of the road, is a prehistoric chamber tomb. Further N., on Doonroe Cliff, is the bivallate promontory fort which gives the cliff its name. ½ m. WSW. of the latter, in Cool West, close to Cooshadawlawn, alias Coosheenadagallaun, is Dún Dá Ghallán, a little promontory fort with pillarstone gate posts (an dá ghallán).

4½ m. SW., in Coarhabeg, are Tobar Ula Bhréanainn (a holy well dedicated to St Brendan) and three rude stone crosses. To the E. are remains of a prehistoric chamber tomb.

7 m. SW. is Bray Head; the cliffs rise to 800 ft. On the S. slope are remains of five clocháns; the site commands lovely views.

¾ m. NW. is the little island, Beginish. Denudation of the covering of blown sand has exposed an ancient system of small fields and remains of eight scattered small houses. Excavation of two of the houses (Nat. Mons.) at the E. end of the island has dated them to the period 1100–1200. A stone with a Runic inscription and an incised cross had been appropriated for use as a door-lintel in one house. The Runic inscription – the fifth found in Ireland – reads: LIR · RISTI · STIN · ThINA [MUNUIKL?]· RISTI· [RUN] ("Lir erected this stone; M . . . carved the runes"). Close to Beginish on the E. (accessible on foot at very low tide) is tiny Church Island. Remains of a cashel, of an oratory of Gallarus (see under Ballyferriter) type, and of clocháns (Nat. Mons.), show that it was the site of a diminutive anchoritic settlement. A fine early cross-pillar found here (now in the Public Museum, Cork) has an ogham inscription imposed on the incised cross.

VENTRY, Co. Kerry (Map 4, B4), is a small village 6 m. WSW. of Dingle, 4½ m. SE. of Ballyferriter, and 5 m. E. of Dunquin. It takes its name from the lovely sandy beach called Fionn Traigh, setting of the early Fionn mac Cumhaill tale, *The Battle of Ventry* (*Cath Fionntrágha*). A local tradition would have it that the country between Ventry and Dingle Harbours was the last foothold of the Norse in Ireland. The countryside hereabouts is almost embarrassingly rich in ancient remains, of which only a very limited selection can be mentioned here.

½ m. NE., on Caherard Hill, is Leaba an Fhir Mhuimhnigh (Labbanirweeny), a chamber tomb.

1 m. NNE., at the ancient church site of Kilcolman (Nat. Mon.), Maumanorig, is a rock with ogham inscription and incised cross. Nearby is St Brendan's Well, where "stations" are made. 1 m. W., in Rahinnane, are ruins of a late castle (Nat. Mon.) which uses a ringfort (with souterrain) as bawn. 2¾ m. NE. of the latter, in Lateevemore, is Templecloonagh (see under Ballyferriter).

1 m. SE., at Faill na Mná, Ballymore West, is a promontory fort.

1¼ m. NW. is Rahinnane castle (above).

To the W. of Ventry Harbour rises Sliabh an Iolair, alias Mount Eagle (1,695 ft). The lower slopes, particularly in the townlands of Caherbullig, Kilvickadownig, Fahan, Glanfahan, Coumeenoole South, and Coumeenoole North, are strewn with the wreckage of the past. Some sixty years ago a survey of these townlands recorded 2 promontory forts, 22 ringforts, 414 clocháns, 12 stone crosses, 18 pillarstones (2 with ogham inscriptions), 19 souterrains, and 29 miscellaneous structures and enclosures. Since then many have been cleared away by farmers, local authorities, and other vandals. The more important monuments are listed below, townland by townland.

3¼ m. SW. of Ventry is the ancient burial ground of Kilvickadownig. In it are a cross-slab and remains of a ringfort-type enclosure. Inside the latter are remains of a clochán and Dáire Donn's Grave, a ridge (marking the site of a souterrain?). In the next field to the S. is Leac na Rae, a large stone with a cross inscribed in a spiral-ended "omega". NW. of the burial ground and on the N. side of the bohereen, is Clochán an Phúca. A short distance W. is another clochán (the Ordnance Survey's Cloghaunaphuca). – 1¼ m. ESE. of Kilvickadownig "village", in Kilfarnoge, is a small promontory fort with seven hut sites. – ¼ m. S. of Kilvickadownig "village" is a good univallate ringfort. 600 yds WSW., in Páirc na Croise, is a heap of stones with a small stone cross. 500 yds WNW. of Páirc na Croise is Fahan "village". Bóthairín na Maoiline leads NNW. up the slope. NE. of the end of this bohereen, in Kilvickadownig, is Cathair na Maoiline, remains of an oval enclosure with the dilapidated ruins of ten diminutive clocháns. Some 700 yds NW. (alt. 1,000 ft) is interesting Clochán an Ardáin, a circular enclosure with three clocháns, the largest of which had a lintelled entrance passage. – ¼ m. S. of Fahan "village" is the interesting promontory fort, Dún Beag (Nat. Mon.). It has quadrivallate earthworks in front of the main, drymasonry, rampart. The latter is terraced, and has guardrooms flanking the entrance. A souterrain passes under this rampart and the path through the outer defences. Inside the fort are remains of a large clochán. (The seaward edges of the fort have been greatly eroded by the sea, and the inturned ends of the stone rampart are by the Board of Works, which did much unrecorded restoration here.) 400 yds NNW. of Dún Beag are remains of Teampall Beag, a church; in the graveyard is a cross-slab. Some 200 yds SW. are remains of Clochán Bóthair an Trasnuig (with a souterrain), two cross-inscribed stones, and a stone with a mass of unintelligible scribings. – ¾ m. NNW. of Fahan "village" is Loc Cabún, alias Clochán Cabún, an enclosure with a three-chamber clochán and an open "yard". 440 yds further WNW. is a group of clocháns, etc. – ¾ m. WSW. of Fahan "village", in Glanfahan, is Caher Conor (Nat. Mon.), a ruined stone ringfort with clocháns (secondary ?), wall-chamber, souterrain, etc. Some 400 yds NNW. is a double clochán with remains of a forecourt. ¼ m. W. of Caher Conor is Cathair na Mairtíneach (Nat. Mon.), an interesting stone ring-fort with "gate-lodge", clocháns (secondary ?), etc. Some 600 yds WNW. of this fort is Glanfahan "village". 200 yds N. is Clochán Ais, a five-chamber clochán with open forecourt; to the S. is a "bed-recess"; further S. is a clochán. 250 yds W. is Cathair Bán, a clochán complex with two souterrains. 300 yds SW. is Clochán Nua, a fine D-shaped clochán. – 600 yds SSW. of Glanfahan "village" is Caher Murphy, alias Caher Glanfahan (Nat. Mon.) a unique stone ringfort, unfortunately much restored. In it is a five-chamber clochán complex; in the second-largest (or S.) chamber is the entrance to a souterrain. A pillarstone, with crosses, etc., on both faces, an ogham inscription, and a barbaric *Crucifixion* (?), found here in the last cent., is now in the National Museum. Some 400 yds W. is Cathair an dá Dhorus, alias Cathair Sayers (Nat. Mon.), a three-chamber clochán with external chamber flanking the entrance. In the main chamber is the entrance to a souterrain. A short distance NE. is An Clochán Mór, a large double clochán. 170 yds NW. of Cathair an dá Dhorus is Clochán Sileóid, alias Clochán Sgológa (Nat. Mon.), a quadruple clochán. The antiquities of Coumeenoole South, next townland to the W., are listed under Dunquin (*q.v.*).

VIRGINIA, Co. Cavan (Map 2, E6), a market village – gay with flowers – on the Kells (11 m.)-Ballyjamesduff (6 m.) road, stands on the N. shore of lovely Lough Ramor. It dates from the Plantation of Ulster and is called after Elizabeth I, the "Virgin Queen".

1½ m. WSW. (by boat), on a promontory projecting from the lake shore, is Knockatemple motte-and-bailey.

1½ m. NE. is the site of Cuilcagh House, home of the Rev. Thomas Sheridan (1687–1738), schoolmaster, friend of Swift, and author of a charming translation of Persius. He was father of Thomas Sheridan (1719–88), author, lexicographer, actor, manager of Smock Alley Theatre, Dublin, and grandfather of Richard Brinsley Sheridan (1751–1816), the playwright. Swift wrote *Gulliver's Travels* at Cuilcagh House, 1726.

WARRENPOINT, Co. Down (Map 3, C6), is a seaside resort very beautifully situated on the N. shore of Carlingford Lough, between Newry (6 m.) and Rostrevor (3 m.). The Catholic church has a three-light window (*Christ the King*) by Michael Healy (1928).

2 m. NW., on the lough, is very attractively maintained Narrow Water Castle (tower and small bawn; Nat. Mon.), built by one of the Magennises of Iveagh about 1560. With the defeat of the Stuart and Irish cause in 1691, the castle passed to the Halls. Open to the public: 1 April to 30 Sept.: Mon. to Sat., 10–1, 2–6; Sun., 2–6; 1 Oct. to 31 March: Sat., 10–1, 2–4; Sun., 2–4; closed on Christmas Day. Admission, adults 6d., school children 3d. 3½ m. N., by the roadside near Milltown bridge, is Carnanbane, an overgrown court cairn.

WATERFORD, Co. Waterford (Map 6, B6), on the tideway of the Suir, is a manufacturing town (bacon, meat, footwear, iron, glass, etc.) and seaport, 14 m. SW. of New Ross, 17 m. SE. of Carrick-on-Suir, and 29 m. NE. of Dungarvan. It is the cathedral town of the diocese of Waterford and Lismore and of the Church of Ireland dioceses of Cashel, Waterford, and Lismore.

Like several other Irish seaports, it traces its origin to the Vikings, whose fleets appeared in the harbour in 914 and 915, and who made a settlement here shortly afterwards. The English name of the town preserves the Norse name of the harbour, Vethrafjörthr. (The Irish name is Port Láirge.) By the close of the 11th cent. the Scandinavians had become Christians, but, rejecting the authority of the Irish see of Lismore, established their own little diocese. Their first bishop was Máel-Ísa ("Malchus") Ó hAinmire, an Irish Benedictine of Winchester, whom they had consecrated (1096) at Canterbury with the approval of High-king Muirchertach O Brien. As a Norse city-state, Waterford was nominally dependent on the King of Munster, but in 1137 Díarmait III (Mac Murrough) of Leinster, aided by his Norse dependencies of Dublin and Wexford, blockaded the town by land and sea and forced it to acknowledge his suzerainty. Like Dublin, Waterford later repudiated Díarmait and, like Dublin, it fell an early victim to his Anglo-Norman hirelings. On 25 Aug. 1170, it was taken by Strongbow and Raymond le Gros at the third assault, and its citizens butchered. Shortly afterwards Strongbow was married to Díarmait's daughter, Aoífe, in the cathedral. (The purpose of the marriage was to invent a claim for Strongbow to be heir to Leinster and its dependencies.) In 1171 Henry II of England declared Waterford a royal city, and throughout the Middle Ages it remained inflexibly loyal to the English Crown. In 1487 it withstood a six-week siege by the adherents of Lambert Simnel, and in 1495 a twelve-day siege by Perkin Warbeck. (Henry VII rewarded it with the motto *Urbs intacta manet Waterfordia*). By this period it had become one of the chief ports in the country. Subsequently, however, the prosperity of the town declined, largely as a result of the adherence of its citizens to the Old Faith during the Reformation era. During the period of the Confederation of Kilkenny it was one of the Catholic strongholds and, on 24 Nov. 1649, Cromwell sat down before the walls. The town was ably defended by Ulster troops under Lieut.-Gen. O Farrell, and after eight days Cromwell withdrew. He returned on 29 May 1650; but the town held out until 10 Aug., when it surrendered on honourable terms to his son-in-law, Ireton.

In the 16th and 17th centuries Waterford produced a group of remarkably gifted men, several of whom played significant roles in the struggle of Catholic Ireland for survival. Among them were: Luke Wadding (1588–1657), Franciscan scholar and historian, professor of theology at Salamanca, and agent of the Confederate Catholics at the papal court; Michael Wadding, alias Miguel Godinez (1591–1644), Jesuit theologian and missionary to the Indians of Mexico; Peter Lombard (1554–1625), Franciscan professor of philosophy and of theology at Louvain, member of the celebrated papal *Congregatio de Auxiliis*, and Archbishop of Armagh. Other natives of Waterford were: the Rev. Francis Hearn (d. 1801), professor of rhetoric at Louvain and "saviour of the Flemish language"; Thomas Francis Meagher (1823–67), Young Ireland leader condemned to death in 1848, who escaped to America – where he fought at Fort Sumter and Fredericksburg and became Governor of Montana; Dorothy Jordan (1762–1816), actress; Charles Kean (1811–68), actor; William Vincent Wallace (1813–68), composer of *Maritana*, *Lurline*, etc.; Robert West (d. 1770), artist.

In the 18th cent. Waterford was one of the leading centres of the famous Irish glass industry, and its products are eagerly sought by connoisseurs. The industry was revived in 1947, and already the factory is one of the largest of its kind in the world.

The major feature of Waterford is the great ¾-m. quay. East of the Suir bridge it is called successively Merchants' Quay, Meagher's Quay, Coal Quay, Custom House Quay, the Parade, and Adelphi Terrace.

Grey Friars, off the Parade, recalls the Franciscans whose friary here was founded about 1240 by Sir Hugh Purcell. It was in the friary that, 25 April 1395, Turloch O Conor Don of Connacht and Brian O Brien of Thomond bent the knee to Richard II of England. The remains (Nat. Mon.) comprise nave, chancel, massive 15th cent. tower, and Lady Chapel (S. transept) of the austere friary church. The transept was built by the Powers of Dunhill as their place of sepulture. At the Dissolution the friary passed to the Crown, and in 1545 was sold to Patrick Walsh, who founded the Holy Ghost Hospital – Master, Brethren (four secular priests to say Mass), and Paupers (at least sixty) – in the friary. The paupers were housed in apartments constructed under the roof of the nave, while the floor of the nave and choir was set aside to provide burial places for subscribers to the charity. In 1695 the Corporation assigned the choir to Huguenot refugees to serve as their parish church; hence the popular name of the ruin, "The French Church". Thomas Francis Meagher's father was Master of the Hospital, 1850–55. In 1888 the Hospital was transferred to the Cork road (*see below*).

The Mall, a fine Georgian street, joins the quay at the junction of the Parade and Adelphi Terrace. Here 12th/13th cent. Reginald's Tower (re-edified 1819; museum) marks the NE. angle of both the Norse and the medieval towns. The triangle bounded by the quay, the Mall, Spring Garden Alley, Michael St, Broad St, and Barron Strand St approximates to the extent of the Norse town, whose main E.–W. axis is represented by narrow High St.

SW. of Reginald's Tower, on the Mall, are the City Hall and Theatre Royal, erected as Exchange and Assembly Rooms in 1788 to the design of John Roberts (1749–94), a native of the city and great-grandfather of the Victorian Field Marshal, Lord Roberts of Waterford and Kandahar. Here may be seen the civic insignia and muniments (including a unique illustrated charter roll of 1390); likewise paintings by Kneller, Cosway, Van der Hagen, and Shee; also the sword presented to Thomas Francis Meagher by the Napper Tandy Light Artillery of the American Union Army and the flags carried by Meagher's Irish Brigade in the heroic assault on Fredericksburg, 13 Dec. 1862, when only 280 of the 1,200 Irish survived. In the Council Chamber is a splendid chandelier of 18th cent. Waterford glass. The Theatre Royal occupies the site of the 18th cent. Lower Assembly Room.

The Luke Wadding centenary statue (1958) in the Mall is by Gabriel Hayes.

Catherine St leads from the Mall to the Court House and the People's Park. The Court House (1849 Classical; by Sir Richard Morrison?) occupies the site of St Catherine's Priory of Canons Regular of St Augustine. It takes the place of a court house in Broad St by Morrison's master, James Gandon.

In the Palace (*below*) garden beside the

Theatre Royal the town wall (running SW. from Reginald's Tower) appears as a terrace; it continues SW. behind the houses in Spring Garden Alley as far as the orphanage.

Palace Lane leads from the Mall to Cathedral Sq. dominated by the Protestant cathedral, Christchurch (alias Trinity Cathedral), built 1770–79 to the design of John Roberts. Partly destroyed by fire in 1815, it was restored in 1818; in 1891 it was re-edified under the direction of Sir Thomas Drew. It occupies the site of 12th cent. Romanesque–Transitional Christchurch and its medieval enlargement, which survived until 1770. Of the medieval cathedral only a small crypt and some miscellaneous fragments survive. The few medieval monuments include a 1469 Rice tombstone and an early 16th cent. tomb with the effigy of an armoured knight. S. of the cathedral is the Palace, formerly residence of the Protestant bishops, since 1920 seat of the Bishop Foy School (formerly the Blue Coat School; founded 1707). This fine house has been attributed to Richard Cassels, but is probably by John Roberts. NE. of the cathedral is the 18th cent. Deanery; under one of the buildings is a medieval crypt. W. of the cathedral are the graveyard and the Clergymen's Widows' Apartment (1702).

Further W., in Francis St, the Franciscan church (1834; enlarged 1906–8) occupies the site of medieval St Mary's Chapel; the 1626 holy water stoup with the arms of White impaling Walsh came from "The French Church" (*above*). A short distance N. is St Olave's Church, 1734 successor of a Norse foundation. It has a good 18th cent. pulpit and bishop's throne.

High St., at the N. end of Olave's St, leads W. to Blackfriars, called after St Saviour's Dominican friary founded in 1226. The church tower and other fragments of the friary survive, but are mostly incorporated in modern structures.

N. of Blackfriars, on the E. side of Barron Strand St, is the Cathedral of the Holy Trinity, popularly known as the Big Chapel and the Great Chapel ever since its erection in Penal times (1793–96); the site was granted by the Corporation, at that time a Protestant body, and the building itself was one of the last works of John Roberts, a Protestant. The sanctuary was extended at some time between 1829 and 1837, the apse added in 1854, the high altar erected and the ceiling decorated in 1881. The spirit of Penal times required the cathedral to be unobtrusive, and it was in fact masked by houses on Barron Strand St. From the first, however, Roberts had provided for an appropriate portico. This was never completed, and the dull façade is an 1893 affair. The cathedral has some interesting 17th and 18th cent. altar plate, including a chalice which belonged to Seathrún Céitinn (*see* Tubbrid *under* Cahir) and a "throne" monstrance of 1729. More important artistically are the vestments discovered during the demolition of medieval Christchurch and magnanimously presented to the Catholic bishop by the Protestant bishop, Dr Chenevix. These comprise four copes and a complete set of High Mass vestments. All are of brocaded velvet on cloth of gold (late-15th cent. Italian ?) and have figure-embroidered orphreys of linen (Flemish ?).

At the S. end of Barron Strand St is Broad St, off which Great George's St opens on the W. The Chamber of Commerce and Harbour Commissioners occupy the charming town house (noteworthy staircase) of the Morrises of Rosduff; about 1795, by John Roberts. St Patrick's Church, oldest Catholic church in the town, originated as a Penal-times chapel in a Jenkins Lane corn store.

At the S. end of Broad St, Patrick St leads W. to the gaol and Ballybricken Green. The boundary between the gaol and St Patrick's churchyard incorporates part of the medieval town wall; there are remains of an angle tower at the NE. corner of the gaol; further E., supporting a water tank, is the square Beach Tower. St Patrick's Church (C. of I.) dates from 1727.

NW. of the gaol, on Thomas's Hill, is St Thomas's Churchyard, with the chancel arch of one of the oldest of the city churches. 350 yds NW., in Bridge St, is St Saviour's Church (Dominican; 1874–78; by Goldie, Child, and Goldie of London). A small oak figure of Our Lady (17th cent. Seville school) preserved here is thought to have reached Waterford during one of the Stuart phases of connivance at the practice of Catholicism.

S. of Patrick St the town wall (fine tower) forms the W. side of St Stephen's School grounds. It continues S. past Bachelor's Walk to Newgate St. 200 yds SW. of Newgate St, in Barrack St, are Mount Sion monastery (1864–66) and schools. It was here that, in 1802, Edmund Ignatius Rice (1762–1844) established his first community. A prosperous Waterford merchant, Rice had sold his possessions to devote himself to the education of the neglected poor. In 1806 he and his companions formed themselves into the Irish Christian Brothers, a teaching congregation which has spread throughout the English-speaking world and beyond. ½ m. SW., in Slievekeal Rd, is the Presentation Convent (1848) by Augustus Welby Pugin.

S. of Newgate St the town wall continues to the French Tower at the W. end of Castle St. Further on it follows the N. side of Castle St before doubling back to a square tower and the rear of the houses. Beyond Manor St is another stretch, with a battlemented circular tower overlooking Railway Sq.

Manor St leads SW. to the Cork road. Here is the 1888 Holy Ghost Hospital, where are preserved a painting (a 16th/17th cent. Altar frontal?) and eight figures from the original hospital in Grey Friars (*above*). In order of date these are: Enthroned Virgin, oak, 13th cent.?; Saint or Angel, oak, Italian, 15th cent.?; St Catherine, alabaster panel, English, 15th cent.; St Saviour, oak, 15th cent.?; St John the Baptist, 15th/16th cent.; Head of John the Baptist, stone, 15th cent.?; St Stephen, oak, late 15th cent.?; St Bonaventure (St Patrick?), 17th cent.

The N. end of Manor St is the junction of John's St, Parnell St, and St John's Lane. In the latter is St John's Churchyard, with remains of the church of the Benedictine priory-hospital of St John (like the Benedictine hospital of Cork, a dependency of Bath Abbey, England). St John's Church, Parnell St, is a Perpendicular essay (1842–50) by Joseph B. Keane: John George McCarthy of Cork designed the 1863 tower, whose upper part and spire have had to be taken down. The E. boundary of the churchyard is the town wall, which continues on towards Parnell St.

John's St ends at John's Bridge across the little John's River. 350 yds SSE. of the bridge is the Infirmary (by John Roberts, 1780); formerly called the Leper Hospital, this is the lineal descendant of the medieval Leper Hospital of St Stephen, which stood in Stephen's St. 600 yds S., on John's Hill, is St John's College, built 1867–71 to the design of Goldie. – 700 yds SE. of the Infirmary, on Passage Rd, is Newtown School (Quakers). The nucleus is the Georgian residence of the Wyse family. Sir Thomas Wyse (1791–1862) married Napoleon's niece, Letitia.

On the N. side of the Suir is the suburb of Ferrybank. Abbey Church and its graveyard (Abbey Rd) mark the site of St Mary's de Bello Portu, an abbey of Augustinian canonesses said to have been founded by Díarmait Mac Murrough as a cell of St Mary de Hogge, Dublin, which he founded in 1163. There was an earlier foundation hereabouts, Cill Chailchín (Kilculliheen).

3½ m. NE. is Slieveroe, Co. Kilkenny. The Catholic church is a Gothic Revival building by Ashlin and Coleman. 1 m. N., in Nicholastown, are the Three Friars, pillarstones. In nearby Attateemore was the birthplace of the great Irish scholar, John O Donovan (1806–66; see Dunkitt, below).

6 m. NE. are the remains of Kilcolumb (Co. Kilkenny) church. 50 yds N. is Cloch Cholaim (Colm's Stone), a boulder with bullauns locally believed to be the imprint of the saint's head and knees. Persons subject to headaches resort to the bullauns.

4 m. SE., in Mount Druid demesne, Ballygunner Temple, is the Druid's Altar, remnant of a chamber tomb or a cist grave.

6 m. SSE. is Ballyganner (see Clohernagh under Tramore).

2¼ m. S. is Ballindud Cromlech, a chamber tomb. 3 m. SSW. is Carriglong (see under Tramore).

4 m. SSW. is Knockeen Cromlech, a magnificent portal dolmen (Nat. Mon.).

5½ m. SW., in Gaulstown, is a splendid portal dolmen (Nat. Mon.). In adjoining Pembrokes-town are a chamber tomb and a motte. 2½ m. ESE. of Gaulstown is Munmahoge (see Carricklong under Tramore). 1 m. S. of Pembrokestown are Ballymoat "Moat" and pillarstone. In Ballyvellon, the adjoining townland on the S., are pillarstones. ⅔ m. S. of Ballyvellon is Matthewstown (see Fennor under Tramore).

8 m. SW. is Dunhill (see Fennor under Tramore).

10½ m. SW., via the Bunmahon road, is Savagetown portal dolmen. 2 m. ESE. is Ballynageeragh portal dolmen (see Fennor under Tramore).

5 m. WSW., by the Suir, are Mount Congreve House and demesne. The house dates from the early 18th cent. The dining-room, originally the entrance hall, is decorated with chiaroscuro paintings on canvas pasted to the walls. Some of these may have come from Whitfieldcourt (Whitfieldstown), a small Georgian house 2m. SW. The Mount Congreve gardens and woodlands are open to the public, April to Sept., Sun., 2.30–5.30 p.m.; other days by arrangement; admission 2/6. 2 m. NW. of Mount Congreve House are the remains of Kilmeedan castle, a Power stronghold taken by Cromwell in 1649.

2¼ m. WNW., on the N. bank of the Suir in Granny, Co. Kilkenny, are the ruins (Nat. Mon.) of a le Poer castle granted to James, Earl of Ormond, in 1375 following the attainder of Eustace fitz Arnold le Poer. It had two wards, a 13th cent. (?) curtain with four circular flankers, and a later square tower to which a 16th cent. hall was attached; one wall (with small oriel window) of the hall survives. In 1650 the Ormondist garrison surrendered to the Cromwellian regicide, Col. Axtel. 3 m. SW. is the five-storey tower of Curluddy castle, a Grant stronghold. 2 m. WNW. of Curluddy is the well-preserved motte-and-bailey of Portnascully, erected probably by Strongbow's follower, Milo, son of Bishop David of St David's, Wales. Nearby are a manorial mill site and remains of a manorial nave-and-chancel church. At the churchyard stile is a bullaun.

3½ m. NW. is Dunkitt (Co. Kilkenny), a village which takes its name from a nearby ringfort, the Ráth of Dunkitt. There are remains of a medieval nave-and-chancel church, at the S. side of which are the graves of the father (Edmund O Donovan "de Ata-Temoria", d. 1817) and other ancestors of the great Irish scholar, John O Donovan (see Attateemore, above).

7¾ m. WNW., via Granny (above) is Pollrone (see Fiddown under Piltown).

WATERVILLE, Co. Kerry (Map 4, B5), is a beautifully situated angling resort 8¾ m. NNW. of Caherdaniel and 11 m. S. of Cahersiveen.

1½ m. N., in Spunkane, is Caherhone, a stone ringfort. SE. is a stone circle; further SE. is a small ringfort.

2 m. NNE., in Termons, to the W. of Termons Lake, are remains of a small, ancient, anchoritic enclosure with a cross-slab (incised crosses on both faces) and the ruins of a clochán. ½ m. ENE. is a tall pillarstone, a short distance from which are megalithic remains. ¾ m. NE. of the pillarstone, in Caherbarnagh, are remains of another anchoritic enclosure, with an early cross-slab and a ruinous clochán. ¼ m. S. of this is St Fíonán's Well. ¾ m. E. of the well, in Dromkeare, is an unenclosed, ancient burial ground; there is a cross-inscribed ogham stone here. ¾ m. ENE. of Dromkeare bridge, on the S. side of the road, is Caher-savane, a stone ringfort (with rampart stair-ways) which gives its name to the townland.

1 m. NE., by the lakeshore in Beenbane, is Lisoven, a "horse-shoe" ringfort with a system of souterrains; outside it is a ruined clochán (Nat. Mons.). The fields to the N. are littered with remains of houses, clocháns, etc., including two pillarstones; W. of the second pillar-stone are two small chamber tombs, etc. Further N. is an ancient burial ground with a small stone cross, a souterrain, and the remains of a fine clochán; not far away are two other clocháns; all Nat. Mons. NE. of these, on a promontory, is another pillarstone.

14 m. NE. (3 m. from the road), in Cloon West (close to the head of Cloon Lough), is an ancient church-site with two cross-pillars.

2 m. ENE., in Lough Currane, alias Lough Leagh, is Inis Úasal, alias Church Island. The remains (Nat. Mons.) of St Fíonán's Church, of three clocháns (one called St Fíonán's Cell), and of an enclosing cashel, represent a monastery allegedly founded by St Máel-M'Áedhóg after his expulsion from Bangor (q.v.) in 1127. The church is a small, nave-and-chancel, Romanesque building; doorway very much restored. In the graveyard are two pillar-stones and eight early gravestones and cross-slabs, two with inscriptions: A Ω IHS XPS BENNACHT F[OR] ANMAIN ANMCH-ADA ("Alpha Omega Jesus Christ. A blessing on the soul of Anmchad"), IHS XPS MARIA BENNACHT F[OR] ANMAIN GILLE-IN-CHOIMDE I BUICNE ADBUR RI CIAR-RAIDI . . . ("Jesus Christ. Mary. A blessing on the soul of Gilla-in-Choimded Ó Búicne, a royal prince of Ciarraidhe . . .").

In Ballybrack, the adjacent townland to the SE. of Waterville, is a large chamber tomb with cup marks on the capstone.

¾ m. ESE., in Eightercua, is the ancient church site, Templenakilla. NNE. four pillar-stones look like the façade of the adjacent long cairn. – ¾ m. ENE. is a pillarstone. – 5 m. E., in Inchfarrannagleragh Glebe (S. of the road and SE. of Iskanagahiny Lough), is a small, un-enclosed burial ground; there is an early cross-pillar here. NE. is a pillarstone; NW. a small ringfort with central souterrain.

1¼ m. S., in Ardkearagh, is an ancient enclosure with a souterrain and a cross-pillar. 1¾ m. further S., in Loher (60 yds W. of the old road to Darrynane), is Kildreenagh, an oval enclosure with remains of a small oratory (on a platform) and of a clochán. S. of the oratory are three early cross-pillars; the W. pillar, An Leac Chaol, has A and Ω under the arms of the cross. There are several stone ringforts hereabouts; also clocháns on the slope to the E. of the road.

WELLINGTON BRIDGE, alias **DROI-CHEAD EOIN**, Co. Wexford (Map 6, C6), is a village on the Bridgetown (11 m.)–New Ross (17 m.) road. It is named after the Iron Duke (see Trim). 1¼ m. W. is Nelson's Bridge. 1½ m. SE. of the latter, at the head of Bannow Bay, is the site of the medieval town of Clon-mines. Though in ruins by 1684, it continued to return two members to the Dublin Parlia-ment until the Union, when the proprietors were bought out by the British Government. There are remains of four castles and three churches. The latter include St Nicholas's Church – a unique, castle-like parish church – and the choir, S. aisle, and tower (inserted) of a late 14th cent. friary of Austin Hermits.

3½ m. SE., in Coolehull, is an unusual, small, late 16th cent. castle. 1½ m. SSW. is Cullens-town, a small seaside resort which has a good beach.

5 m. SSW. (on the E. side of Bannow Bay) are Bannow Island and Bannow Strand. About 1 May 1169, Robert FitzStephen and Hervey de Montmorency, uncle of Strongbow, arrived in the bay with thirty "milites", sixty mail-clad horsemen, and 300 archers. Next day they were joined by Maurice de Prendergast with another strong force of archers, and they all landed on Bannow Island, at that time still cut off from the mainland. Here they waited ("and the Irish set no store by them"; Four Masters) until joined by Díarmait Mac Murrough, King of Leinster and the Danes, with 500 men. The combined forces then attacked Wexford. – On the mainland are the ruins of St Mary's, a simple, 13th cent., nave-and-chancel church with later N. and S. porches; the battlements and E. window are 14th cent. This and the remains of a small chapel (St Brendan's Chantry founded by Hervey de Montmorency ?) are all that survive of the "lost city of Bannow", the first Anglo-Norman corporate town in Ireland. As early as 1684 the town had been quite ruined by drifting sands; but it continued to return two members to the Dublin House of Commons until the Union, though all they had to repre-sent in the end were the church and a chimney. In 1798 the Earl of Ely was paid £15,000 to compensate him for the extinction of the representation. Near the church is the Long Stone, a pillarstone with cup marks and other devices.

WESTPORT, Co. Mayo (Map 1, C4), is a market town and small seaport on the Ballin-robe (20 m.)–Newport (8 m.) road, at the head of Westport Bay (SE. corner of Clew Bay). It is a convenient centre for touring some of the loveliest mountain country of the West. The finest circuits are probably round the Sheeffry Hills via Westport – Louisburgh – Doo Lough – Glen -- Liscarney – Westport; or Westport – Louisburgh – Doo Lough – Killary – Aasleagh – Erriff bridge – Liscarney – Westport.

It is a well laid-out little town (planned by James Wyatt about 1780), with a pleasant tree-lined Mall. The Catholic church has *opus sectile* Stations of the Cross by Hubert Mc Goldrick (*c.* 1930). The Protestant church (*c.* 1880) is a good period piece with *art nouveau* carvings and other noteworthy details; "George A. Bermingham" (Canon J. Hannay, 1865–1952), the novelist, was rector here for many years.

Adjoining the town (entrance from the Quay) is the mutilated demesne (open to the public, 26 May to 30 Sept., 2–6 p.m.; house and grounds 3/-, children 1/6; grounds only, 6d.) of Westport House (Marquess of Sligo), with ornamental waters achieved by controlling the tides of an inlet of Clew Bay. The house (about 1730) is by Richard Cassels; 1778 additions and alterations by James Wyatt. Among its former treasures were the ornamental pillars from the so-called Treasury of Atreus, alias the Tomb of Agamemnon, at Mycenae. They had been brought home by the 2nd Marquess (1788–1845) and erected at a side-door of Westport House. Their fate remained a mystery to archaeologists until 1910, when they were sold to the British Museum.

2½ m. ENE., close to the Castlebar road and commanding a very fine view, is Sheeaun, a hill-top (382 ft) tumulus. Daniel O Connell's great meeting here still lives in folk memory. 2 m. SE., in Dooncastle, are the ruins of a castle of the Mac Philbin branch of the Mac William *Íochtair* Burkes. 3 m. SE. of this, in Aille, are remains of Mac Philbin's Castle. Less than ½ m. S. Tóchar Phádraig – an ancient pilgrims' road to Croagh Patrick (*below*) via Aghagower, 1½ m. W. (*below*) – led W. from the Aille River (which disappears underground in silted-up Aille Caves, ½ m. away).

4½ m. SE. on Tóchar Phádraig (*above*), is Aghagower. St Patrick is said to have founded a church here, which he confided to Bishop Seanach. Later there was a monastery here, but by the 15th cent. the church was parochial. There are ruins (Nat. Mons.) of a 12th (?) cent. Round Tower and of a 12th/13th cent. church with 15th cent. features. Near the SE. corner of the churchyard is Leaba Phádraig, an over-grown modern enclosure with remains of an ancient tree. Outside the W. wall of the church-yard (NW. of the tower), in an overgrown en-closure, is Tobar na nDeochán, "Well of the Drinks" (dried up). N. of this, in the angle of the road, is Dabhach Phádraig, "Patrick's Vat", an enclosed well, also dried up. "Stations" are still made at *leaba* and wells on Crom Dubh's (Garland) Friday and Sunday; *see* Croagh

Patrick pilgrimage (*below*). 300 yds NE. of the road junction, on the W. side of Tóchair Phádraig, are the last remnants of Teampall na bhFiacal, "Church of the Teeth", traditionally the church founded by St Patrick; 300 yds N. is a bullaun ("holy well"). ¼ m. ENE. of this, on the S. side of the *tóchar*, was Leacht Tomaltaigh, "Tomaltach's Memorial". – Tóchar Phádraig continued W. of Aghagower via Lahardaun ford to Cloghan bridge (1¾ m. SW.), thence through Lankill, Lanmore, and Boheh to the Owenwee and so to Croagh Patrick. 1½ m. WNW. of Cloghan bridge is Knappamanagh graveyard (*below*). ¾ m. SW. of Cloghan bridge, in Lankill, is a 7-ft pillarstone (Nat. Mon.) with incised cross and concentric circles; (fake ?). Nearby is an ancient churchyard with Tober-brendan, "Brendan's Well". ¾ m. WNW. of the latter, in Lanmore, is Cloch Phádraig, "Patrick's Stone", alias Cloch Fhada, "Long Stone", a pillarstone. 2¼ m. WSW. of Cloch Phádraig is Boheh killeen (*below*).

3¾ m. S. is Lankill pillarstonè (*above*).

2¾ m. SSW., in Knappamanagh, is an ancient circular churchyard. A small stone here has an incised anthropomorphic cross design and other devices. The altar is said to have been used in Penal times. Outside the churchyard are the remains of small circular Feart.

4½ m. SSW., in Boheh, are St Patrick's Chair and Killeen. St Patrick's Chair is a heap of stones with concentric-circle cup marks, etc. The killeen is an ancient churchyard. Tóchar Phádraig continued W. past them to the Owenwee.

1¾ m. SW., in Knockfin, is Finn Mac Cool's Grave. ¾ m. WSW., in Churchfield, is the site of Oughaval, an early monastery (attributed to Columcille) which gave its name to Westport parish. NE. of the churchyard is St Columcille's Well.

4 m. WSW., by the seashore in Gortbraud, are pillarstones, a stone alignment, and remains of an enclosure.

5½ m. WSW., to the N. of the Louisburgh road, are the remains of Murrisk "Abbey" (Nat. Mon.), a small Augustinian friary founded in 1457 by Tadhg O Malley, "Captain of his nation". There was a tower over the W. end of the church.

6 m. WSW. is Croagh Patrick (2,510 ft), Ireland's Holy Mountain. A beautiful quartzite ridge and cone, it rises steeply from the S. shore of Clew Bay, and in clear weather offers magni-ficent views. St Patrick is said to have fasted on the mountain top for forty days, and every year thousands of devout pilgrims climb to the summit before dawn on Domhnach Chrom Dubh, "Crom Dubh's Sunday" (last Sunday of July; down to the early part of the last century the pilgrimage took place on Aoine Chrom Dubh, *i.e.* the preceding Friday). The ascent is begun in Murrisk; the final climb is over the bare scree of the upper cone, or *crúach* proper. At the base of the upper cone is the first pilgrim's "station", Leacht Mhionnáin, "St

Benignus's Monument", where seven *deiseal* praying circuits are made. The climb continues W. up Casán Phádraig "Patrick's Path" to the summit, where the pilgrims kneel and pray. At the last traces of Teampall Phádraig, "Patrick's Church", further prayers are said, followed by fifteen *deiseal* circuits (over 2 m.) of a circular path around the summit. The next "station" is Leaba Phádraig, "Patrick's Bed", now a mere heap of stones NE. of the modern chapel. Prayers are said inside it, after which seven *deiseal* circuits are made. The last "station" is Roilig Mhuire, "St Mary's Cemetery", alias An Garraí Mór, "the Great Garden", with its three mounds of stones, ½ m. WSW.; seven circuits are made at each mound, followed by seven circuits around the *roilig*. (Some pilgrims complete their *turas* at Kilgeever near Louisburgh, *q.v.*) At the N. foot of the cone, below Leacht Mhionnáin, is Log na nDeamhan, a hollow into which St Patrick is said to have driven demons. Near the S. base of the mountain is Lough na Corra, into which he is said to have driven the demon Corra, thereby causing the lake to burst forth from the earth.

WEXFORD, Co. Wexford (Map 6, C6), the county town, is attractively situated at the mouth of the Slaney in Wexford Harbour, 24 m. S. of New Ross and 11 m. NW. of Rosslare. Once a busy seaport, it is today a manufacturing (agricultural machinery, brewing) and marketing centre, as well as a place of considerable attraction to the tourist and the antiquarian.

The town owes its origin to the Norse, who founded a trading settlement here in the 9th or early 10th cent. In May 1169 it was captured by Díarmait na nGall and his Anglo-Norman allies, the first town in Ireland to fall into Anglo-Norman hands. Díarmait promptly granted it to Robert fitz Stephen and Maurice fitz Gerald. On Díarmait's death in 1171 the townsfolk burned the town, and fitz Stephen fled to Carrick-on-Slaney (*see* Beggerin *and* Ferrycarrig, *below*). In 1172 Henry II reserved the town to the English Crown, but subsequently assigned it to Strongbow. In the 14th cent., having outgrown its old defences, the town was enclosed by a new towered wall with five gates. Thereafter little of moment is recorded until 1649, when Cromwell massacred the inhabitants in breach of the agreed terms of surrender. In 1798 the town was stormed and held for nearly a month by the Insurgents, some of whom disgraced a bravely fought cause by the murder of ninety-one of their enemies.

Like many an old walled town, Wexford is one of quaint, but inconveniently narrow, streets. Of the town wall, however, only some fragments and the West Gate remain (near the principal railway station).

Near the West Gate are the ruins (Nat. Mon.) of the 13th/14th (?) cent. church of the Augustinian Priory of SS Peter and Paul, commonly called Selskar (*i.e.* Holy Sepulchre)

Abbey. The priory – where Henry II of England spent the Lent of 1172 doing penance for the murder of St Thomas à Becket – was founded by the local branch of the Norman Roches. The remains comprise the double nave (the W. windows are insertions) and the battlemented square tower (14th cent. ?) which intervened between it and the choir. A Protestant church (unroofed 1961) was built on the site of the chancel in the last century. At the W. side of the churchyard is a fragment of the town wall (Nat. Mon.).

At the intersection of Abbey St, Main St, and Quay St is the Bull Ring, scene of one of the worst episodes of the Cromwellian massacre. Its name recalls the once popular pastime of bull-baiting. The 1798 memorial (1905) is by Oliver Sheppard, R.H.A. To the W., in the angle of John's Lane and John St, is St John's Graveyard. This is the site of a priory-hospital of the Knights of St John of Jerusalem founded about 1211 by Strongbow's son-in-law, William the Marshal I. The Irish Commandery of the Order had its seat there until the acquisition of Kilmainham (Dublin City, SW.).

The Church of the Immaculate Conception, Rowe St, W. of Main St, is by Robert Pierce (*see* Church of the Assumption, Bride St, *below*).

On the Crescent (Quay), east of Main St, is a 1956 statue (by the American sculptor, Wheeler Williams) of Commodore John Barry (1745–1803), "father" of the United States Navy. Barry was a native of Ballysampson (*see under* Rosslare).

The interesting small 18th cent. Theatre, McSweeny St, has been restored and is now the focus of the annual Wexford Festival of music, drama, and the arts (last Sunday of October to first Sunday of November).

In the Franciscan church, School St, are the enshrined remains of the Roman boy-martyr, St Adjutor. The church occupies the site of a Franciscan friary founded in 1230 by Strongbow's grandson, William the Marshall II, on the site of the Knights Templar priory-hospital of SS John and Brigid founded by his father. After the Cromwellian triumph the remains of the friary were given to Capt. William Ivory. In 1688 Ivory's son, John, restored the site to the Franciscans. They erected a Mass house which served as the parish church from 1690 to 1858.

At the S. end of McSweeny St–Patrick St are the remains of St Patrick's Church, like Selskar Abbey a double-nave edifice. A short distance SE., between Main St and Bride St, is a fragment of St Mary's Church.

The Church of the Assumption, Bride St (two-light 1920 window by Harry Clarke: *Our Lady, SS Patrick, George*) and the Church of the Immaculate Conception, Rowe St, are called the Twin Churches because built at the same time, 1851–58, to the designs of the same architect, Robert Pierce, pupil and assistant of Augustus Welby Pugin. Pugin himself designed the excellent Chapel of St Peter's College, Summerhill Rd.

Wexford was the birthplace or the home of several famous or interesting persons. Jane Frances Elgee, Oscar Wilde's eccentric mother, better known as Speranza, was born (1826) at the old rectory in South Main St. Sir John Mac Clure (1807–73), who discovered the North-West Passage (1851), was born in North Main St in the house next to White's Hotel. The mother of Thomas Moore, the song-writer, lived in the Cornmarket.

Outside the town, on the New Ross road, a copy of Pompey's Pillar at Alexandria commemorates the British conquest of Egypt. It was erected in 1841 by Gen. Brown-Clayton, who took part in the campaign.

4½ m. N. (via Castlebridge) is pretty Glen of Eden with cascades on the little River Sow. (Partly private; apply for permission to Eden Vale House.)

4 m. NE., in Wexford Harbour, is Beggerin Island, now joined to the mainland as a result of reclamation works. The name is a corruption of Beag Éire, Little Éire. (Alternative names were Inis Fáil and Inis Ibair.) There was an early monastic church here, attributed to a "pre-Patrician" Bishop Ibar, who is described as one of the most obdurate of St Patrick's rivals. The monastery was plundered by the Vikings in 813. Despite the Viking settlement nearby, it survived, and in 1182 was granted by the Wexford Roches to St Nicholas's Monastery, Exeter. The remains include the ruins of a small church and some early gravestones. They are still resorted to by pilgrims. In 1171 the Wexford folk took refuge on the island, bringing with them fitz Stephen and their other Anglo-Norman prisoners, and forced Strongbow to withdraw by threatening to behead the captives.

6 m. NE. is the quiet little resort of Curracloe with a 6-m. sandy beach.

3¾ m. S. are the interesting tower and bawn of Kiliane castle, sometime seat of a branch of the Cheevers of Ballyhally which succeeded the Hays here. 3 m. SW. (½ m. NW. of the Kilmore road) is the picturesque castle of Rathmacknee (Nat. Mon.), one of the best preserved of the many 15th cent. castles of S. Wexford. It and the manorial church were built inside a large ring-work by the Rosseters, a family of Lincolnshire origin which had its home here from the 14th, if not from the 12th, cent. onwards (see baronies of Forth and Bargy under Bridgetown). The remains comprise a well-preserved tower and a five-sided bawn.

4½ m. SW. is Johnstown Castle, an excellent 19th cent. Gothic mansion which incorporates the remains of an Esmonde castle. The Esmonde castle was dismantled, and the property confiscated, by the Cromwellians. They were sold to John Grogan of York in 1683. In 1856 the last Grogan (Mrs Grogan-Morgan) married Sir Thomas Esmonde, and the place returned to the Esmondes. More recently the castle was the home of Lady Maurice Fitzgerald, sister of Lord Granard. In 1944 her grandson presented it to the nation, and it is now a research

station of the Agricultural Institute. The grounds and gardens are open to the public on week days, 10 a.m.–6 p.m.

The road from Wexford SW. to Wellington Bridge (q.v.) runs along the S. slope of Forth Mountain (779 ft), which affords extensive views of land and sea.

3 m. W. is Three Rock Hill, site of one of the principal insurgent encampments in 1798.

2½ m. WNW. is Ferrycarrig, where the Slaney forces its way through a narrow gorge. Above, the river is broad and still; here it is a rapid torrent. On a spur of rock on the N. bank is the tall tower of a 15th cent. castle absurdly attributed to Robert fitz Stephen. There was a skirmish between Insurgents and British troops at Ferrycarrig in 1798. The tower on the S. bank commemorates the Wexfordmen who fell in the Crimean War. The high earthen bank and broad ditch nearby, which cut off a level space on the riverside rock, almost certainly represent fitz Stephen's fort of Carrick on Slaney, that "first Norman castle in Ireland", in which fitz Stephen took refuge when forced to abandon Wexford on the death of Díarmait na nGall in 1171. 3½ m. NW., on the E. bank of the Slaney, is the Deeps' Castle, alias Kyle Castle.

WHITEHEAD, Co. Antrim (Map 3, D4), is a seaside resort on the N. shore of Belfast Lough, 5 m. NE. of Carrickfergus and 9 m. SE. of Larne. It is the most convenient place for exploring Island Magee (q.v.). N. of the railway station is the stump of Castle Chichester (Nat. Mon.), a small tower built by Sir Moses Hill about 1604.

2½ m. NW., in Ballycarry village, are the ruins of Templecorran church, with a memorial (about 1720) to the Rev. Edward Brice, the first Presbyterian minister ordained (1613) to preach in Ireland. In the churchyard is the grave of James Orr (1770–1816), "Bard of Ballycarry", and a member of the United Irishmen. ½ m. N. is Red Hall, a Clannaboy O Neill castle which passed in 1609 to Sir William Edmonston, who remodelled it. The interior has interesting 17th cent. stucco ceilings.

WICKLOW, Co. Wicklow (Map 6, D4), county town of the county to which it gives its name, is a small seaport and seaside resort at the mouth of the Vartry, 32 m. SE. of Dublin. It is a convenient base for touring the beauty spots of the Wicklow Mountains.

The town takes its English name from a 9th cent. Norse settlement (Vikingaló); its Irish name (Cill Mhantáin) from a church founded by St Mantán, reputedly a disciple of St Patrick. Both Palladius and St Patrick are said to have landed at the mouth of the Vartry, only to be driven away by the local ruler.

At the Anglo-Norman conquest the town and district were granted to Maurice fitz Gerald, ancestor of the barons of Naas, who remained nominal lords of the place until 1350, when the castle became an English royal fortress. Nevertheless, from about 1430 to 1542 town and castle lay at the mercy of the O Byrnes, who exacted "Black Rents" from the English townsfolk. In 1542 the O Byrnes indentured with Henry VIII to cease to exact their tributes. In October 1580 they razed both castle and town. The castle was, however, re-garrisoned by the Crown the following year, and by the close of the century Irish power in the county was at an end. In 1641 the place was seized by Confederate Catholics under Luke O Toole, but was taken after a siege by the Parliamentarian, Sir Charles Coote I.

The 18th cent. Protestant church occupies the site of the medieval parish church of St Patrick. Built into the S. porch are fragments of a 12th cent. Romanesque doorway. To the N. is the Round Mount, a motte; some think it is a relic of the Viking defences.

In the garden of the parish priest's residence is the Abbey, remnant of a small, poor, Franciscan friary founded, presumably by the Naas Fitzgeralds, in the 13th cent., and extended or rebuilt by the O Byrnes in the 15th.

In the Market Sq. is a 1798 memorial (statue of the valiant Billy Byrne of Ballymanus); in Fitzwilliam Sq. a monument to Capt. Robert C. Halpin (1836–94) of Wicklow, captain of the *Great Eastern*, which laid the first Transatlantic cable.

On a cliff-promontory E. of the town are the ruins of Black Castle, successor to Maurice fitz Gerald's castle of 1178.

1½ m. SE., near Bride's Head, is Bride's Well. In a cleft of Bride's Head is the Penal-times Catholic chapel of St Bride.

2½ m. SE. is Wicklow Head (245 ft). The middle, and second oldest, of the three light-houses is now an An Óige (Irish Youth Hostel Association) hostel.

4 m. S., by the little Three Mile Water, is Ennisboyne (Inis Bhaíthín, Bheóithín). There was an early ecclesiastical foundation here, beautifully sited on a plateau. Legend associates it with St Patrick's landing. At the close of the 6th cent. the relics of SS Sylvester and Solinus were brought there. 1¾ m. S. of the church-site is Jack's Hole, a small, sandy cove. 1¾ m. W. of the latter, in Castletimon townland, is the Long Stone, a ruined chamber tomb. Not far away are the ruins of Castletimon church; there are fragments of a stone cross here. By the road-side is an ogham stone (Nat. Mon.). 1¼ m. WNW. are the ruins of Dunganstown castle.

6½ m. S. is Brittas Bay, with its lovely 2¼-m. beach backed by sand dunes.

5¾ m. SSW. are the ruins of Dunganstown castle.

WOODFORD, Co. Galway (Map 5, C2), is a village at the intersection of the Portumna (9 m.)–Ennis (36 m.) and Loughrea (14 m.)–Mountshannon (10 m.) roads. It was here that Wilfred Scawen Blunt (1840–1922), English author, politician, and champion of the op-pressed, was arrested in October 1887, after

organizing a Mass Protest Meeting of the ten-ants on the Clanricarde estates (*see* Portumna). He was imprisoned for two months in Galway and Kilmainham gaols. His *In Vinculis* (1889) describes his experiences.

YOUGHAL, Co. Cork (Map 5, D6), is an interesting old market town and fishing port at the W. side of the Blackwater estuary, 17 m. E. of Midleton, 18 m. S. of Lismore, and 19 m. SW. of Dungarvan. It is also a popular seaside resort with a good, safe, 5-m. strand. At Monatrea, on the opposite side of the estuary in Co. Waterford, is another good bathing beach.

Nothing is known of the history of Youghal prior to the foundation of a baronial town by the Anglo-Normans in the 13th cent. (The barony – Inchiquin – was part of fitz Stephen's share of the Kingdom of Cork; *see* Cork.) The town changed ownership several times in the 13th, 14th, and 15th centuries. By 1358 the citizens had acquired municipal liberties, which were enlarged in 1413/20 by a charter from the then proprietor, the Earl of Ormond. Sub-sequently the town passed to the Earls of

Irish Tourist Board

Tomb of the Great Earl of Cork,
St Mary's Church, Youghal

Desmond. Outside the walls were two friaries, Dominican on the N., Franciscan on the S. On 15 Nov. 1579, the Rebel Earl of Desmond sacked and burned the town; and when the Earl of Ormond arrived with an English force ten weeks later he found it altogether deserted (save for one solitary friar) and the walls overthrown. At the Plantation of Munster the town was included in the vast grant made to Sir Walter Raleigh. The Guide Books and local "tradition" notwithstanding, Raleigh spent little time in the place. (His duties as Mayor, 1588–89, were discharged by a deputy.) He neither built nor lived in Raleigh's House (below); nor did he plant the first Irish potatoes in its garden. In Dec. 1602 he sold out to the notorious Richard Boyle, afterwards Earl of Cork (1566–1643). Boyle built a new College House (below) and made it his residence. At the outbreak of the 1641–52 war he strengthened the town's defences and made it one of the more important English bases in Munster. In the summer of 1645 it was blockaded for ten weeks by a Confederate Catholic army under the command of Lord Castlehaven. A Parliamentarian flotilla, commanded by William Penn, tried to relieve the town, but could do little more than lie off the harbour for a month. When Cromwell reached New Ross in Nov. 1649, the English garrison of Youghal went over to the Parliamentarian side, and on 6 Dec. Cromwell laid up his army in winter quarters in the town.

South Abbey St, at the S. end of the old town, preserves the memory of vanished "South Abbey", the first Franciscan friary in Ireland. It was founded in 1224 by Maurice Fitzgerald, 2nd Baron O ffaly, and completed by his son, Thomas. Several earls of Desmond were buried there. Nearby is the Presentation Convent, noted for its lace (pointe d'Irlande). The Carnegie Library, Ashe St, has a small collection of local antiquities.

The Clock Gate, South Main St, is a 1771 replacement (architect, William Meade) of the medieval Iron Gate, alias Trinity Castle, between the upper and lower towns. It served as the town gaol until 1837. The Water Gate ("Cromwell's Arch"), nearby in Quay Lane, is an early 19th cent. "restoration".

On the E. side of North Main St is Tynte's Castle, formerly Walsh's Castle, a much-altered, ruinous, 15th cent. tower-house. On the opposite side of the street is the Red House, a brick building with Dutch Renaissance details. It was built (1706–15) for the Uniackes by a Dutch builder named Leuventhen.

Also on the W. side of North Main St, close to the Munster and Leinster Bank, is the much-altered gable of St John's House, a hospital (founded 1360) belonging to the Benedictine priory-hospital of St John the Evangelist, Waterford. Also in North Main St are almshouses for six poor Protestant widows, founded in 1634 by Richard Boyle and re-edified early in the last century.

To the W. of North Main St is St Mary's Church (Protestant), erected about 1250 on the site of an older edifice. (Some fragments of older – including Romanesque ? – work are incorporated in the W. gable of the nave proper, in the N. walls of the N. aisle and N. transept aisle, and in the basement of the tower.) Partly wrecked by Desmond's followers in 1579, neglected by Richard Boyle in breach of his covenant, savaged by 18th cent. churchwardens, and unhappily "restored" (1852–54) by a local architect and antiquary, Edward Fitzgerald (1820–93), it remains, for all that, a building of interest. It is a cruciform structure with aisled nave of five bays, aisled N. transept, aisleless S. transept, long chancel, and massive bell-tower at the NW. angle of the N. transept. It has lost its rood-loft, a circular tower (which stood at the W. gable of the nave), N. and S. porches, a sacristy (off the N. side of the choir), and two chantry chapels (one a W. prolongation of the S. aisle, the other an insertion between the S. aisle and the S. transept). The ugly candle-snuffer roof, which smothers nave, transepts, and aisles, is the work of Edward Fitzgerald, who swept away the battlemented parapets of the nave walls. Nave, transepts, and tower are basically mid-13th cent. work, but the nave walls were considerably modified in the 15th cent., probably around 1464, when Thomas, 7th Earl of Desmond, established a college (warden, eight fellows, and eight singing men) to supply the church services. It was, no doubt, this foundation which brought about the enlargement of the chancel to its present size. The church has a good 14th/15th cent. font and a number of interesting tombs and monuments. The sword-rest (1684) for the Corporation's Sword of State is the only surviving Irish example. Of particular interest are the monuments in the S. transept (Cork Transept), founded by Richard Benet and his wife, Ellis Barry, as the chantry of St Saviour. Wrecked by Desmond's men in 1579, it was tardily re-edified by Richard Boyle in 1619. (The endowments of the college had been given into his clutches on condition of repairing the church and the college house for Protestant use.) Boyle restored the tomb of the 13th cent. founders, and furnished it with the polychrome effigies in 17th cent. costume. He also erected the grandiose Renaissance monument (by Edmund Tingham of Chapelizod ?; restored 1848) to himself, his wives, his mother, and nine of his sixteen children; the effigies are very good. (Another Tingham monument was erected by Boyle in St Patrick's Cathedral, Dublin, SW.) The churchyard is partly enclosed by a portion of the town wall (repaired more than once in the 17th and 18th centuries).

E. of the church is New College House, 1781–82 successor of Richard Boyle's house of 1608, itself the successor of the 15th cent. college (residence of the parish clergy). The flanking towers are relics of the defences constructed by Boyle, 1641–42; the only other relic of Boyle's house is an elaborate chimney-piece.

Myrtle Grove, Youghal

Near by, with a fine view of town and harbour, is a terrace built by Boyle to mount a battery.

NW. of New College House is Myrtle Grove, alias Sir Walter Raleigh's House, alias Sir Lawrence Parsons's House, a much-altered Elizabethan house (not open to public). It may have been built by Sir Thomas Norreys, English Lord President of Munster. Some interesting original features survive inside.

Near the N. end of North Main St are the remnants (Nat. Mon.) of North Abbey, church of a Dominican friary founded in 1268 by Thomas Fitzgerald.

3¼ m. NW. are the ruins of Kilnatoora castle (Nat. Mon.), a MacSheehy stronghold granted to Sir Walter Raleigh and sold by him to Richard Boyle. In 1645 it surrendered to Lord Castlehaven after bombardment.

2 m. N., at Rinncrew, magnificently sited above the confluence of the Blackwater and Tourig, are the fragmentary remains of a cell of the Knights Hospitaller preceptory of Mourne Abbey, Co. Cork (*see under* Mallow).

1½ m. further N., at the confluence of the Blackwater and the little Glendine River, are remains of Templemichael castle (Fitzgerald) and St Michael's Well. 2 m. N. of Templemichael is Ballynatray House (1795 onwards), home of the Holroyd-Smyths. Penelope Smyth, whose Gretna Green marriage (1836) to Charles Frederick Borbone, brother of notorious Ferdinand II of the Two Sicilies, was made a bone of international contention by Lord Palmerston (British Foreign Secretary), was of this family. ¼ m. away, on an island in the Blackwater (causeway approach), are the ruins of Dairinis Augustinian priory. St Máel-Anfaidh ("Molana"), abbot of Lismore, founded an anchoritic settlement here in the 6th/7th cent. A charming anecdote is told of the saint in the *Félire* of Oengus the Culdee (*see* Clonenagh *under* Mountrath): "Máel-Anfaidh, abbot of Dairinis, a cell of Mo-Chuda's Lismore . . . This is the Máel-Anfaidh who one day saw a little bird weeping and lamenting. 'O my God,' said he, 'what has happened to that creature?

Plate 17. Near Carraroe, Co. Galway

I swear,' said he, 'that I will eat no food until it is revealed to me.' So abiding there he beheld an angel approaching. 'Hail, cleric,' said the angel, 'let the trouble of this vex you no longer. Mo-Lúa, son of Oche, has died. And the creatures lament him because he never killed any creature, little or big. And men bewail him no more than do the other creatures, including the tiny bird you see.' " A monk of Dairinis, Rubin mac Connadh, "Scribe of Munster" (d. 725), was one of the compilers – the other being Cú-Chuimne *Sapiens* of Iona (d. 747) – of the celebrated *Collectio canonum Hibernensis*. (This, a collection of aphorisms and enactments dealing with church discipline, the religious life, and the government of souls, had widespread European influence.) Fer-dá-chrích (d. 747), Abbot of Dairinis, was one of the leaders of the 8th cent. reform movement. (Máel-Rúáin of Tallaght, *q.v.*, was a disciple of his.) At the 12th cent. Reformation, Dairinis was one of the numerous ancient Irish foundations which, in conformity with a decree of the Lateran Council (1139), adopted the Rule of the Augustinian Canons Regular. Raymond le Gros is believed to have been a patron of the reformed foundation, and to have been buried there. In the later Middle Ages the priory had a famous statue, which was burned at the Reformation by one, Bluett, of Youghal. The priory and its properties were among the acquisitions of Sir Walter Raleigh which passed into the possession of Richard Boyle. The remains comprise a ruined church and fragments of the claustral buildings. The church consisted of short, early nave and later (*i.e.* early 13th cent.) chancel. The chancel, in Augustinian fashion, is longer than the nave. Opening off the N. side of the chancel is the later, two-storeyed, prior's lodging (?).

7 m. N., on the Blackwater, is Strancally (*see* Okyle *under* Cappoquin).

3 m. ENE., is Grange, Co. Waterford (*see under* Ardmore).

1 m. S., at Kilcoran, was the home of Edmund Spenser's wife, Elizabeth Boyle, golden-haired daughter of a kinsman of Richard Boyle's. It was for her that Spenser wrote his *Amoretti* sonnets and *Epithalamium*. After Spenser's death she married Sir Robert Tynte of Ballycrenane (*see* Ballymacoda *and* Kilcredan *under* Castlemartyr).

6 m. WSW. are remnants of the 13th cent. circular keep of Inchiquin castle, *caput* of the Anglo-Norman barony to which it gave its name.

Visitors to Ireland are advised to study *The Angler's Guide*, published by the Irish Tourist Board; booklets are also available on Game, Coarse, and Sea Fishing. The following are some of the principal fisheries of the country with their specialities.

WATERS	Spring salmon	Grilse	Sea trout	Brown trout	Coarse	CENTRES
Co. Antrim						
Bann		★	★			Coleraine
Bush		★	★			Bushmills
Dun	★			★		Cushendun
Glenarm		★	★			Glenarm
Glenariff		★	★			Cushendall
L. Neagh	★	★	★	★		Antrim
Co. Carlow						
Barrow			★		★	Carlow & Borris
Co. Cavan						
Erne & L. Erne				★	★	Belturbet, Cavan, Killeshandra & Arvagh
Glyde	★					Kingscourt
L. Ramor				★	★	Virginia & Granard
L. Sheelin				★	★	Virginia
L. Sillan				★	★	Cootehill
Co. Clare						
L. Derg	★	★	★	★	★	Mountshannon, Scarriff & Killaloe
Fergus & L. Fergus				★	★	Corrofin & Ennis
Co. Cork						
L. Allua	★			★		Inchigeela
Allow				★		Kanturk
Argideen			★			Courtmacsherry
Awbeg				★		Buttevant
Bandon	★		★	★		Ballineen–Enniskean, Bandon, & Dunmanway
Blackwater	★	★	★		★	Fermoy, Mallow, & Millstreet
Bride	★			★	★	Ballincollig & Cookstown
Brinny	★		★	★		Ballineen–Enniskean
Carrigaline			★			Crosshaven
Dalua				★		Kanturk
Funshion				★		Glanworth
Glanmire			★	★		Cork
Glengariff	★	★	★	★		Bantry

WATERS	Spring salmon	Grilse	Sea trout	Brown trout	Coarse	CENTRES
Co. Cork (*cont.*)						
Ilen		★	★			Skibbereen
Lee	★	★			★	Ballincollig, Cork, Crookstown, Macroom, & Inchigeela
Owenacurra				★		Midleton
Owvane		★	★			Bantry
Co. Derry						
Bann	★	★	★	★	★	Coleraine
Co. Donegal						
Bundrowes	★					Bundoran
Clady		★	★			Gweedore
Crana		★	★			Buncrana
Culdaff			★			Culdaff
Crolly		★	★			Bunbeg
Erne		★	★			Ballyshannon & Bundoran
L. Fern	★					Milford & Rathmelton
L. Glen		★	★			Carrigart
Gweebarra			★			Dungloe
Lackagh		★	★			Rosapenna & Carrigart
Lennan	★					Rathmelton & Milford
L. Melvin	★					Donegal
Oily		★	★			Dunkineely
Owenea		★	★			Ardara & Glenties
Owentocker		★	★			Ardara & Glenties
L. Swilly			★			Portsalon
Co. Down						
Ballynahinch				★		Ballynahinch
Co. Dublin						
Liffey	★	★		★	★	Dublin
Co. Fermanagh						
Erne		★	★	★		Enniskillen
Erne					★	Lisnaskea
Co. Galway						
Ballynahinch	★	★	★			Clifden & Ballynahinch
Claregalway	★	★	★		★	Galway
Corrib	★	★	★	★	★	Cong, Galway, & Oughterard
Costelloe (Casla)		★	★			Maum & Galway
Dawros		★	★	★		Leenane, Renvyle, & Letterfrack
L. Derg		★	★	★	★	Portumna

WATERS	Spring salmon	Grilse	Sea trout	Brown trout	Coarse	CENTRES
Co. Galway (*cont.*)						
Erriff		★	★			Leenaun
L. Fee	★			★		Leenaun
Galway	★	★	★			Galway
L. Gowla		★	★			Cashel
Inver		★				Cashel
L. Kylemore		★	★			Kylemore
Loughrea				★		Loughrea
Screebe		★	★			Maum Cross
Spiddal		★				Spiddal & Galway
Suck				★	★	Ballinasloe
Co. Kerry						
Anascaul				★		Anascaul
Caragh & L. Caragh	★	★	★	★		Glenbeigh, Glencar, &
						Waterville
L. Coomasaharn				★		Glenbeigh
Feale		★	★	★		Listowel & Ballybunnion
Killarney Lakes	★		★	★		Killarney
Laune	★	★	★	★		Killorglin
Roughty		★	★	★		Kenmare
L. Waterville	★	★	★	★		Waterville
Co. Kildare						
Barrow				★	★	Athy
Co. Kilkenny						
Barrow				★	★	Graiguenamanagh &
						Goresbridge
Nore	★			★	★	Kilkenny & Thomastown
Co. Laois						
L. Ballyfin					★	Mountrath
Barrow				★	★	Portarlington
Nore	★				★	Abbeyleix & Mountrath
Co. Leitrim						
Bonet	★		★			Dromahaire
L. Garadice				★	★	Ballinamore
L. Macnean				★	★	Manorhamilton
L. Melvin	★			★		Kinlough
Shannon				★	★	Carrick-on-Shannon
Co. Limerick						
Deel	★	★		★		Askeaton & Rathkeale
Feale	★	★	★	★		Abbeyfeale

WATERS	Spring salmon	Grilse	Sea trout	Brown trout	Coarse	CENTRES
Co. Limerick (*cont.*)						
Maigue	★	★		★		Adare, Croom, & Limerick
Mulcaire	★	★		★		Limerick
Shannon	★	★	★	★	★	Limerick & Castleconnell
Co. Longford						
Inny				★		Ballymahon
L. Kilglass				★	★	Longford
L. Ree				★	★	Lanesborough
Shannon			★	★	★	Longford
L. Sheelin				★	★	Granard & Virginia
Co. Louth						
Dee	★			★	★	Ardee
Fane	★					Dundalk
Glyde	★			★		Dundalk
Co. Mayo						
L. Beltra		★	★			Newport & Mallaranny
Bunowen			★			Louisburgh
Burrishoole		★	★			Newport
L. Carra				★	★	Ballinrobe, Castlebar,
						Tourmakeady, & Cong
L. Castlebar					★	Castlebar
Carrownisky		★				Louisburgh
L. Conn	★	★	★	★	★	Pontoon, Crossmolina, &
L. Cullen	★		★	★	★	Crossmolina [Foxford
L. Feeagh		★				Newport & Mallaranny
L. Levally					★	Pontoon
L. Mask					★	Ballinrobe, Castlebar,
						Tourmakeady, & Cong
Moy	★	★	★			Ballina & Pontoon
L. Nafooey					★	Leenaun & Cong
Newport		★	★			Newport
Owenduff ⎫		★	★			⎫
Owengarve ⎬			★			⎬ Mallaranny
Owenmore ⎭		★	★			⎭
Palmerston			★			Killala
Co. Meath						
Boyne	★					Drogheda, Slane, & Navan
Co. Monaghan						
L. Muckno				★	★	Castleblayney
L. Ross				★	★	Monaghan

WATERS	Spring salmon	Grilse	Sea trout	Brown trout	Coarse	CENTRES
Co. Offaly						
Shannon	★	★		★	★	Banagher
Co. Roscommon						
L. Arrow				★	★	Boyle
Ballaghadereen local waters				★		Ballaghadereen
Boyle					★	Boyle
L. Gara				★	★	Boyle
L. Key				★	★	Boyle
Suck					★	Castlerea, Roscommon, & Ballinasloe
Co. Sligo						
L. Arrow				★	★	Ballinafad
Ballysadare		★	★			Ballysadare & Sligo
Drumcliff	★	★	★			Sligo & Rosses Point
Easky		★				Easky
L. Gill	★	★	★	★	★	Sligo
Sligo (Garavogue)	★					Sligo
Co. Tipperary						
Aherlow				★		Tipperary
Ara				★		Tipperary
L. Derg	★	★		★	★	Nenagh & Dromineer
Suir	★	★		★	★	Clonmel, Cahir, Thurles, & Cashel
Tar				★		Clogheen
Co. Tyrone						
L. Catherine		★		★	★	Newtown Stewart
L. Blackwater				★		Caledon
L. Neagh				★	★	Dungannon
Co. Waterford						
Blackwater	★	★	★	★	★	Lismore & Cappoquin
Co. Westmeath						
L. Derravarragh				★	★	Mullingar & Castlepollard
L. Ennel				★	★	Mullingar
L. Owel				★	★	Mullingar
L. Ree				★	★	Athlone
Shannon				★	★	Athlone
Co. Wexford						
Ballyteige		★	★		★	Kilmore Quay
Barrow	★				★	New Ross

WATERS	Spring salmon	Grilse	Sea trout	Brown trout	Coarse	CENTRES
Co. Wexford (*cont.*)						
Nore	⋆	⋆	⋆	⋆	⋆	New Ross
Owenavarra			⋆			Courtown Harbour
Slaney	⋆					Enniscorthy & Bunclody
Sow			⋆			Wexford
Co. Wicklow						
Lake of the Liffey						
hydro-electric works				⋆		Blessington
Avonmore				⋆		Laragh

Appendix 2 · Irish Golf Clubs

Clubs	Holes
Co. Antrim	
Ballycastle	18
Ballyclare	9
Ballymena (2½ m.)	9
Belfast–	
Balmoral	18
Belvoir Park	18
Cliftonville	9
Fortwilliam	18
The Knock (Dundonald)	18
Malone	18
Ormeau	9
Royal Belfast (Craigavad, 6 m., *see* Co. Down)	
Shandon Park	18
Bushfoot (Bushmills 1½ m.)	9
Cairndhu (Ballygalley, Larne)	9
Carrickfergus	9
Cushendall	9
Dunmurry	9
Greenisland	9
Larne (Islandmagee)	9
Lisburn	9
Massareene (Antrim)	9
Royal Portrush –	
Two championship courses	18
Third course	9
Whitehead	9
Co. Armagh	
Armagh	9
Lurgan	9
Portadown (2 m.)	9
Tanderagee	9
Co. Carlow	
Borris	9
Carlow	18
Co. Cavan	
Belturbet	9
Cavan	9
Virginia	9
Co. Clare	
Dromoland (Newmarket-on-Fergus 2½ m.)	18
Ennis	18
Kilkee	9
Kilrush	9
Lehinch	18
Spanish Point (Miltown Malbay)	9
Co. Cork	
Bandon	9
Charleville	9

Clubs	Holes
Co. Cork – *cont.*	
Cork City –	
Douglas	18
Little Island	18
Muskerry (Carrigrohane)	18
Doneraile	9
Fermoy	9
Glengarriff	9
Kanturk	9
Kinsale (Ringnanean 2 m.)	9
Macroom	9
Mallow	9
Mitchelstown	9
Monkstown	9
Skibbereen and West Carbery	9
Youghal	9
Co. Derry	
Castlerock	18
City of Derry (1½ m.)	18
Kilrea	9
Portstewart (1 m.) –	
Strand Course	18
Old Course	18
Co. Donegal	
Buncrana	9
Bundoran	18
Dunfanaghy	18
Greencastle	9
Gweedore	9
Letterkenny	9
Naran-Portnoo	9
North West (Lisfannon Strand)	18
Otway (Rathmullan 3 m.)	9
Portsalon	18
Rosapenna (Carrickart 1¾ m.)	18
Rossnowlagh	9
Rosses (Burtonport)	9
Tantallon (Mountcharles)	9
Co. Down	
Ardglass	9
Banbridge	9
Bangor	18
Carnalea (Bangor Municipal, Bangor 1 m.)	18
Clandeboye (Bangor 2½ m.)	18
Cuan (Strangford)	9
Donaghadee (1 m.)	18
Downpatrick	9
Helen's Bay	9
Holywood	18
Kilkeel	9
Kirkistown Castle (Ardkeen)	18

Clubs	Holes
Co. Down – *cont.*	
Mahee Island (Comber 6 m.)	9
Royal Belfast (Craigavad)	18
Royal Co. Down (Newcastle) –	
Championship Course	18
No. 2 Course	18
Scrabo (Newtownards 1½ m.)	9
The Spa (Ballynahinch 2¼ m.)	9
Warrenpoint	18
Co. Dublin	
Balbriggan	9
Carrickmines	9
Corballis	18
Donabate	18
Dublin City –	
Castle (Rathfarnham)	18
Clontarf	18
Edmondstown	9
Elm Park (Donnybrook)	18
Grange (Rathfarnham)	18
Hermitage (near Lucan)	18
Milltown	18
Newlands (Clondalkin)	18
Rathfarnham	9
Royal Dublin (Dollymount)	18
St Anne's (Dollymount)	18
Dún Laoghaire	18
Foxrock	9
Howth	18
The Island (Malahide)	18
Killiney	9
Lucan	9
Malahide	9
Portmarnock	18
Rush	9
Skerries	9
Sutton (near Howth)	9
Woodbrook (near Bray)	18
Co. Fermanagh	
Enniskillen	9
Co. Galway	
Athenry	9
Ballinasloe	9
Galway (at Salthill, 2 m.)	18
Rockfield (Gort)	9
Loughrea	9
Mountbellew	9
Portumna	9
Tuam	9

Clubs	Holes	Clubs	Holes	Clubs	Holes
Co. Kerry		**Co. Louth**		**Co. Tipperary**	
Ballybunnion	18	Ardee	9	Carrick-on-Suir	9
Castleisland	9	County Louth (Baltray)	18	Clonmel (2½ m.)	9
Dingle (2 m.)	9	Dundalk (Blackrock)	18	Nenagh (3 m.)	9
Dooks, Glenbeigh	9	Greenore	18	Roscrea	9
Kenmare	9			Tipperary	9
Killarney	18	**Co. Mayo**		Thurles (Turtulla)	18
Parknasilla	9	Ballina	9		
Tralee	9	Ballinrobe	9	**Co. Tyrone**	
Waterville	9	Ballyhaunis (2 m.)	9	Dungannon	9
		Belmullet (2 m.)	9	Fintona	9
Co. Kildare		Castlebar	9	Killymoon (Cookstown)	9
Athy (2 m.)	9	Claremorris (1½ m.)	9	Omagh (1 m.)	9
Cill Dara (Kildare)	9	Swineford	9	Newtownstewart	9
Curragh	18	Westport	9	Strabane (1 m.)	9
Co. Kildare (Naas)	9				
		Co. Meath		**Co. Waterford**	
Co. Kilkenny		Bellinter Park (Navan 4 m.)	9	Dungarvan (3 m.)	9
Callan	18	Headfort (Ceanannus Mór)	9	Tramore	18
Castlecomer	9	Laytown and Bettystown	18	Waterford (see Co.	
Kilkenny	18			Kilkenny)	
Thomastown	9	**Co. Monaghan**			
Waterford (Waterford City		Clones (2 m.)	9	**Co. Westmeath**	
½ m.)	18	Rossmore (Monaghan		Athlone (see Co.	
		2 m.)	9	Roscommon)	
Co. Laois				Moate	9
Abbeyleix	9	**Offaly**		Mullingar	18
The Heath (Portlaoise		Birr	18		
4 m.)	9	Edenderry	9	**Co. Wexford**	
Mountrath	9	Portarlington	9	Bunclody (Newtownbarry)	9
Portarlington (2 m.)	9	Tullamore (2 m.)	18	Courtown (Gorey 4 m.)	9
Rathdowney	9			Enniscorthy (1 m.)	9
		Co. Roscommon		New Ross (1 m.)	9
Co. Leitrim		Athlone (2 m.)	18	Rosslare Strand	18
Carrick-on-Shannon		Ballaghaderreen	9		
(Woodbrook 5 m.)	9	Boyle	9	**Co. Wicklow**	
		Castlerea	9	Arklow	9
Co. Limerick		Roscommon	9	Baltinglass	9
Adare Manor, Adare	9			Bray	9
Castletroy (Limerick 3 m.)	18	**Co. Sligo**		Delgany	18
Limerick (at Ballyclough,		Inishcrone	9	Greystones	18
3 m.)	18	Rosses Point (Sligo		Wicklow	9
Newcastle West	9	County)	18	Woodenbridge	9
		Strandhill	9		
Co. Longford					
Longford	9				

Appendix 3 · The Irish Language and Irish Place-Names

Irish (Gaelic) is a Celtic language. It was brought to Ireland by Celtic invaders in the first millennium B.C. There are some indications that it may have been preceded by a Britannic dialect of Celtic, i.e. by one akin to the ancestor of Welsh, Cornish, and Breton. Between the second and fifth centuries A.D. colonists from Ireland brought the Gaelic language to Scotland, Man, and North and South Wales. In Wales it secured no lasting footing, but in Man it survived until the present century, and in Ireland and Scotland it still maintains a precarious hold on the Atlantic fringes.

The earliest documents in Irish are Ogham (see Glossary) inscriptions on pillar-stones. Ogham, which is based on the Latin alphabet, possibly originated about the fourth century A.D. among the Irish colonists of South Wales, who were in contact with Roman funerary and other inscriptions.

Written (as distinguished from oral) Irish literature dates from the sixth century and had already grown to considerable proportions by the eighth.

While most Irish place-names are Gaelic, many are demonstrably pre-Celtic, some doubtless pre-Indo-European. After the Gaelic names, English names are the most numerous. Many of these, however, are either translations or corruptions (see, for example, *Roundstone* and *Dog's Bay* under the Roundstone entry in the Gazetteer) of Gaelic ones. Other "English" names are of Scandinavian origin, deriving from Viking seafarers and colonists, but only a proportion of these ever replaced the older names on the lips of Irish speakers: compare ENG. *Waterford* (NORSE *Vethra-fjörthr*) and IR. *Port Láirge*, ENG. *Howth* (NORSE *höfuth*, "head") and IR. *Beann Éadair*. A few "English" place-names are Norse-Gaelic hybrids, e.g. *Ul-ster*, *Lein-ster*, where the first elements represent Irish *Ulaidh* and *Laighin* respectively, while the second represents Norse *staor*, "settlement". The English name of the country itself is just such a hybrid: *Ire-land*, from Norse *Ira-land*, representing *Éire-land*. (*Éire* itself may be pre-Indo-European.)

The official English spelling of Gaelic place-names in Ireland, stabilized more than a century ago by the Ordnance Survey, has proved a sad misfortune. It has led not only to the obscuring of meanings, but also to distortions of pronunciation.

The following list illustrates the "English" renderings of some of the more frequent elements in surviving Gaelic place-names; also some less frequent ones which happen to figure in this *Guide*.

a, agh(a), augh, a(u)gh(e)y. IR. *achadh*, field; e.g. *Achonry*, Conaire's field; *Ardagh(y)*, high field; *Aghaboe*, cow field.

a, aw, ou, ow. IR. *abha*, river; e.g. *Anna Liffey*, river of the (district called) Life; *Awbeg*, little river; see also *ow(e)n*.

aglish, eglis(h), heagles. IR. *eaglais* (from LAT. *ecclesia*), church; e.g. *Glennahaglish*, valley of the church.

a(h), ath, aw. IR. *áth*, ford; e.g. *Adare*, ford of the oak; *Athlone*, Lúan's ford; *Athenry*, ford of the kings.

ahane, ahaun, aghan. IR. *áthán*, diminutive of preceding.

an(n)a(gh), eanna. IR. *eanach*, marshy ground; e.g. *Annaghdown*, marshy ground of the ring-fort; *Rinneanna*, point of the marsh.

ar(d). IR. *ard*, high, height; e.g. *Armagh*, Macha's height; *Ardmore*, great height.

ardaun, ardawn. IR. *ardán*, diminutive of preceding.

a(a)s, a(a)ssa(a), sa, so. IR. *eas*, waterfall; e.g. *Asseylin*, O Flynn's waterfall; *Ballysadare*, the townland of the waterfall of the oak.

avon, see *ow(e)n*.

bal, ballagh, bally. IR. *bealach*, path, way; e.g. *Baltinglass* (IR. *Bealach Con Glais*), the path of Cú Ghlas; *Ballaghaderreen*, the path of the little oak wood. In compounds the *b* is lenited, resulting in English forms with *v*; e.g. *Moyvally*, plain of the path.

bal(l), balla, balli, bally, plural *balty*. IR. *baile*, plural *bailte*, steading, settlement, townland; e.g. *Ballybough(t)*, poor steading. As the second element of compound names *baile* becomes *bhaile*, represented by forms like *vally, ville, willow*; e.g. *Lavally*, half-townland; *Bauville*, cow townland.

475

balleen, balteen. IR. *bailín, bailtín,* diminutive of preceding.

bal(l), bel(l). IR. *béal,* mouth, entrance; e.g. *Belfast,* mouth of the sandspit; *Ballina,* mouth of the ford.

bane, baun, bawn. IR. *bán,* white; e.g. *Carnanbane,* white little cairn.

barn(a), barnes. IR. *bearna, bearnas,* gap, defile; e.g. *Barnderg,* red gap; *Bearnasmore,* great defile.

beg(g), big. IR. *beag,* small; e.g. *Drombeg,* little ridge; *Beggary,* little Éire.

ben, bin, pin. IR. *beann,* peak, mountain; e.g. The Twelve Bens (Pins).

boher, bor, booter, batter. IR. *bóthar,* cow track, road; e.g. *Boherboy,* yellow road; *Borderreen,* road of the little oak wood; *Batterstown.* In compounds *bóthar* becomes *bhóthar* rendered *voher,* etc.; e.g. *Ballinvoher,* townland of the road.

bohreen, boreen, borheen. IR. *bóithrín,* diminutive of preceding.

boley, boola, booley, boula, plural *boulty,* etc. IR. *buaile,* plural *buailte* (see Glossary); e.g. *Booleyglass,* green buaile; *Knocknaboley,* hill of the buaile. In compounds *buaile* becomes *bhuaile* represented by *voley, vool(y),* etc.; e.g. *Ballyvooly,* townland of the buaile.

bon, bun. IR. *bun,* foot, lowest reach, of a river; e.g. *Bunclody,* lowest reach of the Clody.

boy, bwee. IR. *buidhe,* yellow; e.g. *Mullaghboy,* yellow summit.

caher, cahir. IR. *cathair* (from LAT. *castrum*), fort; e.g. *Cahersiveen,* Little Sive's fort.

ca(i)rn. IR. *carn,* heap; e.g. *Carnmore,* great heap.

carna(u)n. IR. *carnán,* diminutive of preceding.

can, see *ken(n).*

cappa(gh), cappo. IR. *ceapach,* a tillage plot; e.g. *Cappoquin,* Conn's plot.

carhoo, carrow. IR. *ceathramha,* a quarter of a townland, etc.; e.g. *Carrowkeel,* narrow quarter.

carrick, carrig, corrig. IR. *carraig,* rock; e.g. *Carrickfergus,* Fergus's rock.

carrow, see *carhoo.*

cashel, castle. IR. *caiseal* (from LAT. *castellum*), fort; e.g. *Cashelnavean,* fort of the Fianna; *Ballycastle,* townland of the fort. In the genitive plural after the definite article *caiseal* becomes *gcaiseal,* rendered *goshel;* e.g. *Knocknagoshel,* hill of the forts; see also *desart, disert, dysert.*

cashlaun. IR. *caisleán,* diminutive of preceding; castle.

cel, see *kil(l).*

claddagh. IR. *cladach,* a flat beach.

clifden, see *clogha(u)n.*

clogher. IR. *clochar,* a stone structure, a stony place.

clon(e), cloon(e), plural *cloonta, cloonty, clinty.* IR. *cluain,* plural *cluainte,* meadow; e.g. *Clones,* meadow of Eos; *Cloontyclogher,* meadows of the stony place.

clo(o)neen. IR. *cluainín,* diminutive of preceding.

cloonta, cloonty, see *clon(e).*

clo(u)gh. IR. *cloch,* a stone, a stone structure; e.g. *Cloghaneely,* Ceann Faoladh's stone.

clogha(u)n, cloghan(e), clifden. IR. *clochán,* diminutive of preceding, stepping stones, a dry-masonry hut.

cool(e). IR. *cúl,* back; e.g. *Coolbally,* back townland.

corrig, see *carrick.*

croagh. IR. *cruach,* a rick, a rick-like hill or mountain; e.g. *Croagh Patrick,* Patrick's rick.

cro(a)ghan. IR. *cruachán,* diminutive of preceding.

crock, see *knock.*

curra(gh), curry. IR. *currach,* a level low-lying plain, a marsh, etc.; e.g. *Currabeha,* marsh of the birches.

da(w). IR. *dá,* two; e.g. *Glendalough,* valley of the two lakes; *Slievedaeane,* mountain of the two birds.

dangan, dingin, dingle. IR. *daingean,* stronghold; e.g. *Ballindangan,* townland of the stronghold.

darry, derry, derri. IR. *doire,* oak tree, oak wood; e.g. *Derrybawn,* white oak wood.

derreen. IR. *doirín,* diminutive of preceding.

derg. IR. *dearg,* red; e.g. *Barnderg,* red gap.

desart, disert, dysert (corruptly *tristle,* which may become *castle*). IR. *díseart* (from LAT. *desertum*), hermitage ; e.g. *Dysertenos,* Aonghus's hermitage.

dingle, see *dangan.*

donagh, donough, dun. IR. *domhnach* (from LAT. *ecclesia dominica*), a large church; e.g. *Donaghpatrick,* Patrick's church ; *Dunshaughlin,* Seachlann's (=Seachnall's, i.e. Secundinus's) church.

doo, dou, dub, duff, duv. IR. *dubh,* black; e.g. *Doolough,* black lake; *Douglas,* black stream; *Dublin,* black pool; *Duvillaun,* black island.

do(o)n, down, dun. IR. *dún,* a fort; e.g. *Donegal,* fort of the foreigners; *Downamona,* fort of the bog.

dooneen, downeen, downing(s). IR. *dúinín,* diminutive of preceding.

drehid, droghed, drohid, drought, driet, droit, tred. IR. *droichead,* a bridge; e.g. *Drogheda,* bridge of the ford; *Carrigadrohid,* rock of the bridge; *Kildrought* (alias *Celbridge*), church of the bridge.

drim, see *drom.*

droghed, drohid, see *drehid.*

drom, drum, drim. IR. *druim,* ridge; e.g. *Drumadrehid,* ridge of the bridge.

drought, see *drehid.*

dub, see *doo.*

duff, see *doo.*

dun, see *donagh* and *do(o)n.*

duv, see *doo.*

(e)ighter. IR. *íochtar,* lower, northern part; e.g. *Eighterard,* high northern part; cf. *oughter.*

emlagh, emly. IR. *imleach,* land bordering on a lake or marsh.

ennis, see *inch(y).*

farran. IR. *fearann*, land; e.g. *Farranmacbride*, MacBride's land.

fau, see *no(o)*.

fee, feigh, feth, few, fi(d), fith. IR. *fiodh*, plural *feadha*, wood; e.g. *The Fews of Athlone; Fethard*, high wood; *Fiddown*, wood of the fort.

feth, see *fee*.

fews, see *fee*.

fi(d), see *fee*.

glan, glen, glin, glyn(n). IR. *gleann*, a valley; e.g. *Glandine*, deep valley; *Ballinglanna*, townland of the glen.

glenna(u)n, glentane, glantaun. IR. *gleannán, gleanntán*, diminutives of preceding.

gort, gurt. IR. *gort*, tillage field; e.g. *Gortaganniff*, field of the sand.

gorteen, gortin, gurteen. IR. *goirtín*, diminutive of preceding.

goshel, see *cashel*.

ighter, see *(e)ighter*.

illa(u)n. IR. *oileán*, island; e.g. *Illauntannig*, Seanach's island.

inch(y), inis(h), ennis, nish. IR. *inis, inse*, island; e.g. *Inishowen*, Eóghan's island; *Lehinch(y)*, peninsula; *Feenish*, wood island; *Inisfree*, heather isle.

keel, kill. IR. *caol*, narrow; e.g. *Carrowkeel*, narrow quarter; *Killary*, narrow salt water.

ken(n), kin, can. IR. *ceann, cinn*, head; e.g. *Kenmare*, head of the sea; *Kinvara*, head of the sea.

kil(e), kyle, kill, plural *keelty, kilti, kilty, quilty, cultia*, etc. IR. *coill*, plural *coillte*, a wood; e.g. *Kylemore*, great wood; *Quilty*, woods.

kil(l), cel. IR. *cill* (from LAT. *cella*), cell, church; e.g. *Kilcolman*, Colmán's cell (or church); *kill* may also represent IR. *coill*, a wood (see *kil(e)*) and IR. *caol*, narrow (see *keel*).

killeen. IR. *cillín*, diminutive of *kill*, cell, church.

knock, crock, cruck. IR. *cnoc*, hill; e.g. *Knockfierna*, hill of truth; *Crocknagapple*, hill of the horses.

knockan(e), knockaun, knockeen, crockeen, etc., diminutives of preceding.

lack, leck, leek, lick, plural *lacka*. IR. *leac*, plural *leaca*, a flagstone; e.g. *Ballinalack*, the mouth of the ford of the flagstones; *Belleek*, the (ford-)mouth of the flagstone.

lacken, lackan. IR. *leacán*, stony hill-slope.

la(h) le. IR. *leath, leith*, half; e.g. *Lavally*, half townland; *Lehinch(y)*, peninsula.

letter, plural *latteragh, lettera(gh), lettery*. IR. *leitir*, plural *leitreacha, leatracha*, a wet hillside; e.g. *Lettermullen*, Meallán's hill-slope.

lew, lieve, see *(s)lew*.

lis(s). IR. *lios*, enclosure (of a ringfort, etc.); e.g. *Lissonuffy*, enclosure of the O Duffys. Variant forms of the genitive of *lios* are exemplified by *Moylish(a)*, plain of the enclosure, *Gortalassa*, tillage field of the enclosure, *Ballinliss*, townland of the enclosure.

lisheen, lissan(e), lissaun. IR. *lisín, liosán*, diminutives of preceding.

lo(u)gh, low. IR. *loch*, lake, sea-inlet; e.g. *Lough Corrib*, Oirbsean's lake; *Carlow*, fourfold lake.

loughan(e), loughaun. IR. *lochán*, diminutive of preceding.

low, see *lo(u)gh*.

maghera, maghery. IR. *machaire*, a plain.

ma(y), moy, maw, muff. IR. *magh*, an open plain; e.g. *Mallow*, plain of the (river) Ealla; *Maynooth*, Nuadha's plain. In compounds *magh* becomes *mhagh*, represented by *voy* in *Finvoy*, fair plain.

moan, mon(e). IR. *móin*, genitive *móna*, a peat bog; e.g. *Monabraher*, friars' bog; *Kilnamona*, church of the bog.

monaster. IR. *mainistear*, monastery; e.g. *Monasternenagh*, monastery of the public assembly (place).

more. IR. *mor*, big, great; e.g. *Baltimore*, townland of the big house.

moy, see *ma(y)*.

muff, see *ma(y)*.

mullagh. IR. *mullach*, topmost part, crown; e.g. *Mullaghareirk*, summit of the prospect.

mullen, mullin. IR. *muileann*, mill; e.g. *Mullinavat*, mill of the stick. In compounds *muileann* becomes *mhuileann*, represented by *vullen, willi(a)n*; e.g. *Killavullen, Killawillin*, church of the mill.

munter. IR. *muintear* (from LAT. *monasterium*), family; e.g. *Munterloney*, O Luinigh family.

nish, see *inch(y)*.

no(o), (n)ou, fau. IR. *nua*, new; e.g. *Portnoo*, new port; *Nohaval, Oughaval, Faughaval*, new foundation.

ou, see *a, aw* and *no(o)*.

oughter, wa(ugh)ter. IR. *úachtar*, upper part, southern part; e.g. *Lough Oughter*, the lake of the upper part; *Wateraughey*, the upper part of the field; cf. *(e)ighter*.

ow, see *a, aw*.

ow(e)n, avon. IR. *abhainn*, dative case of *abha* (see *a, aw*), river; e.g. *Owencam*, crooked river; *Avonmore*, great river; also represents *abhann*, genitive case of *abha*; e.g. *Ballinahown*, steading of the river.

quilty, see *kil(e)*.

ra(th), ra(g)h, raw, ray, roe. IR. *ráth*, ringfort; e.g. *Rathnew*, Naoi's fort; *Roemore*, big fort.

raheen. IR. *ráithín*, diminutive of preceding.

ray, see *ra(th)*.

re(e)n, ring, rin(n), rine. IR. *rinn*, point; e.g. *Renvyle*, Míl's point; *Ringville*, tree point; *Rineanna*, point of the marsh.

roe. IR. *ruadh*, red; e.g. *Roeillaun*, red island; see also *ra(th)*.

see. IR. *suidhe*, seat; e.g. *Seefin*, Fionn's seat.

shan. IR. *sean*, old; e.g. *Shanbally*, old steading.

(s)lew, (s)lieve. IR. *sliabh*, mountain; e.g. *Slievenacallee*, mountain of the hag. In compounds the initial of *sliabh* becomes aspirate, whence English spellings like *Curlew* (= *Corr-shliabh*), conical mountain, *Killevy* (= *Cill Shléibhe*, church of the mountain).

(s)ta, (s)ti, ta(u)gh. IR. *teach, tigh*, house, monastery, church; e.g. *Stabannon*, Benignus's house (church); *Stillorgan*, Lorcán's

house (church); *Ta(u)ghmon*, Munnu's house (church); *Timolin*, Mo-Ling's house (church); *Tiscoffin*, Scuithín's house (church).

tample, tempal, temple. IR. *teampall* (from LAT. *templum*), church; e.g. *Templebreedy*, Brigid's church.

tee, ti, ty. IR. *tighe*, genitive singular of *teach, tigh*, house; e.g. *Baltimore*, townland of the big house; *Attidermot*, site of Dermot's house.

tibber, tibret, tipper, tubbert, tubbrid. IR. *tiobra(id)*, a well; e.g. *Tibberaghny*, Fachtna's well; *Tipperary*, the well of Ára; *Clontibret*, the meadow of the well; *Kiltubbrid*, church of the well.

tir, tyr. IR. *tír*, country, territory; e.g. *Tyrawley*, Amhalghaidh's territory; *Tyrone*, Eóghan's country.

tob(b)er, tubber. IR. *tobar*, a well; e.g. *Tobercurry*, the well of the whirlpool; *Ballintober*, townland of the well.

to(o)m, tu(a)m. IR. *tuaim*, tomb; e.g. *Tomgraney*, Grian's tomb.

toor, tour, tore. IR. *túar*, milking enclosure, bleach green; e.g. *Ballitore*, mouth of the ford of the bleach green.

tra(gh), traw, tray. IR. *tráigh*, strand; e.g. *Tramore*, great strand; *Ventry*, fair strand.

tristle, see *desart*.

tul(lagh), tullig, tullow, tully. IR. *tulach*, a small hill; e.g. *Kiltullagh*, church of the hillocks.

vally, see *bal(l), balla* and *bal*.

ville, see *bal(l), balla* (can also represent *bhile*, lenited form of *bile*, tree).

voher, see *boher*.

voley, vool(y), see *boley*.

voy, see *ma(y)*.

vullen, see *mullen*.

wa(ugh)ter, see *oughter*.

willi(a)n, see *mullen*.

willow, see *bal(l), balla*.

Glossary

Ambry, aumbry. A wall cupboard.

Antae. Pilaster-like projections of the side walls of a building.

Bachall. A short, crozier-like staff.

Bailey. A ward or enclosure of a castle; *see also* motte-and-bailey.

Barge-boards. Boards or rafters finishing off a gable immediately beneath the roof edge.

Batter. The sloping inwards, from bottom to top, of a wall face.

Bawn. A fortified enclosure.

Berm. Level ground between a fosse and a mound or a rampart.

Bivallate. Having two ramparts.

Bohereen. A country lane, a minor road.

Booley(ing). *See* **Buaile.**

Brehon. A Gaelic professional jurist.

Buaile, "booley". Milking place, particularly of summer hill-pastures; hence "booleying", transhumance which removed cattle and other livestock from the arable (unfenced) land between spring and harvest.

Bullaun. An artificial, basin-like hollow in a boulder; used for grinding; a feature of early monastic sites.

Caoine, "keen". A mourning lamentation of a traditional kind.

Cashel. A ringfort of dry masonry; the vallum or rampart of such a ringfort.

Céle Dé, "culdee". Lit. "a companion (client, vassal) of God"; *see* p. 27.

Chamber tomb. A prehistoric burial chamber large enough to enter; it is (was) covered by or buried in a tumulus or cairn. Irish chamber tombs are always megalithic. *See* **Court grave, Gallery grave, Passage grave,** *and* **Portal grave,** *below*.

Chantry. A chapel or altar endowed for anniversary and other Masses.

Chevaux-de-frise. An abbatis or defence zone made of close-set stakes or comparable obstacles.

Chi-rho. A monogram formed from the initials, X (chi) and P (rho), of the Greek form of *Christus*; in a simple form it is represented by a cross with a small lateral hook or loop at the top right.

Clochán. A corbel-roofed hut of dry masonry; usually beehive-shaped.

Coarb, IR. *comharba*, "heir". Originally the successor in office of an early founding abbot; later the rector of a church originally monastic, or the hereditary farmer of church lands originally monastic.

Collegiate church. One staffed by priests (secular canons, chaplains, or chantry priests) living in community.

Coracle. A primitive type of river boat formed by stretching a hide over a wickerwork frame; *see also* **Currach.**

Court cairn. Properly the cairn of a court grave (q.v.). The name is often applied to graves whose cairn and/or court(s) have largely disappeared.

Court grave. A segmented gallery grave (q.v.) set in a long cairn and entered from a forecourt (open or closed) at or towards the end, or (rarely) at the centre, of the cairn. Central courts gave access to more than one grave. Dual-court monuments had a court and grave at each end of the cairn.

Crannóg, lit. "timber structure", etc., from IR. *crann* "tree, timber". In archaeology the name is applied to lake-, river-, and marsh-dwellings, which often present the form of artificial islands; despite the name, crannógs were not constructed exclusively of timber.

Cross-pillar. A pillarstone/standing stone with one or more crosses.

Cross-slab. A stone slab with one or more crosses; often an early gravestone.

Currach, in Co. Kerry *naomhóg*. A primitive type of keel-less sea boat of tarred canvas (formerly of hide) stretched over a framework of laths; *see also* **Coracle.**

Deiseal. Right-hand-wise, sun-wise; the opposite to *tuathal*, "widdershins".

Dolmen. *See* **Portal grave.**

Erenagh, IR. *airchinneach*, "superior". Originally a monastic official; later an hereditary farmer of parish – originally monastic – lands, for which he paid rent to the bishop and contributed to the maintenance of the fabric of the parish church.

Gaeltacht. A district where Irish survives as the vernacular.

Gallery grave. A rectangular or wedge-shaped chamber tomb without a passage; it may be segmented, i.e. divided into compartments, by jamb-stones projecting from the walls, or by septal stones rising from the floor, or by both.

Gallo(w)gla, IR. *gallóglách*, "foreign soldier". Initially applied to Gaelic-speaking Hebridean mercenaries; *see* p. 35.

Garderobe. Latrine.

Garland Sunday. *See* **Lughnasa.**

Halberd (Bronze Age). A dagger-like blade mounted at right angles to its handle.

Henge monument. A "ritual" enclosure with a ditch *inside* the rampart.

High Cross. A tall ring-headed cross of stone, usually with figure and/or other carving.

Hill-fort. A fort whose defences circle the top of a hill, usually adhering (more or less) to the same height (contour).

Lughnasa. A harvest-time festival, originally in honour of the god, Lugh. In early times Aonach Tailteann (*see* Teltown *under* Donaghpatrick) was one of the major public assemblies connected with it. In recent folk practice the celebration took place, often on the last Sunday of July, at traditional hill-sites and other places. Some of the surviving gatherings have long had the form of Christian pilgrimages. Of these the best known is the pilgrimage to Croagh Patrick (*see under* Westport). In the West, Garland (alias Garlic) Sunday is a well-known name in English for the Sunday in question; other English names include Bilberry Sunday and Fraughan (IR. *fraochán*, "heatherberry") Sunday. The surviving Irish names include Domhnach Chrom Dubh, "Crom Dubh's Sunday"; Crom was a deity who figures in Patrician legend.

Motte-and-bailey. The earthwork remains of a primitive castle: the motte a steep-sided, flat-topped, round mound; the bailey an enclosure at the foot of the mound. Both motte and bailey were stockaded; the motte carried a wooden tower and the bailey enclosed a dwelling hall and other buildings.

Multivallate. Having multiple ramparts.

Ogham. A 4th/5th cent. adaptation (lines and notches) of the Latin alphabet to the purpose of cutting inscriptions on sticks; subsequently used for inscriptions on memorial stones and the like; it may have been invented in one of the Gaelic colonies in Wales (40 ogham stones) and been brought home to Ireland (300-odd inscriptions, mostly in Counties Waterford, Cork, and Kerry).

Orthostat. A stone set on end.

Passage grave. A chamber tomb with a passage (sometimes used for burials) leading to the chamber(s); *see also* **V-passage grave.**

Pátrún, "pattern" (cf. Breton *pardon*). Celebrations of the festival of a patron saint.

Pillarstone, standing stone. A menhir, or prehistoric, single, upright, large stone.

Piscina. A basin for washing liturgical vessels; usually in a wall-niche close to the altar.

Plantation castle. A type of "stronghouse and bawn" characteristic of the Ulster Plantation; features of the Scottish variety are crow-stepped gables and conical-roofed turrets corbelled out on the angles of the tower.

Portal grave, portal dolmen. A simple-chamber, megalithic tomb whose entrance is flanked by a pair of tall portal stones.

Promontory fort. A promontory or a hill spur protected by defences across the neck from one cliff or slope to another.

Ring-barrow. A burial mound, usually low, encircled by a low earthen ring.

Ringfort. An enclosure, commonly ring-shaped, bounded by one or more ramparts and (usually) ditches; the simplest, and much the most numerous, type has a single bank inside a (quarry) ditch, and represents a farmyard rather than a fort.

Round Tower. A tall, free-standing, circular belfry-cum-stronghouse with a conical stone roof.

Sedilia. Wall seats for the use of celebrant, deacon, and sub-deacon during High Mass.

Sheila-na-gig. An obscene female figure of uncertain significance.

Sinn Féin, lit. "We ourselves". A nationalist movement founded by Arthur Griffith and mistakenly credited by the British authorities with responsibility for the Republican insurrection of Easter 1916.

Souterrain. An underground series of chambers of undetermined purpose.

Station(s). *See* **Turas.**

Sweathouse, IR. *teach alluis.* A stone structure (usually small, simple, and with a single opening) used for sweat baths. It was heated by a fire drawn before the bather entered. The procedure commonly ended with a cold plunge.

Trabeate. Having a straight, single-stone lintel.

Transitional. Transitional from Romanesque to Gothic.

Trivallate. Having three ramparts.

Turas, lit. "journey". The making of "rounds" of prayers and penitential exercises at "stations" often marked by ancient monastic (or comparable) remains.

Urnes style. An art style characterized by distinctive interlaced beasts, often in pairs or enmeshed in serpents; a classic motif is the combat between a great beast and serpents; called after the 11th cent. church at Urnes, Norway.

V-passage grave. A passage grave with diverging side walls, i.e. one in which the "chamber" is simply a widening of the "passage", neither element being distinguishable from the other.

Voussoir. One of the wedge-shaped stones of an arch.

Weepers. Properly refers to the figures of mourners on a tomb-chest or other monument, but is also used of similarly placed figures of angels and saints.

Zoomorphic. Of animal form.

Bibliography

General History

Bieler, Ludwig. *Ireland, Harbinger of the Middle Ages*. London, New York, Toronto, Oxford University Press, 1963. German edition, Urs Graf Verlag, Olten, Lausanne, Freiburg i. Breisgau, 1961.

Bournequel, Camille. *Irlande*. Paris, Editions du Seuil, 1955.

Carty, James, ed. *Ireland, a Documentary Record, 1607–1782*. Dublin, Fallon, 1947.

Carty, James, ed. *Ireland, a Documentary Record, 1783–1850*. Dublin, Fallon, 1949.

Carty, James, ed. *Ireland, a Documentary Record, 1851–1921*. Dublin, Fallon, 1951.

Chauviré, Roger. *Histoire de l'Irlande*. Paris, Presses Universitaires de France, 1949.

Coonan, Thomas L. *The Irish Catholic Confederacy and the Puritan Revolution*. Dublin, Clonmore & Reynolds; London, Burns, Oates & Washbourne; New York, Columbia University Press; 1954.

Curtis, Edmund. *A History of Medieval Ireland*. London, Methuen, 1938.

Curtis, Edmund. *A History of Ireland*. London, Methuen, 1950.

Daniel-Rops, Henry. *Le Miracle Irlandais*. Paris, Laffont, 1956.

Gougaud, Dom Louis. *Christianity in Celtic Lands*. London, Sheed & Ward, 1932.

Gwynn, Denis. *The History of Partition*. Dublin, Browne & Nolan, 1950.

Holt, Edgar. *Protest in Arms: the Irish Troubles 1916–1923*. London, Putnam, 1960.

Hughes, Kathleen. *The Church in Early Irish Society*. London, Methuen, 1966.

Kenny, James F. *The Sources for the Early History of Ireland*. Vol. I. *Ecclesiastical*. New York, Columbia University Press, 1929.

Lecky, William E. H. *A History of Ireland in the 18th Century*. Vols. I–V. London, Longmans, 1895.

Macardle, Dorothy. *The Irish Republic*. 4th ed. Dublin, Irish Press, 1951.

MacLysaght, Edward. *Irish Life in the 17th Century*. Cork University Press, 1950.

MacNeill, Eoin. *Phases of Irish History*. Dublin, Gill & Son, 1919.

Mansergh, Nicholas. *The Commonwealth and the Nations*. London, Royal Institute of International Affairs, 1948.

Mansergh, Nicholas. *The Irish Question, 1840–1921*. Rev. ed. London, Allen and Unwin, 1965.

O Faoláin, Seán. *The Great O Neill*. London, Longmans, 1942.

O Hegarty, P. S. *A History of Ireland under the Union, 1800–1922*. London, Methuen, 1952.

Pakenham, Francis. *Peace by Ordeal*. London, Cape, 1935.

Senior, Hereward. *Orangism in Ireland and Britain, 1795–1836*. London, Routledge and Kegan Paul; Toronto, The Ryerson Press; 1966.

Shearman, Hugh. *Ulster*. London, Hale, 1949.

Folklore, Literary and Social History, etc.

Arensberg, Conrad M., & Kimball, Solon T. *Family and Community in Ireland*. Cambridge, Mass., Harvard U.P., 1940.

Boyd, Ernest A. *Ireland's Literary Renaissance*. London, Grant Richards, 1923.

Carney, James, ed. *Early Irish Poetry*. Cork, Mercier Press, 1965.

Corkery, Daniel. *The Hidden Ireland*. Dublin, Gill & Son, 3rd impr., 1941.

Cross, Tom Peete, & Slover, Clark Harris, eds. *Ancient Irish Tales*. London, Harrap, 1936.

Dillon, Myles. *The Cycle of the Kings*. London, Oxford University Press, 1946.

Dillon, Myles, ed. *Early Irish Literature*. Chicago University Press, 1948.

Dillon, Myles, ed. *Early Irish Society*. Dublin, Cultural Relations Committee, 1959.

Dillon, Myles, ed. *Irish Sagas*. Dublin, Stationery Office, 1959.

Ellis-Fermor, Una. *The Irish Dramatic Movement*. London, Methuen, 2nd ed., 1954.

Evans, E. Estyn. *Irish Folk Ways*. London, Routledge & Kegan Paul, 1957.

Flower, Robin. *The Irish Tradition*. Oxford, Clarendon Press, 1948.

Flower, Robin. *The Western Island, or The Great Blasket*. London, Oxford University Press, 1944.

Hyde, Douglas. *The Story of Gaelic Literature*. Dublin, Talbot Press, 1938.

Kavanagh, Peter. *The Irish Theatre*. Tralee, The Kerryman, 1946.

Kiely, Benedict. *Modern Irish Fiction*. Dublin, Golden Eagle Books, 1950.

King, F. C., ed. *Public Administration in Ireland*. 3 Vols. Dublin, Parkside Press, 1944–54.

Knott, Eleanor, and Murphy, Gerard. *Early Irish Literature*. London, Routledge & Kegan Paul, 1966.

McClintock, H. F. *Old Irish Dress*. Dundalk, Dundalgan Press, 1950.

McDonagh, Thomas. *Literature in Ireland*. Dublin, Talbot Press, 1916.

McDowell, R. B., ed. *Social Life in Ireland, 1800–1845*. Dublin, Cultural Relations Committee, 1957.

481

Mac Neill, Máire. *The Festival of Lughnasa.* London, Oxford University Press, 1962.

Murphy, Gerard. *Early Irish Lyrics.* Oxford, Clarendon Press, 1956.

O Connor, Frank. *Kings, Lords, and Commons: an Anthology from the Irish.* New York, Knopf, 1959; London, Macmillan, 1961.

Ó Cuiv, Brian, ed. *Seven Centuries of Irish Learning.* Dublin, Stationery Office, 1961.

O Faoláin, Seán. *Irish Journey.* London, 1940.

O Keefe, James G., and O Brien, Art. *A Handbook of Irish Dances.* Dublin, Gill, 1934.

Ó Súilleabháin, Seán. *A Handbook of Irish Folklore.* Dublin, Educational Co., 1942.

O Sullivan, Donal. *Irish Folk Music and Song.* Dublin, Cultural Relations Committee, 1952.

O Sullivan, Donal. *Songs of the Irish.* Dublin, Browne & Nolan, 1960.

Praeger, R. Lloyd. *The Natural History of Ireland.* London, Collins, 1950.

Praeger, R. Lloyd. *The Way that I Went.* Dublin, Hodges, Figgis, 1937.

Seymour, St John D. *Anglo-Irish Literature, 1200–1582.* Cambridge University Press, 1929.

Sjoestedt, Marie-Louise. *Dieux et Héros celtiques.* Paris, Presses Universitaires, 1940.

Sjoestedt, Marie-Louise. *Gods and Heroes of the Celts,* translated by Myles Dillon. London, Methuen, 1949.

Webb, David A. *An Irish Flora.* Dundalk, Tempest, 1951.

Archaeology, Architecture, Topography, etc.

Ancient Monuments in Northern Ireland in State charge. Belfast, H.M.S.O., 1962.

Ancient Monuments in Northern Ireland not in State charge. Belfast, H.M.S.O., 1952.

Charlesworth, J. K. *The Geology of Ireland.* Edinburgh, Oliver & Boyd, 1953.

Chart, D. A., ed. *A Preliminary Survey of the Ancient Monuments of Northern Ireland.* Belfast, H.M.S.O., 1940.

Coleman, J. C. *The Caves of Ireland.* Tralee, Anvil Books, 1965.

Craig, Maurice. *Dublin, 1660–1860.* Dublin, Hodges, Figgis; London, The Cresset Press; 1952.

De Paor, Máire and Liam. *Early Christian Ireland.* London, Thames & Hudson, 2nd ed., 1960.

Evans, E. Estyn. *Mourne Country Landscape and Life in South Down.* Dundalk, Tempest, 1957.

Freeman, T. W. *Ireland, its Physical, Historical, Social and Economic Geography.* London, Methuen, 1950.

Harvey, John. *Dublin, a Study in Environment.* London, Batsford, 1949.

Henry, Francoise. *Art Irlandais.* Dublin, Cultural Relations Committee, 1954.

Henry, Françoise. *L'Art Irlandais.* Vols. I–III. Paris, Zodiaque, La Nuit des Temps, 1963–4.

Henry, Françoise. *Irish Art in the Early Christian Period to 800 A.D.* London, 1965.

Joyce, P. W. *The Origin and History of Irish Names of Places.* Vols. I–III. Dublin, Gill, 1893–1913.

Leask, Harold G. *Irish Castles and Castellated Houses.* Dundalk, Dundalgan Press, 3rd ed., 1951.

Leask, Harold G. *Irish Churches and Monastic Buildings. I. The first phase and the Romanesque. II. Gothic architecture in A.D. 1400. III. Medieval Gothic – the last phase.* Dundalk, Dundalgan Press, 1955, 1958, 1960.

Powell, T. G. E. *The Celts.* London, Thames & Hudson, 1959.

Raftery, Joseph. *Prehistoric Ireland.* London, Batsford, 1951.

Strickland, Walter G. *A Dictionary of Irish Artists.* Vols I and II. Dublin, 1913.

White, James, & Wynne, Michael. *Irish Stained Glass.* Dublin, Gill & Son, 1963.

Sport

The Angler's Guide to Ireland. Dublin, Irish Tourist Board, 5th ed., 1957.

Dagg, T. S. C. *Hockey in Ireland.* Tralee, The Kerryman, 1944.

Drought, J. B. *A Sportsman Looks at Éire.* London, Hutchinson, 1947.

Gaelic Athletic Association. *Sixty Glorious Years of the G.A.A.* Dublin, 1947.

Gwynn, Stephen. *The Happy Fisherman.* London, Country Life, 1936.

Hanna, Thos. J. *Fly-fishing in Ireland.* London, Witherby, 1933.

Lynch, Stanislaus. *Echoes of the Hunting Horn.* Dublin, Talbot Press, 1946.

Redlich, Anna. *The Dogs of Ireland.* Dundalk, Tempest, 1949.

Sinclair, C. E. R. *Coarse Fishing in Ireland.* London, Witherby, 1949.

Wall, W. C. *Mountaineering in Ireland.* Dublin, Irish Tourist Association, 1939.

General

Éire. *Bunreacht na h-Éireann. Constitution of Ireland.* Dublin, Stationery Office, 1937.

Thom's *Directory of Ireland.* Published annually.

Bibliography

Best, Richard Irvine. *Bibliography of Irish Philology and Printed Irish Literature.* London, H.M.S.O., 1913.

Best, Richard Irvine. *Bibliography of Irish Philology and Printed Irish Literature. Publications 1913–41.* Dublin, Inst. of Advanced Studies, 1942.

Carty, James. *Bibliography of Irish History 1870–1911.* Dublin, National Library, 1940.

Carty, James. *Bibliography of Irish History 1912–1921.* Dublin, National Library, 1936.

Cultural Relations Committee. *Leabhra ar Éirinn. Books on Ireland.* Dublin, Three Candles, 1953.

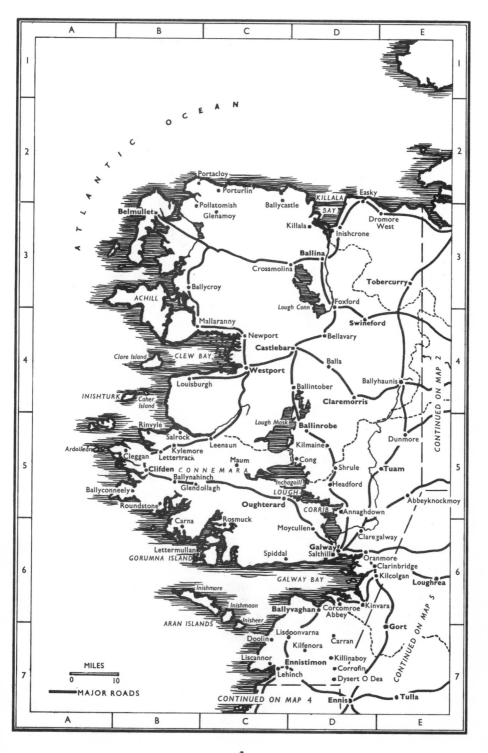

1

MAJOR ROADS

MILES
0   10

MALIN HEAD

TORY ISLAND

Malin
Culdaff
Ballyliffin
Clonmany
Carndonagh
Portsalon
Moville
Carrigart
LOUGH
FOYLE
Dunfanaghy
Buncrana
Creeslough
Rathmullan
Gortahork
Millford
Muff
Gweedore
Rathmelton
Kilmacrenan
Newtown Cunningham
Derry
Limavady
ARAN ISLAND
Letterkenny
Manor
Cunningham
St Johnstown
Claudy
Dungiven
Dunglow
Raphoe
Dunnamanagh
Lifford
Portnoo
Strabane
Naran
Glenties
Ballybofey
Plumb Bridge
Ardara
Castlederg
Glencolumbkille
Newtown Stewart
Killybegs
Donegal
Carrick
Dunkineely
Lough
Derg
Drumquin
Omagh
Carrickmore
Ballintra
Pettigoe
DONEGAL BAY
Ballyshannon
Kesh
Dromore
Fintona
Ballygawley
Bundoran
Belleek
LOUGH ERNE
Irvinestown
Cliffoney
Kinlough
Augher
INISHMURRAY
Grange
Garrison
Clogher
Monea
Raghly
Drumcliff
Tempo
Enniskillen
Manorhamilton
Belcoo
SLIGO BAY
Lisnaskea
Monaghan
Sligo
Blacklion
Dromard
Dromahaire
Newtown
Butler
Newbliss
Beltra
Ballysadare
Dowra
Clones
Coolaney
Collooney
Ballintogher
Lough Allen
Riverstown
Ballyconnell
Belturbet
Cootehill
Ballymote
Ballyfarnan
Ballinamore
Ballyhaise
Ballinafad
Kilmactranny
Drumshanbo
Killeshandra
Tobercurry
Leitrim
Cavan
Kilfree
Bailieborough
Boyle
Carrick-on-Shannon
Ballaghaderreen
Drumsna
Arvagh
Ballinagh
Frenchpark
Elphin
Ballinamuck
Ballyjamesduff
Bellanagare
Rathcroghan
Newtown
Forbes
Virginia
Ballyhaunis
Castlerea
Tulsk
Strokestown
Granard
Oldcastle
Kells
Ballintober
Longford
Castlepollard
Ballymoe
Oran
Edgeworthstown
Roscommon
Multyfarnham
Ballymahon
Tuam
Athleague
Lecarrow
Rathconrath
Mullingar
Lough Ree
Auburn
Ballymore
Kinnegad

CONTINUED ON MAP 3

CONTINUED ON MAP 1

CONTINUED ON MAP 6

2

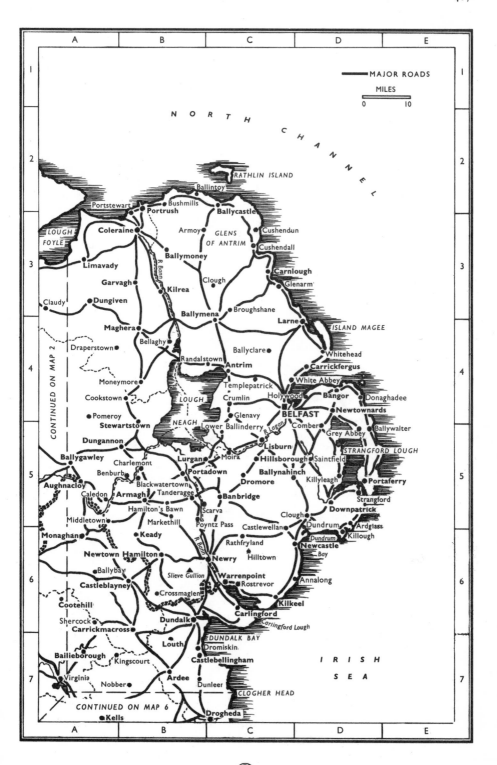

3

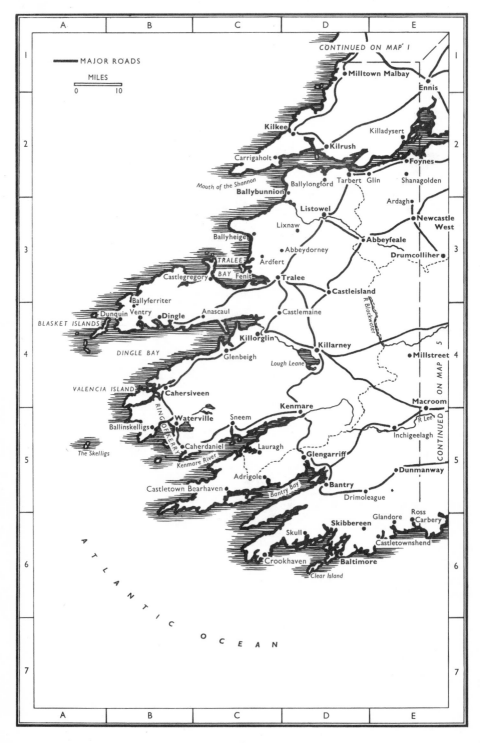

MAJOR ROADS

MILES
0   10

CONTINUED ON MAP 1

Milltown Malbay

Ennis

Killadysert

Kilkee

Kilrush

Carrigaholt

Foynes

Mouth of the Shannon

Ballylongford   Tarbert Glin

Shanagolden

Ballybunnion

Listowel

Ardagh

Lixnaw

Newcastle
West

Ballyheige

Abbeydorney

Abbeyfeale

Ardfert

Drumcolliher

TRALEE

Castlegregory   *BAY* Fenit

Tralee

Castleisland

Ballyferriter

Castlemaine

R. Blackwater

Dunquin Ventry

Dingle

Anascaul

BLASKET ISLANDS

Killorglin

Killarney

Millstreet

DINGLE BAY

Glenbeigh

Lough Leane

VALENCIA ISLAND

Cahersiveen

Macroom

Waterville

Sneem

Kenmare

R. Lee

RING OF KERRY

Ballinskelligs

Inchigeelagh

Caherdaniel

Lauragh

The Skelligs

Kenmare River

Glengarriff

Dunmanway

Adrigole

Castletown Bearhaven

Bantry

Bantry Bay

Drimoleague

Ross
Carbery

Glandore

Skibbereen

Skull

Castletownshend

ATLANTIC

Crookhaven

Baltimore

Clear Island

OCEAN

CONTINUED ON MAP 5

489

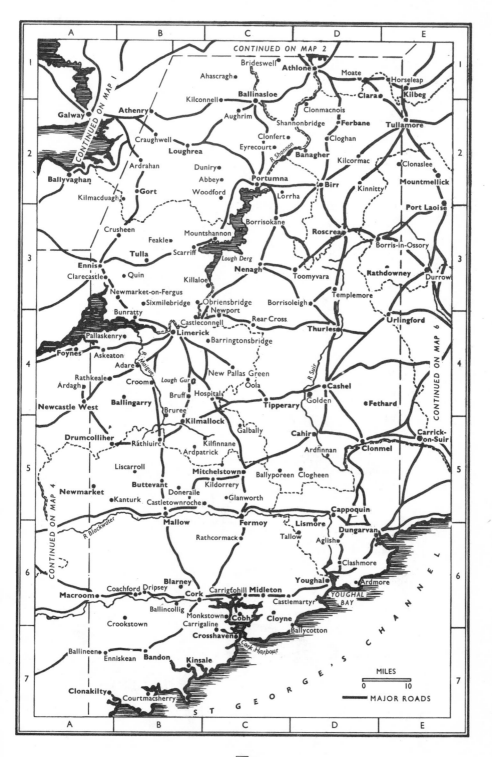

5

Index

To avoid unnecessary repetition, the main entries in the Gazetteer have not been included in this Index. Page numbers in *italic type* indicate illustrations.